DISPUTE RESOLUTION AND LAWYERS

Fifth Edition

■ ■ ■

by

Leonard L. Riskin
Chesterfield Smith Professor of Law
University of Florida Levin College of Law

James E. Westbrook
Earl F. Nelson and James S. Rollins Professor of Law, Emeritus
University of Missouri School of Law

Chris Guthrie
Dean & John Wade-Kent Syverud Professor of Law
Vanderbilt University Law School

Richard C. Reuben
James Lewis Parks Professor of Law
University of Missouri School of Law

Jennifer K. Robbennolt
Professor of Law and Psychology
University of Illinois College of Law

Nancy A. Welsh
William Trickett Faculty Scholar and Professor of Law
Penn State University
Dickinson School of Law

AMERICAN CASEBOOK SERIES®

Mat #41348973

American Casebook Series is a trademark registered in the U.S. Patent and Trademark Office.

COPYRIGHT © 1987 WEST PUBLISHING
© West, a Thomson business, 1997, 2005
© 2009 Thomson Reuters
© 2014 LEG, Inc. d/b/a West Academic
      444 Cedar Street, Suite 700
      St. Paul, MN 55101
      1-877-888-1330

West, West Academic Publishing, and West Academic are trademarks of West Publishing Corporation, used under license.

Printed in the United States of America

ISBN: 978-0-314-28590-4

To Casey, Andrew, & Barney and to the memory of Minnie Hauser, with love. L.L.R.

To my wonderful grandchildren: Daniel, Jimmy, Collin and Laura. JEW

To my parents, who taught me most of what I know about conflict resolution. C.P.G.

To Robin, with gratitude, and to Patrick and Daniel, with hope for the future. R.C.R.

To Grant, Dale, and Jake, with love. J.K.R.

To Eric, Sean, and Daniel, with so much love. N.A.W.

PREFACE

This book is premised upon the idea that the essential task of lawyering is to help clients and society solve problems well. To do this, the lawyer must be able not only to grasp and promote legal rights and positions; he or she also must be able to identify and articulate underlying interests and the motives or goals that impel people to act. In addition, the lawyer must know the nature and potential advantages and disadvantages of various methods of managing or resolving disputes.

Trial, of course, is one way to resolve disputes, and many courses in law school are devoted to this approach. But there are other methods, such as mediation and arbitration, that have expanded significantly over the last few several decades. Historically, these methods were referred to as ADR for "Alternative Dispute Resolution." Today, however, they are more commonly called Dispute Resolution, reflecting that the resolution of legal problems properly embraces many different methods, including trial, as well as the fact that these processes have become mainstreamed and institutionalized within legal culture. For this reason, some people consider the "A" in "ADR" to refer to Appropriate Dispute Resolution.

These methods, and how they compare to, and interact with trial and appellate processes form the central focus of this book. One of our principal goals in teaching about dispute resolution is to prepare law students to select and carry out, in particular cases or categories of cases, the most suitable methods of dispute resolution.

Such a grounding has become increasingly essential to law practice since the publication of the first edition of *Dispute Resolution and Lawyers* in 1987. Today, mediation, arbitration, and other alternatives to trial affect the practices of the bulk of lawyers in most parts of the United States and have virtually transformed law practice in some geographic and substantive areas. In addition, many lawyers have found great satisfaction working as dispute resolution neutrals, and as advocates in these processes.

Yet ADR continues to present unique challenges for lawyers. The legal tradition historically has emphasized formal processes and adversarial practices and perspectives. Alternatives to trial, however, tend to be informal and to require such interpersonal skills as understanding, consensus-building, and accommodation, which necessitate a very different mindset. This book seeks to help law students meet these challenges by introducing them to the nature of conflict and disputes, the fundamental principles of dispute resolution, the wide array of dispute resolution options, the law that affects these processes, the ethical problems they present, and the bases upon which one may discern which process is most appropriate for a particular dispute. In so doing, it recognizes that conflict can present opportunities for significant change and growth, and that the best lawyering will strive to achieve such benefits.

This Fifth Edition is the most significant revision of the book in a decade, and begins a generational change for the book that corresponds with the evolution of the field. The first two editions, by Professors Leonard L. Riskin and James E. Westbrook, established the book's orientation, framework, core content, and tone. Dean Chris Guthrie and Professors Jennifer K. Robbennolt and Richard C. Reuben joined the book for the Third Edition, and introduced several new themes, including conflict and conflict management, greater emphasis on the empirical literature that has come to support the field, and the importance of self-awareness and emotional intelligence for lawyers as participants in these processes. The Fourth Edition provided important updates, and welcomed a new coauthor, Nancy A. Welsh.

In this Fifth Edition, we make a subtle but important shift, away from a book that seeks to be an historical record of the field and toward a sharper, clearer, more concise, and more user-friendly presentation of the materials. We still view the history as important, and many of the historical materials that were once main readings continue to inform our understanding in the notes, to reflect their weight more properly and to provide space for the issues and cases that are more significant today. As a result, despite many new cases and readings, the book continues to be approximately the same length.

As with the Third Edition, we have also introduced new materials thematically that help better integrate the law that attends to dispute resolution processes, the ethical questions for practitioners that arise uniquely within them, as well as the psychological phenomena that influences participants in these processes. For example, the chapters on The Attorney Client Relationship, Negotiation, Mediation, and Arbitration all include materials and problems on confidentiality, ethics, and the abundant case law that has emerged about those processes. As the field has evolved, we believe such issues are important fully inform and prepare students to meet the challenges of practicing dispute resolution competently, ethically, and professionally.

We have made every effort to introduce these changes in a way that maintains the consistency of the book's orientation, structure, and tone, so as to make the transition as seamless for users as the evolution of the field itself. Teachers and others who have worked with previous editions will recognize many familiar landmarks, and should find the need to revise their teaching plans to be fairly minimal. They should also find the book much fresher, and closer to the field's cutting edge.

Chapter I provides an overview of conflict and dispute resolution, and sets up the main theme of the book: effective conflict management, especially by lawyers, through the use of the most appropriate methods of dispute resolution. The book continues its central focus on the role and perspectives of lawyers, beginning with the emphasis on client interviewing and counseling in Chapter II. In Chapters III, IV, and V, we continue the book's tradition of addressing the nature, varieties, and advantages and disadvantages of the primary alternative dispute resolution processes—negotiation, mediation, and arbitration. We emphasize the importance of innovation, adaptation, and creativity in the field in Chapter VI, addressing these qualities in the courts and administrative agencies, as well as in the private sector. Chapter VII addresses the choice, design, and evaluation of dispute resolution methods and programs.

Finally, Chapter VIII, Looking Ahead, connects the dispute resolution movement with other similar developments in the law, and provides guidance on how readers may further their interest in dispute resolution. Chapter VIII also emphasizes the importance of emotional intelligence and present-moment non-judgmental awareness, and the use of mindfulness meditation as a means of cultivating such qualities in a dispute resolution professional.

We also have a web site for the casebook on The West Education Network (TWEN). It includes many important documents in an Online Appendix that complements the book's main appendix, as well as role play instructions and new cases, policies, and other developments. To access the *Dispute Resolution and Lawyers, 5th Ed.*, web site, follow these instructions:

1. Go to http://lawschool.westlaw.com and click the TWEN tab

2. Enter either your West OnePass Username and Password or your Westlaw password in the appropriate field(s) and click GO.

3. Once you are signed on to TWEN click Drop/Add a Course.

4. Select the check box next to *Dispute Resolution and Lawyers, 5th Ed.*

5. Click Submit at the bottom of the page to return to the TWEN home page. The site you added is now displayed on your TWEN home page.

6. Click *Dispute Resolution and Lawyers 5th ed.* to view information related to the book.

As usual, we are publishing this edition in both hardcover and abridged paperback versions, each of which has a variety of potential uses. The hardcover edition is suitable for a dispute resolution survey course for three or four credits as well as for courses that include Interviewing, Counseling, Negotiation, and Mediation. The abridged edition is especially appropriate for integrating dispute resolution instruction into standard courses. The first abridged edition was the foundation for the program to integrate dispute resolution into all first-year courses at the University of Missouri School of Law.[1] In addition, it is suitable for two- or three-credit courses that include Interviewing, Counseling, Negotiation, and Mediation.

The online Instructor's Manual contains scores of exercises and problems prepared by professors at more than a dozen law schools, as well as suggestions for teaching dispute resolution as a separate course and for integrating such material into standard first-year law school courses. The Instructor's Manual is available through the book's TWEN site.

In addition, the book offers general information for several role play exercises for which demonstration videotapes are available on the book's

---

[1] The project to integrate dispute resolution into all standard first-year courses was developed under a grant from the National Institute for Dispute Resolution and a series of grants from the U.S. Department of Education's Fund for the Improvement of Post-Secondary Education (FIPSE) to the Center for the Study of Dispute Resolution at the University of Missouri-Columbia School of Law. In addition to the first two editions of this book, the project produced the Dispute Resolution and Lawyers Videotape Series (West 1991). An early history and description of the project appears in Leonard L. Riskin and James E. Westbrook, *Integrating Dispute Resolution into Standard First-Year Courses: The Missouri Plan*, 39 J. LEG. EDUC. 509 (1989).

In 1995, the Center received another grant from FIPSE to work with six other law schools that wished to develop adaptations of this program. Each of these schools—DePaul, Hamline, Inter-American, Ohio State, Tulane, and the University of Washington—began with unique circumstances and goals; as we anticipated, each produced a one-of-a-kind adaptation, some of which focus on integrating dispute resolution into the advanced, rather than the first-year curriculum. Some of the exercises prepared at these schools appear in the Instructor's Manual for this book. For an overview and analysis of the Missouri program to integrate dispute resolutions into first-year courses as well as programs at the other six participating law schools, see *Symposium, Dispute Resolution in the Law School Curriculum: Opportunities and Challenges*, 50 FLA. L. REV. 583 (1998).

In 2004, for a variety of complex reasons, the University of Missouri School of Law shifted emphasis from the integrated approach to a required, first-year course called *Lawyering: Problem-Solving and Dispute Resolution*. We have used the abridged Third Edition to teach this course.

TWEN site. Confidential instructions for these role plays are found on the book's TWEN site.

We have inserted three asterisks (* * *) to indicate omissions in reprinted material. However, we have omitted most footnotes, parenthetical references to authorities, and some citations to cases and statutes without so indicating. In the few instances where we retained footnotes, we kept their original numbering. Footnotes prepared by the authors of this book are marked by asterisks.

To avoid awkward language, we generally use either masculine or feminine pronouns to include their opposites.

We are grateful to many people who helped produce this new edition. The deans, faculty, and library staff at the University of Missouri School of Law have been endlessly supportive. We are also thankful to our invaluable research assistants: Daniel Coffman, K'iara Cross, Christian Gordon, Larry Lambert, Jamie Myers, and Patrick Reuben (Missouri), Amanda Gavin, Brian Brodeur, Katie Rimpfel, and Stephanie Sweenie (Penn State/Dickenson) Laura Coleman provided crucial administrative assistance, and Karen Neylon helped with the graphics. We also appreciate the skillful handling of the book by our editors at West, Jim Cahoy and Laura Holle, and remain grateful for similar contributions by their predecessors, Staci Herr and Ryan Pfeiffer.

Finally, Chris, Jen, Jim, Nancy, and Len give special thanks to Richard, who performs the essential role of executive editor with a wonderful blend of editorial skill, enthusiastic optimism, humor, and dogged persistence.

L.L.R.
J.E.W.
C.P.G.
R.C.R.
J.K.R.
N.A.W.

January 2014

ACKNOWLEDGEMENTS

We gratefully acknowledge the permission extended to reprint the works listed below.

CH. I

BERNARD MAYER, THE DYNAMICS OF CONFLICT RESOLUTION: A PRACTITIONER'S GUIDE 4–5. COPYRIGHT © 2000 JOSSEY–BASS, INC. REPRINTED WITH PERMISSION OF JOHN WILEY & SONS, INC.

RICHARD MILLER & AUSTIN SARAT, GRIEVANCES, CLAIMS AND DISPUTES: ASSESSING THE ADVERSARY CULTURE, 15 LAW & SOC'Y REV. 524, 544 (1980–81).

OWEN FISS, AGAINST SETTLEMENT. REPRINTED BY PERMISSION OF THE YALE LAW JOURNAL COMPANY AND FRED B. ROTHMAN & COMPANY FROM THE YALE LAW JOURNAL, VOL. 93, PP. 1073, 1075, 1076–78, 1082–90 (1984).

CARRIE MENKEL–MEADOW, WHOSE DISPUTE IS IT ANYWAY? A PHILOSOPHICAL AND DEMOCRATIC DEFENSE OF SETTLEMENT (IN SOME CASES), 83 GEO. L.J. 2663, 2663–71, 2692 (1995). REPRINTED WITH THE PERMISSION OF THE PUBLISHER, GEORGETOWN LAW JOURNAL. COPYRIGHT © 1995 GEORGETOWN UNIVERSITY.

FRANK E.A. SANDER, VARIETIES OF DISPUTE PROCESSING, ADDRESS DELIVERED AT THE NATIONAL CONFERENCE ON THE CAUSES OF POPULAR DISSATISFACTION WITH THE ADMINISTRATION OF JUSTICE, 70 F.R.D. 111, 112, 130–133 (1976).

LEONARD L. RISKIN, MEDIATION AND LAWYERS, 43 OHIO ST. L.J. 29, 43–48, 57–59 (1982).

CH. II

ROBERT D. DINERSTEIN, CLIENT–CENTERED COUNSELING: REAPPRAISAL & REFINEMENT, 32 ARIZ. L. REV. 501, 503–04, 506–09 (1991).

ROBERT F. COCHRAN, JR., JOHN M.A. DIPIPPA, & MARTHA M. PETERS, THE COUNSELOR-AT-LAW: A COLLABORATIVE APPROACH TO CLIENT INTERVIEWING AND COUNSELING 6–7 (1999). COPYRIGHT © 1999 MATTHEW BENDER & COMPANY, INC., A MEMBER OF THE LEXISNEXIS GROUP. ALL RIGHTS RESERVED.

MODEL RULES OF PROFESSIONAL CONDUCT RULES PREAMBLE, 1.2, 1.4, 2.1 (2004). COPYRIGHT © 2004 AMERICAN BAR ASSOCIATION. REPRINTED BY PERMISSION.

HERBERT M. KRITZER, THE JUSTICE BROKERS: LAWYERS AND ORDINARY LITIGATION 60–65 (1990), OXFORD UNIVERSITY PRESS.

ROBERT H. MNOOKIN, SCOTT PEPPET & ANDREW S. TULUMELLO, BEYOND WINNING: NEGOTIATING TO CREATE VALUE IN DEALS AND DISPUTES 70–71 (THE BELKNAP PRESS OF HARVARD UNIVERSITY PRESS, 2000). COPYRIGHT © 2000 BY THE PRESIDENT AND FELLOWS OF HARVARD COLLEGE. REPRINTED BY PERMISSION OF HARVARD UNIVERSITY PRESS. ALL RIGHTS RESERVED.

JANICE NADLER RAPPORT IN NEGOTIATION AND CONFLICT RESOLUTION, 87 MARQUETTE L. REV. 875, 875–76 (2004).

SANA LOUE, A GUIDE TO BETTER CLIENT INTERVIEWS, 89–07 IMMIGR. BRIEFINGS 1 (1989). WITH PERMISSION OF WEST PUBLISHING.

DAVID MAISTER, CHARLES GREEN & ROBERT GALFORD, THE TRUSTED ADVISOR, AM. LAW., OCT. 2000, AT 65, 65–66.

ROBERT DINERSTEIN, STEPHEN ELLMAN, ISABELLE GUNNING & ANN SHALLECK, CONNECTION CAPACITY AND MORALITY IN LAWYER–CLIENT RELATIONSHIPS, 10 CLINICAL L. REV. 755, 758–62 (2004).

LEONARD L. RISKIN, THE CONTEMPLATIVE LAWYER: ON THE POTENTIAL CONTRIBUTIONS OF MINDFULNESS MEDITATION TO LAW STUDENTS, LAWYERS, AND THEIR CLIENTS, 7 HARV. NEGOT. L. REV. 1, 49–53 (2002).

ROY M. SOBELSON, INTERVIEWING CLIENTS ETHICALLY, 37 PRAC. LAW. 13, 18–21 (1991).

JENNIFER GERARDA BROWN, CREATIVITY AND PROBLEM–SOLVING, 87 MARQUETTE L. REV. 697, 699–702, 703–4, 705, 706 (2004).

ROBERT PIRSIG, ZEN AND THE ART OF MOTORCYCLE MAINTENANCE 278–79, 285–86 (WILLIAM MORROW & CO., C/O HARPERCOLLINS 1975).

JEFFREY M. SENGER, DECISION ANALYSIS IN NEGOTIATION, 87 MARQ. L. REV. 723, 723, 729–33 (2004).

ATUL GAWANDE, COMPLICATIONS: A SURGEON'S NOTES ON AN IMPERFECT SCIENCE 210–11, 211–12, 219–22 (2002).

DAVID A. BINDER, PAUL BERGMAN & SUSAN C. PRICE, LAWYERS AS COUNSELORS: A CLIENT-CENTERED APPROACH 348–50 (2D ED. 1991).

ROBERT F. COCHRAN, JR., INTRODUCTION: THREE APPROACHES TO MORALS ISSUES IN LAW OFFICE COUNSELING, 30 PEPP. L. REV. 591, 592, 593, 594–95, 595–97, 597–98, 598–99, 600 (2003).

LINDA F. SMITH, MEDICAL PARADIGMS FOR COUNSELING: GIVING CLIENTS BAD NEWS, 4 CLINICAL L. REV. 391, 391–92, 417–19, 421–22, 423–24 (1998).

NANCY A. WELSH, INTEGRATING "ALTERNATIVE" DISPUTE RESOLUTION INTO BANKRUPTCY: AS SIMPLE (AND PURE) AS MOTHERHOOD AND APPLE PIE?, 11 NEV. L. J. 397, 402–408 (2011).

CH. III

G. RICHARD SHELL, BARGAINING FOR ADVANTAGE: NEGOTIATION STRATEGIES FOR REASONABLE PEOPLE 8, 9–12, 43–49, 119 (2D ED. 2006). USED BY PERMISSION OF VIKING PENGUIN, A DIVISION OF PENGUIN GROUP (USA) INC.

NANCY A. WELSH, THE REPUTATIONAL ADVANTAGES OF EEMONSTRATING TRUSTWORTHINESS: USING THE REPUTATION INDEX WITH LAW STUDENTS, 28 NEGOT. J. 117, 136–139 (2011).

RUSSELL KOROBKIN, A POSITIVE THEORY OF LEGAL NEGOTIATION, 88 GEO. L.J. 1789, 1792–94 (2000). REPRINTED WITH PERMISSION OF THE PUBLISHER, GEORGETOWN LAW JOURNAL. COPYRIGHT © 2000 BY THE GEORGETOWN LAW JOURNAL ASSOCIATION AND RUSSELL KOROBKIN.

CARRIE J. MENKEL–MEADOW, TOWARD ANOTHER VIEW OF LEGAL NEGOTIATION: THE STRUCTURE OF PROBLEM SOLVING, 31 U.C.L.A. L. REV. 754, 755–61, 795–801 (1984). ORIGINALLY PUBLISHED IN 31 U.C.L.A. L. REV. 754. COPYRIGHT © 1984 THE REGENTS OF THE UNIVERSITY OF CALIFORNIA. ALL RIGHTS RESERVED.

GARY GOODPASTER, A PRIMER ON THE COMPETITIVE BARGAINING, 1996 J. DISP. RESOL. 325, 342–43.

DAN ORR & CHRIS GUTHRIE, ANCHORING, INFORMATION, EXPERTISE, AND NEGOTIATION: NEW INSIGHTS FROM META–ANALYSIS, 21 OHIO ST. J. ON DISP. RESOL. 597, 597–98, 621–22 (2006).

ROBERT B. CIALDINI, INFLUENCE: SCIENCE AND PRACTICE 36–39, 65, 4E, PUBLISHED BY ALLYN & BACON, BOSTON, MA. COPYRIGHT © 2001 BY PEARSON EDUCATION. REPRINTED BY PERMISSION OF THE PUBLISHER.

CARRIE MENKEL–MEADOW, KNOW WHEN TO SHOW YOUR HAND, 10 NEGOT. 1, 1–3 (JUNE 2007).

THOMAS C. SCHELLING, THE STRATEGY OF CONFLICT, 21–25 (HARVARD UNIVERSITY PRESS). COPYRIGHT © 1960, 1980 BY THE PRESIDENT AND FELLOWS OF HARVARD COLLEGE, COPYRIGHT RENEWED 1988 BY THOMAS C. SCHELLING. REPRINTED WITH PERMISSION OF HARVARD UNIVERSITY PRESS. ALL RIGHTS RESERVED.

ROGER FISHER, WILLIAM URY & BRUCE PATTON, GETTING TO YES: NEGOTIATING AGREEMENT WITHOUT GIVING IN 10–12, 14, 44 (2D ED. 1991). COPYRIGHT © 1981, 1991 BY ROGER FISHER & WILLIAM URY. REPRINTED BY PERMISSION OF PUBLISHER.

DOULAS STONE, BRUCE PATTON & SHEILA HEEN, DIFFICULT
    CONVERSATIONS: HOW TO DISCUSS WHAT MATTERS MOST, 163–67, 167–
    68 (1999). LEARNING: LISTEN FROM THE INSIDE OUT BY DOUGLAS STONE
    AND BRUCE M. PATTON, SHEILA HEEN, FROM DIFFICULT
    CONVERSATIONS BY DOUGLAS STONE, BRUCE M. PATTON AND SHEILA
    HEEN, COPYRIGHT A 1999 BY DOUGLAS STONE, BRUCE M. PATTON &
    SHEILA HEEN. USED BY PERMISSION OF VIKING PENGUIN, A DIVISION OF
    PENGUIN GROUP (USA) INC.

DANIEL L. SHAPIRO, TEACHING STUDENTS HOW TO USE EMOTIONS AS THEY
    NEGOTIATE, 22 NEGOT. J. 105, 106–7 (2006).

DEEPAK MALHOTRA & MAX H. BAZERMAN, INVESTIGATIVE NEGOTIATION,
    HARV. BUS. REV. 73, 74–75 (SEPTEMBER 2007).

DAVID E. MATZ, IGNORANCE AND INTERESTS, 4 HARV. NEGOT. L. REV. 59, 63–
    65 (1999).

ROBERT H. MNOOKIN, SCOTT PEPPET & ANDREW S. TULUMELLO, BEYOND
    WINNING: NEGOTIATING TO CREATIVE VALUE IN DEALS AND DISPUTES
    (HARVARD UNIVERSITY PRESS) 14–15, 64–65, 83–86, 226, 240–42.
    COPYRIGHT © 2000 THE PRESIDENT AND FELLOWS OF HARVARD
    COLLEGE. REPRINTED BY PERMISSION OF THE PUBLISHER.

CARRIE MENKEL–MEADOW, AHA? IS CREATIVITY POSSIBLE IN LEGAL
    PROBLEM SOLVING AND TEACHABLE IN LEGAL EDUCATION? 6 HARV.
    NEGOT. L. REV. 97, 105–06, 109–11 (2001).

ROGER FISHER, COMMENT, 34 J. LEGAL EDUC. 120, 121–23 (1984).

JAMES E. WESTBROOK, HOW TO NEGOTIATE WITH A JERK WITHOUT BEING
    ONE, 1992 J. DISP. RESOL. 443, 444–46.

JEFFREY J. RACHLINSKI, GAINS, LOSSES, AND THE PSYCHOLOGY OF
    LITIGATION, 70 S. CAL. L. REV. 113, 128–29 (1996).

JENNIFER K. ROBBENOLT, APOLOGY—HELP OR HINDRANCE? AN EMPIRICAL
    ANALYSIS OF APOLOGIES' INFLUENCE ON DECISION–MAKING, DISP.
    RESOL. MAG., SPRING 2004, AT 33–34.

RUSSELL KOROBKIN, MICHAEL MOFFITT & NANCY WELSH, THE LAW OF
    BARGAINING, 87 MARQ. L. REV. 839, 839–44 (2004).

MODEL RULE OF PROFESSIONAL RESPONSIBILITY 4.1 TRUTHFULNESS IN
    STATEMENTS TO OTHERS (2013).

JAMES J. WHITE, MACHIAVELLI AND THE BAR: ETHICAL LIMITATIONS ON
    LYING IN NEGOTIATION, 1980 AM. B. FOUND. RES. J. 926, 927–29, 931–
    35.

JONATHAN R. COHEN, WHEN PEOPLE ARE THE MEANS: NEGOTIATING WITH
    RESPECT, 14 GEO. J. LEGAL ETHICS 739, 741–43, 749–51 (2001).

JAYNE SEMINARE DOCHERTY, CULTURE AND NEGOTIATION: SYMMETRICAL
ANTHROPOLOGY FOR NEGOTIATORS, 87 MARQ. L. REV. 711, 712–13, 713–
14, 714–17 (2004).

LEONARD L. RISKIN, OBEY THE RULE: JUST SAY "NO, NO, NO," CHI. TRIB.,
JUNE 25, 1992, AT C19.

CARRIE MENKEL-MEADOW, WHAT DIFFERENCE DOES "GENDER
DIFFERENCE" MAKE?, 18 NO. 3 DISP. RESOL. MAG. 4, 5–7 (2012).

ANDREA SCHNEIDER, EFFECTIVE RESPONSES TO OFFENSIVE COMMENTS, 10
NEGOTIATION J. 107, 111–13 (1994).

IAN AYRES, FAIR DRIVING: GENDER AND RACE DISCRIMINATION IN RETAIL
CAR NEGOTIATIONS, 104 HARV. L. REV. 817, 817–19, 827–33 (1991).

CH. IV

LEONARD L. RISKIN, UNDERSTANDING MEDIATORS' ORIENTATIONS,
STRATEGIES, AND TECHNIQUES: A GRID FOR THE PERPLEXED, 1 HARV.
NEGOT. L. REV. 7, 8–13, 17–39, 41–48 (1996).

LEONARD L. RISKIN, REPLACING THE MEDIATOR ORIENTATION GRIDS,
AGAIN: THE NEW NEW GRID SYSTEM, 23 ALTERNATIVES TO THE HIGH
COST OF LITIG. 127–132 (SEPT. 2005).

ROBERT A. BARUCH BUSH & JOSEPH FOLGER, THE PROMISE OF MEDIATION:
THE TRANSFORMATIVE APPROACH TO CONFLICT 45–46, 49–56, 59, 60,
62, 65–66, 68, 72, 75, 78–81 (REVISED ED. 2005). COPYRIGHT © 2005
JOHN WILEY & SONS. REPRINTED WITH PERMISSION.

GARY FRIEDMAN & JACK HIMMELSTEIN, CHALLENGING CONFLICT:
MEDIATION THROUGH UNDERSTANDING XXIX–XXXI, XXXV–XXXVI (2008).

HANK DE ZUTTER, PROPONENTS SAY ADR SPELLS RELIEF, ILL. LEGAL
TIMES, JAN. 1988, AT 1.

ANDERSON J. LITTLE, MAKING MONEY TALK: HOW TO MEDIATE INSURED
CLAIMS AND OTHER MONETARY DISPUTES XI - XII, 1–10, 14–20, 22, 24–
30 (2007).

FRANK J. SCARDILLI, SISTERS OF THE PRECIOUS BLOOD V. BRISTOL-MYERS
CO.

ALANA S. KNASTER & PHILIP J. HARTER, THE CLEAN FUELS REGULATORY
NEGOTIATION, INTERGOVERNMENTAL PERSPECTIVE, SUMMER 1992, AT
20.

TEXAS CASE STUDY ONE: MURDER–VICTIM AND OFFENDER PERSPECTIVES
IN MARK S. UMBREIT, ET. AL., FACING VIOLENCE: THE PATH OF
RESTORATIVE JUSTICE AND DIALOGUE 45–52 (2003).

MODEL RULES OF PROF'L CONDUCT R. 1.12 (2004). COPYRIGHT © 2004
AMERICAN BAR ASSOCIATION. REPRINTED BY PERMISSION.

MODEL RULES OF PROF'L CONDUCT R. 2.2 (2001). COPYRIGHT © 2004 AMERICAN BAR ASSOCIATION. REPRINTED BY PERMISSION.

MODEL RULES OF PROF'L CONDUCT R. 2.4 (2004). COPYRIGHT © 2004 AMERICAN BAR ASSOCIATION. REPRINTED BY PERMISSION.

J.H. WADE, LIABILITY OF MEDIATORS FOR PRESSURE, DRAFTING AND ADVICE: TAPOOHI V. LEWENBERG, BOND DISP. RESOL. NEWS (JAN. 2004).

J. MICHAEL KEATING JR., GETTING RELUCTANT PARTIES TO MEDIATE: A GUIDE FOR ADVOCATES, 13 ALTERNATIVES TO HIGH COST LITIG. 9 (CPR INSTITUTE FOR DISPUTE RESOLUTION, N/K/A THE INTERNATIONAL INSTITUTE FOR CONFLICT PREVENTION AND RESOLUTION, 1995).

DANIEL BOWLING AND DAVID HOFFMAN, BRINGING PEACE INTO THE ROOM: HOW THE PERSONAL QUALITIES OF THE MEDIATOR IMPACT THE PROCESS OF CONFLICT RESOLUTION 14, 17–18, 21–24 (2003).

TOM ARNOLD, 20 COMMON ERRORS IN MEDIATION ADVOCACY, 13 ALTERNATIVES TO THE HIGH COST OF LITIG. 69. (CPR INSTITUTE OF DISPUTE RESOLUTION, N/K/A THE INTERNATIONAL INSTITUTE FOR CONFLICT PREVENTION AND RESOLUTION, 1995). COPYRIGHT © 1995 BY CPR INSTITUTE FOR DISPUTE RESOLUTION, 575 LEXINGTON AVENUE, NEW YORK, NY 10022. REPRINTED WITH PERMISSION. ALL RIGHTS RESERVED.

LEONARD L. RISKIN, THE REPRESENTED CLIENT IN A SETTLEMENT CONFERENCE: THE LESSONS OF G. HEILEMAN BREWEING CO. V. JOSEPH OAT CORP., 69 WASH. U. L.Q. 1059, 1098–1106 (1991). REPRINTED WITH PERMISSION.

JEFF KICHAVEN, AVOIDABLE SINS: WHEN A MEDIATOR STEPS BEYOND THE BOUNDARIES, 22 ALTERNATIVES TO HIGH COST LITIG. 77, 91–92 (2004). (CPR INSTITUTE OF DISPUTE RESOLUTION, N/K/A THE INTERNATIONAL INSTITUTE FOR CONFLICT PREVENTION AND RESOLUTION).

GARY FRIEDMAN & JACK HIMMELSTEIN, DEAL KILLER OR DEAL SAVER: THE CONSULTING LAWYER'S DILEMMA, DISP. RESOL. MAG., WINTER 1997, AT 7.

JAMES R. COBEN & PETER N. THOMPSON, MEDIATION LITIGATION TRENDS: 1999–2007, 1 WORLD ARBITRATION & MEDIATION REV. 395, 395–97, 399, 401–05, 407–09, 411–14 (2007).

UNIFORM MEDIATION ACT PREFATORY NOTE & SEC. 4–6 (2003). PERMISSION GIVEN BY THE NATIONAL CONFERENCE OF COMMISSIONERS ON UNIFORM STATE LAWS.

NANCY A. WELSH, THE THINNING VISION OF SELF–DETERMINATION IN COURT–CONNECTED MEDIATION: THE INEVITABLE PRICE OF INSTITUTIONALIZATION?, 6 HARV. NEGOT. L. REV. 1, 3–7 (2001).

RICHARD DELGADO, CHRIS DUNN, PAMELA BROWN, HELENA LEE & DAVID HUBBERT, FAIRNESS AND FORMALITY: MINIMIZING THE RISK OF PREJUDICE IN ALTERNATIVE DISPUTE RESOLUTION, 1985 WIS. L. REV. 1359, 1387–91, 1400–04.

MICHELLE HERMANN, ET AL., METROCOURT PROJECT FINAL REPORT: A STUDY OF THE EFFECTS OF ETHNICITY AND GENDER IN MEDIATED AND ADJUDICATED CASES AT THE METROPOLITAN COURT MEDIATION CENTER VIII–XII (1993).

LEONARD L. RISKIN & NANCY A. WELSH, WHAT'S IT ALL ABOUT?: FINDING THE APPROPRIATE PROBLEM DEFINITION IN MEDIATION, 15 DISP. RESOL. MAG. 19 (SUMMER 2009).

TRINA GRILLO, THE MEDIATION ALTERNATIVE: PROCESS DANGERS FOR WOMEN, 100 YALE L.J. 1545, 1549–50, 1600–08, 1610 (1991).

JOSHUA D. ROSENBERG, IN DEFENSE OF MEDIATION, 33 ARIZ. L. REV. 467, 468–69, 492–500, 503–05 (1991). COPYRIGHT © 1991 BY THE ARIZONA BOARD OF REGENTS. REPRINTED BY PERMISSION.

NANCY VER STEEGH, YES, NO, AND MAYBE: INFORMED DECISION MAKING ABOUT DIVORCE MEDIATION IN THE PRESENCE OF DOMESTIC VIOLENCE, 9 WM & MARY J. WOMEN & L. 145, 186–88 (2003).

JOAN B. KELLY, MEDIATED AND ADVERSARIAL DIVORCE: RESPONDENTS' PERCEPTIONS OF THEIR PROCESSES AND OUTCOMES, MEDIATION Q., SUMMER 1989, AT 71, 84–86.

THE RED DEVIL DOG MEDIATION (ROLE PLAY) INSTRUCTIONS. THIS ROLE PLAY WAS PREPARED BY PROFESSOR NANCY ROGERS AND IS BASED ON THE FACTS OF VIDEOTAPE III IN THE DISPUTE RESOLUTION AND LAWYERS VIDEOTAPE SERIES (WEST PUBLISHING CO. 1991) AND DALE A. WHITMAN, THE MISSING TENANT: A NEGOTIATION EXERCISE FOR PROPERTY LAW, IN LEONARD L. RISKIN AND JAMES E. WESTBROOK, INSTRUCTOR'S MANUAL FOR DISPUTE RESOLUTION AND LAWYERS, 3RD ED. (2005).

PROSANDO V. HIGH TECH (ROLE PLAY) INSTRUCTIONS. THIS EXERCISE WAS CREATED FOR THE INTERNATIONAL INSTITUTE FOR CONFLICT PREVENTION AND RESOLUTION, INC., BY CATHY CRONIN–HARRIS, VICE PRESIDENT, AND PROFESSOR STEPHEN GOLDBERG AS A BASIS FOR CPR'S 36–MINUTE VIDEOTAPE, MEDIATION IN ACTION: RESOLVING A COMPLEX BUSINESS DISPUTE (1994). THE VIDEOTAPE IS AVAILABLE FROM THE CPR INSTITUTE, 575 LEXINGTON AVENUE, 14TH FLOOR, NEW YORK, NY 10022 (212) 949–6490, OR ON CPR'S WEBSITE AT WWW.CPRADR.ORG. COPYRIGHT 1994 BY THE CPR INSTITUTE FOR DISPUTE RESOLUTION N/K/A INTERNATIONAL INSTITUTE FOR CONFLICT PREVENTION AND RESOLUTION. REPRINTED WITH THE PERMISSION OF CPR.

DANCE INNOVATION ROLE PLAY MEDIATOR'S INSTRUCTIONS. COPYRIGHT © 2001, CENTER FOR MEDIATION IN LAW. REPRINTED WITH PERMISSION.

CH. V

STEPHEN HAYFORD & RALPH PEEPLES, COMMERCIAL ARBITRATION IN EVOLUTION: AN ASSESSMENT AND CALL FOR DIALOGUE, 10 OHIO ST. J. ON DISP. RESOL. 343, 367–71, 375–76 (1995).

THEODORE O. ROGERS, JR. & JUDITH P. VLADECK, ADDRESS AT THE SYMPOSIUM ON ARBITRATION IN THE SECURITIES INDUSTRY, 63 FORDHAM L. REV. 1613, 1617–22, 1625–26 (1995).

KRISTEN BLANKELY, TAMING THE WILD WEST OF ARBITRATION ETHICS, 60 KAN. L. REV. 925, 925–942 (2012).

W. LAURENCE CRAIG, SOME TRENDS AND DEVELOPMENTS IN THE LAWS AND PRACTICE OF INTERNATIONAL COMMERCIAL ARBITRATION, 30 TEX. INT'L L.J. 1, 3–4, 6–7, 8–9, 10, 11, 57 (1995).

CHARLES N. BROWER, THE GLOBAL COURT: THE INTERNATIONALIZATION OF COMMERCIAL ADJUDICATION AND ARBITRATION, 26 U. BALT. L. REV. 9, 11–12, 13 (1997).

YVES DELAZAY AND BRYANT GARTH, FUSSING ABOUT THE FORUM: CATEGORIES AND DEFINITIONS AS STAKES IN A PROFESSIONAL COMPETITION, 21 L. & SOC'Y REV. 285, 295–99 (1996).

CH. VI

CHARLES POU JR., "WHEEL OF FORTUNE" OR "SINGLED OUT?": HOW ROSTERS "MATCHMAKE" MEDIATORS, DISP. RESOL. MAG., SPRING 1997, AT 10, 12. COPYRIGHT © 1997 AMERICAN BAR ASSOCIATION. REPRINTED BY PERMISSION.

BOBBI MCADOO, NANCY A. WELSH & ROSELLE L. WISSLER, INSTITUTIONALIZATION: WHAT DO EMPIRICAL STUDIES TELL US ABOUT COURT MEDIATION? 9 DISP. RESOL. MAG., WINTER 2003, AT 8, 8–9. COPYRIGHT © 2003 AMERICAN BAR ASSOCIATION. REPRINTED BY PERMISSION.

DORCAS QUECK, MANDATORY MEDIATION: AN OXYMORON? EXAMINING THE FEASIBILITY OF IMPLEMENTING A COURT–MANDATED MEDIATION PROGRAM, 11 CARDOZO J. CONFLICT RESOL. 479, 480–89, 498–500 (2010).

LAUREL WHEELER, COMMENT, MANDATORY FAMILY MEDIATION AND DOMESTIC VIOLENCE, 26 S. ILL. U. L. J. 559, 563–70 (2002).

JOHN LANDE, USING DISPUTE SYSTEM DESIGN METHODS TO PROMOTE GOOD–FAITH PARTICIPATION IN COURT–CONNECTED MEDIATION PROGRAMS, 50 UCLA L. REV. 69, 70, 86–89, 93–95, 98–99, 102–04, 106–08 (2002).

THOMAS D. LAMBROS, THE SUMMARY JURY TRIAL AND OTHER ALTERNATIVE METHODS OF DISPUTE RESOLUTION, 103 F.R.D. 461, 468–69 (1984). REPRINTED FROM 103 F.R.D. 461 WITH PERMISSION OF WEST PUBLISHING COMPANY.

JOSHUA D. ROSENBERG & H. JAY FOLBERG, ALTERNATIVE DISPUTE RESOLUTION: AN EMPIRICAL ANALYSIS, 46 STAN. L. REV. 1487, 1488, 1489–92, 1493 (1994). COPYRIGHT © 1994 THE BOARD OF TRUSTEES OF THE LELAND STANFORD JUNIOR UNIVERSITY.

GEORGE W. CONK, DIVING INTO THE WRECK: BP AND KENNETH FEINBERG'S GULF COAST GAMBIT, 17 ROGER WILLIAMS L. REV. 137 (2012).

PHILIP J. HARTER, NEGOTIATING REGULATIONS: A CURE FOR THE MALAISE, 71 GEO. L. J. 1, 28–31 (1982).

LISA BINGHAM, MEDIATION AT WORK: TRANSFORMING WORKPLACE CONFLICT AT THE UNITED STATES POSTAL SERVICE, IBM CENTER FOR THE BUSINESS OF GOVERNMENT 5, 12–23 (2003).

RICHARD C. REUBEN, DEMOCRACY AND DISPUTE RESOLUTION: THE PROBLEM OF ARBITRATION, 67 L. & CONTEMP. PROBS., WINTER/SPRING 2004, AT 279, 279–82, 285–95.

ERIC D. GREEN, CORPORATE ALTERNATIVE DISPUTE RESOLUTION, 1 OHIO ST. J. ON DISP. RES. 203, 238–242 (1986).

BARLOW F. CHRISTENSEN, PRIVATE JUSTICE: CALIFORNIA'S GENERAL REFERENCE PROCEDURE, 1982 AM. B. FOUND. RES. J. 79, 79–82. COPYRIGHT © 1982 UNIVERSITY OF CHICAGO PRESS.

STEPHEN B. GOLDBERG, THE MEDIATION OF GRIEVANCES UNDER A COLLECTIVE BARGAINING CONTRACT: AN ALTERNATIVE TO ARBITRATION, 77 NW. U. L. REV. 270, 281–84 (1982). REPRINTED BY SPECIAL PERMISSION OF NORTHWESTERN UNIVERSITY SCHOOL OF LAW, NORTHWESTERN UNIVERSITY LAW REVIEW.

PHILIP J. HARTER, OMBUDS—A VOICE FOR THE PEOPLE, DISP. RESOL. MAG., WINTER 2005, AT 5, 5–6. COPYRIGHT © 2005 AMERICAN BAR ASSOCIATION. REPRINTED BY PERMISSION.

JOHN LANDE, POSSIBILITIES FOR COLLABORATIVE LAW: ETHICS AND PRACTICE OF LAWYER DISQUALIFICATION AND PROCESS CONTROL IN A NEW MODEL OF LAWYERING, 64 OHIO ST. L.J. 1315, 1315–30 (2003).

JOHN G. BICKERMAN, PARTNERING IN THE CONSTRUCTION INDUSTRY: TEAMING UP TO PREVENT DISPUTES, PROB. & PROP. MAR./APR. 1995, AT 61, 61, 61–63, 64. COPYRIGHT © 1995 AMERICAN BAR ASSOCIATION. REPRINTED BY PERMISSION.

LOUIS DEL DUCA, COLIN RULE & ZBYNEK LOEBL, FACILITATING EXPANSION OF CROSS–BORDER E–COMMERCE DEVELOPING A GLOBAL ONLINE

DISPUTE RESOLUTION SYSTEM,1 PENN. ST. J. L. & INT'L AFF. 59, 59–74 (2012).

CH. VII

NATIONAL INSTITUTE FOR DISPUTE RESOLUTION, PATHS TO JUSTICE: MAJOR PUBLIC POLICY ISSUES OF DISPUTE RESOLUTION 3–4, 8–18, 30–34–35. (REPORT OF THE AD HOC PANEL ON DISPUTE RESOLUTION AND PUBLIC POLICY, NATIONAL INSTITUTE FOR DISPUTE RESOLUTION, 1983). THIS PROJECT WAS SUPPORTED IN PART BY A GRANT (NO 83–NI–AX–0002) FROM THE FEDERAL JUSTICE RESEARCH PROGRAM, U.S. DEPARTMENT OF JUSTICE. POINTS OF VIEW OR OPINIONS STATED IN THIS DOCUMENT ARE THOSE OF THE AUTHOR AND DO NOT NECESSARILY REPRESENT THE OFFICIAL POSITION OR POLICIES OF THE U.S. DEPARTMENT OF JUSTICE.

NANCY A. WELSH, MAKING DEALS IN COURT–CONNECTED MEDIATION: WHAT'S JUSTICE GOT TO DO WITH IT? 79 WASH. U. L.Q. 787, 817–26, 826–27 (2001).

JEAN R. STERNLIGHT, ADR IS HERE: PRELIMINARY REFLECTIONS ON WHERE IT FITS IN A SYSTEM OF JUSTICE, 3 NEV. L.J. 289, 297–300 (2002/2003).

HARRY EDWARDS, ALTERNATIVE DISPUTE RESOLUTION: PANACEA OR ANATHEMA?, 99 HARV. L. REV. 668, 671–72, 675–82 (1986).

FRANK E. A. SANDER & STEPHEN B. GOLDBERG, FITTING THE FORUM TO THE FUSS: A USER–FRIENDLY GUIDE TO SELECTING AN ADR PROCEDURE, 10 NEGOTIATION J. 49, 60–61 (1994).

TRACEY E. GEORGE & CHRIS GUTHRIE, INDUCED LITIGATION, 98 NW. U. L. REV. 545, 555–56 (2004).

JEANNE M. BRETT, STEPHEN B. GOLDBERG & WILLIAM L. URY, DESIGNING SYSTEMS FOR RESOVING DISPUTES IN ORGANIZATIONS, 45 AM. PSYCHOLOGIST 162, 162–63, 165–69 (1990).

CATHY COSTANTINO, USING INTEREST–BASED TECHNIQUES TO DESIGN CONFLICT MANAGEMENT SYSTEMS, 12 NEGOTIATION J. 207, 207–14 (1996).

LISA B. BINGHAM, SELF–DETERMINATION IN DISPUTE SYSTEM DESIGH AND EMPLOYMENT ARBITRATION, 56 U. MIAMI L. REV. 873, 879–80, 881–86 (2002).

DONNA STIENSTRA, EVALUATING AND MONITORING ADR PROCEDURES, 7 FJC DIRECTIONS, DEC. 1994, AT 24, 24–25.

ROBERT J. MACCOUN, E. ALLAN LIND, DEBORAH HENSLER, DAVID L. BRYANT & PATRICIA A. EBENER, ALTERNATIVE ADJUDICATION: AN EVALUATION OF THE NEW JERSEY AUTOMOBILE ARBITRATION PROGRAM V–XI (1988)

ROSELLE L. WISSLER, BARRIERS TO ATTORNEYS' DISCUSSION AND USE OF ADR, 19 OHIO ST. J. ON DISP. RESOL. 459, 462–68, 470–72, 493–97, 500 (2004).

MODEL RULES OF PROFESSIONAL CONDUCT 1.2, 1.4, 2.1 (2013).

FRANK E.A. SANDER & LUKASZ ROZDEICZER, MATCHING CASES AND DISPUTE RESOLUTION PROCEDURES: DETAILED ANALYSIS LEADING TO A MEDIATION–CENTERED APPROACH, 11 HARV. NEGOT. L. REV. 1, 10–29 (2006).

KATHLEEN M. SCANLON & HARPREET K. MANN, INSIDE GUIDE TO MULTI–STEP DISPUTE RESOLUTION CLAUSES, ADR COUNSEL IN–BOX, NO. 8, 20 ALTERNATIVES (CENTERFOLD PULLOT SEPTEMBER 2002). COPYRIGHT © 2003 CPR INSTITUTE FOR DISPUTE RESOLUTION. REPRINTED WITH PERMISSION OF JOHN WILEY & SONS.

CH. VIII

SUSAN DAICOFF, THE COMPREHENSIVE LAW PRACTICE: OVERVIEW OF THE MOVEMENT, THE VECTORS, AND THEIR COMMON GROUND 49–61 (2011).

LEONARD L. RISKIN, MINDFULNESS: FOUNDATIONAL TRAINING FOR DISPUTE RESOLUTION, 54 J. LEGAL EDUC. 79 (2004).

JAMES J. ALFINI & ERIC GALTON, ADR PERSONALITIES AND PRACTICE TIPS 6–8, 13–14, 50–53, 104–07, 136–39 (1998). COPYRIGHT © 1998 AMERICAN BAR ASSOCIATION. REPRINTED BY PERMISSION.

APPENDICES

MODEL RULES OF PROFESSIONAL CONDUCT 1.1, 1.2, 1.4, 1.6, 1.7, 1.9, 2.1, 2.4, 4.1, 8.4.

UNIFORM MEDIATION ACT (2003). PERMISSION GIVEN BY THE NATIONAL CONFERENCE OF COMMISSIONERS ON UNIFORM STATE LAWS.

UNIFORM ARBITRATION ACT (1997). NATIONAL CONFERENCE OF COMMISSIONERS ON UNIFORM STATE LAWS.

AMERICAN ARBITRATION ASSOCIATION, COMMERCIAL ARBITRATION RULES AND MEDIATION PROCEDURES (INCLUDING PROCEDURES FOR LARGE, COMPLEX COMMERCIAL DISPUTES) (2013).

SUMMARY OF CONTENTS

TABLE OF CONTENTS

TABLE OF CASES

The principal cases are in bold type.

DISPUTE RESOLUTION AND LAWYERS
Fifth Edition

CHAPTER I

OVERVIEW OF DISPUTE RESOLUTION & CONFLICT MANAGEMENT

■ ■ ■

Conflict and disputes pervade society. They touch every individual, every family, every organization, and every relationship between and among these individuals and groups. Most lawyers are closely involved with conflict and disputes. Trial lawyers, for example, use the law and courts to resolve specific disputes between specific parties. Public interest lawyers, too, often use individual disputes to address more fundamental issues of social conflict. Resolving disagreement over the terms and conditions of contracts is daily grist for transactional lawyers. Even navigating within our practices can present lawyers with conflict challenges.

In recent years it has become clear that a range of methods, such as negotiation, mediation, and arbitration, are often viable and appropriate for resolving particular disputes. Collectively, these methods are commonly called "Alternative Dispute Resolution," "Appropriate Dispute Resolution," or simply "ADR." In our view, the best term to describe this full array of processes, including litigation, is simply "dispute resolution."

In the context of this broad range of options for resolving disputes, the tasks of the lawyer are to determine—ordinarily in consultation with the client—which method is most appropriate for a given dispute and to work effectively within that process. This book seeks to enhance this capacity by providing a better understanding of three sets of issues:

    A.   The nature of conflict, and the disputes that conflicts produce, as well as the various processes available for resolving such disputes appropriately;

    B.   The significant legal, policy, and ethical issues surrounding these processes; and

    C.   The varied and complementary roles of lawyers in managing and resolving disputes, as well as the unique challenges that lawyers face as participants in conflict and disputes.

In addressing these issues, we draw upon a wide range of resources. The field of dispute resolution is broad, and has been informed not only by the teachings of law, but also of psychology, anthropology, economics, and political science, among other disciplines.

A. THE NATURE OF CONFLICT AND DISPUTES

Awareness of the sources, structure, and dynamics of the conflicts that give rise to legal and other disputes improves the capacity of lawyers to steer conflict toward processes and outcomes that are more constructive, and away from conflict's more destructive consequences.

1. SOURCES OF CONFLICT

People tend to use the words "conflict" and "dispute" interchangeably. This is usually adequate in lay conversation. However, for lawyers and dispute resolution professionals, a more precise understanding of these phenomena is helpful. Conflict, as we use the term, is an actual or perceived clash of interests or aspirations. Disputes arise out of those sources of conflict, and are the concrete manifestations of the underlying conflict. Put another way, a dispute is a conflict that has been acted upon, a product of the conflict.

There are many theories about why conflict arises. In our view, no single perspective provides a complete explanation. Rather, different theories help inform our understanding of the tensions that may underlie a particular dispute. The following materials provide a brief overview of the different theoretical perspectives on the sources of conflict and then offer a helpful way of analyzing different dimensions of any particular dispute.

a. Theoretical Underpinnings

Different theories about the sources of conflict may be generally organized into three sets: individual characteristics theories, social process theories, and social structure theories. JAMES A. SCHELLENBERG, CONFLICT RESOLUTION: THEORY, RESEARCH, AND PRACTICE 39–102 (1996).

The first theories relate to individual characteristics of people, entities, and institutions. Needs theory is a prominent example, and suggests that conflict arises from any one of a number of unmet human needs, ranging from physical needs for food and shelter to psychological needs for love and self-actualization *See, e.g.*, ABRAHAM MASLOW, HIERARCHY OF NEEDS (1954). Similarly, modern identity theory holds that conflict arises from threats to individual and social identity, or a sense of self and self-worth. *See generally* SOCIAL IDENTITY AND INTERGROUP RELATIONS (Henri Tajfel, ed. 2010). Social process theories build on individual characteristics theories, but emphasize the relationships between parties, particularly along distributional lines. For a social process theorist, conflict is the result of the competition for resources. This was essentially the view of economist Adam Smith, who argued that people seek to maximize their rational self-interest, and that conflict arises when these interests collide. *See* WEALTH OF NATIONS (E. Cannon Ed., 1937) (1776). Today, rational choice and public choice theorists sound similar themes in explaining social phenomena ranging from economic markets to legislative behavior. For accessible accounts, see Chris Guthrie, *Prospect Theory, Risk Preference, and the Law,* 97 Nw. U. L. Rev. 1115, 1115–20 (2003); Russell B. Korobkin & Thomas S. Ulen, *Law and Behavioral Science: Removing the Rationality Assumption from Law and Economics,* 88 Cal. L. Rev. 1051, 1060–66 (2000).

Finally, social structure theories of conflict emphasize the institutionalized structures organizing a society, holding that conflict arises from the nature of the social system itself, particularly as it relates to disparities of power and influence. Karl Marx, for example, saw conflict as resulting from the competition between "haves" and "have nots", with the "haves" being the propertied elite seeking to preserve the status quo and the "have nots" being the subservient working class seeking greater wealth. KARL MARX & FREDERICK ENGELS, MANIFESTO OF THE COMMUNIST PARTY (Int'l Publishers, 1948 Ed.) (1848). Social structure theory often finds its expression today in critical theory, which looks to power and other disparities between genders, races, and other classes to explain social conflict. *See, e.g.,* DERRICK BELL, AND WE ARE NOT SAVED: THE ELUSIVE QUEST FOR RACIAL JUSTICE (1987); JUDITH SHKLAR, AMERICAN CITIZENSHIP: THE QUEST FOR INCLUSION 64 (1991).

Lawyers often deal with disputes that are manifestations of these underlying conflicts. Landlord-tenant disputes over unsafe conditions and withheld rent, employer-employee disputes over hiring and promotion decisions, disputes between cell phone manufacturers over proprietary design features, and disputes regarding the prosecution and punishment of criminal acts are all manifestations of some underlying conflict.

NOTES AND QUESTIONS

1.   Disputes are not the only manifestations of conflict. In an organization, for example, conflict can be manifested in a variety of other ways, including unhealthy competition, inefficiency or a lack of productivity, low morale, and withholding knowledge. CATHY A. COSTANTINO & CHRISTINA SICKLES MERCHANT, DESIGNING CONFLICT MANAGEMENT SYSTEMS: A GUIDE TO CREATING PRODUCTIVE AND HEALTHY ORGANIZATIONS 5–6 (1996). What other indicia or manifestations of unresolved conflict have you experienced that might be added to this list?

2.   People often view conflict as undesirable. But clearly that is not always the case. For example, many would say that the desegregation of public schools ordered by the U.S. Supreme Court in *Brown v. Board of Education,* 349 U.S. 294, 75 S.Ct. 753, 99 L.Ed. 1083 (1955), elevated

American society with respect to race relations. Conflict theorists, such as Morton Deutsch and Lewis Coser, often distinguish between constructive and destructive conflict. *See generally* LEWIS COSER, FUNCTIONS OF SOCIAL CONFLICT (1954); MORTON DEUTSCH, THE RESOLUTION OF CONFLICT: CONSTRUCTIVE AND DESTRUCTIVE PROCESSES (1973). Consider the following:

> As conflict—difference—is here in the world, as we cannot avoid it, we should, I think, use it. Instead of condemning it, we should try to set it to work for us. Why not? What does the mechanical engineer do with friction? Of course his chief job is to eliminate friction, but it is true that he also capitalizes on friction. The transmission of power by belts depends on friction between the belt and the pulley. The friction between the driving wheel of the locomotive and the track is necessary to haul the train. All polishing is done by friction. The music of the violin we get by friction. We left the savage state when we discovered fire by friction. So in business, too, we have to know when to try to capitalize it, when to see what work we can make it do.

Mary Parker Follett, *Constructive Conflict, in* DYNAMIC ADMINISTRATION: THE COLLECTED PAPERS OF MARY PARKER FOLLETT 30–31 (Henry C. Metcalf & L. Urwick eds.) (1940). In your view, what are some of the differences between constructive and destructive conflict? Can you think of a situation in your life in which conflict has been beneficial? Would this result have been possible without the conflict?

b.   An Analytical Approach

The foregoing discussion articulates different ways of understanding the conflict dynamics that lead to specific disputes. In the following passage, Bernard Mayer, a well-known mediator and scholar, suggests that people experience conflict in different ways, all of which are important to the ultimate resolution of conflict.

BERNARD MAYER, THE DYNAMICS OF CONFLICT
RESOLUTION: A PRACTITIONER'S GUIDE
4–5 (2000)

Conflict may be viewed as occurring along cognitive (perception), emotional (feeling), and behavioral (action) dimensions. This three-dimensional perspective can help us understand the complexities of conflict and why a conflict sometimes seems to proceed in contrary directions.

Conflict as Perception

As a set of perceptions, conflict is a belief or understanding that one's own needs, interests, wants, or values are incompatible with someone else's. There are both objective and subjective elements to this cognitive dimension. If I want to develop a tract of land into a shopping center, and you want to preserve it as open space, then there is an objective incompatibility in our wants. If I believe that the way you desire to guide our son's educational development is incompatible with my philosophy of parenting, then there is at least a significant subjective component. What if only one of us believes an incompatibility to exist, are we still in conflict? As a practical matter, I think it useful to think of conflict as existing if at least one person believes it to exist. If I believe us to have incompatible interests, and act accordingly, then I am engaging you in a conflict process whether you share this perception or not.

Conflict as Feeling

Conflict also involves an emotional reaction to a situation or interaction that signals a disagreement of some kind. The emotions felt might be fear, sadness, bitterness, anger, or hopelessness, or some amalgam of these. If we experience these feelings in regard to another person or situation, we feel that we are in conflict—and therefore we are. As a mediator, I have sometimes seen people behave as if they were in great disagreement over profound issues, yet I have not been able to ascertain exactly what they disagreed about. Nonetheless, they were in conflict because they felt they were. And in conflicts, it does not take two to tango. Often a conflict exists because one person feels in conflict with another, even though those feelings are not reciprocated by or even known to the other person. The behavioral component may be minimal, but the conflict is still very real to the person experiencing the feelings.

Conflict as Action

Conflict also consists of the actions that we take to express our feelings, articulate our perceptions, and get his or her needs met in a way that has the potential for interfering with someone else's ability to get our needs met. This conflict behavior may involve a direct attempt to make something happen at someone else's expense. It may be an exercise of power. It may be violent. It may be destructive. Conversely, this behavior may be conciliatory, constructive, and friendly. But, whatever its tone, the purpose of the conflict behavior is either to express the conflict or to get one's needs met. Again, the question of reciprocity exists. If you write letters to the editor, sign petitions, and consult lawyers to stop my shopping center, and I do not even know you exist, are we in conflict? Can you be in conflict with me if I am not in conflict with you? Theory aside, I think the practical answer to both of these questions is yes.

NOTES AND QUESTIONS

1.   Mayer argues that "the dimensions of *resolution* parallel the dimensions of conflict. The process of resolution occurs along cognitive, emotional, and behavioral dimensions." In other words, cognitive resolution turns on a disputant's perceptions and beliefs about a conflict, emotional

resolution turns on the nature and intensity of the disputants' feelings about the conflict, and behavioral resolution has to do with the extent to which the disputants have "discontinue[d] the conflict behavior and . . . institut[ed] actions to promote resolution." Mayer argues that "[f]ull resolution of conflict only occurs when there is a resolution along all three dimensions: cognitive, emotional, and behavioral. But . . . sometimes disputants are happy to call a conflict resolved when they have achieved significant resolution on one or two dimensions." BERNARD MAYER, THE DYNAMICS OF CONFLICT RESOLUTION 98–108 (2000) (emphasis added).

2.   Think of a dispute in which you have been involved—with a friend, relative, co-worker, teacher, or anyone else. Using Mayer's framework, see whether you can discern behavioral, cognitive, and emotional dimensions. In other words, what behaviors, thoughts, and emotions affected the development and evolution of the conflict? Did all parties experience the three dimensions similarly?

3.   A deeper understanding of conflict is particularly helpful for attorneys in their roles as client counselors. Do you think lawyers can be effective in exploring all three dimensions with their clients? What dimensions, if any, may be best addressed through litigation? Which dimensions are ordinarily discussed in traditional law school courses? How might a lawyer counsel a client to address the other issues?

2.   THE LIFE CYCLE OF A DISPUTE

Dispute resolution scholars have identified what may be described as a life cycle of disputes. Disputes begin with some divergence between the interests, aspirations, preferences, and desires of two or more parties—a "perceived injurious event." Many perceived injurious events are minor and simply brushed aside as part of the normal wear and tear of social life. Some, however, are deemed to be more significant, worthy of recognizing (naming), assigning fault (blaming), and sometimes even seeking recompense (claiming). William L. F. Felstiner, Richard L. Abel & Austin Sarat, *The Emergence and Transformation of Disputes: Naming, Blaming, Claiming . . .* , 15 Law & Soc'y Rev. 631 (1981). Some of these perceived injurious events may be resolved informally, through avoidance, discussion, or negotiation. Others, however, may lead to a more formalized dispute resolution process, such as the assertion of a grievance or the initiation of a lawsuit. There are far more perceived injurious events than there are formalized disputes and even fewer disputes persist into later stages of the process.

Disputes may either escalate or stabilize, in whole or in part, depending upon a wide array of conditions, such as the parties' tactics and responses during the dispute, the level of trust between the parties, and group and social norms that may affect the conflict. DEAN G. PRUITT & SUNG HEE KIM, SOCIAL CONFLICT: ESCALATION, STALEMATE, AND

SETTLEMENT 121–151 (3d ed. 2004). When a dispute escalates, it is likely to entail a greater commitment of resources (including time and money), more confrontational tactics, and involve more issues and participants. Skillful lawyers manage both conflict and disputes effectively by working with each of these dimensions of expansion to prevent the inappropriate escalation or persistence of conflict.

A Dispute Pyramid: The General Pattern
No. per 1000 Grievances

Court Filings	50
Lawyers	103
Disputes	449
Claims	718
Grievances	1000

Richard Miller & Austin Sarat, *Grievances, Claims and Disputes: Assessing the Adversary Culture*, 15 Law & Soc'y Rev. 524, 544 (1980–81).

Lawyers, however, often get involved in disputes well after a dispute has formalized and escalated. While escalation can and should still be managed, the emphasis at the point of attorney intervention often shifts to how the dispute may be resolved. Lawyers may also be involved before a particular dispute has formalized as they attempt to help clients prevent and plan for managing future disputes. The primary methods for resolving disputes may be seen as falling on a continuum that is based on who will determine the outcome of the dispute. At one end of the continuum are *adjudicatory* methods, in which a third party decides how to resolve the dispute. At the other end of the continuum are *consensual* methods of dispute resolution, in which the parties resolve the disputes themselves. Such a continuum might look like this:

Dispute Resolution Continuum

Consensual Processes   *Adjudicatory Processes*

negotiation   mediation   arbitration   trial

Trial as a dispute resolution method is the focus of much of the law school experience. But trial has never been the only method for resolving disputes and recent empirical studies indicate that the proportion of cases resolved by trial has decreased significantly in the second half of the twentieth century—a phenomenon now known as the "vanishing trial." Marc Galanter, *The Vanishing Trial: An Examination of Trials and Related Matters in State and Federal Courts*, 1 J. Empirical Legal Stud. 459 (2004). This book emphasizes other processes for resolving disputes.

B. AN INTRODUCTION TO PROCESSES FOR RESOLVING DISPUTES

The "ADR movement" that began in the late 1970s has been one of the most significant developments in American law and practice in recent history.* Much of the initial energy and innovation came from non-lawyers, who created a variety of dispute-resolution vehicles in which lawyers play a minor role or none at all. As the movement took root, the legal community became active, too, with leadership from all three branches of the federal government, presidents of the American Bar Association, and state and local bar groups. Lawyers for large corporations have also been especially active, as has the criminal bar.

Five motives, often intermingled, spark most of the interest in alternatives to traditional litigation: 1. saving time and money, and possibly rescuing an overloaded judicial system; 2. using "better" processes—more open, flexible and responsive to the unique needs of the participants; 3. achieving "better" results—outcomes that serve the real needs of the participants or society; 4. enhancing community involvement in the dispute resolution process; and 5. broadening access to "justice." A sixth motive, sometimes subconscious, is to protect turf for oneself, an institution, or a profession.

These motives are intricately intertwined for most people who are involved in dispute resolution and, when squared with other professional values and responsibilities, can make lawyers, judges, and others involved in dispute resolution deeply ambivalent. The judge who considers annexing a dispute resolution program to speed up case processing, for instance, may be compelled in part by a perception that the public will not long tolerate extensive delays without imposing changes upon the courts. Her concern about judicial overload may be mixed with desire to protect the court's authority. She may also appreciate that informal processes outside the courts have reduced the court's caseload, have sometimes been more satisfying to participants, and have yielded results better suited to their needs. Yet her enthusiasm for informal processes on all these counts may be tempered by a belief in the importance of courts as articulators of public policy and as guarantors of public and private rights. Lawyers and their clients may experience similarly mixed motives and feelings.

Brief descriptions of the major methods of dispute processing are set forth below. We begin with the "primary processes"—adjudicative and

---

* For a discussion of previous periods of strong interest in "informal justice," see JEROLD S. AUERBACH, JUSTICE WITHOUT LAW? RESOLVING DISPUTES WITHOUT LAWYERS (1983). For a discussion of the use of arbitration, mediation, and negotiation in Anglo–Saxon England during the earliest stages of English legal history, see Valerie A. Sanchez, *Towards a History of ADR: The Dispute Processing Continuum in Anglo–Saxon England and Today*, 11 OHIO ST. J. ON DISP. RESOL. 1 (1996).

consensual—and then describe "mixed processes," which combine features of the primary processes. We exclude other important forms of dispute processing such as voting, fighting, and avoidance. As we will see as we learn more about each process, there are many variants of each process and processes that are analytically distinct can, in particular cases, operate almost identically in practice. Thus, a small claims court judge, who has authority to impose a solution, may in fact seek to facilitate an agreement between the parties and then announce it as his decision. Some arbitrators do the same. Lawyers representing individuals are sometimes said to "mediate" when they seek a negotiated solution. And there are mediators who, in effect, impose a solution through the force of their own convictions or techniques or because of the power they exercise outside the mediation. In addition, within almost any institution that deals with disputes, many different dispute resolution processes are employed. Despite these tendencies, and perhaps because of them, it is important to understand and maintain these basic distinctions among the processes.

1. ADJUDICATIVE PROCESSES

Court and Administrative Adjudication

Adjudication, the most familiar process to lawyers, features a third party with power to impose a solution upon the disputants, such as in public trials and appeals in courts and in administrative adjudication by government agencies. Adjudication usually produces a "win/lose" result. Parties have the opportunity to present evidence and arguments, and usually do so through representatives, ordinarily lawyers.

Arbitration

In arbitration, the parties at least theoretically agree to submit their dispute to a neutral party whom they have selected to make a decision—a decision that may be either binding or nonbinding. Arbitration is used extensively in industrial labor relations and in commercial and consumer disputes. The parties can select an arbitrator with background and experience suitable for dealing with the particular issues in dispute. Because the parties can customize the proceedings to suit their needs, arbitration has the potential to be less formal, faster, and less expensive than the judicial process. The parties can agree that less importance be given to following or establishing precedent and more importance be given to other factors, such as community, industry, or workplace norms or expectations. We devote Chapter V to a fuller consideration of the arbitration process.

Private Tribunals

In some jurisdictions, statutes or rules of court permit a court to refer cases to privately selected and paid third-party neutrals ("rent-a-judge").

The private judge's decision is entered as the judgment of the court. Therefore, unlike an arbitrator's award, a judgment entered by a private judge may be appealed. The parties voluntarily submit to such tribunals in order to select their own decision maker, or in the hope of eliminating delay or gaining the ability to exclude the public from the proceedings. For further discussion, see Chapter VI, beginning at p. 852.

2. CONSENSUAL PROCESSES

Negotiation

In negotiation, parties seek to resolve a disagreement or plan a transaction through discussions conducted by the parties themselves or through representatives. Much negotiation in law practice, particularly negotiation involved in resolving disputes, is based on adversarial or value distributing assumptions—that is, that the purpose of the negotiation is to divide a limited resource. Since the early 1980s, however, scholars have argued that problem-solving or value-creating approaches to negotiation, long-used in putting together business deals and other transactions, can and should be applied to dispute resolution. These problem-solving approaches, which emphasize the underlying interests and concerns of the parties, make up an important part of this book. We explore negotiation in great detail in Chapter III.

Mediation

Mediation is an informal process in which an impartial third party helps the parties to resolve a dispute or plan a transaction but does not impose a solution. In other words, mediation is facilitated negotiation. The parties often enter into mediation voluntarily, but many courts have programs that require parties to mediate before proceeding to trial. The desired result is an agreement uniquely suited to the needs and interests of the parties. Normally the agreement is expressed in a contract or release and is enforceable according to the rules of contract law. Apart from negotiation, mediation has come to be the predominant alternative method of dispute resolution. We address it comprehensively in Chapter IV.

Conciliation

The term "conciliation" is sometimes used interchangeably with "mediation," particularly in international settings. But it also has other meanings. For example, when the federal Equal Employment Opportunity Commission determines that an employer has engaged in a prohibited practice, it frequently recommends that the employer and the affected employee or employees meet informally to try to resolve their differences. Sometimes those conciliations involve a third party mediator, thus taking the form of a mediation. But they can also involve just the parties, in which case the process more resembles a negotiation. Most broadly, conciliation generally refers to a less formal consensual process (e.g., where the neutral acts as a "go-between") or to a less active role for the neutral.

3. MIXED PROCESSES

Disputing parties frequently use so-called mixed processes, which combine elements of more than one of the primary dispute resolution process. The following are the most common forms of mixed processes, and are considered more fully in Chapter VI.

Mediation–Arbitration

"Med-arb" begins as mediation. If the parties do not reach an agreement, they proceed to arbitration, which may be performed either by the mediator or by another neutral. This process is commonly used in arenas such as labor-management relations and commercial disputes.

Arbitration–Mediation

"Arb-med" begins as arbitration, but converts to mediation after the presentation of evidence to the arbitrator. The arbitrator makes and records a decision, which is withheld from the parties while they attempt to mediate the dispute. If the parties reach a settlement, the arbitrator's decision is not disclosed to the parties. If the parties do not settle, the arbitrator's award is disclosed to and binding upon the parties.

Mediation–Arbitration

"Med-arb" begins as mediation. If the parties do not reach an agreement, they proceed to arbitration, which may be performed either by the mediator or by another neutral. This process is commonly used in arenas such as labor-management relations and commercial disputes.

Arbitration–Mediation

"Arb-med" begins as arbitration, but converts to mediation after the presentation of evidence to the arbitrator. The arbitrator makes and records a decision, which is withheld from the parties while they attempt to mediate the dispute. If the parties reach a settlement, the arbitrator's decision is not disclosed to the parties. If the parties do not settle, the arbitrator's award is disclosed to and binding upon the parties.

Mediation–Arbitration

"Med-arb" begins as mediation. If the parties do not reach an agreement, they proceed to arbitration, which may be performed either by the mediator or by another neutral. This process is commonly used in arenas such as labor-management relations and commercial disputes.

The Primary Dispute Resolution Processes*

	Court	Arbitration	Mediation	Negotiation
Nature	Formal adversarial hearings	Informal adversarial hearings	Informal meetings with parties or representatives and third party neutral	Informal meetings with parties or representatives
Decision Maker	Judge or jury	Arbitrator	Parties	Parties
Third Party Role	Decide based on application of law to facts	Decide based on terms of agreement to arbitrate	Facilitate negotiation between parties	NA
Basis for Decision	Law	Standards provided by arbitration agreement— e.g. industry practices	Interests or positions of parties	Interests or positions of parties
Desired Result	Reasoned decision	Award	Settlement agreement	Settlement agreement
Confidential	Generally no	Generally yes	Generally yes	Generally yes
Binding	Yes. Court decree	Yes. Confirmation of arbitration award	Yes. Settlement agreement enforced as a contract	Yes. Settlement agreement enforced as a contract
Appeal	Yes.	Generally no substantive review	NA	NA

* Note: This chart presents a simple overview of the primary dispute resolution processes. As we will see throughout the book, in actual practice there are many variations and nuances in the characteristics described above.

Arbitration–Mediation

"Arb-med" begins as arbitration, but converts to mediation after the presentation of evidence to the arbitrator. The arbitrator makes and records a decision, which is withheld from the parties while they attempt to mediate the dispute. If the parties reach a settlement, the arbitrator's decision is not disclosed to the parties. If the parties do not settle, the arbitrator's award is disclosed to and binding upon the parties.

Mini-trial

"Mini-trials," or "structured settlement negotiations," refer to specially designed processes to resolve complex business disputes that would otherwise be the subject of protracted litigation. In the most common model, lawyers for both sides present their cases in abbreviated form to a panel composed of decision-making executives of the two organizations and a neutral advisor, who usually is a lawyer with expertise in relevant areas of law. Next, the executives retire to negotiate a settlement, with or without the neutral advisor. The neutral advisor may kick off these negotiations by giving her opinion about what would happen if the matter were litigated, or she may provide her opinion only if the principals fail to reach an agreement.

The mini-trial was a popular form of ADR in the early 1990s, but is costly and cumbersome, and has been less common more recently as mediation and other processes have become more popular.

Summary Jury Trial

Summary jury trial is an adaptation of some mini-trial concepts to cases that would be tried before a jury. Lawyers give brief presentations of their cases to a jury that has no authority, but whose members are drawn from the same pool as real jurors. The jury's nonbinding verdict helps the parties better understand their cases and, thus, facilitates settlement. Like the mini-trial, the summary jury trial's popularity has waned since the early 1990s in favor of mediation and other processes. For more detail, see Thomas D. Lambros, *The Summary Jury Trial and Other Methods of Alternative Dispute Resolution*, 103 F.R.D. 461 (1984).

Early Neutral Evaluation

Early neutral evaluation (ENE) seeks to reduce pretrial costs and delay by requiring the parties to confront the strengths and weaknesses of their cases at an early stage. A neutral identifies issues on which the parties agree and disagree and provides an evaluation of each side's case. The neutral may predict the probable outcome if the case were to go to trial and estimate a range of likely damages if the plaintiff were to win. The neutral may also offer to assist the parties in settlement discussions. ENE combines elements of mediation and nonbinding arbitration. For a discussion of the relationship between ENE and mediation, see Wayne D.

Brazil, *Early Neutral Evaluation or Mediation? When Might ENE Deliver More Value?*, 14 Disp. Resol. Mag. 10 (2007).

Fact-finding

In this process, a neutral makes findings on contested issues of fact, such as the valuation of property. This can aid in negotiation, mediation, or adjudication.

Ombuds

An ombuds is an official, appointed by a public or private institution, whose job is to receive complaints and either prevent disputes or facilitate their resolution within that institution. Methods include investigating, publicizing, and recommending. Although ombuds sometimes mediate or perform other dispute resolution functions, the more classic model involves assisting complainants, directing them to other processes that might be appropriate.

C. WHAT PROCESS IS APPROPRIATE? THE GREAT DEBATE OVER SETTLEMENT AND ADR

The real value of understanding the nature of conflict and disputes and the methods by which they may be addressed is that such understanding can inform the selection of the most appropriate method for resolving a particular dispute. The classic work is Frank E.A. Sander & Stephen B. Goldberg, *Fitting the Forum to the Fuss: A User–Friendly Guide for Selecting an ADR Procedure*, 10 Negot. J. 49 (1994). The title sums up a proposition that may seem simple at first blush, but it raises deep and fundamental questions. How do we determine which method of resolution is appropriate for a particular dispute? Who should decide? What interests does society have in the resolution of disputes, particularly those between seemingly private disputants? What should be the relationship between "litigation" and "ADR"?

Further complicating these questions is the fact that one can approach dispute resolution from any number of perspectives: those of the client, of individual lawyers, of the legal profession, of courts, and of society in general. Yet these are not distinct, unified perspectives. Every case, every client, and every judge is unique. While bar associations, for example, may adopt positions, individual lawyers have widely divergent opinions. Each dispute resolution process promotes and threatens different values or interests, and attitudes about each process depend, in part, on where one sits. The fact that each process includes many variations adds a further complication.

In this section, we focus on macro-level questions raised by the "great settlement debate" and the institutionalization of ADR. Should disputes be resolved by settlement or through litigation? What kinds of cases, should move through which kinds of processes? As you read the pieces in this section, recall the principal goals that seem to motivate people who are interested in ADR. What seems to animate these authors?

ADR evokes a wide range of views on its desirability and the extent to which it is justified. Some, for example, might believe ADR is generally inappropriate when there is a public system of law available, while others might favor the use of alternative methods of dispute resolution as the first option. The issues and concerns that arise from this debate resonate throughout the many policy issues affecting ADR.

1. THE STRONG VIEW

OWEN M. FISS, AGAINST SETTLEMENT
93 Yale L.J. 1073, 1075–78, 1082–90 (1984)

The advocates of ADR are led to . . . exalt the idea of settlement more generally because they view adjudication as a process to resolve disputes. They act as though courts arose to resolve quarrels between neighbors who had reached an impasse and turned to a stranger for help. Courts are seen as an institutionalization of the stranger and adjudication is viewed as the process by which the stranger exercises power. The very fact that the neighbors have turned to someone else to resolve their dispute signifies a breakdown in their social relations; the advocates of ADR acknowledge this, but nonetheless hope that the neighbors will be able to reach agreement before the stranger renders judgment. Settlement is that agreement. It is a truce more than a true reconciliation, but it seems preferable to judgment because it rests on the consent of both parties and avoids the cost of a lengthy trial.

In my view, however, this account of adjudication and the case for settlement rest on questionable premises. I do not believe that settlement as a generic practice is preferable to judgment or should be institutionalized on a wholesale and indiscriminate basis. It should be treated instead as a highly problematic technique for streamlining dockets. Settlement is for me the civil analogue of plea bargaining: Consent is often coerced; the bargain may be struck by someone without authority; the absence of a trial and judgment renders subsequent judicial involvement troublesome; and although dockets are trimmed, justice may not be done. Like plea bargaining, settlement is a capitulation to the conditions of mass society and should be neither encouraged nor praised.

THE IMBALANCE OF POWER

By viewing the lawsuit as a quarrel between two neighbors, the dispute-resolution story that underlies ADR implicitly asks us to assume a rough equality between the contending parties. It treats settlement as the anticipation of the outcome of trial and assumes that the terms of settlement are simply a product of the parties' predictions of that outcome. In truth, however, settlement is also a function of the resources available to each party to finance the litigation, and those resources are frequently distributed unequally. Many lawsuits do not involve a property dispute between two neighbors, or between AT&T and the government (to update the story), but rather concern a struggle between a member of a racial minority and a municipal police department over alleged brutality, or a claim by a worker against a large corporation over work-related injuries. In these cases, the distribution of financial resources, or the ability of one party to pass along its costs, will invariably infect the bargaining process, and the settlement will be at odds with a conception of justice that seeks to make the wealth of the parties irrelevant.

The disparities in resources between the parties can influence the settlement in three ways. First, the poorer party may be less able to amass and analyze the information needed to predict the outcome of the litigation, and thus be disadvantaged in the bargaining process. Second, he may need the damages he seeks immediately and thus be induced to settle as a way of accelerating payment, even though he realizes he would get less now than he might if he awaited judgment. All plaintiffs want their damages immediately, but an indigent plaintiff may be exploited by a rich defendant because his need is so great that the defendant can force him to accept a sum that is less than the ordinary present value of the judgment. Third, the poorer party might be forced to settle because he does not have the resources to finance the litigation, to cover either his own projected expenses, such as his lawyer's time, or the expenses his opponent can impose through the manipulation of procedural mechanisms such as discovery. It might seem that settlement benefits the plaintiff by allowing him to avoid the costs of litigation, but this is not so. The defendant can anticipate the plaintiff's costs if the case were to be tried fully and decrease his offer by that amount. The indigent plaintiff is a victim of the costs of litigation even if he settles.

* * *

Of course, imbalances of power can distort judgment as well: Resources influence the quality of presentation, which in turn has an important bearing on who wins and the terms of victory. We count, however, on the guiding presence of the judge, who can employ a number of measures to lessen the impact of distributional inequalities. He can, for example, supplement the parties' presentations by asking questions, calling his own witnesses, and inviting other persons and institutions to participate as amici. These measures are likely to make only a small contribution toward moderating the influence of distributional inequalities, but should not be ignored for that reason. Not even these small steps are possible with settlement. There is, moreover, a critical difference between a process like settlement, which is based on bargaining and accepts inequalities of wealth as an integral and legitimate component of the process, and a process like judgment, which knowingly struggles against those inequalities. Judgment aspires to an autonomy from distributional inequalities, and it gathers much of its appeal from this aspiration.

THE ABSENCE OF AUTHORITATIVE CONSENT

The argument for settlement presupposes that the contestants are individuals. These individuals speak for themselves and should be bound by the rules they generate. In many situations, however, individuals are ensnared in contractual relationships that impair their autonomy: Lawyers or insurance companies might, for example, agree to settlements that are in their interests but are not in the best interests of their clients, and to which their clients would not agree if the choice were still theirs. But a deeper and more intractable problem arises from the fact that many parties are not individuals but rather organizations or groups. We do not know who is entitled to speak for these entities and to give the consent upon which so much of the appeal of settlement depends.

* * *

THE LACK OF A FOUNDATION FOR CONTINUING
JUDICIAL INVOLVEMENT

The dispute-resolution story trivializes the remedial dimensions of lawsuits and mistakenly assumes judgment to be the end of the process. It supposes that the judge's duty is to declare which neighbor is right and which wrong, and that this declaration will end the judge's involvement (save in that most exceptional situation where it is also necessary for him to issue a writ directing the sheriff to execute the declaration). Under these assumptions, settlement appears as an almost perfect substitute for judgment, for it too can declare the parties' rights. Often, however, judgment is not the end of a lawsuit but only the beginning. The involvement of the court may continue almost indefinitely. In these cases, settlement cannot provide an adequate basis for that necessary continuing involvement, and thus is no substitute for judgment.

The parties may sometimes be locked in combat with one another and view the lawsuit as only one phase in a long continuing struggle. The entry of judgment will then not end the struggle, but rather change its terms and the balance of power. One of the parties will invariably return to the court and again ask for its assistance, not so much because conditions have changed, but because the conditions that preceded the lawsuit have unfortunately not changed. This often occurs in domestic-relations cases, where the divorce decree represents only the opening salvo in an endless series of skirmishes over custody and support.

The structural reform cases that play such a prominent role on the federal docket provide another occasion for continuing judicial involvement. In these cases, courts seek to safeguard public values by restructuring large-scale bureaucratic organizations. The task is enormous, and our knowledge of how to restructure on-going bureaucratic organizations is limited. As a consequence, courts must oversee and manage the remedial process for a long time—maybe forever. This, I fear, is true of most school desegregation cases, some of which have been pending for twenty or thirty years. It is also true of antitrust cases that seek divestiture or reorganization of an industry.

* * *

Settlement also impedes vigorous enforcement, which sometimes requires use of the contempt power. As a formal matter, contempt is available to punish violations of a consent decree. But courts hesitate to use that power to enforce decrees that rest solely on consent, especially when enforcement is aimed at high public officials, as became evident in the Willowbrook deinstitutionalization case and the recent Chicago desegregation case. Courts do not see a mere bargain between the parties as a sufficient foundation for the exercise of their coercive powers.

* * *

JUSTICE RATHER THAN PEACE

The dispute-resolution story makes settlement appear as a perfect substitute for judgment, as we just saw, by trivializing the remedial dimensions of a lawsuit, and also by reducing the social function of the lawsuit to one of resolving private disputes: In that story, settlement appears to achieve exactly the same purpose as judgment—peace between the parties—but at considerably less expense to society. The two quarreling neighbors turn to a court in order to resolve their dispute, and society makes courts available because it wants to aid in the achievement of their private ends or to secure the peace.

In my view, however, the purpose of adjudication should be understood in broader terms. Adjudication uses public resources, and employs not strangers chosen by the parties but public officials chosen by a process in which the public participates. These officials, like members of the legislative and executive branches, possess a power that has been defined and conferred by public law, not by private agreement. Their job is not to maximize the ends of private parties, nor simply to secure the peace, but to explicate and give force to the values embodied in authoritative texts such as the Constitution and statutes: to interpret those values and to bring reality into accord with them. This duty is not discharged when the parties settle.

In our political system, courts are reactive institutions. They do not search out interpretive occasions, but instead wait for others to bring matters to their attention. They also rely for the most part on others to investigate and present the law and facts. A settlement will thereby deprive a court of the occasion, and perhaps even the ability, to render an interpretation. A court cannot proceed (or not proceed very far) in the face of a settlement. To be against settlement is not to urge that parties be "forced" to litigate, since that would interfere with their autonomy and distort the adjudicative process; the parties will be inclined to make the court believe that their bargain is justice. To be against settlement is only to suggest that when the parties settle, society gets less than what appears, and for a price it does not know it is paying. Parties might settle while leaving justice undone. The settlement of a school suit might secure the peace, but not racial equality. Although the parties are prepared to live under the terms they bargained for, and although such peaceful coexistence may be a necessary precondition of justice, and itself a state of affairs to be valued, it is not justice itself. To settle for something means to accept less than some ideal.

* * *

THE REAL DIVIDE

To all this, one can readily imagine a simple response by way of confession and avoidance: We are not talking about *those* lawsuits. Advocates of ADR might insist that my account of adjudication, in contrast to the one implied by the dispute-resolution story, focuses on a rather narrow category of lawsuits. They could argue that while settlement may have only the most limited appeal with respect to those cases, I have not spoken to the "typical" case. My response is twofold.

First, even as a purely quantitative matter, I doubt that the number of cases I am referring to is trivial. My universe includes those cases in which there are significant distributional inequalities; those in which it is difficult to generate authoritative consent because organizations or social groups are parties or because the power to settle is vested in autonomous agents; those in which the court must continue to supervise the parties after judgment; and those in which justice needs to be done, or to put it more modestly, where there is a genuine social need for an authoritative interpretation of law. I imagine that the number of cases that satisfy one of these four criteria is considerable; in contrast to the kind of case portrayed in the dispute-resolution story, they probably dominate the docket of a modern court system.

Second, it demands a certain kind of myopia to be concerned only with the number of cases, as though all cases are equal simply because the clerk of the court assigns each a single docket number. All cases are not equal. The Los Angeles desegregation case, to take one example, is not equal to the allegedly more typical suit involving a property dispute or an automobile accident. The desegregation suit consumes more resources, affects more people, and provokes far greater challenges to the judicial power. The settlement movement must introduce a qualitative perspective; it must speak to these more "significant" cases, and demonstrate the propriety of settling them. Otherwise it will soon be seen as an irrelevance, dealing with trivia rather than responding to the very conditions that give the movement its greatest sway and saliency.

Nor would sorting cases into "two tracks," one for settlement, and another for judgment, avoid my objections. Settling automobile cases and leaving discrimination or antitrust cases for judgment might remove a large number of cases from the dockets, but the dockets will nevertheless remain burdened with the cases that consume the most judicial resources and represent the most controversial exercises of the judicial power. A "two track" strategy would drain the argument for settlement of much of its appeal. I also doubt whether the "two track" strategy can be sensibly implemented. It is impossible to formulate adequate criteria for prospectively sorting cases.

* * *

Civil litigation is an institutional arrangement for using state power to bring a recalcitrant reality closer to our chosen ideals. We turn to the courts because we need to, not because of some quirk in our personalities. We train our students in the tougher arts so that they may help secure all that the law promises, not because we want them to become gladiators or because we take a special pleasure in combat.

To conceive of the civil lawsuit in public terms as America does might be unique. I am willing to assume that no other country . . . has a case like *Brown v. Board of Education* in which the judicial power is used to eradicate the caste structure. I am willing to assume that no other country conceives of law and uses law in quite the way we do. But this should be a source of pride rather than shame. What is unique is not the problem that we live short of our ideals, but that we alone among the nations of the world seem willing to do something about it. Adjudication American-style is not a reflection of our combativeness but rather a tribute to our inventiveness and perhaps even more to our commitment.

2. THE RESPONSES

Fiss's powerful article, which articulates concerns about settlement and alternative methods of dispute resolution that continue to be felt throughout the legal community, drew a generation of responses. The following excerpt, for example, takes on a core component of Fiss's argument: that settlement is inappropriate because of the public's overriding interest in the resolution of private disputes for purposes of shaping future behavior. Other responses follow in the notes and questions.

CARRIE MENKEL–MEADOW, WHOSE DISPUTE IS IT ANYWAY?: A PHILOSOPHICAL AND DEMOCRATIC DEFENSE OF SETTLEMENT (IN SOME CASES)

83 Geo. L.J. 2663, 2663–71, 2692 (1995)

In the last decade or so, a polarized debate about how disputes should be resolved has demonstrated to me once again the difficulties of simplistic and adversarial arguments. Owen Fiss has argued "Against Settlement"; Trina Grillo and others have argued against mediation (in divorce cases and other family matters involving women); Richard Delgado and others have questioned whether informal processes are unfair to disempowered and subordinated groups; Judith Resnik has criticized the (federal) courts' unwillingness to do their basic job of adjudication; Stephen Yeazell has suggested that too much settlement localizes, decentralizes, and delegalizes dispute resolution and the making of public law; Kevin C. McMunigal has argued that too much settlement will make bad advocates; and David Luban and Jules Coleman, among other philosophers, have criticized the moral value of the compromises that are thought to constitute legal settlements. On the other side, vigorous proponents of alternative dispute resolution, including negotiation, mediation, arbitration, and various hybrids of these forms of preadjudication settlement, criticize the economic and emotional waste of adversarial processes and the cost, inefficiency, and political difficulties of adjudication, as well as its draconian unfairness in some cases.

In my view, this debate, while useful for explicitly framing the underlying values that support our legal system, has not effectively dealt with the realities of modern legal, political, and personal disputes. For me, the question is not "for or against" settlement (since settlement has become the "norm" for our system), but *when, how, and under what circumstances* should cases be settled? When do our legal system, our citizenry, and the parties in particular disputes need formal legal adjudication, and when are their respective interests served by settlement, *whether public or private?*

* * *

The difficulty with the debate about settlement vs. adjudication is that there are many more than two processes, as well as other variables that affect the processes, to consider. The diverse interests of the participants in the dispute, the legal system, and society may not be the same. Issues of fairness, legitimacy, economic efficiency, privacy, publicity, emotional catharsis or empathy, access, equity among disputants, and lawmaking may differ in importance for different actors in the system, and they may vary by case—this is the strength of our common law system.

* * *

[H]ow can we decide which settlements to be for and which to be against? In other words, how can we tell good settlements from bad ones, and when should we prefer adjudication to settlement? Like others who have written on this subject, both recently and in the past, I do not think there are easy answers to this question; but more problematically, I want to suggest that it will be very difficult for us to specify in advance criteria for allocation to particular processes. In the words of current academic cachet, much depends on the context—of disputes, of disputants, and of the system being considered. I will here complexify and problematize Luban's seemingly easy proposition—that democratic discourse requires full disclosure of legal dispute information. In this essay, I will make a case for settlement by arguing that there are philosophical, as well as instrumental, democratic, ethical, and human justifications for settlements (at least in some cases).

Those who criticize settlement suffer from what I have called, in other contexts, "litigation romanticism," with empirically unverified assumptions about what courts can or will do. More important, those who privilege adjudication focus almost exclusively on structural and institutional values and often give short shrift to those who are actually involved in the litigation. I fear, but am not sure, that this debate can be reduced to those who care more about the people actually engaged in disputes versus those who care more about institutional and structural arrangements. I prefer to think that we need both adjudication and settlement. These processes can affect each other in positive, as well as negative ways, but in my view, settlement should not be seen as "second best" or "worst case" when adjudication fails. Settlement can be justified on its own moral grounds—there are important values, consistent with the fundamental values of our legal and political systems that support the legitimacy of settlements of some, if not most, legal disputes. These values include consent, participation, empowerment, dignity, respect, empathy and emotional catharsis, privacy, efficiency, quality solutions, equity, access, and yes, even justice.

Though some have argued that compromise itself can be morally justified, I will here argue, as well, that compromise is not always necessary for settlement and that in fact, some settlements, by not requiring compromise, may produce better solutions than litigation. In particular, my own arguments for settlements (of particular kinds) have been often misstated or oversimplified, for the purpose of argument, so that they begin to strike me as strawpersons and cause me to question whether we are really able to understand each other when we "sharpen" the argument by "narrowing" it.

To summarize, it seems to me that the key questions implicated in the ongoing debate about settlement vs. adjudication are:

1. In a party-initiated legal system, when is it legitimate for the parties to settle their dispute themselves, or with what assistance from a court in which they have sought some legal-system support or service?

2. When is "consent" to a settlement legitimate and "real," and by what standards should we (courts and academic critics) judge and permit such consent?

3. When, in a party-initiated legal system, should party consent be "trumped" by other values—in other words, when should public, institutional, and structural needs and values override parties' desire to settle or courts' incentives to promote settlement? In short, when is the need for "public adjudication" or . . . "public settlement" more important (to whom?) than what the parties may themselves desire?

* * *

I have here tried to make the following arguments on behalf of the "best" aspects of settlement:

1. Settlements that are in fact consensual represent the goals of democratic and party-initiated legal regimes by allowing the parties themselves to choose processes and outcomes for dispute resolution.

2. Settlements permit a broader range of possible solutions that may be more responsive to both party and system needs.

3. What some consider to be the worst of settlement, that is, compromise, may actually represent a moral commitment to equality, precision in justice, accommodation, and peaceful coexistence of conflicting interests.

4. Settlements may be based on important nonlegal principles or interests, which may, in any given case, be as important or more important to the parties than "legal" considerations. Laws made in the aggregate may not always be appropriate in particular cases, and thus settlements can be seen as yet another "principled" supplement to our common law system.

5. Settlement processes may be more humanely "real," democratic, participatory, and cathartic than more formalized processes, permitting in their best moments, transformative and educational opportunities for parties in dispute as well as for others.

6. Some settlement processes may be better adapted for the multiplex, multiparty issues that require solutions in our modern society than the binary form of plaintiff-defendant adjudication.

7. Despite the continuing and important debates about discovery and information exchange in the litigation process, some settlement processes (mediation and some forms of neutral case evaluation and

scheduling) may actually provide both more and better (not just legally relevant) information for problem-solving, as well as "education" of the litigants.

8. When used appropriately, settlement may actually increase access to justice, not only by allowing more disputants to claim in different ways, but also by allowing greater varieties of case resolutions.

NOTES AND QUESTIONS

1.   Do you think Fiss or Menkel–Meadow has the better view? How does one measure and compare the justice provided in adjudication and alternative processes? What does justice mean to you?

2.   Professor Menkel–Meadow responds primarily to Fiss's public realm argument. Jethro Lieberman and James Henry offer several other critiques of Fiss's central thesis, emphasizing the uniqueness of individual cases and contexts, and the reasons for which ADR can be socially desirable in some cases.

* * * One short answer to Fiss is that most ADR proponents make no claim for shunting all, or even most, litigation into alternative forums. The ADR movement of the 1980s does not suppose that every legal dispute has a non-judicial solution. Indeed, the ADR literature recognizes that some types of cases are not suited to resolution outside the courtroom, including in particular cases in which the plaintiff seeks a declaration of law by the court. Fiss overlooks this accepted limitation of ADR because he assumes, at least implicitly, that all cases resemble *Brown v. Board of Education*. But, of course, they do not. It seems obvious that large classes of cases are not so consequential, and do not call for the definitive ruling of a judge or the imprimatur of an official organ of the state. Automobile accidents, uncontested divorces, breaches of contract, and other common types of suits do not cry out to be memorialized in the official reports, and, in any event, most are settled far short of trial.

A second response to Fiss's critique is that his "conspiracy theory" of ADR is dubious. Many people who seek to use ADR are scarcely "powerful" economic interests—ADR is not limited to adoption by Fortune 500 companies. Moreover, ADR does not dispense with community norms. All dispute resolution takes place with an eye toward existing alternatives—including litigation. Finally, the choice to employ ADR is made by parties who have determined that the injustice resulting from delay and the prohibitive costs of pursuing a case through the courts (direct expenditures for lawyers and expenses, as well as significant indirect expenditures, like lost opportunity costs) far outweigh any putative injustice stemming from the decision to forgo judgment by the court.

A third response to Fiss is that not all questions need to be answered. An open society needs the tension of open questions; parties who settle do not thereby foreclose answers at some later time when matters of principle are truly at stake and the issues cannot be compromised. Fiss agrees that avoidance has a value to society, "which sometimes thrives by masking its basic contradictions." He questions, however, whether settlement will result in too much avoidance. But we know of no way to measure the appropriateness of avoidance. Furthermore, Fiss's concern is one-sided. We should be equally concerned to prevent courts from rendering judgment when settlement is more appropriate.

Finally, Fiss's position is seriously weakened by his failure to offer proof that court judgments are more just. He says, for example, that "[a]djudication is more likely to do justice than conversation, mediation, arbitration, settlement, rent-a-judge, mini-trials, community moots or any other contrivance of ADR, precisely because it vests the power of the state in officials who act as trustees for the public, who are highly visible, and who are committed to reason."

Does ADR reach a just result or merely an expedient one? How can one measure the justice of a private settlement? The question is important, but it has not been well discussed in the ADR literature—no doubt because it is so difficult a proposition to test. Whatever the answer, it seems fair to ask the same questions of courts. In theory, courts are committed to reason, but in practice much stands in their way. Some judges are dispassionate and disinterested seekers after justice, but not all are. And all judges are busy; it is a fair assumption that they do not have sufficient time to devote to any single case. Moreover, the maneuvering of partisan lawyers alone is often enough to ensure that justice will *not* be done.

A perhaps more controversial response to Fiss's argument about the quality of outcomes is that in certain important classes of cases—cases involving public institutions like schools, hospitals, and prisons (the very cases that particularly interest Fiss)—courts themselves invoke processes that are firmly lodged in the ADR arsenal. Stories that describe litigation over unconstitutional prison conditions, inhumane mental hospital conditions, and segregated schools frequently depict the judge acting as mediator, helping the parties to negotiate the remedy the court will impose by consent decree. If the courts themselves find these processes useful or even necessary, chances are good that the same processes can be as beneficial when invoked outside the courts.

Jethro K. Lieberman & James F. Henry, *Lessons From the Alternative Dispute Resolution Movement,* 53 U. Chi. L. Rev. 424, 432, 433–35 (1986). How might Fiss respond to these arguments?

3. The settlement debate raises important questions about the goals of ADR. Earlier in this chapter, we listed the goals of ADR as including the

saving of time and money, having better processes, achieving better results, enhancing community involvement, and broadening access to justice. Are these goals always compatable? Are they socially desirable? Consider, for example, the goals of efficiency and access to justice. Is it possible to construct a dispute resolution process that saves time and money but threatens the goal of access to justice? See the discussion of mandatory arbitration in Chapter V.

4.   ADR proponents often cast their arguments in terms of efficiency, especially the capacity of parties to save time and money through the use of ADR processes. But the empirical evidence has been mixed. *See e.g.,* Roselle Wissler, *The Effectiveness of Court–Connected Dispute Resolution in Civil Cases*, 22 Conflict Res. Q. 55 (2004). Under what circumstances or conditions might a particular ADR method promote efficiency? Under what circumstances might an ADR method undermine efficiency? Should the desirability of ADR turn only on whether it is economically efficient, or are other factors equally or more important? We will revisit these questions in Chapter VII.

5.   In his article, Fiss indicates that he believes the movement's principal objective is to relieve court congestion. In a response, Professors McThenia and Shaffer say Fiss missed the soundest argument in favor of ADR: its capacity to foster reconciliation. For them, justice is not something we get from government but something we give to each other. Andrew W. McThenia & Thomas L. Shaffer, *For Reconciliation*, 94 Yale L.J. 1660 (1985). In his reply, Fiss faults McThenia and Shaffer for giving a partial view of the ADR movement and for failing to understand that "the more general ADR version" is just another assault on the activist state, another form of the deregulation movement. Owen M. Fiss, *Out of Eden*, 94 Yale L.J. 1669 (1985). He pleads that the reader give credit to the aspirations behind litigation and asserts that adjudication is more likely than ADR to realize its aspirations. With which side do you agree?

6.   For discussion of the dimensions on which the merits of settlement might be assessed (party preference, cost-reduction, superior outcomes, and other effects), the empirical evidence that speaks to them, and the difficulties inherent in making such empirical assessments, see Marc Galanter & Mia Cahill, *"Most Cases Settle": Judicial Promotion and Regulation of Settlement*, 46 Stan. L. Rev. 1339 (1994).

D. THE INSTITUTIONALIZATION OF ADR

Assuming, as we do, that settlement and ADR are legitimate, socially desirable processes that may be beneficial in appropriate cases, questions remain over whether and how they fit within our traditional system of law. Over time, the institutionalization of ADR has proceeded in both the public and private spheres, and has raised many significant questions that we touch on briefly here and explore more deeply in later chapters.

1. INSTITUTIONALIZATION IN THE COURTS

Courts have been an important venue of ADR institutionalization. Today, significant ADR initiatives can be found in most federal and state trial courts and in all federal and many state appellate courts as well. *See* DONNA STIENSTRA, ADR IN THE FEDERAL DISTRICT COURTS: AN INITIAL REPORT (2011); ROBERT J. NIEMIC, MEDIATION & CONFERENCE PROGRAMS IN THE FEDERAL COURTS OF APPEALS (2d ed., 2006). Most of these initiatives are mediation programs, which deal with a wide range of civil disputes, including family, employment, commercial, and environmental matters. Many criminal courts also work with victim-offender mediation programs that bring perpetrators of crimes together with their victims, or the survivors of victims, to discuss restitution and other matters.

Judicial support for ADR has been crucial since its earliest days. Indeed, the birth of modern ADR is commonly pegged at 1976, the date of the so-called "Pound Conference," organized by U.S. Supreme Court Chief Justice Warren Burger. The conference invoked a speech presented to the ABA by Harvard Law School Dean Roscoe Pound on August 29, 1906, entitled "The Causes of Popular Dissatisfaction with the Administration of Justice." The 1976 conference revisited such causes, as well as ways in which the justice system could be made more efficient and effective. The highlight of the conference was a presentation by a Harvard law professor, Frank E.A. Sander, calling for courts to use other methods of dispute resolution besides trial. While Professor Sander did not use the words, the speech has come to be known as "the multi-door courthouse speech," and is widely credited for kicking off the modern ADR movement.

FRANK E. A. SANDER, VARIETIES OF DISPUTE PROCESSING
70 F.R.D. 79, 113–114, 118–119, 121, 127–133

A second way of reducing the judicial caseload is to explore alternative ways of resolving disputes outside the courts, and it is to this topic that I wish to devote my primary attention. By and large we lawyers and law teachers have been far too single-minded when it comes to dispute resolution. Of course, as pointed out earlier, good lawyers have always tried to prevent disputes from coming about, but when that was not possible, we have tended to assume that the courts are the natural and obvious dispute resolvers. In point of fact there is a rich variety of different processes, which, I would submit, singly or in combination, may provide far more "effective" conflict resolution.

Let me turn now to the two questions with which I wish to concern myself:

1) What are the significant characteristics of various alternative dispute resolution mechanisms (such as adjudication by courts,

arbitration, mediation, negotiation, and various blends of these and other devices)?

2) How can these characteristics be utilized so that, given the variety of disputes that presently arise, we can begin to develop some rational criteria for allocating various types of disputes to different dispute resolution processes?

One consequence of an answer to these questions is that we will have a better sense of what cases ought to be left in the courts for resolution, and which should be "processed" in some other way. But since this inquiry essentially addresses itself to developing the most effective method of handling disputes it should be noted in passing that one by-product may be not only to divert some matters now handled by the courts into other processes but also that it will make available those processes for grievances that are presently not being aired at all. We know very little about why some individuals complain and others do not, or about the social and psychological costs of remaining silent. It is important to realize, however, that by establishing new dispute resolution mechanisms, or improving existing ones, we may be encouraging the ventilation of grievances that are now being suppressed. Whether that will be good (in terms of supplying a constructive outlet for suppressed anger and frustration) or whether it will simply waste scarce societal resources (by validating grievances that might otherwise have remained dormant) we do not know. The important thing to note is that there is a clear trade-off: the price of an improved scheme of dispute processing may well be a vast increase in the number of disputes being processed.

Criteria

Let us now look at some criteria that may help us to determine how particular types of disputes might best be resolved. [Professor Sander proceeds to focus on the nature of the dispute (single issue or "polycentric"), the relationship between the disputants, the amount in dispute, cost of dispute processing, and speed as primary considerations in selecting a dispute resolution process from the available options. *Ed.*]

Implications

1.   At one time perhaps the courts were the principal public dispute processors. But that time is long gone. With the development of administrative law, the delegation of certain problems to specialized bodies for initial resolution has become a commonplace. Within the judicial sphere, too, we have developed specialized courts to handle family problems and tax problems, among others.

* * *

4.   What I am thus advocating is a flexible and diverse panoply of dispute resolution processes, with particular types of cases being assigned

to differing processes (or combinations of processes), according to some of the criteria previously mentioned. Conceivably such allocation might be accomplished for a particular class of cases at the outset by the legislature; that in effect is what was done by the Massachusetts legislature for malpractice cases. Alternatively one might envision by the year 2000 not simply a court house but a Dispute Resolution Center, where the grievant would first be channeled through a screening clerk who would then direct him to the process (or sequence of processes) most appropriate to his type of case. The room directory in the lobby of such a Center might look as follows:

Screening Clerk	Room 1
Mediation	Room 2
Arbitration	Room 3
Fact–Finding	Room 4
Malpractice Screening Panel	Room 5
Superior Court	Room 6
Ombudsman	Room 7

Of one thing we can be certain: once such an eclectic method of dispute resolution is accepted there will be ample opportunity for everyone to play a part. Thus a court might decide of its own to refer a certain type of problem to a more suitable tribunal. Or a legislature might, in framing certain substantive rights, build in an appropriate dispute resolution process. Institutions such as prisons, schools, or mental hospitals also could get into the act by establishing indigenous dispute resolution processes. Here the grievance mechanism contained in the typical collective bargaining agreement stands as an enduring example of a successful model. Finally, once these patterns begin to take hold, the law schools, too, should shift from their preoccupation with the judicial process and begin to expose students to the broad range of dispute resolution processes.

5.   I would be less than candid if I were to leave this idyllic picture without at least brief reference to some of the substantial impediments to reform in this area. To begin with there is always the deadening drag of status quoism. But I have reference to more specific problems. First, particularly in the criminal field, cries of "denial of due process" will undoubtedly be heard if an informal mediational process is sought to be substituted for the strict protections of the adversary process. In response to this objection it must be asserted candidly that many thoughtful commentators appear agreed that we may have over-judicialized the system, with concomitant adverse effects on its efficiency as well as its

accessibility to powerless litigants. This is not the place to explore that difficult issue, but we clearly need to address ourselves more fully to that question.

A related concern is the one that will be voiced by Judge Higginbotham concerning the need to retain the courts as the ultimate agency capable of effectively protecting the rights of the disadvantaged. This is a legitimate concern which I believe to be consistent with the goals I have advocated. I am not maintaining that cases asserting novel constitutional claims ought to be diverted to mediation or arbitration. On the contrary, the goal is to reserve the courts for those activities for which they are best suited and to avoid swamping and paralyzing them with cases that do not require their unique capabilities.

Finally, we are robbed of much-needed flexibility by the constitutional requirement of jury trial. . . . In view of the desperate state of some of our civil calendars, it seems to me that the burden of persuasion should shift to those who maintain that the high costs are justified by unique advantages afforded by jury trials. Here again we must try to shun the endless abstract discussions of pros and cons, and seek instead to explore whether there are specific types of cases in which juries make more or less sense, so that we might opt ultimately for a constitutional amendment that would give greater flexibility to the legislature on this question.

Conclusion

It seems appropriate to end this fragmentary appraisal on a modest note. There are no panaceas; only promising avenues to explore. And there is so much we do not know. Among other things, we need far better data than are presently available in many states on what is in fact going on in the courts so that we can develop some sophisticated notion of where the main trouble spots are and what types of cases are prime candidates for alternative resolution.

We need more evaluation of the comparative efficacy and cost of different dispute resolution mechanisms. And we need more data on the role played by some of the key individuals in the process (e.g., lawyers). Do they exacerbate the adversary aspects of the case and drag out the proceedings (as many family law clients believe), or do they serve to control otherwise overly litigious clients (as trial lawyers often assert)? What is the optimal state of a country's grievance machinery so that festering grievances can be readily ventilated without unduly flooding the system and creating unreasonable expectations of relief?

Above all, however, we need to accumulate and disseminate the presently available learning concerning promising alternative resolution mechanisms, and encourage continued experimentation and research. In this connection we must continue to forge links with those from other disciplines who share our concerns. Their differing orientation and background often give them a novel perspective on the legal system.

NOTES AND QUESTIONS

1.   As compelling as this vision might be, only a few multi-door courthouses were ever established. Why do you think this might be the case? While Sander's vision of a "multi-door courthouse" has not come to pass, dispute resolution processes have become deeply rooted within the federal and state courts. Most courts now have mediation programs, and others incorporate other methods of alternative dispute resolution.

2.   The Pound Conference's primary organizer was Chief Justice Warren Burger, who later came to champion ADR both as a member of the Supreme Court deciding arbitration cases, as well as in his capacity as chief justice of the United States. In 1982, he used his Annual Report on the State of the Judiciary to promote ADR. He entitled his report "Isn't There A Better Way?", and said:

> The obligation of our profession is, or long has been thought to be, to serve as healers of human conflicts. To fulfill our traditional obligation means that we should provide mechanisms that can produce an acceptable result in the shortest possible time, with the least possible expense and with a minimum of stress on the participants. That is what justice is all about.

> The law is a tool, not an end in itself. Like any tool, particular judicial mechanisms, procedures, or rules can become obsolete. Just as the carpenter's handsaw was replaced by the power saw and his hammer was replaced by the stapler, we should be alert to the need for better tools to serve our purposes.

* * *

> Abraham Lincoln once said: "Discourage litigation. Persuade your neighbors to compromise whenever you can. Point out to them how the nominal winner is often the real loser—in fees, expenses, and waste of time." In the same vein, Judge Learned Hand commented: "I must say that, as a litigant, I should dread a lawsuit beyond almost anything else short of sickness and death."

* * *

> We, as lawyers, know that litigation is not only stressful and frustrating, but expensive and frequently unrewarding for litigants. . . . The plaintive cry of many frustrated litigants echoes what Learned Hand implied: "There must be a better way."

> We must now use the inventiveness, the ingenuity and the resourcefulness that have long characterized the American business and legal community, to shape new tools. The paradox is that we already

have some very good tools and techniques ready and waiting for imaginative lawyers to adapt them to current needs.

Burger's speech gave an important boost to the movement Sander's speech ignited. That was more than a quarter of a century ago. How far has the ADR movement come? How much farther does it have to go? Will it get there?

3. Professor Reuben contends this development has constitutional implications in that the situating of alternative dispute resolution within the courts means that it is operating under the aegis of state action, therefore requiring, in his words, at least "minimal but meaningful" due process protections. Such a notion runs counter to the common belief in ADR as privatized justice. *See* Richard C. Reuben, *Constitutional Gravity: A Unitary Theory of Alternative Dispute Resolution and Public Civil Justice*, 47 UCLA L. Rev. 949 (2000). For a counter-argument, see Sarah Rudolph Cole, *Arbitration and State Action*, 2005 B.Y.U. L. Rev. 1. If Reuben is right, what does due process require in a mediation or other dispute resolution process?

2. INSTITUTIONALIZATION IN GOVERNMENT AGENCIES

Alternative dispute resolution has also become commonplace in federal and state agencies for a wide variety of disputes, ranging from disputes over internal employment and procurement matters to administrative rulemaking on public policy issues delegated to agencies by the legislature. The Administrative Dispute Resolution Act of 1990 (ADRA) requires all federal agencies to adopt ADR policies and to provide departmental ADR leadership and training. 5 U.S.C. § 571 (2000). The U.S. Postal Service is often held out as an example of the capacity of ADR to improve relationships within an agency (for further discussion of the Service's REDRESS program, see Chapter VI) and all major branches of the U.S. military have instituted extensive ADR programs.

While states lag behind the federal government with respect to the use of administrative dispute resolution, there is still a considerable amount of activity. These and other administrative developments are discussed further in Chapter VI, beginning at p. 817.

3. INSTITUTIONALIZATION IN THE PRIVATE SPHERE

The private sector has also been an important focus of ADR institutionalization. Many businesses have incorporated alternative methods of dispute resolution into their workplace management systems, as well as their procedures for dealing with other types of disputes. *See* David B. Lipsky, *How Corporate America Uses Conflict Management: The Evidence From a New Survey of the Fortune 1000*, Alt. High Cost of Litig. (2012). The fundamental premise of this vehicle of institutionalization is contract—that is, parties privately agree to use ADR methods to resolve their differences, rather than turning to courts. "For many businesses, for example, tailoring of dispute resolution approaches most appropriate to resolving particular issues 'is an integral part of corporate policy' and an important measure for achieving corporate objectives." Thomas J. Stipanowich, *Contract and Conflict Management,* 2001 Wis. L. Rev. 831.

The use of ADR processes in the private sector raises a variety of questions about the role of "privatized justice." Some ADR advocates, of course, think of ADR processes as wholly removed from the reach of the law, especially when the path into dispute resolution is through private contract. However, that plainly is not the case. All contracts are subject to judicial review and potential invalidation. Moreover, as the materials in the following chapters illustrate, all of these processes are subject to and influenced by the positive law that may affect the dispute. Even private negotiations are said to operate in the "shadow of the law," meaning that parties assess the desirability of their negotiated settlements against the possible outcomes before a court. Robert H. Mnookin & Lewis Kornhauser, *Bargaining in the Shadow of the Law: The Case of Divorce,* 88 Yale L.J. 950, 968–69 (1979). At the same time, however, settlements also occur in the shadow of other privately bargained settlements. See Ben Depoorter, *Law in the Shadow of Bargaining: The Feedback Effect of Civil Settlements,* 95 Cornell L. Rev. 957 (2010). What other legal constraints might influence purely private negotiations? For further discussion, see Chapter III, beginning at p. 246.

As in the public sphere, ADR raises significant questions in the private sphere that remain largely unresolved. For example, does it effectively create a two-tier system of civil justice in which the civil justice system is limited to those with the money and power to access it, while those of less means are limited "alternative" forms of dispute resolution that may compromise important legal rights in the name of harmony. See, e.g., LAURA NADER, HARMONY IDEOLOGY: JUSTICE AND CONTROL IN A ZAPOTEC MOUNTAIN VILLAGE (1991). In the same way, perhaps, does ADR simply provide elites a vehicle to dispose of and shield their mischief from public view? Does it simply reinforce or even exploit inherent power imbalances between the parties? Such tensions are created by the fundamental trade-off of the formality of the rule of law in favor of ADR's practicality and potential for personalized justice, and animate many of the deepest policy, doctrinal, and practice challenges that the field continues to face.

E. DISPUTE RESOLUTION AND LAWYERS

Our goal is to prepare lawyers to help their clients and communities choose (or design) and use the most appropriate methods to resolve a dispute or consummate a transaction. This, to us, is appropriate dispute resolution. In this regard, we see lawyers managing disputes, helping contain underlying conflict, and steering disputes toward as constructive an outcome as circumstances will reasonably allow.

To do so, lawyers must understand the available processes, their advantages and disadvantages in different contexts, and the many different ways each can be implemented. She must also appreciate the impact the process will have on those who will be affected—her clients, other involved or affected parties, or the community. The danger of incomplete knowledge is substantial. The lawyer who has a superficial grasp of the alternatives may steer his clients into alternatives that are ill-suited to their needs and may be an ineffective agent within those procedures.

1. HEADWINDS AND TAILWINDS: THE INVOLVEMENT OF LAWYERS IN ALTERNATIVES TO LITIGATION

There are forces that complicate the involvement of lawyers in ADR. First, some lawyers may still be unfamiliar with alternative processes. In practice, lawyers still often confuse the different ADR processes, even arbitration and mediation. Some lawyers may resist the unfamiliar or fear that they might make less money or lose control of the dispute if they use alternative processes. But in the nearly 40 years since the onset of the modern ADR movement, these processes have become an important part of our justice system. It is regularly taught in law schools, offered by courts, sought by clients, and prominent at bar association conferences and other professional gatherings. Many major law firms have established dispute resolution units, have assigned lawyers solely or principally to help their colleagues resolve disputes, and are publicizing their ADR capabilities. And most lawyers want to respond appropriately to the needs of their clients and communities. For this task, an understanding of the alternative processes is essential, and this is increasingly understood and accepted within the legal profession.

Even so, lawyers are still fundamentally trained to be advocates, and many lawyers still define that quite narrowly in terms of legal arguments and strategies in courts of law. But this kind of advocacy is simply one approach to dealing with a problem. And, the adversarial perspective, so valuable in some settings, often constricts the way lawyers function in settings where a problem-solving approach might be more appropriate. As Leonard Riskin describes below, the adversarial perspective—or the "lawyer's standard philosophical map," which is its frequent companion— can keep lawyers from appreciating the value of negotiation, mediation, and other consensual models of dispute resolution. But by developing an understanding of alternative modes of resolving disputes, lawyers can be more responsive and effective.

LEONARD L. RISKIN, MEDIATION AND LAWYERS
43 Ohio St. L.J. 29, 43–48, 57–59 (1982)

A. THE LAWYER'S STANDARD PHILOSOPHICAL MAP

E.F. Schumacher begins his *Guide for the Perplexed* with the following story:

> On a visit to Leningrad some years ago, I consulted a map * * * but I could not make it out. From where I stood, I could see several enormous churches, yet there was no trace of them on my map. When finally an interpreter came to help me, he said: "We don't show churches on our maps." Contradicting him, I pointed to one that was very clearly marked. "That is a museum," he said, "not what we call a 'living church.' It is only the 'living churches' we don't show."

> It then occurred to me that this was not the first time I had been given a map which failed to show many things I could see right in front of my eyes. All through school and university I had been given maps of life and knowledge on which there was hardly a trace of many of the things that I most cared about and that seemed to me to be of the greatest possible importance to the conduct of my life.

The philosophical map employed by most practicing lawyers and law teachers, and displayed to the law student—which I will call the lawyer's standard philosophical map—differs radically from that which a mediator must use. What appears on this map is determined largely by the power of two assumptions about matters that lawyers handle: (1) that disputants are adversaries—*i.e.,* if one wins, the other must lose—and (2) that disputes may be resolved through application, by a third party, of some general rule of law. These assumptions, plainly, are polar opposites of those which underlie mediation: (1) that all parties can benefit through a creative solution to which each agrees; and (2) that the situation is unique and therefore not to be governed by any general principle except to the extent that the parties accept it.

The two assumptions of the lawyer's philosophical map (adversariness of parties and rule-solubility of dispute), along with the real demands of the adversary system and the expectations of many clients, tend to exclude mediation from most lawyers' repertoires. They also blind lawyers to other kinds of information that are essential for a mediator to see, primarily by riveting the lawyers' attention upon things that they must see in order to carry out their functions. The mediator must, for instance, be aware of the many interconnections between and among disputants and others, and of the qualities of these connections; he must be sensitive to emotional needs of all parties and recognize the importance of yearnings for mutual respect, equality, security, and other such non-material interests as may be present.

On the lawyer's standard philosophical map, however, the client's situation is seen atomistically; many links are not printed. The duty to represent the client zealously within the bounds of the law discourages concern with both the opponents' situation and the overall social effect of a given result.

Moreover, on the lawyer's standard philosophical map, quantities are bright and large while qualities appear dimly or not at all. When one party wins, in this vision, usually the other party loses, and, most often, the victory is reduced to a money judgment. This "reduction" of nonmaterial values—such as honor, respect, dignity, security, and love—to amounts of money, can have one of two effects. In some cases, these values are excluded from the decision makers' considerations, and thus from the consciousness of the lawyers, as irrelevant. In others, they are present but transmuted into something else—a justification for money damages. Much like the church that was allowed to appear on the map of Leningrad only because it was a museum, these interests—which may in fact be the principal motivations for a lawsuit—are recognizable in the legal dispute primarily to the extent that they have monetary value or fit into a clause of a rule governing liability.

The rule orientation also determines what appears on the map. The lawyer's standard world view is based upon a cognitive and rational outlook. Lawyers are trained to put people and events into categories that are legally meaningful, to think in terms of rights and duties established by rules, to focus on acts more than persons. This view requires a strong development of cognitive capabilities, which is often attended by the under-cultivation of emotional faculties. This combination of capacities joins with the practice of either reducing most nonmaterial values to amounts of money or sweeping them under the carpet, to restrict many lawyers' abilities to recognize the value of mediation or to serve as mediators.

The lawyer's standard philosophical map is useful primarily where the assumptions upon which it is based—adversariness and amenability to solution by a general rule imposed by a third party—are valid. But when mediation is appropriate, these assumptions do not fit. The problem is that many lawyers, because of their philosophical maps, tend to suppose that these assumptions are germane in nearly any situation that they confront as lawyers. The map, and the litigation paradigm on which it is based, has a power all out of proportion to its utility. Many lawyers, therefore, tend not to recognize mediation as a viable means of reaching a solution; and worse, they see the kinds of unique solutions that mediation can produce as threatening to the best interests of their clients.

* * *

I do not mean to imply that all lawyers see only what is displayed on the lawyer's standard philosophical map. The chart I have drawn exaggerates certain tendencies in the way many lawyers think. Any good lawyer will be alert to a range of nonmaterial values, emotional considerations, and interconnections. Many lawyers have "empathic, conciliatory" personalities that may incline them to work often in a mediative way. And other lawyers, though they may be more competitive, would recognize the value of mediation to their clients. I do submit, however, that most lawyers, most of the time, use this chart to navigate.

* * *

I do not mean to indict the lawyers' standard philosophical map. In many cases, lawyers must use it. Most clients and judges expect them to. Moreover, the adversary-rule perspective from which the standard map is drawn has real strengths. It promotes a loyalty to clients. It encourages vigorous presentation of competing positions and interests. The rule orientation fosters in the lawyer an allegiance to the system of laws, which in turn serves to unify society, to provide a measure of security of expectations, and to keep open possibilities of fairness between persons irrespective of status and of vindication of the rights of the downtrodden. But at the same time, the lawyer's conventional view of the world permits a great deal of misery. It does this by dominating the professional consciousness of most lawyers and legal educators too fully, crowding or crowding out other views.

An enormous percentage of potential consumers of legal services are either ill-served or not served at all by our legal system. Many people can afford a lawyer only when a contingent fee arrangement is feasible. Those who can get into the litigation process will find it enormously time consuming, expensive, uncertain, and unpleasant unless their lawyers can arrange settlements. And much of this results directly from the over-zealousness with which many lawyers routinely embrace their adversarial roles. Many lawyers tend to delay and obscure the truth in the service (usually) of their clients' financial interest. Often they "exacerbate and prolong the contest rather than * * * arrive at a quiet compromise."

That this situation persists can be attributed in no small measure to the strength of the lawyer's standard philosophical map. The atomistic perspective, the inclination to accept the adversary system as it is and assume that it is useful, the focus on legal rights and interests (often reduced to monetary terms), the assumption of an adversary stance—all these tendencies combine to permit the working lawyer to ignore, at least while he is working, the well-known adverse conditions that I set forth above.

A lawyer who has experienced the mediational perspective would have difficulty keeping on his adversarial blinders and would be more likely, therefore, to acknowledge the serious difficulties in our current adversary system. The mediation experience also may encourage the lawyer to come up with creative solutions to systemic as well as individual problems. Mediation training and practice can help lawyers question the many (often unconscious) value presuppositions that underlie normal lawyer behavior—for example, assumptions about adversariness and rules, how lawyers behave, and what clients want—from which we tend to operate automatically. Mediation training, in other words, may help lawyers break out of the "mental grooves and compartments" characteristic of the lawyer's conventional world view. This can lead not just to mediation but to legal services that are more responsive to the needs of clients and of society.

NOTES AND QUESTIONS

1. Has law school pushed your thinking toward what Professor Riskin describes as the "lawyer's standard philosophical map"? Consider an example: Has law school changed the way you view injuries or catastrophes? Imagine that a neighbor tells you she just heard on the radio that a bus crashed in a part of the United States with which you have no connections. What are your subjective reactions? What questions would you ask? Would you try to elicit information that would enable you to place the event into a category you learned about in law school? Would you have had a similar reaction before law school?

2. In his article, Professor Riskin raised the possibility that mediation might change the nature of legal practice and the ways in which lawyers view disputes and the possibility that lawyers would "legalize" mediation and shape the process to the norms of the profession. Over the intervening years, both have occurred. *See* Leonard L. Riskin & Nancy Welsh, *Is That All There Is?: "The Problem" in Court–Oriented Mediation*, 15 Geo. Mason L. Rev. 863 (2008). Which influence do you imagine has been stronger? *See also* Jeff Goldfien & Jennifer K. Robbennolt, *What if the Lawyers Have Their Way? An Empirical Assessment of Conflict Strategies and Attitudes Toward Mediation Styles,* 22 Ohio St. J. Dispute Resol. 277 (2007). Interaction between the lawyer's standard philosophical map and mediation processes also raises the possibility that lawyers and others might embrace a process called "mediation" but use the process in ways that are antithetical to the values underlying mediation. We return to this issue in Chapter IV.

2. THE ROLES AND SKILLS OF THE LAWYER

The roles of the lawyer in dispute processing are many. Lawyers come to understand—and sometimes resolve—disputes and their underlying conflicts through the processes of interviewing and counseling their clients. Lawyers anticipate and seek to prevent, limit, and manage disputes through careful planning, client advising, targeted negotiation, and document drafting. They act as advocates and problem solvers in negotiating deals and settlements. They represent or advise parties in trials, arbitration, mediation, and negotiation. Lawyers also function in neutral capacities, as arbitrators, mediators, and fact-finders. As legislators or as leaders of the bar, community organizations, or government agencies, they define what conflicts will be addressed, as well as the means by which they will be addressed, including the design and implementation of programs for the resolution of particular disputes.

These myriad roles, and the many others that lawyers play in our society, require a range of skills. Some of these skills are at the forefront of much of legal education—researching and analyzing the law, advocating on behalf of a client, writing and speaking clearly and persuasively, and managing the process for the client or clients. But other skills are required as well.

Effective lawyers are skilled and creative problem-solvers. Indeed, problem solving is the overriding mission of lawyering. "A good problem solver must take the problem, transaction, or matter presented by the client, analyze what the problem or situation requires, and then use creative abilities to solve, resolve, arrange, structure, or transform the situation so it is made better for the client, not worse." Carrie Menkel–Meadow, *When Winning Isn't Everything: The Lawyer As Problem Solver,* 28 Hofstra L. Rev. 905, 915 (2000). Innovative lawyers are able to craft inventive solutions to specific disputes and also to pioneer new processes of dispute resolution. *See* Jennifer Gerarda Brown, *Creativity and Problem–Solving, in* THE NEGOTIATOR'S FIELDBOOK: THE DESK REFERENCE FOR THE EXPERIENCED NEGOTIATOR 407 (Andrea Kupfer Schneider & Christopher Honeyman eds., 2006); Julie Macfarlane, *ADR and the Courts: Renewing Our Commitment to Innovation,* 95 Marq. L. Rev. 927 (2012).

Good communication is also central to working effectively with clients, other parties and lawyers, mediators, judges, and others to resolve disputes. Attorneys who can communicate clearly, understand the potential for miscommunication and dissembling, take the perspective of others, use and accurately interpret nonverbal communication, and successfully build trust and rapport will be more successful lawyers. *See* JENNIFER K. ROBBENNOLT & JEAN R. STERNLIGHT, *Interpersonal Communication, in* PSYCHOLOGY FOR LAWYERS: UNDERSTANDING THE HUMAN FACTORS IN LITIGATION, NEGOTIATION, AND DECISION MAKING 141 (2012). In particular, the ability to ask good questions and the ability to listen carefully to the answers are important to any process for resolving disputes. We explore these crucial skills in detail in Chapters II and III.

It is also important for lawyers to be skilled at dealing with emotion. Being aware of your own emotions and the emotions of others, understanding the ways in which emotions arise and interact, using emotions as information and a source of motivation, managing your emotions and their expression, and helping others to regulate their emotions can all contribute to more effective lawyering. *See* DAVID R. CARUSO & PETER SALOVEY, THE EMOTIONALLY INTELLIGENT MANAGER (2004); JENNIFER K. ROBBENNOLT & JEAN R. STERNLIGHT, *Emotion, in* PSYCHOLOGY FOR LAWYERS: UNDERSTANDING THE HUMAN FACTORS IN LITIGATION, NEGOTIATION, AND DECISION MAKING 141 (2012).

As lawyers engage in each of the tasks involved in resolving disputes, cultivating the ability to be present and aware helps lawyers be more effective by facilitating better communication, improved attention, focus, and memory, greater self-awareness and empathy for others, a more effective approach to emotion, increased cognitive flexibility, and improved decision making. *See* Daphne M. Davis & Jeffrey A. Hayes, *What Are the Benefits of Mindfulness? A Practice Review of Psychotherapy–Related Research,* 48 Psychotherapy 198 (2011); Symposium, *The Mindful Lawyer,* 61 J. Legal Educ. 634 (2012). We address mindfulness in greater detail in Chapter VIII.

NOTES AND QUESTIONS

1. The role of the lawyer is the subject of much debate and controversy. Among the more interesting writings that call into question the adequacy of the adversarial perspective are: ELIZABETH DVORKIN, JACK HIMMELSTEIN & HOWARD LESNICK, BECOMING A LAWYER: A HUMANISTIC PERSPECTIVE ON LEGAL EDUCATION AND PROFESSIONALISM (1981); ROBERT H. MNOOKIN, SCOTT R. PEPPET & ANDREW S. TULUMELLO, BEYOND WINNING: NEGOTIATING TO CREATE VALUE IN DEALS AND DISPUTES (2000); THOMAS SHAFFER, ON BEING A CHRISTIAN AND A LAWYER (1981); Warren Lehman, *The Pursuit of a Client's Interest,* 77 Mich. L. Rev. 1078 (1979); William Simon, *The Ideology of Advocacy,* 1978 Wis. L. Rev. 29.

2. Law professor Marjorie Shultz and psychologist Sheldon Zedek have done extensive empirical research designed to identify the competencies of effective lawyers. Their research has identified the following important skills: analysis and reasoning; creativity and innovation; problem solving; practical judgment; researching the law; fact finding; questioning and interviewing; influencing and advocating; writing; speaking; listening; strategic planning; organizing and managing the lawyer's own work; organizing and managing others; negotiating; seeing the world through the eyes of others; networking and developing business; providing advice and counsel and building relationships with clients; developing relationships within the legal profession; evaluation, development, and mentoring; passion and engagement; diligence; integrity and honesty; stress management; community involvement and service; and self-development. MARJORIE M.

SCHULTZ & SHELDON ZEDEK, FINAL REPORT: IDENTIFICATION, DEVELOPMENT, AND VALIDATION OF PREDICTORS FOR SUCCESSFUL LAWYERING (2008). How might each of these skills be important for resolving disputes? How effective are law schools at cultivating these qualities?

3.   Ethical issues are often challenging for lawyers and the legal profession, but can be especially so for lawyers acting in the roles contemplated by alternative methods of dispute resolution. This, in part, is because ethics rules have generally been drafted under an adversarial understanding of the practice of law. Thus, existing ethics rules may be better suited for adjudicative processes for resolving disputes than for more evaluative or consensual processes. Ethics are further challenged when engaging in dispute resolution cross-culturally with lawyers trained in different legal systems and with different conceptions of their role. *See* Symposium, *Ethics in the Expanding World of ADR: Considerations, Conundrums, and Conflicts,* 49 S. Tex. L. Rev. 787 (2008); Robert C. Bordone, *Fitting the Ethics to the Forum: A Proposal for Process–Enabling Ethical Codes,* 21 Ohio St. J. on Disp. Resol. 1 (2005); Carrie Menkel–Meadow, *Ethics in ADR: The Many "Cs" of Professional Responsibility and Dispute Resolution,* 28 Fordham Urb. L.J. 979 (2001); CATHERINE ROGERS, ETHICS IN INTERNATIONAL ARBITRATION (forthcoming 2013); Nancy Welsh, *Integrating "Alternative" Dispute Resolution Procedures into Bankruptcy: As Simple (And Pure) as Motherhood and Apple Pie?,* Nev. L. J. 101 (2011). Ethics issues as they manifest in dispute resolution contexts are considered throughout this textbook.

4.   Finally, consider the role of law in dispute resolution. On the one hand, the law is *everywhere* in dispute resolution. Substantive legal rules and available legal procedures will be factors to consider in counseling clients. In some contexts, people negotiate, mediate, or arbitrate only because the law—e.g., a court rule, statute, or contract provision—requires or incentivizes them to do so. The law grants evidentiary privileges to participants in certain dispute resolution procedures. The law of arbitration is extensive, with rules related to the enforceability and scope of arbitral clauses and the judicial review of arbitral awards. And, the law governs the legal duties owed by lawyers to clients.

At the same time, you will see that law and legal solutions do not and should not entirely preempt other ways of understanding and resolving disputes. Good lawyers use the law, of course, but they also seek to understand and respond to their clients' underlying personal, relational, and financial needs. Good lawyers also consider the use of both legal and non-legal procedures. ("Non-legal," by the way, does not mean "illegal.") As you read this book, participate in your dispute resolution class, and enter the practice of law, take care to avoid the incomplete view of the world that is offered by the "lawyer's standard philosophical map."

CHAPTER II

THE ATTORNEY-CLIENT RELATIONSHIP

▪ ▪ ▪

This chapter introduces the attorney-client relationship, which is central to your representation of your client in negotiation, mediation, arbitration and other dispute resolution processes. Skillful interviewing and counseling foster the development of a strong and productive attorney-client relationship. With your help, for example, your client is more likely to make a thoughtful, fully-informed decision regarding her objectives. In turn, you are more likely to understand the needs, goals and limitations that inform your client's objectives, and this knowledge will enable you to be more effective in assisting your client in achieving those objectives. Given the importance of the attorney-client relationship, we will address it repeatedly throughout the book.

Interviewing is the principal means by which the lawyer comes to understand the client and the problems and issues that brought the client to the lawyer. In counseling, the lawyer helps the client decide whether and how to address these problems and issues, a discussion that may include selecting a method for resolving a dispute or planning a transaction.

Interviewing and counseling are dispute resolution processes in their own right. After an interview or a counseling session with a lawyer, for instance, a client may decide not to bring a legal claim, may take alternative non-legal action, or may seek some other form of professional help. In addition, many disputes are transformed or redefined during interviewing and counseling. Sometimes the transformation is from an ill-defined human problem to a legal dispute. Other times the reverse occurs. A client comes in wishing to sue, but learns that other approaches may be more appropriate.

Lawyers' interviewing and counseling also are critical components of other dispute resolution or planning processes, including negotiation, mediation, arbitration, and litigation. The lawyer-negotiator will interview and counsel her client before a negotiation, for example, but also between negotiation sessions as she gains new insight into what negotiated outcomes are possible.

Interviewing and counseling are distinct but closely related activities. We study them separately in this chapter to better understand each process. But we also study them together because in practice they usually occur together, and ideally in sequence, as part of a process of problem solving.

Our main objectives for this chapter are to emphasize the importance of the attorney-client relationship, highlight the allocation of authority between lawyer and client, and introduce the goals, strategies, and techniques of interviewing and counseling. We will return to some of these strategies and techniques again, in the context of negotiation and mediation.

Section A describes three models of the attorney-client relationship and introduces lawyers' ethical obligations. Sections B and C discuss interviewing and counseling. Section D examines some of the legal issues that can arise out of difficulties in the attorney-client relationship. Finally, as a prelude to the remaining chapters in this book, Section E explores whether the lawyer, as part of her role as counselor, has a duty to advise her clients about dispute resolution alternatives. Section F provides the general instructions for a role play exercise for practicing the skills discussed in this chapter.

A. PRELIMINARY CONSIDERATIONS

1. BASIC MODELS

Most of us carry a model or idealized vision of the attorney-client relationship around in our heads. Formed in various ways—from television, movies, and books, to real encounters with lawyers and clients—this image informs our understanding of the way lawyers and clients are supposed to relate to one another.

The following two excerpts explore three models of the attorney-client relationship. In the first excerpt, Professor Robert Dinerstein describes both the traditional model, in which the lawyer exercises broad control over the relationship, and the client-centered model, in which the client plays a much larger role. In the second excerpt, Professors Robert Cochran, Jr., John DiPippa, and Martha Peters describe their more recently developed collaborative model of the attorney-client relationship, which falls somewhere between the extremes of the traditional and client-centered approaches.

ROBERT D. DINERSTEIN, CLIENT–CENTERED COUNSELING: REAPPRAISAL AND REFINEMENT
32 Ariz. L. Rev. 501, 503–04, 506–09 (1990)

Legal counseling inevitably raises questions about the proper role of the lawyer with respect to her client and the degree of the client's participation in the decisionmaking process. Who should decide what actions to take—lawyer, client, or a combination of the two? Is the lawyer's professional role to make decisions for the client, advise the client about what decision the client should make, or simply lay out the options and let the client decide? Should client decisions be judged by an informed consent standard? These questions are not unique to the attorney-client relationship—in some sense they arise in all professional/layperson relationships—but they have particular salience within that relationship.

The traditional view of legal counseling (and the attorney-client relationship generally) maintains that the client should make the critical decisions concerning the overall goals of the representation, with the lawyer exercising a great deal of influence over how such decisions are made and what the actual decisions are. This view holds that the client should stand by passively while the lawyer lays out all relevant legal considerations for the decision and indicates what decision he believes, as a matter of his professional judgment, the client ought to make. The lawyer then urges the client to make the recommended decision. The client-centered or participatory model of counseling, with the client empowered to make decisions for him or herself, is a response to this traditional model.

* * *

A.   *The Traditional Model*

Traditional legal counseling reflects an absence of meaningful interchange between lawyer and client. The client comes to the lawyer with some idea about his problem. The lawyer asks questions designed to adduce the information necessary to place the client's problem within the appropriate conceptual box. At the proper time, he counsels the client by essentially conducting a monologue: the lawyer tells the client about the course of action he recommends. The lawyer may go into great detail about the rationale for his advice. Alternatively, she may provide a relatively terse recitation of technical advice and let the client decide how to proceed. The lawyer is concerned with the client's reaction to his advice but tends not to value client input, for he believes that the client has little of value to contribute to the resolution of his legal problem. Lawyer and client are likely to talk at, rather than with, each other. Any assurance that the lawyer provides to the client—and it could be substantial—is likely to be based on the client's perception that the lawyer is "taking care of matters" rather than on a belief that the lawyer truly tried to understand the client as a whole, complex person.

In general, the traditional legal counseling model assumes that clients should be passive and delegate decisionmaking responsibility to their lawyers; that ineffective professional service is relatively rare; that professionals give disinterested service and maintain high professional standards; that effective professional services are available to all who can pay; and that professional problems tend to call for technical solutions beyond the ken of laypersons.

B. The Binder and Price Counseling Model

Client-centered counseling is a critical component of client-centered lawyering. Client-centered counseling may be defined as a legal counseling process designed to foster client-decisionmaking. Its goal is not only to provide opportunities for clients to make decisions themselves but also to enhance the likelihood that the decisions are truly the client's and not the lawyer's. To accomplish these goals, client-centered counselors must attend to the means they employ in the counseling process, as well as the end of client decisionmaking they attempt to achieve.

Binder and Price describe a relatively straightforward, but highly structured, legal counseling model to be used in litigation contexts. With respect to the basic decision about whether to litigate, the lawyer first sets out the legal alternatives for the client. Next, she solicits the client's input in generating additional alternatives. Then, the lawyer engages the client in a discussion of the positive and negative consequences of the options. These consequences include not only the legal consequences, as to which the lawyer is enjoined to make predictions of the most likely outcome of each alternative, but the social, psychological and economic consequences as well. Finally, the lawyer assists the client in weighing these consequences with an eye towards having the client make the final decision.

ROBERT F. COCHRAN, JR., JOHN M. A. DIPIPPA & MARTHA M. PETERS, THE COUNSELOR-AT-LAW: A COLLABORATIVE APPROACH TO CLIENT INTERVIEWING AND COUNSELING
6–7 (1999)

We believe that the authoritarian [traditional] model provides too small a role for clients, the client-centered approach provides too small a role for lawyers, and that clients will be best served when lawyers and clients resolve problems in the law office through collaborative decision making. Under this model, the client would control decisions, but the lawyer would structure the process and provide advice in a manner that is likely to yield wise decisions.

This model would be likely to avoid the problems of the authoritarian model. The client's control of the decisions would ensure client dignity. It would also be likely to yield superior results to the authoritarian model. Rosenthal found that the more varied forms of client participation and the more persistently the client employed them, "the better his chances of protecting his emotional and economic interests in the case outcome." We share Rosenthal's call for lawyers and clients to engage in "mutual participation in a cooperative relationship in which the cooperating parties have relatively equal status, are equally dependent, and are engaged in activity 'that will be in some ways satisfying to both [parties].' "

A collaborative client counseling model would also avoid the weaknesses of the client-centered counselors. It would provide the lawyer and client with an opportunity to consider the effects of their decisions on other people. It would provide the flexibility to counsel the client in a wide variety of ways. Finally it would enable the client and lawyer to engage in a collaborative deliberation that would be likely to yield practical wisdom.

NOTES AND QUESTIONS

1.   The distinction between the client-centered model and the collaborative model is subtle. Here is a helpful way to think about it:

> The client-centered approach seeks to promote client autonomy by making the client an active participant in the decision-making process. The lawyer tries to identify the client's problem from the client's perspective and then enlists the client's aid in identifying potential solutions and the likely consequences of each solution. Ultimately, counsel encourages the client to make all decisions that are likely to have a substantial legal or non-legal impact on the client's case. The client-centered model emphasizes client feelings, stresses the importance of lawyer empathy, and insists that lawyers accept client values when rendering advice. Lawyers' recommendations, therefore, shall be designed to promote the client's best interests as defined by that client. As Cochran and his compatriots pointed out, "whereas the client has a very limited role in the authoritarian model, the lawyer has a very limited role in the client-centered model." * * *

> [With the collaborative decision-making model, Cochran and his co-authors] looked to Douglas Rosenthal who urged lawyers and clients to engage in "mutual participation in a cooperative relationship." To Cochran and his colleagues, the collaborative model is superior to the client-centered model because it increases counsel's flexibility, promotes equality, and encourages an attorney-client dialog about the effects that case decisions may have on others. Thus, in Cochran's collaborative model, "the client would control decisions, but the lawyer would structure the process and provide advice in a manner that is likely to yield wise decisions."

> Cochran and his colleagues trumpet the collaborative model because they believe that lawyers following this approach are more likely to achieve what Dean Anthony Kronman calls practical wisdom. To Kronman, the key to being a good lawyer is the ability to exercise practical wisdom. To exercise such wisdom, a lawyer must "combine the opposing qualities of sympathy and detachment." Acting as a counselor

and friend, the good lawyer strives to help her clients make sound judgments. To render the good advice her client needs, counsel must also seek to understand the client. Ultimately, "it is only through a process of joint deliberations, in which the lawyer imaginatively assumes his client's position, and with sympathetic detachment begins to examine the alternatives for himself, that the necessary understanding can emerge." Using this process then, the good lawyer is better able to assist her client in making the "deliberatively wise choice" among alternatives. Thus, not only does the good lawyer exercise practical wisdom, but she helps her client make wise judgments as well.

Rodney J. Uphoff, *Relations between Lawyer and Client in* Damages*: Model, Typical, or Dysfunctional?*, 2004 J. Disp. Resol. 145, 152–54.

2.   Which model of the attorney-client relationship do you think is most appropriate? Who should decide—you or your client—how you will carry out your representation of the client? What factors might help you decide which model is more appropriate? The type of client? The nature of your relationship with the client? The type of knowledge required to solve the problem? Your knowledge of your client's needs and goals? The client's ability or inability to make a decision?

3.   Recall Mayer's argument from Chapter I that it is helpful to understand conflict and conflict resolution along three dimensions: behavioral, cognitive, and emotional. Which model of the attorney-client relationship is most likely to address conflict along all three dimensions?

4.   What impact might the choice of model have on whether conflict de-escalates, stabilizes, or escalates?

5.   Professor Katherine Kruse has elaborated on the client-centered model by identifying five distinct approaches within it: the holistic approach (focusing on the client as a whole instead of the client's legal issues to prevent lawyer misdiagnosis or narrow legal framing of the client's problems); narrative integrity approach (focusing on the client rather than the lawyer's construction of the client to prevent lawyer distortion of the client narrative in legal storytelling); client empowerment approach (focusing on the client as a whole rather than the client's stated wishes to prevent misdiagnosis of what the client "really wants"); partisan advocacy approach (focusing on the client as a whole rather than third parties to prevent the loss of the client's legal rights and interests); and client-directed approach (focusing on the client rather than the client's best interests to prevent lawyer paternalism). *See* Katherine R. Kruse, *Fortress in the Sand: The Plural Values of Client-Centered Representation*, 12 Clinical L. Rev. 369, 420–26 (2006). Professor Baruch Bush has recently suggested that because an "important aim for the client-centered lawyer is to conduct the representation in a manner that supports and facilitates client participation and empowerment[,]" client-centered lawyering shares fundamental premises with transformative mediation. We discuss transformative mediation in Chapter IV, *infra. See*

Robert A. Baruch Bush, *Mediation Skills and Client–Centered Lawyering: A New View of the Partnership*, 19 Clinical L. Rev. 429, 448–50 (2013).

6.   For the lawyer and client who wish to conduct their relationship in accord with the client-centered model or the collaborative model, what impediments might prevent them from doing so? From the client's side, active participation in the relationship may be difficult for several reasons. The client may not wish to devote the time or energy required for participation. He may strongly embrace a traditional model of attorney-client relationships. He may be unable to master enough knowledge or muster enough judgment to make a wise decision.

The lawyer may also have problems helping the client participate effectively. The lawyer may assume that the client wants or needs the lawyer to take charge. She may worry about losing time or money. She may feel anxious about the possibility of losing control. As Douglas Rosenthal put it:

> Lawyers, and perhaps most professionals, seem to have two human needs in disproportionately great measure: the desire to control their environment and aggressive (and competitive) feelings. * * * The traditional model serves the function of a professional ideology, justifying the control the lawyer wants, affirming his status and competence, and defining as legitimate a role of client passivity and uncritical trust. The traditional model resolves unilaterally the conflicts inherent in the lawyer's role. It is a way lawyers can cope with the strains of practice.

DOUGLAS ROSENTHAL, LAWYER AND CLIENT: WHO'S IN CHARGE? 173, 174 (1974). *See also,* Nancy A. Welsh, *Looking Down the Road Less Traveled: Challenges to Persuading the Legal Profession to Define Problems More Humanistically,* 2008 J. Disp. Resol. 45, 49–57 (2008) (discussing the psychological, professional, and business factors that deter lawyers from adopting a humanistic approach to lawyering).

7.   The traditional model, in which the lawyer takes broad control over the decision-making process, might make sense if: (a) the solutions may require knowledge or expertise within the lawyer's exclusive control; (b) the lawyer fully understands the needs and values of the client; (c) the lawyer can be neutral; and (d) the client is unwilling or unable to make a decision. These factors exist in some situations, especially where the lawyer and the client have a continuing relationship. But in many other situations they may be absent. For an example of a client who prefers to have a professional make a difficult decision, *see* Atul Gawande, *Complications: A Surgeon's Notes on an Imperfect Science, infra.*

8.   A relatively new area of legal practice, Collaborative Law, offers another model of the attorney-client relationship. In this model, the lawyers and clients on both sides agree to use a problem-solving approach in their negotiation. Both sides enforce this commitment by agreeing that the lawyers will withdraw from their representation of the clients if either party chooses to proceed to litigation. As long as the clients provide their informed consent

(as required by Rule 1.2(c) of the Model Rules of Professional Conduct, *infra*) this arrangement has been found not to violate lawyers' ethical obligations under Rule 1.7. *See* ABA Ethics Opinion 07–447. We examine Collaborative Law in some detail in Chapter VI, *infra*.

2. ETHICS ISSUES

Attorneys are required to comply with the professional responsibility rules adopted by the state where the attorney is licensed. More than forty states have now patterned their professional responsibility rules after the ABA Model Rules of Professional Conduct.

Among other things, the ABA Model Rules of Professional Conduct address the appropriate role for the lawyer to play in the attorney-client relationship. For purposes of this chapter, we urge you to review Rules 1.1 (Competence), 1.2 (Scope of Representation and Allocation of Authority Between Client and Lawyer), 1.4 (Communications), 1.6 (Confidentiality of Information), 1.7 (Conflict Of Interest: Current Clients), and 2.1 (Advisor). You will find these rules in Appendix 2. Some of the notes and questions in this chapter will require you to consider and apply these rules to the processes of interviewing and counseling. Once you begin to practice law, real clients will present novel situations that require you to turn to the rules of the state (or states) where you are licensed.

As you read through the rules listed above, consider how they apply to the traditional model of the attorney-client relationship, the client-centered model, and the collaborative model. Also be sure to read the Model Rules' Preamble. We have included the Preamble and Rule 1.2(a) below because they graphically illustrate the difficult but essential "creative tension" that can arise for any lawyer as she confronts a demanding client and tries to find the appropriate balance in simultaneously serving her client, the legal system and our society's need for justice.

PREAMBLE: A Lawyer's Responsibilities

[1] A lawyer, as a member of the legal profession, is a representative of clients, an officer of the legal system and a public citizen having special responsibility for the quality of justice.

[2] As a representative of clients, a lawyer performs various functions. As advisor, a lawyer provides a client with an informed understanding of the client's legal rights and obligations and explains their practical implications. As advocate, a lawyer zealously asserts the client's position under the rules of the adversary system. As negotiator, a lawyer seeks a result advantageous to the client but consistent with requirements of honest dealings with others. As an evaluator, a lawyer

acts by examining a client's legal affairs and reporting about them to the client or to others. . . .

Rule 1.2 Scope of Representation and Allocation of Authority Between Client and Lawyer

(a) Subject to paragraphs (c) and (d), a lawyer shall abide by a client's decisions concerning the objectives of representation and, as required by Rule 1.4, shall consult with the client as to the means by which they are to be pursued. A lawyer may take such action on behalf of the client as is impliedly authorized to carry out the representation. A lawyer shall abide by a client's decision whether to settle a matter. In a criminal case, the lawyer shall abide by the client's decision, after consultation with the lawyer, as to a plea to be entered, whether to waive jury trial and whether the client will testify. . . .

MODEL RULES OF PROF'L CONDUCT (2013).

The law also addresses various aspects of the attorney-client relationship, including the question of authority. If a lawyer exceeds the scope of his authority in negotiating an agreement on a client's behalf, will the client be legally bound by the terms of the agreement? If the client suffers damage as a result of the agreement, will the client be able to sue the lawyer for malpractice or breach of fiduciary duty? Later in this chapter, we will turn to these and other knotty questions as we examine the law of the attorney-client relationship.

3.   ALLOCATION OF AUTHORITY

The following excerpt uses empirical research to provide a picture of the attorney-client relationship, particularly regarding how lawyers and clients interact when decisions must be made.

HERBERT M. KRITZER, THE JUSTICE BROKER: LAWYERS AND ORDINARY LITIGATION

60–65 (1990)

The idea of professional autonomy suggests that it is the professional who is dominant in the [attorney-client] relationship; [however,] norms for lawyer responsibility dictate that the client be advised and consulted at important junctures and that final decisions on important matters (e.g., filing a court case, rejecting or accepting an offer of settlement) be the responsibility of the client. While this ambiguity may suggest that it will be impossible to arrive at any kind of definitive statement on who dominates the relationship, the analysis shows very clearly that control rests largely with the lawyer, particularly when the client is an individual.

From the Lawyer's Viewpoint

* * *

THE NATURE OF CLIENT INVOLVEMENT

Concerning the nature of the explicit or ongoing understandings regarding the client's role, lawyers were asked to characterize them in terms of one of the following categories.

> The client would play a major decision-making role, providing (the lawyer) with instructions on some matters.

> The client would not play a major decision-making role, but (its) approval would be required on most decisions.

> (The lawyer) and the client would discuss matters, but (the lawyer) would make most of the decisions.

> The client would pretty much turn the case over to (the lawyer).

Not surprisingly, the largest groups of lawyers placed the understanding in the two intermediate categories (35 percent and 26 percent), with 19 percent describing the content as falling into each of the two extreme categories.

> Things shift somewhat when the lawyers describe the actual role taken by their clients. The actual role taken in 90 percent or more of the dyads where there was an understanding was consistent with that understanding, but when there was a discrepancy, there was a slight tendency for the actual role to be one of less involvement than called for by the understanding. Client involvement tended to be substantially lower when no agreement about that involvement was reached:

> - Only 20 percent of clients having an understanding with their lawyers about their involvement played no significant role at all, while 44 percent of the clients without an understanding played no significant role.

> - In 19 percent of the dyads where there was an understanding, the client's involvement fell at the high end versus only 8 percent where there was no understanding.

In general, the likely organizational clients tended to play a larger role than the likely individual clients, regardless of whether or not there was an explicit understanding . . .

> This pattern is confirmed, at least from the lawyer's viewpoint, by the responses to a second question: "To what degree was your client involved in determining case strategy other than in settlement negotiations?" Sixty-seven percent of the lawyers said that their clients had little or no role in determining case strategy, and only 13 percent said that the clients had been "very much" involved in strategic planning.

Again, the level of involvement among likely individual litigants was much lower than that among likely organizational litigants, with 59 percent of the likely organizations having little or no involvement compared to 79 percent of the likely individuals.

* * *

From the Client's Viewpoint

* * *

ALLOCATING RESPONSIBILITY

If the picture from the lawyers' side of the relationship is described as a substantial amount of autonomy being retained by the lawyer, that picture is quite consistent with what the clients report in terms of allocation of responsibility, reporting, and decision making. First, a majority of both organizational (52 percent) and individual (78 percent) litigants report that there were *no* discussions at all concerning allocation of responsibilities between the lawyer and the litigant. At least a part of this may reflect the existence of a prior relationship between the lawyer and the client in which explicit discussions had taken place or implicit understandings had been arrived at regarding responsibilities. Ninety-five of the 141 organizational litigants who reported no discussions concerning responsibilities and 50 of the 180 individual litigants so situated had had a prior professional relationship with their lawyer. If one makes the strong (and probably unwarranted) assumption that some prior discussion or agreement about responsibilities governed the relationship if the lawyer had worked for the litigant previously (and there was no explicit discussion for this particular case), then only 15 percent of the organizations were dealing with a lawyer where allocation of responsibilities had not been brought up or previously settled; the comparable figure for individuals is much, much higher at 57 percent. In actuality, the two figures for each type of litigant (15 percent and 52 percent for organizations, and 57 percent and 78 percent for individuals), provide an upper and lower bound for the likelihood that allocation of responsibilities had been deal with "up front".

* * *

STAYING INVOLVED AND INFORMED

This picture of greater involvement by organizations than individuals carries over to reporting practices from the lawyer to the client. Sixty-nine percent of the organizational litigants reported receiving regular written reports from their lawyer, compared to only 50 percent of the individual litigants. For the individuals receiving such reports, only 10 percent explicitly requested them—90 percent of the time, the reports were sent on the lawyer's own initiative; only 51 percent of the organizations said that the lawyer took the initiative in sending reports, with the rest indicating that they requested written reports or that such reports were simply part of the standard procedure.

While the level of involvement of the litigants in the major decisions in the case (filing the lawsuit, going to trial) seems to be quite high, these are the kinds of decisions that the lawyer would expect the client to be involved with. In fact, it is somewhat surprising that clients reported decisions being made entirely, or mostly, by the lawyers as often as they were; it is not surprising, given the other patterns I have described here, that lawyer dominance was greater with individual clients than with organizational clients. Seventy-six organizations reported that the suit was filed on their behalf; only 20 percent said that their lawyer (or "mostly" their lawyer) made the decisions, and another 18 percent said that their own involvement had been equal to that of their lawyer. One hundred and sixty-four individuals reported that the suit had been filed on their behalf; 29 percent said it was their lawyer's decision (or "mostly" the lawyer's decision), and 22 percent reported equal involvement by themselves and their lawyer. Thus, the litigant dominated the decision to file 62 percent of the time when that litigant was an organization, but only 49 percent of the time when it was an individual.

NOTES

1.   Many of the examples in this book deal with civil transactions and disputes, in which problems in the attorney-client relationship can lead to malpractice claims or attempts to vacate agreements. The attorney-client relationship is also extraordinarily important in the criminal context. Professors Rodney Uphoff and Peter Wood found that public defenders have varying levels of commitment to the concept of client-centered decision-making. Most of the lawyers surveyed strongly agreed that the following four decisions should involve the client's consent: waiving a jury trial; entering into or rejecting a plea bargain; having the client testify at trial; and waiving a preliminary hearing. There was a sharp division among the lawyers, though, on whether the client's consent was needed to decide whether to: talk to the prosecutor about a possible plea bargain, raise an affirmative defense or request a lesser included instruction. *See* Rodney J. Uphoff & Peter B. Wood, *The Allocation of Decisionmaking Between Counsel and Criminal Defendant: An Empirical Study of Attorney–Client Decisionmaking*, 47 U. Kan. L. Rev. 1, 34 (1998).

2.   Professor Kritzer reports that organizational clients tend to exercise more control in the attorney-client relationship than do individual clients. Professor David Wilkins asserts that today's corporate clients can wield incentives in such a manner that they have the ability to "hold their lawyer-agents to full-throated standards of partisan advocacy." This is due to the "logic of power," which emphasizes the ability of corporate clients to coerce their counsel into taking certain positions or engaging in certain behaviors.

Professor Wilkins further asserts, however, that the "logic of power" has failed to deliver fully on its promises of lawyering quality and reduced costs, and therefore corporate clients are now moving to a "logic of embeddedness." Law firms' lawyers now may be located inside certain corporate clients' offices. The firms may invite their most significant corporate clients to participate in interviews of potential associates. The goal is to emphasize reciprocity and mutual trust in the relationship between lawyer and client "for the production of joint gains." Professor Wilkins acknowledges that this model of the attorney-client relationship is not consistent with the principal-agent template and "arguably threatens the ability of outside counsel to function as public-regarding gatekeepers" but he asserts that:

> the logic of embeddedness is no more corrosive of public-regarding values than the logic of power that now typifies the relationship between companies and their outside firms. Indeed, this logic has the potential to be significantly less corrosive—particularly if we move away from ethical and regulatory structures based on a principal-agent model that serves only to entrench the ability of powerful corporate-principals to impose their will on increasingly vulnerable lawyer-agents. Indeed as a wag like Bentham might say, current market conditions have largely turned the traditional justification for the agency model on its head. By withholding information and manipulating incentives, sophisticated corporate clients now have the power to pressure their lawyers into taking risky or unethical actions that threaten to throw their law firms "into confusion" in the form of legal peril or financial ruin. "Innocent" lawyers who do not want to participate in such actions have no recourse other than to resign—or be fired. At the same time, "guilty" lawyers who have no interest in standing up to client pressure are given a pass on the ground that they are not responsible for the ends of the representation and are required to follow the client's direction so long as it is technically within the letter of the law. A model of the attorney-client relationship that recognizes that both clients and lawyers have reciprocal obligations of disclosure, forbearance, and fair dealing of the kind characteristic of strategic alliances, I will argue, provides a better foundation for dealing with these increasingly important problems.

David B. Wilkins, *Team of Rivals? Toward a New Model of the Corporate Attorney–Client Relationship*, 78 Fordham L. Rev. 2067, 2071–72 (2010). How does the "logic of embeddedness" fit with the traditional, client-centered and collaborative models of the attorney-client relationship?

3. The allocation of authority between lawyers and their clients has both ethical and legal implications. Review Rule 1.2 of the Model Rules of Professional Conduct, *supra*. We will deal with potential legal issues *infra*. For now, though, consider these questions:

a. Imagine that you represent a young woman who has been charged with assaulting a police officer. She claims that she is innocent of any crime. Indeed, she tells you that the officer tackled her and put her in a chokehold simply because she encouraged her 7–year–old neighbor to go into the house and get his mother after the officer started asking the young boy some questions. You believe that your client is telling you the truth. But you also think that it is very unlikely that the prosecutor or judge will believe her. Without consulting your client, you contact the prosecutor to ask about reducing the felony charges to misdemeanors. Have you stayed within the scope of your authority according to the Model Rules of Professional Conduct?

     b.   Now imagine that you represent an entrepreneur in the negotiation of a business deal. During negotiations with the other party's lawyer, you see a solution that strikes you as wise and even elegant. You have not discussed this negotiated solution with your client. Ethically, may you indicate to the other lawyer that your client agrees to be bound by this resolution? According to the Model Rules of Professional Conduct what course of action are you obligated to take? Practically speaking, what course of action seems advisable?

4.   INCENTIVES IN THE ATTORNEY-CLIENT RELATIONSHIP

     Whether traditional, client-centered, collaborative, or some combination of these, the relationship between a client and lawyer is generally understood as a classic example of a principal-agent relationship. The client, as principal, retains the lawyer, as her agent, to carry out her wishes. As the following excerpt explains, all agency relationships, including the attorney-client relationship, can have complicated dynamics.

ROBERT H. MNOOKIN, SCOTT R. PEPPET & ANDREW S. TULUMELLO, BEYOND WINNING: NEGOTIATING TO CREATE VALUE IN DEALS AND DISPUTES*
70–71 (2000)

     Agency relationships are everywhere. We constantly delegate authority to others so that they may act in our place. We ask lawyers to represent us; we give money managers authority to make our investments; we ask doctors to take responsibility for our medical care; we depend on employees to do the work we assign; and we elect public officials to legislate on our behalf. Indeed, it is hard to imagine how society could function at all without agents acting on behalf of principals—diplomats on behalf of nations; labor leaders on behalf of unions; sports agents on behalf of players; literary agents on behalf of authors.

     When a principal hires an agent to act on his behalf in negotiations across the table with another party, he may expect—naively—that the agent will be motivated solely to serve the principal's interests. This is

---

how principal-agent relations would work ideally. But in the real world, agents always have interests of their own. As a result, the principal-agent relationship is rife with potential conflicts that demand skillful management behind the table.

For example, a client and his lawyer may need to negotiate how the lawyer will be paid; how the other side will be approached; what information will be sought from or disclosed to the other side; at what point to accept the other side's offer, and so on. If these issues are left unacknowledged and unaddressed, they can adversely affect the negotiation across the table. For all of these reasons, effective negotiation requires a good understanding of the benefits and risks of the agency relationship and how it can best be managed.

NOTES AND QUESTIONS

1.   As the excerpt from Professor Mnookin and his colleagues suggests, clients hire lawyers because they can offer certain advantages or benefits in dispute resolution. Below, we explore three "agency benefits" offered by lawyers: "rationality," expertise, and strategic advantages.

a.   *"Rationality."* Lawyers may offer their clients a more rational perspective, which may be of particular value in highly-charged disputes like contentious divorce disputes, employment disputes, corporate dissolutions, and so on.

> Most lawyers, perhaps by personality as well as by training and practice, approach the world in an abstract, analytical way. Lawyers are deemed so rational and analytical, in fact, that "brain researchers have selected lawyers when they wished to test an occupational group that is characteristically analytical in its preferred mode of thought." Scholars using a variety of methodologies have demonstrated that lawyers are analytically inclined. Researchers using a brain-dominance testing instrument, for instance, have found that nearly 90% of lawyers are "left-brain dominant," indicating an analytical orientation. Researchers have also used the Myers–Briggs Type Indicator (MBTI) to assess lawyers' personalities. The MBTI, which is based on Jungian psychology, measures four dimensions of personality, including whether one is inclined toward "thinking" or "feeling." Thinkers "make decisions more analytically and impersonally" than Feelers. "When making decisions, they place more value on consistency and fairness than on how others will be affected. They look for flaws and fallacies, excelling at critiquing conclusions and pinpointing what is wrong with something." Researchers from the 1960s to the 1990s have found that lawyers are substantially more inclined toward the "thinking" orientation than the population as a whole. Lawyers, in short, "tend to be more logical, unemotional, rational, and objective" than others and place a "great emphasis on logic, thinking, rationality, justice, fairness, rights, and rules."

Chris Guthrie, *The Lawyer's Philosophical Map and the Disputant's Perceptual Map: Impediments to Facilitative Mediation and Lawyering*, 6 Harv. Negot. L. Rev. 145, 156–57 (2001). Consider the interaction between a lawyer's rationality and the ethical obligation to provide "independent professional judgment" and "candid advice" to clients.

b.   *Expertise and Relationships.* Lawyers also offer their clients special knowledge. As the following excerpt explains, this expertise can take several forms:

> *Substantive knowledge.* A tax attorney or accountant knows things about the current tax code that make it more likely that negotiations with an IRS auditor will benefit the client as much as possible. Similarly, a divorce lawyer, an engineering consultant, and a real estate agent may have substantive knowledge in a rather narrow domain of expertise, and this expertise may redound to the client's benefit.
>
> *Process expertise.* Quite apart from the specific expertise they may have in particular content areas, agents may have skill at the negotiation *process,* per se, thereby enhancing the prospects of a favorable agreement. A skillful negotiator—someone who understands how to obtain and reveal information about preferences, who is inventive, resourceful, firm on goals but flexible on means, etc.—is a valuable resource. Wise principals would do well to utilize the services of such skilled negotiators, unless they can find ways of developing such process skills themselves.
>
> *Special influence.* A Washington lobbyist is paid to know the "right" people, to have access to the "corridors of power" that the principals themselves are unlikely to possess. Such "pull" can certainly help immensely, and is yet another form of expertise that agents may possess, although the lure of this "access" often outweighs in promise the special benefits that are confirmed in reality.

Jeffrey Z. Rubin & Frank E. A. Sander, *When Should We Use Agents? Direct vs. Representative Negotiation*, 4 Negotiation J. 395, 396 (1988).

c.   *Strategic Advantages.* Lawyers also may offer their clients certain strategic advantages. The following excerpt identifies some specific strategic advantages lawyers might offer their clients in negotiation:

> The use of agents allows various gambits to be played out by the principals, in an effort to ratchet as much as possible from the other side. For example, if a seller asserts that the bottom line is $100,000, the buyer can try to haggle, albeit at the risk of losing the deal. If the buyer employs an agent, however, the agent can profess willingness to pay that sum but plead lack of authority, thereby gaining valuable time and opportunity for fuller consideration of the situation together with the principal. Or an agent for the seller who senses that the buyer may be especially eager to buy the property can claim that it is necessary to go back to the seller for ratification of the deal, only to return and up the price, profusely apologizing all the while for the behavior of an

"unreasonable" client. The client and agent can thus together play the hard-hearted partner game.

Conversely, an agent may be used in order to push the other side in tough, even obnoxious, fashion, making it possible—in the best tradition of the "good cop/bad cop" ploy—for the client to intercede at last, and seem the essence of sweet reason in comparison with the agent. Or the agent may be used as a "stalking horse," to gather as much information about the adversary as possible, opening the way to proposals by the client that exploit the intelligence gathered.

Id. at 397–98. In a related vein, Professors Ronald Gilson and Robert Mnookin have suggested that clients who do not trust each other may nonetheless have an interest in signaling their desire to negotiate cooperatively. They may accomplish this by hiring a lawyer or firm with a reputation for cooperative behavior. *See* Ronald J. Gilson & Robert H. Mnookin, *Disputing Through Agents: Cooperation and Conflict Between Lawyers in Litigation*, 94 Colum. L. Rev. 509, 522–523 (1994). Similarly, clients seeking a sustainable long-term relationship could signal this intent by hiring lawyers with reputations for negotiating durable contracts. *See* Jamison Davies, *Formalizing Legal Reputation Markets*, 16 Harv. Negot. L. Rev. 367 (2011) (proposing a secondary or "prediction market" essentially based on the sale of derivative contracts that would monetize predictions regarding the primary contract's durability).

2.   Notwithstanding the benefits identified above, lawyers may impose certain disadvantages or costs on their clients as well. Below, we explore three agency costs: rationality, conflicting interests, and misaligned incentives.

a.   *Rationality.* Lawyers are famously rational or analytical in their approach to disputes. As noted above, this orientation often works to the benefit of clients. In some circumstances, though, it can pose significant problems:

[L]awyers' analytical prowess is "purchased at the price of a loss of concrete information" because abstract analysis necessarily reduces complexity. When information is too complex or too subtle to lend itself to abstract reduction, lawyers often have difficulty understanding, interpreting, and working with such information. One task that requires "a gestalt appreciation of an unedited set of concrete data, rather than abstract analytical reduction," is the "recognition and interpretation of subtle displays of emotion."

For all their analytical skills, most lawyers seem fairly uninterested in, and unskilled at, dealing with emotional and interpersonal content. Researchers using the MBTI, for example, have found not only that lawyers are more inclined toward the "thinking" orientation than the population as a whole, but also that lawyers are substantially less inclined toward the "feeling" orientation. Feelers "make decisions more subjectively [than Thinkers], according to their values or what is more important to them. They also place greater emphasis on how other people will be affected by their choices and actions. . . . It is possible for them to decide whether something is acceptable or agreeable without needing logical reasons." Professors John Barkai and Virginia Fine administered the Truax Accurate Empathy Scale to law students and found that even after undergoing empathy training, law students obtained an average score below Level Five on the scale, "the minimum level of facilitative interpersonal functioning." Professor G. Andrew Benjamin and his colleagues, who undertook a comprehensive study of the mental health and well-being of law students and lawyers, found elevated levels of mental distress and speculated that this could be due to the "[u]nbalanced development of [law] student interpersonal skills." Professor James Hedegard, in his study of BYU law students found "drops in sociability and, more generally, interest in people" during the first year of law school. And Professor Sandra Janoff, who studied the moral reasoning of law students before and after the first year of law school, found that law students became less "caring" during their first year of formal legal education.

On balance, this research suggests that lawyers are "less interested in people, in emotions, and interpersonal concerns" than others.

Chris Guthrie, *The Lawyer's Philosophical Map and the Disputant's Perceptual Map: Impediments to Facilitative Mediation and Lawyering*, 6 Harv. Negot. L. Rev. 145, 158–60 (2001).

Lawyers' traditional approach to rationality may be particularly counterproductive for certain types of clients. In the transactional context, for example, lawyer Scott Edward Walker has developed a list of the top ten reasons that entrepreneurs hate—or at least complain about—lawyers. Topping the list is: "Because they are deal killers." Walker explains:

> Lawyers are often viewed as deal-killers because of their failure to set a positive tone and their annoying habit of raising all sorts of reasons why a particular deal won't close or why a particular idea won't work. One of the better lawyers I worked with at a firm often said: "Good lawyers are able to identify significant potential legal problems; great lawyers provide solutions to those problems."

> As James Freund, a professor and retired partner at Skadden Arps in New York, points out, "In a transactional practice, nothing comes easy. There are invariably two opposing points of view on significant issues, and the parties will even clash . . . over a circumstance that may never come to pass. Every disputed issue has to be resolved in order for the deal to take place. And the business lawyers bear the primary responsibility for getting it done. Viewed in its broader context, this activity falls under the rubric of problem solving. Unless you're a problem solver, you're unlikely to be an effective business lawyer. And the problems that stand in your way aren't limited to transactional matters . . . they can involve dealings

with regulatory agencies, tax planning, strategizing about how to protect intellectual property, and on and on."

Scott Edward Walker, *Top 10 Reasons Why Entrepreneurs Hate Lawyers*, available at http://venturehacks.com/articles/hate-lawyers. Several of Walker's other reasons that entrepreneurs "hate" lawyers suggest that lawyers could do better in communicating and demonstrating understanding of their clients' most important interests:

- "Because they don't communicate clearly or concisely"
- "Because they don't keep me informed"
- "Because they have poor listening skills"
- "Because they spend too much time on insignificant issues"
- "Because they don't genuinely care about me or my matter"
- "Because they are unresponsive"

Id. The Law School Admission Project: Looking Beyond the LSAT, led by principal investigators Marjorie Shultz and Sheldon Zedeck, has identified the following 26 lawyering effectiveness factors: analysis and reasoning, creativity/innovation, practical judgment, researching the law, passion and engagement, questioning and interviewing, influencing and advocating, writing, speaking, integrity/honesty, ability to see the world through the eyes of others, self-development, organizing and managing others, negotiation skills, networking and business development, building client relationship including advice and counsel, organizing and managing own work, developing relationships, evaluation/development/mentoring, problem solving, stress management, fact finding, diligence, listening, community involvement and service, and strategic planning. Several of the factors identified by Shultz and Zedeck suggest that effective lawyers display interest in people, emotions and interpersonal relations. See Marjorie M. Shultz and Sheldon Zedeck, Final Report: Identification, Development, and Validation of Predictors for Successful Lawyering (September 2008).

     b. *Conflicting Interests and Identities.* Despite the requirement that lawyers act on their clients' behalf, consult with them and abide by their decisions on certain matters, lawyers and clients may encounter conflicting interests:

> In theory, it is clear that the principal calls the shots. Imagine, however, an agent who is intent on applying the GETTING TO YES (Fisher and Ury, 1981) approach by searching for objective criteria and a fair outcome. Suppose the client simply wants the best possible outcome, perhaps because it is a one-shot deal not involving a future relationship with the other party. What if the agent (a lawyer, perhaps) *does* care about his future relationship with the other *agent,* and wants to be remembered as a fair and scrupulous bargainer? How *should* this conflict get resolved and how, in the absence of explicit discussion, *will* it be resolved, if at all? Conversely, the client, because of a valuable long-

term relationship, may want to maintain good relations with the other side. But if the client simply looks for an agent who is renowned for an ability to pull out all the stops, the client's overall objectives may suffer as the result of an overzealous advocate.

This issue may arise in a number of contexts. Suppose that, in the course of a dispute settlement negotiation, a lawyer who is intent on getting the best possible deal for a client turns down an offer that was within the client's acceptable range. Is this proper behavior by the agent? The Model Rules of Professional Conduct for attorneys explicitly require (see Rules 1.2(a), 1.4) that every offer must be communicated to the principal, and perhaps a failure to do so might lead to a successful malpractice action against the attorney if the deal finally fell through.

Jeffrey Z. Rubin & Frank E. A. Sander, *When Should We Use Agents? Direct vs. Representative Negotiation*, 4 Negotiation J. 395, 399–40 (1988). This would be a good time to review Rules 1.2, 1.4 and 1.7 of the Model Rules of Professional Conduct. See Appendix 2 *infra*. We will look at the potential for malpractice and breach of fiduciary duty claims, *infra*.

c.   *Misaligned Incentives.* Conflicting interests can lead to conflicting economic incentives. Misaligned incentives, in turn, can lead lawyers to take actions that might not be in the client's best interests, as the following excerpt explains:

> The economic literature on agency, and scholarship relating to transaction cost economics, teaches that an agent's incentives cannot be perfectly aligned with those of her principal. Using an agent allows the principal the benefits of the agent's special knowledge, skills, and resources. However, the interests of an agent negotiating on behalf of a principal may be a barrier to reaching an agreement that would benefit the principal. For example, critics often claim that litigators are themselves a barrier to the efficient resolution of business disputes through early settlement. High discovery costs surely contribute to the income of partners in many large American defense law firms. Similarly, the fact that plaintiffs' lawyers paid on contingency largely bear the costs of trial surely leads to some settlements that are not in the clients' interests.

Ronald J. Gilson & Robert H. Mnookin, *Foreword: Business Lawyers and Value Creation for Clients*, 74 Or. L. Rev. 1, 11–12 (1995).

3.   In what circumstances do the agency benefits of the attorney-client relationship outweigh the agency costs? Which of the agency benefits is most important? Which of the agency costs is most troubling?

4.   What strategies might clients and lawyers employ to maximize agency benefits but to minimize agency costs? Professor Scott Peppet recommends six "principles" for managing the agency relationship in negotiation:

Principle One: If possible, use agents (and work for principals) whose preferences are known and acceptable to you.

* * *

Principle Two: If possible, use agents (and work for principals) whose preferences are known to the other side.

* * *

Principle Three: If possible, change the structure of the negotiation to align the incentives of principal and agent.

* * *

Principle Four: Share information between principal and agent to the extent necessary to effect the principal's strategy.

* * *

Principle Five: Treat role coordination and authority delegation as an ongoing negotiation, not a one-time event.

* * *

Principle Six: Rely most heavily on an agent when psychological biases or emotional risks cloud the principal's decision making.

Scott R. Peppet, *Six Principles for Using Negotiating Agents to Maximum Advantage, in* THE HANDBOOK OF DISPUTE RESOLUTION 189, 194–98 (Michael L. Moffitt & Robert C. Bordone eds. 2005).

5.   Professor Peppet recommends aligning incentives between the principal and agent. Some fee arrangements, like contingency fees, are designed to improve the alignment of the lawyer's and client's incentives. But such alignment can disappear when the lawyer thinks the client should settle a case, and the client wants to continue to litigate. There also can be times when a lawyer may find it difficult to anticipate or understand the incentives motivating her client due to differences between the lawyer and client in terms of their life experiences, social identities, cultures or vulnerabilities. *See e.g.*, Lucie E. White, *Subordination, Rhetorical Survival Skills, and Sunday Shoes: Notes on the Hearing of Mrs. G.*, 38 Buff. L. Rev. 1, 46–51 (1990) (exploring why client did not speak at hearing as she and her lawyer had planned); *see also* Carla D. Pratt, *Way to Represent: The Role of Black Lawyers in Contemporary American Democracy*, 77 Fordham L. Rev. 1409, 1410–11 (2009) (urging that black lawyers enhance black citizens' participation in democracy, in part by serving an interpretive function in translating both the language of democracy and the concerns of members of the black community).

6.   How does Professor Wilkins' "logic of embeddedness," described *supra* in Section A.3. (on the allocation of authority), deal with the alignment

of incentives? Do the Model Rules of Professional Conduct, *supra*, assume a *complete* alignment of incentives between lawyer and client?

7. Consider the following hypothetical. Jim, a solo practitioner specializing in personal injury, is representing Sandy, a retail department store clerk, in a personal injury matter on a contingency basis, in which Jim will keep 33% of Sandy's recovery. Sandy was in a car accident in which her car was totaled by the driver of a major overnight shipping company, who was hurrying to meet a drop-off deadline. Sandy's actual damages were $30,000 for the cost of replacing her car, plus another $10,000 in medical expenses. During the discovery process, however, Jim learns that the shipping company has very tight drop-off deadlines for drivers, and that the accident rate for the company's drivers is ten times higher than the industry standard. The shipping company has offered a settlement of $45,000, which Jim knows Sandy might be willing to accept to put the matter behind her. However, Jim thinks Sandy's claim will be more valuable if he uses it to pursue a class action against the shipper. How are Jim's and Sandy's interests aligned? How are they inconsistent? When you consider the models of the attorney-client relationship identified *supra*, which do you think is most likely to enhance the alignment of Jim's and Sandy's interests?

8. Consider Jim and Sandy once again. How do the Model Rules of Professional Conduct, *supra*, apply to their situation?

B. INTERVIEWING

In this section, we introduce our version of client interviewing, which is based on insights developed by proponents of both the Binder, Bergman & Price client-centered model of interviewing and the Cochran, DiPippa & Peters collaborative model of interviewing.

We believe that the lawyer's primary task is to understand the client's situation and interests as well as legally relevant facts (i.e., facts that might help establish a cause of action or defense). Of course, it is typically important for the lawyer to understand and develop the relevant legal theories. However, over-emphasis on law particularly in the early stages of the consultation can obscure the client's interests and non-legal concerns, unduly narrow the subject matter of the attorney-client relationship, and cut off opportunities for finding the best processes and solutions.

1. OVERVIEW OF THE PROCESS

What follows is an overview of an interviewing process that will help you acquire the information you need to help your client define the problem and develop options that meet her interests (and perhaps the interests of others). The interviewing process we recommend has six stages: a. introduction; b. preliminary problem identification; c. detailed problem identification; d. exploration of interests; e. theory development; and f. next steps.

a. Introduction

During the initial moments of the interview, the lawyer seeks to build trust and establish rapport with the client by introducing herself, exchanging pleasantries (or "icebreaking"), and discussing the terms of the representation. The lawyer should take steps to put the client at ease without minimizing the concerns that may have brought the client to the lawyer's office.

In the following excerpt, Professor Janice Nadler details the elements that contribute to the development of rapport:

JANICE NADLER, RAPPORT IN NEGOTIATION AND CONFLICT RESOLUTION
87 Marq. L. Rev. 875, 875–76 (2004).

Interpersonal rapport has been described as a state of mutual positivity and interest. The development of rapport has been characterized by three dynamic components: (1) mutual attention and involvement; (2) positivity; and (3) coordination. These will be considered in turn.

First, mutual attention and involvement are exemplified by the simple idea that my focusing attention on you makes you feel involved in the interaction, and vice-versa. An important component of rapport is when we both simultaneously attend to one another and both feel involved in the interaction. Mutual attention and involvement are signaled by the physical orientation of participants in the interaction. For example, spontaneous formation of a circular or semi-circular configuration in a group, forward lean, uncrossed arms, and eye contact are all signals of attention, and, in turn, foster feelings of involvement in the interaction.

Second, rapport is characterized by participants in an interaction having positive attitudes toward one another. Such mutual positivity is signaled by particular nonverbal behaviors such as forward lean, eye contact, smiling, and gestures

Third, most definitions of rapport include in their descriptions the feeling of being "in sync" with the other persons in the interaction. Rapport-related coordination includes smooth turn taking in conversation, in which the listener acknowledges understanding, agreement, or attention with forward lean, head nods, and brief verbal responses (e.g., "uh-huh"). In addition to smooth turn taking, rapport-related coordination is characterized by nonconscious mimicry, which occurs when one person imitates the behaviors of another. Without even realizing it, when people interact they tend to mirror one another in posture, facial expression, tone of voice, and mannerisms. On the surface, it might seem that mimicking would be annoying—almost like a form of mockery. The type of mimicry that is involved in everyday social encounters, however, is quite subtle—people do not usually recognize when it is happening. At the same time, powerful effects of mimicry result in greater liking and rapport in an interaction. For example, in one study, half the participants were mimicked by the other person in the interaction and half were not. Participants who were mimicked rated the interaction as more smooth and harmonious than those who were not. Additionally, when people are motivated to create an affiliation with another person, they automatically and unconsciously increase their mimicry behavior to accomplish this goal. When two people are mirroring one another, their movements become a choreographed dance. To the extent that our behaviors are synchronized with those of others, we feel more rapport, and this increases our trust in those with whom we communicate.

NOTES AND QUESTIONS

1. Professor Nadler was writing in the context of conflict resolution. However, rapport is also important in the attorney-client relationship. What does the reading suggest to you might be effective ways of building rapport with a new client?

2. With new clients and others, "icebreakers" are often particularly helpful in terms of cultivating rapport. Why do you this might be the case. Are there any topics that are particularly good icebreakers? Bad icebreakers?

3. Consider someone with whom you have especially good rapport. Which of the Nadler components do you think help explain why the two of you have good rapport? How? Now consider someone with whom you do not have good rapport, and ask yourself which of the Nadler factors seem to provide an explanation. Finally, suppose you seek better rapport with that person. Do the Nadler considerations offer any suggestions for improving the rapport between the two of you?

We view the techniques of active listening and looping as "all purpose" negotiation techniques, even though we have followed convention by including them among the techniques associated with the problem-solving strategy.

4. Increasingly, lawyers and clients use the "lean medium" of email to communicate, which requires the development of different and intentional strategies for developing rapport. *See* Leigh Thompson & Janice Nadler, *Judgmental Biases* in *Conflict Resolution and How to Overcome Them*, in HANDBOOK OF CONFLICT RESOLUTION 228–29 (Morton Deutsch & Peter Coleman eds., 2000) (describing the effectiveness of beginning email interaction with personal interaction or "schmoozing"); Noam Ebner, Anita D. Bhappu, Jennifer Gerarda Brown, Kimberlee K. Kovach & Andrea Kupfer

Schneider, *You've Got Agreement: Negoti@ting via Email*, in RETHINKING NEGOTIATION TEACHING 89 (2009).

b. Preliminary Problem Identification

During the preliminary problem identification stage of the interview, the lawyer seeks to develop a basic notion of what brought the client into the office and what the client would like to happen. Typically, the lawyer would use open-ended questions, such as, "How can I help you?" and "What brought you here?"

Suppose, for example, that a client explains he is an executive with Hays Corp., a manufacturer of water filtration equipment, and that the firm wants to sue Hovercamp Brewery for failure to make certain payments due under a contract. He wants you to tell him whether Hays has a strong claim. That's plenty of information for the preliminary problem identification, but it might not be enough for the lawyer to understand how she can most appropriately help the client.

Some lawyers might, at least temporarily, allow the client's first definition of the problem to set the parameters of the representation. Such lawyers might then gather the information needed to answer the client's question. This might lead to a discussion of solutions that focus narrowly on what would happen in court.

Under the approach we recommend, however, the lawyer would try to slow down the process in order to learn more about what happened and the client's situation, interests, and goals.

c. Detailed Problem Identification

During this stage, the lawyer asks the client to start at the beginning and describe the events that led to the situation at hand—whether an automobile accident or negotiations to start a new joint venture. Generally, the lawyer leads the client gently during this stage, interrupting principally to obtain essential clarifications or—if the client is rambling excessively (a reasonable amount of rambling can be helpful)—to get the client back on track. Ordinarily, this approach yields the bulk of the basic information that the lawyer will need.

During this stage, the Hays executive would describe the two corporations and the history of their relationship. He would set forth the events, as he saw them, leading up to the contract under which Hays developed and installed a water purification system for Hovercamp Brewing. He would explain that the system did not work as expected because the water contained debris of the sort that Hays did not anticipate; that Hovercamp knew of the debris but did not tell Hays; that Hays tried to correct the problem but was unable to do so; and that he has heard that Hovercamp eventually hired another company that was able to correct the problem. Finally, the Hays executive might explain that Hovercamp has withheld $100,000 of the payments due under the contract.

d.   Exploration of Positions and Interests

During this stage, the lawyer probes to understand, and to make sure the client understands, not merely his *positions* but also his *interests*.

A client's *position* is what he says he wants. A client who feels he has been defamed, for instance, may demand $1 million. A client's *interests* are the motivations or needs that impel him to assert that position. These interests may be substantive, procedural, or psychological. The client may be motivated to repair his reputation; to "punish" the newspaper editor; to get the newspaper to change its reporting practices; to support his family; to maintain his business; or to buy a new sailboat. These are interests. Looking at your client's interests along with the interests of the other side makes it easier to come up with solutions.

It is clear that the Hays executive wishes to assert the *position* that Hays is legally entitled to the $100,000 payment that Hovercamp has withheld. But the lawyer should explore to the extent the client is willing to do so the client's underlying interests as well. So, for instance, the lawyer might ask the Hays executive about the firm's current situation, its short- and long-term goals, and any significant new developments in the services or products it provides. The client might explain that Hays wishes to expand its services to the brewing and bottling industries and that it has developed but has not found an opportunity to test a new technology that probably will deal with the problem in the system it installed for Hovercamp. As the lawyer and client discuss the situation, the client may reach a new understanding of the problem or at least recognize that the problem can be defined in a different way.

The lawyer might ask what attempts Hays has made to negotiate a settlement with Hovercamp, and what has stood in the way. Consequently, she might, for instance, learn about personality problems or communication difficulties or hurt feelings. The lawyer would seek to learn how the other side—the Hovercamp executives—might see this situation and what their interests and goals might be as well.

e.   Development of Legal Theory

Now that the lawyer understands the client's interests, the lawyer is in a much better position to determine what she might do for the client. To the extent legal remedies seem appropriate—here, for instance, a breach of contract suit against Hovercamp may be a real possibility—the lawyer makes sure she has or requests the facts necessary to develop her legal theory. In this case, for instance, she would want a copy of the contract and any other relevant document, would want to understand the course of dealings between Hays and Hovercamp, and would want to know the customary practices in this industry.

f.   Next Steps

Finally, before terminating the interview, the lawyer and client discuss what they will do next. In some instances, the matter could end at this point; the interview may lead the client to determine that legal representation is not what he needs or may lead the lawyer to decide she will not represent the client. In other instances, the lawyer and client will decide to work together to address the client's problem. At this point, the lawyer makes clear what she intends to do next and may ask the client for assistance—e.g., providing documents and so forth.

NOTES AND QUESTIONS

1.   Lawyers have to make judgments about the problem(s) confronting their clients. Many refer to this assessment as "theory development" and focus on determining a legal theory or theories that could govern the case in court. Others view this assessment process as "problem setting," which can include identifying a legal theory but also can be much broader and quite demanding:

> In real-world practice, problems do not present themselves to the practitioner as givens. They must be constructed from the materials of problematic situations which are puzzling, troubling, and uncertain. In order to convert a problematic situation to a problem, a practitioner must do a certain kind of work. He must make sense of an uncertain situation that initially makes no sense.

* * *

> When we set the problem, we select what we will treat as the "things" of the situation, we set the boundaries of our attention to it, and we impose upon it a coherence which allows us to say what is wrong and in what directions the situation needs to be changed. Problem setting is a process in which, interactively, we *name* the things to which we will attend and *frame* the context in which we will attend to them.

DONALD A. SCHON, THE REFLECTIVE PRACTITIONER: HOW PROFESSIONALS THINK IN ACTION 40 (1983).

2.   Although lawyers must help "set" or diagnose the client's problems, they must strive to avoid premature diagnosis. There is a true story about a medical resident working in an emergency room who was interviewing a middle aged man who complained of chest pain. Immediately the resident asked, "Have you ever had heart trouble?"

"No."

"Have your parents had heart trouble?"

"No."

"How about your siblings or other relatives?"

"No, Doc," the patient answered. "How come you're asking all these questions about heart trouble?"

"Because I think that the reason you are having chest pain is that you are having a heart attack," said the resident.

"Well, Doc," replied the patient, "I think the reason I am having chest pain is that a tractor ran over my chest this afternoon."

The same kind of premature diagnosis can take place in a law office. It is easy for a lawyer to mentally transform a client, a human being, into a "rear-ender" or a "breach of contract." The interviewing approach delineated above should help the lawyer avoid this problem.

3.   Although it is important not to jump to conclusions about the problem confronting the client, it is also important to attend carefully to the disclosures the client makes early in the interview. In her empirical study of attorney-client interviews, Professor Gay Gellhorn found "a pattern of revelation of key, emotion-laden information in the opening moments of the interview. . . ." Gay Gellhorn, *Law and Language: An Empirically–Based Model for the Opening Moments of Client Interviews*, 4 Clinical L. Rev. 321, 326 (1998).

4.   The interview is often an ongoing process rather than a single event, with the lawyer and the client continuing to communicate about new issues as they arise, and preferences as they develop.

2.   QUESTIONING AND LISTENING

In interviews, the lawyer attempts to obtain relevant information from the client about the problems that have brought her to the lawyer. The lawyer is attentive to the client, strives to develop trust, and works to cultivate a productive relationship. This means, of course, that lawyers need to develop good communication skills to become effective interviewers. The two communication skills most directly relevant to interviewing are questioning and listening. These two skills facilitate the information-gathering required of effective interviewing. At the same time, the lawyer who asks and listens well demonstrates empathy, which will facilitate the development of a trusting and productive working relationship between her and her client. Good questioning and listening skills are also important to lawyers' counseling of their clients, as well as other dispute resolution processes we will discuss in this book.

a.   Questioning

The primary purpose of client interviews is for the lawyer to elicit information from the client. To do so effectively, lawyers must cultivate their questioning skills. Generally speaking, lawyers should begin an interview with *open* or *open-ended* questions to gather general information and subsequently ask *specific* or *closed* questions to clarify understandings.

Open-ended questions. Open-ended questions are broad enough to permit the respondent to choose the subject matter:

"What prompted you to see a lawyer?"

"What brings you here today?"

"What happened?"

An open-ended question can enhance the client's willingness to talk and ability to choose the topics to be discussed. If accompanied by effective listening, an open-ended question can thus increase rapport and elicit substantial information.

> Open inquiry is encouraged to take advantage of its potential to communicate that clients are important, essential resources in the information-gathering process. It also provides maximum opportunities for lawyers to listen to their clients and build rapport by demonstrating they heard and understood what was being said. Using open questions may avoid the damage to rapport resulting from focused inquiry posed prematurely on topics that are likely to threaten clients. Contemporary interviewing literature acknowledges that an effective interviewer must consider the motivational realities of human communication, and one of these realities is that questions seeking certain types of information can inhibit complete disclosure. Open inquiry is also recommended because it has the information-gathering advantage of letting clients respond from their frames of reference and relevance. Open inquiry is particularly suggested for beginning interviews when lawyers should invite their clients to talk freely about their situations and what they want to do about them.

DON PETERS & MARTHA M. PETERS, MAYBE THAT'S WHY I DO THAT: PSYCHOLOGICAL TYPE THEORY, THE MYERS–BRIGGS TYPE INDICATOR, AND LEARNING LEGAL INTERVIEWING 169, 186 (1990).

In some circumstances, however, broad open-ended questions may engender discomfort, or draw information that is insufficiently relevant. When that happens, the lawyer should temporarily abandon such questions and opt for closed questions.

Closed questions are designed to elicit particular pieces of information:

"Where were you born?"

"How much is your rent?"

"What happened to your car after the accident?"

A subset of closed questions permits only a "yes" or "no" answer:

"Was the door ajar?"

In some situations, closed questions can increase the client's comfort level, improve rapport, and stimulate recollections. In other situations, however, they may stem the flow of information or make the client feel cut off. These negative consequences are more likely to occur if closed questions are used too early, or if they take the form of *leading questions* (e.g., "The door was ajar, wasn't it?").

The following reading explores the relative advantages and disadvantages of open-ended and closed questions in the context of immigration interviews:

SANA LOUE, A GUIDE TO BETTER CLIENT INTERVIEWS*
89–07 Immigration Briefings 1 (1989)

Probing for Information

You must be able to motivate your client to answer your questions, and you must ask your questions in a way that allows your client to give you the information you seek. The timing, form and direction of your questions are all important.

Timing. Your opening question at the beginning of the interview is crucial because your client does not know yet what is expected. Your first question should not be difficult and should not touch on a traumatic or embarrassing area. . . .

Form. Questions can be "open" or "closed." Open questions are more appropriate if the client may not have formulated an opinion or if you wish to learn about the client's frame of reference and how he or she arrived at a particular point of view. A closed question is more appropriate if there is a known range of possible responses and within that range there are clearly defined points representing each client's position.

Case Illustration: You are interviewing an asylum applicant and want to determine if she fears persecution upon return to her country. Compare:

Open question: "What do you think will happen to you if you go back?"

Closed question: "Are you afraid of being persecuted upon your return?"

In this situation, the open question is likely to yield significantly more information. The closed question presumes that the client defines

---

* With permission of West Publishing.

and understands "afraid" and "persecuted" as you do and will answer accurately. It further presumes that the only valid answers are "yes" and "no," thereby foreclosing further inquiry into the client's particular situation.

Case Illustration: You are interviewing a Section 212(c) applicant for evidence of rehabilitation.

Open question: "Have you had any trouble with the police since your last conviction?"

Closed question: "Have you been arrested or detained by any law enforcement officer since your last conviction?"

In this case, the closed question is more likely to yield an accurate answer, "yes" or "no." The open question may yield an inaccurate or partial response because the client's definition of "trouble" is not the same as yours.

NOTES AND QUESTIONS

1. Lawyers can use questions to improve the accuracy of the information obtained. For example, lawyers can ask questions directed at uncovering interviewee's assumptions, shading of the facts, or faulty memory. Asking open ended questions before asking specific questions can aid interviewee memory, as can asking the interviewee to tell her story in both chronological and reverse chronological order, asking the interviewee to close his eyes as he tries to remember, and making sure not to interrupt. The questioning process can also be used to explore the veracity of the interviewee:

[V]ery few of us are in fact able to accurately and consistently detect lying. Thus, rather than rely on our own—likely erroneous—ability to detect lying based on body movement, facial tics, or other mannerisms, it is usually better to focus on keeping an open mind, withholding judgment about the client or witness's veracity while seeking additional information through further questioning and from other witnesses or documents.

. . . Although many people believe that liars avert their gaze, engage in lots of movement (e.g., shifting position, hand or foot movements), smile, and have more disturbed speech (e.g., hesitation, pauses, slower speech), many of these anticipated cues do not turn out to be associated with lying. The characteristics that do seem more closely linked to lying include offering fewer details, giving accounts that are less plausible and coherent, and speaking with somewhat more vocal tension and higher pitch. However, because these speech characteristics can be present for other reasons (for example, simple nervousness or stress), we suggest that they should be seen as a signal to probe further or to seek additional verification rather than as a reliable indication of lying. And, of course, the lack of these cues is no guarantee that the speaker is telling the truth.

The literature on lie detection also suggests that attorneys can stay alert to changes in the behavior of an interviewee. . . . [And, a]ttorneys can also ask interviewees to tell their stories in reverse chronological order, which increases the difficulty of maintaining a lie and increases the likelihood that any lies will be detected.

JENNIFER K. ROBBENNOLT & JEAN R. STERNLIGHT, PSYCHOLOGY FOR LAWYERS: UNDERSTANDING THE HUMAN FACTORS IN NEGOTIATION, LITIGATION, AND DECISION MAKING 207–208 (American Bar Association, 2012).

2.   Questioning is obviously only one way that lawyers gather information. Some clients will provide additional information in response to a non-committal acknowledgment, such as "I see" or "Uh-huh," or simple encouragement, such as "Please go on" or "And then?" Silence can also be powerful; most people will feel a need to speak to avoid the discomfort that silence evokes. Lawyers can also gather information through their review of documents provided by the client or as a result of formal and informal discovery. Consider how different means of gathering information may have different implications for the development of rapport.

3.   Our proposed approach to interviewing is general. In some contexts, lawyers may need to deviate from this approach due to the unique characteristics of the client, the nature of the client's problem, and so forth. Lawyers interviewing clients who have been victims of domestic abuse, for example, may find that these clients are not particularly forthcoming with relevant information. In such a context, Linda Lopez suggests using specific, focused questions such as:

   a.   Have you ever gone to the hospital or a doctor as a result of your partner's behavior?

   b.   Did you or anyone else ever call the police about problems occurring in your household?

   c.   Has your partner ever been physical with any of the children?

   d.   Are you or the children afraid of your partner? If so, why?

   e.   Has your partner ever forced you to do any sexual acts that you are uncomfortable with?

   f.   Have there been any incidents of violence during the holidays?

   g.   Did your partner do or say things to you that made you feel embarrassed, humiliated, or belittled?

Linda Lopez, *Interviewing the Domestic Violence Victim*, in NEW YORK PRACTICE SKILLS COURSE HANDBOOK SERIES 345–348 (Sept. 27, 2000).

b. Listening

1. *The Basic Skill*

A lawyer's questioning skills are only as good as her listening skills; only if she listens well will she understand the facts and feelings a client communicates. Moreover, the lawyer who demonstrates that she is listening carefully conveys understanding, empathy, and interest in her client, and this, in turn, furthers the attorney-client relationship and increases the likelihood of information-sharing.

Listening is beneficial not only to clients but also to lawyers themselves. In the next two readings, though, we limit our focus to the potential benefits to clients.

DAVID MAISTER, CHARLES GREEN & ROBERT GALFORD, THE TRUSTED ADVISOR*

Am. Law., Oct. 2000, at 65, 65–66

Jack Welch, CEO of General Electric Company, has high praise for Steven Volk, a corporate lawyer to whom Welch turned when GE's subsidiary NBC acquired Financial News Network in 1991. "He is really a great adviser," says Welch. "He listens better than anybody else."

Effective, trusted advisers are (without a single exception, in our experience) very good listeners. Listening is not a sufficient condition by itself, but it is a necessary one. Listening is essential to earn the right to comment on and be involved with the client's issues. We must listen effectively, and be *perceived* to be listening effectively, *before* we can proceed with any advisory process. Cutting to the chase without having earned the right to do so will usually be interpreted as arrogance.

Jim Copeland is the CEO of Deloitte & Touche and someone who very effectively builds lasting, deep relationships. In 1989 Deloitte, Haskins & Sells merged with Touche, Ross & Co. Copeland had been with Deloitte. He describes the first five minutes of a nine-hour meeting with the CEO of a key Touche, Ross client, a fiery character who was not at all pleased at having to "train" a whole new accounting firm.

> He leads with power, energy, wants to overwhelm you, to let you know who's in charge. And I didn't fight that. I just kept saying, "Tell me more about that problem. How did it happen, how did it come about, what's going on?" I wanted to know why he was upset and what it would take to fix things. Basically I was there for him and let him know that. You just start with an attitude that, by gosh, you are going to set things right, and to do that you have to totally focus on the client and the client's problems.

There are many aspects of Copeland's demeanor in this meeting that explain why it was the genesis of a very long and successful relationship. But in that first meeting, none mattered more than his ability to listen. Listening earned him the right to deliver on quality content, to cross-sell, to demonstrate problem-solving capabilities, and to speak about his people. None of that would have happened had he not earned the right through listening (thereby finding out what was going on).

Why is "being listened to" so important? The answer is not only about the need for a rational understanding of the issues. Our desire to be heard also flows from our need for respect, empathy, and involvement. The trusted adviser recognizes this and always ensures that the self-esteem of the client is protected. A trusted adviser might say, "What I like about your idea is *X;* now help me understand how we can use it to accomplish *Y.*" Through such language, the adviser constantly lets the client know that the client is respected and that the two of them are free to discuss with great candor the specific merits of the idea at hand.

* * * Listening to earn the right is very much an emotional as well as a rational process. Here's the rest of Copeland's story:

> So he got the message that I cared about him, and wouldn't let things go by that weren't right for him. Years later, we had a chance to pitch a project to him, $5 million, a pretty big project in those days, and at the end of the pitch, he just looked at me and said, "Do *you* think I should do this?" Meaning that if I could look him in the eye and say, "You bet," then he had me on the line to do the right thing for him. And he knew that if I didn't believe that, I wouldn't look him in the eye and say so, because he knew he could trust me. And I was able to say, in this case, "Absolutely you should do it; you need this, and we'll do great work for you."

NOTE AND QUESTIONS

The authors make a strong case for the importance of good listening. What does that look like? In other words, what would you say are the qualities and characteristics of good listening? Conversely, what are the characteristics of bad listening?

c. Active Listening

There are many variations of listening. Relatively straightforward paraphrasing can be effective as a means to demonstrate understanding of key content. But *reflective* or *active listening* is an especially effective device for conveying non-judgmental empathetic understanding, developing trust, and eliciting additional information. In active listening, the interviewer restates both the content and the feelings she believes are associated with the statement. The following excerpt explains and illustrates active listening.

ROBERT DINERSTEIN, STEPHEN ELLMAN, ISABELLE GUNNING & ANN SHALLECK, CONNECTION, CAPACITY AND MORALITY IN LAWYER–CLIENT RELATIONSHIPS

10 Clinical L. Rev. 755, 758–62 (2004)

Active listening is a particular form of listening that involves conveying to the speaker, here your client, that you have heard both the substance of what she has said as well as its emotional content. You do this by "mirroring" or paraphrasing what you have heard said explicitly, and by putting into words the implicit feelings emanating from the speaker; sometimes you may answer on only one of these levels (addressing explicit content or implicit feelings, but not both), but often you will need to respond both to the client's words and to his emotions. It is important to note that you will or should use active listening from the moment you meet your client, and consistently thereafter, as a way to verify for yourself and your client that you understand what he has told you and as a way of demonstrating your respect for and sympathy with his concerns.

Consider these examples:

In the first dialogue, Harriet Long, a family lawyer, is a divorced African American woman in her 50's. Her client, Betty Ann Jackson, is also in her 50s, but Caucasian. Jackson seeks Long's help for a divorce and custody matter.

L1: Mrs. Jackson, good to finally meet you in person. Please sit. How may I help you today?

C1: Hello, Ms. Long. Well after 25 years of marriage, of putting him through dental school and raising his children, my husband has found someone younger, thinner and childless and I need to decide how to kill him and get away with it.

L2: Ah Mrs. Jackson. . . . I see. After all you have done in this marriage, you fear this affair will break it up.

C2: I guess that is fair. Although he has said that he wants to leave me for . . . her, so it seems like the marriage is pretty much over.

(A few minutes later in the conversation):

L3: So, Mrs. Jackson. . . . After many years of marriage where you have been an enormous support and helpmate to your husband and mother to his and your children, your husband has made it clear that this recent affair will break up your marriage and you are hurt and angry.

C3: Yes. I can't believe that this is happening. He was never a cheat . . . and I guess I thought if he did he would be like my friends' husbands who will stay in the marriage but this. . . . That he would really leave after all these years!

L4: Okay. So you may well be facing a divorce. And we can talk about the specifics of that. I recognize that this kind of circumstance is bound to cause some very strong feelings in you and I want us to address those. But let's agree to put the killing issue aside, shall we? Tell me more about how you are feeling about what your husband said and what you think, now, you would like to do about it?

Here attorney Long immediately learns from her new client that a divorce matter is the likely legal object of this representation and that her client is quite bitter and unhappy. She uses active listening to show her client that she has heard the gist of what the client has said. Long's response at L2 both paraphrases some of the facts—"after all you have done"—and names one of the possible emotions involved, fear. When an attorney should do a summary of facts that appear most important, along with a more complete restatement of the client's emotions as the lawyer has heard them, is a judgment call that turns on how the rest of the conversation has progressed, but you should certainly consider making such a statement to your client. Attorney Long summarizes her understanding of the facts and emotions at L3 where she paraphrases all the facts—the marriage has been long, the wife has taken care of the husband in some respects and there are children—and names the emotions—hurt and anger—that underlie the assertion "I need to decide how to kill him and get away with it."

The lawyer's restatement of "killing him" as "hurt and anger" demonstrates several characteristics of active listening. First, her response was not a "stupid" or literal paraphrase of the client's statement. Long does not say "Ah Mrs. Jackson, you want to take out a contract on your husband's life and need my help in drawing up the particulars." The lawyer understands that the client's words are much more likely an expression of emotion than of criminal intent, and she rightly avoids attributing to the client a literal meaning that is extreme and offensive. Second, however, while the phrase "kill him" probably is a figure of speech, the lawyer also picks up on the acute ethical issue that would be raised if there is any literal truth to the assertion, and she puts herself on record immediately as discouraging the client from even thinking about pursuing such a course of action. And third, notice that in lightly discouraging the client from thinking that killing would be appropriate, the attorney is disagreeing with her client. Young lawyers and students sometimes think that active listening and the support it conveys means never disagreeing with your client. However, you will have occasions to disagree with clients; and many of those times clients will expect to hear your differing opinions.

Sometimes the client's feelings will be farther from the surface than in our first example. In the following dialogue, Allen Anderson, an employment discrimination attorney, is a white male in his 40's who, due to a shooting, cannot walk and uses a wheel chair. His client, Anthony Braxton, is also a white male and in a wheel chair, but in his late 20's.

L1: Mr. Braxton, it is a pleasure to meet you. I see you were given coffee. So . . . make yourself comfortable and please tell me what employment matter I can help you with?

C1: Well Mr. Anderson, where to begin? Well for one thing I just learned this morning that all of my coworkers at the brokerage firm I work at, Burnham and Block, make almost twice as much money as I do and I figured I should talk with a lawyer about my options.

L2: All right, Mr. Braxton. You learned something today that you had not known before, which is that you are apparently the lowest paid employee at your job and you feel that this fact, if true, is unfair and want to know if the law can help.

C2: Well it's true. And it's not just unfair. I have worked hard, gotten the highest evaluations and gone through . . . well, just not gotten any kind of support at that office.

L3: It sounds as if with your work record and evaluations you should be at or near the top of the pay scale and so you are feeling quite angry and maybe even surprised by this revelation.

C3: Yes, but maybe not entirely surprised.

L4: Please tell me more. How did you discover this and why aren't you surprised?

Here attorney Anderson, while given facts, is not given much emotional content to work with based upon what his client tells him. In an actual interview, of course, there may be any number of nonverbal cues that convey the client's emotional state, like the tone or intensity of his voice, facial expressions, the color of the eyes or skin, and the movements of different parts of the body. Still, despite the (possible) paucity of information, the attorney forges ahead and both describes the facts he has heard ("you learned something today . . . you are apparently the lowest paid") and attaches a likely emotional state ("you feel this is unfair"). The inferences the lawyer makes about the client's emotional reaction are plausible; they fit with the juxtaposition of the client's discovery of his low pay and his seemingly immediate consultation with a lawyer. But the lawyer could be wrong.

Indeed in this case, the client does not really feel that "unfair" quite captures his feelings. Like most clients, however, the client does not hold the lawyer's inability to "mind read" (or "heart read") against him. He corrects the lawyer by providing him with more information. That information still emerges as a factual account rather than a direct assertion of feelings. But the new facts—the client's hard work and excellent evaluations—lead the lawyer more confidently to identify and label some of Braxton's feelings as anger and surprise. In addition, the client's cryptic and incomplete reference to having "gone through" something, followed by a pause and then a statement about lack of "support," suggest to the attorney the strength and color of the client's emotions, despite the client's difficulty in speaking about them.

Although active listening is a critical tool to underscore that you are listening to your client, it is generally not seen by the novice as a very natural or comfortable way to respond. The young attorney or law student sometimes feels that it is difficult to come up with true active listening responses and that the client will view his awkward attempts as phoniness. Effective active listening responses are difficult for many new interviewers to imagine or to formulate on the spot and so require practice. While early and self-conscious efforts at active listening may have a feeling of "phoniness," it is our own view and experience that clients sense phoniness and can tell it apart from the authentic feeling communicated by the lawyer regardless of how smoothly or awkwardly she speaks. A sincere attempt to understand the client's factual statement and feelings, no matter how stiff and even off base, will usually be met with appreciation by clients for the effort made by the attorney—even if the client ends up having to correct what you have said.

NOTES AND QUESTIONS

1.   Active listening is a way of conveying empathy to a client. Empathy is a complicated construct with emotional, cognitive, and behavioral components. It is valuable in the doctor-patient relationship and no doubt in the attorney-client relationship as well:

> Emotional empathy amounts to feeling what others feel; cognitive empathy amounts to understanding what others feel by virtue of first having an open-mind to attain that understanding; and behavioral empathy amounts to displaying emotional empathy to the other person with some measure of cognitive empathy.

> A completely "other-aware" person will be able to achieve the three dimensions of empathy in relation to another person. Numerous experiments in medical contexts suggest that the presence of emotional, cognitive, and behavioral empathy in doctors for their patients is crucial to patients' speedy recovery and healing, both emotionally and physically. Studies repeatedly prove that when doctors communicate with patients in a way that conveys understanding of the patient's feelings, patients are "enabled" to recover, and recover more readily. In her classic study on empathy and healing, Saint Edith Stein described this process as "grasp[ing] the Other as a living body and not merely as a

physical body." ... Empathy thus enables physicians to "grasp the content of first-person reports of bodily disorder, and to comprehend the meaning of illness as lived." Appropriately, there is now a renewed call to incorporate empathy training into medical school curricula.

Valerie A. Sanchez, *Back to the Future of ADR: Negotiating Justice and Human Needs*, 18 Ohio St. J. on Disp. Resol. 669, 726–28 (2003). Applying empathy to active listening, David Maister argues:

> [I]f the message carries any emotional flavor at all (and most do), then *not* to use emotive colorings or tones in our acknowledgments sends the message that we are not listening. A client who says, "We do 300,000 transactions a day here" has a feeling about that number. It is not enough to know whether 300,000 is above or below the competition, or higher or lower than last month. The client may be proud of that number, or proud simply of knowing it. Or he may be bored by the number, or embarrassed by it, or any number of things. The adviser who listens passively (using only "mm-hmm") is sending a message that only the rational content matters, that the feelings of the one conveying the information are irrelevant. The effective adviser knows that the emotional data is every bit as valid and important as the rational data. Each plays its role in successfully adding value and changing a client organization.

> There are even circumstances when a reaction from the adviser is not just good to have, but essential. For example, a CEO who complains that a former key employee is selling trade secrets to the enemy deserves more than mere "mm-hmm." The adviser might appropriately respond, "You must be outraged. I wish I had a button to push to resolve this for you instantly, but I don't. I don't think anyone does."

DAVID MAISTER CHARLES GREEN & ROBERT GALFORD, THE TRUSTED ADVISOR 100 (Free Press, 2001).

3. Some law students find active listening difficult because it feels artificial, contrived or manipulative. Consider this response by Professors Binder and Price:

> The use of active listening skills is in part the use of a technique to gain information. However, you do not employ active listening simply out of a voyeuristic interest in a client's private feelings. Rather, active listening is one among many techniques you employ in order to assist a client in finding an adequate solution to a problem. If any technique which produces information that a client might not otherwise reveal is to be denounced as "manipulative," then perhaps such standard practices as putting clients at ease with a bit of chit-chat and cup of coffee, eliciting information in chronological fashion, probing for details with closed rather than open questions, and showing clients documents to refresh their recollection are all unfairly "manipulative."

> For us, the answer to the claim that active listening is unfairly "manipulative" is this: Clients come to you for assistance and advice, and

a client's full participation is necessary if you are to help a client find a solution that addresses all dimensions of a problem. Active listening, which provides non-judgmental understanding, is an essential technique for gaining full client participation.

DAVID A. BINDER & SUSAN C. PRICE, LEGAL INTERVIEWING AND COUNSELING: A CLIENT CENTERED APPROACH 32–36 (1977).

4.   Perhaps you are uncomfortable at the prospect of saying to a client that he sounds "angry" or "hurt." Remember that your sincerity matters, and you can use less intense language, such as observing that the situation sounds "extremely challenging" for the client or "very difficult." This may be sufficient acknowledgement for your client to feel "heard."

5.   To practice the concepts addressed in this section, choose a classmate or friend and spend ten minutes actively listening to him as he describes a dispute in which he was involved. Then let him actively listen to you as you spend ten minutes describing a dispute in which you were involved. Was active listening easy or difficult? To the extent it was difficult, what made it difficult? How was it different from a normal conversation, or a more formal interview? Did you feel that your counterpart really understood the facts involved in your dispute? Did you feel that your counterpart really understood how you felt about the dispute?

6.   There is a vast psychological literature about *procedural justice*. Research in this area convincingly demonstrates the importance of decision-making and dispute resolution processes that people judge to be fair. Notice that we're focusing here on the fairness of the procedure, separate from the fairness of the outcome. If people judge a process to be fair, they are more likely to perceive the procedure's outcome as fair and to comply with that outcome—even if that outcome is unfavorable to them. Allowing clients the opportunity to express themselves ("voice"), demonstrating sincere consideration of what they have to say, and treating them in an even-handed, dignified manner can contribute to clients' experience of procedural justice. Do you see a possible relationship between effective listening and procedural justice? Who are the primary beneficiaries of an interviewing or counseling session that proceeds in a procedurally fair manner? For more on procedural justice, *see generally* E. ALLAN LIND & TOM R. TYLER, THE SOCIAL PSYCHOLOGY OF PROCEDURAL JUSTICE (1988); Nancy A. Welsh, *Perceptions of Fairness*, in THE NEGOTIATOR'S FIELDBOOK: THE DESK REFERENCE FOR THE EXPERIENCED NEGOTIATOR 165 (Andrea K. Schneider & Christopher Honeyman, eds. 2006); Nancy A. Welsh, *Making Deals in Court–Connected Mediation: What's Justice Got To Do With It?*, 79 Wash. U. L.Q. 787, 859–61 (2001). For more detailed discussion about the application of procedural justice to lawyers' interviewing and counseling of clients, *see* JENNIFER K. ROBBENNOLT & JEAN R. STERNLIGHT, PSYCHOLOGY FOR LAWYERS: UNDERSTANDING THE HUMAN FACTORS IN NEGOTIATION, LITIGATION, AND DECISION MAKING (American Bar Association, 2012). We will return to a discussion of procedural justice in Chapter VII.

3. Other Listening Skills

Active listening is an important technique for improving our listening skills, but it is not the only one. In this subsection, we offer two more techniques that can be very helpful. The first is the Loop of Understanding, which is a step-by-step process for ensuring listening accuracy by demonstrating understanding. The second is the cultivation of mindfulness, which enhances listening by cultivating focused attention and the ability to eliminate distractions.

a) The Loop of Understanding

The "loop of understanding," commonly called "looping," is a way of focus the dialogue and develop understanding that can be used in client counseling, negotiation, mediation, or any other situation in which accurate communication is essential. Although the technique is similar to and borrows much from the active listening method we discussed earlier, looping extends it much further. In active listening, we reflect back to the speaker our sense of what they were saying in terms of both the facts and the speaker's emotional sense of the experience. The loop of understanding takes the additional step of confirming having the speaker confirm or correct the listener's understanding. There are four steps to the process:

1. The speaker says what he or she is going to say.

2. The listener reflects back that what he or she understood, both the facts and emotional content. (This is essentially active listening.)

3. The listener then seeks confirmation from the speaker that the listener fully understood the speaker

4. The speaker confirms the accuracy of the listener's understanding, or corrects it by providing more information and beginning the loop again (steps 1–3). This loop continues until the speaker is fully satisfied that the listener completely understands the listener.

The loop of understanding is relatively simple to understand, but takes time and practice to master. It is well worth the effort, however, as the successful looping can produce many benefits beyond enhancing accurate understanding—no small achievement by itself. Critically, looping also *communicates to the speaker* that the listener actually understands what the speaker said and how the speaker felt about it. This demonstration of understanding eliminates doubt in the mind of the speaker and allows for a deeper connection between the speaker and the listener. Similarly, it also allows the speaker to correct the listener if the listener is wrong, and to do so by focusing precisely on the point of misunderstanding. Interestingly, it can also clarify and deepen the speaker's own thoughts in that the listener may have accurately reflected back what the speaker was communicating, only for the speaker to find that there was more to it than he or she thought, factually, emotionally, or both.

The co-authors of *Beyond Winning* offer some additional advice for looping:

> There is no single formula for demonstrating understanding. But we can suggest some helpful questions for eliciting the other person's story and showing them that you're trying to understand. These include:
>
> - "Is this the problem as you see it?"
> - "Will you clarify what you mean by . . . My understanding is . . . Is that right?"
> - "What I understand you to say is . . . Is that right?"
> - "As I understand it, the problem is . . . Am I hearing you correctly?"
> - "To summarize, the main points as I heard them are . . . Have I understood you right?"
> - "What am I missing?"
> - "Is there anything about how you see this that we haven't talked about yet?"
>
> The precise formulation is less important than trying to check the accuracy of what you have understood. Demonstrating understanding requires paraphrasing, checking your understanding, and giving the other person a chance to respond.

ROBERT MNOOKIN, SCOTT PEPPET & ANDREW S. TULUMELLO, BEYOND WINNING: NEGOTIATING TO CREATE VALUE IN DEALS AND DISPUTES 64–65 (2000).

NOTE

As these suggestions indicate, it important to be natural when looping a speaker, and so much of the advice we gave about active listening also applies with equal force to the loop of understanding. Like active listening, looping may well seem a little contrived when you first try it. But with practice it can quickly become much more natural as we adapt the principles to our own styles and personalities. But it does take practice. We suggest you start the next time you have a relatively minor dispute, disagreement, or conflict with someone where you get the sense that the two of you are just talking past each other. At that point, make a conscious effort to go through the loop and see how it goes. You might be surprised at the results.

b) *Mindful Awareness*

As we have seen, good listening is hard for a lot reasons, including the fact that it is difficult to control the focus of our attention. This is due to at least two qualities of the human mind.

First, the human mind wanders, almost incessantly. As a result, we have trouble keeping our attention where we want it to be. If you have any doubt about this, think about a time you were reading a book or a case and, after a few pages, realized you had no idea what you had read. Your eyes covered the words, but your mind was elsewhere, perhaps imagining time on the beach, or replaying a recent conversation, or planning for a trip to the supermarket. Or try this: Get into a comfortable seated position and close your eyes. Bring your attention to your breath. Specifically, focus on either the sensation the breath makes when it enters or leaves your nostrils or the sensation of the rising and falling of your belly as you inhale and exhale. Once you have focused, begin counting your breaths—but keep most of your attention on the sensations of breathing. Count up to ten exhalations. Once you reach ten or lose track of your count, begin again at one and count up to ten. Do this for five minutes. If you are like many smart, disciplined people, you may have trouble reaching ten even one time!

Second, we not only have difficulty focusing our attention where we want it to be, we are often unaware of where our attention is actually focused. Our minds seem to have a mind of their own. To illustrate, try resuming the breathing exercise, but this time, when you become aware that your mind has wandered, notice where it has gone and then return your attention to your breath. To the extent you are able to do this exercise (and it is often surprisingly difficult), you probably will have noticed a wide range of thoughts, bodily sensations, and emotions. In addition, you may have observed that many of the thoughts were about you, and they concerned making things better for you getting more pleasure or avoiding pain.

Since 1998, several scholars and practitioners have begun to teach law students and lawyers a way to pay attention called "mindfulness." This is a skill that anyone can develop through mindfulness meditation and then deploy in everyday life, including law study or practice. Mindfulness meditation is given greater consideration in Chapter VIII, *supra*. However, in the following excerpt, Professor Riskin explains how mindfulness can facilitate better listening.

LEONARD L. RISKIN, THE CONTEMPLATIVE LAWYER:
ON THE POTENTIAL CONTRIBUTIONS OF MINDFULNESS
MEDITATION TO LAW STUDENTS, LAWYERS,
AND THEIR CLIENTS
7 Harv. Negot. L. Rev. 1, 49–53 (2002)

Good listening means paying attention both to the interaction
between the lawyer and client and to what is going on inside the lawyer.
But this kind of attention takes a high degree of self-awareness and
empathy, along with self-confidence, motivation, patience, and emotional
self-control—the very capacities that mindfulness can produce. Thus,
mindfulness could help lawyers improve their ability to listen deeply—to
themselves and others—and to respond appropriately, rather than react
automatically based on established mind-sets and habits. This is how
mindfulness has improved the listening skills of one bankruptcy attorney:

> When Stacey is practicing mindfully and a colleague or opponent flies
> off the handle she tries to simply notice the feelings that come up for
> her without responding reflexively. Instead, she waits until she's
> ready. Oftentimes, she chooses to look more deeply, to consider what
> might be behind the outburst. Maybe there's an illness in the
> person's family, or perhaps someone just told him off.
>
> In the past, when an interview with a client was getting off track,
> Stacey became self-critical; internal voices told her she really didn't
> know what she was doing and even questioned her choice of work.
> Now when that happens, she just watches it happening, often
> noticing that her stomach is knotting up. She lets herself be aware of
> it all without having to get attached to it. She doesn't fight the voices
> or the physical sensations, so they have no real power over her.
> Suddenly she becomes aware that she can choose to work with the
> client in a different way. She stops, takes a mindful breath, and
> thinks about how she might connect with the person in her office in a
> way that helps them both find their way.*

Simply by listening carefully, deeply, and openly, a lawyer can
relieve some clients' suffering and establish a connection that would be
satisfying to both. Such listening also can be essential if the lawyer is to
help the client make wise decisions. Through such attentive listening, the
lawyer can help the client understand her own needs and then select the
most appropriate methods for addressing them. Mindfulness can help
lawyers overcome barriers to attentive listening, including distracting
thoughts and emotions, "personal agendas," and bias and prejudice based
on the speaker's appearance, ethnicity, gender, speech or manner.

---

* STEVEN KEEVA, TRANSFORMING PRACTICES: FINDING JOY AND SATISFACTION IN THE LEGAL
LIFE 70 (1999).

NOTES AND QUESTIONS

1. It can be challenging for anyone to acknowledge and deal with difficult internal emotions. Lawyers in particular have been shown to prefer to process information and make decisions through the application of rules rather than dealing with their own and others' difficult negative emotions. Professor Leonard Riskin suggests that lawyers may find it helpful to consider their own internal reactions through a metaphor that recognizes the multiplicity of selves existing within each of us and then acknowledges the legitimate roles that these different "parts" of our self play, the needs and emotions of these different "parts," and the "parts alliances," "divisions," etc. *See* Leonard L. Riskin, *Managing Inner and Outer Conflict: Selves, Subpersonalities, and Internal Family Systems*, 18 Harv. Negot. L. Rev. 1 (2013).

2. To be a good interviewer, it helps to be curious. Dean Chris Guthrie asks whether someone who "isn't naturally curious about her counterpart [can] become that way?" Focusing on "situational" curiosity, which is triggered by a particular activity or transaction, Dean Guthrie suggests the following curiosity-enhancing strategies: 1) set "listening goals, because researchers have found that people are more likely to be curious if they are trying to meet a challenge or goal;" 2) remember why it is helpful to listen "because researchers have found that people are more likely to remain interested in a task when they focus on the purposes served by performing it;" and 3) vary the means used to elicit information, "because researchers have found that people are more likely to remain interested and engaged in a task if they vary the way they perform it." Chris Guthrie, *I'm Curious: Can We Teach Curiosity*, in RETHINKING NEGOTIATION TEACHING: INNOVATIONS FOR CONTEXT AND CULTURE 63, 65–67 (James Coben, Giuseppe De Palo & Christopher Honeyman, eds., 2009). What "listening goals" would you set for yourself?

3. Now that you have learned about the importance of listening and the different approaches that can help you be an effective listener, you may want to return to the section on questioning. How will you combine good listening and good questioning?

3. EVALUATING YOUR INTERVIEWING TECHNIQUES

In the following excerpt, Roy Sobelson offers lawyers a way to evaluate their client interviewing skills.

ROY M. SOBELSON, INTERVIEWING CLIENTS ETHICALLY
37 Prac. Law. 13, 18–21 (1991)

There are two common myths about interviewing. One is that everyone can do it and that training is unnecessary. This myth is encouraged by traditional legal training which makes no attempt to teach the three skills most often used in practice: interviewing, counseling, and negotiating. The second myth is that people are born as good or bad interviewers and that training is a waste of time.

My own experience tells me that neither one of these myths is true. You can and should learn proper interviewing techniques. Since it's never too late to learn, here are some questions that may prove helpful in evaluating your own interviewing techniques. Every "no" answer points to a potential problem.

Did I "Break the Ice" First?

Studies indicate that people may fear going to lawyers as much as opposing them. Lawyers need to "acknowledge" the fear by making explicit attempts to put people at ease by "reducing the strangeness" of the experience.

Did I Explain the Interview Process to the Client Before We Got Started?

Was there really a process at all? Once I explained the process, did I live up to the "contract" to conduct the interview in the manner promised? If not, did I acknowledge the reason for varying from my stated format?

* * *

Did I Explain Confidentiality?

There is little, if any, evidence that confidentiality plays a major role in the attorney-client relationship. Nevertheless, you must make the client understand that a relationship of trust is partly supported by the promise of confidentiality.

Did I Give the Client My Undivided Attention?

Think about possible distractions here. They may range from the papers on the desk to the ringing telephone to a client's peculiar habits, looks, speech, etc. Notes are often nothing more than a distracting crutch. Do you listen more than you talk?

Did I Control the Interview Without Being "Controlling"?

Lawyers often approach clients as if they were "cases" that can be handled by using a checklist, whether that list is in the lawyer's head or on paper. Consider who determined what subjects were covered in the interview and at what time.

Did I Ask Mostly Open–Ended Questions Before Closed–End Questions?

Open-ended questions and narrative answers elicit more information than closed-ended or directed questions and answers. Although open-ended questions are generally better at getting the conversation started, they may not always be preferable. Varying the types of questions is helpful.

Did I Periodically Check My Understanding with the Client?

Summaries are valuable. They tend to: show the client you are listening; keep the interview on track; aid memory; and clarify things for the speaker and the listener.

Did I Avoid Concluding Too Early in the Interview What the Problem Was?

The danger of the "premature diagnosis" is a very real one. It can mislead and stifle the process.

Did I Find Out What the Client's Real Objective Was?

Find out exactly what it is that the client wants. Lawyers think in terms of legal solutions and approach problems accordingly. The fact that a client has sought a lawyer's help does not mean that the best solution is a legal one.

Did the Client and I Nonjudgmentally Explore Alternative Solutions?

Did I Recognize the Existence of Non-legal Problems or Solutions?

Brainstorming with the client is essential.

Did I Communicate Empathy and Understanding?

The evidence is overwhelming that clients are more likely to be complete, accurate, and honest if they believe the listener is empathic.

Did I Effectively Handle Questions I Was Unable To Answer Immediately?

Did I Say "I Don't Know" When I Didn't Know? Did I Say "No" Instead of "Maybe" When the Answer Should Have Been "No"? Did I Make Sure That Important Questions or Concerns Were Adequately Addressed?

Did I "Hear" Things the Client Didn't Say?

Did I Pay Attention to "When" and "How" Things Were Said?

Pay particularly close attention to: word emphasis; unresponsiveness; adjectives; and gestures.

Did I Acknowledge and Respect My Client's Feelings?

Although you are not expected to be a therapist, remember that feelings are facts. Even if you can't make the problems go away, you can at least acknowledge them. This will help in your honest evaluation of your client's strengths and weaknesses, as well as showing the client that her feelings "count." Try to focus on "what" questions instead of "why" questions.

Did I Leave the Situation Where Fairness and Honesty Demand That It Be Left?

Sometimes the hardest thing to do is to say "no." Considerations of fairness and honesty, as well as potential liability, demand that you give clients the bad news when it is warranted.

Did I Deal With the "Hard Stuff" Myself?

Some lawyers don't like to talk about money with their clients, leaving fee agreements, etc. up to their secretaries, paralegals, assistants, or (even worse) the mail!

Did I Pay Attention to the "Environmental" Factors?

These factors include proximity, lighting, and seating. They are very powerful in communicating messages about importance, sharing of responsibilities, etc. Are they communicating the messages you want them to communicate?

Do My Client and I Have a Relationship Based on Mutual Respect, Trust, and Understanding?

Keep in mind that although the client is the boss and you are the employee, this relationship is unique and requires open communication.

Does My Client Know What His "Role" Is?

Clients should not be treated as passive recipients of services. Give them a stake in the enterprise and they will be more likely to help you. They'll also be more likely to accept responsibility if things don't turn out exactly as planned.

NOTES

1.   Sobelson dismisses the use of checklists during client interviews, but we think the issue is not so easily addressed. Certainly it is ideal for the lawyer to be open, empathetic, sophisticated and natural in his handling of the demands of the initial interview. And indeed, some attorneys may be naturally adept right from the start. However, this is an acquired skill for many of us, requiring practice and time, and checklists can be very helpful in keeping us on track and ensuring that we handle the initial interview effectively—including getting the information we need to proceed properly with the representation.

2.   Consider again the Model Rules of Professional Conduct provided in this chapter, *supra*. Would regular use of Sobelson's list of questions help a lawyer meet some of these ethical obligations? All of them?

C. COUNSELING

Interviewing and counseling are inextricably linked. Lawyers interview their clients to obtain information about the problems that have brought them to seek legal help. Armed with this information, lawyers then help clients in counseling sessions determine how to address the problems confronting them.

Here we propose a five-step counseling model. This model assumes that the lawyer has interviewed the client, perhaps multiple times, and understands both the relevant facts and the objectives of the representation. Armed with that information, the lawyer and client should follow a five-step counseling process: 1. clarifying issues and interests; 2. considering the relevant law; 3. identifying options; 4. exploring the likely consequences of each option; and 5. facilitating decision making.

1. CLARIFYING ISSUES AND INTERESTS

The first step in the counseling process is to clarify the issues that are important to the client, as well as the client's interests. If the counseling session occurs immediately after an interview following the model proposed above, the lawyer should have a good idea about the issues that require attention, as well as the client's interests. Regardless, the lawyer should start by saying something like, "It seems to me that you are concerned about *issue* and hope to come to a resolution that is consistent with *interest x, interest y, and interest z*, is that right?" Assuming the client confirms this, then the lawyer might ask, "Is there anything else that is important to you in this process, or is there anything I've missed?"

2. CONSIDERING THE RELEVANT LAW

The client has come to the lawyer *because* she is a lawyer. At this point, the lawyer has probably identified one or more legal theories that may be relevant for problem-solving. She should describe the relevant law and its potential application to the client's situation. It will be important, of course, for her to describe the law and its application in a manner that is understandable to her client. The degree of detail that she shares is likely to vary, depending upon her client's level of sophistication, his mental state and the amount of time available to both the lawyer and her client. Further, the level of certainty expressed by the lawyer will depend upon many factors. The prudent lawyer will nearly always acknowledge some degree of uncertainty.

While it is important, talking about the law can be challenging. For one, legal concepts can be difficult and sometimes counter-intuitive for clients. Just imagine trying to explain the potential for a renewed motion for judgment as a matter of law (Rule 50 of the Federal Rules of Civil Procedure) to a client who is considering whether to go to trial. Similarly, even if a client generally understands legal concepts, the client may not understand how these concepts will apply to his case. Professor Marjorie Aaron says "the lawyer must become a master translator, adept at the art of translating from legal language, concept, and context, to the client's." MARJORIE CORMAN AARON, CLIENT SCIENCE: ADVICE FOR LAWYERS ON COUNSELING CLIENTS THROUGH BAD NEWS AND OTHER REALITIES 37 (2012).

Once the lawyer has clarified the client's interests and shared her thoughts regarding the application of the relevant law, then the lawyer can move the counseling session into its problem-solving phase.

3. IDENTIFYING OPTIONS

During the second stage of the counseling process, the lawyer and client work together to identify alternative courses of action that might meet the client's interests. The following readings explore different ways of accomplishing this objective. Alex Osborn begins by describing what he calls "brainstorming" to identify options. Dean Jennifer Gerarda Brown then discusses several other techniques that might be used to generate creative options. Finally, Robert Pirsig demonstrates how simply "being" with a problem can enable people to generate creative options, in an excerpt from his famous novel, ZEN AND THE ART OF MOTORCYCLE MAINTENANCE (1975).

ALEX F. OSBORN, APPLIED IMAGINATION: PRINCIPLES AND PROCEDURES OF CREATIVE PROBLEM–SOLVING
151–52, 155–56 (3d ed. 1963)

The modern brainstorm session is nothing more than a creative conference for the sole purpose of producing a checklist of ideas—ideas which can serve as leads to problem-solution—ideas which can *subsequently* be evaluated and further processed.

* * *

Idea-producing conferences are relatively fruitless unless certain rules are understood by all present, and are faithfully followed. Here are four basics:

(1) *Criticism is ruled out.* Adverse judgment of ideas must be withheld until later.

(2) *"Free-wheeling" is welcomed.* The wilder the idea, the better; it is easier to tame down than to think up.

(3) *Quantity is wanted.* The greater the number of ideas, the more the likelihood of useful ideas.

(4) *Combination and improvement are sought.* In addition to contributing ideas of their own, participants should suggest how ideas of others can be turned into *better* ideas; or how two or more ideas can be joined into still another idea.

JENNIFER GERARDA BROWN, CREATIVITY AND PROBLEM–SOLVING

87 Marq. L. Rev. 697, 699–702, 703–4, 705, 706 (2004)

A. Wordplay

Once an issue or problem is articulated, it is possible to play with the words expressing that problem in order to improve understanding and sometimes to yield new solutions.

1. Shifting Emphasis

To take a fairly simple example, suppose that two neighbors are in a dispute because cigarette butts and other small pieces of trash, deposited by Mr. Smith in his own front yard, are blowing into Mr. Jones's yard, and those that remain in Mr. Smith's yard are detracting from the appearance of the neighborhood (at least as Mr. Jones sees it). Mr. Jones might ask himself (or a mediator at the neighborhood justice center), "How can I get Mr. Smith to stop littering in his yard?" Shifting the emphasis in this sentence brings into focus various aspects of the problem and suggests possible solutions addressing those specific aspects. Consider the different meanings of the following sentences:

"How can *I* get Mr. Smith to stop littering in his yard?"

"How can I get *Mr. Smith* to stop littering in his yard?"

"How can I get Mr. Smith to stop *littering* in his yard?"

"How can I get Mr. Smith to stop littering in *his* yard?"

"How can I get Mr. Smith to stop littering in his *yard*?"

As the focus of the problem shifts, so too different potential solutions might emerge to address the problem as specifically articulated.

2. Changing a Word

Sometimes changing a word in the sentence helps to reformulate the problem in a way that suggests new solutions. In the example above, Mr. Jones might change the phrase "littering in his yard" to something else, such as "neglecting his yard" or "hanging out in his yard." It may be that something besides littering lies at the root of the problem, and a solution will be found, for example, not in stopping the littering, but in more regularized yard work.

3. Deleting a Word

Through word play, parties can delete words or phrases to see whether broadening the statement of the problem more accurately or helpfully captures its essence. Mr. Jones might delete the phrase "Mr. Smith" from his formulation of the problem, and thereby discover that it is not just Mr. Smith's yard, but the entire street, that is looking bad. Focusing on Mr. Smith as the source of the problem may be counterproductive; Mr. Jones might discover that he needs to organize all of the homeowners on his block to battle littering in order to make a difference. Deleting words sometimes spurs creativity by removing an overly restrictive focus on the issue or problem.

4. Adding a New Word

A final form of word play that can spur creative thinking is sometimes called "random word association." Through this process, participants choose a word randomly and then think of ways to associate it with the problem. Suppose Mr. Jones and Mr. Smith were given the word "work" and asked how it might relate to their dispute. Here are some possible results:

Work (time, effort): Mr. Smith will try to work harder to keep his yard looking nice, and he will check Mr. Jones's yard every Saturday to make sure there are no cigarette butts or other pieces of trash in it.

Work (being operational or functional): What the neighborhood needs is a sense of cohesion; Mr. Jones and Mr. Smith will organize a neighborhood beautification project to try to instill a sense of community among their neighbors.

Work (job): Although Mr. Smith's odd working hours sometimes lead him to smoke on his front porch and chat with his friends or family late at night (after Mr. Jones has gone to bed), Mr. Smith will stay in the back of his house after 10 p.m., further from Mr. Jones's bedroom window.

As the different meanings and resulting associations of "work" are explored by the parties, they discover new ways to solve their shared problem. Other seemingly unrelated words might trigger still more associations and more potential solutions.

Adding words can also be helpful if participants insert adjectives that narrow the problem so it appears more manageable. Mr. Jones might ask, "How can I get Mr. Smith to stop littering in his *front* yard?" Narrowing the problem from all of Mr. Smith's property to the front yard might suggest agreements that could keep Mr. Smith's front yard looking nice but still permit him to use other parts of his property (such as a side or back yard) as he wishes. This approach to word play builds upon the insight that many creative solutions are incremental. The problem will not seem so daunting to the parties when it is narrowed, and they can address the larger issues step by step.

These techniques of word play (especially random word association) are designed to "force the mind to 'jump across' its usual pathways (mental ruts), or make new connections between old pathways in order to create a new idea out of two seemingly disparate ideas." The exercises might feel mechanical to the parties at first, but if adopted with some energy and good faith, they could help the parties to enhance the creativity of their thinking.

* * *

D.   ATLAS OF APPROACHES

. . . Using the Atlas of Approaches technique, participants adopt the perspectives of professionals from a variety of fields. By asking themselves, for example, "What would a journalist do?", "What would an economist do?", "How would a psychologist view this?", and so on, negotiators are able to form a more interdisciplinary view of their problem. With this more complete picture of the issues and potential outcomes, they might be able to connect disciplines in ways that give rise to creative solutions.

E.   VISUALIZATION

When parties use the visualization technique, they take time to imagine the situation they desire, one in which their problem is solved. What do they see? What specific conditions exist, and how might each of those conditions be achieved? Weinstein and Morton suggest that parties can engage in visualization simply by closing their eyes and thinking about the problem in terms that are visual rather than abstract. Another approach is to "look at the problem from above, and see things otherwise invisible." The goal is to deploy a variety of the brain's cognitive pathways (verbal, visual, spatial and abstract), the better to make connections that give rise to creative solutions.

F.   "WWCD": WHAT WOULD CROESES DO?*

This process requires a participant to take the perspective of an unconstrained actor. What solutions suggest themselves if we assume no limit to available money, time, talent, technology, or effort? In some ways, one could think of the WWCD method as a more specific application of brainstorming. As the proponents of brainstorming are quick to point out, creativity and the free flow of ideas can be impeded by criticism or assessment. WWCD takes off the table any assessment based on

---

*   Editor's Note: Croesus was the last king of Lydia (560–546 B.C.), and was famous for his great wealth, which he acquired through the conquest of foreign lands and then opening trade and establishing commerce, rather than enslaving the conquered people as was common at the time. As a result, Croesus was a beloved leader, even by those he had conquered.

constraints—financial, technological, etc. If we assume that we can afford and operationalize any solution we can come up with, what might we discover?

A second phase of this approach requires participants to think about the extent to which their unconstrained solution might be modified to make it workable given the existing constraints.

* * *

H. FLIPPING OR REVERSAL

With this technique, one asks whether flipping or reversing a given situation will work. As Edward de Bono explains:

> In the reversal method, one takes things as they are and then turns them round, inside out, upside down, back to front. Then one sees what happens . . . one is not looking for the right answer but for a different arrangement of information which will provoke a different way of looking at the situation.

Chris Honeyman sometimes uses this technique in his work as a neutral when he asks parties to put forward some really *bad* ideas for resolving the conflict. When people offer ideas in response to a call for "bad" ideas, they may free themselves to offer the ideas they partially or secretly support; again, as in brainstorming, they disclaim ownership of the ideas. It is also possible that the instruction to offer bad ideas stimulates creative thinking because it can seem *funny* to people. Humor is a good stimulant for creativity.

* * *

I. IDEA ARBITRAGE

With idea arbitrage, parties see an existing solution in one context and ask themselves where else it might work. A great example of this from the field of consumer products design is the electric toothbrush with rotating bristles. Nalebuff and Ayres point out that this terrific invention actually grew out of a much more trivial discovery the rotating lollipop! The inventors of the lollipop knew they had a good thing, so they looked for new places to put it to use. Similar stories can be told about velcro or polycarbonate wheels. This building upon prior discovery is the root of creativity in art and science. With idea arbitrage, the creativity stems from solutions that is, expanding the problem to which an existing solution may be applied, rather than from a focus on the problems themselves. This approach assumes that there are solutions in search of problems, rather than the other way around.

ROBERT PIRSIG, ZEN AND THE ART OF MOTORCYCLE MAINTENANCE
278–79, 285–86 (1975)

Stuckness. That's what I want to talk about today . . .

A screw sticks, for example, on a side cover assembly. You check the manual to see if there might be any special cause for this screw to come off so hard, but all it says is "Remove side cover plate" in that wonderful terse technical style that never tells you what you want to know. There's no earlier procedure left undone that might cause the cover screws to stick.

If you're experienced you'd probably apply a penetrating liquid and an impact driver at this point. But suppose you're inexperienced and you attach a self-locking plier wrench to the shank of your screwdriver and really twist it hard, a procedure you've had success with in the past, but which this time succeeds only in tearing the slot of the screw.

Your mind was already thinking ahead to what you would do when the cover plate was off, and so it takes a little time to realize that this irritating minor annoyance of a torn screw slot isn't just irritating and minor. You're stuck. Stopped. Terminated. It's absolutely stopped you from fixing the motorcycle.

This isn't a rare scene in science or technology. This is the commonest sense of all. Just plain *stuck*. In traditional maintenance this is the worst of all moments, so bad that you have avoided even thinking about it before you come to it.

* * *

The book's no good to you now. Neither is scientific reason. You don't need any scientific experiments to find out what's wrong. It's obvious what's wrong. What you need is an hypothesis for how you're going to get that slotless screw out of there and scientific method doesn't provide any of these hypotheses. It operates only after they're around.

This is the zero moment of consciousness. Stuck. No answer. Honked. Kaput. It's a miserable experience emotionally. You're losing time. You're incompetent. You don't know what you're doing. You should be ashamed of yourself. You should take the machine to a *real* mechanic who knows how to figure these things out.

* * *

Let's consider a reevaluation of the situation in which we assume that the stuckness now occurring, the zero of consciousness, isn't the worst of all possible situations, but the best possible situation you could be in. After all, it's exactly this stuckness that Zen Buddhists go to so much trouble to induce; through koans, deep breathing, sitting still and the like. Your mind is empty, you have a "hollow-flexible" attitude of "beginner's mind." You're right at the front end of the train of knowledge, at the track of reality itself. Consider, for a change, that this is a moment to be not feared but cultivated. If your mind is truly, profoundly stuck, then you may be much better off than when it was loaded with ideas.

* * *

But now consider the fact that no matter how hard you try to hang on to it, this stuckness is bound to disappear. Your mind will naturally and freely move toward a solution. Unless you are a real master at staying stuck you can't prevent this. The fear of stuckness is needless because the longer you stay stuck the more you see the Quality-reality that gets you unstuck every time. What's *really* been getting you stuck is the running from the stuckness through the cars of your train of knowledge looking for a solution that is out in front of the train.

Stuckness shouldn't be avoided. It's the . . . predecessor of all real understanding. An egoless acceptance of stuckness is a key to an understanding of all Quality, in mechanical work as in other endeavors. It's this understanding of Quality as revealed by stuckness which so often makes self-taught mechanics appear so superior to institute-trained men who have learned how to handle everything except a new situation.

NOTES AND QUESTIONS

1.   Brainstorming and the other processes described in the excerpts from Dean Brown's article and Robert Pirsig's novel are all devices that can enable lawyers and clients to generate options for the client. To illustrate, suppose you are a lawyer, and a new client, Albert, tells you he loaned his $900 mountain bicycle to Bernice and she has refused to return it. He wants to know what to do. As an exercise, you might want to write down the first thoughts that come to your mind.

Suppose you ask a few questions and learn that Albert and Bernice had been neighbors and close "platonic" friends for several years until Bernice moved to another town fifty miles away, that Bernice may be angry at Albert because he borrowed $200 from her several months ago, and that Albert is in debt, does not need the bicycle, and would like to resume a friendship with Bernice.

What options do you see now? Take two or three minutes to think about them. As you do, notice that the "interests" of your client have broadened from those he first mentioned. Although he would like the bicycle back, he also wants to resume a relationship with Bernice, and he owes her money.

2.   To be a good problem solver, you also must learn and respond to Bernice's interests. Why is she keeping the bike? What does she want from Albert? Recognition? Money? Does she need transportation? Are there other ways for her to get around? Take a moment to write down your ideas.

The following is a list of ideas that might have come from brainstorming or another process designed to stimulate creative thinking:

Albert helps himself and takes the bicycle.

Albert offers to pay the $200 in exchange for the bicycle.

Bernice keeps the bicycle.

Bernice keeps the bicycle and forgives the debt.

Bernice keeps the bicycle, forgives the debt, and gives some money ($200? $400?) to Albert.

Albert visits the D.A. and seeks to have Bernice prosecuted.

Albert ceases contact with Bernice and gives up trying to get the bicycle.

Negotiation

—Albert and Bernice negotiate.

—Albert's lawyer negotiates with Bernice.

—Albert's lawyer negotiates with Bernice's lawyer.

Letter writing

—Albert (or his lawyer) sends a letter to Bernice

    —asking for return of the bicycle.

    —asking to meet.

    —proposing one of the solutions described above.

—Albert or his lawyer writes or telephones others, such as Bernice's employer, parent, roommate

Third-party assistance

—Small claims court

—Mediation (formal)

    —Neighborhood justice center

    —Prosecutor's mediation program

    —Other forums, such as Christian Conciliation Service

—Mediation (informal)

    —Intervention by a mutual friend

3. Notice that this list is disorganized; it resulted from a free-association process. Sometimes you can enhance your creativity by ignoring rigid categories. But before analyzing the options, you would want to group them. Some of the items—such as Bernice keeping the bicycle and paying money to Albert—are proposals for specific solutions to the problem. Others suggest a process for developing a solution. Still others combine elements of process and content.

4.   To try your hand at brainstorming, work with a group of friends and identify a problem that affects you all. This could be, for example, a class scheduling or room allocation issue at your law school. Or it could be something affecting your larger community, such as school bullying, or neighborhood blight. Now give yourselves 30 minutes to brainstorm possible solutions. Be sure follow the guidelines set forth above, and note which are easier to comply with, and which are harder.

5.   Is brainstorming always a suitable means of creative problem-solving? What conditions do you think are important for brainstorming to work? On the other hand, when do you think brainstorming is likely to be ineffective?

4. EXPLORING CONSEQUENCES

After identifying viable options, the lawyer and client should attempt to assess the likely consequences of each of these options and then determine whether each consequence is advantageous or disadvantageous to the client.

Lawyers normally (but not always) are more skilled at predicting the likely outcome of legal processes like trials: How long they will take, how much they will cost, the chances of a judgment for a given amount, the degree of publicity, and the like. Clients typically (but not always) are better able to characterize these consequences as advantages or disadvantages. Also, the client may be better at predicting non-legal or social outcomes, such as the effect of various actions on her emotional state, employment, and family and social relationships. The lawyer's job is to help the client bring out, understand, and evaluate such outcomes.

Dean Chris Guthrie and Professor David Sally have issued a bit of a warning, though, to those who place unqualified faith in people's ability to identify the underlying interests or goals that are most important to them:

Researchers from an emerging movement within psychology— labeled "positive psychology" or "hedonic psychology"—have learned a great deal in recent years about what people really want. Of greatest relevance ... researchers have discovered that people are often mistaken about what they want or what will make them happy.

It is not that people are entirely unaware of what they want or how they will feel. In fact, people are generally quite skilled at predicting whether they will feel positively or negatively about some event or item. People accurately predict, for example, that they will feel favorably about a promotion and unfavorably about a demotion. Likewise, people are generally pretty good at predicting the specific emotion(s) they will experience upon obtaining some item or experiencing some event. People anticipate, for instance, that they will feel pride and joy upon being promoted and anger and embarrassment upon being demoted.

What people struggle with, however, is predicting both the intensity and duration of their emotional reactions to an event or outcome. . . . Unfortunately people have a tendency to overestimate the impact of future events on their emotional well-being. Psychologists Daniel Gilbert and Timothy Wilson refer to this phenomenon as the "impact bias."

* * *

Researchers are not entirely sure why people have such difficulty assessing the emotional impact of various life events and outcomes, but they have identified several potential explanations. First, when predicting reactions to a future event, people tend to ignore the impact that other events are likely to have on their sense of well-being. Researchers refer to this as "focalism" or a "focusing illusion." Relatedly, when choosing between items, people tend to ignore the features the items share in common and overestimate the emotional impact that distinct features of the chosen option will have on their well-being. People are prone, in other words, to an "isolation effect." Also, people underestimate the extent to which they use "sense-making processes" to dampen the emotional impact of an experience or outcome. People "inexorably explain and understand events that were initially surprising and unpredictable, and this process lowers the intensity of emotional reactions to the events." In advance, however, they fail to appreciate that they are equipped with this "psychological immune system."

Chris Guthrie & David F. Sally, *Miswanting*, in THE NEGOTIATOR'S FIELDBOOK 277–78 (Schneider & Honeyman, eds., 2006). Dean Guthrie and Professor Sally recommend that lawyers counteract the effects of the impact bias on their clients by: 1) educating their clients (and themselves) about default options; 2) using cooling off periods to reduce the "cognitive load" and potential emotionality of decision-making; and 3) remembering the power of framing, described *supra*. *Id*. at 280–81.

Let us return to Albert, Bernice and the bicycle. Albert expresses interest in using the small claims court. How might he and the lawyer analyze this?

First, the lawyer could explain the process how one goes about filing, the expense, time, and likely result. In abbreviated form, it might go something like this: "It would cost $100 for filing and service of process. The hearing would be held within two months. You probably would get an order against Bernice requiring that she return the bike. However, there is a good chance that she would assert her claim against you for the money you borrowed, and she probably would get a judgment against you for that amount." The lawyer also would help the client understand the process by which a judgment would be executed, and the potential for the decision to be appealed.

Next the lawyer might inquire about predictions the client could make. How is Bernice likely to react? Would the notice from the court soften her attitude in negotiations or harden her resistance, and increase her possible anger about the money? What is the likely impact of instituting this action upon the client's feelings toward Bernice? What about their relationships with mutual friends?

In this example, the small claims court may be a plausible option, but not necessarily the best option in terms of maximizing client interests. An analysis of the consequences would make that plain to most clients. If the lawyer is to be a problem solver, he must help the client consider how the other side would interpret any action the client takes.

Lawyer and client might go through a similar dialogue regarding each of the alternatives that seemed superficially plausible. This would narrow the numerous options to a few: probably a contact through a mutual friend, a letter, or a telephone call by the client or attorney.

5. FACILITATING DECISION MAKING

a. Deciding How to Decide

Often, after the client and lawyer have developed options and identified likely consequences, the client can easily tell the lawyer his choice. Many times, however, the lawyer will have to review options, help the client revisit or re-clarify his objectives, or give the client time to think over the choices, perhaps after discussing them with friends, relatives or colleagues. And sometimes the client will ask the lawyer for his opinion about what to do.

Deciding how to decide as a pair can be difficult, as the following readings attest. The first, by Dr. Atul Gawande, tells a very personal story illustrating this difficulty in the doctor-patient relationship; the second, by Professors Binder, Bergman, and Price, describes this difficulty in the attorney-client relationship.

ATUL GAWANDE, COMPLICATIONS: A SURGEON'S NOTES ON AN IMPERFECT SCIENCE
210–11, 211–12, 219–22 (2002)

Little more than a decade ago, doctors made the decisions; patients did what they were told. Doctors did not consult patients about their desires and priorities, and routinely withheld information—sometimes crucial information, such as what drugs they were on, what treatments they were being given, and what their diagnosis was. Patients were even forbidden to look at their own medical records: too fragile and simple-minded to handle the truth, let alone make decisions. And they suffered for it. People were put on machines, given drugs, and subjected to operations they would not have chosen. And they missed out on treatments that they might have preferred.

My father recounts that, through the 1970s and much of the 1980s, when men came to see him seeking vasectomies, it was accepted that he would judge whether the surgery was not only medicinally appropriate but also personally appropriate for them. He routinely refused to do the operation if the men were unmarried, married but without children, or "too young." In retrospect, he's not sure he did right by all these patients, and, he says, he'd never do things this way today. In fact, he can't even think of a patient in the last few years whom he has turned down for a vasectomy.

One of the reasons for this dramatic shift in how decisions are made in medicine was a 1984 book, THE SILENT WORLD OF DOCTOR AND PATIENT, by a Yale doctor and ethicist named Jay Katz. It was a devastating critique of traditional medical decision making, and it had wide influence. In the book, Katz argued that medical decisions could and should be made by the patients involved.

* * *

Eventually, medical schools came around to Katz's position. By the time I attended, in the early 1990s, we were taught to see patients as autonomous decision makers. "You work for them," I was often reminded. There are still many old-school doctors who try to dictate from on high, but they are finding that patients won't put up with that anymore. Most doctors, taking seriously the idea that patients should control their own fates, lay out the options and the risks involved. A few even refuse to make recommendations, for fear of improperly influencing patients. Patients ask questions, look up information on the Internet, seek second opinions. And they decide.

In practice, however, matters aren't so straightforward. Patients, it turns out, make bad decisions, too. Sometimes, of course, the difference between one option and another isn't especially significant. But when you see your patient making a grave mistake, should you simply do what the patient wants? The current medical orthodoxy says yes. After all, whose body is it, anyway?

* * *

The new orthodoxy about patient autonomy has a hard time acknowledging an awkward truth: patients frequently don't want the freedom that we've given them. That is, they're glad to have their autonomy respected, but the exercise of that autonomy means being able to relinquish it. Thus, it turns out that patients commonly prefer to have others make their medical decisions. One study found that although 64 percent of the general public thought they'd want to select their own treatment if they developed cancer, only 12 percent of newly diagnosed cancer patients actually did want to do so.

This dynamic is something I only came to understand recently. My youngest child, Hunter, was born five weeks early, weighing barely four pounds, and when she was eleven days old she stopped breathing. She had been home a week and doing well. That morning, however, she seemed irritable and fussy, and her nose ran. Thirty minutes after her feeding, her respiration became rapid, and she began making little grunting noises with each breath. Suddenly, Hunter stopped breathing. My wife, panicked, leaped up and shook Hunter awake, and the baby started breathing again. We rushed her to the hospital.

Fifteen minutes later, we were in a large, bright, emergency department examination room. With an oxygen mask on, Hunter didn't quite stabilize—she was still taking over sixty breaths a minute and expending all her energy to do it—but she regained normal oxygen levels in her blood and held her own. The doctors weren't sure what the cause of her trouble was. It could have been a heart defect, a bacterial infection, a virus. They took X rays, blood, and urine, did an electrocardiogram, and tapped her spinal fluid. They suspected—correctly, as it turned out—that the problem was an ordinary respiratory virus that her lungs were too little and immature to handle. But the results from the cultures wouldn't be back for a couple of days. They admitted her to the intensive care unit. That night, she began to tire out. She had several spells of apnea—periods of up to sixty seconds in which she stopped breathing, her heartbeat slowed, and she became pale and ominously still—but each time she came back, all by herself.

A decision needed to be made. Should she be intubated and put on a ventilator? Or should the doctors wait to see if she could recover without it? There were risks either way. If the team didn't intubate her now, under controlled circumstances, and she "crashed"—maybe the next time she would not wake up from an apneic spell—they would have to perform an emergency intubation, a tricky thing to do in a child so small. Delays could occur, the breathing tube could go down the wrong pipe, the doctors could inadvertently traumatize the airway and cause it to shut down, and then she might suffer brain damage or even die from lack of oxygen. The likelihood of such a disaster was slim but real. I myself had seen it happen. On the other hand, you don't want to put someone on a ventilator if you don't have to, least of all a small child. Serious and detrimental effects . . . happen frequently. And, as people who have been hooked up to one of these contraptions will tell you, the machine shoots air into and out of you with terrifying, uncomfortable force; your mouth becomes sore; your lips crack. Sedation is given, but the drugs bring complications, too.

So who should have made the choice? In many ways, I was the ideal candidate to decide what was best. I was the father, so I cared more than any hospital staffer ever could about which risks were taken. And I was a doctor, so I understood the issues involved. I also knew how often problems like miscommunication, overwork, and plain hubris could lead physicians to make bad choices.

And yet when the team of doctors came to talk to me about whether to intubate Hunter, I wanted them to decide—doctors I had never met before. The ethicist Jay Katz and others have disparaged this kind of desire as "childlike regression." But that judgment seems heartless to me. The uncertainties were savage, and I could not bear the possibility of making the wrong call. Even if I made what I was sure was the right choice for her, I could not live with the guilt if something went wrong. Some believe that patients should be pushed to take responsibility for decisions. But that would have seemed equally like a kind of harsh paternalism in itself. I needed Hunter's physicians to bear the responsibility; they could live with the consequences, good or bad.

I let the doctors make the call, and they did so on the spot. They would keep Hunter off the ventilator, they told me. And, with that, the bleary-eyed, stethoscope-collared pack shuffled onward to their next patient. Still, there was the nagging question: if I wanted the best decision for Hunter, was relinquishing my hard-won autonomy really the right thing to do? Carl Schneider, a professor of law and medicine at the University of Michigan, recently published a book called THE PRACTICE OF AUTONOMY, in which he sorted through a welter of studies and data on medical decision making, even undertaking a systematic analysis of patients' memoirs. He found that the ill were often in a poor position to make good choices: they were frequently exhausted, irritable, shattered, or despondent. Often, they were just trying to get through their immediate pain, nausea, and fatigue; they could hardly think about major decisions. This rang true to me. I wasn't even the patient, and all I could do was sit and watch Hunter, worry, or distract myself with busywork. I did not have the concentration or the energy to weigh the treatment options properly.

Schneider found that physicians, being less emotionally engaged, are able to reason through the uncertainties without the distortions of fear and attachment. They work in a scientific culture that disciplines the way they make decisions. They have the benefit of "group rationality"—norms based on scholarly literature and refined practice. And they have the key relevant experience. Even though I am a doctor, I did not have the experience that Hunter's doctors had with her specific condition.

In the end, Hunter managed to stay off the ventilator, although she had a slow and sometimes scary recovery.

NOTES AND QUESTIONS

1.   Suppose you are Gawande's lawyer and he calls you for your advice before authorizing the doctors to make the decision. What advice will you give him? If your advice is purely legal—on issues such as the hospital's or doctor's potential liability, or Gawande's potential civil or criminal liability as a parent what do you think his reaction will be?

2.   Former Stanford Law Dean Paul Brest says lawyers must take care to be attentive both to legal *and* non-legal considerations, noting:

> Counseling lies at the heart of the professional relationship between lawyer and client. A client comes to a lawyer rather than, say, an accountant, an engineer, or a psychologist because the client perceives his problem to have a legal component. But most real-world problems do not conform to the neat boundaries that define and divide different disciplines, and a good lawyer must be able to counsel clients and serve their interests beyond the confines of his technical expertise to integrate legal considerations with the business, personal, political, and other nonlegal aspects of the matter.
>
> In counseling a client about a strategic decision, negotiating or drafting an agreement, or dealing with an organizational problem, the lawyer's work may be constrained, facilitated, or even driven, by the law; but it often calls for judgment and even expertise not of a strictly legal nature. Thus, good lawyers bring more to bear on a problem than legal knowledge and lawyering skills. They bring creativity, common sense, practical wisdom, and that most precious of attributes, good judgment. Paul Brest, *The Responsibility of Law Schools: Educating Lawyers as Counselors and Problem Solvers*, 58 Law & Contemp. Probs. 5, 8 (1995). *See also* Larry O. Natt Gantt, *More Than Lawyers: The Legal and Ethical Implications of Counseling Clients on Nonlegal Considerations*, 18 Geo. J. Legal Ethics 365 (2005) (arguing that attorneys should counsel clients regarding non-legal considerations but that they should also be mindful of other ethical obligations that might be implicated by the giving of such advice).

3.   Do the Model Rules of Professional Conduct permit lawyers to counsel their clients regarding non-legal issues? Look particularly at Rule 2.1, *supra*.

b.   Giving Bad News

As the Gawande reading suggests, sometimes lawyers are forced to give their clients bad news—perhaps the judicial approval of an unwanted divorce or the rejection of a final settlement offer or the prospect of incarceration. In the following excerpt, Professor Linda Smith borrows from medicine a model for delivering bad news to clients.

LINDA F. SMITH, MEDICAL PARADIGMS FOR COUNSELING: GIVING CLIENTS BAD NEWS

4 Clinical L. Rev. 391, 391–92, 417–19, 421–22, 423–24 (1998)

The dominant paradigm for legal counseling focuses on giving the client choice. The "Ethical Lawyer" explains the situation sufficiently for the client to make an informed decision. The "Client–Centered Lawyer" identifies alternatives, predicts consequences, and assists the client in choosing the course of action that best meets the client's goals. This orientation has been, no doubt, an appropriate corrective to the paradigm of the controlling professional who knows best and decides what the client needs.

But sometimes there are no choices that will achieve the client's goals. The abandoned spouse cannot prevent the divorce or avoid an order for visitation, the thief cannot stay out of jail, the business cannot escape paying damages, and the tenant will be evicted. Of course, the amount of the visitation, jail time or damages can be greater or smaller and the eviction may be delayed a bit; but the outcome the client wants to avoid is inevitable. These are particularly hard cases for the lawyer-counselor where the formula of identifying alternatives and predicting consequences can seem like a cruel joke. In these cases the lawyer must also be able to tell the client "bad news." At these junctures, the skill of informing and explaining empathically takes priority over the paradigm of offering the client choice.

* * *

B.   A Model for Legal Counseling About "Bad News"

* * *

1) Be Prepared. Because clients will usually desire (and may need) a good deal of information, the lawyer should avoid communicating "bad news" until she is prepared to fully explain the situation. In most instances, this may mean delaying the "bad news" counseling until after the interview and providing it during a follow-up counseling session. Even when the lawyer may know early in an interview that a client's goal cannot be achieved, it will be wise to delay that discussion. Time will allow the lawyer not only to prepare a comprehensive explanation, but to engage in creative problem-solving. The lawyer will be able to consider whether there may be alternatives to achieving the most important aspects of the client's goals.

If, during the interview, the lawyer hears a client insist upon an outcome that seems highly unlikely, the lawyer should decline to tell the client how hopeless the case is. Instead, the lawyer should empathize with the underlying feeling and encourage the client to explore what the most important aspects of a solution might be. For example, imagine a client whose spouse has left, telling the client he wants a divorce and intends to marry "the other woman":

> Client: There is no way I'll let him have a divorce. Let them live in sin, but there is no way I'm agreeing to a divorce.

> Lawyer: Well, since the "no fault" statute there really isn't anything you can do to prevent him from getting a divorce. If he files for divorce, he'll get one. Of course we can try to hit him up for alimony and the house, so he won't enjoy his freedom.

While the lawyer may be correct in this legal advice, providing this information to the client at this time is not necessary. The lawyer would be better advised to empathize and explore the rationale of the client's underlying goal of remaining married:

> Lawyer: I can tell you are quite angry at him and don't want to just agree to his demands. Could you tell me some more about what's gone on to get to this point? Have there been problems for some time? What if any counseling have you or he had?

Alternatively, the lawyer might discuss the client's immediate needs and offer her choices about short-term goals:

> Lawyer: I can see you are quite angry with him at this point. Can you tell me what's going on with the children and the bills, and what you'd like to see done in the immediate future to help you and your kids have some stability?

2) Be Self–Aware. Ironically, being overly prompt with bad news may come from the laudable goals of providing the client with information (e.g., no consent is required for a no-fault divorce) and performing effective service (e.g., obtaining alimony). Yet the client who is still in denial about the separation and divorce is not emotionally ready to consider this information or to make such a decision. The attorney must help her process the "bad news" that her marriage is over before they can consider various realistic options.

Sarat and Felstiner [*see supra* this section] criticize their domestic relations lawyers for just such a "tutorial posture toward the world of law" and their "strategic" movement of clients "toward positions they deem to be reasonable and appropriate." If these lawyers are to alter their counseling, it would be well if they understood why they feel the need to take such a posture and pursue such strategies. Similarly, Sarat and Felstiner conclude that these lawyers "resist" clients' attempts to "expand the conversation agenda to encompass a broader picture of their lives, experiences, and needs." In order to change such behavior, the lawyer must know how she reacts to clients in pain—whether she wants to rescue them or to "talk some sense into" them. Only by becoming self-aware will the lawyer be able to interact supportively with a client instead of reacting to a client in pain.

3) Conduct the counseling session in person, in private, and with sufficient time. Once it is clear that "bad news" must be conveyed and the lawyer is prepared to do so, the lawyer should arrange a personal counseling session with ample time for the difficult conversation.

4) Be clear, direct and candid in giving information. The lawyer should open with a "warning shot," control the conversation and get to the point promptly.

* * *

5) Convey empathy and caring. Of course, while divulging this information, the lawyer should show empathy for the client and take note of the client's concerns and agendas. In fact, such empathy may be necessary to help the client take in the "bad news."

A counseling session with a tenant facing a certain eviction may include the following information exchange:

Lawyer: I need to explain the legal situation you face. Since your lease requires rent be paid on the first of the month, and you were unable to make that payment three weeks ago, under your lease, here in paragraph 15, your landlord is entitled to go to court and ask that the judge order you out of your apartment.

Client: But it is so unfair—I lost my job and couldn't possibly pay this month.

Lawyer: It certainly is unfortunate that you are facing an eviction on top of your job loss. And it certainly would be a decent thing for the landlord to give you a little while to get work and catch up on the rent. But I've talked to the landlord's lawyer and he says that unless you can come up with the rent by the end of the week, they want to go ahead with the eviction case.

Client: I've told you I have no cash, no job, no one to borrow from, and I'm behind on my utilities anyway. Why can't the judge understand that?

Lawyer: It seems like they're kicking you when you're down. But the judge is required to enforce the laws on the books. The statute says that if you are behind in your rent and don't immediately catch up, the landlord is entitled to his apartment back so he can rent it to someone else. And that is almost certainly what the judge will order, even if you explain your situation.

It is most important for the client to understand the legal standard and how it applies to his case. Linking the law with the facts allows the client to understand, and requires the client to rely less upon the lawyer's forcefulness or estimated risk (99%) of loss. Moreover, in those cases where the lawyer may have performed a perfunctory interview and misunderstood some crucial facts, this presentation will enable the client to correct the lawyer and the two to reach a better analysis.

6) Attend and respond to the client's level of knowledge.

7) Attend and respond to the client's emotional reactions. Once they hear "bad news," clients, like patients, will respond in a variety of ways. In fact, studies suggest that how much patients know about the condition or treatment influences their reaction and even whether they consider the news to be "bad." Accordingly, the lawyer should be calm and empathetic, but not signal an opinion that the legal situation is a dire one. For example, a career criminal may not see incarceration as so terrible, and a tenant who can move in with relatives may prefer moving out to keeping an apartment which she cannot afford. Instead, the lawyer must listen to the client's concerns during the counseling session.

Patients frequently respond with disbelief or denial; and clients who feel wronged may also respond by expressing disbelief. The lawyer should understand this as the client's emotional difficulty in accepting the situation, rather than an argument over the lawyer's analysis. Accordingly, the lawyer should empathize with the client who feels unfairly treated. The lawyer should explore the client's feelings if they are unclear. If the client needs further information to understand the law and how it applies in his case, of course the lawyer should explain.

* * *

8) Conclude with a proposed plan which takes into account the client's personal perspective. As doctors turn to the treatment plan following the information, once the lawyer has conveyed the essence of the "bad news" he should discuss how the case can be handled. Here alternatives will be discussed—but in light of the crucial information about the weakness of the client's case.

* * *

With this approach the lawyer-counselor should be able to engage in counseling sessions which, of necessity, involve telling clients that their goal is probably impossible and the outcome they most fear is likely to be ordained under the law.

c.   The Place of Values and Morals

Suppose that Gawande asks you, as clients often do, "What would you do?" How would you answer this question? Should you answer it at all? Suppose further that you take Dean Brest's advice and decide to address the non-legal issues that obviously are in play. What would you use as the source of your advice? Would you consider values? Morals? If yes, whose values and morals? Gawande's? Yours? Society's?

The next two readings deal with these issues and demonstrate the importance of ensuring that you fully understand your client's values before you offer advice. At the same time, these readings also urge you to be clear regarding your own unique and important role as a lawyer and civic professional. Now would be a good time to re-read the Preamble to the Model Rules of Professional Conduct, *supra*.

DAVID A. BINDER, PAUL BERGMAN & SUSAN C. PRICE, LAWYERS AS COUNSELORS: A CLIENT–CENTERED APPROACH

348–50 (2d ed. 1991)

Responding to client requests for your opinion about what to do primarily concerns not whether, but how and when you give it.

A. GIVING ADVICE BASED ON CLIENTS' VALUES

When you give an opinion, client-centeredness suggests that you usually do so on the basis of each client's unique mix of values and attitudes towards the consequences at stake. Thus, if a client asks for your opinion early on, you should normally withhold it until after you have engaged the client in a thorough counseling dialogue. However, explain your desire to postpone giving your opinion in an empathic manner which indicates that you are aware of the client's request and will respond to it. A dialogue conveying such an explanation may go as follows:

> Lawyer: Next, Diana, why don't we turn to the question I asked you to think about, whether to insist on a personal guarantee from the officers?

> Client: I've been thinking about it a lot, and I'm still not sure what to do. What do you suggest?

> Lawyer: I hate to sound like a lawyer, but there's not one right answer. A lot depends on the unique circumstances of your situation. What I suggest is this. Let's discuss the likely pros and cons both of having and not having personal guarantees. We'll even prepare a chart of the likely consequences. If you still want my opinion after we've done that, I'll certainly give it to you. But by postponing my view, I'll be able to take what you say into account in giving you my opinion. Does that sound all right?

> Client: Sure.

Sometimes clients will not agree to a counseling dialogue. For example, after the explanation above, instead of "Sure," Diana might have said:

> Client: That sounds like it'll take some time, and frankly I don't want to devote the time or money to it. You're a lawyer, and I'm sure you've come across these situations lots of times. I'll go along with what you think is best.

Here, the client refuses the invitation to go through the counseling process, and again asks for your opinion. Should you give it? The answer depends on whether the client has had a "reasonable opportunity" to make the decision. That, in turn, entails consideration of, among other things, the relative importance of the decision in the framework of the client's problem and the content and extent of your prior discussions with Diana. Assuming you believe that Diana has had a reasonable opportunity to decide, you might respond as follows:

> Lawyer: I'm not sure that I know what's best. But you tell me if I'm wrong. My sense is that your primary objective is for this deal to go through and that you feel the company itself is pretty solid. If I'm right about those things, probably you're better off not insisting on personal guarantees. Is that a decision you're comfortable with?

Note that you couch the advice in terms of the client's apparent values, invite the client to disagree if you have the values wrong, and conclude by giving the client room to have the last word. Thus, when you do give advice, you do so as much as possible based on the client's values.

In a second type of scenario, clients make (or renew) requests for your opinion after a thorough counseling dialogue has taken place. In these situations, you are at least confident that a client has had a reasonable opportunity to decide.

* * *

[T]he advice remains tied to the client's values. But since a full counseling dialogue has already taken place, you have a richer data base from which to operate, and can give advice on what the client has actually said.

B.   OFFERING OPINIONS BASED ON YOUR PERSONAL VALUES

[C]lients may ask for and are entitled to receive opinions based on your own personal values. That is, they want to know what you personally would do if you faced the same decision as they do.

Assume that a client asks, "What would you do personally?" or, "I want to do what's right. Do you think I'm doing the right thing?" These questions are ambiguous in terms of what sort of reply the client expects. You should ask a question such as the following to clarify the ambiguity:

"Just so I'm clear, do you want to know what I'd do if I were in your shoes, or what I would personally do, given my own values and objectives?"

In response, a client may say one or the other, or both. In any event, when a client does want to know what you personally would do, be sure to mention the values and attitudes on which you rest your decision. That way, clients can compare their attitudes to yours when deciding how much weight to give your opinion.

ROBERT F. COCHRAN, JR., INTRODUCTION: THREE APPROACHES TO MORALS ISSUES IN LAW OFFICE COUNSELING

30 Pepp. L. Rev. 591, 592, 593, 594–95, 595–97, 597–98, 598–99, 600 (2003)

One of the most important challenges to lawyers and clients is addressing issues that are not controlled by law. Will the client take steps (legal steps) that will harm other people? Will the officers of a corporation consider the effects of its actions on workers, on consumers, on the community, on the environment? In a divorce, will the client take actions that will harm a child or spouse? What role should the lawyer play regarding these questions? The way lawyers address such issues may do more to determine whether their practice is socially useful or socially harmful than any rule governing the profession. The way lawyers address these issues is also likely to have a great deal to do with whether they find the practice of law personally satisfying.

* * *

A.   The Directive Approach

The first school of lawyering advocates a directive lawyer, a lawyer who is willing to assert control of moral issues that arise during legal representation.

* * *

There are troubling aspects of the directive approach. First, there is the danger that, as to moral issues arising in the representation, the lawyer will be wrong. Humility is justified when approaching such issues. These issues are likely to be difficult. I do not suggest that there are not objective moral standards, but none of us has perfect ability to discern those standards or to determine how they should apply. There is a danger that lawyers will be confident of their moral judgment when confidence is not justified. Generally, two consciences in conversation are more likely to get to moral truth than one.

A second concern is that the directive lawyer is likely to impose her values on the client. Directive lawyering is inconsistent with client dignity. There is no place in the directive lawyer's office for the morals of the client. The lawyer robs the client of the opportunity to grow morally. People grow morally through exercising moral judgment. They develop virtues through practice, as an athlete develops physical skills through practice. Lawyers who prevent clients from moral exercise—from deliberating, making moral judgments, and acting on them—deny clients the opportunity to become better people.

* * *

B.   The Client–Centered Approach

In the client-centered view, the lawyer should not act in ways that would influence the client's choice. The lawyer should be "neutral" and "nonjudgmental." Whereas the client has a very limited role in resolving moral issues under the directive model, the lawyer has a very limited role in resolving such issues under the client-centered model. The danger for the client-centered lawyer is that she becomes merely a hired gun in the hands of the client.

* * *

The client-centered counselors' framework claims to be neutral, but in fact, it steers the client toward a particular method of moral analysis, consequentialism. Decision-making under the client-centered counselor model is a matter of cost-benefit analysis. The client-centered counselors' framework excludes the moral imperatives and virtues that are a part of the moral framework of many. Under some standards of morality, one should do the right thing in spite of the negative consequences.

In addition, the client-centered counselors' framework steers clients toward making self-serving choices. The client considers only "Consequences to the Client." This ignores the importance of other people. In the illustration that only one client-centered book gives of its counseling method, a client is considering suing his neighbor over a zoning violation. Among the "consequences for client" of filing suit are: "Time and effort required," "[m]oney to pay for fees and expenses," "[e]xposure to deposition and trial examination," and "[s]train on relationship with [the neighbor]." The client is to consider the consequences to the neighbor solely in light of the effect that they will have on the client; the neighbor has no independent moral significance. The client-centered approach imposes a framework of client selfishness. It may advance the autonomy of clients, but that autonomy comes at the expense of the autonomy of other people. It is likely to advance the autonomy of those who can afford lawyers at the expense of those who cannot.

* * *

C. The Collaborative Approach

* * *

Under the collaborative model, the lawyer and client resolve moral issues together through moral discourse. The client makes the ultimate decision, but the lawyer is actively involved in the process. Thomas Shaffer, who represents the collaborative approach in this symposium, uses the traditional notion of friendship to describe how a lawyer might raise and discuss moral issues with clients. A lawyer should approach moral issues with a client in the same way that she would approach such issues with a friend, raising such issues for serious discussion, but not imposing her will on the client.

* * *

Lawyers cannot become friends with every client, but they might discuss moral issues with clients in the way that they discuss moral issues with friends. Central to the traditional notion of friendship was a moral component: friends help friends become better people. People today generally think of friendship in terms of pleasure, but the traditional notion of friendship as a moral relationship is not entirely lost. Imagine that a close friend comes to you and confesses that he has embezzled something from his employer. You are likely neither to push your friend to confess, nor to ignore the wrong that your friend has done. You are likely to try and help your friend think through the matter. You might offer an opinion, but you would be likely to do so in a tentative fashion, respecting the dignity of your friend. As Aristotle said, friends collaborate in the good. A friend is unlikely to impose his or her will on a friend, but neither will a friend sit by and let a friend go down a wrong path.

The lawyer as friend engages in moral conversation with the client but generally leaves decisions to the client. One of the best ways to raise such issues is by asking questions that come naturally in the course of decision-making. As to each alternative under consideration, the lawyer can ask the client, "what will be its effect on other people?" The lawyer and client should consider all of the consequences that might arise from various alternatives, not merely the consequences to the client. When it comes time to make a choice among alternatives, the lawyer can ask, "What would be fair?" Note that this question does not impose the lawyer's values on clients; it calls on clients to draw on their own sources of moral values.

* * *

As with other models of lawyering, there are difficulties with the collaborative model. To raise and discuss moral problems thoughtfully with another requires wisdom, a quality that comes in part with age and experience. It is difficult to combine the sympathy and detachment that is the heart of good lawyering (it may be that the lawyers for Enron erred too much on the side of sympathy and were not able to give the dispassionate advice that their clients needed). In addition, we live in an individualistic age—we do not collaborate very well. That may be why each of the other models of client counseling identifies one of the parties to the relationship as the party in charge. Moral counsel also requires time, a scarce commodity in the hourly billing-driven practice of the corporate lawyer or the heavy case-load practice of the legal aid lawyer.

In addition, differences in power between lawyer and client may make collaboration difficult. There is a danger that either the lawyer or the client will dominate the other. In many lawyer/client relationships, the lawyer is in the dominant position. The lawyer has the knowledge of the law and the trappings of power. The lawyer sits behind the big desk in the elevated chair. But in another world of lawyering, the client is likely to be in the position of power. The lawyer may be little more than an employee of the corporate client. If the lawyer is in-house counsel she is an employee of the corporate client. The CEO is likely to sit behind the bigger desk, in the more elevated chair. The power within the relationship can also be a function of a host of other factors: age, education, experience, sex, social class, race, and status. The lawyer in either situation may have to work to attain a level of mutuality with the client. She may need to empower the weak client; she may need to assert herself with the strong client.

NOTES AND QUESTIONS

1.   The approach to counseling presented by Binder, Bergman and Price should help the lawyer and client avoid selecting the first solution that occurs to them. This is one of the major problems facing both parties in the legal counseling situation and is a first cousin to the "premature diagnosis" problem in interviewing, discussed *supra*.

The crux of the problem is that a person who thinks he knows the answer is likely to become too rigidly wed to that answer and pass up other opportunities. This is the point of the following story, familiar in religious circles, about a man sitting on the roof of his home as a flood swept through his town.

> The water was well up to the roof when along came a rescue team in a rowboat. They tried hard to reach him and finally when they did, they shouted, "Well, come on. Get into the boat!" And he said, "No, no. God will save me." So the water rose higher and higher and he climbed higher and higher on the roof. The water was very turbulent, but still another boat managed to make its way to him. Again they begged him to get into the boat and to save himself. And again he said, "No, no, no. God will save me! I'm praying. God will save me!" Finally the water was

almost over him, just his head was sticking out. Then along came a helicopter. It came down right over him and they called, "Come on. This is your last chance! Get in here!" Still he said, "No, no, no. God will save me!" Finally his head went under the water and he drowned. When he got to heaven, he complained to God, "God, why didn't you try to save me?" And God said, "I did. I sent you two rowboats and a helicopter."

CHARLOTTE JOKO BECK, EVERYDAY ZEN 70 (1989).

2. Unfortunately, many lawyers choose to limit their counsel to matters involving substantive law and legal procedures. This can work to the detriment of their clients. The following reading describes findings from a study of attorney-client interactions in divorce cases:

> Throughout their interactions, lawyers and clients mark conversational space as a way of defining the appropriate scope of the legal divorce. Clients often seek to expand the conversational agenda to encompass a broader picture of their lives, experiences, and needs. In so doing, they contest the ideology of separate spheres that lawyers seek to maintain. Lawyers, on the other hand, passively resist such expansion. They close down the aperture; they are interested only in those portions of the client's life that have tactical significance for the prospective terms of the divorce settlement or the conduct of the case. Although O'Gorman reports that over two-thirds of the lawyers in his sample described themselves as counselors who considered it to be their "job . . . to ascertain the nature of the client's problem and then work toward a solution that is fair to both parties," the lawyers that we studied did not take a broad perspective on their professional mission. They did not act as "counselors for the situation" nor did they try to provide psychological, emotional, or moral support or guidance for their clients.

AUSTIN SARAT & WILLIAM L. F. FELSTINER, DIVORCE LAWYERS AND THEIR CLIENTS: POWER AND MEANING IN THE LEGAL PROCESS 144 (1995). But *see* Nancy A. Welsh, *Looking Down the Road Less Traveled: Challenges to Persuading the Legal Profession to Define Problems More Humanistically*, 2008 J. Disp. Resol. 45, 56–57 (2008) (suggesting that even though clients may appreciate good communication and caring from lawyers, they may not be able to afford the attendant costs). You may want to take another look at Rule 2.1 of the Model Rules of Professional Conduct in Appendix 2.

3. Does Professor Cochran's analysis of moral issues in legal counseling prompt you to re-evaluate which of the three approaches is most appropriate? Does the situation or context matter? For an article arguing that lawyers have an obligation to provide moral counseling to their clients, *see* Deborah L. Rhode, *Moral Counseling*, 75 FORDHAM L. REV. 1317 (2006).

4. Imagine that Gawande's daughter had died, and he came to you for advice regarding his legal options. Would that discussion be likely to involve values and morals? Whose? Which model of the attorney-client relationship would you be most likely to use? Why?

d. Formal Decision Analysis

Emotions, expectations, ambiguity and a wide variety of other factors can make it difficult for a client to make a clear decision about their case. Formal decision analysis can help improve their understanding of their case, as well as the risks involved and the probable impact of those risks, as Jeffrey Senger explains.

JEFFREY M. SENGER, DECISION ANALYSIS IN NEGOTIATION

87 Marq. L. Rev. 723, 723, 729–33 (2004)

[I]magine you are the plaintiff in a lawsuit where the defendant has filed a motion to dismiss the case. You believe you probably will win the motion, and you believe you probably will win the trial as well. The damage award from the trial would be $100,000. The defendant has offered to pay you $40,000 to settle the case. Should you accept the offer?

In order to answer this question, you need to provide a mathematical probability that represents the value of the word "probably." This requires making your best estimate of how likely you are to win the motion and the trial. Assume you decide your chances of winning in each instance are 75%. Would you accept the offer in these circumstances?

In this example, you must prevail in both the motion and the trial in order to win any money. Decision analysis under these circumstances involves multiplying the probability of winning the motion by the probability of winning the trial, 0.75 x 0.75, which is 0.5625. This result is then multiplied by the payoff that results ($100,000), which yields an expected value of $56,250. Under this scenario, the $40,000 offer is too low, and the plaintiff should continue with the lawsuit. This case is represented in Figure 4.

Figure 4

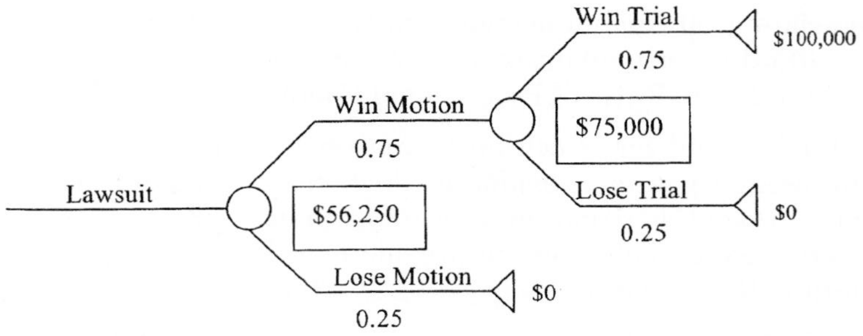

It is worthwhile to examine the effect of attorney fees on this analysis. In the example above, the expected outcome of the case is $56,250. Thus, on average, the plaintiff can expect to receive $56,250 from litigation, and the defendant can expect to pay $56,250. However, assume that both sides would face attorney fees of $10,000 if they took the matter all the way through trial. In this case, the expected income from the lawsuit would be only $46,250 for the plaintiff ($56,250 reduced by $10,000 in fees), and the expected cost of the lawsuit would be $66,250 for the defendant ($56,250 in addition to $10,000 in fees).

This difference in expected outcome creates opportunities for the parties to settle. Any settlement amount greater than $46,250 would represent an improvement for the plaintiff over litigation, and any settlement amount less than $66,250 is better for the defendant. The $20,000 range between these two numbers is a zone of potential agreement. In this case, it is in the economic best interest of both parties to settle somewhere in that range. Decision analysis can be a valuable tool in this regard to show both parties in a lawsuit how they benefit from reaching a settlement.

Decision analysis can be particularly powerful in complex cases. Consider the multiple stages of proof involved in a Title VII discrimination lawsuit. First, in order to survive a motion for summary judgment, the plaintiff must produce evidence sufficient to prevent the defendant from establishing that there is no genuine disputed issue of material fact. At trial, the plaintiff then must establish a prima facie case indicating discrimination. If that burden is met, the defendant must articulate a legitimate, non-discriminatory reason for its actions. In order to prevail, the plaintiff must then establish that this reason is pretextual.

In a hypothetical Title VII case, the plaintiff makes the following estimates: the chance of surviving the motion for summary judgment is 75%, the chance of establishing a prima facie case is 90%, and the chance of establishing that the defendant's explanation is pretextual is 67%. To analyze likely jury awards, the plaintiff estimates that there is a 10% chance that the jury will award $35,000, an 80% chance the jury will award $100,000, and a 10% chance that the jury will award $300,000. This type of calculation is difficult to do by hand and almost impossible to do accurately by means of a hunch. A computer, however, can calculate the result in an instant, as shown in Figure 5.

This analysis shows that the expected value of the case at the beginning of litigation is $51,330. It also shows the value of the case as litigation proceeds. The second chance node (immediately after the summary judgment stage) has a value of $68,440, indicating that if the plaintiff wins the summary judgment motion, the case rises in worth by almost $20,000. At the final stage (when the jury is deliberating), the case is worth $113,500.

* * *

Decision analysis is not a perfect tool. The probabilities that parties place on the likelihood of various events are not magically accurate. The final result of an analysis is only as reliable as the data that parties use to create it, and the data are usually uncertain and subjective. Indeed, the figure that results from a decision analysis can appear artificially precise. Parties must recognize that it represents only an estimate based on the information available at the time.

FIGURE 5

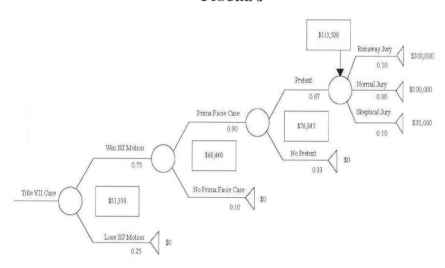

Nonetheless, decision analysis can be a valuable tool to enable parties to make more accurate predictions in negotiation. Assessing the future outcomes is uncertain and subjective no matter what method is used. Predictions based on hunches or intuition are no more accurate than those based on decision analysis, and they may be less so. The advantage of decision analysis is that it allows parties to combine several individual hunches in a rigorous, mathematical manner.

NOTES AND QUESTIONS

1.   While decision analysis is a very helpful tool, it can also look so precise that it lulls the lawyer and client into a false sense of security. When working with decision analysis, it is crucial to remember that every number represents a guess, even if it is an educated guess, and lawyers—like all human beings—can be overoptimistic.

In a 2010 study of 481 lawyers from across the United States, practicing attorneys with civil or criminal cases that were expected to go trial within six to 12 months, were asked "What would be a win situation in terms of your minimum goal for the outcome of this case?" In other words, what was the worst outcome that they would nonetheless categorize as a "win." Attorneys were then asked "From 0 to 100%, what is the probability that you will receive this outcome or something better?" With this question, the researchers sought the attorneys' level of confidence that they would achieve their minimum "win." The object of the study was to see how well the lawyers' predictions squared with the actual outcome. The final case outcome matched the goal set by the lawyers only 32% of the time. The lawyers did better than they thought they would in 24% of the cases, but in 44% of the cases did worse than they expected—or were overconfident. There was no difference in calibration rates between civil and criminal lawyers, and more experienced lawyers did not demonstrate more accurate calibration rates. *See* Jane Goodman–Delahunty, P.A. Granhag, Maria Hartwig & Elizabeth F. Loftus, *Insightful or Wishful: Lawyers' Ability to Predict Case Outcomes*, 16 PSYCHOL., PUB. POL'Y, & L. 133 (2010). Professors Jennifer Robbennolt and Jean Sternlight summarize as follows: "Attorneys were overconfident but didn't realize it." JENNIFER K. ROBBENNOLT & JEAN R. STERNLIGHT, PSYCHOLOGY FOR LAWYERS: UNDERSTANDING THE HUMAN FACTORS IN NEGOTIATION, LITIGATION, AND DECISION MAKING 68 (2013).

Why might this dynamic exist? Do you think you might be susceptible to this trap? How might you correct for it?

2.   Attorneys can improve the accuracy of their predictions by consulting with colleagues. Taking the time to talk with even one colleague in the same firm or practice group provides the opportunity to get a more objective outsider's view. Consulting with multiple colleagues can make an attorney's predictions even more accurate. *See* Jonas Jacobson et al., *Predicting Civil Jury Verdicts: How Attorneys Use (and Misuse) a Second Opinion*, 8 J. Empirical Legal Stud. 99 (2011). Professors Jennifer Robbennolt and Jean Sternlight observe: "[A]veraging multiple individual predictions or judgments is a powerfully effective way in which to improve accuracy. In part because of the representativeness heuristic, people tend to believe that averaging leads to average performance. But it turns out that the *wisdom of crowds* can actually lead to improved performance." JENNIFER K. ROBBENNOLT & JEAN R. STERNLIGHT, PSYCHOLOGY FOR LAWYERS: UNDERSTANDING THE HUMAN FACTORS IN NEGOTIATION, LITIGATION, AND DECISION MAKING 80 (American Bar Association, 2012).

3.   Try working your way through the math of decision analysis with the following relatively simple hypotheticals. Notice that we have provided you with the estimates of your chances of achieving different degrees of "wins." These are just the sorts of estimates you will need to make when you advise your client regarding likely decisions by the assigned judge or a local jury. Based on what you have learned, perhaps you will want to consult with your colleagues in your firm or practice group.

a.   Jane has brought a contract action against Acme Stores. Based on the discovery that has been done, her lawyer tells her that she has a 20% chance of winning $100,000, a 40% chance of winning $50,000 and a 40% chance of losing. What is the expected value of Jane's case?

b.   Jane has brought a contract action against Acme Stores. Based on the discovery that has been done, her lawyer tells her that she has a 40% chance of losing on summary judgment. If she survives summary judgment, she then has a 20% chance of winning $100,000, a 40% chance of winning $50,000 and a 40% chance of losing. What is the expected value of Jane's case?

c.   Assume the same facts as in b. Jane has already paid her lawyer $5,000 in attorney's fees. Jane's lawyer expects that it will cost another $10,000 to take her case to trial. Now what is the expected value of Jane's case?

d.   How does the result change if Jane's lawyer is working on a contingency fee basis and will receive 33% of any amount that Jane wins? (Notice how this calculation becomes much more complicated if Jane's attorney charges a 25% contingency fee if the case settles before formal discovery, 35% if it settles after formal discovery, and 45% if the case goes to trial.)

4.   We will examine expected value analysis and relevant cognitive bin more detail in Chapter III.

D. THE LAW OF THE LAWYER–CLIENT RELATIONSHIP

1. THE LAWYER'S AUTHORITY TO BIND THE CLIENT TO AN AGREEMENT

The following cases explore the problems that can arise between lawyers and clients as they consider whether the client should enter into a settlement or transactional agreement. Focus on the attorney-client relationship here, and whether the clients had given authority to their lawyers to enter into the agreements at issue. In *Gatto*, the question is whether the lawyer had *express* authority. In *Fennell*, the court asks whether the lawyer had *apparent* authority. What is the difference between express and apparent authority? Does the difference matter?

Like most events reported in judicial opinions, these cases ultimately represent cautionary tales. You may want to review the ethics provisions in this chapter, *supra,* and in Appendix B for their guidance regarding the allocation of authority between lawyer and client and the management of tensions in the attorney-client relationship. Also consider whether lawyers' approach to interviewing and counseling could reduce (or enhance) the likelihood of litigation over issues of authority.

GATTO v. VERIZON PENNSYLVANIA, INC.

United States District Court, W.D. Pennsylvania, 2009
Slip Copy 2009 WL 3062316

CONTI, DISTRICT JUDGE.

* * *

FINDINGS OF FACT

[Plaintiff, a former Verizon employee, filed two separate lawsuits against Verizon in the United States District Court for the Western District of Pennsylvania, claiming discrimination, violations of the Americans with Disabilities Act (ADA) and the Pennsylvania Human Relations Act (PHRA), and retaliation. The court ordered consolidation. Gatto also was simultaneously involved in an arbitration with Verizon.]
* * *

The October 8, 2008 mediation ended with a proposed $25,000 settlement offer ("the mediation offer") from Verizon that included a full and complete release of all claims Gatto had against Verizon, an agreement not to reapply with Verizon, nondisparagement, and confidentiality. Uncomfortable with the terms, Gatto asked Verizon for additional time to consider the offer, and was granted until October 13, 2008. On October 13, 2008, Gatto rejected the $25,000 settlement offer and asked Holmes to move forward with her case. Gatto did not tell Holmes to cease negotiations with Verizon.

* * *

Holmes testified that Gatto gave him authority to settle for $50,000 sometime after October 17, 2008, but before October 20, 2008. Holmes testified that Gatto told him that she did not think Verizon would accept $50,000, so she was willing to counteroffer with that amount. Later in his testimony, Holmes remembered Gatto's comments slightly differently: Holmes recalled Gatto saying, "Well I don't think they will come up much higher. Lets [sic] do 50."

After speaking with Gatto, Holmes sent an email to Ryan noting that Gatto rejected the $30,000 settlement offer. In a phone conversation later that day, Holmes reiterated Gatto's rejection to Ryan, but indicated that Gatto would be willing to settle for $50,000.

Ryan contacted Verizon regarding the rejection of the $30,000 offer and the availability of the $50,000 offer from Gatto. Verizon directed Ryan to accept the $50,000 offer. * * *

After speaking with Ryan, Holmes left a message on Gatto's answering machine which Gatto played for the court. Gatto claimed that Holmes stated in the message that he "received a counteroffer." Holmes claimed that he said, "I received our counteroffer." After Gatto played the tape, the following exchange took place with respect to the tape:

(Whereupon, the tape was played.)

MISS GATTO: Now, as you just heard, that's October 20th, 2008 at 4:07 p.m. He left a message on my machine, stating he received a counteroffer from the defendant.

THE COURT: I didn't hear that.

MISS GATTO: Sure. Can I play it again?

THE COURT: My recollection was, some important information.

(Whereupon, the tape was played.)

* * *

MISS GATTO: He says, I have a counteroffer. Does anybody need to hear that again?

THE COURT: Well—

THE WITNESS: [Holmes] I'll answer questions. I believe I said, I said, I received our counteroffer.

BY MISS GATTO: Q. It says, I have a counteroffer.

A.   [Holmes] Okay. I think it's—it speaks for itself, but, okay.

In a follow-up phone conversation with Gatto, Holmes claimed that Verizon accepted a $50,000 offer, subject to the same terms and conditions initially discussed by the parties during mediation. According to Holmes, Gatto expressed concern to Holmes over releasing her separate claims against Verizon. Gatto claimed that Holmes said that he had received an offer of $50,000 from Verizon, and that he tried to talk her into taking the offer during that phone conversation.

Meanwhile, Ryan reduced the settlement agreement to writing and forwarded it to Holmes on October 21, 2008. * * *

* * *

When Holmes spoke with Gatto on October 21, 2008, he told her that Verizon believed the $50,000 agreement was finalized. Gatto, however, thought the $50,000 was Verizon's offer, leaving her with the right of refusal. Gatto told Holmes to call Ryan the following day to inform Verizon that she never authorized the $50,000 demand. Gatto never executed the settlement agreement.

After the refusal by Gatto to sign the settlement agreement, the relationship between Holmes and Gatto rapidly devolved. An email from Gatto to Holmes on October 28, 2008 stated in part: "Many things that you have stated have been false and inaccurate. Specifically, I never agreed to a settlement amount of $50,000 or to include my arbitration case as part of any settlement with Verizon." That email was in response to a letter sent by Holmes to Gatto on October 24, 2008, in which Holmes stated in relevant part:

> As we discussed, I think it is quite clear that we had a rather large misunderstanding or miscommunication. As everything stands now, we have a settlement agreement with Verizon for $50,000 to settle not only the discrimination and retaliation case, but also your arbitration case. . . .

> * * *

I disagree with your recollection of the events leading up to Verizon accepting our offer of $50,000. I believe that I did, with your permission, have authority to settle the case for $50,000. More specifically, I recall us offering that amount after Verizon offered $30,000, because neither of us believed that Verizon would increase their amount by $20,000. . . . * * *

> * * *

[A]fter the motion to enforce the settlement is filed, and Verizon will be filing it, if the case moves on I will be withdrawing with your permission.

* * * [On] . . . November 18, 2008, Holmes stated:

> [W]e are going through this ordeal because you did not, as you claim, understand what an offer and acceptance is. With that said, we made a valid offer and they accepted. . . .

> * * *

> Despite the fact that I strongly disagree with the fact that you never gave me authority to make an offer, I've made a good faith effort to make an argument on your behalf. . . . You refuse to let me do my job, and when I do, you claim I do so without your "authority." I've had your authority in everything. And your claim that you did not know that the settlement included release of all of your claims and meant no reinstatement is simply not true. Within the first 10 minutes at the mediation . . . it was made quite clear to you that these things were non-negotiable.

Shortly thereafter, Holmes and Gatto severed their attorney-client relationship.

At the hearing on the motion to enforce settlement, which began on February 6, 2009 [and lasted three days], Gatto elected to represent herself. During the course of the three-day hearing, Holmes and Gatto presented conflicting testimony about whether Holmes had express authority to settle any of Gatto's claims against Verizon.

> * * *

. . . Under Pennsylvania law, "an attorney must have express authority in order to bind a client to a settlement agreement." "The rationale for this rule stems from the fact that parties settling legal disputes forfeit substantial legal rights, and such rights should only be forfeited knowingly."

* * *

It is clear to the court that the terms and conditions of the mediation offer were understood by both parties at the time of the mediation. With respect to the mediation offer, it was understood that any settlement agreement would include a full release of all claims Gatto had against Verizon, an agreement not to reapply with Verizon, a nondisparagement agreement, and a confidentiality agreement. It is also clear to the court that Holmes entered into an agreement on his client's behalf for $50,000, including those terms. The issue before this court, however, is whether Holmes had Gatto's express authority to enter into a settlement agreement on those terms.

Both parties presented conflicting evidence from Gatto and Holmes with respect to the issue of express authority and this court is charged with determining which witness is credible. In order to make credibility determinations, the court was able to observe the witnesses' demeanor and reactions when they were being questioned, to compare the testimony with the exhibits, to listen to the telephone recordings, and to review the transcripts for inconsistencies. There were substantial inconsistencies in both witnesses' testimony and neither witness was viewed as being especially credible with respect to the issue of express authority. At the very least there was a breakdown in the clarity of the communications between attorney and client.

* * * The recording was difficult to hear, and the court was unable to discern exactly what Holmes said. The court, however, notes it is awkward to tell someone that the other side has accepted your offer by saying, "I received our counteroffer." That kind of statement is not consistent with someone who had his client's express authority to settle a case and was telling his client the good news.

The court concludes that it was more likely than not that Gatto's interpretation was correct and Holmes said, "I have a counteroffer." This is consistent with Gatto's theory that Holmes received a counteroffer from Verizon.

When Holmes later talked to Gatto and learned that she would not accept the $50,000 offer, he realized he already told Verizon's counsel that there was a settlement and tried to talk Gatto into accepting the offer. The court, however, is convinced that Gatto did know Holmes was trying, with her permission, to obtain a higher offer from Verizon. The burden of proof with respect to this issue, however, is placed squarely on Verizon.

"Under Pennsylvania law, enforceability of a settlement agreement is governed by principles of contract law." The burden of proof is on the party attempting to enforce the settlement agreement. * * * The party with the burden must prove, in light of all the evidence, that what he or she claims is more likely so than not so. In other words, if the evidence favorable to one party and the evidence favorable to the other party were placed on opposite sides of the scales of justice, the party with the burden would have to make the scales tip somewhat on his or her side.

* * *

Based upon the evidence presented, the court does not find Holmes or Gatto to have accurately remembered the events. It is debatable that Gatto wanted a higher offer, but did not want to give up her other claims to obtain that higher amount. Under these circumstances, the court finds the scales of justice remain evenly balanced on the issue whether Gatto expressly authorized the settlement and Verizon failed to meet its burden of proving that Holmes had the express authority of his client when he settled this case with Verizon for $50,000. Verizon's motion to enforce the settlement agreement is denied and Gatto's motion to deny enforcement of the settlement agreement is granted.[2]

FENNELL v. TLB KENT COMPANY
United States Court of Appeals, Second Circuit, 1988
865 F.2d 498

MAHONEY, CIRCUIT JUDGE:

* * * [Fennell sued his employer in federal district court,] alleging wrongful discharge because of his race and age in violation of 42 U.S.C. § 1981 (1982). Fennell was represented by C. Vernon Mason and several of his associates, including Fred K. Brewington.

The case was on Judge Stanton's ready calendar on January 6, 1987. On January 16, 1987, however, Brewington and Eugene Frink, defendants' attorney, agreed to settle the case for $10,000 during a telephone conversation. The settlement was reported to the court by both attorneys in a telephone conference call on January 20, 1987. The district court issued an order of dismissal on the same day which provided that either party could apply to the court by letter to restore the case to the court's calendar within sixty days of the order. The settlement was conditioned upon Fennell signing a general release and a stipulation of discontinuance being filed with the court, which never occurred.

---

[2] This case is a good example of why the final proposed terms of a mediation offer should be memorialized in writing and for subsequent offers to be communicated in writing between counsel and between counsel and his or her client. The difficulties encountered in this case would likely not have existed had the terms been clearly communicated in writing.

Fennell expressed his dissatisfaction with the settlement in a letter to the district court dated March 28, 1987. * * *

On February 27, 1987, Fennell wrote Mason expressing his dissatisfaction with the settlement agreement and indicating that he had "no further use of [Mason's] services." * * * On March 20, 1987, Brewington wrote to the district court requesting that the "matter be restored to the calendar as the settlement which was authorized and accepted by our client is no longer acceptable to him," and that Mason and his associates be released by the court as counsel to Fennell.

Following a status conference on June 5, 1987, the district court held a hearing on June 16, 1987 to determine whether Fennell's case should be restored to the calendar. At the conclusion of the hearing, the district court dismissed the action and approved the settlement. This ruling was based upon a finding that Fennell's attorney had been clothed with "apparent authority" when he settled the case, and the court's expressed view that "[t]o allow a client to reject a settlement which has been agreed upon by his attorney with apparent authority is to open the door to a mild form of chaos."

* * *

We begin with the undisputed proposition that the decision to settle is the client's to make, not the attorney's. On the other hand, if an attorney has apparent authority to settle a case, and the opposing counsel has no reason to doubt that authority, the settlement will be upheld.

The district court made the following findings concerning the issue of apparent authority: 1) that Mason and his associates represented Fennell "in dealing with the other side," 2) that they were authorized to appear at conferences for him, 3) that Fennell knew that settlement was being discussed, 4) that Fennell did not tell his counsel not to continue discussing settlement, 5) that Fennell would have accepted a higher settlement figure ($50,000–75,000), and 6) that Fennell did not tell defendants' counsel that the authority of plaintiff's counsel was limited in any way. The district court concluded that Fennell's counsel "had every appearance of being authorized to make a binding agreement with [defendants' counsel]." The district court then applied the common law principle that an agent clothed with apparent authority binds the principal as to actions taken within the scope of that authority, together with the principle favoring settlement agreements, to conclude that Fennell was bound by the settlement agreement.

Apparent authority is "the power to affect the legal relations of another person by transactions with third persons, professedly as agent for the other, arising from and in accordance with *the other's manifestations* to such third persons." Restatement (Second) of Agency § 8 (1958) (emphasis added). Further, in order to create apparent authority, the *principal must manifest to the third party* that he "consents to have the act done on his behalf by the person purporting to act for him." *Id.* § 27. Second Circuit case law supports the view that apparent authority is created only by the representations of the principal to the third party, and explicitly rejects the notion that an agent can create apparent authority by his own actions or representations.

In this case, taking the facts as the district court found them, Fennell made no manifestations to defendants' counsel that Mason and his associates were authorized to settle the case. Fennell's attorneys accordingly had no apparent authority to settle the case for $10,000 without Fennell's consent. The district court's findings that Mason and his associates represented Fennell, and that they were authorized to appear at conferences for him, do not prove otherwise. A client does not create apparent authority for his attorney to settle a case merely by retaining the attorney.

Further, the court's findings that Fennell knew settlement was being discussed, did not ask his attorneys not to discuss settlement, would have accepted a higher settlement figure, and did not tell defendant's counsel that the authority of plaintiff's counsel was limited in any way, do not lead to a different outcome. These findings involve only discussions between Fennell and his attorneys or things that Fennell did not say to opposing counsel. None of these findings relates to positive actions or manifestations by Fennell to defendants' counsel that would reasonably lead that counsel to believe that Fennell's attorneys were clothed with apparent authority to agree to a definitive settlement of the litigation.

* * *

We realize that the rule we announce here has the potential to burden, at least occasionally, district courts which must deal with constantly burgeoning calendars. A contrary rule, however, would have even more deleterious consequences. Clients should not be faced with a Hobson's choice of denying their counsel all authority to explore settlement or being bound by *any* settlement to which their counsel might agree, having resort only to an action against their counsel for malpractice. In any event, even if we were to consider such a rule advisable, the applicable precedents and settled principles of agency law would preclude its adoption.

Reversed and remanded for further proceedings not inconsistent herewith.

NOTES AND QUESTIONS

1. It is worth recalling the procedural posture of *Fennell*. The court dismissed the original action after learning of its settlement, but provided 60 days for restoration of the action to the court's calendar. The dismissal,

therefore, did not represent a final judgment. However in *In re Artha Management, Inc.*, 91 F.3d 326 (2d Cir. 1996), the Second Circuit revisited the issue of a lawyer's authority to bind his client to a settlement agreement and reversed the burden of proof for actions taken by an attorney-of-record:

> Nevertheless, because of the unique nature of the attorney-client relationship, and consistent with the public policy favoring settlements, we presume that an attorney-of-record who enters into a settlement agreement, purportedly on behalf of a client, had authority to do so. In accordance with that presumption, any party challenging an attorney's authority to settle the case under such circumstances bears the burden of proving by affirmative evidence that the attorney lacked authority. *International Bhd.*, 986 F.2d at 20 (stating that "[t]he burden of proving that an attorney entered into a settlement agreement without authority is not insubstantial"); *Gilbert v. United States,* 479 F.2d 1267, 1268–69 (2d Cir.1973) (noting, but not relying on, other courts' placement of the burden of proof on the party challenging the attorney's authority to settle a case). To the extent that our recitation of that rule in *International Bhd.* was not an express holding, we now join several of our sister circuits and so hold. *See, e.g., Greater Kansas City Laborers Pension Fund v. Paramount Indus.,* 829 F.2d 644, 646 (8th Cir.1987) (holding that burden of proof is on party challenging attorney-of-record's authority to settle case); *Edwards,* 792 F.2d at 390 (same); *Mid–South Towing v. Har–Win, Inc.,* 733 F.2d 386, 392 (5th Cir.1984) (same); *Thomas v. Colorado Trust Deed Funds,* 366 F.2d 136, 139 (10th Cir.1966) (same).

Id. at 329.

Note that the Second Circuit's cites are all to federal courts that have adopted this rule as a matter of federal common law, applicable to lawyers' representation of clients on federal claims.

2. In *Anand v. California Department of Developmental Services*, 626 F. Supp.2d 1061 (E.D. Ca. 2009), a federal district court found no compelling reason to apply federal common law rather than California's law of agency. According to the court, California requires an attorney to have express authority in order to settle his client's claims and does not have a presumption that a settlement agreed to by the attorney is binding upon the client. The court further observed in *Anand* that California law requires an evidentiary hearing on the lawyer's authority to enter into the contested settlement. Importantly, however, the *Anand* court then required the client to show that her lawyer did not have the authority to settle her claims or that she should not otherwise be bound by her attorney's acts through her subsequent ratification. Even without an explicit presumption, does this allocation of the burden of proof tend to favor the lawyer's settlement of the case? Incidentally, the challenged settlement in *Anand* involved significant email negotiation, as well as significant email communication between plaintiff and her lawyer.

3. Pennsylvania, like California, requires an attorney to have express authority in order to bind a client to a settlement agreement. This rule was affirmed in *Reutzel v. Douglas*, 870 A.2d 787 (Pa. 2005). In that case, a plaintiff's lawyer negotiating the settlement of his client's medical malpractice claim left the following voicemail for the hospital's lawyer:

> Before I have a knockdown drag out of any kind with [the doctor's lawyer], my thought is if you could talk to her first, you guys get us a hundred, contribute what you want, I will make it go away. I don't have client consent, but I'm not going to come back to you and say $125,000, I can guarantee you that. A hundred and it all goes poof!

Defendants subsequently agreed to pay $100,000 to settle the matter. Plaintiff was dissatisfied with this settlement. When plaintiff's lawyer tried to resume the negotiations, defense counsel petitioned to enforce the settlement agreement defendants understood they had reached.

In reversing the lower courts' enforcement of the settlement, the Pennsylvania Supreme Court explained:

> The law in this jurisdiction is clear and well-settled that an attorney must have express authority in order to bind a client to a settlement agreement. The rationale for this rule stems from the fact that parties settling legal disputes forfeit substantial legal rights, and such rights should only be forfeited knowingly. As such, a client's attorney may not settle a case without the client's grant of express authority, and such express authority can only exist where the principal specifically grants the agent the authority to perform a certain task on the principal's behalf. *See* Restatement (Second) of Agency § 7 cmt. c (1958).

In a concurring opinion, Chief Justice Cappy urged Pennsylvania's adoption of the doctrine of apparent authority "due to its recognition of the practical difficulties inherent in negotiating and enforcing settlements, and its proper balancing of the competing policies of the client's right to control settlement, protection of third parties, and our strong public policy in favor of settlement." In another concurring opinion, Justice Eakin observed that the majority opinion should be considered advisory because the Reutzels' lawyer clearly did not have express authority to settle the case: "[T]he attorney stated 'I don't have client consent' in the very voicemail construed below as an 'offer.' As such, the majority's thoughtful analysis balancing the equities in this case is an unnecessary step—the absence of express authority ends the inquiry."

4.   In determining whether lawyers possess apparent authority to bind their clients, note the importance of courts' local rules. Some require that the lawyers attending pretrial settlement conferences or mediation sessions possess full settlement authority. *See e.g., Hallock v. State,* 64 N.Y.2d 224 (1984) described *supra* in *Fennell; see also, Alvarez v. City of New York,* 146 F.Supp.2d 327 (S.D.N.Y.2001) (finding apparent authority based in part on plaintiff's appearance at the judicial settlement conference and the impression created that his attorney had authority to speak for him).

Public documents also can be helpful in specifying who does and does not possess settlement authority. In rejecting the claim that a faxed offer was enough to create apparent authority, a federal district court said: [T]he City of New York has made plain in its Charter that there is only one official with settlement authority in litigated cases: the Comptroller of the City of New York. *See* N.Y. City Charter § 93[i] ("the comptroller shall have the power to settle and adjust all claims in favor of or against the city"). * * * *Kleine v. City of New York*, 547 F.Supp.2d 315 (S.D.N.Y. 2008) (citing N.Y. City Charter § 394[c]).

5. Recalling our discussion of the different incentives of lawyers and clients, is it possible for a lawyer to be tempted to exceed the scope of her authority in negotiating a settlement on behalf of a client? Consider, for the following examples:

    a.   You are a plaintiff's lawyer working on a contingency fee basis in an employment discrimination case. Discovery has revealed that your client's claims are not as strong as you originally thought, and defense counsel indicates that his client wishes to use every available basis to contest your discovery requests. Pursuing this client's claims will be much more time-consuming—and expensive for you—than you anticipated. You have encouraged your client to settle his case for a relatively nominal sum, along with the promise of reform of the employer's procedures. Your client prefers to fight. He tells you that he wants to know what happened and why, and he also wants his day in court. You have litigated against the defendant's lawyer before, and have always found him to be reasonable and trustworthy.

    b.   Imagine yourself as the defendant-employer's lawyer. You see the merits of the plaintiff's case and have strongly urged your client's CEO to settle the case and reform the company's procedures, Your client, however, insists that his company did nothing wrong. He requires you to fight every discovery request and engage in every possible procedural maneuver to contest plaintiff's claims. Against your advice, the CEO even places the plaintiff under heightened surveillance. You find yourself morally offended by the CEO's views and actions. You have litigated against the plaintiff's lawyer before, and have always found him to be reasonable and trustworthy.

6.   It can be even more difficult for a lawyer to determine his authority when he represents multiple clients in a single lawsuit. Consider, for example, a lawyer representing 100 plaintiffs. In order to reduce the difficulty and the attendant costs when a lawyer requires authority from multiple clients, should clients be able to waive the right to approve the terms of an aggregate settlement negotiated on their behalf by their lawyer? See Association of the Bar of the City of New York Committee on Professional and Judicial Ethics, Formal Opinion 2009–6 (waiver not permitted due to requirement of individual informed consent); *see also* Elizabeth Chamblee Burch, *Adequately Representing Groups,* 81 Fordham L. Rev. 3043 (2013).

2. SETTLEMENT AND LEGAL MALPRACTICE

In the following case, the clients claim that their lawyer did not provide sufficient advice regarding the consequences of entering into a potential settlement agreement. The clients sue for malpractice. The lawyer responds that the clients are barred from making their claims because they did not first engage in self-help, by attempting to vacate the settlement. The court finds that attempted vacatur is not a condition precedent to the legal malpractice claim.

GUIDO v. DUANE MORRIS LLP
Supreme Court of New Jersey, 2010
202 N.J. 79, 995 A.2d 844

JUSTICE RIVERA–SOTO delivered the opinion of the Court.

We need not recite at length the rather tortured factual history of this appeal, as its procedural history is more germane to the issues on appeal. Suffice it to note that plaintiff Joseph Guido was the majority shareholder and chairman of the board of directors of Allstates Worldcargo, Inc. (Allstates). In October 2004, plaintiff sued Allstates and several of its officers and directors, alleging certain corporate governance concerns. On October 27, 2004, the day before the return date on plaintiff's order to show cause, James J. Ferrelli, Esq., a lawyer with and a partner in defendant Duane Morris, LLP (the Law Firm), wrote to plaintiff and explained as follows:

> I previously faxed you a copy of the Voluntary Dismissal without Prejudice, and will file that with the Court tomorrow morning per our discussion this afternoon. That will end the current case against the defendants and would enable you to reinitiate action in the event that you do not come to written terms with the defendants, or assert other claims as you advised you may want to do.

> As we discussed this afternoon, *we advise against any agreement* with [the president and also a member of the board of directors of Allstates] and the [other] defendants *that includes as a term any limitation on your rights as majority shareholder of Allstates,* whether to change the composition of the Board of Directors, otherwise amend the By–Laws, or take other action. In essence, *by requesting that you agree to such terms, [the president of Allstates] is taking away your ability to control the company, which substantially undermines your majority ownership.*

Ferrelli's letter was prophetic. He explained further that "[i]f the case is not dismissed or settled on the record, the Court will order mediation." He noted that, "[i]f mediation were to proceed, an impartial mediator would be appointed to help the parties reach an agreement." He reasoned that "[t]his would be one way for you to obtain a better settlement with [the president of Allstates], one that protects your interests and does not diminish the value of your stock." He remarked further:

> We understand that [the president of Allstates] is talking about extending your employment agreement for five (5) years and increasing your salary. He also wants you to enter into an agreement not to vote your stock in any way that would increase the Board without the consent of all Board members.

> *A binding agreement limiting how you vote your stock severely diminishes the value of your stock,* which we understand is your primary asset. [The president of Allstates] is not offering to pay you for this. Rather, in return for an agreement which will reduce and possibly destroy the value of your stock, [the president of Allstates] is offering a five (5) year employment contract and a to-be-determined raise.

> *In lieu of an agreement not to change the board of directors, we believe that you should be exploring other alternatives,* including a sale of the company and/or the sale of your stock. If [the president of Allstates] wants to control the company and limit your rights as majority shareholder to do so, he should pay you for that by buying your stock or arranging for a sale of the company. Such options could be pursued through mediation.

Ferrelli's letter concluded as follows:

> The ultimate decision is, of course, yours. However, we recommend that if you settle, you do so without undermining your ability and right as majority shareholder to change the board of directors, amend the By–Laws, or take other appropriate action, and that you take all steps to protect, to the greatest extent possible, the value of your stock. You should also obtain repayment of your attorneys' fees, as provided in your Employment Agreement.

The next day, on October 28, 2004 and as foreseen by Ferrelli, the trial court denied plaintiff's request for temporary restraints and referred the matter to mediation; the parties entered into a voluntary dismissal without prejudice, as provided in Rule 4:37–1(a); and entered into a settlement that was placed on the record. The parties, however, were unable to reduce the settlement terms to writing and, ultimately, Allstates "withdr[e]w [its] settlement proposal and elect[ed] to proceed with the litigation of this matter."

As a result, in February 2005, plaintiff filed a second suit against Allstates, again seeking injunctive relief; that complaint was filed by the Law Firm, was signed by defendant Frank A. Luchak, and was verified by plaintiff. The trial court also referred that action to mediation, which ultimately resulted in the settlement plaintiff now claims was inadequate due to defendant's failure to represent plaintiff in a competent manner.

That settlement incorporates all of the items that caused concern to, and were counseled against by, Ferrelli in his letter to plaintiff. At a hearing held on April 5, 2005 where plaintiff was represented by Luchak and defendant Patricia Kane Williams, both of whom were lawyers from the Law Firm, the terms of the settlement reached before the mediator were placed on the record. Following that, the trial court addressed plaintiffs as follows: [transcript in which Guido aknoweldges he "had settlement discussions on [his] own, and [ ]also had the assistance of [retired] Judge Havey in mediating this and bring[ing] closure in accordance with the terms that were described in court, and that he did "understand" and "agree to be bound by . . . the terms."]

Almost two years later, on February 15, 2007, plaintiffs filed their legal malpractice complaint against the Law Firm, Luchak and Williams, claiming that defendants "failed to exercise the knowledge, skill and ability ordinarily possessed and exercised by members of the legal profession similarly situated, and failed to employ reasonable care and prudence in connection with their representation of" plaintiffs. Based on that claimed breach of duty, plaintiffs sought both compensatory damages and a refund of approximately $358,000 in legal fees plaintiffs paid defendants; plaintiffs also sought "attorneys' fees, costs of suit, and such other and further relief as the Court deems just and proper."

Defendants moved for summary judgment, pursuant to pursuant to *Rules* 4:46–1 and –2. By a letter opinion and order dated June 11, 2008, the trial court entered summary judgment in favor of defendants and dismissed plaintiffs' complaint with prejudice. Acknowledging that "there is a genuine issue of material fact as to whether or not the defendants adequately advised plaintiffs of the impact the voting agreement would have on the value of their shares, and whether or not the failure to do so constitutes legal malpractice[,]" the trial court nevertheless concluded that "a [p]laintiff must take reasonable steps to avoid the consequences of a former attorney's tortious conduct before suing the attorney for malpractice." It reasoned that plaintiffs "testified before [the settlement hearing judge] that they understood and agreed to be bound by the terms of the settlement agreement." It noted that "[plaintiffs] never sought to vacate or set aside the underlying settlement, nor did they take any reasonable steps to remedy the purported negligence of their attorneys. Instead, [plaintiffs] filed this malpractice action[.]" Believing that efforts to vacate a prior settlement are an indispensable condition precedent to an action which alleges that the prior settlement was the result of legal malpractice, the trial court granted defendants' motion for summary judgment and dismissed plaintiffs' complaint "in its entirety with prejudice[.]"

* * *

Outright rejecting "the rule . . . that a dissatisfied litigant may not recover from his or her attorney for malpractice in negotiating a settlement that the litigant has accepted unless the litigant can prove actual fraud on the part of the attorney[,]" the Court in *Ziegelheim* concluded that "[t]he fact that a party received a settlement that was 'fair and equitable' does not mean necessarily that the party's attorney was competent or that the party would not have received a more favorable settlement had the party's incompetent attorney been competent." That said, the Court tempered its conclusion with the recognition that it was "not open[ing] the door to malpractice suits by any and every dissatisfied party to a settlement." The Court "acknowledge[d] that attorneys who pursue reasonable strategies in handling their cases and who render reasonable advice to their clients cannot be held liable for the failure of their strategies or for any unprofitable outcomes that result because their clients took their advice [,]" explaining that "[t]he law demands that attorneys handle their cases with knowledge, skill, and diligence, but it does not demand that they be perfect or infallible, and it does not demand that they always secure optimum outcomes for their clients."

* * *

An application of those precepts leads to the conclusion that plaintiffs' malpractice claim should not be barred. Here, unlike in *Puder*, plaintiffs did not represent to the court that they were satisfied with the settlement, or that the settlement was fair and adequate. The entirety of the colloquy between the court and plaintiffs concerning the settlement addressed but two questions: whether plaintiffs understood and agreed to abide by the settlement terms, and whether plaintiffs were subject to any impediments in understanding those terms. Glaringly absent is any representation by plaintiffs that the settlement was "fair" and "adequate," a representation deemed crucial in [prior cases].

In addition, and provided that they are supported by sufficient credible evidence in the record, we are bound by the trial court's factual findings. * * *

Defendants and amici have urged, nevertheless, that as a condition precedent to the filing of a malpractice case arising from a judicially accepted settlement, this Court should require that the malpractice plaintiff first try to vacate the settlement, and that a malpractice claim should lie only if those efforts fail. * * *

The facts in this case mandate that we reject defendants' and amici's blanket invitation. Here, as the Appellate Division aptly concluded, "plaintiffs had no reasonable expectation of success on a motion to set aside the General Equity settlement, and consequently had no obligation to make such an application." Because " 'the law does not compel one to do a useless act [,]' " requiring that a malpractice plaintiff first engage in what may well be the barren exercise of seeking to vacate a settlement is both wasteful and unnecessary. No doubt, there may be circumstances in which a malpractice plaintiff's failure to mitigate his or her damages by seeking to vacate the settlement that gives rise to the malpractice claim may be relevant. However, because that action logically cannot be a prerequisite for all malpractice claims based on a settlement, it also cannot rise to the level of a condition precedent to a malpractice suit. * * *

NOTES AND QUESTIONS

1.   In discussing the potential for legal malpractice arising out of settlement, the court in *Guido* quotes *Ziegelheim v. Apollo*, 128 N.J. 250, 607 A.2d 1298 (1992) for the following:

> "[A]ttorneys who pursue reasonable strategies in handling their cases and who render reasonable advice to their clients cannot be held liable for the failure of their strategies or for any unprofitable outcomes that result because their clients took their advice[,]" explaining that "[t]he law demands that attorneys handle their cases with knowledge, skill, and diligence, but it does not demand that they be perfect or infallible, and it does not demand that they always secure optimum outcomes for their clients.

This language should be reassuring, at least to some degree. Lawyers' potential liability for legal malpractice in the settlement context depends primarily on whether they demonstrated sufficient knowledge of the relevant substantive and procedural law and whether the client can demonstrate that he suffered harm as a result of the lawyer's negligent representation. *See e.g.*, *McWhirt v. Heavey*, 550 N.W.2d 327 (Neb. 1996) (finding that the client's settlement did not bar a malpractice claim when such claim involved allegations that the lawyer had made misrepresentations and lacked sufficient knowledge of divorce law to judge the various settlement offers made by the other party).

2.   Suppose you are one of a small handful of lawyers in a boutique commercial law firm. The Chief Executive Officer of one of your corporate clients calls to tell you that she and her husband of 25 years have decided to divorce amicably. She wants you to assist her and her husband with the negotiation of all the terms of their divorce. You have no expertise with family law issues. You have found the CEO to be brilliant, but frequently preoccupied and somewhat inadequate in terms of her communication skills. Based on the cases you have just read, would you have any concerns regarding the potential for legal liability? Now recall Rules 1.1, 1.4 and 1.7 of the Model Rules of Professional Conduct, *supra*. Would have any ethical concerns? Do the rules provide any guidance regarding handling these concerns?

3.   Breach of fiduciary duty claims also may arise out of settlements. Unlike legal malpractice claims, though, these claims do not require a showing of proximate cause based on the "trial-within-a-trial test." See e.g., *Crist v. Loyacono*, 65 So.3d 837 (Miss. 2011) (reversing summary judgment

that had been granted to lawyers in claim brought by clients against their lawyers for premature settlement of cases, allegedly in order to maximize attorneys' fees).

4.   Recent Supreme Court jurisprudence has "constitutionalized" criminal defense lawyers' provision of advice to their clients during plea bargaining. In *Missouri v. Frye*, 132 S. Ct. 1399 (2012), a lawyer failed to convey two possible plea bargains to his client. The offers then expired. Less than a week before the preliminary hearing, the client was arrested again. He pled guilty with no underlying plea agreement and was sentenced to a longer prison term than would have been required by one of the plea offers.

The Supreme Court held that as a general rule, defense counsel has a duty to communicate formal offers from the prosecution to the client. Further, the Court held that in this case, defense counsel had not met the standard of effective assistance required by the Constitution. In order to win relief, however, the client still had to show he was prejudiced by the ineffective assistance of his counsel. The evidence showed a reasonable probability that the client would have accepted the plea offer, but the Court remanded to permit him to demonstrate the additional required showings— i.e., a reasonable probability that the prosecution would have maintained the offer, and that the trial court would have accepted it.

In a companion criminal case, *Lafler v. Cooper*, 132 S. Ct. 1376 (2012), the Court found another instance of constitutionally ineffective assistance of counsel. The criminal defendant had rejected a favorable plea offer based on his lawyer's recommendation, which relied upon an inaccurate description of a legal standard. The Court determined that the appropriate remedy in that case was to order the State to reoffer the more favorable plea that had been rejected. *Id.* at 1382.

5.   Professor Steven Zeidman has warned against using an extreme model of client-centered lawyering in criminal cases, in which the lawyer *refuses* to advise a course of action to her client. Professor Zeidman's concerns are based largely on *Boria v. Keane*, 90 F.3d 36 (2d Cir. 1996), which held that a criminal defendant had a "constitutional right to be advised whether or not the offered bargain 'appeared to be desirable.'" Because the defense attorney never actually advised his client whether or not he should accept the plea offer, he failed to provide the requisite effective assistance of counsel. *See* Steven Zeidman, *To Plead or Not to Plead: Effective Assistance and Client–Centered Counseling*, 39 B.C. L. Rev. 841, 847–48 (1998).

Several courts have distinguished or disagreed with the *Boria* decision, including the Second Circuit itself in a subsequent case. *Purdy v. U.S.*, 208 F.3d 41 (2d Cir. 2000) (distinguishing and limiting the *Boria* holding)*; see also Jones v. Murray*, 947 F.2d 1106, 1110 (4th Cir. 1991) (refusing to find ineffective assistance of counsel in a capital case where defense counsel neither recommended nor attempted to persuade defendant to enter into a plea agreement); *Bright v. State*, 4 S.W.3d 568 (Mo. Ct. App. 1999) (distinguishing *Boria*).

E. A LAWYER'S DUTY TO ADVISE CLIENTS ABOUT DISPUTE RESOLUTION OPTIONS

The rest of this book is devoted to the various dispute resolution processes to which the client and her lawyer might turn, including negotiation, mediation, arbitration, and mixed processes. Litigators are likely to find themselves advising clients about these processes before commencing litigation or at some point during the lengthy litigation process. Transactional lawyers, meanwhile, may need to advise their clients about the inclusion of dispute resolution clauses in all sorts of contracts.

Do lawyers have an ethical duty to advise their clients about potential dispute resolution processes? Should they have such a duty? Rules 1.1, 1.2, 1.4 and 2.1 of the Model Rules of Professional Conduct, *supra*, are relevant in responding to these questions.

NANCY A. WELSH, INTEGRATING "ALTERNATIVE" DISPUTE RESOLUTION INTO BANKRUPTCY: AS SIMPLE (AND PURE) AS MOTHERHOOD AND APPLE PIE?
11 Nev. L. J. 397, 402–408 (2011)

[The client, XYZ Corporation, seeks reorganization under Chapter 11. However, there are 1,000 pending asbestos-related lawsuits that name XYZ as a defendant, and the continued existence of these lawsuits has the potential to hinder the client's ability to secure funding and solicit potential buyers, among other things. XYZ's CEO has asked for our legal advice on how to deal with the pending lawsuits.]

Rule 1.1 states: "A lawyer shall provide competent representation to a client." It further defines "competent representation" as "requir[ing] the legal knowledge, skill, thoroughness and preparation reasonably necessary for the representation." Comment 2 is particularly helpful here:

> A lawyer need not necessarily have special training or prior experience to handle legal problems of a type with which the lawyer is unfamiliar. . . . Some important legal skills, such as the analysis of precedent, the evaluation of evidence and legal drafting, are required in all legal problems. Perhaps the most fundamental legal skill consists of determining what kind of legal problems a situation may involve, a skill that necessarily transcends any particular specialized knowledge. A lawyer can provide adequate representation in a wholly novel field through necessary study. . . .

Clearly, we must have sufficient knowledge about the dispute resolution options available to our client. The most frequently used "alternative" procedures are negotiation, mediation, and arbitration. Based on the limited information currently available, it seems that any of these could be appropriate here. Potentially, we also could advise XYZ to use med-arb, which is a hybrid of mediation and arbitration. We could even recommend a tiered—or three step—procedure: offer and exchange as the first step (consisting of a plaintiff's submission, a responsive take-it-or-leave-it settlement offer from XYZ, and plaintiff's decision whether or not to take the offer), followed by sixty days for mediation as the second step, if the offer and exchange do not result in settlement, and a third step of binding arbitration in the event that mediation does not produce a settlement. We will need to do more research regarding our client, its insurance, likelihood of liability, extent of damages, and the impact of our Chapter 11 posture in order to choose the most appropriate procedure.

* * *

Do we need to advise XYZ regarding these procedures and the differences among them? According to Rule 1.2, we must abide by XYZ's decisions regarding the objectives of our representation, but are required only to "consult" with our client regarding the means by which we will try to achieve these objectives. Rule 1.4(a)(2) elaborates that "[a] lawyer shall . . . reasonably consult with the client about the means by which the client's objectives are to be accomplished," while Rule 2.1 provides that "a lawyer shall exercise independent professional judgment and render candid advice." Comment 5 to Rule 2.1 specifically references the counseling of clients regarding the potential use of dispute resolution:

> In general, a lawyer is not expected to give advice until asked by the client. However, when a lawyer knows that a client proposes a course of action that is likely to result in substantial adverse legal consequences to the client, the lawyer's duty to the client under Rule 1.4 may require that the lawyer offer advice if the client's course of action is related to the representation. Similarly, when a matter is likely to involve litigation, it may be necessary under Rule 1.4 to inform the client of forms of dispute resolution that might constitute reasonable alternatives to litigation. A lawyer ordinarily has no duty to initiate investigation of a client's affairs or to give advice that the client has indicated is unwanted, but a lawyer may initiate advice to a client when doing so appears to be in the client's interest.

These rules suggest that we certainly will not violate our ethical obligations if we choose to advise XYZ about the potential use of dispute resolution procedures that might assist with its planned reorganization. At the same time, the conditional language of Comment 5 makes it less than clear that we have an affirmative obligation to provide this advice. Some states, on the other hand, have found such an obligation.

If we decide to provide this advice to XYZ, how much does the CEO need to know? The significant differences among dispute resolution procedures, described *supra*, suggest the importance of ensuring that clients are sufficiently informed about the procedures and their potential consequences. Rule 1.4(b) provides that "[a] lawyer shall explain a matter to the extent reasonably necessary to permit the client to make informed decisions regarding the representation." Comment 5 to Rule 1.4 expands upon this requirement and muddies the waters:

> The client should have sufficient information to participate intelligently in decisions concerning the objectives of the representation and the means by which they are to be pursued, to the extent the client is willing and able to do so. Adequacy of communication depends in part on the kind of advice or assistance that is involved. For example, when there is time to explain a proposal made in a negotiation, the lawyer should review all important provisions with the client before proceeding to an agreement. In litigation a lawyer should explain the general strategy and prospects of success and ordinarily should consult the client on tactics that are likely to result in significant expense or to injure or coerce others. On the other hand, a lawyer ordinarily will not be expected to describe trial or negotiation strategy in detail. The guiding principle is that the lawyer should fulfill reasonable client expectations for information consistent with the duty to act in the client's best interests, and the client's overall requirements as to the character of representation.

In deferring to "reasonable client expectations" and "the client's overall requirements as to the character of representation," Comment 5 unfortunately seems to substitute the ethics of the marketplace for a general professional ethic that is consistently applicable. Sophisticated clients with substantial experience with dispute resolution options are likely to know enough to demand advice regarding the potential legal consequences of using a particular procedure within a particular context, regardless of the cost or time restrictions. Unsophisticated clients—or clients swept up in financial turmoil—are much less likely to make this demand or even know they could make it. And then, of course, a lawyer who would prefer to operate autonomously may question whether such client expectations are objectively "reasonable," especially if time is short and the client has no resources to fund the research that will be required.

NOTES AND QUESTIONS

1. Some states' ethics codes require or strongly recommend that lawyers advise their clients about ADR options. The Virginia Rules of Professional Conduct are particularly comprehensive:

- Rule 1.2, Comment 1 provides: "Both lawyer and client have authority and responsibility in the objectives and means of representation.... [A] client also has a right to consult with the lawyer about the means to be used in pursuing those objectives. In that context, a lawyer shall advise the client about the advantages, disadvantages, and availability of dispute resolution processes that might be appropriate in pursuing these objectives."

- Rule 1.4, Comment 1 provides: "This continuing duty to keep the client informed includes a duty to advise the client about the availability of dispute resolution processes that might be more appropriate to the client's goals than the initial process chosen. For example, information obtained during a lawyer-to-lawyer negotiation may give rise to consideration of a process, such as mediation, where the parties themselves could be more directly involved in resolving the dispute."

- Rule 2.1, Comment 2 provides: "Advice couched in narrowly legal terms may be of little value to a client, especially where practical considerations, such as cost or effects on other people, are predominant. Purely technical legal advice, therefore, can sometimes be inadequate. It could also ignore, to the client's disadvantage, the relational or emotional factors driving a dispute. In such a case, advice may include the advantages, disadvantages and availability of other dispute resolution processes that might be appropriate under the circumstances."

Michigan Ethics Opinion RI–262 interprets the Michigan Rules of Professional Conduct to hold, within the spirit and intent of these Rules, that: "A lawyer has an obligation to recommend alternatives to litigation when an alternative is a reasonable course of action to further the client's interests, or if the lawyer has any reason to think that the client would find the alternative desirable." Some courts' rules require lawyers to advise their clients regarding ADR. *See e.g.,* Supreme Court Rule 17.02 of the Missouri Rules Governing the Missouri Bar and the Judiciary; Rule 114.03 of the Minnesota General Rules of Practice for the District Courts.

2.   Other states' ethics provisions encourage lawyers to advise their clients regarding ADR, but do not require it. *See e.g.,* Colorado Rules of Professional Conduct, Rule 2.1 ("a lawyer should advise the client . . ."); Hawaii Rules of Professional Conduct, Rule 2.1 ("a lawyer should advise a client . . ."), Rule 1.4, Comment 5 of Massachusetts Rules of Professional Conduct (" 'a lawyer should advise a client . . .' ").

3.   Some ethics opinions or provisions specifically require lawyers to advise their clients if the other side has proposed the use of ADR. *See e.g.,* Mich. Eth. Op. RI–255 (1996); Pa. Eth. Op. 90–125 (1991).

4.   Besides legal and ethical requirements, what other reasons would counsel in favor of a practice of discussing ADR options with clients?

5.   Should lawyers who fail to advise their clients face potential liability for legal malpractice? *See* Robert F. Cochran, *Must Lawyers Tell Their Clients About ADR?,* Arb. J., June 1993, at 8.

6.   Assuming you believe that it is necessary or appropriate to discuss dispute resolution options with a client, how would you do it? That question underlies much of what appears in this book, and we expect that your understanding of it will develop as you proceed through these materials. Chapter VII will provide suggestions on how to deploy in a particular case the knowledge you have developed about dispute resolution options.

F. INTERVIEWING AND COUNSELING EXERCISE

A FIGHT OVER AMY

The following are general instructions for an interviewing and counseling role play about child custody in the divorce context. The confidential instructions for Alice, Bob, and the attorneys are available from the instructor, and may also be downloaded from the casebook web site, at www.lawschool.westlaw.com. A password is required to download the confidential instructions.

General Information for All Parties

Alice and Bob divorced five years ago when their daughter, Amy, was three years old. They amicably reached an agreement, the terms of which the court entered in its decree ordering that: Alice was sole owner of the family home, Alice had the right of custody and the responsibility for bringing up Amy, and Bob had the "right of reasonable visitation with Amy, including full time for a two-week vacation period each summer."

For three years the family cooperated comfortably under this arrangement, but last year Alice objected to Bob taking Amy to Florida for two weeks in July, saying it was too hot. Alice refused to give up Amy at the last minute, and Bob went without her. This year Bob informed Alice a month in advance, when he bought the supersaver plane tickets, that he would take Amy to New York City during his vacation. Alice phoned him about two days ahead and indicated she did not think that was a good idea, but Bob told her he would pick Amy up at 7:00 p.m. the night before the scheduled plane departure. Alice said, "Don't come." When Bob arrived at 7:00 p.m., Alice met him at the edge of the front porch and told him not to come any further and that he could not take Amy to New York because it was too dangerous for her there. Bob could see Amy peering through the screen door and brushed by Alice, walking to the door. Alice stepped in front of him and gently pushed him back to the edge of the porch. When Bob tried to move forward again, Alice pushed harder, and Bob fell down the steps breaking his wrist. Amy was crying.

The next morning, both Alice and Bob called for appointments with their respective attorneys, who are *not* the same persons who represented them in the divorce. At the beginning of their office visit, both Alice and Bob recount the above sequence of events.

CHAPTER III

NEGOTIATION

■ ■ ■

Negotiation is an interpersonal process through which we make arrangements with others to resolve disputes or plan transactions, often by reconciling conflicting—or apparently conflicting—interests. It involves communication—through the use of words or actions—of demands, wishes, and perspectives.

Most lawyers spend a major part of their professional lives engaged in this process. Lawyers negotiate, usually with other lawyers, to plan transactions and to resolve disputes. In addition, negotiation makes up an important part of other dispute resolution processes. Mediation, for instance, is negotiation that is facilitated by a third party. Several of the mixed processes discussed in Chapter VI—court-annexed (nonbinding) arbitration, the mini-trial, and the summary jury trial—are intended to help parties negotiate better. So many cases in litigation are actually settled through negotiation that Professor Marc Galanter finds it useful to consider the two processes as one "litigotiation" process. Marc Galanter, *World of Deals: Using Negotiation to Teach About Legal Process*, 34 J. Legal Educ. 268, 268 (1984). Professor Gary Goodpaster has gone a step further and suggested that we could learn much by looking at litigation as part of the negotiation process. Gary Goodpaster, *Lawsuits as Negotiations*, 8 Negot J. 221 (1992).

Lawyers do not merely negotiate with other lawyers, however. In their professional lives, lawyers also negotiate with their bosses, partners, subordinates, and with providers of supplies and services. Lawyers also spend a significant portion of their professional lives negotiating with their clients about various aspects of their representation. And in their personal lives, lawyers, like all people, negotiate constantly—with their family, friends, physicians, clergy, taxi drivers, and so on.

Because negotiation takes place in such a wide variety of situations, and relies significantly on intuition and judgment, some argue that negotiation skills cannot be taught. We believe, however, that anyone can improve his or her negotiating skills by learning from experience and by planning, practicing, and reflecting on negotiation.

In this chapter, we cannot hope to cover the many situations in which lawyers negotiate. For that reason, we attempt to deal with the basics—a set of concepts and suggestions that will help you understand the various negotiation situations in which you may find yourself. In Section A, we begin by focusing on individual negotiator style. In Section B, we introduce the negotiation process and provide a basic framework for thinking about how a typical negotiation might proceed. Then, in Section C, we explore how negotiators might approach this process by setting forth two major approaches to (or conceptualizations of) negotiation, which we label "adversarial" and "problem-solving." The former approach focuses on positions while the latter focuses on the underlying interests at the core of the dispute. Believing that nothing is more practical than a good theory, we hope that this section will give you a solid foundation for understanding the approaches that you and your counterparts employ in negotiations. In Section D, we elaborate on these approaches by identifying strategies and tactics associated with each. In Section E, we turn our attention explicitly to legal negotiations, exploring the roles of law, lawyers, and clients in the negotiation process. Finally, in Section F, we examine the potential impact of culture, gender and race on the negotiation process.

A. NEGOTIATOR STYLE

Because negotiation is an interpersonal process that begins with some sort of conflict, a negotiator's general tendencies in responding to conflict represent a critically important component of negotiation. Professor G. Richard Shell provides the following thought experiment to help negotiators discern which of five approaches to conflict most fit them.

1. YOUR INITIAL APPROACH

G. RICHARD SHELL, BARGAINING FOR ADVANTAGE: NEGOTIATION STRATEGIES FOR REASONABLE PEOPLE
8, 9–12 (2d ed. 2006)

Your personal negotiation style is a critical variable in bargaining. If you don't know what your instincts and intuitions will tell you to do under different conditions, you will have a great deal of trouble planning effective strategies and responses.

* * *

To begin our exploration of your bargaining strengths, try the following thought experiment. Imagine you are one of ten people, all of whom are strangers, sitting at a big round table in a conference room. Someone comes into the room and makes the following offer: "I will give a prize of one thousand dollars to each of the first two people who can persuade the person sitting opposite to get up, come around the table, and stand behind his or her chair."

Do you have that picture in mind? You are one of ten strangers at the table. You can see the person sitting opposite you, and that person is looking at you. The first two people who can persuade the person sitting opposite to get up, come around the table, and stand behind his or her chair gets $1,000. Everyone else gets nothing.

What strategy would you use to respond to this strange offer? You will need to move quickly because everyone else is also thinking about what to do.

Before reading on, close your eyes and think of your response. Note what strategy comes to your mind first and write it down. Then see what other responses you can think of. The possibilities will help me introduce five generic negotiating strategies, which will, in turn, lead us to a deeper look at your personality as a negotiation variable.

One reaction is to sit tight and do nothing, suspecting a trick or worrying that you might look like a fool running around a table in response to a stranger's offer. "I don't like to negotiate, so I don't do it unless I have to," you might say. This is the **avoiding** response. . . . Some people might say that avoiding a negotiation is a cop-out, not a bargaining strategy. But you do not have to look very far to notice that many important negotiations are marked by one side or the other studiously avoiding coming to the table. The North Koreans successfully avoided negotiating over their nuclear weapons programs for years—and built up bargaining leverage in the meantime. Presidential candidates in the United States who find themselves ahead in the polls frequently decline to negotiate when their opponents want to increase the number of presidential debates. In general, avoiding is a good strategy when you are happy with the status quo—but it may not be the best approach to the table problem.

Perhaps the most obvious response is to offer the person sitting opposite you $500 if he or she will race around and stand behind your chair. This is the **compromise** solution. Each person agrees to share the gains equally between them. Compromise is a simple, fair, fast strategy that resolves many negotiations amicably. But is it a good strategy for the table problem? You and your partner may arrive at a quick agreement to split the money evenly, but which of you should run and who should sit? During the few seconds it takes to address this issue, other people are already racing around the table. There is no compromise solution to the question of which of you should run—so a simple compromise does not fully solve the problem. An additional strategy is needed.

That strategy is our third candidate—**accommodation**. You could simply get up and run behind your opponent's chair. If you do this in response to your partner's offer to split the money, you can refer to that promise as a bargaining standard in any subsequent negotiation over the money. But there may be no money to split. The people who implemented the 100 percent accommodating strategy took off as soon as they heard the stranger's offer and got to their partners' chairs before you did. But they face a problem, too. The lucky people who were the beneficiaries of the accommodating strategy now have $1,000 and the people who ran have nothing. These helpful negotiators must trust the people for whom they earned the money to share it—without the benefit of a prior commitment on how it will be shared. And remember—everyone at the table is a stranger who never expects to see their counterpart again.

The fourth response embodies the **competitive** strategy. The idea here is to obtain the entire $1,000 as well as the power to decide how it will be shared. One way might be to offer to split the money 50–50 and then later refuse to do so—to renege on your promise. That would obviously be unethical, but some people might do it. After all, there was no mention of a court system to litigate disputes about who said what. An even more aggressive stance would be to lie and say you have a broken leg so you can't move, begging your partner to run as quickly as possible. Are all competitive strategies as ethically dubious as these two? No. We will see examples of many competitive strategies in the pages ahead that are perfectly ethical under any system of morals. But the table problem is not structured well for a strategy that is both ethical and competitive. Moreover, this strategy, like the compromise approach, may take too long to implement.

The final strategy is the most imaginative, given the terms of the offer. You get out of your chair, start running, and scream: "Let's both get behind each other's chairs! We can each make a thousand dollars!" This can work—if you are quick enough. This is the **collaborative** or **problem-solving** strategy. Instead of trying to figure out how to divide $1,000 two ways, the person using this approach has the insight to see that there is a way for *both parties* to get $1,000 out of the situation.

The collaborative strategy is often the hardest to implement. It seeks to discover the underlying problem through good analysis and candid disclosure of interests, find the most elegant solution by brainstorming many options, and resolve tough issues using fair standards and criteria. In many ways, it represents an ideal. As we shall see, problem-solving strategies are especially useful in complex negotiations, such as those faced by international diplomats or corporate negotiators doing mergers or acquisitions. They can also play a useful role in family negotiations, where it is vitally important to avoid having "winners" and "losers." But many obstacles stand in the way of collaborative approaches, such as lack of trust between the parties, greed, personality, cultural differences, and simple lack of imagination.

* * *

Your personal bargaining styles are nothing more (or less) than your inclinations or predispositions to make certain moves when you are negotiating. These inclinations can come from many sources—childhood, family, early professional experiences, mentors, ethical systems or beliefs, and so on. And your inclinations can change over time as your knowledge of negotiation grows and you gain more confidence in a wider range of skills. But I genuinely believe that most of us have a set of core personality traits that make radical changes in our basic bargaining preferences difficult.

NOTES AND QUESTIONS

1.   What is *your* most likely response to conflict? Your *least* likely response? Learning about responses to conflict and one's own tendencies provides a negotiator with a general framework for understanding themselves and their counterparts, and for making sense of their interactions.

2.   What do you think happens when two negotiators using the "competing" approach negotiate with one another? Two negotiators using the "avoiding" approach? Two negotiators using the "compromising" approach? How about a "competing" negotiator and an "accommodating" negotiator? A "competing" negotiator and an "avoiding" negotiator?

3.   Robert R. Blake and Jane Srygley Mouton identified five approaches to managing conflict—competing, accommodating, avoiding, compromising, and collaborating—in the mid–1960s. *See* ROBERT R. BLAKE & JANE SRYGLEY MOUTON, THE MANAGERIAL GRID: KEY ORIENTATIONS FOR ACHIEVING PRODUCTION THROUGH PEOPLE (1964). Professors Kenneth Thomas and Ralph Kilmann developed an instrument, called the Thomas–Kilmann Instrument or TKI, to test for these approaches. *See* Ralph H. Kilmann & Kenneth W. Thomas, *Developing a Forced–Choice Measure of Conflict–Handling Behavior: The "Mode" Instrument*, 37 Educ. Testing & Measurement 309 (1977).

Professor Melissa Nelken administered the TKI to a group of lawyers and a large sample of law students enrolled in negotiation courses at California law schools. She found that both lawyers and law students scored highest on the "compromising" style (i.e., average scores of 8.1 for lawyers and 7.5 for law students) and lowest on the "competing" style (i.e., average scores of 5.0 for lawyers and 5.4 for law students). Interestingly, business executives' dominant approach was also compromising, but they were substantially more likely than law students to use a collaborative approach. *See* Melissa L. Nelken, *The Myth of the Gladiator and Law Students' Negotiation Styles*, 7 Cardozo J. Conflict Resol. 1, 14, 18 (2005).

4.   Professor Shell's example of a competitive approach includes unethical conduct (e.g., reneging on a promise, lying about a broken leg). If you use a competitive approach, is it inevitable that you will behave unethically? In this chapter, *infra*, we will introduce the ethics requirements

that apply to lawyers' negotiations, growing empirical research regarding lawyers' conduct, and some commentators' views on the values and morals that ought to apply to negotiation.

5.   Professor Shell says that "problem solving strategies are especially useful in complex negotiations, such as those faced by international diplomats or corporate negotiators doing mergers and acquisition. They can also play a useful role in family negotiations, where it is vitally important to avoid having 'winners' and 'losers.'" Do you think there is a role for a problem-solving response in dealing with personal injury cases? Employment discrimination claims? *See* Leonard L. Riskin & Nancy A. Welsh, *Is That All There Is?: "The Problem" in Court–Oriented Mediation*, 15 Geo. Mason L. Rev. 863 (2008) (arguing that in court-oriented mediations in "ordinary" civil cases, the parties should be allowed to opt for a problem-solving approach that creates customized value).

6.   The TKI is not behaviorally validated, so we cannot be sure that negotiators' behaviors are consistent with their self-assessments. Some research suggests that negotiators do exhibit fairly consistent styles. That said, many negotiators find that their responses to conflict vary by context, and from situation to situation within a particular context. *See* Robert H. Mnookin, Scott R. Peppet & Andrew S. Tulumello, *Negotiators' Empathy and Assertiveness*, 14 Alternatives to the High Cost of Litig. 133, 145 (1996).

Do you think you respond in the same manner in professional settings as in personal settings? Is your natural response the same when you are negotiating on your own behalf as when you are negotiating for someone else? What other contextual factors might—or should—influence your response to conflict? When Dean Jennifer Gerarda Brown asks her students to complete the TKI, she instructs them to think in terms of the relationship in which they can be their "'truest self' . . . in which you do not assume an artificial *persona* specific to the relationship." She then reminds them that the response demanded by their role—e.g., representing a client in a legal negotiation—"may be a departure from what they identified as authentic, instinctive, or reflexive." Jennifer Gerarda Brown, *Empowering Students to Create and Claim Value Through the Thomas–Kilmann Conflict Mode Instrument*, 28 Negot. J. 79, 84–85 (2012).

7.   Professor Leonard Riskin has argued that negotiators who practice mindfulness meditation are likely to gain insight into their own personalities, moods, and the way they respond to conflict and, consequently, perform better. *See* Leonard L. Riskin, *The Contemplative Lawyer: On the Potential Contributions of Mindfulness Meditation to Law Students, Lawyers, and Their Clients*, 7 Harv. Negot. L. Rev. 1 (2002). For further discussion of mindfulness meditation, *see* Chapter VIII, *infra*. Dean Jennifer Brown, meanwhile, has observed that "our reflexive response to conflict is likely to affect our comfort with [the different negotiation strategies of] value creating and claiming" but she adds: "Still, we are not stuck with our reflexes. We can choose to follow or defy our reflexive responses, and we will choose more wisely if we are mindful of those tendencies" and "[d]eparting from reflexes

requires energy: preparation, mindfulness, and conscious effort." Jennifer Gerarda Brown, *Empowering Students to Create and Claim Value Through the Thomas–Kilmann Conflict Mode Instrument*, 28 Negotiation. J. 79, 81 (2012). Fortunately, each of us can control whether we will prepare, whether we will try to be mindful, and whether we will try to make a conscious effort to control our reflexes. And practice will help us to become more effective.

2. THE IMPACT OF STYLE

Although related, there is a difference between negotiation *style* and negotiation *strategy* or *approach*. Your strategy, or plan for proceeding in the negotiation, is based on underlying assumptions about whether there are only limited resources that you and the other negotiator must divide, or whether you and the other negotiator can work together to expand the available resources. As you will see, *infra*, Professor Carrie Menkel–Meadow describes the first approach or strategy as "adversarial" and the second as "problem-solving."

Your negotiation *style* involves your sense of yourself and your relationship with the other negotiator, independent of the resources available to resolve your dispute. More specifically, do you treat the other negotiator in a cooperative manner, or do you behave in a manner that is competitive or aggressive? It is easy to imagine a negotiator with a cooperative style who pursues a problem-solving strategy. But other pairings are also possible. A lawyer can have a cooperative *style*, for example, while pursuing an adversarial *approach* or *strategy*. As that example suggests, the relationship—and difference—between style and strategy are not always obvious. In addition, the terminology that has arisen in the study of negotiation muddies the waters. *See generally*, Andrea Kupfer Schneider, *Teaching A New Negotiation Skills Paradigm*, 39 Wash. U. J. L. & Pol'y 13 (2012).

The following excerpt examines this relationship. It begins, however, with a description of available research on lawyers' assessments of their colleagues' effectiveness as negotiators and the apparent influence that style exerts upon these assessments.

NANCY A. WELSH, THE REPUTATIONAL ADVANTAGES OF DEMONSTRATING TRUSTWORTHINESS: USING THE REPUTATION INDEX WITH LAW STUDENTS
28 Negot. J. 117 (2011)

The best-known research in this area [on legal negotiators' evaluations of each other's effectiveness in the short term and long term] was conducted by the Brigham Young University Legal Negotiation Project. Gerald Williams and other researchers there aimed to discern the characteristics of lawyer negotiators perceived by their peers as effective or ineffective. Based on surveys of randomly selected active lawyers in the

Denver and Phoenix metropolitan areas, the researchers concluded that lawyer negotiators' behaviors are clustered into three perceived patterns, labeled as "cooperative," "aggressive" (or "competitive"), and "no pattern."

Most frequently (65 percent), lawyers' behaviors were perceived to fit the cooperative pattern; 24 percent of the time, their behaviors fit the aggressive pattern; and 11 percent of the time, they fit "no pattern." Much more importantly for the purposes of this article, however, lawyer respondents did not perceive *any single pattern* as having "a monopoly on effectiveness." Some percentage of the time, cooperative *and* aggressive *and* even "no pattern" patterns of behavior were perceived as effective. And, some percentage of the time, each of the three patterns was perceived as *ineffective.*

A striking finding from Williams and his colleagues' research was that even though lawyers perceived effective and ineffective negotiators within each pattern as sharing many of the same key *objectives,* the *implementation* of those objectives separated the effective negotiators from the ineffective ones. All the effective negotiators, regardless of the pattern into which they fit, were perceived as observant and disciplined professionals, skilled in the craft of lawyering and operating within the profession's ethical constraints. In other words, as lawyer respondents identified effective legal *negotiators,* they noticed whether their opposing counsel were effective *lawyers.*

In contrast, lawyer respondents perceived ineffective legal negotiators as allowing their personal egos, emotions, and insecurities to be given excessive play. Ineffective cooperative negotiators were not just trustworthy but trustful. They were not just personable but gentle, obliging, patient, and forgiving. Ineffective aggressive negotiators were not just dominating but irritating. They did not just reveal information gradually and strategically; they withheld information and were rigid. The lawyer respondents' assessments reveal their perception that ineffective negotiators failed to exercise sufficient self-control and failed to moderate their behaviors based on their observations of opposing counsel's responses. Williams has observed that with the ineffective legal negotiators, "we have . . . a description of the extremes of both styles (cooperative and aggressive), both of them ineffective, but in quite opposite ways. . . . [W]e can assume that negotiators at the ineffective level are either omitting essential aspects of the strategies, or else they are defeating their own strategies by going too far with them or otherwise negating their effectiveness."

It is also interesting, and certainly significant, that lawyer respondents perceived the occurrence of substantially more cooperative legal negotiation than aggressive legal negotiation, and were much more likely to assess those who fit the cooperative pattern as effective. Fifty-nine percent of those perceived as cooperative were also described as effective; 45 percent of those fitting no pattern were described as effective; only 25 percent of those perceived as aggressive were described as effective. Williams has argued that those using a cooperative pattern "are self-monitors who do not want to go beyond what would be fair to both sides." But the lawyer respondents perceived that effective lawyers using a cooperative pattern had maximization of their own clients' settlement as one of their top objectives. Therefore, it might be more accurate to say that these effective lawyers apparently sought both a good result for their own clients—and something fair enough for the other side.

Nonetheless, it is also certainly significant that the lawyer respondents sometimes saw the value and effectiveness of the aggressive pattern when it was implemented intelligently and successfully. Indeed, it might be helpful to understand effective aggressive negotiators as "competitors" or "worthy foes," while ineffective aggressive negotiators could be understood as mere "bullies." Those in the former group may be trusted, at least to some degree, as professionals; those in the latter group should be distrusted. . . .

More recently, Andrea Kupfer Schneider conducted a similar survey of lawyer negotiators in Milwaukee and Chicago. Like Williams and his colleagues, Schneider asked the lawyer respondents to assess their negotiation counterparts. Although Schneider used different labels to identify the patterns her research uncovered, she found that the traits and objectives associated with effective negotiators in one cluster (which she labeled "problem-solving") overwhelmingly tracked those included in Williams' effective "cooperative" pattern. Perhaps due to the addition of new choices in the survey instruments, Schneider found some differences between her "adversarial" cluster and the "aggressive" pattern identified by Williams. Nonetheless, there were many general similarities, with "egotistical," "demanding," and "ambitious" showing up as top adjectives in Schneider's study, while "tough," "dominant," "forceful," "ambitious," and "egotist" were among the top traits of effective negotiators who fit the "aggressive" pattern cited by respondents in Williams' study.

Schneider's respondents also reported that effective lawyers in the problem-solving and adversarial clusters shared two traits: "experienced" and "confident." The top bipolar descriptions and goals reported for both groups revealed several additional areas of overlap:

> Both effective problem-solvers and effective adversarials were perceived as being interested in the needs of their clients, acting consistently with the best interest of their client, and representing their client zealously and within the bounds of the law. Both were also perceived as intelligent. Finally, the goals in common were maximizing the settlement for the client, seeing that the client's needs were met, and taking satisfaction in the exercise of legal skills.

It is easy to see . . . what effective lawyers have in common. They are assertive, smart and prepared (Schneider 2002: 188–189).

Once again, lawyer respondents perceived effective legal negotiators as skilled lawyers.

Some commentators have closely examined Williams' and Schneider's research results to urge that lawyers' perceptions of effectiveness are based more on negotiation *style* than on negotiation *approach* or *strategy*. It is to this important set of concepts that this article now turns.

Negotiation Style Versus Negotiation Approach, Strategy, and Tactics

Donald Gifford has asserted that lawyers need:

to distinguish style from strategy in a real negotiation for two reasons. First, many of the disadvantages of *competitive tactics*—the possibilities of deadlock and a premature breakdown of negotiation, and of generating ill-will and distrust with the other negotiator—can be mitigated if the *style* of the negotiator is friendly. Even when the substance being communicated to the other negotiator is very demanding and competitive, friendliness, courtesy and politeness help to preserve a positive working relationship. Conversely, the beginning lawyer needs to be able to identify *competitive tactics* even when the style of the negotiator is *friendly*. Often, lawyers will be misled by the polite and friendly style of the other lawyer and assume that he is using *cooperative tactics*, i.e., that his goals include a fair and just agreement and a positive, trusting working relationship between the parties. To the extent that the negotiator confuses friendly style for cooperative substance, she may be inclined to reciprocate, and the resulting agreement will disadvantage her client.

Gifford has observed that the adjectives used in Williams' research combine characteristics of style with specific negotiating behaviors or tactics. For example, traits such as "tough" or "aggressive" or "attacking" actually represent "style elements," while other traits—such as "made a high opening demand" or "revealed information gradually"—have more to do with tactics. If a negotiator understands that he/she can and should make a choice regarding his/her style separate from his/her choice regarding his/her approach or strategy or tactics, he/she immediately doubles his/her options and may exponentially expand his/her effectiveness.

Charles Craver has made a similar point in a series of articles and books (generally written alone but sometimes written in collaboration with Williams). For example, Craver and Williams wrote in 2007:

Effective cooperative/problem-solver negotiators and effective competitive/adversarial negotiators share one trait that is most often associated with competitive/adversarial bargainers—they hope to *maximize settlements* for their *own clients*. This may suggest that many effective negotiators are not entirely cooperative/problem-solving or competitive/adversarial, but a combination of both styles. These individuals seek to advance client interests (competitive/adversarial goal), but do so in a courteous and professional manner (cooperative/problem-solving approach). They are also concerned about the interests of opposing parties and hope to achieve agreements that maximize the joint returns enjoyed by both sides (cooperative/problem-solving goal). This hybrid approach may account for the fact that lawyers rated far more cooperative/problem-solvers as effective negotiators than competitive/adversarials. If we could create a third category consisting of *competitive/problem-solvers*, this group might encompass a substantial portion of the lawyers labeled effective cooperative/problem-solvers.

* * *

Some very recent research results further support the conclusion that negotiation style plays a significant role in perceptions of effectiveness. This research suggests that the manner in which negotiators treat each other is correlated with the perceived fairness of negotiated outcomes, the willingness to accept such outcomes and the likelihood of achieving integrative solutions. More specifically, researchers found that in a bargaining situation that permitted *only* distributive outcomes, a negotiator was more likely to perceive the quantitative outcome as fair—even if relatively unfavorable—if his/her negotiation counterpart had treated him/her in a procedurally fair manner. Perceptions of procedurally fair treatment were highly correlated with perceptions that the other negotiator had listened, behaved in a courteous manner, respected the rights of the respondent negotiator's client, demonstrated concern about that client's satisfaction, was trustworthy, and shared information. The assessment of fair treatment also correlated significantly, but negatively, with "whether the other party used deception." If his/her negotiation counterpart had treated him/her in a procedurally fair manner, the respondent negotiator was more likely to accept (or recommend acceptance of) the outcome, thus signaling greater likelihood of compliance. Note that the negotiator behaving in this fair manner did not necessarily achieve a *more* favorable distributive outcome for himself/herself or his/her client. Rather, the researchers found *no* relationship, positive or negative, between the negotiator's procedurally fair behavior and his/her own objective, quantitative results. In terms of the bottom line—the distributive outcome—it neither hurt nor helped to behave in a procedurally just manner.

In a second study, the researchers found that if the bargaining situation permitted the development of integrative outcomes, thus maximizing *joint* gains, the achievement of such outcomes was positively correlated with a procedurally fair negotiation process. Such maximization of joint gain was correlated with perceptions of the negotiation as collaborative, and collaborative negotiation was correlated with procedurally just behaviors. The maximization of joint gain created the potential for both parties to experience additional *individual* gain. Interestingly, if both negotiators behaved in a procedurally just manner, the researchers found that the negotiators were likely to divide the gain equally. Ultimately, the researchers concluded that the disclosures necessary to achieve integrative solutions were more likely to be made in a procedurally just process.

Although this research is framed in terms of procedural fairness, I include it here because the behaviors that correlated with procedural justice—listening, behaving in a courteous manner, demonstrating respect for the rights of the other client, signaling care for the other client, sharing information, not deceiving the other negotiator—are consistent with a cooperative style. Also, the researchers found the relationship between perceptions of procedural fairness and perceptions of the other attorney's trustworthiness to be particularly strong, which is consistent with other research showing that perceptions of trustworthiness help facilitate meaningful and productive disclosures (or "voice") despite the uncertainty and risk that almost inevitably characterize negotiation and other dispute resolution processes. (This research is discussed in greater detail below.) Trustworthiness facilitates the quality of "voice," which also helps explain why integrative solutions are so likely to be correlated with cooperative behavior.

The mutually reinforcing relationships among procedural justice, trustworthiness, cooperative style, and the development of integrative solutions also are consistent with Morton Deutsch's "crude law of social relations," which states that "the characteristic processes and effects elicited by a given type of social relationship also tend to elicit that type of social relationship."

NOTES AND QUESTIONS

1.   Professors Gerald Williams and Charles Craver recommend the following approach to negotiation:

> We believe that attorneys should work diligently to advance the interests of their own clients, but should not allow this objective to negate other equally important considerations, such as behaving ethically and professionally and seeking fair settlements that maximize the joint returns achieved by both sides. Once negotiators obtain what they think is appropriate for their own clients, they should look for ways

to accommodate the non-conflicting interests of their opponents. They should seek what Ronald Shapiro and Mark Jankowski (2001) call "WIN-win" results—both parties obtain beneficial results, but their side obtains more generous terms. They should do this not only for altruistic reasons, but also for their own benefit. First, they have to provide opponents with sufficiently generous terms to induce those parties to accept agreements over their nonsettlement alternatives. Second, they hope to ensure that opponents will not develop post-negotiation "buyer's remorse" and try to overturn the agreements reached. Finally, they are likely to interact with opposing counsel in the future. If they are remembered favorably, their subsequent encounters are likely to be pleasant and mutually productive. On the other hand, if they are remembered negatively as nasty competitive/adversarials who sought to exploit and even embarrass their opponents, those lawyers will seek retribution during their future interactions with these difficult negotiators[.]

GERALD WILLIAMS & CHARLES CRAVER, LEGAL NEGOTIATING 53–54 (2007).

More recently, Professor Craver has observed that effective negotiators, whether cooperative/problem solvers or competitive/problem solvers, "recognize the crucial fact that persons work most diligently to satisfy the needs of opponents they like personally" and "enjoy interacting with these pleasant and professional persons," which enables "these subtly manipulative persons . . . to induce unsuspecting opponents to lower their guard and make greater concessions. They also generate positive moods that promote cooperative behavior and the attainment of more efficient joint agreements."

Admittedly, it is a little jarring to see "pleasant and professional" negotiators reframed as "subtly manipulative." Nonetheless, Professor Craver observes quite perceptively that those who "exude competitiveness and manipulation and . . . behave in a rude manner" are much less likely to be liked—and thus will (intentionally or unintentionally) forfeit associated advantages. Indeed, Professor Craver has noted that in his courses, "[c]ompetitive/adversarial advocates generate more *nonsettlements* than their cooperative/problem-solving cohorts. The extreme positions taken by competitive/adversarial bargainers and their frequent use of manipulative and disruptive tactics make it easy for their opponents to accept the consequences associated with nonsettlements." Professor Craver suggests that, in contrast, competitive negotiators who are perceived as problem-solving—due to their cooperative style—are likely to achieve settlement, maximization of their own side's returns, mutually efficient terms, and mutually satisfactory results See Charles B. Craver, *What Makes A Great Legal Negotiator*, 56 Loy. L. Rev. 337, 348 (2010); Charles Craver, SKILLS AND VALUES: LEGAL NEGOTIATING 103 (2009).

2.   Professor Robert Mnookin, Professor Scott Peppet, and Andrew S. Tulumello argue that there is tension between two components of a negotiator's approach—assertiveness and empathy—that seem to parallel the distinction between a competitive/aggressive style and cooperative style.

They define empathy as "demonstrating an understanding of the other side's needs, interests, and perspective, without necessarily disagreeing." On the other hand, they define assertiveness as "[the] advocacy of one's own needs, interest, and perspective." Robert H. Mnookin, Scott R. Peppet, & Andrew S. Tulumello, BEYOND WINNING 47 (2000).

Are these qualities really in tension? Can negotiators exhibit both empathy and assertiveness? (It is worth observing that empathy has affective, cognitive, and behavioral dimensions. Professor Mnookin and his colleagues focus on the latter two dimensions.) Recent experimental research suggests that negotiators able to exercise the cognitive component of empathy—that is, perspective-taking—obtain superior outcomes in negotiation. *See* Adam D. Galinsky, William W. Maddux, Debra Gilin & Judith B. White, *Why It Pays To Get Inside the Head of Your Opponent: The Differential Effects of Perspective Taking and Empathy in Negotiations*, 19 Psychol. Sci. 378 (2008). Consider another definition of empathy, by Professor Ian Gallacher " '[t]he power of projecting one's personality into (and so fully comprehending) the object of contemplation' "—to urge that "[a] lawyer who can project him or herself into the thoughts of another and understand how that person . . . is thinking, has the ability to calibrate language, posture, and gesture in a manner calculated to persuade the subject to believe whatever argument the lawyer is making." Ian Gallacher, *Thinking Like Non–Lawyers: Why Empathy Is A Core Lawyering Skill and Why Legal Education Should Change to Reflect Its Importance*, 8 Legal Comm. & Rhetoric: JALWD 109 (2011). In other words, those who are skilled at empathizing are likely to be more persuasive—or perhaps more manipulative.

3.   Other commentators have focused on the effect of negotiators' personalities and interpersonal abilities through other lenses. Professor Don Peters has used the Myers–Briggs Type Indicator and its four personality dimensions (sensing-intuitive, thinking-feeling, judging-perceiving, and extroverted-introverted) as a way of understanding the impact that personality variables can have on negotiation. *See, e.g.,* Don Peters, *Forever Jung: Psychological Type Theory, The Myers–Briggs Type Indicator and Learning Negotiation*, 42 Drake L. Rev. 1 (1993).

Professors Bruce Barry and Raymond Friedman studied the impact of the "five-factor model" of personality on negotiation (extroversion, agreeableness, conscientiousness, emotional stability vs. neuroticism, and openness to experience) and found that two of the five factors—extroversion and agreeableness—can be liabilities in distributive negotiation (or negotiation involving the division of a good in which any gains made by one side are at the expense of the other). Bruce Barry & Raymond A. Friedman, *Bargainer Characteristics in Distributive and Integrative Negotiation*, 74 J. of Personality & Soc. Psychol. 345 (1998).

Research in this area continues. For example, a recent meta-analysis reported that negotiators with greater cognitive ability achieve better individual and joint economic outcomes and rate their outcomes as having higher subjective value. Interestingly, negotiators who score high in emotional intelligence were found to achieve lower economic outcomes, but to report greater subjective value. The researchers hypothesize that enhanced relational capital may have long-term economic benefits. None of the big-five personality factors was found to predict individual or joint economic gain overall, but extroversion was associated with lower outcomes in distributive negotiation and higher outcomes in negotiations with integrative potential. *See* Sudeep Sharma, William Bottom & Hillary Anger Elfenbein, *On the Role of Personality, Cognitive Ability, and Emotional Intelligence in Predicting Negotiation Outcomes: A Meta–Analysis*, June 20, 2013, available at http://ssrn.com/abstract=2282251. *See also*, Roderick W. Gilkey & Leonard Greenhalgh, *The Role of Personality in Successful Negotiating*, 2 Negot. J. 245 (1986).

4. Although our focus is on negotiation style, it is useful to acknowledge here that emotion and mood has been shown to affect negotiation behavior—which may translate into style. *See e.g.,* Clark Freshman, Adele Hayes & Greg Feldman, *The Lawyer–Negotiator as Mood Scientist: What We Know and Don't Know About How Mood Relates to Successful Negotiation*, 2002 J. Disp. Resol. 1; Daniel L. Shapiro, *Emotions in Negotiation: Peril or Promise?*, 87 Marq. L. Rev. 737 (2004); Chia–Jung Tsay & Max H. Bazerman, *A Decision–Making Perspective to Negotiation: A Review of the Past and a Look into the Future*, 25 Negotiation. J. 467 (2009); JENNIFER K. ROBBENNOLT & JEAN R. STERNLIGHT, PSYCHOLOGY FOR LAWYERS: UNDERSTANDING THE HUMAN FACTORS IN NEGOTIATION, LITIGATION, AND DECISION MAKING 45–66 (2013); *see also* Ellen Waldman, *The Baby Doe Regulations and Tragic Choices at the Bedside: Accepting the Limits of "Good Process,"* 25 Ga. St. U. L. Rev. 1019 (2009) (raising concerns about the substantive results of empowering families to express their emotions in negotiation or mediation with medical professionals). Some commentators have specifically considered the ethics, advantages and disadvantages of expressing negative emotions even if one is not actually experiencing them. *See e.g.,* Delee Fromm, *Emotion in Negotiation: Part II*, The Negotiator Magazine, Jan. 2008, available at http://www.negotiatormagazine.com/article 408.html.

5. It can be challenging for anyone to acknowledge and deal with difficult emotions. Lawyers in particular, however, have been shown to prefer to process information and make decisions through the application of rules rather than dealing with their own and others' difficult negative emotions. *See* Susan Swaim Daicoff, *Expanding the Lawyer's Toolkit of Skills and Competencies: Synthesizing Leadership, Professionalism, Emotional Intelligence, Conflict Resolution, and Comprehensive Law*, 52 Santa Clara L. Rev. 795, 834–35 (2012); Susan Daicoff, *Lawyer, Know Thyself: A Review of Empirical Research on Attorney Attributes Bearing on Professionalism*, 46 Am. U. L. Rev. 1337, 1381, 1394, 1411–12 (1997). Professor Leonard Riskin suggests that negotiators who find themselves dealing with their own internal conflict may find it helpful to use the mental model of Internal Family Systems to gain awareness of, access to, and a means to manage their internal process. IFS begins by encouraging us to look at the personality as if

it were composed of "subpersonalities" or "parts," and then to acknowledge the parts' roles, needs and perspectives, ability to learn and interact with one another, and even their ability to negotiate. At a minimum, IFS provides a metaphor that can help us see the many possibilities that exist within each of us, including our potential to choose our negotiation behaviors. *See* Leonard L. Riskin, *Managing Inner and Outer Conflict: Selves, Subpersonalities, and Internal Family Systems*, 18 Harv. Negot. L. Rev. 1 (2013).

6.   Some research suggests that in certain contexts, a reputation as a very aggressive legal negotiator can produce superior outcomes for clients. In other contexts, aggressiveness seems to make no difference or to be counterproductive. The devil is in the details, though. Aggressiveness might be defined in terms of a particular bargaining style or, instead, be associated with making aggressive use of legal procedures and developing other options. *See* D. James Greiner, Cassandra Wolos Pattanayak, & Jonathan Hennessy, *The Limits of Unbundled Legal Assistance: A Randomized Study in a Massachusetts District Court and Prospects for the Future*, 126 Harv. L. Rev. 901, 919 (2013).

B. THE NEGOTIATION PROCESS

Every negotiation is unique, but most negotiations follow a fairly predictable path. In the following excerpt, Professor Shell argues that negotiations typically include four steps or stages.

G. RICHARD SHELL, BARGAINING FOR ADVANTAGE: NEGOTIATION STRATEGIES FOR REASONABLE PEOPLE
119 (2d ed. 2006)

Negotiation is a dance that moves through four stages or steps. . . . Let's look at a simple example from real life to see how the four-step sequence works in practice.

Imagine you are approaching a traffic intersection in your car. You notice that another car is nearing the intersection at the same time. What do you do?

Most experienced drivers start by slowing down to assess the situation. Next, they glance toward the other driver to make eye contact, hoping to establish communication with the other person. With eye contact established, one driver waves his or her hand toward the intersection in the universally recognized "after you" signal. Perhaps both drivers wave. After a little hesitation, one driver moves ahead and the other follows.

Note the four-step process: preparation (slowing down), information exchange (making eye contact), proposing and concession making (waving your hand), and commitment (driving through). This may seem like a unique case, but anthropologists and other social scientists have observed a similar four-stage process at work in situations as diverse as rural African land disputes, British labor negotiations, and American business mergers. The four stages form an unstated and often unseen pattern just below the surface of negotiations.

Notes and Questions

1.   Professor Shell describes this four-step process as an "important truth" about negotiation. Do you think all negotiations include these four steps?

2.   The first step in Professor Shell's four-step process is preparation or planning. How should a negotiator prepare for an upcoming negotiation?

3.   Some negotiators focus their preparation primarily on the positions they expect to advocate—and the positions they expect their counterparts to advocate—in the negotiation. This approach to planning is more consistent with an "adversarial" approach to negotiation. *See* Chapter III, *infra*.

4.   Other negotiators reject this approach to negotiation planning as too narrow:

> Many people feel prepared if they know what they want and what they'll settle for. But if our preparation consists of creating a wish list, with a minimum fall-back position, the only thing we will be ready to do in the negotiation is to state demands and make concessions. Position preparation leads to positional negotiation. By focusing on what we will ask for and what we will give up, we set ourselves up for an adversarial, zero-sum kind of negotiation. But this kind of preparation often prevents us from finding creative solutions that expand the pie before splitting it, or from working side by side to solve some joint problem.

> Positional preparation is the greatest source of stress and anxiety during negotiations. We might think that if we invest time and energy planning our demands and concessions we will feel more confident as we make them. But the reality of the matter is that a positional negotiator, even one who has thought about what positions to take and what concession to make, has little basis for deciding when to make a concession. Making a concession when the other side won't simply rewards their bad behavior. Yet not making one can precipitate a contest as to who can be more stubborn. Preparing only by making a list of demands and concessions is preparation for a bad negotiation.

ROGER FISHER & DANNY ERTEL, GETTING READY TO NEGOTIATE: THE "GETTING TO YES" WORKBOOK 5 (1995).

Professor Fisher and Mr. Ertel recommend, instead, that negotiators focus on seven keys during preparations: interests, options, alternatives, legitimacy, communication, relationship, and commitment. *Id*. at 6. Their approach to preparation is more consistent with a "problem-solving" approach to negotiation. *See* Chapter III, *infra*.

5.   Studies have corroborated the important role that research can play in negotiation. In a study of auto negotiations, for example, Professors John and Debora Seiter found that sales managers initially offered to sell a car for substantially less money to consumers armed with invoice information from *Consumer Reports* than to those without such information. *See* John S. Seiter & Debora L. Seiter, *Consumer Persuasion: The Use of Evidence When Negotiating the Price of a New Automobile*, 35 J. Applied Social Psychol. 686, 691 (2005).

6.   Professor Shell's depiction of the negotiation process as four steps can be viewed as a bare minimum. Others parse the process more finely. For example, Professor Thomas Guernsey argues that negotiations generally include ten stages: (a) preparation and planning; (b) ice breaking; (c) agenda control; (d) information bargaining; (e) proposals, offers, demands; (f) persuasion/justification; (g) concessions/reformulation; (h) crisis (i.e., resolution or deadlock); (i) closing; and (j) memorialization. THOMAS F. GUERNSEY, A PRACTICAL GUIDE TO NEGOTIATION 12 (1996).

7.   Professor Shell does acknowledge that negotiators might vary the sequencing and pacing of the process:

> Of course, in complex bargaining encounters, people vary the sequence and pacing of these steps. They may reach an impasse in the concession-making stage, so they go back to exchanging information. And some aspects of a deal may move faster than others—commitments may come on issues "A" and "B" while information exchange and concession making continue on issue "C."

G. RICHARD SHELL, BARGAINING FOR ADVANTAGE: NEGOTIATION STRATEGIES FOR REASONABLE PEOPLE 119 (2D ED. 2006).

C. APPROACHES TO NEGOTIATION

The humorist Robert Benchly declared that "[t]here may be said to be two classes of people in the world: those who constantly divide the people of the world into two classes, and those who do not." Paul Dickson, *The Official Rules,* The Washingtonian, Nov. 1978, at 152. Many commentators have developed systems for dividing approaches to negotiation into two (and sometimes more) categories. We have chosen to use the following dichotomy between two basic and widely held orientations toward negotiation: adversarial and problem-solving. These two approaches often work together; they can also be in tension with one another.

The adversarial approach is grounded upon the assumption that there is a limited resource—such as money, golf balls, or lima beans—and the parties must decide whether and how to divide it. In such a situation, the parties' positions conflict; what one gains, the other must lose. The negotiators are, in a word, adversaries. An adversarial approach naturally fosters strategies designed to maximize the client's position with respect to the resource in question. And the typical tactics include those designed to uncover as much as possible about the other side's situation and simultaneously mislead the other side as to your own situation.

The problem-solving approach is quite different. The negotiators acknowledge that they share, and must solve, a problem. This approach seeks to meet the interests or underlying needs of all parties to the dispute or transaction, and, accordingly, tends to produce strategies designed to promote the disclosure and relevance of these underlying needs. The recommended techniques include those intended to increase the number of issues for bargaining or to "expand the pie" before dividing it.

We introduce both approaches below. The first excerpt, by Professor Russell Korobkin, reflects an adversarial orientation to negotiation. The second excerpt, by Professor Carrie Menkel–Meadow, reflects a problem-solving orientation. Legal negotiators should be acquainted with both approaches because they certainly will encounter and use both in practice. While we may generally prefer the problem-solving approach, we also recognize that negotiation often requires the use of some degree of adversarial tactics.

1. ADVERSARIAL NEGOTIATION

RUSSELL KOROBKIN, A POSITIVE THEORY OF LEGAL NEGOTIATION

88 Geo. L. J. 1789, 1792–94 (2000)

In any negotiation, the maximum amount that a buyer will pay for a good, service, or other legal entitlement is called his "reservation point" or, if the deal being negotiated is a monetary transaction, his "reservation price" (RP). The minimum amount that a seller would accept for that item is her RP. If the buyer's RP is higher than the seller's, the distance between the two points is called the "bargaining zone." Reaching agreement for any amount that lies within the bargaining zone is superior to not reaching an agreement for both parties, at least if they are concerned only with the transaction in question.

For example, suppose Esau, looking to get into business for himself, is willing to pay up to $200,000 for Jacob's catering business, while Jacob, interested in retiring, is willing to sell the business for any amount over $150,000. This difference between Esau's and Jacob's RPs creates a $50,000 bargaining zone. At any price between $150,000 and $200,000, both parties are better off agreeing to the sale of the business than they are reaching no agreement and going their separate ways.

The same structure used to describe a transactional negotiation can be used to describe a dispute resolution negotiation. Suppose that Goliath has filed suit against David for battery. David is willing to pay up to $90,000 to settle the case out of court—essentially, to buy Goliath's legal right to bring suit—while Goliath will "sell" his right for any amount over $60,000. These RPs create a $30,000 bargaining zone between $60,000 and $90,000. Any settlement in this range would leave both parties better off than they would be without a settlement.

In contrast, if the seller's RP is higher than the buyer's RP, there is no bargaining zone. In this circumstance, there is no sale price that would make both parties better off than they would be by not reaching a negotiated agreement. Put another way, the parties would be better off not reaching a negotiated agreement. If Jacob will not part with his business for less than $150,000 and Esau will not pay more than $100,000 for it, there is no bargaining zone. If David will pay up to $50,000 to settle Goliath's claim, but Goliath will not accept any amount less than $60,000, again there is no bargaining zone. An agreement in either case would leave at least one party, and possibly both parties, worse off than if they were to decide not to make a deal.

Knowledge of the parameters of the bargaining zone, which is created by the two parties' reservation points, is the most critical information for the negotiator to possess. Those parameters tell the negotiator both whether any agreement is possible and, if so, identify the range of possible deal points. At the same time, the negotiator has an interest in adjusting the parameters of the bargaining zone to his advantage. A buyer not only wants to know his and the seller's RP, he wishes to make both lower, or at least make both *appear* lower to the seller. This shifts the zone of possible deal points lower, increasing the chances that the seller will ultimately agree to a relatively low price. Experimental evidence in fact confirms that negotiators with more favorable RPs (that is, lower for buyers, higher for sellers) reach more profitable agreements than negotiators with less favorable RPs.

Esau wants to know his and Jacob's RPs, but he also would like to shift both numbers, and therefore the bargaining range, lower. Assuming Esau knows his RP is $200,000 and learns Jacob's is $150,000, Esau knows that an agreement is possible for some amount greater than the latter figure and less than the former. If he could reduce Jacob's RP to $120,000 and his own to $170,000, however, the bargaining zone would remain the same size, but its changed parameters would suggest that Esau would be likely to buy the business for a lower price. Esau could achieve the same advantage if Jacob *believes* the parties' RPs are $120,000 and $170,000 respectively, even if the RPs objectively are $150,000 and $200,000.

The existence of a bargaining zone is necessary for a negotiated agreement, and the parameters of the bargaining zone—defined by both parties' RPs—define the set of possible "deal points."

NOTES AND QUESTIONS

1.   The adversarial approach is based on certain assumptions:

- That the principal goal of each party is to maximize its own economic gain;

- That the outcome of the negotiation will likely be determined by two separate, individualistic cost-benefit analyses, rather than through any joint exploration of what is most suitable for both parties;

- That the process will be closed and deceptive, with each party trying to mislead or at least to conceal information about its own position while seeking to learn as much as it can about the other's position; and

- That "deal points" fall along a continuum, and movement favorable to one party is inevitably unfavorable to the other.

Are these assumptions accurate? Universal for all negotiations? What other assumptions are embedded in this approach?

2.   We have labeled this the "adversarial" approach to negotiation. Other commentators have used other terms. For an example of the "adversarial" approach being described as "positional," see ROGER FISHER, WILLIAM URY & BRUCE PATTON, GETTING TO YES: NEGOTIATING AGREEMENT WITHOUT GIVING IN (2d ed. 1991). To see it described as "distributive," see DAVID LAX & JAMES SEBENIUS, THE MANAGER AS NEGOTIATOR: BARGAINING FOR COOPERATION AND COMPETITIVE GAIN (1986); HOWARD RAIFFA, THE ART AND SCIENCE OF NEGOTIATION (1982). For the term "value-claiming", see ROBERT H. MNOOKIN, SCOTT R. PEPPET & ANDREW S. TULUMELLO, BEYOND WINNING: NEGOTIATING TO CREATE VALUE IN DEALS AND DISPUTES (2000); DAVID LAX & JAMES SEBENIUS, THE MANAGER AS NEGOTIATOR: BARGAINING FOR COOPERATION AND COMPETITIVE GAIN (1986) (discussing "claiming value"). Regardless of the label employed, this approach posits that negotiation is a zero-sum game in which the gains one side receives are at the expense of the other.

2.   PROBLEM–SOLVING NEGOTIATION

CARRIE J. MENKEL–MEADOW, TOWARD ANOTHER VIEW OF LEGAL NEGOTIATION: THE STRUCTURE OF PROBLEM SOLVING

31 UCLA L. Rev. 754, 755–61, 795–801 (1984)

* * *

In order to contrast the adversarial model with the problem-solving model several key concepts must be defined and criteria for evaluation of the models made explicit. The negotiation models described here may seem unduly polarized, yet they represent the polarities of approach exemplified both by the conceptions of negotiation we construct as well as by the strategies and behaviors we choose. The models described here are based on orientations to negotiation, that is, how we approach our purpose in negotiation, rather than on the particular strategies or tactics we choose. It must be noted, however, that the tactics and strategies we choose may well be affected by our conception of negotiation. A general model demonstrates the relationship of negotiation orientations to negotiation results:

Orientation→Mind-set→Behavior→Results.

The orientation (adversarial or problem solving) leads to a mind-set about what can be achieved (maximizing individual gain or solving the parties' problem by satisfying their underlying needs) which in turn affects the behavior chosen (competitive or solution searching) which in turn affects the solutions arrived at (narrow compromises or creative solutions).

The primary, but not exclusive, criterion for evaluation of a negotiation model is the quality of the solution produced. This includes the extent to which the process utilized contributes to or hinders the search for "quality" solutions.

In elaborating on approaches to negotiation I shall consider the following criteria of evaluation:

1.   Does the solution reflect the client's total set of "real" needs, goals and objectives, in both the short and the long term?

2.   Does the solution reflect the other party's full set of "real" needs, goals and objectives, in both the short and long term?

3.   Does the solution promote the relationship the client desires with the other party?

4.   Have the parties explored all the possible solutions that might either make each better off or one party better off with no adverse consequences to the other party?

5.   Has the solution been achieved at the lowest possible transaction costs relative to the desirability of the result?

6.   Is the solution achievable, or has it only raised more problems that need to be solved? Are the parties committed to the solution so it can be enforced without regret?

7.   Has the solution been achieved in a manner congruent with the client's desire to participate in and affect the negotiation?

8.   Is the solution "fair" or "just"? Have the parties considered the legitimacy of each other's claims and made any adjustments they feel are humanely or morally indicated?

A. The Underlying Principles of Problem Solving: Meeting Varied and Complementary Needs

Parties to a negotiation typically have underlying needs or objectives—what they hope to achieve, accomplish, and/or be compensated for as a result of the dispute or transaction. Although litigants typically ask for relief in the form of damages, this relief is actually a proxy for more basic needs or objectives. By attempting to uncover those underlying needs, the problem-solving model presents opportunities for discovering greater numbers of and better quality solutions. It offers the possibility of meeting a greater variety of needs both directly and by trading off different needs, rather than forcing a zero-sum battle over a single item.

The principle underlying such an approach is that unearthing a greater number of the actual needs of the parties will create more possible solutions because not all needs will be mutually exclusive. As a corollary, because not all individuals value the same things in the same way, the exploitation of differential or complementary needs will produce a wider variety of solutions which more closely meet the parties' needs.

* * *

It is also important to recognize that *both* parties have such needs. For example, in the personal injury case above, the defendant may have the same need for vindication or retribution if he believes he was not responsible for the accident. In addition, the defendant may need to be compensated for his damaged car and injured body. He will also have needs with respect to how much, when and how he may be able to pay the monetary damages because of other uses for the money. A contract breaching defendant may have specific financial needs such as payroll, advertising, purchases of supplies, etc.; defendants are not always simply trying to avoid paying a certain sum of money to plaintiffs. In the commercial case, the defendant may have needs similar to those of the plaintiff: lost income due to the plaintiff's failure to pay on the contract, and, to the extent the plaintiff may seek to terminate the relationship with the defendant, a steady source of future business.

* * *

To the extent that negotiators focus exclusively on "winning" the greatest amount of money, they focus on only one form of need. The only flexibility in tailoring an agreement may lie in the choice of ways to structure monetary solutions, including one shot payments, installments, and structured settlements. By looking, however, at what the parties desire money for, there may be a variety of solutions that will satisfy the parties more fully and directly. For example, when an injured plaintiff needs physical rehabilitation, if the defendant can provide the plaintiff directly with rehabilitation services, the defendant may save money and the plaintiff may gain the needed rehabilitation at lower cost. In addition, if the defendant can provide the plaintiff with a job that provides physical rehabilitation, the plaintiff may not only receive income which could be used to purchase more rehabilitation, but be further rehabilitated in the form of the psychological self-worth which accompanies such employment. Admittedly, none of these solutions may fully satisfy the injured plaintiff, but some or all may be equally beneficial to the plaintiff, and the latter two may be preferable to the defendant because they are less costly.

Understanding that the other party's needs are not necessarily as assumed may present an opportunity for arriving at creative solutions. Traditionally, lawyers approaching negotiations from the adversarial model view the other side as an enemy to be defeated. By examining the underlying needs of the other side, the lawyer may instead see opportunities for solutions that would not have existed before based upon the recognition of different, but not conflicting, preferences.

An example from the psychological literature illustrates this point. Suppose that a husband and wife have two weeks in which to take their vacation. The husband prefers the mountains and the wife prefers the seaside. If vacation time is limited and thus a scarce resource, the couple may engage in adversarial negotiation about where they should go. The simple compromise situation, if they engage in distributive bargaining, would be to split the two weeks of vacation time spending one week in the mountains and one week at the ocean. This solution is not likely to be satisfying, however, because of the lost time and money in moving from place to place and in getting used to a new hotel room and locale. In addition to being happy only half of the time, each party to the negotiation has incurred transaction costs associated with this solution. Other "compromise" solutions might include alternating preferences on a year to year basis, taking separate vacations, or taking a longer vacation at a loss of pay. Assuming that husband and wife want to vacation together, all of these solutions may leave something to be desired by at least one of the parties.

By examining their underlying preferences, however, the parties might find additional solutions that could make both happy at less cost. Perhaps the husband prefers the mountains because he likes to hike and engage in stream fishing. Perhaps the wife enjoys swimming, sunbathing and seafood. By exploring these underlying preferences the couple might find vacation spots that permit all of these activities: a mountain resort on a large lake, or a seaside resort at the foot of mountains. By examining their underlying needs the parties can see solutions that satisfy many more of their preferences, and the "sum of the utilities" to the couple as a whole is greater than what they would have achieved by compromising.

In addition, by exploring whether they attach different values to their preferences they may be able to arrive at other solutions by trading items. The wife in our example might be willing to give up ocean fresh seafood if she can have fresh stream or lake trout, and so, with very little cost to her, the couple can choose another waterspot where the hikes might be better for the husband. By examining the weight or value given to certain preferences the parties may realize that some desires are easily attainable because they are not of equal importance to the other side. Thus, one party can increase its utilities without reducing the other's. This differs from a zero-sum conception of negotiation because of the recognition that preferences may be totally different and are, therefore, neither scarce nor in competition with each other. In addition, if a preference is not used to "force" a concession from the other party (which as the example shows is not necessary), there are none of the forced reciprocal concessions of adversarial negotiation.

The exploitation of complementary interests occurs frequently in the legal context. For example, in a child custody case the lawyers may learn that both parties desire to have the children some of the time and neither of the parties wishes to have the children all of the time. It will be easy, therefore, to arrange for a joint custody agreement that satisfies the needs of both parties. Similarly, in a commercial matter, the defendant may want to make payment over time and the plaintiff, for tax purposes or to increase interest income, may desire deferred income.

NOTES AND QUESTIONS

1.   As with the adversarial approach to negotiation, the problem-solving approach is also based on certain assumptions:

- That the principal goal for each party is to meet its underlying needs and interests rather than maximizing economic gain;

- That the outcome of the negotiation will likely be determined by a joint exploration of what is most appropriate for both parties;

- That the process will be an open and creative one in which each party shares information with the other about its underlying needs and interests; and

- That parties can produce joint gains by capitalizing on both shared and different interests.

Again we ask: Are these assumptions accurate? Universal for all negotiations? What other assumptions are embedded in this approach?

2.   We have labeled this the "problem-solving" approach to negotiation. Other commentators have used different terms for this approach. To see the "problem-solving" approach referred to as "principled," see ROGER FISHER, WILLIAM URY & BRUCE PATTON, GETTING TO YES: NEGOTIATING AGREEMENT WITHOUT GIVING IN (2D ED. 1991). To see it described as "integrative," see DAVID LAX & JAMES SEBENIUS, THE MANAGER AS NEGOTIATOR: BARGAINING FOR COOPERATION AND COMPETITIVE GAIN (1986); HOWARD RAIFFA, THE ART

AND SCIENCE OF NEGOTIATION (1982). To see it described as "value-creating," see ROBERT H. MNOOKIN, SCOTT R. PEPPET & ANDREW S. TULUMELLO, BEYOND WINNING: NEGOTIATING TO CREATE VALUE IN DEALS AND DISPUTES (2000); DAVID LAX & JAMES SEBENIUS, THE MANAGER AS NEGOTIATOR: BARGAINING FOR COOPERATION AND COMPETITIVE GAIN (1986) (discussing "creating value"). Regardless of the label employed, this approach posits that negotiation is a collaborative exercise in which the parties work together to satisfy their interests and create joint gains.

3. Which of these approaches—adversarial or problem-solving—seems better able to address conflict on the different dimensions in which it operates (i.e., behavioral, cognitive, and emotional)?

4. Some, if not many, negotiations require the use of a combination of adversarial and problem-solving elements. For example, imagine that you begin with an adversarial approach, the other negotiator responds in kind, and you now face impasse. You may change to a problem-solving strategy, in order to expand the resources available for distribution. Now imagine that you begin with the problem-solving approach, and your negotiating counterpart responds in kind. Together, you realize the largest possible *joint* gain. Then, you switch to an adversarial approach in order to claim the largest possible share of the expanded resources for your client. Do you see any advantages in using this sequence of strategies? Do you see any dangers?

5. The tit for tat approach offers another way to sequence. With this approach, a negotiator always cooperates (i.e., uses a problem-solving approach) on his first move. The technical term for this is being "nice." After that, though, he mirrors whatever choice has been made by his negotiation counterpart. If the counterpart defects (i.e., makes an adversarial move), the negotiator also defects. This is called being "provokable." In this way a negotiator rewards cooperation with cooperation and punishes defection with defection. ROBERT AXELROD, THE EVOLUTION OF COOPERATION 31–40 (1984).

Here is a bit more about tit for tat:

> In both empirical investigations with human subjects and computer simulations of repeated-play prisoner dilemmas, tit for tat is superior to other strategies. It is not just a satisfactory, "satisficing" strategy; playing against a multiplicity of other strategies, it is the best (Axelrod 1984). Moreover, the general principle of cooperating with another agent prior to knowing how that agent will respond, and then reciprocating either cooperation or defection, appears from casual observation to be one many people adopt to their advantage outside the experimental laboratory as well as within it. Be friendly, cooperative, and nice [Editor's note: please translate this into "use a problem-solving approach and a cooperative style"] when initiating an interaction or negotiation, but don't hesitate to counterpunch if the other party punches first; moreover, having a reputation for adopting this policy may obviate the need to counterpunch (and hence the pain of initially being punched). Tit for tat works.

Robyn M. Dawes & John M. Orbell, *The Benefit of Optional Play in Anonymous One-Shot Prisoner's Dilemma Games*, in BARRIERS TO CONFLICT RESOLUTION 63 (Kenneth Arrow et al., eds., 1995).

Tit for tat's reactive form of sequencing has been found to be superior to other strategies when used in an "iterated sequence"—i.e., when there are multiple rounds of negotiation with uncertainty regarding the timing of the last round. Many negotiations, including legal negotiations, fit this description. Even after trial has begun or the jury has announced its verdict, negotiations can continue. In the immortal words of Yogi Berra, "It ain't over till it's over."

Tit for tat can also be a very helpful strategy for negotiators who prefer a cooperative negotiation to foster problem solving and mininze the risk of exploitation. If the negotiator starts "nice," and the counterpart responds nicely, then the negotiator knows she can probably expect a more problem-solving negotiation. On the other hand, if the negotiator starts nice, and her counterpart responds with adversarial tactics, the negotiator should respond in kind with adversarial tactics rather than continuing to use cooperative tactics. The risk of exploitation is thus reduced, and the counterpart may "learn" that the negotiator is willing to engage in adversarial tactics if provoked. Indeed, he may decide to switch his tune and adopt a more problem solving strategy. Playing tit for tat, the negotiator would respond in kind with problem-solving tactics of her own, thus establishing momentum for a problem-solving rather than adversarial negotiation. ROBERT AXELROD, THE EVOLUTION OF COOPERATION 145–92 (1984).

D. NEGOTIATION STRATEGIES AND TACTICS

In this section, we move from discussion of general negotiation "approaches" to the strategies and tactics deployed in the actual negotiation process. At this point, we will refer to "strategies" rather than "approaches" because a "strategy" is an overall plan that you develop in order to achieve your (or your client's) goals in a negotiation. While an "approach" may be unconscious, a "strategy" should be intentional. A "tactic" is a particular move designed to further the strategy you have chosen.

Below, we discuss tactics and associate them with either the adversarial strategy or the problem-solving strategy. Please note that in real life, many of these tactics will be associated with both the adversarial and problem-solving strategies. Your underlying assumptions and goals, rather than your use of a particular tactic, will determine the strategy guiding a particular negotiation.

1. ADVERSARIAL STRATEGY AND TACTICS

The adversarial approach assumes that negotiation is a zero-sum game in which any gains one side gets are inevitably at the expense of the other. This approach to negotiation suggests a straightforward strategy or plan of action: negotiators should attempt to maximize their gains at the bargaining table. The following excerpt by Professor Gary Goodpaster articulates this strategy and introduces the primary tactics associated with it.

GARY GOODPASTER, A PRIMER ON COMPETITIVE BARGAINING
1996 J. Disp. Resol. 325, 342–43

In competitive negotiation or distributive bargaining, the parties' actual or perceived respective aims or goals conflict. In this context, the negotiator's aim is to maximize the realization of its goals. Since the goals conflict, either in fact or supposition, one party's gains are the other party's losses. Therefore, a negotiator's goal is to win by gaining as much value as possible from the other party. The basic idea is that the negotiation is about a fixed good or sum that must be divided between the parties. Not only is the competitive negotiator out to gain as much as he or she can, but he or she will take risks, even the risk of non-agreement, to secure a significant gain.

The competitive negotiator adopts a risky strategy which involves the taking of firm, almost extreme positions, making few and small concessions, and withholding information that may be useful to the other party. The intention, and hoped-for effect, behind this strategy is to persuade the other party that it must make concessions if it is to get agreement. In addition to this basic strategy, competitive negotiators may also use various ploys or tactics aimed at pressuring, unsettling, unbalancing or even misleading the other party to secure an agreement with its demands.

In an important sense, the competitive negotiator plays negotiation as an information game. In this game, the object is to get as much information from the other party as possible while disclosing as little information as possible. Alternatively, a competitive negotiator sometimes provides the other party with misleading clues, bluffs, and ambiguous assertions with multiple meanings, which are not actually false, but nevertheless mislead the other party into drawing incorrect conclusions that are beneficial to the competitor.

The information the competitive negotiator seeks is the other party's bottom line. How much he will maximally give or minimally accept to make a deal. On the other hand, the competitive negotiator wants to persuade the other side about the firmness of the negotiator's own *asserted* bottom line. The competitive negotiator works to convince the other party that it will settle only at some point that is higher (or lower, as the case may be) than its *actual* and unrevealed bottom line.

NOTES

1.   Several tactics are commonly associated with the adversarial negotiation theory and strategy. For lists of adversarial tactics, see, for example, HARRY EDWARDS & JAMES J. WHITE, THE LAWYER AS NEGOTIATOR 112–21 (1977); ROBERT H. MNOOKIN, SCOTT R. PEPPET & ANDREW S. TULUMELLO, BEYOND WINNING: NEGOTIATING TO CREATE VALUE IN DEALS AND DISPUTES (2000); Michael Meltsner & Philip G. Schrag, *Negotiating Tactics for Legal Services Lawyers*, 7 Clearinghouse Rev. 259 (1973); D. James Greiner, Cassandra Wolos Pattanayak, & Jonathan Hennessy, *The Limits of Unbundled Legal Assistance: A Randomized Study in a Massachusetts District Court and Prospects for the Future*, 126 Harv. L. Rev. 901, 919 (2013).

2.   Professor Goodpaster identifies the central adversarial tactics, including extreme opening positions, few and small concessions, withholding information, and staking out commitments. To be sure, all negotiations require some action along each of these dimensions. As a result, even negotiators who prefer the problem-solving approach will find that they must make opening offers and concessions and manage the flow of information. It is the underlying "zero sum" set of assumptions that gives these tactics their adversarial character. Below, we examine each of these adversarial tactics in turn.

a.   Extreme Opening Offers

Negotiators using the adversarial approach often begin with extremely self-serving positions at the bargaining table. Research suggests that negotiators who begin with extreme but justifiable positions often fare quite well due to a phenomenon psychologists call "anchoring."

DAN ORR & CHRIS GUTHRIE, ANCHORING, INFORMATION, EXPERTISE, AND NEGOTIATION: NEW INSIGHTS FROM META-ANALYSIS

21 Ohio St. J. on Disp. Resol. 597, 597–98, 621–22 (2006)

Suppose that we asked you whether the average temperature in San Francisco was higher or lower than 558 degrees. Do you think this question would influence your estimate of the average temperature in the city? Suppose instead that we asked you whether the average price of a college textbook was higher or lower than $7,128.53. Would this question have an impact on your estimate of the average price of such a text? What if we asked you whether the number of "top 10" Beatles' records was higher or lower than 100,025? Would this affect your estimate of the number of Beatles' albums that did make the top 10?

You wouldn't think so, but you would probably be wrong. Due to a phenomenon that psychologists call "anchoring," we are often unduly influenced by the initial figure we encounter when estimating the value of an item. This initial value serves as a kind of reference point or benchmark that anchors our expectations about the item's actual value.

Negotiation and dispute resolution scholars have observed that this phenomenon could have an impact on negotiation. In a number of studies, researchers have shown that opening offers and demands, insurance policy caps, statutory damage caps, negotiator aspirations, and other "first numbers" can influence negotiation outcomes in transactions and settlements. What no researcher has done, however, is assess how potent this phenomenon is.

In this article, we attempt to do just that by conducting a "meta-analysis" of studies that have tested the impact of an opening figure in a negotiation experiment. Meta-analysis . . . is a statistical method that allows scholars to analyze all available studies to measure the impact of one variable—in this case, opening offers, demands or other starting figures—on another variable—in this case, negotiation outcomes.

* * *

Our meta-analysis demonstrates that anchoring has a powerful influence on negotiation outcomes. Across the studies in our sample, we find a correlation of 0.497 between the initial anchor and the outcome of the negotiation. At first blush, this result may be unsurprising; after all, none of the 16 articles and 19 outcomes included in our meta-analysis reported an effect size lower than 0.30. However, by the standards commonly applied in the social and behavioral sciences, our finding is striking because it is unusually "large."

In lay terms, the 0.497 correlation means that every one dollar increase in an opening offer is associated with an approximate fifty-cent increase in the final sale price. A simple conversion provides another estimate of the impact anchoring can have on a negotiation. The square of a correlation provides an estimate of the amount of variance that it explains. The r-squared value of the correlation in our study is 0.247. In general terms, this mean that nearly 25 percent of the difference in outcomes among negotiations can be accounted for as a function of an opening offer or other initial anchor. (This finding is consistent with other research showing that an opening offer and initial counteroffer account for 57.6 percent of the variance in negotiated outcomes.)

NOTES AND QUESTIONS

1.   Psychological research indicates that anchoring may benefit negotiators in two ways. First, as the above excerpt suggests, one negotiator may use an extreme opening position as an anchor to induce her counterpart to agree to terms more favorable to the proposer. Second, a negotiator who anchors herself on a more optimistic goal is likely to achieve a better objective outcome than a negotiator who anchors on a less optimistic goal. *See* Russell

Korobkin, *Aspirations and Settlement*, 88 Cornell L. Rev. 1 (2002). On the other hand, that same negotiator is likely to experience less *subjective* satisfaction with that objectively superior outcome. *See, e.g.,* Adam D. Galinsky, Thomas Mussweiler & Victoria Husted Medvec, *Disconnecting Outcomes and Evaluations: The Role of Negotiator Focus*, 83 J. Personality & Social Psychol. 1131, 1139 (2002) ("Across three experiments . . . [f]ocusing on a target price produced superior negotiated outcomes but lowered satisfaction with those outcomes, compared with focusing on a lower bound or minimally acceptable point."). On the importance of subjective outcomes in negotiation, see generally Jared R. Curhan, Hillary Anger Elfenbein & Heng Xu, *What Do People Value When They Negotiate? Mapping the Domain of Subjective Value in Negotiation*, 91 J. Personality & Social Psychol. 493 (2006).

2.   Does the work on anchoring suggest that a negotiator using the adversarial approach should make the initial demand or offer in negotiation?

3.   Professor Shell recommends that if a negotiator has decided to open, she should offer "the highest (or lowest) number for which there is a supporting standard or argument enabling [her] to make a presentable case." G. RICHARD SHELL, BARGAINING FOR ADVANTAGE: NEGOTIATING STRATEGIES FOR REASONABLE PEOPLE 160 (2nd ed. 2006). Professor Andrea Schneider explains why it important to use objective criteria even when making extreme opening offers:

> First, negotiators will be more likely to succeed in convincing their adversary to reach an agreement based on their aspiration level if they can argue that such an outcome is derived from objective criteria. . . . The objective criteria include what a court would decide, standard business practice, fair market value, or other legitimate criteria, such as the painting that a granddaughter wants from her grandmother's estate is one the granddaughter helped pick out at the gallery.

> The availability of objective criteria also makes it easier for the negotiator to justify a refusal to make concessions. Demands that are not realistically grounded are harder to hold onto during the bargaining process. Imagine two scenarios—one in which a seller would like to get $500,000 for her house because it is a nice round number and she could use it to buy another house, versus one in which the seller lists her house for $500,000, based on the fair market value of the house in comparison to other houses in the neighborhood. In the latter case, the seller has fair and convincing arguments for why she will not accept less and is less likely to move quickly off her list price.

> Demands that lack an objective justification also encourage the opposing negotiator to make unprincipled counter demands. If financial desire is the justification for the seller's list price, then the buyer could just as easily respond with a lowball offer citing their limited ability to get a mortgage. A justifiable list price of $500,000 instead should lead to the more appropriate counteroffer of $450,000 based on the objective

criteria that the roof needs to be replaced or that the kitchen should be updated.

An additional reason that aspirations should be justifiable is that overly aggressive aspirations can lead to a negotiation impasse even when mutually beneficial agreements are possible.

Andrea Kupfer Schneider, *Aspirations*, in THE NEGOTIATOR'S FIELDBOOK 273 (Schneider & Honeyman, eds., 2006). Notice how justifying an aspiration requires sufficient preparation, including research regarding the relevant substantive law, careful consideration of procedural alternatives, and determination of the value of "comparables" (e.g., houses in the same neighborhood, businesses in the same industry and geographic area, lawsuits involving similar legal issues and parties). Your preparation also may include taking steps to improve the "comparables" available to your client.

4. What are the risks associated with making an extreme opening offer?

5. Are there circumstances in which negotiators might profit by starting not with an extremely self-serving position but rather with a position that is extremely charitable to the other side? Consider the following excerpt:

A quotation on the cover of my Morocco travel guide reads, "From the moment you land, adventure assails you." This curiously ominous accolade turned out to be true: my fellow-travelers and I, conspicuously American tourists in an impoverished country, were continually beset by hucksters who wished to sell us undesirable goods or services. We were all at our most vulnerable in the ancient marketplaces, where, for a few pennies, you could have your photograph taken with a large snake draped over your shoulders, and then, for a few dollars, have the snake (now slowly wrapping itself around your neck) removed.

My guidebook also informed me that the prices in the markets are highly negotiable, and that tourists should haggle aggressively. I dutifully bargained a little at one vender's stall—and bought my son a key chain attached to a chunk of plastic in which a scorpion had been embedded—but I hated the feeling that I was fighting over a trivial sum with a man who clearly needed every dirham he could lay his hands on. Suddenly, I had a conceptual breakthrough: instead of bargaining down, why not bargain up? I tried my idea first in a taxi, which I was sharing with two other sportswriters. When the driver told us that the fare was eighty dirhams (about seven dollars), I said, "No! A hundred!" He did a perfect cartoon double take, then looked at me with deep suspicion. I said, in halting French, "You are an excellent driver. Eighty is not enough. A hundred and ten!" He then not only laughed but also drove us all the way across a busy intersection in the middle of which he had previously seemed inclined to abandon us. A little later, in a maze-like souk [marketplace], I reverse-haggled over the price of a leather purse for my daughter ("The work is so beautiful!" I said. "Your price is too low!") and ended up with a free second purse and an invitation to spend Ramadan with the family of the shopkeeper (I think).

David Owen, *Swinging in Morocco*, THE NEW YORKER, May 21, 2001, at 52, 53–54.

b. Making Few and Small Concessions

Negotiators using the adversarial approach not only prefer to start with extreme opening positions, they also prefer to make few and small concessions from those opening positions. As Howard Raiffa explains it, "The most common pattern of concessions (for a maximizer) is monotone decreasing—that is, the intervals between your decreasing offers become successively smaller, signaling that you are approaching your limit." HOWARD RAIFFA, THE ART AND SCIENCE OF NEGOTIATION 128 (1982).

Concession making rests on the so-called "reciprocity norm," which Professor Robert Cialdini explains below.

ROBERT B. CIALDINI, INFLUENCE: SCIENCE AND PRACTICE[*]
36–39 (4th ed. 2001)

I was walking down the street when I was approached by an 11– or 12–year–old boy. He introduced himself and said he was selling tickets to the annual Boy Scouts Circus to be held on the upcoming Saturday night. He asked if I wished to buy any tickets at $5 apiece. Since one of the last places I wanted to spend Saturday evening was with the Boy Scouts, I declined. "Well," he said, "if you don't want to buy any tickets, how about buying some of our chocolate bars? They're only $1 each." I bought a couple and, right away, realized that something noteworthy had happened. I knew that to be the case because (a) I do not like chocolate bars; (b) I do like dollars; (c) I was standing there with two of his chocolate bars; and (d) he was walking away with two of my dollars.

To try to understand precisely what had happened, I went to my office and called a meeting of my research assistants. In discussing the situation, we began to see how the reciprocity rule was implicated in my compliance with the request to buy the candy bars. The general rule says that a person who acts in a certain way toward us is entitled to a similar return action. We have already seen that one consequence of the rule, however, is an obligation to make a concession to someone who has made a concession to us. As my research group thought about it, we realized that was exactly the position the Boy Scout had put me in. His request that I purchase some $1 chocolate bars had been put in the form of a concession on his part; it was presented as a retreat from his request that

---

    *   From Robert B. Cialdini, Influence: Science and Practice, 4e, published by Allyn and Bacon, Boston, MA. © 2001 by Pearson Education. Reprint by permission of the publisher.

I buy some $5 tickets. If I were to live up to the dictates of the reciprocation rule, there had to be a concession on my part. As we have seen, there was such a concession: I changed from noncompliant to compliant when he moved from a larger to a smaller request, even though I was not really interested in *either* of the things he offered.

It was a classic example of the way a weapon of influence can infuse a compliance request with its power. I had been moved to buy something, not because of any favorable feelings toward the item, but because the purchase request had been presented in a way that drew force from the reciprocity rule. It had not mattered that I do not like chocolate bars; the Boy Scout had made a concession to me, *click*, and *whirr*, I responded with a concession of my own. Of course, the tendency to reciprocate with a concession is not so strong that it will work in all instances on all people; none of the weapons of influence considered in this book is that strong. However, in my exchange with the Boy Scout, the tendency had been sufficiently powerful to leave me in mystified possession of a pair of unwanted and overpriced candy bars.

Why should I feel obliged to reciprocate a concession? The answer rests once again in the benefit of such a tendency to the society. It is in the interest of any human group to have its members working together toward the achievement of common goals. However, in many social interactions the participants begin with requirements and demands that are unacceptable to one another. Thus, the society must arrange to have these initial, incompatible desires set aside for the sake of socially beneficial cooperation. This is accomplished through procedures that promote compromise. Mutual concession is one important such procedure.

The reciprocation rule brings about mutual concession in two ways. The first is obvious; it pressures the recipient of an already-made concession to respond in kind. The second, while not so obvious, is pivotally important. Because of a recipient's obligation to reciprocate, people are freed to make the *initial* concession and, thereby, to begin the beneficial process of exchange. After all, if there were no social obligation to reciprocate a concession, who would want to make the first sacrifice? To do so would be to risk giving up something and getting nothing back. However, with the rule in effect, we can feel safe making the first sacrifice to our partner, who is obligated to offer a return sacrifice.

Because the rule for reciprocation governs the compromise process, it is possible to use an initial concession as part of a highly effective compliance technique. The technique is a simple one that we will call the rejection-then-retreat technique, although it is also known as the door-in-the-face technique. Suppose you want me to agree to a certain request. One way to increase the chances that I will comply is first to make a larger request of me, one that I will most likely turn down. Then, after I have refused, you make the smaller request that you were really interested in all along. Provided that you structured your requests skillfully, I should view your second request as a concession to me and should feel inclined to respond with a concession of my own—compliance with your second request.

Was that the way the Boy Scout got me to buy his candy bars? Was his retreat from the $5 request to the $1 request an artificial one that was intentionally designed to sell candy bars? As one who has still refused to discard even his first Scout merit badge, I genuinely hope not. Whether or not the large-request-then-small-request sequence was planned, its effect was the same. It worked! Because it works, the rejection-then-retreat technique can and will be used *purposely* by certain people to get their way. First let's examine how this tactic can be used as a reliable compliance device. Later we will see how it is already being used. Finally we can turn to a pair of little-known features of the technique that make it one of the most influential compliance tactics available.

Remember that after my encounter with the Boy Scout, I called my research assistants together to try to understand what had happened to me—and, as it turned out, to eat the evidence. Actually, we did more than that. We designed an experiment to test the effectiveness of the procedure of moving to a desired request after a larger preliminary request had been refused. We had two purposes in conducting the experiment. First, we wanted to see whether this procedure worked on people besides me. (It certainly seemed that the tactic had been effective on me earlier in the day, but then I have a history of falling for compliance tricks of all sorts.) So the question remained, "Does the rejection-then-retreat technique work on enough people to make it a useful procedure for gaining compliance?" If so, it would definitely be something to be aware of in the future. Our second reason for doing the study was to determine how powerful a compliance device the technique was. Could it bring about compliance with a genuinely sizable request? In other words, did the *smaller* request to which the requester retreated have to be a *small* request? If our thinking about what caused the technique to be effective was correct, the second request did not actually have to be small; it only had to be smaller than the initial one. It was our suspicion that the critical aspect of a requester's retreat from a larger to a smaller favor was its appearance as a concession. So the second request could be an objectively large one—as long as it was smaller than the first request—and the technique would still work.

After a bit of thought, we decided to try the technique on a request that we felt few people would agree to perform. Posing as representatives of the "County Youth Counseling Program," we approached college students walking on campus and asked if they would be willing to chaperon a group of juvenile delinquents on a day trip to the zoo. This idea of being responsible for a group of juvenile delinquents of unspecified age for hours in a public place without pay was hardly an inviting one for these students. As we expected, the great majority (83 percent) refused. Yet we obtained very different results from a similar sample of college students who were asked the very same question with one difference. Before we invited them to serve as unpaid chaperons on the zoo trip, we asked them for an even larger favor—to spend two hours per week as counselors to juvenile delinquents for a minimum of two years. It was only after they refused this extreme request, as all did, that we made the small, zoo-trip request. But presenting the zoo trip as a retreat from our initial request, our success rate increased dramatically. Three times as many of the students approached in this manner volunteered to serve as zoo chaperons.

Be assured that any strategy able to triple the percentage of compliance with a substantial request (from 17 to 50 percent in our experiment) will be used often in a variety of natural settings. Labor negotiators, for instance, often use the tactic of making extreme demands that they do not expect to win but from which they can retreat and draw real concessions from the opposing side. It would appear, then, that the procedure would be more effective the larger the initial request, since there would be more room available for illusory concessions. This is true only up to a point, however. Research conducted at Bar Ilan University in Israel on the rejection-then-retreat technique shows that if the first set of demands is so extreme as to be seen as unreasonable, the tactic backfires. In such cases, the party who has made the extreme first request is not seen to be bargaining in good faith. Any subsequent retreat from that wholly unrealistic initial position is not viewed as a genuine concession and, thus, is not reciprocated. The truly gifted negotiator, then, is one whose initial position is exaggerated just enough to allow for a series of small reciprocal concessions and counteroffers that will yield a desirable final offer from the opponent.

NOTES AND QUESTIONS

1. Do you see how a negotiator using the adversarial strategy can employ both anchoring (starting with an extreme opening offer) and the reciprocity rule (specifically, the rejection-then-retreat strategy Cialdini describes above) to induce her counterpart to reach agreement?

2. The rejection-then-retreat tactic that Cialdini describes above suggests that a negotiator using the adversarial approach can offer a concession as a way to induce her counterpart to do the same. Making concessions is not so easy, however, and the two negotiators are not likely to value their respective concessions in the same way. Psychologists have found that individuals experience more pain from a loss than they experience pleasure from a gain of the same size—a phenomenon known as *loss aversion*. As applied to negotiation, one result can be *concession aversion*, in which a negotiator experiences his own concessions as "losses" from his prior position.

He will see those concessions as being bigger than will his opponent, who experiences them as "gains."

Imagine a Double Whopper with cheese. No onions. Now imagine your Whopper accompanying you to the negotiation table, where I, your counterpart, take it from you and eat it. You have just lost a Whopper.

Imagine a second scenario. You come to the negotiation table with no food of your own and I, your counterpart, of my own accord, offer you that very same type of sandwich. You have just gained a Whopper. How would you value these otherwise identical sandwiches?

A loss aversion approach would predict that most individuals would "hate" the loss of the Whopper in the first scenario considerably more than they would "love" the gain of an equivalent product in the second. You may be wondering, "How can anyone compare the value of the loss of a Whopper with the value of its gain in terms of 'love' and 'hate'?" Indeed, love and hate, although certainly expressing value, are not readily quantified. Consider, therefore, the following alternatives to a love-hate relationship with your sandwich:

How much money would you require in order to lose your Whopper in the first scenario, if I asked for it?

If, on the other hand, I offered you a Whopper when you did not have one, how much would you be willing to pay in order to gain it?

The loss aversion prediction is that you would ask me to pay a considerably larger proportion of money to part with your Whopper than you would be willing to pay if I offered you mine.

Alexander Dobrev, *Concession Aversion: Can Fast Food Slow Down Successful Negotiations?*, Convenor Conflict Resolution, *available at* http://www.convenor.com/madison/dobrev.htm (last visited Feb. 17, 2005).

3.   The endowment effect is also related to loss aversion. Consider the following example:

An attractive object (e.g., a decorated mug) is distributed to one-third of the students. The students who have been given mugs are *sellers*—perhaps better described as owners. They are informed that there will be an opportunity to exchange the mug for a predetermined amount of money. The subjects state what their choice will be for different amounts, and thereby indicate the minimal amount for which they are willing to give up their mug. Another one-third of the students are *choosers*. They are told that they will have a choice between a mug like the one in the hands of their neighbor and an amount of cash; they indicate their choices for different amounts. The remaining students are *buyers*: they indicate whether they would pay each of the different amounts to acquire a mug. In a representative experiment, the median price set by sellers was $7.12, the median cash equivalent set by the choosers was $3.12, and the median buyer was willing to pay $2.88 for the mug.

Daniel Kahneman & Amos Tversky, *Conflict Resolution: A Cognitive Perspective*, in BARRIERS TO CONFLICT RESOLUTION 54–56 (Kenneth J. Arrow, Robert M. Mnookin, Lee Ross, Amos Tversky & Robert B. Wilson eds., 1995).

4. What implications do loss aversion, concession aversion, loss aversion and the endowment effect have for the rejection-then-retreat strategy Cialdini described above? In other words, is a negotiator likely to accept a proposal made by her counterpart if that proposal appears to be a concession (or "retreat") from a prior proposal? Or will the concession be devalued and therefore either rejected or not reciprocated?

5.   Making concessions is also complicated by "reactive devaluation." Research on this phenomenon suggests that negotiators may devalue proposals simply because they have been offered by their "opponent."

In one classic study conducted during the days of Apartheid, researchers solicited students' evaluations of two university plans for divestment from South Africa. The first plan called for partial divestment, and the second increased investments in companies that had left South Africa. Both plans, which fell short of the students' demand for full divestment, were rated before and after the university announced that it would adopt the partial divestment plan. The results were dramatic: students rated the university plan less positively after it was announced by the university and the alternative plan more positively.

We hasten to note that the source of an offer may be diagnostic of its quality. It may be reasonable to view an offer more critically when the source is one's opponent, particularly if there is an unpleasant history between the parties. However, evidence from the aforementioned studies suggests that people tend to experience a knee-jerk overreaction to the source of the offer. If negotiators routinely undervalue concessions made by their counterparts, it will inhibit their ability to exploit tradeoffs that might result in more valuable agreements.

Consider an example of how reactive devaluation might manifest itself in a negotiation between lawyers. Imagine a simplified environmental cleanup action in which the parties are a government enforcement agency (represented by a single person) and a single responsible polluter. There may be two solutions to their problem. In one, the government effectuates the cleanup and sends a bill to the polluter. In the second, the polluter does the cleanup and the government inspects. Perhaps solution one meets more of the polluters' interests than solution two. One might suppose that the polluter would prefer this solution regardless of how it emerges as the agreed method. However, studies of reactive devaluation suggest that once the government tentatively agrees to that particular solution, the polluter may view the alternative solution more favorably. The apparent thought process is "if they held it back, it must be worse for them and therefore better for me than the one offered." The polluter may irrationally reorder her priorities and reject a deal simply because it was offered freely by an opponent.

Richard Birke & Craig R. Fox, *Psychological Principles in Negotiating Civil Settlements*, 4 Harv. Negot. L. Rev. 1, 48–49 (1999).

6. In addition to reciprocity (and commitments, described *infra*), adversarial negotiators can use several other psychological techniques to persuade their counterparts to make valuable concessions:

- Liking—"People prefer to comply with requests made by those they know and like. People tend to like those who are physically attractive; those with whom they share something in common; those with whom they are familiar; and those who pay them compliments." Chris Guthrie, *Courting Compliance* in THE NEGOTIATOR'S FIELDBOOK 371, 372 (Christopher Honeyman & Andrea Schneider eds., 2006).

- Social proof—People "view a behavior as correct in a given situation to the degree that we see others performing it." ROBERT B. CIALDINI, INFLUENCE: SCIENCE AND PRACTICE 100 (4TH ed. 2001).

- Authority—"Individuals often feel an obligation to comply with those who are in real or perceived authority positions." Guthrie, *Courting Compliance supra* at 374.

- Scarcity—" '[O]pportunities seem more valuable to us when they are less available.' " Scarcity induces compliance in large part because it threatens our freedom of choice ('If I don't act now, I will lose the opportunity to do so.')" *Id.* at 374 (quoting Cialdini, *supra* at 205).

The power of these and other psychological tools is due to their appeal to the "peripheral" route to persuasion. Professor Donna Shestowsky explains.

> According to psychologists, a widely accepted way of understanding the psychology of persuasion stems from the Elaboration Likelihood Model (ELM), which characterizes persuasion as occurring by the relative operation of either of two routes. These two routes are differentiated by the level of cognitive processing (i.e., amount of conscious examination or "elaboration" of the message) that is undertaken by the person exposed to a persuasive communication. . . . [O]ne route to persuasion, called the "central" route, involves engaging in extensive processing of issue-relevant information in order to make judgments. Negotiators who engage in central processing will carefully consider the merits of your proposals and be persuaded by relevant and logical arguments. By contrast, the other route to persuasion—the "peripheral" route—is marked by a relative lack of effortful processing. Negotiators persuaded by this route will tend to consider your proposals in a more superficial way, and thus will often be swayed by how you "package" or "frame" them rather than by their intrinsic merit.

Donna Shestowsky, *Psychology and Persuasion*, in THE NEGOTIATOR'S FIELDBOOK 361, 362 (Christopher Honeyman & Andrea Schneider, eds., 2006). *See also* DANIEL KAHNEMAN, THINKING FAST AND SLOW (2011) (examining the dichotomy between System 1 and System 2 thinking, with

System 1 characterized by fast, instinctive, emotional thinking and System 2 by slower, deliberative, logical thinking).

c.   Limited Disclosure of Information

Negotiators using the adversarial approach tend to keep their private information close to the vest, though they often seek to discover the private information their counterparts possess. In other words, they seek to exploit "information asymmetries." Professors Ian Ayres and Jennifer Gerarda Brown elaborate on this concept, and also introduce us to the idea of a BATNA, or Best Alternative to a Negotiated Agreement. While the BATNA is discussed more fully later in this section, the central idea is that negotiators use their BATNA—that is, their best alternative if they can't reach a deal—as a way of assessing the deal they are being offered. As many negotiation teachers have advised, "If your deal isn't better than your BATNA, you might as well walk away."

IAN AYRES & JENNIFER GERARDA BROWN, ECONOMIC RATIONALES FOR MEDIATION
80 Va. L. Rev. 324, 331, 332–33 (1994)

Potential buyers and sellers . . . often have private information about how much they individually value a particular good or service. Because each party's reservation price (or BATNA) is not publicly known, each party has "hidden information" that can give rise to adverse selection [or inefficient outcomes caused by information asymmetries].

* * *

The parties might strategically withhold or misrepresent the private information . . . in order to increase their private returns. When the parties have private knowledge of their own reservation prices, sellers will have an incentive to overstate their valuations in order to negotiate a higher price and buyers will have an incentive to understate their valuations in order to negotiate a lower price. . . . Just as sick people have an incentive to convince insurance companies that they are healthy when negotiating an insurance premium, high-valuing buyers have an incentive to convince sellers that they are low-valuing when negotiating the contract price. In both cases, the asymmetric information gives the party with private information an incentive to pretend to be a different type in negotiating a contract.

NOTES AND QUESTIONS

1.   Some negotiators in some circumstances can use information asymmetries to their advantage. In major league baseball negotiations, for example, agents representing players—including Scott Boras, one of the most

prominent agents in the business—are often able to take advantage of private information on behalf of their clients:

> Agents benefit from what business-school types refer to as "information asymmetry," because they are in touch with multiple teams, who are, in turn, forbidden to communicate with one another. Controlling the flow of that information—between the teams, the media, and the players—is an essential component of the Boras methodology. "In terms of negotiation, this guy is an absolute special-forces guy," a competitor said of Boras. "The prison interrogations—he's one of those." Boras is a skilled manipulator of the media, and shows the kind of patience, as deadlines approach, that derives from great self-confidence. (This spring, he cut his negotiations with the Arizona Diamondbacks over the pitcher Max Scherzer so close to the wire that the A.P. reported, at 4:42 A.M., "Diamondbacks fail to sign No. 1 pick Scherzer," only to reverse course at 5:32 A.M., with a description of a four-year deal.)

Ben McGrath, *The Extortionist*, THE NEW YORKER 56, 60 (Oct. 29, 2007).

2.   Other times, however, information asymmetries can lead to impasse. Consider, for example, the following analysis of strikes:

> In the spring of 1988, television and movie writers went out on strike. The strike, which lasted for twenty-two weeks, was rhetorically bitter and economically destructive: it cost an estimated half billion dollars in lost revenues and wages and sent network ratings down by nine per cent. But the walkout had only limited impact at the negotiating table: when an agreement was finally reached, it looked very much like a deal that could have been made five months earlier. The strike almost certainly cost both sides more than the sums they had been fighting over.

> Twenty years later, entertainment writers are on the picket lines once again. They may do better this time, but history is against them. Walkouts may call to mind labor triumphs like the Flint sitdown strike of 1936–37, which gained union recognition for the United Automobile Workers at G.M., but most don't end that well—nor do they generally end as badly as the 1981 air-traffic controllers' strike, in which everyone got fired. Instead, strikes often end tepidly, with no major gains or rollbacks, and economists have found that, on average, strikes these days have little, if any, impact on what workers get paid. (Paradoxically, unions raise worker wages, but strikes generally don't.) Given the negative economic consequences—lost paychecks for workers and lost business for employers—the economically rational thing for both sides is usually to settle before the walkout strikes. So why don't they?

> One obvious hurdle to a settlement is that neither side knows what the other side's true position is. In economists' terms, strikes happen as a result of "asymmetric information"—when one side knows more than the other about the real economics of the situation. Entertainment writers, for instance, want a share of the revenue generated from their

work in new media, including programs streamed on the Internet. Producers insist that they need flexibility with regard to new technologies and that it's too early to know how much they can afford to pay for streaming programs. This may be just a bluff, or it may contain some truth—it's hard for the writers to know the difference. Going on strike is one way to find out. If a company concedes quickly, that's a sign that it was just bluffing. If it's willing to endure a long strike, that may be a sign that it meant what it said. That's why the longer a strike lasts, the less likely it is to produce a big victory for either side: you're willing to cut a deal after a long strike that you wouldn't have been willing to cut before in part because the strike has told you that the other side wasn't just bluffing.

James Surowiecki, *Striking Out*, THE NEW YORKER 42, 42 (Nov. 19, 2007).

3.   Given that negotiators who provide limited information to their counterparts will sometimes benefit from the resulting information asymmetry and sometimes suffer, what information should a negotiator disclose? What information should she withhold? In the following excerpt, Professor Menkel–Meadow provides sage advice:

CARRIE MENKEL–MEADOW, KNOW WHEN TO SHOW YOUR HAND
10 Negot. 1, 1–3 (June 2007)

Suppose that two entrepreneurs, a marketing expert and an IT specialist, are thinking about merging their consulting firms to create a greater synergy of services. As their talks unfold, each wonders how much information to disclose. Should they bring up discussions with other potential partners? When should they share proprietary business data? What if one is planning to retire in two years, and the other is starting a family—should they share this personal information?

* * *

In all your negotiations, you must calculate the risks and rewards of sharing information with your counterpart. Here, I will show you which factors to consider when making such decisions, when to ask for information directly, and when to seek it elsewhere.

A wealth of useful information

Before talks begin—and, if possible, even before your initial contact with your counterpart—list the information you need to resolve your dispute or to build a strong deal. Also anticipate the information the other side will want from you, and consider how you'll respond to these queries.

Information typically falls into these categories:

- **Facts:** Information about relevant past events, goods, and services; ongoing obligations and liabilities; parties needed to conclude talks; and so forth.

- **Opinions, values, and predictions:** Information subject to different interpretations, such as a company's value, the likely income from a new product, the outcome of a future court decision, or whether the dollar will rise or fall.

- **Preferences:** Information that negotiators express as their needs, interests, goals, objectives, desires, bottom lines, and reservation prices.

Once you have identified the information you need and may be asked to reveal, you're ready to consider the reasons you and your counterpart might choose to disclose or to conceal it.

When to show your hand

For legal, ethical, and strategic reasons, you might choose to disclose these four types of information:

1. Information required by law.

The last thing you want is for a good deal to be voided in post hoc legal proceedings. To fulfill legal standards (and your own code of ethics), research what you must disclose in a particular jurisdiction or realm of negotiation.

Pertinent laws include those on fraud and misrepresentation, disclosure law in securities and real estate, and consumer protection statutes. Mandatory disclosure rules can be national (such as the Sarbanes–Oxley Act), state, or local (such as those concerning hazardous-waste disposal).

In addition, ethics and disclosure rules apply to various professions. Lawyers and accountants may have to reveal adverse financial data and irregularities, real-estate brokers must reveal known defects in a property, and underwriters must disclose many conditions of a public offering.

2. Information in the public domain.

In the age of Google searches and international networking, much information that was formerly hidden is now at our fingertips. Before deciding to conceal a piece of information, consider whether your counterpart is likely to discover it anyway. Here are some types of information to which the other side (and you, too!) may have access:

- Public information available on the Internet, including financial statements of public companies, disclosure statements for smaller companies and nonprofits, news reports, professional biographies, and lawsuit settlements.

- Proprietary information available from private investigators and sources who have dealt with you in the past.

- Information extracted through subpoenas, depositions, discovery, and other legal processes or made public through press leaks.

3.   Information that could inspire reciprocation.

In most negotiations, a pattern of reciprocity tends to develop. If you don't reveal key information, your counterpart may withhold in response. Failure to disclose can prevent you from getting the information you need.

Concealing information may be especially unwise when you're trying to build a relationship. Returning to the case of the two entrepreneurs, suppose that Mindy, the marketing expert, is trying to decide whether to reveal to Paul, the IT specialist, that she plans to retire in two years. Paul might view this information as a chance to grow the business on his own—or as a betrayal of the partnership. Hiding her plans not only could sour the relationship and the merger but also could damage Mindy's reputation in the industry and the community.

4.   Potentially damaging facts and needs.

It may sound counterintuitive, but sometimes you can benefit from revealing information that seems too risky to disclose. Consider how a trial lawyer might handle the possible revelation of damaging information about her client: by bringing it up during direct examination so as to minimize the odds of a disaster during cross-examination. Similarly, skillful negotiators choose to reveal and explain carefully information that might trouble the other side.

As social psychologist George Homans pointed out in the early 1960s, revealing preferences often illuminates complementary (rather than competing) goals and values. Mindy certainly would choose to disclose her impending retirement if she's looking for someone to carry on her business and suspects that Paul would love such an opportunity.

When to hold your cards

Now let's consider four types of information that may be best kept under wraps.

1.   Sensitive or privileged information.

It can be tough to decide whether to disclose private or sensitive information, such as trade secrets and financial data, as well as your preferences (targets, reservation prices, needs, and interests). This information is often necessary to identify tradeoffs and create value, but there's also the risk that your counterpart will take advantage of your disclosure. If Mindy reveals her retirement plans to Paul, he may try to bargain for a greater share of future profits.

* * *

2.   Information that isn't yours to share.

When you negotiate as someone's agent—whether as a lawyer, a broker, or your firm's representative—disclosure decisions may not be yours to make. Instead, you'll first need to discuss the risks and benefits discussed here with your principal. Even if information doesn't technically "belong" to someone else, disclosure might hurt that person. Suppose you're negotiating a purchase from one supplier. You could be tempted to disclose another supplier's bottom line—but it might be wise to consult this party first.

3.   Information that diminishes your power.

If you have less power than your counterpart, think through the potentially negative consequences of making "information concessions." Physically injured plaintiffs often are tempted to offer information about their current injuries in return for an early settlement, though they might procure greater damage awards later if longer-term injuries emerge. And in an overheated real-estate market, the bidder who expresses the greatest desire for a given house risks being exploited by a seller with multiple offers. Evaluate whether your desire for a given outcome might cause you to reveal too much and be exploited.

4.   Information that may fluctuate.

"Facts" may change over time; prices and preferences certainly will. When important information seems unstable, you might choose to wait to reveal it or else seek a deal provision to later modify the information you share. Contractual contingencies allow you and your counterpart to "bet" on your differing predictions; you also can add clauses that permit renegotiation should facts or conditions change. Mindy and Paul might decide that if their joint company nets a certain profit in several years, she will take a percentage as retirement income but put off retirement if this goal is not realized.

d.   Commitments

Negotiators using the adversarial strategy also tend to make commitment statements in negotiation. Effective commitment statements are clear, specific, and final. For example, "we must have a 10% volume discount next month, or we will sign with an alternative supplier" is a more effective commitment statement than "if we don't get a volume discount, there will be trouble." In a negotiation, commitment statements communicate a negotiator's capacities, limitations, preferences and other important information, and can be used strategically to induce the other party to respond in a certain way. In the example, *supra*, the negotiator is communicating clearly, specifically, and finally what she needs to continue the business relationship. Such a commitment statement is designed to persuade the other party to either provide the discount or make a responsive counter-proposal.

THOMAS C. SCHELLING, THE STRATEGY OF CONFLICT[*]
21–25 (1980)

A bargain is struck when somebody makes a final, sufficient concession. Why does he concede? Because he thinks the other will not. "I must concede because he won't. He won't because he thinks I will. He thinks I will because he thinks I think he thinks so. . . ." There is some range of alternative outcomes in which any point is better for both sides than no agreement at all. To insist on any such point is pure bargaining, since one always *would* take less rather than reach no agreement at all, and since one always *can* recede if retreat proves necessary to agreement. Yet if both parties are aware of the limits to this range, *any* outcome is a point from which at least one party would have been willing to retreat and the other knows it! There is no resting place.

There is, however, an outcome; and if we cannot find it in the logic of the situation we may find it in the tactics employed. The purpose of this chapter is to call attention to an important class of tactics, of a kind that is peculiarly appropriate to the logic of indeterminate situations. The essence of these tactics is some voluntary but irreversible sacrifice of freedom of choice. They rest on the paradox that the power to constrain an adversary may depend on the power to bind oneself; that is, in bargaining, weakness is often strength, freedom may be freedom to capitulate, and to burn bridges behind one may suffice to undo an opponent.

* * *

How does one person make another believe something? The answer depends importantly on the factual question, "Is it true?" It is easier to prove the truth of something that is true than of something false. To prove the truth about our health we can call on a reputable doctor; to prove the truth about our costs or income we may let the person look at books that have been audited by a reputable firm or the Bureau of Internal Revenue. But to persuade him of something false we may have no such convincing evidence.

When one wishes to persuade someone that he would not pay more than $16,000 for a house that is really worth $20,000 to him, what can he do to take advantage of the usually superior credibility of the truth over a

---

[*]   Reprinted with permission of Harvard University Press. All rights reserved.

false assertion? Answer: make it true. How can a buyer make it true? If he likes the house because it is near his business, he might move his business, persuading the seller that the house is really now worth only $16,000 to him. This would be unprofitable; he is no better off than if he had paid the higher price.

But suppose the buyer could make an irrevocable and enforceable bet with some third party, duly recorded and certified, according to which he would pay for the house no more than $16,000, or forfeit $5,000. The seller has lost; the buyer need simply present the truth. Unless the seller is enraged and withholds the house in sheer spite, the situation has been rigged against him; the "objective" situation—the buyer's true incentive—has been voluntarily, conspicuously, and irreversibly changed. The seller can take it or leave it. This example demonstrates that if the buyer can accept an irrevocable *commitment*, in a way that is unambiguously visible to the seller, he can squeeze the range of indeterminacy down to the point most favorable to him. It also suggests, by its artificiality, that the tactic is one that may or may not be available; whether the buyer can find an effective device for committing himself may depend on who he is, who the seller is, where they live, and a number of legal and institutional arrangements (including, in our artificial example, whether bets are legally enforceable).

If both men live in a culture where "cross my heart" is universally accepted as potent, all the buyer has to do is allege that he will pay no more than $16,000, using this invocation of penalty, and he wins—or at least he wins if the seller does not beat him to it by shouting "$19,000, cross my heart." If the buyer is an agent authorized by a board of directors to buy at $16,000 but not a cent more, and directors cannot constitutionally meet again for several months and the buyer cannot exceed his authority, and if all this can be made known to the seller, then the buyer "wins"—if, again, the seller has not tied himself up with a commitment to $19,000. Or, if the buyer can assert that he will pay no more than $16,000 so firmly that he would suffer intolerable loss of personal prestige or bargaining reputation by paying more, and if the fact of his paying more would necessarily be known, and if the seller appreciates all this, then a loud declaration by itself may provide the commitment. The device, of course, is a needless surrender of flexibility unless it can be made fully evident and understandable to the seller.

NOTES

1. The Schelling excerpt describes how negotiators using the adversarial strategy can employ commitment to constrain their own behavior in negotiation. As Mnookin and his colleagues explain it, a negotiator who commits to a particular position "ties one's hands, thus forcing the other side to accommodate." ROBERT MNOOKIN, SCOTT PEPPET & ANDREW S.

Tulumello, Beyond Winning: Negotiating to Create Value in Deals and Disputes 24 (2000).

2. In addition to using commitment tactics to constrain their own behavior, negotiators using the adversarial strategy may also attempt to induce their counterparts to make commitments as a way of constraining their counterparts' behavior. Consider the following excerpt from Professor Cialdini:*

If I can get you to make a commitment (that is, to take a stand, to go on record), I will have set the stage for your automatic and ill-considered consistency with that earlier commitment. Once a stand is taken, there is a natural tendency to behave in ways that are stubbornly consistent with the stand.

* * *

Charitable organizations, for instance, will often use progressively escalating commitments to induce individuals to perform major favors. Research has shown that such trivial first commitments as agreeing to be interviewed can begin a "momentum of compliance" that induces such later behaviors as organ or bone marrow donations (Carducci, Deuser, Bauer, Large, & Ramaekers, 1989; Schwartz, 1970).

Many business organizations employ this approach regularly as well. For the salesperson, the strategy is to obtain a large purchase by starting with a small one. Almost any small sale will do because the purpose of that small transaction is not profit, it is commitment. Further purchases, even much larger ones, are expected to flow naturally from the commitment. * * *

* * *

The tactic of starting with a little request in order to gain eventual compliance with related larger requests has a name: the foot-in-the-door technique. Social scientists first became aware of its effectiveness in 1966 when psychologists Jonathan Freedman and Scott Fraser published an astonishing set of data. They reported the results of an experiment in which a researcher, posing as a volunteer worker, had gone door to door in a residential California neighborhood making a preposterous request of homeowners. The homeowners were asked to allow a public-service billboard to be installed on their front lawns. To get an idea of the way the sign would look, they were shown a photograph depicting an attractive house, the view of which was almost completely obscured by a very large, poorly lettered sign reading DRIVE CAREFULLY. Although the request was normally and understandably refused by the great majority of the residents in the area (only 17

---

* From Robert B. Cialdini, Influence: Science and Practice, 4e, published by Allyn and Bacon, Boston, MA. © 2001 by Pearson Education. Reprint by permission of the publisher.

percent complied), one particular group of people reacted quite favorably. A full 76 percent of them offered the use of their front yards.

The prime reason for their startling compliance has to do with something that had happened to them about two weeks earlier: They had made a small commitment to driver safety. A different "volunteer worker" had come to their doors and asked them to accept and display a little three-inch-square sign that read BE A SAFE DRIVER. It was such a trifling request that nearly all of them had agreed to it, but the effects of that request were enormous. Because they had innocently complied with a trivial safe-driving request a couple of weeks before, these homeowners became remarkably willing to comply with another such request that was massive in size.

ROBERT B. CIALDINI, INFLUENCE, SCIENCE AND PRACTICE 65 (4TH ED. 2001).

3.   Although commitment tactics can help negotiators reach agreement on favorable terms, they can also backfire. Consider the following excerpt from Professor Jeffrey Rubin:

> Negotiators often find it tempting, particularly when discussions bog down and things appear not to be going the way they would like, to commit themselves to tough negotiating positions from which they swear they will never retreat. Like the players in the proverbial game of "chicken", each negotiator threatens not to turn aside (to concede) until the other does so first. There are several problems with such bold, seemingly irrevocable commitments. First, if they work—that is, if they succeed in eliciting some long-sought concession—the adversary is likely to think twice before sitting down to negotiate again. Why deliberately elect to walk into a buzz saw if one can help it? On the other hand, should the negotiation commitment fail to work—that is, should the adversary refuse to knuckle under—then the perpetrator is likely to be confronted with a nasty choice: To go back on one's stated commitment is to run the risk of losing credibility in the eyes of the adversary, while opening the way to subsequent exploitation by the other; on the other hand, to carry through a commitment to intransigence, in light of the adversary's determination to resist concession, is in turn to run the risk of engineering unnecessary havoc for both sides.

Jeffrey Rubin, *Negotiation: An Introduction to Some Issues and Themes*, 27 Am. Behav. Scientist 135, 142 (1983).

2.   PROBLEM–SOLVING STRATEGY AND TACTICS

In contrast to the adversarial negotiation strategy, which posits that negotiation is a zero-sum game in which any gains one side receives are necessarily at the expense of the other, the problem-solving strategy views negotiation as a collaborative problem-solving exercise in which the parties work side-by-side to satisfy their interests and produce joint gains.

The most popular explanation of a problem-solving strategy appears in ROGER FISHER, WILLIAM URY & BRUCE PATTON, GETTING TO YES: NEGOTIATING AGREEMENT WITHOUT GIVING IN (2d ed. 1991). The authors call their strategy "principled negotiation" or "negotiation on the merits," and they contrast it with adversarial negotiation (which they label "hard positional bargaining" and "soft positional bargaining"). They describe the problem-solving strategy and its primary tactics in the following excerpt.

ROGER FISHER, WILLIAM URY & BRUCE PATTON, GETTING TO YES: NEGOTIATING AGREEMENT WITHOUT GIVING IN
10–12, 14 (2d ed. 1991)

At the Harvard Negotiation Project we have been developing an alternative to positional bargaining: a method of negotiation explicitly designed to produce wise outcomes efficiently and amicably. This method, called *principled negotiation* or *negotiation on the merits*, can be boiled down to four basic points.

These four points define a straightforward method of negotiation that can be used under almost any circumstance. Each point deals with a basic element of negotiation, and suggests what you should do about it.

People: Separate the people from the problem.

Interests: Focus on interests, not positions.

Options: Generate a variety of possibilities before deciding what to do.

Criteria: Insist that the result be based on some objective standard.

The first point responds to the fact that human beings are not computers. We are creatures of strong emotions who often have radically different perceptions and have difficulty communicating clearly. Emotions typically become entangled with the objective merits of the problem. Taking positions just makes this worse because people's egos become identified with their positions. Hence, before working on the substantive problem, the "people problem" should be disentangled from it and dealt with separately. Figuratively if not literally, the participants should come to see themselves as working side by side, attacking the problem, not each other. Hence the first proposition: *Separate the people from the problem.*

The second point is designed to overcome the drawback of focusing on people's stated positions when the object of a negotiation is to satisfy their underlying interests. A negotiating position often obscures what you really want. Compromising between positions is not likely to produce an agreement which will effectively take care of the human needs that led people to adopt those positions. The second basic element of the method is: *Focus on interests, not positions.*

The third point responds to the difficulty of designing optimal solutions while under pressure. Trying to decide in the presence of an adversary narrows your vision. Having a lot at stake inhibits creativity. So does searching for the one right solution. You can offset these constraints by setting aside a designated time within which to think up a wide range of possible solutions that advance shared interests and creatively reconcile differing interests. Hence the third basic point: Before trying to reach agreement, *invent options for mutual gain.*

Where interests are directly opposed, a negotiator may be able to obtain a favorable result simply by being stubborn. That method tends to reward intransigence and produce arbitrary results. However, you can counter such a negotiator by insisting that his single say-so is not enough and that the agreement must reflect some fair standard independent of the naked will of either side. This does not mean insisting that the terms be based on the standard you select, but only that some fair standard such as market value, expert opinion, custom, or law determine the outcome. By discussing such criteria rather than what the parties are willing or unwilling to do, neither party need give in to the other; both can defer to a fair solution. Hence the fourth basic point: *Insist on using objective criteria.*

* * *

To sum up, in contrast to positional bargaining, the principled negotiation method of focusing on basic interests, mutually satisfying options, and fair standards typically results in a *wise* agreement. The method permits you to reach a gradual consensus on a joint decision *efficiently* without all the transactional costs of digging in to positions only to have to dig yourself out of them. And separating the people from the problem allows you to deal directly and empathetically with the other negotiator as a human being, thus making possible an *amicable* agreement.

NOTES

1.   As formulated by Professor Fisher, and Mssrs. Ury & Patton, negotiators using the problem-solving strategy should attempt to achieve a wise, efficient, and amicable outcome, not merely maximize gains. In contrast to the adversarial strategy—which focuses solely on the substance of the negotiation—the problem-solving strategy focuses on the substance, the process, and the relationship between the negotiators. Recall, though, how a cooperative *style* can "soften the edges" of the adversarial *strategy*.

2.   Below, we focus on the four primary tactics, or principles, of the problem-solving strategy. With respect to each, we identify what we believe is the key (though certainly not the only) skill a negotiator needs to develop to use the tactic successfully.

a.   "Separating the People From the Problem" (Listening)

Negotiators using the problem-solving strategy recognize that negotiators are people first and that "people problems" can become entangled with the substantive issues under discussion. To minimize entanglement, negotiators using the problem-solving strategy are attentive to the people and relationship issues inherent in negotiation.

People problems can arise due to misconceptions on the part of the negotiators, emotional issues, communication difficulties, or situational constraints. Regardless of the source of these problems, negotiators using the problem-solving strategy can best address them by attempting to listen carefully to their counterparts. Through good listening, negotiators can identify and overcome misperceptions, acknowledge emotional issues or difficult situations, and facilitate good communication.

DOUGLAS STONE, BRUCE PATTON & SHEILA HEEN, DIFFICULT CONVERSATIONS: HOW TO DISCUSS WHAT MATTERS MOST*
163–67 (1999)

Andrew is visiting his Uncle Doug. While Doug is on the phone, Andrew tugs on his uncle's pant leg, saying, "Uncle Doug, I want to go outside."

"Not now, Andrew, I'm on the phone," says Doug.

Andrew persists: "But Uncle Doug, I want to go outside!"

"Not now Andrew!" comes Doug's response.

"But I want to go out!" Andrew repeats.

After several more rounds, Doug tries a different approach: "Hey, Andrew. You really want to go outside, don't you?"

"Yes," says Andrew. Then without further comment, Andrew walks off and begins playing by himself. Andrew, it turns out, just wanted to know that his uncle understood him. He wanted to know he'd been heard.

Andrew's story demonstrates something that is true for all of us: we have a deep desire to feel heard, and to know that others care enough to listen.

Some people think they are already good listeners. Others know they are not, but don't much care. If you're in either group you might be tempted to skip this chapter. Don't. Listening well is one of the most powerful skills you can bring to a difficult conversation. It helps you

---

understand the other person. And, importantly, it helps them understand you.

LISTENING TRANSFORMS THE CONVERSATION

A year ago, Greta's mother learned she had diabetes and was ordered to follow a strict regimen of medication, diet, and exercise. Greta is concerned that her mother is not following the regimen, but Greta has had little success encouraging her mother to do so. A typical conversation between them goes like this:

GRETA: Mom, you need to stay on the exercise plan. I worry that you don't understand how important it is.

MOM: Greta, please stop hounding me about this. You don't understand. I'm doing the best I can.

GRETA: Mom, I do understand. I know that exercising can be difficult, but I want you to stay well. I want you to be around for your grandchildren.

MOM: Greta, I really don't like these conversations. It's all very hard for me, the diet, the exercise.

GRETA: I know it's hard. Exercising is no fun, but the thing is, after a week or two, it gets easier, and you start to look forward to it. We can find you some sort of activity that you'll really enjoy.

MOM: [choked up] You don't realize. . . . It's very stressful. I'm just not going to talk about it anymore. That's all there is to it

Not surprisingly, these conversations leave Greta feeling frustrated, powerless, and deeply sad. Greta wonders how she might be more assertive, how she can persuade her mother to change.

But assertiveness isn't Greta's problem. What's missing from her stance is curiosity. In a follow-up conversation, Greta shifts her goal from persuasion to learning. To do this she limits herself to listening, asking questions, and acknowledging her mother's feelings:

GRETA: I know you don't like talking about your diabetes and exercising.

MOM: I really don't. It's very upsetting to me.

GRETA: When you say it's upsetting, what do you mean? In what ways?

MOM: Greta, the whole thing. Do you think it's fun for me?

GRETA: No, Mom, I know it's really hard. I just don't know much about what you think about it, what it means to you, what you feel about it.

MOM: I'll tell you, if your father were alive, it would be different. He was so sweet when I would get sick. Having to follow all these complicated rules, that's what he would have been good at. He would have taken care of the whole thing. Being sick, it just makes me miss him so much.

GRETA: It sounds like you've been feeling really lonely without Dad.

MOM: I have friends, and you've been wonderful, but it's not the same as having your father here to help. I suppose I really do feel lonely, but I hate to talk about that. I don't want to be a burden on you kids.

GRETA: You feel like if you tell us you're lonely, it will be a burden? We'll worry?

MOM: I just don't want you to have to go through what my mother went through. You know *her* mother died of diabetes.

GRETA: I didn't know. Wow.

MOM: It's scary to be told you have what your grandmother died of. It's hard for me to accept. I know the medications are better now, which is why I should be following all those rules, but if I follow all those rules, it just makes me feel like some sick old lady.

GRETA: So keeping to the regimen would feel like accepting something that you don't totally accept yet?

MOM: It's irrational. I'm not saying it's not. [choked up] It's just very frightening and overwhelming.

GRETA: I know it is, Mom.

MOM: I'll tell you something else. I don't even understand what I'm supposed to be doing. The eating, the exercise. If you do one, it affects the other, and you have to keep track. It's complicated, and the doctor isn't terribly helpful in explaining it. I don't know where to begin. Your father would know.

GRETA: Maybe that's something I could help you with.

MOM: Greta, I don't want to be a burden.

GRETA: I want to help. It would actually make me feel better. Not so powerless.

MOM: If you could, that would take a big load off my mind. . . .

Greta was astonished and delighted at how much better her conversations became after she began truly listening to her mother. She came to see the issues from her mother's point of view, how much deeper they ran than she suspected, and how she might be able to help her mother in ways that her mother wanted to be helped. This is perhaps the most obvious benefit of listening: learning about the other person. But there is a second, more surprising benefit as well.

LISTENING TO THEM HELPS THEM LISTEN TO YOU

Ironically, when Greta shifted away from trying to persuade her mother to exercise and toward simply listening and acknowledging, she ended up achieving the goal that had eluded her up to that point. This is not an accident. One of the most common complaints we hear from people engaged in difficult conversations is that the other person won't listen. And when we hear that, our standard advice is "*You* need to spend more time listening to *them*."

When the other person is not listening, you may imagine it is because they're stubborn or don't understand what you're trying to say (If they did, they'd understand why they should listen to it.) so you may try to break through that by repeating, trying new ways to explain yourself, talking more loudly, and so forth.

On the face of it, these would seem to be good strategies. But they're not. Why? Because in the great majority of cases, the reason the other person is not listening to you is not because they are stubborn, but because *they* don't feel heard. In other words, they aren't listening to you for the same reason you aren't listening to them: they think *you* are slow or stubborn. So they repeat themselves, find new ways to say things, talk more loudly, and so forth.

If the block to their listening is that they don't feel heard, then the way to remove that block is by helping them feel heard—by bending over backwards to listen to what they have to say, and perhaps most important, by demonstrating that you understand what they are saying and how they are feeling.

If you don't quite believe this, try it. Find the most stubborn person you know, the person who never seems to take in anything you say, the person who repeats himself or herself in every conversation you ever have—and listen to them. Especially, listen for feelings, like frustration or pride or fear, and acknowledges those feelings. See whether that person doesn't become a better listener after all.

NOTES AND QUESTIONS

1.   The focus of the above excerpt is on "difficult conversations" in general, but such conversations include difficult negotiations. How might the authors' advice apply to negotiations between lawyers representing clients who are in conflict?

2.   Recall the Loop of Understanding that we introduced you to in Chapter II *supra*. This technique calls for us to go through a series of steps in which we seek understanding, demonstrate understanding and seek the other side's confirmation of the understanding we expressed. While we first described it in the context of promoting attorney-client understanding, it can

be just as effective when used in a negotiation to foster understanding between the negotiators, especially on difficult issues.

Looping in negotiation is structurally the same as in attorney client context. But the fact that the negotiators are in a dispute, or representing parties in a dispute, can change the dynamic. It is therefore important to take care in the looping process, and we offer a couple of suggestions.

First, you may need to be assertive to engage the looping process. Parties in negotiation—especially early on, as they are getting a feel for how the negotiation is going to unfold—are often prone to speaking for a long period of time. A lot of this is useful information at this stage, especially about the parties' different perceptions about the dispute, and it may help to politely ask your counterpart to pause so you can clarify your understanding—and begin the looping process. Done well, there should be no need to worry about interrupting; everyone likes to be understood better.

Second, save your looping for points in the negotiation when there is a significant and true disparity in understanding. Looping every little issue can appear strange, if not annoying, in a negotiation. Moreover, if you have understanding and are looping to to try to overcome disagreement on substantive issues, your counterpart may perceive you as being disingenuous for using the frame of understanding to persuade them to your way of thinking.

For Stone and his colleagues, then, negotiators should adopt a "learning stance" and attempt to have "learning conversations" where the goal is to understand, not dispute with, the other side.

3.   Emotions often cause the people problems that arise in negotiation. In *Beyond Reason: Using Emotions as You Negotiate*, Fisher and his co-author, Daniel Shapiro, develop and propose a framework for addressing emotions at the negotiating table. In the following article excerpt, Shapiro explains the various ways in which emotion can influence negotiation and summarizes the "core concerns" framework he and Fisher have developed for dealing with them:

DANIEL L. SHAPIRO, TEACHING STUDENTS HOW TO USE EMOTIONS AS THEY NEGOTIATE

22 Negot. J. 105, 106–7 (2006)

[E]motions are:

- **Unavoidable:** A negotiator cannot avoid emotions any more than he or she can avoid thoughts. Suppressing the expression of emotions tends to consume mental resources, affect the cardiovascular system, and, surprisingly, even lead to increased blood pressure in one's social partner.

- **Numerous:** In any single interaction, a negotiator may experience dozens of emotions such as anger, pride, frustration, and enthusiasm.

- **Fluid:** Emotions often change from moment to moment such as from annoyance to anger, excitement to anxiety, resignation to resentment.

- **Multilayered:** You can feel multiple emotions at once—even multiple "opposite emotions" such as love for your spouse and anger toward him or her for not consulting you on an important issue.

- **Varied in impact:** The impact of emotions varies from person to person, negotiator to negotiator. (Person A may be angered easily, while Person B may be more even-keeled.)

- **Triggered by multiple possible causes:** The source of an emotion is not always easy to identify. The emotion may be triggered by a thought, a new situation, another person's action, or by the levels of specific neurochemicals present in the negotiator's brain.

* * *

In *Beyond Reason*, we suggest a simple framework for circumventing the complexities of emotion. We suggest that negotiators *not* focus on every emotion that arises in themselves and in the other party—such a process is overwhelming. Rather, we advise negotiators to turn their attention to five *core concerns*, matters that are important to most of us much of the time. These core concerns can be used as a "lens" to understand the emotional terrain in a negotiation and as a "lever" to stimulate helpful emotions. As a result, cooperative behavior becomes more likely.

The five core concerns we have considered in depth are appreciation, autonomy, affiliation, status, and role. Each is a dimensional concept:

- **Appreciation:** Are our thoughts, feelings, and actions devalued, or are they acknowledged as having merit?

- **Autonomy:** Is our freedom to make decisions impinged upon, or is it respected?

- **Affiliation:** Are we treated as an adversary and kept at a distance, or are we treated as a colleague?

- **Status:** Is our standing treated as inferior to others, or is it given full recognition where deserved?

- **Role:** Are the many roles we play meaningless, or are they personally fulfilling?

. . . [W]e suggest that instructors and students concentrate on learning how to use these five core concerns as both lenses and as levers.

NOTES AND QUESTIONS

1.   Recall a dispute with one other person in which you are currently or were recently involved. Which of your core concerns were unsatisfied? How did that manifest in emotions? Which of the other person's core concerns were unsatisfied? How did that manifest in emotions?

2.   Fisher and Shapiro recommend that a negotiator strive to develop positive emotions (which would foster better negotiation), by expressing appreciation; building affiliation; fostering autonomy; acknowledging status; and developing meaningful roles. Might any such moves have been helpful in the conflict you recalled?

3.   How might the core concerns construct help one deal with a conflict between long-time business partners whose working and personal relationships have deteriorated to the point that they cannot communicate directly, even though they share an office? See Leonard L. Riskin, *Annual Saltman Lecture: Further Beyond Reason: Mindfulness, Emotions, and the Core Concerns in Negotiation*, 10 Nev. L.J. 289–337 (2010). For a discussion of how the core concerns could fit into the problem-definition in the mediation context, see Leonard L. Riskin & Nancy A. Welsh, *Is That All There Is?: "The Problem" in Court–Oriented Mediation*, 15 Geo. Mason L. Rev. 863–932 (2008).

4.   What are the sources of our core concerns? For the suggestion that, some core concerns might be associated with "subpersonalitities" or "parts" of our personalities, see Leonard L. Riskin, *Managing Inner and Outer Conflict: Selves, Subpersonalities, and Internal Family Systems*, 18 Harv. Negot. L. Rev. 1 (2013).

b.   "Focus on Interests" (Asking)

Problem-solving negotiators focus on interests rather than positions in negotiation. As we discussed in Chapter I, *supra*, interests are a negotiator's underlying needs, wants, fears, and motivations; positions are the negotiator's translation of those interests into particular demands or offers. In a personal injury dispute, for instance, a plaintiff might demand $500,000 to settle the case (her position). The plaintiff may have adopted that position in order to satisfy such interests as paying her medical bills, obtaining a measure of financial security, receiving some vindication for the pain she has suffered, and so on. In short, interests are a negotiator's *ends*, while the position she adopts is merely one *means* of obtaining those ends:

> Before entering a negotiation, one needs to be clear what it is that one seeks from the deal. Although this may appear to be simple, most knowledgeable observers suggest that it is not. Goals determination

involves more than describing a desired end position; it also requires assessing why one seeks a particular goal or goals. As Roger Fisher and William Ury, in their classic exposition on negotiation, *Getting to Yes*, so insightfully observe, those who negotiate over positions without focusing on the underlying interests behind the positions, create enormous and unnecessary obstacles to reaching effective agreements. Identifying and sharing interests with one's opponent injects a substantial degree of flexibility into a negotiation because there are typically a number of ways to satisfy interests, many of which both sides find completely compatible. For example, two sides that vie for a tract of land may find that one wants it for logging purposes and the other to convert it into a pasture for raising livestock. In this case, the parties should be able to accommodate each other's interests without substantial conflict. Unless they reveal their interests to one another, however, they may never get past their competing positions.

Robert S. Adler & Elliot M. Silverstein, *When David Meets Goliath: Dealing with Power Differentials in Negotiations*, 5 Harv. Negot. L. Rev. 1, 62–63 (2000).

1. Open and Closed Questions

Negotiators often become so caught up in the positions they are advancing that they neglect to identify their own interests and to elicit their counterparts' interests. To identify interests, negotiators need to become skilled questioners and information gatherers.

As we saw in Chapter II, there are two basic types of questions: open and closed. Negotiators ask open questions to elicit broad information. For example, "what do you hope to accomplish?" or "what can we do for you?" or "what will enable us to put this deal together?" are examples of open questions.

Negotiators ask closed questions to discover more specific information and to clarify their understanding of previously elicited information. Some closed questions are subject-specific—for example, "what are your client's medical bills?" Other closed questions call for yes-no answers—for example, "has your client incurred any medical bills?" is a yes-no question. Finally, some closed questions seek to lead one's counterpart to a particular answer—for example, "your client has incurred $10,000 in medical bills, right?" is a leading question.

Fisher, Ury & Patton contend that two questions, in particular, are likely to help negotiators uncover their own and their counterparts' interests in negotiation: "why?" and "why not?" Consider the following excerpt:

ROGER FISHER, WILLIAM URY & BRUCE PATTON, GETTING TO YES: NEGOTIATING AGREEMENT WITHOUT GIVING IN

44 (2d ed. 1991)

The benefit of looking behind positions for interests is clear. How to go about it is less clear. A position is likely to be concrete and explicit; the interests underlying it may well be unexpressed, intangible, and perhaps inconsistent. How do you go about understanding the interests involved in a negotiation, remembering that figuring out *their* interests will be at least as important as figuring out *yours*?

Ask "Why?" One basic technique is to put yourself in their shoes. Examine each position they take, and ask yourself "Why?" Why, for instance, does your landlord prefer to fix the rent—in a five-year lease—year by year? The answer you may come up with, to be protected against increasing costs, is probably one of his interests. You can also ask the landlord himself why he takes a particular position. If you do, make clear that you are asking not for justification of this position, but for an understanding of the needs, hopes, fears, or desires that it serves. "What's your basic concern, Mr. Jones, in wanting the lease to run for no more than three years?"

Ask "Why not?" Think about their choice. One of the most useful ways to uncover interests is first to identify the basic decision that those on the other side probably see you asking them for, and then to ask yourself why they have not made that decision. What interests of theirs stand in the way? If you are trying to change their minds, the starting point is to figure out where their minds are now.

NOTES

1.   When asking "why" and "why not," it is important to use a tone that is exploratory, inquisitive, and non-accusatory. If asked in the wrong way, these questions might put your counterpart on the defensive. Consider how you will convey the appropriate tone if you are using email to negotiate.

2.   In the following excerpt, Professors Deepak Malhotra and Max Bazerman provide a concrete illustration of how asking the question "why" can facilitate information-gathering about interests:

DEEPAK MALHOTRA & MAX H. BAZERMAN, INVESTIGATIVE NEGOTIATION

Harv. Bus. Rev. 73, 74–75 (September 2007)

Consider the dilemma facing Richard Holbrooke in late 2000, when he was the U.S. ambassador to the United Nations. At the time, the United States was more than $1 billion in arrears to the UN but was unwilling to pay it unless the UN agreed to a variety of reforms. As a result, U.S. representatives were being sidelined in UN committee meetings, and the country faced losing its vote in the General Assembly. Meanwhile, U.S. senators were calling for a withdrawal from the organization.

Why the turmoil? For decades the United States had paid 25% of the regular UN budget. Believing that was too large a share, Congress decided to hold the $1 billion hostage until the UN agreed to, among other changes, reduce the U.S. assessment from 25% to 22% of the budget. The other UN member states saw this as a nefarious tactic.

Ambassador Holbrooke faced a tough challenge. According to UN regulations, a change in the allocation of dues needed the approval of all 189 members. What's more, a hard deadline was fast approaching. The Helms–Biden bill, which had appropriated close to $1 billion to cover much of what the United States owed, stipulated that if a deal was not struck by January 1, 2001, the money would disappear from the federal budget.

Holbrooke's team had hoped that Japan and some European countries would absorb most of the U.S. reductions. Unfortunately, the Japanese (who were already the second-highest contributors) rejected that idea outright. The Europeans also balked. How could Holbrooke break the impasse?

With the clock ticking, he and his team decided to concentrate less on persuading member states of the need for change and more on better understanding their perspectives. Whenever a member resisted an increase, Holbrooke, instead of arguing, would push further to discover precisely why it could not (or would not) pay more. Soon, one entirely unanticipated reason became salient: Many countries that might otherwise agree to increase their contributions did not have room to do so in their 2001 budgets, because they had already been finalized. The January 1 deadline was making the deal unworkable.

This new understanding of the problem gave rise to a possible solution. Holbrooke's proposal was to immediately reduce U.S. assessments from 25% to 22% to meet Congress's deadline but delay the increase in contributions from other nations until 2002. (The 2001 shortfall was covered by CNN founder and philanthropist Ted Turner, who agreed to make a onetime personal contribution of $34 million to the UN.) The key to resolving the conflict, however, was discovering that the dispute entailed not one issue but two: the timing of assessments as well as their size. Once the negotiators broadened their focus to include the issue of the timing, they could strike a deal that allowed each side to get what it wanted on the issue it cared about most.

2. Knowing What We Want

The advice to focus on interests assumes that negotiators are able to identify what it is they want to get out of a negotiation. When asked why they want something, negotiators are expected to know this (even if they choose not to disclose it). But is this as easy as it sounds? As discussed in Chapter II, *supra*, research regarding the impact bias indicates that people can make accurate predictions about their general preferences, but they may miscalculate exactly how happy they will be or how long their happiness will last. This is likely to be particularly true for "one-shot" negotiators. See Chris Guthrie & David F. Sally, *Miswanting* in The Negotiator's Fieldbook 277–78 (Schneider & Honeyman, eds., 2006).

Professor David Matz has also identified four reasons why it may be difficult for a negotiator (or a mediator) to really "know" the other party's interests:

> First, parties have an incentive to lie. As almost all disputes have a significant, often dominant, distributive aspect, parties can rationally conclude that sharing their interests with their negotiating opponent can be detrimental to their cause. This incentive to lie, while often lamented, is well documented.

> * * *

> Second, * * * a further disadvantage in knowing a party's interests [is that a] demand as expressed . . . can "stand for" a variety of interests. Almost all the interests . . . , for example, can be expressed as money. Compounding the difficulty of knowing which interests are "real" is the fact that it is more culturally acceptable to express some interests than others (e.g. money is acceptable, vengeance is not).

> Third, most parties in disputes are not isolated negotiators. They have constituencies, "second tables," organizational contexts, or significant others. Any of these influences may be part of the negotiator's concerns, an audience to which she will later have to appeal. * * * Moreover, if the negotiator is representing an organization, the interests within that group may be unfocused, conflicted, or evolving. The classic line "I'd love to but my boss won't let me," captures the . . . problem well. Is the boss real or a dodge? An interest or a convenience?

> The final source of difficulty is the hardest to describe, but it is also perhaps the most important. Conventionally, a party has interests in the same sense that she has car keys: they are objective, discrete things. Moreover, in this view, the party has, at least vaguely, a sense of their order of importance to her, and it is the mediator's job to help the party list those interests and articulate or

change their priority. This picture seems to me inaccurate. The interests of a party are much more like a kaleidoscope than they are like a collection of discrete things. The surface clarity, the publicly stated "position," masks an active fluidity. There are in the kaleidoscope some recognizable elements, but the boundaries among the elements keep shifting. * * * This change may result from a party's strategic sense of what to emphasize and downplay; it may result from the party's changing realization of what is important to the other side or to herself; and it may result from the interplay of power between the parties which influences their sense of what is possible in the negotiation.

David E. Matz, *Ignorance and Interests*, 4 Harv. Negot. L. Rev. 59, 63–65 (1999)

NOTES AND QUESTIONS

1.   Professor Matz goes on to suggest that because a party's understanding of her interests should be understood as "fluid," it is wise to continue to probe for such interests throughout the mediation (or negotiation) process: "Though this fluidity might reflect an inadequate preparation [by the party, or negotiator] . . . it could also reflect a healthy open-mindedness, a willingness to use the mediation [or negotiation] process to distinguish the possible from the not-possible. Thus, even when a party comes to the table with a well thought out list of needs and priorities, the power of the process may well—and often must, if a settlement is to be made—revise not only the priorities, but the contents of the items on the list." *Id.*

2.   Do you agree with Matz' assessment of the subjectivity and fluidity of interests, or would you say they are more objectively determinable?

3.   Fully understanding our own client's interests, much less those of the other negotiator and his client, can be extremely challenging. What does it take to achieve this task? To the extent that conflict often tends to evoke emotions, what impact are such emotions likely to have on our ability to understand and advance our interests? Consider how your behavior in negotiation may reduce—or enhance—the other negotiator's sense of conflict, emotional reaction, and ability and willingness to identify and share emotions. See the earlier discussion of the relationships among negotiator style, procedural justice and the uncovering of integrative potential, *supra*.

4.   Can you uncover the other party's interests without asking about them directly? Can the other party's reactions to your proposals signal the existence and priority of underlying interests? Cross-cultural negotiation research suggests that negotiators from high context cultures are more skilled at discerning their counterparts' interests from their responses to a sequence of proposals. *See* Wendi Lyn Adair & Jeanne M. Brett, *Culture and Negotiation Processes, in* THE HANDBOOK OF NEGOTIATION AND CULTURE 168–69 (Michele J. Gelfand & Jeanne M. Brett eds., 2004).

3. Creating Value Through Differences

Problem-solving negotiation theorists encourage negotiators to try to uncover each other's interests in order to "create value" in negotiation. Negotiators can create value by capitalizing on "shared" interests. Divorcing spouses, for example, are likely to share an interest in the physical, emotional, and mental well-being of their children, and they may be able to use this shared interest to construct a value-creating divorce settlement.

Less intuitively, though perhaps more importantly, negotiators can also create value by capitalizing on "different" or "conflicting" interests. Consider the following excerpt:

ROBERT H. MNOOKIN, SCOTT R. PEPPET & ANDREW S. TULUMELLO, BEYOND WINNING: NEGOTIATING TO CREATE VALUE IN DEALS AND DISPUTES*
14–15 (2000)

The notion that differences can create value is counter-intuitive to many negotiators, who believe that they can reach agreement only by finding common ground. But the truth is that differences are often more useful than similarities in helping parties reach a deal. Differences set the stage for possible gains from trade, and it is through trades that value is most commonly created. Consider the following five types of differences:

Different Resources: In the simplest example, two parties may simply trade resources. A vegetarian with a chicken and a carnivore with a large vegetable garden may find it useful to swap what they have. . . .

Different Relative Valuations: Even if both parties have chickens and vegetables, and both prefer chicken to some extent, they can still make useful trades. To put it in economic terms, if the two parties attach different *relative* valuations to the goods in question, trades should occur that make both better off. The party who more strongly prefers chicken to vegetables should be willing to pay a high enough price—in terms of vegetables—to induce the other party to give up at least some of her chickens.

Different Forecasts: Parties may have different beliefs about what the future will hold. In the entertainment industry, for example, performers, agents, and concert halls often have different predictions about the likelihood of various attendance levels. Performers are often convinced of their ability to draw huge crowds, while concert halls may be much less sanguine. By trading on these different forecasts—perhaps through contingent fee arrangements—the parties can resolve these differences to mutual advantage. A singer who expects to draw a standing-room-only

---

crowd might agree to a guaranteed fee based on 80 percent attendance, plus a percentage of any profits earned from higher attendance. Such arrangements allow the parties to place bets on their different beliefs about the future.

Different Risk Preferences: Even if the parties have identical forecasts about a particular event, they might not be equally risk-tolerant with regard to that event. My life insurance company and I might have similar expectations about what the odds are that someone my age will die within the next year. But we will probably have very different risk preferences regarding that possibility. I will be risk-averse, knowing that my family will face financial hardship if I die. Therefore, I might pay the insurance company to absorb that risk. The insurance company, by pooling my risk with the risk of others, can offer me insurance based on costs averaged over the entire pool. In effect, I have shifted the risk of my early demise to the more efficient risk carrier—the insurance company. Negotiators often create value in this way. A car buyer might purchase an extended warranty, or a start-up company might sell shares to a wealthy investor in exchange for needed capital. In each case, by allocating risk to the more risk-tolerant party for an acceptable price, the parties create a more beneficial agreement.

Different Time Preferences: Negotiators often value issues of timing differently—when an event will occur or a payment will be made. For example, a law school graduate and his wife fell in love with a condominium in Washington, D.C. Because he was going to be clerking for a federal judge for two years, his salary during that time was not sufficient to cover the mortgage payments. After the clerkship, however, he knew that he would be joining a large D.C. law firm, at more than twice his clerkship salary. He could then easily afford the house. The solution lay in structuring a mortgage schedule so that there were small payments for the first two years—less than even the interest costs—and larger payments thereafter. Although he had to pay a premium for agreeing to this tiered payment schedule, in the meantime he was able to "afford" his dream home.

* * *

These five types of differences—in resources, relative valuations, forecasts, risk preferences, and time preferences—are all potential sources of value creation. They all support the same basic principal: trades can create value.

NOTES

1. A value-creating deal seeks to approach a "Pareto-efficient" outcome, i.e., one in which the negotiated deal, "when compared to other possible *negotiated* outcomes, either makes both parties better off or makes

one party better off without making the other party worse off." *Id.* at 12. A "Pareto-optimal" outcome is one in which both parties end up as well off as they possibly can.

2. Despite the widespread endorsement of the problem-solving approach in negotiation, some scholars have questioned theorists' contention that integrative opportunities are as abundant as suggested. *See, e.g.,* Russell Korobkin, *A Positive Theory of Legal Negotiation*, 88 Geo. L.J. 1789 (2000); Gerald Wetlaufer, *The Limits of Integrative Bargaining*, 85 Geo. L.J. 369 (1996).

3. Certainly, full-blown problem-solving negotiation is not possible in every situation. After all, not every issue or relationship merits the amount of time and other resources required to engage in a thorough review of interests and development of options. But you might be surprised.

Imagine you are beginning a negotiation with a negotiation counterpart you do not know, and have to decide whether to invest any time or energy in using any of the techniques associated with problem-solving negotiation. The procedural justice research suggests it may be worthwhile to invest at least some energy in procedurally just negotiation behaviors, such as providing the other negotiator with the opportunity for voice, demonstrating sincere and trustworthy consideration, treating the other negotiator in an open-minded and dignified manner.

One study, for example, found that such behaviors did not have a negative impact on a negotiator's distributive outcomes when there was no integrative potential, but did lead to information disclosure that allowed for the maximization of joint gains when there was integrative potential. In other words, there were no distributive downsides to using procedurally just negotiation behaviors in terms of worse outcomes, but there were upsides in terms of better outcomes. Moreover, the authors say their results suggest that "using fair procedures is one way to move beyond the fixed-pie bias and facilitate the development of integrative bargaining. Similarly, using fair procedures helps to prevent one of the parties in bilateral negotiation from hogging the whole surplus that integrative bargaining creates." Rebecca Hollander–Blumoff & Tom R. Tyler, *Procedural Justice in Negotiation: Procedural Fairness, Outcome Acceptance, and Integrative Potential*, 33 Law and Social Inquiry 473, 490 (2008); *see also,* Rebecca Hollander–Blumoff, *Just Negotiation*, 88 Wash. U. L. Rev. 381 (2010).

c. "Consider a Variety of Options" (Inventing)

Negotiators using the problem-solving approach seek to generate a variety of options in negotiation to increase the likelihood they have mutually attractive options from which to choose. Consider the following excerpt by Professor Menkel–Meadow:

Carrie Menkel–Meadow, Aha? Is Creativity Possible in Legal Problem Solving and Teaching in Legal Education?

6 Harv. Negot. L. Rev. 97, 109–11 (2001)

One can structure a problem solving approach to negotiation by focusing on a three step process in which first, the lawyer identifies multiple classes of needs, objectives, interests or goals from one's own client. Then, s/he proceeds to do the same for other parties involved, using information available from public knowledge, research, client knowledge and from the negotiation session. Finally, the negotiator examines and matches loci of complementary and then conflicting needs and interests of the parties, in a systematic way, in order to craft solutions that maximize joint gain or Pareto-optimal solutions. . . .

* * *

Often a solution to a negotiated problem may be illuminated by exploring the characteristics of the "problem" mapped over parties' particular needs and interests. WHAT is the problem about? (What is the res? What is at stake? Can the thing itself be altered in any way?) WHO is involved? Are there stakeholders other than the parties formally at the table? Does adding parties facilitate a solution, or, as in the case of bringing in an insurer, does one increase those who can contribute to a solution, or, as in the case of the IRS, which is always a party to a legal negotiation, do tax concerns change the dynamics and suggest other solutions? WHERE is the transaction/dispute/res located? Does jurisdiction matter for the problem? What about the location is alterable? (e.g. employment disputes with multiple offices or government agencies can offer transfer opportunities). WHEN does the dispute or transaction have to be resolved? This factor has led to the important and structural solutions of annuity payments in tort cases, installment payment contracts, contingency pricing and risk allocations, as well as continuing options, accelerated or graduated payments and duties and a whole host of substantive time-based solutions for trials, contingencies and terminable-upon-conditions arrangements. HOW may the matter be negotiated? Must solutions be conventional payments of money? Are other more creative solutions possible? In-kind trades? Apologies? Percentage of gross or net, instead of fixed sums? Contingent agreements? Secured obligations? Guarantors? Third party reviews? Can dispute resolution procedures themselves be altered? These framing questions for legal solutions to negotiated problems are a way of increasing the resources available for solving problems and probing for non-obvious solutions.

Note and Questions

1.   Contingent agreements, mentioned above, represent a means for "genuinely held disagreements about the future" to generate "an important

opportunity for negotiators to discover an attractive exchange." Michael L. Moffitt, *Contingent Agreements*, in THE NEGOTIATOR'S FIELDBOOK 455 (Schneider & Honeyman, eds., 2006). As Dean Moffitt notes, "[t]he simplest contingent deals are those in which the future has only two possible relevant conditions. X will happen, or it will not. If X happens, the terms of our deal are ABD; if not, we will do DEF." *Id.* Negotiators can provide for incentives to increase the likelihood that X will occur; they can also agree upon contingent sanctions. Agreements can include variable terms, like an interest rate that fluctuates based on a mutually-selected benchmark.

While contingent arrangements can be helpful, Dean Moffitt warns that certain types of contingent agreements can create conditions of moral hazard, in which one party is able to behave in a manner that will adversely affect the other party's ability to gain the benefit of the contingent agreement. For example: "Moral hazard arises when, toward the end of the season, a team notices that the athlete is only a few points away from the triggering contingent event. Will the team structure its play to enable the athlete to achieve the statistical goal, or will the prospect of this contingent payment encourage the team's management to focus its efforts on a different player during the remaining games?" *Id.* at 457. Clearly, it is important for negotiators to consider the potential for moral hazard in any contingent agreement. They may choose to include provisions for transparency and disclosure (i.e., "trust but verify").

2.   A wrongdoer may consider another option that will provide vindication to an injured party and increase the chances that a reasonable financial settlement offer will be accepted: Apologize. See Professor Jennifer Robbennolt's empirical research, regarding apologies' effect on settlement decisionmaking, when this chapter turns specifically to negotiated settlements *infra*.

3.   One way that negotiators using the problem-solving strategy can generate options is through the brainstorming process we introduced in Chapter II. In this process, negotiators generate as many options as possible, without judging them. Should parties brainstorm prior to negotiation as a way of preparing for the negotiation? Should they brainstorm with their counterparts at the bargaining table? Both?

4.   Does brainstorming work in the real world? Consider the following excerpt, which describes brainstorming sessions organized by Nathan Myhrvold, a former Microsoft executive who recently founded a company called Intellectual Ventures (I.V.) to generate, patent, and license ideas and products:

> How useful is it to have a group of really smart people brainstorm for a day? When Myhrvold started out, his expectations were modest. Although he wanted insights like Alexander Graham Bell's, Bell was clearly one in a million, a genius who went on to have ideas in an extraordinary number of areas—sound recording, flight, lasers, tetrahedral construction, and hydrofoil boats, to name a few. The

telephone was his obsession. He approached it from a unique perspective, that of a speech therapist. He had put in years of preparation before that moment by the Grand River, and it was impossible to know what unconscious associations triggered his great insight. Invention was its own algorithm: genius, obsession, serendipity, and epiphany in some unknowable combination. How can you put that in a bottle?

But then, in August of 2003, I.V. held its first invention session, and it was a revelation. "Afterward, Nathan kept saying, 'There are *so* many inventions,'" Wood [Myhrvold's friend and colleague, Lowell Wood] recalled. "'He thought if we came up with a half-dozen good ideas it would be great, and we came up with somewhere between fifty and a hundred. I said to him, 'But you had eight people in that room who are seasoned inventors. Weren't you expecting a multiplier effect?' And he said, 'Yeah, but it was more than multiplicity.' Not even Nathan had any idea of what it was going to be like."

The original expectation was that I.V. would file a hundred patents a year. Currently, it's filing five hundred a year. It has a backlog of three thousand ideas. Wood said that he once attended a two-day invention session presided over by Jung [Myhrvold's friend and colleague, Edward Jung], and after the first day the group went out to dinner. "So Edward took his people out, plus me," Wood said. "And the eight of us sat down at a table and the attorney said, 'Do you mind if I record the evening?' And we all said no, of course not. We sat there. It was a long dinner. I thought we were lightly chewing the rag. But the next day the attorney comes up with eight single-spaced pages flagging thirty-six different inventions from dinner. *Dinner*."

Malcolm Gladwell, *In the Air*, THE NEW YORKER 50, 54 (May 12, 2008).

5.   What are the advantages of option-generation processes like brainstorming?

6.   Do you see any potential drawbacks? Dean Chris Guthrie observes:

[R]ational models of choice assume that negotiators will assign a subjective value to each option based solely on the characteristics of that option, rank-order the options in the choice set, and then select the one they should prefer. Rational models assume, in other words, that irrelevant options or irrelevant characteristics of a set of options will *not* induce negotiators to select an option other than the one they most prefer. Unfortunately, however, this assumption is often wrong because the addition of options to a choice set can induce negotiators to make non-value-maximizing decisions. Specifically, the addition of options can give rise to four phenomena that tend to occur in the following order:

The first phenomenon arises when a choice set grows from one option to two or more options. When a choice set expands from the original option under consideration to more than one option, negotiators tend to devalue the initial option (assuming that the options in the set have both advantages and disadvantages relative to one another). Thus, the first option cost the Article explores below is *option devaluation.*

The second phenomenon arises when a choice set consisting of two or more options grows by one. When an option is added to a choice set consisting of two or more options, negotiators tend to reconsider their relative ranking of the options already under consideration even when the additional option sheds no new light on those options. Negotiators do *not*, in other words, make context-*in*dependent decisions. Thus, the second option cost the Article explores below is *context dependence.*

The third phenomenon arises when a choice set grows to include a large number of options, perhaps ten, fifteen, or twenty options. When a choice set includes a large number of options, negotiators tend to abandon compensatory decision-making strategies that take all options and attributes into account in favor of simplified decision strategies that consider only some of the available information. Thus, the third option cost the Article explores below is *non-compensatory* or *partial decision making.*

The fourth and final phenomenon arises after the decision has been made. Following a decision, negotiators tend to feel greater regret when they have selected one option over another than when they have simply selected the sole available option. Thus, the fourth option cost the Article explores below is *decision regret.*

Although the prescriptive literature on negotiation is certainly correct that option generation offers potential benefits to negotiators, the four phenomena identified above and described below suggest that option generation poses potential costs as well. Negotiators who generate multiple options may be induced by the very availability of those options to make decisions that run contrary to their true preferences and that induce negative post-decision emotions.

Chris Guthrie, *Panacea or Pandora's Box? The Costs of Options in Negotiation*, 88 Iowa L. Rev. 601, 607–08 (2003).

d.   "Insist on Outcomes Tied to Objective Criteria" (Referencing)

The problem-solving strategy advises negotiators to tie their proposed outcomes to legitimate, objective criteria, like fair market value, precedent, professional standards, and the like. Rather than rely solely on pressure to persuade their counterparts to reach agreement, negotiators appeal to principle. In the following excerpt, Professor Shell explains why negotiators can benefit by tying their proposed outcomes to legitimate, objective criteria.

G. RICHARD SHELL, BARGAINING FOR ADVANTAGE: NEGOTIATION STRATEGIES FOR REASONABLE PEOPLE
43–44 (2d ed. 2006)

Why are standards and norms—particularly standards the other side has adopted—such an important part of bargaining? Because, all else being equal, people like to be seen as consistent and rational in the way they make decisions.

Psychologists have a name for this need-to-appear-reasonable phenomenon. They call it "the consistency principle." Social psychologists have discovered that people have a deep need to avoid the disjointed, erratic, and uncomfortable psychological states that arise when our actions are manifestly inconsistent with previously expressed, long-held, or widely shared standards and beliefs.

Most of us have complex "consistency webs" that are interconnected at many levels of our personality. Because we like to keep these webs intact, we rationalize our actions so they appear (at least in our own eyes) to be consistent with our prior beliefs. We are also more open to persuasion when we see a proposed course of action as being consistent with a course we have already adopted.

Negotiations are fertile ground for observing the consistency principle at work. Whether we are aware of it or not, we sometimes feel a tug to agree with the other party when the standards or norms he or she articulates are consistent with prior statements and positions we ourselves have taken. We also feel uncomfortable (though we may keep this to ourselves) when the other side correctly points out that we have been inconsistent in one of our positions or arguments. In short, standards and norms are—or can be—more than just intellectual pawns in bargaining debates. They can be strong, motivating factors in the way negotiations proceed.

QUESTION

What should negotiators using the problem-solving strategy do when they disagree over the appropriate objective criterion to use to resolve a particular issue in negotiation? The authors of *Getting to Yes* argue that, "When each party is advancing a different standard, look for an objective basis for deciding between them, such as which standard has been used by the parties in the past or which standard is more widely applied. Just as the substantive issue itself should not be settled on the basis of will, neither should the question of which standard applies." ROGER FISHER, WILLIAM URY & BRUCE PATTON, GETTING TO YES: NEGOTIATING AGREEMENT WITHOUT GIVING IN 89–90 (2d ed. 1991).

e.   The BATNA and Power in Negotiation

As we discussed briefly in Chapter II, *supra*, objective criteria provide negotiators with some power in negotiation. So, too, does the negotiator's "best alternative to a negotiated agreement," or BATNA. As Professor Fisher, and Mssrs. Ury and Patton put it, "People think of negotiating power as being determined by resources like wealth, political connections, physical strength, friends, and military might. In fact, the relative negotiating power of two parties depends primarily upon how attractive to each is the option of not reaching agreement." *Id.* at 102.

For example, it is fairly easily understood that one has more power in a job interview if her or she already has another other job or offer. But the same principle obtains in less obvious situations. Consider, for example, that you want to buy a 60–inch high-definition 3D LCD television. You go into your nearby box store and find just what you are looking for at a cost of $2,999, plus installation kit. You can give yourself additional power in the negotiation with the store by learning how much you would pay if you purchased the item elsewhere, such as through an online retailer. If you have a cell phone with a bar code scanning application, you can also quickly determine the price that a nearby store charges for the same TV, and then exercise your power by asking the retailer if it will match the price you found elsewhere.

In the following excerpt, Professor Korobkin offers the important observation that it is one's *perceived* BATNA, as opposed to one's *actual* BATNA, that is the true source of power in negotiation.

> Strictly speaking, it is not the actual, objective quality of the negotiator's BATNA that determines his degree of bargaining power, but what the counterpart believes that the negotiator believes about the quality of his BATNA. For example, when an employee receives a job offer from a competing firm and asks his boss for a raise, whether the employee has power depends on whether the boss believes that the employee believes it is in the employee's best interest to accept the competing offer if the demand for a raise is not met. The credibility of the employee's threat to walk away from the negotiation and accept the competing offer if his demand is not met is unaffected by the fact that neither the boss nor any of the employee's colleagues would prefer the competing offer to the employee's current job at his current salary. Where power is concerned, the beauty of a BATNA is in the eye of the beholder, and eccentricity is not penalized as long as it is perceived to be genuine. The employee's threat of impasse will be credible to the boss, thus giving the employee power, even if the employee himself actually would not prefer the competing offer, so long as the boss thinks the employee would prefer that offer.

> An objectively strong BATNA is helpful, of course, because a BATNA that appears strong renders the negotiator's claim that he

believes his BATNA is strong more credible. The employee's threat of impasse will more likely translate into bargaining power if his competing job offer is a $300,000 per year CEO position than if it is a $15,000 per year mailroom attendant position. But either a phantom BATNA (i.e., a nonexistent alternative) or a real BATNA with phantom *value* (i.e., an existent but undesirable alternative) can be a source of power in the hands of a persuasive negotiator.

Russell Korobkin, *Bargaining Power as Threat of Impasse*, 87 Marq. L. Rev. 867, 869–70 (2004).

NOTE

1. In the transactional context, you will determine your BATNA (or your "perceived" BATNA) by looking at your "comparables"—e.g., other acceptable houses in the neighborhood in which you wish to live, other acceptable positions in the sorts of firms you wish to join, other potential business partners for the commercial venture you hope to start. Of course, you will need to determine the cost of achieving your BATNA. For example, if the house requires $60,000 in repairs, you must add that amount to the purchase price of the house. If the job will require you to move, you must consider the financial cost of the move and perhaps the emotional cost of leaving friends and family behind. Your BATNA, supplemented by these transactional costs that are required to achieve your BATNA, will determine your "walkaway point" or "reservation point." Notice we have used the term "point" rather than "price." That is because your reservation point, just like your BATNA, may include both monetary and non-monetary items.

2. In the litigation context, your BATNA is generally going to trial—and this is so even though we have already shared with you how infrequently cases go to trial. You will need to determine the likely value of trial in order to know when to walk away from a settlement offer. In other words, you will need to determine the "expected value" of settlement. We discuss "expected value" in Chapter II. We will discuss it a bit more, *infra*, when we examine litigation settlement more closely:

3. Despite the importance of this concept, the BATNA is not the only source of power available to a negotiator who is using the problem solving approach. *See, e.g.*, ROGER FISHER, WILLIAM URY & BRUCE PATTON, GETTING TO YES: NEGOTIATING AGREEMENT WITHOUT GIVING IN 177–87 (2d ed. 1991) (responding to questions about power in principled negotiation); Roger Fisher, *Negotiating Power: Getting and Using Influence*, 27 Am. Behav. Scientist 149 (1983) (proposing six different sources of power in negotiation: possessing negotiating skill, a thorough knowledge of relevant facts and issues, a good working relationship involving trust and effective mutual communication, a good BATNA, and a negotiation position that is overtly fair or in accordance with law and legal precedent; authoring an elegant solution to the conflict that equally benefits the parties; and specifying what one is willing or unwilling to do, thus establishing parameters for negotiation).

4. We can think of power in negotiation as the ability to get what we want. *See, e.g.*, Peter T. Coleman, *Power and Conflict,* in THE HANDBOOK OF CONFLICT RESOLUTION (Morton Deutsch, Peter T. Coleman & Eric C. Marcus eds., 2nd ed. 2006). A related concept is leverage—that is, the ability to use power or the situation to your advantage in a negotiation. Professor Shell offers the following easy-to-remember test to assess which party has more leverage in a negotiation:

> *Ask yourself, as of the moment when you make the assessment, which party has the most to lose from no deal. The party with the most to lose has the least leverage; the party with the least to lose has the most leverage; and both parties have roughly equal leverage when they both stand to lose equivalent amounts should the deal fall through.*

G. RICHARD SHELL, BARGAINING FOR ADVANTAGE: NEGOTIATION STRATEGIES FOR REASONABLE PEOPLE 105 (2ND ED. 2006) (emphasis in original).

f.   Critiques of the Problem-Solving Approach

Now that you know the two primary theoretical approaches to negotiation and the strategies and tactics that accompany them, which approach would you prefer to use as a general matter? Under what circumstances are you more likely to prefer one over the other? When would you, by necessity, employ some combination of the two approaches? This section critically explores each approach to enable you to make better-informed decisions about which to employ or when to favor one approach over the other.

In the following exchange—which occurred after the first edition of GETTING TO YES was published—Professors James White and Roger Fisher debate the relative merits of adversarial and problem-solving approaches.

JAMES J. WHITE, THE PROS AND CONS OF "GETTING TO YES"
34 J. Legal Educ. 115–16 (1984)

GETTING TO YES is a puzzling book. On the one hand it offers a forceful and persuasive criticism of much traditional negotiating behavior. It suggests a variety of negotiating techniques that are both clever and likely to facilitate effective negotiation. On the other hand, the authors seem to deny the existence of a significant part of the negotiation process, and to oversimplify or explain away many of the most troublesome problems inherent in the art and practice of negotiation. The book is frequently naive, occasionally self-righteous, but often helpful.

* * *

The book's thesis is well summarized by the following passage:

> Behind opposed positions lie shared and compatible interests, as well
> as conflicting ones. We tend to assume that because the other side's
> positions are opposed to ours, their interests must also be opposed. If
> we have an interest in defending ourselves, then they must want to
> attack us. If we have an interest in minimizing the rent, then their
> interest must be to maximize it. In many negotiations, however, a
> close examination of the underlying interests will reveal the
> existence of many more interests that are shared or compatible than
> ones that are opposed (p. 43).

This point is useful for all who teach or think about negotiation. The
tendency of those deeply involved in negotiation or its teaching is
probably to exaggerate the importance of negotiation on issues where the
parties are diametrically opposed and to ignore situations where the
parties' interests are compatible. By emphasizing that fact, and by
making a clear articulation of the importance of cooperation, imagination,
and the search for alternative solutions, the authors teach helpful
lessons. The book therefore provides worthwhile reading for every
professional negotiator and will make sound instruction for every tyro.

Unfortunately the book's emphasis upon mutually profitable
adjustment, on the "problem solving" aspect of bargaining, is also the
book's weakness. It is a weakness because emphasis of this aspect of
bargaining is done to almost total exclusion of the other aspect of
bargaining, "distributional bargaining," where one for me is minus one for
you. Schelling, Karrass and other students of negotiation have long
distinguished between that aspect of bargaining in which modification of
the parties' positions can produce benefits for one without significant cost
to the other, and on the other hand, cases where benefits to one come only
at significant cost to the other. They have variously described the former
as "exploring for mutual profitable adjustments," "the efficiency aspect of
bargaining," or "problem solving." The other has been characterized as
"distributional bargaining" or "share bargaining." Thus some would
describe a typical negotiation as one in which the parties initially begin
by cooperative or efficiency bargaining, in which each gains something
with each new adjustment without the other losing any significant
benefit. Eventually, however, one comes to bargaining in which added
benefits to one impose corresponding significant costs on the other. For
example, in a labor contract one might engage in cooperative bargaining
by the modification of a medical plan so that the employer could engage a
less expensive medical insurance provider, yet one that offered improved
services. Each side gains by that change from the old contract. Ultimately
parties in a labor negotiation will come to a raw economic exchange in
which additional wage dollars for the employees will be dollars subtracted

from the corporate profits, dollars that cannot be paid in dividends to the shareholders.

One can concede the authors' thesis (that too many negotiators are incapable of engaging in problem solving or in finding adequate options for mutual gain), yet still maintain that the most demanding aspect of nearly every negotiation is the distributional one in which one seeks more at the expense of the other. My principal criticism of the book is that it seems to overlook the ultimate hard bargaining. Had the authors stated that they were dividing the negotiation process in two and were dealing with only part of it, that omission would be excusable. That is not what they have done. Rather they seem to assume that a clever negotiator can make any negotiation into problem solving and thus completely avoid the difficult distribution of which Karrass and Schelling speak. To my mind this is naive. By so distorting reality, they detract from their powerful and central thesis.

ROGER FISHER, COMMENT
34 J. Legal Educ. 120, 121–23 (1984)

Are distributional issues amenable to joint problem solving? The most fundamental difference between White's way of thinking and mine seems to concern the negotiation of distributional issues "where one for me is minus one for you." We agree on the importance of cooperation, imagination, and the search for creative options where the task is to reconcile substantive interests that are compatible. White, however, sees the joint problem-solving approach as limited to that area. In his view, the most demanding aspect of nearly every negotiation is the distributional one in which one seeks more at the expense of the other. Distributional matters, in his view, must be settled by the ultimate hard bargaining. He regards it as a distortion of reality to suggest that problem solving is relevant to distributional negotiation.

Here we differ. By focusing on the substantive issues (where the parties' interests may be directly opposed), White overlooks the shared interest that the parties continue to have in the process for resolving that substantive difference. How to resolve the substantive difference is a shared problem. Both parties have an interest in identifying quickly and amicably a result acceptable to each, if one is possible. How to do so is a problem. A good solution to that process-problem requires joint action.

The guts of the negotiation problem, in my view, is not who gets the last dollar, but what is the best process for resolving that issue. It is certainly a mistake to assume that the only process available for resolving distributional questions is hard bargaining over positions. In my judgment it is also a mistake to assume that such hard bargaining is the best process for resolving differences efficiently and in the long-term interest of either side.

Two men in a lifeboat quarreling over limited rations have a distributional problem. One approach to resolving that problem is to engage in hard bargaining. *A* can insist that he will sink the boat unless he gets 60 percent of the rations. *B* can insist that he will sink the boat unless he gets 80 percent of the rations. But *A*'s and *B*'s shared problem is not just how to divide the rations; rather it is how to divide the rations without tipping over the boat and while getting the boat to safer waters. In my view, to treat the distributional issue as a shared problem is a better approach than to treat it as a contest of will in which a more deceptive, more stubborn, and less rational negotiator will tend to fare better. Treating the distributional issue as a problem to be solved ("How about dividing the rations in proportion to our respective weights?" or "How about a fixed portion of the rations for each hour that one of us rows?") is likely to be better for both than a contest over who is more willing to sink the boat.

Objective criteria. It is precisely in deciding such distributional issues that objective criteria can play their most useful role. Here is a second area of significant disagreement. White finds it useful to deny the existence of objective standards: "The suggestion that one can find objective criteria (as opposed to persuasive rationalizations) seems quite inaccurate." To his way of thinking the only approach is for a negotiator first to adopt a position and later to develop rationalizations for it: ". . . every able negotiator rationalizes every position that he takes."

No one has suggested that in most negotiations there is a single objective criterion that both parties will quickly accept as determinative. The question is rather what should be treated as the essence of the negotiation, and what attitude should be taken toward arguments advanced in the discussion. White thinks it better to treat positions of the parties as the essence of the negotiation, and objective standards advanced by either party as mere rationalizations. That is one approach. A different approach is possible and, I believe, preferable.

Two judges, in trying to reach agreement, will be looking for standards that should decide the case. They may have their predispositions and even strongly-held views, but they will jointly look for an agreed basis for decision. Each will typically advance law, precedent, and evidence not simply as rationalizations for positions adopted for other reasons, but honestly, as providing a fair basis for decision. White's example of litigation is the very one I would advance to demonstrate that however great the disagreement, the wise approach is to insist upon using objective criteria as the basis for decision. It is better for the parties in court to be advancing objective standards which they suggest ought to be determinative than to be telling the court that they won't take less (or pay more) than so many dollars. The same, I believe, is true for negotiators.

Two negotiators can be compared with two judges, trying to decide a case. There won't be a decision unless they agree. It is perfectly possible for fellow negotiators, despite their self-interest, to behave like fellow judges, in that they advance reasoned arguments seriously, and are open to persuasion by better arguments. They need not advance standards simply as rationalizations for positions, but as providing a genuine basis for joint decision.

What we are suggesting is that in general a negotiator should seek to persuade by coming up with better arguments on the merits rather than by simply trying to convince the other side that he is the more stubborn. A good guideline is for a negotiator to advance arguments as though presenting them to an impartial arbitrator, to press favorable bases for decision, but none so extreme as to damage credibility. (On the receiving side, a good guideline is for a negotiator to listen to arguments as though he were an impartial arbitrator, remaining open to persuasion despite self-interest and preconceptions.) My experience suggests that this method is often more efficient and amicable than hard positional bargaining and more often leads to satisfactory results for both parties.

NOTES AND QUESTIONS

1. Who gets it right? Is problem-solving negotiation hopelessly naive? Or is adversarial negotiation hopelessly pessimistic? Neither? Both?

2. William Ury published a book addressing concerns, like those raised by White, about problem-solving negotiation. *See* WILLIAM URY, GETTING PAST NO: NEGOTIATING WITH DIFFICULT PEOPLE (1991). Professor James Westbrook explains Ury's recommendations for dealing with so-called hard-bargaining in a book review:

JAMES E. WESTBROOK, HOW TO NEGOTIATE WITH A JERK WITHOUT BEING ONE
1992 J. Disp. Resol. 443, 444–46

One of the most persistent questions about [GETTING TO YES] has been whether the principled negotiation approach will work if the other side takes an adversarial approach. Will the proponent of principled negotiation have to change to an adversarial approach? If she doesn't, will an impasse result? Will a negotiator using the adversarial approach take advantage of a negotiator who tries to engage in principled negotiations? Ury wrote GETTING PAST NO to respond to questions such as these. Of course, not everyone who takes an adversarial approach to negotiation is a jerk. I used the word jerk in my title to get your attention and because I believe it sums up a fear by many persons who are called upon to negotiate but who want to do so in a way that is consistent with their notion of appropriate conduct. Approaches such as principled negotiation appeal to these persons, but they fear that they or their client will be taken advantage of if they take such an approach. I suspect that one of their greatest concerns is that they may have to act like a jerk in order to deal effectively with a bully, a liar, or someone who is both astute and obnoxious. *Getting Past No* asserts that there is an effective alternative to relying on techniques such as deception, stonewalling, or threatening.

AN OVERVIEW OF THE BREAKTHROUGH STRATEGY

Ury recommends what he calls a "breakthrough strategy" for overcoming barriers to cooperation. He concedes that this strategy is counter-intuitive. You are called upon to do the opposite of what you might naturally do. You go around your opponent's resistance instead of meeting it head on.

The first step in the breakthrough strategy is to "go to the balcony." Instead of reacting to your opponent's tactics without thinking, you find a way to buy time. Use the time to recognize your opponent's tactics, figure out your interests, and identify your best alternative to a negotiated agreement. Much of the discussion in the chapter on going to the balcony is about the danger of making important decisions without adequate reflection and about ways of buying time for this reflection.

Second, you "step to their side" in order to create a more favorable negotiating climate. You disarm your opponent before discussing substantive issues. Ury provides a variety of ways to do this, such as asking for more information and reflecting back what you hear, acknowledging points without agreeing with them, focusing on issues on which you agree, and speaking about yourself rather than your opponent by describing the impact of the problem on yourself or your client. The chapter includes an interesting discussion about the value of an apology.

Third, reframe whatever your opponent has said as an attempt to deal with the problem. Since rejecting your opponent's position will usually reinforce it, recast what she says in a way that directs attention to satisfying interests. Ask her for advice, ask why she wants something, bring up what you think her interests are and ask her to correct you if you are wrong, ask "what if" questions, reframe your opponent's position as one possible option among many, and ask why she thinks her position is fair. Throughout, ask questions that cannot be answered by "no" by prefacing them with "how," "why," and "who." Not only do you reframe positions, but you reframe tactics. For example, if your opponent lays down a rigid deadline, reinterpret it as a target to strive for. If this cannot be done, you turn from negotiating substance to negotiating how the negotiations are to proceed. The goal here is to change the game from positional to problem-solving negotiation.

Fourth, make it easy for your opponents to say yes by "building them a golden bridge." The golden bridge chapter contains a multitude of ideas and techniques for involving your opponent in developing your proposal and for presenting it in a way that makes it easier for her to accept. Guide rather than push her toward an agreement. Consider her interests, involve her in developing your proposal, ask for and use her ideas where possible, and offer her choices. Ury suggests ways of expanding the pie by looking for low-cost, high-benefit trades and using an "if-then" formula, which deals with difficult issues by building flexible provisions into the agreement. Help her save face by showing how circumstances have changed since she adopted her position, asking for a third party recommendation, or urging reliance on a standard of fairness. Ury explains the dangers of trying to go too fast and the value of breaking the negotiation into steps.

The fifth and final step is to "make it hard to say no." This chapter contains a discussion of what to do if your opponent still resists your proposals after you have gone through the first four steps. Ury emphasizes persuasion rather than force or threats. He argues that force or threats often backfire. He suggests that you educate your opponent about the costs of not agreeing, that you warn rather than threaten, and that you demonstrate your best alternative to a negotiated agreement (BATNA). Such a demonstration shows what you will do without your actually carrying it out. Ury points out that, Power, like beauty, exists in the eyes of the beholder. If your BATNA is to have its intended educational effect of bringing your opponent back to the table, he needs to be impressed with its reality.

If you must use your BATNA, Ury recommends using as little power as possible, exhausting alternatives before escalating, and using only legitimate means. He explains the value of employing third parties where possible. As you try to persuade your opponent and as you resort to your BATNA, you need to remind her regularly of the golden bridge available to her.

NOTE

Most commentators agree that "although competition and collaboration are antagonistic processes, both necessarily occur in virtually all negotiations." Gary Lowenthal, *A General Theory of Negotiation Process, Strategy and Behavior*, 31 U. Kan. L. Rev. 69, 75 n.31 (1982). Like these commentators, we believe that many negotiations require negotiators to use both problem-solving and adversarial approaches to resolve a dispute successfully. We also believe that negotiators should look for certain reasons to determine whether to favor one approach over the other as they almost invariably balance the two. What factors do you think are likely to suggest adversarial negotiation is more appropriate? What factors are likely to point toward problem-solving negotiation?

2.   As you consider whether and how to combine the adversarial and problem-solving strategies, be aware that earning a reputation as an

extremely effective adversarial negotiator can have reputational effects. In some circles, the negotiator may be feared, and this may work to her advantage. In others, however, there may be reputational costs. This excerpt describes the significance of trust and distrust in negotiation, and how an adversarial negotiator's reputation for effectiveness can reduce other negotiators' willingness to trust and make disclosures to her, thus reducing her ability to be effective.

NANCY A. WELSH, THE REPUTATIONAL ADVANTAGES OF DEMONSTRATING TRUSTWORTHINESS: USING THE REPUTATION INDEX WITH LAW STUDENTS
28 Negot. J. 117, 136–139 (2011)

Exploring trustworthiness requires an initial look at the general concept of trust. Roger Mayer and his colleagues performed foundational work by developing a model of the relationships among antecedents to trust, trust, perceptions of risk, and risk taking. They defined trust as "the willingness of a party to be vulnerable to the actions of another party based on the expectation that the other will perform a particular action important to the trustor, irrespective of the ability to monitor or control that other party," and observed that "[b]eing vulnerable implies that there is something of importance to be lost[.]" * * *

Researchers have found in other professional, nonlegal contexts that the ability to create "an environment of trust" will play a significant role in achieving a negotiation's integrative potential. One hears echoes here of the research regarding the effects of perceptions of procedural justice in integrative negotiator and not negatively correlated with his/her effectiveness as a distributive negotiator. This suggests that there is no disadvantage to behaving in a manner that is consistent with procedural justice and trustworthiness.

But the reality of legal negotiation—in which lawyers must play the simultaneous and conflicting roles of both adversaries and professional colleagues—suggests that lawyers will find it very difficult, if not ethically impossible, to offer *unconditional* trustworthiness to each other. Must lawyers, therefore, leave consideration of trustworthiness behind? Williams has urged for example that the legal negotiators who fit the aggressive pattern are hesitant to extend trust to anyone. They "recognize that one way to avoid being too soft is always to be hard negotiators; that way, they are never in danger of being too trusting. This saves them from the more difficult task of figuring out when and whom to trust[.]"

For these and other lawyers, Roy Lewicki, David Saunders, and Bruce Barry have helpfully distinguished between two different types of trust—calculus-based trust and identification-based trust—involving different types or degrees of vulnerability. Efficient commercial relations and well-functioning polities generally exhibit calculus-based trust, or consistent delivery of promised and desirable behaviors, based on cost-benefit analysis—for example, the trust that if you pay for an extended warranty for your washing machine, the seller will meet its contractual obligations because it wants your future business or fears the cost of litigation or loss of business that could result from its failure to honor its obligations. Similarly, if you cast your vote in a public election and have calculus-based trust, you believe your vote will be counted in just the same way as anyone else's vote, based on the social and political benefits to governmental actors if they fulfill voters' expectations, or because of their fear of litigation or social unrest if they fail to fulfill this expectation. You are unlikely to view the seller of the washing machine or the governmental actors as unconditionally trustworthy, but instead as sufficiently trustworthy.

Identification-based trust involves more personal vulnerability and can almost connote enmeshment or self-other merging; it certainly involves a presumption of benevolence. This form of trust is based on such complete identification, understanding, and appreciation of the other's interests, desires, and intentions that one person can act for the other. The relationship between lawyer and client ideally represents something akin to identification-based trust.

Lewicki and his colleagues have also written about another separate and valuable dimension that would seem to be the opposite of trust but is not necessarily so—*distrust*, both calculus-based and identification-based—which may coexist with trust. Indeed, research in other professional, nonlegal contexts suggests that a degree of distrust can and does coexist quite rationally with a degree of trust. Deepak Malhotra and others have found that negotiators are more likely to extend trust—and make themselves vulnerable—when they calculate the resulting risk of being harmed as relatively low. The need to calculate suggests a rational, self-protective degree of distrust.

Legal negotiation is rife with conflicting relationships that have the potential to pull lawyers in opposing directions and suggest the value of thinking in terms of both calculus-based trust and even a degree of rational distrust. The relationship between lawyer and client can easily conflict with lawyers' shared commitments to their profession, to their colleagues in that profession, and to the justice system. Interestingly, the degree of this conflict may depend upon a lawyer's perception of how "deep" or "shallow" his/her relationship is with the profession, with other lawyers, and with the justice system—and whether "the profession" or "the justice system" is separate from, and has significance beyond, the individual lawyers (and judges) who are part of it. Perhaps paradoxically, the degree of the conflict also may depend upon the clarity with which society, the legal profession,disciplinary bodies, and courts have declared the lawyer's relationship with his/her client to be primary.

Regardless of these larger issues, and focusing once again upon what constitutes a positive reputation for legal negotiators, research suggests that possessing a strong reputation as a very effective *distributive* negotiator actually may trigger rational distrust, and thus hinder the negotiator's ability to create the environment of trust needed to maximize both joint and individual gains. Research by Catherine Tinsley and her colleagues showed that negotiators facing counterparts identified as skilled distributive negotiators tended to share less information about their specific interests, needs, and priorities, and spent more time discussing procedural issues. Also, the negotiators who were identified as skilled distributive negotiators failed to do as well—both in terms of individual gains and the achievement of joint gains—as those negotiators who had not been so identified beforehand. The researchers concluded that assigning a distributive reputation induced a "Pygmalion" effect, with "negotiators' expectations and interpretations of their 'distributive' counterparts' behaviors, and their own distributive behavior (in response), induc(ing) their counterparts to behave more distributively than counterparts in the control condition[.]"

Recall, once again, Lewicki's description of calculus-based trust involving a cost-benefit calculation. Even if the negotiator with the strong distributive reputation is no more self-interested than the average negotiator, his/her effectiveness makes disclosing potentially sensitive information to him/her a greater risk than disclosing the same information to a less effective negotiator. Reflexively perhaps, he/she will use that information for his/her own benefit.

The bottom line for lawyers, then, seems to be that having a very strong distributive reputation—perhaps also considered a reputation as a very effective competitive negotiator—is likely to reduce a lawyer's effectiveness in negotiation. But the devil is always in the details. In their research, Tinsley and her colleagues defined someone skilled at distributive bargaining as being "particularly adept at . . . the art of claiming a lot of value for themselves[,]" which implied "being a bargainer who prizes claiming value over other goals[.]" There is little nuance in this description. The negotiations were conducted through the "lean medium" of e-mail rather than in person; the context was transactional, rather than involving the settlement of pending litigation; the negotiation had the potential for joint gains, rather than being purely distributive; the negotiators were business school students negotiating for their companies, rather than lawyers or law students negotiating on behalf of clients; and the negotiators were students who had completed three weeks ("novices") or ten weeks ("experts") of a negotiation course, rather than professionals with substantial real-life negotiating experience.

Nonetheless, the research is provocative. Recall that Williams' and Schneider's studies showed that lawyer respondents perceived *some* aggressive/competitive/adversarial negotiators to be skilled lawyers, effective negotiators, and aware of the constraints imposed by their professional ethics. They were effective as negotiators and worthy of calculus-based trust, that is, "sufficiently trustworthy" or "trustworthy enough." Of course, the legal profession's ethics rules express normative values and compromises but that does not matter. It is the fact that they are the profession's *rules*, with expressive and coercive power, that matters. The effective negotiators who fit the aggressive pattern were capable of restraining themselves from taking certain actions because such restraint was required.

Meanwhile, the Williams and Schneider studies also showed that while effective negotiators who fit the cooperative/problem-solving pattern (and exhibited a cooperative style) were perceived as caring about the achievement of fair outcomes, they also were perceived as skilled lawyers committed to maximizing settlement results for their clients. In other words, these effective negotiators were similarly ready, able, and professionally required to behave in a manner that might not be entirely consistent with an *unconditional* concern for or fairness toward the other party. Ultimately, these effective negotiators, too, were "sufficiently trustworthy" or "trustworthy enough" to be deserving of calculus-based trust—although their behaviors and reputation might also signal and create the opportunity for something more.

E. LAW, LAWYERS, AND CLIENTS IN NEGOTIATION

Most people conduct most of their negotiations without help from lawyers or other agents. *See, e.g.*, ROBERT C. ELLICKSON, ORDER WITHOUT LAW: HOW NEIGHBORS SETTLE DISPUTES (1991). Even in disputes involving potentially legally actionable claims, people seldom retain lawyers to represent them. One famous study is illustrative. Richard Miller and Austin Sarat contacted individuals by telephone to inquire about potentially legally remediable injuries that members of their households had suffered. Out of every 1,000 such instances, individuals hired lawyers on only 100 occasions. *See* Richard E. Miller & Austin Sarat, *Grievances, Claims, and Disputes: Assessing the Adversary Culture*, 15 Law & Soc'y Rev. 525, 534–46 (1980–81). A more detailed discussion and charts based on this research appear in Chapter I, *supra*.

Despite the relative infrequency with which individuals hire lawyers, lawyers nonetheless represent many clients in transactional negotiations and dispute settlement. Thus, this section explores the role of lawyer-negotiators in these settings. We begin in Subsection 1 below by exploring the primary domain in which lawyers represent disputants, i.e., in litigation and settlement. In Subsection 2, we explore some of the legal and ethical obligations imposed upon lawyer-negotiators in both dispute settlement and transactional negotiations.

1. SETTLEMENT

a. In General

Clients often retain lawyers to represent them in litigation. In civil litigation, our primary thrust, lawyers are retained either to file claims against another party or to defend against same. Most civil cases—something on the order of two-thirds of them—settle through negotiation.

MARC GALANTER & MIA CAHILL, "MOST CASES SETTLE": JUDICIAL PROMOTION AND REGULATION OF SETTLEMENTS
46 Stan. L. Rev. 1339, 1339–40, 1341–42 (1994)

"Most cases settle" has become a commonplace in discussions of civil justice. It is a welcome corrective to the naive tendency to speak as if every case were tried and subjected to appellate review.

* * *

[I]t should be noted that the simple observation 'most cases settle' requires some qualification. While settlement is the most frequent disposition of civil cases in the United States, its predominance should not be exaggerated. Oft-cited figures estimating settlement rates of between 85 and 95 percent are misleading; those figures represent all civil cases that do not go to trial. But that is not quite the same as limiting the definition of cases that 'settle' to those resolved solely by agreement between the parties without any decision by an authoritative decisionmaker. Cases may be disposed of by authoritative decisions in ways other than by trial. Herbert Kritzer, analyzing 1649 cases in five federal judicial districts and seven state courts, found that although only 7 percent of cases went to trial and reached a jury verdict or court decision, another 15 percent terminated through some other form of adjudication, such as arbitration or dismissal. Another 9 percent settled following a ruling on a significant motion.

In the two-thirds of cases that do settle without a definitive judicial ruling, judges are by no means absent. Rather, they are a ghostly but influential presence, through their rulings in adjudicated cases and their anticipated response to the case at hand.

* * *

[M]ost cases that enter the system are resolved short of full-dress adjudication by a process of maneuver and bargaining 'in the shadow of the law.' Rather than two separate tracks—adjudication on the one hand and negotiation and settlement on the other—there is a single process of pursuing remedies in the presence of courts. For mnemonic purposes, we attach to it the fanciful neologism 'litigotiation.'

The whole 'litigotiation' system has been growing as part of a general expansion of the legal world. As the legal system has grown, the settlement component has increased in prominence while the portion of cases that run the whole course to trial has shrunk.

NOTES AND QUESTIONS

1.   Settlement is now so common and trials are so rare that the ABA Section on Litigation recently commissioned a report entitled "The Vanishing Trial," and several law journals have devoted entire issues to the topic. See e.g., Symposium, The Vanishing Trial, 1 J. Empirical Leg. Stud. 459 (2004). Individual courts' bench-bar committees have also written reports devoted to this topic. See e.g., Civil Jury Trial Bench/Bar Task Force of the United States District Court for the Middle District of Pennsylvania, Final Report (October 2, 2008). For more on this topic, review the discussion in Chapter I, supra.

2.   Settlement is so common, in fact, that many observers and participants in the civil justice system often view trials as failures. According to Professors Gross and Syverud:

A trial is a failure. Although we celebrate it as the centerpiece of our system of justice, we know that trial is not only an uncommon method of resolving disputes, but a disfavored one. With some notable exceptions, lawyers, judges, and commentators agree that pretrial settlement is almost always cheaper, faster, and better than trial. Much of our civil procedure is justified by the desire to promote settlement and avoid trial. More important, the nature of our civil process drives parties to settle so as to avoid the costs, delays, and uncertainties of trial, and, in many cases, to agree upon terms that are beyond the power or competence of courts to dictate. These are powerful forces, and they produce settlement in a very high proportion of litigated disputes.

Samuel R. Gross & Kent D. Syverud, *Getting to No: A Study of Settlement Negotiations and the Selection of Cases for Trial*, 90 Mich. L. Rev. 319, 320 (1991). *But see* Robert J. Rhee, *A Price Theory of Legal Bargaining: An Inquiry Into the Selection of Settlement and Litigation Under Uncertainty*, 56 Emory L.J. 619 (2006) (arguing that commentators have misunderstood the relative merits of trial versus settlement).

3.   The civil justice system favors settlement and disfavors trial, and also favors lawyers' negotiations over procedural issues. This may be seen in several procedural and evidentiary rules designed to encourage both negotiation and settlement. Consider, for example, the following:

- Rule 16 of the Federal Rules of Civil Procedure permits judges to facilitate settlements during pretrial conferences. The rule also permits the court to order the use of "special procedures to assist in resolving the dispute" but only "when authorized by statute or local rule[.]" Such procedures are most likely to involve mediation, settlement conferences with magistrate or senior judges, or early neutral evaluation. Professor Judith Resnik describes judicial intervention in settlement as "managerial judging," and notes: "Both before and after the trial, judges are playing a critical role in shaping litigation and influencing results." Judith Resnik, *Managerial Judging*, 96 Harv. L. Rev. 376, 376–77 (1982).

- Lawyers negotiate throughout the litigation process. They may need to reach agreement on extensions of filing deadlines, the scope of production in response to a discovery request, the dates for upcoming depositions, etc. It makes sense—and is consistent with lawyers' professional ethics—to work together to expedite the litigation process. But sometimes, lawyers refuse to negotiate with each other, particularly in the context of hard-fought disagreements over the discovery that is due or the legitimacy of innovative claims and defenses. As a result, Rules 11, 26 and 37 of the Federal Rules of Civil Procedure actually *require* lawyers to confer together and attempt to reach an agreement—presumably through negotiation—as a condition precedent to filing a discovery plan or certain motions with the court.

- Rule 41 of the Federal Rules of Civil Procedure allows a plaintiff to dismiss his lawsuit as a matter of right, with the filing of a stipulation of dismissal signed by all parties who have appeared. Otherwise, such dismissal requires a court order, on terms the court considers proper. Not surprisingly, dismissal is nearly always a condition of settlement. On occasion, though, a plaintiff will assign his claim to a defendant as part of a settlement, rather than dismiss the claim. (Note that if a plaintiff dismisses his claim voluntarily and without a settlement, and then seeks to bring the claim again, he may first be required to meet certain conditions, such as payment of the other side's costs.)

- Rule 68 of the Federal Rules of Civil Procedure provides that a defendant may make a settlement offer to the plaintiff. If the plaintiff rejects the offer and fares less well at trial, she must pay the post-offer costs the defendant incurred.

- Rule 408 of the Federal Rules of Evidence excludes portions of settlement discussions from admission at trial, although there are also significant exceptions to this general rule.

b.   Approaches to Settlement

Lawyers generally play a central role in settling civil cases, and two dominant approaches to settlement have emerged: the "expected-value" approach (sometimes called "net-expected value") and the "interest-based" approach. The former approach is generally more consistent with the adversarial approach to negotiation, while the latter is more consistent with the problem-solving approach. We consider both below.

1. Expected Value

Lawyers who use an expected-value approach rely on basic economic principles to determine whether, or under what circumstances, their clients should settle. Using this approach, lawyers calculate the expected value of trial and then attempt to negotiate a settlement for their clients higher than that value.

To illustrate, suppose that a plaintiff has filed a breach of contract suit against a defendant for $100,000. Suppose further that the lawyers representing both litigants believe, based on the facts of the case and the legal research they have conducted, that the plaintiff has a 50% of winning. Finally, suppose that both litigants will have to spend $10,000 more to litigate the case to a verdict than they will to settle.

To calculate the expected value of trial for the plaintiff, her lawyer multiplies the probability of prevailing (50%) by the anticipated judgment ($100,000) and subtracts the costs of trial ($10,000). The expected value of trial for the plaintiff is thus $40,000 [(50% x $100,000) + (50% x $0)—$10,000].

To calculate the expected value of trial for the defendant, her lawyer multiplies the probability of the plaintiff prevailing (50%) by the anticipated judgment (-$100,000) and subtracts the costs of trial ($10,000). The expected value of trial for the defendant under these circumstances is thus –$60,000 [(50% x—$100,000) + (50% x $0)—$10,000].

Based on these calculations, the plaintiff should be willing to settle for a minimum of $40,000, and the defendant should be willing to pay a maximum of $60,000 to settle. Thus, the lawyers should attempt to negotiate a settlement within this $20,000 bargaining range.

NOTES AND QUESTIONS

1.   To calculate the expected value of trial, a lawyer must predict how a judge or jury will apply governing principles of law to the facts of the case. If a settlement offer exceeds that expected value, she will advise her client to settle; if it does not, she will recommend trial. Thus, a lawyer employing the expected-value approach to settlement bargains "in the shadow of the law."

Robert H. Mnookin & Lewis Kornhauser, *Bargaining in the Shadow of the Law: The Case of Divorce*, 88 Yale L.J. 950 (1979).

2.   Even though determining expected value is an important part of preparation, there is no guarantee that it will determine the settlement amount or even that settlement will occur. What accounts for this? In the following excerpt, Professors Russell Korobkin and Chris Guthrie observe that scholars have proposed three explanations for settlement breakdowns:

> In attempting to create a general framework for explaining why settlement attempts fail and trials occur, commentators have developed two primary explanations, both of which assume that disputants are rational actors. Proponents of the standard economic models of settlement hypothesize that because settlement is almost always less costly than trial, parties will reach agreement out of court as long as they agree on the expected value of a trial; the litigation costs they save represent joint gains of trade achieved through settlement, which the litigants can then distribute between themselves. Conversely, trials will occur when one or both parties miscalculate the likely outcome of the trial. Other commentators—focusing on the distributive bargaining issues that arise when the parties recognize that they would create joint gains by reaching out-of-court agreement but must determine how to divide that savings—hypothesize that disputants fail to settle when one or both parties employ rational distributive bargaining strategies that lead to impasse, as they will on some occasions.
>
> We have no quarrel with either of these theories, but we believe that they fail to explain the full range of litigation negotiation failures. While they are elegant in their simplicity, their explanatory power is limited by the narrow assumptions about human behavior on which they rely. When individuals engaged in litigation must choose between settling a lawsuit out of court and seeking a trial verdict, we predict that they will not always act in the rational way that the economic and strategic bargaining models assume. We hypothesize that even in the absence of miscalculation and strategic bargaining, psychological processes create barriers that preclude out-of-court settlements in some cases.

Russell Korobkin & Chris Guthrie, *Psychological Barriers to Litigation Settlement: An Experimental Approach*, 93 Mich. L. Rev. 107, 108–09 (1994).

3.   As Korobkin and Guthrie suggest, lawyers need to be aware of the psychological processes that can prevent cases from settling even when settlement would make sense in terms of expected value. The following notes identify some of those psychological processes.

a.   *Framing Effects.* When faced with risk or uncertainty—like when deciding whether to settle a case or go forward to trial—people tend to make risk-averse decisions when choosing between options that appear to be gains and risk-seeking decisions when choosing between options that appear to be losses. Professor Jeffrey Rachlinski and other legal scholars have applied this insight—formalized by Professors Daniel Kahneman and Amos Tversky in "prospect theory"—to litigation and settlement.

Most decisions concerning the course of litigation involve risk. As a result, litigation decisions are influenced by the risk preferences of the parties, which, in turn, are determined by the character of the decision as a gain or as a loss. Predicting the behavior of litigants therefore requires an understanding of whether a party views their decision from the perspective of a gain or loss.

Settlement choices seem particularly vulnerable to framing effects. Consider the litigation setting . . .

Version 1.

Imagine you are the plaintiff in a copyright infringement lawsuit. You are suing for the $400,000 that the defendant allegedly earned by violating the copyright. Trial is in two days and the defendant has offered to pay $200,000 as a final settlement. If you turn it down, you believe that you will face a trial where you have a 50% chance of winning a $400,000 award. Do you agree to accept the settlement?

Version 2.

Imagine you are the defendant in a copyright infringement lawsuit. You are being sued for the $400,000 that the defendant allegedly earned by violating the copyright. Trial is in two days and the plaintiff has offered to accept $200,000 as a final settlement. If you turn it down, you believe that you will face a trial where you have a 50% chance of losing a $400,000 award. Do you agree to pay the settlement?

[B]oth versions represent economically identical outcomes. Both parties in the problem above choose between keeping $200,000 for sure and a gamble with a 50% chance of winning $400,000 or $0. The context of litigation, however, sets up the defendant as the stakeholder, making it appear that the defendant chooses among losses while the plaintiff chooses among gains.

As a simple demonstration that framing influences risk preferences in litigation, I presented this hypothetical to first-year law school students at Cornell Law School. Of the 13 students evaluating the plaintiff's perspective, 10, or 77%, chose to settle, while only 4 of the 13, or 31%, of the students evaluating the defendant's perspective chose to settle. Despite the small sample size, the difference in settlement rates was both striking and statistically significant.

Jeffrey J. Rachlinski, *Gains, Losses, and the Psychology of Litigation*, 70 S. Cal. L. Rev. 113, 128–29 (1996)

b. *Self–Serving Biases.* When evaluating their respective cases, litigants and lawyers may overestimate their chances of prevailing at trial due to "self-serving" or "egocentric" biases. The following excerpt explains:

People tend to make judgments about themselves and their abilities that are "egocentric" or "self-serving." People routinely estimate, for example, that they are above average on a variety of desirable characteristics, including health, driving, professional skills, and likelihood of having a successful marriage. Moreover, people overestimate their contribution to joint activities. For example, after a conversation both parties will estimate that they spoke more than half the time. Similarly, when married couples are asked to estimate the percentage of household tasks they perform, their estimates typically add up to more than 100%.

Egocentric biases occur for several reasons. First, of course, is self-presentation. People may not really believe that they are better than average, but they will nonetheless tell researchers that they are. Second, people engage in confirmatory mental searches for evidence that supports a theory they want to believe, such as that their marriage will succeed. They have no comparable data on the nature of strangers' marriages, so the only evidence they find suggests that theirs is more likely than others' to be successful. Third, memory is egocentric in that people remember their own actions better than others' actions. Thus, when asked to recall the percentage of housework they perform, people remember their own contribution more easily and, consequently tend to overestimate it. Finally, many of the constructs involved in egocentric biases are ambiguous, and thus, people can define success differently. For example, safe driving means different things to different people, and as a result, everyone really can drive safer than average, at least as measured by their own standards.

Egocentric biases can be adaptive, but they can also have an unfortunate influence on the litigation process. Due to egocentric biases, litigants and their lawyers might overestimate their own abilities, the quality of their advocacy, and the relative merits of their cases. These views, in turn, are likely to undermine settlement efforts. In one study, for example, Professor George Loewenstein and his colleagues asked undergraduates and law students to assess the value of a tort case in which the plaintiff had sued the defendant for $100,000 in damages arising from an automobile-motorcycle collision. These researchers assigned some participants to play the role of plaintiff and others the role of defendant, but they provided both sets of participants with identical information about the case. Nevertheless, the participants interpreted the facts in self-serving ways. When asked to predict the amount they thought the judge would award in the case, the participants evaluating the case from the perspective of the plaintiff predicted that the judge would award $14,527 more than the defendant-participants predicted. When asked to identify what they perceived to be a fair settlement value, plaintiff-participants selected a value $17,709 higher than the value selected by defendant-participants. These results suggest that self-serving or egocentric biases can lead to bargaining impasse and wasteful litigation.

Chris Guthrie, Jeffrey J. Rachlinski & Andrew J. Wistrich, *Inside the Judicial Mind*, 86 Cornell L. Rev. 777, 811–13 (2001).

    c.   *Equity–Seeking*. Even litigants and lawyers attempting to maximize their net-expected-outcomes in litigation may seek to accomplish non-monetary objectives, such as obtaining vindication from the other side or restoring equity to a damaged relationship. As the following excerpt indicates, concerns for these non-monetary goods may prevent litigants from maximizing their net-expected outcomes.

    Many researchers assume, quite logically, that litigants seeking to restore equity may behave "irrationally"—that is, they may fail to select options with the highest expected monetary value. We attempted to bolster these assumptions with empirical data. Accordingly, we designed a hypothetical litigation scenario to study the extent to which a litigant's sense that she has been treated unjustly by an adversary, in and of itself, impedes the resolution of legal disputes. Such a study would be difficult to conduct using actual litigation data because in many legal disputes the relative blameworthiness of the disputants affects their legal rights and remedies. Using our experimental method, however, we were able to test for the effects of perceived inequitable treatment while controlling for legal rights.

    We provided subjects with a simple landlord-tenant dispute. Subjects were told that they signed a six-month lease to live in an off-campus apartment beginning September 1. After two months the heater broke down. Although they immediately notified the landlord and requested repair, the landlord failed to fix the heater. As a result, according to the scenario, the subjects spent four winter months in a cold apartment attempting to keep warm with a space heater before moving out at the end of the lease period. Throughout this time period, the subjects had continued to pay $1,000 per month in rent. After moving out, they learned from a student legal service lawyer that "there was a good chance" of recovering a portion of the $4,000 in rent paid over that four-month period of time. The lawyer gave neither a specific prediction of the likelihood of success nor any estimate of the exact magnitude of a judgment. Subjects learned that, with the assistance of their attorney, they had filed an action in small claims court against the landlord. Prior to the court date, the landlord offered to settle the case out of court for $900.

    The variable tested in this scenario was the landlord's reason for failing to repair the heater in spite of the tenant's prompt request that he do so. Group A subjects learned that they had made a number of calls to the landlord, to no avail. "The landlord promised to fix your heater, but he never did. A week later, you called him again. Again, he promised to fix it, but he never did. Over the next several weeks, you called him a half-dozen times, but he did not return your calls." Group B participants received a different explanation: After the second call to the landlord, "[y]ou learned that he had left the country unexpectedly due to a family emergency and that he was expected to be gone for several months. . . ."

The given explanation had a significant impact on how likely subjects were to accept the settlement offer and forgo their day in court. Knowing that the landlord did not fix the heater because he was out of the country due to a family emergency, most Group B (Family Emergency) subjects were willing to accept the landlord's offer and let the matter rest. Their mean response was 3.41 [on a 5–point scale where 1 = "definitely reject" and 5 = "definitely accept"]. Group A subjects (Broken Promise), in contrast, were more likely to reject the $900 offer and risk a less favorable decision in small claims court than to accept the offer. Their average score was 2.60. The difference between the two groups is highly significant. Fifty-nine percent of the Family Emergency subjects said they would "definitely" or "probably" accept the settlement offer, while only 35% of the Broken Promise subjects provided those same responses. Thirty percent of the Broken Promise subjects said they would "definitely reject" the $900 settlement offer in favor of small claims court, while only 9% of the Family Emergency subjects would "definitely reject" the offer. . . .

The very different responses of the Family Emergency and Broken Promise subjects provide empirical support for the hypothesis that litigant victims seek more than just monetary damages from the legal system. They seek to restore equity to inequitable relationships. When litigants feel they have been treated badly by the other side, the chances of settlement decrease because litigants are more likely to seek retaliation or vindication of their moral position in addition to monetary damages.

Russell Korobkin & Chris Guthrie, *Psychological Barriers to Litigation Settlement: An Experimental Approach*, 93 Mich. L. Rev. 107, 144–47.

d.   *Attribution Theory.* Attribution theory provides another explanation for the dynamic described by Professor Korobkin and Dean Guthrie. Attribution theory is the study of how we interpret the actions of others. When another person's action hurts us, we search for the cause. Was the other person's action intentional or not? Was it caused by the person's disposition or the circumstance in which the person found herself? How much control did the person have over what happened? Interestingly, we tend to underestimate the extent to which people's behavior is influenced by the circumstances in which they find themselves. Instead, we tend to emphasize explanations that focus on the general disposition and intentions of the person. This is called the *fundamental attribution error*—fundamental because we all do it and error because empirical study establishes that situational influences have more sway than we are inclined to think. Lee Ross, *The Intuitive Psychologist and His Shortcomings: Distortions in the Attribution Process?*, in Leonard Berkowitz (ed.), 10 Advances in Experimental Social Psychology 174, 184–87 (1977). Michael W. Morris, Richard P. Larrick & Steven K. Su, *Misperceiving Negotiation Counterparts:*

When Situationally Determined Bargaining Behaviors Are Attributed to Personality Traits, 77 J. Personality & Soc. Psychol. 52 (1999).

As an example, Professor Keith Allred notes: ". . . [R]esearch indicates that in observing a person at an airport yelling at an airline agent, one tends to overattribute the behavior to bad temper and underattribute it to circumstances, such as having recently been the victim of recurring unfair treatment by the airline." Keith C. Allred, *Anger & Retaliation in Conflict: The Role of Attribution*, in THE HANDBOOK OF CONFLICT RESOLUTION: THEORY AND PRACTICE 237, 240–41 (Coleman, Deutsch et al. eds., 2nd ed. 2006). At the same time, we are more likely to take into account situational factors when making attributions about our own behavior than we are when we are thinking about other people—a phenomenon known as the *actor-observer effect*. Edward E. Jones & Richard E. Nisbett, *The Actor and the Observer: Divergent Perceptions of the Causes of Behavior*, in ATTRIBUTION: PERCEIVING THE CAUSES OF BEHAVIOR 82 (Edward E. Jones et al. eds., 1972). Similarly, research further indicates that if that person in the airport is not a member of your own social group, you are even more likely to attribute such behavior to the person's character or disposition.

Interestingly, Professor Allred has suggested that when someone behaves in a procedurally just manner—and in particular if she provides the other person with an opportunity for voice and genuinely listens and considers the other's perspective—she is more likely to be effective in maintaining the sort of trusting and cooperative relations that can reduce the effect of the fundamental attribution error. *See* Keith G. Allred, *Relationship Dynamics in Disputes: Replacing Contention with Cooperation*, in THE HANDBOOK OF DISPUTE RESOLUTION 85 (Michael Moffitt & Robert Bordone, eds., 2005).

As a final note, research indicates that the fundamental attribution error is less powerful in those cultures (and, presumably, subcultures) where "the concept of the individual person as agentic is less absolute." Michael W. Morris & Michele J. Gelfand, *Cultural Differences and Cognitive Dynamics: Expanding the Cognitive Perspective on Negotiation*, in THE HANDBOOK OF NEGOTIATION AND CULTURE 53 (Michele J. Gelfand & Jeanne M. Brett, eds., 2004).

4. Given various impediments to economically rational settlements—i.e., rational miscalculation, strategic behavior, and such psychological barriers as framing effects, self-serving biases and the fundamental attribution error, equity-seeking lawyers may find it helpful to use the tools of formal decision analysis to guide their clients through an expected-value approach to litigation. See Chapter II, *supra*, regarding decision analysis.

2. *Value Creation*

Lawyers who pursue the interest-based approach to settlement attempt to convert the litigation into a deal-making opportunity by focusing on the parties' underlying interests and attempting to make value-creating trades. Professor Mnookin and his colleagues describe this approach as follows:

ROBERT H. MNOOKIN, SCOTT R. PEPPET & ANDREW S. TULUMELLO, BEYOND WINNING: NEGOTIATING TO CREATE VALUE IN DEALS AND DISPUTES*
240–42 (2000)

. . . [H]ow do you switch to the interest-based table if the situation might permit turning the dispute into a deal? And once at the interest-based table, what do you do?

Moving to the Interest–Based Table

Inviting opposing counsel to explore the opportunity for creating value at the interest-based table can feel risky. Both sides may be reluctant to share interests once they are entrenched in litigation. The interest-based table presents a new concept that may be difficult for some lawyers and clients to accept: that dispute resolution may be an opportunity to find value-creating trades as well as a time for waging war.

For this reason, we advise lawyers interested in moving to the interest-based table to deliver three explicit messages to their counterparts. First, looking for trades may be good for both sides. Moving to the interest-based table may strengthen the parties' relationship, facilitate value-creating deals, and ease distributive tensions at the net-expected-outcome table. Second, looking for trades does not require or imply a ceasefire. Litigation can continue, and a party need not disclose information at the interest-based table that he feels will undermine his position at the net-expected-outcome table. Finally, discussing interests does not signal weakness. Indeed, a willingness to broaden the scope of negotiations can be framed as a sign of strength and confidence.

Searching for Trades

If the other side is willing to try to convert your dispute into a deal, you must first negotiate a process. If you have thought carefully about the other side's interests and come up with options that meet those interests, you may be tempted to unveil all your ideas at once, as in: "I know what you really want, and I've got the solution that gives you what you want." This is a dangerous tendency, and it is unlikely to work. Even if you have guessed right about the other side's interests, he is likely to reject what you propose, either because he has not been given an opportunity to speak for himself or because of reactive devaluation.

Instead, jointly explore what each side cares about and why, and what each side hopes the lawsuit will accomplish. Think broadly—don't

---

just include obvious interests related to the lawsuit, such as "settle quickly" or "receive fair compensation." Also consider interests beyond the scope of the litigation. If two businesses are involved, what are their general business interests? To sell more product? Attract more customers? Expand geographically? Specialize in some area? Reduce costs? What are the interests of the individuals who run those businesses? What synergies exist? Can one side provide the other side with goods or services in a mutually advantageous way? What differences exist between the parties in resources, capabilities, and preferences? How can they trade on those differences?

In some cases, the parties may have important interests beyond the dollar amount of damages at issue. A defendant in an employment discrimination suit may worry about its reputation. Plaintiffs bringing a civil rights complaint against a police department may be interested in an admission of wrongdoing and changing police practices and policies in the future. The seller in a long-term supply contract may have an interest in establishing a more flexible delivery schedule in order to respond to market changes.

Also consider involving clients more at the interest-based table than at the net-expected-outcome table. Of course, if an attorney is accustomed to negotiations that focus on assessing the net expected outcome of litigation, she may not be comfortable with having her clients play an active role at the bargaining table. Relinquishing control can be difficult. But as we have noted, clients often understand their interests and the relative priorities among those interests better than their lawyers do, and they can often be very helpful at the interest-based table.

Finally, consider involving nonparties in searching for trades. The tendency in legal dispute resolution is to focus only on those people or institutions that are named parties in the litigation and to forget that each side has many other relationships that may be affected by the lawsuit. Adding some of these players at the interest-based table can be helpful. If, for example, a building owner and a general contractor are having a dispute over payment, they might bring in an official from the lending institution underwriting the project to assist with their negotiation. If they find a value-creating trade that requires additional lending, this official will be indispensable to making their creative solution possible. Similarly, in a dispute among coauthors over copyright issues, it may be helpful to bring in a representative of the publisher. As the frame of the negotiation widens, outside parties may be essential to devising sophisticated trades.

NOTES AND QUESTIONS

1. Under what circumstances are lawyer-negotiators most likely to employ the interest-based approach to settlement discussions? What

difference might it make if the disputing clients expect to have an ongoing relationship? Will it matter whether the litigants are "one-shotters" or "repeat players" in litigation? What difference might the relationship between the attorneys make?

2.   Does law play a more prominent role in interest-based settlement negotiations or in expected-value settlement negotiations? Relative to other factors—such as the economic consequences of each course of action, the relationship between the parties, psychological factors, time constraints, and so on—how important is law likely to be to the settlement process?

3.   Is the dichotomy between the expected-value approach to settlement and the interest-based approach to settlement a false one? In other words, do skilled lawyer-negotiators need to use both approaches? If yes, why and how? Should they be used in a particular sequence? Should their use or sequence depend on circumstances? Which circumstances matter?

4.   How central *should* law be to the settlement process? Some believe that settlements should reflect what a court of law would decide; others believe that settlement should simply reflect the parties' preferences. Others, like lawyer-mediator Gary Friedman believe that law (in both negotiation and mediation) is relevant but that it should not be assumed to be determinative—i.e., that " 'the law' may point to relevant principles or values which the parties might want to consider in approaching their own resolution of the issues." Gary J. Friedman, Center for the Development of Mediation in Law Training Materials, Memo #6 (1983).

Reflecting this latter view at a more fundamental level, Professor Mnookin says negotiators "bargain in the shadow of the law." Writing in the context of divorce negotiations, he says:

> Divorcing parents do not bargain over the division of family wealth and custodial prerogatives in a vacuum; they bargain in the shadow of the law. The legal rules governing alimony, child support, marital property, and custody give each parent certain claims based on what each would get if the case went to trial. In other words, the outcome that the law will impose if no agreement is reached gives each parent certain bargaining chips—an endowment of sorts.

> A simplified example may be illustrative. Assume that in disputed custody cases the law flatly provided that all mothers had the right to custody of minor children and that all fathers only had the right to visitation two weekends a month. Absent some contrary agreement acceptable to both parents, a court would order this arrangement. Assume further that the legal rules relating to marital property, alimony, and child support gave the mother some determinate share of the family's economic resources. In negotiations under this regime, neither spouse would ever consent to a division that left him or her worse off than if he or she insisted on going to court. The range of negotiated outcomes would be limited to those that leave both parents as well off as they would be in the absence of a bargain.

If private ordering were allowed, we would not necessarily expect parents to split custody and money the way a judge would if they failed to agree. The father might well negotiate for more child-time and the mother for less. This result might occur either because the father made the mother better off by giving her additional money to compensate her for accepting less child-time, or because the mother found custody burdensome and considered herself better off with less custody. Indeed, she might agree to accept less money, or even to pay the father, if he agreed to relieve her of some child-rearing responsibilities. In all events, because the parents' tastes with regard to the trade-offs between money and child-time may differ, it will often be possible for the parties to negotiate some outcome that makes both better off than they would be if they simply accepted the result a court would impose.

Robert H. Mnookin and Lewis Kornhauser, *Bargaining in the Shadow of the Law*, 88 Yale L. J. 950, 968–69 (1979). Settlement plays such a significant role in the disposition of cases that some commentators now assert that settlement occurs primarily in the shadow of other settlements, not in the shadow of law. *See* J. Maria Glover, *The Federal Rules of Civil Settlement*, 87 N.Y.U. L. Rev. 1713, 1725–50 (2012); Rhonda Wasserman, *Secret Class Action Settlements*, 31 Rev. Litig. 889, 919 (2012). Professor Mnookin and his colleagues recommend that clients play a more active role in interest-based settlement discussions than in expected-value settlement negotiations. For a detailed discussion of the benefits and costs of including clients in settlement negotiations, see Leonard L. Riskin, *The Represented Client in a Settlement Conference: The Lessons of* G. Heileman Brewing Co. v. Joseph Oat Corp., 69 Wash. U. L.Q. 1059, 1097–1105 (1991). Both Collaborative Law and mediation also assume the participation of the clients. *See* Chapter VI, *infra*, on Collaborative Law and Chapter IV, *infra*, on mediation.

5.   Some commentators have argued that the mindset required for litigating a case to verdict is so different from the mindset required for settlement that clients might benefit from hiring special "settlement counsel." Indeed, some clients do retain counsel to play this sole role. Consider the following excerpt:

Clients, courts, and the public yearn for a less adversarial approach to dispute resolution. Lawyers are frequently blamed for the current state of affairs. However, lawyers are, for the most part, reacting rationally and in good faith to existing incentives and expectations. The current approach imposes a duty on lawyers to resolve cases quickly, while ignoring the real constraints on settlement and incentives to delay resolution.

The constraints are of several sorts. One is our view of how lawyers resolve disputes. Some people see lawyers romantically—as knights in shining armor, or as hired guns. Others see them realistically, using the litigation process to try to pound opponents into a favorable settlement. But each of these models has elements that make it difficult to settle cases quickly. Conversely, the model of the lawyer as a problem-solver, which could encourage efficient resolution, is neither as clearly defined nor as widely known.

Aside from the fact that problem-solvers are breaking new ground, there are significant incentives for lawyers not to embrace early settlement. These incentives include the need to market services, the desire not to appear weak, the obligation to represent a client zealously, the thirst for justice, and last, but perhaps not least, the desire to maximize income. In addition, it is extremely difficult, psychologically, for an attorney to act as an effective advocate and, at the same time, to encourage settlement. In the face of these obstacles, a poorly defined and toothless "duty to settle" is not likely to bring about the behavior which critics seek.

When a lawyer is hired for the sole purpose of determining if a fair resolution is possible without litigation—i.e., to act as settlement counsel—the lawyer's interests are aligned with the goal of achieving early settlement. Settlement counsel should be in a better position to use interest-based bargaining techniques and should be better able to avoid some of the common obstacles to early settlement. Because settlement counsel is encouraged to use "value-creating" techniques before "value-claiming" begins, the prospect of early settlement should improve.

William F. Coyne, Jr., *The Case for Settlement Counsel*, 14 Ohio St. J. on Disp. Resol. 367, 369–70 (1999). *See also,* Jim Golden, H. Abigail Moy & Adam Lyons, *The Negotiation Counsel Model: An Empathetic Model for Settling Catastrophic Personal Injury Cases*, 13 Harv. Negot. L. Rev. 211 (2008) (describing a "negotiation counsel" model that places a primacy on early, proactive, relational, and empathetic efforts to assist claimants and resolve disputes).

c. Apology and Settlement

One issue that often comes up in dispute resolution is a felt need by one or both of the parties for an apology. This makes sense given the definition of conflict we discussed in Chapter I in terms of a real or perceived belief of one or more of the parties that the other person is interfering with their ability to attain their interests or aspirations. With this interference often comes a sense of being wronged, and many people have a dignitarian interest in having this harm acknowledged. Indeed, it can be the most important issue to address, regardless of how the dispute actually presents itself.

Yet as most of us can probably appreciate from our personal experience, not all apologies are effective. In fact, some apologies can make the situation worse. So for the negotiator who senses an apology may be appropriate, it is important to consider the nature of the apology and its value to the parties in reaching settlement. In the following excerpt, Professor Robbennolt reports on her empirical study of these questions. For a fuller discussion, see Jennifer K. Robbennolt, *Apologies and Legal Settlement: An Empirical Examination*, 102 Mich. L. Rev. 460 (2003).

JENNIFER K. ROBBENNOLT, APOLOGY—HELP OR HINDRANCE? AN EMPIRICAL ANALYSIS OF APOLOGIES' INFLUENCE ON SETTLEMENT DECISION MAKING
Disp. Resol. Mag., Spring 2004, at 33–34

Recently, I conducted a series of experimental studies designed to begin a systematic examination of whether, in what ways and under what conditions apologies might affect settlement decisionmaking. The findings described here are based on the results of two experimental studies in which 506 participants were asked to read a vignette describing a pedestrian-bicycle accident, to take on the role of the injured party, to indicate whether or not they were likely to accept a settlement offer and to respond to a series of questions about the situation.

All participants reviewed the same basic scenario and evaluated the same settlement offer. However, some participants evaluated a version of the scenario in which no apology was offered; a second group evaluated a version of the scenario in which the other party offered a partial apology that merely expressed sympathy for the potential claimant's injuries (i.e., 'I am so sorry that you were hurt.'); and a third group of participants evaluated a version of the scenario in which the other party offered a full apology that took responsibility for causing the injuries (i.e., 'I am so sorry that you were hurt. The accident was all my fault.'). Thus, the only difference between the three groups was the nature of the apology offered.

Apologies Affect Settlement

In the first, study, even though all participants were told that they had suffered the same injuries and received the same offer of settlement, the nature of the apology offered influenced recipients' willingness to accept the offer. Receipt of a full, responsibility-accepting apology increased the likelihood that the offer would be accepted. In contrast, a partial, sympathy-expressing apology increased participants' uncertainty about whether or not to accept the offer.

Specifically, when no apology was offered, 52 percent of respondents indicated that they would definitely or probably accept the offer, while 43 percent would definitely or probably reject the offer, and 5 percent were unsure. When a partial apology was offered, only 35 percent of respondents were inclined to accept the offer, 25 percent were inclined to reject it and 40 percent indicated that they were unsure. In contrast, when a full apology was offered, 73 percent of respondents were inclined to accept the offer, with only 14 percent inclined to reject it and 14 percent unsure.

In addition, a full apology resulted in more positive ratings of numerous variables that are thought to underlie settlement decision making than did either a partial apology or no apology. Where there were differences in participants' responses across conditions, the differences follow a strikingly similar pattern: failing to offer an apology or offering a partial apology elicited equivalent responses on these measures that were both different from the responses elicited when a full apology was offered.

Thus, as compared to offenders who offered either a partial apology or no apology, an offender who offered a full apology was seen as:

- having offered a more sufficient apology

- experiencing more regret

- being more moral

- being more likely to be careful in the future

- believing that he or she was more responsible for the incident, and

- having behaved less badly.

In addition, participants who received a full apology, as opposed to a partial apology or no apology, expressed:

- greater sympathy for the offender

- less anger, and

- more willingness to forgive the offender.

Finally, participants who received a full apology, as opposed to a partial apology or no apology, anticipated:

- less damage to the parties' relationship, and

- that the settlement offer would better make up for their injuries.

These underlying judgments provided the mechanism by which apologies influenced settlement decisions. Beyond their effect on decisions regarding a particular offer, such judgments might also be expected to influence the willingness and ability of litigants to engage in settlement negotiations more generally.

NOTES AND QUESTIONS

1. Is there a place for apology in the expected value approach to settlement?

2. While "full" apologies have the most consistently positive effects on disputant perceptions, simple expressions of sympathy can sometimes have beneficial effects as well. Statements that are not fully apologetic may be difficult to interpret and signals about the sincerity with which they are offered may be particularly important. *See* Jennifer K. Robbennolt, *Apologies and Settlement Levers*, 3. J. Empirical Studies 333 (2006). Think about how

you might advise a client. Under what circumstances would you advise a client to apologize? Express sympathy?

3.   Additional research has found that while attorneys understand the content of apologies in ways that are similar to the ways in which disputants understand them, attorneys are more attuned to the strategic value of apologies—that is, they are more likely to see the apology as an admission—than are disputants. *See* Jennifer K. Robbennolt, *Attorneys, Apologies, and Settlement Negotiation*, 13 Harv. Negot. L. Rev. 349 (2008). How might this different perspective influence the way in which an attorney might counsel a client? How might it affect negotiation with the other side?

4. Despite the benefits of appropriate apology, many lawyers may be reluctant to counsel their clients to take this step, even when warranted, out of concerns for liability. For a discussion, see Jonathan R. Cohen, *Advising Clients to Apologize*, 72 S. Cal. L. Rev. 1009 (1999). Several states have enacted so-called "benevolent gesture" legislation specifically designed to address this concern. For more on this, see Jeffrey S. Helmreich, *Does `Sorry' Incriminate? Evidence, Harm and the Protection of Apology*, Cornell J. L. Pub. Pol'y. 567, 577–79 (2012); Jonathan R. Cohen, *Legislating Apology: The Pros and Cons*, 70 U. Cin. L. Rev. 819 (2002).

5. While apology can be effective in negotiations and mediations, they have been found to be less effective in trials. See Jeffrey J. Rachlinski, Chris Guthrie & Andrew J. Wistrich, *Contrition in the Courtroom: Do Apologies Affect Adjudiction,* 98 Cornell. L. Rev. 1189 (2013).

2.   LEGAL AND ETHICAL OBLIGATIONS

a.   In General

When negotiating, lawyers are subject to several rules governing their conduct, including common law rules, certain context-specific rules, and the ethical rules governing the legal profession. The following excerpt introduces these three sources of regulation of lawyer-negotiator behavior.

RUSSELL KOROBKIN, MICHAEL MOFFITT & NANCY WELSH, THE LAW OF BARGAINING

87 Marq. L. Rev. 839, 839–44 (2004)

I.   COMMON LAW LIMITS ON BARGAINING BEHAVIOR

When a negotiated agreement results from false statements made during the bargaining process, the common law of tort and contract sometimes holds negotiators liable for damages or makes their resulting agreements subject to rescission. The common law does not, however, amount to a blanket prohibition of all lying. Instead, the common law principles are subject to the caveats that false statements must be material, the opposing negotiator must rely on the false statements, and such reliance must be justified. Whether reliance is justified depends on the type of statement at issue and the statement's specificity. A seller's specific false claim ("this car gets eighty miles per gallon gas mileage") is actionable, but his more general claim ("this car gets good gas mileage") is probably not, because the latter statement is acknowledged as the type of "puffing" or "sales talk" on which no reasonable buyer would rely.

While it is often said that misrepresentations of fact are actionable but misrepresentations of opinion are not, this statement is not strictly accurate. Statements of opinions can be false, either because the speaker does not actually have the claimed opinion ("I think this Hyundai is the best car built in the world today") or because the statement implies facts that are untrue ("I think this Hyundai gets the best gas mileage of any car"). But statements of opinion are less likely to induce justified reliance than are statements of specific facts, especially when they are very general, such as a claim that an item is one of "good quality."

Whether reliance on a statement of fact or opinion is justified depends significantly on the context of the negotiation and whether the speaker has access to information that the recipient does not. A seller "aggressively" promoting his product whose stated opinions imply facts that are not true is less likely to find himself in legal difficulty if the veracity of his claims are easily investigated by an equally knowledgeable buyer than if his customer is a consumer unable to evaluate the factual basis of the claims. The case for liability is stronger still when the negotiator holds himself out as being particularly knowledgeable about the subject matter that the expressed opinion concerns. Whether a false statement can be insulated from liability by a subsequent disclaimer depends on the strength and clarity of the disclaimer, as well as on the nature of the false statement. Again, the standard is whether the reasonable recipient of the information in total would rely on the statement at issue when deciding whether to enter into an agreement.

It is universally recognized that a negotiator's false statements concerning how valuable an agreement is to her or the maximum she is willing to give up or exchange in order to seal an agreement (the negotiator's "reservation point," or "bottom line") are not actionable, again on the ground that such false statements are common and no reasonable negotiator would rely upon them. So an insurance adjuster who claimed that $900 was "all he could pay" to settle a claim is not liable for fraud, even if the statement was false. The law is less settled regarding the status of false statements concerning the existence of outside alternatives for a negotiator. A false claim of an offer from a third party is relevant because it implies a strong reservation point, so a negotiator might logically argue that such a claim is no more actionable than a claim as to the reservation point itself. But courts have occasionally ruled that false claims of a specific outside offer are actionable, on the ground that they are material to the negotiation and that the speaker has access to information that cannot be easily verified by the listener's independent investigation.

The most inscrutable area of the law of deception concerns when a negotiator may be held legally liable for failing to disclose information that might weaken his bargaining position (rather than affirmatively asserting a false claim). The traditional laissez-faire rule of caveat emptor eroded in the twentieth century, with courts placing greater disclosure responsibility on negotiators. It is clear that any affirmative action taken to conceal a fact, including the statement of a "half-truth" that implies a false fact, will be treated as if it were an affirmative false statement. Beyond this point, however, the law becomes murky. Although the general rule is probably still that negotiators have no general disclosure obligation, some courts require bargainers (especially sellers) to disclose known material facts not easily discovered by the other party.

Just as the law places some limits on the use of deceptive behavior to seal a bargain, so too does it place some limits upon negotiators' ability to use superior bargaining power to coerce acquiescence with their demands. In general, negotiators may threaten to withhold their goods and services from those who will not agree to their terms. Courts can invoke the doctrine of duress, however, to protect parties who are the victims of a threat that is "improper" and have "no reasonable alternative" but to acquiesce to the other party's demand, such as when one party procures an agreement through the threat of violence, or through the threat to breach a prior agreement after using the relationship created by that agreement to place the victim in a position in which breach would cause noncompensable damage. Judicial intervention is most likely when the bargaining parties' relationship was not arms-length. For example, the common law provides the defense of undue influence to negotiators who can show that they were dependent upon and thus vulnerable to the other, dominant negotiator.

II. CONTEXT–SPECIFIC REGULATION OF NEGOTIATORS' BEHAVIOR

Beyond the general common law constraints on negotiators' behavior, the law imposes particularized parameters on bargainers engaged in negotiations in some specific contexts. For example, labor law places a number of procedural restrictions on negotiating behavior. Compared with their counterparts in non-unionized settings, employers, employees, and their representatives involved in collective bargaining all have considerable limits on their ability to adopt certain approaches to negotiating the terms and conditions of employment.

While federal and state laws proscribe a range of behaviors in collective bargaining contexts, the most vivid encapsulation of these requirements is the duty imposed on both sides by the National Labor

Relations Act to bargain in "good faith." The concept of "good faith" bargaining lacks clear parameters, but a "totality of conduct" standard has given way to a list of proscribed behaviors, such as disengaging from the negotiations and presenting take-it-or-leave-it offers.

In other contexts, the law imposes affirmative duties of disclosure rather than attempting to define the parameters of negotiation behavior. For example, in residential real estate transactions in many states, sellers have a legal obligation to disclose a range of information even if the buyer does not request it. Supplanting the baseline principle of caveat emptor, many states have judged that real estate transactions require different foundational principles.

Finally, in certain bargaining contexts that seem unusually prone to exploitation, the law provides paternalistic protection for potential victims. For example, certain legal disputes involving seamen on the high seas and their employers require judicial approval, because of the perceived power imbalance between seamen and ship owners. Similarly, most jurisdictions require court ratification of divorce agreements. To protect principal parties with little ability to monitor their agents, settlements of class action and shareholder derivative suits also require a judicial finding of fairness. Rather than judicial oversight, many jurisdictions give consumers in certain vulnerable contexts the self-help remedy of unilaterally rescinding an agreement within several days of acceptance, such as when they accept a bargain proposed by telemarketers or door-to-door salespersons. Finally, the law sometimes establishes alternative dispute resolution mechanisms for contexts frequently characterized by dissatisfaction with negotiated agreements. For example, lemon laws anticipate that some percentage of negotiations over used car purchases will result in unhappy consumers. In states with lemon laws, consumers who are dissatisfied with their purchase need not establish one of the traditional bases for rescinding a contract or ceasing performance (for example fraud, duress, or material breach). Instead, consumers have a streamlined system for demonstrating eligibility for the laws' protection after the fact.

III. PROFESSIONAL AND ORGANIZATIONAL CONSTRAINTS ON BARGAINING BEHAVIOR

Some negotiators operate not only within the legal constraints applicable to the general public, but also within the parameters of professional or organizational codes of conduct. These parameters can provide another layer of substantive constraints on negotiating behavior (in addition to those provided by generally applicable law), additional or enhanced enforcement mechanisms, or both.

As an example, attorneys are subject not only to generally applicable legal constraints on negotiating behavior but also to [applicable rules of professional responsibility, which in most jurisdictions are based upon]

the American Bar Association's *Model Rules of Professional Conduct.*
Model Rule 4.1(a) provides that "[i]n the course of representing a client a
lawyer shall not knowingly. . . . Make a false statement of material fact or
law to a third person." The commentary to the rule suggests that the
scope of the rule roughly parallels the common law. For example,
estimates of "price or value" are not considered material, thus permitting
lawyers in general to "puff" as well as lie outright about their reservation
prices. One important difference, however, between the administrative
law governing lawyer-negotiators and the common law governing all
bargainers is the absence of the requirements of reliance and damages in
the regulatory context. To sustain a tort or contract action, the victim
must actually suffer harm. Although punishment for transgressions in
bargaining outside of the doors of the courthouse is a relatively rare
occurrence, lawyers can face disciplinary action for making material
misrepresentations even if no legally cognizable damage results.

NOTES AND QUESTIONS

1.   Professors Korobkin, Moffitt, and Welsh identify several examples
of heightened legislative and regulatory protection for certain groups of
people, as well as people in certain contexts, who are unusually likely to be
vulnerable to exploitation or pressure tactics. Query whether such legislation
or regulation would have been necessary if the courts were less skeptical of
parties' claims of coercion, undue influence, and unconscionability? *See*
Nancy A. Welsh, *The Thinning Vision of Self–Determination in Court–
Annexed Mediation: The Inevitable Price of Institutionalization?*, 6 Harv.
Negot. L. Rev. 1, 63–78, 85–86 (2001)

2.   Recently, Professor Hila Keren has examined the physical, social
and psychological literature regarding stress. Professor Keren argues that an
"informed evaluation of stress arguments is not only pragmatically necessary,
but conceptually required for any legal system that, like contract law, relies
on the power of choice and consent." Hila Keren, *Consenting Under Stress*, 64
Hastings L. J. 679, 679 (2013).

3.   Although our primary focus is on lawyers' involvement in
negotiating civil litigation settlement and transactions, lawyers also
negotiate constantly in the criminal context. Professors Korbkin, Moffit, and
Welsh discuss coercion in the negotiation of civil matters, but claims of
coercion also arise in connection with plea bargaining. The seminal case in
this area is *Brady v. United States*, 397 U.S. 742 (1970). Brady holds that
when a defendant negotiates a guilty plea and thus waives the constitutional
right to trial, such waiver "not only must be voluntary but must be [a]
knowing, intelligent act[ ] done with sufficient awareness of the relevant
circumstances and likely consequences." *Id.* at 748.

4.   In *Bordenkircher v. Hayes*, 434 U.S. 357 (1978), the defendant was
indicted on a charge of passing a forged check in the amount of $88.30, an
offense punishable by two to ten years in prison. During plea negotiations,

the prosecutor stated that he would recommend a sentence of five years if the defendant pled guilty. If the defendant refused to "save[ ] the court the inconvenience and necessity of a trial," however, the prosecutor threatened to re-indict him under a habitual offender law that carried a life sentence. *Id.* at 359. The defendant refused to plead guilty, and the prosecutor did as promised. The defendant was sentenced to life in prison. The Supreme Court held that the defendant's due process rights had not been violated, observing that "in the 'give-and-take' of plea bargaining, there is no such element of punishment or retaliation so long as the accused is free to accept or reject the prosecution's offer." *Id.* at 363.

5.   Interestingly, Professor Andrea Schneider's research, described generally *supra*, suggests that prosecutors perceive defense lawyers as among the most problem-solving of lawyers. See Andrea Kupfer Schneider, *Cooperating or Caving In: Are Defense Attorneys Shrewd or Exploited in Plea Bargaining Negotiations?*, 91 Marq. L. Rev. 145, 156–57 (2007). Professor Schneider suggests that these results may be due to: the extent of repeat play and reputational development in this area of practice; a docket load that requires settlement to move the work along; the clear and punitive nature of the alternative to negotiation; prosecutors' incentive to maximize their conviction rate by going to trial only with sure winners; reduced involvement of lawyers with clients and victims; and defendants' loss aversion.

b.   Ethical Obligations

Lawyers are subject to ethical rules governing the profession, and these rules impose obligations on legal negotiators that may appear to be in tension with the obligations the lawyer faces as an advocate for her client.

Attorneys are required to comply with the professional responsibility rules adopted by the state where the attorney is licensed. More than forty states have now patterned their professional responsibility rules after the ABA's Model Rules of Professional Conduct. For more information, see JAMES R. DEVINE, WILLIAM FISCH & STEPHEN EASTON, PROBLEMS, CASES AND MATERIALS IN PROFESSIONAL RESPONSIBILITY 7–12 (3d ed. 2004).

Recall that the preamble to the Model Rules, in Chapter II *supra*, provides that a lawyer is "a member of the legal profession," "a representative of clients, an officer of the legal system and a public citizen having special responsibility for the quality of justice," and that "[a]s negotiator, a lawyer seeks a result advantageous to the client but consistent with requirements of honest dealings with others." Model Rules of Prof'l Conduct Preamble (2013).

The more specific requirements of honest dealing are embedded in Model Rule 4.1:

RULE 4.1 Truthfulness in Statements to Others

In the course of representing a client a lawyer shall not knowingly:

(a) make a false statement of material fact or law to a third person; or

(b) fail to disclose a material fact to a third person when disclosure is necessary to avoid assisting a criminal or fraudulent act by a client, unless disclosure is prohibited by Rule 1.6.

MODEL RULES OF PROF'L CONDUCT R. 4.1 (2013).

The Comments accompanying this rule attempt to define two of the most vexing terms included in Rule 4.1: "misrepresentation" and "statements of fact." See Appendix B.

NOTES AND QUESTIONS

1.   Professors Art Hinshaw and Jess Alberts presented lawyers with an ethical dilemma involving the continuation of misrepresentation, the truth of which, if known, would have severely compromised what would otherwise have been a substantial claim. Here's what they found:

> The aggregated results of the survey, which report the findings from 734 respondents from the Phoenix, Arizona and St. Louis, Missouri metropolitan areas, found that in response to the client's initial request to refrain from [providing the true information], 62 percent of the respondents said that they would not agree to such a request, while 19 percent said they would agree to the client's request. The remaining 19 percent of the respondents indicated they were not sure how they would respond if placed in this situation. The responses to the client's second request—to disclose [the true information] only if directly asked [about it]—revealed similar results. Sixty-four percent of these respondents (592 respondents) indicated they would refuse the request, 13 percent indicated that they would agree, and 23 percent replied that they were not sure what they would do.

> Focusing on the client's first request, we asked those who indicated they would agree with this request to rate the importance of a number of potential justifications for their decision to agree with the client's request. Using a 10 point scale, with 1 being "not at all important" and 10 being "very important," this subset of respondents gave only three proposed rationales importance ratings higher than the midpoint: "The information is protected by the professional rules of conduct regarding client confidences" (mean = 9.63), "[t]he information is protected by attorney-client privilege" (mean = 9.60), and "[t]he client has specifically requested that this information not be disclosed" (mean = 8.19). For those who indicated they would not agree to the client's request, we asked them to rate the importance of a number of potential justifications to refuse the client's request. Using a 10 point scale, with 1 being "not at all important" to 10 being "very important," all but one proffered

rationale was rated above the midpoint with the following three being rated as very important: "My integrity is too important" (mean = 9.65), "[t]o do so may violate the rules of professional conduct" (mean = 9.54), and "[m]y moral compass will not allow me to do so" (mean = 9.18).

When combining the results of the client's two requests, we found that 30 percent of the respondents agreed to engage in the fraudulent settlement negotiation scheme in violation of Rule 4.1, 50 percent of the respondents refused both client requests, thereby following the proper course of action, and the remaining 20 percent responded that they were unsure how to respond to one or both requests. The study also revealed that potential reasons for this problem include considerable confusion among some attorneys regarding the elements of Rule 4.1. That is, just more than a quarter of the respondents failed to recognize that refraining from disclosing the [true information] constituted a misrepresentation, and many were unable to properly identify various material facts in the hypothetical negotiation. The study also revealed that many attorneys believe that confidentiality concerns, such as client confidentiality and the attorney-client privilege, trump the Model Rule's dictates to refrain from assisting clients in fraudulent conduct.

Art Hinshaw & Jess K. Alberts, *Gender and Attorney Negotiation Ethics*, 39 Wash. U. J.L. & Pol'y 145, 155–157 (2012). For an in-depth description of the research, see Art Hinshaw & Jess K. Alberts, *Doing the Right Thing: An Empirical Study of Attorney Negotiation Ethics*, 16 Harv. Negot. L. Rev. 95 (2011).

2. You are in-house counsel for a company that offers its employees the option to use mediation, with a particular mediation firm, to resolve employment related disputes. An employee's lawyer calls you to inform you that his client is considering bringing breach of contract and discrimination-related claims, but would prefer to negotiate. Your conversation does not produce a resolution. Both of you think, however, that mediation might be helpful. The lawyer says that his client might be willing to consider using the process. But, first, he asks you how your company chose this mediation firm, and how significant a client your company is. You know that the mediation firm's principal mediator is the cousin of your company's CEO. Further, you know that right now, your company is the mediation firm's only repeat client. What will you say in response to the other lawyer?

3. Consider Rule 8.4 of the Model Rules, in Appendix B. How does it apply to your negotiations on your own behalf?

c. Misrepresentation and Omission

The rules governing candor and deception take a lawyer only so far, of course. Most lawyer-negotiators base their conduct not only on the governing ethical rules but also on their own sense of right and wrong. In the following reading, Professor James White describes the circumstances under which he thinks it is acceptable for a lawyer-negotiator to deceive his counterpart.

JAMES J. WHITE, MACHIAVELLI AND THE BAR: ETHICAL LIMITATIONS ON LYING IN NEGOTIATION

1980 Am. B. Found. Res. J. 926, 927–29, 931–35

[In this excerpt, Professor White is commenting on a proposed ethical rule that would have required, in part, that lawyers "be fair in dealing with others."]

On the one hand the negotiator must be fair and truthful; on the other he must mislead his opponent. Like the poker player, a negotiator hopes that his opponent will overestimate the value of his hand. Like the poker player, in a variety of ways he must facilitate his opponent's inaccurate assessment. The critical difference between those who are successful negotiators and those who are not lies in this capacity both to mislead and not to be misled.

Some experienced negotiators will deny the accuracy of this assertion, but they will be wrong. I submit that a careful examination of the behavior of even the most forthright, honest, and trustworthy negotiators will show them actively engaged in misleading their opponents about their true positions. That is true of both the plaintiff and the defendant in a lawsuit. It is true of both labor and management in a collective bargaining agreement. It is true as well of both the buyer and the seller in a wide variety of sales transactions. To conceal one's true position, to mislead an opponent about one's true settling point, is the essence of negotiation.

Of course there are limits on acceptable deceptive behavior in negotiation, but there is the paradox. How can one be "fair" but also mislead? Can we ask the negotiator to mislead, but fairly, like the soldier who must kill, but humanely?

TRUTHTELLING IN GENERAL

The obligation to behave truthfully in negotiation is embodied in the requirement of Rule 4.2(a) that directs the lawyer to "be fair in dealing with other participants."

* * *

The comment on fairness under Rule 4.2 makes explicit what is implicit in the rule itself by the following sentence: "Fairness in negotiation implies that representations by or on behalf of one party to the other party be truthful." Standing alone that statement is too broad. Even the Comments contemplate activities such as puffing which, in the broadest sense, are untruthful. It seems quite unlikely that the drafters intend or can realistically hope to outlaw a variety of other nontruthful behavior in negotiations.

* * *

FIVE CASES

[I]t is probably important to give more than the simple disclaimer about the impossibility of defining the appropriate limits of puffing that the drafters have given in the current Comments. To test these limits, consider five cases. Easiest is the question that arises when one misrepresents his true opinion about the meaning of a case or a statute. Presumably such a misrepresentation is accepted lawyer behavior both in and out of court and is not intended to be precluded by the requirement that the lawyer be "truthful." In writing his briefs, arguing his case, and attempting to persuade the opposing party in negotiation, it is the lawyer's right and probably his responsibility to argue for plausible interpretations of cases and statutes which favor his client's interest, even in circumstances where privately he has advised his client that those are not his true interpretations of the cases and statutes.

A second form of distortion that the Comments plainly envision as permissible is distortion concerning the value of one's case or of the other subject matter involved in the negotiation. Thus the Comments make explicit reference to "puffery." Presumably they are attempting to draw the same line that one draws in commercial law between express warranties and "mere puffing" under section 2–313 of the Uniform Commercial Code. While this line is not easy to draw, it generally means that the seller of a product has the right to make general statements concerning the value of his product without having the law treat those statements as warranties and without having liability if they turn out to be inaccurate estimates of the value. As the statements descend toward greater and greater particularity, as the ignorance of the person receiving the statements increases, the courts are likely to find them to be not puffing but express warranties. By the same token a lawyer could make assertions about his case or about the subject matter of his negotiation in general terms, and if those proved to be inaccurate, they would not be a violation of the ethical standards. Presumably such statements are not violations of the ethical standards even when they conflict with the lawyer's dispassionate analysis of the value of his case.

A third case is related to puffing but different from it. This is the use of the so-called false demand. It is a standard negotiating technique in collective bargaining negotiation and in some other multiple-issue negotiations for one side to include a series of demands about which it cares little or not at all. The purpose of including these demands is to increase one's supply of negotiating currency. One hopes to convince the other party that one or more of these false demands is important and thus successfully to trade it for some significant concession. The assertion of and argument for a false demand involves the same kind of distortion that is involved in puffing or in arguing the merits of cases or statutes that are not really controlling. The proponent of a false demand implicitly or explicitly states his interest in the demand and his estimation of it. Such behavior is untruthful in the broadest sense; yet at least in collective bargaining negotiation its use is a standard part of the process and is not thought to be inappropriate by any experienced bargainer.

Two final examples may be more troublesome. The first involves the response of a lawyer to a question from the other side. Assume that the defendant has instructed his lawyer to accept any settlement offer under $100,000. Having received that instruction, how does the defendant's lawyer respond to the plaintiff's question, "I think $90,000 will settle this case. Will your client give $90,000?" Do you see the dilemma that question poses for the defense lawyer? It calls for information that would not have to be disclosed. A truthful answer to it concludes the negotiation and dashes any possibility of negotiating a lower settlement even in circumstances in which the plaintiff might be willing to accept half of $90,000. Even a moment's hesitation in response to the question may be a nonverbal communication to a clever plaintiff's lawyer that the defendant has given such authority. Yet a negative response is a lie.

It is no answer that a clever lawyer will answer all such questions about authority by refusing to answer them, nor is it an answer that some lawyers will be clever enough to tell their clients not to grant them authority to accept a given sum until the final stages in negotiation. Most of us are not that careful or that clever. Few will routinely refuse to answer such questions in cases in which the client has granted a much lower limit than that discussed by the other party, for in that case an honest answer about the absence of authority is a quick and effective method of changing the opponent's settling point, and it is one that few of us will forego when our authority is far below that requested by the other party. Thus despite the fact that a clever negotiator can avoid having to lie or to reveal his settling point, many lawyers, perhaps most, will sometime be forced by such a question either to lie or to reveal that they have been granted such authority by saying so or by their silence in response to a direct question. Is it fair to lie in such a case?

Before one examines the possible justifications for a lie in that circumstance, consider a final example recently suggested to me by a lawyer in practice. There the lawyer represented three persons who had been charged with shoplifting. Having satisfied himself that there was no significant conflict of interest, the defense lawyer told the prosecutor that two of the three would plead guilty only if the case was dismissed against the third. Previously those two had told the defense counsel that they would plead guilty irrespective of what the third did, and the third had said that he wished to go to trial unless the charges were dropped. Thus the defense lawyer lied to the prosecutor by stating that the two would plead only if the third were allowed to go free. Can the lie be justified in this case?

How does one distinguish the cases where truthfulness is not required and those where it is required? Why do the first three cases seem easy? I suggest they are easy cases because the rules of the game are explicit and well developed in those areas. Everyone expects a lawyer to distort the value of his own case, of his own facts and arguments, and to deprecate those of his opponent. No one is surprised by that, and the system accepts and expects that behavior. To a lesser extent the same is true of the false demand procedure in labor-management negotiations where the ploy is sufficiently widely used to be explicitly identified in the literature. A layman might say that this behavior falls within the ambit of "exaggeration," a form of behavior that while not necessarily respected is not regarded as morally reprehensible in our society.

The last two cases are more difficult. In one the lawyer lies about his authority; in the other he lies about the intention of his clients. It would be more difficult to justify the lies in those cases by arguing that the rules of the game explicitly permit that sort of behavior. Some might say that the rules of the game provide for such distortion, but I suspect that many lawyers would say that such lies are out of bounds and are not part of the rules of the game. Can the lie about authority be justified on the ground that the question itself was improper? Put another way, if I have a right to keep certain information to myself, and if any behavior but a lie will reveal that information to the other side, am I justified in lying? I think not. Particularly in the case in which there are other avenues open to the respondent, should we not ask him to take those avenues? That is, the careful negotiator here can turn aside all such questions and by doing so avoid any inference from his failure to answer such questions.

What makes the last case a close one? Conceivably it is the idea that one accused by the state is entitled to greater leeway in making his case. Possibly one can argue that there is no injury to the state when such a person, particularly an innocent person, goes free. Is it conceivable that the act can be justified on the ground that it is part of the game in this context, that prosecutors as well as defense lawyers routinely misstate what they, their witnesses, and their clients can and will do? None of these arguments seems persuasive. Justice is not served by freeing a guilty person. The system does not necessarily achieve better results by trading two guilty pleas for a dismissal. Perhaps its justification has its roots in the same idea that formerly held that a misrepresentation of one's state of mind was not actionable for it was not a misrepresentation of fact.

In a sense rules governing these cases may simply arise from a recognition by the law of its limited power to shape human behavior. By tolerating exaggeration and puffing in the sales transaction, by refusing to make misstatement of one's intention actionable, the law may simply have recognized the bounds of its control over human behavior. Having said that, one is still left with the question, Are the lies permissible in the last two cases? My general conclusion is that they are not, but I am not nearly as comfortable with that conclusion as I am with the conclusion about the first three cases.

Taken together, the five foregoing cases show me that we do not and cannot intend that a negotiator be "truthful" in the broadest sense of that term. At the minimum we allow him some deviation from truthfulness in asserting his true opinion about cases, statutes, or the value of the subject of the negotiation in other respects. In addition some of us are likely to allow him to lie in response to certain questions that are regarded as out of bounds, and possibly to lie in circumstances where his interest is great and the injury seems small. It would be unfortunate, therefore, for the rule that requires "fairness" to be interpreted to require that a negotiator be truthful in every respect and in all of his dealings. It should be read to allow at least those kinds of untruthfulness that are implicitly and explicitly recognized as acceptable in his forum, a forum defined both by the subject matter and by the participants.

NOTES AND QUESTIONS

1.   Is Professor White correct that a negotiator "must be fair and truthful" on the one hand but that he "must mislead his opponent" on the other?

2.   Do you agree with Professor White's view that there are permissible and impermissible lies? Consider the following excerpt from Professor Gerald Wetlaufer arguing that lawyer-negotiators cannot distinguish between types of lies:

> For purposes of this Article, 'lying' will be defined to include all means by which one might attempt to create in some audience a belief at variance with one's own. These means include intentional communicative acts, concealments and omissions. The exact boundaries of 'lying' as defined, is a subject to which we will, in due course, devote a good deal of attention.
>
> It has been suggested that this definition of lying is too broad and that one should, at this early stage of the inquiry, acknowledge a distinction between lying and other lesser deceptions. My reasons for not doing so are three. First, it is perfectly appropriate, at least in American usage, to define lying as I have done. Second, as is made clear in the new OXFORD ENGLISH DICTIONARY, there is a strong measure of euphemism in our habit of reserving 'lying' for only the most serious offenses. This

tendency toward euphemism can bring considerable confusion to the inquiry at hand. Third, the desire to distinguish lying from lesser deceptions rests on the assumption that there is a moral or ethical distinction between these two categories of conduct.

Gerald Wetlaufer, *The Ethics of Lying in Negotiations*, 75 Iowa L. Rev. 1219, 1223 (1990).

3.   In each of the five cases Professor White discusses, do you agree with his conclusions about whether it is permissible to mislead your opponent?

4.   From Professor White's perspective, how would you respond to the following: Assume you represent a plaintiff in a personal injury case who sustained a back injury. You have had a series of negotiations with the insurance company claims adjuster in which you indicated, truthfully, that because of the back injury, your client has had to give up all vigorous activity for an indefinite period of time. Yesterday, your client told you he had played two sets of tennis in each of the last two weeks, with only minor soreness. This indicates he is recovering much more quickly than anyone anticipated. Would you volunteer this information at the next meeting with the claims adjuster? How would you respond if the claims adjuster asked, "Is your client able to exercise at all?" *See* Thomas F. Guernsey, *Truthfulness in Negotiation*, 17 U. Rich. L. Rev. 99, 113–23 (1982); David Luban, *Bargaining and Compromise: Recent Work on Negotiation and Informal Justice*, 14 Phil. & Pub. Aff. 397 (1985).

5.   Empirical studies indicate that many practicing lawyers have difficulty in applying the ethics rules to their negotiations. Professor Art Hinshaw reports that in one study, "[n]early one-third of attorney respondents indicated that they would agree to engage in a fraudulent settlement scheme if a client asked them to do so. Two other studies showed that approximately one-quarter of attorney respondents were unable to correctly identify the proper ethical response in four run-of-the-mill negotiation situations." Art Hinshaw, *Teaching Negotiation Ethics*, 63 J. of Legal Educ. 82 (2013); Art Hinshaw & Jess K. Alberts, *Doing the Right Thing: An Empirical Study of Negotiation Ethics*, 16 Harv. Negot. L. Rev. 95, 117–20 (2011); Art Hinshaw, Andrea Schneider & Peter Reilly, *Attorneys and Negotiation Ethics: A Material Misunderstanding*, 29 Neg. J. (forthcoming 2013); Peter Reilly, *Was Machiavelli Right? Lying in Negotiation and the Art of Defensive Self–Help*, 24 Ohio St. J. on Disp. Resol. 481 (2010).

6.   Professor Peter Reilly recommends the following self-help measures: conduct a thorough background check on the other parties to the negotiation; network for potential negotiation counterparts; create rapport; demand the use of objective standards but avoid being hamstrung by them; strategically limit information revelation; recognize and thwart tactics of evasion; establish long-term relationships and watch for signs of deception; and use "come clean" questions strategically. *See* Peter Reilly, *Was Machiavelli Right?*

Lying in Negotiation and the Art of Defensive Self–Help, 24 Ohio St. J. on Disp. Resol. 481, 525–532 (2010).

7.   Professor Korobkin and his colleagues, *supra*, introduced the law of misrepresentation generally. In the following case, we examine in some detail allegations of a lawyer's misrepresentation during litigation-related negotiation. As we noted in Chapter II, these sorts of cases represent cautionary tales. As you read the Minnesota Supreme Court's opinion here, consider how you would have responded to the question asked. Consider how your choice of negotiation strategy—adversarial, problem-solving, tit-for-tat—would interact with your ethical obligations and the relevant law.

HOYT PROPERTIES, INC. V. PRODUCTION RESOURCE GROUP, L.L.C.
736 N.W.2d 313 (Minn. Sup. Ct., 2007)

PAGE, JUSTICE.

[In 2001, Hoyt Properties engaged in a multi-million dolar commercial lease with Entolo. When Entolo defaulted, Hoyt filed an unlawful detainer action, and on the day of the eviction hearing Hoyt and Entolo reached a settlement that included a liability release for Entolo's parent corporation. Hoyt alleges it agreed to the release because of a misrepresentation by PRG's attornies on the day of the eviction hearing.

According to Hoyt, upon learning that PRG was concerned about being sued after the fact, Hoyt asked, "I don't know of any reason how we could pierce the veil, do you?" Hoyt alleges that PRG's attorney responded, "There isn't anything. PRG and Entolo are totally separate." However, Hoyt later learned of a lawsuit brought by a third party against Entolo that alleged breach of contract by Entolo but sought to hold its parent company, PRG, liable by piercing the corporate veil. The complaint alleged, among other things, that Entolo failed to observe corporate formalities, was operated by PRG as a division rather than a separate corporation, and was undercapitalized by PRG.

Hoyt filed this action to rescind the settlement agreement and to pierce the corporate veil to hold PRG liable for Entolo's breach of the lease. Hoyt alleges the PRG representations were false and that the attorney either knew or should have known that the representations were false.]

* * *

When reviewing a grant of summary judgment, we review the record to determine: "(1) whether there are any genuine issues of material fact for trial; and (2) whether the trial court erred in its application of the law." We review the evidence in the light most favorable to the nonmoving party, in this case, Hoyt.

To make out a claim for fraudulent misrepresentation, the plaintiff must establish that:

(1) there was a false representation by a party of a past or existing material fact susceptible of knowledge; (2) made with knowledge of the falsity of the representation or made as of the party's own knowledge without knowing whether it was true or false; (3) with the intention to induce another to act in reliance thereon; (4) that the representation caused the other party to act in reliance thereon; and (5) that the party suffer[ed] pecuniary damage as a result of the reliance. Appellants argue that the statements at issue do not amount to statements of past or present material fact as required under the first prong of our fraudulent misrepresentation standard.

As the court of appeals noted, abstract statements of law or pure legal opinions are not actionable; however, a mixed statement of law and fact may be actionable "if it amounts to an implied assertion that facts exist that justify the conclusion of law which is expressed" and the other party would ordinarily have no knowledge of the facts. * * * Thus, according to the Restatement, one who says, ' "I think that my title to this land is good, but do not take my word for it; consult your own lawyer,' " cannot be reasonably understood as asserting any fact with respect to the title. However, a legal statement in the form of an expression of opinion may still be actionable if it carries "with it by implication the assertion that the facts known to the maker are not incompatible with his opinion or that he does know facts that justify him in forming it." For example, a statement that one mortgage has priority over another may imply an assertion that one was made before the other; and a statement that a corporation has the legal right to do business in a state may carry with it an assurance that it has as a matter of fact taken all of the steps necessary to be duly qualified.

In order to evaluate the statement at issue in this case, it is helpful to review the standard courts use to determine whether to pierce the corporate veil. A court may pierce the corporate veil to hold a shareholder liable for the debts of the corporation when the shareholder is the alter ego of the corporation. When using the alter ego theory to pierce the corporate veil, courts look to the "reality and not form, with how the corporation operated and the individual defendant's relationship to that operation." Factors relevant to that inquiry include insufficient capitalization for purposes of corporate undertaking, failure to observe corporate formalities, nonpayment of dividends, insolvency of debtor corporation at time of transaction in question, siphoning of funds by dominant shareholder, nonfunctioning of other officers and directors, absence of corporate records, and existence of corporation as merely facade for individual dealings.

Appellants assert that the representations PRG's attorney allegedly made were statements of the attorney's legal opinion only and thus were not actionable. Appellants argue that Steve Hoyt's question, "I don't know of any reason how we could pierce the veil, do you?," solicited the view of PRG's attorney regarding a legal claim, to which PRG's attorney responded with the legal opinion "There isn't anything." As to the second part of the alleged representation, "PRG and Entolo are totally separate," appellants argue that this was also a legal opinion, and that the word "separate" is a legal term of art that "does not describe a particular factual predicate in a piercing-the-veil case, but rather, a general legal conclusion that piercing is not warranted." Hoyt asserts that the representation that "There isn't anything" "implied that PRG's and Entolo's business operations justified [the attorney's] conclusion that there was not 'anything' to a good-faith piercing claim" and that the representation that "PRG and Entolo are totally separate" was a direct factual statement bolstering the assertion that there were no facts supporting a veil-piercing claim. Hoyt further asserts that Steve Hoyt had no knowledge of the facts underlying PRG's corporate relationship with Haas and Entolo.

* * * When viewed in the light most favorable to Hoyt, as is required under the summary judgment standard, the representation "There isn't anything" is a representation that no facts exist that would support a piercing claim against PRG—for example, no facts indicating that Entolo did not maintain corporate formalities. Even if we assume, as appellants argue, that the alleged statement made by PRG's attorney was an expression of his legal opinion, that representation implies that the attorney was aware of facts supporting that opinion, namely, that there were no facts to support a claim to pierce the corporate veil. Because the representation was not an expression of pure legal opinion (for example, "I do not think someone could pierce the veil but I am not sure"), but rather a statement implying that facts existed that supported a legal opinion, we conclude that the representation is actionable.

We conclude that the second alleged representation, "PRG and Entolo are totally separate," is also actionable. Again viewed in the light most favorable to Hoyt, the second representation constitutes a direct factual assertion that the relationship between PRG and Entolo is such that no facts exist that would allow the corporate veil to be pierced; for example, that no facts existed that would demonstrate that Entolo was a façade for PRG's own dealings. As such, it is the kind of representation that we have traditionally held to be actionable.

* * *

The record is sufficient for us to conclude that there are also genuine issues of material fact for trial as to whether PRG's attorney made the representations at issue without knowing whether they were true or false. * * * In his deposition, PRG's attorney also admitted that when he made the alleged representations at issue he had not yet formed an opinion, one way or the other, about the facts alleged in the complaint. Given these admissions, a finder of fact could conclude that when PRG's attorney responded to Steve Hoyt's question he did not know whether his representations were true. As such, there is a genuine issue of material fact for trial as to whether he made the representations "without knowing whether [they were] true or false."

III.

Finally, we address the district court's finding that "Hoyt's reliance on opposing counsel's remarks was unreasonable as a matter of law." * * * To prevail on a claim of fraudulent misrepresentation, the complaining party must set forth evidence demonstrating both actual and reasonable reliance. * * * To establish actual reliance, Hoyt offered Steve Hoyt's deposition testimony that he agreed to release PRG from liability because he relied on the representations PRG's attorney made regarding piercing the corporate veil. On this record, Steve Hoyt's testimony is sufficient to defeat summary judgment on the question of actual reliance. * * *

Because we hold that Hoyt established genuine issues of material fact for trial as to the required elements of a fraudulent misrepresentation claim, we affirm the court of appeals' decision and remand to the district court for further proceedings.

Affirmed.

ANDERSON, PAUL H., JUSTICE (dissenting).

I respectfully dissent.

* * *

The first element of a claim for fraudulent misrepresentation is only met if the false factual representation by the party involves a "fact susceptible of knowledge." When this standard is applied to the facts in this case, it is difficult to see how PRG's attorney's representations can be actionable. First, in order for PRG's attorney to imply facts that "[t]here isn't anything" to a veil-piercing claim, the attorney would have to imply a factual assertion that the second prong of the claim is met—that the claim is "necessary to avoid injustice or fundamental unfairness." Because this is a subjective inquiry made by a court, it is not a "fact susceptible of knowledge," and even if it was, it is unreasonable to conclude that PRG's attorney *falsely* implied that a veil-piercing claim in this case would not meet this prong. In other words, if PRG's attorney was to evaluate the claim and decide that it was viable, the attorney would have to conclude that it would be unjust and fundamentally unfair for the attorney's client to escape liability. Those are not the type of conclusions we can expect, or even desire, a legal advocate to make, and they are generally not susceptible of the attorney's knowledge.

The majority also accepts the characterization of PRG's attorney's statement that "PRG and Entolo are totally separate" as a "direct factual statement bolstering the assertion that there were no facts supporting a veil-piercing claim." But because the two-prong test for piercing the corporate veil is a subjective test applied by the court, PRG's attorney could not be in a position to know (1) what facts any particular court or factfinder might find significant, and (2) which factors under the first prong the court might apply, since the enumerated factors in case law are not exhaustive. Therefore, it is difficult to see how PRG's attorney could as a matter of law represent that "no facts" exist to support a veil-piercing claim because a court could find a fact significant that no other court ever had in the past.

* * *

But even if the first element is actionable, I conclude that as a matter of law, Hoyt Properties cannot meet the fourth element of fraudulent misrepresentation: "that the representation caused the other party to act in reliance thereon." * * * The majority's conclusion ignores Hoyt Properties' burden of production, which is to create a genuine issue of material fact by presenting evidence sufficiently probative to permit reasonable persons to draw different conclusions.

My review of the record reveals little about the legal basis for Steve Hoyt's reliance on PRG's attorney's statements. In his deposition, Steve Hoyt asserted that "at least in this city * * * I think lawyers are pretty forthright and honest." He further stated, "I think when somebody asks a question, if the other person chooses to respond, * * * I think they have a duty to tell the truth. * * * [W]hether that response is a legal opinion or whatever, I think it's a duty to tell the truth or say nothing."

We have concluded that in actions where a party attempts to rescind an agreement based on fraud, "the question is whether the representations were of such a character and were made under such circumstances that they were reasonably calculated to deceive, not the average man, but a person *of the capacity and experience of the particular individual who was the recipient of the representations.*" The record before us reveals that the district court found the following facts with respect to Steve Hoyt:

- he is an attorney who practiced in the area of general business law;

- he is a sophisticated commercial businessman with significant experience, having formed 30 business entities in order to limit liability;

- he is a significant shareholder and board member of Real Estate Trust, a company worth over a billion dollars;

- he has testified as an expert regarding real estate matters;

- he has the legal and business experience necessary to understand the intricacies of corporations, corporate liability, and matters relating to piercing the corporate veil;

- he includes a standard clause in all of his leases stating "Consult Your Attorney: This document has been prepared for approval of your attorney";

* * *

- in this case, he was accompanied by counsel when settlement negotiations occurred before the agreement was signed;

* * *

In light of Steve Hoyt's extensive legal and business background, his documented practice of relying on his own legal counsel in his business practices, and his standard lease clause advising others to do the same, I conclude that on this record, Hoyt Properties fails to establish reasonable reliance on PRG's attorney's statements as a matter of law. Steve Hoyt's bare assertions that "lawyers [in this city] are pretty forthright and honest" and "have a duty to tell the truth" are not legally sufficient to establish a genuine issue of material fact regarding *reasonable* reliance. Therefore, I conclude that Hoyt Properties cannot establish the fourth element of fraudulent misrepresentation.

Finally, I also share the policy concerns of amicus curiae Minnesota Defense Lawyers Association that the majority's decision will have the adverse effect of discouraging settlement among parties, based on a lack of confidence in the enforceability of settlement agreements. Fewer settlement agreements could create further demands on the court system and also create additional risk and expense for parties in litigation. Further, I am concerned that what the majority has done with its opinion is to design a roadmap with a well-defined exit route for parties who experience remorse after entering into a settlement agreement.

For all the foregoing reasons, I would reverse the court of appeals and reinstate the district court's summary judgment ruling in favor of appellants.

NOTES AND QUESTIONS

1. As *Hoyt Properties* illustrates, it can be difficult to determine whether a representation is one of fact or opinion. Comment d to Section 525 of the Restatement (Second) of Torts (1977) provides:

Strictly speaking, "fact" includes not only the existence of a tangible thing or the happening of a particular event or the relationship between particular persons or things, but also the state of mind, such as the entertaining of an intention or the holding of an opinion, of any person, whether the maker of a representation or a third person. Indeed, every assertion of the existence of a thing is a representation of the speaker's state of mind, namely, his belief in its existence. There is sometimes, however, a marked difference between what constitutes justifiable reliance upon statements of the maker's opinion and what constitutes justifiable reliance upon other representations. Therefore, it is convenient to distinguish between misrepresentations of opinion and misrepresentations of all other facts, including intention.

A statement of law may have the effect of a statement of fact or a statement of opinion. It has the effect of a statement of fact if it asserts that a particular statute has been enacted or repealed or that a particular decision has been rendered upon particular facts. It has the effect of a statement of opinion if it expresses only the actor's judgment as to the legal consequence that would be attached to the particular state of facts if the question were litigated. It is therefore convenient to deal separately with misrepresentations of law.

2. The presence or absence of justifiable reliance can be significant in cases involving claims of fraudulent misrepresentation arising out of negotiations between sophisticated parties such as lawyers, businesspersons, and investment bankers. For example, in the case of *Terra Firma Inves. (GP) 2 Ltd. v. Citigroup Inc.*, 716 F3d 296 (2013)—involving Terra Firma's purchase of the financially-troubled EMI—one of the key issues was whether Terra Firma justifiably relied on an assertion by a Citi investment banker regarding the submission of a competing bid when, in fact, no such bid had been or would be made. In that case, a choice of law provision also proved significant in determining who would bear the burden of proof on the question of justifiable reliance. Both sides had agreed that English law applied. The Second Circuit vacated the district court's judgment for defendants and remanded for a new trial after finding that under English law, when a fraudulent misrepresentation is one on which a reasonable person would rely, there is a rebuttable presumption of reliance. The trial judge therefore had erred in instructing the jury that plaintiff Terra Firma bore the burden of proof on the reliance element. The instructions were prejudicial and required reversal.

In a concurring opinion, Judge Lohier noted "the growing number of international commercial disputes" and the "increasing frequency" of the need to determine and apply foreign law. He observed that the federal courts in the U.S. have long dealt with a similar situation when they have been required to determine and apply state law and had developed a process for certifying questions to state courts. He suggested: "In the context of cross-border commercial disputes, there is every reason to develop a similar formal certification process pursuant to which federal courts may certify an unsettled and important question of foreign law to the courts of a foreign country. Fortunately, in this case, the question appears to have been neither unsettled nor especially important to the development of English law."

3.   In general in the U.S., parties have no common law obligation to negotiate in good faith to reach a final agreement. There are some statutory exceptions as described by Professors Korobkin, Moffitt and Welsh, *supra*. In addition, parties may enter into a binding agreement expressing their commitment to negotiate in good faith. A cause of action for breach of the duty to negotiate in good faith therefore requires the following showings: 1) both parties manifested an intention to be bound by an agreement to negotiate in good faith; 2) the terms of the agreement are sufficiently definite to be enforced; and 3) consideration was conferred. See *Flight Sys., Inc. v. Elec. Data Sys. Corp.*, 112 F.3d 124, 130 (3d Cir. 1997), *Bennett v. Itochu International Inc.*, 682 F. Supp.2d 469 (E.D.Pa. 2010) (finding that "non-binding" term sheet nonetheless conferred a bargained-for benefit and was sufficient to give rise to duty to negotiate in good faith).

d.   Confidentiality of Settlement Negotiations

A lawyer involved in negotiations may divulge information that could be detrimental if widely disseminated. Consider whether lawyers using a problem-solving strategy need to be particularly aware of this danger.

Rule 408 of the Federal Rules of Evidence protects the confidentiality of certain statements made during negotiations to some degree, through the regulation of their admissibility in judicial proceedings. The general purpose of the rule is to promote settlement by rendering information exchanged during the settlement discussion inadmissible in subsequent proceedings. The rule is of common law origin, and has also been codified in many states.

Over the years, Rule 408 has evolved. Today, it specifically provides:

(a) Prohibited Uses. Evidence of the following is not admissible— on behalf of any party—either to prove or disprove the validity or amount of a disputed claim or to impeach by a prior inconsistent statement or a contradiction:

(1) furnishing, promising, or offering—or accepting, promising to accept, or offering to accept—a valuable consideration in compromising or attempting to compromise the claim; and

(2) conduct or a statement made during compromise negotiations about the claim—except when offered in a criminal case and when the negotiations related to a claim by a public office in the exercise of its regulatory, investigative, or enforcement authority.

(b) Exceptions. The court may admit this evidence for another purpose, such as proving a witness's bias or prejudice, negating a contention of undue delay, or proving an effort to obstruct a criminal investigation or prosecution.

NOTES AND QUESTIONS

1.   Some courts have found that "when the issue is doubtful, the better practice is to exclude evidence of compromises or compromise offers." *Bradbury v. Phillips Petrol. Co.,* 815 F.2d 1356, 1364 (10th Cir. 1987). Others, however, are more inclined to permit settlement discussion evidence to come in when they feel it necessary for a party to establish their case.

2.   Rule 408 is broad in that it protects not only statements made during settlement, but also evidence of conduct during a settlement discussion. Thus, for example, if the plaintiff in a personal injury case was walking perfectly well as she entered the room where a settlement discussion was taking place, but then limped up to the witness stand at trial, the settlement discussion rule would prohibit the defendant from establishing this point at trial if it was for the purpose of disputing the validity of the plaintiff's claim or impeaching the plaintiff's testimony. Remember that Rule 408 applies only in federal court. State court rules of evidence may handle this issue differently.

3.   Rule 408 raises several definitional questions. At what point, for example, does a "disputed claim" exist? Several federal circuits recognize a dispute's existence even if it has not yet "crystallize[d] to the point of threatened litigation." *See e.g., Weems v. Tyson Foods Inc.,* 665 F.3d 958, 965 (8th Cir. 2011) (finding separation agreement offered to employee after her removal from her position was inadmissible to support her employment discrimination claim even though she had not raised the issue of discrimination and was not contemplating legal action at the time); *Affiliated Mfrs. v. Aluminum Co. of Am.,* 56 F.3d 521, 527 (3d Cir. 1995); *accord Dallis v. Aetna Life Ins. Co.,* 768 F.2d 1303, 1307 (11th Cir. 1985). For Rule 408 purposes, a dispute exists as long as there is "an actual dispute or difference of opinion" regarding a party's liability for or the amount of the claim. *Weems,* 665 F.3d 958 at 965; *Affiliated Mfrs.,* 56 F.3d at 527; *accord Dallis,* 768 F.2d at 1307 (same). *See also, King v. University Health Care System,* 645 F.3d 713, 720 (add ct. 2011) (affirming exclusion of portions of emails that were offered to prove hospital's liability to doctor and the amount of her claims; portions of emails showing that doctor advised hospital of employment discrimination claim, however, were found admissible).

When does an "investigation" or "fact-finding" transform into a "dispute" for purposes of Rule 408? Does such transformation occur as soon as a lawyer becomes involved? In *Communications Services Inc. v. Hagan,* 641 F.3d 112 (5th Cir. 2011), MCI brought an action against a landowner, claiming that the landowner and a backhoe operator were liable for severing an underground cable owned by MCI. The landowner claimed that he called a lawyer after he found an MCI contractor on his property. MCI claimed that the lawyer then called an MCI employee, who was ready to testify that the lawyer told him that the landowner "had been installing a boat ramp and asked what the damage to the cable would cost." *Id.* at 116. The district court excluded the MCI employee's testimony based on Rule 408. On appeal, the Fifth Circuit upheld the exclusion, but not on the basis of Rule 408: "At the point in time the call was placed, there was not yet an actual dispute or a difference of opinion about who caused the damage to MCI's cable and how much the damage was costing MCI. Coudrain [the lawyer] may have intended the call to begin the process of settlement discussions, but because there was not yet an actual dispute his statement likely cannot qualify as a negotiation toward compromise." *Id.* at 117.

Similarly, Rule 408 does not require exclusion of evidence if such evidence is offered for "another purpose, such as proving a witness's bias or prejudice, negating a contention of undue delay, or proving an effort to obstruct a criminal investigation or prosecution." Courts have admitted settlement evidence where it was "offered to show the state of mind of the witnesses," *Croskey v. BMW of N. Am., Inc.,* 532 F.3d 511, 519 (6th Cir. 2008), and where wrongful acts—such as libel, assault, breach of contract, and unfair labor practices—were alleged to have occurred during settlement negotiations, *Uforma/Shelby Bus. Forms, Inc. v. NLRB,* 111 F.3d 1284, 1293–94 (6th Cir. 1997).

4.   A federal agency undertakes an investigation of a company, and collects sensitive corporate information. Based on the information it has collected, the agency determines that the company has violated the law. The agency and company enter into a settlement agreement. A consumer then brings an action against the company and seeks to discover the documents that the agency had collected. Will Rule 408 exclude the documents from discovery? *See In re Subpoena Issued to Commodity Futures Trading Commission,* 370 F. Supp. 2d 201 (D.C. 2005) (finding Rule 408 inapplicable because it deals only with admissibility, not discovery, and declining to find a federal settlement privilege).

5.   The plain language of Rule 408 formerly reflected an exception commonly recognized in the states: that the rule does not preclude the use of statements made, or conduct engaged in, during a settlement discussion if the information was "otherwise discoverable." This exception prevents the settlement discussion from being used to shield otherwise discoverable evidence. In the personal injury example described in Note 2, for example, the defendant would be able to establish that the plaintiff was walking without a limp at times other than during the settlement discussion. While the rule no longer expressly provides for an "otherwise discoverable" exception, it is highly unlikely that courts will reverse precedent and depart from this well-established rule.

e.   **The Place of Values and Morals**

Does the lawyer-negotiator's obligation to her counterpart extend beyond merely being truthful? According to Professor Jonathan Cohen, lawyer-negotiators have a moral duty to treat one another with respect.

JONATHAN R. COHEN, WHEN PEOPLE ARE THE MEANS: NEGOTIATING WITH RESPECT

14 Geo. J. Legal Ethics 739, 741–43, 749–51 (2001)

The topic of negotiation ethics is by no means new. Negotiation has long been a hallmark of social development, and from ancient times writers have been concerned with how negotiation should be practiced. Were the Biblical characters Rebecca and Jacob wrong to deceive Isaac, by masquerading and outright lying, so as to ensure that Isaac's blessing passed to Jacob rather than Esau? If a merchant porting grain by ship from Alexandria to famine-stricken Rhodes overtakes at sea several other vessels also porting grain to Rhodes, should he, upon arriving in Rhodes, reveal the imminent arrival of those other vessels, or should he bargain without revealing that information? To this day the puzzles of deception and disclosure have remained at the heart of most discussions of negotiation ethics within the American legal community, with occasional attention paid to the topic of fairness. Yet there is a fundamental domain within negotiation ethics that relates to, but is distinct from, these topics that has been largely unaddressed. I call this the ethics of orientation. The purpose of this Article is to explore that domain.

To introduce this domain, consider the following question: What distinguishes negotiation from interpersonal interactions generally? A basic difference is that in negotiation, each party attempts to get the other party to do something, or at least explores that possibility. Put differently, in negotiation the other party is a potential means towards one's ends. If two people are chatting about the weather, rarely will their conversation end with an exchange of promises. If they are negotiating the sale of a car, it very well may.

This basic difference between negotiation and most social interactions points to a core question, or tension, lying within the domain of orientation ethics. Usually we think of other people as, well, people. Yet negotiation may pull us towards seeing others as mere instruments for achieving our purposes. To borrow from the language of Martin Buber, in negotiation we are drawn towards reducing the other person from a "Thou" to an "It." Negotiation thus presents an apparent ethical tension that I call the object-subject tension: when negotiating, how is one to reconcile the impulse to treat the other person as a mere means toward one's ends with general ethical requirements for treating people? In response, I argue that in negotiation one should see the other party both as a means toward one's ends and as a person deserving respect. More specifically, the act of negotiation does not relieve one of the moral duty to respect others. This duty of respect implicates both the traditional negotiation ethics topics of deception, disclosure and fairness and also topics such as manipulation, coercion, listening, and autonomy.

* * *

What orientation should one take towards the other party in a negotiation?

A hard-nosed "realist" might claim that, in a negotiation, the other party is a possible means to one's ends, an instrument toward one's goals. This is undoubtedly true and relevant. However, it is only a partial picture. One's stance towards the other party in negotiation should recognize more than just that person's instrumentality.

Sometimes one's relationship with the other party affects what orientation one should take when negotiating. If a parent and child are negotiating over the child's bedtime, one would hope that they see themselves not as adversaries but rather as members of a loving family. A good parent should ask both "What will work for me?" and "What will be best for my child?" Athletes in team sports often face similar situations. "If I pass the ball, my individual scoring 'stats' may be lower, but it might help the team to win. What should I do?" Implicitly, the issue faced is whether the athlete sees her teammates as rivals or as partners, or as a combination of both.

Even if one does not have a prior relationship with the other party, the other party is still a human being, and it is morally relevant to see the other party as such. Skeptics might argue, "What difference does it make what orientation I take towards the other party? That's just a matter of my internal beliefs." Yet beliefs affect actions. Is it wrong to intimidate another person? Then prima facie it should be wrong to intimidate that other person in negotiation. The same applies to deception, coercion, threats, incivility, psychological assaults, manipulation, and so on. If it is wrong to treat people in these ways, then, unless compelling justification is given (e.g., few would say that it was wrong for the Allies to deceive the Nazis about where the Normandy invasion would occur), it remains wrong to do so in negotiation. A fundamental moral challenge in negotiation is seeing the fundamental dignity of people despite their instrumentality.

Note the linkage here between orientation ethics and more traditional topics within negotiation ethics, such as lying, failing to disclose material information, or substantive unfairness in bargaining outcomes. Seeing the other party as a person with fundamental dignity provides a moral basis for refraining from acts such as treating him unfairly, deceiving him, and so on. Derived from the concept of fundamental human dignity, a very high level of care should attach to our interactions with one another. It is no excuse for a hard-nosed person to say, "I treat people as objects, and that is how I expect them to treat me." There may well be other possible moral bases for refraining from such immoral acts (e.g., religious beliefs that God will punish you if you lie), but seeing the other party as a person deserving of respect provides a solid one.

NOTES AND QUESTIONS

1. How does a lawyer-negotiator both see "the other party as a person deserving of respect" and attempt to secure the greatest advantage possible for her client? Is there an irreconcilable tension between a lawyer-negotiator's duty to her client and her ethical obligations to the human being on the other side of the table?

2. What other moral obligations might a negotiator owe her counterpart, in addition to the respect that Professor Cohen suggests?

3. How can rules of law support negotiators who want to demonstrate the sort of respect that Professor Cohen describes?

4. How might the cultivation of mindfulness, introduced in Chapter II, affect a negotiator's moral choices, particularly with respect to her style of negotiation? *See* SCOTT L. ROGERS AND JAN L JACOBOWITZ, MINDFULNESS AND PROFESSIONAL RESPONSIBILITY: A GUIDEBOOK FOR INTEGRATING MINDFULNESS INTO THE LAW SCHOOL CURRICULUM (2012); Scott R. Peppet, *Can Saints Negotiate? A Brief Introduction to the Problems of Perfect Ethics in Bargaining*, 7 Harv. Negot. L. Rev. 83, 84–90 (2002).

F. DEALING WITH DIFFERENCE IN NEGOTIATION

As we have already discussed *supra*, people often make assumptions about the motives and goals of their negotiation counterparts. Sometimes these assumptions are grounded in substantial experience in negotiating with that person or others who seem similar to her. In other cases, these assumptions are grounded in stereotypes, which themselves may be based on substantial (or limited) experience or commonly-held understandings about characteristics of people who belong to a certain social identity group.

At times, these stereotypes will prove useful; at other times, however, they will mislead. There is a growing amount of scholarly work on culture and conflict. There is also a growing recognition of the extent and effects of implicit bias and unconscious bias. *See e.g.*, Anthony G. Greenwald & Linda Hamilton Krieger, *Implicit Bias: Scientific Foundations*, 94 Cal. L. Rev. 945 (2006); Debra Lyn Bassett, *Deconstruct and Superstruct: Examining Bias Across the Legal System*, 46 U.C. Davis L. Rev. 1563 (2013). Recall our discussion *supra* regarding the heuristics upon which we rely so frequently. Also recall our discussion *supra* of the frequently-negative effects of cognitive biases and the fundamental attribution error.

We cannot, and perhaps would not even want to try to, offer here an exhaustive catalogue of the values, strategies and techniques that are likely to characterize negotiators from different cultures or social identities. Rather, we will focus on helping you to develop a way to think about these issues in negotiation. We begin by suggesting the overwhelming importance of approaching these topics with humility and open-mindedness. We can only learn from and about each other if we are willing to listen.

1. CULTURE

"Culture" is not a simple concept. In the following reading, Professor Jayne Seminare Docherty, an anthropologist, describes three different ways of thinking about culture and negotiation. Moving from what she considers to be the least sophisticated to the most sophisticated, these three approaches are the "tip of the iceberg" approach, the "patterns" approach, and the "symmetrical anthropology" approach. After we consider each of these in turn, we will then explore subcultures.

a. A General Approach to Culture

JAYNE SEMINARE DOCHERTY, CULTURE AND NEGOTIATION: SYMMETRICAL ANTHROPOLOGY FOR NEGOTIATORS
87 Marq. L. Rev. 711, 711–722 (2004)

Unfortunately, some negotiation texts—particularly but not exclusively popular books on negotiation—focus almost entirely on the part of the iceberg visible above the surface. In these texts, cultures are presented as lists of do's and don'ts. These lists are rooted in stereotypes and are of dubious value. Teaching negotiators about culture in this manner is of limited value and might actually be dangerous in some settings.

Furthermore, this approach contains a number of faulty assumptions about human beings and about culture. Lists of do's and don'ts: Do not offer your left hand to an Arab; learn how to deeply bow to a Japanese negotiator; understand the protocols for offering refreshment to a Turkish counterpart; treat culture as a superficial overlay that covers a universal human nature or perhaps a universal human culture; deep down, where it counts, all persons are fundamentally the same when it comes to reasoning, emotionality, needs, and desires. This confusion arises because there is a generic human culture, "a species-specific attribute of Homo sapiens, an adaptive feature of our kind on this planet for at least a million years or so." But there are also local cultures—"those complex systems of meanings created, shared, and transmitted (socially inherited) by individuals in particular social groups". It is local cultures that can create problems in negotiation.

A more sophisticated approach to culture in negotiation involves identifying patterns or types of cultures by studying a large group of cultures. Instead of getting inside of a specific culture to understand it, this approach stands outside of cultures and looks for patterns or cultural styles. These are often presented as a list of dichotomous characteristics including: high context/low context; individualism/collectivism; and egalitarian/hierarchical. A high-context culture often relies on indirect communication, because the participants are expected to understand the complex meaning of relatively small non-verbal gestures. A low-context culture will tend to rely on direct statements and formal, clear ratification of written negotiated agreements. Negotiators from individualist cultures may worry less about preserving relationships than negotiators from collectivist cultures. And, negotiators from egalitarian cultures are likely to be less concerned about issues of rank and privilege than negotiators from hierarchical cultures.

* * *

The goal in identifying types of cultures or developing cultural profiles is to alert negotiators to communication patterns and to provide cautionary advice about how to communicate in a particular cultural context or with someone from a particular culture. This way of thinking about culture is more useful for negotiators than lists of traits as long as they recognize the following: these dichotomies are actually continua; within cultures, changes in context (e.g., family versus business setting) will lead people to locate in different places along the continua; there are subcultural variations within any culture; and not all individuals carry their culture in exactly the same way.

At least this approach to culture alerts people to the fact that *they* have a culture too! The issue is not what is wrong with that person from another culture, but where the mismatches are between our cultures. On the other hand, describing cultures as a collection of styles or preferences that impact communication and therefore negotiation still does not get us at the deepest part of the iceberg. Many people who talk about culture this way miss the point that conflict as a domain of social interaction and negotiation as a mechanism for communicating about conflict are both culturally constructed. All cultures have conflict, but not all cultures see the same problems as conflicts, nor do they make the same assumptions about how human beings should respond to conflict. All cultures have processes we can identify as negotiation, but they do not all negotiate the same way.

The most complete and sophisticated way of thinking about culture and negotiation requires that we greatly enrich our definition of culture. Avruch offers the following definition: "For our purposes, *culture* refers to the socially transmitted values, beliefs and symbols that are more or less shared by members of a social group, and by means of which members interpret and make meaningful their experience and behavior (including the behavior of 'others')." He also points out that this definition includes a number of assumptions. First, individuals belong to multiple groups and therefore carry multiple cultures. The implication is that an encounter between two individuals is likely to be a *multicultural* encounter since each participant can draw on more than one culture to make sense of the situation. This includes negotiation encounters. Second, it is important to understand the institutions and mechanisms that transmit culture. Third, culture is almost never perfectly shared by all members of a community or group. Individuals have the capacity to selectively adopt and adapt their multiple cultures, so you cannot assume that a person from culture X will do Y. Each party can draw from, adapt, and modify a multifaceted set of cultural norms and rules; therefore every intercultural encounter is a complex improvisational experience.

It is critically important to remember that our own cultures are largely invisible to us; they are simply our "common sense" understandings of the world. Hence, "conflict is, at essence, the construction of a special type of reality. Most of the time we assume and take for granted that we share a single reality with others, but we do not." We see culture when we are forced to recognize that not everyone experiences and lives in the world the way we do. Perhaps we experience "language shock" when we recognize that someone may be speaking the same language, but we are not sure they live on the same planet we do. Or, we may encounter someone whose "moral order"—their "pattern of . . . compulsions and permissions to act in certain ways and [their] prohibitions against acting in other ways"—differs from our own. In negotiations, these moments of shock and surprise may occur around issues of risk because risk is very much a cultural construct. We may also experience surprise when people use the same language, even the same metaphors, but we discover that their shared language is actually covering over profound differences in their sense of reality. What *we* assume is negotiable may not be negotiable to another person and vice versa.

As negotiators, the recognition that we have a culture too reshapes the reality within which we work. We are forced to grapple with the fact that the very domain of our work—social conflict—is culturally constructed.

* * *

When we encounter cultural differences about when and how to negotiate, we can focus on what the other person is doing "wrong" compared to us. . . . Or, instead of focusing on what is wrong with the other culture, we can become adept at a form of "symmetrical anthropology" that is "capable of confronting not beliefs that do not touch us directly—we are always critical enough of them—but the true knowledge to which we adhere totally." We can subject our own culture(s) to the same scrutiny we apply to the culture(s) of others. That means we will need to become critically aware of our own assumptions about negotiation. What does it mean to say "get beneath positions to interests?" Does everyone share the assumptions about human nature and social relationships on which this approach to finding a "win-win" solution rests?

NOTES AND QUESTIONS

1.   Professor Docherty refers to three different dichotomies that researchers have studied: high-context versus low-context, individualist versus collectivist, and egalitarian versus hierarchical. Researchers categorize the United States as low-context, individualist, and egalitarian. For more on culture and negotiation, *see* Jeanne M. Brett, NEGOTIATING GLOBALLY (2001); Michele J. Gelfand and Jeanne M. Brett, *Integrating Negotiation and Culture Research*, in THE HANDBOOK OF NEGOTIATION AND CULTURE 415 (Gelfand, Brett et al. eds., 2004); Anthony Wanis, *Cultural Pathways in Negotiation and Conflict Management*, in THE HANDBOOK OF DISPUTE RESOLUTION 118–34 (Moffit & Bordone, eds., 2005); RETHINKING NEGOTIATION TEACHING: INNOVATIONS FOR CONTEXT AND CULTURE 281 (Honeyman, Coben, De Palo et al. eds., 2009); VENTURING BEYOND THE CLASSROOM: VOLUME 2 IN THE RETHINKING NEGOTIATION TEACHING SERIES (Coben, DePalo & Honeyman, eds., 2010); EDUCATING NEGOTIATORS FOR A CONNECTED WORLD (Honeyman, Coben & Wei–Min Lee, eds., 2013). For more on culture and dispute resolution more generally, *see* GEERT H. HOFSTEDE, CULTURE'S CONSEQUENCES: INTERNATIONAL DIFFERENCES IN WORK–RELATED VALUES 15 (1980); THE CONFLICT & CULTURE READER 7 (Pat K. Chew ed., 2001); Harold Abramson, *Outward Bound to Other Cultures: Seven Guidelines for U.S. Dispute Resolution Trainers*, 9 Pepp. Disp. Resol. L.J. 437 (2009).

2.   Using these dichotomies, how would you describe the culture of the city in which your law school is located? How does it compare to the culture of the city in which you were born?

3.   Professor Docherty offers several suggestions to those who would like to improve their skills as "symmetrical anthropologists," including broadening one's expectations, attempting to understand our own and others' worldviews, and exploring the metaphors that people embroiled in conflict use in their speech.

4.   How might one handle cultural differences in negotiation? Consider the following suggestion:

What, then, are some implications of this brief essay for more effective negotiation across cultural/national boundaries? First, while cultural/national boundaries clearly *do* exist, much of what passes for such differences may well be the result of expectations and perceptions which, when acted upon, help to bring about a form of self-fulfilling prophecy. Perhaps the best way to combat such expectations is to go out of one's way to acquire as much information as one can beforehand about the way people in other cultures view the kind of problem under consideration. Thus, if we are negotiating with a German about a health care contract, we should try to find out whatever we can about how Germans tend to view health care. Of course, in large countries, there may be regional variations that also need to be taken into account.

Second, it is important to enter into such negotiations with self-conscious awareness of the powerful tendency we share toward stereotyping; this kind of consciousness-raising may, in its own right, help make it a bit less likely that we will slip into a set of perceptual biases that overdetermine what transpires in the negotiations proper.

Third, it is important to enter into negotiations across cultural/national lines by trying to give your counterpart the (cultural) benefit of the doubt. Just as you would not wish others to assume that you are nothing more than an exemplar of people from your culture, try similarly to avoid making the same mistaken assumption about the other person.

Jeffrey Z. Rubin & Frank E. A. Sander, *Culture, Negotiation, and the Eye of the Beholder*, 7 Negot. J. 249, 252 (1991).

b. Subcultures

When negotiating with a person from a substantially different culture, it may be easy to spot some differences in basic approaches to negotiation. However, when negotiating with someone from our own culture but a different subculture—a different ethnic group, business, organization, or even law school—it may be more difficult to observe such differences. The following excerpt illustrates this problem.

LEONARD L. RISKIN, OBEY THE RULE: JUST SAY "NO, NO, NO,"

Chi. Trib., June 25, 1992, at C19

Right after my speech, a tall woman in a gray business suit rushed forward and said she'd like to meet me for breakfast to discuss professional collaboration. The next morning, before I had tasted my fresh-squeezed orange juice, we both realized that our interests did not match. As I wiped the last bits of the $14.25 Eggs Benedict from my beard, my companion did something that brightened my day immeasurably: She asked the waiter to put both checks on one bill. But when she fumbled awkwardly for her cash, I was impelled to ask whether she would be reimbursed. "Yes," she replied, "but it's from a very limited fund." Reflexively, I blurted out, "I'd be glad to pay my share." And she snapped up my offer.

I was stunned. I quickly recovered my composure, however, when I realized that she accepted my offer only because she thought I meant it. And this misapprehension was in no way her fault.

To grasp the complexity of my state of mind, the woman would have had to drop in on a gathering in my parents' plushly carpeted living room in the 1950s, when I was a schoolboy learning the basics of manners.

There she would schmooze with my relatives and my parents' friends, locked into an irregular circle—formed by a shiny green sofa (from which the plastic cover had been removed for the occasion), three folding "bridge" chairs, two wing-back chairs and an old piano bench—with each guest clutching a tall glass embellished with a frosted flower and brimming with what was known in Milwaukee as "white soda." About 9:15, just as my Tante Nettie mumbles, "Time to go home," my mother throws open the sliding door from the kitchen, steps into the living room and announces she's prepared "a little something to eat." This draws a negative cacophony: "Why did you go to all that trouble?" "My stomach has been bothering me." "I'm on a diet." My mother deftly undercuts their positions: "I've done it already. I had everything in the house. It will all go to waste. Just have a bite." Because of the logic and force of my mother's arguments, most of the group moves, with only mild grumbling, into the kitchen, there to encounter a semi-lavish and overabundant presentation of homemade strudel, sweet rolls, cheese, bread and coffee.

Although my mother has won the major battle, she must carry out several "mopping up" operations—one-on-one combat, to ensure that the guests don't just sit there, but eat! At this point, the players act out the principle that muddled up the end of my breakfast: The Rule of Threes. In its simplest formulation, the rule provides that "Any offer worth making—or any refusal meant sincerely—must be extended three times, unless it is accepted first." For instance:

My mother: "Have some strudel." Her friend Rose (who eats like a bird): "No thanks." My mother: "You eat like a bird." Rose: "I am full, and I've been having stomach trouble." My mother: "Oh, a little bit won't hurt you." Rose: "I am really full." My mother: "Are you sure you won't have just a little?" Rose: "Well, maybe a tiny bit."

Rose proceeds to eat more than my cousins Donny and Delores combined.

Now the Rule of Threes was never meant to be followed woodenly. Its legitimate purpose is simply to help you find out what the other person really wants. Since we can never truly understand another person, the Rule of Threes substitutes for that understanding in the same sense that the adversary process in a court substitutes for truth or justice.

But I've seen friends and relatives twist the rule and employ it to serve another precept—that "It is better, much better, to give than to receive." For instance, any time my parents gave my maternal grandmother a gift, she replied (even before she saw the gift): "That's ridiculous. Why did you spend money on me?" After she opened the box and saw the dress—it was always a dress—she insisted that she didn't need it. After protesting for at least five minutes in at least three languages, she caved in: "All right, if it will make you happy, I will keep it."

My analysis: Giving a gift creates an indebtedness from the recipient (my grandmother) to the giver (my mother). This means that the giver has "won" and the recipient lost. But the recipient can dilute the victory by saying she did not need the gift, that she is accepting it only to please the gift giver. In other words, she in fact is bestowing a good on the gift giver, and—by thus demonstrating that she is a superior person—has "won."

In restaurants, dining with friends and relatives, the rules were more complex—because the stakes were much higher. In a restaurant, the question of who picked up the check could have significant financial consequences. So all the rituals were subservient to the general principle that "He who is best off should pay." Usually, this meant my cousin Joe, who was single and almost wealthy, or my Uncle Max, who could sell aluminum siding to homeless people.

But not before virtually everyone at the table reached for that check, or snatched at it with the same blend of aggression and reticence displayed by two golden retrievers locked in a ritualistic battle—lots of snarling and snapping, but no real attempt to make contact.

On at least one occasion, I manipulated the Rule of Threes in a way that now seems cruel, deploying it against a person who was unaware of the rule, an unarmed civilian, so to speak. It was my friend Isidore, from Montreal, who was visiting my wife and me for a week in Washington. Playing the gracious host (and the prosperous American lawyer), I paid for all the food, at home and in restaurants. But on the last night of Isidore's visit, the three of us were sitting in Luigi's restaurant, playing with the hot wax that dripped onto the gingham tablecloth from the candle stuck into the top of a chianti bottle (this was the early '70s). Isidore said he wanted to pay the bill, and he reached for it. But he was no match for me. I snatched the bill before he could get it. And when he protested that I had paid for all the meals, I said he could reciprocate— when we visited him in Montreal. I expected him to keep offering, but he did not; and so I paid.

He looked surprised, as I recall, perhaps hurt. He really wanted to pay, I guess, but he didn't know what it took. I regretted my behavior almost immediately and have continued to regret it for almost 20 years. This is partly because I wanted him to pay, too, and partly because I thought I had robbed him of a measure of dignity. But there is another reason: I went to Montreal last summer with my family, and I thought Isidore would repay my largesse in a good French restaurant. I tried to call him, but he is not listed in the telephone book.

NOTES AND QUESTIONS

1.   This excerpt suggests that, in a variety of settings, people will not always say what they mean or mean what they say. In fact, sometimes a negotiator may say the opposite of what he or she means. Accordingly, the listener, even if he comes from the same general culture, may often misinterpret the intended message. This is less likely to happen when the negotiation is conducted by lawyers or other agents who share a common negotiation culture.

2.   How could you interpret the negotiation described in the foregoing excerpt in terms of the distinction between high and low context cultures? Consider Riskin's "offer" to pay for his breakfast. In the high-context culture of his family, would that offer have been interpreted in the way that he intended it? Why did he assume, if he did, that his breakfast companion would understand his intention?

Can you recall negotiations or even conversations in which you misunderstood or were misunderstood because of the differing assumptions about the context or meaning of a something said or done? How can you, as a negotiator, determine that your counterpart means what he or she says? How can you enhance the likelihood that your counterpart will understand what you mean to convey?

3.   How would you describe the subculture of a workplace in which you have been employed? Your law school? The legal profession in general?

4.   Different religious groups can represent important subcultures. Jeffrey Seul observes, "Religion offers much more to individuals and groups in their effort to construct and maintain secure identities than do most other social institutions, so religion is often at the core of individuals'—and groups'—conceptions of themselves." Jeffrey R. Seul, *Religion and Conflict*, in THE NEGOTIATOR'S FIELDBOOK 323, 325 (Andrea Kupfer Schneider & Christopher Honeyman eds., 2006).

For negotiators involved in a dispute that has a discernible religious element, Mr. Seul has "a few, tentative prescriptions":

● Recognize that religion is central to the identities of some or all of those involved in the conflict. Religion may very well be *the* primary lens through which one sees oneself and the rest of the world, including what is at stake in the conflict. When this is the case, the religious dimension of the conflict must be acknowledged, accepted, and integrated into negotiations and other conflict resolution efforts.

● Recognize that others' beliefs are deeply and sincerely held, regardless of how foreign they may seem from one's own perspective. One is unlikely to persuade another to abandon his or her beliefs (irrespective of the propriety of attempting to do so in the first place).

● Invite religious people involved in the conflict to speak openly about their commitments and the ways in which those commitments influence their perspectives and actions. In social or political conflicts involving multiple stakeholders, invite influential members of all affected religious communities to participate in negotiations and other components of dispute resolution processes.

  • Focus on practical opportunities for cooperation, not ideology. Look for ways the parties can cooperate that are consistent with their respective beliefs. For example, pro-life and pro-choice activists may never agree when life begins, but they might be willing to cooperate to develop programs designed to reduce the number of unwanted pregnancies.

  • Recognize that the identities of individuals and groups typically are multi-faceted, regardless of the salience of any one element, like religion. Look for alternate "points of contact." For instance, two ideological opponents might find a common bond in their respective experiences raising a handicapped child.

  • Appeal to the better nature of all those involved in the conflict. Each of the religious traditions considered in this chapter provides support for nonviolent approaches to engaging in conflict and efforts to resolve conflicts consensually. If you are a party to a conflict, focus on these strains within your own tradition and invite others to focus on the complementary strains within their traditions.

Id. at 331–332.

  5.   Professor Phyllis Bernard suggests that in international trade, the success of those negotiating business deals in developing countries "will turn on making room at the table for moral considerations, including those rooted in faith traditions that have shaped societies in these emerging markets." Phyllis E. Bernard, *Finding Common Ground in the Soil of Culture, in* RETHINKING NEGOTIATION TEACHING: INNOVATIONS FOR CONTEXT AND CULTURE (Christopher Honeyman, James Coben & Giuseppe De Palo, eds., 2009) at 30. She observes that a major international player, the World Bank, "now discourages unfettered private corporate conduct without consideration of public needs" and "has encouraged the inclusion of non-financial constituencies in economic plans, since 'religious leaders and institutions— churches, mosques, and temples—are often the most trusted associations in developing countries.' This traditional, cultural 'infrastructure' may provide the best base for 'promoting sustainable development.[.]' " *Id.* at 33.

  6.   Professor Ilhyung Lee argues that cross-cultural negotiation should be taught in more law schools. He also suggests that lawyers' experience with the dynamics of subcultures should help them appreciate the need to plan for navigating cultural differences in negotiation:

    Litigation lawyers especially know of the notion of a "local culture" that varies from district to district, state to state, and region to region. What many have suspected was confirmed in an illuminating work by Professor Thomas Church, *Examining Local Legal Culture*, which examined the practices of four court systems in disposing of criminal cases. Sharply questioning the general notion that law is law and is applied neutrally by a neutral forum, Professor Church found the presence of shared norms and attitudes by local practitioners, judges, court staff, and law enforcement, resulting in cases being handled differently from court to court. A sense of ethnocentrism was also seen in the four courts, in that there was "not simply a general contentment with the existing pace of litigation in their courts—no matter how fast or slow—but a firm belief that this *pace was really the only proper one*, that any significant slowing down *or* speeding up would almost certainly produce injustice." Some may respond that a local culture that varies from locality to locality, potentially affecting the client's interests and rights, can be addressed simply enough by wise selection of capable local counsel. If cross-cultural negotiation means dealing in a foreign *forum*, whether beyond the home locale, state, or country, advisors familiar with the local culture may be retained to assist in the preparations and negotiations. Moreover, the matter of negotiation with a foreign *party* is not a novel concept, since learning as much as possible about "the other side" and being prepared is a general lesson for any lawyer.

Ilhyung Lee, *In re Culture: The Cross–Cultural Negotiations Course in the Law School Curriculum*, 20 Ohio St. J. on Disp. Resol. 375, 391–92 (2005).

2. GENDER

Gender may also play a role in negotiation. The following excerpt explores some empirically documented differences in the negotiation behavior of men and women. The first portion of the reading highlights negotiation behavior of women in general; the second portion of the reading highlights the behavior of women who negotiate as lawyers or other professionals. As you read this, whether you are male or female, consider whether, in your experience, this rings true.

CARRIE MENKEL–MEADOW, WHAT DIFFERENCE DOES "GENDER DIFFERENCE" MAKE?
18 Disp. Resol. Mag. 4 (2012)

This essay reviews some of the continuing efforts to determine whether gender has any significant or predicable impact on dispute resolution behavior. I continue to think this is an interesting, but inconclusive question, especially because dispute resolution is itself an interactive process involving parties, representatives (lawyers) and dispute resolvers or facilitators (negotiators, mediators, arbitrators and judges, among other roles), so that the mix or context of gendered participants interact with each other and also with the site (court, private mediation, quasi-private arbitration, negotiation) and subject matter of any particular dispute. Although I continue to think that gender somehow matters, sometimes, in some places, more recent research indicates that the difference that gender difference makes is quite variable, depending on case type, context, role of participant (e.g. agent or principal) and now perhaps, different generations of disputants and disputes.

Parties in Disputes

Much of the work on gender in negotiation or legal disputing assumes that disputants, as principal parties, are much affected by their gender. Women are less likely to view disputes and transactions as negotiable events, as Linda Babcock and Sara Laschever noted in "Women Don't Ask: Negotiation and the Gender Divide." Women are also more likely to compromise or give in to the other side, especially when there is some relationship (friend, family member, repeat player, or workplace superior), therefore requiring a slew of self-improvement advice for how to be better and stronger negotiators, although when closely examined, most of the advice doled out in such books is not much different for women than what is offered to all in our negotiation canon in such works as "Getting to YES." Empirical work on women as direct parties in disputes is actually far more complex, with great relevance for what parties want in disputes, and what they ask their lawyers to achieve in represented negotiations, mediations or arbitration, as well as how they behave themselves as parties. Perhaps most important in such studies is to consider if women are negotiating or disputing directly for their own interest (where they are often perceived to be less demanding, conciliatory and compromising) or whether they are working in a more representative capacity (such as a manager of employees, agent for clients, nurse for patients, or mother on behalf of children's needs), where they are also credited for actually having different, and sometimes "better," leadership, problem-solving or representative skills.

Recent work on women as parties in disputes, both in mediation and in court settings, indicates that consistent with procedural justice findings generally, process matters independent of outcomes. In one of the most rigorous studies to date of mediation, Tamara Relis has found that women as litigant-parties in mediation processes were more concerned with emotional, not just compensatory, aspects of their mediated cases, were more likely to want alleged harm doers (defendants) to attend mediation sessions and to hope for direct communication with other parties, not just about legal issues, but about "extra-legal" aspects of their disputes. In an earlier study designed to measure whether both women and minorities fared differently in different dispute resolution processes, researchers in New Mexico rigorously paired cases in litigated settings with court-annexed mediations with different race, ethnic and gendered dispute resolvers (judges and mediators). Among the complex and varied findings of this study was the interesting result that although many women actually fared better in mediation sessions (in relatively small claims matters) they often preferred court adjudication. This was some confirmation of Trina Grillo's important critique of mediation as being an unfair process for disempowered women many years ago. The perception of fairness or other attributes of a dispute resolution process may turn out to be more important than the actual outcomes themselves.

For many years I have been wondering and teaching about the interesting paradox posed by contradictions in both scholarly and popular views of differences in disputing processes. Grillo, Penelope Bryan, Martha Fineman and others have long argued that in situations of informal and non-public or not strong law-enforcing dispute processing (e.g., negotiation, mediation), women are "disempowered" and do less well than they might in more formal, rule and procedure based settings such as full court adjudication (primarily in family and employment matters). But, researchers outside of law have empirically demonstrated that in fact women are more effective at speaking the language of problem solving which is particularly used in such informal settings as mediation. Deborah Tannen's bestselling books on gendered communication in both the workplace and in relational contexts demonstrate that women are more forthcoming in communicating their needs, desires and ideas for problem solving than are men. Thus, in at least some of those informal dispute resolution settings, women are actually more comfortable with the language of psychological needs and problem solving and also potentially more patient. In Tannen's work, men often are impatient to get to a quick and efficient resolution, rather than spend more time on "relational" work or looking at many sides to the problem. Relis' recent research comments on this, noting that some women plaintiffs are less comfortable talking and advocating strongly in mediation settings, but that female lawyers are more likely to engage in problem solving and collaborative behavior in mediation settings, suggesting that the role that gender plays in dispute resolution is strongly tied to role (professional), as well as to place or site of dispute resolution.]

More recent research on women as parties to negotiation or as parties in settings where others represent them recognize more rigorously that context (type of case and setting) and the interactive expectations of opposite parties can affect what happens in a negotiation greatly, so that there is great variance in "performance" in negotiated settings. Borrowing from work in cultural studies, "performativity" in dispute resolution can depend on "triggers," so that women negotiators working with each other may produce different behaviors than if negotiation dyads are mixed and someone (male or female) makes assumptions of nurturing, problem-solving behavior, or in other studies, overly "aggressive" behavior by women. Expectations of stereotypes may "trigger" particular reactions, but with less stereotyping negotiators are freer to just use whatever strategies and problem-solving skills they have. The point here is that stereotypic assumptions produce reactions (both ways) and that more modern negotiators and dispute resolvers can be taught to read, defuse or "turn" (Deborah Kolb's term) these stereotypic behaviors into more productive means of dispute resolution.

Knowledge of these stereotypes is important, but newer research of younger generations of negotiators, or those in particular professional contexts such as lawyers, business people, real estate agents, or brokers, seems to be indicating that change is afoot. Neither gender nor negotiation behaviors are immutable. Professional role, time, levels of education, training, preparation, client relations, and dispute context may trump whatever gender variations might seem to some to be "natural" or innate. Gender difference research for decades has debated, without successful conclusion, the relative weights of "nurture" (socialization and education) and "nature" (biological forces) in forming our understandings of how gender operates, both conceptually and behaviorally. As more women enter professional roles in dispute resolution, more training, experience and knowledge of these research studies may be dampening the perceived earlier gender differences, at least in some contexts. In some other contexts, gender difference may still be salient.

Professionals in Dispute Resolution: Lawyers and Other Representatives

Carol Gilligan's work in the 1980s produced many studies seeking to discern if there were gender differences in different professions, especially the legal profession, and in different decision-making contexts. One of her students studied differences in ethical decision-making by male and female lawyers and learned that when lawyer ethical rules were relatively clear, there were little to no differences in how male and female lawyers decided what was ethically mandated. But when the rules were more ambiguous, such as whether to turn over adverse evidence to a lawyer on the other side of a case, or when actual harm to a person was involved, such as custody issues for children, women lawyers were slightly more likely to consider "justice" to the other side, rather than "pure" zealous advocacy. Later studies by Gilligan have demonstrated some merging of gender differences, that is, more girls moving to the male (clearer "justice" rule-based) mode of decision-making, while a smaller core of girls and young women remain committed to a "care" and relational approach to moral decision making and problem solving, though studies also demonstrate that newer generations engage in more "cross-over" or context specific forms of reasoning.

Earlier work on women in business and other professional settings demonstrates that to the extent women have something particular or different to offer, there must be a "critical mass" (variable in different sectors) for the message to be accepted on its own merits and be "detached" from a gendered representation. Studies of both law students in negotiation classes and now a few of lawyers confirm that negotiated outcomes do not differ by gender. But perceptions of results achieved (e.g., women are more self-doubting and critical, are more likely to take negotiation courses pass/fail) or assumptions that stereotypic behavior is expected continue to document differences between perceptions and assumptions and the actual outcomes and behaviors in negotiation.

Of the more recent studies on lawyer behavior, particularly in the mediation setting, Relis suggests that women lawyers, particularly defense counsel in medical malpractice cases, had greater "extra-legal sensitivity" (the need for non-compensatory items, like apologies, etc.) and concern for parties on the other side of cases than did male attorneys. But Relis also found that more facilitative female mediators, especially non-lawyer mediators, tended to be overpowered by aggressive male litigators in mediation settings, suggesting that some of the earlier observed gender differences are not yet gone. Relis' study also found that female plaintiffs were more likely to be overpowered by male mediators during mediations than male plaintiffs, demonstrating that the interaction of the gender of the party, lawyer or representative and dispute manager professional (mediator or judge) is complex. It often involves, as Relis eloquently states, "differentially experienced parallel worlds" in mediation by parties, lawyers and mediators, where gender differential is still part of the experience.

NOTES AND QUESTIONS

1.   We use generalizations to simplify a complicated world. As such, they are second cousins to the stereotypes, cognitive biases and heuristics introduced throughout this book. As you have seen, and will continue to see, these sorts of "mental shortcuts" are inevitable, usually useful and sometimes very dangerous. Available empirical research affirms that certain categories of people are more likely than others to recognize and grasp opportunities for negotiation. The people who recognize and grasp these opportunities tend to do better. Professor Linda Babcock and Sara Laschever examine this phenomenon through the prism of gender:

> Could it be that women don't get more of the things they want in life in part because they don't think to ask for them? Are there external pressures that discourage women from asking as much as men do—and even keep them from realizing what they can ask? Are women really less likely than men to ask for what they want?

> To explore this question, Linda conducted a study that looked at the starting salaries of students graduating from Carnegie Mellon University with their master's degrees. When Linda looked exclusively at gender, the difference was fairly large: The starting salaries of the men were 7.6 percent or almost $4,000 higher on average than those of the women. Trying to explain this difference, Linda looked next at who had negotiated his or her salary (who had asked for more money) and who had simply accepted the initial offer he or she had received. It

turned out that only 7 percent of the female students had negotiated but 57 percent (eight times as many) of the men had asked for more money.

Linda was particularly surprised to find such a dramatic difference between men and women at Carnegie Mellon because graduating students are strongly advised by the school's Career Services department to negotiate their job offers. Nonetheless, hardly any of the women had done so. The most striking finding, however, was that the students who had negotiated (most of them men) were able to increase their starting salaries by 7.4 percent on average, or $4,053—almost exactly the difference between men's and women's average starting pay. This suggests that the salary differences between the men and the women might have been eliminated if the women had negotiated their offers.

LINDA BABCOCK & SARA LASCHEVER, WOMEN DON'T ASK: NEGOTIATION AND THE GENDER DIVIDE, 1–3 (2003). In a subsequent laboratory experiment designed to study propensity to negotiate, Professor Babcock and two colleagues, Deborah Small and Michele Gelfand, found that "almost *nine times* as many male as female subjects asked for more money." Two subsequent studies suggested that men initiate *four* times as many negotiations as women. The lesson? Regardless of any of your sources of social identity, it is important to ask for what you want.

2.   Recent research suggests, however, that women who behave assertively in negotiation are evaluated more harshly than men who behave similarly. *See* Hannah Riley Bowles, Linda Babcock & Lei Lai, *Social Incentives for Gender Differences in the Propensity to Initiate Negotiations: Sometimes It Does Hurt to Ask*, 103 Organizational Behav. & Human Decision Processes 84 (2007). This line of research counsels that "women who ask" must be ready to make a difficult choice—between being liked and being viewed as competent (known as the backlash effect). *See* Catherine H. Tinsley, Sandra I. Cheldelin, Andrea Kupfer Schneider & Emily T. Amanatullah, *Women at the Bargaining Table: Pitfalls and Prospects*, 25 Negot. J. 233 (2009).

3.   Professor Menkel–Meadow concludes *supra*, however, that other factors besides gender will determine negotiation effectiveness. Recall the studies conducted by Professors Williams and Schneider regarding lawyers' perceptions of their colleagues' negotiation effectiveness. Professor Schneider returned to her dataset, and it suggests that when women lawyers are negotiating on behalf of their clients, they are significantly less likely to confront the backlash effect:

In a study of lawyers rating other lawyers in their most recent negotiation, female lawyers were described in terms that were similar to their male colleagues (ethical, confident, and personable) and both were equally likely to be judged as effective in general. In fact, women lawyers were rated more highly in assertiveness than their male counterparts, and yet did not seem to suffer negative consequences for violating feminine proscriptions. . . . [The] unique features of legal work reduce the perceived incongruity between assertiveness and proscribed feminine behavior thereby attenuating the likelihood of backlash.

Andrea Kupfer Schneider, Catherine H. Tinsley, Sandra Cheldelin & Emily T. Amanatullah, *Likeability v. Competence: The Impossible Choice Faced by Female Politicians, Attenuated by Lawyers*, 17 Duke J. Gender L. & Pol'y 363, 364 (2010). The co-authors also provide advice for female lawyers in other contexts where the backlash effect may be more salient. *See also* Laura J. Kray, *Leading Through Negotiation: Harnessing the Power of Gender Stereotypes*, 50 Cal. Mgt. Rev. 159 (2007).

4.   Professors Babcock and Laschever also report on research comparing the negotiation results achieved by female pairings, male pairings and pairings of men and women:

> If integrative bargaining methods produce superior results in many types of negotiations, and women are more likely than men to use these methods, this should mean that women actually make better negotiators than men. Actually, this appears to be true—at least in situations in which women's cooperative overtures are reciprocated. In one of Linda's negotiation experiments, she and her colleague Hannah Riley asked pairs of MBAs to conduct a multi-issue negotiation that possessed integrative potential. Some possible negotiated agreements could be terrific for both parties, with a wide range of alternatives in between. Linda and Hannah Riley had chosen the issues to be negotiated so that finding the better outcomes requires the negotiators to share information, and when they compared outcomes they discovered that the all-female pairs had outperformed the all-male pairs. The agreements reached by the all-female pairs were better for both negotiators than those reached by the all-male pairs on average. This strongly suggests that the female pairs shared more information and that the male and female pairs used different techniques and behaviors to achieve these results.

* * *

Although we know that the more cooperative approach women bring to negotiation can produce superior results, a good outcome using this approach is not guaranteed. When both negotiators don't share this view of a negotiation—if a man and woman take different "scripts" into a negotiation, with the man approaching it as a win/lose situation and the woman seeing it as a search for outcomes to benefit both parties—the woman's strategy, though potentially superior, can leave her vulnerable.

Linda and Hannah Riley's study mentioned above, in which the all-female pairs outperformed the all-male pairs, produced another interesting finding: The mixed female-male pairs produced agreements that were no better than those produced by the all-male pairs. Not only did the females fare much worse when they were negotiating against men than when they were negotiating with women, but the "pies" that the female/male pairs slit up were *smaller* than the "pies" divided by the all-female pairs. In other words, by sharing information and working together, the all-female pairs were able essentially to "enlarge the pie." By "logrolling" and together taking an integrative approach to the process, they were able to identify hidden benefits for both sides that went unnoticed by the pairs that took a more competitive approach. This suggests that the best outcomes are produced in situations in which both negotiators take a cooperative rather than an adversarial approach to working out a solution—that it takes two women, in other words, or two people trained to "negotiate like women," to produce a superior outcome.

LINDA BABCOCK & SARA LASCHEVER, WOMEN DON'T ASK: NEGOTIATING AND THE GENDER DIVIDE, 170, 172–3 (2003).

5.   What should a woman, a man, or anyone do when encountering identity-based stereotypes and offensive behavior? Babcock and Leschever report, for example, that men make significantly greater use of threats, insults, rigid positions and ultimatums. *Id.* at 170, 172–3. Professor Andrea Schneider offers some suggestions to women dealing with the problem of offensive comments, but as you read this excerpt, consider how you can give it broader application.

ANDREA SCHNEIDER, EFFECTIVE RESPONSES TO OFFENSIVE COMMENTS
10 Negot. J. 107, 111–13 (1994)

Responding

There are four major responses a negotiator can make to an offensive comment-ignoring, confronting, deflecting, or engaging. The response you choose should be based on a number of factors, including an analysis of your own assumptions and the other side's motivation for making such a comment.

Other factors—such as whether there is an audience for the comment, whether it has been repeated over time, and how much the comment personally offends you—may also be important. But the question of most significance in these situations is: What is your purpose in responding and what do you hope to achieve?

The response of ignoring the comment needs little explanation—you choose not to respond in any way. Many people end up doing this automatically in response to a comment that makes them uncomfortable. Instead, ignoring a comment should be a conscious, affirmative decision by you that either the comment does not bother you that much or it is just not worth your time and effort to deal with it.

Similarly, the response of confronting the comment is also relatively simple theoretically. Confronting is a counterattack either on the person or the comment (e.g., "That's racist! How can you say that?" or "What a stupid thing to say!") This response should also be a conscious one, a response made to achieve a purpose, not a response made just because you cannot think of anything else to say. At times, confronting is wholly appropriate and is often a highly useful response, particularly with bullies.

Deflecting means acknowledging the comment and moving on. For example, in response to someone who is bragging, about his or her grandiose office space compared with yours (which could be interpreted as demeaning), you might respond, "Yes, your office is lovely and perhaps we might now move to the subject at hand." Or, in response to someone asking you to get coffee, you might respond, "I'll call my secretary to bring us refreshments. In the meantime, can we review the contract?" Deflecting, more than any other response, is a question of personal style and comfort level. It often demands a sense of humor and even quicker thinking than other responses.

Engaging is the fourth type of response one can make to an inflammatory remark. Engaging means having a conversation about the other side's purpose in making the remark and your feelings upon hearing it. First, you check your assumptions about their intentions by asking what their purpose was in making the comment. After they respond, you can gather additional data about their intentions and ask further questions.

Finally, when you think that you understand their point of view and also have demonstrated the ability to listen to them, you share your perceptions. Explain your reaction and your reasoning (e.g., "When I hear that comment, I usually assume. . . . And it makes me feel, think, etc. . . ."). The purpose of entering into this type of conversation is both to check your own perceptions and to educate the other side about your perceptions in a way that is nonconfrontational and nonthreatening.

Engaging the other side with regard to the objectionable comment has several advantages over the other responses. Since engaging follows a pattern, it can be a learned skill. Having a practiced reaction to a comment that throws you off balance in a negotiation can be a great advantage. Engaging also gives you more time to think since you are asking questions—another advantage when you are surprised.

Engaging allows you the opportunity to check your perceptions and assumptions once again. In particular, if you do not know the other side, running through charts and decision trees in your own mind may not be helpful when you have very little data on which to base your conclusions. Engaging them can help you determine if the comment was conscious or unconscious, prejudice or ignorance.

Since engaging is nonconfrontational, it is more appropriate for professional and long-term relationships. Engaging allows both you and the other side to rethink assumptions without escalating the conflict. The two of you can agree that there was a misunderstanding and move on to the substance of the negotiation rather than continue to disagree about the comment and each other's worth as a person. It is better for the relationship than confronting since it may provide each side with a way out of the conflict. It is also better than ignoring the comment if the comment will fester within you and color your future interactions.

Engaging can be particularly useful with someone using biased comments as a tactic for two reasons. First, it throws them off to be asked a question about why they made the comment, and second, your question lets them know that you know the game they are playing. Engaging also gives you back control over the conversation since you are directing it through your questions.

Engaging does not preclude the responses of confronting or deflecting. Once you learn more about what they are thinking, you can still decide to confront them or deflect the comment based on that additional knowledge.

Engaging is also something that you can do at later date after further reflections upon the comment. You can still bring the comment up the next day if you initially ignored it or deflected it and it continues to bother you or if you confronted the comment but are not pleased with the outcome of that conversation.

For example, a black person responding to a question about his or her family's educational history could start an engaging conversation by asking, "Why did you ask me if I was the first person in my family to graduate college?" The other side might respond, "Well, I just think that it's wonderful that you went to college and did so well." The black person might follow up by acknowledging the compliment and then asking the other negotiator if he or she thinks that it is so rare for black people to go to college. The other side may respond, "No, but when they come from disadvantaged backgrounds, it's much more of an achievement."

Now that the black person understands the other side's intentions and reasoning, he or she can share their feeling: "Well, when people ask me if I am the first in my family it makes me feel as if I were somehow less worthy to go to college because of my race and background. Rather than take it as a compliment, which is how you intended it, I interpret that question as a slur on my family." If the exchange has gone well, the other side may respond, "I never realized that. I did not intend to insult you in any way."

Engaging conversations can be as explosive as confronting situations, depending on the tone of the engager and the attitude of the person who made the original comment. Yet they have the possibility to educate and to change behavior in the future.

A key difference between confronting and engaging is the acceptance of responsibility for whatever feelings or thoughts you may have. For example, in confronting, you often accuse the other side of having a certain type of character or intention. This, of course, can be disputed by them. When you discuss how the comment makes you feel (engaging), there is no room for disagreement. The issue is not what they intended— of which you cannot really be sure—but what you feel—which they cannot dispute.

* * *

3. RACE

Like culture and gender, race may influence negotiation behavior. The following excerpt reports the results of a study of negotiations at car dealerships. Professor Ian Ayres found significant differences in outcomes based on the race and gender of the prospective car buyers.

IAN AYRES, FAIR DRIVING: GENDER AND RACE DISCRIMINATION IN RETAIL CAR NEGOTIATIONS
104 Harv. L. Rev. 817, 817–19, 827–33 (1991)

The civil rights laws of the 1960s prohibit race and gender discrimination in the handful of markets—employment, housing, and public accommodations—in which discrimination was perceived to be particularly acute. In recent years, lawsuits have increasingly presented claims of more subtle and subjective forms of discrimination within these protected markets. Both legislators and commentators, however, have largely ignored the possibility of discrimination in the much broader range of markets left uncovered by civil rights laws. Housing and employment may be the two most important markets in which people participate, but women and racial minorities may also be susceptible to discrimination when spending billions of dollars on other goods and services. Of these unprotected markets, the market for new cars is particularly ripe for scrutiny because, for most Americans, new car purchases represent their largest consumer investment after buying a home. In 1986, for example, more than $100 billion was spent on new cars in the United States.

This Article examines whether the process of negotiating for a new car disadvantages women and minorities. More than 180 independent negotiations at ninety dealerships were conducted in the Chicago area to examine how dealerships bargain. Testers of different races and genders entered new car dealerships separately and bargained to buy a new car, using a uniform negotiation strategy. The study tests whether automobile retailers react differently to this uniform strategy when potential buyers differ only by gender or race.

The tests reveal that white males receive significantly better prices than blacks and women. As detailed below, white women had to pay forty percent higher markups than white men; black men had to pay more than twice the markup, and black women had to pay more than three times the markup of white male testers. Moreover, the study reveals that testers of different race and gender are subjected to several forms of nonprice discrimination. Specifically, testers were systematically steered to salespeople of their own race and gender (who then gave them worse deals) and were asked different questions and told about different qualities of the car.

* * *

II. RESULTS OF THE TEST

The results from the tester surveys provide a rich database for investigating how salespeople bargain and whether they treat testers of a different race or gender differently. This Part presents the results of these tests in three sections. The first section reports disparate treatment regarding the prices that dealerships were willing to offer the testers. This section includes an analysis of both initial and final offers as well as refusals to bargain and differences in the bargaining paths (the sequence of offers made in succeeding rounds). In the second section, nonprice dimensions of the bargaining process are analyzed. The tests reveal that salespeople asked testers different types of questions and used different tactics in attempting to sell the cars. Finally, the third section uses multivariate regression analysis to analyze the determinants of the final offers. The regressions reveal a fairly sophisticated seller strategy. In particular, the size of final offers is sensitive not only to the race and gender of both the tester and the salesperson, but also to the information revealed by the tester in the course of bargaining.

A. Price Discrimination

1. *Final Offers.*—The final offer of each test was the lowest price offered by a dealer after the multiple rounds of bargaining. By comparing these final offers with independent estimates of dealer cost, it was possible to calculate the dealer profit associated with each final offer (final offer minus dealer cost). For a sample of 165 tester visits, the average dealer profits for the different classes of tester are presented in Table 1.

TABLE 1:	
Average Dealer Profit for Final Offers	
White Male	$ 362
White Female	504
Black Male	783
Black Female	1237

Black female testers were asked to pay over three times the markup of white male testers, and black male testers were asked to pay over twice the white male markup. Moreover, race and gender discrimination were synergistic or superadditive: the discrimination against the black female tester was greater than the combined discrimination against both the white female and the black male tester.

The reliability of these results is buttressed by an analysis of the relative unimportance of individual effects. The average dealer profits on the non-white male testers were statistically different from the average profits on the white males at a five percent significance level. The average profits for the three individual white males were, however, not significantly different from each other. This last result lends support to the proposition that the idiosyncratic characteristics of at least the white male testers did not affect the results.

To determine whether the final offer discrimination stemmed from disparate treatment in sellers' initial offers or from disparate treatment in the sellers' subsequent concession rates, we calculated the average offers testers received in each round of bargaining. Graphically, the differences in final offers can be decomposed into differences in the intercept and differences in the slope: different intercepts represent disparate initial offers; different slopes represent disparate rates of concession. We found that the concession rates do not significantly differ across tester type or across bargaining rounds. The average dealer offers in the initial and subsequent rounds of bargaining, however, differed significantly. For example, the average dealer offers made to black females were significantly higher than those made to white males, but the rate of concession was virtually the same. These results indicate that discrimination in early rounds tends to be perpetuated in later rounds: final offer discrimination is caused by disparate initial offers and not by disparate concession rates. Sellers quoted testers disparate initial offers and then made roughly equal concessions.

Arguably, this perpetuation effect may be an artifact of the testers' split the difference bargaining strategy. In particular, the script instructs testers, in calculating their second counteroffer, to split the difference between dealer's cost (the testers' first counteroffer) and the dealer's second offer. Dealer discrimination in early rounds will cause disparate concessions by testers that may preclude equal treatment in final rounds. The possibility that early offers matter, however, is not an embarrassment of design. Bargainers engage in time-consuming initial rounds of bargaining because they individually believe that these rounds will affect the final price. The tests provide strong evidence that if consumers use the same split the difference strategy, they will receive different final offers that are determined by their race and gender.

2. *Initial Offers.* This study also constructed a test of disparate treatment on the basis of the initial offers sellers made to the testers. As noted above, this short test offers more experimental control because the testers asked only a single question. The average dealer profit on initial offers are presented in Table 2.

TABLE 2:
Average Dealer Profit for Initial Offers

White Male	$ 818
White Female	828
Black Male	1534
Black Female	2169

The average dealer profit on offers made to white female testers was not significantly different from the average profit on offers made to white male testers. Sellers, however, offered both black males and black females significantly higher prices: sellers asked black males to pay almost twice the markups they charged white males, and they asked females to pay two and one-half times that markup.

3. *Willingness to Bargain.* Another potentially important form of disparate treatment concerns the sellers' willingness to bargain. Consumers are hurt if the sellers either refuse to bargain or force the consumers to spend more time bargaining to achieve the same price. An analysis of the number of bargaining rounds reveals that the average number of rounds for different types of testers did not differ significantly, as shown in Table 3. The amount of time black male and white female testers spent bargaining (both total and per round) was not statistically longer than the amount spent by white male testers. Although black female testers clearly had to pay the most for cars, it was not because dealers refused to spend time bargaining with them.

TABLE 3:
Differences in Rounds

	Average # Rounds	Average Length of Test (Minutes)	Average Length per Round (Minutes)
White Male	2.43	35.8	14.8
White Female	2.21	32.9	14.9
Black Male	2.32	49.1	21.2
Black Female	3.08	34.6	11.2

Indeed, the sellers' willingness to bargain longer with black men (or for more rounds with black women) may be an indirect attempt to enhance their market power by reducing their potential competition. If the hourly costs to consumers of searching for a car increase with the time spent searching, then the longer a dealership keeps customers bargaining in its showroom, the smaller the possibility that the consumers will visit additional dealerships. In other words, dealers may intentionally try to bargain for more rounds with certain types of consumers, if doing so is particularly like to reduce the chance that they will visit other dealerships.

NOTES AND QUESTIONS

1.   One of the acknowledged limitations of Professor Ayres's study is that it involved only six testers. To address this limitation, Professor Ayres conducted an elaborate follow-up study involving 38 testers. In it, he replicated his earlier results, with one notable exception:

> The results of the expanded audit confirm the previous finding that dealers systematically offer lower prices to white males than to other tester types. But the more comprehensive data reveal a different ordering of discrimination than in the prior study: as in the original study, dealers offered all black testers significantly higher prices than white males, but unlike the original study, the black male testers were charged higher prices than the black female testers.

Ian Ayres, *Further Evidence of Discrimination in New Car Negotiations and Estimates of its Cause*, 94 Mich. L. Rev. 109, 110 (1995).

2.   Several noted scholars have expressed concerns about how less powerful parties or members of disadvantaged groups are likely to fare in consensual dispute resolution processes like negotiation or mediation. Does the Ayres excerpt corroborate their concerns?

3.   Is a transactional negotiation like the one studied by Ayres likely to be different from a negotiation or mediation involving a dispute between the parties? Consider the potential application of Ayres' research to the workplace or the consumer context. Are supervisors more likely to be willing to negotiate with certain employees than others? On what basis? Are financial services companies more likely to be responsive to certain consumers than others? Again, on what basis? *See* Nancy A. Welsh, *I Could Have Been a Contender: Summary Jury Trial As A Means to Overcome* Iqbal's *Negative Effects Upon Pre–Litigation Communication, Negotiation and Early, Consensual Dispute Resolution*, 114 Penn St. L. Rev. 1149 (2010) (hypothesizing that if members of marginalized group lose access to the coercive power of the courts, employers will be less willing to negotiate with employees who are members of such groups); Ian Ayres, Jeff Lingwall, & Sonia Steinway, *Skeletons in the Database: An Early Analysis of the CFPB's Consumer Complaints* available at http://papers.ssrn.com/sol3/papers.cfm?

abstract_id=2295157 (last visited August 29, 2013) (identifying differential treatment of certain demographic groups).

G. NEGOTIATION EXERCISES

1. A TRANSACTION NEGOTIATION: THE CARTON CONTRACT[1]

Glasco Corporation of Cincinnati, Ohio, manufactures and sells glass jars for use in home canning. The company has asked its lawyer to meet with the lawyer for Quality Carton Company of Springfield, Missouri, to negotiate a contract for the delivery of a particular model of honeycomb fiber carton used for shipping the cartons.

If you were one of these lawyers, how would you decide which approach or approaches to use in negotiating this contract?

2. A DISPUTE NEGOTIATION: THE THOMPSON v. DECKER MEDICAL MALPRACTICE CLAIM[2]

GENERAL INFORMATION FOR ALL PARTICIPANTS

This is a summary of the information the attorneys in this case have stipulated to and the information the attorneys still hold in contention.

A. Statement of Claim:

Plaintiff claims $500,000 compensatory and $500,000 punitive damages against defendant for defendant's alleged negligence and battery during the course of medical treatment. Defendant denies liability on both the negligence and battery claims.

B. Undisputed Facts:

1. Ten months ago, plaintiff, a jazz pianist, consulted defendant doctor, a hand specialist, regarding a pain in her right hand. The defendant doctor diagnosed the condition as the early onset of an arthritic condition.

---

[1] This exercise is based upon The Carton Contract, Videotape II in the Dispute Resolution and Lawyers Videotape Series (Distributed by West Publishing Co. (1991)), which was based upon William H. Henning, "The Mason–Dixon (Product) Line: A Transaction Negotiation Exercise" in Leonard L. Riskin and James E. Westbrook, Instructor's Manual for Dispute Resolution and Lawyers 336 (West Publishing Co. 1992). Confidential Information for the role players appears in the Instructor's Manual, and on the casebook TWEN web site at www.lawschool.westlaw.com

[2] This simulation was developed by Deborah Doxsee for the role players in Videotape I: The Thompson v. Decker Medical Malpractice Claim Negotiation (West Publishing Co. 1991). It is based upon Robert M. Ackerman, "The Case of the Weary Hand: A Negotiation Exercise for Torts" in Leonard L. Riskin and James Westbrook, Instructor's Manual for Dispute Resolution and Lawyers (West Publishing Co. 1987). Confidential instructions for the role players appear in the Instructor's Manual, and on the casebook TWEN web site at www.lawschool.westlaw.com

2. Defendant treated plaintiff's arthritis by injecting the drug polynuvoarthromaleate (AR–21) into the palm of plaintiff's right hand.

3. Prior to injecting the AR–21, defendant told plaintiff that she might feel "a little numbness" for a short while after treatment.

4. AR–21 has recently been approved for use by the U.S. Food and Drug Administration. Approximately 10% of all practicing hand specialists use the drug for the treatment of arthritic conditions.

5. Approximately twelve hours after injection of the AR–21 the plaintiff noted a "slight tingling" in her hand, and within thirty-six hours after injection of the drug, plaintiff experienced total numbness in the fingers of her right hand. This numbness lasted eight weeks, during which plaintiff missed twenty-four scheduled performances.

6. Plaintiff received extensive therapy. The numbness has disappeared, and the plaintiff has regained the use of her right hand. Her arthritic condition continues to bother her as it did prior to her consultation with the defendant.

C.   Disputed Issues of Fact:

1. Whether defendant was negligent in treating plaintiff's arthritis with an injection of AR–21.

2. Whether defendant utilized the correct procedures in injecting the AR–21.

3. Whether defendant's injection of AR–21 caused the numbness in the fingers of plaintiff's right hand.

4. Whether defendant fully and adequately informed plaintiff of the risks attendant to the use of AR–21.

D.   Damages: Plaintiff claims the following damages:

1. Medical Expenses: Plaintiff claims $20,000 in damages for the cost of therapy for her right hand. Defendant contends that this sum is an unreasonable amount for the twenty therapy sessions attended by plaintiff, and that the numbness would have disappeared in three months' time without therapy.

2. Lost Income: Plaintiff claims lost income of $60,000, representing the twenty-four canceled engagements, each of which would have netted the plaintiff $2,500.

3. Pain and suffering: Plaintiff claims pain and suffering in the amount of $420,000.

4. Punitive Damages: Plaintiff claims punitive damages in the amount of $500,000 in connection with her battery claim.

Additional Information:

Plaintiff's Witnesses:

1.   Plaintiff will testify on her own behalf as to the treatment performed by the defendant, the therapy she underwent to restore feeling in her right hand, her pain and suffering, and her lost income.

2.   An orthopedic surgeon, Dennis Waller, M.D., from a University Hospital on one side of the state, will testify as to the proper treatment of arthritis. He will state that he never uses AR–21 because the drug often causes numbness in the extremities.

3.   A physical therapist, Rick Abernathy, R.P.T., will testify to the therapy he performed to restore feeling to the plaintiff's right hand, and to the reasonableness of the costs incurred for such therapy.

Defendant's Witnesses:

1.   Defendant will testify as to the appropriateness of the AR–21 for the treatment of arthritis, the care she utilized in injecting the AR–21 into the plaintiff's hand, and the warning she gave the plaintiff as to the possible risks associated with the use of AR–21.

2.   An orthopedic surgeon, John Sullivan, M.D., from a University Hospital on the other side of the state will testify as to the appropriateness of the use of AR–21, the risks associated with the use of AR–21, and the prognosis for persons whose fingers have been numbed by AR–21.

Discovery:

Discovery is now complete. The parties have exchanged interrogatories and summaries of testimony of medical witnesses. Both plaintiff and defendant and all witnesses have been deposed.

Stipulations:

The parties have stipulated that statements made during the course of settlement negotiations shall not be admissible at trial.

Pretrial Conference:

A pretrial conference is scheduled for one week from today. Extensive negotiations are expected prior to that time.

* * *

The following is a "copy" of the brief drug insert enclosed in the packaging of each vial of the drug. Additionally there is a longer drug description included in the vial with the specific pharmacologic properties of the drug, which fulfills the FDA regulations pertaining to the drug inserts.

POLYNUVOARTHROMALEATE
"AR–21"

ANTIRHEUMATIC & ANTI–INFLAMMATORY

Actions and Uses:

A new water soluble synthetic nonionizable preparation consisting of 50% Polynuvoarthro, a low density metallic alloy. Mechanism of action unknown, though recent research indicates that perhaps some disruption of the degenerative process occurs on a cellular level via individual cellular coating by the alloy. The major effect is a reduction of the inflammatory process early on after the onset of the arthritic condition. There is no reparative effect. Usefulness limited to those with active rheumatoid arthritis or debilitating degenerative joint disease. Particularly good results have been reported with use in the hands and feet.

Absorption and Fate:

Readily absorbed from site of injection with limited dissemination to other soft tissues. Rapidly excreted through urine and feces with maximum of 20% remaining in tissue for prolonged period (greater than 48 hours after injection). This drug has an extremely short half-life and is most beneficial for the treatment of acute rheumatic episodes, though prolonged use is not contraindicated, and bi-weekly treatment for extended periods is not uncommon.

Contraindications and Cautions:

Similar to other synthetic low density metallic alloys. Renal insufficiency, diabetes, recent or ongoing radiation therapy, severe impairment of the hepatic, integumentary, hematopoietic or cardiac systems, presence of other chronic debilitating diseases. Safe use in pregnancy is not established.

Adverse Reactions:

G.I.—diarrhea, gastritis, colic. **Dermatologic**—skin rash, urticaria, pruritus. **G.U.**—urinary insufficiency. **CNS**—headache, dizziness, vertigo, nervousness, tinnitus, polyneuritis, transient neuralgias, occasional paralysis reported. **GENERAL**—Disruptions of the hematopoietic system (rate), and angina, hypertension, syncope, anaphylactoid response.

Route and Dosage:

Intramuscular injection; "Z"—track if possible. Adults only. Single dosage administration 25–50 mg weekly or 5–20 mg three times a week. Prolonged continuous use for 6 mos. or more is not recommended.

CHAPTER IV

MEDIATION

∎ ∎ ∎

In mediation, an impartial third party helps others negotiate to resolve a dispute or plan a transaction. Unlike a judge or arbitrator, the mediator lacks authority to impose a solution. In many cultures, mediation is the predominant means of resolving disputes. So, ordinarily, a mediation is a meeting or series of meetings that are informal (compared to court or arbitration proceedings) in which the mediator helps the parties understand the matter at issue and develop ways to address it.

In the United States, the use of mediation has grown enormously since the late 1970s—much faster than other methods of dispute resolution. Thousands of disputes—from virtually every realm of human activity—are mediated each day. We find mediation of disputes involving child-custody, labor and employment relations, personal injury claims, environmental and other public issues, special education, workers compensation, business transactions, professional-client relations, bankruptcy, international relations, racial and ethnic concerns, and many other issues. Mediation, and its close cousin, facilitation, also are used by government administrative agencies, legislatures, and community and political organizations to develop plans, proposals and agreements on a huge range of issues. Formal mediation programs are sponsored by trial and appellate courts, government agencies, bar associations, business organizations, civic and religious groups, and other organizations. Many individuals and firms offer mediation services. Usually entry into mediation is voluntary, but many courts order cases, or categories of cases, into mediation—a practice that is both common and controversial.

In this chapter, we cannot hope to provide a detailed picture of mediation in the U.S. today. We will, however, present a basic introduction to mediation and help you consider the process from the perspectives of various participants:

• A lawyer, who might recommend for or against mediation to a client, represent a client in a mediation, serve as a mediator, or help to develop, promote or regulate the practice of mediation;

• A party to a dispute or potential transaction, who might (or might not) seek advice or representation from a lawyer in connection with a mediation;

• A judge or other public official, who might establish a mediation program or refer cases to mediation; and

• A mediator, who might offer services for a fee or on a pro bono basis.

In viewing mediation from each of these perspectives, this chapter seeks to emphasize three major ideas about mediation:

First, mediation has certain core characteristics: It is a non-binding process in which a third party, aspiring to be impartial, seeks to help others resolve or settle a dispute or plan a transaction.

Second, mediation comes in a huge variety of forms. Thus, mediation can be as varied as dancing, sports, or music. An aspect of the variety is captured through a number of "models" of mediation, but they can only hint at the richness and diversity of actual mediation processes. In addition, the precise characteristics of a particular mediation depend on a combination of factors, such as:

- The setting in which the dispute or potential transaction arose or is being mediated. For example, the fact that a dispute is already the subject of a lawsuit may incline the process toward a focus on legal issues.

- The attitudes and beliefs of the participants about the nature and significance of the dispute, about the nature of mediation, about their respective roles. For example, beliefs about how much the mediator should direct the process or outcome affect the mediator's behavior, which will influence the nature of the mediation.

Third, any of the participants potentially can exercise great influence over the procedures and outcomes of a mediation.

Despite the variety, which we mention above and will explore below, most mediation processes have certain common elements: The participants can include one or more mediators, who preside; parties to the dispute, or representatives (e.g., executives) of organizational parties, such as corporations or government agencies; and, in certain kinds of cases, lawyers representing the parties. Usually mediations are private and confidential, but sometimes observers are allowed. Procedures usually include presentations by the parties or lawyers or both; explorations of the parties' legal claims and underlying interests; development of options for resolution; evaluation of such options; and attempts to reach an agreement that settles the dispute and, ideally, resolves the conflict. Many mediations center around private "caucuses" between the mediator and participants on each side, though some mediators never use such private meetings.

The Chapter is organized as follows: Section A sets out the wide variety of approaches to mediation, sometimes called "models." Section B presents a more detailed look at typical mediation processes. In Section C, we take a closer look at mediation processes by examining the participants—the mediator, the parties, and the lawyers—as well as the mechanisms and forces that regulate their participation in mediation. Section D considers the circumstances in which one should use, refuse or adjust mediation, in the context of the potential risks and advantages of the informality of mediation. Section E contains instructions for three mediation exercises.

A. APPROACHES TO MEDIATION

One way to understand mediation is through "models" that commentators have developed to categorize or promote various approaches to mediation. Usually these models reflect the mediator's orientation to the mediation based on her idea of the nature of the dispute and her role in addressing it. As the following materials demonstrate, there is a wide range of mediator orientations, so it is important that all participants be aware of the orientation the mediator brings to the table for a variety of reasons that will appear throughout this Chapter. It is just as important, however, for participants to be aware that the mediator's orientation need not determine how the mediation will work or the definition of the problem or how to address it.

We begin, in Section 1, with Leonard Riskin's efforts to use grids to map the terrain of orientations to mediation. These grids are descriptive, not prescriptive, in that they simply seek to describe the mediator's orientation to the mediation. In the first reading, Riskin lays out a "grid" that suggests four mediator "orientations" based on (1) the extent to which the mediator tends to define the problem narrowly or broadly; and (2) whether the mediator sees her role as mainly to "evaluate" or "facilitate." The second reading presents a revised approach, which he calls "the New New Grid System." It corrects perceived flaws in the old grid and incorporates the role of participant influence on the mediation. The "New New Grid System" can also be used for broader set of analytical objectives, such as identifying what is going on at a particular time in a mediation, or with respect to a particular issue, and making decisions about how to proceed.

It important to remember that these grids are not a models of mediation, but rather are means of understanding different approaches to mediation—approaches that can vary even a particular mediation as the mediation moves along.

1.　MAPPING MEDIATION ORIENTATIONS

LEONARD L. RISKIN, UNDERSTANDING MEDIATORS' ORIENTATIONS, STRATEGIES, AND TECHNIQUES: A GRID FOR THE PERPLEXED

1 Harv. Negot. L. Rev. 7, 8–13, 17–39 (1996)

Not long ago, a lawyer asked me to conduct a workshop, for his firm and its clients, on how to participate in a mediation. As I began to prepare this program, I realized that my co-trainers and I could not talk sensibly about how, or even whether, to participate in a mediation without knowing the nature of the process the mediator would conduct. But a bewildering variety of activities fall within the broad, generally-accepted definition of mediation—a process in which an impartial third party, who lacks authority to impose a solution, helps others resolve a dispute or plan a transaction. Some of these processes have little in common with one another. And there is no comprehensive or widely-accepted system for identifying, describing, or classifying them. Yet most commentators, as well as mediators, lawyers, and others familiar with mediation, have a definite image of what mediation is and should be.

For these reasons, almost every conversation about mediation suffers from ambiguity, a confusion of the "is" and the "ought." This creates great difficulties when people try to determine whether and how to participate in mediation, and when they grapple with how to select, train, evaluate, or regulate mediators.

The largest cloud of confusion and contention surrounds the issue of whether a mediator may evaluate. "Effective mediation," claims lawyer-mediator Gerald S. Clay, "almost always requires some analysis of the strengths and weaknesses of each party's position should the dispute be arbitrated or litigated." But law school Dean James Alfini disagrees, arguing that "lawyer-mediators should be prohibited from offering legal advice or evaluations." Formal ethical standards have spoken neither clearly nor consistently on this issue.

Other issues also bedevil the mediation field. People of good will argue about whether mediation should be employed in cases involving constitutional rights, domestic violence, or criminal activity. Program planners differ on how to select mediators. Trainers disagree on the place of the private caucus. Commentators debate whether the mediator should bear responsibility for the outcome of environmental mediation. Lawyers and judges argue about whether a judge may order a represented client to attend a settlement conference along with her or his lawyer. Disputants selecting a mediator worry about bias and whether the neutral should have "subject-matter expertise." And many lawyers and clients wonder about what exactly mediation is and how it differs from other dispute resolution processes.

The bulk of these disagreements arise out of clashing assumptions—often unarticulated—about the nature and goals of mediation. Nearly everyone would agree that mediation is a process in which an impartial third party helps others resolve a dispute or plan a transaction. Yet in real mediations, goals and methods vary so greatly that generalization becomes misleading. This is not simply because mediators practice differently according to the type of dispute or transaction; even within a particular field, one finds a wide range of practices. For example, in studying farm-credit mediation, I discerned two patterns of mediation, which I called "broad" and "narrow." These patterns differed so radically that they could both be called mediation only in the sense that noon meals at McDonald's and at Sardi's could both be called lunch.

The confusion is especially pernicious because many people do not recognize it; they describe one form of mediation and ignore other forms, or they claim that such forms do not truly constitute mediation. I do not aim in this Article to favor one type of mediation over another, although, like most mediators, I incline toward a certain approach. Instead, I hope to facilitate discussions and to help clarify arguments by providing a system for categorizing and understanding approaches to mediation. I try to include in my system most activities that are commonly called mediation and arguably fall within the broad definition of the term. I know that some mediators object to such inclusiveness, and fear that somehow it will legitimize activities that are inconsistent with the goals that they associate with mediation. Although I sympathize with this view, I also disagree with it. Usage determines meaning. It is too late for commentators or mediation organizations to tell practitioners who are widely recognized as mediators that they are not, in the same sense that it is too late for the Pizza Association of Naples, Italy to tell Domino's that its product is not the genuine article. Such an effort would both cause acrimony and increase the confusion that I am trying to diminish. Instead, I propose that we try to categorize the various approaches to mediation so that we can better understand and choose among them.

* * *

II.   THE PROPOSED SYSTEM

The system I propose describes mediations by reference to two related characteristics, each of which appears along a continuum. One continuum concerns the goals of the mediation. In other words, it measures the scope of the problem or problems that the mediation seeks to address or resolve. At one end of this continuum sit narrow problems, such as how much one party should pay the other. At the other end lie very broad problems, such as how to improve the conditions in a given community or industry. In the middle of this continuum are problems of intermediate breadth, such as how to address the interests of the parties or how to transform the parties involved in the dispute.

The second continuum concerns the mediator's activities. It measures the strategies and techniques that the mediator employs in attempting to address or resolve the problems that comprise the subject matter of the mediation. One end of this continuum contains strategies and techniques that *facilitate* the parties' negotiation; at the other end lie strategies and techniques intended to *evaluate* matters that are important to the mediation.

The following hypothetical, developed by Professor Charles Wiggins, will help illustrate the system of categorization that I propose.

COMPUTEC

Golden State Savings & Loan NTC is the second largest savings and loan association in the state. Just over a year ago, it contracted with Computec, a computer consulting firm, to organize and computerize its data processing system and to operate that system for a period of ten years. Computec thus became responsible for all of the computer-related activities of the savings and loan, such as account management, loan processing, investment activity, and payroll. Golden State agreed to pay Computec a consulting and administration fee of over one million dollars per year for the term of the contract.

At the end of the first year of operation under this contract, Computec presented Golden State with a bill for approximately $30,000 in addition to the agreed-upon fee. This bill represented costs incurred by Computec staff in attending seminars and meetings related to the installation of computer technology in banks, and costs incurred while meeting with various outside consultants on aspects of the contract with Golden State. Upon receipt of this bill, Golden State wrote to Computec, advising Computec that because Golden State could find no express term in the contract requiring reimbursement for these charges, and because the bank had a strict policy against reimbursement for such expenses incurred by its own employees, it would not reimburse Computec staff for similar expenses. Computec responded quickly, informing Golden State that this type of charge was universally reimbursed by the purchaser of computer consulting services, and that it would continue to look to Golden State for reimbursement.

The conflict is generating angry feelings between these two businesses, who must work together closely for a number of years. Neither party can see any way of compromising on the costs already incurred by Computec, and of course Computec expects to be reimbursed for such charges in the future as well. Under applicable law, reasonable expenses directly related to the performance of a professional service contract are recoverable as an implied term of the contract if it is industry practice that they be so paid. It is unclear, however, whether the purchaser of these services must be aware of the industry practice at the time of contracting.*

A.   *The Problem–Definition Continuum: Goals, Assumptions, and Focuses*

The focus of a mediation—its subject matter and the problems or issues it seeks to address—can range from narrow to broad. Here, I identify four "levels" of a mediation that correspond to different degrees of breadth.

1.   *Level I: Litigation Issues*

In very narrow mediations, the primary goal is to settle the matter in dispute though an agreement that approximates the result that would be produced by the likely alternative process, such as a trial, without the delay or expense of using that alternative process. The most important issue tends to be the likely outcome of litigation. "Level I" mediations, accordingly, focus on the strengths and weaknesses of each side's case.

In a "Level I" mediation of the Computec case, the goal would be to decide how much, if any, of the disputed $30,000 Golden State would pay to Computec. The parties would make this decision "in the shadow of the law."[116] Discussions would center on the strengths and weaknesses of each side's case and on how the judge or jury would likely determine the relevant issues of fact and law.

2.   *Level II: "Business" Interests*

At this level, the mediation would attend to any of a number of issues that a court would probably not reach. The object would be to satisfy business interests. For example, it might be that Golden State is displeased with the overall fee structure or with the quality or quantity of Computec's performance under the contract, and the mediation might address these concerns. Recognizing their mutual interest in maintaining a good working relationship, in part because they are mutually dependent, the companies might make other adjustments to the contract.

Broadening the focus a bit, the mediation might consider more fundamental business interests, such as both firms' need to continue doing business, make profits, and develop and maintain a good reputation. Such a mediation might produce an agreement that, in

---

[116] See Robert H. Mnookin & Lewis Kornhauser, Bargaining in the Shadow of the Law: The Case of Divorce, 88 Yale L.J. 950 (1979).

addition to disposing of the $30,000 question, develops a plan to collaborate on a new business venture. Thus, by exploring their mutual business interests, both companies have the opportunity to improve their situations in ways they might not have considered but for the negotiations prompted by the dispute.

3. Level III: Personal/Professional/Relational Issues

"Level III" mediations focus attention on more personal issues and interests. For example, during the development of the $30,000 dispute, each firm's executives might have developed animosities toward or felt insulted by executives from the other firm. This animosity might have produced great anxiety or a loss of self-esteem. On a purely instrumental level, such personal reactions can act as barriers to settlement. Although Fisher, Ury and Patton tell us to "separate the people from the problem," sometimes the people *are* the problem. Thus, mediation participants often must address the relational and emotional aspects of their interactions in order to pave the way for settlement of the narrower economic issues. In addition, addressing these relational problems may help the parties work together more effectively in carrying out their mediated agreement.

Apart from these instrumental justifications, addressing these personal and relational problems can be valuable in its own right. Focusing on such issues may be important even if the mediation does not produce a solution to the narrower problems. In other words, a principal goal of mediation could be to give the participants an opportunity to learn or to change. This could take the form of moral growth or a "transformation," as understood by Bush and Folger to include "empowerment" (a sense of "their own capacity to handle life's problems") and "recognition" (acknowledging or empathizing with others' situations). In addition, the parties might repair their relationship by learning to forgive one another or by recognizing their connectedness. They might learn to understand themselves better, to give up their anger or desire for revenge, to work for inner peace, or to otherwise improve themselves. They also might learn to live in accord with the teachings or values of a community to which they belong.

4. Level IV: Community Interests

"Level IV" mediations consider an even broader array of interests, including those of communities or entities that are not parties to the immediate dispute. For example, perhaps the ambiguity in legal principles relevant to the Computec case has caused problems for other companies; the participants might consider ways to clarify the law, such as working with their trade associations to promote legislation or to produce a model contract provision. In other kinds of disputes, parties might focus on improving, or "transforming," communities.

Figure 1 illustrates and summarizes the type of problems that appear along the problem-definition continuum. Of course, mediations that employ broader problem-definitions can include resolution of narrower problems that appear to the left on the continuum. Thus, a mediation of the Computec case that addresses the underlying business interests also could resolve the distributive issue—how much of the $30,000, if any, does Golden State pay to Computec? As the problem broadens, however, the distributive issue could become less important. Thus, if the two feuding executives learn to understand each other, instead of deciding how much Golden State will pay to Computec, they might arrive at an agreement that washes away that distributive issue. For example, they might decide to serve the firms' underlying business interests by creating a joint venture to market computer services to financial institutions, with a $30,000 seed-money contribution from Golden State and an employee loaned by Computec. In other words, in moving from narrow to broad definitions of the subject matter of a mediation, one's view of the conflict can change from that of a problem to be eliminated to that of an opportunity for improvement.

FIGURE 1

PROBLEM–DEFINITION CONTINUUM

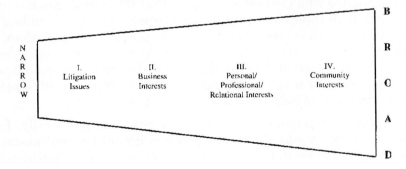

Within a given mediation, a particular problem or issue can have either primary or secondary significance. In a very narrow mediation of Computec, for example, the primary focus is on how much of the $30,000, if any, Golden State will pay. Yet, even in such a mediation, the participants might benefit in secondary, broader ways. They could, for example, feel vindicated, satisfied, or enlightened as to their own situation or that of their counterpart. This might permit greater empathy and the ability to rebuild their working relationship. And any of these developments could transform them, in ways large or small. In a narrow mediation, however, such outcomes claim only secondary importance, as occasional by-products of solving the central, distributive issue. The participants—including the mediator—may not think or care about such outcomes.

B. *The Mediator's Role: Goals and Assumptions Along The Facilitative-Evaluative Continuum*

The second continuum describes the strategies and techniques that the mediator employs to achieve her goal of helping the parties address and resolve the problems at issue. At one end of this continuum are strategies and techniques that *evaluate* issues important to the dispute or transaction. At the extreme of this evaluative end of the continuum fall behaviors intended to direct some or all of the outcomes of the mediation. At the other end of the continuum are beliefs and behaviors that *facilitate* the parties' negotiation. At the extreme of this facilitative end is conduct intended simply to allow the parties to communicate with and understand one another.

The mediator who evaluates assumes that the participants want and need her to provide some guidance as to the appropriate grounds for settlement—based on law, industry practice or technology—and that she is qualified to give such guidance by virtue of her training, experience, and objectivity.

The mediator who facilitates assumes that the parties are intelligent, able to work with their counterparts, and capable of understanding their situations better than the mediator and, perhaps, better than their lawyers. Accordingly, the parties can develop better solutions than any the mediator might create. Thus, the facilitative mediator assumes that his principal mission is to clarify and to enhance communication between the parties in order to help them decide what to do.

To explain the facilitative-evaluative continuum more fully, I must demonstrate how it relates to the problem-definition continuum. The relationship is clearest if we show the problem-definition continuum on a horizontal axis and the facilitative-evaluative continuum on a vertical axis, as depicted in Figure 2. The four quadrants each represent a general orientation toward mediation: evaluative-narrow, facilitative-narrow, evaluative-broad, and facilitative-broad.

C. *The Four Orientations: Strategies and Techniques*

Most mediators operate from a predominant, presumptive or default orientation (although, as explained later, many mediators move along continuums and among quadrants). For purposes of the following explication of mediator orientations, I will assume that the mediator is acting from such a predominant orientation. For this reason, and for convenience, I will refer to the "evaluative-narrow mediator" rather than the more precise, but more awkward, "mediator operating with an evaluative-narrow approach."

A mediator employs strategies—plans—to conduct a mediation. And a mediator uses techniques—particular moves or behaviors—to effectuate those strategies. Here are selected strategies and techniques that typify each mediation orientation.

FIGURE 2

MEDIATOR ORIENTATIONS

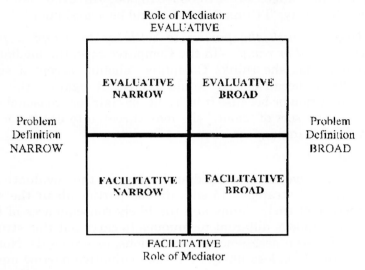

1. *Evaluative–Narrow*

A principal strategy of the evaluative-narrow approach is to help the parties understand the strengths and weaknesses of their positions and the likely outcome of litigation or whatever other process they will use if they do not reach a resolution in mediation. But the evaluative-narrow mediator stresses her own education at least as much as that of the parties. * * *

 a. *Assess the strengths and weaknesses of each side's case.*—In the Computec case, an evaluative mediator might tell Computec's representatives that, even if a court were to interpret the law as they hoped, the firm would have trouble meeting its burden of establishing the existence of an industry custom that purchasers of such services normally pay the related travel expenses of their suppliers. The mediator would explain her reasoning, invoking her experience and knowledge.

 b. *Predict outcomes of court or other processes.*—In Computec, the mediator might predict for Golden State the likely rulings on issues of law and fact, the likely outcome at trial and appeal, and the associated costs.

 c. *Propose position-based compromise agreements.*—A mediator can make such proposals with varying degrees of directiveness. Some mediators might suggest resolution points so gently that they are barely evaluative—for instance, throwing out a figure at which she thinks the parties might be willing to settle, without suggesting that this corresponds to what would happen in court or is otherwise an appropriate settlement point. A slightly more directive proposal might be to ask Computec, "Would you accept $12,000?" or "What about $12,000?" A still more directive proposal would be to suggest that the case might settle within a certain range, say $10,000–$15,000. An even more directive move would be to say, "I think $12,000 would be a good offer."

d. *Urge or push the parties to settle or to accept a particular settlement proposal or range.*—In the Computec case, the mediator might tell Computec that she thinks Computec "should" accept a settlement offer of $12,000 because that would protect it against the risk and expense of litigation or because it is "right" or "fair" or "reasonable." If the mediator has any sort of "clout," she may threaten to use it. Or she may engage in "head-banging."

2. *Facilitative–Narrow*

The facilitative-narrow mediator shares the evaluative-narrow mediator's general strategy—to educate the parties about the strengths and weaknesses of their claims and the likely consequences of failing to settle. But he employs different techniques to carry out this strategy. He does not use his own assessments, predictions, or proposals. Nor does he apply pressure. He is less likely than the evaluative-narrow mediator to request or to study relevant documents. Instead, believing that the burden of decision-making should rest with the parties, the facilitative-narrow mediator might engage in any of the following activities.

a. *Ask questions.*—The mediator may ask questions—generally in private caucuses—to help the participants understand both sides' legal positions and the consequences of non-settlement. The questions ordinarily would concern the very issues about which the evaluative-narrow mediator makes statements—the strengths and weaknesses of each side's case and the likely consequences of non-settlement, as well as the costs of litigation (including expense, delay, and inconvenience).

b. *Help the parties develop their own narrow proposals.*—In the Computec case, for instance, a facilitative-narrow mediator would help each party develop proposals as to how much of the $30,000 Golden State would pay.

c. *Help the parties exchange proposals.*—The mediator might present party proposals in private caucuses or encourage parties to make such proposals in a joint session. In either event, he would encourage participants to provide a rationale for each proposal that might help the other side accept it.

d. *Help the parties evaluate proposals.*—To do this, the mediator might ask questions that would help the parties weigh the costs and benefits of each proposal against the likely consequences of non-settlement.

The facilitative nature of this mediation approach might also produce a degree of education or transformation. The process itself, which encourages the parties to develop their own understandings and outcomes, might educate the parties, or "empower" them by helping them to develop a sense of their own ability to deal with the problems and choices in life. The parties also might acknowledge or empathize with each other's situation. However, in a narrowly-focused mediation, even a facilitative one, the subject matter normally produces fewer opportunities for such developments than does a facilitative-broad mediation.

3. *Evaluative–Broad*

It is more difficult to describe the strategies and techniques of the evaluative-broad mediator. Mediations conducted with such an orientation vary tremendously in scope, often including many narrow, distributive issues, as the previous discussion of the problem-definition continuum illustrates. In addition, evaluative-broad mediators can be more-or-less evaluative, with the evaluative moves touching all or only some of the issues.

The evaluative-broad mediator's principal strategy is to learn about the circumstances and underlying interests of the parties and other affected individuals or groups, and then to use that knowledge to direct the parties toward an outcome that responds to such interests. To carry out this strategy, the evaluative-broad mediator will employ various techniques, including the following (listed from least to most evaluative).

a. *Educate herself about underlying interests.*—The evaluative-broad mediator seeks to understand the underlying legal and other distributive issues by studying pleadings, depositions, and other documents, as well as by allowing the parties (usually through their lawyers) to argue their cases during the mediation. Unlike the narrow mediator, however, the broad mediator emphasizes the parties' underlying interests rather than their positions, and seeks to uncover needs that typically are not revealed in documents. Pleadings in the Computec case, for instance, would not indicate that one of the causes of the dispute was Golden State's interest in protecting the sanctity of its internal policy against reimbursing convention travel expenses of its own employees, let alone that the policy was born when the CEO observed staff members, at a convention in Bermuda, frolicking instead of attending seminars.

* * *

Evaluative-broad mediators expect to construct proposed agreements. For that reason, they generally emphasize their own education over that of the parties. Accordingly, they typically will restrict or control direct communication between the parties; thus, for example, the evaluative-broad mediator would spend more time in private caucuses than in joint sessions.

b. *Predict impact (on interests) of not settling.*—After determining the parties' underlying interests and setting the scope of the problems to be addressed in the mediation, some evaluative-broad mediators would predict how failure to settle would impact important interests. In the Computec case, an evaluative-broad mediator might tell Golden State that unless it reaches an agreement that allows Computec executives to feel appreciated and effective, relations will sour and Computec might become less diligent, thereby impairing Golden State's ability to compete and to serve its customers.

An evaluative-broad mediator also might try to persuade the participants that her assessments are correct by providing objective criteria or additional data.

c. *Develop and offer broad (interest-based) proposals.*—An evaluative-broad mediator's goal is to develop a proposal that satisfies as many of the parties' interests, both narrow and broad, as feasible. Proposals in the Computec case, for example, might range from a payment scheme for Golden State (based on an allocation of costs), to a system for the submission and approval of travel and education expenses in future years, to the formation of a new joint venture.

d. *Urge parties to accept the mediator's or another proposal.*—The evaluative-broad mediator (like the evaluative-narrow mediator) might present her proposal with varying degrees of force or intended impact. If the mediator has clout (the ability to bring pressure to bear on one or more of the parties), she might warn them or threaten to use it.

If the mediator has concluded that the goal of the mediation should include changing the people involved, she might take measures to effectuate that goal, such as appealing to shared values, lecturing, or applying pressure.

4. *Facilitative–Broad*

The facilitative-broad mediator's principal strategy is to help the participants define the subject matter of the mediation in terms of underlying interests and to help them develop and choose their own solutions that respond to such interests. In addition, many facilitative-broad mediators will help participants find opportunities to educate or change themselves, their institutions, or their communities. To carry out such strategies, the facilitative-broad mediator may use techniques such as the following.

a. *Help parties understand underlying interests.*—To accomplish this task, the facilitative-broad mediator will engage in many of the same activities as the evaluative-broad mediator, such as encouraging attendance and participation by the real parties, not just their lawyers, and explaining the importance of interests. Because he expects the parties to generate their own proposals, the facilitative-broad mediator emphasizes the need for the parties to educate themselves and each other more than the mediator. * * *

The facilitative-broad mediator also will help the parties define the scope of the problem to be addressed in the mediation, often encouraging them to explore underlying interests to the extent that they wish to do so. This behavior stands in sharp contrast to that of narrow mediators (even most facilitative-narrow mediators), who tend to accept the obvious problem presented, and that of evaluative-broad mediators, who often define the scope of the problem to be addressed themselves.

Many facilitative-broad mediators especially value mediation's potential for helping parties grow through an understanding of one another and of themselves. These mediators tend to offer the participants opportunities for positive change. One way to look at this is through Bush and Folger's concept of "transformation." In this view, by encouraging the parties to develop their own understandings, options, and proposals, the facilitative-broad mediator "empowers" them; by helping the parties to understand one another's situation, the facilitative-broad mediator provides them opportunities to give "recognition" to one another.

b. *Help parties develop and propose broad, interest-based options for settlement.*—The facilitative-broad mediator would keep the parties focused on the relevant interests and ask them to generate options that might respond to these interests. In the Computec case, the options may include various systems through which the already-incurred expenses could be allocated to the Golden State contract, methods for handling the same issue in the future (informally or by contract amendment), and opportunities to collaborate on other projects (an example of positive change). Next, he would encourage the parties to use these options— perhaps combining or modifying them—to develop and present their own interest-based proposals.

c. *Help parties evaluate proposals.*—The facilitative-broad mediator uses questions principally to help the parties evaluate the impact on various interests of proposals and of non-settlement. In Computec, for instance, a facilitative-broad mediator might ask the Computec representative how a specific settlement would affect the parties' working relationship and how it would alter Computec's ability to deliver appropriate services.

* * *

D. *Movement Along the Continuums and Among the Quadrants: Limitations on the Descriptive Capabilities of the Grid*

Like a map, the grid has a static quality that limits its utility in depicting the conduct of some mediators.

It is true that most mediators—whether they know it or not—generally conduct mediations with a presumptive or predominant orientation. Usually, this orientation is grounded in the mediator's personality, education, training, and experience. For example, most retired judges tend toward an extremely evaluative-narrow orientation, depicted in the far northwest corner of the grid. Many divorce mediators with backgrounds or strong interests in psychology or counseling—and who serve affluent or well-educated couples—lean toward a facilitative-broad approach. Sometimes, the expectations of a given program dictate an orientation; for example, narrow mediation tends to dominate many public programs with heavy caseloads.

Yet many mediators employ strategies and techniques that make it difficult to fit their practices neatly into a particular quadrant. First, some mediators deliberately try to avoid attachment to a particular orientation. Instead, they emphasize flexibility and attempt to develop their orientation in a given case based on the participants' needs or other circumstances in the mediation.

Second, for a variety of reasons, some mediators who have a predominant orientation do not always behave consistently with it. They occasionally deviate from their presumptive orientation in response to circumstances arising in the course of a mediation. * * *

In other cases, a mediator might seek to foster her dominant approach using a technique normally associated with another quadrant. * * *

A narrow mediator who runs into an impasse might offer the parties a chance to broaden the problem by exploring underlying interests. This might lead to an interest-based agreement that would enable the parties to compromise on the distributive issue as part of a more comprehensive settlement. Similarly, a broad mediator might encourage the parties to narrow their focus if the broad approach seems unlikely to produce a satisfactory outcome.

For these reasons it is often difficult to categorize the orientation, strategies, or techniques of a given mediator in a particular case.

NOTES AND QUESTIONS

1. The publication of the grid article drew strong reactions, both favorable and unfavorable. Professor Riskin summarized the problems with the old grid in a popular industry publication as follows:

> Although the problem-definition continuum still works well, the role-of-the-mediator continuum does not, for several reasons, the most important of which is that facilitation is the essence of mediation. Evaluating and facilitating are not really opposites, any more than playing football and kicking a football are opposites. Besides, most mediators use techniques that fall into both these categories. For those reasons, I proffer a "New Old Grid," which is just like the "Old Grid" except that it replaces "evaluative" with "directive" and "facilitative" with "elicitive."

> But I recommend against using that grid, too, because it retains many of the problems of the old grid: It fails to distinguish between the mediator's behavior with respect to substance and procedure; it has a static quality that ignores the dynamic, interactive nature of mediation; and it is grounded on the idea of mediator orientation, an unrealistic notion that excludes attention to many other issues in mediator behavior and ignores the role and influence of the parties.

Leonard L. Riskin, *Replacing the Mediator Orientation Grids, Again: The New New Grid System*, 23 Alternatives to the High Cost of Litig. 127, 127–128 (Sept. 2005).

2. The question of whether a mediator may properly "evaluate" the legal or other aspects of a dispute—e.g., make and communicate assessments of the strengths and weaknesses of one or both parties' sides of a dispute, or predict a judicial outcome—has generated much controversy. Many mediators and commentators believe that such conduct is necessarily inconsistent with the nature of mediation and the mediator's role. Kimberlee K. Kovach & Lela P. Love, *"Evaluative Mediation" is an Oxymoron,* 14 Alternatives to High Cost Litig. 31 (1996). (Since writing this article, Professor Love has acknowledged that evaluation may be part of mediation, provided that it is coupled with informed consent. See Lela P. Love & John W. Cooley, *The Intersection of Evaluation by Mediators and Informed Consent: Warning the Unwary*, 21 OHIO ST. J. ON DISP. RESOL. 45 (2005).) We cover this issue *infra*, Chapter IV.

LEONARD L. RISKIN, REPLACING THE MEDIATOR ORIENTATION GRIDS, AGAIN: THE NEW NEW GRID SYSTEM

23 Alternatives to the High Cost of Litig. 127–132 (Sept. 2005)

This is my last article about mediation grids. I hope.

In 1994 . . . I proposed a system for understanding mediators' orientations that was based on two continuums. One continuum focuses on the mediator's customary approach to problem-definition. It runs from "narrow" to "broad," * * *.

The other continuum, which represents the mediator's notion of the mediator's role, is anchored by "facilitative" and "evaluative." Crossing the two continuums produced ... four quadrants ... each of which, I wrote, represents an "orientation" commonly employed by a segment of mediators.

This grid became the most common method for categorizing approaches to mediation. The grid formed the basis for many training programs. It also provided a framework for academic debates about the nature of mediation and mediation ethics.

In 2003, however, I revisited the grid and published in these pages a critique and a proposal for a new system. But the "new grid system" ... ultimately disappointed and confused me and some others who read it carefully.

And so, later that year, I prepared a more extensive critique of the old grid and proposed a "New New Grid System."

* * *

TWO MATTERS HIGHLIGHTED

The "New New Grid" System is intended to facilitate good mediation decisionmaking by bringing attention to two matters: the enormous range of potential decisions in and about a mediation, and the extent to which various participants could affect these decisions. The system works through a series of grids that—rather than focusing exclusively on the mediator, as did the old grids—give equal attention to all the participants, which ordinarily means the mediator, the parties, and the lawyers. In addition, the grids take account of time and the potentially dynamic nature of decisionmaking.

The system's central focus is on participant "influence" with respect to particular issues. It provides a method for considering the influence that participants aspire to exert, actually exert, and expect others to exert, with respect to any of a wide range of decisions. It does this by dividing mediation decisionmaking into three categories: substantive, procedural, and meta-procedural.

TYPES OF DECISIONMAKING

Substantive decisionmaking includes trying to understand substantive issues, such as what happened to cause the dispute, and trying to make agreements intended to resolve the dispute. It also includes establishing the problem-definition, i.e., the subject of the mediation.

Procedural decisionmaking means deciding what procedures will be employed to reach or address the substantive issues. Here is a list of potential procedural issues, which overlap to some extent.

- Logistics: location; time (dates, starting and ending times, number and length of sessions).

- Pre-mediation submissions: Required or optional? Short letters, mediation briefs, litigation or other documents? Should submissions include: legal analyses, underlying interests, goals for the mediation, or obstacles to achieving these goals? Who receives the submissions: just the mediator, or all participants?

- Attendance and participation: Who attends? Roles of lawyers, clients, experts, others.

- Procedure during the mediation:

  — Opening statements—Which side goes first? Do lawyers and clients speak? What is the focus of these statements?

  — Caucuses—Whether, when, why, and how to call caucuses. Who can call them? Whether to maintain confidentiality of communications?

  — Ending the mediation. Who decides?

- Expressing the agreement in writing: Whether, when, why, how, and by whom? How formal or legally-binding should the document be? Who decides?

- Procedures for defining the problem(s) to be mediated (and/or deciding on the purposes of the mediation): To what extent, if any, will the problem be defined by the parties, e.g., through pre-mediation statements, pre-mediation briefs, or statements made during the mediation? The mediator, e.g., through the questions he asks the other participants? The mediation program managers, designers or sponsors, implicitly or explicitly? All the participants, through dialogue?

- Developing options: Will it happen? If so, when, how, and by whom?

- Developing and presenting proposals: By whom, when, how, where?

- Evaluation: Will/should the mediator evaluate or arrange for evaluation? If so, how, what, why, and under what conditions and standards?

- Reaching agreement: Will the mediator apply pressure on the parties or lawyers to reach a particular settlement? Settlement in general?

- The mediator's role: Will the mediator direct or elicit as to particular procedural and substantive issues? Will the mediator be transparent or obscure about the mediator's behavior? Will the mediator provide food?

Meta-procedural decisionmaking means deciding how subsequent procedural decisions will be made. The participants could make agreements, for instance, about who or what would determine any of a range of procedural issues, such as those mentioned above.

A series of grids appears below. Each grid deals with a particular kind of decision and provides an example of an array of grids we could prepare that would shed light on particular aspects of decisionmaking in mediation. The concept that unifies the system is participant "influence"—the degree of influence that various participants either aspire to exert or actually exert with respect to a particular issue.

On each of these grids, that concept is depicted on the north-south continuum. The north end of that continuum shows that most of the influence comes from the mediator; the south end shows parties and lawyers exerting most of the influence. The east-west axis would depict a particular issue. Thus, the purpose of each grid in this series is to bring attention to the influence that each participant exerts (or would like to exert) with respect to a particular issue. A generic version of this grid appears in Figure 3.

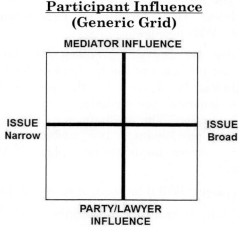

Participant Influence
(Generic Grid)

Figure 3.
Copyright © 2003 Leonard L. Riskin

ILLUMINATING DECISIONMAKING

Here are some examples of how grids could illuminate each of the three kinds of decisionmaking.

Substantive Decisionmaking Grids: Grids of substantive decisionmaking could deal with establishing the problem-definition or with understanding or resolving particular substantive issues. In addressing each of these focuses, I propose two kinds of grids: one deals with participants' predispositions as to how that issue should be resolved and who should contribute to its resolution, and the second focuses on actual influence.

The first grid depicts the participants' beliefs, attitudes or aspirations about a particular issue before the mediation or before the issue arises. Figure 4, for example, shows participant predispositions with respect to the substantive issue of problem-definition and their assumptions about the degree of influence they would, or would like to, exert with respect to this issue.

Substantive Decision-Making

Predisposition re:
Problem-Definition

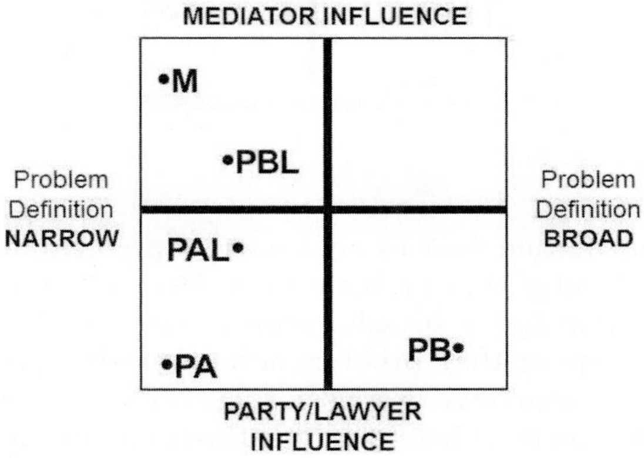

Figure 4.

Copyright © 2003 Leonard L. Riskin

Point M shows that the mediator is predisposed to a narrow problem-definition and assumes that he or she would heavily influence the development of such a problem-definition. Point PA shows that party A is predisposed toward a narrow problem and definition and believes (or assumes) that he would exercise much influence in establishing that problem-definition.

Point PAL shows that party A's lawyer is predisposed toward a slightly broader problem-definition and assumed that his influence, combined with that of the mediator, would move the process toward it. PB shows that party B is predisposed to a broader definition of the problem and assumes that the parties or lawyers would exercise much influence or control over the process of reaching that problem definition. PBL means that party B's lawyer is predisposed toward a problem-definition of the same breadth as was party A's lawyer and expects the mediator to play the strongest role in setting that definition.

The second kind of substantive decisionmaking grid would focus on actual influence. For instance, grids could show the operative problem-definition at various times during a mediation and the influences of the participants in setting that problem-definition, as illustrated in Figure 5.

Substantive Decision-Making

Influence on Problem-Definition at Various Times

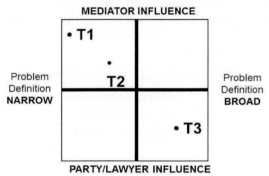

Figure 5
Copyright © 2003 Leonard L. Riskin

At T1, the mediation focuses on a narrow problem, and nearly all of the influence to develop that problem focus has come from the mediator. At T2, the mediation has a broader scope, and although the mediator's influence in developing that problem-definition still predominates, the parties and lawyers also have exercised some influence. At T3, the parties and lawyers have more substantially influenced the development of a broader problem-definition.

Alternatively, we could use separate grids to show the problem-definition at various times. By using individual grids to depict particular moments in a mediation, and considering each as a frame in a motion picture, it would be possible to get a sense of the flow of a mediation with respect to individual issues.

Additional grids could bring attention to understanding and resolving particular substantive issues that fall within the problem-definition. On Figure 6, for instance, point A shows the parties or lawyers mainly influencing the development of understanding about a particular narrow problem, such as how much X will pay Y. Point B shows the mediator influencing the understanding of a broad problem, such as a breakdown in professional and personal relationships between X and Y. A similar figure could show influence in resolving these issues.

Substantive Decision-Making

Influence on Understanding
Particular Problems

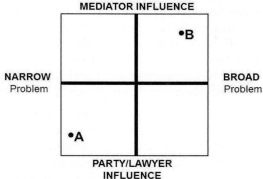

Figure 6.
Copyright © 2003 Leonard L. Riskin

Procedural Decisionmaking Grids: Procedural decisionmaking includes choices about a variety of issues made before or, sometimes moment-to-moment, during a mediation. The decisionmaking influence can come from mediators, parties, and participating lawyers. Sometimes, program administrators or designers make such procedural decisions. Some of these decisions are explicit and carefully determined—part of a formal dispute resolution design process.

In some situations, mediators themselves direct the outcome of certain procedural decisions, either before the mediation or at its inception or during the process; in terms of the "New New Grid" System, we would say that the mediator exercised virtually all the influence over such decisions. In other situations, the mediator might elicit the parties' perspectives and desires, and make a decision that responds either fully or partially to such party desires or perspectives. The new grids would show that both the mediator and the parties exercised some influence over such decisions. Sometimes, the parties assert themselves even if the mediator does not "elicit," and the new grids can depict the influence associated with such assertions.

Procedural decisionmaking grids could address any of a range of procedural issues, such as those listed above. Figure 7 [not included here], for example, shows the influence of the parties/lawyers and the mediator as to whether the mediator would provide an evaluation. Another version of that grid could show predispositions about that issue.

A grid that addresses decisionmaking about the use of private caucuses appears in Figure 8 [not included here].

Meta-Procedural Decisionmaking Grids: Meta-procedural decisionmaking refers to deciding how subsequent procedural decisions will be made. One major issue in meta-procedural decisionmaking is what degree of influence various participants will have over specific procedural issues or over procedural issues in general. On Figure 9 [not included here], the east-west continuum shows participant influence over procedural choices, with party/lawyer influence depicted at the west end and mediator influence depicted at the east end. The north-south continuum depicts participant influence over the meta-procedural decision about how much influence participants will have over subsequent procedural decisions.

Point A shows that the parties/lawyers exercised more influence during the meta-procedural decisionmaking, and that this produced the decision that subsequently the mediator would exercise most of the influence over procedural issues. Point B shows the mediator exerting almost all the influence in meta-procedural decisionmaking, which determined that the parties or lawyers would exert most of the influence over subsequent procedural choices. Point C shows that in the meta-procedural decisionmaking, the mediator exerted slightly more influence than the parties/lawyers, and that this produced an agreement that the parties or lawyers and mediator would have equal influence in deciding subsequent procedural issues. And finally, point D shows that a meta-procedure dominated by the parties/lawyers also produced the outcome that the parties/lawyers and mediator would have equal influence in making procedural choices.

Similar meta-procedure grids could deal with the extent to which various participants would influence decisions about individual procedural issues, such as the use of private caucuses or mediation briefs, mediator evaluation, or the location of the mediation; or the degrees of influence participants would exercise over when procedural choices would be made.

THE NEW NEW GRID SYSTEM

IN PERSPECTIVE

These grids are examples only. The system allows for the development of other grids for specialized purposes. Thus, some may find it useful to produce problem-definition grids that focus on the depth of the problem, rather than on the breadth; the extent to which the mediation would focus on various dimensions of the conflict, such as cognitive, emotional and behavioral; and the extent to which the process would focus on settling the dispute, resolving the dispute, or transforming the parties. Other procedural decisionmaking grids could address the issue of how and when—as opposed to whether—the mediator would evaluate, or on questions regarding the rules under which caucuses would be conducted.

A series of specifically focused grids, such as these, could help foster a high degree of awareness—among mediators, parties, lawyers, program designers, administrators, and evaluators—of the many possible issues for decision and the various degrees to which participants could contribute to understanding or resolving such issues. This awareness would support more active and sophisticated decisionmaking in and about mediation. Such grids also could be useful in evaluating, studying, or reflecting on completed mediations.

* * * [The] principal purpose [of the New New Grid System] is to shed light on what could or did happen in a mediation, and so to facilitate—to make more likely—wise decisionmaking. In other words, the system invites attention to what is and what could be, in order to facilitate decisionmaking about what should be. * * *

THE NEW SYSTEM'S LIMITS

The "New New Grid" System, though far more refined than its predecessors, has several limitations.

First, the grids in the new system, like their precursors, are not mathematically precise in any sense.

Second, as mentioned above, it often will be impossible to know or depict the predisposition or influence of a participant with any degree of certainty. Sometimes, these attitudes or practices will rest on what the participant assumes other participants want or expect, and the outcomes will result from interactions between and among influences that are too complex and subtle to map, even if we could be aware of them. Think, for instance, about a mediator who tries to "successively reframe" the conflict, and parties who may or may not buy into such definition in varying degrees. Sometimes, too, there will be a vast gulf between a participant's intention, and the actual effect of her or his behaviors.

I have considered—and abandoned—a number of ideas and suggestions about depicting the influence of individual participants or the dynamic nature of such influences. These have involved overlaying transparencies, each displaying the influence of a particular participant; using different symbols or colors to denote different participants; adding dimensions; and changing shapes. Each of these ideas has merit, yet each seems to rob the system of the simplicity that I find so valuable. Most important, the weaknesses in the new grid system do not impair its primary function—to enhance understanding, facilitate clear conversations, improve decisionmaking, and bring attention to the subtle relationships among our intentions, our actions, and the effects of these actions.

I hope that the new grid system—the concepts and terminology—will produce similar benefits for participants in real mediations, enabling them to have a more mindful, moment-to-moment awareness that will lead to better decisionmaking.

NOTES AND QUESTIONS

1. For a fuller explanation of the New, New Grid, see Leonard L. Riskin, *Decision-Making in Mediation: The New Old Grid and the New New Grid System*, 79 Notre Dame Law Review 1–53 (2003).

2. Consider the quite common situation, in which participants in a mediation have different pre-dispositions as to problem-definition and as to who should have influence over it. *Damages*, by Barry Werth, an in-depth case study of a Connecticut medical malpractice claim involving a baby born severely damaged, provides a good example. BARRY WERTH, DAMAGES: ONE FAMILY'S LEGAL STRUGGLES IN THE WORLD OF MEDICINE (2001).

In the first mediation described in the book, the parents wanted a broad problem-definition that would afford them recognition for how much they had suffered and how well they had coped, and give them some understanding of what really caused the damage to their child. *See id.* at 310–25. On the other hand, their lawyers seemed to want a narrow problem-definition, limited principally to what was likely to happen in court. *Id.* This desire doubtless was based, at least in part, on the assumption that this focus was best for the client. *Id.* It also seems clear that all the other participants—the mediator, the defendants, and their insurers and lawyers—shared the plaintiffs' lawyers' perspective. *Id.* As a result, the parents exercised no influence over the problem-definition and received none of the recognition they sought. For a fuller discussion of the two mediations described in this book, see Leonard L. Riskin, *Teaching and Learning from the Mediations in Barry Werth's Damages*, 2004 J. Disp. Resol. 119.

3. The purpose of the new grid system, of course, is not to promote any particular behaviors in mediation. Instead, the intention is to enhance awareness of the choices that will be made, explicitly or implicitly, and of the degrees of influence that any of the participants potentially could exercise, so that the participants can make better choices about how to make such decisions. Some of these decisions, such as procedural decisions, could be made during the process of selecting a mediator, which can involve dialogue or negotiation over such issues. More commonly, such decisions, as well as the substantive decisions, are made during the mediation. The new grid system could help participants decide whether to bring up certain issues and try to exercise influence over their determination.

4. As you observe mediations and mediation demonstrations (live or on the screen), try to notice who seems to be exerting influence on various decisions. It will not always be easy to notice. For example, if things are moving in a direction desired by a particular participant, she may exercise influence, in a sense, taking advantage of the existing momentum, by doing nothing.

5. In some mediations, the mediator or the mediation provider organization simply announces what the procedures will be. In others, the procedures are developed through discussion and dialogue. As a lawyer, what do you think should be the proper distribution of influence in substantive, procedural, and meta-procedural decisionmaking in the following kinds of cases:

    a. An automobile accident claim in which you represent

        1. The plaintiff?

        2. The defendant?

    b. A divorce case in which the parties have been married for ten years, have two young children, and are very bitter toward each other?

    c. An anti-trust claim by the U.S. government against a large corporation based on a claim of restraint of trade?

    d. A breach of contract claim between two corporations?

    e. A victim offender mediation? *E.g.*, a session involving the victim of a crime, say a burglary, and a person who has been convicted of, or has confessed to, committing the crime.

6. Should lawyers either be encouraged or required to ask their clients questions to help determine the appropriate focus of the mediation? Should lawyers be required to share the responses with mediators? *See* Leonard L. Riskin & Nancy A. Welsh, What's It All About?: Finding the Appropriate Problem Definition in Mediation, 15 Dispute Resolution Magazine 19 (Summer 2009) *infra* in this chapter for a proposal that would require lawyers or mediators to ask these questions in court-connected mediation; *see also* Leonard L. Riskin & Nancy A. Welsh, *Is That All There Is?: "The Problem" in Court–Oriented Mediation*, 15 Geo. Mason L. Rev. 863 (2008) (more extensive treatment of issue).

2. A FEW PARTICULAR APPROACHES

The Riskin grids are a helpful way of thinking about different approaches to mediation. In this section, we focus on three in particular that, together, help illustrate the wide range of approaches that are in use.

The first of these is reflected in Professor Riskin's training guide, and may be thought of as providing a generic, or "classic," model of mediation for dispute resolution. The second reading presents the transformative model of mediation. It focuses on transforming the conflict and the parties by promoting two kinds of "shifts" in the way they understand themselves and each other: empowerment shifts and recognition shifts. The third introduces us to understanding-based mediation, a model that focuses on deepening the parties' understanding of the dispute, underlying conflict, and the relevant law, as a way to move toward resolution. As you explore these different models, consider where they might fit on the Riskin grids, if at all, as well as the strengths and weaknesses of each approach.

a.   Classic Mediation

LEONARD L. RISKIN, MEDIATION TRAINING GUIDE
(2004) (excerpts)

A.   THE MEDIATOR'S ROLE

The following list provides a way to understand the range of functions a mediator can perform; it arranges the "interventions" very roughly from the least to the most active:

- urging participants to agree to talk

- helping participants understand the mediation process

- providing a suitable environment for negotiation

- carrying messages between participants

- helping participants agree upon an agenda

- setting an agenda

- maintaining order

- clarifying misunderstandings

- identifying issues

- helping participants understand the problem(s)

- defusing unrealistic expectations

- carrying offers back and forth

- rephrasing one participant's perspective or proposals into a form that is understandable and acceptable to the others

- helping participants develop their own proposals

- helping participants negotiate

- expanding resources

- proposing possible solutions

- persuading participants to accept a particular solution

Disagreement abounds concerning the mediator's role, and commentators have described and promoted a variety of models of mediation, each grounded on a particular ideology of mediation or assumptions about what goals are appropriate. [We cover such issues primarily in Section A of this Chapter, though they also arise in many other spots.]

* * *

B.   OVERVIEW OF STAGES, STRATEGIES, AND TACTICS IN MEDIATION

To explain mediation, most writers conceptualize it in terms of stages. For simplicity, I suggest an alternative approach—to understand mediation in terms of five tasks that must be accomplished:

1.   Agreeing to mediate;

2.   Understanding the problem(s);

3.   Generating options;

4.   Reaching agreement;

5.   Implementing the agreement.

A mediation usually addresses these tasks in the above order, hence the implication of stages. On the other hand, sometimes the parties cannot really agree to mediate until they understand the problems or generate options. In any multi-session mediation, each of these tasks is addressed in virtually every session. The agreement to mediate, for instance, almost always is tentative and subject to recission; a party can walk out at any time. Thus, every session involves a new commitment. Participants begin to work at "understanding the problems" immediately; however, new understandings develop continually. Even after fifteen hours of mediation, with the parties on the verge of agreement, or at impasse, suddenly a new insight can emerge. Similarly, parties can reach tentative accords on some issues in the earliest stages, subject to later developments.

Joint Sessions or Private Sessions (Caucuses)

Before explaining the mediation process in more detail, it is important to describe the private caucus. Most mediators use a combination of joint sessions and private sessions (caucuses). A caucus can be employed during any stage of a mediation. It can give a mediator a good chance to develop trust and rapport with a party, to learn the party's real interests or positions, to defuse unrealistic expectations, and to help the party develop or assess proposals. If you caucus with one party, always caucus with the other(s) before returning to a joint session.

Some mediators use the caucus routinely in the belief that parties will speak freely only in private. Other mediators tend to use caucuses only as needed, which often means when the parties are at impasse or the mediator suspects a party is holding back. Mediators who avoid the caucus do so on the theory that one of the great values of mediation is to facilitate <u>direct</u> communication between the parties, which can lead to new understandings and improved relationships. Private meetings can inhibit such direct communication, and something nearly always is lost in the mediator's translation. (One lawyer-mediator feels so strongly about this that he tells parties they may call a caucus with him but that he will not keep from the other party information revealed in a caucus. Gary J. Friedman, A Guide to Divorce Mediation 36–37 (1993)).

1. Agreeing to Mediate

a. Pre-mediation

Some mediations typically begin with or are preceded by private sessions—in person or by telephone—involving the mediator and the individual lawyers or parties. Sometimes the parties do not agree to mediate until after such sessions. Much depends on the nature of the dispute and the types of parties. In most cases, however, it is best to begin with a joint session.

b. The First Joint Session

Goals for the first joint session include: 1) ensuring that the parties understand mediation; 2) helping the parties decide whether they wish to continue with mediation; 3) allowing the mediator to decide whether mediation seems appropriate and whether the mediator can work with these parties and what problems they will face; and 4) setting the tone and structure for future sessions. To achieve these goals, the mediator should undertake the following tasks, while treating all participants equally and with respect:

(1) Seat the participants

Decide in advance where the parties should sit, so as not to exacerbate adversarial tendencies. If the group is small and the room suitable—and tensions are not terribly high—consider sitting in comfortable chairs in a circle rather than at a rectangular table. The seating should reflect equality. For example, the mediator generally should not sit behind a desk. To encourage participation by clients, seat them close to the mediator and put their lawyers further away.

(2) Introduce self and others present

Raise the question of how participants will address one another—by first names or by "Mr.," "Ms.," and the like.

(3) Identify basic nature of dispute

The mediator should ask the parties to state briefly the nature of the dispute and the parties' relationship, for two reasons: first, to be sure the dispute that brought the parties into mediation is still a problem, and, second, to give them an opportunity to speak early in the process, which could relieve tension and reflect the participatory nature of the process. In some cases, especially if the mediator has been in touch with the parties during the pre-mediation process, this step may be unnecessary.

Beware of premature diagnosis of the problem. Avoid letting the parties' initial definition of the problem restrict the issues that later become relevant for discussion, as this might inhibit creativity. In most cases, parties initially will conceive of the problem in adversarial, "win-lose" terms. Sometimes, particularly in a dispute over money, that approach may be appropriate; but the mediator should remain open to the possibilities of expanding the pie, of reaching a problem-solving solution that goes beyond the parties' stated positions and responds to their underlying interests.

(4) Educate Parties About Nature of Mediation Process:
The Mediator's Opening Statement and Initial Dialogue

Explain how mediation generally works and allow opportunities for questions, dialogue, and negotiation about the mediation process. This education process should include information on the following:

(a) Basic explanation of mediation

Mediation is a voluntary process in which a neutral third party helps the disputants reach their own resolution. The mediator (unlike a judge or arbitrator) will not decide the case.

In my view, the appropriate goal is to reach an agreement that satisfies the parties' underlying interests, that is fair to the parties, and that is not unfair to affected third parties. Other mediators have different, sometimes narrower or broader, ideas about the appropriate goals.

(b) The mediator's role

The mediator is impartial. The mediator keeps order, facilitates communication, clarifies issues, and keeps participants moving toward their own agreement. The mediator, unlike judge or arbitrator, does not decide the case.

(c) The roles of lawyers and clients

Address the role of the lawyer. Much will depend on the nature of the case. Some mediations will involve only lawyers, not clients. Other mediations—such as the typical divorce or community mediation—will involve only parties, not lawyers. In private divorce mediations, however, the parties often consult lawyers before finalizing an agreement, whereas this is rarely done in community mediation.

In many mediations, especially those arising in cases in which a lawsuit has been filed, both lawyers and clients attend. It generally facilitates settlement if the clients can speak directly to one another for at least part of the session. Lawyers can play supporting, advisory roles. In some cases, mediators will ask lawyers not to sit at the table, thereby encouraging greater client communication. Another possibility is that the lawyers do some of the talking—e.g., present the clients' legal argument—and the clients do the rest. Many variations are possible.

It is important that the mediator raise the question of the roles of lawyers and clients, so that the parties and lawyers understand that they have to make decisions about this.

The mediator—especially if she is a lawyer—should inform the parties that she does not represent any party, and cannot represent either party in any related matter.

If the mediator determines that one or more of the parties needs legal counsel, she should tell them so and offer to help them find a lawyer, if necessary.

(d) Other participants

As appropriate, the parties or the mediator may include witnesses to an event or other individuals, such as an expert, who might help resolve the conflict.

(e) Mediation procedure

The mediator should present an outline of the steps in mediation, which should include:

[1] Each side has uninterrupted time to make an opening statement about the case and how he would like to see it resolved.

[2] Mediator and other participants discuss what issues must be addressed and how best to address them, i.e., plan an agenda.

[3] Parties (or their lawyers) gather and present in more detail the necessary information (unless it is presented in sufficient detail above).

[4] Parties, lawyers, and mediator develop options to meet the parties' needs.

[5] Parties negotiate and choose among options.

[6] Parties, lawyers, or mediator may incorporate the agreement into a contract.

(f) Agreement to mediate

In some circumstances, and in some jurisdictions, it will be advisable to ask the parties to sign an agreement to mediate. Some agreements—such as those commonly used in private divorce mediation—will include detailed rules of mediation, an explanation of fees, and the like. Others will be brief and will simply state that the parties submit the case to mediation.

(g) Caucuses

Either the mediator or a party may call a private caucus. Statements made during caucuses will be kept confidential except to the extent that the caucusing party permits the mediator to reveal the information. If you plan to hold caucuses immediately after the initial session, it is advisable to announce it at this time.

(h) Confidentiality

Mediation thrives best in an atmosphere of free and open discussion. To foster such discussion requires that information revealed during a mediation be shielded, at least to some extent, against subsequent disclosure both in and out of court. Thus, it may be desirable to protect information against:

1. Admissibility or discoverability in a subsequent judicial proceeding in the same case;

2. Revelation and admissibility through subpoena or depositions in other cases; and

3. Revelation to third parties.

In most jurisdictions, some or all of these results may be achieved by virtue of court rules, statutes, or agreement between the parties. The mediator should ensure that the parties and their lawyers are aware of the protections available and the limitations on these protections. In many jurisdictions, for example, laws that mandate reporting of child abuse may affect the mediator's obligations as to confidentiality. And the mediator may have duties to protect the interests of other third parties. Often mediators ask parties to sign a confidentiality agreement that incorporates applicable rules or establishes additional obligations. Sometimes parties wish to negotiate their own confidentiality agreement. [Confidentiality in mediation is discussed more fully in Chapter IV, *infra*.]

(i) Evidence

Stress informality of the process. Rules of evidence do not apply. Information may be presented by witnesses, documents, or narrative of parties. Within reason, anything the parties deem relevant is relevant. For example, the fact that one party feels offended by the other's conduct toward her is relevant in a mediation though it might not be relevant in a court or arbitration proceeding.

(j) Fees

The mediator should be certain the parties understand the fee arrangements. Most mediators in private practice charge an hourly fee that close to (or the same as) the fee they charge for their other professional services such as law or psychotherapy. Some mediators charge a flat daily rate or an additional administrative fee. Normally mediators who are required to travel expect reimbursement for travel expenses.

Some court connected or community oriented mediation programs charge no fees or minimal fees. Some private mediators will waive or reduce fees in appropriate cases.

(k) Questions

Be sure to allow time for parties to ask questions about the process and to participate in planning how the process will work.

By this point, the parties should have a fundamental understanding of mediation and the mediator should have some insight into the problem and how the parties relate to one another. The mediator should not be surprised at having to repeat much of the above information later.

2.　Understanding the Problems

After the introductory stage, the task is to begin understanding the problems, which can be divided into two types:

Problems inside the mediation. These are problems that will affect the mediation process, such as how well the parties can work with one another or with the mediator. Issues of power imbalance and emotions such as anger, hurt, and pride are important here. In dealing with internal problems, the mediator should consider such questions as:

How will the parties' relationship affect their ability to negotiate?

How openly will the parties speak?

How adversarial or problem-solving are the parties' likely perspectives and behaviors?

How well do the parties understand the difficulties they will face in the mediation process?

What strategies might the mediator employ to deal with problems that affect the process?

Problems that gave rise to the mediation. These are the basic facts, feelings, and perceptions relevant to the conflict. The mediator should consider such questions as:

How do the parties perceive what happened?

How well do they understand each other's perceptions?

What resolution does each party want?

If the parties are taking adversarial "positions," what are the chances of converting the negotiation into a joint problem-solving effort?

Feelings and perceptions are as important as more objective facts, such as how much rent is owed or who did what when. Moreover, in the usual case, the mediator should not only try to understand both sets of problems described above, he also should help all parties understand these problems so that the mediation can foster joint problem-solving.

The mediator should begin gathering information about these problems as soon as he gets involved in the case. The introductory phase, described above, will be a rich source of impressions. A more formal procedure for "understanding the problems" is described below.

a. Parties' opening statements

Each party is allowed time to present his or her view of the problem and to indicate his or her preferred resolution. The other parties should not interrupt the presentation. It is important to allow each speaker room express feelings and raise issues. The mediator may, however, interrupt to keep the presentation focused and to clarify important facts or issues. In making such interventions, the mediator should bear in mind suggestions about interviewing techniques described in Chapter II.

In particular the mediator should strive to identify and make relevant the parties' underlying interests. Thoughtful questioning and active listening will help.

During this time, the mediator should take notes, using brief phrases that will remind him of the ideas he is trying to capture, and try to keep eye contact with the speaker. If there are only two or three parties, you might try having a separate column for each on your note pad, so you may readily compare their outlooks. Do not try to make your own transcript.

b. Post statement information gathering, issue identification, and agenda setting

After the opening presentations, the mediator should work with the parties to identify the issues that must be addressed and to begin to develop a process for addressing them. This may be done by continuing the joint session or by adjourning to private caucuses.

The mediator and the parties should jointly determine the issues to be addressed and the order in which to take them up—i.e., the agenda. The mediator should list the issues on a flip chart or blackboard and work with the parties to order them. Reaching agreement on these points can encourage the parties and help them learn to negotiate.

Ordinarily it is best to begin with the easier issues, so as to generate momentum. Sometimes, however, this is not feasible. It may be essential, for substantive reasons, to settle a difficult issue—at least tentatively—before addressing others. Sometimes a party may wish to address a particularly difficult issue first because it is of overriding importance to her. If the mediator thinks it preferable to postpone this issue, he could acknowledge its importance and explain why he thinks postponement is likely to be beneficial. But a mediator should be flexible and willing to change his thinking as he learns from the parties.

In addition, the mediators should help the parties

- Identify any decisions that must be made immediately.

- Identify additional information that is needed, e.g., written agreements, receipts, depositions. Decide who will provide such information and set deadlines.

- Decide if any witnesses or other participants are needed for the mediation.

- Decide if all the necessary parties are present.

c.   Underlying interests

Here are a number of techniques for bringing out underlying interests that the mediator can use at various points.

- Explain and illustrate the difference between interests and positions and the advantages of interest-based bargaining.

- As part of active listening, try to identify interests that lie behind statements made by the parties. In joint sessions, such active listening can help each participant understand the other's interests.

- Ask questions about plans and then speculate, with the participant, about the participants' interests.

- Float proposals for resolution and measure the parties' responses in terms of the likely interests represented.

- When dealing with a given proposal, ask what interests it fosters or impedes.

- Listen for understanding. [For more on listening, see Chapter II, *supra*, and Note 1, following this excerpt.]

d.   Other approaches to understanding the problems.

(1) Orienting toward future.

At many points during a mediation, a party may talk at great length about what another party did wrong. Although this is sometimes useful, often it causes tensions and non-productive arguments to escalate. The mediator should remind the parties that the purpose of mediation is to plan for the future and that too much rehashing the past can interfere with that goal.

(2) Understanding other perspectives.

Often a party will not understand the way another party perceives the situation. The mediator can help him do so by stressing that the other person's perspective is itself a fact, regardless of whether he agrees with that perspective. The mediator also can ask each party to explain how they think the other actually sees the situation (not how they <u>should</u> see it), and then ask the other to comment. Sometimes it is effective to ask the parties to reverse roles: "Joe, make believe you are Robert. Tell us, in Robert's words, how you think Robert sees this." Such moments may allow for the "recognition" that is a cornerstone of Bush and Folger's notion of "transformation," which they promote as a goal of mediation. ROBERT A. BARUCH BUSH & JOSEPH FOLGER, THE PROMISE OF MEDIATION: THE TRANSFORMATIVE APPROACH TO CONFLICT 2D ED. (2005). [A portion of this book is reprinted *supra* at Chapter IV, *infra*.]

There are, of course, situations in which one participant is unwilling to understand the perspectives of the other; sometimes this occurs when the participant cannot control his rage or fear. In other situations, a participant may fear that if he understood his counterpart's perspective, he might empathize, and, as a decent person, have to change his position. Although many would consider this an important form of moral growth, not everyone wants it. For instance, if you are negotiating with an apparently impoverished merchant, do you really want to know how desperately his large family needs the money? Would you get a "worse" deal, financially, if you did?

(3) Defining the problems to be addressed.

Activities such as the foregoing can help clarify the scope of the problem to be addressed in the mediation. For our purposes, problems may be defined along a continuum ranging from broad to narrow. See Leonard L. Riskin, *Understanding Mediators' Orientations, Strategies and Techniques: A Grid for the Perplexed*, 1 Harv. Negot. L. Rev. 7, 18–23 (1997). [A portion of this article appears earlier in this chapter, beginning at p. 304.]

A narrowly defined problem ordinarily involves just one issue, such as who gets how much of something—money, coffee, cheese. In such a "distributive" negotiation, what one party wins the other loses; there is a fixed pie, so to speak. In these cases, one party may demand $100,000 and the other may offer $20,000. Ideally, and perhaps with the help of the mediator, each will have a rationale for his "position."

A broad conceptualization of the problem may involve more than one issue. Accordingly, there may be room for trade-offs to recognize that parties may attach different values to the same issue. "Problem-solving" negotiation (or "integrative bargaining") seeks to satisfy underlying interests. Thus, if issues of money, prestige, safety, and specific pieces of property are present, many more solutions are possible than if money is the only issue.

In many mediations, parties enter not only with an adversarial attitude but also with a distributive concept of the problem. Often the mediator can best serve the parties by helping them expand the number of issues, and thus the possible solutions.

Sometimes the mediator can help the parties broaden a narrow distributive problem. Imagine a dispute over whether back rent is due. The tenant believes she owes only $300 for one month's rent while the landlord believes she is entitled to $600. Using a distributive approach, the parties cannot settle; their settlement ranges do not overlap. The mediator can help the parties introduce another factor, such as time, which the parties might value differently. A tenant might need her security deposit back before 30 days but might be willing to move immediately. The landlord might want to rent the apartment immediately and would be willing to return the tenant's deposit. Similarly the tenant might be willing to pay more than $300.00 if the payments were extended over time. By making the parties' underlying interests relevant, the mediator can increase the likelihood of agreement.

Even in disputes that obviously have many facets, the mediator can increase the likelihood of an integrative settlement by getting the parties to consider their own and each other's underlying interests and then focusing on developing options that meet them. [See the discussion of underlying interests *supra*, beginning at p. 304.]

3.   Generating Options

The mediator has a number of strategies and techniques for developing options and moving the parties toward solution. For most of these to work, the parties must have some understanding of "problem-solving" negotiation and the differences between positions and interests (discussed *supra*). The mediator may have to explain and illustrate these matters more than once. In addition, it must be clear that the goal is to separate option development from option selection. Because judging, selecting, and choosing interfere with creativity, we postpone them.

Here are some strategies for developing options and moving parties toward agreement.

a.   Dealing with specific proposals by the parties

In true distributive problems, specific proposals about amounts of money (or goods or materials) will be important and often dominant. And note that in late stages of most negotiations, the time comes when distributive questions must be answered; after enlarging the pie, it must be divided.

Sometimes in the early stages of mediation, specific proposals can be counter-productive. On the other hand it is usually more desirable if the parties—rather than the mediator—initiate proposals; this gives the parties a greater sense of psychological "ownership" and allows the mediator to remain more detached and objective. What the mediator should do when a party wishes to make a specific proposal depends upon factors too numerous and subtle to describe, but here are a few suggestions.

1. Treat the proposal as one option.

2. Examine and discuss the proposal to learn what underlying interests of the proponent it is designed to serve and how it affects the underlying interests of others.

3. Listen to the proposal in private caucus and help the party decide whether to (a) modify the proposal to better address underlying needs; (b) present it to the other parties, either directly or through the mediator; (c) delay its presentation; or (d) drop it.

4. Discuss the proposal with the other parties in a joint session or caucus.

b. Brainstorming

In brainstorming the parties are encouraged to suggest virtually any possible solution that comes to mind, and, what is most important, no one—not even the proposer—is allowed to assess or judge any proposal. The mediator should list the ideas on a blackboard or flip chart and then, when brainstorming is completed, lead the parties through assessing the extent to which each alternative meets the parties' underlying needs. Many suggestions will be obviously inappropriate, but sometimes elements of proposals can be combined into new proposals. More likely, the process will reveal several options the parties think are worth further discussion. Brainstorming also may help identify underlying interests.

4. Reaching Agreement

Once various options have been suggested, the next task is deciding about them. Formulas will not help, because everything depends on the precise situation. Here are a number of strategies and tactics:

a. The single negotiating text

The group starts out with one proposal that speaks to all the issues and negotiates to modify it to meet the interests of all concerned. This technique can be very effective in managing negotiations with multiple parties, all of whom might have their own proposals.

b. The BATNA (Best Alternative to a Negotiated Agreement)

The mediator encourages and helps the parties realistically assess their settlement opportunities by understanding and developing their best alternative, such as court or arbitration. (Roger Fisher, William Ury & Bruce Patton, Getting to Yes: Negotiating Agreement without Giving In 97–107 (2d ed. 1991).)

c.   Creating doubts

A mediator can encourage a party to be more flexible by creating doubts about the validity of its position. This normally should be done in private—and with great care—so as not to mislead a party or weaken the parties confidence in the mediator or the mediation process.

d.   Assessing proposed agreements

The mediator can help the parties evaluate the consequences of particular proposals. It is important to help the parties consider social, psychological, and moral consequences as well as financial ones.

e.   Explaining proposals

The mediator should help each party understand the other's proposals and view of the problem. This can be achieved either in joint or private sessions. Again, normally it is best if the parties explain their own ideas, but sometimes the mediator should rephrase ideas to make them easier for the other parties to understand or cope with. For instance, if Party A says, "I think B is a filthy liar and I can't believe a word he says," the mediator can explain that to B as follows: "A has doubts about whether she can rely upon your promises."

f.   Using objective criteria

Fair market value, customary practices, and the like may be readily agreed upon as bases for decision. Experts often will be needed to establish these measures, and the parties may agree on an expert or a process for selecting an expert. Note that there may be a tension between using objective criteria and finding a solution that meets the parties' underlying needs and is fair in the context of their own relationship.

g.   Logrolling

By breaking down the dispute into several issues, the mediator can encourage the parties to trade or "logroll": "I'll give you A and D, if you'll give me B and two-thirds of C." If parties have complementary interests, both might be better off through such a process.

h.   Using deadlines

People ordinarily will not make decisions before they must, so the mediator often can help parties by creating or emphasizing deadlines.

    i.   <u>Different types of agreements</u>

Parties may agree to a resolution that deals with some or all the issues. They may agree to negotiate further and they may set up processes—such as mediation—to deal with issues that may arise in the future. In some cases, it may be appropriate for the mediator to encourage the parties to consider using further professional services, such as those of a counselor or an appraiser.

    5.   <u>Implementing the Agreement</u>

Implementing the agreement means putting it in writing and carrying it out. If the parties consent, a written agreement may be prepared either by the mediator, a party, or a lawyer. Often the parties will reach an oral understanding and will not desire a written agreement. In some cases the parties will agree on the terms and prepare a short memorandum of agreement during the mediation session and plan to work out the precise language later.

In the agreement, the parties should provide for resolving disputes that arise in implementation. Normally, it makes sense to include a clause in the agreement providing that, in the event of a dispute, the parties will return to mediation and, perhaps, if the mediation fails, that they will try another dispute resolution method.

C.   REFERRALS AND OUTSIDE EXPERTS

During the course of the mediation it may become apparent that one or all of the parties in the mediation need additional help in resolving their problems or that the mediator can not adequately address the parties' conflict. In these cases the mediator should refer the parties to appropriate outside agencies or services. It may also be appropriate to arrange for certain kinds of experts—such as accountants or real estate appraisers—to perform their services for both parties.

NOTES AND QUESTIONS

1.   Many other commentators have described how a mediator should go about mediating. Most mediation trainers have their own manuals. But a wide variety of books are available that provide guides to mediation practice. These include: JAMES J. ALFINI, SHARON B. PRESS, JEAN R. STERNLIGHT, & JOSEPH B. STULBERG, MEDIATION PRINCIPLES AND PRACTICE (2nd ed. 2006); MARK D. BENNETT & SCOTT H. HUGHES, THE ART OF MEDIATION (2nd ed. 2005); DWIGHT GOLANN, MEDIATING LEGAL DISPUTES: EFFECTIVE STRATEGIES FOR LAWYERS AND MEDIATORS (1996); DWIGHT GOLANN & JAY FOLBERG, MEDIATION: THE ROLES OF ADVOCATE AND NEUTRAL (2006); KIMBERLEE R. KOVACH, MEDIATION PRINCIPLES AND PRACTICES (3rd ed. 2004); CARRIE MENKEL–MEADOW, LELA PORTER LOVE, & ANDREA KUPFER SCHNEIDER, MEDIATION: PRACTICE, POLICY AND ETHICS (2006); CHRISTOPHER W. MOORE: THE MEDIATION PROCESS: PRACTICAL STRATEGIES FOR RESOLVING CONFLICT

(3d ed. 2003); JOSEPH B. STULBERG, TAKING CHARGE/MANAGING CONFLICT (2nd ed. 2002); JOHN WINSLADE & GERALD MONK, NARRATIVE MEDIATION: A NEW APPROACH TO CONFLICT RESOLUTION (2000); BENNETT G. PICKER, MEDIATION PRACTICE GUIDE: A HANDBOOK FOR RESOLVING BUSINESS DISPUTES (2nd ed. 2003); ANDERSON J. LITTLE, MAKING MONEY TALK: HOW TO MEDIATE INSURED CLAIMS AND OTHER MONETARY DISPUTES (2007); JAMES C. FREUND, ANATOMY OF A MEDIATION (2012).

2. One of the mediator's most important activities is listening and demonstrating understanding. The mediator thus increases the likelihood that the parties will make meaningful progress in resolving their dispute and provides the parties with an "experience of justice." *See* Nancy A. Welsh, *Making Deals in Court–Connected Mediation: What's Justice Got To Do With It?*, 79 Wash. U. L.Q. 787, 791 (2001); Nancy A. Welsh, *Stepping Back Through the Looking Glass: Real Conversations with Real Disputants About Institutionalized Mediation and Its Value*, 19 Ohio St. J. on Disp. Resol 573 (2004).

3. In Chapter II, we introduced you to the process of "looping" as a vehicle to promote attorney-client communication *(supra,* p. 83, and saw how it can also be used to facilitate negotiations between parties in Chapter III *(supra,* p. 199). Veteran loopers and mediation trainers Gary Friedman and Jack Himmelstein offer some particular advice for looping in mediation:

> Our recommendation for looping from the start applies to the mediator's looping the parties, *not* to suggesting that the parties loop each other. Many mediators, drawn by the desire to increase understanding, will turn to the parties early on and ask: What did you understand the other to say? Our advice, generally, is *not yet.* People are much more willing and able to understand one another when they feel understood themselves. To put it another way, believing yourself to be misunderstood is not a good place from which to try to understand another. Parties in conflict are often mired in misunderstood feelings. By establishing some understanding at the start (from the mediator of the parties), the mediator begins to help break the cycle of misunderstanding.

> The mediator:

> 1. Gives each party the experience of being understood;

> 2. Shows each that the other's view, which often seems incomprehensible, can be understood at least by the mediator;

> 3. Restates each party's view in a way that may be easier for the other to hear; and

> 4. Models the art of looping.

> People ensnared in a *conflict trap* tend to want to defend their position, to blame the other, to try to convince a third party that they are

right and the other wrong. The mode is one of defense, persuasion, and coercion.

When conflict takes that form, as is usually the case, misunderstanding prevails. The more the parties feel blamed or vilified by the other, the more they feel misunderstood. The more they feel misunderstood, the more they tend to blame and vilify. The cycle is well known and yet it may feel as inevitable as it is restricting. Looping from the beginning can help soften conflict's powerful hold and suggest a possible way out.

Already this is much more than many mediators (and others) will do in an effort to listen. More often, people make a sincere effort to understand by paying silent attention, nodding agreement, or uttering the catch-all, "I understand what you are saying." These are not bad, but expressing specific understanding goes further. It demonstrates understanding. It does not demonstrate agreement.

* * *

But, at first, it can feel like agreement to many parties. . . . As a result, even this initial effort can become fairly heated, with a share of the heat directed at the mediator. If the parties think understanding means agreeing, looping can all too easily reinforce the *conflict trap*, and the mediator can get caught inside as well. In explaining looping, therefore, the mediator needs to make very clear that understanding is not the same as agreeing.

To guard against parties mistaking understanding for agreement, and jeopardizing their neutrality, some mediators prefer to reserve any outward demonstration of understanding for private meetings, caucuses, where they meet separately with the different parties. For us, understanding each party in the presence of the other does not compromise mediator neutrality. It establishes and validates it.

Looping from the Inside Out

To really understand looping is to recognize that it is more than just a useful skill and that it has an inner life. In that inner life the essential spirit of looping is grounded.

The mediator must truly want to understand the parties in dispute. The mediator needs to listen from the heart when each person is speaking and must make the effort to understand how each experiences the situation, particularly when they are hard to understand or their views easy to criticize. That inner desire to understand is key.

Focusing too much on looping's outer skill, on getting the words right, on learning to rephrase or reframe (which are important skills to learn), can miss the essential point, which is to truly and intentionally understand.

When one party is speaking, the mediator is listening—seeking to understand. When the mediator responds, it's with a genuine desire to communicate his or her understanding. Actually, better said, it is to inquire whether he or she understands. Seeking confirmation is also heartfelt, and the parties' response to "have I understood?" is critical, letting the mediator know whether he or she and the parties are connecting. For looping to truly serve its purpose, each step needs to be grounded in the authentic desire to understand the other, and the mediator and the parties need to know whether they are being successful in that effort.

If the inner desire is lacking, methodically covering each of the four steps (understand parties, express understanding, ask for confirmation, receive confirmation) may well be inadequate. The goal must be to have both the inside and outside processes working together.

GARY FRIEDMAN & JACK HIMMELSTEIN, CHALLENGING CONFLICT: MEDIATION THROUGH UNDERSTANDING 68–71 (2008).

b. Transformative Mediation

ROBERT A. BARUCH BUSH & JOSEPH FOLGER, THE PROMISE OF MEDIATION: THE TRANSFORMATIVE APPROACH TO CONFLICT

45–46, 49–56, 59, 60, 62, 65–66, 68, 72, 75, 78–81 (Revised ed. 2005)

The Transformative Theory of Conflict

The transformative theory of conflict starts by offering its own answer to the foundational question of what conflict means to the people involved. According to transformative theory, what people find most significant about conflict is not that it frustrates their satisfaction of some right, interest, or pursuit, no matter how important, but that it leads and even forces them to behave toward themselves and others in ways that they find uncomfortable and even repellent. More specifically, it alienates them from their sense of their own strength and their sense of connection to others, thereby disrupting and undermining the interaction between them as human beings. This crisis of deterioration in human interaction is what parties find most affecting, significant—and disturbing—about the experience of conflict.

* * *

The transformative theory starts from the premise that interactional crisis is what conflict means to people. And help in overcoming that crisis is a major part of what parties want from a mediator.

* * *

The Picture of Negative Conflict Interaction—and the Evidence Behind It

. . . Conflict, along with whatever else it does, affects people's experience of both self and other. First, conflict generates, for almost anyone it touches, a sense of their own *weakness* and incapacity. . . . This overall sense of "weakening" is something that occurs as a very natural human response to conflict; almost no one is immune to it, regardless of their initial "power position." At the very same time, conflict generates a sense of *self-absorption*: compared to before, each party becomes more focused on self alone—more protective of self, and more suspicious, hostile, closed and impervious to the perspective of the other person. In sum, no matter how strong a person is, conflict propels them into relative weakness. No matter how considerate of others people are, conflict propels them into self-absorption, self-centeredness.

Support for this account of the human experience of conflict comes from work in the fields of cognitive and social psychology, and neurophysiology, among others . . .

* * *

. . . [T]he experiences of weakness and self-absorption . . . reinforce each other in a feedback loop: the weaker I feel myself becoming, the more hostile and closed I am toward you; and the more hostile I am toward you, the more you react to me in kind, the weaker I feel, the more hostile and closed I become, and so on. This vicious circle of *disempowerment* and *demonization* is exactly what scholars mean when they talk about *conflict escalation*. The transformative theory looks at it more as *interactional degeneration*. Before a conflict begins, whatever the context, parties are engaged in some form of decent, perhaps even loving, human interaction. Then the conflict arises and, propelled by the vicious circle of disempowerment and demonization, what started as a decent interaction spirals down into an interaction that is negative, destructive, alienating and demonizing, on all sides.

* * *

What Parties Want From a Mediator: Help in Reversing the Negative Spiral

Taking the transformative view of what conflict entails and means to parties, one is led to a different assumption, compared to other theories of conflict, about what parties want, need and expect from a mediator. If what bothers parties most about conflict is the interactional degeneration itself, then what they will most want from an intervenor is help in reversing the downward spiral and restoring constructive interaction. Parties may not express this in so many words when they first come to a mediator. More commonly, they explain that they what they want is not just agreement but "closure," to get past their bitter conflict experience and "move on" with their lives. However, it should be clear that, to help parties achieve closure and move on, the mediator's intervention must directly address the interactional crisis itself.

The reason for this conclusion is straightforward: if the negative conflict cycle is not reversed, if parties don't regenerate some sense of their own strength and some degree of understanding of the other, it is unlikely they can move on and be at peace with themselves, much less each other. In effect, without a change in the conflict interaction between them, parties are left disabled, even if an agreement on concrete issues is reached. The parties' confidence in their own competence to handle life's challenges remains weakened, and their ability to trust others remains compromised. The result can be permanent damage to the parties' ability to function, whether in the family, the workplace, the boardroom, or the community (Folger and others, 2001). Recognition of this possibility and its ramifications for the workplace was the main reason for the United States Postal Service's decision to employ the transformative model exclusively in their REDRESS Program for mediating workplace conflicts (Bush, 2001; Hallberlin, 2001). * * *

From the perspective of transformative theory, reversing the downward spiral is the primary value mediation offers to parties in conflict. That value goes beyond the dimension of helping parties reach agreement on disputed issues. With or without the achievement of agreement, the help parties most want, in all types of conflict, involves helping them end the vicious circle of disempowerment, disconnection and demonization, alienation from both self and other. Because without ending or changing that cycle, the parties cannot move beyond the negative interaction that has entrapped them and cannot escape its crippling effects.

* * *

The Theory of Mediation as Conflict Transformation

* * * [T]ransformative mediation can best be understood as a process of *conflict transformation*—that is, changing the quality of conflict interaction. In the transformative mediation process, parties can recapture their sense of competence and connection, reverse the negative conflict cycle, re-establish a constructive (or at least neutral) interaction and move forward on a positive footing, with the mediator's help.

Party Capacity for Conflict Transformation: Human Nature and Capacity

To explain this view of mediation, we first return to the concept of interactional degeneration in conflict. How does mediation help parties in conflict reverse the negative conflict spiral? Out of what resource is that kind of transformation generated, and what is the mediator's role in doing so? The first part of the theoretical answer to this question points not to the mediator at all, but to the parties themselves. The critical resource in conflict transformation is the parties' own basic humanity—their essential strength, decency and compassion, as human beings. As discussed earlier, the transformative theory of conflict recognizes that conflict tends to escalate as interaction degenerates, because of the susceptibility we have as human beings to experience weakness and self-absorption in the face of sudden challenge.

However, the theory also posits, based on what many call a *relational theory* of human nature, that human beings have inherent capacities for *strength* (agency/autonomy) and *responsiveness* (connection/understanding), and an inherent *social* or *moral impulse* that activates these capacities when people are challenged by negative conflict, ultimately working to counteract the tendencies to weakness and self-absorption. (Della Noce, 1999) The transformational theory asserts that when these capacities are activated, the conflict spiral can reverse and interaction can regenerate, even without the presence of a mediator as intervenor.

* * *

Conflict is not static. It is an emergent, dynamic phenomenon, in which parties can—and do—move and shift in remarkable ways, even when no third party is involved. They move out of weakness, becoming calmer, clearer, more confident, more articulate and more decisive—in general, *shifting from weakness to strength*. They shift away from self-absorption, becoming more attentive, open, trusting, and understanding of the other party—in general, shifting from self-centeredness to responsiveness to other.

* * *

In transformative theory, these dynamic shifts are called *empowerment* and *recognition* (Bush, 1989a; Bush, 1989b). * * * The stronger I become, the more open I am to you. The more open I am to you, the stronger you feel, the more open you become to me, and the stronger I feel. Indeed the more open I become to you, the stronger I feel in myself, simply because I'm more open; that is, openness not only requires but creates a sense of strength, of magnanimity. So there is also a circling between strength and responsiveness once they begin to emerge. But this is not a vicious circle, it is a "virtuous circle"—a virtuous circle of conflict transformation.

Why conflict transformation? Because as the parties make empowerment and recognition shifts, and as those shifts gradually reinforce in a virtuous circle, the interaction as a whole begins to transform and regenerate. It changes back from a negative, destructive, alienating and demonizing interaction to one that becomes positive, constructive, connecting and humanizing, even while conflict and disagreement are still continuing.

* * *

Mediation as Conflict Transformation: Definitions and Guiding Principles

The previous discussion brings us to the definition of mediation itself, and the mediator's role, in the transformative model. Both of these definitions differ markedly from the normal definitions found in training materials and practice literature—in which mediation is usually defined as a process in which a neutral third party helps the parties to reach a mutually acceptable resolution of some or all the issues in dispute, and the mediator's role is defined as establishing ground rules, defining issues, establishing an agenda, generating options, and ultimately persuading the parties to accept terms of agreement (Stulberg, 1980; Alfini et al., 2003; Moore, 1986; Folberg & Taylor, 1984).

By contrast, in the transformative model

- Mediation is defined as a process in which a third party works with parties in conflict to help them change the quality of their conflict interaction from negative and destructive to positive and constructive, as they explore and discuss issues and possibilities for resolution.

- The mediator's role is to help the parties make positive interactional shifts (empowerment and recognition shifts) by supporting the exercise of their capacities for strength and responsiveness through their deliberation, decision-making, communication, perspective-taking, and other party activities.

- The mediator's primary goals are: (1) to support empowerment shifts, by supporting—but never supplanting—each party's deliberation and decision-making, at every point in the session where choices arise (regarding either process or outcome) and (2) to support recognition shifts, by encouraging and supporting—but never forcing—each party's freely chosen efforts to achieve new understandings of the other's perspective.

* * *

Fourth, even though the mediator's job is to support empowerment and recognition shifts, the transformative model does not ignore the significance of resolving specific issues. Rather, it assumes that, if mediators do the job just described, the parties themselves will very likely make positive changes in their interaction and find acceptable terms of resolution for themselves where such terms genuinely exist. * * *

Empowerment and Recognition: What the Terms Do and Do Not Mean

* * *

[E]mpowerment and recognition are not end states or products of the conflict transformation process. They are *dynamic shifts* from one mode of experiencing self or other to a different mode. In fact, we make it a point today to always use the words empowerment and recognition as *adjectives* attached to the word *"shift."* In an *empowerment shift*, the party moves from weakness to greater strength. In a *recognition shift*, a party moves from self-absorption to greater understanding of other. * * *

The Value of Conflict Transformation: Private and Public

* * *

... [W]hen conflict transformation occurs—because empowerment and recognition shifts were made during mediation—there may also be long term benefits to the parties. These are what some have called *upstream effects* of conflict transformation: impacts of the mediation experience that carry over into future situations. (Hallberlin, 2000) For example, from having made empowerment shifts from confusion to clarity in mediation, parties may carry forward an increased confidence in their ability to clarify and express their views in future situations. Or, having made recognition shifts from suspicion to greater openness, parties may be more willing and able, in other situations, to withhold judgment and give others the benefit of the doubt. The result is that they are more likely to avoid the negative conflict spiral in the future, or to have greater ability to reverse it on their own—important long term benefits of mediation for the parties themselves. * * *

The public value of conflict transformation is overlooked in most discussions of the public benefits of mediation. * * * [S]ome fifteen years ago, one of the authors of this volume explained the public benefits of mediation—beyond systemic efficiency—in the following terms:

Parties to mediation [are affected] in two ways: in terms of their ... capacity for self-determination, and in terms of their ... capacity for consideration and respect for others. And *that itself* is the public value that mediation promotes. In other words, going through mediation is a direct education and growth experience, as to self-determination on the one hand and consideration for others on the other.... Simply put, it is the value of providing a moral and political education for citizens, in responsibility for themselves and respect for others.

NOTES AND QUESTIONS

1. Professors Bush and Folger first elaborated their theory of Transformative Mediation in ROBERT A. BARUCH BUSH & JOSEPH FOLGER, THE PROMISE OF MEDIATION: RESOLVING CONFLICT THROUGH EMPOWERMENT AND RECOGNITION (1994). The most notable effort to implement this approach on a systematic basis is the REDRESS program of the U.S. Postal Service, under which thousands of employment disputes have been mediated. Why do you suppose the Postal Service chose transformative mediation as opposed to, say, the narrow-evaluative approach described in the Riskin excerpt, *supra*? For an analysis of this program, *see* Chapter VI, *infra*.

2. Bush and Folger assert that "interactional crisis is what conflict means to people. And help in overcoming that crisis is a major part of what parties want from a mediator." Do Bush and Folger mean that everyone in every conflict experiences it in this way? To what extent are these thoughts consistent with your own experiences with conflict? With experiences of others with whom you are familiar?

3. For other information about the uses of Transformative Mediation, see Dorothy J. Della Noce, *Special Series: Assuring Mediator Quality: From Practice to Theory to Practice: A Brief Retrospective on the Transformative Mediation Model*, 19 Ohio St. J. on Disp. Resol. 925 (2004); and the web site of the Institute for the Study of Conflict Transformation, Inc., http://www.transformativemediation.org. Although the approach elaborated in the first edition of the Bush & Folger book has attracted many enthusiastic adherents, it also has drawn substantial criticism. Can you imagine what some of those criticisms might be? *See* Carrie Menkel–Meadow, *The Many Ways of Mediation: The Transformation of Traditions, Ideologies, Paradigms, and Practices*, 11 Negot. J. 217 (1995); Robert Condlin, *The Curious Case of Transformative Dispute Resolution: An Unfortunate Marriage of Intransigence, Exclusivity, and Hype*, 14 Cardozo J. Conflict Res. 621 (2013). How well does legal training prepare one for transformative mediation?

4. For a demonstration of the Transformative Model of mediation, see The "Purple" House Conversations: A Demonstration of Transformative Mediation in Action (2003) (video or DVD), available from the web site of the Institute for the Study of Conflict Transformation, Inc., *supra*.

c. Understanding-Based Mediation

GARY FRIEDMAN & JACK HIMMELSTEIN, CHALLENGING CONFLICT: MEDIATION THROUGH UNDERSTANDING
xxix–xxxi, xxxv–xxxvi (2008)

To pursue this path, we work from a base of four interrelated core principles.

- First, we rely heavily on the power of **understanding** rather than the power of coercion or persuasion to drive the process.

- Second, the primary **responsibility** for whether and how the dispute is resolved needs to be with the parties.

- Third, the parties are best served by **working together** and making decisions together.

- Fourth, conflicts are best resolved by **uncovering what lies under** the level at which the parties experience the problem.

* * *

The Power of Understanding

* * *

Understanding proves central along several dimensions of helping parties to deal with their conflict. One, of course, is the substance of the conflict. We support each party in gaining as full an understanding as possible of what is important to him or her in the dispute, as well as what is important to the other party. Understanding is also critical in creating a working relationship between the parties and the mediator that makes sense to all. And understanding can prove crucial in helping the parties to recognize the nature of the conflict in which they are enmeshed and how they might free themselves from its grip.

We want *everything* to be understood that may be important to the parties in resolving their differences, from how we will work together, to the true nature of the conflict in which the parties are enmeshed, where it came from, how it grew, and how they might free themselves from it. We believe the parties should understand the legal implications of their case, but that the law should not usurp or direct our mediation. We put as much weight on the personal-, practical-, or business-related aspects of any conflict as on the legal aspect. In finding a resolution, we want all parties to recognize what is important to them in the dispute and to understand what is important to the others. We strive for a resolution to satisfy each.

Party Responsibility—Let the Parties Own Their Conflict

"Let the parties own their conflict" means it is important to remember and honor that it is the parties' conflict. *They* hold the key to reaching a resolution that best serves them both. And *they* have the power and responsibility, if they are willing, to work together toward that resolution. For us, that does not mean simply that the parties must ultimately agree to any final settlement of their dispute. *Party responsibility* means the parties understand what is substantively at stake for both and craft a resolution best for all. It also means the parties actively participate in shaping the mediation process by making ongoing choices, along with the mediator, as to the course it will take.

* * *

The mediator, too, is responsible. The mediator's responsibility is directed to supporting the parties in *their ability to make choices together based on their growing understanding. Understanding* ensures that those choices will be informed.

* * *

The Non–Caucus Approach

Many other approaches to mediation recommend that the mediator shuttle back and forth between the parties (caucusing), gaining information that he or she holds confidential. Our central problem with caucusing is that the mediator ends up with the fullest picture of the problem and is therefore in the best position to solve it. The mediator, armed with that fuller view, can readily urge or manipulate the parties to the end he or she shapes.

The emphasis in our approach, in contrast, is on *understanding* and *voluntariness* as the basis for resolving the conflict rather than persuasion or coercion. We stress that it is the parties, not the professionals, who have the best *understanding of what underlies* the dispute and thus are in the best position to find the solution. *Meeting together* with the parties (and counsel) follows from these assumptions about people in conflict. * * *

To work in this way is challenging for both the mediator and the parties. The parties' motivation and willingness to work together is critical to the success of this approach. Mediators often assume that the parties (and their counsel) simply do not want to work together, and therefore keep the parties apart. In our experience, many parties (and counsel) simply accept that they will not work together and that the mediator will be responsible for crafting the solution. But once educated about how staying in the same room might be valuable, many are motivated to try it. If the parties (and the mediator) are willing, *working together* throughout can be as rewarding as it is demanding. . . .

NOTES AND QUESTIONS

1. What are the similarities and differences between the transformative and understanding-based approaches?

2. The understanding-based approach is particularly influential in Germany, Austria, and Switzerland, where Friedman and Himmelstein have done a great deal of training.

3. Riskin believes that the Old Grid, mainly because it is static, cannot adequately depict mediation under Transformative and Understanding-Based models. The Old Grid focuses on the mediator's orientation toward the problem-definition and toward the mediator's role (along the evaluative-facilitative continuum). Strictly speaking, however, the transformative mediator should have not have a substantive orientation toward problem-definition because that decision is up to the parties. In the Understanding-Based Model, it is common for the mediator to predict what would happen in court, that is, to evaluate. However, mediator evaluates in a facilitative fashion—to enhance understanding and not to direct the parties toward a particular agreement. In most other ways, the process is very facilitative.

Mediation trainer Nina Meierding, among others, has transcended this problem. She uses the Old Grid to understand what is going on at various moments during a mediation. For example, she might ask, "When the mediator says XYZ, where is he or she on the grid. The New New Grid, in theory, could depict nearly any actual or potential activity in any mediation. Do you see how?

4. Other commentators have developed other systems for classifying approaches to mediation. Professor Ellen Waldman, for instance, has relied on the role played by norms, by describing "norm-generating," "norm-educating," and "norm-advocating" models. Ellen A. Waldman, *Identifying the Role of Social Norms in Mediation: A Multiple Model Approach,* 48 Hastings L. J. 703, 707–10 (1997). *See also* James J. Alfini, *Trashing, Bashing, and Hashing it Out: Is This the End of "Good Mediation?,"* 19 Fla. St. U. L. Rev. 47 (1991) (describing a continuum of "trashing, bashing and hashing it out"); Leonard L. Riskin, *Understanding Mediators' Orientations, Strategies, and Techniques: A Grid for the Perplexed,* 1 Harv. Negot. L. Rev. 7, 14–16 (1996); CHRISTOPHER W. MOORE, THE MEDIATION PROCESS: PRACTICAL STRATEGIES FOR RESOLVING CONFLICT, 41 (2d ed. 1996) (with categories based on the relationship between the mediator and the disputants—e.g., "social network mediators," "authoritative mediators," and "independent mediators"); James Wall & Timothy Dunn, *Mediation Research: A Current Review,* 28 NEG. J. 217 (2012) (recommending consolidation of mediation strategies into "pressing, neutral, relational, analytic, clarification, and multifunctional").

There are also a variety of other, specific models—e.g., the "problem-solving—transformative" approach to mediation (BARBARA ASHLEY PHILLIPS, THE MEDIATION FIELD GUIDE: TRANSCENDING LITIGATION AND RESOLVING CONFLICTS IN YOUR BUSINESS OR ORGANIZATION 59 (2001)); narrative mediation (JOHN WINSLADE & GERALD MONK, NARRATIVE MEDIATION: A NEW APPROACH TO CONFLICT RESOLUTION 31–41 (2000)); the "insight" approach to mediation (CHERYL PICARD, PETER BISHOP, RENA RAMKAY & NEIL SARGENT, THE ART AND SCIENCE OF MEDIATION 120–24 (2004)); the "therapeutic" approach (Susan S. Silbey & Sally E. Merry, Mediator Settlement Strategies, 8 Law & Pol'y 7, 12, 19 (1986)); the "humanistic" approach (MARK S. UMBREIT, HUMANISTIC MEDIATION: A TRANSFORMATIVE JOURNEY OF PEACEMAKING (1997)); the "analytical" approach (John Bickerman, Giving

Mediation Clients What They Want, Nat'l L. J. (Nov. 16, 2009)). Dean Michael Moffit examined the challenges of defining mediation and categorizing different forms of mediation. Michael L. Moffit, *Schmediation and the Dimensions of Definition*, 10 Harv. Negot. L. Rev. 69 (2005).

Each of the models rests on different assumptions about the goals and purposes of a mediation. In terms of the ideas of conflict and dispute resolution described in Chapter I, each has different aspirations and assumptions about which elements of conflict—behavioral, emotional and cognitive—mediation should address, and how deeply beneath the surface of the dispute the mediation could or should reach. Athough each has value for these purposes and others, none of them can fully describe what happens in a real mediation; in that sense, they all distort reality. As many commentators have put it, "[t]he map is not the territory." In George Box's terms, "All models are wrong, but some are useful." G.E.P. Box, *Robustness in the Strategy of Scientific Model Building*, in ROBUSTNESS IN STATISTICS 201, 202 (Robert L. Launer & Graham N. Wilkinson eds., 1979).

For purposes of learning about mediation, however, the models are important for at least three reasons. First, they provide a way of understanding the mental conceptions of mediation—conscious or subconscious—that often influence participants in mediation as well as observers, potential supporters, sponsors, opponents and critics. Second, they should help us begin to think about what kind of process is most appropriate in a particular dispute or category of disputes (e.g., family disputes, "barking dog" cases, commercial contract matters). And third, they can help us be aware of how various participants can influence the development of a particular mediation. In short, as lawyers we need to be aware of the potential variations in mediation processes so we can promote the most appropriate method in particular situations.

B. BRIEF TAKES ON REAL MEDIATIONS

As we hope you can imagine from the foregoing, describing "mediation" generically is nearly as daunting as generically describing dancing or sports. One challenge—in addition to dealing with various models, such as those described above—is that mediation takes place in many different settings, with variations in the types of problems and parties involved, and good mediators respond to these variations, sometimes in ways that do not fit into standard mediation models. For these reasons and others, some mediation processes are so dissimilar that they all can be called mediation only in the same sense that bowling, football, and golf can all be called sports.

Still, for you to understand mediation, it helps to have some sense of how the process works in practice. So, in this section, we set out brief descriptions of five mediations, each from a different field, followed by information about that field and commentary and questions about the issues raised in the mediation described. Within each area in which mediation is practiced, of course, there is so much variety that reading one case study can give you only a small amount of insight. Accordingly, each case study represents the field from which it was drawn only in the limited sense in which an individual "Granny Smith" apple represents the world of apples.

1. PROFESSIONAL MALPRACTICE

HANK DE ZUTTER, PROPONENTS SAY ADR SPELLS RELIEF
Ill. Legal Times, Jan. 1988, at 1

The 62–year–old man had one good testicle and one bad one. A urologist operated and mistakenly removed the good one. The man and wife were outraged: he was impotent.

Time for a lawsuit? Most Americans would think so. An insult so grave, so horrible—mistake or not—would seem to require the most dramatic response: take this doctor to the cleaners. Take him to court.

Then the doctor's insurance company talked them into mediating the matter. Nothing would be binding. Nothing said to the mediator could be part of a future lawsuit, and something might be worked out.

A lawsuit may provide a form of cathartic revenge, but it would prolong the bitterness as well as payment of the claim. The man was 62, and he did have health problems. A trial in the log-jammed Cook County courts was three to five years away. That's three to five years of hating the doctor, hating the insurance company, hating the doctor's lawyer, and wondering about his own lawyer. It would be three to five years of living with the case, of endlessly discussing this hatred and the injustice of it all with sympathetic friends. It would also be three to five years of waiting for financial compensation.

So the man, his wife, and their lawyer showed up earlier this year at the Huron Street office of Resolve Dispute Management Inc., a private dispute settlement firm organized by Brian Muldoon, a successful trial lawyer turned professional mediator.

* * *

Mediation can be seen as a way of improving the quality of our lives. It builds satisfaction in an area that ordinarily mass-produces frustration: it gives clients and their lawyers greater control over their professional and personal lives.

* * *

Though educated and licensed as a lawyer, Muldoon now sees himself as a member of a different profession—a professional in dispute resolution, or a professional mediator.

* * *

He was one of three ADR consultants who recently spoke to a standing-room-only luncheon workshop of the Chicago Bar Association's committee on Arbitration and Alternative Dispute Resolution. And all three described the shift in warm, glowing terms that usually accompany tales of personal transformation.

* * *

The case of the mistaken testicle was resolved one week after the first mediation session. The man accepted a settlement of $75,900. Both parties were happy, Muldoon says, to put the matter behind them and move on.

* * *

The satisfaction, Muldoon says, involved much more than the money. Because the parties—the man, his wife and the doctor—got to resolve the bitter, awkward feelings involved.

Says Muldoon, "The man and his wife got the chance to vent their anger and frustration with the doctor—not just a lawyer or insurance adjustor—there to hear it. It is not very often that you get to tell off a doctor you've sued for malpractice. They had a chance to get it off their chest, a very important step in resolving any conflict. They felt tremendous relief just to get a chance to tell their story."

The doctor, likewise, got a chance to apologize, saying he was proud of his reputation but absolutely mortified that he had made such an error. He said he was wrong and apologized.

The plaintiff then said to the doctor, "I have wanted to hate you and have hated you, but the truth of the matter is that you have been an excellent doctor and I would refer anyone to you. I forgive you." The doctor was so moved that he stayed around to make sure that his insurance company settled the claim.

Muldoon says lawyers, as well as clients, have much to gain through ADR—though some defense lawyers may not think so. "Defense attorneys who charge clients on an hourly fee basis may feel threatened by quick settlements, but once they work out the economics—by charging a flat settlement fee—they will be pushing for it like crazy."

"Lawyers who incorporate mediation as part of their business have more control of their lives, are personally happier, and get paid more regularly," he adds.

"We lawyers have enough problems in our own lives without going through the psychodramas of someone else's life. These psychodramas are exaggerated because of the nature of the adversary system. Every battle we get engaged in is totally black or totally white; we are trained to exaggerate our client's case. The trouble is we begin to believe our exaggerations by the time we get to court. We see our opponents as personal enemies. I've known cases where some lawyers will leave a restaurant if they see an opposition lawyer there."

"Stress infects their lives," Muldoon says. "Divorce among trial lawyers is common. The toll is especially heavy among divorce lawyers."

"Those who seek to avoid the stress through emotional detachment also pay a price. Lawyers are supposed to be their clients' champions, and if they stop seeing themselves that way, they can stop caring for their clients. They can stop caring in other parts of their life—at home—as well. Lawyers have not been very open about the personal price paid in the current advocacy system."

Muldoon says he was initiated to the joys of negotiating settlements when he was appointed by the mayor of Phoenix, where he had his law practice, to head a downtown redevelopment commission. With the help of a veteran lawyer and ace negotiator, Muldoon says in 60 days he negotiated a redevelopment plan involving all the conflicting interests: developers, existing businesses, historic preservationists, and others who were affected.

"It was so exciting I wanted to try to resolve all pending cases in litigation, about a half dozen in all. So I called up my clients, told them I was going to change my system of billing from hourly fees to a 'results achieved' basis, and within 60 days all cases were settled. This done, I needed to figure out a way to make a living. So I took a sabbatical in Puerto Rico and started designing standardized systems for reaching agreement. Then I came back to Chicago [where he had clerked for the U.S. Attorney's office] to start a business specializing in dispute settlement."

* * *

Despite all his talk about the therapeutic benefits of mediating settlements, Muldoon says it's a mistake to regard ADR and mediation as a "dreamy California, let's be nice approach."

It is still a very tough—gentlemanly, but tough—confrontational business. Disputes don't get resolved through mediation because people want to be nice, but because they become educated through the process about the best results available. Mediation takes something that is a matter of principle that people want to fight about and turns it into a business deal-making opportunity.

2. PERSONAL INJURY

ANDERSON J. LITTLE, MAKING MONEY TALK: HOW TO MEDIATE INSURED CLAIMS AND OTHER MONETARY DISPUTES (2007)

p. xi–xii, 1–10, 14–20, 22, 24–30

The Problem

In January of 1992, I [settled in to mediate] a claim for the proceeds of a double indemnity, accidental death insurance policy, [and a] growing sense of frustration took [over], however, as the parties struggled with each other through round after round of monetary proposals and as I tried to apply all I had learned about how to mediate disputes.

* * *

My frustration [in part] stemmed from the process model I had learned in training and was attempting to apply. . . . I was taught to reframe positional bargaining into joint problem solving, but I soon learned that claims for money rarely are resolved with elegant solutions for mutual gain. They are usually settled with prolonged bargaining consisting of numerous rounds of painful concessions. At the end of January of 1992, my understanding of the mediation process collided with the realities of traditional bargaining.

* * *

The Case: The Rear-Ender

The mediator was greeted in plaintiff's lawyer Attorney John Smith's waiting room by his paralegal, Jennifer Ormand, who explained that all the parties to the mediation were assembled in the conference room and were ready to begin. The mediator entered the conference room, greeted everyone, and invited the participants to have a seat for the beginning of the conference. In attendance were the defendant's claims representative, Joseph Moolen Jones; the defendant, was not present because he had been excused from attending by agreement of the lawyers and the mediator.

The mediator knew little about the case but had worked with lawyers Smith and Walker several times in the past. He noted that fact to all in attendance as he easily slipped into his opening remarks and welcomed all to the conference. His remarks were informative but conversational in tone. They included all of the usual subjects: the purpose of the conference, his role and the role of the lawyers, the costs of the litigation, the confidentiality of the process, and statutes covering the inadmissibility of statements made during the conference. * * *

At the end he asked for questions and suggestions about the process. Hearing none, the mediator invited the plaintiff's lawyer Smith to tell the assembled participants what he wanted the others to understand about the case. Smith began:

"My 24-year-old client, Jimmy Young, was driving to work on two-lane NC 101 at 7:30 on a Monday morning in February two years ago. As Young approached a commercial area near the town of Turnersville, he moved into the right-hand lane of the highway that had now widened into four lanes. About four or five car lengths ahead of him was another vehicle that was behind two other cars. The line of traffic ahead of him slowed for the first car to make a right-hand turn. Young slowed also and kept a reasonable distance from the last car in line.

"After the first car turned right, the line of traffic picked up speed without anyone changing into the left-hand lane. Suddenly the car in the front of the line slowed abruptly, apparently considering a right-hand turn at the next intersection. Instead of turning right, the vehicle sped up, slowed down, and then made a sudden turn left across the other lane and into the median crossover. Young and the driver ahead of him came to a quick halt, with plenty of room separating them.

"As he did so, Young heard the sound of screeching tires behind him. He looked into his rearview mirror in time to see a vehicle driven by Allen Jones plow into his rear end. The impact tore loose Young's rear bumper and spare tire assembly at the rear of his truck. The defendant's car came to rest under the rear of Young's frame.

"Closer inspection showed that the frame was bent and that the bed had damaged the body of the cab as it twisted on impact." At the scene, Young complained of neck, back, and left shoulder pain. He also complained of pain in his right knee. * * *

"Two and a half weeks after the collision, Young saw Dr. Angelo, a local orthopedic surgeon, for pain and swelling in his right knee. Dr. Angelo had performed surgery on Young's knee five years earlier to reconstruct the right AC ligament injured in a high school football scrimmage. Records for this recent injury show that Young had suffered swelling and a bruised right knee with pain and tenderness. Dr. Angelo prescribed no physical therapy, only rest.

"Several weeks later, Young sought a second opinion at the urging of his chiropractor. He was referred to Dr. Carlson, an orthopedic surgeon in a nearby town. Dr. Carlson performed arthroscopic surgery on the knee two months after the collision. During surgery, Dr. Carlson discovered sinovitis in the joint, a tear in the meniscus, and a loose AC ligament. Repairs were made and a brief course of physical therapy was prescribed. Young now complains of intermittent pain and swelling in his right knee and says that the injury has completely changed his life. He is no longer able to maintain the unusually high level of physical fitness he was dedicated to before the accident and has gained 50 pounds.

* * *

"Young's medical bills are $7,400. He has lost wages of $3,000.

There is no claim for future loss of wages or medical expenses. In this action, which is set for trial in four months, Young will seek those amounts plus additional damages for pain and suffering and permanent disability. His scarring from the surgery is minimal, and he has elected not to ask for damages due to disfigurement. That's all we have at this time, Mr. Mediator."

The mediator thanked Smith for his comments and invited Jimmy Young to say what he wanted to about the collision or his injuries. Young declined to speak, saying that his lawyer had covered the subject sufficiently; so the mediator reminded him that he could speak later if he wished.

Turning his attention to the defense side of the table, the mediator asked defense lawyer Walker if he wished to give his perspective on the case. Walker spoke briefly, saying to Young directly that his client Allen Jones was sorry that he had been injured in the accident. "We certainly wish that this had not happened, and we have come here today to work hard to settle the claim. Having said that, it's only fair to alert you to the fact that we View this matter a bit differently than you. * * *"

"Now, we're not going to be talking about insurance coverage today. . . . We're also not going to say a lot about liability either, but you should be aware that, if we have to try this case, we'll be talking to the jury about contributory negligence. If the jury finds that you stopped too abruptly or that your stopping constituted a sudden emergency for Mr. Jones, then you won't be able to recover anything for this accident. You and your lawyer can talk about that, but there's a possibility you'll come out of trial with a zero because of the facts of this case.

"It is important to note that the accident was a chain-reaction type of incident. No one's going to get angry with Mr. Jones for his conduct on this occasion. . . . I think every juror who hears this case will believe this to have been an unfortunate occurrence and find that there were really no bad actors here. **It** was an accident, and accidents happen. * * *

* * *

"Now, Mr. Mediator, I'm not going to talk much about the injuries in this matter in the general session. You and I can talk more about them in private. But I would note here that there are some previous injuries in the same knee that Mr. Young injured in this accident. We know we owe something for the injuries we caused, but we don't owe anything for what someone else caused. In particular, we don't believe that we're responsible for permanent disabilities [of 6 percent] arising out of this accident.

* * * Now, Mr. Mediator, we're here to talk and negotiate, but we need to be talking within a reasonable range of settlement. Thank you, Mr. Mediator."

The mediator then asked the claims representative whether he would like to add anything. The representative deferred to Walker's presentation. When it was clear that no one was going to say anything further, the mediator asked the parties whether they would like to speak with him in private. All agreed that private sessions would be useful, and so the mediator led the plaintiff's team to another room on the other side of Smith's suite of offices.

In private session, the mediator discussed the merits of the case with Young and his lawyer. . . . After a lengthy discussion about the value of the case, the mediator asked Smith if they were prepared to make an opening settlement proposal. Smith replied:

"We'd like to hear from them first. They haven't offered a dime in this case."

"Yeah," Young chimed in. "We've been doing all the work. We've given them tons of medical bills and reports; we've answered their picky interrogatories; and I spent the better part of a day being interrogated at a deposition. They haven't done a thing. They don't even care enough to have Jones here. Why should we do all the work!?"

There followed a lengthy discussion about who would "go first" at the settlement conference . . . [after which] Walker asked the mediator:

"What kind of demand did they make?"

The mediator replied: "Bill, I don't have a proposal from them yet. They want to hear from you first. They want to know what kind of range you're talking about."

Walker retorted: "We haven't given them a number because they've never made a demand."

The claims representative added: "Why are they wasting our time? They know how this is done. We're just not going to bid against ourselves." * * *

After much conversation about the pros and cons of "going first," the defense team opened with an offer of $7,400, the amount of Young's medical expenses.

When the mediator conveyed the defense's offer to the plaintiff, Young exclaimed, "That's insulting." His lawyer, too, clearly was not pleased with the offer; it was obvious from their reactions that Young and his lawyer had different expectations about what amount of money was acceptable to settle the case.

The mediator conveyed the defense perspectives on some of the issues in the case, noting in particular that the defense was honing in on the differing disability ratings in the two letters from Young's own doctor. Young and Smith finally settled on $85,000 as an opening proposal, but it was a proposal Smith thought was too high. The mediator returned to the defendant's room to relay the proposal.

"That's ridiculous," the insurance representative said. "That knee was disabled before the accident. It's not clear that we owe anything for the surgery or disability."

* * *

Walker was frustrated also. ". . . Tell Smith to get control of his client."

The mediator . . . invited the defense to make a counterproposal. With some reluctance, the defense countered with a new proposal: $10,400, the total of Young's claim for medical expenses and lost wages.

Young threatened to walk out of the mediation when he heard the proposal and it appeared that the negotiations would collapse. But after much consultation and consternation, the plaintiff's team countered with $80,000.

When the defendant's lawyer heard Young's second proposal, he stood up abruptly. "Well, that's it," he said. "We might as well pack our bags and go home. There's no way this is going to settle; he'll never get realistic."

With the mediator's help and encouragement, however, the defense team decided to remain at the table. For hours, the negotiations continued with round after round of proposal and counterproposal, each arrived at with great agony and deliberation.

Slowly the parties inched toward each other in small increments; and eventually, after 12 complete rounds of proposals, the parties settled at $27,500. The mediator then helped them draw up a memorandum of settlement.

This court-ordered mediation took a total of four hours and 36 minutes. The parties met with each other only once for less than 30 minutes. They said nothing to each other beyond their initial, rather formal presentations. The remaining four hours were spent in private sessions with the mediator.

At the end, the participants signed their agreement, wrote their checks, said their good byes, and went their separate ways. Their interaction was courteous but stiff. Although an agreement was reached at mediation, no one was particularly happy with the settlement or the difficulty with which it was reached.

* * *

Welcome to the world of civil trial court mediation.

NOTES AND QUESTIONS

1. How would you compare the mediations described in these first two "brief takes"? Where would they fit on the Old Riskin Grid? How would you describe the influence patterns using the New New grids? In which would you rather participate as a lawyer? Mediator? Participant? Why?

2. The personal injury mediation excerpt describes much court-oriented mediation and stands in stark contrast to the thrust of much mediation training. Little focuses on the "is" rather than the "ought." Professors Riskin and Welsh address both "is" and "ought" aspects of this "reality" in Leonard L. Riskin & Nancy A. Welsh, *Is That All There Is?: The Problem' in Court-Oriented Mediation*, 15 Geo. Mason L. Rev. 863–932 (2008), infra.

Although they recognize that a primary focus on analysis of the relevant law, litigation realities and monetary damages is appropriate in many cases, they also urge lawyers, mediators and courts to consult with the clients— especially "one shot" litigants—prior to the mediation regarding the issues that the mediation should tackle. Notice that this sort of pre-mediation consultation makes it more likely that the clients will then be able to influence the approach and interventions used in the mediation. Recall Professor Riskin's discussion of different mediation participants' influence in *The New New Grid, supra*. We will see, *infra*, that sophisticated mediation users prefer mediators who are willing to customize the mediation process to fit the needs of the case and clients.

3. Little suggests there is no place for value creation in personal injury mediation. Do believe that is true? If so, why might that be the case? If not, what strategies might you have employed in his mediation to "expand the pie," even if settlement will consist entirely of money? Recall the different valuations of time and risk that create opportunities for value creation as discussed in Chapter III, *supra*.

4. Recall our discussion of apology in Chapter III, *supra*. How might apology affect the medical malpractice and personal injury cases described in these first two "brief take"? Do people in such cases have emotional needs to interact with the other parties? Do our legal system and legal profession discourage fulfillment of these needs? See Jonathan R. Cohen, *Advising Clients to Apologize,* 72 So. Calif. L. Rev. 1009 (1999).

Damages in some civil suits substitute for other kinds of relief, such as an apology, which courts cannot grant. *See* Richard L. Abel, *A Critique of American Tort Law*, 8 Brit. J. of L. & Soc'y 199 (1981).

5. Mediation has come to play an important role in addressing disputes between professionals and their clients. Some writers have praised the possibilities for education and healing. E.g., Ann J. Kellett, Comment, *Healing Angry Wounds: The Roles of Apology and Mediation in Disputes Between Physicians and Patients*, 1987 Mo. J. Disp. Resol. 111. Others have been less optimistic. Andrew McMullen, Comment, *Mediation and Medical Malpractice Disputes: Potential Obstacles in the Traditional Lawyer's Perspective*, 1990 J. Disp. Resol. 371.

A 2007 study of medical malpractice mediations in Ontario found that, despite a rule requiring parties to attend court-connected mediation sessions, lawyers tended to oppose the attendance of physicians, believing that the purpose of mediation is to reach a monetary settlement (or, in the defense lawyers' perspective, to get the plaintiff to abandon the claim) and that physicians do not wish to attend. However, every plaintiff and every defendant physician interviewed believed that physicians should attend because this would allow the parties to communicate, which they thought was a central aspect of mediation. *See* Tamara Relis, *Consequences of Power*, 12 Harv. Negot. L. Rev. 445, 456–59 (2007); *see also* Orna Rabinovich-Einy, *Deconstructing Dispute Classifications: Avoiding the Shadow of the Law in Dispute System Design in Healthcare,* 12 Cardozo J. Conflict Resol. 55 (2013).

Bar associations have established mediation and arbitration programs to deal with fee disputes between lawyers and their clients, and disciplinary bodies have created programs to mediate grievances (generally minor ones) against lawyers. *See* Alan Scott Rau, *Resolving Disputes Over Attorneys Fees: The Role of ADR*, 46 SMU L. Rev. 2005 (1993). Mediation also has found employment with a more prospective outlook in matters of bioethics. *See* NANCY N. DUBLER & CAROL B. LIEBMAN, BIOETHICS MEDIATION: A GUIDE TO SHAPING SHARED SOLUTIONS (2004).

3.   A SHAREHOLDER–MANAGEMENT DISPUTE

FRANK J. SCARDILLI,* SISTERS OF THE PRECIOUS BLOOD v. BRISTOL–MYERS CO.

This case was on appeal from a grant of summary judgment in favor of Bristol–Myers Co., defendant-appellee (hereinafter "Bristol") and against the Sisters of the Precious Blood, plaintiff-appellant (hereinafter "Sisters"). The latter, who owned 500 shares of Bristol stock, started a lawsuit against Bristol under the proxy solicitation section of the Securities Exchange Act of 1934 alleging that a shareholder resolution they proposed was defeated because Bristol's stated opposition to the resolution in the proxy materials distributed to the shareholders was based on serious misrepresentations of fact.

---

*   Frank J. Scardilli is a mediator employed by the Second Circuit Court of Appeals. Mr. Scardilli presented this at a Harvard Faculty Seminar on negotiation on April 13, 1982.

The Sisters were concerned that the company's sales practices in the third world of its infant baby formula were contributing to serious illness, malnutrition and death of infants because of the unsanitary conditions often prevailing there. Frequently the formula is mixed with contaminated water, there is no refrigeration and its use discourages breastfeeding which is clearly healthier in most instances than is the formula.

The Sisters' proposed resolution requested that management report to the shareholders the full extent of its marketing practices of the infant formula in the third world to alert other shareholders to what they perceived was irresponsible business behavior. Their lawsuit was aimed at getting the company to come up with a corrected proxy solicitation to be submitted to a special meeting of the shareholders to be called specifically for that purpose rather than await the next annual meeting of shareholders.

The court declined to grant the relief sought by the Sisters, stating:

> Defendant's proxy solicitation did not result in or have the tendency to threaten or cause plaintiffs irreparable harm sufficient to warrant injunctive relief. Plaintiffs' proposal was precatory only; it sought merely stockholder approval of a "request" that Bristol management issue a report covering the marketing of infant baby formula products in developing countries. Regardless of the outcome of the shareholder vote, management was entirely privileged to ignore the request and retained complete discretion not to make such a report.

The court refused to reach the question of whether Bristol had actually lied in its recommendation to the shareholders to reject the Sisters' proposed resolution, stating:

> To proceed further with the lawsuit would be 'an empty exercise resulting, at most, in a judicial declaration of no practical import.' An evaluation of the objective accuracy of the proxy statement regarding plaintiff's shareholder proposal would be an empty exercise of semantics in the circumstances of this case.

Mediation Efforts on Appeal

The first of four conferences seeking to mediate this dispute was held on July 19, 1977. (The subject of abuses involving infant formulas in the third world seemed relatively new in 1977 but has obviously had considerable media exposure since then.)

First Conference

Apparently because they believed no amicable resolution was possible, counsel who appeared for the parties were very able but had virtually no settlement authority. (The parties' previous negotiations had broken down despite the best efforts of a very able judge who tried to resolve their differences.)

Legal Merits

As is customary, I first explored the arguments of counsel relative to the strengths and weaknesses of their legal positions on appeal. The parties seemed genuinely far apart in their assessment of the likely outcome in our court. The issue on appeal involved some complexity because of the rather technical requirements for suits under Section 14 of the Securities Exchange Act of 1934. While generally appellees have a distinct advantage, if for no other reason than that only about one out of eight cases is reversed on appeal in our court, the outcome of this particular case was hard to predict. Even if the district court decision were deemed technically correct, this could have disturbing policy implications because the decision appeared to create a license for management to lie with impunity whenever it sought to defeat a proposed shareholder resolution, which would virtually always be precatory. The SEC was apparently disturbed by this implication and advised me it was seriously considering filing a brief amicus curiae urging our court to reverse the decision below. In addition, as I pointed out to counsel for Bristol, although a shareholder resolution is precatory in law, in the real world it can and often does have a serious impact on managerial decisions.

Predictably, the parties' respective positions on what might constitute a satisfactory settlement were far apart. The Sisters were adamant on the principle that no settlement terms could be discussed unless Bristol openly admitted that it had lied in its earlier proxy solicitation and that this fact had to be communicated through new proxy solicitations at a special meeting of the shareholders to be convened solely for that purpose. Bristol, of course, insisted it had been truthful all along. It offered, however, to permit the Sisters to make any written statement they wished at the next annual shareholders' meeting, and Bristol would simply state its opposition to the proposal without elaboration. This was unacceptable to the Sisters. Because it was clear I needed parties with more authority and flexibility, I set up a second conference requiring senior counsel to come in with their clients.

Second Conference

The second conference held in the middle of August, 1977 was attended by senior counsel for both sides, the inside General Counsel of Bristol, and a representative of the Advisory Committee of the Interfaith Group for Corporate Responsibility, which was the real moving force behind the Sisters' litigation.

It soon became apparent that there was very deep hostility and profound distrust between the parties. Each was convinced the other was acting in bad faith. The Sisters were outraged by Bristol's insistence that it had not lied. Its distrust of Bristol was total and uncompromising.

At this conference, the Sisters, for the first time, insisted that they would have to be reimbursed for their litigation expenses of approximately $15,000 before any settlement could be effected. After checking with top management, counsel for management flatly refused to pay anything at all to the Sisters.

As a still further condition of settlement, the Sisters wanted Bristol to provide them with a list of the 1000 largest shareholders of the company prior to the next annual meeting. Bristol refused to give the list. I finally disposed of this issue by convincing both parties to allow Delaware law to determine the Sisters' entitlement to the list (Delaware was the state of Bristol's incorporation).

The Parties' Perceptions of Themselves and of Each Other

It became clear that the respective parties' self-image was significantly at variance with the image each had of the other.

Bristol regarded itself as by far the most responsible marketer of infant formula in the third world, far more so than its three major American competitors and the giant Swiss company, Nestle. It claimed it put out a quality nutritional product that was very useful when mothers either could not or chose not to breast feed their infants; that it did not advertise its infant formulas directly to consumers in the third world; that the company policy already sought to minimize the danger or improper use by its labeling. In short, it was convinced that its business practices were both prudent and responsible. Therefore, they were furious that they had been singled out as "baby killers" by the Sisters who had so testified before a Congressional Committee and who had lost few opportunities to criticize them in the media. It was clear they viewed the Sisters as wild-eyed, misguided religious fanatics who were themselves engaging in a distortion of the facts and reckless character assassination.

The Sisters, on the other hand, had spent years accumulating data in affidavits taken throughout the world regarding the enormous peril to infants created by the indiscriminate use of infant formula in the third world. They had witnessed suffering and death and were suffused with the self-righteousness of avenging angels. To them, Bristol was a monster who cared only about profits and not at all about the lives and health of infants.

Restructuring Perceptions of "Bad Faith"

As negotiations proceeded, it became apparent that no meaningful communication could take place until each of the parties realized that its view of the other was a grossly distorted caricature and counter-productive.

I struck often at the theme that it was dangerous to assume that one with whom you disagree violently is necessarily acting in bad faith. Moreover, I stressed to both that I had become fully and firmly convinced that each of the parties was acting in complete good faith, albeit from a different perspective. I strove to get each to view the matter through the eyes of the other.

I found that before I could get the parties to trust each other I had first to get them to trust me. I was aided in this by able and responsible counsel on both sides who though powerful and often uncompromising advocates were more reasonable than their respective constituencies.

Interest of the Parties—Illusion of "Winning" at Law

It was necessary to convince each that its interests were not nearly as incompatible as they perceived them and that the interest of each would be best served by a cooperative problem-solving attitude rather than a litigious one.

I stressed that neither party's true interest would be served by "winning" the appeal.

A "win" by Bristol would not be likely to stop the public attacks in the media which so angered and disturbed them. Likewise, a "win" by the Sisters could mean a remand for an expensive trial with no assurance whatever thereafter that Bristol's marketing practices would be altered in any way.

The point was made forcibly to the Sisters that their insistence that Bristol admit that it had lied was totally unrealistic and that progress was impossible so long as they insisted on humiliating the company's management. They were reminded that their real interest lay in effecting marketing changes in the third world and they could best achieve this in a climate of cooperative good will with management. So long as management perceived them as vindictive it was likely to simply dig in its heels and refuse to budge. I urged that a softening of their attitude would in turn create a more flexible attitude in management.

Bristol in turn was forced to concede that notwithstanding what they viewed as the distasteful stridency of the Sisters there was indeed a real moral issue to be faced and they had a real interest in being perceived as highly ethical, responsible businessmen who were not insensitive to the human tragedy which could result from the improper use of their product in the third world.

Agreement at Last

After considerable negotiation in four face-to-face conferences supplemented by numerous telephone conferences over a period of nearly six months, in the course of which Bristol voluntarily changed some of its marketing practices, the parties finally agreed to resolve their differences as follows:

1.   The Sisters were satisfied that Bristol had already changed some of its marketing practices which the Sisters had regarded as particularly offensive.

2.   The Sisters would be given direct access to Bristol's Board of Directors and other representatives of the company at various times for the purpose of maintaining a first-hand continuing dialogue on the problems of marketing infant formula in the third world.

3.   Bristol and the Sisters would each prepare a separate written statement of its views not to exceed 1500 words to be presented to the shareholders in the next quarterly report of the Company. This would be preceded by an agreed-upon joint preamble which would recite the background of the litigation, its resolution by the parties and that the Sisters and Bristol planned to continue to exchange views in an atmosphere of mutual respect for each other's good faith.

To insure that the statements would not be inflammatory each side was given the right to veto the statement of the other. Agreeing on the principle, however, was easier than its implementation. Numerous drafts were exchanged and when appropriate I mediated between their respective versions.

The final agreement on language was arrived at as a result of a 4½–hour drafting session involving 8 people sitting around a conference table in the court in the afternoon of Christmas Eve of 1977. In a sense of relief and elation, the Chairperson of the Interfaith Group for Corporate Responsibility stated, "It is fitting and perhaps prophetic that we have finally resolved our differences on how best to protect tender infants on this eve when we prepare to celebrate the birth of an Infant who has meant so much to millions of Christians all over the world."

NOTES AND QUESTIONS

1.   Notice that the mediator helped each party see the dispute from the other's perspective and recognize both sides' underlying *interests* in addition to *positions*. Thus, he moved the negotiations from adversarial to problem solving, and the mediation produced an agreement that seemed to respond to the underlying interests. This broadening of the "problem definition" was necessary to achieving a settlement.

2.   Is it socially desirable that this case was settled before the court of appeals had an opportunity to make law? In this case, the mediator pointed out that a victory in court would have benefited neither party. Would "society" have gained if the court had had an opportunity to clarify or make law? In answering this question, consider again the perspective of Professor

Owen M. Fiss, *Against Settlement*, 93 Yale L.J. 1073 (1984), a portion of which is reprinted in Chapter I, *supra*.

3. To what extent did the mediator seem to employ evaluative techniques? A broad or narrow definition of the problem?

4. This mediation involved a dispute between a company's management and shareholders. In a recent article, Professor Scott Peppet argues, using economics and psychology, that a mediator can "add value" to transactions in the same way that a mediator can add value to disputes. The mediator can do this by helping the parties overcome "information asymmetries," which will enable them to reach a more efficient agreement, and to overcome psychological barriers. Scott R. Peppet, *Contract Formation in Imperfect Markets: Should We Use Mediators in Deals?,* 19 Ohio St. J. on Disp. Resol. 283 (2004). In a recent op-ed piece, mediator David Hoffman applied Professor Peppet's ideas to imagine how a mediator could have helped the CEOs of Microsoft and Yahoo to reach a deal:

> With Microsoft offering $33 per share for Yahoo's stock, and Yahoo willing to take $37, was there truly an unbridgeable gulf? The $4 gap seems trivial in comparison to the potential value of the deal. So did Microsoft and Yahoo walk away from a deal that would have made both sides better off? This type of bargaining failure is hardly rare- businesspeople frequently report deals that have come within inches of closing, only to slip away at the last moment, costing their companies plenty.

> In the world of litigation, settlement gaps are routinely bridged with the help of mediators. In the world of foreign policy, mediation—sometimes called "shuttle diplomacy"—is used extensively to resolve conflict. Why, then, are business transactions rarely mediated?

> One theory is that the functions that mediators perform are already handled by transactional lawyers and investment bankers who work hard—and are handsomely rewarded—to close deals. The problem with this theory is that the lawyers and investment bankers often approach the negotiation from a partisan perspective in order to prove their loyalty to their respective clients.

> In the world of diplomacy, it is often the superpowers that intervene when smaller nations quarrel, and court cases are often mediated because a judge insists on it. Indeed, Microsoft mediated its antitrust dispute with the Justice Department only when the court ordered it. In the setting of mergers and acquisitions, however, the key difference is that there is no outside power that can insist on mediation. Accordingly, it is often up to boards of directors or shareholders to push management to mediation.

* * *

Mediators add value by bringing a neutral and independent perspective to the table, buffering the parties' sometimes harsh communications, clarifying their underlying interests, and making sure that all deal options are considered.

In the Microsoft–Yahoo negotiations, a mediator could have helped in several concrete ways.

First, since disagreements about the price of a company usually turn on financial predictions, mediators can help the parties structure creative options for mitigating their risks. Acquisition agreements often contain "earn-out" provisions that award benefits to the seller if the deal turns out to be a winner for the buyer. Without any investment in the outcome, mediators become "honest brokers" who can advance such ideas without the perception that they are seeking an advantage based on secret knowledge.

Second, a mediator can help the parties obtain neutral and independent opinions—as opposed to the potentially partisan opinions of the parties' hired experts, lawyers, and investment bankers.

Third, a "mediator's proposal" can test the waters of compromise. Let's say the mediator asks each side to tell the mediator—on a confidential basis—whether they would accept a deal at $35 per share. This protocol means the mediator will report the answers only if both sides say "yes." Thus, each side can take the risk of saying yes because the other side will never know unless they, too, have said yes.

When deals collapse, conflict often migrates to another venue. Yahoo is already defending lawsuits from disgruntled shareholders, angered by management's failure to accept Microsoft's offer. However, even if there were no possible zone of agreement in the Microsoft–Yahoo case, business managers in other deal negotiations might consider whether calling in mediators, when needed, might save them from bargaining failures and make both sides better off.

David Hoffman, *Microsoft and Yahoo: Where Were the Mediators?*, The Christian Science Monitor, May 12, 2008, at 9.

4.   REGULATORY NEGOTIATION

ALANA S. KNASTER & PHILIP J. HARTER, THE CLEAN FUELS REGULATORY NEGOTIATION

Intergovernmental Perspective, Summer 1992, at 20

Within days after passage of the *Clean Air Act Amendments of 1990,* officials of the U.S. Environmental Protection Agency were confronted with the onerous task of drafting complicated gasoline regulations to meet the November 15, 1991, deadline for promulgation. The act's clean fuels provisions required EPA to issue regulations for the certification of reformulated gasoline, which is to be made available for sale by 1995 in the nine cities experiencing the worst ozone pollution in the country. Other nonattainment areas may take part in this program on petition of the governor to the EPA administrator.

The regulations are intended to reduce emissions of toxic and ozone producing chemicals, to establish procedures for ensuring that the gasoline sold outside these areas is not any worse than that sold before 1990 (the anti-dumping provision), and to address the problem of carbon monoxide. The carbon monoxide rules were to be issued in August 1991 and the program is to be in place by the end of 1992. Adding oxygen to motor fuels reduces the emission of carbon monoxide. The 1990 amendments, therefore, require certain carbon monoxide nonattainment areas to implement a program to secure the use of fuels with an average oxygen content of 2.7 percent. Because only an average is required, the rules needed to provide a means by which it would operate—something easy to describe in principle but difficult to implement in regulations.

The debates over passage of the legislation had been contentious, and it was felt that developing the regulations would be equally controversial. William Rosenberg, EPA's Assistant Administrator for Air Programs, decided to consider using regulatory negotiation to develop the rules. Even though negotiation would be time consuming and would preclude staff from beginning drafting immediately, Rosenberg determined that the process would provide EPA with the expertise, experience, and practical insight of these parties in sorting through the complex issues. And, at least as important, it would develop a consensus on the rules.

Regulatory negotiation—known as "reg neg"—had been used several times by EPA to address difficult, controversial rules. The Congress recently endorsed the process by enacting the *Negotiated Rulemaking Act of 1990* as an amendment to the *Administrative Procedure Act*. Essentially, it provides a structured process by which representatives of the interests that would be substantially affected, including a senior representative of the regulatory agency, come together to negotiate an agreement on the terms of a rule. The negotiations are conducted under the *Federal Advisory Committee Act*, which requires that the meetings be announced in advance and be open to the public.

A consensus in this case means that each interest concurs in the recommended rule when considered as a whole; each interest, therefore, has a veto over the proposal. The agreement also provides that no one participating in the negotiations will do anything to inhibit its adoption or, to the extent the final rule is consistent with the recommended rule, challenge the rule in court. No rule that has been the subject of such a consensus has resulted in court action. The parties participate because they have a direct hand in crafting the rule.

The Convening

EPA contacted the authors, both of whom had experience conducting complex, technical regulatory negotiations, to undertake a feasibility study. This is done during the convening phase of a regulatory negotiation, during which a neutral third party—the convener—identifies potential interests, interviews representatives of those interests, determines what issues they believe will need to be considered and what information is necessary to resolve those issues, determines the willingness of the interests to participate, and ascertains the likelihood that an accommodation can be reached on the key provisions.

EPA initially chose to treat the oxygenated fuels rule and the reformulated gasoline rule separately, with the mediators each assigned the convening for one rule. Since some parties were interested in both rules, interviews and analyses were coordinated as much as possible. The process began with extensive interviews of EPA's Office of Mobile Sources. Using an initial list of potential interests supplied by EPA, the conveners contacted each of the parties to acquaint them with the regulatory negotiations process. The limited amount of time before the rule had to be published was a key concern of nearly all the parties. EPA estimated that the negotiations phase would have to be completed in approximately three months—by mid-June—to give agency staff sufficient time to draft a rule based on the recommendations of the group. The effort would necessitate almost a full-time commitment by many of the participants. The turnaround time for staff to produce notes of the deliberations and draft proposals would be very short.

There was an almost equal concern that the negotiations not reopen the issues that had been debated and resolved during the legislative process. It would be incumbent on the neutral facilitators and the participants themselves to keep the talks productive. Accordingly, the parties were asked to provide their assessment of the feasibility of concluding negotiations in the limited time, the desirability of combining the negotiations, and the willingness to participate in a negotiation of a subset of issues if time constraints or technical complexities made a negotiation of all the issues proposed infeasible.

Accommodating the Interests

It is important to include all the key interests in regulatory negotiation. While one can never hope to get representatives of all the affected interests around the same table, the convener seeks representatives of the major interests and enough others to ensure that the issues will be adequately raised and resolved. In the case of clean fuels, the difficulty lay not in determining what interests needed to be included but in keeping a manageable number of direct participants.

There are several approaches for accommodating additional participants while still keeping the number of negotiators to a minimum, including:

1) Designating alternates to attend as many deliberation sessions as possible and to be ready to substitute for the representative;

2) Setting up technical work groups or subcommittees to do the preparatory work and submit proposals for consideration by the larger advisory committee;

3) Selecting a participating organization's executive director, chief attorney, or another appropriate staff person to represent the group, with staff to serve with one or more member representatives and coordinate the team during the negotiations; and

4) Selecting spokespersons in situations when the parties remain adamant about retaining a greater number of representatives than is ideal for the functioning of the advisory committee, especially when there is great diversity within an interest group and the members reach a compromise.

The *Negotiated Rulemaking Act* suggests that there be a maximum number of 25 members on the Federal Advisory Committee established for each negotiation. In this case, the conveners initial recommendations were in that range, but the parties insisted that the number of "seats at the table" be expanded so that all the key sub-interests within each major organization were represented.

The diversity among members in several key interest groups became an important consideration in the final design of the clean fuels negotiations process. For example, the petroleum refiners had two trade associations, one representing a broad spectrum of the industry, including numerous small refiners, and the other representing major refiners. Differences in market share, geography, and organizational structure between the large and small refiners necessitated that both associations be seated at the table. Representation was complicated further by the diversity among the major refiners, ranging from significant differences in the composition of the crude oil they used to a wide variety of investment strategies that affected companies' position on the content of the regulation. Moreover, several of the major companies were further along in their product reformulations in response to changing, stringent regulations.

To accommodate these differences, it became necessary to allot nine seats for the refining industry on the negotiating committee. Additional representation was afforded through the use of alternates and working group members. Commitments by the facilitators to ensure that alternates were accorded an equal voice in decisionmaking were important in keeping the number to nine.

The oxygenate producers—makers of MBTE, ethanol, and methanol—presented a similar representation problem. Again, although there was considerable overlap in membership among the trade associations, the significance of the rule for individual companies mandated that their representation be expanded to five. One interest, for example, requested a seat even though it was represented by another, broader trade association. With nine major cities subject to the reformulated gasoline provisions (as well as opt-in possibilities) and 40 cities affected by the winter oxygenate requirements, it was important to keep the state and local government interest caucus to a manageable size without sacrificing the ability of the representatives to speak for all the cities and states. The time commitment convinced several cities and states to allow others to participate in the negotiations on their behalf. The willingness of the executive director of the Association of State and Local Air Pollution Control Officials to coordinate the caucus effort and to obtain member input meant that this caucus could accept five seats on the advisory committee. Total representation was expanded in the work groups.

Final Process Design

EPA published a notice in the *Federal Register* announcing its intention to use negotiated rulemaking, outlining the issues involved, and describing the interests that would be represented during the negotiations. The notice made clear that any party that believed it would be significantly affected but was not otherwise represented could request to participate on the committee. A public meeting was held on February 21–22 in Washington. Because of the extensive convening phase, there were no surprises with respect to new interests demanding representation. Two hundred people attended the meeting, at which the conveners presented the results of their interviews, including recommendations for process design and membership on the advisory committee and technical work groups.

"Umbrella" Committee and Work Groups. The conveners proposed that EPA establish an overall policy or "umbrella" committee that would be responsible for developing a consensus on a total package. The conveners recommended allocating the seats on the committee among the various interests that needed to be represented, with the designation of individual representatives left up to the interests (members would be appointed formally by the EPA administrator to form a Federal Advisory Committee). The conveners initially recommended 23 members for the committee, but this was expanded to 31 members. Advisory committee members would designate alternates and work group members. The work groups would develop consensus recommendations for review and consideration by the umbrella committee. The concept of an "umbrella" therefore connoted an oversight role.

Work Group Topics. The participants at the public meeting chose to establish four work groups—fuel certification (combining the issues of testing and modeling); anti-dumping; supply and distribution of oxygenates; and averaging, credits, and enforcement. The participants agreed to schedule meetings to ensure that participants could observe the sessions that were most important to them. After considerable debate, membership on the work groups, with minor exceptions, was kept at approximately 15 individuals. The facilitators agreed to keep observers from usurping the role of official work group members.

The Negotiations Phase

After an initial meeting of the advisory committee in mid-March, the work groups began their discussions in earnest. Each session was scheduled for a full day. Often, meetings would extend into the evening. Progress varied considerably among the different groups, especially in instances when they were waiting for data from EPA researchers and Auto/Oil, the major research consortium jointly sponsored by the petroleum and auto industries. The work groups also enabled the technical experts from the respective interest groups to solve problems collaboratively. Although the members had numerous ideological differences, they were able to develop several key provisions.

In light of the ongoing development of several EPA models and requirements, the negotiators developed provisions for accommodating these changes once they were final, including scheduling future meetings of the key participants to review the EPA products. These types of compromise approaches are unique to negotiated rulemaking.

The debate over the role of modeling versus testing of proposed gasoline formulas was a critical aspect of the negotiations. A strong case could be made that laboratory testing of each gasoline formula to ensure that it met the standard would be both time consuming and costly for the refiners—to the point of making the 1995 deadline difficult to achieve. On the other hand, modeling was not wholeheartedly accepted by all interests because of the gap in existing data on which to base the model. The final agreement incorporated a simpler model than had originally been contemplated. However, the parties established a process for incorporating new data and corresponding time frames that would result in Phase II reformulated gasoline being in the marketplace earlier than was required by the law.

The anti-dumping deliberations clearly demonstrated the advantages of negotiations over the traditional rulemaking process for accommodating the diverse needs of affected interests. The negotiators crafted a hierarchy of approaches for establishing baseline gasoline—against which the anti-dumping provisions in the law would be measured—that began with the use of actual 1990 gasoline data, allowed for variations in the recordkeeping systems of a large number of refiners, and addressed the unique problems of companies that were retrofitting their plants to meet other new gasoline requirements and therefore might not be producing gasoline in 1990. A realistic and enforceable regulatory approach emerged.

Finally, the negotiators crafted an important compromise that enabled the oil companies to agree to reductions that were greater than those contemplated when the process began. To take account of the enormously complex distribution system for gasoline and to enable refineries to smooth out production runs, the committee developed a system by which the standards could be met on an annual average, as opposed to a gallon-by-gallon basis. To meet the concern that one locality could end up with all the dirty fuel, a means was developed by which samples would be taken from around the country, and specific action would be taken if this problem occurred. That provided a creative means of meeting a standard that itself had many creative aspects.

The committee negotiated late into the night of its final meeting, putting together an outline of an entire standard. The various interests could then see the standard as a whole and decide whether they were better off with negotiation or with traditional rulemaking. They also could see how to make the standard work for them—what changes would have to be made and how to package proposed changes so that others would agree to them.

Following that marathon session, the negotiators went back to their constituents for their reactions. Each decided to continue. The bare bones of the outline were fleshed out in a series of smaller meetings that addressed individual issues. The effort culminated in an agreement that was signed by representatives of all the parties on August 16, 1991. Each party "concur[red] in principle to the outline of the proposed rules . . . when considered as a whole," and "not to challenge the . . . rules in court to the extent that the final rules and their preambles have the same substance and effect as the . . . outline concurred in by the Advisory Committee." With the major issues settled by the agreement, the parties could work together to develop specific regulatory language to implement their handiwork.

This rule clearly demonstrated the power of the process: without the direct negotiations among the affected interests, there is very little chance that the rules would have been developed anywhere close to the schedule necessary to meet the ambitious goals of the *Clean Air Act Amendments of 1990*. Although each interest could point to sections they would have preferred to craft differently, the benefits of the final rule in addressing their most important needs clearly outweighed what would otherwise be considered negative features of the resulting regulations.

NOTES AND QUESTIONS

1. For further background on negotiated rulemaking (which is often called "reg-neg"), *see* Chapter VI, *infra*; *Reg.Neg.*, NIDR News, Aug. 1995, at 6; Stephen B. Goldberg, *Reflections on Negotiated Rulemaking: From Conflict to Consensus*, Wash. Law., Sept.–Oct. 1994, at 42.

2. For a critique of negotiated rulemaking, see Cary Coglianese, *Assessing Consensus: The Promise and Performance of Negotiated Rulemaking*, 46 Duke L. J. 1255 (1997), arguing that the process does not save time or reduce litigation. Professor Harter criticized Coglianese's methods and conclusions in Philip J. Harter, *Assessing the Assessors: The Actual Performance of Negotiated Rulemaking*, 9 N.Y.U. Envtl. L.J. 32 (2000). Other positive assessments of the process appear in Laura I. Langbein & Cornelius M. Kerwin, *Regulatory Negotiation versus Conventional Rule Making: Claims, Counterclaims, and Empirical Evidence*, 10 J. Pub. Admin. Res. & Theory 599 (2000); Jody Freeman & Laura I. Langbein, *Regulatory Negotiation and the Legitimacy Benefit*, 9 N.Y.U. Envtl. L.J. 60 (2000).

3. Various forms of mediation and facilitation are used to resolve large public policy disputes, including environmental issues involving many stakeholders. Lawyers also are involved in many of these procedures. *See e.g.*, Barbara Gray & Julia Wondolleck, *Environmental Disputes: Negotiating Over Risks, Values and the Future*, in HANDBOOK OF RESEARCH ON NEGOTIATION (Mara Olekalns & Wendi Adair, eds., forthcoming 2013), Sean F. Nolon, *Negotiating the Wind: A Framework to Engage Citizens in Siting Wind Turbines*, 12 Cardozo J. Conflict Resol. 327 (2011); Susan L. Podziba, CIVIC FUSHION: MEDIATING POLARIZED PUBLIC DISPUTES (2012); Lawrence E. Susskind, *Consensus Building and ADR: Why They Are Not the Same Thing*, in THE HANDBOOK OF DISPUTE RESOLUTION (Michael L. Moffitt & Robert C. Bordone, eds., 2005), THE PROMISE AND PERFORMANCE OF ENVIRONMENTAL CONFLICT RESOLUTION (ROSEMARY O'LEARY & LISA B. BINGHAM, EDS., 2003); THE CONSENSUS BUILDING HANDBOOK: A COMPREHENSIVE GUIDE TO REACHING AGREEMENT (LAWRENCE SUSSKIND ET AL., EDS., 1999); Nancy A. Welsh & Barbara Gray, *Searching for a Sense of Control: The Challenge Presented by Community Conflicts Over Concentrated Animal Feeding Operations*, 10 Penn St. Envtl. L. Rev. 295 (2002).

4. If you were selecting a mediator for a regulatory negotiation, what background and orientation would you seek?

5. VICTIM OFFENDER MEDIATION

TEXAS CASE STUDY ONE: MURDER–VICTIM AND OFFENDER PERSPECTIVES, IN MARK S. UMBREIT, ET AL., FACING VIOLENCE: THE PATH OF RESTORATIVE JUSTICE AND DIALOGUE

45–52 (2003)

The Experience of the Event

Billie Lee Blair, divorced mother of an only child, was awakened by a phone call at 1:00 a.m. The male voice on the other end of the line opened with "Do you know a Bryan Blair?" When she responded with "yes, he's my son," the voice went on: "Somebody shot him a couple of hours ago. You'll need to come to San Antonio to pick up the body." Billie Lee lived alone in a small town some 200 miles from her son's college town. She called her best friend, who drove 50 miles and arrived by 4:00 a.m. Together they made the drive to San Antonio, and began making funeral arrangements.

Billie Lee stood up for herself at the funeral home and insisted on an uninterrupted time alone with her son's body. "It's very important, I feel, that a crime victim get that private time. I personally needed that time with Bryan, that was our time to say goodbye." Her loss was devastating, and there were times she felt suicidal. She had always taken care of Bryan and done what she was supposed to as a mother; now there was nothing more she could do for him. But there were important things she could do for herself. So many things went wrong at the trial of her son's murderer that Billie Lee became an advocate and got involved in victim organizations. She was concerned when she heard that a mediation program for victims of violent crime was being considered. "What if you go talk to that murderer and they tell you, 'Yes, I held that gun on your son, and yes, he was afraid?' And that crime victim that's so alone can't deal with it and they go commit suicide? What if the offender goes back and hangs himself in his cell?"

And, she focused on keeping the offender, James, in prison. Every six months she was at the parole board to make sure he wouldn't be released. James was often moved from one institution to another because of his unruly behavior. Billie Lee wanted to know why they couldn't put him in a more violent prison, where somebody might kill him. She even said they could fix prison overcrowding by just giving them all a loaded gun, locking the door and letting them see who survived.

The offender, James Lewis, who was 17 at the time, tells his experience of that night's events: "I was selling drugs and had two warrants out against me . . . I knew right then they were lookin' for me." So he decided, "I'm gonna try and leave now, I'm not gonna stay and let the law catch me." His plan: to steal a car and flee Texas. He cruised a video arcade; upon seeing Bryan engrossed in a game, he approached him with "say, man, can I get a ride from you?" and told him his mother was sick. Bryan said yes but wanted to finish his game. While Bryan wasn't looking, James pulled his gun out, put three shells in it, and put it back under his shirt. They left together.

As James's directions began getting more and more complicated, Bryan finally protested and pulled the car to a stop, asking James to get out. "I tried to convince him to cut the engine, but he wouldn't. So I guess I was gonna try to wrestle him out of the car, but he reached up like he was gonna get a knife or a pistol or something, and I just blacked out and I turned around and pulled the trigger twice." The car, still running and in gear, crashed into a brick wall. When James regained consciousness he fled the scene, quickly wrapping the pistol in his jacket and stuffing both down a nearby sewer.

James ran home to his mother's house. "She knew I had a burglary warrant but I wasn't man enough to tell her that I just shot somebody." Within three days, police came to the home while he was still sleeping. "I woke up and rolled over and there was two detectives . . . they asked me my name, gave me my rights and told me to get my clothes on." They didn't tell his mother what they were taking him to jail for. At the jail, officers presented him with his pistol and his jacket, both with his fingerprints on them.

James had no idea what he was in for. He heard his victim's mother was trying to get him sentenced to death, but stated he knew she couldn't do it, "because I didn't take nothing from him." He thought he might get 10 years or 15 at the most. He was shocked when his lawyer told him the best he could get was a plea bargain for 40 years, but he took it. And he added, "I don't blame her. Somebody kills my child, I wouldn't feel too much different. In my situation, justice was served."

Introduction to Mediation and Reasons for Participating

For a long time Billie Lee was adamantly against meeting with James. She watched videos of other mediations but felt if she were to meet with James, "nothing's gonna change and I'm not gonna know any more when I leave than when I started." But as her own healing progressed, her anger abated and she began to have reasons to meet with him. She wanted him to know how she felt about her son, and she wanted to make a change in his life. As she put it, "I wanted to make such an impression on him that his life would never, ever be the same. Mine's not, Bryan's isn't, and I told him, 'When you asked Bryan for a ride, our three lives were cemented together for eternity.' "

James was approached by a mediator from the Texas Victim Offender Mediation/Dialogue Program and invited to participate in dialogue with his victim's mother. The mediator was able to bring him a videotape of Billie Lee talking about her experience: "She just explained how she felt, she is real emotional—it's not real easy." It took him a long time to decide he would be willing to meet with her, but he began the preparation process with the mediator and felt this was what changed his mind.

He didn't really think there would be any benefits for himself. He felt the only thing he could give his victim's mother was "answers to why her son was murdered," and to let her know that when he got out he wasn't going to stalk her. He wasn't even sure that telling her he was sorry would make any difference: " 'That's gonna change what happened to her child? That ain't gonna change nothin'.'"

Preparation

The preparation phase in this case lasted for over two years, largely because James was continually in trouble in the prison, was frequently in lock-down, and often had to be moved from one prison to another.

As part of her preparation, Billie Lee studied James's life in detail. She learned where he grew up, read books on the slums he had come out of, and garnered tidbits of information from every source she could find. She came to understand that he had grown up in anger and violence and had never known the kinds of things she had so carefully taught her own son. She learned that as a very young boy he had seen his older brother kill a man. And she felt that his excessive infraction record in the institution was a result of having no life skills, no way of handling any feelings. Out of all this material she carefully drafted an opening statement that she hoped would cause James to *feel* the pain he had created.

Billie Lee found the process of her preparation to be very helpful and deeply appreciated the support of her mediator throughout. She rated her evaluation of the preparation as "somewhat satisfied" because she wished she had been given more detail about the physical setting. She was shocked to discover how tiny the table was separating herself from James in the conference room—it placed her much too close to him for comfort, and she had nowhere to set all the things she had brought with her to share. She recommended that victims be given a chance to see the meeting set-up ahead of time, get a feel for it, and have the opportunity to make changes if possible.

James and the mediator met sporadically over the two-year stretch of the preparation phase. Interruptions were frequent due to his being in lock-down, but at other times they met as often as twice a month. Over time James came to trust the mediator and the process. "He told me, 'I've been doing this quite a while, and so far we never had no one attack their offender.' "

For James, the preparation process was "a healing process, it's like a therapy." He felt preparation was as good as it could have been, though he still was unprepared for how emotional both he and Billie Lee became. The most helpful thing the mediator did was bringing videos of other mediations. "I seen from my own eyes that he's not new at this, he's pretty professional."

The Mediation/Dialogue Session

The session lasted for eight hours, with small breaks and a break for lunch. Present were only Billie Lee, James, the mediator, and the camera crew.

According to Billie Lee, James had brought no opening statement. She began with hers, and shared Bryan's baby book and a large photograph of him. "I asked him if he remembered what Bryan looked like and he said, 'No.' How can you kill somebody that you don't even know?" Fairly quickly she knew she had him where she wanted him. He hung his head and began to cry—and, to her own surprise, she reached for a tissue and wiped his eyes. "I felt compassion for him—my child had those skills, my child was nurtured, this young man had no life skills at all. He was lost." Later in the interview Billie Lee described an even more surprising moment: she herself was crying, and James reached over with a tissue and wiped her tears.

Billie Lee reported that at one point in the mediation James said, "But I don't have anything to give you," and she responded, "Yes you do. You can change. You can be different. I know what your I.Q. is, You're capable of learning." And she gave him a book she had found written by someone else who had grown up in the same ghetto and succeeded. She described his response: "He just cradled the book in his arms, and he said, 'I ain't never had no book come to me before. You can get 'em, but I ain't never had no book."

Billie Lee received a lot of information from James and found it very helpful. He told her how the events of the crime unfolded and he shared Bryan's last words. And she came to understand that he didn't set out to commit murder. "He really didn't want to kill him. He got scared, he panicked. And you can't say it was an accident, because he did have a loaded gun. But I think he thought he'd just shoot Bryan in the arm."

James was surprised that Billie Lee looked almost exactly as he had remembered her from the courtroom many years earlier. He said Billie Lee explained to him all the things she'd been through: her own experience with a violent husband and then raising Bryan without a father, Bryan's life and hopes and dreams, his photograph, and all his baby pictures. When James was asked how this affected him, he responded "There's no way I can sit here and try to describe the feeling, it was so emotional, I looked into her eyes and I couldn't say nothing, for about ten minutes."

James reported that when he told Billie Lee that his own mother had advised him against doing the mediation, she was concerned that he had gone against what his mother said. He responded, "My mother got five kids, all her boys in prison. You only had one son, he's gone forever. She'll probably never know how you feel. That's why I disregarded what she said."

James described how Billie Lee confronted him about his prison behavior. "She said, 'You got a hundred cases, why do you have all these cases?' I explained how when I came to prison I just didn't care. But now I care." And, he told her about his own childhood, about moving from a small town to an urban ghetto as a 10–year–old and getting hooked on drugs. He was stunned when she pulled out a book by someone from his own neighborhood: "She found out how it is livin' in the ghetto and livin' on the streets, 80% of the black families they don't have no father—she gave me this big twenty-one dollar book." She told him she wanted to help him, that she wanted him to get back in the class and get his G.E.D. And when she left, "She smiled, she laughed, and she said, 'James, I could go off filled with hatred—I just don't hate you no more.'"

Outcome and Evaluation

Billie Lee accomplished what she set out to do. James felt the pain she wanted him to feel—perhaps, she thinks, for the first time in his life. She was able to bring him what she had given her own son, and what she felt no one in his life had been able to do for him. And she got a commitment out of him to change. At the time of the interview, she reported James's prison infractions had completely ceased. She worried that he wasn't going as deep as he needed to but was very glad for his behavior change.

When asked to evaluate the impact of the mediation on her outlook on life, Billie Lee rated her outlook as only "somewhat" changed, because of the changes she had already undergone. In particular she felt her spiritual journey had both helped her heal and helped prepare her for her meeting with James. "I just inhale books . . . I began learning tolerance, not so much for Bryan's murder, as for other people. We are all the children of the world, and my spiritual belief is that the power that created us all has put us here to learn lessons."

Billie Lee was extremely pleased with her mediator's role during the session. She knew there were times when he might have wanted to jump in and was impressed that he held back and let her and James handle the process in their own way. She did report that she found it difficult to bring the session to an end, and rated her satisfaction level as "somewhat satisfied." This led her to recommend that preparation could also include thinking about a closing statement: "What would be the last words the victim would want to leave in the offender's ears?" She also found it somewhat unfair that for the preparation phase, mediators can travel to where the offenders are located to meet with them, but victims have to travel to where the mediators are. "It's not balanced."

James could hardly find words for how impactful the meeting has been in his life. "And wow, you know, wow, if I ever get my class back, I'll be helpin' a bunch of kids, so they don't follow in my footprints . . . she's always wanting me to help change other people's lives." Later he added, "I made a commitment. I'm not gonna mess up, I'm gonna do what she told me."

James was deeply impressed with Billie Lee: "She's the strongest woman I ever met." He has seen a video of Billie Lee's debriefing and was very moved: "She was concerned about me, she asked the mediator, 'do you think he'll be all right?' just like I was her child." In fact, he felt she was more concerned about him than his own mother, who had made no contact for two years. "She calls up here every week."

Advice to Others

Billie Lee's words: "I'd encourage anybody to do it if it's appropriate, but not with somebody that's still going to be angry." She felt anyone who decides to meet their offender should get as fully informed about the person and the crime as possible, much in the way she did. She also encouraged participants to ask for a picture of the offender so they won't be surprised at the beginning of the session.

James thought perhaps it might depend on the crime, but in general felt offenders should participate in mediation if their victim wants to, because they never know what they can accomplish—"If you don't try to change your life in here, you're just wasting your time, and when you get out you're gonna come right back. So if you got somebody out there trying to help you, you'd be a fool not to take up on it."

NOTES AND QUESTIONS

1.   More than 300 victim offender mediation (VOM) programs operate in the U.S. and at least 1100 operate abroad. Most focus on juvenile rather than adult crime and tend to address less serious offenses. MARK S. UMBREIT, BETTY VOS, ROBERT B. COATES & KATHERINE A. BROWN, FACING VIOLENCE: THE PATH OF RESTORATIVE JUSTICE AND DIALOGUE 11 (2003). Umbreit and his co-authors describe the usual procedures:

> The process undertaken by most VOM programs is very similar. Trained mediators or facilitators, who may be paid staff members but are more often community volunteers, make contact with the offenders and victims who have been referred and invite their participation, which is always voluntary for the victim and most often voluntary for the

offender. If both parties express interest in meeting, facilitators typically provide at least one "preparation" meeting for both the victim and the offender, in which they explore the participant's experience of the event, the nature of the harm caused, and potential avenues for repairing the harm. Victim and offender are then brought together in a meeting that usually opens with sharing the experience of the crime, and then turns to a discussion of restitution or other resolution. Often family members, support persons, and/or other community members may also be present. Facilitators remain "neutral" in the sense that they support both the victim and the offender in sharing their experience and working toward a resolution. Some programs remain in contact with participants afterwards to monitor compliance with any negotiated agreement; in other programs the referring jurisdiction retains this responsibility.

There is a growing body of empirical research on VOM worldwide * * * [B]oth victims and offenders who have participated in VOM have consistently reported high levels of satisfaction with the process and with the outcome of their meetings. Some studies have found that victims reported reduced levels of fear as a result of their meetings with offenders. In some instances, offender participants have higher rates of restitution compliance than similar offenders whose restitution requirements were not mutually negotiated with victims. And there are encouraging reports of reduced offender recidivism among many VOM programs. It is becoming increasingly clear that the VOM process humanizes the criminal justice experience for both victim and offender, holds offenders directly accountable to the people they victimized, allows for more active involvement of crime victims and community members (as participants or as volunteer mediators) in the justice process,, and can potentially suppress further criminal behaviors in offenders.

Id. at 11–12.

As this excerpt suggests, the parties are not mediating the question of the defendant's guilt or innocence in a victim offender mediation. Many VOM programs require an admission or adjudication of guilt. What is being mediated is restitution, the relationship between the victim and the defendant, or other terms that may be appropriate to the particular case.

2.   Victim offender mediation has faced criticism, too. Dean Jennifer Brown has criticized victim-offender mediation because it inappropriately allows the victim to have some control over the offender's fate. She recommends a complete separation between victim offender mediation and the criminal justice system. Jennifer Gerarda Brown, *The Use of Mediation to Resolve Criminal Cases: A Procedural Critique*, 43 Emory L.J. 1247 (1994). Professor Annalise Acorn has provided an extensive critique of "restorative justice," of which victim offender mediation is a part. She criticizes "much of [the] rhetoric [of restorative justice] and the aspirations it inspires as culpably sentimental and dangerously naïve." ANNALISE ACORN, COMPULSORY COMPASSION: A CRITIQUE OF RESTORATIVE JUSTICE 19 (2004). For a thorough

analysis of restorative justice, see JOHN BRAITHWAITE, RESTORATIVE JUSTICE AND RESPONSIBLE REGULATION (2002); *see also* Susan Szmania & Daniel Mangis, *Finding the Right Time and Place: A Case Study Comparison of the Expression of Offender Remorse in Traditional Justice and Restorative Justice Contexts*, 89 Marq. L. Rev. 335 (2005); Michael O'Hear, *Is Restorative Justice Compatible with Sentencing Uniformity,* 89 Marq. L. Rev. 305 (2005).; Mark Umbreit, Betty Vos, Robert Coates, & Elizabeth Lightfoot, *Restorative Justice in the Twenty-First Century: A Social Movement Full of Opportunities and Pitfalls,* 89 Marq. L. Rev. (2005).

3.   Which dimensions of conflict—behavioral, cognitive, emotional—are typically (or best) addressed through a criminal prosecution? Through a victim offender mediation?

4.   Another way to think about these issues is in terms of what the problem-definition is or should be, in a given mediation. In a victim-offender mediation, such as the one described by Umbreit and his colleagues, to what extent do or should the various participants—the victim, the offender, the mediator—influence the development of the problem-definition? *See* Leonard L. Riskin, *Decisionmaking in Mediation: The New Old Grid and the New New Grid System*, 79 Notre Dame L. Rev. 1 (2003), an excerpt from which appears infra in Chapter IV, *infra.*

5.   For further information on victim-offender mediation, *see generally* MARK S. UMBREIT, VICTIM OFFENDER MEDIATION: CONFLICT RESOLUTION AND RESTITUTION (2012) and the Victim Offender Mediation Association web site, www.voma.org.

NOTE: MEDIATION IN OTHER CONTEXTS AND BY OTHER NAMES

1.   In the U.S., mediation takes place in a great variety of arenas, in addition to those mentioned in this section and in the introduction to this chapter. To give yourself a fuller picture, see JAMES J. ALFINI, SHARON B. PRESS, JEAN R. STERNLIGHT, & JOSEPH B. STULBERG, MEDIATION THEORY AND PRACTICE 513–89 (3rd ed. 2013); DONNA CRAWFORD & RICHARD BODINE, CONFLICT RESOLUTION EDUCATION: A GUIDE TO IMPLEMENTING PROGRAMS IN SCHOOLS, YOUTH SERVING ORGANIZATIONS, AND COMMUNITY AND JUVENILE JUSTICE SETTINGS (1996); DIVORCE AND FAMILY MEDIATION: MODELS, TECHNIQUES, AND APPLICATIONS, (Jay Folberg, Ann L. Milne, & Peter Salem eds., 2004); THE BLACKWELL HANDBOOK OF MEDIATION: BRIDGING THEORY, RESEARCH, AND PRACTICE (Margaret S. Herrman ed., 2006); WHEN TALK WORKS: PROFILES OF MEDIATORS (Deborah M. Kolb ed., 1993); ROGER RICHMAN, ORION F. WHITE, JR., & MICHAUX H. WILKINSON, INTERGOVERNMENTAL MEDIATION: NEGOTIATIONS IN LOCAL GOVERNMENT DISPUTES (1986); JEFFREY M. SENGER, FEDERAL DISPUTE RESOLUTION: USING ADR WITH THE UNITED STATES GOVERNMENT (2004); COMMUNITY MEDIATION: A HANDBOOK FOR PRACTITIONERS AND RESEARCHERS (Karen Grover Duffy, James W. Grosch, & Paul V. Olczak eds., 1991); Wallace Warfield, *Building*

Consensus for Racial Harmony in American Cities: A Case Model Approach, 1996 J. Disp. Resol. 151.

2.   It is common for federal district courts to appoint mediators, sometimes calling them special masters, in complex institutional reform cases, such as those involving segregation in public schools and overcrowding of prisons. *See* Vincent M. Nathan, *The Use of Special Masters in Institutional Reform Litigation*, 10 U. Tol. L. Rev. 419 (1979). For an exploration of the differences between mediators and special masters, see James R. Coben, *Creating a 21st Century Oligarchy: Judicial Abdication to Class Action Mediators*, 5 Y.B. On Arb. & Mediation 162 (2013).

3.   It is increasingly common for mediators to facilitate negotiations among participants on just one side of a dispute. Indeed, "conflict coaching" is on the rise. Sometimes—generally when many individuals will be involved in a mediation—mediators also will provide negotiation training before a mediation begins.

4.   Culture affects mediation, just as it affects negotiation, as we saw in Chapter III. One reason for the variety of mediation practices in the U.S. is that mediations take place among different cultures or subcultures. The culture of personal injury lawyers and their clients is likely to shape a mediation process differently than would the culture of divorce lawyers and clients or the culture of business lawyers and their clients.

It should not be surprising, therefore, that in cultures radically different from ours, "mediation" would have a radically different character. For some examples, see JOHN PAUL LEDERACH, PREPARING FOR PEACE: CONFLICT TRANSFORMATION ACROSS CULTURES (1995); Bruce E. Barnes, *Conflict Resolution Across Cultures: A Hawaii Perspective and a Pacific Mediation Model*, 12 Med. Q. 117 (1995); Ronda Roberts Callister & James A. Wall Jr., *Thai and U.S. Community Mediation*, J. Conflict Resol., Vol. 48, No. 4, Aug. 2004, at 573; Fu Hualing, *Understanding People's Mediation in Post–Mao China*, 6 J. Chinese L. 211 (1992); Michelle LeBaron, *Conflict Resolution in Native Cultures: An Overview*, NIDR Forum, Spr. 1995, at 1; James A. Wall, Jr., *Community Mediation in China and Korea: Some Similarities and Differences*, 9 Negot. J. 141 (1993); Robert Yazzie, *Traditional Navajo Dispute Resolution in the Navajo Peacemaker Court*, NIDR Forum, Spr. 1994, at 5.

5.   The terms "conciliation" and "facilitation" sometimes are used to describe processes that we would call mediation. However, sometimes the terms have different meanings. For example, in some programs, conciliation refers to the process of helping parties agree to mediation. In the international context, conciliation often assumes that the neutral will propose a resolution to the parties. Facilitation, meanwhile, can refer to processes that are less focused (or not focused at all) on resolving a particular dispute. For background on facilitation, and different notions of that process, see SAM KANER, LENNY LIND, CATHERINE TOLDI, SARAH FISK & DUANE BERGER, FACILITATOR'S GUIDE TO PARTICIPATORY DECISION–MAKING (1996);

ROGER M. SCHWARZ, THE SKILLED FACILITATOR: PRACTICAL WISDOM FOR DEVELOPING EFFECTIVE GROUPS (1994); ROGER M. SCHWARZ, ANNE DAVIDSON, PEG CARLSON, & SUE MCKINNEY, THE SKILLED FACILITATOR FIELDBOOK: TIPS, TOOLS, AND TESTED METHODS FOR CONSULTANTS, FACILITATORS, MANAGERS, TRAINERS, AND COACHES (2005).

6.   Mediation is not used as widely in the EU as it is in the United States, but there are many signs that this could change. The London-based Centre for Effective Dispute Resolution (CEDR) has reported that its mediation caseload is growing substantially, due to increased client interest and changes in court rules. In the Netherlands, the Ministry of Justice has institutionalized mediation throughout the country's courts. *See* Bert Niemeijer & Machteld Pel, *Court–Based Mediation in the Netherlands: Research, Evaluation and Future Expectations*, 110 Penn. St. L. Rev. 345 (2005). Other countries, too, have instituted mediation programs. On May 21, 2008, the European Parliament and the Council of the European Union adopted a directive that spurred further development. Designed to promote amicable settlements and the use of mediation in cross-border disputes and civil and commercial matters, the directive requires every Member State except Denmark to encourage: mediator training; the development of quality control mechanisms, including voluntary codes of conduct for mediators and mediation service providers; and the availability of mediation resource information to the general public. Interestingly, Member States must make the enforceability of mediated agreements similar to that of court judgments.

The directive also permits Member States to make the use of mediation mandatory. The response has varied among the states. Italy made mediation a condition precedent to filing a lawsuit, but Italy's Constitutional Court invalidated the compulsory mediation program in October, 2012. Corte Cost., 24 ottobre 2012, n.272, Giur it. 2012 (It.). English courts may refuse to shift costs if they conclude that a party unreasonably refused to participate in mediation. See Jacqueline Nolan–Haley, Mediation Exceptionality, 78 Fordham L. Rev. 1237, 1258 (2009) (describing evolving British jurisprudence on compulsory mediation and imposition of costs); Jacqueline Nolan–Haley, Is Europe Headed Down the Primrose Path with Mandatory Mediation?, 37 N.C. J. Int'l L. & Com. Reg. 981, 998–1006 (2012) (describing the experiences of other nations in mandating mediation); Nancy A. Welsh & Andrea Kupfer Schneider, *The Thoughtful Integration of Mediation into Bilateral Investment Arbitration*, 18 Harv. Negot. L. Rev. 71, 124–26 (2013) (describing the different degrees of intrusion used by various compulsory mediation schemes). Compulsory mediation has been held not to violate Article 6 of the European Convention on Human Rights. *Rosalba Alassini v. Telecom Italia SpA*, 2005 O.J. (C 134) 3.

The directive also provides an evidentiary privilege for mediators' testimony, with very limited exceptions: "Given that mediation is intended to take place in a manner which respects confidentiality, Member States shall ensure that, unless the parties agree otherwise, neither mediators nor those involved in the administration of the mediation process shall be compelled to give evidence in civil and commercial judicial proceedings or arbitration regarding information arising out of or in connection with a mediation process, except: (a) where this is necessary for overriding considerations of public policy of the Member State concerned, in particular when required to ensure the protection of the best interests of children or to prevent harm to the physical or psychological integrity of a person; or (b) where disclosure of the content of the agreement resulting from mediation is necessary in order to implement or enforce that agreement." Member States may enact even stricter measures to protect mediation confidentiality.

The development of mediation throughout the EU and the impact of the directive will be the subjects of a report to be delivered to the European Parliament and Council in 2016. *See Directive 2008/52/EC of the European Parliament and of the Council of 21 May 2008 on certain aspects of mediation in civil and commercial matters.*

For more on mediation in other parts of the world, see NADJA ALEXANDER, GLOBAL TRENDS IN MEDIATION (2006) (including descriptions of mediation in Australia, Austria, Canada, England, The Netherlands, and South Africa).

7.   An increasingly important application of mediation is in the fostering of democracy. *See Special Issue: Developing Mediation Processes in the New Democracies*, 10 Mediation Q. 225 (1993); *Symposium: The Lawyer's Role(s) in Deliberative Democracy: A Commentary by and Responses to Carrie Menkel–Meadow*, 5 Nev. L.J. 347 (2005); Nancy D. Erbe, *Appreciating Mediation's Global Role in Promoting Good Governance*, 11 Harv. Negot. L. Rev. 355 (2006); Jeffrey H. Goldfien, *Thou Shalt Love Thy Neighbor: RLUIPA and the Mediation of Religious Land Use Disputes*, 2006 J. Disp. Resol. 435, 443 (2006); Richard C. Reuben, *Democracy and Dispute Resolution: Systems Design and the New Workplace*, 10 Harv. Negot. L. Rev. 11 (2005). Some commentators have urged reforms in court-connected mediation in the U.S. to help ensure that it operates in a manner consistent with democratic ideals. *See* Nancy A. Welsh, *The Place of Court–Connected Mediation in a Democratic Justice System*, 5 Cardozo J. Conflict Res. 117 (2004).

And, of course, mediation has always been an essential feature of international relations. *See* MARIEKE KLEIBOER, THE MULTIPLE REALITIES OF INTERNATIONAL MEDIATION (1998).

Not surprisingly, mediation and other forms of dispute resolution also take place on-line. *See* Chapter VI, *infra*.

C. THE PARTICIPANTS AND PROCESSES

In Part C, we try to understand the mediation process more fully. We do this by focusing in Section 1 on the Mediator and in Section 2, on the parties and participants. In Section 3, we examine the issue of confidentiality in mediation, which has spawned much controversy, and some legislation in recent years.

1. THE MEDIATOR

A mediator's behavior in and about mediation is affected by many factors, including their personalities, professional training and experience, mediation training and education, their philosophies, beliefs and assumptions about mediation, and potential sources of professional regulation, such as the market for mediation, codes of conduct, and risks of malpractice liability. In this section, we survey a number of these elements.

a. Sources and Backgrounds

Mediators come in many varieties. In community mediation programs and some small-claims court mediation programs, volunteer mediators are drawn from nearly all walks of life and vary greatly in terms of education, socio-economic status, and occupation. In many court-connected mediation programs, however, the mediators must be lawyers or have other specialized education. Indeed, some court-connected mediation programs designate magistrate or senior judges to serve as mediators. Government and business organizations that sponsor mediation programs often have special requirements. For consideration of such requirements, *see* Chapter VI, *infra*.

Many private providers of dispute resolution services maintain rosters of mediators. Some of these are non-profit organizations, such as the American Arbitration Association, the CPR International Institute for Conflict Prevention and Resolution, and state and local bar associations. Others, such as JAMS, are organized for profit. Until it merged with Endispute in 1994, JAMS included only retired judges on its panels. Nearly all mediation programs and providers have substantial training requirements, ranging from sixteen to forty-eight hours, though many of these have "grandfather" exceptions that cover judges or others with substantial dispute resolution experience.

Numerous law firms now provide neutral services, and many small groups have organized solely to offer such services. In addition thousands of people across the U.S. have been trained in mediation. Many of these offer their services directly to the public; some are very busy, while others have little or no mediation work.

b. Training of Mediators

A mediator's training is likely to have a significant impact on her or his performance—though not as significant as many trainers would hope. There are many varieties of mediation training. Organizations offer specialized training to deal with disputes involving such fields as divorce, environmental protection, special education, victim-offender, and attorney-client fee disputes. The training programs vary to some extent with the specialty and with the philosophies of the trainers, including their mental models of mediation, such as those described *supra* in Chapter IV, Section A. These programs generally include certain core elements, however. For an example of a "classic" mediation training guide, see Leonard L. Riskin, Mediation Training Guide, *supra*, p. 328.

c.   Regulation of Mediator Performance

No state requires mediators to be licensed, though virtually all states require licenses for a range of professions and occupations, including taxidrivers, hairdressers, and accountants. So, as a practical matter, anyone can hold herself out as a mediator. In that sense, people become mediators by doing mediation.

But such independence carries costs, for in mediation, as in other areas of regulation, there exists a tension between freedom of contract for the parties and the mediator, on the one hand, and, on the other, society's interest in protecting the parties and other mediation participants. In addition, regulation raises questions about barriers to entry into the "profession" of mediation, while the lack of regulation raises questions about the integrity of the process, which in many contexts is supported by statutes, court rules, and other government policies. This section provides insight into the principal methods of regulating mediator performance by focusing on credentials, ethics standards (with a special focus on mediator impartiality and conflicts of interest, as well as ethical limitations on what mediators may say about the law), and malpractice liability.

1.   *Credentials*

SOCIETY OF PROFESSIONALS IN DISPUTE RESOLUTION, REPORT OF THE SPIDR COMMISSION ON QUALIFICATIONS
(1989)

RATIONALE

The most commonly discussed purposes of setting criteria for individuals to practice as neutrals are (1) to protect the consumer and (2) to protect the integrity of various dispute resolution processes. Many policy makers and professionals in the field are concerned about individuals with little information about or skill in dispute resolution simply "hanging out a shingle" and offering to mediate or arbitrate anyone's dispute. Further, concerns are being raised about poorly trained and inexperienced neutrals offering training to others. The risks are several—the interest of parties may be harmed by incompetent practice and the public's understanding of what it means to request specific dispute resolution services may become confused, leading to public dissatisfaction with the field and claims that mediation and arbitration are merely a form of second class justice.

Proposals to establish qualifications for neutrals also raise considerable controversy, however. Some of the reaction appears to be anxiety among members of a profession newly faced with regulation. Many substantive concerns also have been raised, particularly about mandatory standards of certification, including: (1) creating inappropriate barriers to entry into the field, thus, (2) hampering the innovative quality of the profession, and (3) limiting the broad dissemination of peacemaking skills in society. Even many of those who are persuaded that there is a need for some mandatory standards are concerned that it may not be possible yet to define and measure competence.

* * *

POLICY OPTIONS

There is no single way to promote quality in any professional practice. Among the options are:

     A.   free market

     B.   disclosure requirements

     C.   public/consumer education

     D.   "after the fact" controls, such as malpractice lawsuits

     E.   rosters

     F.   voluntary standards

     G.   codes of professional ethics

     H.   mandatory standards for neutrals

     I.   mandatory standards for programs

     J.   improvements in training for neutrals, including apprenticeship programs

* * *

IV. PRINCIPLES

There is no single answer to what constitutes a qualified neutral or which of the policy options described is appropriate to ensure that those who practice are qualified to do so. SPIDR recommends the following central principles:

     A.   that no single entity (rather, a variety of organizations) should establish qualifications for neutrals;

    B. that the greater the degree of choice the parties have over the dispute resolution process, program or neutral, the less mandatory should be the qualification requirements; and

    C. that qualification criteria should be based on performance, rather than paper credentials.

* * *

7. Knowledge acquired in obtaining various degrees can be useful in the practice of dispute resolution. At this time and for the foreseeable future, however, no such degree in itself ensures competence as a neutral. Furthermore, requiring a degree would foreclose alternative avenues of demonstrating dispute resolution competence. Consequently, no degree should be considered a prerequisite for service as a neutral.

C. Performance-based qualifications

* * *

8–10. SPIDR believes that performance criteria (such as neutrality, demonstrated knowledge of relevant practices and procedures, ability to listen and understand, and ability to write a considered opinion for arbitrators) are more useful and appropriate in setting qualifications to practice than is the manner in which one achieves those criteria (such as formal degrees, training, or experience). * * *

NOTES

    1. After issuing this report, SPIDR continued its interest in competence and qualifications. SOCIETY OF PROFESSIONALS IN DISPUTE RESOLUTION, ENSURING COMPETENCE AND QUALITY IN DISPUTE RESOLUTION PRACTICE (REPORT NO. 2 OF THE SPIDR COMMISSION ON QUALIFICATION 1995). Another report of a SPIDR subcommittee proposed competencies for mediators of public disputes. PUBLIC DISPUTES SECTOR, SOCIETY OF PROFESSIONALS IN DISPUTE RESOLUTION, COMPETENCIES FOR MEDIATORS OF COMPLEX, PUBLIC DISPUTES (1992).

    2. In 2012, the Council of the Dispute Resolution Section approved the following comments and recommendations from the Section's Task Force on Mediator Credentialing:

ALTERNATIVE DISPUTE RESOLUTION SECTION OF THE AMERICAN BAR ASSOCIATION TASK FORCE ON MEDIATOR CREDENTIALING (2012)
Final Report

* * *

Background. Mediator credentialing is an evolving and sometimes controversial field. Many private organizations and some public courts and agencies in the United States offer forms of credentialing or certification, for example by establishing requirements for membership on mediator panels. There is, however, no nationwide system of credentialing, and states and local organizations have reached different conclusions as to its desirability.

Internationally there appears to be a growing interest in credentialing. In recent years private organizations such as the International Mediation Institute of the Hague have created credentialing systems and some European governments have adopted systems to qualify and monitor court-connected and/or private mediators.

The question considered by the Task Force was whether the ADR Section should adopt a policy on this issue and if so what it should be. It should be noted that the issue is not whether the Section itself should provide credentialing services, but rather whether it should support such initiatives by others.

Task Force members reviewed literature and interviewed leaders of domestic and international organizations and experts from states and court systems with different approaches to credentialing. Due to the complexity of the issues raised by credentialing, the Task Force's recommendations are nuanced.

What does "credentialing" mean?

The Task Force agrees that at its core, mediation is a process that includes a mediator, not affiliated with any of the parties, who facilitates the parties' communication and negotiation in a procedurally just manner and helps the parties reach an entirely voluntary agreement. Beyond this general statement, however, there appears to be no common understanding of what a credential means in the context of mediation, either domestically or internationally, or what mediators should specifically be required to do or to demonstrate to obtain a credential.

Most if not all private organizations and court systems which maintain panels of mediators require that members complete a training program. Some provide a credential, or certificate, to anyone who completes training and meets other qualifications, without requiring them to demonstrate specific competencies. Other organizations require candidates to demonstrate specific skills through a testing process. Still others emphasize provision of information, requiring mediators to provide client assessments which are made available to potential users.

The most demanding credentialing programs reviewed by the Task Force require:

- Completion of a training program, typically 30 to 40 hours in duration, which includes significant roleplaying,

- Observation of one or more actual mediations,

- Experience as a co-mediator in one or more actual mediations, and

- An assessment process in which the candidate mediates a roleplayed dispute and is graded on skills by persons knowledgeable in mediation and the assessment process.

What does "competence" mean in the context of mediation?

For a credentialing organization to certify that a mediator possesses certain skills or knowledge requires that the organization define what a successful candidate must demonstrate, and be able to assess whether the candidate has done so. Most Task Force members believe that the mediation community has not reached a consensus concerning a single body of skills and knowledge that skilled mediators must possess, even within a specific subject area, making it difficult or impossible to carry out such an assessment.

Some members of the Task Force believe that while there is no consensus on a single body of mediative skills or knowledge, distinct schools or styles of mediation, for instance "commercial" and "transformative" mediation, have or could arrive at such a consensus for a particular school or style.

Is there a need for credentialing?

Does credentialing have substantive value, either for attorneys and parties who choose mediators, or for neutrals seeking to develop their competence or practice? Task Force members were divided on this issue, with no one expressing a strongly positive or negative view. Some members believe that credentialing can be helpful to users and/or mediators, while other members do not. This may reflect that, as noted, "credentialing" has no precise meaning.

Task force members agree that the need for credentialing is likely to be strongest in certain settings:

1. When a court or public or private entity requires disputants to use, or sponsors or refers disputants to, specific programs or mediators.

Some court systems and public agencies mandate that parties go to mediation through a specific program as a condition of obtaining a hearing. Others sponsor programs or refer disputants to individual mediators, for example by maintaining a panel of approved neutrals. In such situations disputants may reasonably believe that the court or agency has endorsed the competence of the program or providers. When this occurs, courts and agencies have a responsibility to ensure that the program and neutrals in question are competent. Certification is one method to accomplish this.

2. When disputants enter mediation who are not knowledgeable about the process or the qualifications of individual providers and do not have counsel capable of advising them.

Examples of areas in which this may be especially true include marital, small claims, housing, community and foreclosure cases and, more generally, disputes in which one or both parties do not have access to a lawyer. Such "one-time players" often do not have the knowledge or sources of information needed to choose a competent mediator.

3. When lawyers and other professionals who choose mediators do not have a good understanding of mediation or find it difficult to identify competent mediators in a particular field or geographic area.

This may be true, for instance, in regions of the world in which legal mediation is not widely used or well-known to lawyers and the public and potential users cannot evaluate the competence of mediator candidates. In such circumstances certification might be of assistance to users, as well as to mediators wishing to develop their practice.

Task Force members were divided on two points.

1. Some members believe that certification may also be helpful in disputes within the United States in which the parties are represented by lawyers, but counsel does not have sufficient knowledge or resources to identify competent mediators. Examples include smaller tort and contract cases and marital disputes. A majority of the Task Force did not express an opinion about this.

2. A majority of the Task Force believes that in large civil disputes, in which mediators are selected by experienced counsel or other professionals such as insurance adjusters, there is no significant need for credentialing. Such situations, the majority believes, involve repeat users who typically have access to substantial information about candidates and would not find credentialing helpful. A minority believes that even experienced lawyers and other professionals are often not familiar with individual candidates or with the different qualities needed to mediate effectively in different circumstances, and as a result also sees a useful role for credentialing in such disputes.

What should an effective credentialing program include?

The Task Force believes that to be effective, a credentialing program should satisfy the following guidelines. It should:

1. Clearly define the skills, knowledge and values which persons it credentials must possess. Without a clear definition of the skills, knowledge and values a credentialed mediator must possess, credentialing organizations cannot assess whether a candidate possesses them and disputants cannot know what weight to place on a credential. Such definitions should be tailored to a specific form of mediation (family, large commercial, small claims, transformative, etc.) for which the credential is issued.

2. Ensure that candidates have training adequate to instill those skills, knowledge and values. To acquire mediative skills, most if not all candidates require a training program. A task force of the Association for Conflict Resolution recently issued a report on this topic. Such training should include:

- Substantial instruction, including experience acting as mediator in roleplayed disputes of the kind for which the candidate seeks credentials.

- Observation of one or more actual mediations.

- Experience mediating one or more actual cases as co-mediator with a credentialed mediator.

3. Be administered by an organization distinct from the organization which trains the candidate. It is problematic for the same organization both to charge for training and to assess whether its training has been successful. Such dual roles produce a potential conflict of interest. For the same reason that law schools are not permitted to decide whether their graduates will be admitted to the bar, training programs should not be in the position of judging whether their services are effective.

4. Have an assessment process capable of determining with consistency whether or not candidates possess the defined skills, knowledge and values. The Task Force believes that for credentialing to be credible it must be based on a determination whether a candidate has acquired the skills, knowledge and values that comprise the credential. This requires a testing process based on specific criteria and a consistent method of evaluation.

5. Explain clearly to persons likely to rely on its credential what is being certified. Credentialing is justified in large measure by the difficulty that some users have in choosing a competent mediator. For this reason a credentialing program should explain in a clear and understandable manner, to the persons expected to rely on its credential, the skills, knowledge and values its mediators possess. Organizations should make clear in particular whether a credential signifies that a mediator has attained a given level of competence and experience, or simply confirms their attendance at a program, and should describe the form, school or style of mediation the organization is certifying.

6.   Provide an accessible, transparent system to register complaints against credentialed mediators. Promptly and fairly investigate complaints and, if appropriate, de-credential a mediator who fails to comply with standards. Not all credentialed mediators can be expected to display in practice or retain over a career the skills and values required by their credential. Credentialing organizations must have an accessible and transparent mechanism to receive complaints about their mediators. A majority of the Task Force believes organizations should have a process to monitor the performance of credentialed mediators, such as periodic requests for feedback. A minority believes such monitoring is not feasible.

A majority of the Task Force believes that when a complaint is received the organization should have a process to promptly investigate and fairly assess it and, if appropriate, de-credential mediators. A minority believes that at least when users of mediation are "repeat players" such as multi-national corporations, it is sufficient that the substance of any complaints is made available for consideration by potential users.

What should a credentialing system not do?

Credentialing can serve a useful purpose by helping users, especially those who lack experience with mediation, to identify neutrals with basic skills and competence in a particular style of mediation. However, it is also true that a key strength of mediation as a process and a field is its openness to new techniques and approaches, and its commitment to self-determination for disputants.

The Task Force is concerned that credentialing not operate to exclude new methods of resolving disputes or persons with non-traditional backgrounds, or more generally to constrain the evolution and growth of mediation as a method of dispute resolution. Nor should credentialing have the effect of preventing informed disputants from selecting a mediator of their choice. The Section should therefore not support credentialing systems that:

1.   *Operate as mandatory licensing.* Credentialing should provide information about prospective mediators and/or a signal of quality, and organizations should be able to require members of their panels to satisfy requirements. Credentialing should not, however, operate as a de facto licensing system that bars non-credentialed persons from practicing as mediators generally.

2. Bar non-lawyers from becoming credentialed. Effective mediators possess a variety of qualities, some of which are not taught in traditional legal education. Disputants benefit from the opportunity to select mediators with training and experience in fields other than law. Credentialing programs may place value on legal and other academic training, but should not bar non-lawyers from obtaining credentials on *de jure* or *de facto* basis.

3. Bar disputants from selecting a non-credentialed mediator. Self-determination is the first principle of the ABA's Model Standards of Conduct for Mediators and the essence of the process of mediation. It follows that if disputants knowingly decide to select a non-credentialed person to mediate their dispute, they should be able to do so. Thus if courts or other organizations require mediation and/or provide the names of approved mediators to disputants, they should also allow disputants to select non-credentialed mediators by informed, arms-length agreement.

Is there sufficient demand to support an effective credentialing system?

A strong credentialing system as outlined above requires substantial resources to operate. As one example, the National Conflict Resolution Center based in San Diego currently charges candidates $3,500 to $4,000 for participation in its certification program.

If the parties and attorneys who select mediators strongly desired strong credentialing programs, they could demand public funding to pay the cost. Alternatively, if mediators believed credentials were sufficiently valuable, either for personal growth or marketing purposes, they could fund such programs through user fees.

At present, however, neither users nor neutrals in the United States show sufficient demand for mediator credentials to fund a strong credentialing system. The Task Force does not express an opinion about whether sufficient support for such programs exists outside the United States.

Should the Section support mediator credentialing?

The Section should support local initiatives and innovations in the field of credentialing, provided they meet the guidelines set forth in this report. Given, however, the lack of a consensus at this time about the attributes of the mediation process or a process for determining competency, the Section should not support creation of a single nationwide credentialing system.

NOTES AND QUESTIONS

1. At one point, Florida required a law degree for its court-certified mediators. Now, its family and circuit court mediators must have at least a bachelor's degree and must meet a 100 point requirement that is calculated

based on a combination of their mediation training, education/mediation experience and the mentorship they have received. Mediators may earn mentorship points by observing mediations conducted by certified mediators and by conducting mediations under the supervision and observation of certified mediators. *See* FLA. R. CERTIFIED & CT. APP'TED MED., Rule 10.100 (2008).

2. What approach or approaches to regulation seem most appropriate in connection with mediators who focus on matters of divorce, environmental protection and land use, and personal injury claims?

3. The Family Mediation Canada (FMC) program requires substantially more training than U.S. programs of which we are aware: 180 hours for mediating relational issues in family disputes; 230 hours for mediating financial issues in divorce. These resemble mediation certification programs in Germany, Austria, and Switzerland, which have 240–hour training requirements. What would account for this apparent disparity in training obligations between these countries and the U.S.? In what circumstances should mediation training include training in substantive law?

4. A relatively new organization, the International Mediation Institute (IMI), has created an international certification system for commercial mediators. IMI's Independent Standards Commission (ISC) has established seven criteria relating to experience, knowledge, skills, transparency, program integrity, monitoring and commitment to diversity. These criteria are used by approved but independent service providers, trainers, and educational and professional institutions to conduct Qualifying Assessment Programs (QAPs). To become IMI Certified, a mediator must be qualified by one of these QAPs.

After being qualified for IMI Certification through a QAP, mediators construct profiles for inclusion on IMI's online portal. The portal assists potential clients in finding the right mediator for their dispute. Profiles include summaries of feedback from parties who have participated in mediations conducted by IMI–Certified Mediators. Each summary has been prepared by an independent person or institution selected the Mediator.

IMI–Certified Mediators are required to specify the Code of Conduct that is binding upon them, and the disciplinary process that applies. IMI also has its own default Code of Conduct and disciplinary process that IMI Certified Mediators may select.

5. Several attempts to systematize processes of selecting, training, mentoring, and evaluating mediators have emerged over the years. *See* Dorothy J. Della Noce, James R. Antes, Robert A. Baruch Bush, & Judith A. Saul, *Signposts and Crossroads: A Model for Live Action Mediator Assessment*, 23 Ohio St. J. on Disp. Resol. 197 (2008); THE TEST DESIGN PROJECT, PERFORMANCE–BASED ASSESSMENT: A METHODOLOGY FOR USE IN SELECTING, TRAINING, AND EVALUATING MEDIATIONS (National Institute for Dispute Resolution ed., 1995); SAN DIEGO MEDIATION CENTER, MEDIATOR

CREDENTIAL: AN IMPLEMENTATION GUIDE (1992). Mediator Charles Pou, Jr. has argued that we don't need more rules, but better ways of encouraging and helping mediators behave ethically. He has suggested, among other things, creating "ethics hotlines," building support systems, and focusing on the system, rather than just the mediator. Charles Pou, Jr., *Making Ethical Dispute Resolution a Reality*, Disp. Resol. Mag., Winter 2004, at 19. In a related vein, Professor Craig McEwen has asserted that if mediators hope to exercise "collegial control" over their work, they must begin with adhering to established standards of practice and ethical codes. "But because such rules and standards must be general and pose 'often-competing priorities,'" Professor McEwen adds that mediators need to develop "'communities of practice'—groups of practitioners finding regular means of communication with one another and sharing common conceptions about how to deal with everyday decisions." Craig McEwen, *Giving Meaning to Mediator Professionalism*, Disp. Resol. Mag., Spring 2005, at 4. Maryland has used these approaches to encourage best practice among mediators.

6. Assume you were creating a private for-profit organization that would offer services of a number of mediators on a roster that the organization would establish. What credentials would you impose for people to appear on your roster?

2. *Ethics*

This section includes material on ethics standards and on court enforcement of rules dealing with mediator conflicts of interest.

a) *Ethics Standards*

Numerous organizations and courts have promulgated standards of practice and ethics for mediators. One of the most broadly accepted and influential sets of standards is the Model Standards of Conduct for Mediators approved by the American Arbitration Association (AAA), American Bar Association (ABA) and Society of Professionals in Dispute Resolution (now Association for Conflict Resolution) in 1994. In 2005, the same organizations approved a revised set of standards.

The 1994 and 2005 Model Standards have been very influential in that most of the ethical codes adopted by states, court systems and agencies reflect their language. Many ADR providers, including AAA, require their mediators to abide by the 2005 Model Standards. You can find the complete 2005 Model Standards, including applicable introductory notes, prefaces, comments and reporters' notes, in Appendix D.

We have included here the Model Standards' preamble and its standards on self-determination and confidentiality. This is because this chapter will discuss legal challenges to the enforcement of mediated settlement agreements, as well as efforts to breach the confidentiality of mediation sessions.

The other Model Standards are in Appendix D and address: impartiality, conflicts of interest, competence, quality of the process, advertising and solicitation, fees and other charges, and advancement of mediation practice.

MODEL STANDARDS OF CONDUCT FOR MEDIATORS
(2005)

Preamble

Mediation is used to resolve a broad range of conflicts within a variety of settings. These Standards are designed to serve as fundamental ethical guidelines for persons mediating in all practice contexts. They serve three primary goals: to guide the conduct of mediators; to inform the mediating parties; and to promote public confidence in mediation as a process for resolving disputes.

Mediation is a process in which an impartial third party facilitates communication and negotiation and promotes voluntary decision making by the parties to the dispute.

Mediation serves various purposes, including providing the opportunity for parties to define and clarify issues, understand different perspectives, identify interests, explore and assess possible solutions, and reach mutually satisfactory agreements, when desired.

STANDARD I.   SELF–DETERMINATION

A.   A mediator shall conduct a mediation based on the principle of party self-determination. Self-determination is the act of coming to a voluntary, uncoerced decision in which each party makes free and informed choices as to process and outcome. Parties may exercise self-determination at any stage of a mediation, including mediator selection, process design, participation in or withdrawal from the process, and outcomes.

> 1.   Although party self-determination for process design is a fundamental principle of mediation practice, a mediator may need to balance such party self-determination with a mediator's duty to conduct a quality process in accordance with these Standards.

> 2.   A mediator cannot personally ensure that each party has made free and informed choices to reach particular decisions, but, where appropriate, a mediator should make the parties aware of the importance of consulting other professionals to help them make informed choices.

B.   A mediator shall not undermine party self-determination by any party for reasons such as higher settlement rates, egos, increased fees, or outside pressures from court personnel, program administrators, provider organizations, the media or others.

* * *

STANDARD v. CONFIDENTIALITY

A.   A mediator shall maintain the confidentiality of all information obtained by the mediator in mediation, unless otherwise agreed to by the parties or required by applicable law.

> 1.   If the parties to a mediation agree that the mediator may disclose information obtained during the mediation, the mediator may do so.
>
> 2.   A mediator should not communicate to any non-participant information about how the parties acted in the mediation. A mediator may report, if required, whether parties appeared at a scheduled mediation and whether or not the parties reached a resolution.
>
> 3.   If a mediator participates in teaching, research or evaluation of mediation, the mediator should protect the anonymity of the parties and abide by their reasonable expectations regarding confidentiality.

B.   A mediator who meets with any persons in private session during a mediation shall not convey directly or indirectly to any other person, any information that was obtained during that private session without the consent of the disclosing person.

C.   A mediator shall promote understanding among the parties of the extent to which the parties will maintain confidentiality of information they obtain in a mediation.

D.   Depending on the circumstance of a mediation, the parties may have varying expectations regarding confidentiality that a mediator should address. The parties may make their own rules with respect to confidentiality, or the accepted practice of an individual mediator or institution may dictate a particular set of expectations.

NOTES AND QUESTIONS

1.   Interestingly, the Reporter's Notes for the 2005 Model Standards were not specifically approved by any of the sponsoring organizations, and thus are not formally included in them. Nonetheless, the Notes provide very useful commentary regarding the revisions made by the Joint Committee. They are available at http://moritzlaw.osu.edu/programs/adr/msoc/pdf/reportersnotes–092005final.pdf. The Model Standards are very general, and some mediation speciality communities have drafted their own standards as well. For example, the American Bar Association Standards on Family Law and Divorce Mediation (2001) can be found in the online appendix on the TWEN web site for this casebook at www.lawschool.westlaw.com.

2.   The 2005 Model Standards were designed to respond to developments in the field of mediation. One such development was the recognition that mediators are not always entirely truthful. The new Standard VII(A)(4) provides: "A mediator should promote honesty and candor between and among all participants, and a mediator shall not knowingly misrepresent any material fact or circumstance in the course of a mediation."

Professor Kimberlee Kovach has objected that this standard does not go far enough in imposing an adequate obligation of truthfulness and honesty upon mediators and proposes the following, alternative rule: "During the course of a mediation, a mediator shall not knowingly: (a) make a false statement of fact or law to any participant in the process; (b) assist the parties in reaching a resolution that is based, in whole or in part, upon incorrect or fraudulent information; (c) fail to correct a mistake of information when such is directly relevant to the content of the mediation." Kimberlee Kovach, *Musings on Idea(l)s in the Ethical Regulation of Mediators: Honesty, Enforcement, and Education*, 21 Ohio St. J. on Disp. Resol. 123, 137 (2005). With her proposal, Kovach hopes to protect the integrity of the mediation process and promote greater candor and honesty in negotiation. Do you think either the revised standard or Professor Kovach's proposal will accomplish these goals?

3.   Another development involved the rise of contingent fee agreements, in which a mediator and parties agree that the mediator's fee will depend upon the outcome of the mediation. Many ethics codes and court rules prohibit "contingent fee" mediation, but in 2003, Professor Scott Peppet argued against such rigid prohibitions. Scott R. Peppet, *Contractarian Economics and Mediation Ethics: The Case for Customizing Neutrality Through Contingent Fee Mediation*, 82 Tex. L. Rev. 227 (2003). He suggested that parties should be allowed to contract for contingent mediator fees in circumstances where such an agreement would not interfere with the three core functions through which the mediator "adds value": "by discovering whether settlement is possible; by optimizing settlement; and by helping to manage psychological, emotional, and relational barriers." *Id.* at 262. Professor Peppet proposed the following rule as a guide to future ethics codes:

A mediator shall not take a fee contingent on any aspect of a mediation unless

(a) the mediator discloses, in writing, the fee arrangement and its potential consequences, the mediator recommends that the parties consult with counsel about the fee arrangement, and, prior to the mediation, all parties provide informed consent in writing and after an opportunity to consult with counsel;

(b) in court-ordered mediation, the fee arrangement is disclosed to and approved by the court prior to the mediation; and

(c) the fee arrangement does not create an appearance or actuality of partiality toward one party.

Id. at 276. Does this rule satisfy concerns about the risk that the mediator will overreach? Would it protect against partiality? How effective is the provision contained in the 2005 Model Standards?

4. Critics of the 1994 Model Standards had complained that they were too vague and lacked a mechanism to advise practitioners confronting difficult situations. Professor Paula Young has noted that even today, only three states—Florida, Georgia and North Carolina—have installed systems that respond to ethical questions posed by certified or rostered mediators. Paula M. Young, *Rejoice! Rejoice! Rejoice, Give Thanks, and Sing: ABA, ACR and AAA Adopt Revised Model Standards of Conduct for Mediators*, 5 Appalachian J. L. 195, 235 (2006). The ABA Section of Dispute Resolution has established a Committee on Mediator Ethical Guidance to advise mediators regarding the application of the 2005 Model Standards. The Committee issued its first advisory opinion on August 6, 2007. *See* http://www.abanet.org/dch/committee.cfm?com=DR018600.

5. Dean Michael Moffitt was critical of the 1994 Model Standards and is even more concerned about the 2005 Model Standards, which he views as "a series of absolute, hortative prescriptions" that ignore potential internal tensions and fail to provide "an overarching ethical norm—a single value that would trump others." Michael L. Moffitt, *The Wrong Model, Again: Why the Devil Is Not in the Details*, Disp. Resol. Mag., Spring 2006, at 31, 32. He contrasts the 2005 Model Standards with lawyers' ethics which, he says, have established a clearer hierarchy among ethical ideals—e.g., "[a]n attorney's duty to provide competent service to existing clients trumps the duty to provide pro bono services[, a]nd an attorney's duty of candor to the court trumps even the duty of client loyalty." *Id.*

Do you agree with Dean Moffitt that lawyers' ethical obligations are clearer than those that apply to mediators? Was this always the case? Can you imagine situations in which mediators' values of supporting parties' self-determination and informed consent will conflict with the value of maintaining the appearance of impartiality? Do the 2005 Model Standards help reconcile that conflict? Should they do so? How would you change the language or structure of the 2005 Model Standards?

Dean Moffitt is most alarmed by the Note of Construction which he views as compounding the standards' other errors "by inviting the establishment of a dangerous standard of practice." *Id.* He worries that the standards could serve as the basis for malpractice actions against mediators and concludes "that it would be better for mediation to be a practice with no articulation of ethical principles than to have this document be perceived as our shared statement of ethical parameters." *Id.* Consider how legally-binding standards of care have developed in other areas of professional or expert practice. Do you think that Dean Moffitt's concerns are justified? How would you have written the Note of Construction?

For the response of the Reporter for the 2005 Model Standards to Dean Moffitt's concerns, see Joseph B. Stulberg, *The Model Standards of Conduct: A Reply to Professor Moffitt*, Disp. Resol. Mag., Spring 2006, at 34.

6.   Many state courts have also developed codes of ethics for mediators. A smaller number have established formal enforcement mechanisms. Florida has established an elaborate system to regulate the practice of mediation in the court system. For a comprehensive review, see Robert B. Moberly, *Ethical Standards for Court–Appointed Mediators and Florida's Mandatory Mediation Experiment*, 21 Fla. St. U. L. Rev. 701 (1994). In addition to rules for mediator conduct (FLA. R. CERTIFIED & CT. APP'TED MED., RULE 10.200 (2008)), the system includes a Mediator Qualifications Advisory Panel, which provides advice to mediators, and a Mediator Qualifications Board, which handles discipline of certified mediators. Mattox Hair, Sharon Press, & Brooks Rathet, *Ethics Within the Mediation Process,* 1 Am. Arb. Ass'n *ADR Currents*, No. 1, at 9 (1996). The Advisory Board has issued opinions dealing with, inter alia, confidentiality, advertising, and the billing process. *Id.* at 10– 11. *See also* Bruce A. Blitman, *Mediator Ethics: Florida's Ethics Advisory Panel Breaks New Ground*, Disp. Resol. Mag., Spring 2001, at 10 (describing operations of Florida Ethics Review Panel); Sharon Press, *Standards . . . and Results: Florida Provides Forum for Grievances Against Mediators*, Disp. Resol. Mag, Spring 2001, at 8 (discussing Florida's general system of regulating mediators).

Minnesota has an ADR Ethics Board that has promulgated ethics and practice standards as well as dealing with evaluation and other issues. Barbara McAdoo & Nancy Welsh, *The Times They Are a Changin'—Or Are They? An Update on Rule 114,* The Hennepin Lawyer, July–Aug. 1996, at 8; Duane W. Krohnke, *Minnesota Takes up ADR Ethics Challenge*, 14 Alternatives to High Cost Litig. 121 (1996); Duane W. Krohnke, *Decisions Standards Raise Policy Issues as Minnesota Drafts ADR Code of Ethics*, 15 Alternatives to High Cost Litig. 3 (1997). Some professional organizations, such as the Association for Conflict Resolution, also consider ethics complaints against members.

7.   Whether mediation is a profession—or "a set of executive life skills"—is the subject of some debate. *See* Juliana Birkhoff & Robert Rack, *Points of View: Is Mediation Really a Profession?*, Disp. Resol. Mag., Fall 2001, at 10. Is it helpful to frame this as an either-or question? What do you think mediation is, or should be? Mediators who are members of other professions, including law, may be subject to other regulatory regimes. The regulation of mediation practice by lawyers is covered *infra*.

b)   *Mediator Impartiality and Conflicts of Interest*

It is, of course, essential that mediators maintain their impartiality. The 2005 Model Standards address this issue in various provisions by requiring that: mediators may not permit their own interests to undermine parties' self-determination (Standard I.B.), mediators must conduct mediation "in an impartial manner and avoid conduct that gives the appearance of partiality" (Standard II.B.), mediators must withdraw if they cannot conduct a mediation in an impartial manner (Standard II.C.), and mediators may not "charge fees in a manner that impairs their ability to conduct mediation in an impartial manner" (Standard VIII.B.). Standard III is devoted to the avoidance of conflicts of interest and the appearance of such conflicts.

The burden is upon the mediator to make a reasonable inquiry to determine "whether there are any facts that a reasonable individual would consider likely to create a potential or actual conflict of interest" (Standard III.B.), make a disclosure of such conflicts if they exist (Standard III.C.), and proceed with the mediation only if all parties consent (Standard III.C.). Indeed, even if the parties consent, a mediator may not conduct the mediation if she concludes that her conflict could "reasonably be viewed as undermining the integrity of the process." (Standard III.E.). Similar disclosure obligations appear in other ethical standards. *See, e.g.*, MODEL STANDARDS OF CONDUCT FOR MEDIATORS (AAA, ABA, SPIDR 1994), Standard III, which are reprinted in Appendix C; FLA. R. CERTIFIED & CT. APP'TED MED., RULE 10.340 (2008).

Section 9 of the Uniform Mediation Act, in Appendix C, similarly requires inquiry and disclosure by mediators. Indeed, Section 9 provides that a violation of these requirements precludes a mediator from asserting the mediation privilege.

Mediators also must be concerned about conflicts of interest that arise during or after a mediation. The 2005 Model Standards, for instance, provide that "[s]ubsequent to a mediation, a mediator shall not establish another relationship with any of the participants in any matter that would raise questions about the integrity of the mediation." MODEL STANDARDS OF CONDUCT FOR MEDIATORS, STANDARD III.F. (2005). Under the 1994 Model Rules, the mediator's ethical obligation could vary depending upon whether the subsequent relationship involved a matter that was related or unrelated to the mediation: "Without the consent of all the parties, a mediator shall not subsequently establish a professional relationship with one of the parties in a related matter, or in an unrelated matter under circumstances which would raise legitimate question about the integrity of the mediation process." MODEL STANDARDS OF CONDUCT FOR MEDIATORS, STANDARD III. Comments. (1994).

If the mediator is a lawyer, the situation sometimes can become more complicated, requiring consideration of lawyers' ethical obligations. This is the situation presented in the following case.

* * *

McKenzie Construction v. St. Croix Storage

District Court of the Virgin Islands, 1997
961 F.Supp. 857

RESNICK, UNITED STATES MAGISTRATE JUDGE.

Plaintiff McKenzie Construction is a local lumber retail company who brought this damages action against defendants St. Croix Storage Corp. for conversion of lumber. The Court ordered the matter submitted to mediation and later appointed Attorney Lisa Moorehead as mediator. * * * Mediation was unsuccessful and the parties have resumed preparation for trial.

In seeking to disqualify the firm of Rohn & Cusick, defendants claim that the firm's hiring of Attorney Moorehead, who was the mediator appointed by the Court to settle this case, presents an irreparable conflict of interest in contravention of the rules governing the conduct of mediators and attorneys alike. Defendants reason that Moorehead's position as mediator allowed her access to "a wide range of confidential information derived from her private consultations" with the parties. Plaintiffs responded that although Moorehead may be subject to disqualification, she is simply "of counsel" to the law firm of Rohn & Cusick and that, under Virgin Islands law, the disqualification of the law firm is not automatic. Moreover, plaintiffs assert that although no confidences were exchanged in the mediation, the firm had created a "cone of silence" around Moorehead, insulating her from the case. However, defendants countered that since being hired by Rohn & Cusick in September of 1996, Moorehead had inserted herself into the case by meeting with an investigator for defendants concerning the investigator's contact with plaintiff about the case. The Court requested that plaintiffs file a direct response to defendants' allegation. In their response, plaintiffs submit an affidavit of Attorney Moorehead in which she avers that a "cone of silence" has been erected at Rohn & Cusick and admits that she met with the investigator in order to advise him that he could be civilly liable for attempting to settle a case with a represented party. She claims that she did not discuss the merits of the instant case. Defendants also seek the imposition of sanctions against plaintiffs' law firm for filing false affidavits.

After review of the record and the submissions of the parties, this Court concludes that there exists a sufficient basis for resolution of this issue on the pleadings alone. Accordingly, the request for a hearing is denied.

A motion to disqualify counsel requires the court to balance the right of a party to retain counsel of his choice and the substantial hardship which might result from disqualification as against the public perception of and the public trust in the judicial system. *Powell v. Alabama,* 287 U.S.

45, 53, 53 S.Ct. 55, 58, 77 L.Ed. 158 (1932). The underlying principle in considering motions to disqualify counsel is safeguarding the integrity of the court proceedings and the purpose of granting such motions is to eliminate the threat that the litigation will be tainted. *United States Football League v. National Football League,* 605 F.Supp. 1448, 1464 (S.D.N.Y.1985). The district court's power to disqualify an attorney derives from its inherent authority to supervise the professional conduct of attorneys appearing before it. *Richardson v. Hamilton International Corp.,* 469 F.2d 1382, 1385–86 (3d Cir.1972), *cert. denied* 411 U.S. 986, 93 S.Ct. 2271, 36 L.Ed.2d 964 (1973). Disqualification issues must be decided on a case by case basis. *Rogers v. Pittston Co.,* 800 F.Supp. 350, 353 (W.D.Va.1992); *In re Asbestos Cases,* 514 F.Supp. 914, 924 (E.D.Va 1981).

This case presents the question whether a law firm must be disqualified from representing a party when it employs an attorney who was formerly the mediator in the identical litigation. Plaintiffs essentially concede that Attorney Moorehead should be screened from involvement in the case. Indeed, they "do not dispute that Ms. Moorehead, herself, may be subject to disqualification." They argue, however, that the "cone of silence" erected around Attorney Moorehead is sufficient under the rules and case law, and that the facts do not warrant disqualification of the entire firm. Defendants maintain that Moorehead's contact with the investigator, subsequent to the date that the "cone of silence" was reportedly constructed, constitutes a violation of the relevant ethical standards and presents a more compelling case for disqualification.

The leading case on attorney disqualification in this district is *Bluebeard's Castle, Inc. v. Delmar Marketing, Inc.,* 886 F.Supp. 1204, 1207 (D.V.I.1995). In that case, this Court ruled that where an attorney accepts representation of a party adverse to a former client in a substantially related matter, the Court "presumes that confidences were disclosed during the previous relationship and that such confidences would be used against the former client . . . [and] does not require that the moving party be able to show that confidences actually were passed on or to detail their contents." (citations omitted.) The Court went on to find that an attorney faced with such a prospect should, at the least, fully disclose the fact to that party or, at most, refuse such representation. Failure to honor such conflict would result in the disqualification of the attorney and his entire firm. *Id.* at 1208–1210. The Court relied on the Model Rules of Professional Conduct in disqualifying the attorney and his law firm.

* * *

[In footnote 2, the court quoted Rule 1.9 of the ABA MODEL RULES OF PROFESSIONAL CONDUCT:

CONFLICT OF INTEREST: FORMER CLIENT

(a) A lawyer who has formerly represented a client in a matter shall not thereafter represent another person in the same or a substantially related matter in which that person's interests are materially adverse to the interests of the former client unless the former client consents after consultation.

(b) A lawyer shall not knowingly represent a person in the same or substantially related matter in which a firm with which the lawyer formerly was associated had previously represented a client

(1) whose interests are materially adverse to that person; and

(2) about whom the lawyer had acquired information protected by rules 1.6 and 1.9(c) that is material to the matter; (c) A lawyer who has formerly represented a client in a matter or whose present or former firm has formerly represented a client in a matter shall not thereafter

(1) use information relating to the representation to the disadvantage of the former client except as Rule 1.6 or Rule 3.3 would permit or require with respect to a client, or when the information has become generally known; or (2) reveal information relating to the representation except as rule 1.6 or Rule 3.3 would permit or require with respect to a client.]

* * *

The recent case of *Poly Software International, Inc. v. Su,* 880 F.Supp. 1487 (D.Utah 1995), discusses the identical issue presented in the case *sub judice.* In that case, two parties agreed to mediate a copyright action which they were defending. However, soon after the mediated settlement the parties sued each other. One of the parties retained the mediator as his counsel. The other party moved to disqualify the mediator-turned-attorney in light of his prior status as mediator in the previous action. The District Court disqualified the attorney and his law firm from participating in the litigation and held that an attorney who serves as a mediator cannot subsequently represent anyone in a substantially related matter without the consent of the original parties. The court reasoned that mediators routinely receive and preserve confidences in much the same manner as an attorney. The court referred to the Model Rules of Professional Conduct and concluded that where the mediator was privy to confidential information, the applicable ethical rules imposed the same responsibilities as the rules relating to an attorney's subsequent representation of a former client. The court also considered the rule prohibiting judges and other adjudicative officers from representing anyone in connection with a matter in which he or she participated "personally and substantially." Model Rule 1.2.

Likewise, in *Cho v. Superior Court,* 39 Cal.App.4th 113, 45 Cal.Rptr.2d 863 (1995), a former judge and his law firm were disqualified from representing a party in an action in which the former judge had participated in settlement conferences. That court relied on ABA Model Rule 1.12 which prohibits a lawyer who has participated personally and substantially in a matter as a judge or adjudicative officer, from representing anyone in connection with the same matter. *Id.* 45 Cal.Rptr.2d at 867. The Court compared the judge's role in the proceedings to that of a mediator, and found that the position necessarily involved the exchange of confidences going to the merits of the case. The court cautioned that "no amount of assurances or screening procedures, no 'cone of silence' could ever convince the opposing party that the confidences would not be used to its disadvantage." *Id.* 45 Cal.Rptr.2d at 869. The Court concluded that based on the nature of the attorney's prior participation, there is a presumption that confidences were revealed, and the attorney should not have "to engage in subtle evaluation of the extent to which he acquired relevant information in the first representation and of the actual use of that representation." *Id.* Thus, the rule of the cases is that a mediator should never represent a party to the mediation in a subsequent related or similar matter.

It is against this backdrop that this Court must determine whether Attorney Moorehead, who was the mediator in this identical action, may have received confidences which may be used to the disadvantage of defendant in this case, warranting her disqualification and that of her law firm. Guided by the case law and experience, this Court notes that the very nature of mediation requires that confidences be exchanged. Hence, Local Rule of Civil Procedure 3.2(c)(2) provides that a mediator appointed in this jurisdiction must be impartial and is required to disqualify himself or herself "in any action in which he/she would be required under Title 28, USC sec. 455 to disqualify him/herself if he/she were a judge or Magistrate Judge." Title 28, USC sec. 455 requires such a judicial officer to disqualify himself or herself (1) where the attorney served as a lawyer, the associate lawyer, a witness or a judge in the case; or (2) where the attorney has served in governmental employment and participated in the case as a counsel, adviser or material witness.

John Landers, Vice President of defendant St. Croix Storage Corp., states by affidavit that he was present during the mediation conference and met with Attorney Moorehead separately and together with the other parties. He states that he openly discussed "the facts of the matter, the financial status and capability of Sun Storage to either pay a settlement figure or to pay a verdict, the status and degree of involvement of certain of the partners . . . in the management and operation . . . and the trial strategy that was to be employed in the absence of settlement of this matter." Plaintiffs claim that all discussions in the case were done in a group setting and not "confidential". They further argue that any information received would have been discovered during the normal course of litigation.

Plaintiffs' entire argument against disqualification lacks credibility, is unsupported by legal analysis, and completely ignores the existing standards governing attorney conduct. This Court finds, and many commentators agree, that during mediation parties are encouraged to disclose the strengths and weaknesses of their positions, in an effort to arrive at a settlement, Protection of confidences in such a setting strengthens the incentive of parties to negotiate without fear that the mediator will subsequently use the information against them. Additionally, the rules regulating attorney conduct place the onus on the attorney to "remain conscious of the obligation to preserve confidences and maintain loyalty." 886 F.Supp. at 1207. It is clear from the record that the parties met to negotiate a settlement. It is undisputed that the mediation lasted at least one hour. It is not unreasonable to assume that in light of the nature and purpose of the proceeding, that confidential information was disclosed by the parties. Notwithstanding Attorney Moorehead's statements to the contrary, the present situation presents such a serious affront to the policy that forms the basis of the rules, that this Court has no choice but to conclude that Attorney Moorehead must be disqualified.

DISQUALIFICATION OF THE FIRM

This Court further finds that disqualification of Attorney Moorehead should be imputed to the other members of the firm. The cases and Model Rule 1.10(a)[117] require such disqualification. * * *

In addition, the Court is disturbed by Attorney Moorehead's contact with Mr. Pierre Tepie, an investigator associated with this case. Partly in response to a Motion for Sanctions filed by plaintiffs, Mr. Tepie, who is a self-employed investigator and process server, stated, via affidavit that he was hired by Shirryl Hughes, on behalf of a defendant in this case, to attempt to negotiate an out of court settlement. He further stated that after such attempted negotiation, he was contacted by Attorney Moorehead, who attempted to persuade him to discontinue his efforts. Attorney Moorehead responded, also via affidavit, that she contacted Tepie with regard to his attempted negotiation because she "thought it was wise to inform him that he could be civilly liable for contacting a represented party." She claims she did not know whom he worked for. Moorehead, who was reportedly excluded from the case, does not explain in her affidavit, the manner in which she learned about Tepie's

---

[117] The rule states: "While lawyers are associated in a firm, none of them shall knowingly represent a client when any one of them practicing alone would be prohibited from doing so by Rule 1.7, 1.8(c), 1.9 or 2.2."

involvement. In any event, this court finds that Moorehead's contact with an agent of the defendants in this very case, implicates the effectiveness of the measures allegedly adopted by her employer to avoid her involvement in this matter. Accordingly, disqualification of the law firm of Rohn & Cusick is necessary to safeguard the integrity of the ongoing litigation and to eliminate the threat that the proceedings will be tainted.

* * *

CONCLUSION

Based on the foregoing, this Court finds that, as the mediator in this case, Attorney Moorehead is presumed to have received confidential information going to the merits of the case and must be disqualified. This Court also finds that in addition to the mandate of the Model Rules, the screening procedure reportedly employed at the law firm of Rohn & Cusick failed to prevent Moorehead's subsequent involvement in this matter, further bolstering the court's conclusion that the law firm of Rohn & Cusick must also be disqualified. Finally, the Court finds that plaintiffs' affidavits herein do not warrant the imposition of sanctions. Accordingly, none will be imposed.

NOTES AND QUESTIONS

1. The *McKenzie* opinion assumed that the mediator had obtained confidential information during the mediation. Do you suppose the judge assumed that the mediator held private caucuses? If so, does that mean that the result might have been different if there had been no private caucuses, i.e., if the parties, lawyers, and mediator had stayed in joint session at all times, as is the practice in Understanding–Based Mediation?

2. If you were a partner in a large law firm, would you discourage other members of the firm from acting as mediators or arbitrators out of a concern that such practices might disqualify the firm from some potential representations? Or would you prefer to establish procedures that would avoid running afoul of conflict of interest provisions?

For an example of conflict-of-interest concerns prompting the break-up of a law firm that included lawyer-mediators, see *With Conflicts at Issue, Florida Firm and Its Former Partners Restructure ADR—Again*, 15 Alternatives to High Cost Litig. 131 (1997).

3. Lawyer-mediators also must pay attention to rules of professional responsibility dealing with advertising and practicing jointly with a non-lawyer. *See* SARAH R. COLE, NANCY H. ROGERS, & CRAIG A. MCEWEN, MEDIATION: LAW POLICY AND PRACTICE, SEC. 10.3–10.4 (3rd ed. 2013).

* * *

4. In 2002, the ABA modified Model Rule 1.12, which previously dealt only with former judges and arbitrators. The rule now includes mediators and other third-party neutrals:

RULE 1.12   FORMER JUDGE, ARBITRATOR, MEDIATOR OR OTHER THIRD–PARTY NEUTRAL

(a) Except as stated in paragraph (d), a lawyer shall not represent anyone in connection with a matter in which the lawyer participated personally and substantially as a judge or other adjudicative officer or law clerk to such a person or as an arbitrator, mediator or other third-party neutral, unless all parties to the proceeding give informed consent, confirmed in writing.

(b) A lawyer shall not negotiate for employment with any person who is involved as a party or as lawyer for a party in a matter in which the lawyer is participating personally and substantially as a judge or other adjudicative officer or as an arbitrator, mediator or other third-party neutral. A lawyer serving as a law clerk to a judge or other adjudicative officer may negotiate for employment with a party or lawyer involved in a matter in which the clerk is participating personally and substantially, but only after the lawyer has notified the judge or other adjudicative officer.

(c) If a lawyer is disqualified by paragraph (a), no lawyer in a firm with which that lawyer is associated may knowingly undertake or continue representation in the matter unless:

    (1) The disqualified lawyer is timely screened from any participation in the matter and is apportioned no part of the fee therefrom; and

    (2) Written notice is promptly given to the parties and any appropriate tribunal to enable them to ascertain compliance with the provisions of this rule.

(d) An arbitrator selected as a partisan of a party in a multimember arbitration panel is not prohibited from subsequently representing that party.

MODEL RULES OF PROF'L CONDUCT R. 1.12 (2013).

5. Recall that the ABA Model Rules of Professional Responsibility have no binding effect until a particular rule is adopted by an appropriate ethics body, usually a state supreme court.

6. Do you think the screening and notice provisions in Model Rules of Professional Conduct Rule 1.12 provide adequate protection? The Georgia Dispute Resolution Commission thought that even less protection was needed. Because a mediator is pledged to maintain confidentiality, the

commission held that it was not appropriate to impute such knowledge to his firm. *See* Georgia Dispute Resolution Commission, Committee on Ethics, Advisory Opinion 4 (1997).

7.   In the 2013 Detroit bankruptcy case, the federal bankruptcy court appointed a team of mediators, consisting of several judges and one lawyer, to work with the city and its creditors. The city was a former client of the lawyer-mediator. What actions would the Model Standards of Conduct require the mediator to take? Would the Model Rules require him to take any actions? Illinois has adopted a mediation privilege statute patterned after the Uniform Mediation Act. Would that statute require the mediator to take any actions to investigate and avoid conflicts of interest?

8.   Assume that the chief judge of your local trial court appoints you to a committee to study and recommend ways to regulate mediators in the court-ordered mediation program the court is planning to establish. Under that program, judges could order any civil case into mediation, and the parties would be encouraged to select mediators from a roster that the court would maintain. At your upcoming committee meeting, which methods of regulation, if any, would you recommend?

In particular, would you require that mediators have certain degrees? Training?

Would your answer depend on whether parties would have a choice of mediators? On whether parties would pay the mediators, and, if so, how such fees would be determined?

Would you have different requirements for mediators who would deal with family or divorce cases and for those who would handle general civil matters?

If you recommend specific training requirements, would you exempt or "grandfather" retired judges, who have served more than a certain number of years? Why or why not?

What kind of conflict of interest provisions would you use?

Would your answer to any of these questions depend on your own background and expectations about providing or using mediation services?

c)   Limitations on What Mediators May Say About the Law

The question of what a mediator may say about law is hotly debated among some academics, practitioners, and mediation program developers and administrators. To provide windows on such issues, we focus first in subsection a) on a "debate" over whether a mediator may properly "evaluate"—i.e., make predictions about what would happen in court or assessments of how the law applies. We then consider whether certain practices by a mediator, lawyer or non-lawyer, might constitute the practice of law.

3. The Facilitative–Evaluative Debate

The question of whether a mediator may properly "evaluate" the legal or other aspects of a dispute—e.g., make and communicate assessments of the strengths and weaknesses of one or both parties' sides of a dispute, or predict a judicial outcome—has generated much controversy. Many mediators and commentators believe that such conduct is necessarily inconsistent with the nature of mediation and the mediator's role. Kimberlee K. Kovach & Lela P. Love, *"Evaluative" Mediation is an Oxymoron*, 14 Alternatives to High Cost Litig. 31 (1996). In this view, evaluation is a separate process, and therefore should be called by a different name, such as neutral evaluation or non-binding arbitration (these are "mixed" processes, which we cover *infra* in Chapter VI). Professor Love lists 10 reasons why mediators should not evaluate. However, she allows that

> [m]ediators are not foreclosed from engaging in some other process or helping parties design a mixed process. Whatever the service being provided, however, it should be requested by the parties and accurately labeled. When a process is "mixed" and the neutral has multiple roles, he or she is bound by more than one code of ethics, charged with separate goals and tasks. A properly labeled process— or conversely, a label that has a clear meaning—promotes integrity, disputant satisfaction [because expectations are met], and uniform practice.

Lela P. Love, *The Top Ten Reasons that Mediators Should Not Evaluate*, 24 Fla. St. U. L. Rev. 937, 948 (1997).

Florida's ethical rules for mediators address the issue as follows:

Rule 10.370 Advice, Opinions, or Information

(a) Providing Information. Consistent with standards of impartiality and preserving party self-determination, a mediator may provide information that the mediator is qualified by training or experience to provide. * * *

(c) Personal or Professional Opinion. A mediator shall not offer a personal or professional opinion intended to coerce the parties, unduly influence the parties, decide the dispute, or direct a resolution of any issue. Consistent with standards of impartiality and preserving party self-determination however, a mediator may point out possible outcomes of the case and discuss the merits of a claim or defense. A mediator shall not offer a personal or professional opinion as to how the court in which the case has been filed will resolve the dispute.

FLA. R. CERTIFIED & CT. APP'TED MED. 10.370 (2008). Would this approach satisfy the concerns expressed by Professor Love, *supra*?

Many proponents of evaluation in mediation also see its potential problems. Professor Marjorie Corman Aaron, for instance, lists the risks associated with evaluation as follows:

— perceived loss of neutrality;

— assumption of an adversarial relationship;

— loss of "face";

— alienation or division of counsel and client;

— entrenchment of at least one party's bargaining position;

— reduction in the parties' sense of process and outcome ownership; and

— shift in the focus toward winning and away from solving the problem.

Marjorie Corman Aaron, *Evaluation in Mediation*, *in* Dwight Golann, Mediating Legal Disputes: Effective Strategies for Lawyers and Mediators 267, 279 (1996).

Aaron thinks that "the mediation community has been somewhat coy on the issues of mediators providing evaluation of legal disputes." *Id.* at 269. She argues that a mediator may evaluate, if that is what the parties' desire, but only where evaluation is appropriate, noting:

The fundamental diagnostic question a mediator must consider when planning a mediation process and strategy is "What are the barriers to negotiated resolution here?" Where the central barriers to resolution are found in the negotiation dynamics, in poor communication patterns, in asymmetrical information, or in the parties' lack of a sense of empowerment, the mediator should structure the process to address these issues; no evaluation is needed.

Id. at 271.

Aaron supplies thoughtful guidelines for a mediator to consider in attempting to provide a necessary evaluation in such a way as to minimize these risks. These include presenting evaluations in private sessions (after asking and receiving permission), "maintaining a distance" from the evaluation, and acknowledging the limits of the mediator's expertise.

Can you imagine circumstances in which evaluation might foster party self-determination and autonomy? *See* Jacqueline M. Nolan–Haley, *Informed Consent in Mediation: A Guiding Principle for Truly Educated Decisionmaking*, 74 Notre Dame L. Rev. 775 (1999).

Researchers have found that parties perceive mediation as fairer when mediators evaluate the merits of the case. On the other hand, when mediators recommend a particular settlement, non-settling parties feel the mediation process is less fair. Roselle L. Wissler, *Court–Connected Mediation in General Civil Cases: What We Know From Empirical Research*, 17 Ohio St. J. on Disp. Resol. 641, 684 (2002).

Commentators on both sides of this debate share a concern over whether the participants in a mediation get what they expect. Yves Dezalay and Bryant Garth have argued, however, that neither mediation nor arbitration has a fixed meaning and that debates over their definitions derive partially from the desires of practitioners and scholars to promote the forms of these processes that they use or support. Yves Dezalay & Bryant Garth, *Fussing About the Forum: Categories and Definitions as Stakes in a Professional Competition*, 21 Law & Soc. Inquiry 285 (1996).

Issues related to evaluation by a mediator—whether, when, how and why—also arise outside the ethics context. We address such issues, and others, below in discussions of mediation as the practice of law, malpractice by mediators, and party self-determination.

4.   Is Mediation the Practice of Law?

The question of mediator evaluation also implicates the problem of whether that, and a range of other potential mediator activities, might constitute the practice of law. To the extent that mediator activity constitutes the practice of law, it subjects the mediator to regulation by authorities that control the practice of law—ordinarily, regulatory bodies established by the supreme court in each jurisdiction. Lawyers are subject to the ethical obligations of their profession while they are mediating. So they must be concerned about how their conduct is restricted by the rules of the jurisdictions in which they are admitted. In addition, when they are mediating in another jurisdiction, they could *conceivably* be subject to criminal charges for engaging in the unauthorized practice of law. When someone claims that mediation could constitute the practice of law, usually they are imagining that the mediator is not a lawyer.

Ordinarily, mediators—even if they are lawyers—do not believe that they are forming a lawyer-client relationship, with the attendant obligations, when they undertake a mediation. After a good deal of disagreement or confusion on this issue among commentators and ethics authorities, the American Bar Association addressed the issue in 2002 by amending the preamble of the Model Rules of Professional Conduct to state "In addition to these representational functions [advisor, advocate, and negotiator] a lawyer may serve as a third-party neutral, a nonrepresentational role helping the parties to resolve a dispute or other matter." ABA Model Rules of Professional Conduct, Preamble [3] (2002).

The ABA also clarified its stance on whether a lawyer who is mediating is representing the parties, by deleting Rule 2.2 Lawyer as Intermediary and adopting the following new Rule 2.4.

RULE 2.4 LAWYER SERVING AS THIRD–PARTY NEUTRAL

(a) A lawyer serves as a third-party neutral when the lawyer assists two or more persons who are not clients of the lawyer to reach a resolution of a dispute or other matter that has arisen between them. Service as a third-party neutral may include service as an arbitrator, a mediator or in such other capacity as will enable the lawyer to assist the parties to resolve the matter.

(b) A lawyer serving as a third-party neutral shall inform unrepresented parties that the lawyer is not representing them. When the lawyer knows or reasonably should know that a party does not understand the lawyer's role in the matter, the lawyer shall explain the difference between the lawyer's role as a third-party neutral and a lawyer's role as one who represents a client.

ABA, Model Rules of Professional Conduct, Rule 2.4 (2003).

Meanwhile, Standard VI.5. of the 2005 Model Standards of Conduct for Mediators, described *supra*, no longer instructs mediators to avoid providing professional advice. Instead, the standard provides:

Mixing the role of a mediator and the role of another profession is problematic and thus, a mediator should distinguish between the roles. A mediator may provide information that the mediator is qualified by training or experience to provide, only if the mediator can do so consistent with these Standards.

Of course new provisions such as these do not become binding until they are adopted by the highest court in a jurisdiction.

NOTES AND QUESTIONS

1.   Rule 2.4 provides guidance for lawyers engaged in mediation. But what about non-lawyer mediators who provide evaluations? Are they practicing law without a license? As you might imagine, the unauthorized practice of law question has been as controversial as the question of whether lawyers are providing legal services when they mediate cases. Some states, like Virginia and in North Carolina, distinguished between mediators' provision of legal information and legal advice. *See* Geetha Ravindra, *Balancing Mediation with Rules on Unauthorized Practice*, 18 Alternatives to High Cost Litig. 2 (2000). For a critique and comprehensive treatment of the UPL issue, see David A. Hoffman & Natasha A. Affolder, *Mediation and UPL: Do Mediators Have a Well–Founded Fear of Prosecution?*, Disp. Resol. Mag., Winter 2000, at 20.

The ABA Section of Dispute Resolution passed a resolution in 2002 encouraging state UPL statutes and regulations to be informed by the following principles: Mediation is not the practice of law, mediator discussion of legal issues does not create an attorney-client relationship or constitute legal advice, the drafting of settlement agreements does not constitute the practice of law, and mediators have a responsibility to inform the parties in a mediation about the nature of the mediator's role in the process and the limits of that role. ABA Section of Dispute Resolution, Resolution on Mediation and the Unauthorized Practice of Law (2002), available at http://www.americanbar.org/content/dam/aba/migrated/dispute/resolution2002.authcheckdam.pdf (last visited Dec. 3, 2013).

2. For a discussion of whether a mediator should draft a settlement agreement, *see* Harry N. Mazadoorian, *To Draft or Not to Draft: The Rights and Wrongs of Drafting and Signing Settlement Agreements*, Disp. Resol. Mag., Spring 2004, at 31.

3. In a jurisdiction that adopts Rule 2.4 of the ABA Model Rules of Professional Conduct, does the rule obviate any claims that mediation constitutes the practice of law? In a jurisdiction that has neither adopted nor rejected that rule, would the rule nonetheless have some persuasive effect?

Would the rule, if adopted in a jurisdiction, affect the risk that a lawyer-mediator who makes an "incorrect" prediction about a judicial outcome could, in a malpractice action, be held to have breached a duty of care owed to the parties?

4. Rule 2.4 provides that when a lawyer-mediator "knows or reasonably should know" that a party does not understand the lawyer-mediator's role, the lawyer-mediator must explain the difference between the roles of mediator and lawyer. How would you determine whether or not a party understands your role? How and when would you explain the difference between the roles of mediator and lawyer?

5. *Malpractice Liability*

Mediator malpractice liability has not been a significant factor in regulating mediator behavior, in part because it is generally very difficult to establish the standard of care and a breach of that standard of care, causation, and damages, given the enormous variety in mediation. Nonetheless, the possibility of malpractice liability exists and professional mediators commonly have malpractice insurance. The following cases explore mediator liability in two contexts. First, *Wagshal v. Foster* addresses the question of whether mediators should have immunity from causes of action arising out of their service as mediators. Assuming there is no immunity, as is most often the case, *Tapoohi v. Lowenberg* explores issues about whether certain kinds of conduct by a mediator violate the standard of care as well as questions of causation.

WAGSHAL V. FOSTER

United States Court of Appeals, District of Columbia Circuit, 1994
28 F.3d 1249

Before: SILBERMAN, WILLIAMS AND RANDOLPH, CIRCUIT JUDGES
Opinion for the Court filed BY CIRCUIT JUDGE WILLIAMS.

STEPHEN F. WILLIAMS, CIRCUIT JUDGE:

This case presents the issue of whether a court-appointed mediator or neutral case evaluator, performing tasks within the scope of his official duties, is entitled to absolute immunity from damages in a suit brought by a disappointed litigant. The district court found such immunity and we agree.

* * *

In June 1990, appellant Jerome S. Wagshal filed suit in D.C. Superior Court against Charles E. Sheetz, the manager of real property owned by Wagshal. In October 1991 the assigned judge, Judge Richard A. Levie, referred the case to alternative dispute resolution pursuant to Superior Court Civil Rule 16[1] and the Superior Court's alternative dispute resolution ("ADR") program. While the program does not bind the parties (except when they agree to binding arbitration), participation is mandatory. See Superior Court Rules of Civil Procedure 16(j).

Judge Levie chose "neutral case evaluation" from among the available ADR options, and appointed Mark W. Foster as case evaluator.[2] Pursuant to the order of appointment, the parties signed a "statement of understanding" providing (among other things) that the proceedings would be confidential and privileged, and that the evaluator would serve as a "neutral party". Moreover, the parties were not allowed to subpoena the evaluator or any documents submitted in the course of evaluation, and "[i]n no event [could the] mediator or evaluator voluntarily testify on behalf of a party." Wagshal signed in January 1992 (under protest, he alleges).

After Foster held his first session with the parties, Wagshal questioned his neutrality. Foster then asked that Wagshal either waive his objection or pursue it; if Wagshal made no response waiving the objection, Foster would treat it as a definite objection. Receiving no

---

[1] Superior Court Rule 16(b) provides in part: "At [the initial scheduling and settlement] conference the judge will . . . explore the possibilities for early resolution through settlement or alternative dispute resolution techniques. . . . "

[2] We use the terms "case evaluator" and "mediator" interchangeably in this opinion. Each acts as a neutral third party assisting the parties to a dispute in exploring the possibility of settlement, the principal difference being that implicit in the name: the case evaluator focuses on helping the parties assess their cases, while the mediator acts more directly to explore settlement possibilities. See Melinda Ostermeyer, Alternative Dispute Resolution Programs 6 (Superior Court of the District of Columbia, Multi–Door Dispute Resolution Division 1992).

response by the deadline set, and later receiving a communication that he regarded as equivocal, Foster wrote to Judge Levie in February 1992, with copies to counsel, recusing himself. The letter also reported to the judge on his efforts in the case and recommended continuation of ADR proceedings. In particular, Foster said that the case was one "that can and should be settled if the parties are willing to act reasonably", and urged the court to order Wagshal, "as a precondition to any further proceedings in his case, to engage in a good faith attempt at mediation." He also urged Judge Levie to "consider who should bear the defendant's costs in participating" in the mediation to date.

Judge Levie then conducted a telephone conference call hearing in which he excused Foster. Wagshal's counsel voiced the claim that underlies this suit—that he thought Foster's withdrawal letter "indicates that he had certain feelings about the case. Now, I'm not familiar with the mediation process but as I understood, the mediator is not supposed to say, give his opinion as to where the merits are." On that subject, Judge Levie said, "I don't know what his opinions are and I'm not going to ask him because that's part of the confidentiality of the process." Neither Wagshal nor his counsel made any objection or motion for Judge Levie's own recusal.

Judge Levie soon after appointed another case evaluator, and Wagshal and the other parties settled the *Sheetz* case in June 1992. In September 1992, however, Wagshal sued Foster and sixteen others (whom he identified as members of Foster's law firm) in federal district court, claiming that Foster's behavior as mediator had violated his rights to due process and to a jury trial under the Fifth and Seventh Amendments, and seeking injunctive relief and damages under 42 U.S.C. § 1983. Besides the federal claims, he threw in a variety of local law theories such as defamation, invasion of privacy, and intentional infliction of emotional distress. His theory is that Foster's conduct as case evaluator forced him to settle the case against his will, resulting in a far lower recovery than if he had pursued the claim.

The district court granted the defendants' motion to dismiss with prejudice, holding that Foster, like judges, was shielded by absolute immunity. We affirm.

* * *

Foster's first line of defense against the damages claim was the assertion of quasi-judicial immunity. The immunity will block the suit if it extends to case evaluators and mediators, so long as Foster's alleged actions were taken within the scope of his duties as a case evaluator.

Courts have extended absolute immunity to a wide range of persons playing a role in the judicial process. These have included prosecutors,

Imbler v. Pachtman, 424 U.S. 409, 430, 96 S.Ct. 984, 994–95, 47 L.Ed.2d 128 (1976); law clerks, *Sindram v. Suda,* 986 F.2d 1459, 1460 (D.C.Cir.1993); probation officers, *Turner v. Barry,* 856 F.2d 1539, 1541 (D.C.Cir.1988); a court-appointed committee monitoring the unauthorized practice of law, *Simons v. Bellinger,* 643 F.2d 774, 779–82 (D.C.Cir.1980); a psychiatrist who interviewed a criminal defendant to assist a trial judge, *Schinner v. Strathmann,* 711 F.Supp. 1143 (D.D.C.1989); persons performing binding arbitration, *Austern v. Chicago Bd. Options Exch., Inc.,* 898 F.2d 882, 886 (2d Cir.1990); and a psychologist performing dispute resolution services in connection with a lawsuit over custody and visitation rights, *Howard v. Drapkin,* 222 Cal.App.3d 843, 271 Cal.Rptr. 893, 905 (Ct.App.1990). On the other hand, the Supreme Court has rejected absolute immunity for judges acting in an administrative capacity, *Forrester v. White,* 484 U.S. 219, 229, 108 S.Ct. 538, 545, 98 L.Ed.2d 555 (1988), court reporters charged with creating a verbatim transcript of trial proceedings, *Antoine v. Byers & Anderson, Inc.,* 508 U.S. 429, 113 S.Ct. 2167, 124 L.Ed.2d 391 (1993), and prosecutors in relation to legal advice they may give state police, *Burns v. Reed,* 500 U.S. 478, 111 S.Ct. 1934, 114 L.Ed.2d 547 (1991). The official claiming the immunity "bears the burden of showing that such immunity is justified for the function in question." *Antoine,* 508 U.S. at 432–33 n. 4, 113 S.Ct. at 2169–70 n. 4 (citing *Burns v. Reed,* 500 U.S. at 486, 111 S.Ct. at 1939).

We have distilled the Supreme Court's approach to quasi-judicial immunity into a consideration of three main factors: (1) whether the functions of the official in question are comparable to those of a judge; (2) whether the nature of the controversy is intense enough that future harassment or intimidation by litigants is a realistic prospect; and (3) whether the system contains safeguards which are adequate to justify dispensing with private damage suits to control unconstitutional conduct. *Simons v. Bellinger,* 643 F.2d at 778 (citing *Butz v. Economou,* 438 U.S. 478, 512, 98 S.Ct. 2894, 2913–14, 57 L.Ed.2d 895 (1978)).

In certain respects it seems plain that a case evaluator in the Superior Court's system performs judicial functions. Foster's assigned tasks included identifying factual and legal issues, scheduling discovery and motions with the parties, and coordinating settlement efforts. These obviously involve substantial discretion, a key feature of the tasks sheltered by judicial immunity and the one whose absence was fatal to the court reporter's assertion of immunity in *Antoine.* See 508 U.S. at ___, 113 S.Ct. at 2170–71. Further, viewed as mental activities, the tasks appear precisely the same as those judges perform going about the business of adjudication and case management.

Wagshal protests, however, that mediation is altogether different from authoritative adjudication, citing observations to that effect in radically dissimilar contexts. *See, e.g., General Comm. of Adjustment v.*

Missouri–Kan.–Tex. R., 320 U.S. 323, 337, 64 S.Ct. 146, 152–53, 88 L.Ed. 76 (1943) ("The concept of mediation is the antithesis of justiciability."). However true his point may be as an abstract matter, the general process of encouraging settlement is a natural, almost inevitable, concomitant of adjudication. Rule 16 of the Federal Rules of Civil Procedure, for example, institutionalizes the relation, designating as subjects for pre-trial conferences a series of issues that appear to encompass all the tasks of a case evaluator in the Superior Court system: "formulation and simplification of the issues", "the possibility of obtaining admissions of fact and of documents", "the control and scheduling of discovery", and a catch-all, "such other matters as facilitate the just, speedy, and inexpensive disposition of the action." Fed.R.Civ.P. 16(c). Wagshal points to nothing in Foster's role that a Superior Court judge might not have performed under Superior Court Rule 16(c), which substantially tracks the federal model. Although practice appears to vary widely, and some variations raise very serious issues, *See, e.g., G. Heileman Brewing Co. v. Joseph Oat Corp.,* 871 F.2d 648 (7th Cir.1989) (en banc), it is quite apparent that intensive involvement in settlement is now by no means uncommon among federal district judges. *See, e.g.,* Robert J. Keenan, *Rule 16 and Pretrial Conferences: Have We Forgotten the Most Important Ingredient?,* 63 S.Cal.L.Rev. 1449 (1990); Symposium, *The Role of the Judge in the Settlement Process,* 75 F.R.D. 203 (1976).

Wagshal does not assert that a case evaluator is performing a purely administrative task, such as the personnel decisions—demotion and discharge of a probation officer—at issue in *Forrester v. White.* Because the sort of pre-trial tasks performed by a case evaluator are so integrally related to adjudication proper, we do not think that their somewhat managerial character renders them administrative for these purposes.

Conduct of pre-trial case evaluation and mediation also seems likely to inspire efforts by disappointed litigants to recoup their losses, or at any rate harass the mediator, in a second forum. Cf. *Butz v. Economou,* 438 U.S. at 512, 98 S.Ct. at 2913 ("The loser in one forum will frequently seek another, charging the participants in the first with unconstitutional animus."). Although a mediator or case evaluator makes no final adjudication, he must often be the bearer of unpleasant news—that a claim or defense may be far weaker than the party supposed. Especially as the losing party will be blocked by judicial immunity from suing the judge, there may be great temptation to sue the messenger whose words foreshadowed the final loss. Cf. *Sindram v. Suda,* 986 F.2d at 1461 (noting that loser may turn on clerks because unable to reach the judge).

The third of the Supreme Court's criteria, the existence of adequate safeguards to control unconstitutional conduct where absolute immunity is granted, is also present. Here, Wagshal was free to seek relief from any misconduct by Foster by applying to Judge Levie. Alternatively, if he thought Foster's communications might prejudice Judge Levie, he could have sought Levie's recusal under Superior Court R.Civ.P. 63–I, Bias or Prejudice of a Judge. The avenues of relief institutionalized in the ADR program and its judicial context provide adequate safeguards.

Wagshal claims that even if mediators may be generally entitled to absolute immunity, Foster may not invoke the immunity because his action was not taken in a judicial capacity, see *Mireles v. Waco,* 502 U.S. 9, ___, 112 S.Ct. 286, 288, 116 L.Ed.2d 9 (1991) (citing *Forrester,* 484 U.S. at 227–29, 108 S.Ct. at 544–45; *Stump,* 435 U.S. at 360, 98 S.Ct. at 1106–07), and because he acted in complete absence of jurisdiction, see *id.* (citing *Stump,* 435 U.S. at 356–57, 98 S.Ct. at 1104–05; *Bradley,* 13 Wall. at 351). Neither exception applies.

Wagshal's argument that the acts for which he has sued Foster are not judicial (apart from the claim against mediators generally) rests simply on his claim that Foster's letter to Judge Levie, stating that he felt he "must recuse" himself and giving his thoughts on possible further mediation efforts and allocation of costs, breached Foster's obligations of neutrality and confidentiality. We assume such a breach for purposes of analysis. But "if judicial immunity means anything, it means that a judge 'will not be deprived of immunity because the action he took was in error . . . or was in excess of his authority.'" *Mireles,* 502 U.S. at ___, 112 S.Ct. at 288 (quoting *Stump,* 435 U.S. at 356, 98 S.Ct. at 1104–05). Accordingly "we look to the particular act's relation to a general function normally performed by a judge". *Mireles,* 502 U.S. 9–___, 112 S.Ct. at 288–89. Applying the same principle to case evaluators, we have no doubt that Foster's announcing his recusal, reporting in a general way on the past course of mediation, and making suggestions for future mediation were the sort of things that case evaluators would properly do.

Wagshal finally argues that Foster cannot be immune for the statements in his letter made after he stated that he "must recuse" himself. This is frivolous. Even if the letter alone effected a recusal (which is doubtful—Judge Levie clearly saw himself as later excusing Foster from service), the simultaneous delivery of an account of his work was the type of act a case evaluator could properly perform on the way out. In fact, we doubt very much if a modest gap in time between effective recusal and recounting of the events would take the latter out of the immunity.

Nor were Foster's actions "taken in the complete absence of all jurisdiction." Wagshal's claim to the contrary rests primarily on the theory that, although Superior Court Rule of Civil Procedure 16(j) requires parties to "attend . . . any alternative dispute resolution session ordered by the court", there is no explicit authority to *appoint* case evaluators. This contrasts, says Wagshal, with explicit District law authorizing appointment of masters and hearing commissioners. *See,* Superior Court R.Civ.P. 53(a) & (b) (masters); D.C.Code § 11–1732(a) (hearing commissioners).

Whatever merit this claim may have under District law, it does not come within a country mile of showing complete absence of jurisdiction. For such a showing, the judicial officer must "know[ ] that he lacks jurisdiction, or act[ ] despite a clearly valid statute or case law expressly depriving him of jurisdiction." *Mills v. Killebrew,* 765 F.2d 69, 71 (6th Cir.1985) (citing *Rankin v. Howard,* 633 F.2d 844, 849 (9th Cir.1980)). Similarly, in *White by Swafford v. Gerbitz,* 892 F.2d 457, 462 (6th Cir.1989), the court held that a judge enjoyed judicial immunity when, despite procedural defects in his appointment, he "possessed the office of Special City Judge and was discharging the duties of that position under color of authority." Foster was similarly discharging the duties of case evaluator under color of authority.

At no point does Wagshal develop his constitutional attacks on Foster's jurisdiction, which evidently rest on the theory that the District's use of case evaluators for mandatory but non-binding dispute resolution violates the due process clause of the Fifth Amendment and the right to jury trial guaranteed by the Seventh Amendment. We do not normally pass upon claims that a party fails to articulate intelligibly. *Int'l Brotherhood of Teamsters v. Pena,* 17 F.3d 1478, 1487 (D.C.Cir.1994).

* * *

We hold that absolute quasi-judicial immunity extends to mediators and case evaluators in the Superior Court's ADR process, and that Foster's actions were taken within the scope of his official duties. The judgment of the district court is

Affirmed.

NOTES AND QUESTIONS

1.   The idea that mediators should be immune from liability is not widely shared in the mediation community. Caroline Turner English argues, based upon a review of U.S. Supreme Court cases dealing with judicial immunity, that mediators should not have absolute quasi-judicial immunity. She proposes a compromise—qualified immunity, under which they could be held liable for acts that violate the rights of parties. Caroline Turner English, *Mediator Immunity,* 63 Geo. Wash. L. Rev. 759 (1995). Dean Michael Moffitt also believes that *Wagshal v. Foster* was wrong in extending quasi-judicial immunity to court-appointed evaluators and mediators, and believes that if any kind of immunity is appropriate, it should be a qualified one. Michael Moffitt, *Suing Mediators,* 83 B.U. L. Rev. 147, 204 (2003). He writes:

> Former mediation parties are not currently using private litigation as a means to address dissatisfaction with mediators' practices. The fact

that there have been no successful lawsuits against mediators for their mediation conduct should not be mistaken as evidence that mediators are not making mistakes during their service. Instead, the lack of post-mediation legal activity is principally a product of the extraordinary legal obstacles facing any prospective plaintiff. Some mediators enjoy immunity from suits. The difficulty of establishing liability and damages protect mediators who do not enjoy immunity. The challenge of accessing information related to mediations further complicates matters. No traditional basis of recovery is readily available to unhappy mediation consumers and, as a result, lawsuits against mediators are rare.

The uncertainty and rarity of lawsuits against mediators is, in some ways, costly. Victims of substandard mediation practices remain uncompensated for their injuries. Mediators who adopt offensive or harmful approaches to mediation may never be educated about, much less deterred from, those practices. Furthermore, the public—including prospective mediation consumers, potential regulators, and other practitioners—may never learn about the current state of mediation practice in any meaningful way.

The solution to the lack of lawsuits, however, is not a wholesale broadening of liability exposure for all mediators. Instead, appropriate liability treatment demands recognition of some of the unique aspects of mediation practice. Mediation has very few, if any, practices so universally embraced that they would be considered customary. As a result, mediators should face significant exposure only to suits alleging a breach of a duty articulated or established by something other than customary practice. This would shield mediators from excessive second-guessing of those mediation decisions that are fundamentally discretionary judgments. At the same time, shielding mediators from liability in cases in which they breach a duty articulated outside of customary practice serves no persuasive policy. A mediator who engages in egregious behavior, violates contractual or statutory obligations, or breaches separately articulated duties should enjoy no legal or de facto immunity from lawsuits. Simultaneously, courts should favor lawsuits from parties who exercised their judgment in terminating an inadequate mediation. Wise policy and respect for autonomy demand deference both to mediators' subjective judgments and to parties' decisions regarding their continued participation in mediations.

Id. at 206–07.

Do you agree with Moffitt's proposal? Would your answer depend upon any of the following factors: Whether the mediation took place as part of a court program? Was court-ordered? Whether the mediator was a volunteer or was compensated?

The National Standards for Court–Connected Mediation Programs provide:

14.0 Courts should not develop rules for mediators to whom they refer cases that are designed to protect these mediators from liability. Legislators and courts should provide the same indemnity or insurance for those mediators who volunteer their services or are employed by the court that they provide for non-judicial court employees.

NATIONAL STANDARDS FOR COURT–CONNECTED MEDIATION PROGRAMS, STANDARD 14.0, CENTER FOR DISPUTE SETTLEMENT AND THE INSTITUTE FOR JUDICIAL ADMINISTRATION (1992). These standards can be found in the online appendix on the TWEN web site for this casebook, at www.lawschool. westlaw.com.

2. It is unclear how far the belief in mediator immunity extends beyond the mediation community, however. The drafters of the Uniform Mediation Act assumed mediators would be subject to liability for professional malpractice, and ultimately rejected as merely restating the law a provision stating: "[u]nless immunity from liability is extended to mediators by common law, rules of court, or other law of this State, a contractual term purporting to disclaim a mediator's liability is void as a matter of public policy."

Similarly, the 2005 Model Standards' Note on Construction anticipate the possibility of mediator malpractice liability and specifically provides: "These Standards, unless and until adopted by a court or other regulatory authority do not have the force of law. Nonetheless, the fact that these Standards have been adopted by the respective sponsoring entities, should alert mediators to the fact that the Standards might be viewed as establishing a standard of care for mediators."

Professors Cole, McEwen, and Rogers review possible bases for mediator liability, including negligence and breach of confidentiality, and note that other commentators have suggested that a mediator might be held liable for fraud, false advertising, outrageous conduct, breach of fiduciary duty, or tortious interference with contractual relations. SARAH R. COLE, NANCY H. ROGERS & CRAIG A. MCEWEN, MEDIATION: LAW, POLICY AND PRACTICE 11:14, at 605–607 (2012–2013 Edition). Some jurisdictions have enacted immunities for mediators in specific programs. *Id.* at 8–9.

3. Could a mediator who gave an erroneous evaluation be negligent? Would it matter if the parties had their own lawyers? Can you imagine circumstances in which a party could establish causation and damages?

4. In the following opinion, the Supreme Court of Victoria, Australia recognizes the possibility of causes of action for breach of contract and tort duties of care against a mediator, on alleged facts that bear further study. As you read this opinion, pay particular attention to the behavior of the mediator and the lawyers and consider whether, in any of those roles, you might have behaved as they did, or differently.

TAPOOHI V. LEWENBERG

2003 VSC 410 (2003) Supreme Court of Victoria, Australia

[Victorian Unreported Judgments]

[This dispute between sisters Regina Tapoohi and Halina Lewenberg over the disposition of their deceased mother's estate led to a voluntary (i.e., not court-ordered) mediation. At the conclusion of the mediation the mediator dictated an agreement, which was faxed to Tapoohi in Israel, who signed it on the advice of her solicitors (who were at the mediation), had it notarized, and faxed it back. Under this agreement, Tapoohi undertook to pay Mrs Lewenberg $1.4 million and to receive certain properties in exchange. In addition, Mrs Tapoohi was to transfer her shares in EOS Holdings to Mrs Lewenberg. Subsequently Mrs Tapoohi asked the court to set aside this written agreement, essentially on the grounds that it was subject to an oral agreement "that the parties would seek taxation advice concerning the settlement" of the matters in dispute and thereafter "would negotiate in good faith the form of any settlement reached." She also brought a claim against her solicitors, alleging that, if the agreement was binding upon her, the solicitors had breached a duty of care toward her by advising her to sign the agreement and telling her it was not binding. The solicitors, in turn, asserted claims for breach of tort and contract duties against their barrister and the mediator.

The mediator asked the court to dismiss the duty-based claims and moved for summary judgment. In ruling on these motions of the mediator, the court said it had to accept the allegations in the solicitors' affidavits. According to these affidavits,]

[25] At approximately 8.00 pm the parties reached agreement in principle concerning the commercial settlement proposal, which provided that the properties would be transferred to Mrs Tapoohi in return for the payment of $1.4 million and that Mrs Tapoohi would relinquish her interest in the family companies. Mr Shiff [Tapoohi's solicitor] said that these were the only matters agreed and that many others remained outstanding. * * *

[26] Mr Shiff said in his affidavit that when agreement in principle had been reached he said to Mr Denton [his barrister] and Ms Adams [his co-solicitor] that he thought they had done enough for the day. Mr Denton agreed. Both Mr Denton and Mr Shiff said that they did not want to stay late. Mr Shiff said in his affidavit that he was hungry, tired and worn out and did not think that he could deal constructively with the many outstanding issues.

[27] Shortly thereafter, there was a discussion between Mr Golvan [the mediator] and Mr Shiff and Ms Adams. Mr Golvan stated in substance that everyone was to return to the main room so that they could get something down for the parties to sign. Mr Golvan indicated to Mr Shiff

that terms of settlement would be drawn up, which Mr Shiff understood to mean that Mr Golvan was going to reduce to writing the terms of the commercial settlement proposal that had been reached in principle. Either Mr Shiff or Ms Adams said to Mr Golvan words to the effect that it was late. In the ensuing discussion Mr Golvan said such things as:

"You have got to stay, you have got to do the terms of settlement tonight.

No, we are doing it now. We are signing up tonight as that is the way that I do it, that's how I conduct mediations.

Given the acrimony between these two sisters we must go away with something that is written. It is in the interests of all the parties to sign up tonight."

These statements were made forcefully. Both Mr Shiff and Ms Adams took them as a direction from the mediator. Mr Shiff stated that he told Mr Golvan that he was not comfortable with signing that night. Ms Adams said Mr Shiff told Mr Golvan that it had been their intention to leave the mediation at that stage.

[28] Mr Denton also indicated to Mr Golvan that he wished to leave the mediation, however, according to Mr Denton, Mr Golvan asked him to stay to "get down in writing the bones of the commercial agreement." Mr Denton stayed on as requested.

[29] As a result of Mr Golvan's statements, Mr Denton, Mr Shiff and Ms Adams joined the remaining lawyers in the conference room. Mr Shiff said in his affidavit that he "decided to defer to Golvan's advice". He said that he knew Mr Golvan was an experienced mediator and that "his firmness of position weighed heavily on me". He regarded what Mr Golvan had said "as a direction from the mediator about which, effectively, I did not have any choice". Mr Shiff also said that he relied heavily upon both Mr Golvan and Mr Denton agreeing "to proceed to reduce the agreement in principle (to the extent that there was one) to writing because of their experience in these matters". Ms Adams stated that but for Mr Golvan's insistence that terms of settlement be signed that night, she would have departed the mediation when the agreement in principle was reached regarding the transfer of the properties and the payment of $1.4 million.

[30] When he parties had reassembled, Mr Golvan said:

"We will now put together the terms of settlement and I will dictate them."

He also said that someone was needed to write down the terms and Ms Lewenberg agreed to do this. Mr Golvan then proceeded to dictate the proposed terms of settlement. Mr Shiff attempted to raise with Mr Golvan that all terms were subject to seeking taxation advice. Mr Denton and Ms

Adam confirmed this. However, Mr Golvan interrupted Mr Shiff and stated that he wished to continue to dictate the terms. Despite Mr Golvan's assertive dictation of the terms, Mr Shiff reluctantly offered limited observations regarding the terms. Mr Shiff did not accept that the legal representatives of the parties really contributed to the drafting by making alterations to the terms. According to Mr Shiff, Mr Denton and Mr Tsalanidis effectively took no active role in the drafting process. Mr Shiff also stated that Mr Golvan went into far more detail than he had expected in dictating the Terms of Settlement.

[31] Part of the Terms of Settlement included the transfer of shares in EOS Holdings from Mrs Tapoohi to Mrs Lewenberg. When Mr Golvan came to this issue in his dictating, the question of price was raised by him. Ms Lewenberg stated that the amount of consideration for the shares had not yet been addressed. Mr Shiff replied that the amount of consideration could be not be dealt with until advice on the tax implications was sought. Mr Golvan suggested that a figure of $1.00 be provided as nominal consideration for the share transfer. Mr Shiff stated that it was "all subject to review". Although no-one said that the figure of $1.00 was appropriate it was inserted in the Terms. Mr Shiff regarded the insertion of the nominal figure as an indication that there was no binding agreement between the parties, a position that he understood Mr Golvan and Ms Lewenberg to accept because he recollected stating to both of them that he needed to obtain tax advice in relation to the appropriate amount of consideration before any amount could be agreed upon.

[32] Mr Shiff said that after the Terms of Settlement had been drafted they were read "briefly" by both Mr Denton and himself and some minor changes were made. On the contrary, Mr Denton said that he left the mediation without reading or advising on the draft Terms of Settlement. According to Ms Adams, she and Mr Shiff reviewed the Terms of Settlement in private. She said that she did not read the Terms "thoroughly" on that night because she believed that "what was being agreed was only an agreement in principle and not a legally binding agreement". Mr Denton did not join in this private discussion because he had by then left the mediation. According to Mr Shiff, there was no objection to Mr Denton's departure as Mr Shiff did not believe he had to obtain any further instructions from Mrs Tapoohi in relation to a binding agreement.

[33] Ms Adams said that she faxed the Terms of Settlement to Mrs Tapoohi in Israel, on the direction of Mr Golvan. Mr Shiff and Ms Adams discussed the Terms of Settlement with Mrs Tapoohi by telephone. No further amendments were made. The Terms were returned, signed by Mrs Tapoohi.

[34] At the conclusion of the mediation, Mr Golvan provided each party with a copy of the Terms of Settlement, signed by all parties to the Settlement, including the signature of Ms Vivien Lewenberg on behalf of Mr Lewenberg. Mr Golvan then terminated the mediation conference. At this point Ms Adams had a conversation with Ms Vivien Lewenberg, who expressed her concern that her client would be "burdened with tax issues because Tapoohi was an overseas resident." In response, Ms Adams stated that Ms Lewenberg's position would be taken into account once the tax issues had been considered. This conversation took place in the same room in which the Terms of Settlement were prepared.

[35] Thus, Mr Shiff maintained that, at the mediation, he repeatedly informed Mr Golvan that Mrs Tapoohi was not willing to enter into a binding agreement as the matters required expert tax advice that the legal representatives for Mrs Tapoohi were not qualified to provide.

[36] Both Mr Shiff and Ms Adams agreed that that the Terms of Settlement did not contain the express term. Mr Shiff said that he expected that Ms Lewenberg would have recorded the requirement, indicated by Mrs Tapoohi's legal representatives, that tax advice was still to be obtained and was a condition of the Terms of Settlement. However, Mr Shiff stated that given the late hour and the length of time taken to conduct the mediation he failed to observe, when reading over the Terms of Settlement, that such a condition was not included. Mr Shiff did not realise the omission of this condition until some period of time after the mediation's conclusion. Mr Shiff accepted that he did not state to Mr Golvan that there was an express term which had to be included in the Terms of Settlement, but rather indicated to Mr Golvan repeatedly that the Terms were subject to the parties getting tax advice and that once that advice was obtained the Terms required further discussion. Ms Adams said that she did not notice the failure to include the express terms in the Terms of Settlement on the night of the mediation.

[37] According to Mr Shiff, at no time during the mediation did he contemplate that a binding agreement would be entered into. If he had thought that the Terms of Settlement would be considered a binding agreement, Mr Shiff would not have put the document to Mrs Tapoohi. He only did so in reliance on Mr Golvan's firmly expressed views.

[38] Mr Shiff stated that he was aware of Mr Golvan's reputation, when conducting mediations, of being extremely determined to get the parties to reach settlement. However, Mr Shiff said that he did not expect that this approach would result in an agreement being prepared which did not reflect what had been agreed between the respective parties.

* * *

[Tapoohi asserted that the mediator owed and breached contractual and similar common law claims to:]

"(a) exercise all the due care and skill of a senior barrister specialising in commercial litigation and related matters;

(b) exercise all the due care and skill of a senior expert mediator;

(c) reasonably protect the interests of the Parties;

(d) not act in a manner patently contrary to the interests of the Parties, or any of them;

(e) act impartially as between the Parties;

(f) carry out his instructions from the Parties by all proper means; and further or alternatively

(g) not coerce or induce the Parties into settling the Earlier Proceeding when, at the relevant time or times, there was a real and substantial risk that settlement would be contrary to the interests of the Parties, or any of them."

* * *

[In denying the mediator's motions to dismiss and for summary judgment, the court concluded]

it is not beyond argument that some at least of the breaches of the contractual and tortious duties might be made out. I consider that it is possible that a court could find that there was such a breach constituted by the imposition of undue pressure upon resistant parties, at the end of a long and tiring mediation, to execute an unconditional final agreement settling their disputes where it was apparent that they, or one of them, wanted to seek further advice upon aspects of it, or where it was apparent that the agreement was not unconditional, or where the agreement was of such complexity that it required further consideration. I emphasise that it is not for me to conclude that any of these things occurred in the present case and I do not do so. It is sufficient that I conclude, as I do, that on the evidence before me such a contention is not plainly hopeless.

* * *

[The opinion also noted that in the trial, plaintiff Tapoohi would face major causation issues.]

NOTES AND QUESTIONS

1.   Professor John Wade used the factual allegations in *Tapoohi* to describe "familiar negotiation and mediation dynamics":

The facts alleged in the case of *Tapoohi v. Lewenberg* provide a microcosm of events familiar to evaluative and other kinds of mediators, and to lawyers negotiating at the door of a court around the planet. For example:

- Big dollar disputes attract groups of lawyers to share the work and spread the professional risks.

- Ironically, often an essential person (e.g. accountant) or key piece of information (e.g. potential tax liabilities) is missing at early mediation meetings.

- Having assembled so many key people, negotiations tend to go on into the night. Usually, the costs and emotions of adjourning and "meeting again" are daunting. In this case, "night" negotiations had been arranged for the convenience of Mrs T who was in Israeli time zone.

- Mediators (and usually lawyers) make insistent speeches about the necessity of recording any agreements before "ending" the meeting.

- Nevertheless, several participants depart before the final document is signed (in this case, two people left "early").

- Drafting and amending the terms of settlement occurs when people are tired and in a hurry to go home (though no "tiredness" was alleged by anyone in this initial reported case).

- Inevitably, every written settlement overlooks certain contingencies.

- Invariably, those present have different memories of what was said. A memory-battle lurks.

- Large numbers of people present mean that there are numerous conversations occurring, especially during the focused work of drafting (e.g. para 34). Potential "side-bar" or collateral contracts can proliferate.

- All mediated conflicts require some degree of "pressure" or "risk analysis" in order to settle. Without the "pressures" of escalating legal and investigative costs, late hours, inconvenience of missed work, peer disapproval, the fear of post-settlement regrets, the door of the court, uncertain judicial behaviour, delay, adverse publicity etc., someone in the room can procrastinate and plead for "more time to think it over" indefinitely. That is, the concept of "free" consent is illusory. But when does inevitable (and desirable) decision-making pressure cross the line to become "improper"? These judgments about what is "improper" pressure vary between individuals and fact situations. What useful guidelines can emerge on what is "appropriate" pressure from lawyers, judges and mediators in the thousands of different door-of-the-court or mediated settlements which take place around the country each day?

- How much pressure, advice and risk analysis should a mediator offer? Competing answers to this question can be based upon habit, personal ethics, social utility, organisational ethics, market expectation, market reputation and legal risks for the mediator.

There is no such thing as an "adviceless mediator".

- For mediators, organising meetings with multiple people present is often like herding cats. How far is the mediator (or lawyer at the door of the court) being hired to drive the acrimonious, wavering personalities and agendas to an outcome? . . .

- When should the mediator take the lead and dictate or write the first draft, or assist by suggesting wording to be first draft, of any settlement? It is common practice in many parts of Australia, USA, Asia and New Zealand for mediators to assist with drafting. Moreover, in the majority of mediations which take place around Australia and the world, there are no lawyers or professional wordsmiths present. The multi-skilled mediator has no realistic choice but to draft or dictate the first, and often the final draft. To do otherwise would usually disenfranchise the poor and middle class from *any* dispute resolution services. It is folly to suggest that everyone can choose to dine at the Ritz. A few mediators in California dictate settlement terms for unrepresented parties themselves to write out. This appears to be a vain attempt to transfer liability for omissions or commissions from the dictator to the secretary. Nor will reversing the scribe-dictator roles absolve an experienced secretarial mediator from *allegations* or conclusions of blame for scribing "holey" settlements. Nor will exiting the room and leaving inexperienced parties to draft alone create a bright line of moral or legal righteousness for a defensive though experienced mediator.

- When a mediator makes procedural suggestions, younger lawyers and less-experienced clients are often reluctant to assertively question or oppose those suggestions.

J.H. Wade, *Liability of Mediators for Pressure, Drafting and Advice:* Tapoohi v Lewenberg, Bond Dispute Resolution News (Jan. 2004), *available at* http://www.bond.edu.au/law/centres/drc/newsletter/Vol16Jan04.doc.*

2.   Assuming the facts alleged are true, how do you assess mediator Golvan's behavior in terms of the duty of reasonable care that he owed Ms. Tapoohi? In terms of ethics? How does any possible breach of duty by Golvan relate to possible breaches of duty by the lawyers?

3.   Jeff Kichaven, a well-known mediator based in Los Angeles, has strong feelings about this:

If the court's facts as recited are true, we should feel bad for Mr. Golvan personally. He was trying to help and he thought that what he did was right.

But he deserves to be sued. He probably deserves to lose. * * *

As improper as Golvan's bullying was, he still may win this case. That's because the extent to which Golvan was unethical is exceeded

---

* Professor Wade understands that this claim against the mediator and the lawyers was subsequently settled on undisclosed terms.

only by the extent to which Tapoohi's lawyer was incompetent. How dare the lawyer abdicate his responsibilities so completely to a mediator? Didn't he realize that while he owed his client a duty of undivided loyalty, the mediator did not?

* * *

In California, as a matter of law, a client represented by counsel cannot "reasonably" or even "actually" rely on the advice of anyone else on matters within the scope of that counsel's representation * * *

Tapoohi's attorney was profoundly wrong when he allowed, or maybe even required, his client to rely on the advice of another on matters within the scope of his representation. * * *

Jeff Kichaven, *Avoidable Sins: When a Mediator Steps Beyond the Boundaries*, 22 Alternatives to High Cost Litig. 77, 89–90 (2004).

The authors of this book have learned from mediators in Australia that mediator Golvan was in high demand before this case and remained in high demand after it. What would explain that?

4. If somehow you found yourself representing a client like Ms. Tapoohi in a mediation situation such as that alleged in the Tapoohi case, what might you do to protect your client's interests? See the excerpt from Kichaven, *supra* Note 3. If you would like to imagine yourself as the lawyer representing another client in a high-pressure mediation, see Nancy A. Welsh, *The Thinning Vision of Self–Determination in Court–Connected Mediation: The Inevitable Price of Institutionalization?*, 6 Harv. Negot. L. Rev. 1, 9–12 (2001).

5. If you were selecting a mediator for a personal injury case in which you were representing the plaintiff, would you prefer to have the mediator potentially liable for negligence?

6. If you were offering your services as a mediator, would your standard form mediation agreement include a provision in which the parties agree not to hold you liable for negligence? Would courts enforce such an exculpatory clause? Liability insurance for mediation is readily available at rates much lower than for law practice.

7. If you were a judge planning to establish a court-connected mediation program, would you want the mediators to be personally liable for misconduct? Would your answer depend at all on whether the mediators were to volunteer their time or be paid?

2. PARTIES, LAWYERS, AND MEDIATION ADVOCACY

In 1998, when one of the authors was standing in the conference room of the Jerusalem Mediation Center in Israel, which was attached to a small law firm, he noticed two lounge chairs, in full reclining positions, sitting in the corner, some distance from the table. When he inquired about the purpose of this arrangement, the director replied, "That's where we put the lawyers."

This reminds us that at the dawn of the "modern mediation movement" in the U.S.—in the late 1970's and early 1980's—many mediation proponents were motivated by anti-lawyer sentiments. The fundamental idea was that mediation had the potential of freeing people from the narrowness of a traditional legal perspective and from the potentially harmful effects of excessive adversarialism that they thought typified traditional lawyers. (This perspective has been characterized as the "lawyer's standard philosophical map." Leonard L. Riskin, *Mediation and Lawyers*, 43 Ohio St. L.J. 29, 43–48 (1982), which is excerpted in Chapter I, beginning at p. 35, *supra*.) In response to such perspectives, some mediation programs have excluded lawyers or limited their roles. And in some mediation arenas—such as family and community mediation—lawyers' roles are still limited, either for these reasons, or for reasons of economy.

In the last thirty years, however, mediation has become a routine part of law practice in most parts of the U.S. By and large, lawyers have played constructive roles in these processes. Yet, there is still much debate, ambiguity, and confusion about the role of the lawyer for a party in a mediation. The materials in this Section address the roles of lawyers and clients in preparing for and participating in a mediation. For convenience, we divide the subject into five categories: Getting into Mediation, which we cover in section a); Selecting a mediator, the focus of section b); Advocacy and Problem-solving, section c); Good Faith Participation, which we introduce in section d) and elaborate in Chapter VI, *infra*; and the Consulting Lawyer's Role, section e). As you read these materials, keep in mind the tension between adversarial and problem-solving perspectives in negotiation that we discussed in Chapter III, *supra*.

a.   Getting into Mediation

Disputes get into mediation in a variety of ways. Very often, courts order cases into mediation—though in many such programs, parties have opportunities to opt out. In other cases, parties have agreed in advance to mediate disputes that arise under a contract. Sometimes the parties or their lawyers decide to mediate after a dispute has arisen. It is quite common, however, for lawyers to find themselves or their clients wanting to mediate, but facing an adversary who may be unwilling or reluctant. If you were in such a situation, how would you deal with it?

In the following excerpt, Michael Keating, a lawyer who has been mediating full time for more than 25 years, offers suggestions.

J. MICHAEL KEATING, JR., GETTING RELUCTANT PARTIES TO MEDIATE: A GUIDE FOR ADVOCATES

13 Alternatives to High Cost Litig. 9 (CPR Institute for Dispute Resolution, 1995)[*]

* * * The following guide for advocates outlines some persuasive gambits to convince disputants and their counsel to consider mediation.

NATURE OF THE PROCESS

A first group of inducements to mediate relate to the nature of the process.

Control over the substantive outcome. Because mediation is not a binding process (the parties settle their dispute only if the outcome is mutually acceptable), the disputants never have to surrender control over the result to an outsider who may not understand the nature and context of their confrontation. * * *

Parties retain control over the outcome in two senses. First, they retain for themselves the power to define the final result. In addition, they avoid the necessity of handing over to randomly-selected judges or barely-known arbitrators responsibility for crafting a resolution. Binding adversarial processes, on the other hand, deprive the parties of control in both of these senses. * * *

In many commercial disputes, retaining control over the outcome is critical. Astute business people don't want to delegate the resolution of complex and potentially expensive commercial disputes to outsiders who can be ignorant of or indifferent to the realities of business life. The more control business executives preserve over the outcome of their disputes, the more fully a company's interests are likely to be served.

Control over the process. The procedural flexibility of mediation allows parties to fashion a process that responds directly to their needs and concerns. * * *

Opposition to mediation often springs from attorneys' ignorance about its intricacies. One way to overcome that kind of reluctance is by engaging opposing counsel directly in the design of a custom-tailored process. If the other side is convinced that some legal issue needs to be thoroughly aired in the course of the mediation, include the opportunity to do so in the framework of mediation proposed. * * *

Opportunity for better solutions. * * * By shifting the focus and energy of disputants away from the purely legal aspects of their confrontation, facilitative mediation promotes a search for settlement options directly responsive to the commercial interests and concerns of the parties. Mediation promotes a full understanding of underlying

---

[*] Published by the International Institute for Conflict Prevention and Resolution and John Wiley and Sons.

business interests and a search for resolutions that best meet those interests.

NATURE OF THE DISPUTE

Another set of reasons for using mediation in particular cases relates to the nature of the dispute.

Relationship of the parties. Whenever the parties to a dispute anticipate a relationship that will outlast the particular confrontation, mediation ought to be the dispute resolution process of choice. Adversarial alternatives are too divisive and rely too exclusively on demonstrating culpability and liability. Mediation eschews the placing of blame, and concentrates instead on finding solutions that meet the parties' interests, preserve the relationship and cut further losses. * * * *Complexity of the dispute.* Some disputes are so factually dense that litigation would inevitably be prolonged and dubiously probative.* * * Another measure of complexity may be the number of parties on one or another side of a dispute. Most commercial cases involve insurers—at least for one party—and many, such as environmental cases, bring a dozen or more parties to the table. These sorts of cases often involve co-plaintiffs and co-defendants who often differ amongst themselves, as well as with their mutual opponent. When defendants' intramural efforts to fix blame on each other help make the plaintiff's case, mediation clearly makes sense. * * *

Time imperative. Disputes that involve continuing damage to business interests in the absence of quick resolution are particularly appropriate for mediation. * * * Mediation can be activated quickly and is far removed from the plodding pace of litigation, making it powerfully attractive to business adversaries.

Containing damage to reputation. In addition to the direct damage to the bottom line of business entities caught up in litigation, the adversarial struggle often seriously harms the combatants' reputations within their immediate business communities. * * *

NOTES AND QUESTIONS

Some lawyers, for example, have expressed concern about initiating discussions with clients or opposing counsel about mediation or other alternative methods of dispute resolution based on a fear that that the client will consider them less than fully committed to vigorous representation. For demonstrations of how to hold such a conversation, see *Overview of ADR*, Tape IV in the DISPUTE RESOLUTION AND LAWYERS VIDEOTAPE SERIES (West Publishing Co. 1991 (available on the casebook TWEN site at lawschool.westlaw.com).

Some anecdotal reports and research indicates that lawyers who have experienced mediation—even if they were ordered into such mediation—are more likely to recommend mediation to their clients in the future. *See* Roselle L. Wissler, *Court–Connected Mediation in General Civil Cases: What We Know from Empirical Research,* 17 Ohio St. J. on Disp. Resol. 641, 695 (2002). Wissler reached a similar conclusion as to lawyers recommending ADR. Rosselle L. Wissler, *When Does Familiarity Breed Content? A Study of the Role of Different Forms of ADR Education and Experience in Attorneys' ADR Recommendations,* 2 Pepp. Disp. Resol. J. 199 (2002). Does that argue in favor of mandatory mediation programs in courts? For a discussion of court-ordered mediation, see Chapter VI, beginning at p. 775.

Business clients have indicated that they value mediation's potential to maintain or improve relationships. David B. Lipsky, *How Corporate America Uses Conflict Management: The Evidence from a New Survey of the Fortune 1000,* Alternatives to the High Cost of Litigation 1239–142 (July/August 2012); David B. Lipsky, *How Leading Corporations Use ADR to Handle Employment Complaints,* in Nancy Vanderlip, Jay Waks, and David B. Lipsky, eds., Cutting-Edge Advances in Resolving Workplace Disputes (International Institute for Conflict Prevention and Resolution and the Scheinman Institute on Conflict Resolution (2014). The evidence that general civil mediation improves relationships, however, is mixed. *See* Dwight Golann, *Is Legal Mediation a Process of Repair—or Separation? An Empirical Study, and its Implications,* 7 Harv. Negot. L. Rev. 301, 331 (2002); Roselle L. Wissler, *The Effectiveness of Court–Connected Dispute Resolution in Civil Cases,* 22 Conflict Resol. Q. 55, 67 (2004).

One often-overlooked benefit of mediation in comparison to traditional legal negotiation is simply that the parties are more likely to be present as their dispute is discussed and resolved. The opportunity to be present increases the likelihood of participation. In addition, inclusion in mediation allows parties to experience even-handed and respectful treatment and observe both the presentation of their story and the mediator's (and possibly the other parties') consideration of what was said. As a result, parties are likely to perceive mediation as a more procedurally just process than the traditional legal negotiation that excludes them. For more on procedural justice in mediation, see Nancy A. Welsh, *Making Deals in Court–Connected Mediation: What's Justice Got To Do With It?,* 79 Wash. U. L.Q. 787 (2001).

b. Selecting a Mediator

1. Mediator Background and Approach

Who chooses the mediator, or the mediator's approach? Sometimes a court or mediation service provider will propose one or more mediators, giving the parties the opportunity to select or reject any of them. And often parties or lawyers select mediators on their own, either from a list developed by a court or service provider, or simply based on the neutral's reputation. Assuming you have a choice, here are some considerations to keep in mind. The following excerpt is based on the "old grid" of mediator orientations, which assumes that the mediator's "orientation" could be the most significant factor in determining how the mediator will behave in a mediation (an assumption that we question in elsewhere in this chapter.) This reading describes potential advantages and disadvantages of various mediator behaviors and perspectives.

LEONARD L. RISKIN, UNDERSTANDING MEDIATORS' ORIENTATIONS, STRATEGIES, AND TECHNIQUES: A GRID FOR THE PERPLEXED
1 Harv. Negot. L. Rev. 7, 41–48 (1996)

* * *

[An earlier portion of this article, which appears *supra* at p. 304, sets forth the "Computec" hypothetical, which involves a dispute that arose under a service contract between Golden State Savings and Loan and Computec, a computer services company, over Golden State's refusal to reimburse certain travel expenses submitted by Computec.]

A. *The Potential Advantages and Disadvantages of the Various Approaches to Mediation*

Assume that you represent Computec in its dispute with Golden State and that you and your counterpart have agreed (with the consent of both clients) to try mediation. Before considering the characteristics that you would like to see in the mediator and in the mediation process, you need to ask yourself two questions: first, what has blocked the success of the negotiations to date; and, second, what do you hope to achieve through mediation? You must find a mediator whose approach to mediation and other characteristics are most likely to remove obstacles to settlement or otherwise help you accomplish your goals.

To know which orientation on the grid is most appropriate, one must comprehend a great deal about the origins and nature of the dispute, the relationships among the concerned individuals and organizations (both behind and across party lines), and their fears, levels of competence, and goals. Before mediation begins, however, parties and lawyers often will not fully understand these matters; individuals are likely to have different perceptions of what is needed, possible, or desirable in the mediation. These divergent perceptions may interfere with the parties' ability to select the most appropriate form of mediation. Accordingly, and because mediators may fail to test their assumptions about the parties' needs and may thus exercise what Felstiner and Sarat have called "power by indirection," it is important for parties to understand the potential advantages and disadvantages of various points on the two continuums.

1. *The Problem–Definition Continuum*

a. *Narrow Problem–Definition.*—A narrow problem-definition can increase the chances of resolution and reduce the time needed for the mediation. The focus on a small number of issues limits the range of relevant information, thus keeping the proceeding relatively simple. In addition, a narrow focus can avoid a danger inherent in broader approaches—that personal relations or other "extraneous issues" might exacerbate the conflict and make it more difficult to settle.

On the other hand, in some cases the narrow approach can increase the chance of impasse because it allows little room for creative option-generation or other means of addressing underlying interests, which, if unsatisfied, could block agreement. Also, a narrow approach to mediation might preclude the parties from addressing other long-term mutual interests that could lead to long-lasting, mutually-beneficial arrangements.

b. *Broad Problem–Definition.*—A broad problem-definition can produce an agreement that accommodates the parties' underlying interests, as well as the interests of other affected individuals or groups. Such an agreement is substantively superior. Broadening the problem-definition also can both increase the likelihood of settlement and reduce the time necessary for the mediation; when such a process addresses the parties' needs and allows room for creativity, it reduces the likelihood of impasse. In addition, it can provide opportunities for personal change.

In some situations, however, a broad problem-definition can have the opposite effect: it can increase both the probability of an impasse and the time and expense required for mediation by focusing the parties on issues that are unnecessary to the resolution of the narrow issues and that might exacerbate conflict. In addition, broad problem-definition can make parties and lawyers uncomfortable with the process. They may fear the expression of strong emotions and doubt their own abilities to collaborate with the other side and still protect their own interests.

In the Computec case, the parties' mutual dependence and need to work together suggest the desirability of a broad problem-definition. One could also imagine, however, that it might be best simply to resolve the narrow issue, so that the disputants could get on with their work. If we change the facts slightly, we could see the possible virtue of a narrow focus. For instance, if the contract had already terminated, if the parties had no interest in future relations, and if they both believed that the matter could best be handled simply by addressing the issue of whether and how much Golden State should pay, a narrow approach might make great sense. (Of course, the danger here is that the person carrying this narrow vision of the dispute does not fully understand the situations of all concerned, and, for that reason, is unaware of the possibilities for future collaboration.)

2.   The Mediator Role Continuum

a.   The Evaluative Approach.—The evaluative mediator, by providing assessments, predictions, or direction, removes some of the decision-making burden from the parties and their lawyers. In some cases, this makes it easier for the parties to reach an agreement. Evaluations by the mediator can give a participant a better understanding of his "Best Alternative to a Negotiated Agreement" (BATNA), a feeling of vindication, or an enhanced ability to deal with his constituency. If you were Computec's lawyer, for example, and were having trouble educating your client about the weaknesses of its case, you might want a mediator willing to predict credibly what would happen in court.

Yet, in some situations an assessment, prediction, or recommendation can make it more difficult for the parties to reach agreement by impairing a party's faith in the mediator's neutrality or restricting a party's flexibility. As Arthur Chaykin of Sprint Corp. has written:

> Parties often feel [an evaluation] is what they want, until they get it. Once the "opinion" is given, the parties often feel that the mediator betrayed them. They will feel that the mediator's decision on the merits may have been influenced by perceptions of what they would be willing to swallow, not on the "merits" of the case. . . . Nevertheless, the parties should understand that once they involve a third party, and allow that "neutral" to give an opinion on the merits, that determination will almost always have a powerful impact on all further negotiations. After all, how could the "prevailing party" take much less than what the mediator recommended?[118]

Moreover, these evaluative techniques decrease the extent of the parties' participation, and thereby may lower the participants' satisfaction with both the process and the outcome. Of course, such techniques also reduce opportunities for change and growth.

In addition, if the parties or lawyers know that the mediator will evaluate, they are less likely to be candid either with their counterparts or with the mediator. When a mediator asks such parties (in private caucus, for example) to analyze the strengths and weaknesses of their own case or to describe their situation and interests, they may be disinclined to respond honestly. Thus, the prospect that the mediator will render an evaluation can interfere with the parties' coming to understand fully their own and each other's positions and interests, and thereby render the process more adversarial.

---

[118] Arthur A. Chaykin, Selecting the Right Mediator, Disp. Resol. J., Sept. 1994, at 65 n.5.

b. *The Facilitative Approach.*—On the one hand, the facilitative approach offers many advantages, particularly if the parties are capable of understanding both sides' interests or developing potential solutions. It can give them and their lawyers a greater feeling of participation and more control over the resolution of the case. They can fine-tune the problem-definition and any resulting agreement to suit their interests. The facilitative approach also offers greater potential for educating parties about their own and each other's position, interests, and situation. In this way, it can help parties improve their ability to work with others and to understand and improve themselves.

On the other hand, when participants are not sufficiently knowledgeable or capable of developing proposals or negotiating with one another, the facilitative approach holds certain risks. The participants might fail to recognize relevant issues or interests, to fully develop options, or to reach an agreement that is as "good"—by whatever standards—as they would reach with a more evaluative mediator. In addition, a poorly-conducted facilitative approach might waste a great deal of time if it does not respond to underlying interests either in the process or in the outcome.

B. *The Importance of Subject–Matter Expertise*

In selecting a mediator, one would want to consider the relative importance of "subject-matter expertise" as compared to expertise in the mediation process. "Subject-matter expertise" means substantial understanding of the legal or administrative procedures, customary practices, or technology associated with the dispute. In the Computec case, for instance, a neutral with subject-matter expertise could be familiar with the litigation of computer services contract disputes; with the structure, economics, and customary practices of the savings and loan or computer services industries; with computer technology (especially as related to financial services industries); or with all of these.

The need for subject-matter expertise typically increases in direct proportion to the parties' need for the mediator's evaluations. In addition, the kind of subject-matter expertise needed depends on the kind of evaluation or direction the parties seek. If they want a prediction about what could happen in court, they might prefer an evaluative mediator with a strong background in related litigation. If they want ideas about how to structure future business relations, perhaps the mediator should understand the relevant industries. If they want suggestions about how to allocate costs, they may need a mediator who understands the relevant technology. If they need help in sorting out interpersonal-relations problems, they would benefit from a mediator oriented toward such issues, rather than one inclined to shy away from them. If they want to propose new government regulations, they might wish to retain a mediator who understands administrative law and procedure.

In contrast, to the extent that the parties feel capable of understanding their circumstances and developing potential solutions—singly, jointly, or with assistance from outside experts—they might, if they had to choose, prefer a mediator with great skill in the mediation process, even if she lacks subject-matter expertise.

The complexity and importance of a technical issue should influence the nature and extent of the required subject-matter expertise. In almost any mediation, the neutral must at least be able quickly to acquire a minimal level of familiarity with technical matters in order to facilitate discussions or propose areas of inquiry. But to the extent that other participants have this expertise, the need for the mediator to possess it diminishes. In fact, too much subject-matter expertise could incline some mediators toward a more evaluative role, thereby interfering with the development of creative solutions.

C. *The Importance of Impartiality*

The idea that the mediator should be neutral or impartial—both in fact and in appearance—is deeply imbedded in the ethos of mediation, even though observers disagree about the meaning and achievability of the notion. The need for impartiality increases in direct proportion to the extent to which the mediator will evaluate. In other words, the greater the mediator's direct influence on the substantive outcome of the mediation, the greater the risk that one side will suffer as a result of the mediator's biases.

Imagine that you represent Computec and propose mediation to the lawyer representing Golden State. After considering the matter for a few days, she says she is ambivalent but that she would be inclined to agree to mediation if she could be satisfied with the mediator. Eventually, she proposes a neutral who is a lawyer, with substantial practice experience in both the financial services and computer industries, as well as an experienced mediator. She also tells you that the proposed mediator and she were close friends in college and that they occasionally get together for lunch or dinner. You do not know the mediator but are familiar with her fine reputation.

Your response to this proposal likely would depend in part upon your expectation as to the role the mediator would take in the process. If you wanted or expected evaluation, you might worry about this mediator's possible partiality. If you expected facilitation, this mediator might be just what you need, especially since her selection may be the only way to get the case into mediation. Of course, you would want to be certain that the proposed mediator is willing and able to commit to and carry out a facilitative process.

NOTES AND QUESTIONS

1.   Lawyers often want mediators to give their impressions of the strengths and weakness of their cases. *See* Bobbi McAdoo, *A Report to the Minnesota Supreme Court: The Impact of Rule 114 on Civil Litigation Practice in Minnesota*, 25 Hamline L. Rev. 401 (2002); Bobbi McAdoo & Art Hinshaw, *The Challenge of Institutionalizing Alternative Dispute Resolution: Attorney Perspectives on the Effect of Rule 17 on Civil Litigation in Missouri*, 67 Mo. L. Rev. 473, 530–31 (2002). Given the complex set of potential advantages and disadvantages described in the foregoing excerpt, why do you suppose this is the case?

2.   Mediations frequently produce unexpected and unforeseeable activities and insights that redound to the benefit of all the parties. But there is a danger. Suppose you assume, based on what you have read about mediation, that the mediator will not evaluate, i.e., assess the strengths or weaknesses of each side's claims or predict the outcome in court. If your assumption were valid, you might justifiably tell the mediator, in a private caucus, something about your client's underlying interests. In a negligence claim against a physician and hospital, for instance, you or your client might let the mediator know that your client really cares more about reforming hospital procedures than about the money. But if the mediator winds up evaluating—say, recommending a monetary settlement—such information might reduce the ultimate financial outcome for your client.

A contrasting situation presents a contrasting risk. The lawyer or client might assume that the mediator will evaluate; such an assumption could be based on prior experience with mediators who evaluate, or on confusion with arbitration or early neutral evaluation. One or both sides might have chosen mediation precisely because they wanted to get such an assessment in an informal atmosphere. Similarly, an individual who files a complaint in a small claims court or another informal court, and finds the matter referred to a court-connected mediation program, might expect that law will play some role in the resolution and that she will somehow be advised of how a court would likely determine the matter. Jacquelyn M. Nolan–Haley, *Court Mediation and the Search for Justice Through Law*, 74 Wash. U. L.Q. 47 (1996).

In both of these situations, the parties might be disadvantaged, or at least disappointed, by a mediator who does not provide such a service.

So, how might you control for such risks? There are two basic approaches. One is to select a mediator known to take the approach that you desire. The other is to select a mediator who is willing to provide the kind of service that the parties want or need. However, it may be difficult to know in advance what kind of mediation would be most appropriate; generally parties and lawyers learn a great deal during mediations.

How would you find out about a mediator's tendencies and practices and willingness to negotiate about procedures and about issues such as the problem-definition? First, it is generally acceptable for parties to have *ex parte* contact with mediators both before and during a mediation. (Some court-connected programs may not allow this, however.) Thus, you could contact a potential mediator and ask about his practices and ask for references. You might also contact other lawyers, mediators, or mediation trainers who are familiar with the mediator's practices. For a list of questions you might ask a mediator, see Layn R. Phillips, *Laying the Foundation for Successful Mediation: Questions Neutrals and Parties Need to Ask,* 13 Alternatives to High Cost Litig. 132 (1995). In large, complex mediations it has become commonplace for the parties to conduct extensive joint interviews with several candidates before selecting a mediator.

Assuming you have a mediator who is flexible, how would you work with the mediator to decide whether the mediator will evaluate, and if so, how and when? This raises the question of who should or can have influence over a variety of decisions in a mediation (an issue discussed in the next section). Such decisions can be difficult. For instance, what should happen if one side wants evaluation and the other does not—and the mediator tends to evaluate? *See* Joseph B. Stulberg, *Facilitative versus Evaluative Mediator Orientations: Piercing the "Grid" Lock,* 24 Fla. St. U. L. Rev. 985, 992–93 (1997) and Riskin's New New Grid article, supra.

3. A study of 645 mediations of employment discrimination claims that were conducted under the U.S. Equal Employment Opportunity Commission's mediation program concluded that participants (both claimants and respondents) were more satisfied with facilitative mediation than with evaluative mediation but that claimants got more money in evaluative mediations. E. Patrick McDermott & Ruth Obar, *"What's Going On" in Mediation: An Empirical Analysis of the Influence of the Mediator's Style on Party Satisfaction and Monetary Benefit,* 9 Harv. Negot. L. Rev. 75 (2004). Not everyone in the field would agree with the way in which McDermott and Obar determined whether the mediator's self reports showed evaluative or facilitative mediation. Assuming you take their finding seriously, if you were a lawyer representing an employee in an employment discrimination claim, would you necessarily want a mediator who would evaluate? Is evaluation inconsistent with facilitation?

4. More recently, researchers have looked at the question of mediator selection by asking a different question: What do parties want from their mediators? This looks at the question from the standpoint of the parties rather than the mediator. The following excerpt is from a study led by Professor John Lande and mediator Rachel Wohl on behalf of the American Bar Association Section of Dispute Resolution that asked this question in the context of improving mediation quality.

THE ABA SECTION OF DISPUTE RESOLUTION TASK FORCE ON IMPROVING MEDIATION QUALITY
Final Report (2008)

Introduction and Summary

* * *

Methodology

The Task Force organized a series of ten focus group discussions in nine cities across the United States and Canada: Atlanta, Chicago, Denver, Houston, Miami, New York, San Francisco, Toronto, and Washington D.C. (two meetings were held in Washington). For each set of focus groups the Task Force worked with local groups to develop an invitation list. The participants included outside counsel, in-house counsel, and non-attorneys (such as insurance industry managers, risk managers, and human resource managers) whose responsibilities include working for parties in mediation. In later focus group sessions, the Task Force also included small groups of experienced civil mediators, who were asked a slightly different set of questions. In addition to the focus group discussions, the Task Force collected more than 100 responses to questionnaires from mediation users and mediators, and conducted telephone interviews with thirteen individuals who have beenparties in mediation.

This report summarizes the data gathered from the focus groups, questionnaires, and interviewees. * * *

Findings and Observations

Focus group participants, questionnaire respondents, and parties who were interviewed consistently identified the same four issues as important to mediation quality:

- Preparation for mediation by the mediator, parties, and counsel

- Case-by-case customization of the mediation process

- "Analytical" assistance from the mediator

- "Persistence" by the mediator

While the issues identified may not surprise many, we believe they are significant because mediation users consistently identified them as areas where steps could be taken to improve mediation quality. The report will discuss in depth these factors and provide observations, analysis, recommendations, and next steps. We emphasize here, as we do throughout this report, that our conclusions relate only to the arena of private practice civil cases where parties are represented by counsel. We offer no opinion whatsoever about the meaning, if any, of these conclusions for other kinds of mediation.

* * *

II. Discussion of the Task Force of Principal Findings and Observations

A. Preparation by Mediator, Counsel, and Parties

1. Information From Focus Groups, Surveys, and Party Interviews. Many participants in our user focus groups and party interviews identified preparation by the mediator, the parties, and the parties' counsel as important for success in the mediation's outcome. Many focus group participants mentioned liking pre-mediation discussions with the mediator, in part because the discussions prompt them to prepare themselves and their clients for mediation. Actual practice among mediators and among parties and counsel varied widely. Many mediation training programs have traditionally not paid substantial attention to the content of pre-mediation discussions.

A very high percentage of the survey participants endorsed some kind of mediator preparation, although participants disagreed about the preferred method. All but one of the parties interviewed by phone heavily endorsed both significant mediator and party/counsel preparation. The one party who claimed he had not prepared for mediation indicated that he wished he had.

Many mediators in our focus groups stated that it was part of their regular practice to have pre-mediation discussions. We found, however, that some mediators participate in court programs that require the mediator not to communicate with any participant prior to an actual mediation session, and some mediators chose to follow that practice in their private mediation practice. Others, again either by program direction or on their own, communicate their desire or willingness to receive a "mediation statement." These statements may range from totally confidential, to totally non-confidential, to a mix of both. Other mediators engage in a variety of other practices, with some mediators varying their practice with the perceived needs of a particular case. Some include in their preparation, with or without a mediation statement, joint meetings or calls with all counsel (and sometimes parties), private meetings or calls with each counsel (and sometimes parties), and review and analysis of pleadings, motions, briefs, transcripts, exhibits, expert reports, and other documents.

Among respondents to our written survey, more than 96% thought pre-mediation preparation by a mediator was important, very important or essential, and less than 4% thought it only somewhat important. Every single survey participant thought preparation was important. Our survey participants were about evenly divided between preferring private, individual calls with a mediator as opposed to joint calls. Eighty-five percent (85%), however, approved of private calls at least for procedural matters, and 76% for substantive matters. Our survey participants had a very strong preference for calls without parties. (Recall, however, that the survey participants almost all were counsel to parties and not parties themselves.) * * *

* * *

Perhaps the most interesting finding about the preparation phase was that sophisticated repeat mediation users wanted to have substantive input into the mediation process itself.

Traditionally, the mediation process is controlled by the mediator and the outcome is controlled by the parties. We found, however, that in pre-mediation discussions, many users wanted to advise the mediator about process issues such as whether opening statements would be useful in a particular case, or about which issues in the case would best be handled in joint sessions and which in caucuses.

Another element of preparation concerns the goals the representatives, parties, and mediators have for the mediation. Eighty-eight percent (88%) of the users and 92% of the mediators surveyed indicated that in about half or more of their cases their goal is to settle the case. The survey respondents had the goal of minimizing the time, cost, and risk in a slightly smaller proportion of their cases (85% mediation users and 88% mediators indicated that minimizing the time, cost, and risk was a goal in about half or more of their cases). Satisfying the parties' underlying interests is also an important goal for users and mediators in about half or more of their cases (81% mediation users, 92% mediators).

* * *

3. Information and Analysis on Mediator Subject Matter Knowledge. One other aspect of mediator "preparation" warrants discussion here: mediator subject matter knowledge. To a very substantial degree, users endorsed the importance of subject matter knowledge, and in complex areas, subject matter expertise may be preferred. Those who value subject matter knowledge may be influenced in reaching their viewpoint by the understanding that a mediator may provide parties and counsel with opinions, analyses, or evaluations about certain aspects of the case or suggestions or proposals about how to settle—and that those with subject matter knowledge would be better suited to these tasks. Even in cases where users do not want the mediator to provide analytical assistance or to offer opinions, it is still often useful for mediators to have enough subject matter knowledge to understand the details and implications of the dispute, without requiring explanations from the participants during mediation sessions. This does not, however, take precedence over process expertise, which is essential for high quality mediation.

* * *

4. Information and Analysis on Preparation by Counsel and Parties.

In addition to the mediator preparation discussed above, both the participants in the user focus groups and the party interviewees emphasized the importance of preparation by the parties and their counsel. Some counsel stated that one of the benefits of pre-mediation discussions with mediators is to prompt them (the lawyers) to prepare themselves and their clients for the mediation. Participants in our party interviews were especially forceful on the need for party and counsel to be prepared, and they almost universally endorsed the benefits of pre-mediation preparation. Indeed, parties thought it important enough that some indicated that they made decisions to hire (or not hire again) lawyers on the basis of the lawyer's preparation for mediation. At least one said that he expected counsel to be as prepared for mediation as for trial.

* * *

B. Case-by-Case Customization of Mediation Process

1. Information from Focus Groups, Surveys, and Party Interviews. Customization generally occurs during the preparation phase, but the trend towards increasing customization warrants attention as a separate category. Customization is the element of preparation that involves planning a mediation process tailored to the needs of the parties and the dispute. According to focus group participants, the timing of the mediation, exchange of information before the session, and whether to have opening statements, are all elements that can be customized to each dispute. One participant in our first interview group complained that mediators too often handle their cases with a "cookie cutter" approach. Many others voiced essentially the same sentiment, and praised flexibility as a quality desirable in mediators.

In terms of timing of the mediation, the survey respondents indicated that the preferred time for mediation is generally after "critical" discovery is completed, but before full completion of discovery (81% users, 77% mediators). There was disagreement among the mediators and the users about whether mediation would be appropriate before suit is filed (36% percent of the users and 78% of the mediators in our survey sample say that in half or more cases mediation would be appropriate before the suit is filed).

* * *

C. "Analytical" Techniques Used by the Mediator

1. Information from Focus Groups, Surveys, and Party Interviews. The Task Force collected substantial amounts of data about user perceptions of mediators utilizing analytical techniques in mediation. We observed in our focus groups that many reasonably sophisticated mediation users in civil cases want mediators to provide certain services, including analytical techniques. A substantial majority of survey participants (80%) believe some analytical input by a mediator to be appropriate. Other survey questions focused more specifically on user attitudes about specific kinds of input by the mediator. The following percentages of our users surveyed rated the following characteristics important, very important or essential:

- 95%—making suggestions;
- about 70%—giving opinions;

In addition, we asked survey participants to indicate the proportion of cases in which a particular activity would be helpful. The choices included: (1) in all or almost all; (2) most; (3) about half; (4) significant minority; or (5) very few or no cases. The following percentages of users thought the listed activities would be helpful in about half or more of their cases:

- 95%—ask pointed questions that raise issues;
- 95%—give analysis of case, including strengths and weaknesses;
- 60%—make prediction about likely court results;
- 100%—suggest possible ways to resolve issues;
- 84%—recommend a specific settlement; and
- 74%—apply some pressure to accept a specific solution.

On the other hand, nearly half of the users surveyed indicated that there are times when it is not appropriate for a mediator to give an assessment of strengths and weaknesses, and nearly half also indicated that it is sometimes not appropriate to recommend a specific settlement. User reservations on these issues should give pause to mediators who routinely offer such analysis and opinions.

Users had a wide disparity of opinions on how various factors might affect their view of whether it was appropriate for a mediator to provide an assessment of strengths and weaknesses. Anywhere from 25% to 60% of users indicated that the following factors would impact that decision:

- whether assessment is explicitly requested;
- extent of mediator's knowledge and expertise;
- degree of confidence mediator expresses in assessment;

- degree of pressure mediator exerts to accept assessment;
- whether assessment is given in joint session or caucus;
- how early or late in process assessment is given;

* * *

1. Analysis of Information on Analytical Techniques. * * *

* * *

The Task Force has arrived at three principal conclusions concerning analytical techniques used by mediators. First, a substantial majority of lawyers who are repeat mediation users (again, in the arena of civil cases where parties are represented) favor use of what we have described as analytical techniques. Second, for those mediators who use analytical techniques, the fact that a substantial minority of lawyer mediation users and a higher percentage of mediation parties do not want mediator opinions or case analysis should caution mediators to consider the factors listed above before offering their analysis. Third, a different group should undertake to study and make recommendations about quality as it pertains to using these various practice techniques (see Section III. 4. below). It is important that such a group consider the issue in the context of the expectations of participants with particular attention to how mediators and participants can communicate more effectively and clearly about the kinds of analytical techniques the participants expect and the types of analytical inputs a mediator is willing to provide in alignment with mediator ethics.

The Task Force certainly does not purport to take a position on the ever-controversial issue of whether "evaluative" mediation is proper. We do recognize, however, that certain types of practice sometimes characterized in this way occur with great frequency, and that many lawyer users find it desirable, at least in the narrowly viewed field of mediation of civil cases in which parties are represented by lawyers. This conclusion finds overwhelming support in our user focus group discussions and our surveys. * * *

* * *

D. "Persistence" by Mediator

1. Information from Focus Groups, Surveys, and Party Interviews. Many of the participants in our focus groups and interviews discussed several different aspects of the issue of mediator "persistence." These include trying to keep people at the table, trying to get the case settled by exerting some "pressure," and trying to get people back to the table after a mediation session fails to settle the case. In our survey, over 98% of the users thought persistence to be an important, very important or essential quality in a mediator, and 93% identified patience in the same way. Users expressed dissatisfaction with mediators who threw in the towel when negotiations became difficult. They want mediators who are consistently engaged in the process and willing to work hard to help the parties meet their needs and settle their case.

Ninety-three percent (93%) of users thought that if a mediation session ends without agreement but has some potential to reach one, then the mediator should follow-up with each side. Participants in our interview groups generally spoke favorably of mediation follow-up in an effort to resolve a matter that was not resolved at the mediation session, and some participants criticized mediators who did not do so. Eighty-two percent (82%) of users thought "exerting some pressure" was an important trait, very important or essential for a mediator to be effective. We also asked the question in reverse: whether it is important for a mediator to "refrain from using pressure," and we got consistent responses.

2. Analysis of Mediator Persistence. It is clear that mediation users, both parties and lawyers, want mediators to be actively engaged in helping them to settle their dispute. Complaints about "potted plant" mediators were ubiquitous. Mediators need to use and refine their own intuition about when to be quiet and when to work the process. This is perhaps an area in which more mediation training could be useful.

Complaints also abounded about mediators who end mediations because the negotiations have become too difficult, either emotionally or substantively. It is precisely at these junctures that mediation users need mediators to be creative and to hold out the belief that these difficulties can be successfully overcome. Most mediation trainings cover techniques for "breaking impasses." Perhaps more advanced trainings focusing on breaking impasse role-playing could be useful.

The large percentages of buy-in for the use of "pressure" may surprise some. Apparently, some users recognize, expect and even desire this characteristic in mediations, in the context of civil cases where parties are represented. It is important to note, however, the obvious distinction between "pressure" on the one hand, and coercion and intimidation on the other. Pressure may also refer to pressuring the parties to keep on working to achieve settlement rather than pressure to accept a particular outcome. It is important to note that "refraining from applying pressure" received the same percentage of support that "applying pressure" received. This is another instance in which we caution mediators to consider their ethical obligation for self determination by the parties.

Some mediators may not be aware of the user's desire for follow-up after a mediation that fails to settle the case. It is a simple matter for mediators to contact users, after the final session, to ask how things are going and ask whether they may be of any further assistance. In addition, at the conclusion of any "failed" mediation session, the mediator and other participants should consider discussing specific follow-up to be taken by the mediator and/or by counsel or parties. Again, this may be something that trainers will want to give more emphasis. It is clear that persistence is almost uniformly important to mediation users and paying attention to this aspect of mediation practice will help to improve mediation quality.

NOTES AND QUESTIONS

1. Which of the study's findings did you find more surprising, and which did you find less surprising? Why?

2. Notice the composition of the focus groups, and the authors' caution that the results should only be considered significant for "the arena of private practice civil cases where the parties are represented by counsel" and should not be generalized to "other kinds of mediation." Recall, too, the different models of mediation discussed earlier in this chapter. What "kind[] of mediation" do you think the focus group represents? What differences you might expect in "other kinds of mediation"?

3. The study concluded by making the following recommendations. As you read them over, consider: Which do you think are helpful or unhelpful? Practical or impractical? Who should bear the responsibility and cost for implementing them?

- Create comprehensive mediation user guides including a video for parties and their attorneys.

- Consider whether to conduct research similar to the Task Force's research focused on other mediation contexts, such as family mediation, and consider how, if at all, the observations and conclusions of the Task Force concerning preparation, customization, analytical techniques, and persistence might be relevant to those other practice contexts.

- Develop recommendations for how mediation training programs can be responsive to user concerns related to preparation, customization, analytical assistance, and persistence.

- Examine how to use mediator analytical techniques in civil cases in which parties are represented by counsel, consistent with high quality mediation.

- Promote local group discussions with mediation users, similar to those held by the Task Force, conducted by state and local Bar Associations and others.

- Develop brief practical application pamphlets for mediation users (lawyers and parties) and for mediators based upon the Task Force's research efforts, experience, and expertise. The pamphlets will highlight what mediation users or mediators should consider with regard to preparation, customization, analytical assistance, and persistence in order to have high quality mediation.

2. Mediator "Presence"

Have you ever noticed that you feel different in the presence of different people? Feeling calm, excited, bored, or anxious can depend on the person with whom you are having lunch, taking a walk, or playing tennis—an experience that can extend to the professional context. Think for example of doctors who have made you feel comfortable, or uncomfortable, just by their presence and demeanor. In the following excerpt, lawyer-mediators Daniel Bowling and David Hoffman explore how a the importance of the mediator's presence can affect the mediation.

DANIEL BOWLING AND DAVID A. HOFFMAN, BRINGING PEACE INTO THE ROOM: HOW THE PERSONAL QUALITIES OF THE MEDIATOR IMPACT THE PROCESS OF CONFLICT RESOLUTION
14, 17–18, 21–24 (2003)

* * *

[A]s mediators, we have noticed that, when we are feeling at peace with ourselves and the world around us, we are better able to bring peace into the room. Moreover, doing so, in our experience, has a significant impact on the mediation process. * * * This ability arises, in our view, not so much from a particular set of words or behaviors but instead from an array of personal qualities of the mediator that create an atmosphere conducive to resolution.

* * *

. . . [T]here are certain qualities that the mediator's presence brings to the mediation process that exert a powerful influence and enhance the impact of the interventions employed by the mediator. The term presence, of course, has at least two meanings here: (1) the fact that the mediator is physically present and (2) the qualities that his or her physical presence brings into the room. It is the second meaning we are interested in as we explore how the mediator's presence influences the mediation.

* * * [M]ediators need to be aware of the feelings evoked in them by their clients and the nature of the dispute in order to make productive use of those feelings.

* * * [A]nalogies from the field of psychology point to the utility of considering mediation from a systemic perspective, one in which we shift our focus from the interests of the individual parties to the set of interactions and relationships of the parties and the mediator. On the basis of systems theory, the essential properties of an organism, or living system, are properties of the whole, which none of the parts have. They arise from the interactions and relationships among the parts. These properties are destroyed when the system is dissected, either physically or theoretically, into isolated elements. Although we can discern individual parts in any system, these parts are not isolated, and the nature of the whole is always different from the mere sum of its parts. * * * Central to this way of looking at mediation is the recognition that the mediator is not extrinsic to the conflict (any more than the therapist is wholly separate from the issues addressed in therapy).

Such an approach is, to some extent, at odds with prevailing norms in the mediation field, in which the independence (or separateness) of the mediator is viewed as professionally appropriate, perhaps even necessary, if one is to be effective. These norms are expressed in ethical codes that articulate a vision of mediation in which mediators, for the most part, have no prior connections with the parties and maintain a stance of rigorous impartiality.

The view that mediators need to maintain a certain distance from the parties may stem from the professional norms of psychotherapy, law, and other disciplines where ethical principles require the professional to avoid personal involvement that might impair the ability to render independent professional judgments.

However, the values and norms of those other professions may not be completely applicable in the context of mediation. One important difference in the professional roles is that a psychotherapist or lawyer must, in some cases, take responsibility for directing the client's actions by giving professional advice. Most codes of ethics for mediators proscribe offering professional advice. * * *

We are not suggesting abandonment of neutrality or impartiality; far from it. However, being neutral or impartial does not mean that conflict resolvers are separate from the conflict systems they are seeking to help resolve. Because mediators are inextricably involved in the conflicts they mediate, impartial may not be as accurate a description of the mediator's role as the term "omnipartial," which has been proposed by mediator Kenneth Cloke * * *.

> * * *

We are also suggesting that the mediator use his or her own self-awareness by adopting a deeply reflective practice, including the careful observation of the impact that the mediation, the conflict, and the parties have on her or him. Through such a practice, outside the mediation room, the mediator may substantially aid his or her progress in * * * mastering mediation to develop those personal qualities desirable for assisting in the resolution of conflicts. In doing so, mediators should seek to increase their awareness of how they resolve conflict in their own lives in order to lessen any unintended impact of unresolved personal conflict on the mediation process.

NOTES AND QUESTIONS

1.   What are some of the characteristics of the "peaceful quality" that Bowling and Hoffman describe? As a lawyer selecting a mediator, would you look for such a quality in a mediator? If so, how? Would you look for such a quality in the mediator for every case, or would it depend on the nature of the conflict and the participants or other factors? What factors would make it more appropriate to find a mediator with a very different kind of "presence"?

2.   Bowling and Hoffman conclude by suggesting meditation training as a way to deepen self-awareness through reflection. If mediator presence is important, as the authors suggest, and you were responsible for the selection and training of mediators for a mediation program, would you consider incorporating meditation training into your mediation training? *See* Leonard L. Riskin, *Mindfulness: Foundational Training for Dispute Resolution*, 54 J. Legal Educ. 79 (2004) (which is excerpted in Chapter VIII, beginning at p. 1000).

c.   Working With the Mediator and the Other Participants: Advocacy and Problem–Solving

Parties and their lawyers can exercise influence, even control in a mediation, in many ways. This section begins with an older article by Tom Arnold, an intellectual property lawyer and mediator, on ways in which they commonly miss opportunities to exercise influence. It is followed by a piece by Leonard Riskin that addresses the advantages and disadvantages of client participation in a judicial settlement conference, which resembles mediation in several respects. Next, Jeff Kichaven, a lawyer-mediator in Los Angeles, gives advice on what to do when a mediator tries to assert too much power.

TOM ARNOLD, 20 COMMON ERRORS IN MEDIATION ADVOCACY

13 Alternatives to High Cost Litig. 69 (CPR Institute for Dispute Resolution, 1995)*

Trial lawyers who are unaccustomed to being mediation advocates often miss important arguments. Here are 20 common errors, and ways to correct them.

Problem 1: Wrong client in the room

CEOs settle more cases than vice presidents, house counsel or other agents. Why? For one thing, they don't need to worry about criticism back at the office. Any lesser agent, even with explicit "authority," typically must please a constituency which was not a participant in the give and take of the mediation. That makes it hard to settle cases.

A client's personality also can be a factor. A "Rambo," who is aggressive, critical, unforgiving, or self-righteous doesn't tend to be conciliatory. The best peace-makers show creativity, and tolerance for the mistakes of others. Of course, it also helps to know the subject.

Problem 2: Wrong lawyer in the room

Many capable trial lawyers are so confident that they can persuade a jury of anything (after all, they've done it before), that they discount the importance of preserving relationships, as well as the exorbitant costs and emotional drain of litigation. They can smell a "win" in the court room, and so approach mediation with a measure of ambivalence.

Transaction lawyers, in contrast, tend to be better mediation counsel. At a minimum, parties should look for sensitive, flexible, understanding people who will do their homework, no matter their job experience. Good preparation makes for more and better settlements. A lawyer who won't prepare is the wrong lawyer.

Problem 3: Wrong mediator in the room

Some mediators are generous about lending their conference rooms but bring nothing to the table. Some of them determine their view of the case and urge the parties to accept that view without exploring likely win-win alternatives.

The best mediators can work within a range of styles that Leonard L. Riskin developed in a recent issue of Alternatives (September 1994 at p. 111). As Mr. Riskin described them, these styles fall along a continuum, from being totally facilitative, to offering an evaluation of the case. Ideally, mediators should fit the mediation style to the case and the parties before them, often moving from style to style as a mediation progresses.

Masters of the process can render valuable services whether or not they have substantive expertise. When do the parties need an expert? When they want an evaluative mediator, or someone who can cast meaningful lights and shadows on the merits of the case and alternative settlements.

It may not always be possible to know and evaluate a mediator and fit the choice of mediator to your case. But the wrong mediator may fail to get a settlement another mediator might have finessed.

Problem 4: Wrong case

Almost every type of case, from anti-trust or patent infringement to unfair competition and employment disputes, is a likely candidate for mediation. Occasionally, cases don't fit the mold, not because of the substance of the dispute, but because one or both parties want to set a precedent.

For example, a franchisor that needs a legal precedent construing a key clause that is found in 3,000 franchise agreements might not want to submit the case to mediation. Likewise, an infringement suit early in the life of an uncertain patent might be better resolved in court; getting the Federal Circuit stamp of validity could generate industry respect not obtainable from ADR.

Problem 5: Omitting client preparation

Lawyers should educate their clients about the process. Clients need to know the answers to the types of questions the mediator is likely to ask. At the same time, they need to understand that the other party (rather than the mediator) should be the focus of each side's presentation.

In addition, lawyers should interview clients about the client's and the adversary's "best alternative to negotiated agreement," and "worst alternative to negotiated agreement," terms coined by William Ury and Roger Fisher in their book, *Getting to Yes*. A party should accept any offer better than his perceived BATNA and reject any offer seen as worse than his perceived WATNA. So the BATNAs and WATNAs are critical frames of reference for accepting offers and for determining what offers to propose to the other parties. A weak or false understanding of either party's BATNA or WATNA obstructs settlements and begets bad settlements.

Other topics to cover with the client:

- the difference between their interests and their legal positions;
- the variety of options that might settle the case;
- the strengths and weaknesses of their case;
- objective independent standards of evaluation;
- the importance of apology and empathy.

Problem 6: Not letting a client open for herself

At least as often as not, letting the properly coached client do most, or even all, of the opening and tell the story in her own words works much better than lengthy openings by the lawyer.

Problem 7: Addressing the mediator instead of the other side

Most lawyers open the mediation with a statement directed at the mediator, comparable to opening statements to a judge or jury. Highly adversarial in tone, it overlooks the interests of the other side that gave rise to the dispute.

Why is this strategy a mistake? The "judge or jury" you should be trying to persuade in a mediation is not the mediator, but the adversary.

If you want to make the other party sympathetic to your cause, don't hurt him.

For the same reason, plenary sessions should demonstrate your client's humanity, respect, warmth, apologies and sympathy. Stay away from inflammatory issues, which are better addressed by the mediator in private caucuses with the other side.

Problem 8: Making the lawyer the center of the process

Unless the client is highly unappealing or inarticulate, the client should be the center of the process. The company representative for the other side may not have attended depositions, so is unaware of the impact your client could have on a judge or jury if the mediation fails. People pay more attention to appealing plaintiffs, so show them off.

Prepare the client to speak and be spoken to by the mediator and the adversary. He should be able to explain why he feels the way he does, why he is or is not responsible, and why any damages he *caused* are great or only peanuts. But he should also extend empathy to the other party.

Problem 9: Failure to use advocacy tools effectively

You'll want to prepare your materials for maximum persuasive impact. Exhibits, charts, and copies of relevant cases or contracts with key phrases highlighted can be valuable visual aids. A 90–second video showing key witnesses in depositions making important admissions, followed by a readable size copy of an important document with some relevant language underlined, can pack a punch.

Problem 10: Timing mistakes

Get and give critical discovery, but don't spend exorbitant time or sums in discovery and trial prep before seeking mediation.

Mediation can identify what's truly necessary discovery and avoid unnecessary discovery. One of my own war stories: With a mediation under way and both parties relying on their perception of the views of a certain vice president, I leaned over, picked up the phone, called the vice president, introduced myself as the mediator, and asked whether he could give us a deposition the following morning. "No," said he, "I've got a Board meeting at 10:00."

"How about 7:30 a.m., with a one-hour limit?" I asked. "It really is pretty important that this decision not be delayed." The parties took the deposition and settled the case before the 10:00 board meeting.

Problem 11: Failure to listen to the other side

Many lawyers and clients seem incapable of giving open-minded attention to what the other side is saying. That could cost a settlement.

Problem 12: Failure to identify perceptions and motivations

Seek first to understand, only then to be understood. Messrs. Fisher and Ury suggest you brainstorm to determine the other party's motivations and perceptions. Prepare a chart summarizing how your adversary sees the issues.*

Problem 13: Hurting, humiliating, threatening, or commanding

Don't poison the well from which you must drink to get a settlement. That means you don't hurt, humiliate or ridicule the other folks. Avoid pejoratives like "malingerer," "fraud," "cheat," "crook," or "liar." You can be strong on what your evidence will be and still be a decent human being.

All settlements are based upon trust to some degree. If you anger the other side, they won't trust you. This inhibits settlement.

The same can be said for threats, like a threat to get the other lawyer's license revoked for pursuing such a frivolous cause, or for his grossly inaccurate pleadings.

Ultimatums destroy the process, and destroy credibility. Yes, there is a time in mediation to walk out—whether or not you plan to return. But a series of ultimatums, or even one ultimatum, most often is very counterproductive.

Problem 14: The backwards step

A party who offered to pay $300,000 before the mediation, and comes to the mediation table willing to offer only $200,000, injures its own credibility and engenders bad feelings from the other side. Without some clear and dramatic reasons for the reduction in the offer, it can be hard to overcome the damage done.

The backwards step is a powerful card to play at the right time—a walk away without yet walking out. But powerful devices are also dangerous. There are few productive occasions to use this one, and they tend to come late in a mediation. A rule of thumb: unless you're an expert negotiator, don't do it.

Problem 15: Too many people

Advisors—people to whom the decision-maker must display respect and courtesy, people who feel that since they are there they must put in their two bits worth—all delay a mediation immeasurably. A caucus that with only one lawyer and vice president would take 20 minutes, with five people could take an hour and 20 minutes. What could have been a one-day mediation stretches to two or three.

---

*   See chart at the end of this excerpt.

This is one context in which I use the "one martini lunch." Once I think that everyone present understands all the issues, I will send principals who have been respectful out to negotiate alone. Most come back with an expression of oral settlement within three hours. Of course, the next step is to brush up on details they overlooked, draw up a written agreement and get it signed. But usually those finishing touches don't ruin the deal.

Problem 16: Closing too fast

A party who opens at $1 million, and moves immediately to $500,000, gives the impression of having more to give. Rightly or wrongly, the other side probably will not accept the $500,000 offer because they expect more give.

By contrast, moving from $1 million to $750,000, $600,000, $575,000, $560,000, $550,000, sends no message of yield below $500,000, and may induce a $500,000 proposal that can be accepted.

The "dance" is part of communication. Skip the dance, lose the communication, and risk losing settlement at your own figure.

Problem 17: Failure to truly close

Unless parties have strong reasons to "sleep on" their agreement, to further evaluate the deal, or to check on possibly forgotten details, it is better to get some sort of enforceable contract written and signed before the parties separate. Too often, when left to think overnight and draft tomorrow, the parties think of new ideas that delay or prevent closing.

Problem 18: Breaching a confidentiality

Sometimes parties to a mediation unthinkingly, or irresponsibly, disclose in open court information revealed confidentially in a mediation.

When information is highly sensitive, consider keeping it confidential with the mediator. Or if revealed to the adversary in a mediation where the case did not settle, consider moving before the trial begins for an order in limine to bind both sides to the confidentiality agreement.

Problem 19: Lack of patience and perseverance

The mediation "dance" takes time. Good mediation advocates have patience and perseverance.

Problem 20: Misunderstanding conflict

A dispute is a problem to be solved together, not a combat to be won.

To prepare for mediation, rehearse answers to the following questions, which the mediator is likely to ask:

- How do you feel about this dispute or about the other party?
- What do you really want in the resolution of this dispute?

- What are your expectations from a trial? Are they realistic?

- What are the weaknesses in your case?

- What law or fact in your case would you like to change?

- What scares you most?

- What would it feel like to be in your adversary's shoes?

- What specific evidence do you have to support each element of your case?

- What will the jury charge and interrogatories probably be?

- What is the probability of a verdict your way on liability?

- What is the range of damages you think a jury would return in this case if it found liability?

- What are the likely settlement structures, from among the following possibilities: Terms, dollars, injunction, services, performance, product, recision, apology, costs, attorney fees, releases.

- What constituency pressures burden the other party? Which ones burden you?

Part of preparing for mediation is understanding your adversary's perceptions and motivations, perhaps even listing them in chart form. Here is an example, taken from a recent technology dispute.

Plaintiff's Perceptions	Defendant's Perceptions
Defendant entered the business because of my sound analysis of the market, my good judgment and convictions about the technology.	I entered the business based on my own independent analysis of the market and the appropriate technology that was different from Plaintiff's.
Defendant's business plan was based upon confidential information that I provided. He never would have considered it, but for me.	I interviewed nearly 100 market participants before arriving at my market, plan, using my own judgment.
Defendant used me by pretending to be interested in doing business with me.	Plaintiff misled me with exaggerated claims that turned out to be false.
Defendant made a low-ball offer for my valuable technology. Another company paid me my asking price.	I made Plaintiff a fair offer; I later paid less for alternative technology that was better.

NOTE

If you are ordered into mediation, the terms of the order may dictate whether the lawyer or the client must or may attend, and, perhaps, the nature of the participation required. The next excerpt describes various ways in which clients can participate along with their lawyer in settlement conferences, which resemble mediation.

LEONARD L. RISKIN, THE REPRESENTED CLIENT IN A SETTLEMENT CONFERENCE: THE LESSONS OF G. HEILEMANN BREWING CO. V. JOSEPH OAT CORP.

69 Wash. U. L.Q. 1059, 1098–1106 (1991)

A. *Advantages and Disadvantages of Client Attendance in Settlement Conferences*

A client's attendance at a settlement conference can take numerous forms. The following continuum describes one aspect of such involvement:

— Client is available by telephone.

— Client waits outside the conference room.

— Client waits outside the conference room part of the time and sits in on the conference part of the time.

— Client sits in on the conference but does not speak, except perhaps to his lawyer.

— Client sits in on the conference and speaks in response to questions from his lawyer or in response to questions from the other lawyer or judge.

— Client sits in on the conference and speaks and asks questions relatively freely.

— Client and lawyer meet privately with judge.

— Client(s) meet with judge without lawyers.

— Client meets privately with other client, without lawyers.

Add to these variables differences in attorney-client, client-client, and judge-attorney relationships, in the nature of the case, in the type of negotiation conducted and the judicial host's intervention, and you have an inkling of the complexity of the idea of client involvement in a settlement conference. Still, lawyers, judges, and commentators tend to argue about the advantages and disadvantages of client involvement based largely upon unarticulated assumptions about some of these variables.

1.   "Client–Centered" Arguments

One area of debate concerns the effect of the client's participation on the client's own interests. For each potential advantage trumpeted, a corresponding risk or potential disadvantage waits to be sounded:

— The client's presence increases the likelihood that her lawyer will be well-prepared. [But: the client's presence may incline some lawyers to posture, to "show off." In addition, the client may become a great bother, interfering with the lawyer's ability to accomplish her or his work.]

— The client's presence can reduce the risk that interests of the lawyer will prevail over those of the client. For instance, a lawyer might recommend for or against a particular settlement because of the lawyer's own financial or professional needs, which could be related to excessive pressure from the judge. [But: The client's presence may remove tactical advantages. For example, often a lawyer will falsely attribute a stubbornness to the client that will give the lawyer negotiating strength. In addition, it may be strategically useful to delay consideration of an offer from the other side; this is easier to do with an absent client.]

* * *

— The client will feel he has had a chance to tell his story, in his own words, by participating in a settlement conference. [But: to the extent that such a feeling makes it easier for the client to settle, he loses a real day in court.]

— The client can learn much about the strengths and weaknesses of both sides of the case by observing the conduct of the other parties, the lawyers, and the judge; this can soften his attitudes or positions. [But: Some clients might be angered or hardened by exposure to the other side's behavior, making settlement more difficult.]

— If the client actually observes the exchange of monetary offers, he can better assess the strength of the other side's commitment to a position; he may notice things the lawyer misses. Although there may be some lawyers who can fully appreciate and convey to their client the nuances of a settlement negotiation, many are vulnerable to misreading, to oversimplifying, and to too-warmly embracing the virtues of their own side's case. [But: the client may misinterpret the events and affect the lawyer's judgment in an erroneous direction or become more difficult to "control."]

— The client's presence permits more rounds of offers and counter-offers. It permits him to act on new information and allows cooperation and momentum to build. In addition, attendance requires the client to pay attention to the case, which, in itself makes settlement more likely. [But: The client may lose his resolve because of the "crucible effect."]

— The client can clear up miscommunications about facts and interests between lawyers. [But: The client may be too emotionally involved to see the facts clearly.]

— Direct communication between clients can lead to better understanding of each other or of the events that transpired, perhaps even allow a healing of the rift between them. [But: direct communication may cause a flare-up and loss of objectivity. Parties may harden their resolve.]

— The client, because he is more familiar with his situation, may be more able to spot opportunities for problem-solving solutions, which could lead to quicker and more satisfying agreements. [But: the client may give away information about his underlying interests that could leave him vulnerable to exploitation. Moreover, the client might not be sufficiently objective. A lawyer knowledgeable about the client's situation might do a better job at developing problem-solving solutions.]

— Because the client's presence increases the likelihood of a settlement, and a settlement that will be satisfactory to the client, the client's participation will likely result in a savings of time and money for the client. [But: If some of the risks described above materialize, his presence will have caused him to lose time and money.]

— The client would not consider an order to attend a settlement conference as coercive, but rather as an opportunity to participate. [But: the client might react negatively to the coercive nature of the order and be uncooperative.]

These arguments bear two important implications. First, the assertions of both risk and benefit gain strength as the client's actual participation increases. Thus, the client who not only observes the settlement conference, but also talks, may enhance his or her opportunities for developing a problem-solving solution, while simultaneously increasing his or her risks of being exploited, of angering the opponent, or of revealing potentially damaging information. * * *

Second, all the arguments in favor of including the client presume that the client is a competent, reasonably intelligent person with good judgment who will not be pushed into making an agreement. Conversely, the arguments against including the client assume he lacks one or more of these qualities, and that the client's lawyer has them. In other words, the arguments against inclusion of clients are more consistent with Model

I perspectives: a traditional lawyer-client relationship, adversarial negotiation, and coercive intervention by the judicial host. The pro-inclusion arguments are generally consistent with the assumptions that undergird the Model II perspectives: a participatory lawyer-client relationship, problem-solving negotiation, and facilitative intervention by the judicial host.

2. *Lawyers' and Judges' Perspectives*

Although most lawyers apparently believe that the client's presence enhances the prospects for settlement, many judges and lawyers are inclined to exclude clients from active participation in settlement conferences. This inclination is anchored in large part on Model I assumptions: traditional lawyer-client relations and adversarial negotiations under a judge's heavy thumb. These assumptions gain strength from the "lawyer's standard philosophical map" and induce many lawyers and judges to credit the arguments against including clients. Thus, a lawyer may have a reflexive aversion to direct contact between clients because he fears the client may make damaging disclosure. In turn, this fear may impair the lawyer's ability to imagine opportunities for creative problem solving.

Other, more subtle factors also may incline both lawyers and judges toward excluding clients. The client's presence threatens customary hierarchical professional practices. It creates a risk, for instance, that the judge's comments could embarrass the lawyer, a risk that could restrict the judge's perception of his freedom to speak with counsel. It also appears to threaten the lawyer-client relationship. Both lawyer and judge may wish to save the time required to explain to the client what is going on. Lawyers also may resent the loss of certain negotiating techniques, such as the "good-cop/bad-cop" routine.

On the other hand, good lawyers and wise settlement judges do not approach settlement discussions woodenly. Many will recognize particular circumstances in which client involvement, even if contrary to their general predilections, is appropriate. This may occur, for example, when the lawyer encounters "client control problems" or when he recognized that unique characteristics of the case or the client make the client's presence essential.

In addition, the psychological needs of lawyers and judges may be factors in the decision to exclude clients or to suggest, directly or indirectly, that the clients not participate. Take, for example, the personal injury insurance claim mediation described in the beginning of this Article. [Omitted] The clients' presence impaired my ability as mediator to predict and control events. That made me anxious. It called into question my own professional expertise, and, I imagine, that of both of the lawyers. In the mediation of the police brutality claim, at which only professionals were present, we could define the problem simply: finding a settlement agreement acceptable to the clients. The session included only matters that we could handle, in our professional roles, better than could the clients: arguments and discussions about law and fact and predictions about how a judge or jury would behave. The emotional relationship between the parties, which resides in a sphere typically beyond the lawyer's expertise, did not seem important.

Many settlement conferences are sufficiently similar to this kind of nonjudicial mediation that lawyers and judges in those conferences often will have experiences resembling those that the lawyers and I encountered. A lawyer who embraces a Model I vision of professional-client relations may be unsettled by the participation or mere presence of a client in a settlement conference. The lawyer who wants to maintain the mystique of expertise could feel severely threatened by the presence of a client. The client might interpret his uncertainty as incompetence, or, worse, notice that he is unprepared, that the other lawyer is more clever, or that the judge seems not to respect his opinion. Similarly, some judges might feel discomfort about interfering with lawyer-client relations or the possibility of being challenged, questioned, or evaluated by a client who, not being legally trained, might behave less predictably than the lawyer. In short, the presence of clients may breed anxiety and interfere with the lawyers' and judge's feelings of competence and control. This anxiety may cause an unspoken and, perhaps, unconscious conspiracy between lawyers and judges to exclude clients from all or important parts of settlement conferences.

B.   *When Should a Judge Mandate or Otherwise Encourage a Represented Client to Attend a Settlement Conference?*

To the extent that a client's attendance at a settlement conference is likely to be useful to the client, it is more appropriate, and less likely to be an abuse of discretion, for a judicial host to compel such attendance. To the extent that the settlement conference provides for client participation (as opposed to mere attendance) the client's attendance more likely will benefit the client. Additionally, a client more likely will participate in a settlement conference that includes ... participatory lawyer-client relationships, problem-solving negotiation, and judicial interventions emphasizing facilitation rather than pressure. Conversely, the client is less likely to participate when the conference is dominated by ... traditional lawyer-client relations and adversarial bargaining under threats or pressure from the judicial host.

Many of the potential benefits of client involvement, however, are available even in such conferences. Even in a conference in which clients observe but do not speak, in which lawyers dominate, and in which the host attempts to pressure a settlement, the client may feel he benefits from observing both sides' lawyers in action. Such observation may improve his understanding of his legal position. It also may soften his impression of the other side, which could lead to righting the balance between them, to a psychological healing, and perhaps to a final settlement. In addition, the client's "presence," even in the hallway, permits more rounds of offers.

NOTES AND QUESTIONS

1.   Obviously, how one prepares for a mediation must depend on one's expectations about the process. What kind of mediation process do you suppose Tom Arnold imagined when he wrote the article about common errors in mediation advocacy?

2.   As a lawyer, how might your expectations about whether the mediator will evaluate affect how you prepare for and behave during a mediation?

3.   Many of the foregoing readings in this section have related to the issue of the extent to which a lawyer representing a client in a mediation should use adversarial as opposed to problem-solving approaches. You will recall that in Chapter III, we emphasized that an alert negotiator will be constantly aware of the relationship between adversarial and problem solving moves. In a recent, comprehensive book on mediation advocacy, Professor Harold Abramson emphasizes problem-solving, as opposed to adversarial, perspectives in mediation advocacy. HAROLD I. ABRAMSON, MEDIATION REPRESENTATION: ADVOCACY IN A PROBLEM–SOLVING PROCESS (2004). *See also* Harold Abramson, *Problem–Solving Advocacy in Mediations: A Model of Client Representation*, 10 Harv. Negot. L. Rev. 103 (2005). Other commentators on mediation advocacy have paid less attention to that perspective. *See* JOHN W. COOLEY, MEDIATION ADVOCACY (1996); ERIC GALTON, REPRESENTING CLIENTS IN MEDIATION (1994); Jean R. Sternlight, *Lawyers' Representation of Clients in Mediation: Using Economics and Psychology to Structure Advocacy in a Nonadversarial Setting*, 14 Ohio St. J. on Disp. Resol. 269 (1999).

4.   As we all know, advocacy can test the boundaries of honesty. Is a lawyer's obligation to be truthful any different in a mediation than in other processes, such as negotiation or court? As you will recall from Chapter III, Rule 4.1 prohibits a lawyer, while representing a client (which includes negotiating for a client), from making "a false statement of material fact or law to a third person" or failing "to disclose a material fact when disclosure is necessary to avoid assisting a criminal or fraudulent act by a client . . ." ABA MODEL RULES OF PROFESSIONAL RESPONSIBILITY, RULE 4.1 (2013). The Rules, however, provide a higher standard for a lawyer's communication with a tribunal. Rule 3.3(a) provides that: "[a] lawyer shall not knowingly . . . make a false statement of fact or law to a tribunal or fail to correct a false statement of material fact or law previously made to the tribunal by the lawyer." ABA Model Rules of Professional Responsibility, Rule 3.3 (2013).

Notice that this prohibition is not limited to false statements of material fact or law.

Commentators have discussed whether mediation constitutes a tribunal for these purposes. However in 2002, an amendment to the Model Rules defined tribunal for the first time. It "denotes a court, an arbitrator, in a binding arbitration proceeding or a legislative body, administrative agency or other body acting in an adjudicative capacity . . ." *Id.* Rule 1.0(m).

This language indicates that mediation is not a tribunal, and lawyers owe no duty of candor to a mediator. But the language also suggests that lawyers owe no duty of candor to the neutrals involved in other non-adjudicative court-connected processes such as early neutral evaluation, non-binding arbitration, or even summary jury trials.

Rule 3.9, though, makes the situation a bit more confusing because it applies selected portions of Rule 3.3 to *some* non-adjudicative proceedings:

A lawyer representing a client before a legislative body or administrative agency in a nonadjudicative proceeding shall disclose that the appearance is in a representative capacity and shall conform to the provisions of Rules 3.3(a) through (c), 3.4(a) through (c), and 3.5. This suggests that lawyers representing clients in agency-connected mediation owe mediators a duty of candor. Does the duty apply to lawyers representing clients in court-connected mediation? Comment 1 to Rule 3.3 provides that the duty of candor applies "when the lawyer is representing a client in an ancillary proceeding conducted pursuant to the tribunal's adjudicative authority, such as a deposition."

The combination of Rules 1.0, 3.3 and 3.9 indicate that if mediation is considered "an ancillary proceeding conducted pursuant to the . . . adjudicative authority" of a court, lawyers advocating for their clients in *court-connected* mediation or other consensual or evaluation processes will be required to correct or avoid making knowingly false statements of fact or law to the mediator unless such statements run afoul of the lesser standards of Rule 4.1. *Is* mediation ancillary to the courts' adjudicative authority?

JEFF KICHAVEN, AVOIDABLE SINS: WHEN A MEDIATOR STEPS BEYOND THE BOUNDARIES

22 Alternatives to High Cost Litig. 77, 91–92 (2004)

[In the 2003 Australian case, *Tapoohi v. Lowenberg*, 2003 VSC 410 (2003), Supreme Court of Victoria, Australia [Victorian Unreported Judgments], which is described *supra*, beginning at p. 429, lawyers who were sued for malpractice made a claim for contribution against the mediator, George Golvan, whom they accused of a variety inappropriately directive behavior, such as insisting that the lawyers stay into the evening to reduce the agreement to writing even though they wanted to leave, and even controlling some of the content of that agreement. In the following excerpt, Los Angeles lawyer-mediator Jeff Kichaven draws some lessons for lawyers from this case, about selecting and working with mediations.]

1.   Never hire a mediator who believes that "the client is the deal." This Jekyll-and-Hyde character has the capacity to turn into a monstrous bully at the drop of a hat. This bully does not owe your client the same duty of undivided loyalty that you, her lawyer, do. And his hat is likely to be dropped when you are physically and emotionally least able to protect your client from his mindless pursuit of settlement for settlement's sake.

2.   Never ask a mediator to draft a settlement agreement. That's your job, if you are there as a lawyer. If a mediator starts to do so, politely but firmly tell him to stop. Don't even ask the mediator for a form. Bring your own form. Your form is designed to protect your client's interests; the mediator's is not. Your job is to create a settlement agreement that protects your client's rights and promotes her interests. Whatever the mediator's job is, it's not the same as yours.

3.   Limit the help a mediator gives you in drafting a settlement agreement. Good mediators know how to help without crossing the line. Better mediators will use better mediation techniques, asking questions rather than making statements. If the lawyers had been drafting the settlement agreement and hit a snag on this point, Golvan might have asked, "Can we put in a price?" or "What about $1 as a price?"

Of course, these questions must be posed in a spirit of honest curiosity. The lawyers must be free to answer in any way that is consistent with the discharge of their fiduciary obligations to their clients. If the answer is, "I don't know, I have to check with the tax expert and I can't do that until tomorrow, maybe we can't sign this tonight, let's move on to the next point for now," the mediator might just have to accept that.

4.   Know when to call it a day. In some cases, it is appropriate for a mediator to be firm in encouraging—but never forcing—parties to stay until an agreement is signed. In cases where the only, or dominant, issue is "What must the defendant pay as the price of a release from the plaintiff?" the firm approach generally works well. These include, for example, most employment, personal injury, medical malpractice and other cases with consumer plaintiffs. If the mediation of such a case adjourns without a signed "deal," it generally takes all the king's horses and all the king's men to put the deal back together again, even if the adjournment is only overnight. When these plaintiffs go home for the evening and say to their significant others, "I'm about to make a deal," those others rarely say "I'm so happy for you!" Rather, they almost always say "WHAT? After what they have put you through?" and all progress is lost.

But Tapoohi is different. It's more of a business-to-business case, and its settlement involved the negotiation and documentation of a "commercial transaction." It's not good lawyering—or even common sense—to try to document most commercial transactions late at night on the back of a napkin, a legal pad, a laptop computer, or otherwise "on one foot." Neither is it necessary. In the commercial, as opposed to the consumer, context, parties generally are better able to prevent their buyer's or seller's remorse from becoming so severe that it undoes the deal.

And if the deal becomes undone? Well, as mediate.com's Jim Melamed sagely said in one of the first mediation trainings this author attended, "If the deal isn't right on Tuesday, it probably wasn't really right on Monday, either." What kind of lawyer would you be if you allow a mediator to bully you and your client into signing a deal that isn't really right? * * *

d.   Good Faith Participation

Given the range of ideas about whether and how to participate in mediation and the range of mediator practices, it is not surprising that questions have arisen about whether a party to a mediation, usually a court-ordered mediation, has an obligation to participate in "good faith," and if so, what such an obligation might mean and whether a party has met it.

Support for such a proposition is mixed. A number of commentators support establishment and enforcement of strict behavioral standards on good faith participation. *See, e.g.,* Maureen A. Weston, *Checks on Participant Conduct in Compulsory ADR: Reconciling the Tension in the Need for Good–Faith Participation, Autonomy, and Confidentiality*, 76 Ind. L. J. 591 (2001); Kimberlee K. Kovach, *Good Faith in Mediation— Requested, Recommended, or Required? A New Ethic*, 38 S. Tex. L. Rev. 575, 591–96 (1997). Others have cautioned against such rigid standards. *See, e.g, Edward F. Sherman, Court–Mandated Alternative Dispute Resolution: What Form of Participation Should be Required?*, 46 SMU L. Rev. 2079 (1993), arguing that we should see good faith as an aspiration. Professor John Lande emphasizes the importance of process in seeking to fulfill the goals of good faith requirements. John Lande, *Using Dispute System Design Methods to Promote Good–Faith Participation in Court– Connected Mediation Programs*, 50 UCLA L. Rev. 69 (2002). The issue of good faith participation in mediation is complex and important, and we cover it in detail in Chapter VI, *infra*.

e.   The Consulting Lawyer

In most of the foregoing materials in this Section C, we have assumed that lawyers were intimately involved in the decision to mediate and that they participated in the mediation. Frequently, however, that is not the case. In many mediations lawyers are involved in limited ways, or not at all. This happens most often in community mediation and in family and divorce mediation. In many such cases, as well as others, parties may have a specially-tailored relationship with a lawyer. Sometimes, for instance, a party may consult with a lawyer before, during, or after a mediation. When that happens, especially when the consultation comes *after* the mediation, some lawyers may wonder how to serve the client most appropriately. Lawyer-mediators Gary Friedman and Jack Himmelstein provide some advice in the following excerpt.

GARY FRIEDMAN & JACK HIMMELSTEIN, DEAL KILLER OR DEAL SAVER: THE CONSULTING LAWYER'S DILEMMA
Disp. Resol. Mag., Winter 1997, at 7

A client walks into your office, pulls out a document, thrusts it onto your desk and says: "I have just finished mediating a dispute that has been a source of great aggravation to me, and this is our agreement. I just want you to look this over before I sign it. What do you think?"

You glance quickly at the document, and ask your client a few questions. Your first impression is that your client has made a deal that leaves her considerably worse off than if she were to go to court or to have left the negotiation in your hands.

What are you to do? "Simple," you think to yourself: "I should just help my client recognize that she's getting screwed in this mediation. If she leaves this matter in the hands of a competent professional, someone like you who is an expert negotiator, she is much more likely to end up with a better deal."

That's the problem with mediation, you have long suspected. Would your client consider piloting an airplane without sufficient training? This is really no different, and you know it. Important decisions are being made and they require more than a cursory glance at an agreement. They require professional negotiation. That is what you as a lawyer do for a living, and you decide to give her your best legal advice: Bag the deal.

Or maybe you are a lawyer with a different attitude, have taken a mediation training and even meditated with the monks in Marin. After all, you certainly have had enough experience as a litigator to know that not all clients are satisfied with the litigation results, or even negotiation results, that you have been able to obtain for them. And, being honest with yourself, you also know that lawyers on the other side tend to see the likely result as much from what is in their clients' interests as you do from yours, and both of you can't be right at the same time.

While it is true that your client has agreed to a deal that leaves her worse off than what you think you could have gotten, she seems to be pretty satisfied, and she is the one who will have to live with the consequences. Besides, you don't like continually being cast as part of the Evil Empire, the "deal killer." You would like to support the mediation process and are ready, after gulping hard, to soft-pedal your concern about the poor result your client obtained on her own.

Tough Problem, Basic Principles

Whether you are more inclined to deal with the situation as the first lawyer did or the second, from the point of view of a mediator, you have not in either instance served your client well. The job of the consulting lawyer, as we view it, is not to yield to the temptation of either killing the deal because it is different than what you would have recommended, or blindly supporting the mediation process by rubber-stamping the result.

This dilemma is very real, and worthy of much more consideration than is possible here. Still, a few basic principles help begin pointing the way out.

First, you need to have a clear understanding about your role as a consulting lawyer. That role, as we see it, is to be a resource for your client: providing the perspective of an advocate without assuming the role of an advocate.

Second, and this is critical, you need to communicate that understanding to your client and come to a decision together about the parameters of your role. Mediation, correctly done, empowers clients. Supporting mediation as a consulting attorney can do likewise. In litigation, lawyers and clients generally take the lawyer's role for granted. In mediation, it is best that the lawyer's role be the result of explicit agreement. Rather than make assumptions about what your client wants from you, explore directly which responsibilities you can offer and which the client wants you to perform.

Third, you need to carry out those responsibilities in a manner that supports your client's responsibility in the mediation process and for the decisions that she is making. Your responsibilities can include:

- Informing your client of the applicable law, the principles underlying the law, and the likely outcomes in court. Your client is entitled to all of the knowledge of what you think would likely happen in court—and of the risks and costs associated with that strategy. But she is also entitled to your respect and support for her choice to participate in mediation, and to your assessment of how much weight to give to the legal perspective. The law is part of the picture, not the whole picture.

- Assisting your client (to the extent needed) in understanding the practical and legal consequences of what is considered in the mediation, and "reality testing" a proposed agreement to make sure that it will work over time.

- Assisting your client in developing an understanding of what is centrally important to her in the resolution of the dispute, and clarifying the priorities that need to be met for a successful outcome.

- Supporting your client in assuming the responsibility she chooses to take for participation in mediation and the decisions reached there, including advising the client about the negotiation process.

- Ensuring that the written agreement coincides with her understanding of what she thought she agreed to in the mediation.

The Already Done Deal

"So what!" You might say. "All of this would have been great if the client had come in at the start of the mediation, and I'll tell her that the next time she has a mediation. But she walked into my office with an agreement already in hand."

Certainly, it would have been better if the client had come in much earlier. Your task is harder, but it's not too late. And the same basic principles apply.

You need to explain how you see your role and the difficulty of assuming that role in a way that does not appear that you are out to upset the mediation or simply rubber-stamp it. Ascertain your client's priorities and how the proposed agreement does and does not meet them. Explain the applicable law, and respect that it is for your client to decide whether what is important to her in resolving the conflict is the same or differs from what might happen in court. In other words, make sure that the agreement captures what your client intended.

If after that, your client concludes that the agreement really does fail to meet what she intended or what she values, then explore with her how she might, with your support, bring her concerns into the mediation. That must be done with sensitivity to the other party's likely concern that your client could be seen as reneging on the agreement, with you as the deal killer cheering her on.

Your client will then have the difficult task of explaining to her counterpart that she is still willing to negotiate an agreement that serves what is important to both of them. With your help, she might be able to do it in a way that is responsible and seeks to do justice to both of them.

If they have a good mediator, he or she would have counseled them that nothing is final until it is final and this is an opportunity for assuring that they find an agreement that will work for both of them in the future. And, if you have played a part in helping that to come about, you have found a productive way to deal with the tension that you experienced in the beginning.

NOTES AND QUESTIONS

1.   Notice that Friedman and Himmelstein are distinguishing between two accepted roles of the lawyer—advisor and advocate. *See* ABA MODEL RULES OF PROFESSIONAL CONDUCT, Preamble, Rule 2.1 (2004). As a lawyer, would you be comfortable playing the limited role that Friedman and Himmelstein describe? If not, what would be the sources of your discomfort?

2.   Do you agree with this advice? Would your answer depend upon which model of the lawyer-client relationship, discussed in Chapter II, that you use?

3.   Cases are beginning to arise in which clients claim that their lawyers gave them faulty advice during mediation sessions. *See Ramboot Inc. v. Lucas,* 181 N.C. App. 729 (2007). In California, defendant-lawyers have asserted (and won) the protection of California's special evidentiary exclusion for mediation communications. *See e.g., Cassel v. Superior Court of Los Angeles County,* 244 P.3d 1080 (2011); *In re Malcolm,* 2004 Cal. App. Unpub. LEXIS 10675. We discuss California's evidentiary provisions, and the mediation privilege more generally, *infra.* You may wish to consider whether a consulting lawyer could assert either California's evidentiary exclusion or the privilege.

3. MEDIATION LITIGATION

Mediation advocates introduced mediation into the courts in order to help resolve disputes. As a sign of mediation's institutionalization, the process is now also a source of "satellite" litigation. Professors James Coben and Peter Thompson analyzed 1,223 state and federal court mediation decisions available on the Westlaw databases "allstates" and "allfeds" for the years 1999 through 2003. They published their findings in James R. Coben & Peter N. Thompson, *Disputing Irony: A Systematic Look at Litigation About Mediation,* 11 Harv. Negot. L. Rev. 43 (2006). In the following excerpt, Professors Coben and Thompson summarize those findings and also report on more recent years.

JAMES R. COBEN AND PETER N. THOMPSON, MEDIATION LITIGATION TRENDS: 1999–2007

1 World Arbitration & Mediation Rev. 395, 395–97, 399, 401–05, 407–09, 411–14 (2007)

* * *

We reached the following conclusions based on the 1999–2003 data:

- Litigation involving mediation issues increased at a rapid rate from 172 opinions in 1999 to 335 in 2003, a ninety-five percent increase.

- Although there was litigation involving mediation throughout the country, most of the litigation in this five-year period took place in a few states with Texas (178 state and federal opinions), California (134 state and federal opinions), and Florida (112 state and federal opinions) leading the way.

- The subject matter context for disputing about mediation was diverse, including:

  - Commercial or contract (373 opinions)

  - Family law (264 opinions)

  - Employment (153 opinions)

  - Personal injury (153 opinions)

  - Malpractice (41 opinions)

  - Estate/probate (34 opinions)

  - Tax/bankruptcy (23 opinions)

  - IDEA (18 opinions)

  - Miscellaneous (167 opinions)

- Equally diverse was the nature of the disputed mediation issues:

  - Enforcement of mediated settlements (569 opinions)

  - Duty to mediate (279 opinions)

  - Fees (243 opinions)

  - Confidentiality (152 opinions)

  - Condition precedent (123 opinions)

  - Sanctions (117 opinions)

  - Ethics/malpractice (99 opinions)

  - Arbitration-mediation (88 opinions)

  - Miscellaneous (100 opinions)

- Courts frequently consider evidence of what occurs in mediation; indeed, in over three hundred opinions, courts addressed mediation communications without any mention of privilege or mediation confidentiality. Mediators offered testimony in sixty-seven cases, with objections raised only twenty-two times, and the evidence was precluded in only nine cases.

- Nearly half of all court opinions about mediation addressed enforcement of settlement agreements. Traditional contract defenses, although frequently raised in enforcement cases, were rarely successful.

- Very few opinions raised the issue of mediator misconduct; in fact, only seventeen times in five years did parties assert a contract defense based on mediator conduct.

- Courts are inclined to order mediation on their own initiative, and will generally enforce a pre-existing obligation to participate in mediation, whether the obligation was judicially created, mandated by statute or stipulated in the parties' pre-dispute contract.

- Numerous opinions confirm taxation of mediation costs despite the lack of clear statutory or rule authority to do so.

- Opinions about sanctions more than doubled over the five-year period (from thirteen in 1999 to twenty-nine opinions in 2003); courts awarded sanctions in forty-five percent of the cases in which they were sought.

- Disputes about the linkage of mediation and arbitration resulted in courts rendering decisions in eighty-eight opinions during the five-year period covered by the database. Most opinions fell into one of three categories: conflict of interest/disclosure disputes; disputes about the enforcement of pre-dispute mediation/arbitration clauses; and waiver of the right to arbitrate through mediation participation.

- Mediation requests or participation pose complex procedural questions in litigation, ranging from tolling of statutes of limitation, to extension of time for discovery, to exhaustion of administrative remedies.

- Acts or omissions in mediation are increasingly seen as the basis for independent claims, especially in employment disputes where employers' conduct in mediation is, with increasing frequency, invoked as proof of a hostile work environment or retaliation.

* * *

[In a detailed analysis of 966 opinions from 2004–2005, supplemented by more anecdotal review of 2006 cases, the authors generally report continuation of these trends, but they also note some exceptions and further developments, including the following:]

A Recent Increase in Federal Opinions

To a large extent, the increased litigation on mediation issues in 2004–2005 took place in the federal courts. * * * While litigation was up in all categories, federal employment opinions nearly quadrupled from twenty in 2003 to seventy-seven in 2005. Likewise, the number of contract/commercial cases also jumped considerably, from thirty-four in 2003 to seventy-eight in 2005, a 129 percent increase. Several federal jurisdictions that had no reported mediation opinions from 1999–2003 had multiple opinions in 2004–2005.

* * *

The Walls of the Mediation Room Remain Porous

When deciding issues relating to mediations, judges frequently consider what went on or what was said during the mediation, usually without any reference to confidentiality. There may, however, be an emerging trend toward reinvigorating the concern for confidentiality. In 2004–2005, mediators supplied testimony in six percent of the cases, quite similar to the 1999–2003 data, but reliance on other types of mediation evidence (or written mediation communications supplied by the parties) dropped from thirty-three percent in 1999–2003 to twenty-eight percent in the past two-year period.

* * *

Further, in 1999–2003, the claim of privilege was upheld in forty-three percent of the cases in which privilege was raised; but in the recent two years, privilege claims were upheld in fifty-seven percent of the cases in which they were raised.

* * *

Courts Remain Pre-disposed to Enforce Agreements

Nearly half (47%) of the opinions in the 1999–2003 database were enforcement cases where parties were attempting to enforce an alleged agreement arrived at during mediation. While the total number of enforcement cases increased from 140 in 2003 to 194 in 2005, only thirty-nine percent of the 2004–05 cases involved enforcement issues. Again, parties had great success in getting court assistance to enforce an agreement reached during mediation. In 2004–05, the courts enforced a settlement agreement in sixty-two percent of the cases (exactly the same rate as for 1999–2003) and refused to enforce an agreement in twenty percent of the cases (compared to sixteen percent in 1999–2003).

* * *

Contract formation issues were the most common defenses litigated. Claims of no meeting of the minds were raised in forty-three (11%) of the enforcement opinions, "agreement to agree" issues in twenty-two opinions (6%), and various claims of lack of formality including no writing, no signature, and lack of statutorily required language were raised in forty-one (11%) of the enforcement opinions. Many (70) of the disputes simply involved issues of interpretation of the mediation agreement.

* * *

Traditional contract defenses of fraud (26 opinions), duress (20 opinions), or mistake (23 opinions) were raised less frequently. Rarely were any of the defenses successful. The 2004–2005 data is consistent with our previous findings that if there is widespread overreaching and unfairness in the thousands of mediations throughout the country, it is not showing up in great numbers in the reported cases. Parties have some success defending enforcement claims based on contract interpretation issues, or by convincing the court that no enforceable agreement was reached. Rarely are parties successful in defending an enforcement case based on the traditional contract defenses of fraud, mistake, duress, or undue influence.

In only ninety-three of the 569, or sixteen percent of the enforcement opinions, did the court refuse to enforce the agreement from 1999–2003. In the 2004–2005 enforcement opinions, the courts refused to enforce the agreement in seventy-eight of the 384 cases, or in twenty percent of the cases.

* * *

Robust Growth in the Number of "Miscellaneous" Opinions

The most significant growth in any single category of mediation dispute occurred with those opinions we labeled "miscellaneous." * * * In 2004–2005, these "miscellaneous" disputes constituted fourteen percent of the database, increasing from just thirty-six opinions in 2003, to sixty opinions in 2004, to eighty-one opinions in 2005. Such steady growth is clear evidence of mediation's institutionalization. As the process is more frequently utilized, courts grapple with myriad procedural intersections between mediation and the traditional litigation process. Moreover, despite confidentiality limitations, parties' behavior and bargaining patterns in mediation influence court perception and decision on the merits of disputes.

* * *

The Obligation to Mediate

* * * Courts continue to favor mediation on efficiency grounds and are willing to exercise power to compel the attendance of necessary parties. And, courts routinely enforce contractual or statutory obligations to mediate as a condition precedent to litigation. Two categories of exceptions to this general principle, however, have emerged: parties will be foreclosed from enforcing a duty to mediate when they are responsible for previously undermining the mediation effort or where mediation would be moot.

* * *

THE 2006 CASES AND THE FUTURE

* * *

The steady increase in federal court opinions continues. In 2006, federal opinions represented forty-eight percent of all cases in the database (compared to the 1999–2003 average of 32%). [A] considerable amount of litigation seems to focus on mediation expenses—ranging from such issues as how many lawyers does it take to mediate, to who is a prevailing party entitled to statutory attorneys' fees, to penalties for breach of confidentiality.

* * *

There was also a noticeable increase in ethics/malpractice opinions. As before, it was the work of the lawyers, not the mediators, that was the focus of this litigation. That said, several significant challenges to mediator conduct were made with contradictory conclusions on the application of immunity.

* * *

What will 2007 show? It is still too early in the year for systematic conclusions, although gross hits in the Westlaw database January–April, suggest we are on pace for annual growth of at least ten percent.

NOTES AND QUESTIONS

1. Many students are attracted to mediation and ADR courses as alternatives to traditional litigation and legal education. After reading this excerpt, how "alternative" does mediation appear to be? Which law school courses came to mind as you read about the issues that are being litigated as a result of mediation? Is mediation, like discovery before it, being captured by an adversarial mindset and system?

2.   A court may enforce the mediation provision in a contract even when the contract itself has been terminated. *See e.g., The Auchter Company v. Zagloul,* 949 So. 2d 1189 (Fla. App. 2007) (provision that provided for mediation and then arbitration survived termination of contract and thus parties were ordered to mediation).

3.   As noted by Professors Coben and Thompson, parties moving to set aside or avoid enforcement of mediated settlement agreements often allege problems in the formation of contracts as well as the defenses of duress, undue influence, fraudulent inducement and mutual mistake. In the overwhelming majority of cases, courts choose to enforce mediated settlement agreements. *See e.g., In re Marriage of Kieturakis,* 41 Cal. Rptr. 3d 119 (App. 2006) (affirming enforcement of marital settlement agreement incorporated into judgment and decree in the face of claims of fraud, undue influence, duress and non-disclosure); *Chantey Music Publishing, Inc. v. Malaco, Inc.,* 915 So. 2d 1052 (Miss. 2005) (court found defenses of undue influence and meeting of the minds to be without merit due to lack of evidentiary support and principle that parties are responsible for reading the agreements they execute). Indeed, mediation settlement agreements might be classified as "super-contracts." *See generally*, Nancy A. Welsh, *The Thinning Vision of Self–Determination in Court–Annexed Mediation: The Inevitable Price of Institutionalization?*, 6 Harv. Negot. L. Rev. 1, 59–78 (2001) (describing various contract defenses applicable to both mediation and judicial settlement conferences).

On occasion, however, judges or juries refuse to enforce mediated settlement agreements. *See e.g., Lehr v. Afflito,* 382 N.J. Super. 376 (2006) (finding that trial court's determination that parties had reached a binding settlement agreement "was simply not supported by substantial, credible evidence"); *Foreman v. Foreman,* 266 Mich. App. 132 (2005) (affirming jury award finding that husband fraudulently induced wife to enter into property settlement).

4.   Some state statutes and court rules impose additional or heightened requirements on mediated agreements. *See e.g., Williams v. Kansas City Title,* 314 S.W.3d 868 (2010) (pursuant to court rule, agreements arising out of court-ordered mediation must be in writing in order to be enforceable); *Haghighi v. Russian American Broadcasting Co. Inc,* 577 N.W.2d 927 (Minn. 1998) (pursuant to state statute, particular language regarding binding nature of mediation settlement agreement must be included in writing for mediated agreement to be enforceable). Recall the *Gatto* case, *supra*, in Chapter II, which involved a mediation and subsequent agreement. In a footnote, the court expressed a preference for all correspondence regarding the settlement to be in writing.

4.   CONFIDENTIALITY

a.   A Cornerstone, and a Challenge

Confidentiality is often said to be a cornerstone of mediation, for reasons that highlight the uniqueness of mediation as a dispute resolution process. Recall that judges, arbitrators, and other adjudicators preside over the receipt of evidence that the parties present to them, and ultimately make decisions on those cases. Mediators, however, work actively with the parties to help identify, understand, and assess the various underlying interests and concerns that are animating the dispute so that the parties can decide how to resolve the dispute themselves. For this reason, parties in adjudication are likely to guard sensitive information zealously, but in mediation they are encouraged to be more candid about underlying interests, concerns, and other information that is relevant to the dispute.

This candor is often necessary in mediation to get beyond the parties' positions, but can bring to the surface important information that the parties may not want to air publicly. For example, a divorce mediation may uncover such raw emotions as anger and resentment, perhaps even involving third parties, or inappropriate conduct that may be necessary to address in the mediation, but which could be highly prejudicial if the mediation fails and the divorce is litigated. Similarly, businesses engaged in a commercial mediation may need to discuss trade secrets or other proprietary information, the wider dissemination of which could threaten their interests, in order to resolve their immediate dispute. And a participant in a mediation may want or need to disclose information in the mediation that he simply doesn't want to be made public for fear of stigmatization or reputational harm, such as a mental health condition or certain lifestyle issues.

For these reasons and more, candor can be challenging, requiring skill by the mediator and confidence, courage, and commitment by the parties—especially if they are to address underlying interests and achieve resolution along the cognitive and emotional dimensions of the dispute as well as the behavioral dimension. To encourage such candor, Standard V of the Model Standards of Conduct for Mediators, discussed *supra*, provides: "A mediator shall maintain the confidentiality of all information obtained by the mediator in mediation, unless otherwise agreed to by the parties or required by applicable law." In general, mediators also promise confidentiality in agreements to mediate. The parties also may be bound by the obligation of confidentiality, pursuant to court rule, or by their agreement not to disclose mediation discussions to others outside of the room. Finally, courts' rules often provide for confidentiality.

Actually achieving such confidentiality is difficult, however. As a practical matter, mediation confidentiality is in fundamental tension with some basic human instincts in dealing with conflict. As we discussed in Chapter I, *supra*, a dispute that has been formalized to the point of being mediated has been percolating for some time, building its own energy as well as generating collateral effects. Many people have a felt need to discuss the resolution of the dispute with family members, friends, co-workers, or others who may have been consulted or drawn into the dispute along the way. This can be a salutary development. It can allow catharsis for the parties involved in conflict; these trusted third parties also may play the role of counselor or conflict coach, using some of the skills discussed *supra* in Chapter II. Yet, these sorts of disclosures are at odds with the assurance of confidentiality that may be necessary to facilitate the mediation.

More significantly for lawyers, confidentiality in mediation also implicates in a very direct way the often uneasy relationship between mediation and the law. Some participants in the mediation process like to think of mediation as removed from the law, and in some important respects it is. However, as we have seen throughout this book, the law is also relevant to ADR generally, and mediation in particular. A mediation may produce a mediated settlement agreement that is a contract, and that may require judicial enforcement. If a mediation does not result in settlement, the dispute may ultimately require resolution in court.

It is at these points that the tension between public law and private mediation can become most acute, because the integrity of the judicial process depends upon the admission of all relevant evidence—evidence that could include statements made during the mediation. We saw a similar tension when we examined Rule 408, which protects certain settlement-related statements and conduct from admission at trial. The complexity of this tension is compounded, however, by the variety of types and contexts of mediation, as well as the recognition that different mediation participants—parties, mediators, support persons, experts and judges—have different and sometimes competing interests with respect to disclosures of mediation communications.

Some of these tensions are illustrated in *Olam v. Congress Mortgage Co.* The narrow issue before the federal district court was whether a mediator could be compelled to testify about what went on in a mediation, but the case also introduces us to many of the issues that attend to mediation confidentiality.

OLAM V. CONGRESS MORTGAGE CO.

United States District Court, N.D. California, 1999
68 F.Supp.2d 1110

BRAZIL, U.S. MAGISTRATE JUDGE.

[In 1992, Donna Olam applied for and received a loan from Congress Mortgage in the amount of $187,000, which was secured by two single-family homes located in San Francisco. Ms. Olam later said that she never read the 1992 loan documentation, and simply signed where Congress Mortgage's agent told her to sign. She also said she could not afford the monthly payments on the 1992 loan, and when she eventually defaulted, Congress Mortgage began foreclosure proceedings on the properties. After several different follow-up agreements between the parties, and changes of counsel by Mrs. Olam, the matter proceeded to litigation before Judge Brazil.

* * *

Pursuant to a local court rule, the matter was referred to mediation to be conducted by an accomplished mediator who was also the court's ADR program counsel, Howard Herman. The mediation began on September 9, 1998, and lasted more than 12 hours, ending at approximately 1 a.m. with a memorandum of understanding between the parties that was to be later memorialized into a formal settlement agreement. That formal settlement agreement never materialized, however, and several months after the mediation, Congress Mortgage moved to enforce the original Memorandum of Understanding (MOU).

Olam opposed the motion, alleging, *inter alia*, that the MOU was unconscionable and that she was incapable—intellectually, emotionally, and physically—of giving legally viable consent. In particular, Olam, 65 years old at the time of the mediation and allegedly suffering a variety of ailments, claimed she didn't understand the mediation process, and didn't actively participate in the mediation. She further claimed she was pressured into signing the MOU, and that her physical and emotional distress rendered her unduly susceptible to this pressure. As a result, she says, she signed the MOU against her will and without reading and/or understanding its terms.]

* * *

After receiving additional papers from the parties addressing these matters, the court held another status conference on July 21, 1999. At that time counsel for plaintiff confirmed that plaintiff agreed to waive any attorney-client privilege that would attach between her and her former counsel, Phyllis Voisenat. Plaintiff also waived any "mediation privilege" that might attach to any and all communications made during the mediation. Defendants agreed to a limited waiver of their mediation privileges—so that testimony could be taken about both the mediator's and the defendants' interaction with plaintiff and her attorney during the mediation.

As we explain below, it is not at all clear that the waivers by the parties were sufficient to make it lawful to compel testimony from the mediator. * * *

PERTINENT CALIFORNIA PRIVILEGE LAW*

The California legislature has crafted two sets of statutory provisions that must be addressed by courts considering whether they may use in a subsequent civil proceeding any evidence about what occurred or was said during a mediation.

Section 703.5 of the California Evidence Code states, in pertinent part: "No person presiding at any judicial or quasi-judicial proceeding, and no arbitrator or mediator, shall be competent to testify, in any subsequent civil proceeding, as to any statement, conduct, decision, or ruling, occurring at or in conjunction with the prior proceeding, except as to a statement or conduct that could [give rise to contempt, constitute a crime, trigger investigation by the State Bar or the Commission on Judicial Performance, or give rise to disqualification proceedings."

We note, before proceeding, that by its express terms § 703.5 applies (as pertinent here) only to statements or decisions made, or conduct occurring, in connection with a mediation. Read literally, this statute would not apply to perceptions of participants' appearance, demeanor, or physical condition during a mediation. We also note, however, that compelling mediators to testify or otherwise offer evidence about *anything* that occurred or was perceived during a mediation threatens confidentiality expectations of the participants and imposes burdens on mediators—and that such threats and burdens tend, at least in some measure, to undermine interests that the California legislature likely sought to protect when it enacted this statute. In construing and applying this statute, we endeavor to honor the purposes that drive it.

The other directly pertinent provision from the California Evidence Code is § 1119. It states, in pertinent part: "Except as otherwise provided in this chapter: (a) No evidence of anything said or any admission made . . . in the course of, or pursuant to, a mediation . . . is admissible or subject to discovery, and disclosure of the evidence shall not be compelled, in any . . . noncriminal proceeding . . . (b) No writing . . . prepared in the

---

* Editor's Note: While the opinion refers to California "privilege law," the term is used in the generic sense of an evidentiary exclusion. California Ev. Code Section 703.5 is a provision making mediators incompetent to testify about the mediation, while California's mediation confidentiality statute, California Ev. Code Section 1119. is a categorical exclusion, rather than a privilege in a technical sense. The distinction between these approaches is important covered in greater depth *infra*.

course of, or pursuant to, a mediation . . . is admissible or subject to discovery, and disclosure of the writing shall not be compelled in any, . . . noncriminal proceeding . . . (c) All communications . . . by and between participants in the course of a mediation . . . shall remain confidential."

* * *

In the case at bar, the mediator (Mr. Herman) was and is an employee of the federal court (a "staff neutral"). He hosted the mediation at the behest of the court and under this court's ADR rules. These facts are not sufficient to justify ordering him to testify about what occurred during the mediation—even when the parties have waived their mediation privilege and want the mediator to testify. Mr. Herman is a member of the California bar—and no doubt feels bound to honor the directives of California law. He also is a professional in mediation—and feels a moral obligation to preserve the essential integrity of the mediation process—an integrity to which he believes the promise of confidentiality is fundamental.

Out of respect for these feelings, the court chose not to put Mr. Herman in an awkward position where he might have felt he had to choose between being a loyal employee of the court, on the one hand, and, on the other, asserting the mediator's privilege under California law. Instead, the court announced that it would proceed on the assumption that Mr. Herman was respectfully and appropriately asserting the mediator's privilege and was formally objecting to being called to testify about anything said or done during the mediation.

* * *

We turn to the issue of whether, under California law, we should compel the mediator to testify—despite the statutory prohibitions set forth in sections 703.5 and 1119 of the Evidence Code. The most important opinion by a California court in this arena is *Rinaker v. Superior Court,* 62 Cal. App. 4th 155 (Third District 1998). In that case the Court of Appeal held that there may be circumstances in which a trial court, over vigorous objection by a party and by the mediator, could compel testimony from the mediator in a juvenile delinquency proceeding (deemed a "civil" matter under California law). * * *

In essence, the *Rinaker* court instructs California trial judges to conduct a two-stage balancing analysis. The goal of the first stage balancing is to determine whether to compel the mediator to appear at an *in camera* proceeding to determine precisely what her testimony would be. * * *

* * * In [the] second stage the court is to weigh and comparatively assess (1) the importance of the values and interests that would be harmed if the mediator was compelled to testify (perhaps subject to a sealing or protective order, if appropriate), (2) the magnitude of the harm that compelling the testimony would cause to those values and interests, (3) the importance of the rights or interests that would be jeopardized if the mediator's testimony was not accessible in the specific proceedings in question, and (4) how much the testimony would contribute toward protecting those rights or advancing those interests—an inquiry that includes, among other things, an assessment of whether there are alternative sources of evidence of comparable probative value.

* * *

As indicated in an earlier section, the product of the first stage of the analysis was my decision that it was necessary to determine (through sealed proceedings) what Mr. Herman's testimony would be. Reaching that determination involved the following considerations. First, I acknowledge squarely that a decision to require a mediator to give evidence, even *in camera* or under seal, about what occurred during a mediation threatens values underlying the mediation privileges. As the *Rinaker* court suggested, the California legislature adopted these privileges in the belief that without the promise of confidentiality it would be appreciably more difficult to achieve the goals of mediation programs.

* * *

While this court has no occasion or power to quarrel with these generally applicable pronouncements of state policy, we observe that they appear to have appreciably less force when, as here, the parties to the mediation have waived confidentiality protections, indeed have asked the court to compel the mediator to testify—so that justice can be done.

* * *

As the *Rinaker* court pointed out, ordering mediators to participate in proceedings arising out of mediations imposes economic and psychic burdens that could make some people reluctant to agree to serve as a mediator, especially in programs where that service is pro bono or poorly compensated.

This is not a matter of time and money only. Good mediators are likely to feel violated by being compelled to give evidence that could be used against a party with whom they tried to establish a relationship of trust during a mediation. Good mediators are deeply committed to being and remaining neutral and non-judgmental, and to building and preserving relationships with parties. To force them to give evidence that hurts someone from whom they actively solicited trust (during the mediation) rips the fabric of their work and can threaten their sense of the center of their professional integrity. These are not inconsequential matters.

Like many other variables in this kind of analysis, however, the magnitude of these risks can vary with the circumstances. Here, for instance, all parties to the mediation want the mediator to testify about things that occurred during the mediation—so ordering the testimony would do less harm to the actual relationships developed than it would in a case where one of the parties to the mediation objected to the use of evidence from the mediator.

* * *

The magnitude of the risk to values underlying the mediation privileges that can be created by ordering a mediator to testify also can vary with the nature of the testimony that is sought. Comparing the kind of testimony sought in *Rinaker* with the kind of testimony sought in the case at bar illustrates this point. In *Rinaker,* one party wanted to use the mediator's recollection about what another party said during the mediation to impeach subsequent trial testimony. So the mediator was to serve as a source of evidence about what words a party to the mediation uttered, what statements or admissions that party made.

As the Court of Appeal appeared to recognize, this kind of testimony could be particularly threatening to the spirit and methods that some people believe are important both to the philosophy and the success of some mediation processes. Under one approach to mediation, the primary goal is not to establish "the truth" or to determine reliably what the historical facts actually were. Rather, the goal is to go both deeper than and beyond history—to emphasize feelings, underlying interests, and a search for means for social repair or reorientation. In this kind of mediation, what happened between the parties in the past can be appreciably less important than why, than what needs drove what happened or were exposed or defined by what happened, than how the parties feel about it, and than what they can bring themselves to do to move on.

Moreover, the methods some mediators use to explore underlying interests and feelings and to build settlement bridges are in some instances intentionally distanced from the actual historical facts. In some mediations, the focus is on feelings rather than facts. The neutral may ask the parties to set aside pre-occupations with what happened as she tries to help the parties understand underlying motivations and needs and to remove emotional obstacles through exercises in venting. Some mediators use hypotheticals that are expressly and intentionally not presented as accurate reflections of reality—in order to help the parties explore their situation and the range of solution options that might be available. A mediator might encourage parties to "try on" certain ideas or feelings that the parties would contend have little connection with past conduct, to experiment with the effects on themselves and others of expressions of emotions or of openness to concessions or proposals that, outside the special environment of the mediation, the parties would not entertain or admit. All of this, as mediator Rinaker herself pointed out, can have precious little to do with historical accuracy or "truth."[119]

Given these features of some mediations, it could be both threatening and unfair to hold a participant to the literal meaning of at least some of the words she uttered during the course of a mediation. And testimony from the mediator about what those words were during the mediation might constitute very unreliable (actively misleading) evidence about what the earlier historical facts were.

For these reasons, a court conducting the kind of balancing analysis called for by the *Rinaker* court should try to determine what kind of techniques and processes were used in the particular mediation in issue. The more like the processes just described, the more harm would be done by trying to use evidence about what was said or done during the mediation to help prove what the earlier historical facts really were. On the other hand, if the mediation process was closer to an adjudicate/evaluative model, with a clear focus (understood by all participants) on evidence, law, and traditional analysis of liability, damages, and settlement options, use of evidence from the mediation in subsequent civil proceedings might be less vulnerable to criticism for being unfair and unreliable.* * *

The interests that are likely to be advanced by compelling the mediator to testify in this case are of considerable importance. Moreover, as we shall see, some of those interests parallel and reinforce the objectives the legislature sought to advance by providing for confidentiality in mediation.

The first interest we identify is the interest in doing justice. Here is what we mean. For reasons described below, the mediator is positioned in this case to offer what could be crucial, certainly very probative, evidence about the central factual issues in this matter. There is a strong possibility that his testimony will greatly improve the court's ability to determine reliably what the pertinent historical facts actually were. Establishing reliably what the facts were is critical to doing justice (here, justice means this: applying the law correctly to the real historical facts).

---

[119] I found the descriptions in Rinaker's briefs of her mediation process articulate and instructive. *See, Rinaker,* 62 Cal. App. 4th at 170 and 166 (quotations from Ms. Rinaker's briefs).

It is important to acknowledge, however, that there is a broad range of approaches to mediation (people attach the label "mediation" to many different kinds of processes and methods)—and that the "mediations" that occur in at least some federal court ADR programs are likely to be quite a bit more "evaluative" than the purely facilitative model would contemplate. In fact, I suspect that in a good many "mediations" of cases filed in federal court, the parties and the neutral pay considerable attention to evidence and law—and that the negotiations revolve around fairly traditional analysis of positions—as much as the mediators might want to shift focus to underlying interests and to searches for creative solutions.

It is the fundamental duty of a public court in our society to do justice—to resolve disputes in accordance with the law when the parties don't. Confidence in our system of justice as a whole, in our government as a whole, turns in no small measure on confidence in the courts' ability to do justice in individual cases. So doing justice in individual cases is an interest of considerable magnitude.When we put case-specific flesh on these abstract bones, we see that "doing justice" implicates interests of considerable importance to the parties—all of whom want the mediator to testify. From the plaintiff's perspective, the interests that the defendants' motion threatens could hardly be more fundamental. According to Ms. Olam, the mediation process was fundamentally unfair to her—and resulted in an apparent agreement whose terms are literally unconscionable and whose enforcement would render her homeless and virtually destitute. To her, doing justice in this setting means protecting her from these fundamental wrongs.

From the defendants' perspective, doing justice in this case means, among other things, bringing to a lawful close disputes with Ms. Olam that have been on-going for about seven years—disputes that the defendants' believe have cost them, without justification, at least scores of thousands of dollars. The defendants believe that Ms. Olam has breached no fewer than three separate contractual commitments with them (not counting the agreement reached at the end of the mediation)—and that those breaches are the product of a calculated effort not only to avoid meeting legitimate obligations, but also to make unfair use, for years, of the defendants' money.

       * * *

And they are not the only interests that could be advanced by compelling the mediator to testify. According to the defendants' pre-hearing proffers, the mediator's testimony would establish clearly that the mediation process was fair and that the plaintiff's consent to the settlement agreement was legally viable. Thus the mediator's testimony, according to the defendants, would re-assure the community and the court about the integrity of the mediation process that the court sponsored.

That testimony also would provide the court with the evidentiary confidence it needs to enforce the agreement. A publicly announced decision to enforce the settlement would, in turn, encourage parties who want to try to settle their cases to use the court's mediation program for that purpose. An order appropriately enforcing an agreement reached through the mediation also would encourage parties in the future to take mediations seriously, to understand that they represent real opportunities to reach closure and avoid trial, and to attend carefully to terms of agreements proposed in mediations. In these important ways, taking testimony from the mediator could strengthen the mediation program.

In sharp contrast, refusing to compel the mediator to testify might well deprive the court of the evidence it needs to rule reliably on the plaintiff's contentions—and thus might either cause the court to impose an unjust outcome on the plaintiff or disable the court from enforcing the settlement. In this setting, refusing to compel testimony from the mediator might end up being tantamount to denying the motion to enforce the agreement—because a crucial source of evidence about the plaintiff's condition and capacities would be missing. * * *

　　　* * *

In short, there was a substantial likelihood that testimony from the mediator would be the most reliable and probative on the central issues raised by the plaintiff in response to the defendants' motion. And there was no likely alternative source of evidence on these issues that would be of comparable probative utility. So it appeared that testimony from the mediator would be crucial to the court's capacity to do its job—and that refusing to compel that testimony posed a serious threat to every value identified above. * * *

[Based on a review of Olam's testimony and the testimony offered by the mediator and Olam's lawyer, the court concluded that Olam had not proven that her signature on the MOU was the result of undue influence and granted defendant's motion to enforce the mediated agreement as memorialized in the MOU. The Court refused any attempt to expand California law to permit a party's own lawyer to serve as a source of undue influence. The court also ordered the mediator's testimony to be unsealed.] * * *

NOTES AND QUESTIONS

1.　In his discussion, Judge Brazil repeatedly stressed that both of the parties wanted the mediator to testify, albeit for different reasons. What rationales might support an independent power of the mediator to refuse to testify, despite contrary preferences of the parties? Are they sufficient in your mind to justify a categorical rule that trumps the right of the parties to the mediator's evidence in all cases? Would a more nuanced approach be preferable?

2.　Judge Brazil concluded the court needed the mediator's testimony to assess Mrs. Olam's claim that she didn't have the capacity to enter into the mediation agreement, and that she didn't actually participate in the mediation. If these judicial needs were significant enough to overcome the mediator's interests in not testifying in this case, in what type of case might the balance come out the other way?

3.   Citing *Rinaker*, Brazil notes that mediation evidence may not be very reliable when the mediation process is aimed at resolving competing interests rather than truth-finding. Why might this distinction lead mediation evidence to be potentially unreliable? As you reflect back on the Riskin grid of mediator orientations, how might a mediator's approach affect the reliability of mediation communications as an evidentiary matter? Does it matter whether the communication is made by the parties or the mediator?

4. Many within the dispute resolution community view confidentiality as a foundational characteristic of the mediation process. For thoughtful critiques of this viewpoint, however, see Eric D. Green, *A Heretical View of the Mediation Privilege*, 2 Ohio St. J. on Disp. Resol. 1 (1986); Scott H. Hughes, *The Uniform Mediation Act: To the Spoiled Go the Privileges*, 85 Marq. L. Rev. 9 (2001); Christopher Honeyman, *Confidentiality, More or Less: The Reality and Importance of Confidentiality is Often Oversold by Mediators and the Profession*, Disp. Resol. Mag., Winter 1998, at 20.

b.   The Purpose, Meaning, and Structure of Confidentiality

1.   *Purpose*

Olam discusses the central justifications for the legal protection of mediation confidentiality: the promotion of party candor and public confidence in mediation.

As the drafters of the Uniform Mediation Act (UMA) observed in their Prefatory Note:

. . . [M]ediation offers the opportunity for a candid and informal exchange regarding events in the past, as well as the parties' perceptions of and attitudes toward these events, and . . . mediators encourage parties to think constructively and creatively about ways in which their differences might be resolved. This frank exchange can be achieved only if the participants know that what is said in the mediation will not be used to their detriment through later court proceedings and other adjudicatory processes. Such party-candor justifications for mediation confidentiality resemble those supporting other communications privileges, such as the attorney-client privilege, the doctor-patient privilege, and various other counseling privileges. * * * Similarly, public confidence in and the voluntary use of mediation can be expected to expand if people have confidence that the mediator will not take sides or disclose their statements, particularly in the context of other investigations or judicial processes. The public confidence rationale has been extended to permit the mediator to object to testifying, so that the mediator will not be viewed as biased in future mediation sessions that involve comparable parties.

2. *Meaning*

The concept of mediation confidentiality actually embraces two very different contexts in which mediation communications may be revealed. It is important to distinguish between them.

The first context does not involve formal judicial, governmental or arbitral proceedings at all. Consider all of the people to whom mediation communications may be disclosed. Parties may talk with their spouses and other family members, friends, business associates, and even reveal mediation communications to the general public through contacts with news outlets or use of social media. The law typically addresses this type of mediation confidentiality through private contract. That is to say, the parties agree in a contract (typically their agreement to mediate) whether or not to disclose mediation communications to third parties outside of the mediation, and the conditions under which such disclosures may be made if the parties do agree to permit such disclosures. This practice furthers party autonomy, and courts have generally been willing to enforce these types of contracts as a matter of legitimate private ordering. *See, e.g., Cohen v. Cowles Media Co.,* 501 U.S. 663 (1991) (First Amendment does not bar recovery against a newspaper's breach of promise of confidentiality); *Horne v. Patton,* 287 So.2d 824 (Ala. 1973) (physician disclosure may be invasion of privacy, breach of fiduciary duty, breach of contract).

A few states have also enacted statutes, and some courts have adopted local rules, to protect the general confidentiality of mediation communications. The UMA defers to these personal and state law choices in Section 8, stating "Unless subject to the [insert statutory references to open meetings act and open records act], mediation communications are confidential to the extent agreed by the parties or provided by other law or rule of this State." Does the UMA thus defer to the confidentiality provisions contained in county courts' procedural rules? Federal district courts' local rules?

The second disclosure context focuses on the admission of information regarding mediation communications in judicial, administrative, arbitral or other adjudicative proceedings, and related discovery. Here, the tension between mediation and rule of law values is implicated most directly. While parties could, theoretically, contractually agree not to testify in such situations, courts generally are reluctant to uphold such agreements as a matter of public policy. The law generally permits parties the right to relevant evidence to prove their cases, and encroachments on this fundamental principle are generally disfavored and narrowly construed. 8 WIGMORE, EVIDENCE § 2192, at 70 (McNaughton Rev. 1961); *see* SARAH R. COLE, CRAIG A. MCEWEN & NANCY H. ROGERS, MEDIATION: LAW, POLICY, PRACTICE §§ 9.23, 9.25 (3rd ed 2013).

On rare occasions, courts have upheld agreements not to testify. *See, e.g., Addesa v. Addesa*, 919 A.2d 885, 891 (N.J. Super. App. Div. 2007) (citing to the parties' mediation agreement as primary basis for the conclusion that "the first judge should not have ordered or required the mediator to appear and testify as to the communications and disclosures made to him during the mediation"); *Princeton Ins. Co. v. Vergano*, 883 A.2d 44, 52–53 (Del. Ch. 2005) (citing to the UMA as evidence of the strong public policy favoring mediation confidentiality and to the confidentiality provision in the parties' mediation agreement as basis of court's decision not to permit introduction of mediator's testimony). However, deference to parties' agreements is very much the exception, not the rule.

3. Structure

Protections against the subsequent admissibility of mediation communications may be generally classified according to type and structure.

A. *Type*. There are two general classifications of admissibility rules based on type. The first of these classifications includes those rules that are embedded in substantive statutes or court rules and only apply to mediations covered by such provisions. A statute permitting mediation in a farmer-lender dispute would be an example. The second of these classifications includes those rules that apply to all mediations conducted in that state. Many states have both types of regulations.

In states that have only context-specific mediation confidentiality protections, lawyers should be aware that mediation communications are generally not protected from subsequent discovery and admissibility at trial unless they are of the type specified by statute. For example, in a context-specific state in which the only mediation confidentiality provision is in a statute regulating farmer-lender relations, the mediation of a domestic relations dispute would have no direct confidentiality protections. Attorneys in such a case may argue for a judicially-created privilege, but may not be successful, as noted above.

B. *Structure*. There are four basic structures that have been used to regulate the subsequent admissibility of mediation communications: privilege, categorical rule, settlement discussion, and testimonial incapacity.

a) Privilege

The vast majority of the state and federal protections are structured as privileges, such as the UMA. *See, e.g.*, ARIZ. REV. STAT. ANN. § 12–2238 (West 1993); 42 PA. CONS. STAT. § 5949 (2008). Courts are familiar with privileges protecting special relationships, such as the lawyer-client and spousal privileges, and the privilege structure results in a narrow exclusion of potentially relevant evidence because a party must be a valid holder of the privilege in order to assert it. For example, a spousal privilege may be asserted by spouses, not by their children. Moreover, over time, the law has carved out exceptions in which the value of fostering the confidential relationship gives way to other interests, such as the need for personal safety. Holder and exception issues for mediation are discussed further below, *infra*, in the context of the UMA.

Unfortunately for practicing lawyers, however, state admissibility laws vary widely in terms of their scope and exceptions—a dynamic that was the central impetus for the drafting of the Uniform Mediation Act, which had been adopted in 12 jurisdictions as of the end of 2013. Practitioners in non-UMA states are advised to study their state confidentiality laws closely.

Privilege has also been the primary structure for regulating the admissibility of mediation communications at the federal level. There is less there than meets the eye, however.

Only a few lower federal courts have recognized a common law privilege for mediation communications, pursuant to Rule 501 of the Federal Rules of Evidence and a key U.S. Supreme Court decision interpreting that provision, *Jaffee v. Redmond*, 518 U.S. 1, 116 S.Ct. 1923, 135 L.Ed.2d 337 (1996). *See, e.g., Folb v. Motion Picture Industry Pension & Health Plans*, 16 F.Supp.2d 1164, 1181 (C.D.Cal. 1998) (". . . encouraging mediation by adopting a federal mediation privilege . . . will provide a 'public good transcending the normally dominant principle of utilizing all rational means for ascertaining the truth.' "); *United States v. Gullo*, 672 F.Supp. 99 (W.D.N.Y. 1987) (suppressing mediation communications in a criminal proceeding); *NLRB v. Macaluso*, 618 F.2d 51 (9th Cir. 1980) (public interest in maintaining the perceived and actual impartiality of mediators outweighs the benefits derivable from a given mediator's testimony); *Sheldone v. Pennsylvania Turnpike Com'n*, 104 F.Supp.2d 511 (W.D.Pa., 2000), order affirmed (2000) (adopting *Folb* reasoning); *In re RDM Sports Group, Inc.* 277 B.R. 415 (N.D.Ga., 2002) (adopting *Folb* reasoning and scope of privilege announced in *Sheldone*, with mediation privilege operating to protect only those communications made to the mediator, between the parties during mediation, or in preparation for mediation).

To the extent they have been asked, most federal courts have not gone that far, however. *See Hallon v. City of Stockton*, 2012 WL 394200, E.D.Cal., Feb. 06, 2012; *Molina v. Lexmark Int'l, Inc.*, 2008 WL 4447678 (C.D.Cal. 2008) (questioning whether federal mediation privilege exists and observing that "even if a federal mediation privilege exists, its scope and application are unclear"); *Eagle Precision Technologies, Inc. v. Eaton*

Leonard Robolix, Inc. 2005 WL 6453567 (S.D.Cal., 2005) (distinguishing *Folb's* claims based on their jurisdictional basis: federal question and pendant jurisdiction). *See also* Ellen Deason, *Predictable Mediation Confidentiality in the U.S. Federal System,* 17 Ohio St. J. Disp. Resol. 239 (2001–2002); Ellen Deason, *The Quest for Uniformity in Mediation Confidentiality: Foolish Consistency or Crucial Predictability?* 85 Marq. L. Rev. 79 (2001–2002).

As noted in the introduction to this section, courts are reluctant to deny parties access to evidence to prove their cases. *See Branzburg v. Hayes,* 408 U.S. 665, 682 n.21, 92 S.Ct. 2646, 33 L.Ed.2d 626 (1972) (quoting 8 JOHN H. WIGMORE, EVIDENCE § 2286, at 543 (McNaughton rev. 1961)) ("In general, then, the mere fact that a communication was made in express confidence, or in the implied confidence of a confidential relation, does not create a privilege [for the media under the First Amendment] . . . No pledge of privacy or oath of secrecy can avail against the demand for the truth in a court of justice."); *see also, In re Grand Jury Subpoena Duces Tecum,* 112 F.3d 910, 923 (8th Cir. 1997) (then First Lady Hillary "Clinton's reasonable belief that her conversations with White House lawyers were privileged is insufficient to prevent their disclosure."). See generally Charles Ehrhardt, *Confidentiality, Privilege and Rule 408: The Protection of Mediation Proceedings in Federal Court,* 60 La. L. Rev. 91 (1999).

Congress has, however, created a statutory privilege for mediations that take place in the various federal agencies. 5 U.S.C. § 574 (1996). Even then, it is relatively narrow. For example, it applies only to the caucus sessions between the mediator and a party, and does not apply to general sessions in which the mediator meets jointly with the parties. It also includes exceptions for disclosures that are "necessary to (A) prevent a manifest injustice; (B) help establish a violation of law; or (C) prevent harm to the public health and safety. . . ." These exceptions are few, but broad. The act, known as the Alternative Dispute Resolution Acxt of 1996, can be found in the online appendix on the TWEN web site for this casebook, at www.lawschool.westlaw.com.

b) The Settlement Discussion Model

While the privilege structure is clearly the majority rule, a few states have enacted mediation communications protections modeled on the protections traditionally provided for settlement discussions discussed in Chapter III. For example, a Missouri confidentiality statute includes a provision stating "Arbitration, conciliation and mediation proceedings shall be regarded as settlement negotiations . . ." MO. REV. STAT. § 435.014(2) (2008). The settlement discussion rule is of common law origin, but has been codified by many states, and at the federal level by

Rule 408 of the Federal Rules of Evidence, as described in Chapter III, *supra*.

c) Mediator Incompetence

A small handful of states protect against the subsequent admissibility of mediation communications by making mediators incompetent to testify as a matter of law. California has adopted this approach, as we saw in the *Olam* decision. Relatively few other states have followed suit, however, The first, the mediator-incompetency model, makes the mediator incompetent in part because this approach provides no protections for the subsequent admissibility of statements by parties or witnesses in a mediation. It only prevents the mediator from being call in as a tie-breaker. Another weakness to this approach is that, if taken seriously, it renders the mediator incapable of testifying in her own defense if she is sued for malpractice.

d) Categorical Exclusion

The second model is the categorical exclusion, which simply bars the introduction of any evidence relating to the mediation. This is California's primary anti-admissibili ty protection and was at the center of the dispute in *Olam*. CAL. EVID. CODE § 1119 provides:

> Except as otherwise provided in this chapter: (a) No evidence of anything said or any admission made . . . in the course of, or pursuant to, a mediation . . . is admissible or subject to discovery, and disclosure of the evidence shall not be compelled, in any . . . noncriminal proceeding . . . (b) No writing . . . prepared in the course of, or pursuant to, a mediation . . . is admissible or subject to discovery, and disclosure of the writing shall not be compelled in any, . . . noncriminal proceeding . . . (c) All communications . . . by and between participants in the course of a mediation . . . shall remain confidential.

This absolutist approach effectively seeks to build a cocoon around the mediation, and to prevent any communication made in the mediation from getting out. However, because of its rigidity, the categorical model is prone to judicial exception, and indeed, California's approach has been the most litigated of all the vehicles of mediation confidentiality. We will take a closer look at this approach later in this chapter.

NOTES AND QUESTIONS

1.   If you were drafting a statute, which of these approaches would you prefer?

2.   Look up the protections for mediation confidentiality in your state. Are they found in a statute or court rule, or both? Do they apply to all

mediations, or are they subject-matter specific? How are they structured? How have any courts construed the provisions? What exceptions are there to the general rule of confidentiality?

c.   A Closer Look at Privilege: The UMA

Since privilege is the primary structure by which mediation communications are kept from disclosure in subsequent discovery or testimony, it is worth taking a closer look at the privilege structure. The UMA is particularly helpful here because it was drafted at the national level for consideration by individual states, and because it draws upon the experience of the many state privileges.

UNIFORM MEDIATION ACT
(2003)

* * *

SECTION 4. PRIVILEGE AGAINST DISCLOSURE; ADMISSIBILITY; DISCOVERY.

(a) Except as otherwise provided in Section 6, a mediation communication is privileged as provided in subsection (b) and is not subject to discovery or admissible in evidence in a proceeding unless waived or precluded as provided by Section 5.

(b) In a proceeding, the following privileges apply:

(1) A mediation party may refuse to disclose, and may prevent any other person from disclosing, a mediation communication.

(2) A mediator may refuse to disclose a mediation communication, and may prevent any other person from disclosing a mediation communication of the mediator.

(3) A nonparty participant may refuse to disclose, and may prevent any other person from disclosing, a mediation communication of the nonparty participant.

(c) Evidence or information that is otherwise admissible or subject to discovery does not become inadmissible or protected from discovery solely by reason of its disclosure or use in a mediation.

Legislative Note: The Act does not supersede existing state statutes that make mediators incompetent to testify, or that provide for costs and attorney fees to mediators who are wrongfully subpoenaed. See, e.g., Cal. Evid. Code Section 703.5 (West 1994).

* * *

SECTION 6. EXCEPTIONS TO PRIVILEGE.

(a) There is no privilege under Section 4 for a mediation communication that is:

  (1) in an agreement evidenced by a record signed by all parties to the agreement;

  (2) available to the public under [insert statutory reference to open records act] or made during a session of a mediation which is open, or is required by law to be open, to the public;

  (3) a threat or statement of a plan to inflict bodily injury or commit a crime of violence;

  (4) intentionally used to plan a crime, attempt to commit or commit a crime, or to conceal an ongoing crime or ongoing criminal activity;

  (5) sought or offered to prove or disprove a claim or complaint of professional misconduct or malpractice filed against a mediator;

  (6) except as otherwise provided in subsection (c), sought or offered to prove or disprove a claim or complaint of professional misconduct or malpractice filed against a mediation party, nonparty participant, or representative of a party based on conduct occurring during a mediation; or

  (7) sought or offered to prove or disprove abuse, neglect, abandonment, or exploitation in a proceeding in which a child or adult protective services agency is a party, unless the

  [Alternative A: [State to insert, for example, child or adult protection] case is referred by a court to mediation and a public agency participates.]

  [Alternative B: public agency participates in the [State to insert, for example, child or adult protection] mediation].

(b) There is no privilege under Section 4 if a court, administrative agency, or arbitrator finds, after a hearing in camera, that the party seeking discovery or the proponent of the evidence has shown that the evidence is not otherwise available, that there is a need for the evidence that substantially outweighs the interest in protecting confidentiality, and that the mediation communication is sought or offered in:

  (1) a court proceeding involving a felony [or misdemeanor]; or

  (2) except as otherwise provided in subsection (c), a proceeding to prove a claim to rescind or reform or a defense to avoid liability on a contract arising out of the mediation.

(c) A mediator may not be compelled to provide evidence of a mediation communication referred to in subsection (a)(6) or (b)(2).

(d) If a mediation communication is not privileged under subsection (a) or (b), only the portion of the communication necessary for the application of the exception from nondisclosure may be admitted. Admission of evidence under subsection (a) or (b) does not render the evidence, or any other mediation communication, discoverable or admissible for any other purpose.

Legislative Note: If the enacting state does not have an open records act, the following language in paragraph (2) of subsection (a) needs to be deleted: "available to the public under [insert statutory reference to open records act] or".

NOTES AND QUESTIONS

1.   The mediation privilege in the UMA is unique in that it expressly provides for three separate holders: the parties, the mediator(s), and any non-party participants, such as support persons or witnesses. The UMA is the only mediation statute or court rule to expressly cover non-party participants.

2.   Under Section 4, holders of the UMA privilege are entitled to refuse to testify, and in some circumstances may affirmatively prevent, or block, another person from testifying about mediation communications. *See* UNIF. MEDIATION ACT § 4, Comment 4(b) (2001).

Parties have the greatest blocking power under the UMA, and may block discovery or testimony about mediation communications made by anyone in the mediation—including another party, a mediator, or any other participant. Mediators and non-party participants have a more limited privilege. A mediator may block testimony of her own mediation communications, regardless of whether that testimony is being offered by a party or non-party participant. The mediator privilege allows the mediator to block any testimony about the mediator's mediation communications, even if both parties consent to the testimony. Finally, a non-party participant may block evidence of that individual's mediation communications, regardless of who provides the evidence and whether the parties or mediator consent.

3.   Assume an employment discrimination mediation in which Jim, an African–American, claims that he did not receive a promotion because of his race. During the mediation, Jim's boss, Bill, admitted that Jim's race was a factor in the decision not to promote Jim. The mediation is unsuccessful, and a trial ensues in a jurisdiction has adopted the UMA. Can Bill block Jim from testifying about Bill's admission? Can Bill stop the mediator from similarly testifying? Can Bill, Jim, or the mediator prevent similar testimony by Jim's union steward, who was at the mediation and heard the admission?

4.   The UMA exceptions are consistent with mediation privilege exceptions that have been recognized in most jurisdictions by statute or common law. What is unique about the UMA exceptions is that they are divided into two classes, referred to during the drafting process as "above the line" and "below the line" exceptions. The "above the line" exceptions are

found in Section 6(a)(1)–(7), and do not require judicial balancing as a condition of admissibility. If one of these exceptions applies, the mediation communications evidence will be admitted. These include exceptions that would allow the admission of a recorded mediated settlement agreement, evidence of the abuse of vulnerable parties, and evidence of criminal activities.

The "below the line" exceptions, UMA Section 6(b)(1)–(2), require a court to determine the admissibility of the evidence under the unique facts and circumstances of the case in an *in camera* proceeding. Significantly, the statute sets a high standard for admissibility, requiring the proponent of the evidence to show that the evidence is "otherwise unavailable" and "substantially outweighs" the state's strong presumption favoring the confidentiality of mediation communications. This includes exceptions that would allow testimony of mediation communications to be used to establish guilt or innocence in at least felony criminal proceedings (and misdemeanors if states elect to adopt this bracketed language), and that would permit a party to establish that she signed the mediated settlement agreement because of fraud, duress, or some other basis that would render the agreement legally invalid as a matter of contract law.

What is the benefit of requiring judicial balancing before the evidence can be admitted in the matters covered by these two exceptions? Think again about the court's decision in *Olam*. Do you see any of its reasoning reflected here? Also think back to the work product doctrine in Rule 26 of the Federal Rules of Civil Procedure.

5.   Section 6(b) of the UMA requires courts to balance the availability of alternative evidence and the substantiality of a party's need for the evidence against the importance of protecting confidentiality. To date, the case law is under this test is sparse. *See, e.g., State v. Williams*, 877 A.2d 1258, 1265 (N.J. 2005) (affirming a lower court's refusal to admit the mediator's testimony to help establish a self-defense claim in a criminal case); *Wilson v. Wilson*, 653 S.E.2d 702, 706–07 (Ga. 2007) (concluding that a trial court did not err in permitting mediator to testify regarding party's mental and emotional condition), *Lehr v. Afflitto*, 889 A.2d 462, 471–74 (N.J. Super. App. Div. 2006) (finding, inter alia, that trial court erred in permitting mediator to testify because need for mediator testimony did not outweigh public's interest in protecting confidentiality of mediation). Apparently, the mediators involved in these cases did not invoke the protections of Section 6(c) in order to decline to testify.

6.   The drafting of the UMA was an often stormy process, as it implicated some of most cherished values of mediation, and the broad range of views on those issues that are held by mediators, litigators, judges, and other interested parties. There were more than a dozen public meetings in locations around the country over the four year drafting period, with new drafts circulated for public comment before each meeting. In the end, however, the final act was endorsed without opposition by the Uniform Law

Commission, the American Bar Association (on the strength of more than a dozen co-sponsoring ABA sections), all major dispute resolution professional organizations, and by all major providers of dispute resolution services. For a history of the drafting process, see Richard C. Reuben, *The Sound of Dust Settling: A Response to Critics of the UMA*, 2003 J. Disp. Resol. 99. Professor Reuben served as a Reporter for the UMA Project.

7.   Professor Scott Hughes has strongly criticized the UMA. Hughes questions the need for a mediation privilege in general, and criticizes the UMA's privilege in particular, writing:

> To the extent that mediation confidentiality impairs the parties' self-determination, the mediation privilege should yield to self-determination and to the court's ability to determine the truth. If the party's access to justice is hampered, or is so restricted by the UMA as to be virtually non-existent, any relationship between the results achieved in mediation and self-determination will be merely coincidental. This is not acceptable. . . .

> If it is necessary to have a privilege for mediation, certain elements should be adopted. First, the mediation process is not well served by a separate privilege for mediators. Second, clear exceptions should be drafted to cover contractual misconduct. Third, although a procedural step prior to accessing testimony (such as an in camera hearing or sealed proceedings) is appropriate, no substantive hurdles should hinder access to normal common law contract remedies or impair self-determination. Finally, when challenges arise to an agreement reached in mediation, the mediator should be treated like all other mediation participants—he or she should be required to testify. The UMA should not allow the artificial distinction between the mediator malpractice and the contractual misconduct exceptions.

Scott H. Hughes, *The Uniform Mediation Act: To the Spoiled Go the Privileges*, 85 Marq. L. Rev. 9, 77 (2001).

Do you agree? If not, how would you respond to Professor Hughes?

8.   As with any uniform or model law, states that have adopted the UMA may choose to amend its language. Only New Jersey, however, has made a significant change. Legislators there omitted the words "of violence" from the exception to the privilege for a mediation communication that is "a threat or statement of a plan to . . . commit a crime of violence." UMA, Section 6(a)(3). Thus, New Jersey allows the privilege to be breached if a mediation party threatens to commit any sort of crime.

9.   Compare the mediation statute(s) and/or court rule(s) in your state to the UMA. What are the differences between the rules? Which is stronger?

d. The Categorical Rule: An Alternative to Privilege

As we saw in *Olam*, California law provides a categorical exception for mediation. Under this approach, if a communication is made in a mediation that falls within the category of mediations covered by the statute, it simply cannot be introduced in later proceedings. Unlike the privilege, the categorical approach does not require a proper holder to assert the protection, cannot be waived, and generally has few exceptions. As a statute, the categorical approach is therefore simpler than the more nuanced privilege structure.

As noted earlier, however, one challenge with categorical rules is the tendency of courts to create exceptions to them based on the exigencies of particular cases before them. This was certainly the early history of the California statute, which saw trial and appeals courts grant numerous exceptions until the state Supreme Court made it clear this practice was inappropriate.

The path of the statute is recounted in the following case, which raises the difficult question of whether the confidentiality statute can be used as a shield against discovery of evidence of professional malpractice during a mediation. As you read the opinion, recall Chapter II's discussion of the attorney-client relationship and tensions that can arise in the decision-making process.

CASSEL V. SUPERIOR COURT OF LOS ANGELES COUNTY
Supreme Court of California, 2011
244 P.3d 1080

BAXTER, J.

* * *

FACTS AND PROCEDURAL BACKGROUND

[Cassel was a clothing importer who had a license (GML) to use the Von Dutch label, and operated under the name of Von Dutch Originals, L.L.C. (VDO). He lost his claimed ownership of VDO in a 2002 arbitration, but his law firm, Wasserman, Comden, Casselman & Pearson, L.L.P. (WCCP), advised him he could continue to market clothing under the Von Dutch label because he retained the GML. The new owners of VDO sued Cassel for trademark infringement and sought to enjoin Cassel from usng the Von Dutch label. WCCP did not tell Cassel of the request for a preliminary injunction, which the court granted after WCCP failed to oppose the request.

The VDO case went to mediation on Aug. 4, 2004, and the parties entered into a $1.25 million settlement. Cassel later sued WCCP and several of its members for breach of professional, fiduciary, and contractual duties, alleging that WCCP had coerced him into accepting the settlement rather than the $2 million he had instructed them to seek. In that case, which is the case at bar, the WCCP moved to exclude all evidence of Cassel's communications with his lawyers during the 14-hour mediation.]

* * *

DISCUSSION

* * *

Section 1119 governs the general admissibility of oral and written communications generated during the mediation process. Subdivision (a) provides in pertinent part that "[n]o evidence of anything said or any admission made for the purpose of, in the course of, or pursuant to, a mediation . . . is admissible or subject to discovery, and disclosure of the evidence shall not be compelled, in any . . . civil action. . . ." * * * Subdivision (c) of section 1119 further provides that "[a]ll communications, negotiations, or settlement discussions by and between participants in the course of a mediation . . . shall remain confidential." * * *

* * * [T]he purpose of these provisions is to encourage the mediation of disputes by eliminating a concern that things said or written in connection with such a proceeding will later be used against a participant. "Toward that end, 'the statutory scheme . . . unqualifiedly bars disclosure of communications made during mediation absent an express statutory exception.'" Judicial construction, and judicially crafted exceptions, are permitted only where due process is implicated, or where literal construction would produce absurd results, thus clearly violating the Legislature's presumed intent. Otherwise, the mediation confidentiality statutes must be applied in strict accordance with their plain terms. Where competing policy concerns are present, it is for the Legislature to resolve them.

Thus, in Foxgate, we concluded that under the confidentiality provisions of section 1119, and under section 1121, which strictly limits the content of mediators' reports, a mediator may not submit to the court, and the court may not consider, a report of communications or conduct by a party which the mediator believes constituted a failure to comply with an order of the mediator and to participate in good faith in the mediation process. * * *

In Rojas, we confirmed that under the plain language of the mediation confidentiality statutes, all "writings" "'prepared for the purpose of, in the course of, or pursuant to, a mediation,'" are confidential and protected from discovery. We explained that the broad definition of "writings" set forth in section 250, and incorporated by express reference into section 1119, subdivision (b), encompasses such materials as charts, diagrams, information compilations, expert reports, photographs of physical conditions, recordings or transcriptions of witness statements, and written or recorded analyses of physical evidence. * * *.

* * *

Most recently, in Simmons, we held that the judicial doctrines of equitable estoppel and implied waiver are not valid exceptions to the strict technical requirements set forth in the mediation confidentiality statutes for the disclosure and admissibility of oral settlement agreements reached in mediation. * * *

* * *

Here, as in Foxgate, Rojas, Fair, and Simmons, the plain language of the mediation confidentiality statutes controls our result. Section 1119, subdivision (a) clearly provides that "[n]o evidence of anything said or any admission made for the purpose of, in the course of, or pursuant to, a mediation . . . is admissible or subject to discovery. . . ." * * *

The obvious purpose of the expanded language is to ensure that the statutory protection extends beyond discussions carried out directly between the opposing parties to the dispute, or with the mediator, during the mediation proceedings themselves. All oral or written communications are covered, if they are made "for the purpose of" or "pursuant to" a mediation. It follows that, absent an express statutory exception, all discussions conducted in preparation for a mediation, as well as all mediation-related communications that take place during the mediation itself, are protected from disclosure. Plainly, such communications include those between a mediation disputant and his or her own counsel, even if these do not occur in the presence of the mediator or other disputants.

* * * [T]here is no persuasive basis to equate mediation "parties" or "disputants" with mediation "participants," and thus to restrict confidentiality to potentially damaging mediation-related exchanges between disputing parties. In the first place, section 1119, subdivisions (a) and (b), do not restrict confidentiality to communications between mediation "participants." They provide more broadly that "[n]o evidence of anything said", and "[n]o writing", is discoverable or admissible in a legal proceeding if the utterance or writing was "for the purpose of, in the course of, or pursuant to, a mediation. . . ." The protection afforded by these statutes is not limited by the identity of the communicator, by his or her status as a "party," "disputant," or "participant" in the mediation itself, by the communication's nature, or by its specific potential for damage to a disputing party.

* * * Though petitioner urges us to do so, we therefore decline to accept the Court of Appeal's "single participant" characterization, which contradicts the plain import of the statutes.

* * *

The Court of Appeal majority also implied that the mediation confidentiality statutes, in their role as protectors of frank exchanges between the parties to a mediation, were not intended to trump section 958, which eliminates the confidentiality protections otherwise afforded by the attorney-client privilege in suits between clients and their own lawyers. But the mediation confidentiality statutes include no exception for legal malpractice actions by mediation disputants against their own counsel. Moreover, though both statutory schemes involve the shielding of confidential communications, they serve separate and unrelated purposes.

A legal client's personal statutory privilege of confidentiality, applicable to all communications between client and counsel, allows the client to consult frankly with counsel on any matter, without fear that others may later discover and introduce against the client confidences exchanged in the attorney-client relationship. The exception to the privilege set forth in section 958 simply acknowledges that, in litigation between lawyer and client, the client should not be able to use the privilege to bar otherwise relevant and admissible evidence which supports the lawyer's claim, or undermines the client's.

By contrast, the mediation confidentiality statutes do not create a "privilege" in favor of any particular person. Instead, they serve the public policy of encouraging the resolution of disputes by means short of litigation. The mediation confidentiality statutes govern only the narrow category of mediation-related communications, but they apply broadly within that category, and are designed to provide maximum protection for the privacy of communications in the mediation context. A principal purpose is to assure prospective participants that their interests will not be damaged, first, by attempting this alternative means of resolution, and then, once mediation is chosen, by making and communicating the candid disclosures and assessments that are most likely to produce a fair and reasonable mediation settlement. To assure this maximum privacy protection, the Legislature has specified that all mediation participants involved in a mediation-related communication must agree to its disclosure.

Neither the language nor the purpose of the mediation confidentiality statutes supports a conclusion that they are subject to an exception, similar to that provided for the attorney-client privilege, for lawsuits between attorney and client. The instant Court of Appeal's contrary conclusion is nothing more or less than a judicially crafted exception to the unambiguous language of the mediation confidentiality statutes in order to accommodate a competing policy concern—here, protection of a client's right to sue his or her attorney. We and the Courts of Appeal have consistently disallowed such exceptions, even where the equities appeared to favor them.

* * *

We further emphasize that application of the mediation confidentiality statutes to legal malpractice actions does not implicate due process concerns so fundamental that they might warrant an exception on constitutional grounds. Implicit in our decisions in Foxgate, Rojas, Fair, and Simmons is the premise that the mere loss of evidence pertinent to the prosecution of a lawsuit for civil damages does not implicate such a fundamental interest.

* * *

Furthermore, while we pass no judgment on the wisdom of the mediation confidentiality statutes, we cannot say that applying the plain terms of those statutes to the circumstances of this case produces a result that is either absurd or clearly contrary to legislative intent. The Legislature decided that the encouragement of mediation to resolve disputes requires broad protection for the confidentiality of communications exchanged in relation to that process, even where this protection may sometimes result in the unavailability of valuable civil evidence. To this end, the Legislature could further reasonably conclude that confidentiality should extend to "anything" said or written "for the purpose of, in the course of, or pursuant to" a mediation, including mediation-related discussions between a mediation disputant and his own counsel, subject only to express waiver by all mediation "participants" involved in the communication, including such attorneys.

Inclusion of private attorney-client discussions in the mediation confidentiality scheme addresses several issues about which the Legislature could rationally be concerned. * * *

* * *

We express no view about whether the statutory language, thus applied, ideally balances the competing concerns or represents the soundest public policy. Such is not our responsibility or our province. We simply conclude, as a matter of statutory construction, that application of the statutes' plain terms to the circumstances of this case does not produce absurd results that are clearly contrary to the Legislature's intent. Of course, the Legislature is free to reconsider whether the mediation confidentiality statutes should preclude the use of mediation-related attorney-client discussions to support a client's civil claims of malpractice against his or her attorneys.

* * *

We therefore conclude that the evidence the trial court ruled nondiscoverable and inadmissible by reason of the mediation confidentiality statutes was not, as a matter of law, excluded from coverage by those statutes on the mere ground that they were private attorney-client communications which occurred outside the presence or hearing of the mediator or any other mediation participant. Instead, such attorney-client communications, like any other communications, were confidential, and therefore were neither discoverable nor admissible—even for purposes of proving a claim of legal malpractice—insofar as they were "for the purpose of, in the course of, or pursuant to, a mediation. . . ." By holding otherwise, and thus overturning the trial court's exclusionary order, the Court of Appeal erred. We must therefore reverse the Court of Appeal's judgment.

CHIN, J. CONCURRING

I concur in the result, but reluctantly.

The court holds today that private communications between an attorney and a client related to mediation remain confidential even in a lawsuit between the two. This holding will effectively shield an attorney's actions during mediation, including advising the client, from a malpractice action even if those actions are incompetent or even deceptive. Attorneys participating in mediation will not be held accountable for any incompetent or fraudulent actions during that mediation unless the actions are so extreme as to engender a criminal prosecution against the attorney. This is a high price to pay to preserve total confidentiality in the mediation process.

I greatly sympathize with the Court of Appeal majority's attempt to interpret the statutory language as not mandating confidentiality in this situation. But, for the reasons the present majority gives, I do not believe the attempt quite succeeds.

Moreover, although we may sometimes depart from literal statutory language if a literal interpretation "would result in absurd consequences that the Legislature did not intend", I believe, just barely, that the result here does not so qualify. Plausible policies support a literal interpretation. * * *

Accordingly, I agree with the majority that we have to give effect to the literal statutory language. But I am not completely satisfied that the Legislature has fully considered whether attorneys should be shielded from accountability in this way. There may be better ways to balance the competing interests than simply providing that an attorney's statements during mediation may never be disclosed. For example, it may be appropriate to provide that communications during mediation may be used in a malpractice action between an attorney and a client to the extent they are relevant to that action, but they may not be used by anyone for any other purpose. Such a provision might sufficiently protect other participants in the mediation and also make attorneys accountable for their actions. But this court cannot so hold in the guise of interpreting statutes that contain no such provision. As the majority notes, the Legislature remains free to reconsider this question. It may well wish to do so.

* * *

NOTES AND QUESTIONS

1.   Would the communications between the lawyers and client be covered by the attorney-client privilege? If yes, why wouldn't that privilege be sufficient to make testimony regarding these communications inadmissible? Hint: Who is the holder of the attorney-client privilege?

2.   The California Supreme Court approvingly quotes this language from the Court of Appeal's decision in *Wimsatt*: "The stringent result we reach here means that when clients, such as [the malpractice plaintiff in that case], participate in mediation they are, in effect, relinquishing all claims for new and independent torts arising from mediation, including legal malpractice causes of action against their own counsel." Do you view such relinquishment as positive or negative? Now could be a good time to look again at *Guido v. Duane Morris* and the notes following, *supra* in Chapter II.

3.   At various points, we have considered the importance and effects of tone. Imagine that you are a California legislator reading the *Cassel* opinion. How would you describe the tone of the majority opinion? The dissent?

4.   In light of the California Supreme Court's decision, can Mr. Cassel bring a malpractice claim against his lawyers? The Court asserts that this effect of the mediation privilege does not present a due process violation. Specifically, the Court states: "Implicit in our decisions in *Foxgate, Rojas, Fair,* and *Simmons* is the premise that the mere loss of evidence pertinent to the prosecution of a lawsuit for civil damages does not implicate such a fundamental interest." How does the Court reach this legal conclusion? If you have had Constitutional Law, remember that due process comes in two variations: substantive and procedural. Which do you think is implicated here? Do you agree with the Court's assessment?

5.   In states that have adopted the UMA, there is no privilege for mediation communications that are "sought or offered to prove or disprove a claim or complaint of professional misconduct or malpractice filed against a mediator," or against "a mediation party, nonparty participant, or representative of a party based on conduct occurring during a mediation [.]" Does this explicit exception represent an advantage of adopting the UMA?

6.   If mediators are in a state that has not adopted the UMA and are concerned about the potential use of the process to shield legal malpractice, what can they do? Here is one suggestion:

. . . Justice Chin proposed that California's relevant statutes should be amended to "provide that communications during mediation may be used in a malpractice action between an attorney and a client to the extent they are relevant to that action, but they may not be used by anyone for any other purpose. . . ." Rather than waiting for legislators in California or other non-UMA states to heed Justice Chin's words, we mediation proponents could use and improve upon this language to incorporate its objectives into our agreements to mediate. We mediation proponents could even lead by example by including in our agreements to mediate that such mediation communications may also be used in actions against mediators. We would be modeling our willingness and ability to "work mediation" to achieve improved communication, negotiation, and voluntary resolution. We would also be modeling our commitment to a process that, at the very least, does no harm to the people it is supposed to serve.

Nancy A. Welsh, *Musings on Mediation, Kleenex, and (Smudged) White Hats*, 33 U. La Verne L. Rev. 5, 23 (2011).

D. FAIRNESS, FORMALITY, AND SELF–DETERMINATION IN MEDIATION

The question of whether to use mediation in a given case or category of cases is important and complex; although we have referred to it repeatedly in this Chapter, we defer it mainly to Chapter VII, *infra*, to give it the depth of analysis the question deserves. In this section, however, we address one of the controversial issues that arises in this connection: the extent to which mediation threatens or promotes fairness to less powerful individuals or groups or to important public interests.

This issue arises most strikingly in so-called mandatory mediation, that is, where a court orders parties in a particular case or category of cases to mediate. On one hand, mediation has been widely touted for its informality and the possibilities it can offer the parties for self-determination, including the ability to uncover and address their real interests (in addition to their positions, which is the focus of litigation). On the other, some argue that mediation is less able to protect the less powerful, because it typically lacks at least some of the formal protections associated with court—such as a neutral decision-maker and the ability to invoke and even establish legal entitlements and set public policy. These arguments—as well as the counter-arguments—assume the primacy of certain values. They also assume that mediation has certain relatively fixed characteristics, an assumption that is necessarily wrong much of the time.

The underlying question is how to address the potential for unfairness or other risks posed by mediation. There are two basic answers: (1) to discourage or forbid the use of mediation by certain kinds of people or in certain kinds of cases; or (2) to customize mediation so as to lessen or eliminate the risks. We see many examples of the first category in court-connected mediation programs. Courts can allow parties to opt out without cause, or may exclude categories of cases, such as those involving intimate partner violence. In addition, the court could refuse to enforce an agreement made in mediation, based on coercion or other reasons that could serve as the basis for rescinding any contract.

Outside the court-ordered or agency-ordered mediation context, parties only mediate by agreement, so they can avoid mediation simply by not agreeing to mediate. However, it is common to have mediation agreements in contracts, and these agreements could cover a variety of terms, such as how to choose the mediator and what procedures to follow. Courts typically enforce such agreements. *See* SARAH COLE, NANCY H. ROGERS & CRAIG A. McEWEN, MEDIATION: LAW, POLICY, AND PRACTICE SECTIONS §§ 8.1–8.4 (2d ed. 2001).

This section focuses most heavily on the second type of response to the problem of what to do about risks posed by mediation: design the mediation process in order to address its potentially undesirable aspects or outcomes. It begins with an article by Professor Nancy Welsh, who argues that in court-connected mediations, the parties' self-determination may be severely limited by the program's design features, and discusses a series of measures that may address this problem. The next two excerpts—by Professors Richard Delgado and Michele Hermann and their colleagues—demonstrate the fairness risks to minorities and other low-power parties, while also proposing some possible remedies. Professors Len Riskin and Nancy Welsh point out that sophisticated repeat players already expect and receive customization of the mediation process, and urge courts, mediators, and lawyers to make such customization available to "one shot" players as well.

Finally, the potential advantages of mediation—*and* the risks of unfairness and coercion—are especially compelling in the family law context. Professor Trina Grillo cautions about the risks associated with a certain form of mandatory child custody mediation and Professor Joshua Rosenberg counters her argument.

1. GENERAL CONSIDERATIONS

NANCY A. WELSH, THE THINNING VISION OF SELF–DETERMINATION IN COURT–CONNECTED MEDIATION: THE INEVITABLE PRICE OF INSTITUTIONALIZATION?
6 Harv. Negot. L. Rev. 1, 3–7 (2001)

Ethical codes for mediators describe party self-determination as "the fundamental principle of mediation," regardless of the context within which the mediation is occurring. But what exactly does "party self-determination" mean? Does it mean the same thing now in the context of court-connected mediation as it did when it inspired many people to become involved in the "contemporary mediation movement" that arose in the 1970s and early 1980s? Most importantly, if the meaning of this "fundamental" term is changing as mediation adapts to its home in the courthouse, does it matter?

Based on a review of the debate surrounding recently promulgated or revised ethical codes for court-connected mediators in Florida and Minnesota, this Article will demonstrate that the originally dominant vision of self-determination, which borrowed heavily from concepts of party empowerment, is yielding to a different vision in the court-connected context. Perhaps not surprisingly, this vision is more consistent with the culture of the courts.

Believers in the originally dominant vision of self-determination assumed that the disputing parties would be the principal actors and creators within the mediation process. The parties would: 1) actively and directly participate in the communication and negotiation that occurs during mediation, 2) choose and control the substantive norms to guide their decision-making, 3) create the options for settlement, and 4) control the final decision regarding whether or not to settle. The mediator's role was to enable the parties' will to emerge and thus support their exercise of self-determination. Many mediation advocates continue to adhere to this vision.

However, as mediation has been institutionalized in the courts and as evaluation has become an acknowledged and accepted part of the mediator's function, the original vision of self-determination is giving way to a vision in which the disputing parties play a less central role. The parties are still responsible for making the final decision regarding settlement, but they are cast in the role of consumers, largely limited to selecting from among the settlement options developed by their attorneys. Indeed, it is the parties' attorneys, often aided by mediators who are also attorneys, who assume responsibility for actively and directly participating in the mediation process, invoking the substantive (i.e., legal) norms to be applied and creating settlement options. Thus, even as most mediators and many courts continue to name party self-determination as the "fundamental principle" underlying court-connected mediation, the party-centered empowerment concepts that anchored the original vision of self-determination are being replaced with concepts that are more reflective of the norms and traditional practices of lawyers and judges, as well as the courts' strong orientation to efficiency and closure of cases through settlement.

It can be argued that this thinning of the vision of self-determination does not matter. After all, even in its reduced form, self-determination still promises that the mediator will respect, support, and protect the parties' control over the final decision regarding settlement. Unfortunately, however, a disconnect is surfacing between even this more limited promise and the reality of court-connected mediation.

It is quite clear that court-connected mediators are providing evaluations of the parties' positions (e.g., estimates of the strengths and weaknesses of the parties' cases, suggestions regarding settlement options, etc.). When offered in the context of a party-centered, facilitative mediation, evaluation can serve a useful educational function and can aid party self-determination by assisting the parties in making informed decisions. There is growing evidence, however, that at least some court-connected mediators are engaging in very aggressive evaluations of parties' cases and settlement options (i.e., "muscle mediation") with the goal of winning a settlement, rather than supporting parties in their exercise of self-determination. As mediation has become increasingly institutionalized in the courts, a small but growing number of disputants have approached courts and ethical boards, claiming that mediators' aggressive evaluation or advocacy for particular settlements actually coerced them into a settlement.

In response to this challenge to party self-determination, ethical boards in some states have established mechanisms intended to keep evaluative mediation in check. Specifically, Florida and Minnesota, while permitting mediator evaluation in their ethical guidelines, have incorporated safeguards that pronounce party self-determination as the paramount goal of mediators and clearly prohibit coercion by the mediator.

These mechanisms are unlikely to be effective in taming mediator evaluation and in protecting even the narrowed vision of party self-determination. Despite the aspirational language and the good intentions underlying Florida's and Minnesota's ethical guidelines, the narrowed vision of party self-determination that is now institutionalized in these guidelines will be understood as no different than the free will which is to be exercised by parties involved in judicially-hosted settlement conferences. In that context, when parties have alleged that the judge or magistrate presiding over their settlement conference coerced them into reaching a settlement agreement by evaluating the parties' cases or urging a particular settlement, the courts have generally refused to find coercion unless the judge or magistrate engaged in outright threats or issued sanctions. Indeed, one court has written, "We do not agree that a judge should refrain from offering his or her assessment of a case on the eve of trial, solely to avoid the appearance of impropriety. Such a policy would effectively render meaningless a judge's role in the settlement process." It is unlikely that the courts or ethical boards responsible for interpreting and enforcing mediators' ethical guidelines will judge aggressive evaluation as coercive just because it occurred within the context of a mediation rather than in a judicially-hosted settlement conference, especially if the vision of party self-determination in mediation is no longer anchored in the concept of party empowerment.

This Article examines possible means to protect parties' self-determination in mediation and advocates for a particular solution. Specifically, the proposal suggests modifying the current presumptions regarding the finality of mediated settlement agreements and urges the adoption of a three-day, non-waivable cooling-off period before mediated settlement agreements may become enforceable. This modification would permit the continued use of evaluative techniques as a means to educate parties and inform their decision-making while rewarding the use of techniques (often facilitative) that increase parties' commitment to their settlement. The more committed parties are to their settlement, the less likely it is that they will withdraw from the settlement during the cooling-off period. Ultimately, this proposal has the potential to keep "muscle mediation" in check while also allowing the return to a vision of self-determination which is closer to that which first dominated (and inspired) the contemporary mediation movement.

NOTES AND QUESTIONS

1. In order to address concerns about self-determination, Professor Welsh makes several proposals. The first would seek to "clarify the definition of self-determination":

> In response to the concern that the original rich vision of self-determination is being lost, there may be a need to clarify the definition of self-determination in statutes, rules and ethical guidelines. It must be made clear that self-determination is different than parties' free will and requires more protection than parties' free will has received in traditional negotiation or in judicially-hosted settlement conferences. Specifically, statutes, rules, and ethical guidelines regarding self-determination could be rewritten to include: the parties' active and direct participation, communication, and negotiation; the parties' identification and selection of the interests and substantive norms which should guide the creation of settlement options; the parties' creation of potential settlement options; and the parties' control over the final outcome. In other words, the definitions should reference the indicia of party empowerment.

Welsh, *supra* at 80.

Do you think such provisions are likely to affect actual practices?

2.   If the Minnesota rules had been in force in Australia, would the behavior of the mediator in the *Tapoohi* case, *supra*, have been influenced by this provision: "A mediator shall not require a party to stay in the mediation against the party's will"?

Professor Welsh also discusses, among other things, education of mediators and the public, changing the presumption against coercion, and focusing on undue influence rather than coercion. Ultimately, and particularly in the context of mandatory mediation, she recommends the implementation of a three-day "cooling-off" period to allow easy rescission of mediated settlement agreements. Welsh, *supra* at 23–26. To what extent do you think the imposition of any of these requirements would be helpful? We will address mandatory mediation in more detail in Chapter VI, *infra*.

3.   Professor Welsh's concept of self-determination is consistent with larger concepts of more democratic dispute resolution methods and processes. Personal autonomy and respectful consideration of "voice" are central values of democratic governance and civil society, respectively. When fostered in a dispute resolution method, they help to legitimize the sponsoring method of governance. Mediation's potential for the promotion of personal autonomy, along with the opportunity it provides for voice and consideration, likely helps explain why mediation, even court-ordered mediation, has generally been perceived by participants as both satisfying and procedurally just. *See* Richard C. Reuben, *Democracy and Dispute Resolution: The Problem of Arbitration*, 67 Law & Contemp. Probs. 279 (2004); Nancy A. Welsh, *Stepping Back Through the Looking Glass: Real Conversations with Real Disputants About Institutionalized Mediation and Its Value*, 19 Ohio St. J. Disp. Resol. 573 595–600 (2004) (summarizing relevant research).

RICHARD DELGADO, CHRIS DUNN, PAMELA BROWN, HELENA LEE & DAVID HUBBERT, FAIRNESS AND FORMALITY: MINIMIZING THE RISK OF PREJUDICE IN ALTERNATIVE DISPUTE RESOLUTION

1985 Wis. L. Rev. 1359, 1387–91, 1400–04

E.   THE OPTIMAL SETTING FOR THE REDUCTION OF PREJUDICE: FORMAL VS. INFORMAL DISPUTE RESOLUTION

The selection of one mode or another of dispute resolution can do little, at least in the short run, to counter prejudice that stems from authoritarian personalities or historical currents. Prejudice that results from social-psychological factors is, however, relatively controllable. Much prejudice is environmental—people express it because the setting encourages or tolerates it. In some settings people feel free to vent hostile or denigrating attitudes toward members of minority groups; in others they do not.

Our review of social-psychological theories of prejudice indicates that prejudiced persons are least likely to act on their beliefs if the immediate environment confronts them with the discrepancy between their professed ideals and their personal hostilities against out-groups. According to social psychologists, once most persons realize that their attitudes and behavior deviate from what is expected, they will change or suppress them.

Given this human tendency to conform, American institutions have structured and defined situations to encourage appropriate behavior. Our judicial system, in particular, has incorporated societal norms of fairness and even-handedness into institutional expectations and rules of procedure at many points. These norms create a "public conscience and a standard for expected behavior that check *overt* signs of prejudice."[120] They do this in a variety of ways. First, the formalities of a court trial— the flag, the black robes, the ritual—remind those present that the occasion calls for the higher, "public" values, rather than the lesser values embraced during moments of informality and intimacy. In a courtroom trial the American Creed, with its emphasis on fairness, equality, and respect for personhood, governs. Equality of status, or something approaching it, is preserved—each party is represented by an attorney and has a prescribed time and manner for speaking, putting on evidence, and questioning the other side. Equally important, formal adjudication avoids the unstructured, intimate interactions that, according to social scientists, foster prejudice. The rules of procedure maintain distance between the parties. Counsel for the parties do not address one another, but present the issue to the trier of fact. The rules preserve the formality of the setting by dictating in detail how this confrontation is to be conducted.

That the formality of adversarial adjudication deters prejudice is borne out by the few empirical studies that have investigated the question. An experiment conducted by Walker and his colleagues showed that subjects viewed adversarial procedures as "the most preferable and the fairest mode of dispute resolution,"[121] a preference that may even extend to persons in countries that do not use an adversarial system of justice. Another experiment placed subjects in a laboratory setting behind a "veil of ignorance" and asked them to choose among a variety of procedural alternatives. Almost all the subjects chose the adversarial system. The authors concluded that the adversary system introduces a systematic evidentiary bias in favor of the weaker party.

---

[120] G. Allport, The Nature of Prejudice 7, 470 (25th Anniv.Ed.1979).

[121] Thibaut, Walker, LaTour & Houlden, *Procedural Justice as Fairness*, 26 Stan.L.Rev. 1271, 1288 (1974).

Another experiment showed that the "competitive presentation of evidence counteracts decisionmaker bias. . . ."[227] In one experiment, subjects were presented with a test case; they were given a list of both "lawful" and "unlawful" factors, but were told to consider only the "lawful" ones in making a decision. The results showed that in a simulated adversarial framework, even those subjects predetermined to be biased gave less weight to unlawful factors in their decisionmaking. The authors hypothesized that adversarial procedure counteracts decisionmaker bias because it combats the natural human tendency to "judge too swiftly in terms of the familiar that which is not yet fully known."[230] The human propensity to prejudge and make irrational categorizations is thus checked by procedural safeguards found in an adversarial system.

Formality and adversarial procedures thus counteract bias among legal decisionmakers and disputants. But it seems likely that those factors increase fairness in yet a third way—by strengthening the resolve of minority disputants to pursue their legal rights.

F.   DISPUTE RESOLUTION AND THE MINORITY DISPUTANT

Early in life, minority children become aware of themselves as different, especially with respect to skin color. This awareness is often not merely neutral, but associated with feelings of inferiority. Separate studies by psychologists Kenneth Clark and Mary Goodman in which minority children were presented with dolls of various colors illustrate this graphically. For example, when asked to make a choice between a white and black doll, "the doll that looks like you," most black children chose the white doll. A black child justified his choice of the white doll over the black doll as friend because "his feet, hands, ears, elbows, knees, and hair are clean."[235] In another experiment, a black child hated her skin color so much that she "vigorously lathered her arms and face with soap in an effort to wash away the dirt."[236] As minority children grow, they are "likely to experience a long series of events, from exclusion from play groups and cliques to violence and threats of violence, that are far less likely to be experienced by the average member of the majority group."[237] Against a background of "slights, rebuffs, forbidden opportunities, restraints, and often violence . . . the minority group member shapes that

---

[227] Thibaut, Walker & Lind, *Adversary Presentation & Bias in Legal Decisionmaking*, 86 Harv.L.Rev. 386, 401 (1972).

[230] *Id.* at 390, 401.

[235] Clark & Clark, *Racial Identification and Preference in Negro Children*, in READINGS IN SOCIAL PSYCHOLOGY 602, 611 (E. Maccoby, T. Newcomb & E. Hartley, eds. 1958).

[236] M. GOODMAN, RACE AWARENESS IN YOUNG CHILDREN 56 (rev. ed. 1964) (discussing and citing studies).

[237] G. SIMPSON & J. YINGER, RACIAL AND CULTURAL MINORITIES: AN ANALYSIS OF PREJUDICE AND DISCRIMINATION 168 (4th ed.1972).

fundamental aspect of personality—a sense of oneself and one's place in the total scheme of things."[238]

Discriminatory treatment can trigger a variety of responses. Writers identify three main reactions: avoidance, aggression, and acceptance. A minority group member may display one or more of these responses, depending on the setting. In some situations, victims of discrimination are likely to respond with apathy or defeatism; in others, the same individuals may forthrightly and effectively assert their interests. In general, when a person feels "he is the master of his fate, that he can control to some extent his own destiny, that if he works hard things will go better for him, he is then likely to achieve more...."[242] That is, minority group members are more apt to participate in processes which they believe will respond to reasonable efforts. They are understandably less likely to participate in proceedings where the results are random and unpredictable.

Thus, it is not surprising that a favored forum for redress of race-based wrongs has been the traditional adjudicatory setting. Minorities recognize that public institutions, with their defined rules and formal structure, are more subject to rational control than private or informal structures. Informal settings allow wider scope for the participants' emotional and behavioral idiosyncrasies; in these settings majority group members are most likely to exhibit prejudicial behavior. Thus, a formal adjudicative forum increases the minority group member's sense of control and, therefore, may be seen as the fairer forum. This perception becomes self-fulfilling: minority persons are encouraged to pursue their legal rights as though prejudice were unlikely and thus the possibility of prejudice is in fact lessened.

IV. The Left Critique of ADR

Many commentators who have criticized ADR have expressed concerns associated with the "left"—concerns for the unempowered, the poor and other disadvantaged groups. This section canvasses the thoughts of these commentators, in particular objections that informalism (i) solidifies control by capital and the state; (ii) disadvantages "weaker" parties; (iii) expands state control; (iv) deflects energy away from collective action; and (v) promotes law without justice. As we shall see, the political critique of ADR, although based on different premises and couched in different terms, comes to the same general conclusion as the psychological critique: ADR is no safe haven for the poor and powerless.

* * *

---

[238] *Id.* at 192.

[242] Grambs, *Negro Self–Concept Reappraised,* in Black Self–Concept: Implications For Education and Social Science 184 (J. Banks & J. Grambs, eds. 1972).

ADR increases the risk of prejudice toward vulnerable disputants. Our review of social science writings on prejudice reveals that the rules and structures of formal justice tend to suppress bias, whereas informality tends to increase it. The social science findings are reinforced, on a sociopolitical level, by ADR's leftwing critics, who see ADR as increasing the power of authoritarian social institutions over individuals, extending state coercive power into new areas of citizens' lives, and discouraging collective action.

This Part assumes that the social-science and leftwing critiques are at least partly valid—that ADR does indeed increase the risk of unfair treatment for minority disputants, women and the poor. From this it proceeds to address two final questions: (i) How much weight should be assigned to such a risk? and (ii) Can the risk be minimized without forfeiting the benefits and advantages of ADR?

A.   THE IDEAL OF FAIRNESS IN AMERICAN PROCEDURE

If ADR increases the risk of prejudice or bias in adjudication, it does not follow immediately that ADR should be curtailed. Equity concerns are only one value among many; conceivably, the gains in flexibility, speed, and economy that ADR's proponents cite could override moderate losses in fairness. A survey of the role of the ideal of fairness in American procedural law suggests, however, that the balance should be struck on the side of fairness.

American procedural law's history evidences a strong and steady evolution toward fairness, an evolution that has at times overshadowed the impulse toward economy and efficiency. Over a century ago, the Field code simplified pleading rules, largely to eliminate traps for the unwary and to render legal paper work intelligible to ordinary persons. The great procedural reforms of this century, civil discovery and long-arm jurisdiction, were likewise intended to equalize power and opportunity among litigants. Discovery enables litigants of modest means to learn facts about the dispute that might otherwise remain in the exclusive possession of the more powerful party. Long-arm jurisdiction enables citizens injured by corporations and other powerful entities to bring them to account where the injury occurred, instead of being forced to sue where the defendant is found.

Civil and criminal reforms have made access to court cheaper and more readily available to all. * * *

B. STRIKING THE BALANCE: PROTECTING AGAINST PREJUDICE
WITHOUT SACRIFICING THE BENEFITS OF ADR

ADR offers a number of clear-cut benefits. It can shape a decree flexibly so as to protect a continuing relationship between the parties. It is low-cost, speedy, and, for some at least, nonintimidating. Yet there is little benefit for a minority disputant in a quick, painless hearing that renders an adverse decision tainted by prejudice.

Part III showed that the risk of prejudice is greatest when a member of an in-group confronts a member of an out-group; when that confrontation is direct, rather than through intermediaries; when there are few rules to constrain conduct; when the setting is closed and does not make clear that "public" values are to preponderate; and when the controversy concerns an intimate, personal matter rather than some impersonal question. Our review also indicated that many minority participants will press their claims most vigorously when they believe that what they do and say will make a difference, that the structure will respond, and that the outcome is predictable and related to effort and merit.

It follows that ADR is most apt to incorporate prejudice when a person of low status and power confronts a person or institution of high status and power. In such situations, the party of high status is more likely than in other situations to attempt to call up prejudiced responses; at the same time, the individual of low status is less likely to press his or her claim energetically. The dangers increase when the mediator or other third party is a member of the superior group or class. Examples of ADR settings that may contain these characteristics are prison and other institutional review boards, consumer complaint panels, and certain types of cases referred to an ombudsman. In these situations, minorities and members of other out-groups should opt for formal in-court adjudication, and the justice system ought to avoid pressuring them to accept an alternate procedure. ADR should be reserved for cases in which parties of comparable power and status confront each other.

ADR also poses heightened risks of prejudice when the issue to be adjudicated touches a sensitive or intimate area of life, for example, housing or culture-based conduct. Thus, many landlord-tenant, interneighbor, and intrafamilial disputes are poor candidates for ADR. When the parties are of unequal status and the question litigated concerns a sensitive, intimate area, the risks of an outcome colored by prejudice are especially great. If, for reasons of economy or efficiency ADR must be resorted to in these situations, the likelihood of bias can be reduced by providing rules that clearly specify the scope of the proceedings and forbid irrelevant or intrusive inquiries, by requiring open proceedings, and by providing some form of higher review. The third-party facilitator or decisionmaker should be a professional and be acceptable to both parties. Any party desiring one should be provided with an advocate, ideally an attorney, experienced with representation before the forum in question. To avoid atomization and lost opportunities to aggregate claims and inject public values into dispute resolution, ADR mechanisms should not be used in cases that have a broad societal dimension, but forward them to court for appropriate treatment.

Would measures like these destroy the very advantages of economy, simplicity, speed, and flexibility that make ADR attractive? Would such measures render ADR proceedings as expensive, time-consuming, formalistic, and inflexible as trials? These measures do increase the costs, but, on balance, those costs seem worth incurring. The ideal of equality before the law is too insistent a value to be compromised in the name of more mundane advantages. Continued growth of ADR consistent with goals of basic fairness will require two essential adjustments: (1) It will be necessary to identify those areas and types of ADR in which the dangers of prejudice are greatest and to direct those grievances to formal court adjudication; (2) In those areas in which the risk of prejudice exists, but is not so great as to require an absolute ban, checks and formalities must be built into ADR to ameliorate these risks as much as possible. With both inquiries, the preliminary investigations and tentative identifications of troublesome areas made in this Article may prove useful starting points.

MICHELE HERMANN ET AL., METROCOURT PROJECT FINAL REPORT: A STUDY OF THE EFFECTS OF ETHNICITY AND GENDER IN MEDIATED AND ADJUDICATED CASES AT THE METROPOLITAN COURT MEDIATION CENTER

viii–xii (1993)

INTRODUCTION

This study was funded by the Fund for Research in Dispute Resolution to examine how women and minorities fared in mediated and adjudicated small claims civil cases in Albuquerque, New Mexico. The research hypotheses that we examined were:

(1) Whether women and minorities achieve worse results than males and non-minorities in both adjudicated and mediated small claims cases,

(2) Whether that disparity is greater in mediated than in adjudicated cases, and

(3) Whether that disparity is reduced or eliminated when the mediators are women and/or minorities.

These hypotheses were suggested by theoretical writings postulating that informal, flexible, private settings of alternative dispute resolution processes such as mediation are more susceptible to bias and prejudice which impacts disproportionately on ethnic minorities and women.

BACKGROUND

The study was conducted in the Bernalillo County Metropolitan Court, a non-record court which has jurisdiction to hear civil cases where the amount in controversy is $5,000 or less. The court has 3 judges in the civil division who hear a total caseload of approximately 9,000 cases per year. All three judges are male; one is African American, one Hispanic, and one Caucasian. The court contracts with the Albuquerque Mediation Center to administer and operate the court's mediation program.

With the cooperation of the court and the Mediation Center, civil cases were randomly assigned to either adjudication or mediation and followed by the study. The total final sample was 603 cases, 323 of which were adjudicated and 280 of which were mediated. Cases were co-mediated by a pool of mediators who were combined in all-female, all-male, or mixed gender pairs, and all-minority, all-white, or mixed ethnicity pairs.

Telephone interviews were conducted with parties in both mediated and adjudicated cases as soon as possible after the hearing or mediation. A follow-up questionnaire was mailed approximately six months after the initial interview. Parties who did not respond to the follow-up mailings were called on the telephone. A number of mediation sessions and adjudicated hearings also were observed by study researchers.

We sought to evaluate results in mediation and adjudication using two measures: (1) the objective formula for outcome developed by Vidmar, and (2) subjective measures of satisfaction. Vidmar's objective measure defines monetary outcome as the ratio of the final award minus admitted liability divided by the amount claimed minus admitted liability.

RESULTS

As measured by the objective Vidmar outcome ratio, minority claimants consistently received less money than non-minorities in our study cases, while minority respondents consistently paid more. These disparate results were more extreme in mediated than in adjudicated cases. Statistical analysis of the adjudicated cases showed that monetary outcomes were due primarily to case characteristics and secondarily to the ethnicity of the participants, with strong inter-relationships between the two. In mediated cases, however, ethnicity remained significantly more important for predicting outcome, even with the addition of case characteristic variables.

Having found that minority claimants received less and minority respondents paid more in mediated cases, we then explored whether these effects were counteracted by the ethnicity of the mediators. Our results were quite startling, showing that having two minority mediators eliminated the negative impact on the size of monetary outcomes for minorities in mediation. The combination of one minority mediator and one white mediator, however, did not produce a similar result.

The negative outcomes found for minority participants were not replicated when the data were analyzed for gender. Neither the gender of the claimant nor that of the respondent had an effect on monetary outcomes in either adjudicated or mediated cases. The only statistically reliable tendency we found was for female respondents to pay less in mediated than in adjudicated cases, i.e., to do better than males in mediation.

Our examination of subjective outcome and procedural satisfaction produced interesting contrasts to the objective outcome analysis. Despite their tendency to achieve lower monetary awards as claimants and to pay more as respondents, minority claimants were more likely than non-minority claimants to express satisfaction with mediation. Minority claimants and respondents consistently were more positive about mediation than they were about adjudication on all satisfaction and fairness measures. They also reported process satisfaction significantly more often than non-minorities in mediation.

Minority claimants were most satisfied with the mediation process when the two mediators were also minorities. In fact, white as well as minority claimants were more likely to report procedural satisfaction when the mediation involved a minority respondent and two minority mediators.

Looking at satisfaction levels of women, we found very different responses. As both claimants and respondents, compared to all other ethnic/gender groups, white women reported greater satisfaction with adjudicated rather than mediated outcomes. While white female respondents achieved significantly more favorable outcomes in mediation than the other three groups, they actually reported the lowest levels of satisfaction. Furthermore, compared to other mediation respondents, white women were less likely to see the mediation process as fair and unbiased. Minority women, on the other hand, reported the highest level of satisfaction with mediation, despite their tendency to receive less as claimants and to pay more as respondents.

CONCLUSION

The evidence that minority participants generally fare worse than whites in both mediation and adjudication, and that these effects are most severe in mediation, although they are coupled with higher levels of satisfaction in that forum, raises numerous questions concerning cause and implications. While the temptation is to jump to conclusions about bias, prejudice and cultural blindness, the underlying effects may be considerably more complex and should be the subject of further study, analysis and reflection. Similarly, the fact that women fare well in mediation in small claims court does not dispel the concerns about gender bias in mediation in other forums, such as family court in the context of marital dissolution. More study and analysis is required as well to understand the broader implications of gender differences in mediation. Such study also needs to examine the preference which women expressed for adjudication over mediation, and the disproportionate level of dissatisfaction with the mediation process which we found among white females.

NOTES AND QUESTIONS

1. Professor Delgado and his colleagues wrote *Fairness and Formality* in 1985. At one point in the article, they write "American procedural law's history evidences a strong and steady evolution toward fairness, an evolution that has at times overshadowed the impulse toward economy and efficiency," Consider the current state of mediation, as well as negotiation, plea bargaining, arbitration and ADR generally. Be sure to consider both voluntary use of the procedures, and court-ordered and contractually-mandated use. Does recent history continue to evidence "a strong and steady evolution toward fairness?"

2. Does the analysis in the study by Professor Michele Hermann and her colleagues suggest that we can reduce or eliminate concerns about mediation's potential risks for members of minority groups by using a co-mediation model and making sure that one or both of the mediators are also a member of a minority group? Do you suppose that would always be feasible or appropriate? Would it present other problems?

3. The New Mexico study concluded that minority women found mediation more satisfying than adjudication even though they seemed to do worse financially. Some would explain that finding by suggesting that these women were deceived. Can you think of other explanations? Professor Laura Nader suggests, for example, that ADR values harmony over justice, and tends to pacify the discontented rather than help them assert or enforce rights they may have. *See* Laura Nader, *Controlling Processes in the Practice of Law: Hierarchy and Pacification in the Movement to Re–Form Dispute Ideology,* 9 Ohio St. J. on Disp. Resol. 1 (1993). Some procedural justice research suggests that members of minority populations or those who perceive themselves to be of lower status are especially influenced by processes in which they were treated in a fair and respectful manner. Higher status individuals, in contrast, are less likely to allow process fairness to soften the blow of an unfavorable outcome. In fact, for a higher status negotiator, procedural fairness contributes significantly to her satisfaction only if the outcome is also favorable. *See* Nancy A. Welsh, *Making Deals in Court–Connected Mediation: What's Justice Got To Do With It?,* 79 Wash. U. L.Q. 787, 824 (2001); Ya–Ru Chen, Joel Brockner, & Jerald Greenberg, *When Is It "A Pleasure To Do Business With You?" The Effects of Relative Status, Outcome Favorability, and Procedural Fairness*, 92 Organizational Behavior

and Human Decision Processes, 2003, at 1. Individuals who define and evaluate themselves based on their relationships with others, or believe that social interactions should affirm basic moral values, also seem to be influenced more strongly by the procedural fairness (or unfairness) they experience in negotiation (and presumably, mediation). *See* Joel Brockerner, David De Cremer, Kees van den Bos, & Ya–Ru Chen, *The Influence of Interdependent Self–Construal on Procedural Fairness Effects*, 96 Organizational Behavior and Human Decision Processes, 2005, at 155; David De Cremer & Tom Tyler, *Managing Group Behavior: The Interplay Between Procedural Justice, Sense of Self, and Cooperation*, in ADVANCES IN EXPERIMENTAL SOCIAL PSYCHOLOGY (M. Zanna, Ed., 2005).

4. Professor Emily Calhoun has proposed a variation in mediation procedure for cases involving allegations of individual employment discrimination. She suggests the use of a "first-phase" private caucus with plaintiffs in such cases as a way to make it likely that the mediation will include an awareness of the interests of the plaintiff's minority group and of the plaintiff's relationships with that group as well as the plaintiff's relationship with the workplace community. In addition, she argues that cultivation of "group presence" in such cases would enhance the plaintiff's prospects of self-determination and would foster improved problem-solving. Emily M. Calhoun, *Workplace Mediation: The First–Phase, Private Caucus in Individual Discrimination Disputes*, 9 Harv. Negot. L. Rev. 187 (2004). Thus, she urges that "mediators and civil rights advocates should take seriously the group presence in an individual discrimination dispute and take appropriate advantage of the opportunities offered by first-phase caucuses to work with that presence." *Id.* at 219. Would implementation of that proposal ameliorate some of the concerns expressed in the foregoing excerpts by Professor Delgado and his colleagues and by Professor Hermann and her colleagues? *See also* Roderick Swaab & Jeanne Brett, *Caucus with Care: The Impact of Pre–Mediation Caucuses on Conflict Resolution,* IACM Meetings Paper (2007), *available at* http://papers.ssrn.com/sol3/papers.cfm?abstract_id=10806 22 (reporting empirical research and recommending use of pre-mediation caucus to build trust, not to encourage development of settlement proposals).

5. For further related reading, see Isabelle R. Gunning, *Diversity Issues in Mediation: Controlling Negative Cultural Myths*, 1995 J. Disp. Resol. 55; Carol Izumi, *Implicit Bias and the Illusion of Mediator Neutrality*, 34 Wash. U. J.L. & Pol'y 71 (2010). For an overview of critical scholarship on ADR, see Eric K. Yamamoto, *ADR: Where have All the Critics Gone?*, 36 Santa Clara L. Rev. 1055 (1996). For a plea that all procedures, whether traditional or "alternative," should be viewed in a balanced and realistic manner, *see* Michael Moffitt, *Three Things To Be Against ("Settlement" Not Included)*, 78 Fordham L. Rev. 1203 (2009).

LEONARD L. RISKIN & NANCY A. WELSH, WHAT'S IT ALL ABOUT?: FINDING THE APPROPRIATE PROBLEM DEFINITION IN MEDIATION

15 Dispute Resolution Magazine 19 (Summer 2009)

Since at least the early 1980s, a segment of mediation proponents has persistently emphasized one potential advantage of the mediation process: its ability to escape or at least loosen the pinched perspective that typically dominates the settlement of cases that are or are likely to be in the litigation stream. We call these "court-oriented" cases. The idea is that mediation can help the parties exercise autonomy, not only in agreeing to a solution, but also in determining the focus of the mediation ("the problem definition"). Such autonomy can lead to a broader problem definition and to processes and solutions that are better suited to the parties' real needs.

With some notable exceptions, however, court-oriented mediations in "ordinary" civil, nonfamily disputes—such as personal injury matters, employment cases, contract and property damage disputes, and medical malpractice claims—have not fulfilled this great promise of mediation. Without doubt, some mediations deal with the parties' underlying interests and nonlegal issues. However, it appears that the problem definition in most court-oriented mediation sessions is quite narrow, dominated by litigation risk analysis and valuation. Similarly, the outcomes of these mediations do not vary much from those produced by lawyers' traditional bilateral negotiations.

Often, the plaintiffs or defendants in these cases are "one-shot players." They have little or no experience with litigation and the ways of courts (or private ADR providers). For them, involvement in litigation is far from ordinary. Indeed, many resort to the courts only because they have been caught up in once-in-a-lifetime, unique, or catastrophic events. Only the lawyers, mediators, and insurance claims representatives—the "repeat players" in the litigation system—consider such cases "ordinary." The repeat players effectively narrow both the definition of the problem to be addressed and the set of available remedies. They set the scope of inquiry and the procedures, often without any explicit discussion or recognition of the many available alternative formulations and often without the influence of the one-shot players.

The repeat players tend to focus narrowly on two questions: First, what would happen if the parties litigated this case? Second, how much is the defendant willing to pay and the plaintiff willing to accept to avoid the delay, risks, and costs of trial? In other words, they focus on litigation issues. The lawyers and mediators then implement mediation procedures that they think will enable them to address those questions efficiently. Such procedures typically exclude consideration of the parties' motivations and underlying interests, limit opportunities for the parties to speak or listen to each other directly, and emphasize case evaluation. As a result, such mediations foster a bracketed understanding of the dispute and rational-cognitive-legal approaches to resolving it.

For many one-shot players who have chosen (or are likely to choose) litigation to resolve their disputes, this narrow approach may be wholly appropriate and useful. In *some segment* of cases, though, the dominant focus on litigation analysis means that parties miss opportunities for processes and outcomes that could better suit their needs. This suggests that there could be great value in developing a means to permit parties, especially one-shot players, to determine whether they wish to influence the development of the problem definition in their cases and thus capitalize upon one of the unique attributes of mediation.

In this article, we propose four mechanisms to enable mediation participants to explore problems broadly and then to decide what problem definition is most appropriate for the mediation of their case:

• A three-step systematic method for determining the problem to be addressed;

• Two variations of a rule that could be adopted by courts (and private providers) that would require lawyers or mediators to implement this systematic way of working with problem definition; and

• A new rule under which a court (or private) mediation program would offer to customize any mediation in order to seek the most appropriate problem definition.

We offer these mechanisms here to stimulate a dialogue regarding the most effective and administrable approaches that could give parties—especially one-shot players—the opportunity to influence the focus of their mediation sessions.

A Three–Step Method for Identifying and Addressing "the Problem"

In many ways, this three-step systematic method represents a simple distillation of good practices in other mediation arenas. It includes mapping the problem; setting the problem; and addressing the problem.

Step 1: Mapping the Problem

To map the problem in the ordinary case, the parties need to reveal to the mediator—and potentially to the other parties—as much as is feasible and appropriate about all of the issues potentially involved in their court-oriented mediation. Obviously, in these types of cases, there will be litigation issues. In addition, though, there may be personal, relational, business/economic, community, and public policy issues and interests. It also may be helpful for the mediation participants to think about the three dimensions of conflict—behavioral, cognitive, and emotional—that Bernard Mayer has identified as necessary elements of full resolution, as well as the five "core concerns"—appreciation, autonomy, affiliation, status, and role—that Roger Fisher and Daniel Shapiro tell us all negotiators share.

To accomplish this, we propose that parties try to answer questions such as these:

1.   What do you hope to accomplish and what problem(s) would you like to address in this mediation? How can the process, the mediator, or both help you accomplish these goals?

2.   If the mediation focuses on the legal strengths and weaknesses of your case and the likely cost of continuing in litigation, will this be sufficient to help you reach a complete resolution of your dispute with the other party? If not, what other nonlitigation issues need to be addressed? How could they be addressed?

3.   As you imagine settling this dispute, what are your most important needs or goals? (For example, are you most concerned about compensation for expenses? The availability of future medical care for you or your dependents? Training? An apology? Maintaining your reputation?)

4.   What do you think are the most important needs or goals of the other side?

5.   If not already described, is there anything besides the payment of money that would help to resolve this matter?

6.   If not already described, do the parties need to change any behaviors to resolve this conflict? If yes, what behavioral changes are required?

7.   If not already described, are emotions a significant part of this conflict? If yes, what outcome or procedure could help you (or the other party) feel at peace about this dispute and its resolution?

8.   How would you describe the communications or negotiations you have had with each other up until now? Why haven't you been able to reach a resolution?

9.   Do you have any questions about how the mediation process works? Do you have any questions or concerns about your role during the presentations or discussions? Do you have any questions or concerns about your role in making a decision about whether to settle your case?

Step 2: Setting the Problem: Selecting the Issues to Be Addressed in the Mediation Process

Once they have uncovered all of the issues that could be discussed in their mediation, the parties and lawyers must advise the mediator regarding those issues that they affirmatively wish to tackle. The following sorts of questions can help at this step. Should the mediation address:

1.   All of your nonlitigation issues? If not, which nonlitigation issues should be addressed?

2.   All of your underlying needs and goals? If not, which underlying needs and goals should be addressed?

3.   All of the other side's underlying needs and goals? If not, which underlying needs and goals should be addressed?

4.   The needs of individuals or organizations that are not direct parties to this lawsuit or potential lawsuit?

5.   Behavioral changes, if these are an important part of resolving this dispute?

6.   The parties' different understandings of what took place, if these are an important part of resolving this dispute?

7.   The parties' emotions, if these are an important part of resolving this dispute?

8.   All of the above issues explicitly? Alternatively, should the mediation process address certain issues only indirectly? How?

After discussion of such questions, the parties, lawyers, and mediator "set" the problem, that is, specify the issues that will comprise the substance of the mediation.

Step 3: Addressing the Problem

In this step, the parties, lawyers, and mediator establish the mediation process and begin to address the problem or problems they have set. In the mediation of a corporate contract dispute, for instance, in addition to legal issues, the corporate representatives may choose to speak with each other about the personal toll that each has borne and will continue to bear if the dispute is not resolved. They may even discuss their organizations' differing cultural expectations and their mutual need for recognition of and appreciation for their attempts to accommodate each other. In an employment mediation, the employer and a long-time employee may decide to include a discussion of the health needs of the employee's spouse that have affected the employee's autonomy and that also restrict the retirement options available to the employee.

Court (and Private) Initiatives to Encourage Establishment of Appropriate Problem Definition

We do not expect that all or even most parties will choose to go beyond the discussion of litigation issues in their court-oriented mediation sessions. Nonetheless, we believe that explicitly taking the first two steps—mapping the problem and then setting it—will increase the proportion of cases that employ the most appropriate problem definition. In order for that to happen, of course, someone must foster the use of such a three-step process. We propose three initiatives that courts (and private ADR providers) could employ.

A Rule for Lawyers

Courts could adopt a rule requiring lawyers to consult with their clients in the creation of written, premediation responses to questions such as those posed previously and to submit such responses to the mediator in confidence. Although a lawyer could sign this document on her client's behalf, we also suggest a requirement that she certify that the responses represent the result of a thorough discussion with her client. This submission would help the mediator facilitate the first and second steps—mapping and setting the problem. Even if the mediator were not following the three-step approach, the submission would help the mediator identify the issues that the mediation process could and should address.

We are aware, of course, that many mediators and court-connected mediation programs already require the submission of confidential premediation statements. Generally, however, these statements reflect a narrow, litigation-focused problem definition even for those mediators and court programs that ask about nonlitigation issues. We suspect that lawyers often do not comprehend what information the mediator or program is requesting. They may understand "interests" as "positions" despite all of the books, court publications, and training programs that distinguish between these concepts. Our proposed rule provides more guidance to enable lawyers (along with their clients) to take a detailed look at the range of issues that could be addressed in mediation.

Although our proposal provides parties with the opportunity to address a broader version of their dispute, they should, of course, also have the power to address only narrower aspects. We hope that the simple requirement that lawyers and clients *consider and answer* these questions together will enhance lawyer-client dialogues and encourage lawyers and mediators to notice and seek opportunities to address nonlitigation issues, underlying interests, and the cognitive and emotional dimensions of the dispute. At a minimum, the obligation to consider such issues should increase mediators' confidence in the propriety of broadening their inquiry once the mediation begins.

A Rule for Mediators

Under this proposal, courts (and private ADR programs) would require that, in premediation conversations or during mediation sessions, their mediators ask some or all of the mapping and setting questions, and that they be competent to respond appropriately to the answers. Implementation of this proposal, like the one directed at lawyers, would require some work by courts and private ADR providers. This might include training sessions for mediators as well as lawyers. Lawyers would learn that they and their clients would be asked some or all of the mapping and setting questions before or during mediation sessions. Indeed, courts and private ADR providers that furnish educational information to lawyers about mediation for distribution to their clients could include these sorts of questions in their explanation of what to expect in mediation.

A New Program to Offer "Customized" Mediation

Our third proposal is that courts (and private providers) should offer to "customize" every mediation, beginning with some form of mapping and including an explicit process for setting the problem definition. We are *not* proposing that courts offer two mutually exclusive and rigid categories of mediation. Instead, our proposal would allow parties and lawyers to "customize" their mediation or choose—deliberately and knowingly—to avoid all the time and effort that would be required for such customization. Some court programs, such as the Circuit Mediation Office of the U.S. Court of Appeals for the Ninth Circuit and the U.S. District Court for the Northern District of California, already offer such customization routinely. The local rules for the Northern District of California specifically note that "[a] hallmark of mediation is its capacity to expand traditional settlement discussions and broaden resolution options, often by exploring litigant needs and interests that may be formally independent of the legal issues in controversy." Much can be learned from the experience of these courts' programs, particularly the manner in which they have made customization part of their culture. For other courts, however, this undertaking will be quite new and will require the education of mediators, lawyers, and parties.

Likely Concerns About the Proposed Initiatives: The Roles of Lawyers and Courts

Of the many potential objections to our proposals, two seem most significant. The first has to do with the likelihood that lawyers will resist the opportunity to expand mediation's problem definition for the identical reasons that they embrace the focus that currently characterizes court-oriented mediation: The emphasis in most ordinary mediations on knowledge of the law and litigation expertise reinforces lawyers' claims to the privileges of professionalism, including autonomy, status, and substantial fees. A law-and-litigation problem definition also matches most lawyers' psychological preferences for the resolution of disputes based on the application of standards and rules and the avoidance of emotional issues. Most important, lawyers' transformation of their clients' unwieldy disputes and expectations into claims and remedies that can be addressed by the law has real strengths, and often is the best way to protect and foster clients' interests.

The concern about lawyers' resistance is well grounded, but there are interesting hints of change in the legal profession that may both encourage and gain support from courts' and private providers' adoption of our proposals. Many lawyers, for example, express interest in using broader problem definitions, and growing numbers are forming groups of "collaborative" or "cooperative" lawyers who support each other through their practice protocols. New initiatives seek to bring aspects of the "collaborative" or "cooperative" approaches to areas beyond their original home in family law, including the "ordinary" matters that we have been discussing. In addition, certain influential elements of the commercial bar have expressed appreciation for a mediation process that includes litigation analysis, but also explores the parties' underlying interests.

A second objection concerns the appropriate role of the courts. Should the courts offer to broaden the subject matter of a mediation session when access to this public resource has historically been conditioned upon narrowing the subject matter of a dispute in order to make it manageable and consistent with the unique mission of the courts? Further, is it the courts' role to encourage wide-ranging, nonlegal conversations at the same time that the Supreme Court is signaling to judges that they can and should decide early, at the pleadings stage, whether plaintiffs deserve access to the courts—or even a response from defendants? [FN6] Throughout history, courts have evolved in response to the changing needs of society and the emergence of competing, successful models of dispute resolution. Examples abound. In medieval Europe, which had a patchwork of contradictory local laws and business practices, a private system known as the Law Merchant arose to create and apply commerce-facilitating rules and procedures to the resolution of international merchants' disputes. Over time, ordinary courts throughout Europe incorporated the Law Merchant's principles into commercial law. In recent years, U.S. courts have been adapting to the needs of particular subsets of disputants. For example, there are now business courts, mental health courts, juvenile courts, domestic violence courts, drug courts, and community courts. In each of these contexts, courts have concluded that their traditional processes and remedies were not sufficiently effective and have therefore chosen to offer additional services.

Similarly, courts can decide that court-connected mediation should have the capacity to be responsive to those parties who desire or need a more inclusive dispute resolution process. Having this option could enhance these parties' sense of being treated fairly by their courts, which is likely to influence their perceptions of the substantive fairness of their agreements and the institutional legitimacy of the courts. As noted earlier, some courts already invite parties to go beyond a litigation focus in mediation. These courts can serve as models for others.

In addition, though other countries' courts reflect their own procedures, histories, and values, it may be useful for courts in the United States to consider some aspects of the mediation program that the courts of the Netherlands recently institutionalized. There, mediating and judging are understood as different in terms of process *and* problem definition. Dutch judges, who may meet with the parties and lawyers several times to investigate and attempt to resolve the case, are taught to ask, "Will my decision solve your problem?" If the answer is "Yes," then the judge should retain the case, continuing the investigation into its legal merits and issuing a decision. On the other hand, if the parties acknowledge the importance of nonlegal issues, the judge urges them to try mediation, specifically to address those issues.

Litigant Influence on the Process

Through any of our proposals, courts would offer a real "value added" for the disputants and disputes that do not quite fit the mold provided by the standard litigation focus in court-oriented mediation. Indeed, in the United States, where most citizens accessing the courts are one-shot players, it seems quite appropriate that our courts should allow such litigants to influence the design and focus of the process so that it will respond to their unique needs.

NOTES AND QUESTIONS

1.   Professors Riskin and Welsh explain that their proposal is based in part on actual procedures in place in some federal district and circuit courts, specifically the U.S. District Court of the Northern District of California (where Olam was mediated) and the 9th Circuit. Since this article was written, and as a result of Congress' continued underfunding of the federal courts, financial cutbacks have been made to the Northern District of California's program.

2.   How persuasive do you find this proposal by Professors Riskin and Welsh? Do you think that lawyers would ask these questions of their clients? Are these questions consistent with any of the models of the attorney-client relationship discussed in Chapter II?

2. THE PROBLEM WITH FAIRNESS IN FAMILY LAW

TRINA GRILLO, THE MEDIATION ALTERNATIVE: PROCESS DANGERS FOR WOMEN
100 Yale L.J. 1545, 1549–50, 1600–08, 1610 (1991)

[Editor's Note: California is one of numerous states that require mediation of disputed child custody issues in divorce cases. CAL. CIV. CODE § 4607(a) (West Supp.1990). In this excerpt, Professor Trina Grillo—at the time of this writing an active family mediator handling private, voluntary cases—criticizes California's mandatory system, which often excludes lawyers from the mediation sessions.]

Custody mediation under the California system] provides neither a more just nor a more humane alternative to the adversarial system of adjudication of custody, and, therefore, does not fulfill its promises. In particular * * * mandatory mediation can be destructive to many women and some men because it requires them to speak in a setting they have not chosen and often imposes a rigid orthodoxy as to how they should speak, make decisions, and be. This orthodoxy is imposed through subtle and not-so-subtle messages about appropriate conduct and about what may be said in mediation. It is an orthodoxy that often excludes the possibility of the parties speaking with their authentic voices.

* * *

III. MANDATORY MEDIATION AND THE DANGERS OF FORCED ENGAGEMENT

Emma has been in a marriage which in its early years seemed to be a good one for both Emma and her husband. She has been the primary caretaker of the children, and she is very committed to them. She has lived much of her life through her husband and her children, and has not worked outside her home. Increasingly, however, she has begun to feel that she and her husband have grown apart, and that he does not see her as a person but rather as a repository of various roles. After much agony, she has decided to end her marriage. Her departure from the marriage is a first step toward seeing her life as having separate dimensions from her husband's and children's, but her right to individuation does not seem clear to her; in fact, there are many times when it seems selfish and wrong. It is hard for her even to find the language to describe what is propelling her to turn her life, and her children's lives, upside down, but propelling she is. The marital separation was an early step toward defining her own physical and psychological boundaries. She now finds herself, however, feeling guilty, frightened, and unsure of how she will survive in the world alone.

Joan has been in a marriage in which she has been physically abused for ten years. She and her husband David have two children, whom David has never abused. She is afraid, however, that if she leaves David, he will begin to abuse the children whenever he is caring for them. Joan has been afraid to leave her marriage because David has threatened to harm her if she does so. When she separated briefly from him previously, he followed her and continually harassed her. Each time David beats Joan he shows great remorse afterwards and promises never to do it again. He is a man of considerable charm, and she has often believed him on these occasions. Nonetheless, Joan has finally decided to leave her husband. She is worried about what will happen, economically and physically, to her children and herself.

It might be that mediation would help Emma's family disengage and discover ways of relating to one another. Mediation could be useful, even transformative, during the divorce process. Significant possibilities of damage to Emma also exist, however. For example, she might find herself traumatized by a forced engagement with her husband. Or, in the intimate mediation setting, she might find it difficult to withstand criticism of how she is conducting herself in life or in the mediation.

For Joan, the direct confrontation with her husband, with the safety of her children and herself at stake, would surely be psychologically traumatizing and might also put her in physical danger. Because of these possibilities, the chance—even the substantial one—of a beneficial result cannot justify the sort of intrusion by the state that occurs when mediation is mandatory.

While some of mandatory mediation's dangers affect men and women equally, others fall disproportionately on women. A study that compared people who chose to mediate with those who rejected the opportunity found that 44% of the reasons given by women who rejected mediation services offered to them center around their mistrust of, fear of, or desire to avoid their ex-spouse. In contrast, those men who rejected mediation appeared to do so because they were skeptical of the mediation process or convinced they could win in court. Thus, the requirement of mandatory mediation that the parties meet personally with one another, usually without a lawyer present, presents troubling issues for women. Feminist analyses, looked at alone and together, clarify why this is so.

A.   The Ethic of Care in Mediation

As discussed earlier, several feminist scholars have suggested that women have a more "relational" sense of self than do men. The most influential of these researchers, Carol Gilligan, describes two different, gendered modes of thought. The female mode is characterized by an "ethic of care" which emphasizes nurturance, connection with others, and contextual thinking. The male mode is characterized by an "ethic of justice" which emphasizes individualism, the use of rules to resolve moral dilemmas, and equality. Under Gilligan's view, the male mode leads one to strive for individualism and autonomy, while the female mode leads one to strive for connection with and caring for others. Some writers, seeing a positive virtue in the ethic of care, have applied Gilligan's work to the legal system. * * *

The "ethic of care" has also been viewed as the manifestation of a system of gender domination. Nevertheless, it is clear that those who operate in a "female mode"—whether biologically male or female—will respond more "selflessly" to the demands of mediation.

Whether the ethic of care is to be enshrined as a positive virtue, or criticized as a characteristic not belonging to all women and contributing to their oppression, one truth emerges: many women see themselves, and judge their own worth, primarily in terms of relationships. This perspective on themselves has consequences for how they function in mediation.

Carrie Menkel–Meadow has suggested that the ethic of care can and should be brought into the practice of law—that the world of lawyering would look very different from the perspective of that ethic. Some commentators have identified mediation as a way to incorporate the ethic of care into the legal system and thereby modify the harshness of the adversary process. And, indeed, at first glance, mediation in the context of divorce might be seen as a way of bringing the woman-identified values of intimacy, nurturance, and care into a legal system that is concerned with the most fundamental aspects of women's and men's lives.

If mediation does not successfully introduce an ethic of care, however, but instead merely sells itself on that promise while delivering something coercive in its place, the consequences will be disastrous for a woman who embraces a relational sense of self. If she is easily persuaded to be cooperative, but her partner is not, she can only lose. If it is indeed her disposition to be caring and focused on relationships, and she has been rewarded for that focus and characterized as "unfeminine" when she departs from it, the language of relationship, caring, and cooperation will be appealing to her and make her vulnerable. Moreover, the intimation that she is not being cooperative and caring, that she is thinking of herself instead of thinking selflessly of the children can shatter self-esteem and make her lose faith in herself. In short, in mediation, such a woman may be encouraged to repeat exactly those behaviors that have proven hazardous to her in the past.

In the story above, Emma is asked to undergo a forced engagement with the very person from whom she is trying to differentiate herself at a difficult stage in her life. She may find it impossible to think of herself as a separate entity during mediation, while her husband may easily be able to act on behalf of his separate self. "When a separate self must be asserted, women have trouble asserting it. Women's separation from the other in adult life, and the tension between that separation and our fundamental state of connection, is felt most acutely when a woman must make choices, and when she must speak the truth."[122]

Emma will be asked to talk about her needs and feelings, and respond to her husband's needs and feelings. Although in the past her valuing relationships above all else may have worked to the detriment of her separate self, Emma will now be urged to work on the future relationship between herself and her ex-husband. Above all, she will be asked to put the well-being of the children before her own, as if she and her children's well-being were entirely separate. Her problem in addressing her future alone, however, may be that she reflexively puts her children before herself, even when she truly needs to take care of herself in order to take care of her children. For Emma, mediation may play on what are already her vulnerable spots, and put her at a disadvantage. She may begin to think of herself as unfeminine, or simply bad, if she puts her own needs forward. Emma may feel the need to couch every proposal she makes in terms of the needs of her children. In sum, if she articulates her needs accurately, she may end up feeling guilty, selfish, confused, and embarrassed; if she does not, she will be moving backwards to the unbounded self that is at the source of her difficulties.

For Joan, the prescription of mediation might be disastrous. She has always been susceptible to her husband's charm, and has believed him when he has said that he would stop abusing her. She has always been afraid of him. She is likely, in mediation, to be susceptible and afraid once again. She may continue to care for her husband, and to think that she was responsible for his behavior toward her. Joan, and not her husband, will be susceptible to any pressure to compromise, and to compromise in her situation might be very dangerous for both her and her children.

B.   Sexual Domination and Judicial Violence

Women who have been through mandatory mediation often describe it as an experience of sexual domination, comparing mandatory mediation to rape. Catharine MacKinnon's work provides a basis for explaining why, for some women, this characterization is appropriate. MacKinnon has analyzed gender as a system of power relations, evidenced primarily with respect to the control of women's sexuality. While MacKinnon recognizes the sense in which women are fundamentally connected to others, she does not celebrate it. Rather, she sees the potential for connection as invasive and intrusive. It is precisely the potential for physical connection that permits invasion into the integrity of women's bodies. It is precisely

---

[122] West, *Jurisprudence and Gender*, 55 U.CHI.L.REV. 1, 55 (1988).

the potential for emotional connection that permits intrusion into the integrity of women's lives.

Men do not experience this same fear of sexual domination, according to MacKinnon; they do not live in constant fear of having the very integrity of their lives intruded upon. Men may not comprehend their role in this system of sexual domination any more than women may be able to articulate the source of their feeling of disempowerment. Yet both of these dynamics are at work in the mediation setting. It may seem a large leap, from acts of physical violence and invasion to the apparently simple requirement that a woman sit in a room with her spouse working toward the resolution of an issue of mutual concern. But that which may be at stake in a court-ordered custody mediation—access to one's children— may be the main reason one has for living, as well as all one's hope for the future. And because mandatory mediation is a *forced* engagement, ordinarily without attorneys or even friends or supporters present, it may amount to a form of "psychic breaking and entering" or, put another way, psychic rape.

There is always the potential for violence in the legal system: "a judge articulates her understanding of a text, and as a result, somebody loses his freedom, his property, his children, even his life . . . When interpreters have finished their work, they frequently leave behind victims whose lives have been torn apart by these organized, social practices of violence."[123]

The reality of this background of judicial violence cannot be discounted when measuring the potential trauma of the mandatory mediation setting. Although the mediation system is purportedly designed in part to help participants *avoid* contact with the violence that must come from judicial decisions, in significant ways the violence of the contact is more direct. Since the parties are obliged to speak for themselves in a setting to which the culture has not introduced them and in which the rules are not clear (and in fact vary from mediator to mediator), the potential violence of the legal result, combined with the invasiveness of the setting, may indeed end up feeling to the unwilling participant very much like a kind of rape. Moreover, in judging, it is understood that the critical view of the quarrel is that of the judge, the professional third party. Mediation is described as a form of intervention that reflects the *disputants'* view of the quarrel. But having the mediation take place on court premises with a mediator who might or might not inject her prejudices into the process may make it unlikely that the disputants' view will control. Thus, a further sense of violation may arise from having another person's view of the dispute characterized and treated as one's own.

---

[123] Cover, *Violence and the Word*, 95 Yale L.J. 1601, 1601 (1986).

That many reportedly find mediation helpful does not mean everyone does. Consensual sex may take place in a certain setting in one instance but that does not make all sex in that setting consensual; sometimes it is rape. And sometimes it may only seem to be consensual because forced sex is considered par for the course—that is, it is all we know or can imagine.

When I have suggested to mediators that even being forced to sit across the table and negotiate, unassisted, with a spouse might be traumatic, their reaction has been almost uniformly dismissive. Some mediators have denied that this could possibly be the case. Even mediators who acknowledge the possibility of trauma have said, in effect, "So what?" A few hours of discomfort seems not so much to ask in return for a system that, to their mind, serves the courts and the children much better than the alternative. But a few hours of discomfort may not be all that is at stake; the trauma inflicted upon a vulnerable party during mediation can be as great as that which occurs in other psychologically violent confrontations. As such, it should not be minimized. People frequently take months or years to recover from physical or mental abuse, rape, and other traumatic events. Given the psychological vulnerability of people at the time of a divorce, it is likely that some people may be similarly debilitated by a mandatory mediation process.

Moreover, because the mandatory mediation system is more problematic for women than for men, forcing unwilling women to take part in a process which involves much personal exposure sends a powerful social message: it is permissible to discount the real experience of women in the service of someone else's idea of what will be good for them, good for their children, or good for the system.

IV. ALTERNATIVES TO MANDATORY MEDIATION

* * *

With respect to institutional changes, an adequate mediation scheme should not only be voluntary rather than mandatory, but should also allow people's emotions to be part of the process, allow their values and principles to matter in the discussion, allow parties' attorneys to participate if requested by the parties, allow parties to choose a mediator and the location for the mediation, allow parties to choose the issues to mediate, and require that divorcing couples be educated about the availability and logistics of mediation so as to enable them to make an intelligent choice as to whether to engage in it.

The second aspect of reform represents more of a personal dynamic, one which is harder to institutionalize or to regulate. But the mediator must learn to respect each client's struggles, including her timing, anger, and resistance to having certain issues mediated, and also learn to refrain, to the extent he is capable, from imposing his own substantive agenda on the mediation.

CONCLUSION

Although mediation can be useful and empowering, it presents some serious process dangers that need to be addressed, rather than ignored. When mediation is imposed rather than voluntarily engaged in, its virtues are lost. More than lost: mediation becomes a wolf in sheep's clothing. It relies on force and disregards the context of the dispute, while masquerading as a gentler, more empowering alternative to adversarial litigation. Sadly, when mediation is mandatory it becomes like the patriarchal paradigm of law it is supposed to supplant. Seen in this light, mandatory mediation is especially harmful: its messages disproportionately affect those who are already subordinated in our society, those to whom society has already given the message, in far too many ways, that they are not leading proper lives.

Of course, subordinated people can go to court and lose; in fact, they usually do. But if mediation is to be introduced into the court system, it should provide a better alternative. It is not enough to say that the adversary system is so flawed that even a misguided, intrusive, and disempowering system of mediation should be embraced. If mediation as currently instituted constitutes a fundamentally flawed process in the way I have described, it is more, not less, disempowering than the adversary system—for it is then a process in which people are told they are being empowered, but in fact are being forced to acquiesce in their oppression.

NOTE

Professor Joshua D. Rosenberg, a colleague of Professor Grillo's and formerly a mediator in a mandatory court mediation program in California, provides an extensive rebuttal to Grillo's argument. A short excerpt follows:

JOSHUA D. ROSENBERG, IN DEFENSE OF MEDIATION
33 Ariz. L. Rev. 467, 468–69, 492–500, 503–05 (1991)[*]

Professor Grillo's article paints a very effective and very dramatic picture of mediation as a misguided and destructive process. As both a teacher and a student of mediation, I have found that the process is supportive, empowering and enlightening to the participants. Helping parties to feel better about themselves and their interests is one of the most important and most valued of skills among mediators. Studies regularly show that people who go through mandatory mediation are pleased with the process.

How does my colleague's picture of mediation as a monster emerge? Professor Grillo's article distorts the mediation process in four ways: (1) the article tells stories about mediation that are the equivalent of using a series of stories about physicians' rape of patients to paint a picture of the practice of medicine in this country; (2) the article subjects mediation to a series of double-binds, in which anything a mediator does is characterized as bad; (3) mediation is blamed for problems which existed long before mediation; and (4) the article portrays mediation as being both more powerful and more dangerous than it really is.

* * *

Indeed, most of Professor Grillo's mediation horror stories are not from mediation at all. Instead, they involve mediation/evaluation, a process in which the "mediator" also functions as an evaluator and quasi-decision-maker. This process is often more like an informal arbitration or settlement conference than like mediation, a process in which the mediator has no decision-making authority at all. An overwhelming percentage of the mandatory participants (especially the women) prefer even mediation/evaluation to litigation. Nonetheless, it is significantly different from mediation.

* * *

GIVING IN

Another criticism of mediation stems from Professor Grillo's assertion that women are more "relational" than men. In essence, Professor Grillo asserts that women are more concerned with relating to and working with people, while men are often more concerned with dominating other people. Indeed, while Professor Grillo talks about psychological history as a basis for this difference, there is also biological evidence to support the proposition that some of men's tendencies toward dominance and aggression are hormonal. The truth of this proposition, however, does not lead, directly or indirectly, to the conclusion that mandatory mediation should be abandoned.

* * *

While it is true that one parent may do "better" than the other in mediation, it is equally true that the same parent is likely to do better in non-mediated settlements. Indeed, it is likely that during the entire marriage that spouse got things his or her way to a greater extent. Of course, the same reasoning is not limited to marriage. We all know some people who are more strong-willed and who seem able to get what they want; and we know others who, though perhaps equally or more capable, and perhaps more worthy, seem always to just miss getting what they want. Several surveys indicate that negotiating success correlates more highly with certain personality constructs (usually referred to as those that make someone "strong-willed") than it does with intelligence. It was suggested long ago that life is not fair, but it is more fair to those who stand up for what they want.

While it may not be news to suggest that life is not fair, it is no answer for Professor Grillo to suggest that the state should, as a result, be content to sit by and let things proceed unfairly. The state has an undeniably strong interest in intervening to change pre-existing power imbalances (indeed, that is what the state does every time it acts). An action between divorcing spouses engaged in child custody determinations, therefore, might simply be one of many occasions when state intervention is appropriate. An objective analysis of the situation, however, would indicate that it is not. In all relationships, and, as a result, in all marriages, there is, to a greater or lesser extent, some power imbalance caused solely by personality differences (in addition to whatever situation specific external power imbalances might also exist). These imbalances are often most dramatic in intact marriages, because the very filing for divorce is often a sign of change in the power imbalance, and it often acts to drastically realign relationships even more. Despite the relatively high divorce rate of recent years, many people go through years or an entire lifetime feeling stuck in relationships they find oppressive. Either because of feared financial hardship, or because they are afraid of what else might happen if they leave their spouses, people often endure relationships which give them little of what they want or need, and in which they feel at the mercy of their spouses. This kind of relationship is both intolerable for the person and potentially harmful to children of the marriage.

People who remain in these relationships need more assistance in asserting themselves than do people who are leaving them, or than people who are divorcing for other reasons. Unfortunately, this same lack of assertiveness, combined with a lack of understanding of its true roots and consequences, prevents those individuals most in need of assistance from obtaining it. Absent actual or threatened physical abuse, the state does not even consider intervening to help in these cases, where help may be most needed.

* * *

Professor Grillo asserts that some people will nonetheless feel compelled to abide by a tentative agreement. If so, it is only because the mediator does not adequately explain the party's options and the mediator's expectation that the party will take care to evaluate the tentative agreement outside of the mediation session. Concern that a mediator make that expectation clear is appropriate and helpful. To suggest that mandatory mediation ought to be eliminated because of a mediator might not do so is too drastic a remedy.

Professor Grillo suggests that some women may, nonetheless, resist mediation because they fear that they will give in. These women need protection because once in mediation, they will feel obligated to reach an agreement, and once having reached an agreement, they will feel obligated to stick to it regardless of whether or not it is actually binding at that point. In fact, those who become aware prior to mediation of a self-defeating tendency to acquiesce become less likely to actually capitulate once in the mediation. Anyone who is sufficiently aware of her tendency to give in so that she would, if given the opportunity, refuse to participate in mediation, is unlikely to feel compelled to adhere to an admittedly tentative agreement when she is directly advised that she ought to consider the agreement only tentative. This may happen on rare occasions, but to eliminate mandatory mediation would be to take drastic action that affects numerous individuals, to provide only limited benefit for a very small number of individuals who likely need assistance in many areas.

* * *

Finally, even if mediation were impermissible, there would be no guarantee that a court would order a more fair or just result in court. Court determinations on a given set of facts depend on the particular judge and on the quality of the attorney representing each party. Since there is as much fluctuation in the quality and the negotiating ability of attorneys as there is among non-attorneys, judicial results are subject to the same kinds of variation that result from bargaining between the parties.

FORCED ENGAGEMENT AS HORROR

Professor Grillo's final criticism of mandatory mediation is that the very experience of sitting in a room with her former husband may be awful for some women, and the state ought not to require women to go through that experience. Women would have to negotiate with their husbands over the future of their children even in the absence of state intervention, but they might not otherwise have to come in close physical proximity to them in a setting in which they are encouraged to be open and honest, so that mandatory mediation does, in this respect, affirmatively create a problem for some women. The problem, suggests Professor Grillo, is that women are expected to sit across from their husbands, expose their desires, needs and feelings, and listen to the desires, needs and feelings of their husbands. They are also expected to absorb an assortment of judgments from their husbands and the mediator about their ways of being inside and outside the mediation process.

Indeed, goes the argument, some women will find mediation traumatic and will experience it as being as terrible as rape. * * * The analogy of mandatory mediation to rape is somewhat less than compelling. First of all, while mandatory mediation may require a women to sit in the same room as her husband, it cannot be merely the physical proximity that makes the session feel like rape. If it were, the judicial hearing with the parties present would have the same result. What makes the situation so oppressive, according to Professor Grillo, is that a woman may subject herself to listening to and absorbing her husband's concerns and may feel guilty about standing up for her own desires. The choices available to the woman, according to Professor Grillo, are to either stand up for herself and feel intolerably guilty, or to give in and thereby give up what is most important to her—another classic double-bind. Fortunately, much more appealing alternatives are not only available, but are likely. The woman who cooperates for the good of the children is likely to feel good about herself for being concerned with her children and their best interests. She may, for the first time in her life, find her more relational stance being validated and even adopted, and her husband's competitive and noncommunicative stance being rejected by the mediator, a representative of the state. She may be encouraged, for the first time in her life, to stand up to her husband for the good of herself and her children. Her assertion (as opposed to watching someone else attempt to stand up for her) may be a transformative experience. Indeed, if the mediator is any good, the woman will find that she can stand up for herself *and* have her relational stance validated at the same time. If the mother is angry, the mediation is likely to allow her to feel justified in being angry and to encourage her to protect herself in the future.

* * *

Professor Grillo suggests that, at least in court, each party expects that the proceedings will be rough. Each party is therefore likely to have her guard up and be less vulnerable to the judicial violence. In a mediation session, however, the expectation is of cooperation. There, the woman is more likely to be hit with her defenses down. Of course, the woman who is getting divorced and fighting with her husband about child custody is less than likely to go into any kind of session aimed at resolving custody disputes expecting only cooperation and pleasantness. Hopefully, the mediator will be able to de-escalate conflict and allow cooperation to emerge in time. However, neither party is likely [to] be surprised to confront a spouse who is hostile in the beginning of the session, or even a spouse who remains hostile throughout.

Admittedly, one significant difference between court hearings and most mediation sessions is the presence of attorneys at one and not the other. The attorney's presence in court, claims Professor Grillo, protects the women from the psychological damage that a mediation session might cause. Initially, it is important to note that the role of an attorney is limited in a hearing. While she can object to certain questions from the other side, she can do so only for the reasons provided in the rules of evidence, not simply because the questions may cause some psychological harm to her client. Indeed, if anything, the mediator is generally more aware of the parties' psychological states than is a judge. The mediator is trained to attend to that state rather than to the rules of evidence in determining how far to allow questioning to go.

Nor is the presence of an attorney always a good thing for the person who habitually accommodates herself to the wishes of others. The woman who would accommodate the former husband who now opposes her is even more likely to accommodate the wishes of the attorney who is represented as her savior. * * *

On the other hand, the best of both worlds exists when the parties can better negotiate with help from a third party, who sees her role as both protecting the parties and facilitating creative problem-solving, and can also consult with their attorneys prior to making any commitments. This process allows the parties to explore solutions, and to adequately consider those proposed solutions before committing to them.

WHY MANDATORY

The vast majority of women who participate in mandatory mediation are satisfied with the experience and are glad that they have gone through mediation as opposed to a judicial hearing. Nor is there any indication that these women are somehow being duped. They come out with agreements that they believe are good for themselves and for their children. Statistics indicate that court hearings are likely to bring about arrangements that are worse. Not only do fathers "win" contested cases as often as do women, but also even those cases that women "win" are not as tailored or as personalized as are mediated agreements. In addition, mediated agreements are more likely to remain satisfactory to the parties and to continue to be respected and followed than are court-mandated arrangements.

But, goes the argument, if mediation is good, it should not have to be mandatory. All we need to do is tell people about it, or show them a videotape, and those for whom it is helpful will choose it. The unfortunate truth about human behavior, however, is that left to our own devices, we often choose to act in ways that are not profoundly wise. * * *

To the extent that people's views about mediation are subject to influence outside of the judicial system, it is not the educational media, but the opinions of their lawyers, that seems to impact most noticeably. Where mediation is not mandatory, it is likely to be chosen by those whose lawyers recommend it and likely to be rejected by those advised by their attorneys to do so.

In addition, if mediation is not mandatory, it is not then voluntary in any real sense of the word. Instead, under a system of non-mandatory mediation, either parent could force the case to trial by refusing to mediate, regardless of the other party's preference. Evidence indicates that women would not be more likely than men to opt out of mediation. Instead, those most likely to reject mediation are those who are unfamiliar with the process and are generally hesitant to try anything new. Whether those represented by attorneys are likely to accept or reject mediation seems to depend more on the attitudes of the local bar than on any insight on the parties' part. Studies have shown that while in some areas one third of divorcing parents would reject mediation if given the opportunity, when those parents are required to mediate, 75% to 80% of them are satisfied with the process and glad they were ordered to participate. Courts satisfy about half that many. Many people find custody mediation to be tense and unpleasant. These same people find court more tense and more unpleasant, and of those who find the mediation process unpleasant, over three-quarters nonetheless remain satisfied with the process.

NOTES AND QUESTIONS

1.   Notice that Professor Grillo is condemning a particular child custody mediation program with certain characteristics: the mediation is mandatory, the parties have little or no choice of mediators, the mediators have little time to spend on each case and often make recommendations to the court, and lawyers usually are excluded from the mediation sessions. Currently, custody mediation programs in California display great variety. *See* Joan B. Kelly, *Family Mediation Research: Is There Empirical Support for the Field?*, Conflict Resol. Q., Fall–Winter 2004, at 3. Kelly reports that "in thirty-four of California's fifty-eight counties (C. Depner, personal communication, Dec. 8, 2003), mediators are authorized to make recommendations to the court for custody and visitation when parents are at impasse." *Id.* at 5. Donald T. Saposnek, explaining the difficulty of doing empirical research on such programs, states that

> [w]ithin the court system, the definition of and the actual current practices of what is called mediation have parted ways, resulting in serious theoretical and practical inconsistencies. The mandate to mediate is being interpreted and implemented in practice as if the statute read: *Parties in dispute must attend a session with a court counselor who may mediate, arbitrate, recommend, refer or terminate the case.*

Donald T. Saposnek, *Commentary: The Future of the History of Family Mediation Research,* Conflict Resol. Q., Fall 2004, at 37, 43 (2004) (Emphasis in original). And although parties have a right to legal representation, in more than half of such cases, at least one parent does not have legal counsel. Kelly, *supra* at 6. In one brief study, in 76 percent of cases at least one parent reported "interparental violence." *Id.* According to Kelly, "[s]ubsequent legislation provided for separate sessions, opt-outs for parents, and special assessment for families where domestic violence was alleged or had occurred." *Id.* at 5. Would such changes make mediation less objectionable to Grillo? To you? What other changes might you want?

Because of the great variety in mediation processes, in this and other settings, the question of whether a particular dispute ought to be mediated cannot be addressed without considering the types of mediation that might be available.

2.   Professors Grillo and Rosenberg may have been talking about different types of mediation. But setting that aside, do you think Professor Rosenberg would have found Professor Grillo's conclusions less objectionable if she had hedged her language more? Here is the second to last paragraph of that article into which we have inserted qualifiers in brackets:

> Although mediation can be useful and empowering, it presents some serious process dangers that need to be addressed, rather than ignored. When mediation is imposed rather than voluntarily engaged in, its virtues are [often] lost. More than lost: mediation becomes [can become; sometimes becomes] a wolf in sheep's clothing. It relies on force and [often] disregards [can disregard] the context of the dispute, while masquerading as a gentler, more empowering alternative to adversarial litigation. Sadly, when mediation is mandatory it becomes [can become] like the patriarchal paradigm of law it is supposed to supplant. Seen in that light, mandatory mediation is [has the potential to be] especially harmful: its messages [may] disproportionately affect those who are already subordinated in our society, those to whom society has already given the message, in far too many ways, that they are not leading proper lives.

Rosenberg, 33 Ariz. L. Rev., at 505.

In suggesting these modifications are the authors of this book trying to mediate between Professors Grillo and Rosenberg? Does the proposed solution cover up real differences in their beliefs or only create the opportunity to find some "play in the joints?"

3.   For an elaboration of the risks of women's participation in divorce mediation, see Penelope E. Bryan, *Killing Us Softly: Divorce Mediation and the Politics of Power*, 40 Buff. L. Rev. 441 (1992). For a review of studies dealing with whether women tend to be more risk averse and more altruistic than men, see Margaret F. Brinig, *Does Mediation Systematically Disadvantage Women?*, 2 Wm. & Mary J. Women & L. 1 (1995). Professor Brinig concludes that

> [b]ecause mediation is swifter, less expensive and easier on children, it is a good alternative to litigation in many divorce cases. Many women who have tried mediation liked it. However, congested courts cannot justify mandatory mediation in cases where one spouse holds a monopoly on

marital power. No one should order mediation when there has been abuse within the family, substance abuse, or systematic hiding of assets.

Id. at 34.

4. Professor Nancy Ver Steegh, writing in the context of the mediation of divorces for couples that have encountered domestic abuse, suggests ways in which a divorce mediator can address problems of power imbalance:

In some cases, the power imbalance is too severe for mediation to take place. However, in less extreme cases, skilled mediators are equipped to deal with moderate power differentials. One way that mediators deal with power imbalance is through their own exercise of power. The mediator controls the process by:

1. Creating the ground rules.

2. Choosing the topic.

3. Deciding who may speak.

4. Controlling the length of time each person may speak.

5. Allowing and timing the person's response.

6. Determining which spouse may present a proposal to the other.

7. Presenting an interpretation of what the spouse said.

8. Ending the discussion.

9. Writing down the agreement.

The mediator gradually transfers power from himself or herself to the divorcing couple as they become able to use it appropriately. If the mediator retains too much power the couple will not "own" the agreement, but if the mediator relinquishes power prematurely, sessions are unproductive and, in the case of domestic violence, potentially dangerous. Because knowledge is a form of power, special care is taken to share information and verify facts. Power can also be balanced in a neutral fashion by asking probing questions and validating the concerns of the less powerful party. Separate caucuses give the mediator a chance to obtain direct feedback on power and safety issues.

Mediators watch for specific behaviors that indicate power imbalances. These include but are not limited to tone of voice, glaring, insults, passivity, threats, outbursts, and refusal to speak. In addition to behavioral cues, mediators watch for lopsided agreements. "Even if we concede that a mediator will not be able to see how the husband is maneuvering his wife to where he wants to get her, it is simply impossible for the mediator not to see where her husband has brought her."

Additional safeguards in such situations include independent legal advice and, to some extent, judicial review. If necessary, the mediator can end the mediation "on behalf" of the less empowered person.

Some have argued that mediators cannot deal with power imbalance without jeopardizing their neutrality and impartiality. Mediators do remain neutral with respect to the outcome of the mediation but they are not "value-free" with respect to the process and the safety of the participants. For example, as a part of the process of balancing power, mediators ask probing questions and suggest that legal counsel be sought to ensure that the parties are equally informed and fully understand the implications of agreements being considered. The alternative to ignoring power imbalances would essentially amount to siding with the more powerful party. Obviously, the experience of the mediator is key.

Nancy Ver Steegh, *Yes, No, and Maybe: Informed Decision Making about Divorce Mediation in the Presence of Domestic Violence*, 9 Wm & Mary J. Women & L. 145, 186–88 (2003).

She concludes this extensive study as follows:

Should abuse victims mediate their divorces? In some cases, the answer is "no." In others, the answer is "maybe" but only on a voluntary basis with a highly skilled mediator using a specialized procedure. Even then, the decision regarding mediation must be made with regard for the victim's particular situation and the options realistically available. * * *

Thus, mediation should be offered as one option among many. Abuse survivors must be informed of choices, educated about the advantages and disadvantages of each, and counseled with respect to what might work for them. They and their families deserve no less.

Id. at 204. We deal more extensively with this issue in Chapter VI, *infra*.

5.   A study by psychologist Joan Kelly compared attitudes of couples who mediated all their divorce issues (not just the custody issues as in the mandatory custody mediation program that was the subject of the Grillo–Rosenberg debate) with those who used a traditional "adversary" process with two lawyers. On most measures, the mediation groups tended to be happier with its process and outcomes than the adversarial group. Here is an excerpt from that study:

On a separate, global measure of satisfaction, the mediation group was significantly more satisfied with the mediation process and outcomes than the adversarial group was with the adversarial process. At final divorce, 69 percent of mediation respondents were somewhat to very satisfied, compared to only 47 percent of adversarial men and women. There were no significant sex differences.

Discussion

The findings reported in this chapter consistently favor mediation as a method for reaching comprehensive divorce agreements when compared to the adversarial process. All but two of the eighteen significant group differences indicated that those in mediation had more positive perceptions of and greater satisfaction with their divorce experience. Men and women in the adversarial group did not report their divorce process as better, fairer, smoother, more empowering, or more satisfactory on any measure.

In this study, mediation spouses believed that the mediation process had a more beneficial effect on their ability to be reasonable and communicative with each other compared to adversarial respondents who used attorneys. . . . The respondents in the current study also perceived that the mediators had led them to more workable compromises. Whether these perceptions of improved communication will result in reduced conflict and enhanced coparental communication and cooperation postdivorce will be determined in future analyses. We have reported elsewhere (Kelly, Gigy, and Hausman, 1988) that the mediation intervention resulted in greater increases in cooperation between mediation spouses at time 2 than did the adversarial experience. Pearson, Thoennes, and Vanderkooi and Emery and Jackson have also found small improvements in the parental relationship reported by mediation respondents. Preliminary time–3 analyses indicate that while mediation and adversarial clients do not differ in their level of anger at their spouses at final divorce, the mediation group reported less conflict during the divorce, were significantly more cooperative, and perceived their spouses as less angry than did the adversarial group.

The absence of significant group differences on a number of crucial process variables begins to address some of the criticisms leveled against mediation by those who believe that divorcing spouses will be disadvantaged unless they have the legal representation inherent to the adversarial process. The questions assessing adequacy of information produced in the mediation process indicated that, in these particular mediation interventions, mediation respondents did not feel any less informed, unprotected, or heard than did the adversarial group; neither did they believe that their spouses had an advantage over them in the negotiations.

With the exception of child support agreements, the mediation group was more satisfied with all of the outcomes reached. Fairer spousal support, more satisfactory property agreements, and better custody and visiting agreements were more often reported by the mediation group, when compared to the adversarial group. There were no significant sex differences or interaction effects for these variables. The finding that the mediation group was significantly more likely to perceive that they had equal influence over the terms of these agreements compared to adversarial men and women suggests that the mediators did a competent job of balancing power and spouses' needs. Clearly, for some adversarial respondents, the presumed condition of equal power through legal representation was not met.

* * *

Much opposition to mediation currently expressed by legal and political advocates for women derives from the belief that women are less powerful and knowledgeable than men and therefore likely to be disadvantaged in all types of divorce mediation. The findings of this study do not support these concerns. On no single items measuring process or outcome did adversarial women express more satisfaction or more favorable perception of their attorneys, their divorce process, or their agreements. Mediation women are significantly more satisfied than adversarial women on eighteen process and outcome items. Further, women in mediation were equally as satisfied as men with the overall process, mediator impartiality, adequacy and clarity of data, and various mediator techniques.

Joan B. Kelly, *Mediated and Adversarial Divorce: Respondents' Perceptions of Their Processes and Outcomes*, Mediation Q., Summer 1989, at 71, 84–86.

Social scientist Jessica Pearson interviewed more than 300 people who mediated at least some of the issues in their divorce (the other issues were resolved by a judge, by negotiations between the parties' lawyers or by negotiations directly between the parties); all of these respondents—both those in public and in private mediation efforts—were enrolled in programs that were open to mediating more than just the custody issue. Jessica Pearson, *The Equity of Mediated Divorce Agreements*, Mediation Q., Winter 1991, at 179, 180. One of her goals was to determine whether adversarial processes or mediation "produce more equitable results for women"—an issue on which studies had produced conflicting results. Pearson concluded that "mediation is not worse than adversarial and independent decision-making in generating agreements that are perceived to be equitable and fair." *Id.* at 192–93.

6. For further reading on exceptions to compelled participation in mediation, with special relevance to domestic relations and violence, as well as provisions for appropriate screening for intimate partner abuse, *see* Chapter VI, *infra*.

7. What other types of cases are likely to involve legal and personal relationships as intimate and difficult as those found in the domestic relations context? What about employment-related disputes such as discrimination or bullying in the workplace? Elder law matters? Disputes between business partners or co-authors? Special education issues? Medical malpractice claims? Disputes between neighbors?

8. Lawyers did not participate in the mediations discussed by Grillo and Rosenberg. In most parts of the U.S., even when divorcing parties have retained lawyers, the lawyers typically do not attend the divorce or custody mediations. Their attendance may even be precluded by statute or court rule in some jurisdictions. Writing in opposition to this practice, Craig McEwen, Nancy Rogers, and Richard Maiman contend that allowing lawyers to

participate in the mediation process provides low power parties sufficient protections in mandatory divorce mediations to justify the process.

> Lawyers prevent or moderate the effects of a face to face encounter with an abuser, thus diminishing the likelihood of unfairness in domestic violence cases. Maine lawyers attending mediation sessions with their clients report arranging separate sessions, time-outs, and other measures to protect their clients. Past violence, which may be a key factor in determining whether the parties will submit to an unfair settlement or will be forced into a frightening situation, becomes less of a bargaining factor if the parties attend with their lawyers. Lawyers can advise clients to avoid settlements that will allow further opportunities for abuse, or that are unlikely to be obeyed, or that are bad deals. Lawyers can also advise their clients to terminate mediation sessions.

Craig A. McEwen, Nancy H. Rogers & Richard J. Maiman, *Bring in the Lawyers: Challenging the Dominant Approaches to Ensuring Fairness in Divorce Mediation*, 70 Minn. L. Rev. 1317, 1376 (1995).

The authors also suggest that other forms of regulation, such as issue limitations, would also be unnecessary if lawyers are permitted to participate and that "bringing lawyers into the room" would also mitigate concerns about the mediators, such as their qualifications and the impacts of any legal evaluations they may make. Id. at 1377. Still, they concede domestic violence victims should "probably" be allowed to "opt out of joint sessions," and that the mediator should not be permitted to make recommendations to the court. Id.

What do you think? Does "bringing in the lawyers" solve the problems we have identified in these cases? If not, what remedies would you suggest?

9.　　If you were a member of a state supreme court committee charged with developing proposals for establishing divorce mediation programs, how would you answer the following questions:

    a.　Should participation be voluntary or mandatory? If mandatory, should some kinds of cases be excluded?

    b.　Who should pay for such services—the parties or the courts?

    c.　Should the mediation include financial and property issues or only child custody issues?

    d.　Should the participation of lawyers in mediation sessions be encouraged or discouraged?

    e.　Should all meetings be joint, or should private caucuses be routine?

    f.　Should mediators evaluate, i.e., make predictions about what would happen in court? Would your answer depend on whether the mediator was a lawyer? Whether the parties had lawyers? Whether the lawyers attended the mediation?

g. Would your views on the above questions differ if you were a divorce lawyer? A divorce mediator in private practice?

10. For an argument that state statutes and court rules barring lawyers from attending court-annexed mediations are unconstitutional, see Richard C. Reuben, *Constitutional Gravity: A Unitary Theory of Alternative Dispute Resolution and Public Civil Justice*, 47 UCLA L. Rev. 949, 1079–82 (2000).

E. MEDIATION EXERCISES

1. THE RED DEVIL DOG MEDIATION ROLE PLAY*

General Information for the Mediator

You are an attorney in private practice and have agreed to mediate a dispute between a commercial landlord and a prospective tenant. The referral came from the landlord's lawyer. The landlord will pay for the first two hours of mediation. The prospective tenant, who apparently has no lawyer, has agreed to attend, as long as the landlord does not bring a lawyer. Piecing together information provided by the referring lawyer and the prospective tenant, you surmise that the prospective tenant had agreed to rent the premises to operate a local franchise of the well-known Red Devil Dog Restaurant chain. The lease provides for payment of $1,000 per month plus 3 percent of gross sales for a 5–year period. After the landlord made $2,500 in modifications and the tenant moved in boxes of equipment, the news broke that the Red Devil Dog chain had filed for bankruptcy. The prospective tenant then called to cancel the lease and the landlord responded with a letter demanding $80,000. The mediation has been scheduled in the early evening because the prospective tenant works days as a nurse. Your secretary reports that the prospective tenant sounded angry.

Before you begin the mediation, think out your approach. Do you expect any bargaining imbalances? If so, should your approach change in any way? If the disputing parties are angry, how can you get them to focus on possible solutions?

---

*   This role play was prepared by Professor Nancy Rogers and is based on the facts of Videotape III in the *Dispute Resolution and Lawyers Videotape Series* (West Publishing Co. 1991) and Dale A. Whitman, *The Missing Tenant: A Negotiation Exercise for Property Law, in* LEONARD L. RISKIN AND JAMES E. WESTBROOK, INSTRUCTOR'S MANUAL FOR DISPUTE RESOLUTION AND LAWYERS, 3rd ed. (2005). Confidential information for the landlord and the tenant may be found in the Instructor's Manual for this book, in the Instructor's Manual for Videotape III, *supra*, at 43 and on the casebook's TWEN web site at www.lawschool.westlaw.com.

2. PROSANDO V. HIGH–TECH: GENERAL INFORMATION**

Prosando, a German–Argentine joint venture based in Argentina, is a distributor of office and business equipment. High–Tech is a large, well-established computer manufacturer, with its headquarters in southern California.

In January 1990 * * * Prosando entered into an exclusive five-year distribution contract with High–Tech. Prosando agreed to establish a distribution network for High–Tech's Futura A and B minicomputers throughout South America and to use High–Tech's trademark in doing so.

Immediately after the contract was signed, Prosando ordered 50 Futura A computers. High–Tech, however, refused to ship until its legal department had reviewed the contract. Following that review, in June 1990, High–Tech insisted that it retain the right to sell directly in South America. Prosando reluctantly agreed, and in August 1990, High–Tech shipped 50 Futura A computers to Prosando.

In October 1990, Prosando ordered another 20 Futura A computers, which were delivered in December 1990. In January 1991, High–Tech discontinued the Futura A and introduced the Century series, but refused initially to allow Prosando to distribute that series. According to High–Tech, Prosando's distribution contract was limited to the Futura series. In June 1991 (one and one-half years into the contract), High–Tech agreed to allow Prosando to distribute the Century series. In February 1992, Prosando ordered 18 Century series computers.

In June 1992, without prior warning, High–Tech notified Prosando that the contract would be terminated in 30 days because of Prosando's clear and unequivocal breach of contract. According to High–Tech, Prosando had:

1. Failed to use its best efforts to sell the product within the assigned territory to the total dissatisfaction of the Seller, since Prosando had placed orders for only 88 units of product in 24 months.

2. Failed to establish a "distributor" network on or before June 30, 1991. As of June 1992, Prosando had established a total of four distributors, all in Chile.

** This exercise was created for the International Institute for Conflict Prevention and Resolution, Inc., by Cathy Cronin–Harris, Vice President, and Professor Stephen Goldberg as a basis for CPR's 36–minute videotape, *Mediation in Action: Resolving a Complex Business Dispute* (1994). The videotape is available from the CPR Institute, 575 Lexington Avenue, 14th floor, New York, NY 10022 (212) 949–6490, or on CPR's website at www.cpradr.org. Copyright 1994 by the CPR Institute for Dispute Resolution n/k/a International Institute for Conflict Prevention and Resolution. Reprinted with the permission of CPR. Confidential information for attorneys and business executives appears in the Instructor's Manual, and on the casebook's TWEN web site at www.lawschool.westlaw.com.

3.　Failed to submit or negotiate annual purchase commitments.

The relevant provisions of the contract are these:

A.　Prosando shall have the sole right (except for High–Tech) to sell High–Tech Futura A and Futura B minicomputers, and any updates thereto (hereafter "the product") within the assigned territory.

B.　Prosando shall use its best efforts to sell within the assigned territory.

C.　Prosando shall establish a distribution network within the assigned territory to the satisfaction of High–Tech.

D.　Prosando shall have its distribution network in place by June 1991. If it fails to do so, High–Tech shall have the right to terminate Prosando's status as exclusive South American distributor of the product, and to engage other distributors in addition to Prosando.

E.　Prosando must place a noncancellable blanket order for 100 of the product totalling one million U.S. dollars upon execution of this agreement for delivery on or after _____. (Left blank in the contract.)

F.　On each calendar year commencing in _____ (left blank in the contract) the parties will agree on the minimum purchase requirements for the subsequent twelve-month period. If agreement is not achieved, either party may terminate this agreement upon prior 90 days' written notice.

G.　Upon termination of this Agreement becoming effective: (a) Neither party shall be liable to the other for loss of profits or prospective profits of any kind or nature sustained or arising out of or alleged to have arisen out of such termination.

On receiving High–Tech's June 1992 notice of termination, Prosando continued to sell its remaining High–Tech equipment.

In September 1992, Prosando initiated litigation in the U.S. District Court for the Southern District of California, claiming damages for breach of contract and fraud: $1 million for loss of business reputation; $6 million for lost profits; and actual reliance damages of $3 million expended on the contract (including capitalized loans, leasing of premises, personnel, promoting and advertising the product, travel, etc.), a total of $10 million.

High–Tech denied all allegations and counterclaimed for $126,000 for equipment shipped and not paid for.

At the suggestion of the district court, the parties have agreed to attempt to resolve this dispute through mediation.

3. DANCE INNOVATION
Mediator's Instructions*

You had a short conference call with the two lawyers, Joe and Connie, in which you learned the following information prior to your first mediation session. Two years ago, Jackie (who had been a dancer and then a choreographer) was working as an assistant Director for a large New York Dance Company. At that point, Dance Innovation, a smaller Boston Company, hired her/him to become its Artistic Director and resident choreographer (when its founder and previous Artistic Director, Peter George, died suddenly). The three-year contract provided that any works Jackie produced as part of her/his employment were to be considered "work for hire." S/he could be fired with six months' notice.

The mission of Dance Innovation is to support the work of new choreographers. Jackie brought with her/him a work in progress that s/he had been creating (on the side) while at (and with the permission of) her/his former employer. S/he completed that work, MOTIF, while at Dance Innovation (and the company produced it). S/he created a second work, CHORALE, during her/his first year at Dance Innovation (and the company produced it). S/he was working on a third major work, ENSEMBLE, (which was to be produced in the upcoming season) when s/he was fired.

Mickey, Dance Innovation's Chairman and Executive Director, sent Jackie a letter notifying her/him of her/his dismissal on the grounds that s/he focused almost exclusively on the creation of her/his own work (rather than devoting attention to her/his own work <u>and</u> supporting the work of new choreographers) and because s/he was consistently over budget. Mickey also informed Jackie that he/she considered ENSEMBLE virtually complete when Jackie left, needing at most a little final polishing and refinement and that the company is going forward with completing ENSEMBLE which will be the centerpiece of its upcoming season. Mickey further maintained that any works completed by Jackie or that s/he was working on while employed are exclusively the property of Dance Innovation.

---

    *   Copyright © 2001, Center for Mediation in Law. Reprinted with permission. Confidential information for lawyers and parties appears in the Instructors Manual for this book, and on this casebook's TWEN web site at www.lawschool.westlaw.com. A videotape of a mediation based on the information in these instructions, Saving the Last Dance: Mediation Through Understanding, is available from the Program on Negotiation at Harvard Law School, www.pon.org.

The Company views all the works as owned by the company under the contract language and the work-for-hire doctrine. Connie views the works as belonging to Jackie as the creator and threatens to enjoin the upcoming season of Dance Innovation, which has ENSEMBLE as its centerpiece.

The lawyers have agreed to come into mediation with their clients.

CHAPTER V

ARBITRATION

■ ■ ■

Arbitration is a form of adjudication in which the neutral decision maker is not a judge or an official of an administrative agency. Arbitration is normally a private proceeding based on the parties' agreement to arbitrate, although a few state and federal courts have arbitration programs, which is discussed more fully in Chapter VI beginning at p. 799. Unlike in negotiation or mediation, where the disputing parties determine the outcome, in arbitration the arbitrator decides the parties' rights based on evidence or other submissions from them. Thus, an arbitration proceeding is more like litigation than negotiation or mediation. Arbitration is, however, less formal than litigation in that it generally is not conducted according to the same rules of law and procedure as public adjudication.

Arbitration also differs from negotiation and mediation in that it is based more on statutes and case law. In general, there are three types of arbitration that we will discuss in this chapter and each has its own legal basis. The first type are arbitrations between employers and unions, which are governed by § 301 of the National Labor Relations (Taft–Hartley) Act, 29 U.S.C. § 185 (2000). The second type are commercial arbitrations between (i) two or more business entities, (ii) businesses and consumers, or (iii) employers and non-unionized employees, which are generally governed by the Federal Arbitration Act (FAA), 9 U.S.C. § 1, *et seq.* (2000), and related state arbitration laws. The third type are international arbitrations, which are governed primarily by the 1958 U.N. Convention on the Recognition and Enforcement of Foreign Arbitral Awards as adopted by Congress in 9 U.S.C. § 201, *et seq.* (2000).

Most states (thirty-nine jurisdictions) either have adopted or based their arbitration statutes on the Uniform Arbitration Act (UAA), which was promulgated by the National Conference of Commissioners on Uniform State Laws (NCCUSL) in 1955. The UAA was revised in 2000, and 10 states have passed the revised Uniform Arbitration Act (RUAA). *See* Timothy J. Heinsz, *The Revised Uniform Arbitration Act: Modernizing, Revising, and Clarifying Arbitration Law,* 2001 J. Disp. Resol. 1. Our emphasis will be on commercial, employment, and consumer arbitration because these are the areas of greatest growth and the areas lawyers are most likely to encounter in practice. Unlike prior chapters, Chapter V requires more statutory and case analysis.

The use of arbitration has grown tremendously in recent years. At one time, most arbitrations involved either employers and unions or two or more commercial entities. Today arbitration clauses have become ubiquitous—particularly in adhesion situations. (*See infra*, beginning at p. 650.) Undoubtedly any reader who has a credit card or has made an on-line purchase of a product is a party to an arbitration agreement and subject to an arbitration process to resolve any disputes arising under it.

Private arbitration is based on contract and the parties may shape the contours of their arbitration agreement to meet their needs. Typically, parties either agree in advance that designated categories of disputes will be arbitrated (pre-dispute arbitration) or they enter into an ad hoc agreement to arbitrate after a dispute has arisen (post-dispute arbitration). Most private arbitration systems allow the parties to select the arbitrator jointly. Generally, arbitration clauses provide that the arbitrator's decision will be final and binding. Although courts enforce agreements to arbitrate and confirm or vacate arbitration awards, they typically do not review the merits of an arbitrator's decision. Arbitration is normally a confidential process. Because one of the features of private arbitration is that the parties have considerable autonomy in designing the process, the arbitration agreements can provide the substantive standards that arbitrators use in making a decision. Arbitrators generally do not consider themselves bound by the doctrine of precedent. Arbitration awards in some fields are published and arbitrators often look to such awards for guidance, even if they are not binding.

Section A of this chapter surveys the practice and procedures used in private arbitration in the United States. Section B reviews the legal framework of the domestic arbitration process. Section C looks at international commercial arbitration. Section D examines the considerations involved in deciding whether to use arbitration and how to construct arbitration systems.

A. THE PRACTICE AND PROCEDURES OF PRIVATE ARBITRATION

Arbitration is very different than the other processes we have discussed thus far, and in this section, we provide a general orientation to the arbitration process. We begin with a discussion of the contexts in which arbitration is used, and then provide some insight into the people who serve as arbitrators, and conclude Section A with a discussion of the mechanics of the arbitration process.

1. THE USES AND GROWTH OF ARBITRATION

Arbitration has an ancient lineage and an active present. King Solomon, Phillip II of Macedon, and George Washington employed arbitration. *See* ELKOURI & ELKOURI, HOW ARBITRATION WORKS 3–4 Alan

Miles Rubin ed., 6th ed. (2003). Commercial arbitration has been used in England and the United States for hundreds of years. Labor-management arbitration, which has its roots in the late nineteenth century, came to the fore after World War II, as companies expanded and employees unionized. "International commercial arbitration has to a great extent now been institutionalized as the generally accepted private legal process applicable to transnational business disputes." Yves Dezalay & Bryant Garth, *Merchants of Law as Moral Entrepreneurs: Constructing International Justice from the Competition for Transnational Business Disputes*, 29 Law & Soc'y Rev. 27, 59 (1995).

Arbitration takes place in three different institutional contexts: the disputing parties create their own process and make all the arrangements in processing the arbitration; trade associations or exchanges establish arbitration systems to deal with disputes among their members; and groups such as the American Arbitration Association, JAMS, the Federal Mediation & Conciliation Service, and the International Chamber of Commerce provide ready-made systems and panels of arbitrators for disputing parties who agree to use arbitration.

Arbitration is widely used to resolve construction, insurance, securities, and maritime disputes. Arbitration is also used to settle disputes between employers and unions, manufacturers and consumers, shareholders in close corporations, members of families, banks and their customers, attorneys and clients, major league baseball players and their employers, brokers and customers in the securities industry, and physicians and hospitals. Employers have promulgated arbitration plans that cover non-union employees.

The underlying reasons that many parties choose arbitration over litigation are the relative capacities for speed, cost savings, and greater efficiency in the arbitral process. These benefits primarily occur because, unlike trial practice, discovery either does not exist or is much more limited in arbitration. Additionally, most arbitration clauses specify that the arbitrator's decision will be final. As we will see, arbitration statutes provide only limited grounds for a court to overturn an arbitral award. The arbitration process usually is less formal than court proceedings. For instance, in many cases parties represent themselves or are represented by non-lawyers; and the arbitrator need not be a lawyer. Finally, parties often opt for arbitration because they can pick their decision maker, who will likely have expertise in the field in which their dispute arises.

Another factor causing significant growth in arbitration is the favorable legal framework for the process. For many years courts in the United States were hostile to arbitration and refused to enforce arbitration agreements. The underlying basis for this antagonism was that courts looked upon arbitration tribunals as competition that improperly ousted courts of their jurisdiction to hear cases decided under the law of the land, and provided an inferior form of justice. The legal doctrine courts used was that arbitration agreements were executory promises and thus unenforceable. *See, e.g., Red Cross Line v. Atlantic Fruit Co.*, 264 U.S. 109, 120–21, 44 S.Ct. 274, 68 L.Ed. 582 (1924) (noting that "federal courts—like those of the states and of England—have, both in equity and at law, denied, in large measure, the aid of their processes to those seeking to enforce executory agreements to arbitrate disputes."); *Home Insurance Co. v. Morse*, 87 U.S. (20 Wall.) 445, 455, 22 L.Ed. 365 (1874) (adopting so-called English "ouster doctrine" and refusing to enforce pre-dispute agreements to arbitrate). This hostility could be seen at the U.S. Supreme Court, which in *Wilko v. Swan*, 346 U.S. 427, 74 S.Ct. 182, 98 L.Ed. 168 (1953), again refused to enforce a pre-dispute arbitration provision because, it held, the right to a judicial forum could not be waived. *Id.* at 435.

This judicial antagonism first changed in labor-management arbitration when the U.S. Supreme Court in 1957 decided that arbitration agreements were enforceable under § 301 of the NLRA. *Textile Workers Union v. Lincoln Mills*, 353 U.S. 448, 451, 77 S.Ct. 912, 1 L.Ed.2d 972 (1957). Then in 1960, in three cases involving the United Steelworkers Union (referred to as the "Steelworkers Trilogy"), the Court held that the judiciary should favor labor arbitration and give only limited review to the decisions of arbitrators. *United Steelworkers v. American Manufacturing Co.*, 363 U.S. 564, 568–69, 80 S.Ct. 1343, 4 L.Ed.2d 1403 (1960); *United Steelworkers v. Warrior & Gulf Navigation Co.*, 363 U.S. 574, 585, 80 S.Ct. 1347, 4 L.Ed.2d 1409 (1960); *United Steelworkers v. Enterprise Wheel & Car Corp.*, 363 U.S. 593, 599, 80 S.Ct. 1358, 4 L.Ed.2d 1424 (1960).

In the 1980's, in a series of cases beginning with *Southland Corp. v. Keating, see infra* beginning at p. 590, the U.S. Supreme Court applied the same pro-arbitration policy developed in the labor-management area to commercial disputes in interstate commerce subject to the Federal Arbitration Act, and formally overruled *Wilko v. Swan* in the late 1980s. *Rodriguez de Quijas v. Shearson/American Express, Inc.*, 490 U.S. 477, 484, 109 S.Ct. 1917, 104 L.Ed.2d 526 (1989). Today, rather than viewing arbitration as unfriendly competition, federal and state courts have embraced arbitration as a means parties may choose to resolve their disputes and as a beneficial mechanism to divert cases from crowded court dockets. This substantial judicial change, referred to by some as an "arbitration revolution," has fostered the substantial development of this dispute-resolution mechanism. *See* STEPHEN K. HUBER & E. WENDY TRACHTE–HUBER, ARBITRATION: CASES AND MATERIALS 5–6 (1998).

The success of traditional private arbitration has stimulated calls for increased reliance on arbitration. Arbitration has been used or proposed for use in connection with prisoner grievances, environmental disputes, civil rights disputes, divorce proceedings, and medical malpractice cases. The rapid increase in electronic commerce has been accompanied by the development of a number of on-line arbitration systems. As improvements in technology, transportation, and communications make for a global marketplace of goods and services, the role of arbitration can be expected to continue to grow and evolve.

2. THE ARBITRATOR

A primary reason parties decide to use arbitration rather than litigation is because they can select their decision maker. If the parties do not have a particular individual in mind to serve as an arbitrator, they may turn to a number of organizations for assistance in selecting arbitrators.

There is no single, monolithic arbitration profession. To be an arbitrator does not require special training or education. Unlike lawyers, physicians, or accountants, arbitrators are not credentialed by state or national boards. As a result, and because arbitrators are involved in so many diverse areas, their backgrounds vary widely. Professors, attorneys, architects, accountants, clergy, and many others serve as arbitrators. The key to becoming an arbitrator is acceptability by the parties. While some make arbitration a full-time occupation, others devote only part of their time to arbitration.

A study by the National Academy of Arbitrators is indicative of the make-up of the arbitration profession. MICHEL PICHER, RONALD L. SEEBER & DAVID B. LIPSKY, THE ARBITRATION PROFESSION IN TRANSITION: A SURVEY OF THE NATIONAL ACADEMY OF ARBITRATORS (2000). About 40% reported that arbitration was their full-time activity. The average Academy arbitrator was sixty-three years old and had been arbitrating for twenty-six years. Only 12% of NAA arbitrators were women and less than 6% were nonwhite. The predominant education of this group of arbitrators was law. More than 60% had law degrees, while 35% of the remaining NAA arbitrators had master or doctorate degrees in various fields.

Ethical codes for arbitrators have been developed by several organizations. The American Bar Association and AAA have promulgated a Code of Ethics for Arbitrators in Commercial Disputes. A Code of Professional Responsibility for Arbitrators of Labor–Management Disputes has been instituted by AAA, FMCS, and NAA. (See casebook website at www.lawschool.westlaw.com for these materials.) The NAA's Committee on Professional Responsibility and Grievances issues formal advisory opinions on the ethical responsibilities of labor arbitrators.

Arbitrators, like judges, are granted immunity from civil liability when they act in their adjudicative capacity. This immunity is generally based on the common law, but has been codified in the RUAA § 14. (See casebook website at www.lawschool.westlaw.com.) In *Reexamining Arbitral Immunity In an Age of Mandatory and Professional Arbitration*, 88 Minn. L. Rev. 449 (2004), Professor Maureen H. Weston argues for a qualified immunity that balances the arbitrator's need for protection in their decisional roles against the public's need to hold the arbitration industry accountable.

3. ARBITRATION INSTITUTIONS

Arbitral proceedings may be removed from the courts, but they still require many support services that are consistent with those that the courts provide to individual judges. For example, arbitrators need organizations that will help connect them with potential clients, space in which to hold their arbitrations, rules for conducting their arbitrations, as well as billing services for collecting their fees. These functions are performed by entities generally known as arbitral institutions or, provider organizations or just providers. Arbitrators affiliate with these organizations by being selected to serve on their arbitration rosters or panels.

As in other commercial sectors, there are many different providers across the country, but the overwhelming majority of arbitrations are administered by a small handful of large national providers. The oldest of these is the American Arbitration Association (AAA), a non-profit organization founded in 1926, For many years, AAA was the only nationally recognized provider of arbitration services and as such was frequently written into state arbitration statutes and private contracts. More recently, the Judicial Arbitration and Mediation Service (JAMS) has become an equally significant force in the market, especially for complex commercial cases. At one time, the JAMS roster consisted only of former judges. In recent years, however, it has also come to include non-judicial arbitrators as well. The CPR International Institute for Conflict Prevention and Resolution also has a large and prestigious roster of neutrals who serve as arbitrators

AAA, JAMS, and CPR offer general arbitration services. Other providers serve more niche markets. The National Association of Securities Dealers and the New York Stock Exchange maintain panels of arbitrators for securities disputes. The Federal Mediation and Conciliation Service (FMCS) provide panels of labor-management arbitrators.

In addition to arbitration provider agencies, there are also professional organizations to which arbitrators belong. Perhaps the best known is the National Academy of Arbitrators (NAA) for arbiters in the labor-management field. The NAA, founded in 1947, includes the most experienced arbitrators in the profession; its mission is to foster high ethical standards and promote education in labor-management arbitration. Many arbitrators are also members of the Labor and Employment Relations Association.

4.   THE ARBITRATION PROCESS

Generalizing about the arbitration process is difficult because the parties have the autonomy to design their arbitration system. The system proposed in the Commercial Arbitration Rules of the American Arbitration Association is one of those most widely used. (See casebook website at www.lawschool.westlaw.com.) AAA has a separate set of rules for labor arbitration and for a number of special situations such as health care, wills and trusts, patents, the wireless industry, real estate valuation, securities, and domain name disputes.

As an adjudicative process, arbitration is much more akin to litigation than is either negotiation or mediation. Most arbitrations involve a hearing in which attorneys may represent the parties; witnesses are sworn, examined and cross-examined; and exhibits are entered into evidence. In many cases, parties request a transcript of the proceedings and file post-hearing briefs. After all of the evidence and briefs (if filed) are in, the arbitrator will issue a decision. In some instances, such as commercial or securities cases, it is customary for arbitrators to write only an award finding in favor of the claimant or the respondent; in others, such as labor-management or international arbitration, arbitrators will include a reasoned decision along with their award.

Arbitration and litigation differ primarily in the areas of pre-hearing matters, such as discovery, and the applicability of the rules of evidence. The materials that follow discuss these two areas and some of the institutions and persons involved in international commercial arbitration.

STEPHEN HAYFORD AND RALPH PEEPLES, COMMERCIAL ARBITRATION: AN ASSESSMENT AND CALL FOR DIALOGUE
10 Ohio St. J. on Disp. Resol. 343, 367–71, 375–76 (1995)

1.   *Pleadings and Pre–Hearing Motions*

The first major distinguishing characteristic of the commercial arbitration process is the comparative simplicity and brevity of the pleadings and pre-hearing stage. * * *

In a manner analogous to traditional litigation, the commercial arbitration proceeding commences with the filing of the moving party's (claimant's) demand for arbitration, setting forth a concise description of the facts pertinent to the underlying dispute and a description of the relief the claimant seeks. Subsequently, the respondent in arbitration files an answer to the claimant's submission, taking issue with any disputed factual allegations, setting forth any defenses, and articulating any * * * controversy. This pleadings process is largely mechanical and does not require any active intervention by the arbitrator. In fact, the pleadings process is usually complete before the arbitrator is selected.

There is no formal analog in commercial arbitration to the pre-trial motion practice in traditional litigation. This characteristic of the process accounts for a substantial portion of the cost and time savings that can be realized in arbitration. Rule 10 of the AAA Commercial Arbitration Rules does provide for pre-hearing proceedings, including a "preliminary hearing." However, Rule 10 does not expressly contemplate pre-hearing motions addressing the form and content of the pleadings, questions of proper parties and jurisdiction, or attempts to avoid a hearing by achieving dismissal as a matter of law or through adjudication based on undisputed facts.

Rule 4 of the AAA Supplementary Procedures for Large, Complex Disputes does speak to a more extensive preliminary hearing dealing with, among other matters: service by the parties on one another of detailed statements of claims, damages, and defenses; specification of the issues before the arbitrator; and stipulations of fact. Even though this proceeding is labeled a "preliminary hearing," on its face, Rule 4 does not contemplate any form of adjudication by a neutral in the nature of a motion to dismiss or a motion for summary judgment. In the same manner, the emphasis of the relevant pre-hearing portion of the Endispute Comprehensive Arbitration Rules is on the submission of claim, answer, and counterclaim.

The omission of a surrogate for pre-hearing motion practice from the existing framework for commercial arbitration does not mean the concerns underlying that dimension of traditional litigation are not at times present in commercial arbitration. Rather, the Authors believe this circumstance is due to the fact that, to date, the parties and their attorneys generally have been willing to forego pre-hearing motion practice and present their entire cases at hearing. This is likely to continue to be the case in the commercial disputes submitted to arbitration that present relatively simple questions of law (and contract) and application of law to fact.

However, as larger numbers of more complex cases are submitted to arbitration, arbitrators will find themselves frequently confronted with the type of complicated questions of law and application of law to fact that give rise to the pre-trial motions in traditional litigation. These cases seldom turn on simple questions of contract interpretation. Rather, they typically involve numerous and interrelated claims based in common law doctrine or statutory law, or both. Consequently, questions of law and mixed questions of law and fact are often crucial determinations that competent adjudication requires to be made in some fashion, tacitly or expressly, by the arbitration tribunal.

* * *

2.   *The Role and Nature of Discovery*

As with most all of the dimensions of commercial arbitration, it is difficult to generalize as to the extent and nature of pre-hearing discovery. The only reference to pre-hearing discovery contained in the AAA Commercial Arbitration Rules is found at Rule 10, which addresses the Preliminary Conference. Rule 10 authorizes the arbitrator to "establish . . . the extent of and schedule for the production of relevant documents and other information, [and to establish] the identification of any witnesses to be called." Rule 5(b)–(d) of the Association's Supplementary Procedures for Large, Complex Cases grants the arbitrator(s) authority to: direct an exchange of documents, exhibits, and information; limit the nature and extent of discovery; and order the deposition of, or the propounding of written interrogatories to a person possessing material knowledge if that person will not be available to testify at the arbitration hearing. In addition to these matters, Endispute's Comprehensive Arbitration Rule C–13 speaks directly to interrogatories, document exchange, expert witnesses, and the parties' continuing obligation to provide one another with documents they rely upon to supplement their post-pleading responses.

The discovery-related promulgations cited above contemplate a pre-hearing discovery process that focuses on the production of documents and data. Depositions and written interrogatories are accorded a lower level of significance, generally being deemed warranted only if the deponent or the subject of the interrogatories is not able to testify at the hearing, or if the party seeking to depose a hostile witness can convince the arbitrator of a reasonable need for the deposition(s).

* * *

4.   *Hearing Advocacy Tactics and The Rules of Evidence*

One of the primary selling points for the commercial arbitration alternative to traditional litigation is its relative simplicity of procedure and substance. At hearing, this characteristic is reflected by the absence of rigid standards for the admission of evidence. Rule 31 of the AAA Commercial Arbitration Rules states that "conformity to legal rules of evidence shall not be necessary." Instead, the arbitrator is instructed to judge the relevance and materiality of the proffered evidence. Rule 31 does not expressly establish relevance or materiality as criteria for the admissibility of evidence.

* * *

Despite the fluid nature of the evidentiary standards in commercial arbitration, the Authors' collective experience indicates that litigators are seldom able or willing to abandon the standard jury trial *modus operandi*, including the compulsion to continually test the boundaries of the rules of evidence applicable in court while strenuously challenging the same maneuvers by opposing counsel. Generally, admonitions from the arbitrator to counsel to remember that rigid adherence to the rules of evidence are not necessary (because the case is not being presented to a jury of laypersons) go unheeded. At times this adherence to traditional jury trial tactics can result in a highly dysfunctional and unnecessary extension of the proceeding, and a significant diminution in arbitral attention span. It also leads to the application of a wide range of *de facto* evidentiary standards at hearing, depending in large part on the proclivities and the decisional consistency of the presiding arbitrator.

The roadblocks to expeditious adjudication and the inconsistency in *de facto* evidentiary standards that frequently arise at hearings are troubling and indicate a need for a careful scrutiny of this key dimension of the commercial arbitration process. Litigators, arbitrators, and neutral appointing authorities are obliged to confront this reality and openly and thoughtfully debate the utility of the current rudimentary evidentiary standards. If a consensus emerges in favor of a simplified evidentiary standard, it needs to be more clearly defined and attorneys and arbitrators alike must deem themselves obliged to abide by it. If the result is general agreement that something more than the existing evidentiary framework is called for, new standards need to be drafted that fully contemplate the presence of an expert adjudicator who need not be shielded in the same manner as a lay jury.

NOTE

The typical labor arbitration process is quite similar to the Hayford and Peeples description of the commercial process, except that labor arbitrators usually prepare a written opinion explaining their award. Professor Hayford summarized the labor arbitration process as follows in 1992:

> Though there are exceptions, when compared to litigation, the typical private-sector arbitration tribunal is a relatively informal proceeding. But, for contractual provisions requiring full disclosure at the latter stages of the grievance procedure, there is no analog to prehearing discovery. Similarly, prehearing submissions/briefs are an anomaly. The rules of evidence are not applied in any formal sense. The relevant FMCS statistic indicates that transcripts are made in only one of four cases. Further, in most cases we need not be concerned with potential reversal on the merits by an appellate body.

> [Professor] St. Antoine's conceptualization of the arbitrator as the parties' "official contract reader" provides an apt description of the arbitrator's function in the private sector * * *.

Stephen L. Hayford, *The Changing Character of Labor Arbitration,* in Arbitration 1992, IMPROVING ARBITRAL AND ADVOCACY SKILLS, PROCEEDINGS

OF THE FORTY–FIFTH ANNUAL MEETING, NATIONAL ACADEMY OF ARBITRATORS 73–74 (Gladys W. Gruenberg ed., 1992).

The material in Section C suggests that international commercial arbitration is somewhat more formal than either domestic commercial arbitration or labor arbitration.

YVES DEZALAY AND BRYANT GARTH, MERCHANTS OF LAW AS MORAL ENTREPRENEURS: CONSTRUCTING INTERNATIONAL JUSTICE FROM COMPETITION FOR TRANSNATIONAL BUSINESS DISPUTES

29 Law & Soc'y Rev. 27, 30–31 (1995)

When businesses enter into transnational relationships such as contracts for the sale of goods, joint ventures, construction projects, or distributorships, the contract typically calls for arbitration in the event of any dispute arising from the contractual arrangement. The main reason given today for this choice is that it allows each party to avoid being forced to submit to the courts of the other. Another is the secrecy of the process. International arbitration can be "institutional," following the procedural rules of the International Chamber of Commerce in Paris, the American Arbitration Association, the London Court of International Commercial Arbitration, or many others; or it can be ad hoc, often following the rules of the United Nations Commission on International Trade Law (UNCITRAL) used also for the arbitrations by the Iran Claims Tribunal at the Hague.

The arbitrators are private individuals selected by the parties, and usually there are three arbitrators. The parties each select one, and the parties jointly, the arbitrators, or an institutional appointing authority select the third. They act as private judges, holding hearings and issuing judgments. There are few grounds for appeal to courts, and the final decision of the arbitrators, under the terms of a widely adopted 1958 New York Convention, is more easily enforced among signatory countries than would be a court judgment.

There is considerable competition for the business of representing parties, providing institutional support, and serving as arbitrators. The increasing competition is an important aspect of international arbitration today, but it is also essential to see that there are a relatively small number of important institutions, chief among them the International Chamber of Commerce, and of individuals in each country who are the key players both as counsel and as arbitrators. There is a kind of "international arbitration community"—quite often referred to as a "club"—connected by personal and professional relations cemented by conferences, journals, and actual arbitrations. * * *

1.   Would you feel comfortable as a lawyer presenting a case to an arbitrator without some of the procedural rights available in litigation? Would it depend on the type of case?

B. THE LEGAL FRAMEWORK FOR ARBITRATION UNDER THE FAA

In this section, we focus on the legal framework for arbitrations conducted under the Federal Arbitration Act, which will include most commercial, employment, and consumer arbitrations. As we shall see in Section 2, the U.S. Supreme Court has given the FAA broad preemptive effect over related state arbitration law. As you read these materials, ask yourself what policy interests are served and disserved by such a posture. Section 3 then looks at the difficult problem of arbitrability, which is, generally, the question of whether a dispute is subject to an arbitration provision, and who decides that question. In Section 4, we focus on the controversial problem of so-called mandatory, or unilaterally imposed arbitration, with a series of important cases that in part chronicle the U.S. Supreme Court's initial unwillingness to enforce pre-dispute agreements to arbitrate in *Wilko v. Swan*, to the Court's apparent modern embrace of mandatory arbitration in *Gilmer v. Interstate Johnson/Lane*, 500 U.S. 20, 111 S.Ct. 1647, 114 L.Ed.2d 26 (1991), and the related problems of forum fees and class actions.

1.   PRELIMINARY CONSIDERATIONS

a.   A Brief Summary of the FAA

The FAA, 9 U.S.C. § 1 *et seq.* (2000), was enacted in 1925 primarily to reverse legislatively the historic "ouster doctrine," a centuries-old common law doctrine under which courts refused to enforce agreements to arbitrate. For a definitive legislative history of the FAA, see IAN R. MACNEIL, AMERICAN ARBITRATION LAW: REFORMATION, NATIONALIZATION, INTERNATIONALIZATION (1992). In particular, Section 2 of the Act provides that arbitration agreements will be enforced just like any other agreement, as long as the agreement is enforceable as a matter of contract law. Section 4 of the Act further permits a court to compel an unwilling party into arbitration if it is satisfied that there is an enforceable agreement to arbitrate, and Section 3 permits it to stay related legal proceedings. Section 7 of the FAA permits an arbitrator to summon and hear witnesses during the arbitration, while Sections 9 and 13 permit the arbitrator to issue an award that may be entered as a court judgment. After an arbitration, Section 11 authorizes a court to modify or correct an award, while Section 10 allows a court to vacate an award where there was corruption, partiality, or other misconduct by the arbitrator, or where the arbitrator exceeded the scope of his or her authority.

b. Arbitrability

Arbitration is a contractual process. With few exceptions, parties arbitrate because they have agreed to do so, either in a contract entered into before the dispute arose or in an ad hoc agreement after the dispute arose.

In considering arbitrability, it is essential to distinguish between two different levels of analysis. The first level is the substantive issue of *whether* the parties agreed to arbitrate a dispute, and the scope of that agreement. The second level is the more "arcane" procedural level of *who decides* the existence and scope of an arbitration agreement: the "who decides" question.

Unfortunately, the term "arbitrability" has come to embrace—and confuse—a series of similar but analytically distinct issues relating to agreements to arbitrate. The analytical abyss that has inevitably followed does not permit easy synthesis; even simple discussion is often inhibited by the frailty of language in allowing for nuance. As a result, one leading arbitration scholar has mused wistfully that " 'arbitrability' is a word that might well be banned from our vocabulary entirely—or at least restricted, as in other legal systems, to the notion of what society will permit arbitrators to do."

It is therefore helpful to identify the major related but clearly distinct questions that are commonly and crudely clumped together under the general heading of "arbitrability," and to recognize that they operate at both the substantive level and the "who decides" level. These questions principally include:

1. Whether the parties entered into an agreement to arbitrate (and who decides);

2. Whether a specific issue or dispute is included within the scope of the arbitration agreement (and who decides);

3. Whether any conditions that might be necessary to trigger the contractual duty to arbitrate have been satisfied (and who decides).

A related and important concept that is also sometimes included within the rubric of "arbitrability" is the question of whether an arbitrator may decide his or her own jurisdiction, a concept known in international and comparative commercial arbitration as *competence-competence*, or *kompetenz-kompetenz*. * * * Richard C. Reuben, *First Options, Consent to Arbitration, and the Demise of Separability: Restoring Access to Justice for Contracts with Arbitration Provisions*, 56 SMU L. Rev. 819, 832–33 (2003) (emphasis added).

1. Who Decides Questions of Arbitrability?

Arbitrability issues usually arise in court when petitions are filed under § 3 of the FAA to stay litigation or under § 4 to compel arbitration. As we see in the following case, just who decides such issues is a highly nuanced question.

FIRST OPTIONS OF CHICAGO, INC. V. KAPLAN

Supreme Court of the United States, 1965
514 U.S. 938, 115 S.Ct. 1920, 131 L.Ed.2d 985

JUSTICE BREYER delivered the opinion of the Court.

In this case we consider two questions about how courts should review certain matters under the federal Arbitration Act, 9 U.S.C. § 1 *et seq.* (1988 Ed. and Supp. V): (1) how a district court should review an arbitrator's decision that the parties agreed to arbitrate a dispute, and (2) how a court of appeals should review a district court's decision confirming, or refusing to vacate, an arbitration award.

I

The case concerns several related disputes between, on one side, First Options of Chicago, Inc., a firm that clears stock trades on the Philadelphia Stock Exchange, and, on the other side, three parties: Manuel Kaplan; his wife, Carol Kaplan; and his wholly owned investment company, MK Investments, Inc. (MKI), whose trading account First Options cleared. The disputes center on a "workout" agreement, embodied in four separate documents, which governs the "working out" of debts to First Options that MKI and the Kaplans incurred as a result of the October 1987 stock market crash. In 1989, after entering into the agreement, MKI lost an additional $1.5 million. First Options then took control of, and liquidated, certain MKI assets; demanded immediate payment of the entire MKI debt; and insisted that the Kaplans personally pay any deficiency. When its demands went unsatisfied, First Options sought arbitration by a panel of the Philadelphia Stock Exchange.

MKI, having signed the only workout document (out of four) that contained an arbitration clause, accepted arbitration. The Kaplans, however, who had not personally signed that document, denied that their disagreement with First Options was arbitrable and filed written objections to that effect with the arbitration panel. The arbitrators decided that they had the power to rule on the merits of the parties' dispute, and did so in favor of First Options. The Kaplans then asked the Federal District Court to vacate the arbitration award, and First Options requested its confirmation. The court confirmed the award. Nonetheless, on appeal the Court of Appeals for the Third Circuit agreed with the Kaplans that their dispute was not arbitrable; and it reversed the District Court's confirmation of the award against them.

We granted certiorari to consider two questions regarding the standards that the Court of Appeals used to review the determination that the Kaplans' dispute with First Options was arbitrable. First, the Court of Appeals said that courts "should *independently* decide whether an arbitration panel has jurisdiction over the merits of any particular dispute." First Options asked us to decide whether this is so (*i.e.,* whether courts, in "reviewing the arbitrators' decision on arbitrability," should "apply a *de novo* standard of review or the more deferential standard applied to arbitrators' decisions on the merits") when the objecting party "submitted the issue to the arbitrators for decision." Second, the Court of Appeals stated that it would review a district court's denial of a motion to vacate a commercial arbitration award (and the correlative grant of a motion to confirm it) "*de novo.*" First Options argues that the Court of Appeals instead should have applied an "abuse of discretion" standard.

II

The first question—the standard of review applied to an arbitrator's decision about arbitrability—is a narrow one. To understand just how narrow; consider three types of disagreement present in this case. First, the Kaplans and First Options disagree about whether the Kaplans are personally liable for MKI's debt to First Options. That disagreement makes up the *merits* of the dispute. Second, they disagree about whether they agreed to arbitrate the merits. That disagreement is about the *arbitrability* of the dispute. Third, they disagree about *who should have the primary power to decide the second matter*. Does that power belong primarily to the arbitrators (because the court reviews their arbitrability decision deferentially) or to the court (because the court makes up its mind about arbitrability independently)? We consider here only this third question.

Although the question is a narrow one, it has a certain practical importance. That is because a party who has not agreed to arbitrate will normally have a right to a court's decision about the merits of its dispute (say, as here, its obligation under a contract). But, where the party has agreed to arbitrate, he or she, in effect, has relinquished much of that right's practical value. The party still can ask a court to review the arbitrator's decision, but the court will set that decision aside only in very unusual circumstances. Hence, who—court or arbitrator—has the primary authority to decide whether a party has agreed to arbitrate can make a critical difference to a party resisting arbitration.

We believe the answer to the "who" question (*i.e.,* the standard-of-review question) is fairly simple. Just as the arbitrability of the merits of a dispute depends upon whether the parties agreed to arbitrate that dispute, so the question, "who has the primary power to decide arbitrability" turns upon what the parties agreed about *that* matter. Did the parties agree to submit the arbitrability question itself to arbitration?

If so, then the court's standard for reviewing the arbitrator's decision about *that* matter should not differ from the standard courts apply when they review any other matter that parties have agreed to arbitrate. That is to say, the court should give considerable leeway to the arbitrator, setting aside his or her decision only in certain narrow circumstances. If, on the other hand, the parties did *not* agree to submit the arbitrability question itself to arbitration, then the court should decide that question just as it would decide any other question that the parties did not submit to arbitration, namely, independently. These two answers flow inexorably from the fact that arbitration is simply a matter of contract between the parties; it is a way to resolve those disputes—but only those disputes—that the parties have agreed to submit to arbitration.

We agree with First Options, therefore, that a court must defer to an arbitrator's arbitrability decision when the parties submitted that matter to arbitration. Nevertheless, that conclusion does not help First Options win this case. That is because a fair and complete answer to the standard-of-review question requires a word about how a court should decide whether the parties have agreed to submit the arbitrability issue to arbitration. And, that word makes clear that the Kaplans did not agree to arbitrate arbitrability here.

When deciding whether the parties agreed to arbitrate a certain matter (including arbitrability), courts generally (though with a qualification we discuss below) should apply ordinary state-law principles that govern the formation of contracts. The relevant state law here, for example, would require the court to see whether the parties objectively revealed an intent to submit the arbitrability issue to arbitration.

This Court, however, has (as we just said) added an important qualification, applicable when courts decide whether a party has agreed that arbitrators should decide arbitrability: Courts should not assume that the parties agreed to arbitrate arbitrability unless there is "clear and unmistakable" evidence that they did so. In this manner the law treats silence or ambiguity about the question "*who* (primarily) should decide arbitrability" differently from the way it treats silence or ambiguity about the question "*whether* a particular merits-related dispute is arbitrable because it is within the scope of a valid arbitration agreement"—for in respect to this latter question the law reverses the presumption. * * * (" '[A]ny doubts concerning the scope of arbitrable issues should be resolved in favor of arbitration' ").

But, this difference in treatment is understandable. The latter question arises when the parties have a contract that provides for arbitration of some issues. In such circumstances, the parties likely gave at least some thought to the scope of arbitration. And, given the law's permissive policies in respect to arbitration, one can understand why the law would insist upon clarity before concluding that the parties did *not* want to arbitrate a related matter. See Domke § 12.02, p. 156 (issues will be deemed arbitrable unless "it is clear that the arbitration clause has not included" them). On the other hand, the former question—the "who (primarily) should decide arbitrability" question—is rather arcane. A party often might not focus upon that question or upon the significance of having arbitrators decide the scope of their own powers. And, given the principle that a party can be forced to arbitrate only those issues it specifically has agreed to submit to arbitration, one can understand why courts might hesitate to interpret silence or ambiguity on the "who should decide arbitrability" point as giving the arbitrators that power, for doing so might too often force unwilling parties to arbitrate a matter they reasonably would have thought a judge, not an arbitrator, would decide.

On the record before us, First Options cannot show that the Kaplans clearly agreed to have the arbitrators decide (*i.e.,* to arbitrate) the question of arbitrability. First Options relies on the Kaplans' filing with the arbitrators a written memorandum objecting to the arbitrators' jurisdiction. But merely arguing the arbitrability issue to an arbitrator does not indicate a clear willingness to arbitrate that issue, *i.e.,* a willingness to be effectively bound by the arbitrator's decision on that point. To the contrary, insofar as the Kaplans were forcefully objecting to the arbitrators deciding their dispute with First Options, one naturally would think that they did *not* want the arbitrators to have binding authority over them. This conclusion draws added support from (1) an obvious explanation for the Kaplans' presence before the arbitrators (*i.e.,* that MKI, Mr. Kaplan's wholly owned firm, was arbitrating workout agreement matters); and (2) Third Circuit law that suggested that the Kaplans might argue arbitrability to the arbitrators without losing their right to independent court review.

* * *

We conclude that, because the Kaplans did not clearly agree to submit the question of arbitrability to arbitration, the Court of Appeals was correct in finding that the arbitrability of the Kaplan/First Options dispute was subject to independent review by the courts.

* * *

The judgment of the Court of Appeals is affirmed.

NOTES AND QUESTIONS

1.   Why do you think the Kaplans wanted to avoid arbitration? The choice between arbitration and court litigation is discussed *supra*, beginning at p. 562.

2.   Justice Breyer's opinion helpfully delineates the various levels of disputes between the parties. First, there was the dispute over the merits— that is, whether First Options owes the Kaplans the money they seek. There

is no question that the arbitrator had the power to decide this issue and therefore it is not an arbitrability issue. The second level of dispute was over whether they agreed to arbitrate the merits. This was an arbitrability issue because it goes whether the dispute over the merits was included within a valid arbitration agreement, and the parties disagree about that. The third level of dispute was over whether an arbitrator or a court should decide the second dispute, over whether the dispute over the merits was subject to arbitration. Professor Rau has called this "the arbitrability question itself," and it is the only level of dispute addressed by the Court in its opinion. Alan Scott Rau, *The Arbitrability Question Itself*, 10 Am. Rev. Int'l. Arb 287 (1999).

3.   In deciding whether the parties have agreed to arbitrate a dispute, the federal courts are to resolve doubts in favor of arbitration. As the Court stated in *Mitsubishi Motors Corp. v. Soler Chrysler–Plymouth Inc.,* "the parties' intentions control, but those intentions are generously construed as to issues of arbitrability." 473 U.S. 614, 626, 105 S.Ct. 3346, 87 L.Ed.2d 444 (1985). See cases collected in Stephen Hayford & Ralph Peeples, *Commercial Arbitration in Evolution: An Assessment and Call for Dialogue*, 10 Ohio St. J. on Disp. Resol. 343, 357 n.48 (1995).

The presumption of arbitrability in labor-management contract disputes was established in the "Steelworkers Trilogy" in 1960. It was reaffirmed in *AT&T Technologies, Inc. v. Communications Workers*, 475 U.S. 643, 106 S.Ct. 1415, 89 L.Ed.2d 648 (1986), where the Court quoted with approval the following language from *United Steelworkers v. Warrior & Gulf Navigation Co.*, 363 U.S. 574, 80 S.Ct. 1347, 4 L.Ed.2d 1409 (1960), one of the Trilogy cases: "[a]n order to arbitrate the particular grievance should not be denied unless it may be said with positive assurance that the arbitration clause is not susceptible of an interpretation that covers the asserted dispute. Doubts should be resolved in favor of coverage." 475 U.S. at 650, quoting *United Steelworkers v. Warrior & Gulf Navigation Co.*, 363 U.S. at 582–83.

2.   What Issues Are Subject to Arbitration?

While *First Options* dealt with the question of who decides arbitrability decisions, the following case focuses on arbitrability questions about the subject matter of the arbitration—that is, whether the parties intended to submit a particular dispute or class of disputes to arbitration.

HOWSAM V. DEAN WITTER REYNOLDS, INC.

Supreme Court of the United States, 2002
537 U.S. 79, 123 S.Ct. 588, 154 L.Ed.2d 491

JUSTICE BREYER delivered the opinion of the Court.

This case focuses upon an arbitration rule of the National Association of Securities Dealers (NASD). The rule states that no dispute "shall be eligible for submission to arbitration . . . where six (6) years have elapsed from the occurrence or event giving rise to the . . . dispute." NASD Code of

Arbitration Procedure § 10304 (1984) (NASD Code or Code). We must decide whether a court or an NASD arbitrator should apply the rule to the underlying controversy. We conclude that the matter is for the arbitrator.

I

The underlying controversy arises out of investment advice that Dean Witter Reynolds, Inc. (Dean Witter), provided its client, Karen Howsam, when, some time between 1986 and 1994, it recommended that she buy and hold interests in four limited partnerships. Howsam says that Dean Witter misrepresented the virtues of the partnerships. The resulting controversy falls within their standard Client Service Agreement's arbitration clause, which provides:

> all controversies . . . concerning or arising from . . . any account . . . any transaction . . . , or . . . the construction, performance or breach of . . . any . . . agreement between us . . . shall be determined by arbitration before any self-regulatory organization or exchange of which Dean Witter is a member.

The agreement also provides that Howsam can select the arbitration forum. And Howsam chose arbitration before the NASD.

To obtain NASD arbitration, Howsam signed the NASD's Uniform Submission Agreement. That agreement specified that the "present matter in controversy" was submitted for arbitration "in accordance with" the NASD's "Code of Arbitration Procedure." And that Code contains the provision at issue here, a provision stating that no dispute "shall be eligible for submission . . . where six (6) years have elapsed from the occurrence or event giving rise to the . . . dispute."

After the Uniform Submission Agreement was executed, Dean Witter filed this lawsuit in Federal District Court. It asked the court to declare that the dispute was "ineligible for arbitration" because it was more than six years old. And it sought an injunction that would prohibit Howsam from proceeding in arbitration. The District Court dismissed the action on the ground that the NASD arbitrator, not the court, should interpret and apply the NASD rule. The Court of Appeals for the Tenth Circuit, however, reversed. In its view, application of the NASD rule presented a question of the underlying dispute's "arbitrability"; and the presumption is that a court, not an arbitrator, will ordinarily decide an "arbitrability" question.

The Courts of Appeals have reached different conclusions about whether a court or an arbitrator primarily should interpret and apply this particular NASD rule. We granted Howsam's petition for certiorari to resolve this disagreement. And we now hold that the matter is for the arbitrator.

II

This Court has determined that arbitration is a matter of contract and a party cannot be required to submit to arbitration any dispute, which he has not agreed so to submit. Although the Court has also long recognized and enforced a "liberal federal policy favoring arbitration agreements," it has made clear that there is an exception to this policy: The question whether the parties have submitted a particular dispute to arbitration, *i.e.*, the *"question of arbitrability,"* is "an issue for judicial determination unless the parties clearly and unmistakably provide otherwise." We must decide here whether application of the NASD time limit provision falls into the scope of this last-mentioned interpretive rule.

Linguistically speaking, one might call any potentially dispositive gateway question a "question of arbitrability," for its answer will determine whether the underlying controversy will proceed to arbitration on the merits. The Court's case law, however, makes clear that, for purposes of applying the interpretive rule, the phrase "question of arbitrability" has a far more limited scope. The Court has found the phrase applicable in the kind of narrow circumstance where contracting parties would likely have expected a court to have decided the gateway matter, where they are not likely to have thought that they had agreed that an arbitrator would do so, and, consequently, where reference of the gateway dispute to the court avoids the risk of forcing parties to arbitrate a matter that they may well not have agreed to arbitrate.

Thus, a gateway dispute about whether the parties are bound by a given arbitration clause raises a "question of arbitrability" for a court to decide. Similarly, a disagreement about whether an arbitration clause in a concededly binding contract applies to a particular type of controversy is for the court.

At the same time the Court has found the phrase "question of arbitrability" *not* applicable in other kinds of general circumstance where parties would likely expect that an arbitrator would decide the gateway matter. Thus " 'procedural' questions which grow out of the dispute and bear on its final disposition" are presumptively *not* for the judge, but for an arbitrator, to decide. * * * Indeed, the Revised Uniform Arbitration Act of 2000 (RUAA), seeking to "incorporate the holdings of the vast majority of state courts and the law that has developed under the [Federal Arbitration Act]," states that an "arbitrator shall decide whether a condition precedent to arbitrability has been fulfilled." And the comments add that "in the absence of an agreement to the contrary, issues of substantive arbitrability . . . are for a court to decide and issues of procedural arbitrability, *i.e.*, whether prerequisites such as *time limits,* notice, laches, estoppel, and other conditions precedent to an obligation to arbitrate have been met, are for the arbitrators to decide."

Following this precedent, we find that the applicability of the NASD time limit rule is a matter presumptively for the arbitrator, not for the judge. The time limit rule closely resembles the gateway questions that this Court has found not to be "questions of arbitrability." Such a dispute seems an "aspec[t] of the [controversy] which called the grievance procedures into play."

Moreover, the NASD arbitrators, comparatively more expert about the meaning of their own rule, are comparatively better able to interpret and to apply it. In the absence of any statement to the contrary in the arbitration agreement, it is reasonable to infer that the parties intended the agreement to reflect that understanding. And for the law to assume an expectation that aligns (1) decision maker with (2) comparative expertise will help better to secure a fair and expeditious resolution of the underlying controversy—a goal of arbitration systems and judicial systems alike.

We consequently conclude that the NASD's time limit rule falls within the class of gateway procedural disputes that do not present what our cases have called "questions of arbitrability." And the strong pro-court presumption as to the parties' likely intent does not apply.

* * *

IV

For these reasons, the judgment of the Tenth Circuit is

Reversed.

JUSTICE O'CONNOR took no part in the consideration or decision of this case. * * *

[JUSTICE THOMAS' concurring opinion is omitted.]

NOTES AND QUESTIONS

1. The *Howsam* court draws the distinction between "substantive" arbitrability and "procedural" arbitrability. Substantive arbitrability generally addresses the question of whether a particular dispute is covered by an arbitration clause. Procedural arbitrability generally addresses the question of whether the conditions that would trigger the arbitration provision have been met. *See John Wiley & Sons, Inc. v. Livingston*, 376 U.S. 543, 84 S.Ct. 909, 11 L.Ed.2d 898 (1964). For a discussion, see Richard C. Reuben, *First Options, Consent to Arbitration, and the Demise of Separability: Restoring Access to Justice for Contracts With Arbitration Provisions*, 56 SMU L. Rev. 819, 835–36 (2003).

2. Waiver is one area where courts, rather than arbitrators, often make the decision as to enforceability of an arbitration clause. However, because of the public policy favoring arbitration, a court normally will only find a waiver of a right to arbitrate where a party claiming waiver meets the

burden of proving that the waiver has caused prejudice. For instance, where a plaintiff brings an action against a defendant in court, engages in extensive discovery and then attempts to dismiss the lawsuit on the grounds of an arbitration clause, a defendant might challenge the dismissal on the grounds that the plaintiff has waived any right to use of the arbitration clause. *S & R Co. of Kingston v. Latona Trucking, Inc.*, 159 F.3d 80 (2d Cir. 1998). Allowing the court to decide this issue of arbitrability comports with the separability doctrine because in most instances waiver concerns only the arbitration clause itself and not an attack on the underlying contract. It is also a matter of judicial economy to require that a party, who pursues an action in a court proceeding but later claims arbitrability, be held to a decision of the court on waiver.

3. *Who Decides the Validity of Contracts with Arbitration Provisions? The Separability Doctrine*

PRIMA PAINT CORP. V. FLOOD & CONKLIN MFG. CO.
Supreme Court of the United States, 1967
388 U.S. 395, 87 S.Ct. 1801, 18 L.Ed.2d 1270

MR. JUSTICE FORTAS delivered the opinion of the Court.

This case presents the question whether the federal court or an arbitrator is to resolve a claim of "fraud in the inducement," under a contract governed by the United States Arbitration Act of 1925, where there is no evidence that the contracting parties intended to withhold that issue from arbitration.

The question arises from the following set of facts. On October 7, 1964, respondent, Flood & Conklin Manufacturing Company, a New Jersey corporation, entered into what was styled a "Consulting Agreement," with petitioner, Prima Paint Corporation, a Maryland corporation. This agreement followed by less than three weeks the execution of a contract pursuant to which Prima Paint purchased F & C's paint business. The consulting agreement provided that for a six-year period F & C was to furnish advice and consultation "in connection with the formulae, manufacturing operations, sales and servicing of Prima Trade Sales accounts." These services were to be performed personally by F & C's chairman, Jerome K. Jelin, "except in the event of his death or disability." F & C bound itself for the duration of the contractual period to make no "Trade Sales" of paint or paint products in its existing sales territory or to current customers. To the consulting agreement were appended lists of F & C customers, whose patronage was to be taken over by Prima Paint. In return for these lists, the covenant not to compete, and the services of Mr. Jelin, Prima Paint agreed to pay F & C certain percentages of its receipts from the listed customers and from all others, such payments not to exceed $225,000 over the life of the agreement. The agreement took into account the possibility that Prima Paint might encounter financial difficulties, including bankruptcy, but no corresponding reference was made to possible financial problems which might be encountered by F & C. The agreement stated that it "embodies the entire understanding of the parties on the subject matter." Finally, the parties agreed to a broad arbitration clause, which read in part:

> "Any controversy or claim arising out of or relating to this Agreement, or the breach thereof, shall be settled by arbitration in the City of New York, in accordance with the rules then obtaining of the American Arbitration Association . . ."

The first payment by Prima Paint to F & C under the consulting agreement was due on September 1, 1965. None was made on that date. Seventeen days later, Prima Paint did pay the appropriate amount, but into escrow. It notified attorneys for F & C that in various enumerated respects their client had broken both the consulting agreement and the earlier purchase agreement. Prima Paint's principal contention, so far as presently relevant, was that F & C had fraudulently represented that it was solvent and able to perform its contractual obligations, whereas it was in fact insolvent and intended to file a petition under Chapter XI of the Bankruptcy Act, shortly after execution of the consulting agreement. Prima Paint noted that such a petition was filed by F & C on October 14, 1964; one week after the contract had been signed. F & C's response, on October 25, was to serve a "notice of intention to arbitrate." On November 12, three days before expiration of its time to answer this "notice," Prima Paint filed suit in the United States District Court for the Southern District of New York, seeking rescission of the consulting agreement on the basis of the alleged fraudulent inducement. The complaint asserted that the federal court had diversity jurisdiction.

Contemporaneously with the filing of its complaint, Prima Paint petitioned the District Court for an order enjoining F & C from proceeding with the arbitration. F & C cross-moved to stay the court action pending arbitration. F & C contended that the issue presented—whether there was fraud in the inducement of the consulting agreement—was a question for the arbitrators and not for the District Court. Cross-affidavits were filed on the merits. On behalf of Prima Paint, the charges in the complaint were reiterated. Affiants for F & C attacked the sufficiency of Prima Paint's allegations of fraud, denied that misrepresentations had been made during negotiations, and asserted that Prima Paint had relied exclusively upon delivery of the lists, the promise not to compete, and the availability of Mr. Jelin. They contended that Prima Paint had availed itself of these considerations for nearly a year without claiming "fraud," noting that Prima Paint was in no position to claim ignorance of the bankruptcy proceeding since it had participated therein in February of 1965. They added that F & C was revested with its assets in March of 1965.

The District Court, granted F & C's motion to stay the action pending arbitration, holding that a charge of fraud in the inducement of a contract containing an arbitration clause as broad as this one was a question for the arbitrators and not for the court. For this proposition it relied on *Robert Lawrence Co. v. Devonshire Fabrics, Inc.*, 271 F.2d 402 (C.A.2d Cir. 1959), cert. granted, 362 U.S. 909, dismissed under Rule 60, 364 U.S. 801 (1960). The Court of Appeals for the Second Circuit dismissed Prima Paint's appeal. It held that the contract in question evidenced a transaction involving interstate commerce; that under the controlling *Robert Lawrence Co.* decision a claim of fraud in the inducement of the contract generally—as opposed to the arbitration clause itself—is for the arbitrators and not for the courts; and that this rule—one of "national substantive law"—governs even in the face of a contrary state rule. We agree, albeit for somewhat different reasons, and we affirm the decision below.

The key statutory provisions are §§ 2, 3, and 4 of the United States Arbitration Act of 1925. Section 2 provides that a written provision for arbitration "in any maritime transaction or a contract evidencing a transaction involving commerce . . . shall be valid, irrevocable, and enforceable, save upon such grounds as exist at law or in equity for the revocation of any contract." Section 3 requires a federal court in which suit has been brought "upon any issue referable to arbitration under an agreement in writing for such arbitration" to stay the court action pending arbitration once it is satisfied that the issue is arbitrable under the agreement. Section 4 provides a federal remedy for a party "aggrieved by the alleged failure, neglect, or refusal of another to arbitrate under a written agreement for arbitration," and directs the federal court to order arbitration once it is satisfied that an agreement for arbitration has been made and has not been honored.

* * *

Having determined that the contract in question is within the coverage of the Arbitration Act, we turn to the central issue in this case: whether a claim of fraud in the inducement of the entire contract is to be resolved by the federal court, or whether the matter is to be referred to the arbitrators. The courts of appeals have differed in their approach to this question. The view of the Court of Appeals for the Second Circuit, as expressed in this case and in others, is that—*except where the parties otherwise intend*—arbitration clauses as a matter of federal law are "separable" from the contracts in which they are embedded, and that where no claim is made that fraud was directed to the arbitration clause itself, a broad arbitration clause will be held to encompass arbitration of the claim that the contract itself was induced by fraud. The Court of Appeals for the First Circuit, on the other hand, has taken the view that the question of "severability" is one of state law, and that where a State regards such a clause as inseparable a claim of fraud in the inducement must be decided by the court.

With respect to cases brought in federal court involving maritime contracts or those evidencing transactions in "commerce," we think that Congress has provided an explicit answer. That answer is to be found in § 4 of the Act, which provides a remedy to a party seeking to compel compliance with an arbitration agreement. Under § 4, with respect to a matter within the jurisdiction of the federal courts save for the existence of an arbitration clause, the federal court is instructed to order arbitration to proceed once it is satisfied that "the making of the agreement for arbitration or the failure to comply [with the arbitration agreement] is not in issue." Accordingly, if the claim is fraud in the inducement of the arbitration clause itself—an issue, which goes to the "making" of the agreement to arbitrate—the federal court may proceed to adjudicate it. But the statutory language does not permit the federal court to consider claims of fraud in the inducement of the contract generally. Section 4 does not expressly relate to situations like the present in which a stay is sought of a federal action in order that arbitration may proceed. But it is inconceivable that Congress intended the rule to differ depending upon which party to the arbitration agreement first invokes the assistance of a federal court. We hold, therefore, that in passing upon a § 3 application for a stay while the parties arbitrate, a federal court may consider only issues relating to the making and performance of the agreement to arbitrate. In so concluding, we not only honor the plain meaning of the statute but also the unmistakably clear congressional purpose that the arbitration procedure, when selected by the parties to a contract, be speedy and not subject to delay and obstruction in the courts.

There remains the question whether such a rule is constitutionally permissible. The point is made that, whatever the nature of the contract involved here, this case is in federal court solely by reason of diversity of citizenship, and that since the decision in *Erie R. Co. v. Tompkins*, federal courts are bound in diversity cases to follow state rules of decision in matters which are "substantive" rather than "procedural," or where the matter is "outcome determinative." The question in this case, however, is not whether Congress may fashion federal substantive rules to govern questions arising in simple diversity cases. Rather, the question is whether Congress may prescribe how federal courts are to conduct themselves with respect to subject matter over which Congress plainly has power to legislate. The answer to that can only be in the affirmative. And it is clear beyond dispute that the federal arbitration statute is based upon and confined to the incontestable federal foundations of "control over interstate commerce and over admiralty."

In the present case no claim has been advanced by Prima Paint that F & C fraudulently induced it to enter into the agreement to arbitrate "(a)ny controversy or claim arising out of or relating to this Agreement, or the breach thereof." This contractual language is easily broad enough to encompass Prima Paint's claim that both execution and acceleration of the consulting agreement itself were procured by fraud. Indeed, no claim is made that Prima Paint ever intended that "legal" issues relating to the contract be excluded from arbitration, or that it was not entirely free so to contract. Federal courts are bound to apply rules enacted by Congress with respect to matters—here, a contract involving commerce—over which it has legislative power. The question, which Prima Paint requested, the District Court to adjudicate preliminarily to allowing arbitration to proceed is one not intended by Congress to delay the granting of a § 3 stay. Accordingly, the decision below dismissing Prima Paint's appeal is

Affirmed.

[The concurring opinion of MR. JUSTICE HARLAN is omitted.]

* * *

MR. JUSTICE BLACK, with whom MR. JUSTICE DOUGLAS and MR. JUSTICE STEWART join, dissenting.

The Court here holds that the United States Arbitration Act, 9 U.S.C. §§ 1–14, as a matter of federal substantive law, compels a party to a contract containing a written arbitration provision to carry out his "arbitration agreement" even though a court might, after a fair trial, hold the entire contract—including the arbitration agreement—void because of fraud in the inducement. The Court holds, what is to me fantastic, that the legal issue of a contract's voidness because of fraud is to be decided by persons designated to arbitrate factual controversies arising out of a valid contract between the parties. And the arbitrators who the Court holds are to adjudicate the legal validity of the contract need not even be lawyers, and in all probability will be nonlawyers, wholly unqualified to decide legal issues, and even if qualified to apply the law, not bound to do so. I am by no means sure that thus forcing a person to forgo his opportunity to try his legal issues in the courts where, unlike the situation in arbitration, he may have a jury trial and right to appeal, is not a denial of due process of law. I am satisfied, however, that Congress did not impose any such procedures in the Arbitration Act. And I am fully satisfied that a reasonable and fair reading of that Act's language and history shows that both Congress and the framers of the Act were at great pains to emphasize that nonlawyers designated to adjust and arbitrate factual controversies arising out of valid contracts would not trespass upon the courts' prerogative to decide the legal question of whether any legal contract exists upon which to base an arbitration.

* * *

I would reverse this case.

NOTES AND QUESTIONS

1.   Do you agree with the majority or the dissent? Why?

2.   How does *Prima Paint* square with *First Options?* Recall that in *First Options*, the Court held that "courts should not assume that the parties agreed to arbitrate arbitrability unless there is 'clear and unmistakable' evidence that they did so." 514 U.S. at 994. This would suggest that a judicial interpretation of 'clear and unmistakable' waiver cannot be based on implied consent.

On the other hand, implied consent seems crucial to the Supreme Court's finding of separability in *Prima Paint*. As Professor Reuben explains:

> [S]eparability imputes assent and consideration from the container contract to the 'separated' contract for arbitration by virtue of the construction of the FAA, not by the conduct of the parties. * * * It is this imputed consent that makes it theoretically possible for the arbitration provision to survive as an independent contract when the larger contract that contains it is found to be defective by an arbitrator.

Richard C. Reuben, *First Options, Consent to Arbitration, and the Demise of Separability: Restoring Access to Justice for Contract With Arbitration Provisions*, 56 SMU L. Rev. 819, 849–50 (2003).

Professor Rau argues that there is no conflict between *Prima Paint* and *First Options* because *First Options* dealt with the question of who decides arbitrability issues while *Prima Paint* dealt with the question of who decides the merits of fraudulent inducement claims. Alan Scott Rau, *The Arbitrability Question Itself*, 10 Am. Rev. Int'l Arb. 287, 331, 339 (1999). In another article, Rau says Reuben "seems to me to get the point of *Prima Paint* precisely backwards: Any supposed difficulty completely evaporates once one understands that the doctrine's presumption of intent—for example, its presumption of a willingness to entrust a fraudulent inducement claim to arbitration—has no role at all in the absence of a prior finding of an 'agreement' to arbitrate. It is always a court, acting at the threshold as a gatekeeper, that passes on this requisite to arbitral jurisdiction." Alan Scott Rau, *Everything You Really Needed to Know About "Separability" in Seventeen Simple Propositions*, 14 Am. Rev. Int'l. Arb. 1, 29–30 (2003).

Do you agree with Professor Reuben or Professor Rau?

3.   *Prima Paint's* rule of separability is sometimes known as "the federal rule" because nearly half the states refused to follow it at all, or limited its reach either to contracts that were voidable rather than void ab initio, or to the specific fraud in the inducement context presented by the facts in Prima Paint.

The U.S. Supreme Court put a halt to that in 2006 as it reaffirmed the separability doctrine in *Buckeye Check Cashing, Inc. v. Cardegna,* 546 U.S. 440, 126 S.Ct. 1204, 163 L.Ed.2d 1038 (2006).

The case came out of a legal challenge to a payday loan contract that called for an interest rate that would have been usurious under Florida state law. Buckeye Check Cashing responded with a motion to compel arbitration. The trial court denied the motion, holding that a court should resolve a claim that the contract was unlawful and therefore void *ab initio*—i.e., that it didn't exist as a matter of law. The state court of appeal reversed, saying the question was for the arbitrator to decide under the separability doctrine, not the courts. The Florida Supreme Court reversed, reinstating the trial court's decision.

The U.S. Supreme Court reversed on an 8–1 vote, in an opinion by Justice Scalia. The decision relied on both *Prima Paint* and *Southland v. Keating,* 465 U.S. 1 104 S.Ct. 852, 79 L.Ed.2d1 (1984), which held that the Federal Arbitration Act applies in state courts and preempts state laws that are hostile to arbitration. *See infra* 590. Said the court:

> In declining to apply *Prima Paint's* rule of severability, the Florida Supreme Court relied on the distinction between void and voidable contracts. "Florida public policy and contract law," it concluded, permit "no severable, or salvageable, parts of a contract found illegal and void under Florida law." *Prima Paint* makes this conclusion irrelevant. That case rejected application of state severability rules to the arbitration agreement without discussing whether the challenge at issue would have rendered the contract void or voidable. Indeed, the opinion expressly disclaimed any need to decide what state-law remedy was available [citations omitted]. Likewise in *Southland*, which arose in state court, we did not ask whether the several challenges made there—fraud, misrepresentation, breach of contract, breach of fiduciary duty, and violation of the California Franchise Investment Law—would render the contract void or voidable. We simply rejected the proposition that the enforceability of the arbitration agreement turned on the state legislature's judgment concerning the forum for enforcement of the state-law cause of action. So also here, we cannot accept the Florida Supreme Court's conclusion that enforceability of the arbitration agreement should turn on 'Florida public policy and contract law[.]. . . .

> [For emphasis, the court later added:] "We reaffirm today that, regardless of whether the challenge is brought in federal or state court, a challenge to the validity of the contract as a whole, and not specifically to the arbitration clause, must go to the arbitrator."

The court's decision clearly rejected the void *ab initio* exception to the separability doctrine. But what about the other exceptions? Are they still viable after a strong reaffirmation of *Prima Paint*? What policies are served by a strong view of separability that rejects exceptions? What interests might counsel a contrary view? If you were a state attorney general, would you support a strong version of *Prima Paint*? Recall that the court in *Buckeye Check Cashing* held that a state supreme court's determination on the validity of a contract executed and performed within the state was legally "irrelevant" to the question of who decides the merits of the plaintiff's usury claims.

For a critique of *Buckeye Check Cashing* set in the context of the court's larger arbitration jurisprudence, see Margaret L. Moses, *Statutory Misconstruction: How the Supreme Court Created a Federal Arbitration Law Never Enacted by* Margaret L. Moses, *Statutory Misconstruction: How the Supreme Court Created a Federal Arbitration Law Never Enacted by Congress*, 34 Fla. St. U. L. Rev. 99 (2006).

4.   The doctrine of separability announced in *Prima Paint* has been widely criticized by many legal scholars.

According to Professor Stempel, "[m]uch of the atrophy of contract revocation defenses results from *Prima Paint Corp. v. Flood & Conklin Manufactuing Co.* . . . To be heard by courts after *Prima Paint*, a contract revocation defense must specifically address the arbitration clause rather than the entire contract, which at least in the first instance, made the vast bulk of fraud, misrepresentation, illegality, and other traditional recision defenses the province of the arbitrator." Jeffrey W. Stempel, *A Better Approach to Arbitrability*, 65 Tul. L. Rev. 1377, 1390–91 (1991).

Professor Sternlight has argued, "it is difficult to imagine a factual scenario in which a party would use fraud solely to impose an arbitration clause and not to affect other essential terms of a contract." Jean R. Sternlight, *Rethinking the Constitutionality of the Supreme Court's Preference for Binding Arbitration: A Fresh Assessment of Jury Trial, Separation of Powers, and Due Process Concerns*, 72 Tul. L. Rev. 1, 24 (1997).

Professor Reuben had this to say about *Prima Paint*: "For a society steeped in the belief in the right to one's 'day in court,' the separability doctrine is counter-intuitive, and as a result has been difficult for many lower courts to implement, and has simply been rejected by others as bad policy. This has led to massive doctrinal complexity, confusion, and uncertainty. . . ." Richard C. Reuben, *First Options, Consent to Arbitration, and the Demise of Separability: Restoring Access to Justice for Contracts With Arbitration Provisions*, 56 SMU L. Rev. 819, 825 (2003). Professor Reuben provides numerous arguments for the repudiation of separability and points to *First Options,* the next case, as an indication that the Supreme Court may be moving toward a different approach. *Id.* at 883. The Wyoming Supreme Court adopted Professor Reuben's reasoning on separability in *Fox v. Tanner*, 101 P.3d 939 (Wyo. 2004).

State cases recognizing and refusing to recognize some form of the separability doctrine are collected in Comment 4 of Section 6 of RUAA, *infra* Section B(2)(a) following the *Howsam* case, beginning at p. 578.

For a comprehensive defense of *Prima Paint*, see Alan Scott Rau, *Everything You Really Need to Know About "Separability" In Seventeen Simple Propositions*, 14 Am. Int'l Rev. Arb. 1 (2003). Professor Rau asserts that "[i]t should be obvious how frequently the issue of contract validity will be intertwined with the substantive issues underlying the 'merits' of the dispute: The arbitral determination that the parties unquestionably bargained for. . . . Here we can say how abundantly sensible it would be to impute to contracting parties a preference for what has neatly been termed 'the practical advantages of one-stop adjudication.' " *Id.* at 33–34.

5. The separability doctrine raises important questions about arbitration and federalism because application of "the federal rule" necessarily precludes the ability of bringing challenges to arbitrability based on state contract law, as we saw in the *Buckeye Check Cashing* case discussed in Note 3. In the next subsection, we explore further the FAA's implications for federalism.

c.   Which Law Applies? FAA Preemption

The original assumption was that the FAA applied only in federal courts. IAN R. MACNEIL, RICHARD E. SPEIDEL, THOMAS J. STIPANOWICH, FEDERAL ARBITRATION LAW §§ 10.2, 10.3.1, 10.3.2 (1994 ed. & Supp. 1999). This was significant because the application of the FAA in state courts had the potential of invalidating a wide range of state statutes and common law doctrines hostile to arbitration. The Supreme Court indicated in its 1967 decision in *Prima Paint Corp. v. Flood & Conklin Manufacturing Co.,* 388 U.S. 395, 87 S.Ct. 1801, 18 L.Ed.2d 1270 (1967), that the FAA created a body of federal substantive law. *Id.* at 404–05. This conclusion was reaffirmed in the Court's 1983 decision in *Moses H. Cone Memorial Hospital v. Mercury Construction Corp.,* 460 U.S. 1, 103 S.Ct. 927, 74 L.Ed.2d 765 (1983). As we see in the cases that follow, these decisions laid the foundation for what has become a broad rule of FAA preemption of state law.

1.   *The Rationale for Preemption*

SOUTHLAND CORP. V. KEATING
Supreme Court of the United States, 1984
465 U.S. 1, 104 S.Ct. 852, 79 L.Ed.2d 1

CHIEF JUSTICE BURGER delivered the opinion of the Court.

This case presents the questions (a) whether the California Franchise Investment Law, which invalidates certain arbitration agreements covered by the Federal Arbitration Act, violates the Supremacy Clause and (b) whether arbitration under the Federal Act is impaired when a class-action structure is imposed on the process by the state courts.

I

Appellant Southland Corp. is the owner and franchisor of 7–Eleven convenience stores. Southland's standard franchise agreement provides each franchisee with a license to use certain registered trademarks, a lease or sublease of a convenience store owned or leased by Southland, inventory financing, and assistance in advertising and merchandising. The franchisees operate the stores, supply bookkeeping data, and pay Southland a fixed percentage of gross profits. The franchise agreement also contains the following provision requiring arbitration:

> Any controversy or claim arising out of or relating to this Agreement or the breach hereof shall be settled by arbitration in accordance with the Rules of the American Arbitration Association . . . and judgment upon any award rendered by the arbitrator may be entered in any court having jurisdiction thereof.

Appellees are 7–Eleven franchisees. Between September 1975 and January 1977, several appellees filed individual actions against Southland in California Superior Court alleging, among other things, fraud, oral misrepresentation, breach of contract, breach of fiduciary duty, and violation of the disclosure requirements of the California Franchise Investment Law, Cal.Corp.Code § 31000 *et seq.* (West 1977). Southland's answer, in all but one of the individual actions, included the affirmative defense of failure to arbitrate.

In May 1977, appellee Keating filed a class action against Southland on behalf of a class that assertedly includes approximately 800 California franchisees. Keating's principal claims were substantially the same as those asserted by the other franchisees. After the various actions were consolidated, Southland petitioned to compel arbitration of the claims in all cases, and appellees moved for class certification.

The Superior Court granted Southland's motion to compel arbitration of all claims except those claims based on the [California] Franchise Investment Law. The court did not pass on appellees' request for class certification. Southland appealed from the order insofar as it excluded from arbitration the claims based on the California statute. Appellees filed a petition for a writ of mandamus or prohibition in the California Court of Appeal arguing that the arbitration should proceed as a class action.

The California Court of Appeal reversed the trial court's refusal to compel arbitration of appellees' claims under the Franchise Investment Law. That court interpreted the arbitration clause to require arbitration of all claims asserted under the Franchise Investment Law, and construed the Franchise Investment Law not to invalidate such agreements to arbitrate. Alternatively, the court concluded that if the Franchise Investment Law rendered arbitration agreements involving commerce unenforceable, it would conflict with § 2 of the Federal Arbitration Act, 9 U.S.C. § 2 (1976), and therefore be invalid under the Supremacy Clause. The Court of Appeal also determined that there was no "insurmountable obstacle" to conducting an arbitration on a classwide basis, and issued a writ of mandate directing the trial court to conduct class certification proceedings.

The California Supreme Court, by a vote of 4–2, reversed the ruling that claims asserted under the Franchise Investment Law are arbitrable. The California Supreme Court interpreted the Franchise Investment Law to require judicial consideration of claims brought under that statute and concluded that the California statute did not contravene the federal Act. The court also remanded the case to the trial court for consideration of appellees' request for classwide arbitration.

We postponed consideration of the question of jurisdiction pending argument on the merits. We reverse in part and dismiss in part.

* * *

The California Franchise Investment Law provides:

> Any condition, stipulation or provision purporting to bind any person acquiring any franchise to waive compliance with any provision of this law or any rule or order hereunder is void. Cal.Corp.Code § 31512 (West 1977).

The California Supreme Court interpreted this statute to require judicial consideration of claims brought under the state statute and accordingly refused to enforce the parties' contract to arbitrate such claims. So interpreted the California Franchise Investment Law directly conflicts with § 2 of the Federal Arbitration Act and violates the Supremacy Clause.

In enacting § 2 of the federal act, Congress declared a national policy favoring arbitration and withdrew the power of the states to require a judicial forum for the resolution of claims which the contracting parties agreed to resolve by arbitration. The Federal Arbitration Act provides:

> A written provision in any maritime transaction or a contract evidencing a transaction involving commerce to settle by arbitration a controversy thereafter arising out of such contract or transaction, or the refusal to perform the whole or any part thereof, or an agreement in writing to submit to arbitration an existing controversy arising out of such a contract, transaction, or refusal, shall be valid, irrevocable, and enforceable, save upon such grounds as exist at law or in equity for the revocation of any contract. 9 U.S.C. § 2 (1976).

Congress has thus mandated the enforcement of arbitration agreements.

We discern only two limitations on the enforceability of arbitration provisions governed by the Federal Arbitration Act: they must be part of a written maritime contract or a contract "evidencing a transaction involving commerce" and such clauses may be revoked upon "grounds as exist at law or in equity for the revocation of any contract." We see nothing in the Act indicating that the broad principle of enforceability is subject to any additional limitations under state law.

The Federal Arbitration Act rests on the authority of Congress to enact substantive rules under the Commerce Clause. In *Prima Paint Corp. v. Flood & Conklin Manufacturing Corp.*, 388 U.S. 395 (1967), the Court examined the legislative history of the Act and concluded that the statute "is based upon . . . the incontestable federal foundations of 'control over interstate commerce and over admiralty.'" *Id.*, at 405 (quoting H.R.Rep. No. 96, 68th Cong., 1st Sess. 1 (1924)). The contract in *Prima Paint,* as here, contained an arbitration clause. One party in that case alleged that the other had committed fraud in the inducement of the contract, although not of the arbitration clause in particular, and sought to have the claim of fraud adjudicated in federal court. The Court held that, notwithstanding a contrary state rule, consideration of a claim of fraud in the inducement of a contract "is for the arbitrators and not for the courts," 388 U.S. at 400. The Court relied for this holding on Congress' broad power to fashion substantive rules under the Commerce Clause.

At least since 1824 Congress' authority under the Commerce Clause has been held plenary. In the words of Chief Justice Marshall, the authority of Congress is "the power to regulate; that is, to prescribe the rule by which commerce is to be governed." *Ibid.* The statements of the Court in *Prima Paint* that the Arbitration Act was an exercise of the Commerce Clause power clearly implied that the substantive rules of the Act were to apply in state as well as federal courts. As Justice Black observed in his dissent, when Congress exercises its authority to enact substantive federal law under the Commerce Clause, it normally creates rules that are enforceable in state as well as federal courts.

In *Moses H. Cone Memorial Hospital v. Mercury Construction Corp.*, 460 U.S., at 1, 25, and n. 32, we reaffirmed our view that the Arbitration Act "creates a body of federal substantive law" and expressly stated what was implicit in *Prima Paint, i.e.*, the substantive law the Act created was applicable in state and federal court. *Moses H. Cone* began with a petition for an order to compel arbitration. The District Court stayed the action pending resolution of a concurrent state-court suit. In holding that the District Court had abused its discretion, we found no showing of exceptional circumstances justifying the stay and recognized "the presence of federal-law issues" under the federal Act as "a major consideration weighing against surrender [of federal jurisdiction]." We thus read the underlying issue of arbitrability to be a question of substantive federal law: "Federal law in the terms of the Arbitration Act governs that issue in either state or federal court."

Although the legislative history is not without ambiguities, there are strong indications that Congress had in mind something more than making arbitration agreements enforceable only in the federal courts. The House Report plainly suggests the more comprehensive objectives:

The purpose of this bill is to make valid and enforceable [sic] agreements for arbitration contained *in contracts involving interstate commerce* or within the jurisdiction or [sic] admiralty, *or* which may be the subject of litigation in the Federal courts.

This broader purpose can also be inferred from the reality that Congress would be less likely to address a problem whose impact was confined to federal courts than a problem of large significance in the field of commerce. The Arbitration Act sought to "overcome the rule of equity, that equity will not specifically enforce [any] arbitration agreement." The House Report accompanying the bill stated:

> The need for the law arises from ... the jealousy of the English courts for their own jurisdiction.... This jealousy survived for so [long] a period that the principle became firmly embedded in the English common law and was adopted with it by the American courts. The courts have felt that the precedent was too strongly fixed to be overturned without legislative enactment....

Surely this makes clear that the House Report contemplated a broad reach of the Act, unencumbered by state-law constraints. As was stated in *Metro Industrial Painting Corp. v. Terminal Construction Co.*, "the purpose of the act was to assure those who desired arbitration and whose contracts related to interstate commerce that their expectations would not be undermined by federal judges, or ... by state courts or legislatures." Congress also showed its awareness of the widespread unwillingness of state courts to enforce arbitration agreements, and that such courts were bound by state laws inadequately providing for "technical arbitration by which, if you agree to arbitrate under the method provided by the statute, you have an arbitration by statute [;] but [the statutes] [had] nothing to do with validating the contract to arbitrate."

The problems Congress faced were therefore twofold: the old common law hostility toward arbitration, and the failure of state arbitration statutes to mandate enforcement of arbitration agreements. To confine the scope of the Act to arbitrations sought to be enforced in federal courts would frustrate what we believe Congress intended to be a broad enactment appropriate in scope to meet the large problems Congress was addressing.

Justice O'Connor argues that Congress viewed the Arbitration Act "as a procedural statute, applicable only in federal courts." If it is correct that Congress sought only to create a procedural remedy in the federal courts, there can be no explanation for the express limitation in the Arbitration Act to contracts "involving commerce." 9 U.S.C. § 2. For example, when Congress has authorized this Court to prescribe the rules of procedure in the federal courts of appeals, district courts, and bankruptcy courts, it has not limited the power of the Court to prescribe rules applicable only to causes of action involving commerce. We would expect that if Congress, in enacting the Arbitration Act, was creating what it thought to be a procedural rule applicable only in federal courts, it would not so limit the Act to transactions involving commerce. On the other hand, Congress would need to call on the Commerce Clause if it intended the Act to apply in state courts. Yet at the same time, its reach would be limited to transactions involving interstate commerce. We therefore view the "involving commerce" requirement in § 2, not as an inexplicable limitation on the power of the federal courts, but as a necessary qualification on a statute intended to apply in state and federal courts.

Under the interpretation of the Arbitration Act urged by Justice O'Connor, claims brought under the California Franchise Investment Law are not arbitrable when they are raised in state court. Yet it is clear beyond question that if this suit had been brought as a diversity action in a federal district court, the arbitration clause would have been enforceable. *Prima Paint, supra.* The interpretation given to the Arbitration Act by the California Supreme Court would therefore encourage and reward forum shopping. We are unwilling to attribute to Congress the intent, in drawing on the comprehensive powers of the Commerce Clause, to create a right to enforce an arbitration contract and yet make the right dependent for its enforcement on the particular forum in which it is asserted. And since the overwhelming proportion of all civil litigation in this country is in the state courts, we cannot believe Congress intended to limit the Arbitration Act to disputes subject only to *federal*-court jurisdiction. Such an interpretation would frustrate congressional intent to place "[an] arbitration agreement . . . upon the same footing as other contracts, where it belongs."

In creating a substantive rule applicable in state as well as federal courts, Congress intended to foreclose state legislative attempts to undercut the enforceability of arbitration agreements.[11] We hold that § 31512 of the California Franchise Investment Law violates the Supremacy Clause.

* * *

Justice O'Connor, with whom Justice Rehnquist joins in dissenting.

* * *

---

[11] Justice Steven dissents in part on the ground that § 2 of the Arbitration Act permits a party to nullify an agreement to arbitrate on "such grounds as exist at law or in equity for the revocation of any contract." We agree, of course, that a party may assert general contract defenses such as fraud to avoid enforcement of an arbitration agreement. We conclude, however, that the defense to arbitration found in the California Franchise Investment Law is not a ground that exists at law or in equity "for the revocation of *any* contract" but merely a ground that exists for the revocation of arbitration provisions in contracts subject to the California Franchise Investment Law. * * *

One rarely finds a legislative history as unambiguous as the FAA's. That history establishes conclusively that the 1925 Congress viewed the FAA as a procedural statute, applicable only in federal courts, derived, Congress believed, largely from the federal power to control the jurisdiction of the federal courts.

In 1925, Congress emphatically believed arbitration to be a matter of "procedure." At hearings on the Act congressional Subcommittees were told: "The theory on which you do this is that you have the right to tell the Federal courts how to proceed." The House Report on the FAA stated: "Whether an agreement for arbitration shall be enforced or not is a question of procedure. . . ." On the floor of the House Congressman Graham assured his fellow members that the FAA

> Does not involve any new principle of law except to provide a simple method . . . in order to give enforcement . . . It creates no new legislation, grants no new rights, except a remedy to enforce an agreement in commercial contracts and in admiralty contracts.

A month after the Act was signed into law the American Bar Association Committee that had drafted and pressed for passage of the federal legislation wrote:

> The statute establishes a procedure in the Federal courts for the enforcement of arbitration agreements . . . A Federal statute providing for the enforcement of arbitration agreements does relate solely to procedure in the Federal courts . . . [Whether] or not an arbitration agreement is to be enforced is a question of the law of procedure and is determined by the law of the jurisdiction wherein the remedy is sought. That the enforcement of arbitration contracts is within the law of procedure as distinguished from substantive law is well settled by the decisions of our courts.

* * *

The Court, *ante*, at 15–16, rejects the idea of requiring the FAA to be applied only in federal courts partly out of concern with the problem of forum shopping. The concern is unfounded. Because the FAA makes the federal courts equally accessible to both parties to a dispute, no forum shopping would be possible even if we gave the FAA a construction faithful to the congressional intent. * * *

[The court's discussion of jurisdiction and the propriety of superimposing class action procedures on a contract arbitration is omitted. Also omitted is the opinion of JUSTICE STEVENS, who concurred in part and dissented in part.]

NOTES AND QUESTIONS

1. *Southland* was and remains controversial. If you were a state attorney general charged with enforcing your states' civil laws, what would be your reaction to the decision? *See* Barbara A. Atwood, *Issues in Federal–State Relations Under the Federal Arbitration Act*, 37 U. Fla. L. Rev. 61, 102–03 (1985).

If you were a United States Senator would you support legislation that would overrule *Southland*? *See* Jean R. Sternlight, *Panacea or Corporate Tool?: Debunking the Supreme Court's Preference for Binding Arbitration*, 74 Wash. U. L.Q. 637, at 697–701 (1996).

2. The FAA does not apply unless an arbitration provision is part of a written maritime contract or a contract evidencing a transaction involving commerce. Following *Southland*, the lower courts differed on whether this language extended the FAA's coverage to the constitutional limits of Congress' power.

The Supreme Court adopted the expansive interpretation in *Allied–Bruce Terminix Cos. v. Dobson*, 513 U.S. 265, 115 S.Ct. 834, 130 L.Ed.2d 753 (1995). Writing for the Court, Justice Breyer stated that:

> . . . a broad interpretation of this language is consistent with the Act's basic purpose, to put arbitration provisions on "the same footing" as a contract's other terms . . . Conversely, a narrower interpretation . . . would create a new, unfamiliar test lying somewhere in the no-man's land between "in commerce" and "affecting commerce," thereby unnecessarily complicating the law and breeding litigation from a statute that seeks to avoid it.

513 U.S. at 275.

In a concurring opinion in *Allied–Bruce*, Justice O'Connor said, "I continue to believe that Congress never intended the Federal Arbitration Act to apply in state courts . . ." (513 U.S. at 283) but then went on to state:

> Were we writing on a clean slate, I would adhere to that view and affirm the Alabama court's decision. But, as the Court points out, more than 10 years have passed since *Southland*, several subsequent cases have built upon its reasoning, and parties have undoubtedly made contracts in reliance on the Court's interpretation of the Act in the interim. After reflection, I am persuaded by considerations of *stare decisis*, which we have said "have special force in the area of statutory interpretation," . . . to acquiesce in today's judgment. Though wrong, *Southland* has not proved unworkable, and, as always, "Congress remains free to alter what we have done."

Id. at 283–84.

Do you find Justice O'Connor's argument persuasive?

3. For an extended and authoritative critique of *Southland*, *see* IAN R. MACNEIL, AMERICAN ARBITRATION LAW: REFORMATION, NATIONALIZATION,

INTERNATIONALIZATION 92–121 (1992). *See also*, Paul D. Carrington, *Contract and Jurisdiction*, 1996 S. Ct. Rev. 331; David S. Schwartz, *Correcting Federalism Mistakes In Statutory Interpretation: The Supreme Court and the Federal Arbitration Act*, 67 Law & Contemp. Probs. 5 (2004), and Jean R. Sternlight, *Rethinking the Constitutionality of the Supreme Court's Preference for Binding Arbitration: A Fresh Assessment of Jury Trial, Separation of Powers, and Due Process Concerns*, 72 Tul. L. Rev. 1 (1997). Professor David Schwartz argues that the FAA is unconstitutional as it has been applied in Southland and its progeny. He asserts that "the FAA is the only federal statute that is 'substantive' for preemption purposes even though it is really procedural, and procedural for every other purpose." David Schwartz, *The Federal Arbitration Act and the Power of Congress Over State Courts*, 83 Oregon L. Rev. 541, 628 (2004).

Professor Christopher R. Drahozal acknowledges the weakness of Justice Burger's arguments in his *Southland* analysis, but offers alternative rationales in arguing that the court reached the right result in the case. *See* Christopher R. Drahozal, *In Defense of Southland: Reexamining the Legislative History of the Federal Arbitration Act*, 78 Notre Dame L. Rev. 101 (2002).

4.   Despite broad scholarly criticism of *Southland*, the Supreme Court has held steadfastly to its principle of broad preemption of state law when a contract includes an arbitration provision. The Court in 2008 voted 8–1 to extend *Southland* preemption to the administrative context in *Preston v. Ferrer*, 552 U.S. 346, 128 S.Ct. 978, 169 L.Ed.2d 917 (2008).

"When parties agree to arbitrate all questions arising under a contract, the FAA supercedes state laws lodging primary jurisdiction in another forum, whether judicial or administrative. Justice Ginsburg wrote for the court." *Id.* at 987. "The 'mere involvement of an administrative agency in the enforcement of a statute' . . . does not limit private parties' obligation to comply with their arbitration agreements." *Id.* at 986, citing *Gilmer v. Interstate Johnson/Lane Corp.*, 500 U.S. 20, 28–29, 111 S.Ct. 1647, 114 L.Ed.2d 26 (1991).

5.   The Court's decision in *Buckeye Check Cashing, Inc. v. Cardegna*, 546 U.S. 440, 126 S.Ct. 1204, 163 L.Ed.2d 1038 (2006) was also a ringing endorsement of *Southland* preemption. As discussed more fully above at p. 598, the Court's decision the federal separability doctrine preempted Florida usury law was predicated on the fact that the FAA applied in state courts in the first place because of *Southland*.

DOCTOR'S ASSOCIATES, INC. V. CASAROTTO

Supreme Court of the United States, 1996
517 U.S. 681, 116 S.Ct. 1652, 134 L.Ed.2d 902

JUSTICE GINSBURG delivered the opinion of the Court.

This case concerns a standard form franchise agreement for the operation of a Subway sandwich shop in Montana. When a dispute arose between parties to the agreement, franchisee Paul Casarotto sued franchisor Doctor's Associates, Inc. (DAI), and DAI's Montana development agent, Nick Lombardi, in a Montana state court. DAI and Lombardi sought to stop the litigation pending arbitration pursuant to the arbitration clause set out on page nine of the franchise agreement.

The Federal Arbitration Act (FAA or Act) declares written provisions for arbitration "valid, irrevocable, and enforceable, save upon such grounds as exist at law or in equity for the revocation of any contract." 9 U.S.C. § 2. Montana law, however, declares an arbitration clause unenforceable unless "notice that [the] contract is subject to arbitration" is "typed in underlined capital letters on the first page of the contract." Mont.Code Ann. § 27–5–114(4) (1995). The question here presented is whether Montana's law is compatible with the federal Act. We hold that Montana's first-page notice requirement, which governs not "any contract," but specifically and solely contracts "subject to arbitration," conflicts with the FAA and is therefore displaced by the federal measure.

I

Petitioner DAI is the national franchisor of Subway sandwich shops. In April 1988, DAI entered a franchise agreement with respondent Paul Casarotto, which permitted Casarotto to open a Subway shop in Great Falls, Montana. The franchise agreement stated, on page nine and in ordinary type: "Any controversy or claim arising out of or relating to this contract or the breach thereof shall be settled by Arbitration. . . ."

In October 1992, Casarotto sued DAI and its agent, Nick Lombardi, in Montana state court, alleging state-law contract and tort claims relating to the franchise agreement. DAI demanded arbitration of those claims, and successfully moved in the Montana trial court to stay the lawsuit pending arbitration.

The Montana Supreme Court reversed. That court left undisturbed the trial court's findings that the franchise agreement fell within the scope of the FAA and covered the claims Casarotto stated against DAI and Lombardi. The Montana Supreme Court held, however, that Mont.Code Ann. § 27–5–114(4) rendered the agreement's arbitration clause unenforceable. The Montana statute provides:

"Notice that a contract is subject to arbitration . . . shall be typed in underlined capital letters on the first page of the contract; and unless such notice is displayed thereon, the contract may not be subject to arbitration."

Notice of the arbitration clause in the franchise agreement did not appear on the first page of the contract. Nor was anything relating to the clause typed in underlined capital letters. Because the State's statutory notice requirement had not been met, the Montana Supreme Court declared the parties' dispute "not subject to arbitration."

DAI and Lombardi unsuccessfully argued before the Montana Supreme Court that § 27–5–114(4) was preempted by § 2 of the FAA.[1] DAI and Lombardi dominantly relied on our decisions in *Southland Corp. v. Keating,* and *Perry v. Thomas.* In *Southland,* we held that § 2 of the FAA applies in state as well as federal courts, see 465 U.S. at 12, and "withdr[aws] the power of the states to require a judicial forum for the resolution of claims which the contracting parties agreed to resolve by arbitration." We noted in the pathmarking *Southland* decision that the FAA established a "broad principle of enforceability," and that § 2 of the federal Act provided for revocation of arbitration agreements only upon "grounds as exist at law or in equity for the revocation of any contract." In *Perry*, we reiterated: "State law, whether of legislative or judicial origin, is applicable *if* that law arose to govern issues concerning the validity, revocability, and enforceability of contracts generally. A state-law principle that takes its meaning precisely from the fact that a contract to arbitrate is at issue does not comport with [the text of § 2]."

The Montana Supreme Court, however, read our decision in *Volt Information Sciences, Inc. v. Board of Trustees of Leland Stanford Junior Univ.*, 489 U.S. 468, 103 L. Ed. 2d 488, 109 S. Ct. 1248 (1989), as limiting the preemptive force of § 2 and correspondingly qualifying *Southland* and *Perry*. As the Montana Supreme Court comprehended *Volt,* the proper inquiry here should focus not on the bare words of § 2, but on this question: Would the application of Montana's notice requirement, contained in § 27–5–114(4), "undermine the goals and policies of the FAA." Section 27–5–114(4), in the Montana court's judgment, did not undermine the goals and policies of the FAA, for the notice requirement did not preclude arbitration agreements altogether; it simply prescribed "that before arbitration agreements are enforceable, they be entered knowingly."

DAI and Lombardi petitioned for certiorari. Last Term, we granted their petition, vacated the judgment of the Montana Supreme Court, and remanded for further consideration in light of *Allied–Bruce Terminix Cos. v. Dobson*, 513 U.S. 265, 130 L. Ed. 2d 753, 115 S. Ct. 834 (1995). See 515

---

[1] Section 2 provides, in relevant part: "A written provision in . . . a contract evidencing a transaction involving commerce to settle by arbitration a controversy thereafter arising out of such contract or transaction, or the refusal to perform the whole or any part thereof, . . . shall be valid, irrevocable, and enforceable, save upon such grounds as exist at law or in equity for the revocation of any contract."

U.S. 1129 (1995). In *Allied–Bruce,* we restated what our decisions in *Southland* and *Perry* had established:

> "States may regulate contracts, including arbitration clauses, under general contract law principles and they may invalidate an arbitration clause 'upon such grounds as exist at law or in equity for the revocation of *any* contract.' 9 U.S.C. § 2 (emphasis added). What States may not do is decide that a contract is fair enough to enforce all its basic terms (price, service, credit), but not fair enough to enforce its arbitration clause. The Act makes any such state policy unlawful, for that kind of policy would place arbitration clauses on an unequal 'footing,' directly contrary to the Act's language and Congress's intent."

On remand, without inviting or permitting further briefing or oral argument, the Montana Supreme Court adhered to its original ruling. The court stated: "After careful review, we can find nothing in the [*Allied–Bruce*] decision which relates to the issues presented to this Court in this case." Elaborating, the Montana court said it found "no suggestion in *Allied–Bruce*] that the principles from *Volt* on which we relied [to uphold § 27–5–114(4)] have been modified in any way." We again granted certiorari, and now reverse.

II

Section 2 of the FAA provides that written arbitration agreements "shall be valid, irrevocable, and enforceable, save upon such grounds as exist at law or in equity for the revocation of *any* contract." Repeating our observation in *Perry,* the text of § 2 declares that state law may be applied "*if* that law arose to govern issues concerning the validity, revocability, and enforceability of contracts generally." Thus, generally applicable contract defenses, such as fraud, duress, or unconscionability, may be applied to invalidate arbitration agreements without contravening § 2. * * *

Courts may not, however, invalidate arbitration agreements under state laws applicable *only* to arbitration provisions. See *Allied–Bruce*; *Perry.* By enacting § 2, we have several times said, Congress precluded States from singling out arbitration provisions for suspect status, requiring instead that such provisions be placed "upon the same footing as other contracts." Montana's § 27–5–114(4) directly conflicts with § 2 of the FAA because the State's law conditions the enforceability of arbitration agreements on compliance with a special notice requirement not applicable to contracts generally. The FAA thus displaces the Montana statute with respect to arbitration agreements covered by the Act. * * *

The Montana Supreme Court misread our *Volt* decision and therefore reached a conclusion in this case at odds with our rulings. *Volt* involved an arbitration agreement that incorporated state procedural rules, one of which, on the facts of that case, called for arbitration to be stayed pending the resolution of a related judicial proceeding. The state rule examined in *Volt* determined only the efficient order of proceedings; it did not affect the enforceability of the arbitration agreement itself. We held that applying the state rule would not "undermine the goals and policies of the FAA," because the very purpose of the Act was to "ensur[e] that private agreements to arbitrate are enforced according to their terms."

Applying § 27–5–114(4) here, in contrast, would not enforce the arbitration clause in the contract between DAI and Casarotto; instead, Montana's first-page notice requirement would invalidate the clause. The "goals and policies" of the FAA, this Court's precedent indicates, are antithetical to threshold limitations placed specifically and solely on arbitration provisions. Section 2 mandate[s] the enforcement of arbitration agreements, "save upon such grounds as exist at law or in equity for the revocation of any contract." * * * Montana's law places arbitration agreements in a class apart from "any contract," and singularly limits their validity. The State's prescription is thus inconsonant with, and is therefore preempted by, the federal law.

* * *

For the reasons stated, the judgment of the Supreme Court of Montana is reversed, and the case is remanded for further proceedings not inconsistent with this opinion.

It is so ordered.

JUSTICE THOMAS, dissenting. For the reasons given in my dissent last Term in *Allied–Bruce Terminix Cos. v. Dobson*, I remain of the view that § 2 of the Federal Arbitration Act, does not apply to proceedings in state courts. Accordingly, I respectfully dissent.

NOTES AND QUESTIONS

1. The *Casarotto* case is an example of the breadth of the preemption doctrine, and is frequently cited for the proposition that states may not pass laws that are hostile to arbitration. Does the case make you more or less supportive of *Southland* and *Allied–Bruce* (Note 2 p. 597)?

2. The Casarroto case drew numerous amicus briefs including one signed by half of the state attorneys general asking the court to use it to reverse *Southland v. Keating*. If you were a state attorney general, would you have signed on to the brief?

3. Would any of the following state laws or decisions be invalid under the principles laid down in *Southland* and *Allied–Bruce*?

(a) Massachusetts regulations prohibited securities firms from requiring customers to agree to arbitration as a condition precedent to account relationships. *See Securities Industry Ass'n v. Connolly,* 883 F.2d 1114 (1st Cir. 1989).

(b) New York law required arbitration agreements to be express and unequivocal. *See Continental Group, Inc. v. NPS Communications, Inc.,* 873 F.2d 613, 619 n.3 (2d Cir. 1989); and IAN R. MACNEIL, RICHARD E. SPEIDEL & THOMAS J. STIPANOWICH, FEDERAL ARBITRATION LAW § 10.8.3.3, text accompanying n.103 (1994 ed. & Supp. 1999).

(c) A Pennsylvania rule precluded arbitration of bad faith claims against insurance companies. *Brayman Construction Co. v. Home Insurance Co.,* 319 F.3d 622, 627 (3rd Cir. 2003).

2. *The Scope of Preemption*

AT&T MOBILITY LLC v. CONCEPCION

Supreme Court of the United States, 2012
___ U.S. ___, 131 S.Ct. 1740, 179 L.Ed.2d 742

JUSTICE SCALIA delivered the opinion of the Court.

Section 2 of the Federal Arbitration Act (FAA) makes agreements to arbitrate "valid, irrevocable, and enforceable, save upon such grounds as exist at law or in equity for the revocation of any contract." We consider whether the FAA prohibits States from conditioning the enforceability of certain arbitration agreements on the availability of classwide arbitration procedures.

I.

In February 2002, Vincent and Liza Concepcion entered into an agreement for the sale and servicing of cellular telephones with AT&T Mobility LCC (AT&T). The contract provided for arbitration of all disputes between the parties, but required that claims be brought in the parties' "individual capacity, and not as a plaintiff or class member in any purported class or representative proceeding." * * *

The Concepcions purchased AT&T service, which was advertised as including the provision of free phones; they were not charged for the phones, but they were charged $30.22 in sales tax based on the phones' retail value. In March 2006, the Concepcions filed a complaint against AT&T in the United States District Court for the Southern District of California. The complaint was later consolidated with a putative class action alleging, among other things, that AT&T had engaged in false advertising and fraud by charging sales tax on phones it advertised as free.

In March 2008, AT&T moved to compel arbitration under the terms of its contract with the Concepcions. The Concepcions opposed the motion, contending that the arbitration agreement was unconscionable and unlawfully exculpatory under California law because it disallowed classwide procedures. The District Court denied AT&T's motion. It described AT&T's arbitration agreement favorably.... Nevertheless, relying on the California Supreme Court's decision in *Discover Bank v. Superior Court* (Ca. 2005), the court found that the arbitration provision was unconscionable because AT&T had not shown that bilateral arbitration adequately substituted for the deterrent effects of class actions.

The Ninth Circuit affirmed, also finding the provision unconscionable under California law as announced in *Discover Bank*. It also held that the *Discover Bank* rule was not preempted by the FAA because that rule was simply "a refinement of the unconscionability analysis applicable to contracts generally in California." * * *

II

The FAA was enacted in 1925 in response to widespread judicial hostility to arbitration agreements. Section 2, the "primary substantive provision of the Act," provides, in relevant part, as follows:

> A written provision in any maritime transaction or a contract evidencing a transaction involving commerce to settle by arbitration a controversy thereafter arising out of such contract or transaction ... shall be valid, irrevocable, and enforceable, save upon such grounds as exist at law or in equity for the revocation of any contract.

We have described this provision as reflecting both a "liberal federal policy favoring arbitration," and the "fundamental principle that arbitration is a matter of contract." In line with these principles, courts must place arbitration agreements on an equal footing with other contracts, and enforce them according to their terms.

The final phrase of § 2, however, permits arbitration agreements to be declared unenforceable "upon such grounds as exist at law or in equity for the revocation of any contract." This saving clause permits agreements to arbitrate to be invalidated by "generally applicable contract defenses, such as fraud, duress, or unconscionability," but not by defenses that apply only to arbitration or that derive their meaning from the fact that an agreement to arbitrate is at issue. The question in this case is whether § 2 preempts California's rule classifying most collective-arbitration waivers in consumer contracts as unconscionable. We refer to this rule as the *Discover Bank* rule.

Under California law, courts may refuse to enforce any contract found "to have been unconscionable at the time it was made," or may "limit the application of any unconscionable clause." A finding of unconscionability requires "a procedural and a substantive element, the former focusing on 'oppression' or 'surprise' due to unequal bargaining power, the latter on 'overly harsh' or 'one-sided' results."

In *Discover* Bank, the California Supreme Court applied this framework to class-action waivers in arbitration agreements and held as follows:

> "[W]hen the waiver is found in a consumer contract of adhesion in a setting in which disputes between the contracting parties predictably involve small amounts of damages, and when it is alleged that the party with the superior bargaining power has carried out a scheme to deliberately cheat large numbers of consumers out of individually small sums of money, then . . . the waiver becomes in practice the exemption of the party 'from responsibility for [its] own fraud, or willful injury to the person or property of another.' Under these circumstances, such waivers are unconscionable under California law and should not be enforced.

California courts have frequently applied this rule to find arbitration agreements unconscionable.

III.

A.

The Concepcions argue that the *DiscoverBank* rule, given its origins in California's unconscionability doctrine and California's policy against exculpation, is a ground that "exist[s] at law or in equity for the revocation of any contract" under FAA § 2. Moreover, they argue that even if we construe the *Discover Bank* rule as a prohibition on collective-action waivers rather than simply an application of unconscionability, the rule would still be applicable to all dispute-resolution contracts, since California prohibits waivers of class litigation as well.

When state law prohibits outright the arbitration of a particular type of claim, the analysis is straightforward: The conflicting rule is displaced by the FAA. But the inquiry becomes more complex when a doctrine normally thought to be generally applicable, such as duress or, as relevant here, unconscionability, is alleged to have been applied in a fashion that disfavors arbitration. * * *

An obvious illustration of this point would be a case finding unconscionable or unenforceable as against public policy consumer arbitration agreements that fail to provide for judicially monitored discovery. The rationalizations for such a holding are neither difficult to imagine nor different in kind from those articulated in *Discover Bank*. A court might reason that no consumer would knowingly waive his right to full discovery, as this would enable companies to hide their wrongdoing. Or the court might simply say that such agreements are exculpatory-restricting discovery would be of greater benefit to the company than the consumer, since the former is more likely to be sued than to sue. And, the reasoning would continue, because such a rule applies the general principle of unconscionability or public-policy disapproval of exculpatory agreements, it is applicable to "any" contract and thus preserved by § 2 of the FAA. In practice, of course, the rule would have a disproportionate impact on arbitration agreements; but it would presumably apply to contracts purporting to restrict discovery in litigation as well.

* * * The Concepcions suggest that all this is just a parade of horribles, and no genuine worry. Rules aimed at destroying arbitration or demanding procedures incompatible with arbitration, they concede, would be preempted by the FAA because they cannot sensibly be reconciled with Section 2. The grounds available under § 2's saving clause, they admit, should not be construed to include a State's mere preference for procedures that are incompatible with arbitration and 'would wholly eviscerate arbitration agreements.

We largely agree. Although § 2's saving clause preserves generally applicable contract defenses, nothing in it suggests an intent to preserve state-law rules that stand as an obstacle to the accomplishment of the FAA's objectives. As we have said, a federal statute's saving clause "cannot in reason be construed as [allowing] a common law right, the continued existence of which would be absolutely inconsistent with the provisions of the act. In other words, the act cannot be held to destroy itself."

We differ with the Concepcions only in the application of this analysis to the matter before us. We do not agree that rules requiring judicially monitored discovery or adherence to the Federal Rules of Evidence are "a far cry from this case." The overarching purpose of the FAA, evident in the text of §§ 2, 3, and 4, is to ensure the enforcement of arbitration agreements according to their terms so as to facilitate streamlined proceedings. Requiring the availability of classwide arbitration interferes with fundamental attributes of arbitration and thus creates a scheme inconsistent with the FAA.

B

The principal purpose of the FAA is to ensure that private arbitration agreements are enforced according to their terms. This purpose is readily apparent from the FAA's text. Section 2 makes arbitration agreements "valid, irrevocable, and enforceable" as written (subject, of course, to the saving clause); § 3 requires courts to stay litigation of arbitral claims pending arbitration of those claims "in accordance with the terms of the agreement"; and § 4 requires courts to compel arbitration "in accordance with the terms of the agreement" upon the motion of either party to the agreement (assuming that the "making of the arbitration agreement or the failure . . . to perform the same" is not at issue). In light of these provisions, we have held that parties may agree to limit the issues subject to arbitration, to arbitrate according to specific rules, and to limit with whom a party will arbitrate its disputes.

The point of affording parties discretion in designing arbitration processes is to allow for efficient, streamlined procedures tailored to the type of dispute. It can be specified, for example, that the decisionmaker be a specialist in the relevant field, or that proceedings be kept confidential to protect trade secrets. And the informality of arbitral proceedings is itself desirable, reducing the cost and increasing the speed of dispute resolution. * * *

The dissent quotes *Dean Witter Reynolds Inc. v. Byrd* (1985) as " 'reject[ing] the suggestion that the overriding goal of the Arbitration Act was to promote the expeditious resolution of claims.' " That is greatly misleading. After saying (accurately enough) that "the overriding goal of the Arbitration Act was [not] to promote the expeditious resolution of claims," but to "ensure judicial enforcement of privately made agreements to arbitrate," *Dean Witter* went on to explain: "This is not to say that Congress was blind to the potential benefit of the legislation for expedited resolution of disputes. Far from it. . . ." * * *

In the present case, of course, those "two goals" do not conflict—and it is the dissent's view that would frustrate both of them.

Contrary to the dissent's view, our cases place it beyond dispute that the FAA was designed to promote arbitration. They have repeatedly described the Act as "embodying a national policy favoring arbitration," and "a liberal federal policy favoring arbitration agreements, notwithstanding any state substantive or procedural policies to the contrary," Thus, in *Preston v. Ferrer* (2008), holding preempted a state-law rule requiring exhaustion of administrative remedies before arbitration, we said: "A prime objective of an agreement to arbitrate is to achieve streamlined proceedings and expeditious results," which objective would be "frustrated" by requiring a dispute to be heard by an agency first. That rule, we said, would "at the least, hinder speedy resolution of the controversy."

California's *Discover Bank* rule similarly interferes with arbitration. Although the rule does not require classwide arbitration, it allows any party to a consumer contract to demand it ex post. The rule is limited to adhesion contracts, but the times in which consumer contracts were anything other than adhesive are long past.[6] The rule also requires that damages be predictably small, and that the consumer allege a scheme to cheat consumers. The former requirement, however, is toothless and malleable (the Ninth Circuit has held that damages of $4,000 are sufficiently small . . .), and the latter has no limiting effect, as all that is required is an allegation. * * *

---

[6] Of course States remain free to take steps addressing the concerns that attend contracts of adhesion—for example, requiring class-action-waiver provisions in adhesive arbitration agreements to be highlighted. Such steps cannot, however, conflict with the FAA or frustrate its purpose to ensure that private arbitration agreements are enforced according to their terms.

Although we have had little occasion to examine classwide arbitration, our decision in *Stolt–Nielsen* is instructive. In that case we held that an arbitration panel exceeded its power under § 10(a)(4) of the FAA by imposing class procedures based on policy judgments rather than the arbitration agreement itself or some background principle of contract law that would affect its interpretation. We then held that the agreement at issue, which was silent on the question of class procedures, could not be interpreted to allow them because the "changes brought about by the shift from bilateral arbitration to class-action arbitration" are "fundamental." This is obvious as a structural matter: Classwide arbitration includes absent parties, necessitating additional and different procedures and involving higher stakes. Confidentiality becomes more difficult. And while it is theoretically possible to select an arbitrator with some expertise relevant to the class-certification question, arbitrators are not generally knowledgeable in the often-dominant procedural aspects of certification, such as the protection of absent parties. The conclusion follows that class arbitration, to the extent it is manufactured by *Discover Bank* rather than consensual, is inconsistent with the FAA.

First, the switch from bilateral to class arbitration sacrifices the principal advantage of arbitration—its informality—and makes the process slower, more costly, and more likely to generate procedural morass than final judgment. In bilateral arbitration, parties forgo the procedural rigor and appellate review of the courts in order to realize the benefits of private dispute resolution: lower costs, greater efficiency and speed, and the ability to choose expert adjudicators to resolve specialized disputes. But before an arbitrator may decide the merits of a claim in classwide procedures, he must first decide, for example, whether the class itself may be certified, whether the named parties are sufficiently representative and typical, and how discovery for the class should be conducted. * * *

Second, class arbitration requires procedural formality. The AAA's rules governing class arbitrations mimic the Federal Rules of Civil Procedure for class litigation. And while parties can alter those procedures by contract, an alternative is not obvious. If procedures are too informal, absent class members would not be bound by the arbitration. For a class-action money judgment to bind absentees in litigation, class representatives must at all times adequately represent absent class members, and absent members must be afforded notice, an opportunity to be heard, and a right to opt out of the class. At least this amount of process would presumably be required for absent parties to be bound by the results of arbitration.

We find it unlikely that in passing the FAA Congress meant to leave the disposition of these procedural requirements to an arbitrator. Indeed, class arbitration was not even envisioned by Congress when it passed the

FAA in 1925; as the California Supreme Court admitted in *Discover Bank*, class arbitration is a "relatively recent development." And it is at the very least odd to think that an arbitrator would be entrusted with ensuring that third parties' due process rights are satisfied.

Third, class arbitration greatly increases risks to defendants. Informal procedures do of course have a cost: The absence of multilayered review makes it more likely that errors will go uncorrected. Defendants are willing to accept the costs of these errors in arbitration, since their impact is limited to the size of individual disputes, and presumably outweighed by savings from avoiding the courts. But when damages allegedly owed to tens of thousands of potential claimants are aggregated and decided at once, the risk of an error will often become unacceptable. Faced with even a small chance of a devastating loss, defendants will be pressured into settling questionable claims. Other courts have noted the risk of *in terrorem* settlements that class actions entail, and class arbitration would be no different.

Arbitration is poorly suited to the higher stakes of class litigation. In litigation, a defendant may appeal a certification decision on an interlocutory basis and, if unsuccessful, may appeal from a final judgment as well. Questions of law are reviewed de novo and questions of fact for clear error. In contrast, 9 U.S.C. § 10 allows a court to vacate an arbitral award only where the award "was procured by corruption, fraud, or undue means"; "there was evident partiality or corruption in the arbitrators"; "the arbitrators were guilty of misconduct in refusing to postpone the hearing . . . or in refusing to hear evidence pertinent and material to the controversy[,] or of any other misbehavior by which the rights of any party have been prejudiced"; or if the "arbitrators exceeded their powers, or so imperfectly executed them that a mutual, final, and definite award . . . was not made." The AAA rules do authorize judicial review of certification decisions, but this review is unlikely to have much effect given these limitations; review under § 10 focuses on misconduct rather than mistake. And parties may not contractually expand the grounds or nature of judicial review. We find it hard to believe that defendants would bet the company with no effective means of review, and even harder to believe that Congress would have intended to allow state courts to force such a decision. * * *

The dissent claims that class proceedings are necessary to prosecute small-dollar claims that might otherwise slip through the legal system. But States cannot require a procedure that is inconsistent with the FAA, even if it is desirable for unrelated reasons. * * *

Because it "stands as an obstacle to the accomplishment and execution of the full purposes and objectives of Congress," California's *Discover Bank* rule is preempted by the FAA. The judgment of the Ninth

Circuit is reversed, and the case is remanded for further proceedings consistent with this opinion.

JUSTICE THOMAS, concurring.

* * * I write separately to explain how I would find [limits on contract defenses under Section 2] in the FAA's text. As I would read it, the FAA requires that an agreement to arbitrate be enforced unless a party successfully challenges the formation of the arbitration agreement, such as by proving fraud or duress. Under this reading, I would reverse the Court of Appeals because a district court cannot follow both the FAA and the *Discover Bank* rule, which does not relate to defects in the making of an agreement. * * *

Moreover, I think that the Court's [purposes-and-objectives] test will often lead to the same outcome as my textual interpretation and that, when possible, it is important in interpreting statutes to give lower courts guidance from a majority of the Court. Therefore, although I adhere to my views on purposes-and-objectives pre-emption, see Wyeth v. Levine (2009) (opinion concurring in judgment), I reluctantly join the Court's opinion.

[In *Wyeth*, Justice Thomas said "My review of this Court's broad implied pre-emption precedents, particularly its 'purposes and objectives' pre-emption jurisprudence, has increased my concerns that implied pre-emption doctrines have not always been constitutionally applied. Under the vague and potentially boundless doctrine of 'purposes and objectives' pre-emption, for example, the Court has pre-empted state law based on its interpretation of broad federal policy objectives, legislative history, or generalized notions of congressional purposes that are not contained within the text of federal law."]

JUSTICE BREYER, with whom JUSTICE GINSBURG, JUSTICE SOTOMAYOR, and JUSTICE KAGAN join, dissenting

The Federal Arbitration Act says that an arbitration agreement "shall be valid, irrevocable, and enforceable, save upon such grounds as exist at law or in equity for the revocation of any contract." California law sets forth certain circumstances in which "class action waivers" in any contract are unenforceable. In my view, this rule of state law is consistent with the federal Act's language and primary objective. It does not "stan[d] as an obstacle" to the Act's "accomplishment and execution." And the Court is wrong to hold that the federal Act pre-empts the rule of state law.

I

The California law in question consists of an authoritative state-court interpretation of two provisions of the California Civil Code. The first provision makes unlawful all contracts "which have for their object, directly or in-directly, to exempt anyone from responsibility for his own

. . . violation of law." The second provision authorizes courts to "limit the application of any unconscionable clause" in a contract so "as to avoid any unconscionable result." * * *

II

A

The *Discover Bank* rule is consistent with the federal Act's language. It "applies equally to class action litigation waivers in contracts without arbitration agreements as it does to class arbitration waivers in contracts with such agreements." Linguistically speaking, it falls directly within the scope of the Act's exception permitting courts to refuse to enforce arbitration agreements on grounds that exist "for the revocation of any contract." The majority agrees.

B

The *Discover Bank* rule is also consistent with the basic purpose behind the Act. We have described that purpose as one of "ensuring judicial enforcement" of arbitration agreements. As is well known, prior to the federal Act, many courts expressed hostility to arbitration, for example by refusing to order specific performance of agreements to arbitrate. The Act sought to eliminate that hostility by placing agreements to arbitrate "upon the same footing as other contracts." * * *

III

The majority's contrary view (that *Discover Bank* stands as an "obstacle" to the accomplishment of the federal law's objective) rests primarily upon its claims that the *Discover Bank* rule increases the complexity of arbitration procedures, thereby discouraging parties from entering into arbitration agreements, and to that extent discriminating in practice against arbitration. These claims are not well founded.

* * * Unlike the majority's examples, class arbitration is consistent with the use of arbitration. It is a form of arbitration that is well known in California and followed elsewhere. Indeed, the AAA has told us that it has found class arbitration to be "a fair, balanced, and efficient means of resolving class disputes." And unlike the majority's examples, the *Discover Bank* rule imposes equivalent limitations on litigation; hence it cannot fairly be characterized as a targeted attack on arbitration.

Where does the majority get its contrary idea—that individual, rather than class, arbitration is a "fundamental attribut[e]" of arbitration? The majority does not explain. * * *

For another thing, the majority's argument that the *Discover Bank* rule will discourage arbitration rests critically upon the wrong comparison. The majority compares the complexity of class arbitration with that of bilateral arbitration. And it finds the former more complex. But, if incentives are at issue, the relevant comparison is not "arbitration with arbitration" but a comparison between class arbitration and judicial class actions. After all, in respect to the relevant set of contracts, the *Discover Bank* rule similarly and equally sets aside clauses that forbid class procedures—whether arbitration procedures or ordinary judicial procedures are at issue.

Why would a typical defendant (say, a business) prefer a judicial class action to class arbitration? AAA statistics "suggest that class arbitration proceedings take more time than the average commercial arbitration, but may take less time than the average class action in court." Data from California courts confirm that class arbitrations can take considerably less time than in-court proceedings in which class certification is sought. And a single class proceeding is surely more efficient than thousands of separate proceedings for identical claims. Thus, if speedy resolution of disputes were all that mattered, then the *Discover Bank* rule would reinforce, not obstruct, that objective of the Act. * * *

IV.

By using the words "save upon such grounds as exist at law or in equity for the revocation of any contract," Congress retained for the States an important role incident to agreements to arbitrate. Through those words Congress reiterated a basic federal idea that has long informed the nature of this Nation's laws. We have often expressed this idea in opinions that set forth presumptions. But federalism is as much a question of deeds as words. It often takes the form of a concrete decision by this Court that respects the legitimacy of a State's action in an individual case. Here, recognition of that federalist ideal, embodied in specific language in this particular statute, should lead us to uphold California's law, not to strike it down. We do not honor federalist principles in their breach.

NOTES AND QUESTIONS

1.   The decision is clearly a landmark for the Court. But how would you describe the holding?

2.   What influence do you think the fact that the case concerned class actions had on the Court's decision? Put another way, do you think the case might have come out differently if it had not been a class action?

3.   Note that in its *Discover Bank* rule, the California Supreme Court was interpreting the state's unconscionability law—a law of general applicability—in the specific context of a practical waiver of a right to a class action effected by an arbitration clause. What does the U.S. Supreme Court's decision to find it preempted by the FAA suggest about its view of the reach of Section 2's saving's clause, which on its face requires an arbitration agreement to be subject to state law challenges to contract formation and enforcement?

4.   Professor Aronovsky suggests *Concepcion's* application of the court's expansive interpretation of the FAA's "pro-arbitration policy" may be leading toward a "preemptive federal arbitration procedural paradigm," which which little role is left for state law. He suggests Congress should amend the FAA to exclude from its scope pre-dispute arbitration clauses in consumer and employment adhesion contracts. "Rather than making these arbitration agreements unenforceable as a matter of federal law, this proposal would leave pre-dispute arbitration agreements between parties with unequal bargaining power to more accountable state regulation untethered to the Court's interpretation of a federal 'pro-arbitration policy.' The FAA would continue to govern ad hoc arbitration agreements and pre-dispute agreements between contracting parties capable of protecting their procedural interests at the bargaining table." Ronald G. Aronovsky, *The Supreme Court and the Future of Arbitration: Toward a Preemptive Federal Arbitration Procedural Paradigm*, 42 SW L. Rev. 131, 134 (2012).

3.   *Party Choice of the FAA or State Law*

VOLT INFORMATION SCIENCES, INC. V. BOARD OF TRUSTEES OF LELAND STANFORD JUNIOR UNIVERSITY

Supreme Court of the United States, 1989
489 U.S. 468, 109 S.Ct. 1248, 103 L.Ed. 488

CHIEF JUSTICE REHNQUIST delivered the opinion of the Court.

Unlike its federal counterpart, the California Arbitration Act contains a provision allowing a court to stay arbitration pending resolution of related litigation. We hold that application of the California statute is not pre-empted by the Federal Arbitration Act (FAA or Act), in a case where the parties have agreed that their arbitration agreement will be governed by the law of California.

Appellant Volt Information Sciences, Inc. (Volt), and appellee Board of Trustees of Leland Stanford Junior University (Stanford) entered into a construction contract under which Volt was to install a system of electrical conduits on the Stanford campus. The contract contained an agreement to arbitrate all disputes between the parties "arising out of or relating to this contract or the breach thereof."[1] The contract also contained a choice-of-law clause providing that "[t]he Contract shall be governed[2] by the law of the place where the Project is located." During the

---

[1] The arbitration clause read in full as follows:

"All claims, disputes and other matters in question between the parties to this contract, arising out of or relating to this contract or the breach thereof, shall be decided by arbitration in accordance with the Construction Industry Arbitration Rules of the American Arbitration Association then prevailing unless the parties mutually agreed [sic] otherwise.... This agreement to arbitrate ... shall be specifically enforceable under the prevailing arbitration law."

[2] Volt's motion to compel was apparently brought pursuant to s 4 of the FAA, 9 U.S.C. s 4, and the parallel provision of the California Arbitration Act, Cal.Civ.Proc.Code Ann. s 1281.2 (West 1982); the motion cited both Acts as authority, but did not specify the particular sections

course of the project, a dispute developed regarding compensation for extra work, and Volt made a formal demand for arbitration. Stanford responded by filing an action against Volt in California Superior Court, alleging fraud and breach of contract; in the same action, Stanford also sought indemnity from two other companies involved in the construction project, with whom it did not have arbitration agreements. Volt petitioned the Superior Court to compel arbitration of the dispute. Stanford in turn moved to stay arbitration pursuant to Cal.Civ.Proc.Code Ann. § 1281.2(c) (West 1982), which permits a court to stay arbitration pending resolution of related litigation between a party to the arbitration agreement and third parties not bound by it, where "there is a possibility of conflicting rulings on a common issue of law or fact." The Superior Court denied Volt's motion to compel arbitration and stayed the arbitration proceedings pending the outcome of the litigation on the authority of § 1281.2(c).

The California Court of Appeal affirmed. The court acknowledged that the parties' contract involved interstate commerce, that the FAA governs contracts in interstate commerce, and that the FAA contains no provision permitting a court to stay arbitration pending resolution of related litigation involving third parties not bound by the arbitration agreement. However, the court held that by specifying that their contract would be governed by "the law of the place where the project is located," the parties had incorporated the California rules of arbitration, including § 1281.2(c), into their arbitration agreement. Finally, the court rejected Volt's contention that, even if the parties had agreed to arbitrate under the California rules, application of § 1281.2(c) here was nonetheless pre-empted by the FAA because the contract involved interstate commerce.

The court reasoned that the purpose of the FAA was "not [to] mandate the arbitration of all claims, but merely the enforcement . . . of privately negotiated arbitration agreements." While the FAA therefore pre-empts application of state laws which render arbitration agreements unenforceable, "[i]t does not follow, however, that the federal law has preclusive effect in a case where the parties have chosen in their [arbitration] agreement to abide by state rules." To the contrary, because "[t]he thrust of the federal law is that arbitration is strictly a matter of contract," the parties to an arbitration agreement should be "at liberty to choose the terms under which they will arbitrate." Where, as here, the parties have chosen in their agreement to abide by the state rules of arbitration, application of the FAA to prevent enforcement of those rules would actually be "inimical to the policies underlying state and federal arbitration law," because it would "force the parties to arbitrate in a manner contrary to their agreement." The California Supreme Court

upon which reliance was placed. Volt also asked the court to stay the Superior Court litigation until the arbitration was completed, presumably pursuant to s 3 of the FAA, 9 U.S.C. s 3, and the parallel provision of California Arbitration Act, Cal.Civ.Proc.Code Ann. s 1281.2(c)(3) (West 1982).

denied Volt's petition for discretionary review. We postponed consideration of our jurisdiction to the hearing on the merits. We now hold that we have appellate jurisdiction and affirm.

Appellant devotes the bulk of its argument to convincing us that the Court of Appeal erred in interpreting the choice-of-law clause to mean that the parties had incorporated the California rules of arbitration into their arbitration agreement. Appellant acknowledges, as it must, that the interpretation of private contracts is ordinarily a question of state law, which this Court does not sit to review. But appellant nonetheless maintains that we should set aside the Court of Appeal's interpretation of this particular contractual provision for two principal reasons. Appellant first suggests that the Court of Appeal's construction of the choice-of-law clause was in effect a finding that appellant had "waived" its "federally guaranteed right to compel arbitration of the parties' dispute," a waiver whose validity must be judged by reference to federal rather than state law. This argument fundamentally misconceives the nature of the rights created by the FAA. The Act was designed to overrule the judiciary's longstanding refusal to enforce agreements to arbitrate, and place such agreements upon the same footing as other contracts. Section 2 of the Act therefore declares that a written agreement to arbitrate in any contract involving interstate commerce or a maritime transaction "shall be valid, irrevocable, and enforceable, save upon such grounds as exist at law or in equity for the revocation of any contract," and § 4 allows a party to such an arbitration agreement to "petition any United States district court . . . for an order directing that such arbitration proceed in the manner provided for in such agreement."

But § 4 of the FAA does not confer a right to compel arbitration of any dispute at any time; it confers only the right to obtain an order directing that "arbitration proceed in the manner *provided for in [the parties'] agreement*." 9 U.S.C. § 4 (emphasis added). Here the Court of Appeal found that, by incorporating the California rules of arbitration into their agreement, the parties had agreed that arbitration would not proceed in situations, which fell within the scope of Calif.Code Civ.Proc.Ann. § 1281.2(c). This was not a finding that appellant had "waived" an FAA-guaranteed right to compel arbitration of this dispute, but a finding that it had no such right in the first place, because the parties' agreement did not require arbitration to proceed in this situation. Accordingly, appellant's contention that the contract interpretation issue presented here involves the "waiver" of a federal right is without merit.

Second, appellant argues that we should set aside the Court of Appeal's construction of the choice-of-law clause because it violates the settled federal rule that questions of arbitrability in contracts subject to the FAA must be resolved with a healthy regard for the federal policy favoring arbitration. [citations omitted] These cases of course establish that, in applying general state-law principles of contract interpretation to the interpretation of an arbitration agreement within the scope of the Act, due regard must be given to the federal policy favoring arbitration, and ambiguities as to the scope of the arbitration clause itself resolved in favor of arbitration.

But we do not think the Court of Appeal offended the Moses H. Cone principle by interpreting the choice-of-law provision to mean that the parties intended the California rules of arbitration, including the § 1281.2(c) stay provision, to apply to their arbitration agreement. There is no federal policy favoring arbitration under a certain set of procedural rules; the federal policy is simply to ensure the enforceability, according to their terms, of private agreements to arbitrate. Interpreting a choice-of-law clause to make applicable state rules governing the conduct of arbitration-rules which are manifestly designed to encourage resort to the arbitral process-simply does not offend the rule of liberal construction set forth in Moses H. Cone, nor does it offend any other policy embodied in the FAA

The question remains whether, assuming the choice-of-law clause meant what the Court of Appeal found it to mean, application of Cal.Civ.Proc.Code Ann. § 1281.2(c) is nonetheless pre-empted by the FAA to the extent it is used to stay arbitration under this contract involving interstate commerce. It is undisputed that this contract falls within the coverage of the FAA, since it involves interstate commerce, and that the FAA contains no provision authorizing a stay of arbitration in this situation. Appellee contends, however, that §§ 3 and 4 of the FAA, which are the specific sections claimed to conflict with the California statute at issue here, are not applicable in this state-court proceeding and thus cannot pre-empt application of the California statute. While the argument is not without some merit, we need not resolve it to decide this case, for we conclude that even if §§ 3 and 4 of the FAA are fully applicable in state-court proceedings, they do not prevent application of Cal.Civ.Proc.Code Ann. § 1281.2(c) to stay arbitration where, as here, the parties have agreed to arbitrate in accordance with California law.

The FAA contains no express pre-emptive provision, nor does it reflect a congressional intent to occupy the entire field of arbitration. But even when Congress has not completely displaced state regulation in an area, state law may nonetheless be pre-empted to the extent that it actually conflicts with federal law—that is, to the extent that it "stands as an obstacle to the accomplishment and execution of the full purposes and objectives of Congress." The question before us, therefore, is whether application of Cal.Civ.Proc.Code Ann. § 1281.2(c) to stay arbitration under this contract in interstate commerce, in accordance with the terms of the arbitration agreement itself, would undermine the goals and policies of the FAA. We conclude that it would not.

The FAA was designed to overrule the judiciary's long-standing refusal to enforce agreements to arbitrate, and to place such agreements upon the same footing as other contracts. While Congress was no doubt aware that the Act would encourage the expeditious resolution of disputes, its passage was motivated, first and foremost, by a congressional desire to enforce agreements into which parties had entered. Accordingly, we have recognized that the FAA does not require parties to arbitrate when they have not agreed to do so, nor does it prevent parties who do agree to arbitrate from excluding certain claims from the scope of their arbitration agreement. It simply requires courts to enforce privately negotiated agreements to arbitrate, like other contracts, in accordance with their terms.

In recognition of Congress' principal purpose of ensuring that private arbitration agreements are enforced according to their terms, we have held that the FAA pre-empts state laws which require a judicial forum for the resolution of claims which the contracting parties agreed to resolve by arbitration. But it does not follow that the FAA prevents the enforcement of agreements to arbitrate under different rules than those set forth in the Act itself. Indeed, such a result would be quite inimical to the FAA's primary purpose of ensuring that private agreements to arbitrate are enforced according to their terms. Arbitration under the Act is a matter of consent, not coercion, and parties are generally free to structure their arbitration agreements as they see fit. Just as they may limit by contract the issues, which they will arbitrate, so too may they specify by contract the rules under which that arbitration will be conducted. Where, as here, the parties have agreed to abide by state rules of arbitration, enforcing those rules according to the terms of the agreement is fully consistent with the goals of the FAA, even if the result is that arbitration is stayed where the Act would otherwise permit it to go forward.

By permitting the courts to rigorously enforce such agreements according to their terms, we give effect to the contractual rights and expectations of the parties, without doing violence to the policies behind by the FAA.

The judgment of the Court of Appeals is affirmed.

[The vote was 6–2, with JUSTICE O'CONNOR recusing herself for unspecified reasons. The dissent by JUSTICE BRENNAN, joined by JUSTICE MARSHALL, is omitted.]

NOTES AND QUESTIONS

1.   The Court's opinion is a strong endorsement of party autonomy in arbitration in that it effectively allows the parties to opt out of the Federal Arbitration Action, in part or in whole. As the *Volt* court emphasizes, this is perfectly consistent with arbitration's contract law roots.

However, when viewed in light of the Court's larger preemption jurisprudence, it raises a question that goes to the heart of the Court's broad historic distinction between public and private law: Would the Supreme Court uphold a state statute permitting parties to opt out of the FAA? What arguments could be made either way? If you conclude that the Court would likely strike down such a provision as a matter of doctrine, what principle would justify a rule permitting private parties to do something on their own—opt out of the FAA—that a state government cannot authorize them to do? Or does this suggest that the reach of *Volt* is more limited than previously believed?

2. *Mastrobuono v. Shearson Lehman Hutton, Inc.*, 512 U.S. 52, 115 S.Ct. 1212 (1995) is another example of the Court's commitment to enforcing party intent with respect to arbitration, even in the face of apparently contrary law. The case involved an investor's complaint against his stock brokerage company in New York for allegedly mishandling his account. The arbitrator sided with the investor and award punitive damages. The lower courts threw out the punitive damage award on appeal because New York state law does not permit arbitrators to award punitive damages; only courts can award punitive damages. Moreover, the contract's choice-of-law provision specifically provided that the contract would be construed according to the laws of the state of New York.

Writing for the court, Justice John Paul Stevens said the lower courts were wrong for two reasons. First, traditional canons of contract interpretation require standard form contracts to be read against the drafter. Second, in reasoning that resonated in the principal of separability, Stevens said the arbitration clause and the forum-selection clauses had to be read separately, such that the arbitration clause covered the arbitration while the forum-selection clause covered the rest of the contact. Since the arbitration clause did not specifically preclude punitive damages, the arbitrator was free to award them. "[T]he text of the arbitration clause itself surely does not support—indeed, it contradicts—the conclusion that the parties agreed to foreclose claims for punitive damages," he wrote.

2. SECTION 2: THE HEART OF THE FAA

Section 2, 9 U.S.C. § 2 (2000), is the primary substantive provision of the Federal Arbitration Act. In relevant part, it provides:

> A written provision in . . . a contract evidencing a transaction involving commerce to settle by arbitration a controversy thereafter arising out of such contract . . . shall be valid, irrevocable, and enforceable, save upon such grounds as exist at law or in equity for the revocation of any contract.

On the face of it, Section 2 seems relatively innocuous. Indeed, it appears merely to state a truism: that a contract to arbitrate a commercial dispute is an enforceable contract. As noted early, the statute was only necessary because courts historically had refused to enforce agreements to arbitrate as a policy matter under the so-called "ouster doctrine," and when it was enacted in 1925, the FAA provided a statutory basis for specific enforcement of agreements to arbitrate.

When we fast-forward a half-century to the 1970s, however, we see that the commercial environment in which the statute operates has changed dramatically. The personally lawyered contracts of yesteryear have given way to standard form contracts. Society has become more litigious as legal rights, such as the right not to be discriminated against in employment, have expanded. Lawyers advertise on television, and stories of large jury awards are common in news and entertainment. In such a threatening environment, traditional defendants called for relief under various banners, including "tort reform," "punitive damages reform," and "civil justice reform."

It is against this backdrop that arbitration under the FAA went from a small role to center stage in the world of dispute resolution. Lawyers and judges in the 1970s had begun to look for alternative methods of addressing the expansion of rights. In the 1980s, they turned their focus to arbitration as a possibility, in part because of its familiarity as an adjudicatory process, but also in part because of its statutory authorization and its history in the commercial field. Beginning with the securities industry, traditional defendants began to experiment with standard form contract clauses that required disputes to be decided by arbitration rather than by courts—provisions that have come to be known as "mandatory" or "unilaterally imposed" arbitration.

As we will see, the rise of mandatory arbitration has led to an extraordinary expansion of arbitration. But it has been, and remains, hugely controversial, as witnessed by the more than 30 U.S. Supreme Court decisions since 1990. The central question has been whether, and if so, under what circumstances, such provisions are enforceable, since the effect is to foreclose the ability of the parties to have their dispute heard by a court of law. While the question may be raised for all legal claims, some judges and scholars would contend that it is particularly significant for statutory claims because these are legislatively conferred rights, such as the right to be free from job discrimination or to pursue remedies against a particular party. Does this make a difference? What policy interests are advanced by permitting the enforcement of mandatory arbitration provisions, and what are diminished by such enforcement? These materials also recall issues we have already addressed, such as what is the meaning of consent to arbitration? Who should decide whether these clauses are enforceable? The courts? The legislature? What law should apply? State? Federal? These questions and others permeate these provocative materials.

In this subsection, we look at the key cases construing Section 2. The first set of cases construe the language of the section that makes arbitration agreement enforceable. The second set of cases interpret the savings clause of the section, which assures the contractual validity of the arbitration agreement but making it subject to traditional contract defenses to enforcement.

a. Arbitration Agreements 'Shall Be Valid, Irrevocable, and Enforceable . . .'

1. The Shift in Judicial Attitudes

WILKO V. SWAN
Supreme Court of the United States, 1953
346 U.S. 427, 74 S.Ct. 182, 98 L.Ed. 168

[A customer of a securities brokerage firm sought damages under the Securities Act of 1933 in a United States District Court. The customer alleged that he was induced to buy stock because of false representations and a failure to provide relevant information. The brokerage firm argued that the customers agreement to arbitrate waived his right to sue under the Securities Act. The U.S. Supreme Court rejected the waiver argument.]

MR. JUSTICE REED delivered the opinion of the Court.

. . . [W]e think the right to select the judicial forum is the kind of "provision" that cannot be waived under § 14 of the Securities Act. * * *

Even though the provisions of the Securities Act, advantageous to the buyer, apply, their effectiveness in application is lessened in arbitration as compared to judicial proceedings. Determination of the quality of a commodity or the amount of money due under a contract is not the type of issue here involved. This case requires subjective findings on the purpose and knowledge of an alleged violator of the Act. They must be not only determined, but applied by the arbitrators without judicial instruction on the law. As their award may be made without explanation of their reasons and without a complete record of their proceedings, the arbitrators' conception of the legal meaning of such statutory requirements as "burden of proof," "reasonable care" or "material fact," * * * cannot be examined. * * * While it may be true, as the Court of Appeals thought, that a failure of the arbitrators to decide in accordance with the provisions of the Securities Act would "constitute grounds for vacating the award pursuant to section 10 of the Federal Arbitration Act," that failure would need to be made clearly to appear. In unrestricted submission, such as the present margin agreements envisage, the interpretations of the law by the arbitrators in contrast to manifest disregard are not subject, in the federal courts, to judicial review for error in interpretation. The United States Arbitration Act contains no provision for judicial determination of legal issues such as is found in the English law. As the protective provisions of the Securities Act require the exercise of judicial direction to fairly assure their effectiveness, it seems to us that congress must have intended § 14 note 6, supra, to apply to waiver of judicial trial and review.

* * *

Recognizing the advantages that prior agreements for arbitration may provide for the solution of commercial controversies, we decide that the intention of Congress concerning the sale of securities is better carried out by holding invalid such agreement for arbitration of issues arising under the act.

Reversed.

[MR. JUSTICE JACKSON's concurring opinion and MR. JUSTICE FRANKFURTER's dissenting opinion have been omitted.]

NOTE

In *Shearson/American Express, Inc. v. McMahon*, 482 U.S. 220, 233, 107 S.Ct. 2332, 96 L.Ed.2d 185 (1987), the U.S. Supreme Court stated that ". . . the mistrust of arbitration that formed the basis for the *Wilko* opinion in 1953 is difficult to square with the assessment of arbitration that has prevailed since that time." *Wilko* was specifically overruled in *Rodriguez de Quijas v. Shearson/American Express, Inc.*, 490 U.S. 477, 485, 109 S.Ct. 1917, 104 L.Ed.2d 526 (1989). For an interesting behind-the-scenes account of the court's shifting view of *Wilko*, see Ellen E. Deason, *Perspectives on Decisionmaking From the Blackmun Papers: The Cases on Arbitrability of Statutory Claims*, 70 Mo. L. Rev. 1133 (2005).

GILMER V. INTERSTATE/JOHNSON LANE CORP.

Supreme Court of the United States, 1991
500 U.S. 20, 111 S.Ct. 1647, 114 L.Ed.2d 26

JUSTICE WHITE delivered the opinion of the Court.

The question presented in this case is whether a claim under the Age Discrimination in Employment Act of 1967 (ADEA), as amended, can be subjected to compulsory arbitration pursuant to an arbitration agreement in a securities registration application. The Court of Appeals held that it could, and we affirm.

I

Respondent Interstate/Johnson Lane Corporation (Interstate) hired petitioner Robert Gilmer as a Manager of Financial Services in May 1981. As required by his employment, Gilmer registered as a securities representative with several stock exchanges, including the New York Stock Exchange (NYSE). His registration application, entitled "Uniform Application for Securities Industry Registration or Transfer," provided, among other things, that Gilmer "agreed to arbitrate any dispute, claim or controversy" arising between him and Interstate "that is required to be arbitrated under the rules, constitution or by-laws of the organizations with which I register." Of relevance to this case, NYSE Rule 347 provides for arbitration of "any controversy between a registered representative and any member or member organization arising out of the employment or termination of employment of such registered representative."

Interstate terminated Gilmer's employment in 1987, at which time Gilmer was 62 years of age. After first filing an age discrimination charge with the Equal Employment Opportunity Commission (EEOC), Gilmer subsequently brought suit in the United States District Court for the Western District of North Carolina, alleging that Interstate had discharged him because of his age, in violation of the ADEA. In response to Gilmer's complaint, Interstate filed in the District Court a motion to compel arbitration of the ADEA claim. In its motion, Interstate relied upon the arbitration agreement in Gilmer's registration application, as well as the Federal Arbitration Act (FAA). The District Court denied Interstate's motion, based on this Court's decision in *Alexander v. Gardner–Denver Co.,* and because it concluded that "Congress intended to protect ADEA claimants from the waiver of a judicial forum." The United States Court of Appeals for the Fourth Circuit reversed, finding "nothing in the text, legislative history, or underlying purposes of the ADEA indicating a congressional intent to preclude enforcement of arbitration agreements." We granted certiorari, to resolve a conflict among the Courts of Appeals regarding the arbitrability of ADEA claims.

II

* * *

It is by now clear that statutory claims may be the subject of an arbitration agreement, enforceable pursuant to the FAA. Indeed, in recent years we have held enforceable arbitration agreements relating to claims arising under the Sherman Act, § 10(b) of the Securities Exchange Act of 1934; the civil provisions of the Racketeer Influenced and Corrupt Organizations Act (RICO)*;* and § 12(2) of the Securities Act of 1933. In these cases we recognized that "by agreeing to arbitrate a statutory claim, a party does not forgo the substantive rights afforded by the statute; it only submits to their resolution in an arbitral, rather than a judicial, forum."

Although all statutory claims may not be appropriate for arbitration, "having made the bargain to arbitrate, the party should be held to it unless Congress itself has evinced an intention to preclude a waiver of judicial remedies for the statutory rights at issue." In this regard, we note that the burden is on Gilmer to show that Congress intended to preclude a waiver of a judicial forum for ADEA claims. If such an intention exists, it will be discoverable in the text of the ADEA, its legislative history, or an "inherent conflict" between arbitration and the ADEA's underlying purposes. Throughout such an inquiry, it should be kept in mind that "questions of arbitrability must be addressed with a healthy regard for the federal policy favoring arbitration."

III

Gilmer concedes that nothing in the text of the ADEA or its legislative history explicitly precludes arbitration. He argues, however, that compulsory arbitration of ADEA claims pursuant to arbitration agreements would be inconsistent with the statutory framework and purposes of the ADEA. Like the Court of Appeals, we disagree.

A

Congress enacted the ADEA in 1967 "to promote employment of older persons based on their ability rather than age; to prohibit arbitrary age discrimination in employment; [and] to help employers and workers find ways of meeting problems arising from the impact of age on employment." To achieve those goals, the ADEA, among other things, makes it unlawful for an employer "to fail or refuse to hire or to discharge any individual or otherwise discriminate against any individual with respect to his compensation, terms, conditions, or privileges of employment, because of such individual's age." This proscription is enforced both by private suits and by the EEOC. * * *

As Gilmer contends, the ADEA is designed not only to address individual grievances, but also to further important social policies. We do not perceive any inherent inconsistency between those policies, however, and enforcing agreements to arbitrate age discrimination claims. It is true that arbitration focuses on specific disputes between the parties involved. The same can be said, however, of judicial resolution of claims. Both of these dispute resolution mechanisms nevertheless also can further broader social purposes. The Sherman Act, the Securities Exchange Act of 1934, RICO and the Securities Act of 1933 all are designed to advance important public policies, but as noted above, claims under those statutes are appropriate for arbitration. "So long as the prospective litigant effectively may vindicate [his or her] statutory cause of action in the arbitral forum, the statute will continue to serve both its remedial and deterrent function."

We also are unpersuaded by the argument that arbitration will undermine the role of the EEOC in enforcing the ADEA. An individual ADEA claimant subject to an arbitration agreement will still be free to file a charge with the EEOC, even though the claimant is not able to institute a private judicial action. Indeed, Gilmer filed a charge with the EEOC in this case. In any event, the EEOC's role in combating age discrimination is not dependent on the filing of a charge; the agency may receive information concerning alleged violations of the ADEA "from any source," and it has independent authority to investigate age discrimination. Moreover, nothing in the ADEA indicates that Congress intended that the EEOC be involved in all employment disputes. Such disputes can be settled, for example, without any EEOC involvement. Finally, the mere involvement of an administrative agency in the enforcement of a statute is not sufficient to preclude arbitration. For example, the Securities Exchange Commission is heavily involved in the enforcement of the Securities Exchange Act of 1934 and the Securities Act of 1933, but we held that claims under both of those statutes may be subject to compulsory arbitration.

Gilmer also argues that compulsory arbitration is improper because it deprives claimants of the judicial forum provided for by the ADEA. Congress, however, did not explicitly preclude arbitration or other nonjudicial resolution of claims, even in its recent amendments to the ADEA. "If Congress intended the substantive protection afforded [by the ADEA] to include protection against waiver of the right to a judicial forum, that intention will be deducible from text or legislative history." Moreover, Gilmer's argument ignores the ADEA's flexible approach to resolution of claims. The EEOC, for example, is directed to pursue "informal methods of conciliation, conference, and persuasion," which suggests that out-of-court dispute resolution, such as arbitration, is consistent with the statutory scheme established by Congress. In addition, arbitration is consistent with Congress' grant of concurrent jurisdiction over ADEA claims to state and federal courts, because arbitration agreements, "like the provision for concurrent jurisdiction, serve to advance the objective of allowing [claimants] a broader right to select the forum for resolving disputes, whether it be judicial or otherwise."

B

In arguing that arbitration is inconsistent with the ADEA, Gilmer also raises a host of challenges to the adequacy of arbitration procedures. Initially, we note that in our recent arbitration cases we have already rejected most of these arguments as insufficient to preclude arbitration of statutory claims. Such generalized attacks on arbitration "rest on suspicion of arbitration as a method of weakening the protections afforded in the substantive law to would-be complainants," and as such, they are "far out of step with our current strong endorsement of the federal statute favoring this method of resolving disputes." Consequently, we address these arguments only briefly.

Gilmer first speculates that arbitration panels will be biased. However, "we decline to indulge the presumption that the parties and arbitral body conducting a proceeding will be unable or unwilling to retain competent, conscientious and impartial arbitrators." In any event, we note that the NYSE arbitration rules, which are applicable to the dispute in this case, provide protections against biased panels. The rules require, for example, that the parties be informed of the employment histories of the arbitrators, and that they be allowed to make further inquiries into the arbitrators' backgrounds. In addition, each party is allowed one peremptory challenge and unlimited challenges for cause. Moreover, the arbitrators are required to disclose "any circumstances which might preclude [them] from rendering an objective and impartial determination." The FAA also protects against bias, by providing that courts may overturn arbitration decisions "where there was evident partiality or corruption in the arbitrators." There has been no showing in this case that those provisions are inadequate to guard against potential bias.

Gilmer also complains that the discovery allowed in arbitration is more limited than in the federal courts, which he contends will make it difficult to prove discrimination. It is unlikely, however, that age discrimination claims require more extensive discovery than other claims that we have found to be arbitrable, such as RICO and antitrust claims. Moreover, there has been no showing in this case that the NYSE discovery provisions, which allow for document production, information requests, depositions, and subpoenas, will prove insufficient to allow ADEA claimants such as Gilmer a fair opportunity to present their claims. Although those procedures might not be as extensive as in the federal courts, by agreeing to arbitrate, a party "trades the procedures and opportunity for review of the courtroom for the simplicity, informality, and expedition of arbitration." Indeed, an important counterweight to the reduced discovery in NYSE arbitration is that arbitrators are not bound by the rules of evidence.

A further alleged deficiency of arbitration is that arbitrators often will not issue written opinions, resulting; Gilmer contends, in a lack of public knowledge of employers' discriminatory policies, an inability to obtain effective appellate review, and a stifling of the development of the law. The NYSE rules, however, do require that all arbitration awards be in writing, and that the awards contain the names of the parties, a summary of the issues in controversy, and a description of the award issued. In addition, the award decisions are made available to the public. Furthermore, judicial decisions addressing ADEA claims will continue to be issued because it is unlikely that all or even most ADEA claimants will be subject to arbitration agreements. Finally, Gilmer's concerns apply equally to settlements of ADEA claims, which, as noted above, are clearly allowed.

It is also argued that arbitration procedures cannot adequately further the purposes of the ADEA because they do not provide for broad equitable relief and class actions. As the court below noted, however, arbitrators do have the power to fashion equitable relief. Indeed, the NYSE rules applicable here do not restrict the types of relief an arbitrator may award, but merely refer to "damages and/or other relief." The NYSE rules also provide for collective proceedings. But "even if the arbitration could not go forward as a class action or class relief could not be granted by the arbitrator, the fact that the [ADEA] provides for the possibility of bringing a collective action does not mean that individual attempts at conciliation were intended to be barred." Finally, it should be remembered that arbitration agreements will not preclude the EEOC from bringing actions seeking class-wide and equitable relief.

C

An additional reason advanced by Gilmer for refusing to enforce arbitration agreements relating to ADEA claims is his contention that there often will be unequal bargaining power between employers and employees. Mere inequality in bargaining power, however, is not a sufficient reason to hold that arbitration agreements are never enforceable in the employment context. Relationships between securities dealers and investors, for example, may involve unequal bargaining power, but we nevertheless held in *Rodriguez de Quijas* and *McMahon* that agreements to arbitrate in that context are enforceable. As discussed above, the FAA's purpose was to place arbitration agreements on the same footing as other contracts. Thus, arbitration agreements are enforceable "save upon such grounds as exist at law or in equity for the revocation of any contract." "Of course, courts should remain attuned to well-supported claims that the agreement to arbitrate resulted from the sort of fraud or overwhelming economic power that would provide grounds 'for the revocation of any contract.'" There is no indication in this case, however, that Gilmer, an experienced businessman, was coerced or defrauded into agreeing to the arbitration clause in his registration application. As with the claimed procedural inadequacies discussed above, this claim of unequal bargaining power is best left for resolution in specific cases.

* * *

V

We conclude that Gilmer has not met his burden of showing that Congress, in enacting the ADEA, intended to preclude arbitration of claims under the Act. Accordingly, the judgment of the Court of Appeals is

Affirmed.

JUSTICE STEVENS, with whom JUSTICE MARSHALL joins, dissenting.

* * *

III

Not only would I find that the FAA does not apply to employment-related disputes between employers and employees in general, but also I would hold that compulsory arbitration conflicts with the congressional purpose animating the ADEA, in particular. As the Court previously has noted, authorizing the courts to issue broad injunctive relief is the cornerstone to eliminating discrimination in society. The ADEA, like Title VII, authorizes courts to award broad, class-based injunctive relief to achieve the purposes of the Act. Because commercial arbitration is typically limited to a specific dispute between the particular parties and because the available remedies in arbitral forums generally do not provide for class-wide injunctive relief, I would conclude that an essential purpose of the ADEA is frustrated by compulsory arbitration of employment discrimination claims. Moreover, as Chief Justice Burger explained:

> Plainly, it would not comport with the congressional objectives behind a statute seeking to enforce civil rights protected by Title VII to allow the very forces that had practiced discrimination to contract away the right to enforce civil rights in the courts. For federal courts to defer to arbitral decisions reached by the same combination of forces that had long perpetuated invidious discrimination would have made the foxes guardians of the chickens.

In my opinion, the same concerns expressed by Chief Justice Burger with regard to compulsory arbitration of Title VII claims may be said of claims arising under the ADEA. The Court's holding today clearly eviscerates the important role played by an independent judiciary in eradicating employment discrimination.

IV

When the FAA was passed in 1925, I doubt that any legislators who voted for it expected it to apply to statutory claims, to form contracts between parties of unequal bargaining power, or to the arbitration of disputes arising out of the employment relationship. In recent years, however, the Court "has effectively rewritten the statute," and abandoned its earlier view that statutory claims were not appropriate subjects for arbitration. Although I remain persuaded that it erred in doing so, the Court has also put to one side any concern about the inequality of bargaining power between an entire industry, on the one hand, and an individual customer or employee, on the other. Until today, however, the Court has not read § 2 of the FAA as broadly encompassing disputes arising out of the employment relationship. I believe that additional extension of the FAA is erroneous. Accordingly, I respectfully dissent.

NOTES AND QUESTIONS

1.   One of the recurring arguments against compelling the arbitration of a statutory claim is that the arbitration process is "an inferior system of justice, structured without due process, rules of evidence, accountability of judgment or rule of law." The relative merits of litigation and alternative processes is a continuing issue. Arbitration is criticized by Professor Stephen Goldberg for being too much like litigation. Defenses of arbitration focus at times on ways that arbitration systems are similar to the legal system. Recall, for example, Justice White's discussion in *Gilmer* of NYSE rules on discovery and the powers of arbitrators to fashion equitable relief. Is arbitration too much like litigation or not enough like litigation? If your answer is "it depends," on what does it depend?

2.   The court's opinion in *Gilmer* was viewed by many practitioners as a broad endorsement of mandatory arbitration. Do you read it that broadly? Could one argue that it is more of a case about presumptions regarding arbitration and the evidence that is required to support or refute such assumptions? *See* Joseph R. Grodin, *Arbitration of Employment Discrimination Claims: Doctrine and Policy in the Wake of* Gilmer, 14 Hofstra Lab. L.J. 1 (1996). The scholarly literature critical of *Gilmer* is voluminous. *See, e.g.,* David S. Schwartz, *Enforcing Small Print to Protect Big Business: Employee and Consumer Rights Claims in an Age of Compelled Arbitration,* 1997 Wis. L. Rev. 33; Jean R. Sternlight, *Panacea or Corporate Tool?: Debunking the Supreme Court's Preference for Binding Arbitration,* 74 Wash. U. L.Q. 637 (1996); Katherine Van Wezel Stone, *Mandatory Arbitration of Individual Employment Rights: The Yellow Dog Contract of the 1990's,* 73 Denv. U. L. Rev. 1017 (1996); Reginald Alleyne, *Statutory Discrimination Claims: Rights "Waived" and Lost in the Arbitration Forum,* 13 Hofstra Lab. L. J. 381 (1996); Robert A. Gorman, *The* Gilmer *Decision and the Private Arbitration of Public–Law Disputes,* 1995 U. Ill. L. Rev. 635. For scholarly commentary defending *Gilmer,* see Dennis R. Nolan, *Employment Arbitration After* Circuit City, 41 Brandeis L.J. 853 (2003); Samuel Estreicher, *Pre-dispute Agreements to Arbitrate Statutory Employment Claims,* 72 N.Y.U. L. Rev. 1344 (1997).

3.   Mandatory arbitration provisions are now common in a wide variety of areas, including securities, health care, financial services, consumer goods and service, and employment, to name just a few. Professor Hensler and Linda Demaine analyzed 161 consumer contracts in a variety of industries, and discovered nearly a third of them, fifty-one, included mandatory arbitration provisions. *See* Linda J. Demaine & Deborah R. Hensler, *"Volunteering" to Arbitrate through Pre-dispute Arbitration Clauses: The Average Consumer's Experience,* 67 Law & Contemp. Probs. 55, 61 (2004). Demaine and Hensler further found

> The prevalence of arbitration clauses is highest (69.2%) in the financial category (credit cards, banking, investment, and accounting/tax consulting), and lowest (0) in the food and entertainment category

(grocery stores, restaurants, theme parks, and cultural/sports events). This pattern is not surprising, as the financial category is characterized by industries that rely heavily on written contracts, often for ongoing services, whereas the food and entertainment category is characterized by industries that engage in isolated transactions with no written contract between businesses and consumers. A similar pattern holds to some extent across industries. The auto insurance and health insurance industries, for example—both of which typically provide ongoing services under written contract—are more likely to require arbitration than are the auto repair/maintenance and health-care-provider industries. This pattern is not universal, however. For example, none of the home protection companies and only one health club surveyed required arbitration, although consumers usually contract in writing for these ongoing services. Customary practice and industry regulations likely explain some of the patterns found.

Id. at 62.

4.   In a study of the use of arbitration clauses in the consumer finance and telecommunications industries, Professor Theodore Eisenberg and colleagues analyzed "26 consumer agreements drafted by 21 companies and 164 negotiated [non-consumer] contracts entered into by the same companies" in 2007. They found 76.9% (20 of 26) of the consumer contracts included arbitration clauses, but only 6.1% (9 of 147) of the non-employment contracts included arbitration clauses. Theodore Eisenberg, Geoffrey P. Miller & Emily Sherwin, *Arbitration's Summer Soldiers: An Empirical Study of Arbitration Clauses in Consumer and Nonconsumer Contracts*, 41 U. Mich. J.L. Reform 871 (2008).

5.   While it was an FAA employment law case, the Court ultimately held that *Gilmer* also overruled an important collective bargaining case, *Gardner–Denver*. In that case, the Court held that the inclusion of an arbitration provision in a collective bargaining agreement did not preclude a worker from going to court to vindicate a statutory right, such as employment discrimination. In 2009, however, the Court held that Gardner–Denver was superseded by Gilmer and that arbitration under collective bargaining was an exclusive remedy. *14 Penn. Plaza v. Pyett*, 556 U.S. 247, 129 S.Ct. 1456 (2009)

6.   Congress endorsed arbitration and other alternative processes in the Civil Rights Act of 1991, 42 U.S.C. § 1981 (2000), and the Americans with Disabilities Act, 42 U.S.C. § 12212 (2000). Referring to the Civil Rights Act of 1991, the D.C. Circuit stated "the language of the statute in no way suggests that the rule of *Gilmer* should no longer apply." *Benefits Communication Corp. v. Klieforth*, 642 A.2d 1299, 1305 (D.C. 1994).

7.   Consider the following comments by Theodore O. Rogers, Jr., a management lawyer, and Judith P. Vladeck, an attorney who represents employees, in *Symposium on Arbitration in the Securities Industry*, 63 Fordham L. Rev. 1507 (1995). Rogers takes the first shot:

I believe there has been a well-orchestrated public relations campaign over the course of the last nine or ten months against arbitration of employment discrimination claims. I think it has been unfair and I think the motives of many of the people who are behind it are quite suspect.

* * *

[T]he court system is broken.

Page one of today's New York Times reports on the U.S. Judicial conference's recommendation that employment discriminations claims somehow be thrown out of the federal courts or at least be subject to some preliminary screenings by the Equal Employment Opportunity Commission.

The federal judges realize that they cannot handle the tidal wave of employment discrimination claims. Their suggestion that the EEOC handle it is a difficult one to fathom because those of us with experience with the EEOC know that they're swamped and what they're doing is trying to shuttle cases over to the federal courts.

The Dunlop Commission, the commission formed by the current administration to consider worker-management relations, issued a fact-finding report in May of 1994.

* * *

[T]he report found that litigation is expensive and that complicated court processes make it difficult for employees to pursue claims; the report also found that from 1971 to 1991 the overall number of civil cases brought in federal court has risen by 110%, but the number of employment claims rose by 430%. And those figures are from before the Americans with Disabilities Act and the 1991 Civil Rights Act became effective, so by now presumably, the increase in discrimination cases is much larger.

As for costs, the Commission found that substantially over one dollar in costs, attorneys' fees, and other just wasted money is spent for each one dollar that goes to a claimant in compensation for a court finding of discrimination. The Commission found that the costs, the difficulty, and the complication of employment litigation ultimately restrict litigation to upper-level professionals, usually complaining of their termination.

Jury verdicts, the Commission noted, are often lottery-like in their results. The problem of unpredictable jury decisions is one that everyone seems to be considering these days. Last night on the eleven o'clock news, I saw a report that the City of New York is going to propose some way whereby claims against the City could be determined in a forum without a jury.

In other words, the current litigation process is just broken. * * *

Now, I want to address a few of the specific criticisms that have been raised against arbitration of employment discrimination claims. First, it is often claimed that arbitrators have no training in employment law. That's wrong. The NYSE does train arbitrators in the law. The NASD, I know, does an excellent job in its training efforts. * * *

Those who criticize the supposed lack of legal training by arbitrators ignore the fact that juries have no training in discrimination law, and there is no reason to suppose that a judge's instruction to a jury concerning the law leaves the jury any more informed on these issues than arbitrators who have received some training and have the benefit of the competing arguments and evidence submitted by counsel. * * *

The second criticism that's been raised in this ongoing P.R. campaign against arbitration is that arbitration rules are unfair to employees. That's wrong again. The New York Stock Exchange bends over backwards to afford employees an opportunity to present their case. * * *

Finally, another subtext that underlies all of the criticisms of arbitration is the claim that employees cannot win. Mr. Clemente may have more accurate or more updated statistics, but the ones I have prove this is just not right. The GAO report from March of 1994 studied eighteen cases that went to a decision, and of those the claimant won in ten of them. A fifty-five percent success rate for claimants is not evidence of a biased forum. Now, some may try to minimize that substantial success by claimants by stating that a number of the winning employees may have wanted more than they even got. But I don't think that's anything that distinguishes arbitration from any other litigation forum. * * *

Theodore O. Rogers Jr., *Employment Discrimination*, 63 Fordham L. Rev. 1613, 1617–22 (1995).

Judith Vladeck responds:

If I take a woman into the federal court who has a legitimate, meritorious case of discrimination, she is entitled to certain protection, she is entitled to a fair hearing, entitled to due process. If she wins, she gets whatever money she's lost in back wages, she gets enough in attorneys' fees so that she nets whatever it is of the damages provided, and if she has suffered emotional distress, under the Act she can get damages for that. * * *

Let me ask you all: How ready are you to let all of your IRS matters be arbitrated? The IRS doesn't like some filing you've done. It gives it to an arbitrator. You don't get to pick. You don't get to choose. The arbitrator doesn't have to be bound by the law. He thinks you earn too damn much money anyway. Not only don't you get a refund, but you get a penalty imposed with no explanation and no right to appeal. What are we doing with our public rights, giving them to untrained arbitrators? Do you really want to do that with major pieces of your life? You know, you could be there some day. This is not simply for women who complain of sexual harassment. It is for executives, too, who have been cheated.

Judith P. Vladeck, *Employment Discrimination*, 63 Fordham L. Rev. 1613, 1625–26.

8.   Professor Jeffrey Stempel has argued that the rise of mandatory arbitration has led to "new" "mass" arbitration that is very different from "old" arbitration. Jeffrey W. Stempel, *Mandating Minimum Quality in Mass Arbitration*, 76 U. Cin. L. Rev.383 (2007). "Old" arbitration is typically restricted to a trade or industry, involves commercial actors who are familiar to the system, is limited to disputing over commercial issues, and usually concerns contractual interpretation. "New" "mass" arbitration, however, involves claimants such as consumers and employees going against large, repeat-players, and disputing over personal issues instead of commercial ones. In the "old" system, players expect and typically prefer to be subject to arbitration, whereas the "new" system commonly forces persons unknowingly or unwillingly into arbitration.

Stempel argues that certain problems, particularly insufficient levels of fairness and quality control, are prevalent in "new" arbitration. He proposes full judicial review for "new" arbitrations that do not meet certain minimum qualifications, including: arbitral neutrality and expertise, evenly balanced arbitration clauses, remedies that are equivalent to those available in litigation, procedures for cost-sharing, and access to legal services. What do you think of Stempel's proposal? How would it impact the arbitration process?

2.   The Role of the Courts

The scheme set forth in the Federal Arbitration Act provides a narrow but vital role in the execution of the statute's central mission of enforcing agreements to arbitrate. Under Sections 3 and 4, the courts are to determine whether the agreement to arbitrate is valid. If it is, then the court must enforce it; there is no discretion. This, of course, is an arbitrability issue like the ones discussed in Subsection B(1)(a). We treat it here, however, to provide greater focus on this function as one of the central battlegrounds of mandatory arbitration.

RENT–A–CENTER WEST, INC. V. JACKSON

Supreme Court of the United States, 2010
___ U.S. ___, 130 S.Ct. 2772, 177 L.Ed.2d 403

JUSTICE SCALIA delivered the opinion of the Court.

We consider whether, under the Federal Arbitration Act (FAA or Act), a district court may decide a claim that an arbitration agreement is unconscionable, where the agreement explicitly assigns that decision to the arbitrator.

I

On February 1, 2007, the respondent here, Antonio Jackson, filed an employment-discrimination suit under Rev. Stat. § 1977, 42 U.S.C. § 1981, against his former employer in the United States District Court for the District of Nevada. The defendant and petitioner here, Rent–A–Center, West, Inc., filed a motion under the FAA to dismiss or stay the proceedings, and to compel arbitration, Rent–A–Center argued that the Mutual Agreement to Arbitrate Claims (Agreement), which Jackson signed on February 24, 2003 as a condition of his employment there, precluded Jackson from pursuing his claims in court. * * *

Jackson opposed the motion on the ground that "the arbitration agreement in question is clearly unenforceable in that it is unconscionable" under Nevada law. Rent–A–Center responded that Jackson's unconscionability claim was not properly before the court because Jackson had expressly agreed that the arbitrator would have exclusive authority to resolve any dispute about the enforceability of the Agreement. It also disputed the merits of Jackson's unconscionability claims.

The District Court granted Rent–A–Center's motion to dismiss the proceedings and to compel arbitration. The court found that the Agreement " ' "clearly and unmistakenly [sic]" ' " gives the arbitrator exclusive authority to decide whether the Agreement is enforceable, and, because Jackson challenged the validity of the Agreement as a whole, the issue was for the arbitrator. * * *

Without oral argument, a divided panel of the Court of Appeals for the Ninth Circuit reversed in part, affirmed in part, and remanded. The court reversed on the question of who (the court or arbitrator) had the authority to decide whether the Agreement is enforceable. It noted that "Jackson does not dispute that the language of the Agreement clearly assigns the arbitrability determination to the arbitrator," but held that where "a party challenges an arbitration agreement as unconscionable, and thus asserts that he could not meaningfully assent to the agreement, the threshold question of unconscionability is for the court." * * *

We granted certiorari.

II

A

The FAA reflects the fundamental principle that arbitration is a matter of contract. Section 2, the "primary substantive provision of the Act," *Moses H. Cone Memorial Hospital v. Mercury Constr. Corp.*, provides:

> A written provision in ... a contract evidencing a transaction involving commerce to settle by arbitration a controversy thereafter

arising out of such contract ... shall be valid, irrevocable, and enforceable, save upon such grounds as exist at law or in equity for the revocation of any contract.

The FAA thereby places arbitration agreements on an equal footing with other contracts, and requires courts to enforce them according to their terms. Like other contracts, however, they may be invalidated by "generally applicable contract defenses, such as fraud, duress, or unconscionability."

* * * The Agreement here contains multiple "written provision[s]" to "settle by arbitration a controversy," Two are relevant to our discussion. First, the section titled "Claims Covered By The Agreement" provides for arbitration of all "past, present or future" disputes arising out of Jackson's employment with Rent–A–Center." Second, the section titled "Arbitration Procedures" provides that "[t]he Arbitrator ... shall have exclusive authority to resolve any dispute relating to the ... enforceability ... of this Agreement including, but not limited to any claim that all or any part of this Agreement is void or voidable." The current "controversy" between the parties is whether the Agreement is unconscionable. It is the second provision, which delegates resolution of that controversy to the arbitrator, that Rent–A–Center seeks to enforce. Adopting the terminology used by the parties, we will refer to it as the delegation provision.

The delegation provision is an agreement to arbitrate threshold issues concerning the arbitration agreement. We have recognized that parties can agree to arbitrate "gateway" questions of "arbitrability," such as whether the parties have agreed to arbitrate or whether their agreement covers a particular controversy. This line of cases merely reflects the principle that arbitration is a matter of contract.[1] * * * The question before us, then, is whether the delegation provision is valid under § 2.

B

There are two types of validity challenges under § 2: One type challenges specifically the validity of the agreement to arbitrate, and the other challenges the contract as a whole, either on a ground that directly affects the entire agreement (e.g., the agreement was fraudulently

---

[1] There is one caveat. *First Options of Chicago, Inc. v. Kaplan* held that "[c]ourts should not assume that the parties agreed to arbitrate arbitrability unless there is 'clea[r] and unmistakabl[e]' evidence that they did so." The parties agree the heightened standard applies here. * * * [The dissent, however,] mistakes the subject of the *First Options* "clear and unmistakable" requirement. It pertains to the parties' manifestation of intent, not the agreement's validity. As explained in *Howsam v. Dean Witter Reynolds, Inc.*, it is an "interpretive rule," based on an assumption about the parties' expectations. In "circumstance[s] where contracting parties would likely have expected a court to have decided the gateway matter," we assume that is what they agreed to. Thus, "[u]nless the parties clearly and unmistakably provide otherwise, the question of whether the parties agreed to arbitrate is to be decided by the court, not the arbitrator." * * *

induced), or on the ground that the illegality of one of the contract's provisions renders the whole contract invalid. In a line of cases neither party has asked us to overrule, we held that only the first type of challenge is relevant to a court's determination whether the arbitration agreement at issue is enforceable.[2] See *Prima Paint* [and progeny]. * * * As a matter of substantive federal arbitration law, an arbitration provision is severable from the remainder of the contract.

But that agreements to arbitrate are severable does not mean that they are unassailable. If a party challenges the validity under § 2 of the precise agreement to arbitrate at issue, the federal court must consider the challenge before ordering compliance with that agreement under § 4. In *Prima Paint*, for example, if the claim had been "fraud in the inducement of the arbitration clause itself," then the court would have considered it. "To immunize an arbitration agreement from judicial challenge on the ground of fraud in the inducement would be to elevate it over other forms of contract," * * *

Here, the written provision to settle by arbitration a controversy that Rent–A–Center asks us to enforce is the delegation provision-the provision that gave the arbitrator "exclusive authority to resolve any dispute relating to the . . . enforceability . . . of this Agreement," The remainder of the contract is the rest of the agreement to arbitrate claims arising out of Jackson's employment with Rent–A–Center. To be sure this case differs from *Prima Paint, Buckeye,* and *Preston*, in that the arbitration provisions sought to be enforced in those cases were contained in contracts unrelated to arbitration—contracts for consulting services. In this case, the underlying contract is itself an arbitration agreement. But that makes no difference. Application of the severability rule does not depend on the substance of the remainder of the contract. * * *

C

The District Court correctly concluded that Jackson challenged only the validity of the contract as a whole. Nowhere in his opposition to Rent–A–Center's motion to compel arbitration did he even mention the delegation provision. * * *

As required to make out a claim of unconscionability under Nevada law, he contended that the Agreement was both procedurally and substantively unconscionable. It was procedurally unconscionable, he argued, because it "was imposed as a condition of employment and was non-negotiable." But we need not consider that claim because none of Jackson's substantive unconscionability challenges was specific to the delegation provision. * * *

---

[2] The issue of the agreement's "validity" is different from the issue whether any agreement between the parties "was ever concluded," and, as in *Buckeye Check Cashing, Inc. v. Cardegna* (2006), we address only the former.

* * *

We reverse the judgment of the Court of Appeals for the Ninth Circuit.

JUSTICE STEVENS, with whom JUSTICE GINSBURG, JUSTICE BREYER, and JUSTICE SOTOMAYOR join, dissenting.

Neither petitioner nor respondent has urged us to adopt the rule the Court does today: Even when a litigant has specifically challenged the validity of an agreement to arbitrate he must submit that challenge to the arbitrator unless he has lodged an objection to the particular line in the agreement that purports to assign such challenges to the arbitrator-the so-called "delegation clause."

The Court asserts that its holding flows logically from *Prima Paint Corp. v. Flood & Conklin Mfg. Co.* (1967), in which the Court held that consideration of a contract revocation defense is generally a matter for the arbitrator, unless the defense is specifically directed at the arbitration clause, We have treated this holding as a severability rule: When a party challenges a contract, "but not specifically its arbitration provisions, those provisions are enforceable apart from the remainder of the contract." *Buckeye Check Cashing, Inc. v. Cardegna* (2006). The Court's decision today goes beyond *Prima Paint*. Its breezy assertion that the subject matter of the contract at issue-in this case, an arbitration agreement and nothing more "makes no difference" is simply wrong. This written arbitration agreement is but one part of a broader employment agreement between the parties, just as the arbitration clause in *Prima Paint* was but one part of a broader contract for services between those parties. Thus, that the subject matter of the agreement is exclusively arbitration makes all the difference in the *Prima Paint* analysis.

I

Under the Federal Arbitration Act (FAA), parties generally have substantial leeway to define the terms and scope of their agreement to settle disputes in an arbitral forum. Arbitration is, after all, "simply a matter of contract between the parties; it is a way to resolve those disputes—but only those disputes-that the parties have agreed to submit to arbitration." *First Options of Chicago, Inc. v. Kaplan* (1995). The FAA, therefore, envisions a limited role for courts asked to stay litigation and refer disputes to arbitration.

Certain issues—the kind that "contracting parties would likely have expected a court to have decided"—remain within the province of judicial review. These issues are "gateway matters" because they are necessary antecedents to enforcement of an arbitration agreement; they raise questions the parties "are not likely to have thought that they had agreed that an arbitrator would" decide. Quintessential gateway matters include "whether the parties have a valid arbitration agreement at all." It would be bizarre to send these types of gateway matters to the arbitrator as a matter of course, because they raise a " 'question of arbitrability.' "

"[Q]uestion[s] of arbitrability" thus include questions regarding the existence of a legally binding and valid arbitration agreement, as well as questions regarding the scope of a concededly binding arbitration agreement. In this case we are concerned with the first of these categories: whether the parties have a valid arbitration agreement. This is an issue the FAA assigns to the courts.

Two different lines of cases bear on the issue of who decides a question of arbitrability respecting validity, such as whether an arbitration agreement is unconscionable. Although this issue, as a gateway matter, is typically for the court, we have explained that such an issue can be delegated to the arbitrator in some circumstances. When the parties have purportedly done so, courts must examine two distinct rules to decide whether the delegation is valid.

The first line of cases looks to the parties' intent. In *AT&T Technologies*, we stated that "question[s] of arbitrability" may be delegated to the arbitrator, so long as the delegation is "clear and unmistakable." We reaffirmed this rule, and added some nuance, in *First Options*. Against the background presumption that questions of arbitrability go to the court, we stated that federal courts should "generally" apply "ordinary state-law principles that govern the formation of contracts" to assess "whether the parties agreed to arbitrate a certain matter (including arbitrability)." But, we added, a more rigorous standard applies when the inquiry is whether the parties have "agreed to arbitrate arbitrability": "Courts should not assume that the parties agreed to arbitrate arbitrability unless there is clear and unmistakable evidence that they did so." Justice Breyer's unanimous opinion for the Court described this standard as a type of "revers[e]" "presumption"[4] —one in favor of a judicial, rather than an arbitral, forum. Clear and unmistakable "evidence" of agreement to arbitrate arbitrability might include, as was urged in *First Options*, a course of conduct demonstrating assent, or, as is urged in this case, an express agreement to do so. In any event, whether such evidence exists is a matter for the court to determine.

The second line of cases bearing on who decides the validity of an arbitration agreement, as the Court explains, involves the *Prima Paint* rule. That rule recognizes two types of validity challenges. One type challenges the validity of the arbitration agreement itself, on a ground arising from an infirmity in that agreement. The other challenges the validity of the arbitration agreement tangentially-via a claim that the

---

[4] It is a "revers[e]" presumption because it is counter to the presumption we usually apply in favor of arbitration when the question concerns whether a particular dispute falls within the scope of a concededly binding arbitration agreement.

entire contract (of which the arbitration agreement is but a part) is invalid for some reason. Under *Prima Paint*, a challenge of the first type goes to the court; a challenge of the second type goes to the arbitrator. The *Prima Paint* rule is akin to a pleading standard, whereby a party seeking to challenge the validity of an arbitration agreement must expressly say so in order to get his dispute into court.

In sum, questions related to the validity of an arbitration agreement are usually matters for a court to resolve before it refers a dispute to arbitration. But questions of arbitrability may go to the arbitrator in two instances: (1) when the parties have demonstrated, clearly and unmistakably, that it is their intent to do so; or (2) when the validity of an arbitration agreement depends exclusively on the validity of the substantive contract of which it is a part.

II

We might have resolved this case by simply applying the *First Options* rule: Does the arbitration agreement at issue "clearly and unmistakably" evince petitioner's and respondent's intent to submit questions of arbitrability to the arbitrator?[6] The answer to that question is no. Respondent's claim that the arbitration agreement is unconscionable undermines any suggestion that he "clearly" and "unmistakably" assented to submit questions of arbitrability to the arbitrator. * * *

In other words, when a party raises a good-faith validity challenge to the arbitration agreement itself, that issue must be resolved before a court can say that he clearly and unmistakably intended to arbitrate that very validity question. This case well illustrates the point: If Respondent's unconscionability claim is correct—i.e., if the terms of the agreement are so one-sided and the process of its making so unfair—it would contravene the existence of clear and unmistakable assent to arbitrate the very question petitioner now seeks to arbitrate. Accordingly, it is necessary for the court to resolve the merits of respondent's unconscionability claim in order to decide whether the parties have a valid arbitration agreement under § 2. Otherwise, that section's preservation of revocation issues for the Court would be meaningless.

* * * This is, in essence, how I understand the Court of Appeals to have decided the issue below. I would therefore affirm its judgment, leaving, as it did, the merits of respondent's unconscionability claim for the District Court to resolve on remand.

---

[6] Respondent has challenged whether he "meaningfully agreed to the terms of the form Agreement to Arbitrate, which he contends is procedurally and substantively unconscionable." Even if *First Options* relates only to "manifestations of intent," as the Court states, whether there has been meaningful agreement surely bears some relation to whether one party has manifested intent to be bound to an agreement.

III

Rather than apply *First Options*, the Court takes us down a different path, one neither briefed by the parties nor relied upon by the Court of Appeals. In applying *Prima Paint*, the Court has unwisely extended a "fantastic" and likely erroneous decision.[8]

As explained at the outset, this case lies at a seeming crossroads in our arbitration jurisprudence. It implicates cases such as *First Options*, which address whether the parties intended to delegate questions of arbitrability, and also those cases, such as *Prima Paint*, which address the severability of a presumptively valid arbitration agreement from a potentially invalid contract. The question of "Who decides?"—arbitrator or court—animates both lines of cases, but they are driven by different concerns. In cases like *First Options*, we are concerned with the parties' intentions. In cases like *Prima Paint*, we are concerned with how the parties challenge the validity of the agreement. * * *

The *Prima Paint* rule has been denominated as one related to severability. Our opinion in *Buckeye*, set out these guidelines:

> First, as a matter of substantive federal arbitration law, an arbitration provision is severable from the remainder of the contract. Second, unless the challenge is to the arbitration clause itself, the issue of the contract's validity is considered by the arbitrator in the first instance.

Whether the general contract defense renders the entire agreement void or voidable is irrelevant. All that matters is whether the party seeking to present the issue to a court has brought a discrete challenge to the validity of the arbitration clause.

Prima Paint and its progeny allow a court to pluck from a potentially invalid contract a potentially valid arbitration agreement. Today the Court adds a new layer of severability—something akin to Russian nesting dolls—into the mix: Courts may now pluck from a potentially invalid arbitration agreement even narrower provisions that refer particular arbitrability disputes to an arbitrator. I do not think an agreement to arbitrate can ever manifest a clear and unmistakable intent to arbitrate its own validity. But even assuming otherwise, I certainly would not hold that the *Prima Paint* rule extends this far.

In my view, a general revocation challenge to a standalone arbitration agreement is, invariably, a challenge to the making of the arbitration agreement itself, therefore, under *Prima Paint*, must be

---

[8] Justice Black quite reasonably characterized the Court's holding in *Prima Paint* as "fantastic," (dissenting opinion), because the holding was, in his view, inconsistent with the text of § 2 of the FAA, as well as the intent of the draftsmen of the legislation. Nevertheless, the narrow holding in that case has been followed numerous times, and, as the Court correctly notes today, neither party has asked us to revisit those cases.

decided by the court. A claim of procedural unconscionability aims to undermine the formation of the arbitration agreement, much like a claim of unconscionability aims to undermine the clear-and-unmistakable-intent requirement necessary for a valid delegation of a "discrete" challenge to the validity of the arbitration agreement itself. Moreover, because we are dealing in this case with a challenge to an independently executed arbitration agreement-rather than a clause contained in a contract related to another subject matter-any challenge to the contract itself is also, necessarily, a challenge to the arbitration agreement. They are one and the same.

* * *

3. The Costs of Arbitration

One of the differences between public adjudication and private arbitration is that with public adjudication the costs of the judge, the courtroom, the clerk's office, and the other necessary components of a public court are paid by the government. With private arbitration, however, those costs must be borne by the parties, including the costs of the arbitrator's time and the costs of administering the case. The *Cole* and the *Green Tree* cases that follow examine the implications of this dynamic in the context of mandatory arbitration.

COLE V. BURNS INTERNATIONAL SECURITY SERVICES
United States Court of Appeals, District of Columbia Circuit, 1997
105 F.3d 1465

HARRY T. EDWARDS, CHIEF JUDGE:

This case raises important issues regarding whether and to what extent a person can be required, *as a condition of employment,* to (1) waive all rights to a trial by jury in a court of competent jurisdiction with respect to any dispute relating to recruitment, employment, or termination, including claims involving laws against discrimination, and (2) sign an agreement providing that, at the employer's option, any such employment disputes must be arbitrated. At its core, this appeal challenges the enforceability of conditions of employment requiring individuals to arbitrate claims resting on statutory rights. The issues at hand bring into focus the seminal decision of *Gilmer v. Interstate/Johnson Lane Corp.,* and call into question the limits of the Supreme Court's holdings in that case.

In this case, the appellant, Clinton Cole, seeks to overturn an order of the District Court dismissing his complaint under Title VII of the Civil Rights Act of 1964, as amended, and compelling arbitration of his disputes with Burns International Security Services ("Burns" or "Burns Security"). Although Cole seemingly raised a viable action under Title

VII, the District Court held that his statutory claims of employment discrimination should be dismissed pursuant to the Federal Arbitration Act ("FAA" or "Act"). * * *

[W]e find that the disputed arbitration agreement is valid. In doing so, we are mindful of the clear distinctions between arbitration of labor disputes under a collective bargaining agreement and mandatory arbitration of individual statutory claims outside of the context of collective bargaining. We are also cognizant of the numerous concerns that have been voiced by arbitrators, legal commentators, the Equal Employment Opportunity Commission ("EEOC"), and National Labor Relations Board ("NLRB") regarding the potential inequities and inadequacies of arbitration in individual employment cases, as well as their concerns about the competence of arbitrators and the arbitral forum to enforce effectively the myriad of public laws protecting workers and regulating the workplace. Nonetheless, in this case, we are constrained by *Gilmer* to find the arbitration agreement enforceable. We do not read *Gilmer* as mandating the enforcement of *all* mandatory agreements to arbitrate statutory claims; rather, we read *Gilmer* as requiring the enforcement of arbitration agreements that do not undermine the relevant statutory scheme. The agreement in this case meets that standard.

We note that this case raises an issue not directly presented in *Gilmer* or any other Supreme Court case to date: can an employer require an employee to arbitrate all disputes and also require the employee to pay all or part of the arbitrators' fees? We hold that it cannot. In *Gilmer* and other securities industry cases, the employers routinely paid *all* arbitrators' fees, so the matter was not in dispute. However, there is no reason to think that the Court would have approved a program of mandatory arbitration of statutory claims in *Gilmer* in the absence of employer agreement to pay arbitrators' fees. Because public law confers both substantive rights and a reasonable right of access to a neutral forum in which those rights can be vindicated, we find that employees cannot be *required* to pay for the services of a "judge" in order to pursue their statutory rights. In this case, the parties' contract does not address explicitly the payment of the arbitrators' fees; however, because ambiguity in a contract should be resolved against the drafter—here, the employer—and ambiguity should be resolved in favor of a legal construction of the parties' agreement, we interpret the arbitration agreement at issue as requiring Burns to pay all arbitrators' fees associated with the resolution of Cole's claims. So construed, the contract is valid.

* * *

[W]e are unaware of any situation in American jurisprudence in which a beneficiary of a federal statute has been required to pay for the services of the judge assigned to hear her or his case. Under *Gilmer,* arbitration is supposed to be a reasonable substitute for a judicial forum. Therefore, it would undermine Congress's intent to prevent employees who are seeking to vindicate statutory rights from gaining access to a judicial forum and then require them to pay for the services of an arbitrator when they would never be required to pay for a judge in court.

* * *

In sum, we hold that Cole could not be required to agree to arbitrate his public law claims as a condition of employment if the arbitration agreement required him to pay all or part of the arbitrator's fees and expenses. In light of this holding, we find that the arbitration agreement in this case is valid and enforceable. We do so because we interpret the agreement as requiring Burns Security to pay all of the arbitrator's fees necessary for a full and fair resolution of Cole's statutory claims.

* * *

For the foregoing reasons, we affirm the District Court's order dismissing the complaint and compelling arbitration.

NOTES

1.   The *Cole* case appears to be an example of what Professor Gorman recommended in 1995, when he said a code of due process for public law arbitration should be "articulated by the courts through a 'common law' type of evolutionary development." Robert A. Gorman, *The Gilmer Decision and the Private Arbitration of Public Law Disputes*, 1995 U. Ill. L. R. 635, 639.

2.   As a practical matter, the *Cole* decision resolved the problem of forum fees. Those who impose arbitration upon employees, consumers, and others almost always pay the costs of the arbitral forum. No circuit court has reached a conclusion contrary to the D.C. Circuit's in *Cole*, and it is unlikely the issue will be presented with the issue in the future.

3.   We will revisit the holding in *Cole* after you read the next case.

GREEN TREE FINANCIAL CORP. V. RANDOLPH

Supreme Court of the United States, 2000
531 U.S. 79, 121 S.Ct. 513, 148 L.Ed.2d 373

CHIEF JUSTICE REHNQUIST delivered the opinion of the Court.

In this case we first address whether an order compelling arbitration and dismissing a party's underlying claims is a "final decision with respect to an arbitration" within the meaning of § 16(a)(3) of the Federal Arbitration Act, 9 U.S.C. § 16(a)(3), and thus is immediately appealable pursuant to that Act. Because we decide that question in the affirmative, we also address the question whether an arbitration agreement that does not mention arbitration costs and fees is unenforceable because it fails to affirmatively protect a party from potentially steep arbitration costs. We conclude that an arbitration agreement's silence with respect to such matters does not render the agreement unenforceable.

I

Respondent Larketta Randolph purchased a mobile home from Better Cents Home Builders, Inc., in Opelika, Alabama. She financed this purchase through petitioners Green Tree Financial Corporation and its wholly owned subsidiary, Green Tree Financial Corp.—Alabama. Petitioners' Manufactured Home Retail Installment Contract and Security Agreement required that Randolph buy Vendor's Single Interest insurance, which protects the vendor or lienholder against the costs of repossession in the event of default. The agreement also provided that all disputes arising from, or relating to, the contract, whether arising under case law or statutory law, would be resolved by binding arbitration.

Randolph later sued petitioners, alleging that they violated the Truth in Lending Act (TILA), 15 U.S.C. § 1601 *et seq.,* by failing to disclose as a finance charge the Vendor's Single Interest insurance requirement. She later amended her complaint to add a claim that petitioners violated the Equal Credit Opportunity Act, 15 U.S.C. §§ 1691—1691f, by requiring her to arbitrate her statutory causes of action. She brought this action on behalf of a similarly situated class. In lieu of an answer, petitioners filed a motion to compel arbitration, to stay the action, or, in the alternative, to dismiss. The District Court granted petitioners' motion to compel arbitration, denied the motion to stay, and dismissed Randolph's claims with prejudice. The District Court also denied her request to certify a class. She requested reconsideration, asserting that she lacked the resources to arbitrate, and as a result, would have to forgo her claims against petitioners. The District Court denied reconsideration. Randolph appealed.

The Court of Appeals for the Eleventh Circuit first held that it had jurisdiction to review the District Court's order because that order was a final decision. The Court of Appeals looked to § 16 of the Federal Arbitration Act (FAA), which governs appeal from a district court's arbitration order, and specifically § 16(a)(3), which allows appeal from "a final decision with respect to an arbitration that is subject to this title." The court determined that a final, appealable order within the meaning of the FAA is one that disposes of all the issues framed by the litigation, leaving nothing to be done but execute the order. The Court of Appeals found the District Court's order within that definition.

The court then determined that the arbitration agreement failed to provide the minimum guarantees that respondent could vindicate her statutory rights under the TILA. Critical to this determination was the court's observation that the arbitration agreement was silent with respect to payment of filing fees, arbitrators' costs, and other arbitration expenses. On that basis, the court held that the agreement to arbitrate posed a risk that respondent's ability to vindicate her statutory rights would be undone by "steep" arbitration costs, and therefore was unenforceable. We granted certiorari, and we now affirm the Court of Appeals with respect to the first conclusion, and reverse it with respect to the second.

II

* * *

The District Court's order directed that the dispute be resolved by arbitration and dismissed respondent's claims with prejudice, leaving the court nothing to do but execute the judgment. That order plainly disposed of the entire case on the merits and left no part of it pending before the court. The FAA does permit parties to arbitration agreements to bring a separate proceeding in a district court to enter judgment on an arbitration award once it is made (or to vacate or modify it), but the existence of that remedy does not vitiate the finality of the District Court's resolution of the claims in the instant proceeding. The District Court's order was therefore "a final decision with respect to an arbitration" within the meaning of § 16(a)(3), and an appeal may be taken.

* * *

III

We now turn to the question whether Randolph's agreement to arbitrate is unenforceable because it says nothing about the costs of arbitration, and thus fails to provide her protection from potentially substantial costs of pursuing her federal statutory claims in the arbitral forum. Section 2 of the FAA provides that "[a] written provision in any maritime transaction or a contract evidencing a transaction involving commerce to settle by arbitration a controversy thereafter arising out of such contract . . . shall be valid, irrevocable, and enforceable, save upon such grounds as exist at law or in equity for the revocation of any contract." In considering whether respondent's agreement to arbitrate is unenforceable, we are mindful of the FAA's purpose "to reverse the longstanding judicial hostility to arbitration agreements . . . and to place arbitration agreements upon the same footing as other contracts."

In light of that purpose, we have recognized that federal statutory claims can be appropriately resolved through arbitration, and we have enforced agreements to arbitrate that involve such claims. We have likewise rejected generalized attacks on arbitration that rest on "suspicion of arbitration as a method of weakening the protections afforded in the substantive law to would-be complainants." These cases demonstrate that even claims arising under a statute designed to further important social policies may be arbitrated because " 'so long as the prospective litigant effectively may vindicate [his or her] statutory cause of action in the arbitral forum,' " the statute serves its functions.

In determining whether statutory claims may be arbitrated, we first ask whether the parties agreed to submit their claims to arbitration, and then ask whether Congress has evinced an intention to preclude a waiver of judicial remedies for the statutory rights at issue. In this case, it is undisputed that the parties agreed to arbitrate all claims relating to their contract, including claims involving statutory rights. Nor does Randolph contend that the TILA evinces an intention to preclude a waiver of judicial remedies. She contends instead that the arbitration agreement's silence with respect to costs and fees creates a "risk" that she will be required to bear prohibitive arbitration costs if she pursues her claims in an arbitral forum, and thereby forces her to forgo any claims she may have against petitioners. Therefore, she argues, she is unable to vindicate her statutory rights in arbitration.

It may well be that the existence of large arbitration costs could preclude a litigant such as Randolph from effectively vindicating her federal statutory rights in the arbitral forum. But the record does not show that Randolph will bear such costs if she goes to arbitration. Indeed, it contains hardly any information on the matter. As the Court of Appeals recognized, "we lack ... information about how claimants fare under Green Tree's arbitration clause." The record reveals only the arbitration agreement's silence on the subject, and that fact alone is plainly insufficient to render it unenforceable. The "risk" that Randolph will be saddled with prohibitive costs is too speculative to justify the invalidation of an arbitration agreement.

To invalidate the agreement on that basis would undermine the "liberal federal policy favoring arbitration agreements." It would also conflict with our prior holdings that the party resisting arbitration bears the burden of proving that the claims at issue are unsuitable for arbitration. We have held that the party seeking to avoid arbitration bears the burden of establishing that Congress intended to preclude arbitration of the statutory claims at issue. Similarly, we believe that where, as here, a party seeks to invalidate an arbitration agreement on the ground that arbitration would be prohibitively expensive, that party bears the burden of showing the likelihood of incurring such costs. Randolph did not meet that burden. How detailed the showing of prohibitive expense must be before the party seeking arbitration must come forward with contrary evidence is a matter we need not discuss; for in this case neither during discovery nor when the case was presented on the merits was there any timely showing at all on the point. The Court of

Appeals therefore erred in deciding that the arbitration agreement's silence with respect to costs and fees rendered it unenforceable.

The judgment of the Court of Appeals is affirmed in part and reversed in part.

It is so ordered.

JUSTICE GINSBURG, with whom JUSTICE STEVENS and JUSTICE SOUTER join, and with whom JUSTICE BREYER joins as to Parts I and III, concurring in part and dissenting in part.

I

I join Part II of the Court's opinion, which holds that the District Court's order, dismissing all the claims before it, was a "final," and therefore immediately appealable, decision. *Ante,* at 4–8. On the matter the Court airs in Part III, *ante,* at 8–12—allocation of the costs of arbitration—I would not rule definitively. Instead, I would vacate the Eleventh Circuit's decision, which dispositively declared the arbitration clause unenforceable, and remand the case for closer consideration of the arbitral forum's accessibility.

II

The Court today deals with a "who pays" question, specifically, who pays for the arbitral forum. The Court holds that Larketta Randolph bears the burden of demonstrating that the arbitral forum is financially inaccessible to her. Essentially, the Court requires a party, situated as Randolph is, either to submit to arbitration without knowing who will pay for the forum or to demonstrate up front that the costs, if imposed on her, will be prohibitive. As I see it, the case in its current posture is not ripe for such a disposition.

The Court recognizes that "the existence of large arbitration costs could preclude a litigant such as Randolph from effectively vindicating her federal statutory rights in the arbitral forum." But, the Court next determines, "the party resisting arbitration bears the burden of proving that the claims at issue are unsuitable for arbitration" and "Randolph did not meet that burden." In so ruling, the Court blends two discrete inquiries: First, is the arbitral forum *adequate* to adjudicate the claims at issue; second, is that forum *accessible* to the party resisting arbitration.

Our past decisions deal with the first question, the *adequacy* of the arbitral forum to adjudicate various statutory claims. These decisions hold that the party resisting arbitration bears the burden of establishing the inadequacy of the arbitral forum for adjudication of claims of a particular genre. It does not follow like the night the day, however, that the party resisting arbitration should also bear the burden of showing that the arbitral forum would be financially inaccessible to her.

The arbitration agreement at issue is contained in a form contract drawn by a commercial party and presented to an individual consumer on a take-it-or-leave-it basis. The case on which the Court dominantly relies, *Gilmer,* also involved a nonnegotiated arbitration clause. But the "who pays" question presented in this case did not arise in *Gilmer.* Under the rules that governed in *Gilmer*—those of the New York Stock Exchange—it was the standard practice for securities industry parties, arbitrating employment disputes, to pay all of the arbitrators' fees. Regarding that practice, the Court of Appeals for the District of Columbia Circuit recently commented:

> In *Gilmer,* the Supreme Court endorsed a system of arbitration in which employees are not required to pay for the arbitrator assigned to hear their statutory claims. There is no reason to think that the Court would have approved arbitration in the absence of this arrangement. Indeed, we are unaware of any situation in American jurisprudence in which a beneficiary of a federal statute has been required to pay for the services of the judge assigned to hear her or his case.

Id. at 1484.

III

The form contract in this case provides no indication of the rules under which arbitration will proceed or the costs a consumer is likely to incur in arbitration. Green Tree, drafter of the contract, could have filled the void by specifying, for instance, that arbitration would be governed by the rules of the American Arbitration Association (AAA). Under the AAA's Consumer Arbitration Rules, consumers in small-claims arbitration incur no filing fee and pay only $125 of the total fees charged by the arbitrator. All other fees and costs are to be paid by the business party. Other national arbitration organizations have developed similar models for fair cost and fee allocation. It may be that in this case, as in *Gilmer*, there is a standard practice on arbitrators' fees and expenses, one that fills the blank space in the arbitration agreement. Counsel for Green Tree offered a hint in that direction. ("Green Tree does pay [arbitration] costs in a lot of instances. . . ."). But there is no reliable indication in this record that Randolph's claim will be arbitrated under any consumer-protective fee arrangement.

As a repeat player in the arbitration required by its form contract, Green Tree has superior information about the cost to consumers of pursuing arbitration. In these circumstances, it is hardly clear that Randolph should bear the burden of demonstrating up front the arbitral forum's inaccessibility, or that she should be required to submit to arbitration without knowing how much it will cost her.

As I see it, the Court has reached out prematurely to resolve the matter in the lender's favor. If Green Tree's practice under the form contract with retail installment sales purchasers resembles that of the employer in *Gilmer,* Randolph would be insulated from prohibitive costs. And if the arbitral forum were in this case financially accessible to Randolph, there would be no occasion to reach the decision today rendered by the Court. Before writing a term into the form contract, as the District of Columbia Circuit did, see *Cole,* 105 F.3d, at 1485, or leaving cost allocation initially to each arbitrator, as the Court does, I would remand for clarification of Green Tree's practice.

The Court's opinion, if I comprehend it correctly, does not prevent Randolph from returning to court, postarbitration, if she then has a complaint about cost allocation. If that is so, the issue reduces to when, not whether, she can be spared from payment of excessive costs. Neither certainty nor judicial economy is served by leaving that issue unsettled until the end of the line.

For the reasons stated, I dissent from the Court's reversal of the Eleventh Circuit's decision on the cost question. I would instead vacate and remand for further consideration of the accessibility of the arbitral forum to Randolph.

NOTES AND QUESTIONS

1.   Does the decision of the Supreme Court in *Green Tree Financial Corp.* cast doubt on the *Cole* opinion and Professor Gorman's argument for development by the courts of a code of due process for public law arbitration?

2.   An important question is whether an arbitration clause can be used to defeat a class action. Those who try to use arbitration clauses to defeat class actions assert that class actions are used to extort settlements from innocent defendants. They argue that arbitration cases must proceed individually and they sometimes draft arbitration clauses that specifically prohibit class actions. Employee and consumer advocates point out that many claimants lack the resources to pursue individual claims and that allowing arbitration to defeat class actions will allow defendants guilty of illegal conduct to defeat valid claims. These advocates argue for allowing class actions in arbitration and against foreclosing class actions when defendants have succeeded in inserting an arbitration clause in their contract with the claimant. This issue is treated more fully *infra,* at 698. See generally Jean R. Sternlight, *As Mandatory Binding Arbitration Meets the Class Action, Will the Class Action Survive?,* 42 Wm. & Mary L. Rev. 1, 78 (2000).

3.   Does the cost issue make you more reticent about *Gilmer?* Choose one of the positions described below and be prepared to defend your position in class.

(a) *Gilmer* should be overturned by the U.S. Supreme Court or by an amendment to the FAA.

(b) The FAA should be amended to:

(1) prohibit enforcement of pre-dispute arbitration agreements that employees are required to accept in order to obtain a job; or

(2) prohibit companies from using arbitration clauses to preclude class actions; or

(3) require arbitrators to prepare a written opinion giving reasons for their award when cases turn on the interpretation and application of federal statutes; or *specifically authorize,*

(4) de novo review of arbitral interpretations of federal statutes.

(c) There is no need to amend the FAA. However, the courts should develop a code of due process for public law arbitration on a case by case basis.

See Thomas J. Stipanowich, *Contract and Conflict Management*, 2001 Wisc. L. Rev. 831, 909–916, for discussion of some of the issues underlying these choices.

b. '. . . Save Upon Such Grounds as Exist in Law and Equity for the Revocation of Any Other Contract.'

Section 2's savings clause assures that arbitration agreements are subject to standard contractual formation defenses, just like any other contract. In this subsection, we review how the U.S. Supreme Court has treated such defense.

1. Fraud

In the arbitrability section of this chapter, we introduced you to the so-called "separability doctrine" of *Prima Paint*, see *infra* p. 582, and we strongly encourage you to review that case and the notes that follow as the starting point for your consideration of defenses to the enforcement of an agreement to arbitrate.

As you recall, the doctrine calls for the arbitration provision in a larger contract—such as the sale of a house—to be treated as a presumptively valid contract that is separate from the larger contract. The implications of this treatment are significant because Sections 3 and 4 of the Federal Arbitration Act require a court to enforce an agreement to arbitrate when the court is satisfied that an agreement to arbitrate has been made—and *Prima Paint* construed that to mean the arbitration provision itself, not the larger substantive contract. Under the separability doctrine, the agreement to the arbitration provision is presumptively valid merely by virtue of entering into the larger contract. *Prima Paint* thus allocates to the courts the question of whether the arbitration provision is valid (which it presumptively is), and the allocates to the arbitrator the question of whether the larger agreement is valid (assuming the arbitration provision is a typical broad arbitration clause submitting all disputes under the agreement to the arbitrator).

The facts in *Prima Paint* illustrate the point well. The case involved a contract between a contractor and a paint manufacturer that the contractor alleged was fraudulently induced. Applying the doctrine of separability, the Supreme Court said the consultant's fraud allegation was for the arbitrator to decide because the contract's arbitration provision was a separate contract that was presumptively valid, and because the arbitration clause called for all disputes under the brokerage agreement to be decided by arbitration—including the question of whether the consulting agreement had been fraudulently induced.

As you might suspect, the way this plays out in the real world is that most fraud cases in contracts with arbitration provisions are decided by arbitrators because most of them are directed at the larger substantive contract, rather than the narrow arbitration provision. Further, since separability assumes the arbitration provision is a separate and valid contract, the only time courts will decide fraud challenges is when the allegation is that the arbitration provision itself was fraudulently induced. This of course is possible, but uncommon because in most situations the fraud is directed at the larger contract—that is, the substantive subject of the agreement.

2. *Unconscionability*

Perhaps the most common defense associated with arbitration provisions is that of unconscionability—that the provision is substantively and procedurally too one-sided or unfair to be enforced by a court of law as a matter of policy. Courts will generally require a fact-intensive showing that an arbitration provision is both substantively and procedurally unconscionable before striking it down. *See generally Graham v. Scissor–Tail, Inc.,* 28 Cal. 3rd 807 (1981) and *Armendariz v. Foundation Health Psychcare Services, Inc.,* 24 Cal.4th 83 (2000).

Procedural unconscionability is commonly shown by demonstrating that the provision is oppressive in that there was no meaningful opportunity to turn it down, such as its inclusion in a standard form contract that is offered on a "take it or leave it" basis. Procedural unconscionability can also be shown by establishing surprise, such as the placement of the arbitration provision in an obscure part of the larger contract between the parties. Substantive arbitrability can be established by showing an arbitration provision is too one-sided, overly harsh, shocks the conscience, or in some cases, frustrates the reasonable expectations of the parties. Clauses most likely to be found substantively unconscionable include those that impose a biased arbitrator, excessive costs, limit remedies, and treat the parties disparately, or use a combination of these techniques. *See generally* IAN R. MACNEIL, RICHARD E. SPEIDEL & THOMAS

J. STIPANOWICH, FEDERAL ARBITRATION LAW § 19.3 (1994 ed and Supp. 1999).

In recent years, the courts have become more receptive to claims that mandatory arbitration provisions are unconscionable and therefore unenforceable, although many such claims are still unsuccessful. For a discussion with extensive case citations, see F. PAUL BLAND JR. ET AL., NATIONAL CONSUMER LAW CENTER, CONSUMER ARBITRATION AGREEMENTS §§ 4.1–4.4 (4th ed. 2005). In this Section, we look at unconscionability claims in the contexts of employment and consumer goods and services. All of the excerpted cases arise from mandatory arbitration situations, but it is certainly possible for unconscionability claims to be presented in situations in which there has been actual bilateral agreement to arbitration.

a) *In General*

CHAVARRIA V. RALPH'S GROCERY CO.

2013 WL 5779337 (CTA 9 Cal.)

Defendant Ralphs Grocery Company appeals the district court's denial of its motion to compel arbitration. Plaintiff Zenia Chavarria filed an action alleging violations of the California Labor Code and California Business and Professions Code §§ 17200 *et seq*. She asserted claims on behalf of herself and a proposed class of other Ralphs employees. Ralphs moved to compel arbitration of her individual claim pursuant to its arbitration policy, to which all employees acceded upon submitting applications for employment with Ralphs. The district court denied the motion, holding that Ralphs' arbitration policy was unconscionable under California law and therefore unenforceable.

[1] Ralphs argues that its policy is not unconscionable under California law and in the alternative that the Federal Arbitration Act ("FAA") preempts California law. The FAA provides that arbitration agreements must be enforced except "upon such grounds as exist at law or in equity for the revocation of any contract." The FAA preempts a contract defense, such as unconscionability, that may be generally applicable to any contract but disproportionately impacts arbitration agreements. *AT & T Mobility LLC v. Concepcion,* ___ U.S. ___, 131 S.Ct. 1740, 179 L.Ed.2d 742 (2011).

We affirm. We conclude that Ralphs' arbitration policy is unconscionable under California law, and that the state law supporting that conclusion is not preempted by the FAA.

I. Background

Plaintiff Zenia Chavarria completed an employment application seeking work with Defendant Ralphs Grocery Company. Chavarria obtained a position as a deli clerk with Ralphs and worked in that capacity for roughly six months. After leaving her employment with Ralphs, Chavarria filed this action, alleging on behalf of herself and all similarly situated employees that Ralphs violated various provisions of the California Labor Code and California Business and Professions Code §§ 17200 *et seq.* Ralphs moved to compel arbitration of her individual claim pursuant to an arbitration policy incorporated into the employment application. Chavarria opposed the motion, arguing that the arbitration agreement was unconscionable under California law.

By completing an employment application with Ralphs, all potential employees agree to be bound by Ralphs' arbitration policy. The application contains an acknowledgment that the terms of the mandatory and binding arbitration policy have been provided for the applicant's review. Ralphs' policy contains several provisions central to this appeal.

Paragraph 7 governs the selection of the single arbitrator who will decide the dispute. It provides that, unless the parties agree otherwise, the arbitrator must be a retired state or federal judge. It explicitly prohibits the use of an administrator from either the American Arbitration Association ("AAA") or the Judicial Arbitration and Mediation Service ("JAMS").

If the parties do not agree on an arbitrator, the policy provides for the following procedure:

> (1) Each party proposes a list of three arbitrators;
>
> (2) The parties alternate striking one name from the other party's list of arbitrators until only one name remains;
>
> (3) The party "who has not demanded arbitration" makes the first strike from the respective lists; and
>
> (4) The lone remaining arbitrator decides the claims.

In practice, the arbitrator selected through this process will invariably be one of the three candidates nominated by the party that did not demand arbitration.

Paragraph 10 concerns attorney and arbitration fees and costs. It specifies that each party must pay its own attorney fees, subject to a later claim for reimbursement under applicable law. The provision regarding arbitration fees, including the amount to be paid to the arbitrator, is more than a little convoluted. Ultimately, it provides that the arbitrator's fees must be apportioned at the outset of the arbitration and must be split evenly between Ralphs and the employee unless a decision of the U.S. Supreme Court directly addressing the issue requires that they be apportioned differently.

Paragraph 13 of the policy permits Ralphs to unilaterally modify the policy without notice to the employee. The employee's continued employment constitutes acceptance of any modification.

* * *

II. Discussion

Ralphs argues that the district court erred when it held that the arbitration policy was unconscionable under California law. Ralphs also contends that federal law requires that the policy be enforced in accordance with its terms, even if the policy is unconscionable under California law, and that therefore the district court was required to compel arbitration. We review de novo the denial of a motion to compel arbitration.

The FAA provides that any contract to settle a dispute by arbitration shall be valid and enforceable, "save upon such grounds as exist at law or in equity for the revocation of any contract." This provision reflects both that (a) arbitration is fundamentally a matter of contract, and (b) Congress expressed a "liberal federal policy favoring arbitration." Arbitration agreements, therefore, must be placed on equal footing with other contracts.

Like other contracts, arbitration agreements can be invalidated for fraud, duress, or unconscionability. A defense such as unconscionability, however, cannot justify invalidating an arbitration agreement if the defense applies "only to arbitration or [derives its] meaning from the fact that an agreement to arbitrate is at issue." The U.S. Supreme Court has held that state rules disproportionately impacting arbitration, though generally applicable to contracts of all types, are nonetheless preempted by the FAA when the rule stands as an obstacle to the accomplishment of Congress's objectives in enacting the FAA.

No single rule of unconscionability uniquely applicable to arbitration is at issue in this case. We must therefore apply California's general principle of contract unconscionability. * * *

A. Unconscionability under California Law

Under California law, a contract must be both procedurally and substantively unconscionable to be rendered invalid. California law utilizes a sliding scale to determine unconscionability—greater substantive unconscionability may compensate for lesser procedural unconscionability. Applying California law, the district court held that the arbitration agreement in this case was both procedurally unconscionable and substantively unconscionable. We agree.

1. Procedural Unconscionability

Procedural unconscionability concerns the manner in which the contract was negotiated and the respective circumstances of the parties at that time, focusing on the level of oppression and surprise involved in the agreement. Oppression addresses the weaker party's absence of choice and unequal bargaining power that results in "no real negotiation." Surprise involves the extent to which the contract clearly discloses its terms as well as the reasonable expectations of the weaker party.

The district court held that Ralphs' arbitration policy was procedurally unconscionable for several reasons. The court found that agreeing to Ralphs' policy was a condition of applying for employment and that the policy was presented on a "take it or leave it" basis with no opportunity for Chavarria to negotiate its terms. It further found that the terms of the policy were not provided to Chavarria until three weeks after she had agreed to be bound by it. This additional defect, the court held, multiplied the degree of procedural unconscionability.

Ralphs argues that the policy is not procedurally unconscionable because Chavarria was not even required to agree to its terms. Ralphs bases this contention on a provision in the employment application that provides, "Please sign and date the employment application . . . to acknowledge you have read, understand & agree to the following statements." The word "please," Ralphs contends, belies any suggestion of a requirement. Ralphs argues that Chavarria could have been hired without signing the agreement.

Ralphs' argument ignores the terms of the policy itself, which bound Chavarria regardless of whether she signed the application. The policy provides that "[n]o signature by an Employee or the Company is required for this Arbitration Policy to apply to Covered Disputes." That Ralphs asked nicely for a signature is irrelevant. The policy bound Chavarria and all other potential employees upon submission of their applications.

These circumstances are similar to others where we have held agreements to be procedurally unconscionable. . . . [We have] held that an arbitration agreement was procedurally unconscionable under California law because it was imposed upon employees as a condition of their continued employment. We explained, "where . . . the employee is facing an employer with 'overwhelming bargaining power' who 'drafted the contract and presented it to [the employee] on a take-it-or-leave-it basis,' the clause is procedurally unconscionable." Likewise . . . we held that "a contract is procedurally unconscionable under California law if it is 'a standardized contract, drafted by the party of superior bargaining strength, that relegates to the subscribing party only the opportunity to adhere to the contract or reject it.' "Chavarria could only agree to be bound by the policy or seek work elsewhere. Ralphs' policy meets the standard under which we have previously found arbitration provisions in employment contracts to be procedurally unconscionable.

Further, we have held that the degree of procedural unconscionability is enhanced when a contract binds an individual to later-provided terms. Ralphs did not provide Chavarria the terms of the arbitration policy until her employment orientation, three weeks after the policy came into effect regarding any dispute related to her employment. The employment application merely contains a one-paragraph "notice" of the policy. The policy itself is a four-page, single-spaced document with several complex terms. Ralphs' arbitration policy fits squarely within these decisions, so the district court did not err when it held that the policy was procedurally unconscionable.

2. Substantive Unconscionability

Chavarria must also demonstrate that Ralphs' arbitration policy is substantively unconscionable under California law. A contract is substantively unconscionable when it is unjustifiably one-sided to such an extent that it "shocks the conscience."

The district court found that several terms rendered Ralphs' arbitration policy substantively unconscionable. First, the court noted that Ralphs' arbitrator selection provision would always produce an arbitrator proposed by Ralphs in employee-initiated arbitration proceedings. Second, the court cited the preclusion of institutional arbitration administrators, namely AAA or JAMS, which have established rules and procedures to select a neutral arbitrator. Third, the court was troubled by the policy's requirement that the arbitrator must, at the outset of the arbitration proceedings, apportion the arbitrator's fees between Ralphs and the employee regardless of the merits of the claim. The court identified this provision as "a model of how employers can draft fee provisions to price almost any employee out of the dispute resolution process." The combination of these terms created a policy, according to the court, that "lacks any semblance of fairness and eviscerates the right to seek civil redress. . . . To condone such a policy would be a disservice to the legitimate practice of arbitration and a stain on the credibility of our justice system."

Ralphs contests the district court's conclusion and argues that the policy is not unconscionable. Indeed, Ralphs goes a step further and argues that the provisions relied upon by the district court actually disadvantage Ralphs and are intended to benefit the employee. Ralphs' strained construction of its policy is unpersuasive. In fact, the policy includes further provisions that add to its unconscionability.

Regarding the arbitrator selection provision, Ralphs does not deny that its policy precludes the selection of an arbitrator proposed by the party demanding arbitration. Nor does it deny that the party selecting the arbitrator gains an advantage in subsequent proceedings. . . . Ralphs simply argues that it won't always be the party that is guaranteed an arbitrator of its choosing.

In particular, Ralphs argues that the district court erred in assuming that an employee will always be the party that demands arbitration. Ralphs contends that the opposite is true. In Ralphs' view, Chavarria, the employee in this case, will wind up with an arbitrator of her choosing because it is Ralphs that demanded arbitration. Ralphs' logic is thus:

(1) Chavarria brought a claim in federal court;

(2) Ralphs filed a motion to compel arbitration;

(3) If the court grants the motion, then the case will go to arbitration; and

(4) Ralphs will have "demanded" arbitration and thereby relinquished the first strike to Chavarria.

Chavarria will, under Ralphs' scenario, strike all three of the arbitrators on Ralphs' list, and the last remaining arbitrator will necessarily be from Chavarria's list.

It doesn't take a close examination of Ralphs' argument to reveal its flaws. To begin with, Ralphs' argument invites an employee to disregard the arbitration policy and to file a lawsuit in court, knowing that the claim is subject to arbitration. Even if Ralphs is willing to waste its time and money for that detour, it is not one that makes any sense for the court. We cannot endorse an interpretation that encourages the filing of an unnecessary lawsuit simply to gain some advantage in subsequent arbitration.

* * *

Even if it were the case that Ralphs' policy does not guarantee that Ralphs will always be the party with the final selection, the selection process is not one designed to produce a true neutral in any individual case. As noted above, Ralphs has not argued that the selection process is fair, acknowledging that the process "disadvantages the party seeking arbitration." Ralphs simply argues that sometimes the process may work to its disadvantage. But that is no consolation to the individual employee who is disadvantaged in her one and only claim. * * *

Ralphs also argues that there is nothing of concern in its cost allocation provision because it simply follows the "American Rule" that each party shall bear its own fees and costs. Ralphs misses the point. The troubling aspect of the cost allocation provision relates to the arbitrator fees, not attorney fees.

The policy mandates that the arbitrator apportion those costs on the parties up front, before resolving the merits of the claims. Further,

Ralphs has designed a system that requires the arbitrator to apportion the costs equally between Ralphs and the employee, disregarding any potential state law that contradicts Ralphs' cost allocation. . . . There is no justification to ignore a state cost-shifting provision, except to impose upon the employee a potentially prohibitive obstacle to having her claim heard. Ralphs' policy imposes great costs on the employee and precludes the employee from recovering those costs, making many claims impracticable.

The significance of this obstacle becomes more apparent through Ralphs' representation to the district court that the fees for a qualified arbitrator under its policy would range from $7,000 to $14,000 per day. Ralphs' policy requires that an employee pay half of that amount—$3,500 to $7,000—for each day of the arbitration just to pay for her share of the arbitrator's fee. This cost likely dwarfs the amount of Chavarria's claims.

The specific allocation of costs distinguishes this arbitration agreement from the provision we [previously] upheld. In that case, plaintiffs asserted only two arguments supporting unconscionability: (1) that a class waiver provision was unconscionable under California law; and (2) that students may not be able to afford arbitration fees. The first argument was expressly foreclosed by the U.S. Supreme Court in *Concepcion*. We rejected the second argument because the Court has held that the mere risk that a plaintiff will face prohibitive costs is too speculative to justify invalidating an arbitration agreement. But in this case, not only does the cost provision stand beside other unconscionable terms, there is nothing speculative about it. Ralphs' term requires that the arbitrator impose significant costs on the employee up front, regardless of the merits of the employee's claims, and severely limits the authority of the arbitrator to allocate arbitration costs in the award.

* * *

3. The Sliding Scale of Unconscionability

Excessive procedural or substantive unconscionability may compensate for lesser unconscionability in the other prong. But here we have both. Ralphs has tilted the scale so far in its favor, both in the circumstances of entering the agreement and its substantive terms, that it "shocks the conscience." Accordingly, Ralphs' arbitration policy cannot be enforced against Chavarria under California law.

B. Preemption by the FAA

Federal law preempts state laws that stand as an obstacle to the accomplishment of Congress's objectives. *Concepcion*. Accordingly, the FAA preempts state laws that in theory apply to contracts generally but in practice impact arbitration agreements disproportionately.

California's unconscionability doctrine applies to all contracts generally and therefore constitutes "such grounds at law or in equity for the revocation of [a] contract." But specific application of rules within that doctrine may be problematic. *Concepcion.*

In this case, California's procedural unconscionability rules do not disproportionately affect arbitration agreements, for they focus on the parties and the circumstances of the agreement and apply equally to the formation of all contracts. The application of California's general substantive unconscionability rules to Ralphs' arbitration policy, however, warrants more discussion.

The Supreme Court's recent decision in *American Express Corp. v. Italian Colors Restaurant,* ___ U.S. ___, 133 S.Ct. 2304, 186 L.Ed.2d 417 (2013), does not preclude us from considering the cost that Ralphs' arbitration agreement imposes on employees in order for them to bring a claim. In that case, plaintiffs argued that the class waiver term of the arbitration agreement at issue effectively foreclosed vindication of the plaintiffs' federal rights: specifically, their rights under the Sherman Antitrust Act. Plaintiffs could not pursue their antitrust claims, they argued, because the experts required to prove an antitrust claim would cost hundreds of thousands of dollars, while the individual recovery would not exceed $40,000. The class waiver provision did not foreclose effective vindication of that right, the Court reasoned, because "the fact that it is not worth the expense involved in *proving* a statutory remedy does not constitute an elimination of the *right to pursue* that remedy." The Court explicitly noted that the result might be different if an arbitration provision required a plaintiff to pay "filing and administrative fees attached to arbitration that are so high as to make access to the forum impracticable."

Ralphs' arbitration policy presents exactly that situation. In this case, administrative and filing costs, even disregarding the cost to prove the merits, effectively foreclose pursuit of the claim. Ralphs has constructed an arbitration system that imposes non-recoverable costs on employees just to get in the door.

The Supreme Court's holding that the FAA preempts state laws having a "disproportionate impact" on arbitration cannot be read to immunize all arbitration agreements from invalidation no matter how unconscionable they may be, so long as they invoke the shield of arbitration. Our court has recently explained the nuance: "*Concepcion* outlaws discrimination in state policy that is *unfavorable* to arbitration." * * *

This case illustrates the distinction. In addition to the problematic cost provision, Ralphs' arbitration policy contains a provision that unilaterally assigns one party (almost always Ralphs, in our view, as explained above) the power to select the arbitrator whenever an employee brings a claim. Of course, any state law that invalidated this provision would have a disproportionate impact on arbitration because the term is arbitration specific. But viewed another way, invalidation of this term is agnostic towards arbitration. It does not disfavor arbitration; it provides that the arbitration process must be fair.

If state law could not require some level of fairness in an arbitration agreement, there would be nothing to stop an employer from imposing an arbitration clause that, for example, made its own president the arbitrator of all claims brought by its employees. Federal law favoring arbitration is not a license to tilt the arbitration process in favor of the party with more bargaining power. California law regarding unconscionable contracts, as applied in this case, is not unfavorable towards arbitration, but instead reflects a generally applicable policy against abuses of bargaining power. The FAA does not preempt its invalidation of Ralphs' arbitration policy.

b) *Consumer Goods and Services*

HILL v. GATEWAY 2000, INC.

United States Court of Appeals, Seventh Circuit, 1997
105 F.3d 1147

EASTERBROOK, CIRCUIT JUDGE.

A customer picks up the phone, orders a computer, and gives a credit card number. Presently a box arrives, containing the computer and a list of terms, said to govern unless the customer returns the computer within 30 days. Are these terms effective as the parties' contract, or is the contract term-free because the order-taker did not read any terms over the phone and elicit the customer's assent?

One of the terms in the box containing a Gateway 2000 system was an arbitration clause. Rich and Enza Hill, the customers, kept the computer more than 30 days before complaining about its components and performance. They filed suit in federal court arguing, among other things, that the product's shortcomings make Gateway a racketeer (mail and wire fraud are said to be the predicate offenses), leading to treble damages under RICO for the Hills and a class of all other purchasers. Gateway asked the district court to enforce the arbitration clause; the judge refused, writing that "[t]he present record is insufficient to support a finding of a valid arbitration agreement between the parties or that the plaintiffs were given adequate notice of the arbitration clause." Gateway took an immediate appeal, as is its right.

The Hills say that the arbitration clause did not stand out: they concede noticing the statement of terms but deny reading it closely enough to discover the agreement to arbitrate, and they ask us to conclude that they therefore may go to court. Yet an agreement to arbitrate must be enforced "save upon such grounds as exist at law or in equity for the revocation of any contract." 9 U.S.C. § 2. *Doctor's Associates, Inc. v. Casarotto* holds that this provision of the Federal Arbitration Act is inconsistent with any requirement that an arbitration clause be prominent. A contract need not be read to be effective; people who accept take the risk that the unread terms may in retrospect prove unwelcome. Terms inside Gateway's box stand or fall together. If they constitute the parties' contract because the Hills had an opportunity to return the computer after reading them, then all must be enforced.

ProCD, Inc. v. Zeidenberg holds that terms inside a box of software bind consumers who use the software after an opportunity to read the terms and to reject them by returning the product. Likewise, *Carnival Cruise Lines, Inc. v. Shute* enforces a forum-selection clause that was included among three pages of terms attached to a cruise ship ticket. *ProCD* and *Carnival Cruise Lines* exemplify the many commercial transactions in which people pay for products with terms to follow; *ProCD* discusses others. The district court concluded in *ProCD* that the contract is formed when the consumer pays for the software; as a result, the court held, only terms known to the consumer at that moment are part of the contract, and provisos inside the box do not count. Although this is one way a contract could be formed, it is not the only way: "A vendor, as master of the offer, may invite acceptance by conduct, and may propose limitations on the kind of conduct that constitutes acceptance. A buyer may accept by performing the acts the vendor proposes to treat as acceptance." Gateway shipped computers with the same sort of accept-or-return offer ProCD made to users of its software. *ProCD* relied on the Uniform Commercial Code rather than any peculiarities of Wisconsin law; both Illinois and South Dakota, the two states whose law might govern relations between Gateway and the Hills, have adopted the UCC; neither side has pointed us to any atypical doctrines in those states that might be pertinent; *ProCD* therefore applies to this dispute.

Plaintiffs ask us to limit *ProCD* to software, but where's the sense in that? *ProCD* is about the law of contract, not the law of software. Payment preceding the revelation of full terms is common for air transportation, insurance, and many other endeavors. Practical considerations support allowing vendors to enclose the full legal terms with their products. Cashiers cannot be expected to read legal documents to customers before ringing up sales. If the staff at the other end of the phone for direct-sales operations such as Gateway's had to read the four-page statement of terms before taking the buyer's credit card number, the droning voice would anesthetize rather than enlighten many potential buyers. Others would hang up in a rage over the waste of their time. And oral recitation would not avoid customers' assertions (whether true or feigned) that the clerk did not read term X to them, or that they did not remember or understand it. Writing provides benefits for both sides of commercial transactions. Customers as a group are better off when vendors skip costly and ineffectual steps such as telephonic recitation, and use instead a simple approve-or-return device. Competent adults are bound by such documents, read or unread. For what little it is worth, we add that the box from Gateway was crammed with software. The computer came with an operating system, without which it was useful only as a boat anchor. Gateway also included many application programs. So the Hills' effort to limit *ProCD* to software would not avail them factually, even if it were sound legally—which it is not.

For their second sally, the Hills contend that ProCD should be limited to executory contracts (to licenses in particular), and therefore does not apply because both parties' performance of this contract was complete when the box arrived at their home. This is legally and factually wrong: legally because the question at hand concerns the *formation* of the contract rather than its *performance*, and factually because both contracts were incompletely performed. *ProCD* did not depend on the fact that the seller characterized the transaction as a license rather than as a contract; we treated it as a contract for the sale of goods and reserved the question whether for other purposes a "license" characterization might be preferable. All debates about characterization to one side, the transaction in *ProCD* was no more executory than the one here: Zeidenberg paid for the software and walked out of the store with a box under his arm, so if arrival of the box with the product ends the time for revelation of contractual terms, then the time ended in *ProCD* before Zeidenberg opened the box. But of course ProCD had not completed performance with delivery of the box, and neither had Gateway. One element of the transaction was the warranty, which obliges sellers to fix defects in their products. The Hills have invoked Gateway's warranty and are not satisfied with its response, so they are not well positioned to say that Gateway's obligations were fulfilled when the motor carrier unloaded the box. What is more, both ProCD and Gateway promised to help customers to use their products. Long-term service and information obligations are common in the computer business, on both hardware and software sides. Gateway offers "lifetime service" and has a round-the-clock telephone hotline to fulfill this promise. Some vendors spend more money helping customers use their products than on developing and manufacturing them. The document in Gateway's box includes promises of future performance that some consumers value highly; these promises bind Gateway just as the arbitration clause binds the Hills.

* * *

At oral argument the Hills propounded still another distinction: the box containing ProCD's software displayed a notice that additional terms were within, while the box containing Gateway's computer did not. The difference is functional, not legal. Consumers browsing the aisles of a store can look at the box, and if they are unwilling to deal with the prospect of additional terms can leave the box alone, avoiding the transactions costs of returning the package after reviewing its contents. Gateway's box, by contrast, is just a shipping carton; it is not on display anywhere. Its function is to protect the product during transit, and the information on its sides is for the use of handlers * * * rather than would-be purchasers.

Perhaps the Hills would have had a better argument if they were first alerted to the bundling of hardware and legal-ware after opening the box and wanted to return the computer in order to avoid disagreeable terms, but were dissuaded by the expense of shipping. What the remedy would be in such a case—could it exceed the shipping charges?—is an interesting question, but one that need not detain us because the Hills knew before they ordered the computer that the carton would include *some* important terms, and they did not seek to discover these in advance. Gateway's ads state that their products come with limited warranties and lifetime support. How limited was the warranty—30 days, with service contingent on shipping the computer back, or five years, with free onsite service? What sort of support was offered? Shoppers have three principal ways to discover these things. First, they can ask the vendor to send a copy before deciding whether to buy. The Magnuson–Moss Warranty Act requires firms to distribute their warranty terms on request; the Hills do not contend that Gateway would have refused to enclose the remaining terms too. Concealment would be bad for business, scaring some customers away and leading to excess returns from others. Second, shoppers can consult public sources (computer magazines, the Web sites of vendors) that may contain this information. Third, they may inspect the documents after the product's delivery. Like Zeidenberg, the Hills took the third option. By keeping the computer beyond 30 days, the Hills accepted Gateway's offer, including the arbitration clause.

The Hills' remaining arguments, including a contention that the arbitration clause is unenforceable as part of a scheme to defraud, do not require more than a citation to *Prima Paint Corp. v. Flood & Conklin Mfg. Co.* Whatever may be said pro and con about the cost and efficacy of arbitration (which the Hills disparage) is for Congress and the contracting parties to consider. Claims based on RICO are no less arbitrable than those founded on the contract or the law of torts. The decision of the district court is vacated, and this case is remanded with instructions to compel the Hills to submit their dispute to arbitration.

NOTES AND QUESTIONS

1.   What arguments would you make on behalf of the Hills?

2.   In Jean R. Sternlight, *Panacea or Corporate Tool? Debunking the Supreme Court's Preference for Binding Arbitration*, 74 Wash. U. L.Q. 637 (1996), Professor Sternlight argues at length that large companies can use arbitration clauses to take advantage of employees and consumers. *Id.* at 677–97. She says that, "(1) procedural factors influence and sometimes determine substantive outcomes; (2) the party that drafts an agreement will try to draft it so as to achieve maximum advantage for itself, which may well entail imposing disadvantage on the opposing party; and (3) competitors will neither prevent businesses from taking advantage of little guys nor insure that gains from lower liability exposure will be passed on to the little guys." *Id.* at 680. For an argument that employees should unionize to deal with the power imbalance, see Michael Z. Green, *Opposing Executive Use of Employer Bargaining Power in Mandatory Arbitration Agreements Through Collective Employee Actions*, 10 Tex. Wesleyan L.Rev. 77 (2003).

3. In response to concerns about mandatory consumer arbitration, the American Arbitration Association in 1997 created the National Consumer Dispute Advisory Committee to adapt the previously enacted Employment Due Process Protocols to the consumer context. As with the Employment Due Process Protocols, the Consumer Due Process Protocols are primarily procedural, and include such assurances as independent and impartial arbitrators, the right to counsel, adequate discovery, and reasonable costs, hearing locations, and time limits. After analyzing 301 AAA cases, Professor Christopher Drahozal and Samantha Zyontz concluded that the protocols were effective. They found that more than 76 percent of the consumer arbitration clauses in those cases complied with the standards, that AAA successfully identified nearly all of the non-complying clauses, that business frequently waived non-complying clauses, and that AAA refused to administer 9.4 percent of the 1378 consumer cases it docketed in 2007. See Christopher R. Drahozal and Samantha Zyontz, Private Regulation of Consumer Arbitration, 79 Tenn. L. Rev. 289 (2012). Do these results affect your views about the mandatory arbitration of consumer disputes?

3.   *General Duty of Good Faith and Fair Dealing*

HOOTERS OF AMERICA, INC. V. PHILLIPS

United States Court of Appeals, Fourth Circuit, 1999
173 F.3d 933

WILKINSON, CHIEF JUDGE:

Annette R. Phillips alleges that she was sexually harassed while working at a Hooters restaurant. After quitting her job, Phillips threatened to sue Hooters in court. Alleging that Phillips agreed to arbitrate employment-related disputes, Hooters preemptively filed suit to compel arbitration under the Federal Arbitration Act. Because Hooters set up a dispute resolution process utterly lacking in the rudiments of even-handedness, we hold that Hooters breached its agreement to arbitrate. Thus, we affirm the district court's refusal to compel arbitration.

I.

Appellee Annette R. Phillips worked as a bartender at a Hooters restaurant in Myrtle Beach, South Carolina. She was employed since 1989 by appellant Hooters of Myrtle Beach (HOMB), a franchisee of appellant Hooters of America (collectively Hooters).

Phillips alleges that in June 1996, Gerald Brooks, a Hooters official and the brother of HOMB's principal owner, sexually harassed her by grabbing and slapping her buttocks. After appealing to her manager for help and being told to "let it go," she quit her job. Phillips then contacted Hooters through an attorney claiming that the attack and the restaurant's failure to address it violated her Title VII rights. Hooters responded that she was required to submit her claims to arbitration according to a binding agreement to arbitrate between the parties.

This agreement arose in 1994 during the implementation of Hooters' alternative dispute resolution program. As part of that program, the company conditioned eligibility for raises, transfers, and promotions upon an employee signing an "Agreement to arbitrate employment-related disputes." The agreement provides that Hooters and the employee each agree to arbitrate all disputes arising out of employment, including "any claim of discrimination, sexual harassment, retaliation, or wrongful discharge, whether arising under federal or state law." The agreement further states that

> the employee and the company agree to resolve any claims pursuant to the company's rules and procedures for alternative resolution of employment-related disputes, as promulgated by the company from time to time ("the rules"). Company will make available or provide a copy of the rules upon written request of the employee.

The employees of HOMB were initially given a copy of this agreement at an all-staff meeting held on November 20, 1994. HOMB's general manager, Gene Fulcher, told the employees to review the agreement for five days and that they would then be asked to accept or reject the agreement. No employee, however, was given a copy of Hooters' arbitration rules and procedures. Phillips signed the agreement on November 25, 1994. When her personnel file was updated in April 1995, Phillips again signed the agreement.

After Phillips quit her job in June 1996, Hooters sent to her attorney a copy of the Hooters rules then in effect. Phillips refused to arbitrate the dispute.

Hooters filed suit in November 1996 to compel arbitration under 9 U.S.C. § 4. Phillips defended on the grounds that the agreement to arbitrate was unenforceable. Phillips also asserted individual and class counterclaims against Hooters for violations of Title VII and for a declaration that the arbitration agreements were unenforceable against the class. In response, Hooters requested that the district court stay the proceedings on the counterclaims until after arbitration.

In March 1998, the district court denied Hooters' motions to compel arbitration and stay proceedings on the counterclaims. The court found that there was no meeting of the minds on all of the material terms of the agreement and even if there were, Hooters' promise to arbitrate was illusory. In addition, the court found that the arbitration agreement was unconscionable and void for reasons of public policy. Hooters filed this interlocutory appeal, 9 U.S.C. § 16.

II.

* * *

The threshold question is whether claims such as Phillips' are even arbitrable. The EEOC as amicus curiae contends that employees cannot agree to arbitrate Title VII claims in predispute agreements. We disagree. The Supreme Court has made it plain that judicial protection of arbitral agreements extends to agreements to arbitrate statutory discrimination claims. In *Gilmer v. Interstate/Johnson Lane Corp.,* the Court noted that " '[b]y agreeing to arbitrate a statutory claim, a party does not forgo the substantive rights afforded by the statute; it only submits to their resolution in an arbitral, rather than a judicial, forum.' " Thus, a party must be held to the terms of its bargain unless Congress intends to preclude waiver of a judicial forum for the statutory claims at issue. Such an intent, however, must "be discoverable in the text of the [substantive statute], its legislative history, or an 'inherent conflict' between arbitration and the [statute's] underlying purposes." *Id.*

The EEOC argues that in passing the Civil Rights Act of 1991, Congress evinced an intent to prohibit predispute agreements to arbitrate claims arising under Title VII. This circuit, however, has already rejected this argument. The Civil Rights Act of 1991 provided that "Where appropriate and to the extent authorized by law, the use of alternative means of dispute resolution, including . . . arbitration, is encouraged to resolve disputes arising under [Title VII]." In *Austin,* we stated that this language "could not be any more clear in showing Congressional favor towards arbitration." We also noted that the legislative history did not establish a contrary intent nor was there an "inherent conflict" between the Civil Rights Act and arbitration. This holding is in step with our sister circuits which have also rejected the EEOC's argument.

III.

Predispute agreements to arbitrate Title VII claims are thus valid and enforceable. The question remains whether a binding arbitration agreement between Phillips and Hooters exists and compels Phillips to submit her Title VII claims to arbitration. The FAA provides that agreements "to settle by arbitration a controversy thereafter arising out of such contract or transaction ... shall be valid, irrevocable, and enforceable, save upon such grounds as exist at law or in equity for the revocation of any contract." 9 U.S.C. § 2. "It [i]s for the court, not the arbitrator, to decide in the first instance whether the dispute [i]s to be resolved through arbitration." In so deciding, we " 'engage in a limited review to ensure that the dispute is arbitrable—i.e., that a valid agreement to arbitrate exists between the parties and that the specific dispute falls within the substantive scope of that agreement.' " *Glass v. Kidder Peabody & Co.*, 114 F.3d 446, 453 (4th Cir.1997) (quoting *PaineWebber Inc. v. Hartmann*, 921 F.2d 507, 511 (3d Cir.1990)).

Hooters argues that Phillips gave her assent to a bilateral agreement to arbitrate. That contract provided for the resolution by arbitration of all employment-related disputes, including claims arising under Title VII. Hooters claims the agreement to arbitrate is valid because Phillips twice signed it voluntarily. Thus, it argues the courts are bound to enforce it and compel arbitration.

We disagree. The judicial inquiry, while highly circumscribed, is not focused solely on an examination for contractual formation defects such as lack of mutual assent and want of consideration. Courts also can investigate the existence of "such grounds as exist at law or in equity for the revocation of any contract." 9 U.S.C. § 2. However, the grounds for revocation must relate specifically to the arbitration clause and not just to the contract as a whole. In this case, the challenge goes to the validity of the arbitration agreement itself. Hooters materially breached the arbitration agreement by promulgating rules so egregiously unfair as to constitute a complete default of its contractual obligation to draft arbitration rules and to do so in good faith.

Hooters and Phillips agreed to settle any disputes between them not in a judicial forum, but in another neutral forum—arbitration. Their agreement provided that Hooters was responsible for setting up such a forum by promulgating arbitration rules and procedures. To this end, Hooters instituted a set of rules in July 1996.

The Hooters rules when taken as a whole, however, are so one-sided that their only possible purpose is to undermine the neutrality of the proceeding. The rules require the employee to provide the company notice of her claim at the outset, including "the nature of the Claim" and "the specific act(s) or omissions(s) which are the basis of the Claim." Hooters, on the other hand, is not required to file any responsive pleadings or to notice its defenses. Additionally, at the time of filing this notice, the employee must provide the company with a list of all fact witnesses with a brief summary of the facts known to each. The company, however, is not required to reciprocate.

The Hooters rules also provide a mechanism for selecting a panel of three arbitrators that is crafted to ensure a biased decisionmaker. The employee and Hooters each select an arbitrator, and the two arbitrators in turn select a third. Good enough, except that the employee's arbitrator and the third arbitrator must be selected from a list of arbitrators created exclusively by Hooters. This gives Hooters control over the entire panel and places no limits whatsoever on whom Hooters can put on the list. Under the rules, Hooters is free to devise lists of partial arbitrators who have existing relationships, financial or familial, with Hooters and its management. In fact, the rules do not even prohibit Hooters from placing its managers themselves on the list. Further, nothing in the rules restricts Hooters from punishing arbitrators who rule against the company by removing them from the list. Given the unrestricted control that one party (Hooters) has over the panel, the selection of an impartial decision maker would be a surprising result.

Nor is fairness to be found once the proceedings are begun. Although Hooters may expand the scope of arbitration to any matter, "whether related or not to the Employee's Claim," the employee cannot raise "any matter not included in the Notice of Claim." Similarly, Hooters is permitted to move for summary dismissal of employee claims before a hearing is held whereas the employee is not permitted to seek summary judgment. Hooters, but not the employee, may record the arbitration hearing "by audio or videotaping or by verbatim transcription." The rules also grant Hooters the right to bring suit in court to vacate or modify an arbitral award when it can show, by a preponderance of the evidence, that the panel exceeded its authority. No such right is granted to the employee.

In addition, the rules provide that upon 30 days notice Hooters, but not the employee, may cancel the agreement to arbitrate. Moreover, Hooters reserves the right to modify the rules, "in whole or in part," whenever it wishes and "without notice" to the employee. Nothing in the rules even prohibits Hooters from changing the rules in the middle of an arbitration proceeding.

If by odd chance the unfairness of these rules were not apparent on their face, leading arbitration experts have decried their one-sidedness. George Friedman, senior vice president of the American Arbitration Association (AAA), testified that the system established by the Hooters rules so deviated from minimum due process standards that the Association would refuse to arbitrate under those rules. George Nicolau, former president of both the National Academy of Arbitrators and the

International Society of Professionals in Dispute Resolution, attested that the Hooters rules "are inconsistent with the concept of fair and impartial arbitration." He also testified that he was "certain that reputable designating agencies, such as the AAA and Jams/Endispute, would refuse to administer a program so unfair and one-sided as this one." Additionally, Dennis Nolan, professor of labor law at the University of South Carolina, declared that the Hooters rules "do not satisfy the minimum requirements of a fair arbitration system." He found that the "most serious flaw" was that the "mechanism [for selecting arbitrators] violates the most fundamental aspect of justice, namely an impartial decision maker." Finally, Lewis Maltby, member of the Board of Directors of the AAA, testified that "This is without a doubt the most unfair arbitration program I have ever encountered."

In a similar vein, two major arbitration associations have filed amicus briefs with this court. The National Academy of Arbitrators stated that the Hooters rules "violate fundamental concepts of fairness . . . and the integrity of the arbitration process." Likewise, the Society of Professionals in Dispute Resolution noted that "[i]t would be hard to imagine a more unfair method of selecting a panel of arbitrators." It characterized the Hooters arbitration system as "deficient to the point of illegitimacy" and "so one sided, it is hard to believe that it was even intended to be fair."

We hold that the promulgation of so many biased rules—especially the scheme whereby one party to the proceeding so controls the arbitral panel—breaches the contract entered into by the parties. The parties agreed to submit their claims to arbitration—a system whereby disputes are fairly resolved by an impartial third party. Hooters by contract took on the obligation of establishing such a system. By creating a sham system unworthy even of the name of arbitration, Hooters completely failed in performing its contractual duty.

Moreover, Hooters had a duty to perform its obligations in good faith. * * * By agreeing to settle disputes in arbitration, Phillips agreed to the prompt and economical resolution of her claims. She could legitimately expect that arbitration would not entail procedures so wholly one-sided as to present a stacked deck. Thus we conclude that the Hooters rules also violate the contractual obligation of good faith.

Given Hooters' breaches of the arbitration agreement and Phillips' desire not to be bound by it, we hold that rescission is the proper remedy. Generally, "rescission will not be granted for a minor or casual breach of a contract, but only for those breaches which defeat the object of the contracting parties." As we have explained, Hooters' breach is by no means insubstantial; its performance under the contract was so egregious that the result was hardly recognizable as arbitration at all. We therefore permit Phillips to cancel the agreement and thus Hooters' suit to compel arbitration must fail.

IV.

We respect fully the Supreme Court's pronouncement that "questions of arbitrability must be addressed with a healthy regard for the federal policy favoring arbitration." Our decision should not be misread: We are not holding that the agreement before us is unenforceable because the arbitral proceedings are too abbreviated. An arbitral forum need not replicate the judicial forum. "[W]e are well past the time when judicial suspicion of the desirability of arbitration and of the competence of arbitral tribunals inhibited the development of arbitration as an alternative means of dispute resolution."

Nor should our decision be misunderstood as permitting a full-scale assault on the fairness of proceedings before the matter is submitted to arbitration. Generally, objections to the nature of arbitral proceedings are for the arbitrator to decide in the first instance. Only after arbitration may a party then raise such challenges if they meet the narrow grounds set out in 9 U.S.C. § 10 for vacating an arbitral award. In the case before us, we only reach the content of the arbitration rules because their promulgation was the duty of one party under the contract. The material breach of this duty warranting rescission is an issue of substantive arbitrability and thus is reviewable before arbitration. This case, however, is the exception that proves the rule: fairness objections should generally be made to the arbitrator, subject only to limited post-arbitration judicial review as set forth in section 10 of the FAA.

By promulgating this system of warped rules, Hooters so skewed the process in its favor that Phillips has been denied arbitration in any meaningful sense of the word. To uphold the promulgation of this aberrational scheme under the heading of arbitration would undermine, not advance, the federal policy favoring alternative dispute resolution. This we refuse to do.

The judgment of the district court is affirmed, and the case is remanded for further proceedings consistent with this opinion.

NOTE AND QUESTIONS

1.   The *Hooters* court's decision was technically based on breach of contract, but the provision at issue includes the kind of one-sided provisions that other courts have found to be unconscionable. *See, e.g., Ting v. AT&T,* 319 F.3d 1126 (9th Cir. 2003).

2.   Which of the shortcomings in the *Hooters* arbitral process would have been sufficient, standing alone, to justify granting the rescission remedy? Which do you find most offensive? Least troubling?

3.   Assuming that Hooters' management wanted a strong arbitration clause during the drafting of the provision at issue in this case, how might Hooters' lawyers have drafted the clause to have avoided this result? What arguments would it have made to management?

4.   Critics of mandatory arbitration had argued that employees were exempted from coverage under the FAA because of the following language in § 1 of the FAA: ". . . nothing herein contained shall apply to contracts of employment of seamen, railroad employees, or any other class of workers engaged in foreign or interstate commerce." *See, e.g.,* Matthew W. Finken, *"Workers' Contracts" Under the United States Arbitration Act: An Essay in Historical Clarification,* 17 Berkeley J. Empl. & Lab. L. 282 (1996).

The U.S. Supreme Court rejected this argument as a matter of textual interpretation in *Circuit City Stores, Inc. v. Adams,* 532 U.S. 105, 121 S.Ct. 1302, 149 L.Ed.2d 234 (2001) Writing for the 5–4 court, Justice Kennedy said:

> The wording of § 1 calls for the application of the maxim *ejusdem generis,* the statutory canon that "[w]here general words follow specific words in a statutory enumeration, the general words are construed to embrace only objects similar in nature to those objects enumerated by the preceding specific words." Under this rule of construction, the residual clause should be read to give effect to the terms "seamen" and "railroad employees," and should itself be controlled and defined by reference to the enumerated categories of workers which are recited just before it; the interpretation of the clause pressed by respondent fails to produce these results.

5.   In a closely watched case arising in the financial services industry, *Badie v. Bank of America,* 67 Cal.App.4th 779, 79 Cal.Rptr.2d 273 (1998), the California Court of Appeals used this good faith duty as a basis for refusing to enforce the addition of a mandatory arbitration provision to the "terms and conditions" of the customer's deposit account signature card, ruling that a change in the dispute resolution forum was not consistent with the terms to which the customer had initially agreed when signing the deposit card. *Id.* at 790–97.

Since the initial customer agreement had not included a dispute resolution term, it was beyond the customer's reasonable expectation that the lender's right to change the terms of the signature agreement unilaterally would include a term limiting the presumptive right to court access. Rather, the court held that the bank's right to change terms unilaterally was limited to those terms expressly included within the initial agreement, such as purchases and cash advances requirements and limitations, credit limits, finance charges, membership fees, late charges and other fees, calculation of balances and finance charges, payments, etc.

> Where, as in this case, a party has the unilateral right to change the terms of a contract, it does not act in an 'objectively reasonable' manner when it attempts to 'recapture' a forgone opportunity by adding an entirely new term which has no bearing on any subject, issue, right, or

obligation addressed in the original contract and which was not within the reasonable contemplation of the parties when the contract was entered into. That is particularly true where the new term deprives the other party of the right to a jury trial and the right to select a judicial forum for dispute resolution.

Id. at 796.

6.   In Paul D. Carrington and Paul Y. Castle *The Revocability of Contract Provisions Controlling Resolution of Future Disputes Between the Parties*, 67 Law & Contemp. Probs. 207 (2004), the authors argued that pre-dispute arbitration agreements should be revocable when contained in contracts of adhesion, "at least until a dispute to which they purport to apply has been submitted in writing to the specified forum or procedure." *Id.* at 207.

3.   SECTION 10: JUDICIAL REVIEW OF ARBITRATION AWARDS

a.   In General

Most parties voluntarily comply with arbitration awards. Courts impose sanctions for failure to comply with an award only if a court has confirmed it. Federal and state statutes authorize courts to confirm, vacate, and modify awards. Courts do not routinely review the merits of an award in deciding whether to confirm, vacate, or modify. If they did, agreements to arbitrate would result in more rather than less time and money being devoted to processing disputes. As the Supreme Court said in a labor arbitration case, the "policy of settling labor disputes by arbitration would be undermined if courts had the final say on the merits of the awards." *United Steelworkers v. Enterprise Wheel & Car Corp.*, 363 U.S. 593, 80 S.Ct. 1358, 4 L.Ed.2d 1424 (1960). Limitation of judicial review is part of the strong federal pro-arbitration policy. *See* IAN R. MACNEIL, RICHARD E. SPEIDEL, THOMAS J. STIPANOWICH, FEDERAL ARBITRATION LAW § 40.14 (1994 ed. & Supp. 1999). Successful challenges of arbitration awards are relatively rare. Yet courts and commentators agree that there is a need at times to modify or vacate arbitration awards. The materials that follow focus on the difficult issues raised by attacks in court on arbitration awards.

SOBEL V. HERTZ, WARNER & CO.
United States Court of Appeals, Second Circuit, 1972
469 F.2d 1211

Before MOORE, FEINBERG and MULLIGAN, CIRCUIT JUDGES.

FEINBERG, CIRCUIT JUDGE:

This is an interlocutory appeal from an order of the United States District Court for the Southern District of New York, Milton Pollack, J., that remanded an arbitration proceeding to the arbitrators to fulfill their "obligation to furnish some explanation of the ultimate findings embodied in their decision." We hold that in the circumstances of this case the arbitrators have no such obligation to explain their award, and we reverse the order of the district court.

I

The arbitration that led to this appeal was first requested in November 1967 by appellee Herbert Sobel, who was a customer of appellant Hertz, Warner & Co., a stock brokerage firm and a member of the New York Stock Exchange. As a customer, Sobel had the right under Article VIII of the Constitution of the New York Stock Exchange to demand arbitration of any controversy he might have with a member firm growing out of its "business." Briefly, Sobel claimed that between December 1965 and March 1966 he had purchased 10,200 shares of the common stock of Hercules Galion Products, Inc., upon the recommendation of his long-time broker, Edward Wetzel, and Michael Geier, both then employed by Hertz, Warner, and that Wetzel and Geier had made fraudulent misstatements and omissions of material facts on which Sobel had relied to his detriment. As their employer, Hertz, Warner was, according to Sobel, liable for the damages he had suffered. Sobel continued to hold his Hercules shares until Hertz, Warner demanded, in connection with the arbitration, that they be sold to fix damages. This was done in May 1968, and Sobel thereafter claimed a direct loss of about $34,000.

In 1970, both parties signed a formal submission to arbitration pursuant to the provisions of the Stock Exchange Constitution and the rules of the Board of Governors. Under the Constitution, Sobel's claim was heard by a panel consisting of two persons "engaged in the securities business" and three not so engaged. The panel held two hearings at which it heard the testimony of three witnesses and received documentary evidence. At the hearings, of which there is a full transcript, both sides were ably represented by counsel.

In May 1971, the panel issued the following decision:

> We, the undersigned, being the arbitrators selected to hear and determine a matter in controversy between the above-mentioned claimant and respondents set forth in a submission to arbitration signed by the parties on April 6, 1970 and April 10, 1970 respectively;

> And having heard and considered the proofs of the parties, have decided and determined that the claim of the claimant be and hereby is in all respects dismissed;

> That the costs, $240.00, be and hereby are assessed against the claimant.

After an unsuccessful request to the arbitrators for reconsideration, Sobel moved in the Southern District under 9 U.S.C. § 10 to vacate the arbitration award on the grounds that it had been "procured by undue means" and "that the Award is contrary to public policy, in that the arbitrators refused to make their Award in accordance with the applicable Federal Securities laws." Judge Pollack heard argument on the motion to vacate and concluded, in an exhaustive opinion, that he could not decide the question without "an indication, now wholly lacking from the record, of the basis on which the petitioner's claim was dismissed." Holding that "a District Court is justified in requiring some statement of the facts the arbitrators found decisive," the judge remanded the controversy to the arbitrators for that purpose. Thereafter, he certified as an interlocutory appeal the question whether his action was proper, and we permitted the appeal.

II

Although Sobel's claims before the arbitrators rested on state statutory law and common law fraud concepts, as well as on federal securities acts, only the last are significant on this appeal. The district judge was clearly disturbed by Sobel's claim that the arbitrators must have ignored the prohibitions of sections 12(2) and 17(a) of the Securities Act of 1933, 15 U.S.C. §§ 77l(2), 77q(a), section 10(b) of the Securities Exchange Act of 1934, 15 U.S.C. § 78j(b), and Rule 10b–5 promulgated thereunder. The judge's opinion emphasized that Wetzel and Geier had been indicted in 1967—not long after the transactions complained of by Sobel—for conspiring to create market activity in the Hercules shares and to induce the purchase of the security by others, and that in 1971 Wetzel had pleaded guilty to the conspiracy charge and Geier had been found guilty of that and other counts after a jury trial. Sobel argued to the district court that unless the arbitrators explained their decision, there was no way of telling whether it was in "manifest disregard" of the provisions of the securities acts. The quotation is from *Wilko v. Swan*, which—oddly enough, in the context of Sobel's use of it here—stands primarily for the proposition that certain kinds of claims cannot be forced to arbitration despite a pre-dispute agreement to arbitrate. *Wilko v. Swan* held that an agreement to arbitrate future controversies was an impermissible waiver of the plaintiff-customer's right to have his claim of securities act violations heard in court. In the course of its opinion, however, the Court also said:

> Power to vacate an award is limited. While it may be true, as the Court of Appeals thought, that a failure of the arbitrators to decide in accordance with the provisions of the Securities Act would "constitute grounds for vacating the award pursuant to section 10 of the Federal Arbitration Act," that failure would need to be made clearly to appear. In unrestricted submissions, such as the present margin

agreements envisage, the interpretations of the law by the arbitrators *in contrast to manifest disregard* are not subject, in the federal courts, to judicial review for error in interpretation.

The district judge agreed with Sobel that unless the arbitrators in this case stated the basis of their decision, the judge could not determine whether it was in "manifest disregard" of the law.

The first issue before us is what is the issue before us. In one portion of his memorandum opinion certifying an interlocutory appeal, the district judge described the question as

> whether an arbitration award in a case involving federal securities law standards which fails to provide some indication of the basis of the arbitration panel's decision may be set aside and resubmitted to the arbitration panel pursuant to 9 U.S.C. § 10(d) and (e), * * *.

* * *

From this, Sobel argues that Judge Pollack's order merely requires a clarification from the arbitrators when the court finds no indication of the basis of the decision and that Judge Pollack's decision does not require arbitrators to write opinions in the first instance. Such a ruling, says Sobel, is not at all unusual. The latter part of the argument puzzles us. It does not make any real difference whether an arbitrator is ordered to write an opinion in the first instance or in the second instance. The issue is whether the requirement is proper in either case. As to the point that the judge sought only "clarification," if this version of the question were correct we doubt whether the appeal would have been certified by the district judge or accepted by this court. Sobel's description of the narrow effect of Judge Pollack's order is at variance with other portions of both his original opinion and his supplemental memorandum. In the latter, the judge phrased the question in the manner set forth in the first paragraph of this opinion. And, in the judge's earlier opinion before certifying the interlocutory appeal, he characterized the arbitrators' decision several times as inadequate because lacking an explanation of its basis. (sic) Moreover, whatever may be the power of a court to require clarification of an arbitration award, on the ample record in this case "clarification" can only mean setting forth the reasons for decision. Under these circumstances, we believe that the issue before us is whether the arbitrators here are required to disclose the reasoning underlying their award.

The question so phrased, of course, is still a narrow one. We are not asked to decide whether arbitration was an inappropriate forum here in the first place. Nor must we determine all the circumstances in which a court may vacate an arbitrator's award.

Nonetheless, the extent of an arbitrator's obligation to explain his award is necessarily related to the scope of judicial review of it. That issue, insofar as it leads to attempts to define "manifest disregard," is particularly troublesome. But if the arbitrators simply ignore the applicable law, the literal application of a "manifest disregard" standard should presumably compel vacation of the award. The problem is how a court is to be made aware of the erring conduct of the arbitrators. Obviously, a requirement that arbitrators explain their reasoning in every case would help to uncover egregious failures to apply the law to an arbitrated dispute. But such a rule would undermine the very purpose of arbitration, which is to provide a relatively quick, efficient and informal means of private dispute settlement. The sacrifice that arbitration entails in terms of legal precision is recognized, and is implicitly accepted in the initial assumption that certain disputes are arbitrable. Given that acceptance, the primary consideration for the courts must be that the system operate expeditiously as well as fairly.

Presumably based upon the foregoing considerations, the Supreme Court has made it clear that there is no general requirement that arbitrators explain the reasons for their award. In *Wilko v. Swan, supra,* just before the language quoted above the Court pointed out that an award by arbitrators "may be made without explanation of their reasons and without a complete record of their proceedings * * *." This statement is especially significant because Mr. Justice Frankfurter in dissent made exactly the opposite point. A little over two years later, the Court observed that "Arbitrators * * * need not give their reasons for their results. * * *." These statements were, of course, known to the district judge; he even quoted them in his opinion. The argument, then, must be that there is something about this particular case that justifies the extraordinary requirement of the district court's order. We fail to see what that is. There was a complete transcript here of the arbitration proceeding. The arbitrators—and the district court—also had the benefit of an extremely detailed submission to arbitration, including Sobel's Statement of Claim and Hertz, Warner's Reply, excellent memoranda of law and summations of counsel, all of which indicate a number of theories upon which the arbitrators may have decided. It is true that claims under the securities acts are frequently complicated, although those made here seem less so than usual. And the same public interest that led to the enactment of the securities acts makes it desirable that such claims be decided correctly. But there is also a public interest, manifested in the United States Arbitration Act, in the proper functioning of the arbitral process. It would be destructive of that process if we approved the district judge's requirement here that the arbitrators give reasons for their decision. Arbitration may not always be the speedy and economical remedy its admirers claim it is—this case is proof enough of that. But forcing arbitrators to explain their award even when grounds for it can be gleaned from the record will unjustifiably diminish whatever efficiency the process now achieves.

Sobel cites a number of cases in support of the district court order. Courts have, on occasion, remanded awards to arbitrators for clarification, but they generally have done so to find out whether an issue has already been decided in arbitration rather than to discover whether the arbitrators had good reasons for their award.

* * *

In short, we believe that the district court erred in remanding the arbitration proceeding to the arbitrators. We do not agree with its conclusion that "the present state of the record is not sufficient to justify final determination of the issues petitioner has raised." Those issues are whether the arbitration award was procured by "undue means," 9 U.S.C. § 10(a), or is void as against public policy. Both parties have urged us to decide those questions. While we are tempted to do so in order to bring this litigation to an end, orderly administration suggests that the district court should rule upon them first.

Case remanded for further proceedings consistent with this opinion.

NOTES AND QUESTIONS

1.   The *Sobel* court finds that arbitrators have no duty to explain their decisions. Yet, written and reasoned opinions are becoming more common, and are now expressly provided for in rules of major providers of arbitration services. *See, e.g.*, AM. ARBITRATION ASSOC., NATIONAL RULES FOR THE RESOLUTION OF EMPLOYMENT DISPUTES § 34(c) (rev. ed. 2005); CPR INT'L. INST. FOR CONFLICT PREVENTION & RESOLUTION, NON–ADMINISTERED ARBITRATION RULES, Rule 15.2 (rev. ed. 2007); JUDICIAL ARBITRATION AND MEDIATION SERVS., COMPREHENSIVE ARBITRATION RULES AND PROCEDURES, Rule 24(h) (rev. ed. 2007). Why might these providers have taken this step? What are the arguments for and against requiring arbitrators to explain an award?

2.   *Statutory grounds for vacatur.* A full appreciation of the issues raised in *Sobel* requires a basic understanding of the vacatur scheme of the Federal Arbitration Act.

There are four statutory grounds for vacating an arbitration award under the FAA, all of which are found in Section 10(a) of the FAA. All four set a high bar for proponents to meet, furthering the FAA's vision of arbitration as a final and binding dispute resolution process.

Section 10(a)(1) provides for an award to be vacated "where the award is procured by corruption, fraud, or undue means." The standard is high. For example, fraud under this section "must (1) be established by clear and convincing evidence, (2) materially relate to an issue in the arbitration, [and] (3) neither have been brought to the attention of the arbitrator and the issue handled by them, nor have been discoverable upon the exercise of due diligence prior to the arbitration." IAN R. MACNEIL, RICHARD E. SPEIDEL, AND

THOMAS J. STIPANOWICH, FEDERAL ARBITRATION LAW: AGREEMENTS, AWARDS, AND REMEDIES UNDER THE FEDERAL ARBITRATION ACT, § 40.2.2 (1994 ed. and Supp. 1999).

Section (10)(a)(2) provides that an arbitral award may be vacated "where there was evident partiality or corruption in the arbitrators, or either of them." In applying this provision, the courts have distinguished between "active" and "passive" partiality. "Active partiality" refers to actions by the arbitrator indicating that he or she is predisposed in favor or against one of the parties. "Passive" partiality refers to circumstances surrounding the arbitrator that may give rise to inferences of partiality, even where there is no demonstration of active partiality, such as an arbitrator's relationship with one of the parties. A Florida appeals court distinguished between the two in *Gaines Construction Co. v. Carol City Utilities, Inc.*, 164 So.2d 270 (Fla. App. 1963), rejecting the arbitrator's dominance and control of one of the parties as a basis to vacate because of "active" partiality, but agreeing that a business relationship between the arbitrator and one of the parties was cause to vacate on the ground of "passive" partiality.

Section 10(a)(3) provides that an arbitral award may be vacated "where the arbitrators were guilty of misconduct in refusing to postpone the hearing, upon sufficient cause shown, or in refusing to hear evidence pertinent and material to the controversy; or of any other misbehavior by which the rights of any party have been prejudiced." This ground allows for objections to the way in which the arbitrator actually conducted the hearing, such as claims that one was denied a fundamentally fair hearing, was denied the right to counsel, was prejudiced by an ex parte hearing or the refusal of the arbitrator to grant a subpoena or discovery request. The high threshold requires proponents to show that the misbehavior, in the words of one court, "so prejudiced the rights of a party that it denies the party to a fundamentally fair hearing." *Apex Fountain Sales, Inc. v. Kleinfeld*, 818 F.2d 1089, 1094 (3rd Cir. 1987). Such prejudice is ordinarily not found unless the aggrieved party's right to be heard is "grossly and totally blocked." *Cofinco, Inc. v. Bakrie & Bros.*, 395 F. Supp. 613, 615 (S.D.N.Y 1975).

Section 10(a)(4) provides that an arbitral award may be vacated "where the arbitrators exceeded their powers, or so imperfectly executed them that a mutual, final, and definite award upon the subject matter submitted was not made." Arbitrators exceed their powers when they issue an award on an issue not presented to them in the submission to arbitration, or when they fail to adhere to other constraining criteria prescribed by the parties, such as arbitration rules that the parties may have drafted into their arbitration provisions or a choice-of-law provision. It is well-established that arbitrators do not exceed their powers by misconstruing contracts or making errors of law or fact, even when the mistake is serious. As the U.S. Supreme Court recently reiterated, "A party seeking relief under [Section 10(a)(4)] bears a heavy burden. . . . [T]he sole question for us is whether the arbitrator (even arguably) interpreted the parties' contract, not whether he got its meaning right or wrong." *Oxford Health Plans LLC v. Sutter*, 133 S.Ct. 2064, 186

L.Ed.2d 113, 81 USLW 4382 (2013). "[A]s long as the arbitrator is even arguably construing or applying the contract and acting within the scope of his authority, that a court is convinced he committed serious errors does not suffice to overturn his decision." *United Paperworkers Int'l Union v. Misco, Inc.*, 484 U.S. 29, 38 (1987).

3. *Non-statutory grounds: Manifest disregard and public policy exceptions.* For many years, much of the discussion around statutory grounds for vacating arbitration awards centered on the degree to which it was appropriate for courts to depart from the specifically enumerated statutory grounds, such as when an arbitral award violates public policy or is in manifest disregard of the law. *See, e.g.*, Stephen L. Hayford, *Law in Disarray: Judicial Standards for Vacatur of Commercial Arbitration Awards*, 30 Ga. L. Rev. 734 (1996).

a. *Manifest disregard. Sobel* raises the issue of manifest disregard, by far the most significant non-statutory ground for vacatur. The claim with manifest disregard is that the arbitrator's award contradicted clearly controlling law, that the arbitrator knew what the law was, and deliberately disregarded it. This doctrine is discussed more fully below at p. 694.

b. *Public Policy.* The notes of the Revised Uniform Arbitration Act also provide a sense of the history of the public policy exception to the general rule of limited review of arbitral awards.

> The origin and essence of the 'public policy' ground for vacatur is well captured in the Tenth Circuit's opinion in *Seymour v. Blue Cross/Blue Shield*, 988 F.2d 1020, 1023 (10th Cir. 1993). *Seymour* observed: '[I]n determining whether an arbitration award violates public policy, a court must assess whether 'the specific terms contained in [the contract] violate public policy, by creating an 'explicit conflict with other 'laws and legal precedents.' " *Id.* at 1024 (citing *United Paperworkers Int'l Union v. Misco*, 484 U.S. 29, 43 (1987)).

> Like the "manifest disregard of the law" nonstatutory ground, vacatur under the "public policy" ground requires something more than a mere error or misunderstanding of the relevant law by the arbitrator. Under all of the articulations of this nonstatutory ground, the public policy at issue must be a clearly defined, dominant, undisputed rule of law. * * * For a full discussion of the evolution and application of the public policy exception in the labor arbitration sphere, see Stephen L. Hayford and Anthony V. Sinicropi, *The Labor Contract and External Law: Revisiting the Arbitrator's Scope of Authority*, 1993 J. Disp. Resol. 249. R.U.A.A. § 23, cmt. C (2000).

c. *Other non-statutory grounds.* Courts have also vacated arbitration awards that are arbitrary and capricious or are irrational. Again, the bar is high for both standards. To establish that an arbitration award is arbitrary and capricious, a party must demonstrate that the legal ground for the arbitrator's decision cannot be inferred from the facts of the case, that the decision is not grounded in the contract, or, more commonly, that the reasoning is so faulty that no judge or group of judges could ever have conceivably made such a ruling. *Safeway Stores v. American Bakery and Confectionery Workers, Local 111*, 390 F.2d 79, 82 (5th Cir.1968) The party seeking vacatur has a heavy burden of proof, being required to refute every rational basis on which the arbitrators could possibly have relied. Similarly, for awards alleged to be irrational, the complaining party must show that the arbitrator's award is not at least rationally inferable, if not obviously drawn, from the letter and purpose of the agreement. Put another way, the award must only, in some logical way, be derived from the wording or purpose of the contract.

Stephen L. Hayford has argued, "with the arguable exception of the 'manifest disregard' of the law standard and the 'public policy' ground, the non-statutory grounds for vacatur of commercial arbitration awards are without a legitimate legal, doctrinal or theoretical basis." Stephen L. Hayford, *Law in Disarray: Judicial Standards For Vacatur of Commercial Arbitration Awards*, 30 Ga. L. Rev. 731, 833 (1996).

4.   *Sobel* indicates that there is no general requirement that arbitrators explain the reasons for their award. *See, e.g., Monscharsh v. Heily & Blase*, 3 Cal.4th 1, 10 Cal.Rptr.2d 183, 832 P.2d 899 (1992) (arbitrator's decision is not generally reviewable for errors of fact or law, whether or not such error appears on the face of the award and causes substantial injustice to the parties). Findings of fact by arbitrators receive the same deference. Do you agree that an arbitration award should receive more deferential review than a decision of a lower court? Would a more expansive review "destroy the very thing the parties bargained for, namely, a non-judicial process"? DAN B. DOBBS, HANDBOOK ON THE LAW OF REMEDIES 942 (1973). Would it result in greater delay and higher costs? *See* Jon O. Newman, *Rethinking Fairness: Perspectives on the Litigation Process*, 94 Yale L.J. 1643 (1985), in which the author, a judge on the U.S. Court of Appeals for the Second Circuit, argues that our litigation system has become slower and more expensive in part because of the elaborate lengths to which we go to avoid making a mistake in individual cases.

Compare this view to the following from Jay R. Sever, *The Relaxation of Inarbitrability and Public Policy Checks on U.S. and Foreign Arbitration: Arbitration Out of Control?*, 65 Tul. L. Rev. 1661, 1696–97 (1991):

> Yet, limited judicial review may prove essential to the health and survival of both domestic and international arbitration. The most progressive arbitration statutes, such as France's statute of 1981, openly recognize this reality. There is no reason why the very threat of limited judicial review cannot benefit arbitration. As one commentator has noted:
>
>> The national court judge as 'guarantor of arbitral integrity' remains an indispensable factor in the international arbitration system. * * * Review of arbitral awards * * * involves an important psychological aspect. The constant threat of judicial review along clearly defined

criteria leads arbitrators to pay due regard to the interests of the parties and factual and legal setting of the case, thus further contributing to more legality in arbitral proceedings.

5. In 2001, the U.S. Supreme Court again admonished the lower courts not to review arbitrator's decisions on the merits even when faced with serious errors on the arbitrator's part. *Major League Baseball Players Assoc. v. Garvey*, 532 U.S. 504, 121 S.Ct. 1724, 149 L.Ed.2d 740 (2001). The following is from the per curiam opinion for the Court:

> Judicial review of a labor-arbitration decision pursuant to such an agreement is very limited. Courts are not authorized to review the arbitrator's decision on the merits despite allegations that the decision rests on factual errors or misinterprets the parties' agreement. * * * We recently reiterated that if an " 'arbitrator is even arguably construing or applying the contract and acting within the scope of his authority,' the fact that 'a court is convinced he committed serious error does not suffice to overturn his decision.' " * * * (quoting *Misco, supra,* at 38, 108 S.Ct. 364). It is only when the arbitrator strays from interpretation and application of the agreement and effectively "dispense[s] his own brand of industrial justice" that his decision may be unenforceable. * * * When an arbitrator resolves disputes regarding the application of a contract, and no dishonesty is alleged, the arbitrator's "improvident, even silly, factfinding" does not provide a basis for a reviewing court to refuse to enforce the award. * * *

> In discussing the courts' limited role in reviewing the merits of arbitration awards, we have stated that "courts . . . have no business weighing the merits of the grievance [or] considering whether there is equity in a particular claim." * * * When judiciary does so, "it usurps a function which . . . is entrusted to the arbitration tribunal." ("It is the arbitrator's construction [of the agreement] which was bargained for. . . .") Consistent with this role, we said in *Misco* that "[e]ven in the very rare instances when an arbitrator's procedural aberrations rise to the level of affirmative misconduct, as a rule the court must not foreclose further proceedings by settling the merits according to its own judgment of the appropriate result." * * * That step, we explained, "would improperly substitute a judicial determination for the arbitrator's decision that the parties bargained for" in their agreement. Instead, the court should "simply vacate the award, thus leaving open the possibility of further proceedings if they are permitted under the terms of the agreement."

> To be sure, the Court of Appeals here recited these principles, but its application of them is nothing short of baffling. The substance of the court's discussion reveals that it overturned the arbitrator's decision because it disagreed with the arbitrator's factual findings, particularly those with respect to credibility. The Court of Appeals, it appears, would have credited Smith's 1996 letter, and found the arbitrator's refusal to do so at worst "irrational" and best "bizarre." *Garvey I,* 203 F.3d, at 590–

91. But even "serious error" on the arbitrator's part does not justify overturning his decision, where as here, he is construing a contract and acting within the scope of his authority.

Id. at 509–10.

6. Arbitrators routinely award punitive damages even when the agreement of the parties may not expressly authorize them. STEPHEN J. WARE, ALTERNATIVE DISPUTE RESOLUTION 107 (2nd ed. 2007). However, some courts, following New York's lead, have held that arbitrators can never award punitive damages. Some have held that arbitrators can award punitive damages only if they are specifically provided for in the parties' agreement. Others have held that arbitrators can award punitive damages unless they are explicitly excluded in the parties' agreement. See the discussion of case law in *Ratheon Co. v. Automated Business Systems, Inc.*, 882 F.2d 6, 11–12 (1st Cir.1989), and the discussion of policy issues in Thomas J. Stipanowich, *Punitive Damages in Arbitration:* Garrity v. Lyle Stuart, Inc. Reconsidered, 66 B.U. L. Rev. 953, 998–1010 (1986). Writing in 1994, Stephen J. Ware argued that the New York rule was preempted by the FAA. Steven J. Ware, *Punitive Damages in Arbitration: Contracting Out of Government's Role in Punishment and Federal Preemption of State Law*, 63 Fordham L. Rev. 529, 571 (1994). In *Mastrobuono v. Shearson Lehman Hutton, Inc.*, 514 U.S. 52, 115 S.Ct. 1212, 131 L.Ed.2d 76 (1995), the U.S. Supreme Court indicated that courts cannot use state law as a basis for refusing to enforce arbitral punitive damage awards unless the parties incorporate state arbitration law to this effect into their agreement. The Court said that, "in the absence of contractual intent to the contrary, the FAA would preempt the *Garrity* rule [the New York rule holding arbitrators cannot award punitive damages]." *Id.* at 59.

For a discussion of a proposal by the National Association of Securities Dealers to modify its arbitration rules to impose multiple caps on punitive damages by NASD arbitrators, see Thomas J. Stipanowich, *Punitive Damages and the Consumerization of Arbitration*, 92 Nw. U. L. Rev. 1 (1997).

Section 21 (C) of the RUAA provides that if the arbitrator awards punitive damages, she shall "specify in the award that basis in fact justifying and the basis in law authorizing the award and state separately the amount of the punitive damages or other exemplary relief."

7. In *Gilmer v. Interstate/Johnson Lane Corporation*, 500 U.S. 20, 111 S.Ct. 1647, 114 L.Ed.2d 26 (1991), the Court indicated that limited judicial scrutiny of arbitration awards was "sufficient to ensure that arbitrators comply with" statutory requirements. *Id.* at 31 n.4 (quoting *Shearson American Express, Inc. v. McMahon*, 482 U.S. 220, 232, 107 S.Ct. 2332, 96 L.Ed.2d 185 (1987)). Under the "manifest disregard" standard of review, it appears that a court could confirm an arbitrator's award that was based on an erroneous interpretation of a federal statute as long as the arbitrator did not know that the award conflicted with the statute. Does the obvious tension between such a result and the statements in *Gilmer* and *McMahon* suggest

that the "manifest disregard" standard will be modified in cases where arbitrators base awards on federal statutes? See *Cole v. Burns International Security Services*, 105 F.3d 1465 (D.C. Cir. 1997), where the Court indicated that in cases involving novel or difficult legal issues, courts can review an arbitrator's award to ensure that its resolution of public law issues is correct. Would such a result support or undermine the arbitration process?

8.   Labor arbitration awards may be vacated for reasons similar to those set forth in Sections 10 and 11 of the FAA. *See, e.g., Ludwig Honold Manufacturing. Co. v. Fletcher*, 405 F.2d 1123, 1127 (3d Cir. 1969). Another important basis for judicial review of labor arbitration awards is the "essence" test laid down in *United Steelworkers v. Enterprise Wheel & Car Corp.*, 363 U.S. 593, 80 S.Ct. 1358, 4 L.Ed.2d 1424 (1960). The fundamental responsibility of a labor arbitrator is to interpret the collective bargaining contract negotiated by labor and management. The Supreme Court repeatedly has stressed that when courts are asked to enforce or vacate a labor arbitration award, they should not overturn the award merely because they believe the arbitrator was mistaken in his interpretation of the contract. This deference to the arbitrator's decision on the merits has limits. The "essence" test, found in *Enterprise Wheel*, articulates these limits:

> [A]n arbitrator is confined to interpretation and application of the collective bargaining agreement; he does not sit to dispense his own brand of industrial justice. He may of course look for guidance from many sources, yet his award is legitimate only so long as it draws its essence from the collective bargaining agreement. When the arbitrator's words manifest an infidelity to his obligation, courts have no choice but to refuse enforcement of the award.

Id. at 597.

The case reports are filled with decisions that have applied the "essence" test to challenged labor arbitration awards. Numerous commentators have interpreted and evaluated these decisions. *See, e.g.*, Charles Morris, *Twenty Years of Trilogy: A Celebration, Proceedings of the 33rd Annual Meeting*, NAT'L ACAD. OF ARBITRATORS, 331, 355–56 (1981); Dennis R. Nolan & Roger I. Abrams, *American Labor Arbitration: The Maturing Years,* 35 U. Fla. L. Rev. 557, 591 (1983); Theodore J. St. Antoine, *Judicial Review of Labor Arbitration Awards: A Second Look at Enterprise Wheel and Its Progeny*, 75 Mich. L. Rev. 1137, 1148–49 (1977). Some of the commentators have concluded that the courts frequently fail to honor the policy underlying the "essence" test. Instead they scrutinize the merits of an arbitration award under the guise of determining whether the award drew its "essence" from the contract. *See, e.g.*, Lewis B. Kaden, *Judges and Arbitrators: Observations on the Scope of Judicial Review*, 80 Colum. L. Rev. 267, 270–71, 274 (1980). On the other hand, there are cases in which courts vigorously resist requests by losing parties to reconsider the merits. *See Hill v. Norfolk & Western Railway Co.*, 814 F.2d 1192, 1194–95 (7th Cir. 1987).

Courts also refuse to enforce labor arbitration awards when they are contrary to public policy. In *United Paperworkers International Union, AFL–CIO v. Misco, Inc.*, 484 U.S. 29, 108 S.Ct. 364, 98 L.Ed.2d 286 (1987), the Supreme Court limited the public policy doctrine to situations where, "the contract as interpreted would violate 'some explicit public policy' that is 'well defined and dominant, and is to be ascertained' by reference to the law and legal precedents and not from general considerations of supposed public interest." *Id.* at 43. Lower courts don't always adhere to the Supreme Court's admonition not to rely on general considerations of public interest. *See, e.g., U.S. Postal Service v. National Ass'n of Letter Carriers*, 839 F.2d 146 (3d Cir. 1988). The federal courts disagree on the meaning of *Misco*. For example, the D.C. and Eleventh Circuits reached opposite conclusions in two cases that were indistinguishable on the facts. In *Northwest Airlines, Inc. v. Air Line Pilots Ass'n*, 808 F.2d 76 (D.C. Cir. 1987), an arbitration panel reinstated an airline pilot who had served as a co-pilot while intoxicated on condition that he regain FAA certification to fly, concluding that the award did not violate public policy as expressed in positive law. The court said that "[i]t would be the height of judicial chutzpa for us to second-guess the present judgment of the FAA recertifying Morrison for flight duty." *Id.* at 83. The Eleventh Circuit, on the other hand, held that enforcement of an award arising out of a similar situation would violate public policy. *Delta Air Lines, Inc. v. Air Line Pilots Ass'n*, 861 F.2d 665 (11th Cir. 1988). These two cases and others are analyzed in Arlus J. Stephens, Note, *The Sixth Circuit's Approach to the Public–Policy Exception to the Enforcement of Labor Arbitration Awards: A Tale of Two Trilogies?*, 11 Ohio St. J. on Disp. Resol. 441 (1996).

9.   Professor David Feller, a former president of the National Academy of Arbitrators, has asserted that courts are more apt to set aside labor arbitration awards than commercial arbitration awards. DAVID E. FELLER, PRESIDENTIAL ADDRESS, PROCEEDINGS OF THE 46TH ANNUAL MEETING, NAT'L ACAD. OF ARBITRATORS 6–9 (1993). Although there are differences between labor and FAA arbitration, courts use concepts developed in one category in cases arising in the other. For example, the "essence" test, developed in labor arbitration cases, is used in commercial arbitration cases. *See, e.g., Michigan Mutual Insurance Co. v. Unigard Security Insurance Co.*, 44 F.3d 826, 830–32 (9th Cir. 1995); *Maxus, Inc. v. Sciacca*, 598 So.2d 1376, 1381 (Ala. 1992). Under the essence test, the arbitral award will be deemed within the scope of the arbitration agreement if it draws its essence from that agreement. The public policy rationale developed in *United Paperworkers International Union, AFL–CIO v. Misco, Inc.*, 484 U.S. 29, 108 S.Ct. 364, 98 L.Ed.2d 286 (1987), a labor arbitration case, was relied on in *PaineWebber, Inc. v. Agron*, 49 F.3d 347, 350 (8th Cir. 1995), a securities arbitration case. IAN R. MACNEIL, RICHARD E. SPEIDEL & THOMAS J. STIPANOWICH, FEDERAL ARBITRATION LAW § 40 (1994 ed. & Supp. 1999) urges caution in cross citing FAA and labor arbitration cases. "The purposes lying behind a number of LMRA § 301 principles respecting vacation are simply not applicable to the typical FAA arbitration." *Id.* at § 40.51.

10. Claim and issue preclusion are the two parts of res judicata law. They promote the policy of finality—putting an end to disputes. Claim preclusion prohibits relitigation of a claim or cause of action that was dealt with in a proceeding that produced a final judgment on the merits. Courts give claim preclusion effect to arbitration awards under appropriate circumstances. If they did not, parties could ignore demands to arbitrate and could relitigate when they lose in arbitration. IAN R. MACNEIL, RICHARD E. SPEIDEL & THOMAS J. STIPANOWICH, FEDERAL ARBITRATION LAW § 39.2.3 (1994 ed. & Supp. 1999).

Issue preclusion (collateral estoppel) prohibits relitigation of issues argued and decided in a prior proceeding. It is more difficult to determine when an arbitration award should be given an issue preclusion effect. Courts do give issue preclusion effect to arbitration awards at times, but the relative informality of arbitration proceedings and the fact that arbitrators don't always explain their awards make it more difficult to generalize about when it is appropriate to do so. Courts have considerable discretion and proceed case by case in deciding whether an award should have issue preclusion effect. *Id.* at § 39.3.1.2–1.5. Professor Motomura argues that "a better approach to arbitral collateral estoppel than the case-by-case method is a rule that arbitral findings never have collateral estoppel effect, unless the arbitration agreement clearly and expressly provides for it." Hiroshi Motomura, *Arbitration and Collateral Estoppel: Using Preclusion to Shape Procedural Choices*, 63 Tul. L. Rev. 29, 81 (1988). Compare Professor Motomura's views with G. Richard Shell, *Res Judicata and Collateral Estoppel Effects of Commercial Arbitration*, 35 UCLA L. Rev. 623, 673–74 (1988).

11. May violation of constitutional rights provide a basis for judicial review at arbitral awards? In the excerpt that follows, Professor Edward Brunet discusses the relationship between arbitration and constitutional rights and suggests that parts of the FAA text could be relied upon to expand the rights of parties in arbitration proceedings:

The relationship between constitutional rights and arbitration is uneasy. Classical arbitration theory rejects the application of definite constitutional rights in an arbitration hearing. Such rights would needlessly judicialize what is supposed to be an informal process. Moreover, the parties have opted out of the formal, judicial process by contracting to arbitrate and have voluntarily removed any "state action" nexus, which would mandate the application of constitutional rights.

The classical view holds true when applied to parties who are experienced, repeat players in arbitration. Any argument of wholesale waiver of procedural rights, however, which applies to all arbitration fails to account for the explosive growth of arbitration. Arbitration has grown into areas such as consumer purchases or consumer loans where rookie signatories to arbitration clauses are unlikely to waive constitutional rights intentionally or intelligently. The doctrine of waiver of constitutional rights is, at this time, simply inadequate to explain the absence of constitutional rights in all arbitration settings.

How can increased procedural protections find their way into both the arbitration hearing and judicial review of arbitration awards? The lack of a traditional basis of state action makes it improbable that courts will mandate the application of constitutional rights. A much more attractive legal ground is a historically accurate reading of the FAA which requires courts to protect "rights" of arbitral parties. The FAA's text provides a basis for vacating awards obtained by "undue means" and to safeguard "the rights" of parties to an arbitration. To date, courts have largely ignored these phrases, perhaps because of a general feeling that courts should avoid review of arbitral awards.

Edward Brunet, *Arbitration and Constitutional Rights*, 71 N.C. L. Rev. 81, 119 (1992).

Professor Reuben challenges the traditional distinction between public and private processes and asserts that contract-based arbitration under the FAA is state action. After discussing what he describes as "minimal but meaningful due process standards," Professor Reuben concludes that:

> Despite the arguments against its adoption, there is an air of inevitability about the recognition of state action in some seemingly private ADR processes, if not the embrace of a more fully developed unitary theory of public civil dispute resolution. The more court-related ADR expands, the more reasonable it is to expect questions to be raised in judicial forums over due process, the First Amendment, equal protection, and possibly other constitutional issues. The more those constitutional questions are raised in the court-related context, the greater the likelihood that courts will recognize that those processes are driven by state action and therefore compel at least rudimentary notions of due process as a constitutional imperative. In time, the illogic of having different standards of fundamental fairness applicable in the court-related and contractual contexts—especially given that the same neutrals frequently serve in both spheres—may lead to the crumbling of that wall in practice if not in theory. At that point, the wall between the public and private dispute resolution systems will become imperceptibly thin, the elements of a unitary system of dispute resolution will begin to align, and the best promises of ADR will be well on their way to being finally fulfilled.

Richard C. Reuben, *Constitutional Gravity: A Unitary Theory of Alternative Dispute Resolution and Public Civil Justice*, 47 UCLA L. Rev. 949, 1104 (2000).

What would be the consequences for judicial review of accepting the proposals of Brunet and Reuben?

12. Section 11 of the FAA authorizes modification or correction of an award in the following circumstances:

(a) Where there was an evident material miscalculation of figures or an evident material mistake in the description of any person, thing, or property referred to in the award.

(b) Where the arbitrators have awarded upon a matter not submitted to them, unless it is a matter not affecting the merits of the decision upon the matter submitted.

(c) Where the award is imperfect in matter of form not affecting the merits of the controversy.

The order may modify and correct the award, to effect the intent thereof and promote justice between the parties.

b. Contracted Judicial Review

Finality is one of the hallmarks of the arbitration process. As we have seen, in practice this means that arbitration awards are generally not subject to substantive judicial review. Rather, judicial review is limited to impropriety on the part of the arbitrator under Section (10)(a) of the Federal Arbitration Act.

But what if the parties want the arbitrator to follow the law, and to have courts review the arbitral award for legal error? As arbitration has grown and has become more popular for sophisticated business disputes, some parties have chosen to include judicial review provisions in their arbitration clauses. The federal courts of appeal quickly divided on whether the FAA permits parties to opt back into the public system of law for purposes of judicial review. Some, led for some time by the 9th U.S. Circuit Court of Appeal, held that parties could contract for judicial review as long as the review didn't call for courts to use unfamiliar standards. *Lapine Tech. Corp. v. Kyocera Corp.*, 130 F.3d 884, 891 (9th Cir. 1997) vacated, *Kyocera Corp. v. Prudential–Bache Trade Servs., Inc.*, 341 F.3d 987 (9th Cir. 2003) (en banc). Concurring in the first Kyocera case, Judge Alex Kozinski famously said he "would call the case differently if the agreement provided that the district judge would review the award by flipping a coin or studying the entrails of a dead fowl." *Id.* at 891. Other courts, led by Judge Richard Posner of the 7th Circuit, held that parties could not contract for judicial review because federal jurisdiction cannot be established by contract. *Chicago Typographical Union No. 16 v. Chicago Sun–Times, Inc.*, 935 F.2d 1501 (7th Cir. 1991).

The U.S. Supreme Court resolved that conflict in the following case. As you read the opinion, consider whether it goes farther than merely mending the conflict between the circuits.

HALL STREET ASSOCIATES, L.L.C. v. MATTEL, INC.

Supreme Court of the United States, 2008
128 S.Ct. 1396, 170 L.Ed.2d 254

JUSTICE SOUTER delivered the opinion of the Court.

The Federal Arbitration Act (FAA or Act), 9 U.S.C. § 1 et seq., provides for expedited judicial review to confirm, vacate, or modify arbitration awards. §§ 9–11. The question here is whether statutory grounds for prompt vacatur and modification may be supplemented by contract. We hold that the statutory grounds are exclusive.

I

['The case arises from an environmental dispute between a landlord, Hall Street, and a tenant, Mattel. After a trial court sustained Mattel's right to terminate its lease with petitioner Hall Street, the parties proposed to arbitrate Hall Street's claim for indemnification of the costs of environmental clean up. The District Court approved, and entered as an order, the parties' arbitration agreement, which, *inter alia,* required the court to vacate, modify, or correct any award if the arbitrator's conclusions of law were erroneous. The arbitrator decided for Mattel, but the District Court vacated the award for legal error, expressly invoking the agreement's legal-error review standard and citing the Ninth Circuit's *LaPine* decision for the proposition that the FAA allows parties to draft a contract dictating an alternative review standard. On remand, the arbitrator ruled for Hall Street, and the District Court largely upheld the award, again applying the parties' stipulated review standard. The Ninth Circuit reversed, holding the case controlled by its Kyocera decision, which had overruled *LaPine* on the ground that arbitration-agreement terms fixing the mode of judicial review are unenforceable, given the exclusive grounds for vacatur and modification provided by FAA §§ 10 and 11.]

II

* * * The [Federal Arbitration] Act ... supplies mechanisms for enforcing arbitration awards: a judicial decree confirming an award, an order vacating it, or an order modifying or correcting it. §§ 9–11. An application for any of these orders will get streamlined treatment as a motion, obviating the separate contract action that would usually be necessary to enforce or tinker with an arbitral award in court. § 6. Under the terms of § 9, a court "must" confirm an arbitration award "unless" it is vacated, modified, or corrected "as prescribed" in §§ 10 and 11. Section 10 lists grounds for vacating an award, while § 11 names those for modifying or correcting one.[4]

---

[4]   Title *9 U.S.C. § 10(a)* provides:

The Courts of Appeals have split over the exclusiveness of these statutory grounds when parties take the FAA shortcut to confirm, vacate, or modify an award, with some saying the recitations are exclusive, and others regarding them as mere threshold provisions open to expansion by agreement.[5] As mentioned already, when this litigation started, the Ninth Circuit was on the threshold side of the split, see *LaPine,* from which it later departed en banc in favor of the exclusivity view, see *Kyocera,* which it followed in this case. We now hold that §§ 10 and 11 respectively provide the FAA's exclusive grounds for expedited vacatur and modification.

III

Hall Street makes two main efforts to show that the grounds set out for vacating or modifying an award are not exclusive, taking the position, first, that expandable judicial review authority has been accepted as the law since *Wilko v. Swan,* 346 U.S. 427, 74 S. Ct. 182, 98 L. Ed. 168 (1953). This, however, was not what *Wilko* decided, which was that *§ 14* of the

---

"(a) In any of the following cases the United States court in and for the district wherein the award was made may make an order vacating the award upon the application of any party to the arbitration—

"(1) where the award was procured by corruption, fraud, or undue means;

"(2) where there was evident partiality or corruption in the arbitrators, or either of them;

"(3) where the arbitrators were guilty of misconduct in refusing to postpone the hearing, upon sufficient cause shown, or in refusing to hear evidence pertinent and material to the controversy; or of any other misbehavior by which the rights of any party have been prejudiced; or

"(4) where the arbitrators exceeded their powers, or so imperfectly executed them that a mutual, final, and definite award upon the subject matter submitted was not made."

Title *9 U.S.C. § 11 (2000 ed.)* provides:

"In either of the following cases the United States court in and for the district wherein the award was made may make an order modifying or correcting the award upon the application of any party to the arbitration—

"(a) Where there was an evident material miscalculation of figures or an evident material mistake in the description of any person, thing, or property referred to in the award.

"(b) Where the arbitrators have awarded upon a matter not submitted to them, unless it is a matter not affecting the merits of the decision upon the matter submitted.

"(c) Where the award is imperfect in matter of form not affecting the merits of the controversy.

"The order may modify and correct the award, so as to effect the intent thereof and promote justice between the parties."

[5]   The Ninth and Tenth Circuits have held that parties may not contract for expanded judicial review. See *Kyocera Corp. v. Prudential–Bache Trade Servs., Inc.,* 341 F.3d 987, 1000 (CA9 2003); *Bowen v. Amoco Pipeline Co.,* 254 F.3d 925, 936 (CA10 2001). The First, Third, Fifth, and Sixth Circuits, meanwhile, have held that parties may so contract. See *Puerto Rico Tel. Co. v. U.S. Phone Mfg. Corp.,* 427 F.3d 21, 31 (CA1 2005); *Jacada (Europe), Ltd. v. International Marketing Strategies, Inc.con,* 401 F.3d 701, 710 (CA6 2005); *Roadway Package System, Inc. v. Kayser,* 257 F.3d 287, 288 (CA3 2001); *Gateway Technologies, Inc. v. MCI Telecommunications Corp.,* 64 F.3d 993, 997 (CA5 1995). The Fourth Circuit has taken the latter side of the split in an unpublished opinion, see *Syncor Int'l Corp. v. McLeland,* 120 F.3d 262 (1997), while the Eighth Circuit has expressed agreement with the former side in dicta, see *UHC Management Co. v. Computer Sciences Corp.,* 148 F.3d 992, 997–998 (1998).

Securities Act of 1933 voided any agreement to arbitrate claims of violations of that Act, a holding since overruled by *Rodriguez de Quijas v. Shearson/American Express, Inc.*, 490 U.S. 477, 484, 109 S. Ct. 1917, 104 L. Ed. 2d 526 (1989). Although it is true that the Court's discussion includes some language arguably favoring Hall Street's position, arguable is as far as it goes.

The *Wilko* Court was explaining that arbitration would undercut the Securities Act's buyer protections when it remarked (citing FAA § 10) that "[p]ower to vacate an [arbitration] award is limited," and went on to say that "the interpretations of the law by the arbitrators in contrast to manifest disregard [of the law] are not subject, in the federal courts, to judicial review for error in interpretation[.]" Hall Street reads this statement as recognizing "manifest disregard of the law" as a further ground for vacatur on top of those listed in § 10, and some Circuits have read it the same way. Hall Street sees this supposed addition to § 10 as the camel's nose: if judges can add grounds to vacate (or modify), so can contracting parties.

But this is too much for *Wilko* to bear. Quite apart from its leap from a supposed judicial expansion by interpretation to a private expansion by contract, Hall Street overlooks the fact that the statement it relies on expressly rejects just what Hall Street asks for here, general review for an arbitrator's legal errors. Then there is the vagueness of *Wilko*'s phrasing. Maybe the term "manifest disregard" was meant to name a new ground for review, but maybe it merely referred to the § 10 grounds collectively, rather than adding to them. Or, as some courts have thought, "manifest disregard" may have been shorthand for § 10(a)(3) or § 10(a)(4), the subsections authorizing vacatur when the arbitrators were "guilty of misconduct" or "exceeded their powers." We, when speaking as a Court, have merely taken the *Wilko* language as we found it, without embellishment, see *First Options of Chicago, Inc. v. Kaplan*, and now that its meaning is implicated, we see no reason to accord it the significance that Hall Street urges.

Second, Hall Street says that the agreement to review for legal error ought to prevail simply because arbitration is a creature of contract, and the FAA is "motivated, first and foremost, by a congressional desire to enforce agreements into which parties ha[ve] entered." But, again, we think the argument comes up short. Hall Street is certainly right that the FAA lets parties tailor some, even many features of arbitration by contract, including the way arbitrators are chosen, what their qualifications should be, which issues are arbitrable, along with procedure and choice of substantive law. But to rest this case on the general policy of treating arbitration agreements as enforceable as such would be to beg the question, which is whether the FAA has textual features at odds with enforcing a contract to expand judicial review following the arbitration.

To that particular question we think the answer is yes, that the text compels a reading of the §§ 10 and 11 categories as exclusive. [Court's statutory analysis omitted.] * * *

That aside, expanding the detailed categories would rub too much against the grain of the § 9 language, where provision for judicial confirmation carries no hint of flexibility. On application for an order confirming the arbitration award, the court "must grant" the order "unless the award is vacated, modified, or corrected as prescribed in sections 10 and 11 of this title." There is nothing malleable about "must grant," which unequivocally tells courts to grant confirmation in all cases, except when one of the "prescribed" exceptions applies. This does not sound remotely like a provision meant to tell a court what to do just in case the parties say nothing else.

* * * Instead of fighting the text, it makes more sense to see the three provisions, §§ 9–11, as substantiating a national policy favoring arbitration with just the limited review needed to maintain arbitration's essential virtue of resolving disputes straightaway. Any other reading opens the door to the full-bore legal and evidentiary appeals that can "rende[r] informal arbitration merely a prelude to a more cumbersome and time-consuming judicial review process," and bring arbitration theory to grief in post-arbitration process. . . .

IV

In holding that §§ 10 and 11 provide exclusive regimes for the review provided by the statute, we do not purport to say that they exclude more searching review based on authority outside the statute as well. The FAA is not the only way into court for parties wanting review of arbitration awards: they may contemplate enforcement under state statutory or common law, for example, where judicial review of different scope is arguable. But here we speak only to the scope of the expeditious judicial review under §§ 9, 10, and 11, deciding nothing about other possible avenues for judicial enforcement of arbitration awards.

* * *

Although we agree with the Ninth Circuit that the FAA confines its expedited judicial review to the grounds listed in 9 U.S.C. §§ 10 and 11, we vacate the judgment and remand the case for proceedings consistent with this opinion.

It is so ordered.

[Dissents by JUSTICE STEVENS and KENNEDY, and JUSTICE BREYER, are omitted.]

NOTES AND QUESTIONS

1.   The *Hall Street Associates* opinion makes clear that the grounds for vacatur under the Federal Arbitration Act are limited to those specified in Section 10. What does that portend for the non-statutory grounds discussed in Note 3 to the *Sobel* case on p. 671, such as manifest disregard, public policy, arbitrary and capriciousness, and irrationality?

Manifest disregard is considered more fully on p. 694. But for now consider the public policy exception. As you recall from earlier discussion p. 678, courts have been willing to set aside arbitration awards that the award violates clearly established public policy. But that is a non-statutory ground, and *Hall Street* is quite clear in holding that the statutory grounds are exclusive under the Federal Arbitration Act. If so, then there can be no public policy ground for vacatur anymore. But can that result be taken seriously? How should a court rule on an arbitration award that requires one of the parties to do an illegal act? Is there a persuasive and principled argument that *Hall Street* should not be applied so rigidly?

Irrationality and arbitrary and capricious as non-statutory grounds raise similar questions. Suppose an arbitrator is hearing an intentional tort claim between two former friends who got into a fight over a borrowed motorcycle that was not returned, and that the submission to arbitration did not limit the arbitrator to applying the law in deciding the case but does call for the arbitrator to issue a written decision. Suppose further that as the arbitration hearing proceeded that the person who borrowed the bike thought he had a right to the bike because the other party didn't pay as agreed on a drug deal between the two. Finally, suppose the parties both ask the arbitrator not to mention anything about the drug deal in any way, and the arbitrator decides the dispute in favor of the person who took the motorcycle and writes an opinion grounded exclusively in the facts of the motorcycle dispute—facts that, in the absence of knowledge about the underlying drug deal, would lead most reasonably prudent readers of the award to conclude the bike ownwer should have won the case rather than the bike borrower. The bike owner then goes to court asking for the award to be reversed as either irrational or arbitratry and capricious in light of the facts determined by the arbitrator. What should the trial court do after *Hall Street?*

2.   *Hall Street* left open the question of whether parties could obtain substantive judicial review by arguing that the arbitrator exceeded her powers by failing to apply the law when so instructed by the parties. Indeed, the court seemed to have tacitly endorsed that possibility by acknowledging ". . . as some courts have thought, 'manifest disregard' may have been shorthand for § 10(a)(3) or § 10(a)(4), the subsections authorizing vacatur when the arbitrators were 'guilty of misconduct' or 'exceeded their powers.' "

However, in 2013 the court appeared to forclose this argument when it rejected a similar claim in *Oxford Health Plans LLC v. Sutter,* 133 S.Ct. 2064 (2013). In that case, a class action, physicians sued Oxford for failing to pay for certain treatments. As a preliminary matter, the arbitrator determined that the parties agreed to permit class actions when they entered into the contract containing the arbitration provision.

After the arbitrator's ruling on that question, the U.S. Supreme Court held that class actions could only be maintained in arbitration if they were author*ized by the parties. Stolt Nielsen, S.A. v. AnimalFeeds Int'l Corp.*, 599 U.S. 662 (2010). Following that decision, Oxford asked the arbitrator to reconsider his ruling in light of *Stolt–Nielsen*, essentially arguing that the parties did not *explicitly* agree to class arbitration, and that *Stolt–Nielsen* precluded an arbitrator from finding an *implied* agreement to arbitrate class actions. When the arbitrator reaffirmed his ruling, Oxford appealed to the U.S. Supreme Court, contending that the arbitrator had misapplied *Stolt–Nielsen.*

The high court unanimously rejected that argument and reiterated the limited scope of Section 10(a)(4) review. "the sole question for us is whether the arbitrator (even arguably) interpreted the parties' contract, not whether he got its meaning right or wrong." Justice Elena Kagan wrote for the court. "Twice . . . the arbitrator did what the parties had asked: He considered their contract and decided whether it reflected an agreement to permit class proceedings. That suffices to show that the arbitrator did not 'exceed[ ] [his] power[ ]' under § 10(a)(4)."

3.   The court's opinion is limited to judicial review of arbitration awards by public courts. Parties may, however, seek private review of their arbitration awards—in effect, arbitrations of the arbitral award. The American Arbitration Association approved new optional rules in November, 2013, to facilitate this possibility. http:// www. adr.org/aaa/ShowProperty? nodeId=/UCM/ADRSTAGE2016218&revision=latestreleased.   (last   visited Dec. 16, 2013). Would this be of interest to you? What are the arguments for and against including such a provision? Are there situations in which it might make more sense? Less sense?

4.   In Part IV of its opinion, the court suggests parties seeking expanded judicial review "may contemplate enforcement under state statutory or common law." Recall, though, the preemptive breadth the court has given the FAA in *Southland, Doctor's Associates, Buckeye Check Cashing*, and, most recently, in *Concepcion* court, where the court said the FAA preempts state laws that interfere with the "purposes and objectives" of the FAA.

a.   How can the tension between these two propositions be reconciled? Does the answer lie in the nature of the claims? *Southland, Doctor's Associates, Buckeye Check Cashing,* and *Concepcion* were all Section 2 enforcement claims, while *Hall Street Associates* focuses on the vacatur and modification provisions of Sections 9–11. Are there reasons that might justify greater deference to state law for purposes of judicial review than for purposes of the initial enforcement of the arbitration award?

b.   Would a state law permitting parties to contract for judicial review be preempted by the FAA? Under what theory might it be valid? For insight into this question, see Maureen A. Weston, *The Other Avenues of Hall Street and Prospects for Judicial Review of Arbitration Awards*, 14 Lewis & Clark L. Rev. 929 (2010) (arguing, inter alia, that parties who want judicial review of arbitration awards can agree to opt out of the Federal Arbitration).

c.   Assuming such a statute were valid and that parties specified that state law would govern the arbitration proceeding, would the availability of judicial review make state courts a more attractive forum for enforcement of arbitration awards? Under what conditions might you advise a client to include a judicial review provision?

d.   Courts have been found to have the "inherent power" to "manage their own affairs so as to achieve the orderly and expeditious resolution of their cases." *Chambers v. NASCO*, 501 U.S. 32, 43 (1991). This inherent power has been held to include the power to discipline attorneys who practice before it, to issue contempt citations, and to vacate its own judgment upon proof that a fraud has been perpetuated upon it. Under what circumstances might a court have the inherent power to correct legal errors by an arbitrator?

5.   Claims for judicial review also press the question of just when an arbitrator is required to apply the law to begin with, much less correctly. Practicing arbitrators are deeply split on this issue. Some will contend that an arbitrator is always bound to apply the law and that this obligation arises from the fact that they are interpreting a legal document. Under this view, the obligation to apply the law is an implied term of the contract or is least an expectation of the parties that they have to comply with as a practical matter to assure the legitimacy of their award.

Others, however, will contend that there is no inherent obligation to apply the law, and that the very nature of the arbitration process calls for the arbitrator to apply their best judgment, and that the basis for that judgment may be something other than legal standards, such as industry norms or the informal practices of a particularly company. Under this view, the arbitrator's obligation to apply the law must be expressly invoked by the parties in the submission to the arbitration agreement.

Which side do you think has the better view? Why? If you tend to side with those who call for the obligation to apply the law to be explicit, how explicit does the statement have to be? What if the arbitration clause is in a contract that also includes a choice of law provision stating: "This contract shall be governed by the law of the state of Delaware." Is that enough to obligate an arbitrator to apply Delaware law in deciding the dispute submitted to him?

6.   In rejecting the freedom of contract argument, the *Hall Street* court said "limited review" was needed "to maintain arbitration's essential virtue of resolving disputes straightaway. Any other reading opens the door to the full-

bore legal and evidentiary appeals that can rende[r] informal arbitration merely a prelude to a more cumbersome and time-consuming judicial review process, and bring arbitration theory to grief in post-arbitration process." What arbitration process virtues would be compromised by a ruling that would permit such broad appeals? *See* Richard C. Reuben, *Process Purity and Innovation: A Response to Professors Stempel, Cole, and Drahozal*, 8 Nev. L. J. 271, 293–296 (2007).

7.   The court in *Hall Street Associates* discusses the "vagueness" of the phrase "manifest disregard," but unfortunately does not provide any clarification, other than to say that manifest disregard does not mean that courts can review arbitration awards for legal errors, as *Hall Street Associates* had argued. We look more closely at the manifest disregard doctrine in the next section.

c.   Manifest Disregard of the Law

As brief and inconclusive as it was, the court's discussion of manifest disregard in *Hall Street Associates* is its most extensive to date. The doctrine raises fundamental questions about the nature of the arbitration process, and its relationship to the rule of law, and is worth more focused attention.

The doctrine generally holds that an arbitral award may be reversed if it was in "manifest disregard of the law," and emanates from dictum in the U.S. Supreme Court's decision in *Wilko v. Swan*, excerpted above at p. 620. In deciding that judicial forum rights were not the kind of rights that could be waived, the court also noted in passing:

> While it may be true . . . that a failure of the arbitrators to decide in accordance with the provisions of the Securities Act would "constitute grounds for vacating the award pursuant to section 10 of the Federal Arbitration Act," that failure would need to be made clearly to appear. In unrestricted submissions, such as the present margin agreements envisage, the interpretations of the law by the arbitrators in contrast to manifest disregard are not subject, in the federal courts, to judicial review for error in interpretation.

The court's dictum was ambiguous, and unpacking the language does help us understand it better, if only by a bit. By an "unrestricted submission," the court is re referring to the fact that the submission to arbitration did not require the arbitrator to apply the law in the matter before it. Therefore, read without the reference to manifest disregard, the passage is simply a reaffirmation of the time-honored, bedrock principle that errors of law—in this case—the interpretation of the Securities Act of 1933—are not subject to review for errors of law.

By adding the phrase "manifest disregard," however, the court implied that some legal-error claims could succeed—specifically, those in which the claim was that the arbitral award was legally erroneous because it was in "manifest disregard" of the law. The court, however, did not specify what the phrase meant, and left it to the lower courts to work out. By 1999, all of the federal courts of appeal and some state courts had adopted the manifest disregard doctrine in some form. While not uniform, there was general agreement that the phrase refers to situations in the arbitrator knew what the law was that controlled the facts before her and deliberately ignored it in reaching a decision that was contrary to that rule. See Michael H. LeRoy, *Are Arbitrators Above the Law? The "Manifest Disregard of the Law" Standard*, 52 B.C.L. REV. 137, 158–171 (2011) (circuit by circuit analysis of cases).

The U.S. Supreme Court has not adopted that interpretation, however. To the contrary, with rare candor, the justices in *Hall Street* all but threw up their hands in admitting they didn't know what the phrase means or how it fits within the statutory vacatur framework of the FAA. Said Justice Souter about "the vagueness of *Wilko*'s phrasing":

> Maybe the term "manifest disregard" was meant to name a new ground for review, but maybe it merely referred to the § 10 grounds collectively, rather than adding to them. Or, as some courts have thought, "manifest disregard" may have been shorthand for § 10(a)(3) or § 10(a)(4), the subsections authorizing vacatur when the arbitrators were "guilty of misconduct" or "exceeded their powers."

The federal courts have deeply split on the question of whether "manifest disregard" survives *Hall Street* as a ground for vacatur. Some circuits have held that *Hall Street*'s limitation of judicial review to the FAA's statutory grounds effectively abolishes the doctrine. See, e.g., *Citigroup Global Mkts., Inc. v. Bacon*, 562 F.3d 349, 355 (5th Cir. 2009) (overruling circuit precedent recognizing manifest disregard doctrine). Others circuits have held that the doctrine survives, relying on the fact that the *Hall Street* court did not explicitly overrule the manifest disregard doctrine in *Hall Street* when it clearly could have. See, e.g. *Coffee Beanery, Ltd. v. WW, L.L.C.*, 300 F. App'x 415, 418–19 (6th Cir. 2008) (*Hall Street* "significantly reduced the ability of federal courts to vacate arbitration awards for reasons other than those specified in 9 U.S.C. § 10, but it did not foreclose federal courts' review for an arbitrator's manifest disregard of the law.")

Even if manifest disregard is found to survive *Hall Street*, Manifest disregard claims are rarely successful. *Montes v. Shearson Lehman Bros, Inc.*, 128 F.3d 1456 (11th Cir. 1997), is an often-cited example of the rare case accepting a manifest disregard challenge. In that case, counsel specifically asked the arbitrators to ignore the law in her closing arguments. Under these circumstances, the court said it was "able to clearly discern from the record that this is one of those cases where manifest disregard of the law is applicable, as the arbitrators recognized that they were told to disregard the law (which the record reflects they knew) in a case in which the evidence to support the award was marginal. Thus, there is nothing in the record to refute the suggestion that the law was disregarded. Nor does the record clearly support the award." *Id.* at 1462.

Similarly in *Halligan v. Piper Jaffray, Inc.*, 148 F.3d 197, 203–04 (2nd Cir. 1998), the Second Circuit found manifest disregard because Halligan had presented overwhelming evidence of age discrimination, both parties had agreed upon the law governing the claim and explained it to the arbitrator, and the arbitrator still ruled against the age discrimination claim in a decision unaccompanied by a written and reasoned decision. Said the court: "In view of the strong evidence that Halligan was fired because of his age and the agreement of the parties that the arbitrators were correctly advised of the applicable legal principles, we are inclined to hold that they ignored the law or the evidence or both." In the absence of an opinion explaining the award, the court went on to express its "firm belief that the arbitrators have manifestly disregarded the law or the evidence or both." *Id.* at 204.

NOTES AND QUESTIONS

1.   The split in the federal circuit courts suggests that the vitality (and meaning) of manifest disregard is ripe for resolution by the U.S. Supreme Court. Do you think that will happen? Are there reasons why the Supreme Court would not want to decide this question? Are there reasons it would? What is the harm that the doctrine seeks to address? How would frame your argument to the court if you were seeking to get it to review the doctrine in a factually appropriate case? If you were opposing *certiorari*?

2.   Scholars have proposed several approaches for dealing with manifest regard in the wake of *Hall Street*. What are the pros and cons of the following suggestions:

a. Professor Reuben argues that the doctrine should be abolished for good. "Manifest disregard has no place in the modern structure of arbitration for general submissions to arbitration," he contends. Reuben calls it "a paternalistic remnant of the era of judicial strust of arbitration that undermines personal autonomy, relies on an unsupported rationale, and ultimately is nonsensical." Richard C. Reuben, *Personal Autonomy and Vacatur After Hall Street*, 113 Penn. St. L. Rev. 1103, 1147 (2009).

b. Professor Moses counters that in an age of mandatory arbitration by "private citizen arbitrators," manifest disregard is necessary to assure "that the process is fair, and that arbitral awards resolving statutory claims will not stand upon erroneous conclusions of law." Margaret L. Moses, *Arbitration Law: Who Is In Charge?*, 40 Set. Hall. L. Rev., 147, 189 (2010).

c. Professor Drahozal suggests that the Federal Arbitration Act be modified to include manifest disregard as a statutory ground for vacatur. Christopher R. Drahozal, *Codifying Manifest Disregard*, 8 Nev. L. Rev. 234 (2008). He contends that codification is necessary to ensure the integrity of the judicial process, and is concerned that without manifest disregard review, courts would have to confirm awards that on their face openly refuse to follow established law. He warns this would undermine the legitimacy of the judicial system and "could result in a political backlash against the arbitration process."

d. Dean Bales proposes that manifest disregard of the law should be replaced with the standard of "manifest disregard of the agreement." Under this approach, a court may vacate an arbitration award only if the award fails to "draw[ ] its essence" from the construction of the contract. MyLinda Sims and Richard A. Bales, *Much Ado About Nothing: The Future of Manifest Disregard After* Hall Street, 62 S.C. L. Rev. 407, 408 (2010).

3.   The RUAA drafters opted against codifying manifest disregard, and against codifying a public policy exception, stating:

here are reasons for the RUAA not to embrace either the "manifest disregard" or the "public policy" standards of court review of arbitral awards. The first is presented by the omission from the FAA of either standard. Given that omission, there is a very significant question of possible FAA preemption of such a provision in the RUAA, should the Supreme Court or Congress eventually confirm that the four narrow grounds for vacatur set out in Section 10(a) of the federal act are the exclusive grounds for vacatur. The second reason for not including these vacatur grounds is the dilemma in attempting to fashion unambiguous, "bright line" tests for these two standards. The case law on both vacatur grounds is not just unsettled but also is conflicting and indicates further evolution in the courts. As a result, the Drafting Committee concluded not to add these two grounds for vacatur in the statute. A motion to include the ground of "manifest disregard" in Section 23(a) was defeated by the Committee of the Whole at the July, 2000, meeting of the National Conference of Commissioners on Uniform State Laws. R.U.A.A. § 23, cmt. C(5) (2000).

4.   Georgia is the only state that has codified the manifest disregard standard. O.C.G.A. § 9–9–13(b)(5)(2011) For a critique, see Brent S. Gilfedder, *"A Manifest Disregard of Arbitration? An Analysis of Recent Georgia Legislation Adding 'Manifest Disregard of the Law' to the Georgia Arbitration Code as a Statutory Ground for Vacatur"*, 39 Ga. L. Rev. 259 (2004); David Boohaker, *Note, The Addition of the "Manifest Disregard of the Law" Defense to Georgia's Arbitration Code and Potential Conflicts with Federal Law*, 21 Ga. St. U. L. Rev. 501 (2004).

C. SPECIAL TOPICS

1. CLASS ACTIONS

STOLT NEILSEN SA V. ANIMALFEEDS INT'L. CORP.

Supreme Court of the United States, 2010
559 U.S. 662, 130 S.Ct. 1758, 176 L.Ed.2d 605

JUSTICE ALITO delivered the opinion of the Court.

We granted certiorari in this case to decide whether imposing class arbitration on parties whose arbitration clauses are "silent" on that issue is consistent with the Federal Arbitration Act (FAA).

I

A

Petitioners are shipping companies that serve a large share of the world market for parcel tankers—seagoing vessels with compartments that are separately chartered to customers wishing to ship liquids in small quantities. One of those customers is AnimalFeeds International Corp. (hereinafter AnimalFeeds), which supplies raw ingredients, such as fish oil, to animal-feed producers around the-world. AnimalFeeds ships its goods pursuant to a standard contract known in the maritime trade as a charter party. Numerous charter parties are in regular use, and the charter party that AnimalFeeds uses is known as the "Vegoilvoy" charter party. * * *

Adopted in 1950, the Vegoilvoy charter party contains the following arbitration clause:

> Arbitration. Any dispute arising from the making, performance or termination of this Charter Party shall be settled in New York, Owner and Charterer each appointing an arbitrator, who shall be a merchant, broker or individual experienced in the shipping business; the two thus chosen, if they cannot agree, shall nominate a third arbitrator who shall be an Admiralty lawyer. Such arbitration shall be conducted in conformity with the provisions and procedure of the United States Arbitration Act [i.e., the FAA], and a judgment of the Court shall be entered upon any award made by said arbitrator.

In 2003, a Department of Justice criminal investigation revealed that petitioners were engaging in an illegal price-fixing conspiracy. When AnimalFeeds learned of this, it brought a putative class action against petitioners in the District Court for the Eastern District of Pennsylvania, asserting antitrust claims for supracompetitive prices that petitioners allegedly charged their customers over a period of several years.

* * * The parties agree that as a consequence of the [ ] judgments and orders [in this and other proceedings that compelled the cases into

arbitration], AnimalFeeds and petitioners must arbitrate their antitrust dispute.

B

In 2005, AnimalFeeds served petitioners with a demand for class arbitration, designating New York City as the place of arbitration and seeking to represent a class of "[a]ll direct purchasers of parcel tanker transportation services globally for bulk liquid chemicals, edible oils, acids, and other specialty liquids from [petitioners] at any time during the period from August 1, 1998, to November 30, 2002." The parties entered into a supplemental agreement providing for the question of class arbitration to be submitted to a panel of three arbitrators who were to "follow and be bound by Rules 3 through 7 of the American Arbitration Association's Supplementary Rules for Class Arbitrations (as effective Oct. 8, 2003)." These rules (hereinafter Class Rules) were developed by the American Arbitration Association (AAA) after our decision in *Green Tree Financial Corp. v. Bazzle* (2003), and Class Rule 3, in accordance with the plurality opinion in that case, requires an arbitrator, as a threshold matter, to determine "whether the applicable arbitration clause permits the arbitration to proceed on behalf of or against a class." The parties selected a panel of arbitrators and stipulated that the arbitration clause was "silent" with respect to class arbitration. Counsel for AnimalFeeds explained to the arbitration panel that the term "silent" did not simply mean that the clause made no express reference to class arbitration. Rather, he said, "[a]ll the parties agree that when a contract is silent on an issue there's been no agreement that has been reached on that issue."

After hearing argument and evidence, including testimony from petitioners' experts regarding arbitration customs and usage in the maritime trade, the arbitrators concluded that the arbitration clause allowed for class arbitration. They found persuasive the fact that other arbitrators ruling after *Bazzle* had construed "a wide variety of clauses in a wide variety of settings as allowing for class arbitration," but the panel acknowledged that none of these decisions was "exactly comparable" to the present dispute. Petitioners' expert evidence did not show an "inten[t] to preclude class arbitration," the arbitrators reasoned, and petitioners' argument would leave "no basis for a class action absent express agreement among all parties and the putative class members."

The arbitrators stayed the proceeding to allow the parties to seek judicial review, and petitioners filed an application to vacate the arbitrators' award in the District Court for the Southern District of New York. The District Court vacated the award, concluding that the arbitrators' decision was made in "manifest disregard" of the law insofar as the arbitrators failed to conduct a choice-of-law analysis. Had such an analysis been conducted, the District Court held, the arbitrators would have applied the rule of federal maritime law requiring that contracts be interpreted in light of custom and usage.

AnimalFeeds appealed to the Court of Appeals, which reversed. * * *

We granted certiorari.

II

A

Petitioners contend that the decision of the arbitration panel must be vacated, but in order to obtain that relief, they must clear a high hurdle. It is not enough for petitioners to show that the panel committed an error—or even a serious error. In that situation, an arbitration decision may be vacated under § 10(a)(4) of the FAA on the ground that the arbitrator "exceeded [his] powers," for the task of an arbitrator is to interpret and enforce a contract, not to make public policy. In this case, we must conclude that what the arbitration panel did was simply to impose its own view of sound policy regarding class arbitration.[3]

B

1

In its memorandum of law filed in the arbitration proceedings, AnimalFeeds made three arguments in support of construing the arbitration clause to permit class arbitration:

> The parties' arbitration clause should be construed to allow class arbitration because (a) the clause is silent on the issue of class treatment and, without express prohibition, class arbitration is permitted under *Bazzle*; (b) the clause should be construed to permit class arbitration as a matter of public policy; and (c) the clause would be unconscionable and unenforceable if it forbade class arbitration.

The arbitrators expressly rejected AnimalFeeds' first argument, and said nothing about the third. Instead, the panel appears to have rested its decision on AnimalFeeds' public policy argument. Because the parties agreed their agreement was "silent" in the sense that they had not reached any agreement on the issue of class arbitration, the arbitrators' proper task was to identify the rule of law that governs in that situation. Had they engaged in that undertaking, they presumably would have looked either to the FAA itself or to one of the two bodies of law that the parties claimed were governing, i.e., either federal maritime law or New York law. But the panel did not consider whether the FAA provides the rule of decision in such a situation; nor did the panel attempt to determine what rule would govern under either maritime or New York law in the case of a "silent" contract. Instead, the panel based its decision

---

[3] We do not decide whether " 'manifest disregard' " survives our decision in *Hall Street Associates, L.L.C. v. Mattel, Inc.* (2008), as an independent ground for review or as a judicial gloss on the enumerated grounds for vacatur set forth at 9 U.S.C. § 10. * * *

on post-*Bazzle* arbitral decisions that "construed a wide variety of clauses in a wide variety of settings as allowing for class arbitration." The panel did not mention whether any of these decisions were based on a rule derived from the FAA or on maritime or New York law. * * *

Rather than inquiring whether the FAA, maritime law, or New York law contains a "default rule" under which an arbitration clause is construed as allowing class arbitration in the absence of express consent, the panel proceeded as if it had the authority of a common-law court to develop what it viewed as the best rule to be applied in such a situation. Perceiving a post-*Bazzle* consensus among arbitrators that class arbitration is beneficial in "a wide variety of settings," the panel considered only whether there was any good reason not to follow that consensus in this case. The panel was not persuaded by "court cases denying consolidation of arbitrations," by undisputed evidence that the Vegoilvoy charter party had "never been the basis of a class action," or by expert opinion that "sophisticated, multinational commercial parties of the type that are sought to be included in the class would never intend that the arbitration clauses would permit a class arbitration." Accordingly, finding no convincing ground for departing from the post-*Bazzle* arbitral consensus, the panel held that class arbitration was permitted in this case. The conclusion is inescapable that the panel simply imposed its own conception of sound policy.[7] * * *

2

* * * In sum, instead of identifying and applying a rule of decision derived from the FAA or either maritime or New York law, the arbitration panel imposed its own policy choice and thus exceeded its powers. As a result, under § 10(b) of the FAA, we must either "direct a rehearing by the arbitrators" or decide the question that was originally referred to the panel. Because we conclude that there can be only one possible outcome on the facts before us, we see no need to direct a rehearing by the arbitrators.

III

A

The arbitration panel thought that *Bazzle* "controlled" the "resolution" of the question whether the Vegoilvoy charter party "permit[s] this arbitration to proceed on behalf of a class," but that understanding was incorrect. * * *

When *Bazzle* reached this Court, no single rationale commanded a majority. The opinions of the Justices who joined the judgment—that is, the plurality opinion and Justice Stevens opinion—collectively addressed

---

[7] The dissent calls this conclusion "hardly fair," noting that the word " 'policy' is not so much as mentioned in the arbitrators' award." But just as merely saying something is so does not make it so, the arbitrators need not have said they were relying on policy to make it so.

three separate questions. The first was which decision maker (court or arbitrator) should decide whether the contracts in question were "silent" on the issue of class arbitration. The second was what standard the appropriate decision maker should apply in determining whether a contract allows class arbitration. (For example, does the FAA entirely preclude class arbitration? Does the FAA permit class arbitration only under limited circumstances, such as when the contract expressly so provides? Or is this question left entirely to state law?)

The final question was whether, under whatever standard is appropriate, class arbitration had been properly ordered in the case at hand.

The plurality opinion decided only the first question, concluding that the arbitrator and not a court should decide whether the contracts were indeed "silent" on the issue of class arbitration. * * * The plurality did not decide either the second or the third question noted above. * * *

B

Unfortunately, the opinions in *Bazzle* appear to have baffled the parties in this case at the time of the arbitration proceeding. * * *

As we have explained, however, *Bazzle* did not establish the rule to be applied in deciding whether class arbitration is permitted. The decision in *Bazzle* left that question open, and we turn to it now.

IV

While the interpretation of an arbitration agreement is generally a matter of state law, the FAA imposes certain rules of fundamental importance, including the basic precept that arbitration "is a matter of consent, not coercion."

A

In 1925, Congress enacted the United States Arbitration Act, as the FAA was formerly known, for the express purpose of making "valid and enforceable written provisions or agreements for arbitration of disputes arising out of contracts, maritime transactions, or commerce among the States or Territories or with foreign nations." * * *

Whether enforcing an agreement to arbitrate or construing an arbitration clause, courts and arbitrators must "give effect to the contractual rights and expectations of the parties." In this endeavor, "as with any other contract, the parties' intentions control." This is because an arbitrator derives his or her powers from the parties' agreement to forgo the legal process and submit their disputes to private dispute resolution. * * *

We think it is also clear from our precedents and the contractual nature of arbitration that parties may specify with whom they choose to arbitrate their disputes. It falls to courts and arbitrators to give effect to these contractual limitations, and when doing so, courts and arbitrators must not lose sight of the purpose of the exercise: to give effect to the intent of the parties.

B

From these principles, it follows that a party may not be compelled under the FAA to submit to class arbitration unless there is a contractual basis for concluding that the party agreed to do so. In this case, however, the arbitration panel imposed class arbitration even though the parties concurred that they had reached "no agreement" on that issue. * * * The panel's conclusion is fundamentally at war with the foundational FAA principle that arbitration is a matter of consent.

In certain contexts, it is appropriate to presume that parties that enter into an arbitration agreement implicitly authorize the arbitrator to adopt such procedures as are necessary to give effect to the parties' agreement. Thus, we have said that "procedural" questions which grow out of the dispute and bear on its final disposition' are presumptively not for the judge, but for an arbitrator, to decide. This recognition is grounded in the background principle that "[w]hen the parties to a bargain sufficiently defined to be a contract have not agreed with respect to a term which is essential to a determination of their rights and duties, a term which is reasonable in the circumstances is supplied by the court."

An implicit agreement to authorize class-action arbitration, however, is not a term that the arbitrator may infer solely from the fact of the parties' agreement to arbitrate. This is so because class-action arbitration changes the nature of arbitration to such a degree that it cannot be presumed the parties consented to it by simply agreeing to submit their disputes to an arbitrator. In bilateral arbitration, parties forgo the procedural rigor and appellate review of the courts in order to realize the benefits of private dispute resolution: lower costs, greater efficiency and speed, and the ability to choose expert adjudicators to resolve specialized disputes. But the relative benefits of class-action arbitration are much less assured, giving reason to doubt the parties' mutual consent to resolve disputes through class-wide arbitration

Consider just some of the fundamental changes brought about by the shift from bilateral arbitration to class-action arbitration. An arbitrator chosen according to an agreed-upon procedure, no longer resolves a single dispute between the parties to a single agreement, but instead resolves many disputes between hundreds or perhaps even thousands of parties. Under the Class Rules, "the presumption of privacy and confidentiality" that applies in many bilateral arbitrations "shall not apply in class arbitrations," thus potentially frustrating the parties' assumptions when they agreed to arbitrate. The arbitrator's award no longer purports to bind just the parties to a single arbitration agreement, but adjudicates the rights of absent parties as well. And the commercial stakes of class-action arbitration are comparable to those of class-action litigation, even though the scope of judicial review is much more limited. We think that the differences between bilateral and class-action arbitration are too great for arbitrators to presume, consistent with their limited powers under the FAA, that the parties' mere silence on the issue of class-action arbitration constitutes consent to resolve their disputes in class proceedings.[10]

* * * Here, where the parties stipulated that there was "no agreement" on this question, it follows that the parties cannot be compelled to submit their dispute to class arbitration.

V

For these reasons, the judgment of the Court of Appeals is reversed, and the case is remanded for further proceedings consistent with this opinion.

JUSTICE GINSBURG, with whom JUSTICE STEVENS and JUSTICE BREYER join, dissenting.

When an arbitration clause is silent on the question, may arbitration proceed on behalf of a class? The Court prematurely takes up that important question and, indulging in de novo review, overturns the ruling of experienced arbitrators.

The Court errs in addressing an issue not ripe for judicial review. Compounding that error, the Court substitutes its judgment for that of the decisionmakers chosen by the parties. I would dismiss the petition as improvidently granted. Were I to reach the merits, I would adhere to the strict limitations the Federal Arbitration Act (FAA) places on judicial review of arbitral awards. Accordingly, I would affirm the judgment of the Second Circuit, which rejected petitioners' plea for vacation of the arbitrators' decision.

* * *

II

I consider, first, the fitness of the arbitrators' clause-construction award for judicial review. The arbitrators decided the issue, in accord with the parties' supplemental agreement, "as a threshold matter." Their decision that the charter-party arbitration clause permitted class arbitration was abstract and highly interlocutory. The panel did not decide whether the particular claims AnimalFeeds advanced were suitable for class resolution; much less did it delineate any class or

---

[10] We have no occasion to decide what contractual basis may support a finding that the parties agreed to authorize class-action arbitration. Here, as noted, the parties stipulated that there was "no agreement" on the issue of class-action arbitration.

consider whether, "if a class is certified, . . . members of the putative class should be required to 'opt in' to th[e] proceeding."

The Court does not persuasively justify judicial intervention so early in the game or convincingly reconcile its adjudication with the firm final-judgment rule prevailing in the federal court system. * * *

Section 16 of the FAA, governing appellate review of district court arbitration orders, lists as an appealable disposition a district court decision "confirming or denying confirmation of an award or partial award." Notably, the arbitrators in the matter at hand labeled their decision "Partial Final Clause Construction Award." It cannot be true, however, that parties or arbitrators can gain instant review by slicing off a preliminary decision or a procedural order and declaring its resolution a "partial award."

Lacking this Court's definitive guidance, some Courts of Appeals have reviewed arbitration awards "finally and definitely dispos[ing] of a separate independent claim." Another confirmed an interim ruling on a "separate, discrete, independent, severable issue."

Receptivity to review of preliminary rulings rendered by arbitrators, however, is hardly universal.

While lower court opinions are thus divided, this much is plain: No decision of this Court, until today, has ever approved immediate judicial review of an arbitrator's decision as preliminary as the "partial award" made in this case.

III

Even if Stolt–Nielsen had a plea ripe for judicial review, the Court should reject it on the merits. Recall that the parties jointly asked the arbitrators to decide, initially, whether the arbitration clause in their shipping contracts permitted class proceedings. The panel did just what it was commissioned to do. It construed the broad arbitration clause (covering "[a]ny dispute arising from the making, performance or termination of this Charter Party," and ruled, expressly and only, that the clause permitted class arbitration. The Court acts without warrant in allowing Stolt–Nielsen essentially to repudiate its submission of the contract-construction issue to the arbitration panel, and to gain, in place of the arbitrators' judgment, this Court's de novo determination.

A

The controlling FAA prescription, § 10(a), authorizes a court to vacate an arbitration panel's decision "only in very unusual circumstances." The four grounds for vacatur codified in § 10(a) restate the longstanding rule that, "[i]f [an arbitration] award is within the submission, and contains the honest decision of the arbitrators, after a full and fair hearing of the parties, a court . . . will not set [the award] aside for error, either in law or fact."

The sole § 10 ground Stolt–Nielsen invokes for vacating the arbitrators' decision is § 10(a)(4). The question under that provision is "whether the arbitrators had the power, based on the parties' submissions or the arbitration agreement, to reach a certain issue, not whether the arbitrators correctly decided that issue. The parties' supplemental agreement, referring the class-arbitration issue to an arbitration panel, undoubtedly empowered the arbitrators to render their clause-construction decision. That scarcely debatable point should resolve this case.

B

The Court's characterization of the arbitration panel's decision as resting on "policy," not law, is hardly fair comment, for "policy" is not so much as mentioned in the arbitrators' award. Instead, the panel tied its conclusion that the arbitration clause permitted class arbitration to New York law, federal maritime law, and decisions made by other panels pursuant to Rule 3 of the American Arbitration Association's Supplementary Rules for Class Arbitrations.

* * * Emphasizing the breadth of the clause in question—" 'any dispute arising from the making, performance or termination of this Charter Party' shall be put to arbitration," the panel noted that numerous other partial awards had relied on language similarly comprehensive to permit class proceedings "in a wide variety of settings." The panel further noted "that many of the other panels [had] rejected arguments similar to those advanced by [Stolt–Nielsen]." * * *

The question properly before the Court is not whether the arbitrators' ruling was erroneous, but whether the arbitrators "exceeded their powers" [under FAA § 10(a)(4)]. The arbitrators decided a threshold issue, explicitly committed to them, about the procedural mode available for presentation of AnimalFeeds' antitrust claims. That the arbitrators endeavored to perform their assigned task honestly is not contested. "Courts . . . do not sit to hear claims of factual or legal error by an arbitrator as an appellate court does in reviewing decisions of lower courts." The arbitrators here not merely "arguably," but certainly "constru[ed] . . . the contract" with fidelity to their commission. This Court, therefore, may not disturb the arbitrators' judgment, even if convinced that "serious error" infected the panel's award. * * *

NOTES AND QUESTIONS

1. To date, all of the Supreme Court's class arbitration cases have gone against the class arbitration claimant. In 2013, for example, the court held, on a 5–3 vote with Justice Sonya Sotomayor abstaining, that a court could

not invalidate a prospective waiver of class arbitration, even if the costs of proceeding individually effectively precluded prosecution of the action. *American Express Co. v. Italian Colors Restaurant,* 133 S.Ct. 2304 (2013). The case involved an antitrust action against American Express by merchants accepting American Express cards, and Justice Antonin Scalia, writing for the court, eliminated an exception to the enforcement of an arbitration provision if the statutory rights at stake could not be effectively vindicated. "[T]he fact that it is not worth the expense involved in *proving* a statutory remedy does not constitute the elimination of the *right to pursue* that remedy," Scalia wrote. *Id.* at 2311.

2. In *Paying the Price of Process: Judicial Regulation of Consumer Arbitration Agreements,* 2001 J. Disp. Resol. 89, 99–100, Professor Stephen J. Ware contends that arguments for greater regulation of consumer arbitration should factor into their analysis the effect of such regulations on consumer prices.

> The previous section of this article discussed judicial decisions that raise prices (and interest rates) by requiring arbitration to: (1) allow for class actions, (2) subsidize the consumer's fees, (3) include substantial discovery, and (4) encompass both parties' claims. Whether these price increases are worth incurring, i.e., whether the judicial decisions are good policy, plainly depends on a number of factors including the amount of the price increase caused by each category of judicial decision. And different observers will certainly have different views about the value of, for example, class actions and litigation-like discovery. This article makes no attempt to assess the merits of those different views. Rather it argues that any such assessment should consider the influence consumer arbitration law has on the prices consumers pay. Failure to address price inevitably biases any assessment of consumer arbitration law. It is easy to insist upon "due process" in consumer arbitration, indeed "due process is as widely-cherished as 'mom and apple pie,' but the hard thinking begins when one asks who pays the price of process and how much they pay."

See also Christopher R. Drahozal, *Privatizing Civil Justice: Commercial Arbitration and the Civil Justice System,* 9 Kan. J.L. & Pub. Pol'y. 578, 587–88 (2000); but see Jean R. Sternlight & Elizabeth J. Jensen *Using Arbitration to Eliminate Consumer Class Actions: Efficient Business Practice or Unconscionable Abuse?* 67 Law & Contemp. Probs. 75, 92–99 (2004); (repudiating that argument).

Professor Mark E. Budnitz concluded as follows in *The High Cost of Mandatory Consumer Arbitration,* 67 Law & Contemp. Probs. 133, 161 (2004):

> The costs of arbitration can be so high that they deny consumers access to a forum in which to air their disputes. Costs can be excessive whether one considers the consumer's ability to pay, the absolute cost of arbitration, or the cost of arbitration compared to the cost of litigation.

The problem is only exacerbated by agreement terms restricting remedies, class actions, and venue that make the actual cost of arbitration greater than the direct fees charged. Nevertheless, consumers face tremendous obstacles in proving that arbitration agreements should not be enforced because of those high costs. These obstacles arise from several sources. First, to avoid having to pay costs, the consumer must mount her challenge before the arbitration takes place, forcing her in many situations to estimate what the costs might be. In addition, the rules and fee schedules of the arbitration service providers and the common terms of arbitration agreements often makes this estimation extremely difficult, if not impossible. This is only made worse by the courts' disagreement over what factors to consider in estimating the costs of arbitration and what standard to use in determining if those costs are too high.

3.   Recall that in *Green Tree, supra,* the Supreme Court recognized that arbitration costs could preclude a claimant from effectively vindicating her statutory rights, but went on to hold that a plaintiff has the burden of showing a likelihood of incurring a prohibitively expensive financial burden.

Could you fashion an effective argument under *Green Tree* that an arbitration clause cannot be used to prohibit a class action by a large number of consumers with small claims? *See* Sternlight, *Class Action,* at 57–65.

Professor Christopher Drahozal has studied cost cases after *Green Tree,* finding that courts reject cost-based challenges roughly 75% of the time. He further contends that contingency fee arrangements could be used to help plaintiffs of lesser means bring claims in arbitration. Christopher R. Drahozal, *Arbitration Costs and Contingent Fee Contracts,* 59 Vand. L. Rev. 729 (2006).

4.   Professor Maureen Weston calls for Congress and the courts to take steps to provide parties in class arbitrations at least minimal levels of due process protection as well, including notice, a chance for participants to opt out or participate, and adequate representation. In order to protect absent class members and guard against bias, she further argues that courts should handle class certification, supervise the selection of arbitrators, and monitor the adequacy of representation. She also urges Congress to amend the Federal Arbitration Act to incorporate the due process requirements of Rule 23 and to clarify the roles of the arbitrator and court in class action arbitrations. Maureen A. Weston, *Universes Colliding: The Constitutional Implications of Arbitral Class Actions,* 47 WM. & MARY L. REV. 1711 (2006). For an argument that the *Bazzle* decision significantly reduces the role of courts with respect to class arbitration, see Carole J. Buckner, *Toward a Pure Arbitral Paradigm of Classwide Arbitration: Arbitral Power and Federal Preemption,* 82 Den. U. L. Rev. 301 (2004).

2.　CONFIDENTIALITY

As we have discussed, parties may be attracted to arbitration because it is a private and confidential process. It is private because the parties to the arbitration may choose to exclude non-parties from participating in or observing the arbitration hearing, in stark contrast to the public's right to attend public trials. It is confidential because the parties may generally choose to prevent the release of documents and other arbitration communications arising from the arbitration into the public domain—again in strong contrast to the public documents produced during a public trial. *See generally* Amy J. Schmitz, *Untangling the Privacy Paradox in Arbitration*, 54 Kan. L. Rev. 1211 (2006).

But how far do privacy and confidentiality go? How far should they go? Should, for example, arbitration communications be shielded from discovery and admissibility in other proceedings? Consider the following court's answer to that question.

UNITED STATES V. PANHANDLE EASTERN CORP.

United States District Court, D. Delaware, 1988
118 F.R.D. 346

LATCHUM, SENIOR DISTRICT JUDGE.

I.　INTRODUCTION

The present matter arises out of a civil action brought by the United States of America, on behalf of the Maritime Administration, demanding monetary, equitable and declaratory relief from Panhandle Eastern Corporation ("PEC") and its affiliates. . . . The case is currently in the discovery stage. Presently before the Court is the Motion of Defendant Panhandle Eastern Pipe Line Co. ("PEPL") for Protective Order, pursuant to Rule 26(c) of the Federal Rules of Civil Procedure. By its motion, PEPL attempts to prevent the disclosure of documents relating to arbitration proceedings which were held in Geneva, Switzerland between PEPL and Sonatrach, the Algerian National Oil and Gas Company ("Sonatrach Arbitration"). In support of its motion, PEPL essentially argues that disclosure to third parties of documents related to the Sonatrach Arbitration would severely prejudice defendants' ongoing business relationship with both Sonatrach and the Algerian Government. Nevertheless, because the Court finds that PEPL has failed to satisfy the "good cause" requirement of Rule 26(c) of the Federal Rules of Civil Procedure . . . its motion will be denied.

II.　FACTS PERTAINING TO THIS MOTION

The facts needed to be reviewed for an accurate assessment of the present motion are traceable back to May 8, 1987. On that date plaintiff, United States, served PEC with Plaintiff's First Request for Production of

Documents ("Request for Production"). Included within plaintiff's Request for Production were:

> All documents relating to the Sonatrach Arbitration ("Sonatrach Arbitration documents"), including, but not limited to: briefs, correspondence and other papers filed with or submitted to the arbitrators, or their delegates; communications between any and all of the defendants; depositions or other witness statements; transcripts of all hearings before the arbitrators, or their delegates; proposals to settle the arbitration; and, inter- or intra-company documents.

* * *

[T]his Court . . . ordered PEC to produce the requested documents by November 12, 1987, unless the parties mutually agreed to a different time, date or place of production. After the issuance of that order, PEC unsuccessfully sought plaintiff's agreement to a protective order to preserve the "confidentiality" of the Sonatrach Arbitration documents . . . PEC had offered to make the Sonatrach Arbitration documents available . . ., so long as plaintiff would refrain from copying them or taking notes. Plaintiff declined to accept this offer . . . Finally, on December 4, 1987, defendant PEPL filed its motion for a protective order to preserve the alleged "confidentiality of documents" submitted in the Sonatrach Arbitration.

III. ANALYSIS

The standard for issuing a protective order has been clearly articulated by the Third Circuit Court of Appeals in *Cipollone v. Liggett Group, Inc.,* 785 F.2d 1108 (3d Cir.) (*"Cipollone I"*), *on remand,* 113 F.R.D. 86 (D.N.J.1986), *aff'd,* 822 F.2d 335 (3d Cir.1987). In *Cipollone I* the court of appeals stated that Rule 26(c) of the Federal Rules of Civil Procedure places the burden of persuasion on the party seeking the protective order. The rule mandates that to successfully carry this burden "the party seeking the protective order must show good cause by demonstrating a particular need for protection." In order to substantiate the claim, the movant must provide specific examples of the harm that will be suffered because of the disclosure of information; broad-sweeping allegations are insufficient under Rule 26(c). Furthermore, the harm thereby demonstrated "must be significant, not a mere trifle."

Rule 26(c) of the Federal Rules of Civil Procedure reads in pertinent part: Upon motion by a party or by the person from whom discovery is sought, and for good cause shown, the court in which the action is pending . . . may make any order which justice requires to protect a party or person from annoyance, embarrassment, oppression, or undue burden or expense, including one or more of the following: (1) that the discovery not be had; (2) that the discovery may be had only on specified terms and conditions, including a designation of the time or place; (3) that the discovery may be had only by a method of discovery other than that selected by the party seeking discovery; (4) that certain matters not be inquired into, or that the scope of the discovery be limited to certain matters; (5) that discovery be conducted with no one present except persons designated by the court; (6) that a deposition after being sealed be opened only by order of the court; (7) that a trade secret or other confidential research, development, or commercial information not be disclosed or be disclosed only in a designated way. . . .

In light of the foregoing requirements, it is clear that PEPL has failed to carry its burden of showing good cause. The only foundation that PEPL has provided in support of its motion is the affidavit of Louis Begley ("affidavit"), who served as lead counsel for PEPL and Trunkline LNG Co. ("TLC") in the Sonatrach Arbitration. The affidavit first presents the argument that the applicable Rules of the Court of Arbitration of the International Chamber of Commerce ("ICC Rules") require the Sonatrach Arbitration documents to be kept confidential. In support of this argument Begley cites to various rules, including one which states that "[t]he work of the Court of Arbitration is of a confidential character which must be respected by everyone who participates in that work in whatever capacity." However, this rule, as well as another which the affidavit quotes for support, have been culled from Appendix II of the Rules, which is entitled: "Internal Rules of the Court of Arbitration." These rules are therefore meant to be applied internally, governing the members of the Court of Arbitration. They do not apply to the parties to arbitration proceedings or to the independent arbitration tribunal which conducts those proceedings. Furthermore, even if the internal rules somehow applied to the parties, they would govern only those proceedings which take place within the Court of Arbitration, as opposed to those proceedings conducted by arbitrators who were appointed by the Court of Arbitration. As the ICC Rules themselves state: "The Court of Arbitration does not itself settle disputes. Insofar as the parties shall not have provided otherwise, it appoints, or confirms the appointment of, arbitrators in accordance with the provisions of this Article." Therefore, the rules governing the internal functioning of the Court of Arbitration are not applicable here, and provide no support for PEPL's motion.

As support for the other claim, that disclosure will cause PEPL to suffer economic injury, Begley makes the same type of conclusory allegations, which the Third Circuit has held to be insufficient to meet the stringent requirements of Rule 26(c). For example, the affidavit states that at the outset of the Sonatrach Arbitration "a general understanding was reached by counsel . . . that the pleadings and related documents in the [a]rbitration would be kept confidential." However, this assertion is of questionable significance. First, Begley fails to point to any actual agreement of confidentiality, documented or otherwise. Instead, he merely gives his opinion that a "general understanding" existed. Secondly, the affidavit conveniently fails to indicate whether the understanding, if in fact it existed, was reached at Sonatrach's or PEPL's request. This distinction is significant, because elsewhere in the affidavit Begley asserts that he "became aware that Sonatrach is extremely sensitive to revelations of information it considers private." Based on his experience with Sonatrach, Begley "formed the opinion" that privacy and confidentiality were essential to successful business dealings with Sonatrach. Despite Begley's opinion to this effect, however, he never affirmatively asserts that Sonatrach actually sought an understanding as to confidentiality.

Even assuming that an understanding existed, the affidavit fails to provide specific examples of the harm that will befall PEPL upon disclosure. For instance, Begley suggests that by disclosing to third parties certain derogatory statements which defendants may have made about Sonatrach in the arbitration proceedings, defendants would have run the risk of "offending the sensitivities" of Sonatrach and the Algerian Government. Begley concludes that, in his opinion, such disclosures would have been prejudicial to any prospects for a possible settlement to the Sonatrach Arbitration. However, since the settlement has already taken place and been implemented, it is impossible to imagine how present disclosure would harm PEPL in this respect. In any event, if any such potential harm exists, Begley has failed to point it out.

Additionally, Begley asserts that the disclosures would severely prejudice future business negotiations "as to price, quantities and term of deliveries" under a new contract between PEC affiliates and a Sonatrach subsidiary. However, such broad allegations of economic injury, without more, are insufficient to show good cause. Rather, good cause requires a showing that the "disclosures will work a clearly defined and serious injury." Begley's affidavit simply fails to provide such a showing. . . .

IV. CONCLUSION

The Motion of Defendant Panhandle Eastern Pipe Line Co. for Protective Order is predicated upon Rule 26(c) of the Federal Rules of Civil Procedure. The Third Circuit clearly holds that under Rule 26(c) the burden of persuasion falls on the party seeking the protective order. To successfully carry that burden, the movant must show good cause by demonstrating a particular need for protection, substantiated by specific examples of the harm to be suffered upon the disclosure of information. The affidavit which PEPL offers as the sole support for its motion fails to satisfy the good cause requirement of Rule 26(c). Consequently, PEPL has failed to carry its burden of persuasion. . . . In view of all these factors, PEPL's motion will be denied.

An order will be entered in accordance with this Memorandum Opinion.

Notes and Questions

1.   Are you persuaded by the court's analysis? Note that the court finds that the relevant ICC rules limit confidentiality obligations to confidentiality within the Court of Arbitration. The court also finds insufficient evidence of a general understanding that the arbitration would be confidential. Is it possible to give the arbitral rules a broader read than the court gave them? Is it plausible that the parties really did have a general understanding that the arbitration was confidential? What evidence might you use to prove this general understanding? What are the arguments for and against the admissibility of arbitration communications as a matter of policy?

2.   Unlike mediation, confidentiality in arbitration has been given scant attention by legislatures. In a study of arbitration confidentiality statutes and court rules, Professor Reuben found:

> There is surprisingly little protection for arbitration confidentiality in the states. Fewer than half of the states address the issue in either statutes or court rules; a couple of jurisdictions even make it clear that arbitrations are not confidential. This is in stark contrast to the more than 250 state statutes and court rules affecting mediation confidentiality.

> Only seventeen states have statutes that provide any protection to arbitration confidentiality with respect to discovery and admissibility. Of these, only four have statutes that apply to arbitrations generally, regardless of subject matter: Arkansas, California, Missouri, and Texas. The other thirteen states have enacted legislation providing such protections for specific types of arbitrations, such as court-related, consumer, or health-care arbitrations: California, Connecticut, Georgia, Kansas, Maryland, Missouri, Nebraska, New Jersey, North Carolina, South Carolina, Tennessee, Utah, Virginia, and Wisconsin. Both general and subject-matter-specific statutes include exceptions that vary widely. Not one has been interpreted judicially as of this writing.

> Court rules are similarly sparse: only sixteen states have at least one court rule affecting arbitration confidentiality, many of which are limited to attorneys fees, or in the case of South Carolina, law firm disputes. Also, court rules whose protections are limited to court-related non-binding arbitration programs show up in five states: Georgia, Indiana, New Hampshire, Rhode Island, and Vermont.

> The context limitations of the court rules are significant. While several are in states that also provide some statutory protections, arbitrations in those states that have only court rules have no prohibitions on discovery or admissibility for arbitrations that are not specifically covered by the court rule. The same holds true for subject matter specific statutes. For example, the state of New York—a major

locus of U.S. arbitration—has no statutory protections, and its statewide court rule is limited to arbitrations of disputes over attorneys fees. This means that communications arising from commercial, consumer, employment, and other arbitrations covered under the FAA may be fully discoverable and admissible in New York.

In sum, the pattern in the states appears to be that the discovery and admissibility of arbitration communications is generally unconstrained by statutes, with the exception of some court-related arbitration and attorney-fee dispute programs. Only a small handful of states provide general protections by statute, while several provide limited protections in subject-matter-specific statutes and court rules, and the rest—the large majority of states—leave the issue to the common law.

Richard C. Reuben, *Confidentiality in Arbitration: Beyond the Myth*, 54 Kan. L. Rev. 1255, 1261–63 (2007)

3.   *Panhandle Eastern* is one of only a small handful of federal and state judicial decisions that have addressed the question of the admissibility of arbitration communications. Most have followed the Panhandle Eastern approach. Professor Reuben summarized the state of the doctrine as follows:

It is difficult to generalize from such a small handful of state and federal cases. In assessing whether arbitration communications are discoverable and admissible, the courts appear mindful of the tension between the judicial system's need for relevant evidence, and the parties' expectations of confidentiality. The judicial system's need for relevant evidence generally has prevailed, especially when there is no confidentiality clause in the agreement to arbitrate or other clear evidence of the parties' expectation of confidentiality. Internal arbitration rules may be a consideration in a court's determination, but have not been persuasive evidence of the parties' expectations. However, where there is evidence of party expectations, such as through the securing of a protective order, courts may be more willing to defer to the protective order if it otherwise meets relevant standards, such as the good cause requirement in Federal Rule of Civil Procedure 26(c). Where statutory law clearly precludes the discovery and admissibility of arbitration communications, such protective orders are likely to be upheld. This sketch of the terrain only provides an initial impression of what the emerging case law on this issue might look like. Many details remain to be filled in by future cases.

Richard C. Reuben, *Confidentiality in Arbitration: Beyond the Myth*, 54 Kan. L. Rev. 1255, 1271 (2007).

4.   As we know from prior discussion, confidentiality is considered a cornerstone of the mediation process. But can the same be said for arbitration? What are some of the process differences distinguishing arbitration and mediation that might be relevant to the question of the discovery and admissibility of arbitration communications? For example, how

does the role of the arbitrator differ from that of a mediator, and how might that difference affect the question of whether arbitration communications should be protected from discovery and admissibility? For a discussion, see Richard C. Reuben, *Confidentiality in Arbitration: Beyond the Myth*, 54 Kan. L. Rev. 1255, 1274–81 (2007).

3. ETHICS

KRISTEN BLANKLEY, TAMING THE WILD WEST OF ARBITRATION ETHICS
60 Kan. L. Rev. 925, 925–942 (2012)

In arbitration's perceived "anything goes" atmosphere, increasing concerns arise regarding ethical conduct within the forum. This concern is particularly valid given the extraordinarily limited review available after an arbitrator renders an award.[1] Although a number of scholars have commented on arbitrator misconduct, the literature is surprisingly devoid of commentary on the issue of attorney misconduct in the arbitral forum. In fact, codes of conduct for arbitrators have existed since the 1970s,[3] but

---

[1] Under the Federal Arbitration Act (FAA), a district court can vacate an award in any of the following limited circumstances:

    (1) where the award was procured by corruption, fraud, or undue means;

    (2) where there was evident partiality or corruption in the arbitrators, or either of them;

    (3) where the arbitrators were guilty of misconduct in refusing to postpone the hearing, upon sufficient cause shown, or in refusing to hear evidence pertinent and material to the controversy; or of any other misbehavior by which the rights of any party have been prejudiced; or

    (4) where the arbitrators exceeded their powers, or so imperfectly executed them that a mutual, final, and definite award upon the subject matter submitted was not made.

9 U.S.C. §10(a) (2006).

The Uniform Arbitration Act—adopted by the vast majority of states—similarly allows for vacatur in the following events:

    (1) The award was procured by corruption, fraud, or other undue means;

    (2) There was evident partiality by an arbitrator appointed as a neutral or corruption in any of the arbitrators or misconduct prejudicing the right of any party;

    (3) The arbitrators exceeded their powers;

    (4) The arbitrators refused to postpone the hearing upon sufficient cause being shown therefor or refused to hear evidence material to the controversy or otherwise so conducted the hearing, contrary to the provisions of Section 5, as to prejudice substantially the rights of a party; or

    (5) There was no arbitration agreement and the issue was not adversely determined in proceedings under Section 2 and the party did not participate in the arbitration hearing without raising the objection; but the fact that relief was such that it could not or would not be granted by a court of law or equity is not ground for vacating or refusing to confirm the award.

Unif. Arbitration Act §12(a) (1956).

The Revised Uniform Arbitration Act—adopted by a handful of states—provides a similar, but expanded, set of review provisions, including the review for "corruption, fraud, or other undue means." Revised Unif. Arbitration Act §23(a) (2000).

[3] See Am. Bar Ass'n & Am. Arbitration Ass'n, Code of Ethics for Arbitrators in Commercial Disputes (2004). . . . In 1977, the American Bar Association (ABA) and the American Arbitration Association (AAA) jointly created the Code of Ethics for Arbitrators in Commercial Disputes, which was a comprehensive and well regarded set of standards for arbitrators. Id. In 2004, the

no similar standards have ever existed for arbitration participants. Attorney misconduct in the arbitral forum is an especially deep quagmire given the potential inapplicability of criminal penalties and sanctions commonly used in litigation to ensure that the attorneys act ethically, the witnesses testify truthfully, and the proper evidence remains available.[4]

These ethical concerns permeate popular media, as well as case law. For instance, in 2007, the Financial Industry Regulatory Authority (FINRA) issued $12.5 million in sanctions against Morgan Stanley for intentionally withholding e-mail evidence from arbitration claimants and falsely claiming that the e-mail communications had been destroyed in the September 11, 2001 terrorist attacks on the World Trade Center. * * *

More recently, questions have arisen regarding Floyd Landis and his testimony under oath in a doping arbitration. Landis won the 2006 Tour de France after falling behind in Stage Sixteen, only to rally to a miraculous comeback in Stage Seventeen of the Tour. Following the race, the International Cycling Union—the governing body for cycling—confirmed that Landis tested positive for performance enhancing drugs in violation of anti-doping rules. Landis denied taking any illegal substances and challenged the allegations in an arbitration against the United States Anti-Doping Agency under the World Anti-Doping Code. Landis engaged in a public arbitration of epic proportion to defend his alleged innocence. After a multi-day hearing, Landis lost by a 2–1 decision. More than two years after the announcement of the decision, Landis admitted to using banned substances, detailing "extensive, consistent use of the red blood cell booster erythropoietin (commonly known as EPO), testosterone, human growth hormone and frequent blood transfusions, along with female hormones and a one-time experiment with insulin, during the years he rode for the U.S. Postal Service and Switzerland-based Phonak teams."

Despite the admission of lying under oath at arbitration, no serious inquiry has been conducted as to whether Landis committed perjury in the arbitral forum. In stark contrast, consider the testimony of Barry Bonds before a grand jury regarding whether he ever used performance enhancing drugs. Bonds vehemently denied taking steroids under oath. Now that baseball's steroid scandal is in the public light, Bonds has stood

---

ABA and the AAA updated the Code of Ethics to reflect the changing nature of arbitration practice, particularly in consumer and employment arbitration. Id. * * * Of course, these provider rules do not have the force of law, but many courts use them as guidance on issues of arbitrator conduct. * * *

    [4] . . . [T]he 2002 changes to the Model Rules of Professional Conduct now explicitly apply to attorneys engaged in arbitration practice. See Model Rules of Prof'l Conduct R. 1.0(m) (2003) (including representation before an arbitral tribunal as part of the definition of "tribunal"). These rules, of course, only apply to attorneys and not to other arbitration participants. Other common rules of litigation ethics—regarding perjury, suborning perjury, document tampering, or document destruction—have not yet been extended to arbitration. * * *

trial for his testimony before the grand jury. As will be discussed in more detail, the current state of perjury laws helps explain why these two otherwise similar situations were handled so differently.

* * *

III. Questionable Practices in Arbitration and Whether "Court"–Designed Rules Apply

Although the limited role of courts in the arbitral process creates many efficiencies, [it] also creates certain ethical loopholes in the administration of justice. * * *

A. Why Perjury Laws Generally Do Not Apply to Arbitral Proceedings

This section seeks to answer a relatively straightforward question: Do perjury laws and ethical rules apply to arbitration at all? Surprisingly, a fifty-state survey of perjury laws reveals that these laws do not, in fact, apply to arbitration—or at least not by their plain language. By contrast, however, the attorney ethics rules do prohibit attorneys from suborning perjury, but no consequences appear to befall a lying witness. Similarly, a fifty-state survey of document destruction rules reveals that outside of the realm of attorney ethics, no sanctions exist for clients and other individuals guilty of evidentiary spoliation.

1. Perjury Statutes Almost Never Explicitly Apply to Arbitration

The purpose of perjury laws is to encourage truth-telling in official matters by providing criminal consequences for lying under oath. * * * The exact same concerns exist in arbitration. Adjudication based on false information undermines the system—whether it occurs in the litigation system or the arbitral system.

. . . [W]hether a person commits perjury by lying under oath in arbitration largely depends on whether arbitration is considered an "official proceeding" covered by the perjury statutes. The term "official proceeding" stems from the 1976 definition of perjury in the Model Penal Code (MPC), adopted by a majority of states. Arbitration is simply not mentioned in the MPC chapter regarding perjury.

* * *

a. The Widely Used "Official Proceedings" Language Is Ambiguous in Its Applicability to Arbitration

Unsurprisingly, a large number of state legislatures enacted perjury laws in line with the MPC. Under the MPC, a person is guilty of perjury "if in any official proceeding, he makes a false statement under oath or equivalent affirmation, or swears or affirms the truth of a statement previously made, when the statement is material and he does not believe it to be true." The MPC defines "official proceeding" as "a proceeding heard or which may be heard before any legislative, judicial, administrative or other governmental agency or official authorized to take evidence under oath, including any referee, hearing examiner, commissioner, notary or other person taking testimony or deposition in connection with any such proceeding." The terms "arbitration" and "arbitrator" are not found anywhere in this definition.

* * *

Courts are split on whether arbitration falls under the MPC definition of "official proceeding."[66] If courts apply traditional rules of statutory interpretation, then the MPC definition of "official proceeding" should not include an arbitral forum. To the extent that this ambiguous phrase at the end of the definition needs to be interpreted, it should be interpreted in line with the previously enumerated proceedings, i.e., judicial proceedings, legislative proceedings, administrative proceedings, depositions associated with the same, and the like. Additionally, the ambiguous phrase "any other person" is arguably limited by the phrase "governmental agency or official." Contractual arbitrations, for the most part, take place outside of the realm of the government. Accordingly, the crime of perjury under the MPC likely does not extend to the arbitral forum.

b. The Statutes Prohibiting Lying "Under Oath" Are Also Ambiguous

Other states have adopted more generic perjury laws that simply prohibit lying under oath or making false sworn statements. If the statute prohibits lying under oath, and arbitral testimony is given under oath, then presumably these statutes would apply to arbitration. Courts, however, do not universally accept this interpretation.

* * *

Compared to the MPC definition of perjury, this broader definition more easily extends to arbitration. Because the statute does not limit perjury to "official proceedings," arbitration should fall squarely within the definition, even if not explicitly mentioned in the statute. This interpretation is far from assured given the ambiguities in the wording of the statutes. . . . [T]the clearest definition of perjury would explicitly reference arbitration; but for statutes that are deliberately vague, remaining vague will likely be the best statutory option.

---

[66] For instance, numerous Florida cases granted arbitration witnesses immunity, noting the perjury consequences for falsely testifying under oath in arbitration. See Kidwell v. Gen. Motors Corp., 975 So. 2d 503, 505 (Fla. Dist. Ct. App. 2007) (applying witness immunity in part because "[a]n arbitration hearing, although informal, is a judicial or quasi-judicial proceeding") . . . * * * In contrast, Nebraska perjury law only applies to a non-judicial "official proceeding" if the legislature requires that the procedure be given under oath. State v. Douglas, 388 N.W.2d 801, 807 (Neb. 1986). Unlike the Washington statute, see supra note 64, the Nebraska statute defining "official proceeding" is the exact same, facially broad definition found in the MPC. The Nebraska Supreme Court's judicial gloss on this definition is not necessarily dictated by the text of the statute.

c. A Minority of States Have Statutes Explicitly Applying to Arbitration or Only to Judicial Proceedings

A small minority of states have more specific perjury statutes than the ones discussed previously. * * *

Wisconsin is the only state that specifically mentions arbitration in its perjury statute. The arbitration provision, however, is quite limited in its scope. Under Wisconsin law, a person commits perjury if he makes a false material statement under oath, knowing the statement to be false, in a court, before a magistrate, before an agency, or before "[a]n administrative agency or arbitrator authorized by statute to determine issues of fact." Again, because contractual arbitration falls outside of the legal system, this statute would not expressly extend to private, contractual arbitration. The specific inclusion of a hearing before an arbitrator "authorized by statute to determine issues of fact" likely means that any other arbitration would be interpreted as falling outside the scope of the statute. For being the state with the only mention of arbitration in the statute, the statute appears to have less effect than some more general perjury statutes.

* * * On the other side of specificity, some state perjury statutes are specifically limited to litigation procedures. For instance, perjury in Georgia is limited to statements made "in a judicial proceeding." The Louisiana perjury law only applies in a "judicial proceeding" before a board "authorized to take testimony" or in legislative proceedings. The Massachusetts law applies solely in a "proceeding in a court of justice" and does not extend to testimony at a labor arbitration. * * *

Federal law also falls within this category of statutes. The general perjury statute applies to witnesses "having taken an oath before a competent tribunal, officer, or person, in any case in which a law of the United States authorizes an oath to be administered."[110] Nothing in the FAA speaks to the ability to administer oaths, permissive or otherwise. Without a direct mention of an oath within the statute, arbitrations cannot be tribunals "in which a law of the United States authorizes an oath to be administered." Thus, federal law provides no support for a truth-telling requirement in arbitration, and this law, too, will need a revision to apply to the arbitral forum.

2. Attorney Ethics Rules on Truthfulness Generally Apply to Arbitration

While perjury statutes provide criminal consequences to witnesses who lie under oath, attorneys have additional obligations to be truthful toward a tribunal. All attorneys are bound by ethical rules that govern their behavior, and each state promulgates its own ethical rules. Most states' ethical rules model the version of the Model Rules of Professional

---

[110] 18 U.S.C. §1621(1) (2006).

Conduct (the Model Rules) published in 2002. Unlike the MPC, the Model Rules of Professional Conduct explicitly apply to arbitration proceedings and other alternative dispute resolution processes.[114]

The "Ethics 2000" revisions, changes made to the Model Rules by the ABA's Commission on Evaluation of the Rules of Professional Conduct, contained a number of revisions to the ethical rules specifically targeted at alternative dispute resolution. * * * One of the ways that the Ethics 2000 Commission included arbitration practice within the parameters of the general rules was to define a previously undefined term: "tribunal." Under the revisions, a tribunal includes "a court, an arbitrator in a binding arbitration proceeding or a legislative body, administrative agency or other body acting in an adjudicative capacity." * * * For the states adopting this definition, any portion of the ethical rules referencing a tribunal now applies to arbitration—or at least binding arbitration. For the states that have not adopted this definition, whether the ethics rules referencing tribunal—including the truthfulness rules—apply to arbitration at all is unclear.

NOTES AND QUESTIONS

1. As we know, arbitration is a less formal process than trial. Is there something about the informality of the arbitration process that gives you less concern about the possibility of perjury? More concern? If you were an arbitrator and learned that there had been perjury in a case you decided, what would you do?

2. The spoliation of evidence is another area in which there is a gap between treatment of behavior that occurs in arbitration and in trial. In public courts, tampering with evidence can lead to criminal charges. Not so, however, in arbitration—although it is at least theoretically possible that a party could bring a civil action for evidence tampering in arbitration. There is case law permitting arbitrators to shift certain burdens when evidence has been destroyed, altered, concealed, or otherwise spoliated. For a discussion, see id. at 943–555.

3. Blankley ultimately concludes that the criminal law of perjury should be extended to arbitration? Do you agree? Or does the fact that arbitration is a private process give you any concern about criminalizing behavior within that process? If so, what would you propose as possible remedies for perjury and spoliation of evidence?

4. What other ethical challenges do you see for arbitrators?

5. Attorneys are subject to their ethical obligations as attorneys in arbitrations, just as they are in trial. However, parties and witnesses in arbitration are not covered by any ethical rules or subject to sanctions for misconduct in arbitrations. If the misconduct occurs during the arbitration,

---

[114] Model Rules of Prof'l Conduct R. 2.4 cmt. 5 (2002).

what power, if any, does the arbitrator have to deal with it? What if it occurs afterward?

4. INTERNATIONAL COMMERCIAL ARBITRATION

Thus far, we have been discussing arbitration in the domestic context, and even then primarily under the Federal Arbitration Act. However, arbitration is also widely used in the international commercial context, and, apart from negotiation, may be the most commonly used dispute resolution mechanism for settling private international disputes. While international commercial arbitration shares many of the same characteristics as domestic arbitration, there are also very significant differences.

Section 1 provides a general overview of the field, beginning with a comparison of international and domestic arbitration. The first two excerpts by W. Laurence Craig and Charles Brower, help explain the popularity of arbitration for resolving international commercial disputes, and introduce us to the key treaty affecting the area, the Convention on the Recognition and Enforcement of Foreign Arbitral Awards (the New York Convention). The article by Yves Dezalay and Bryant Garth describes the culture of international commercial arbitration, as well as the unique form of informal precedent known as the *lex mercatoria*.

Section 2 then discusses the legal framework of international commercial arbitration, focusing first on arbitrability, forum selection, and choice of law issues, and then concluding with discussion of enforceability and review of international commercial arbitration awards. As you work through these materials, consider how the similarities and differences between the domestic and international contexts would affect your decision to recommend arbitration to a client, and how it might affect your preparation for the arbitration.

a. Overview and Comparison With Domestic Arbitration

"[I]nternational arbitration is a consensual means of dispute resolution, by a non-governmental decision maker, that produces a legally binding and enforceable ruling." GARY BORN, INTERNATIONAL COMMERCIAL ARBITRATION 1 (2001). Although international arbitration is based on an agreement of the disputing parties, it works as well as it does because of national arbitration legislation, international conventions and treaties, several institutions, such as the International Chamber of Commerce (ICC), that administer international commercial arbitration proceedings, and a group of experienced advocates and arbitrators.

International arbitration is similar to domestic arbitration in many ways. Both are based on an agreement of the disputing parties, are normally conducted in private, and require the assistance of courts at times. Issues of arbitrability and judicial enforcement and review of awards arise in both kinds of arbitration. Both international and domestic arbitration have experienced explosive growth in recent years.

As noted earlier in this chapter, domestic arbitration is often sold based on alleged speed, lower costs, and greater informality. That is hardly the case with respect to international arbitration. Indeed, the differences between international arbitration and other kinds of arbitration illustrate our point in Section D, *infra*, that each type of arbitration should be analyzed and evaluated in light of the context in which the process will be used. Although arbitration occurs between nations and between nations and private parties, the emphasis in this section is primarily on arbitration between private parties, where the great bulk of cases likely to confront lawyers arise.

The materials that follow illustrate differences between domestic and international arbitration, indicate why arbitration is the preferred method of dealing with international commercial disputes, and provide background on relevant sources of law and those who practice in this field.

W. LAURENCE CRAIG, SOME TRENDS AND DEVELOPMENTS IN THE LAWS AND PRACTICE OF INTERNATIONAL COMMERCIAL ARBITRATION

30 Tex. Int'l L.J. 1, 3–4, 6–7, 8–9, 10, 11, 57 (1995)

I. HISTORICAL MILESTONES

A. Normalcy of International Commercial Arbitration

* * *

[W]hile speed, informality, and economy have had some influence on the growth of international commercial arbitration, the essential driving force has been the desire of each party to avoid having its case determined in a foreign judicial forum. Parties seek to avoid these forums for fear that they will be at a disadvantage due to unfamiliarity with the jurisdiction's language and procedures, preferences of the judge, and possibly even national bias.

While the viewpoint outlined above may be stark and simplified, it seems likely that thoughts of this nature, if not necessarily of this degree, frequently motivate parties to choose international arbitration. Concerns about litigation in a foreign country are not limited to the result obtained in the court of first instance. There is the additional risk that a national court judgment will be subject to one or more layers of appellate review, causing further delay and uncertainty in the ultimate disposition of the matter. And even if a foreign court's decision is satisfactory, there is often doubt about whether the decision can be enforced in another country.

The absence of any multilateral convention for the recognition of foreign judgments, and the existence of very few bilateral treaties with such provisions, makes the arbitral solution not only attractive but compelling. This is due to the existence of an international mechanism for the enforcement of foreign arbitral awards. The Convention on the Recognition and Enforcement of Foreign Arbitral Awards (New York Convention), which entered into effect in 1958, has put into place a system which assures the recognition in member countries of arbitral awards rendered abroad and which excludes any judicial review of the merits of the arbitral award by the court where enforcement is sought. In the absence of any international court for the resolution of private international disputes, arbitration has provided the participants in international commerce with a decision-making process which, if not international in the legal sense, is a least internationalized, and which leads to an award which will ordinarily be enforceable internationally. It is for this reason that commercial arbitration is much more common in international dispute resolution than in domestic dispute resolution. Nicholas Katzenbach, former Attorney General of the United States and former General Counsel for IBM, commented on the importance of the private international dispute resolution system in dealing with the increase in world trade, investment, and finance, and the underlying technological developments which made multinational activities both inevitable and desirable:

As national laws of contract, property, commercial paper developed and grew domestically to make a variety of types of promises enforceable in national courts in accordance with common commercial understanding, so too has it become essential to the same activities that promises and understandings on international or transnational scale be enforced in the same way. While we have experienced commercial arbitration in domestic trade for many years and this has been successful and helpful in a variety of ways, I suggest that arbitration in international commerce is really of a wholly different order of importance. Here to get effective and reasonably predictable and fair resolutions arbitration has become essential in a way it never has been in domestic matters. It is fair to say that arbitration in international commercial matters is today—and certainly should be—the norm, not the exception.

. . . While much can be said for arbitration in domestic transactions as an effective alternative to litigation, it is an alternative—a choice. Commercial promises can usually be effectively enforced in national courts. But in international matters the risks of failure of effective enforcement are considerable and the existence of predictable commercial results far less. . . . [L]awyers and businessmen who are not experts in international transactions must acquire an understanding of the enormous advantages of arbitration in most circumstances.

* * *

B.   *Arbitration as a Self–Contained Process*

* * *

Especially in the case of arbitration under the auspices of a specialized arbitral institution between members of a close-knit trade or professional group, it is intended and confidently expected that the contractually chosen procedure will be definitive and will replace all recourse to courts. These arbitration proceedings are viewed by the parties as being an essentially independent process, and not the adjunct of any court system. Having agreed to participate in an arbitral process to resolve a dispute, the parties agree to carry out the resulting award, and to respect that award as final and binding between them. Indeed, where two parties have agreed to submit their dispute to a wise outsider for resolution, how can one of them later refuse to defer to the wisdom applied?

The same spirit which motivated the choice of arbitration by close-knit professional groups has also motivated its promotion by broader arbitration associations. In its early attempts to promote arbitration, the International Chamber of Commerce (ICC), which has become the foremost international arbitration association in the world, did not foresee the need to provide for judicial enforcement of awards. The ICC Arbitration Rules of 1923 provided only that the parties were "honor bound" to carry out the award of the arbitrators. It was expected that moral norms and "the force that businessmen of a country can bring to bear upon a recalcitrant neighbor" would be sufficient to ensure respect of arbitral awards.

While this view may seem somewhat quaint today, the success of international arbitration as a self-contained process should not be underestimated. The vast majority of disputes which go to arbitration are resolved without any judicial recourse whatsoever. This may be due to settlement negotiations during the course of the proceedings or by the rendition of an award and its satisfaction. The ICC estimates that more than 90% of its awards are satisfied voluntarily. Evidence is not available as to the voluntary settlement of awards in ad hoc arbitrations, but at least where these arbitration proceedings are specifically agreed to after the dispute arises—and hence where the parties have agreed to submit a defined dispute to a designated tribunal—it would stand to reason that voluntary respect of awards would be even greater than in the case of arbitration pursuant to a preexisting arbitration clause.

* * *

Conceptually, the desire to obtain an award enforceable by the courts—both nationally and internationally—lies at the heart of a conflict inherent in the arbitral process. Designed as a system of private justice, arbitration is a creation of contract, and parties may, through arbitration agreements, dispose of their right to sue in court to the same extent that they can, through other contracts, dispose of other legal rights. The contractual origin of arbitration proceedings allows for great flexibility. This flexibility is threatened, however, by the desire of the winning party to enlist the power of the state to compel compliance with the award. This requires recourse to the courts because only national courts have the power of the state to compel performance and execute against a party's assets. * * * The requirement of enforceability has both national and international consequences. During the early postwar period, the first priority of the international business community was to assure international recognition of agreements to arbitrate and of arbitral awards. On the international level, this could be accomplished only by treaty.

* * *

The New York Convention was prepared and entered into force in 1959. Among the early parties to the Convention were France, Russia, Morocco, India, Israel, Egypt, Czechoslovakia, and the Federal Republic of Germany. The United States was a relative latecomer, ratifying the New York Convention only in 1970. As of April 1994, ninety-six states have ratified the New York Convention, making it the cornerstone upon which the value of international arbitral awards is based.

The New York Convention requires both the recognition of agreements to arbitrate and the recognition and enforcement of arbitral awards. The means for assuring recognition of arbitration agreements is the Convention's requirement that national litigation be stayed in favor of Convention arbitration and that the parties be referred to arbitration. This is spelled out in article II(3), which provides: "The court of a Contracting State, when seized of an action in a matter in respect of which the parties have made an agreement within the meaning of this article, shall, at the request of one of the parties, refer the parties to arbitration, unless it finds that the said agreement is null and void, inoperative or incapable of being performed."

* * *

The New York Convention was designed to give international currency to arbitral awards. Any award rendered and binding in a New York Convention country can, under the Convention, be enforced in any other New York Convention signatory. What the Convention did not do, however, was provide any international mechanism to insure the validity of the award where rendered. This was left to the provisions of local law.

The Convention provides no restraint whatsoever on the control functions of local courts at the seat of arbitration.

* * *

Concluding Points: Diversity or Convergence?

1.   Despite all the developments in arbitration laws and practice, most international arbitrations will proceed as a self-contained process. The parties will conduct their proceedings according to rules that they have agreed to by contract. These actions will not be substantially impacted by the contents of national procedural law at the seat of arbitration or elsewhere. This will be particularly the case where the counsel who assisted in drafting the arbitration clause took care to choose as the seat of arbitration a jurisdiction whose arbitration law gives wide freedom to the parties, or to the arbitrators, to determine how arbitral proceedings shall be conducted. International arbitrations can in this respect be compared to an iceberg: Above the surface is a small visible mass representing those cases where arbitrations intersect with national courts through ancillary proceedings, judicial recourse, enforcement actions, and disputed issues of applicable procedural law. Below the surface is the great preponderance of cases which proceed in a self-contained private system of justice, as they were intended to do.

2.   This very partial survey shows substantial convergence in modern arbitration laws with respect to the procedures to be followed in arbitration and the standards for judicial recourse therefrom. The common denominator is the specific recognition, by the law of the place of arbitration, of a wide degree of party autonomy to agree to rules of arbitral procedure. This degree of convergence may be explained by the fact that the laws have been designed to accommodate themselves to international arbitral practices, and not vice versa. These arbitral practices have been developed under both institutional rules, such as the ICC Rules, and noninstitutional rules, such as the UNCITRAL Rules, and have been designed to accommodate the specific needs of international business. This is not only true of the Model Law but also of a number of the recently modified arbitration laws in countries such as France, Switzerland, and the Netherlands.

3.   One of the surprising effects of the legislative reform movement has been to reinforce the concept of the territorial application of arbitration law and the importance of the law of the seat of arbitration. The insistence on the application of the arbitration law of the place of arbitration has not, however, been deleterious to international arbitration, because the contents of the law have been designed to attract international arbitration, to be user-friendly, and to specifically empower the parties to contractually specify arbitral procedures.

* * *

Charles N. Brower, The Global Court: The Internationalization of Commercial Adjudication and Arbitration
26 U. Balt. L. Rev. 9, 11–12, 13 (1997)

* * *

Any arbitration necessarily is subject to the national law of the state in which it takes place. Statutes in major industrial jurisdictions have been modernized so as to minimize state intervention in the arbitral process itself, while offering judicial review to the extent necessary to ensure the integrity of the process by which the arbitral tribunal arrived at its award. To the same end UNCITRAL in 1985 fashioned a Model Law on International Commercial Arbitration designed to provide an "off the shelf" statute for adoption by less sophisticated jurisdictions and to encourage greater convergence, if not uniformity, on the part of others. It has been adopted, albeit with variations, in a considerable number of jurisdictions.

At the same time, the international community has adopted a series of conventions and treaties ensuring mutual and uniform enforcement of agreements to arbitrate, and also of the resulting awards, of which the New York Convention of 1958 is the most prominent. In 1965 the World Bank went so far as to establish, pursuant to convention, the International Centre for Settlement of Investment Disputes (ICSID), and with it, a completely self-contained regime for deciding investment disputes. So effective are these systems that today an international arbitral award is worth far more than a judgment of a national court abroad; the former is subject to comparatively automatic enforcement, whereas the latter must be made the subject of a plenary suit.

This three-tiered and essentially global system, consisting of private adjudication under agreed rules, supported by only the most limited national regulation necessary to ensure its integrity, and an international exercise of state power to the extent required to guarantee enforcement of the results, is based on the parties' reciprocal mistrust of state power. This mistrust takes a special form, however. It is not mistrust of state power per se; rather it is the lack of faith on the part of each party that the courts of the other party's state of nationality in fact will administer justice fairly and impartially. In short, neither party wishes to be judged in the other's "backyard." In addition, relative detachment of the process from state power facilitates a degree of internationalization, and consequent uniformity, which has its own merits for international commerce, but which otherwise would be unattainable.

This trend goes much deeper, however, than the adjudicatory process itself; it goes also to the heart of the matter, the applicable substantive law. Just as trading partners who are foreign to each other eschew each other's courts, so, too, do they prefer not to be judged by each other's national legal norms. This concern is highest, of course, where one of the parties is itself a state or a peristaltic enterprise. In such circumstances the parties, with increasing frequency, will concoct for themselves a jurisprudential corpus that either is divorced from any national system of law or combines a relevant national legal system with another body of law to supplement or modify it and which any national court system would have considerable difficulty to apply. For example, under the 1955 Libyan Petroleum Law, the law applicable to oil concession agreements in that country (some of which still are in effect), it is provided that the applicable law is "the law[ ] of Libya and such rules and principles of international law as may be relevant but only to the extent that such rules and principles are not inconsistent with and do not conflict with the laws of Libya."

* * *

The fact that this "global court" works, and works well, is proven by its consistent triumph over adversity. Numerous arbitrations against foreign parties, including pariah governments such as, in recent years, Libya, have proceeded to a conclusion, with payment being achieved, notwithstanding the most determined efforts of some defendants to disrupt, or even to abort, the proceedings. Tactics to this end have included failure to appoint an arbitrator, or appointment of a patently biased arbitrator; refusal to appear, or alternating sporadic appearances with demonstrative "walkouts" and other intentional absences; unwarranted objections to jurisdiction; unjustified challenges to the service of particular arbitrators, or even attempts to intimidate them; and all manner of lesser forms of abuse of the process. In one famous case at the Iran–United States Claims Tribunal two Iranian judges even assaulted an elderly Swedish colleague. In the end, none of these tactics succeeds, however, because all modern sets of arbitral rules provide the means for demolishing or overlooking such obstacles and are backed, as noted a moment ago, by indispensable attachment to state power.

* * *

NOTES AND QUESTIONS

1.   Charles Brower and Laurence Craig, practitioners in the field of international arbitration, give several reasons why parties prefer international arbitration. "Neither party wishes to be judged in the other's backyard." *Brower, supra* at p. 727. They also mentioned a desire for uniformity and doubts about the enforcement of judgments by courts from other countries. Nicholas Katzenbach, quoted in *Craig, supra* at p. 723, said, "to get effective and reasonably predictable and fair resolutions arbitration has become essential in a way it never has been in domestic matters." Ian MacNeil and his co-authors point out other reasons: international arbitration

allows parties to select a location for arbitration most beneficial to the parties; the international arbitration establishment is used to handling problems arising from differing languages; and arbitration provides a way to avoid problems created by judges unfamiliar with the applicable law by selecting arbitrators who are experts in the applicable law. IAN R. MACNEIL, RICHARD E. SPEIDEL & THOMAS J. STIPANOWICH, FEDERAL ARBITRATION LAW § 44.3 (1994 ed. & Supp. 1999).

2.   Why is enforcement of international arbitration awards generally more effective than enforcement of judgments of courts from various countries? *See* Christine Tecuyer–Thieffry & Patrick Thieffry, *Negotiating Settlement of Disputes Provisions in International Business Contracts: Recent Developments in Arbitration and Other Processes*, 45 Bus. Law. 577, 585–88 (1990); W. Lawrence Craig, *Some Trends and Developments in the Laws and Practice of International Commercial Arbitration*, 30 Tex. Int'l L.J. 1 (1995).

YVES DEZALAY & BRYANT GARTH, FUSSING ABOUT THE FORUM: CATEGORIES AND DEFINITIONS AS STAKES IN A PROFESSIONAL COMPETITION
21 Law & Soc. Inquiry 285, 295–99 (1996)

In the past 20 years, "international commercial arbitration" has shifted from an informal, compromise-oriented justice dominated by European academics to a U.S.-style, formalized, "offshore litigation." Despite dramatic practical changes, it is still called "international commercial arbitration," and the major institutions still have the same identities. The specific term of arbitration and some of the most general characteristics are, after all, passed on through the activities of individual carriers and through the activities of the institutions long identified with arbitration. Scholarly accounts of international commercial arbitration, furthermore, reinforce the story of continuity by counting cases and discussing growth as if the process has essentially remained the same. It is clear, however, that what is now generally understood by the term is significantly different.

International commercial arbitration's recent history began with the activities after World War II of a small group of gentlemen idealists— mainly Continental legal academics schooled in international law— connected with the International Chamber of Commerce in Paris. These idealists cultivated good relations with the business world and promoted the distinctiveness of international commercial arbitration as an alternative to national litigation. Through academic writing, conferences, and activity that promoted the virtues of arbitration, they gained credibility for arbitration as a means to resolve transnational business disputes. They promoted arbitration as relatively inexpensive, informal, and capable of meeting the needs of businesses increasing their international activities and investing in third world countries. They developed an elegant academic legal doctrine, which they termed the new *lex mercatoria,* and they also sought to make their decisions conform to the particular needs of business. One need they met was the business desire to avoid giving state enterprises advantages over private parties. The *lex mercatoria* governed all such business relations by the private norms of contract.

The promoters of the *lex mercatoria* also emphasized the importance of using arbitration as a way to bring the parties to an acceptable solution consistent with general business expectations. The success of these academic mediators reveals the advantage of a portfolio combining high status and academic sophistication. The formulators of the *lex mercatoria* could play a rather successful double game in dispute resolution. As academic authors of the rules of the game applicable substantively, they would also be the best ones to decide when the rules did and did not apply. Accordingly, they could shape their rulings to particular situations without losing the claim of universalism for the *lex mercatoria.* The success at finding tailored solutions was such that commentators active in international arbitration could emphasize that, in contrast to litigation, arbitration could help parties preserve a long-term contractual or other business relationship. Tailored settlements and the *lex mercatoria* coexisted perfectly.

There were not many arbitrations, however, even though the pioneers did succeed in promoting the idea and placing arbitration clauses in many contracts. They developed a niche, but no one could have predicted that business disputes that invoked these clauses would suddenly proliferate and open up this very small market. External factors helped bolster the demand.

The large construction and infrastructure projects that took place after the increase in the price of oil in the early 1970s can be seen as a key catalyst for change. The projects gave rise to numerous disputes and—because of the success of the pioneers in promoting arbitration clauses—many more international commercial arbitrations. New entrants sought to gain a foothold in the growing arbitration market, and they began to compete with the senior generation of gentlemen arbitrators. The terms of the competition, however, reflected the particular kind of market that existed and the way that arbitration had been defined by the gentlemen scholars.

Those pioneer idealists, who still possessed considerable power in the arbitral institutions and in the recommending of arbitrators, had succeeded in defining the terms of entry into the field of arbitration so that entry was virtually barred to individuals who did not purport to promote the long term interests of arbitration as a dispute resolution device for international conflicts. Under these rules, for example, it was difficult for self-promoters to gain the credibility to advance as arbitrators or lawyers in arbitration. There was no explicit advertising, and it would not have helped to gain entry into this cartelized community—sometimes termed a club or even a mafia.

The competition was therefore expressed in terms of what would best make arbitration legitimate and acceptable to businesses and to other potential constituencies. It was a competition in ideas organized around theoretical and scholarly debates about what international commercial arbitration must be in order to retain its legitimacy. The ideas were also closely related to the individuals seeking dominance in the business. Theorists and practitioners—quite often the same people—debated in academic terms that also reflected their own positions in arbitration.

Competitors thus sought to define international commercial arbitration—and the leading institutions, especially the ICC—in terms that privileged their own skills and attributes. The senior generation defended the status quo of informal, compromise-oriented arbitration close to business and the *lex mercatoria,* insisting that only very experienced and scholarly individuals, selected on the basis of their excellent legal careers, had the stature and judgment to resolve such cases. A younger generation criticized the vagueness and uncertainty of the *lex mercatoria* on scholarly grounds and emphasized the vital importance of technical sophistication about arbitration. The technocrats argued that arbitration could only be successful and legitimate if practiced in a more legalized fashion. Common law lawyers bolstered the technocrats by adding their criticisms of the vagueness of the academic *lex mercatoria* that was supposedly being applied by the Continental academics, and they hinted strongly that the English commercial court was a better forum for commercial disputes. Continental academics, in turn, emphasized the importance of arbitration detached from any national laws and legal systems.

Most significantly, however, American litigators—whose domestic power was just becoming established—insisted in this domain that the arbitrators needed to pay more attention to the facts, indulge more motions and adversarial behavior in the interests of their clients, and in general allow the litigators to employ their legal weaponry as if they were arguing in a U.S. court. They promoted the idea that arbitration could serve legitimately for international business transactions only if it became a courtlike substitute for national (meaning, to them, U.S.) courts.

Each group, in short, competed with theory and practice on behalf of the characteristics that its members had to offer to resolve international business disputes. The already-established prominence of international commercial arbitration led them to play within the rules of the arbitration field rather than to challenge it directly with some newly minted and defined process. They promoted their visions and theories of arbitration as what arbitration was and was supposed to be—in particular, offshore litigation on the side of one major group, a compromise-oriented academic affair on the other.

As it turned out, an alliance between the U.S. litigators and the technocrats gained the upper hand, although the other groups remain far from absent, and the competition continues. The champions of formalism succeeded in part because they promoted a kind of arbitration that could process more cases than could be handled by the charisma of the grand old men. They also succeeded because they were allied with the U.S. litigators empowered both by the resources of the large law firms and the powerful clients who employed those firms.

International commercial arbitration therefore became something very different from what it had been in the 1950s and 1960s. The center of power shifted from the small group of Continental academics to the U.S. law firms and their allies. Despite this important shift, however, it is important also to recognize the continuity. The International Chamber of Commerce remained the central institution, even though redefined by battles fought from within the institution. The practice of appointing private individuals to serve as "arbitrators" charged with deciding the cases also continued, but "international commercial arbitration" undeniably changed fundamentally from 1970 to 1990.

During this period of intense competition, furthermore, there was also cooperation. All the players in this field—and those who wanted to be taken seriously in the field—continued in their writing and activities to promote "international commercial arbitration" as the preferred method for resolving transnational business disputes. They adhered to the rules of the game while they fought to modify the rules to favor the position or positions that they occupied. Indeed, outsiders impressed by the public shows of unanimity about international commercial arbitration might believe that the members of the club were united around a stable set of practices.

On the contrary, practices were not stable, and as the practice of arbitration changed, so finally even the accepted definition of arbitration changed so as to define an almost entirely different process. The terminology—now reified in many scholarly publications and definitions—reflected the change in practice and in the balance of power. We now tend to accept the fact that international commercial arbitration is simply a quasi-judicial form of dispute resolution that substitutes for national courts but not court-like processes. The point, to repeat, is that we should not accept the latest scholarly representation as the essence of arbitration—as if such a thing existed in the abstract. The definition is but the linguistic evidence of the power of the promoters of that particular representation of international commercial arbitration. They played within the rules—established by the pioneers who built up the modern institutions—until they succeeded in redefining the game and the key institutions.

The legitimacy of international commercial arbitration is no longer built on the fact that arbitration is informal and close to the needs of business; rather legitimacy now comes more from a recognition that arbitration is *formal* and close to the kind of resolution that would be produced through litigation—more precisely, through the negotiation that takes place in the context of U.S.-style litigation. Litigators, in other words, maintained the name of international commercial arbitration, but they appropriated it as a place for the practice of large commercial litigation.

NOTES AND QUESTIONS

1.   Dezalay and Garth suggest that processes such as arbitration do not have a fixed content. They believe that the process is changed as parties try to change rules and practices to help them compete for business. They view the increased formalism of international arbitration as one indication of the success of U.S. litigators in persuading affected parties that arbitration should become more like national courts (especially U.S. courts).

2.   Is there an analogous situation with respect to the way mediation is conducted? See John Lande, *How Will Lawyering and Mediation Practices Transform Each Other?*, 24 Fla. St. U. L. Rev. 839, 849–54 (1997).

b.   The Legal Framework

1.   *Arbitrability, Forum Selection, Choice of Law*

ROBY V. CORPORATION OF LLOYD'S

United States Court of Appeals, Second Circuit, 1993
996 F.2d 1353

MESKILL, CHIEF JUDGE:

[A group of American citizen or residents (referred to as "Roby Names" in the Court's opinion) sued the corporation of Lloyds (Loyds) in a United States District Court, alleging that they had suffered severe financial loss as a result of violations by Loyds and Lloyds entities of the 1933 Securities Act, the 1934 Securities Exchange Act, and the Racketeer Influenced and Corrupt Organizations Act. The Roby Names argued that their claim should be litigated in the United States in spite of contract clauses that provided for arbitration in England under English law. Syndicates compete within Loyds for insurance underwriting business. The plaintiffs Roby Names were solicited in the United States by various Lloyds entities and representatives. Eighty percent of Lloyds 26,000 Names are English; about 2,500 Names are American. Roby Names selected from a list of syndicates and decided how much to invest in each one. Names earn profits in proportion to their capital contributions and bear unlimited liability for their proportionate losses in each syndicate they join.

The District Court dismissed the Roby Names complaint and its judgment and order was affirmed on appeal.]

* * *

DISCUSSION

The Roby Names present us with two basic arguments as to why these suits should be litigated in the United States: (1) the contract clauses, by their terms, apply neither to the substance of their claims nor to certain defendants; and (2) the clauses are unenforceable due to the public policy codified in the securities laws. We find neither of these arguments persuasive.

* * *

Paragraph 2.2 of the General Undertaking states, in pertinent part:

Each party hereto irrevocably agrees that the courts of England shall have exclusive jurisdiction to settle any dispute and/or controversy of whatsoever nature arising out of or relating to the [Name's] membership of, and/or underwriting of insurance business at, Lloyd's.

Paragraph 2.1 is equally broad and provides for the application of English law. The syndicates are third-party beneficiaries of this agreement.

* * *

Disputes Covered

"[A] party cannot be required to submit to arbitration any dispute which he has not agreed so to submit." The Roby Names contend essentially that the forum selection and arbitration clauses apply only to disputes arising from the conduct of the defendants as managers, representatives or regulators. Because this conduct can occur only after the "securities" have been sold, the Roby Names claim that they did not agree to arbitration of, or English jurisdiction over, complaints pertaining to the sale of those "securities." They present two basic arguments: (1) because the choice of law clauses require the application of English law, the Roby Names' United States statutory claims cannot possibly be covered under the agreements, and (2) resolution of their claims does not require the construction of the agreements because the Roby Names have not alleged any breach of contract, and the language of the arbitration and forum selection clauses is not broad enough to cover their claims. We reject both arguments.

1. *Application of English Law*

It defies reason to suggest that a plaintiff may circumvent forum selection and arbitration clauses merely by stating claims under laws not recognized by the forum selected in the agreement. A plaintiff simply would have to allege violations of *his country's* tort law or *his country's* statutory law or *his country's* property law in order to render nugatory any forum selection clause that implicitly or explicitly required the application of the law of another jurisdiction. We refuse to allow a party's solemn promise to be defeated by artful pleading. In the absence of other considerations, the agreement to submit to arbitration or the jurisdiction of the English courts must be enforced even if that agreement tacitly includes the forfeiture of some claims that could have been brought in a different forum.

2. *Scope of the Agreements*

Of course, the Roby Names are quite right that if the *substance* of their claims, stripped of their labels, does not fall within the scope of the clauses, the clauses cannot apply. However, they must make this argument in the face of strong public policy in favor of forum selection and arbitration clauses. Indeed, an order to arbitrate "should not be denied unless it may be said with positive assurance that the arbitration clause is not susceptible of an interpretation that covers the asserted dispute."

There is ample precedent that the scope of clauses similar to those at issue here is not restricted to pure breaches of the contracts containing the clauses. * * *

In the instant case the conduct surrounding the underwriting activities at Lloyd's is integrally related to the sale of Lloyd's "securities" because the "security" is essentially equivalent to the underwriting of risk or the pledging of capital. * * *

It is perhaps even more persuasive that the agreements are in fact not limited to the conduct of business but also cover the raising of capital. * * *

Similarly, and even more forcefully, the broad language of the forum selection clause of the General Undertaking covers the Roby Names' claims at least against Lloyd's' governing bodies. Those claims are undoubtedly related to the Roby Names' "membership of, and/or underwriting of insurance business at, Lloyd's."

Application of the Securities Laws

The Roby Names argue that the public policy codified in the antiwaiver provisions of the securities laws renders unenforceable any agreement that effectively eliminates compliance with those laws. The Securities Act provides that "[a]ny . . . stipulation . . . binding any person acquiring any security to waive compliance with any provision of this subchapter . . . shall be void." Similarly, the Securities Exchange Act states, "[a]ny . . . stipulation . . . binding any person to waive compliance with any provision of this chapter or of any rule or regulation thereunder . . . shall be void." According to the undisputed testimony of a British attorney, neither an English court nor an English arbitrator would apply the United States securities laws, because English conflict of law rules do not permit recognition of foreign tort or statutory law. From this, the Roby Names conclude that the contract clauses work to waive compliance with the securities laws and therefore are void.

We note at the outset that *Wilko v. Swan* held that an agreement to arbitrate future controversies was void under the anti-waiver provision of the Securities Act. We do not doubt that judicial hostility to arbitration has receded dramatically since 1953 and that the arbitral forum is perfectly competent to protect litigants' substantive rights. In the words of the *Mitsubishi* Court, quoted by both the *Rodriguez* and *McMahon* Courts, "[b]y agreeing to arbitrate a statutory claim, a party does not forgo the substantive rights afforded by the statute; it only submits to their resolution in an arbitral, rather than a judicial, forum." 473 U.S. at 628, 105 S.Ct. at 3354. If the Roby Names objected merely to the choice of an arbitral rather than a judicial forum, we would reject their claim immediately, citing *Rodriguez* and *McMahon*. However, the Roby Names argue that they have been forced to forgo the *substantive* protections afforded by the securities laws, not simply the judicial forum. We therefore do not believe that *Rodriguez* and *McMahon* are controlling and must look elsewhere to determine whether parties may contract away their substantive rights under the securities laws.

The Tenth Circuit recently addressed this exact issue in a similar context in *Riley v. Kingsley Underwriting Agencies, Ltd.,* 969 F.2d 953 (10th Cir.). Relying primarily on four Supreme Court precedents, the *Riley* Court concluded that "[w]hen an agreement is truly international, as here, and reflects numerous contacts with the foreign forum, the Supreme Court has quite clearly held that the parties' choice of law and forum selection provisions will be given effect." While we agree with the ultimate result in *Riley,* we are reluctant to interpret the Supreme Court's precedent quite so broadly.

A.   *Presumption of Validity*

The Supreme Court certainly has indicated that forum selection and choice of law clauses are presumptively valid where the underlying transaction is fundamentally international in character. In *The Bremen,* the Court explained that American parochialism would hinder the expansion of American business and trade, and more generally, interfere with the smooth functioning and growth of global commerce. Forum selection and choice of law clauses eliminate uncertainty in international commerce and insure that the parties are not unexpectedly subjected to hostile forums and laws. Moreover, international comity dictates that American courts enforce these sorts of clauses out of respect for the integrity and competence of foreign tribunals. In addition to these rationales for the presumptive validity of forum selection and choice of law clauses, the Court has noted that contracts entered into freely generally should be enforced because the financial effect of forum selection and choice of law clauses likely will be reflected in the value of the contract as a whole.

This presumption of validity may be overcome, however, by a clear showing that the clauses are " 'unreasonable' under the circumstances." The Supreme Court has construed this exception narrowly: forum selection and choice of law clauses are "unreasonable" (1) if their incorporation into the agreement was the result of fraud or overreaching; (2) if the complaining party "will for all practical purposes be deprived of his day in court," due to the grave inconvenience or unfairness of the selected forum; (3) if the fundamental unfairness of the chosen law may deprive the plaintiff of a remedy; or (4) if the clauses contravene a strong public policy of the forum state.

In this case, we can easily dispose of the first two factors. The Roby Names do not contend that they were fraudulently induced into agreeing to the forum selection, choice of law or arbitration clauses. Nor do we believe it gravely inconvenient for the Roby Names to litigate in London; they found it convenient enough to travel there for their mandatory interviews, and, in any event, many of them presently are prosecuting actions there. Moreover, nothing in the record suggests that the English courts would be biased or otherwise unfair, and United States courts consistently have found them to be neutral and just forums. Finally, the Roby Names have not presented any convincing evidence that the chosen arbitral forum would be biased in any way.

As to the third factor, we note that it is not enough that the foreign law or procedure merely be different or less favorable than that of the United States. Instead, the question is whether the application of the foreign law presents a danger that the Roby Names "will be deprived of *any* remedy or treated unfairly." As we explain below in section C, we believe the Roby Names have ample remedies under English law.

B. *Public Policy*

We depart somewhat from the *Riley* Court with respect to the fourth factor. We believe that there is a serious question whether United States public policy has been subverted by the Lloyd's clauses. In this section, we explain our concerns; in section C below, we resolve those concerns. Ultimately, we hold that the presumption of validity has not been overcome.

The Supreme Court in *The Bremen* wrote, "[a] contractual choice-of-forum clause should be held unenforceable if enforcement would contravene a strong public policy of the forum in which suit is brought." By including anti-waiver provisions in the securities laws, Congress made clear its intention that the public policies incorporated into those laws should not be thwarted.

The framers of the securities laws were concerned principally with reversing the common law rule favoring "caveat emptor." To this end, the securities laws are aimed at prospectively protecting American investors from injury by demanding "full and fair disclosure" from issuers. Private actions exist under the securities laws not because Congress had an overwhelming desire to shift losses after the fact, but rather because private actions provide a potent means of deterring the exploitation of American investors. We believe therefore that the public policies of the securities laws would be contravened if the applicable foreign law failed adequately to deter issuers from exploiting American investors.

* * *

We are concerned in the present case that the Roby Names' contract clauses may operate "in tandem" as a prospective waiver of the statutory remedies for securities violations, thereby circumventing the strong and expansive public policy in deterring such violations. We are cognizant of the important reasons for enforcing such clauses in Lloyd's' agreements. Lloyd's is a British concern, which raises capital in over 80 nations. Its operations are clearly international in scope. There can be no doubt that the contract clauses mitigate the uncertainty regarding choice of law and forum inherent in the multinational affairs of Lloyd's. Comity also weighs in favor of enforcing the clauses. Yet we do not believe that a United States court can in good conscience enforce clauses that subvert a strong national policy, particularly one that for over fifty years has served as the foundation for the United States financial markets and business community. In this case, the victims of Lloyd's' alleged securities violations are hundreds of individual American investors, most of whom were actively solicited in the United States by Lloyd's representatives. We believe that if the Roby Names were able to show that available remedies in England are insufficient to deter British issuers from exploiting American investors through fraud, misrepresentation or inadequate disclosure, we would not hesitate to condemn the choice of law, forum selection and arbitration clauses as against public policy. For the reasons set forth in section C below, however, we conclude that the Roby Names have failed to make such a showing.

C. *Availability of Adequate Remedies*

We are satisfied not only that the Roby Names have several adequate remedies in England to vindicate their substantive rights, but also that in *this* case the policies of ensuring full and fair disclosure and deterring the exploitation of United States investors have not been subverted. We address the fraud and misrepresentation claims first.

1. *Fraud and Misrepresentation*

English common law provides remedies for knowing or reckless deceit, negligent misrepresentation, and even innocent misrepresentation. Moreover, the Misrepresentation Act of 1967 provides some additional statutory remedies. *Id.* * * *

In any event, the available remedies are adequate and the potential recoveries substantial. This is particularly true given the low scienter requirements under English misrepresentation law (*e.g.,* negligence, "innocence"). Moreover, together with the contractual obligations imposing certain fiduciary and similar duties on Members' and Managing Agents, we believe that the available remedies and potential damages recoveries suffice to deter deception of American investors.

* * *

Moreover, even the Corporation of Lloyd's is not exempt for acts "done in bad faith." Furthermore, as a self-regulating organization, we cannot say that Lloyd's' own bylaws will not insure the honesty and forthrightness that American investors deserve and expect. We conclude that the Roby Names have adequate remedies in England to vindicate their statutory fraud and misrepresentation claims.

2. *Disclosure*

We turn now to address whether adequate remedies are available to deter issuers from issuing securities without disclosing sufficient information to permit investors to make informed decisions. We believe that this policy concern is somewhat diluted in this case because the SEC consistently has exempted Lloyd's from the registration requirements of the securities laws. Apparently the SEC has decided that Lloyd's' means test meets the requirements of Regulation D. We are extremely reluctant to dispute the SEC's apparent judgment that the Roby Names are sophisticated enough that they do not need the disclosure protections of the securities laws.

* * *

While we do not doubt that the United States securities laws would provide the Roby Names with a greater variety of defendants and a greater chance of success due to lighter scienter and causation requirements, we are convinced that there are ample and just remedies under English law. Moreover, we cannot say that the policies underlying our securities laws will be offended by the application of English law. In this case, the Roby Names have entered into contracts that require substantial disclosure by both the Members' and Managing Agents. The specter of liability for breach of contract should act as an adequate deterrent to the exploitation of American investors. The well developed English law of fraud and misrepresentation likewise adequately requires that the disclosure be "fair."

* * *

CONCLUSION

For the foregoing reasons we hold that the Roby Names' contract clauses cover the scope of, and the parties named in, the complaint and that the Roby Names have remedies under English law adequate not only to vindicate their substantive rights but also to protect the public policies established by the United States securities laws.

The judgment and order of the district court are affirmed.

NOTES AND QUESTIONS

1. In *Mitsubishi Motors Corp. v. Soler Chrysler–Plymouth*, 473 U.S. 614, 105 S.Ct. 3346, 87 L.Ed.2d 444 (1985), the U.S. Supreme Court said that the liberal federal policy favoring arbitration applied with special force in international commerce. "Concerns of international comity, respect for the capacities of foreign and transnational tribunals, and sensitivity to the need of the international commercial system for predictability in the resolution of disputes, all require enforcement of the arbitration clause in question, even assuming a contrary result would be forthcoming in a domestic context." *Id.* at 629. Do you agree?

2. Why was it important for Lloyds' to provide for the arbitration of disputes in England with English law governing the disputes?

The International Chamber of Commerce recommends that parties stipulate in the arbitration clause the law governing the contract, the location of the arbitration, and the language of the hearing. COMMERCIAL ARBITRATION AT ITS BEST: SUCCESSFUL STRATEGIES FOR BUSINESS USES 331 (STIPANOWICH AND KASKELL EDS, CPR INST. DISP. RES. AND ABA SECTIONS OF BUSINESS LAW AND DISPUTE RESOLUTION) (2001).

3. See CHARLES S. BALDWIN IV, RONALD A. BRAND, DAVID EPSTEIN, & MICHAEL WALLACE GORDON, INTERNATIONAL CIVIL DISPUTE RESOLUTION 627 (2004) for a list of issues to consider in drafting an arbitration provision for an international business contract. IAN R. MACNEIL, RICHARD E. SPEIDEL & THOMAS J. STIPANOWICH, FEDERAL ARBITRATION LAW § 44.7 (1994 ed. & Supp. 1999) also discusses issues to consider and cite to numerous articles and treatises that would be helpful in drafting such an arbitration provision.

4. Foreign investment treaties have provided an important context for international arbitration in recent years, with more than 2,500 such treaties signed by approximately 175 countries as of the end of 2005. These treaties typically involve investments in the infrastructure of developing nations. The

numbers are huge, with about $1.6 trillion expected to be invested in foreign investments by 2012. World Investment Prospects Survey: 2012–2014 (2012), available at http://unctad.org/en/PublicationsLibrary/webdiaeia2012d21_en. pdf.

The treaties essentially safeguard the investor's investment by providing certain substantive and procedural safeguards that commonly include a right of arbitration against the host government for state actions that negatively affect the investment.

In an important empirical study of foreign investment treaty arbitration, Professor Susan Franck found that there has been an increase in treaty arbitrations, that costs associated with arbitration can be substantial, that settlement was relatively uncommon, and that few of the arbitrators were female. She also found that investors did not win more disputes than governments, large damage awards were rare, and that the majority of arbitrators did not have repeat appointments. Susan D. Franck, *Empirically Evaluating Claims About Investment Treaty Arbitration*, 86 N.C. L. Rev. 1 (2007). *See also* Susan D. Franck, *Integrating Investment Treaty Conflict and Dispute Systems Design*, 92 Minn. L. Rev. 161 (2007) (discussing other dispute resolution options); Tai–Heng Cheng, *Precedent and Control in Investment Treaty Arbitration*, 30 Fordham Int'l L.J. 1014 (2007); Eric Gottwald, *Leveling the Playing Field: Is it Time for a Legal Assistance Center for Developing Nations in Investment Treaty Arbitration?*, 22 Am. U. Int'l L. Rev. 237 (2007).

c.   Enforcement and Review of Awards

Section 13 of the Federal Arbitration Act permits federal courts to enforce valid arbitration awards, and to review them for arbitral misconduct and ultra vires acts. As we know from the readings in the preceding section, however, international commercial arbitration is not supported by a unified judicial system. The following readings explore the problems created by the interplay between international treaties and the domestic law of a particular nation with respect to enforcement and review of international commercial arbitration awards.

YUSUF AHMED ALGHANIM & SONS V. TOYS "R" US, INC.

United States Court of Appeals, Second Circuit, 1997
126 F.3d 15

MINER, CIRCUIT JUDGE.

Appeal from a judgment entered in the United States District Court for the Southern District of New York (McKenna, J.) denying respondents' cross-motion to vacate or modify an arbitration award and granting the petition to confirm the award. The court found that while the petition for confirmation was brought under the Convention on the Recognition and Enforcement of Foreign Arbitral Awards, respondents' cross-motion to vacate or modify the award was properly brought under the Federal Arbitration Act, and thus those claims were governed by the Federal Arbitration Act's implied grounds for vacatur. Nonetheless, the court granted the petition to confirm the award, finding that respondents' allegations of error in the arbitral award were without merit.

For the reasons that follow, we affirm.

BACKGROUND

In November of 1982, respondent-appellant Toys "R" Us, Inc. (collectively with respondent-appellant TRU (HK) Limited, "Toys 'R' Us") and petitioner-appellee Yusuf Ahmed Alghanim & Sons, W.L.L. ("Alghanim"), a privately owned Kuwaiti business, entered into a License and Technical Assistance Agreement (the "agreement") and a Supply Agreement. Through the agreement, Toys "R" Us granted Alghanim a limited right to open Toys "R" Us stores and use its trademarks in Kuwait and 13 other countries located in and around the Middle East (the "territory"). Toys "R" Us further agreed to supply Alghanim with its technology, expertise and assistance in the toy business.

From 1982 to the December 1993 commencement of the arbitration giving rise to this appeal, Alghanim opened four toy stores, all in Kuwait. According to Toys "R" Us, the first such store, opened in 1983, resembled a Toys "R" Us store in the United States, but the other three, two of which were opened in 1985 and one in 1988, were small storefronts with only limited merchandise. It is uncontested that Alghanim's stores lost some $6.65 million over the 11–year period from 1982 to 1993, and turned a profit only in one year of this period.

* * *

On July 20, 1992, Toys "R" Us purported to exercise its right to terminate the agreement, sending Alghanim a notice of non-renewal stating that the agreement would terminate on January 31, 1993. Alghanim responded on July 30, 1992, stating that because its most recently opened toy store had opened on January 16, 1988, the initial term of the agreement ended on January 16, 1993. Alghanim asserted that Toys "R" Us's notice of non-renewal was four days late in providing notice six months before the end of the initial period. According to Alghanim, under the termination provision of the agreement, Toys "R" Us's failure to provide notice more than six months before the fifth year after the opening of the most recent store automatically extended the term of the agreement for an additional two years, until January 16, 1995.

On September 2, 1992, Toys "R" Us sent a second letter. Toys "R" Us explained that, on further inspection of the agreement, it had determined that the initial term of the agreement expired on December 31, 1993, and it again gave notice of non-renewal. In this letter, Toys "R" Us also directed Alghanim not to open any new toy stores and warned that failure to comply with that direction could constitute a breach of the agreement.

* * *

On December 20, 1993, Toys "R" Us invoked the dispute-resolution mechanism in the agreement, initiating an arbitration before the American Arbitration Association. Toys "R" Us sought a declaration that the agreement was terminated on December 31, 1993. Alghanim responded by counterclaiming for breach of contract.

On May 4, 1994, the arbitrator denied Toys "R" Us's request for declaratory judgment. The arbitrator found that, under the termination provisions of the agreement, Alghanim had the absolute right to open toy stores, even after being given notice of termination, as long as the last toy store was opened within five years. The parties then engaged in substantial document and expert discovery, motion practice, and a 29–day evidentiary hearing on Alghanim's counterclaims. On July 11, 1996, the arbitrator awarded Alghanim $46.44 million for lost profits under the agreement, plus 9 percent interest to accrue from December 31, 1994. The arbitrator's findings and legal conclusions were set forth in a 47–page opinion.

Alghanim petitioned the district court to confirm the award under the Convention on the Recognition and Enforcement of Foreign Arbitral Awards of June 10, 1958 ("Convention"). Toys "R" Us cross-moved to vacate or modify the award under the Federal Arbitration Act ("FAA"), arguing that the award was clearly irrational, in manifest disregard of the law, and in manifest disregard of the terms of the agreement. The district court concluded that "[t]he Convention and the FAA afford overlapping coverage, and the fact that a petition to confirm is brought under the Convention does not foreclose a cross-motion to vacate under the FAA, and the Court will consider [Toys "R" Us's] cross-motion under the standards of the FAA." By judgment entered December 20, 1996, the district court confirmed the award, finding Toys "R" Us's objections to the award to be without merit. This appeal followed.

DISCUSSION

I. *Availability of the FAA's Grounds for Relief in Confirmation Under the Convention*

Toys "R" Us argues that the district court correctly determined that the provisions of the FAA apply to its cross-motion to vacate or modify the arbitral award. In particular, Toys "R" Us contends that the FAA and the Convention have overlapping coverage. Thus, Toys "R" Us argues, even though the petition to confirm the arbitral award was brought under the Convention, the FAA's implied grounds for vacatur should apply to Toys "R" Us's cross-motion to vacate or modify because the cross-motion was brought under the FAA. We agree that the FAA governs Toys "R" Us's cross-motion.

A.   Applicability of the Convention

Neither party seriously disputes the applicability of the Convention to this case and it is clear to us that the Convention does apply. The Convention provides that it will apply to the recognition and enforcement of arbitral awards made in the territory of a State other than the State where the recognition and enforcement of such awards are sought, and arising out of differences between persons, whether physical or legal. It shall also apply to arbitral awards *not considered as domestic awards* in the State where their recognition and enforcement are sought.

* * *

The Convention's applicability in this case is clear. The dispute giving rise to this appeal involved two nondomestic parties and one United States corporation, and principally involved conduct and contract performance in the Middle East. Thus, we consider the arbitral award leading to this action a non-domestic award and thus within the scope of the Convention.

B.   Authority Under the Convention to Set Aside An Award Under Domestic Arbitral Law

Toys "R" Us argues that the district court properly found that it had the authority under the Convention to apply the FAA's implied grounds for setting aside the award. We agree. Under the Convention, the district court's role in reviewing a foreign arbitral award is strictly limited: "The court shall confirm the award unless it finds one of the grounds for refusal or deferral of recognition or enforcement of the award specified in the said Convention." Under Article V of the Convention, the grounds for refusing to recognize or enforce an arbitral award are:

> (a) The parties to the agreement . . . were . . . under some incapacity, or the said agreement is not valid under the law . . . ; or (b) The party against whom the award is invoked was not given proper notice of the appointment of the arbitrator or of the arbitration proceedings . . . ; or (c) The award deals with a difference not contemplated by or not falling within the terms of the submission to arbitration, or it contains decisions on matters beyond the scope of the submission to arbitration . . . ; or (d) The composition of the arbitral authority or the arbitral procedure was not in accordance with the agreement of the parties . . . ; or (e) The award has not yet become binding on the parties, or has been set aside or suspended by a competent authority of the country in which, or under the law of which, that award was made.

Convention art. V(1). Enforcement may also be refused if "[t]he subject matter of the difference is not capable of settlement by arbitration," or if "recognition or enforcement of the award would be contrary to the public policy" of the country in which enforcement or recognition is sought. *Id.* art. V(2). These seven grounds are the only grounds explicitly provided under the Convention.

In determining the availability of the FAA's implied grounds for setting aside, the text of the Convention leaves us with two questions: (1) whether, in addition to the Convention's express grounds for refusal, other grounds can be read into the Convention by implication, much as American courts have read implied grounds for relief into the FAA, and (2) whether, under Article V(1)(e), the courts of the United States are authorized to apply United States procedural arbitral law, i.e., the FAA, to nondomestic awards rendered in the United States. We answer the first question in the negative and the second in the affirmative.

1. Availability Under the Convention of Implied Grounds for Refusal

We have held that the FAA and the Convention have "overlapping coverage" to the extent that they do not conflict. However, by that same token, to the extent that the Convention prescribes the exclusive grounds for relief from an award under the Convention, that application of the FAA's implied grounds would be in conflict, and is thus precluded.

In *Parsons & Whittemore Overseas Co. v. Societe Generale de L'Industrie du Papier (RAKTA)*, 508 F.2d 969 (2d Cir.1974), we declined to decide whether the implied defense of "manifest disregard" applies under the Convention, having decided that even if it did, appellant's claim would fail. *See id.* at 977. Nonetheless, we noted that "[b]oth the legislative history of Article V and the statute enacted to implement the United States' accession to the Convention are strong authority for treating as exclusive the bases set forth in the Convention for vacating an award." *Id.* (citation and footnote omitted).

There is now considerable case law holding that, in an action to confirm an award rendered in, or under the law of, a foreign jurisdiction, the grounds for relief enumerated in Article V of the Convention are the only grounds available for setting aside an arbitral award. This conclusion is consistent with the Convention's pro-enforcement bias. We join these courts in declining to read into the Convention the FAA's implied defenses to confirmation of an arbitral award.

2. Nondomestic Award Rendered in the United States

Although Article V provides the exclusive grounds for refusing confirmation under the Convention, one of those exclusive grounds is where "[t]he award ... has been set aside or suspended by a competent authority of the country in which, or under the law of which, that award was made." Convention art. V(1)(e). Those courts holding that implied defenses were inapplicable under the Convention did so in the context of petitions to confirm awards rendered abroad. These courts were not presented with the question whether Article V(1)(e) authorizes an action to set aside an arbitral award under the domestic law of the state in which, or under which, the award was rendered. We, however, are faced head-on with that question in the case before us, because the arbitral award in this case was rendered in the United States, and both confirmation and vacatur were then sought in the United States.

We read Article V(1)(e) of the Convention to allow a court in the country under whose law the arbitration was conducted to apply domestic arbitral law, in this case the FAA, to a motion to set aside or vacate that arbitral award. The district court in *Spector v. Torenberg*, reached the same conclusion as we do now, reasoning that, because the Convention allows the district court to refuse to enforce an award that has been vacated by a competent authority in the country where the award was rendered, the court may apply FAA standards to a motion to vacate a nondomestic award rendered in the United States.

The Seventh Circuit has agreed, albeit in passing, that the Convention "contemplates the possibility of the award's being set aside in a proceeding under local law." Likewise, the United States District Court for the District of Columbia has found that, in an arbitration conducted in Egypt and under Egyptian law, nullification of the award by the Egyptian courts falls within Article V(1)(e).

Our conclusion also is consistent with the reasoning of courts that have refused to apply non-Convention grounds for relief where awards were rendered outside the United States. For example, the Sixth Circuit in *M & C* concluded that it should not apply the FAA's implied grounds for vacatur, because the United States did not provide the law of the arbitration for the purposes of Article V(1)(e) of the Convention. Similarly, in *International Standard*, the district court decided that only the state under whose procedural law the arbitration was conducted has jurisdiction under Article V(1)(e) to vacate the award, whereas on a petition for confirmation made in any other state, only the defenses to confirmation listed in Article V of the Convention are available.

This interpretation of Article V(1)(e) also finds support in the scholarly work of commentators on the Convention and in the judicial decisions of our sister signatories to the Convention. There appears to be no dispute among these authorities that an action to set aside an international arbitral award, as contemplated by Article V(1)(e), is controlled by the domestic law of the rendering state. As one commentator has explained:

> The possible effect of this ground for refusal [Article V(1)(e)] is that, as the award can be set aside in the country of origin on *all* grounds

contained in the arbitration law of that country, including the public policy of that country, the grounds for refusal of enforcement under the Convention may indirectly be extended to include all kinds of particularities of the arbitration law of the country of origin. This might undermine the limitative character of the grounds for refusal listed in Article V . . . and thus decrease the degree of uniformity existing under the Convention.

van den Berg, *supra,* at 355 * * *. The defense in Article V(1)(e) incorporates the entire body of review rights in the issuing jurisdiction. . . . If the scope of judicial review in the rendering state extends beyond the other six defenses allowed under the New York Convention, the losing party's opportunity to avoid enforcement is automatically enhanced: The losing party can first attempt to derail the award on appeal on grounds that would not be permitted elsewhere during enforcement proceedings.

Indeed, many commentators and foreign courts have concluded that an action to set aside an award can be brought *only* under the domestic law of the arbitral forum, and can never be made under the Convention. ("[T]he fact is that setting aside awards under the New York Convention can take place only in the country in which the award was made.").

There is no indication in the Convention of any intention to deprive the rendering state of its supervisory authority over an arbitral award, including its authority to set aside that award under domestic law. The Convention succeeded and replaced the Convention on the Execution of Foreign Arbitral Awards ("Geneva Convention"), Sept. 26, 1927. The primary defect of the Geneva Convention was that it required an award first to be recognized in the rendering state before it could be enforced abroad, * * *.

The Convention eliminated this problem by eradicating the requirement that a court in the rendering state recognize an award before it could be taken and enforced abroad. In so doing, the Convention intentionally "liberalized procedures for enforcing foreign arbitral awards."

Nonetheless, under the Convention, the power and authority of the local courts of the rendering state remain of paramount importance. "What the Convention did not do . . . was provide any international mechanism to insure the validity of the award where rendered. This was left to the provisions of local law. The Convention provides no restraint whatsoever on the control functions of local courts at the seat of arbitration." Another commentator explained:

Significantly, [Article V(1)(e)] fails to specify the grounds upon which the rendering State may set aside or suspend the award. While it would have provided greater reliability to the enforcement of awards under the Convention had the available grounds been defined in some way, such action would have constituted meddling with national procedure for handling domestic awards, a subject beyond the competence of the Conference.

Leonard V. Quigley, *Accession by the United States to the United Nations Convention on the Recognition and Enforcement of Foreign Arbitral Awards,* 70 Yale L.J. 1049, 1070 (1961). From the plain language and history of the Convention, it is thus apparent that a party may seek to vacate or set aside an award in the state in which, or under the law of which, the award is rendered. Moreover, the language and history of the Convention make it clear that such a motion is to be governed by domestic law of the rendering state, despite the fact that the award is nondomestic within the meaning of the Convention as we have interpreted it in *Bergesen.* * * *

In sum, we conclude that the Convention mandates very different regimes for the review of arbitral awards (1) in the state in which, or under the law of which, the award was made, and (2) in other states where recognition and enforcement are sought. The Convention specifically contemplates that the state in which, or under the law of which, the award is made, will be free to set aside or modify an award in accordance with its domestic arbitral law and its full panoply of express and implied grounds for relief. *See* Convention art. V(1)(e). However, the Convention is equally clear that when an action for enforcement is brought in a foreign state, the state may refuse to enforce the award only on the grounds explicitly set forth in Article V of the Convention.

II. *Application of FAA Grounds for Relief*

Having determined that the FAA does govern Toys "R" Us's cross-motion to vacate, our application of the FAA's implied grounds for vacatur is swift. The Supreme Court has stated, "that courts of appeals should apply ordinary, not special, standards when reviewing district court decisions upholding arbitration awards." We review the district court's findings of fact for clear error and its conclusions of law *de novo.*

"[T]he confirmation of an arbitration award is a summary proceeding that merely makes what is already a final arbitration award a judgment of the court." The review of arbitration awards is "very limited . . . in order to avoid undermining the twin goals of arbitration, namely, settling disputes efficiently and avoiding long and expensive litigation." Accordingly, "the showing required to avoid summary confirmance is high."

More particularly, "[t]his court has generally refused to second guess an arbitrator's resolution of a contract dispute." As we have explained: "An arbitrator's decision is entitled to substantial deference, and the arbitrator need only explicate his reasoning under the contract 'in terms that offer even a barely colorable justification for the outcome reached' in order to withstand judicial scrutiny."

However, awards may be vacated, *see* 9 U.S.C. § 10, or modified, *see id.* § 11, in the limited circumstances where the arbitrator's award is in manifest disregard of the terms of the agreement, or where the award is in "manifest disregard of the law." We find that neither of these implied grounds is met in the present case.

A. *Manifest Disregard of the Law*

Toys "R" Us argues that the arbitrator manifestly disregarded New York law on lost profits awards for breach of contract by returning a speculative award. This contention is without merit. "[M]ere error in the law or failure on the part of the arbitrator[ ] to understand or apply the law" is not sufficient to establish manifest disregard of the law. For an award to be in "manifest disregard of the law,"

> [t]he error must have been obvious and capable of being readily and instantly perceived by the average person qualified to serve as an arbitrator. Moreover, the term "disregard" implies that the arbitrator appreciates the existence of a clearly governing legal principle but decides to ignore or pay no attention to it.

In the instant case, the arbitrator was well aware of and carefully applied New York's law on lost profits. The arbitrator specifically addressed *Kenford Co. v. County of Erie,* which contains New York's law on the subject and upon which Toys "R" Us relied in its arguments, and concluded:

> I do not think the Kenford case rules out damages in this case. Kenford disallowed damages based on future profits from concessions in a domed stadium that was never built. . . . In this case [Alghanim], which is forced into the estimating posture because of [Toys "R" Us's] breach, bases its damages not on its own experience but on [Toys "R" Us's]. [Toys "R" Us] has hundreds of toy stores worldwide. Since it has been found that the Agreements require [Toys "R" Us] to provide a wide variety of services, similar to what it provides its own toy stores, I find that [Alghanim's] method of estimating damages is reasonable and believable, and provides a sound basis on which to fashion the award.

We find no manifest disregard of the law in this analysis.

* * *

B. *Manifest Disregard of the Agreement*

Toys "R" Us also argues that the district court erred in refusing to vacate the award because the arbitrator manifestly disregarded the terms of the agreement. In particular, Toys "R" Us disputes the arbitrator's interpretation of four contract terms: (1) the termination provision; (2) the conforming stores provision; (3) the non-assignment provision; and (4) the deletion provision. We find no error.

Interpretation of these contract terms is within the province of the arbitrator and will not be overruled simply because we disagree with that interpretation. We will overturn an award where the arbitrator merely "mak[es] the right noises—noises of contract interpretation—"while ignoring the clear meaning of contract terms. We apply a notion of "manifest disregard" to the terms of the agreement analogous to that employed in the context of manifest disregard of the law.

As to each of these contract provisions, Toys "R" Us merely takes issue with the arbitrator's well-reasoned interpretations of those provisions, and simply offers its own contrary interpretations. Toys "R" Us does not advance a convincing argument that the arbitrator manifestly disregarded the agreement. We will not overturn the arbitrator's award merely because we do not concur with the arbitrator's reading of the agreement. For the reasons stated by the district court, we find the arbitrator's interpretation of the contractual provisions supportable.

We have carefully considered Toys "R" Us's remaining contentions and find them all to be without merit.

CONCLUSION

For the foregoing reasons, the judgment of the district court is affirmed.

NOTES AND QUESTIONS

1.   What was the primary defect in the Geneva Convention that was eliminated in the New York Convention?

2.   In what situations does the New York Convention apply? See Convention Art. 1(1) cited in the *Yusuf* case. Grounds for non-enforcement of the Convention are set out in Article VI. American courts construe these grounds for non-enforcement narrowly. *See* CHRISTOPHER R. DRAHOZAL, COMMERCIAL ARBITRATION: CASES AND PROBLEMS 549 (2d ed. 2006).

3.   Chapter 2 of the FAA implements the U.S. obligations under the New York Convention. Section 207 of the FAA provides that any court having jurisdiction may confirm an arbitrator's award unless the award falls under one of the grounds for refusal of recognition set out in the Convention. Section 203 of the FAA grants subject matter jurisdiction in federal court over an action falling under the convention. Section 205 of the FAA authorizes removal from state courts of cases falling under the Convention.

On the other hand, an action to vacate an international award can be brought only at the arbitration situs or in the country whose law was selected by the parties. For discussions of the notion of "de-localizing" arbitration awards, a criticism of the arbitral situs rule, see *id.* at 555; William W. Park,

Book Review, 82 Am. J. Int'l L. 616, at 622–23 (1988) (reviewing ALAN REDFERN & MARTIN HUNTER, LAW AND THE PRACTICE OF INTERNATIONAL COMMERCIAL ARBITRATION (1996)).

4. Where does one look for the applicable standards for vacating an arbitration award? Is it proper to consider both explicit and implied grounds when deciding whether to vacate an award?

Where does one look for the applicable standards for confirmation and enforcement of an arbitration award? Is it proper to consider both explicit and implied grounds in deciding whether to confirm and enforce an arbitration award?

CHAPTER VI

MIXED PROCESSES, ADAPTATIONS, AND OTHER INNOVATIONS

■ ■ ■

If any one quality characterizes the alternative dispute resolution movement, it may well be innovation. As we have seen, the movement was born out of a felt need by many inside and outside the legal profession to expand beyond traditional public adjudication in the resolution of disputes, and the development of the processes themselves has been a dynamic process of experimentation and adaptation.

In this chapter, we look at this evolution in terms of innovative types of dispute resolution processes, as well as the seemingly inevitable expansion of alternative dispute resolution processes into new contexts. In particular, we look at "mixed" processes, which combine elements of negotiation, mediation, fact finding, or adjudication—the primary dispute resolution processes—as well as three different contexts in which both traditional and mixed processes have been used: public courts, administrative agencies, and the private sector. Each process and context provides different challenges, and opportunities, with regard to many of the questions we have been exploring throughout this book, including the suitability of a dispute resolution process for a particular dispute, and the lawyer's role in helping the client select an appropriate dispute resolution process. You should continue to keep these questions in mind as you read the following materials. Also consider whether and why a mixed process may be more appropriate for a given dispute or dispute resolution system, as well as any arguments against the use of mixed processes, such as confusion, complexity, or cost. Finally, consider how you might combine or adapt the primary processes creatively to address other situations or contexts.

This chapter broadly distinguishes between the public and private spheres, beginning with the public sphere. Section A–1 focuses on the use of primary processes, mixed processes, and other innovations in public courts, and Section B addresses their use in administrative agencies. Section B also looks at their use in the private sphere, including both traditional contexts, such as labor-management relations, as well as such new contexts as online dispute resolution.

A. THE PUBLIC SPHERE

1. THE COURTS

a. The Big Picture

One of the first, and most important, places in which the modern ADR movement took roots was in the courts. This served a critical education function, as judges, court administrators, lawyers, and parties would need to learn about alternative processes in order to be willing and able to use them.

In some respects, courts were willing partners for ADR advocates, out of efficiency concerns for litigant time and cost, as well as their own burgeoning court dockets. Courts also recognized the inherent weaknesses of the law in terms of resolving legal problems, and the potential for ADR to provide much greater access to more meaningful outcomes for more of the litigants who came before them. Yet they also recognized that this potential forced them to rethink deeply cherished principles of justice and the rule of law.

This struggle, as well as such practical issues as who will pay for court-related ADR services, continues to endure and animate court-related ADR programs. It is readily seen the main reading for this section, the most recent report for federal judges on federal court ADR, and further explored in the notes that follow.

DONNA STIENSTRA, ADR IN THE FEDERAL DISTRICT COURTS: AN INITIAL REPORT
Federal Judicial Center (November 2011)

* * *

History of ADR Development in the Federal District Courts

Although the federal district courts started designing and testing ADR procedures as long ago as the 1970s, the biggest growth in ADR came in response to the Civil Justice Reform Act of 1990. Below is a short chronology of ADR developments.

During the late 1970s and the 1980s, several district courts experimented with mediation; one district court created a new procedure called the summary jury trial, and another district court created a new procedure called early neutral evaluation. Three district courts, selected by the Judicial Conference, experimented in the early 1980s with mandatory court-annexed arbitration, which resulted in a 1988 statute authorizing ten district courts to mandate arbitration for a specified subset of civil cases and ten district courts to offer voluntary use of arbitration.

In December 1990, Congress passed the Civil Justice Reform Act of 1990, which required the federal district courts to develop cost and delay reduction plans. The statute directed the courts to consider adoption of six case management principles, the sixth of which was alternative dispute resolution. Many of the ninety-four district courts developed ADR procedures in response to this statute. The CJRA offered monetary incentives for implementation of the act's requirements, and during the CJRA period a number of courts hired professional staff to manage their ADR programs.

* * *

A year after the CJRA sunset, Congress passed another act regarding ADR in the federal district courts. Whereas the CJRA simply encouraged the district courts to adopt ADR, the ADR Act of 1998 mandated that these courts provide ADR services to civil litigants. This act remains in effect; * * *

* * *

The most recent development in ADR in the federal district courts is the emergence of mediation programs for pro se litigants. This type of case has traditionally been exempt from court ADR programs because the needs of pro se litigants can put ADR neutrals at risk of appearing biased in the pro se's favor. * * *

Some thirty years after the first experiments with ADR and twenty years since the major statutory push to develop these procedures, ADR is now an established part of many districts', or many judges', regular case management practices. Even so, of course, ADR use varies from district to district, as we will see below.

ADR in the Federal District Courts Today

The tables in this section summarize various features of the ADR programs currently authorized by the district courts. The information in the tables is based on my review of local rules, general orders, CJRA plans, internal operating procedures, web sites, and any other written source I could find that describes a district's ADR procedures. * * *

* * *

Types of ADR Programs Authorized by the Federal District Courts

Table 1 shows the types of ADR programs adopted by the district courts. * * * Table 1 shows that the greatest number of districts—thirty-four, or a little more than a third of the district courts—offer multiple forms of ADR. Typically, such a district authorizes mediation and arbitration, or mediation and early neutral evaluation, or perhaps all three. Of these thirty-four districts, fourteen authorize three or more distinct forms of ADR. Another third of the districts offer only one form of

ADR, the most common being mediation, which twenty-five districts, or more than a quarter of the districts, authorize as their sole form of ADR.

Table 1
Number of District Courts by Types of ADR Procedures They Have Authorized

Type of ADR Procedures Authorized	Number and Percent of District Courts	
	Number	Percent
Multiple Forms of ADR[a]	34	36.2
Mediation Only[b]	27	28.7
General Authorization Only	12	12.8
Settlement Conference Only	10	10.6
General Authorization[c] and Settlement Conference Only	3	3.2
Early Neutral Evaluation (ENE) Only	3	3.2
Summary Jury Trial Only	1	1.1
Case Evaluation[d] Only	1	1.1
Other	3	3.2
Total	94	100.1

* * * Note that no district court authorizes only arbitration. Although for a short period in the mid-1980s to mid-1990s arbitration was the most visible ADR procedure in the federal district courts, with thousands of cases referred to the process, today it plays a much smaller role.

The second-largest group of districts—thirty-six, or more than a third—mention settlement conferences in their ADR provisions (including the ten districts that authorize only settlement conferences). We can be certain that a greater number of districts use settlement conferences, but

---

[a] A district is counted in this category only if it authorizes two or more types of distinct ADR procedures—e.g., mediation, arbitration, early neutral evaluation, summary jury or bench trials. * * *

[b] Where the word "only" is used in this table it means a district's written ADR documents mention only that one distinct form of ADR. Some of the districts that authorize only one of the distinct forms of ADR—e.g., mediation or early neutral evaluation—also include settlement conferences and/or a general authorization for ADR in their ADR documents.

[c] "General authorization" means the district authorizes use of ADR or authorizes an "open track" or "general track" for ADR. These districts may mention specific forms of ADR, such as mediation and early neutral evaluation, but their written documents do not provide details that suggest authorization of a court-administered ADR program.

[d] This arbitration-like process is authorized for certain types of cases arising under state law and uses a state tribunal.

many very likely do not mention this procedure in their ADR provisions. Although Table 1 showed that no district courts authorize only arbitration, Table 2 shows that twenty-three districts, or nearly a quarter, include it among other forms of authorized ADR. * * *

Table 2
Number of District Courts in Which Each Type of ADR Procedures is Authorized

Type of ADR Procedure Authorized	Number and Percent of District Courts That Have Authorized the ADR Procedure[a]	
	Number	Percent[b]
Mediation	63	67.0
Settlement Conferences	36	38.3
General Authorization	27	28.7
Arbitration	23	24.5
Early Neutral Evaluation	23	24.5
Pro Se Mediation Program[c]		
Non-Prisoner Pro Se Litigants	18	19.2
Prisoner Pro Se Litigants	11	11.7
Summary Jury or Bench Trial	14	14.9
Mini-Trial	5	5.3
Case Evaluation[d]	3	3.2
Settlement Week[e]	2	2.1
Med/Arb[f]	1	1.1

Table 2 offers a different way to look at the types of ADR authorized by the district courts. The table reports the total number of ADR procedures authorized across all the district courts. Of the ninety-four

---

[a] A district is counted as authorizing a procedure if that procedure is mentioned as a distinct ADR procedure and not as one among several included in a general authorization to use ADR.

[b] As a percent of ninety-four district courts.

[c] Many of the pro se mediation programs are new and experimental and not yet recorded in court local rules or other ADR documents. * * *

[d] This arbitration-like process is authorized for certain types of cases arising under state law and uses a state tribunal.

[e] During settlement week, the court's facilities are devoted to mediation of a roster of trial-ready cases. Attorneys from the district's bar serve as mediators.

[f] In this procedure, a case first uses mediation and, if it does not settle, proceeds to arbitration.

district courts, for example, the greatest number—sixty-three, or a little more than two-thirds of the district courts—authorize referral to mediation.

Table 2 also shows greater authorization for early neutral evaluation than Table 1 suggested. While only three districts authorize ENE as their sole procedure, twenty-three districts, or nearly a quarter, authorize it as one among two or more ADR options.

Table 3

Number of Districts That Authorize Each Type of Referral Process by Type of ADR Procedure Authorized

	Number of Districts That Authorize Each Type of Referral Process[a]			
ADR Procedure (Number of Districts That Authorize)	Consent by All Parties Needed	Judge May Order Without Party Consent	District Mandates Referral for All or Specified Cases	No Information
Mediation (63)	11	46	12	0
Arbitration (23)	11	9	4[b]	0
ENE (23)	7	13	5	1
General Authorization (27)[c]	13	13	0	2

Although few of the district court ADR documents available at court web sites reflect the newly emerging mediation programs for pro se litigants, at least twenty-one districts have set up such programs. Eighteen of these twenty-one districts offer mediation to non-prisoner pro se litigants, and eleven offer it to prisoner pro se litigants. * * * At this time, we have no details about how they are administered or which pro se litigants they are serving.

---

[a] The total number of districts authorizing referral processes may be greater than the number of districts authorizing each type of ADR procedure because some districts authorize more than one type of referral process (for example, a district may authorize mandatory referral for some types of cases and voluntary referral for other types of cases).

[b] Three of the original ten mandatory arbitration districts continue to require use of arbitration for all eligible cases; one includes it as an option in a program where use of some form of ADR is presumed.

[c] For each of the three distinct types of ADR—mediation, arbitration, and ENE—the majority of districts authorize some degree of required use, either by giving judges the authority to refer cases on their own initiative without party consent or by mandating referral for some or all civil cases. This approach is especially apparent for mediation, where fifty-eight districts authorize required use of mediation, including twelve districts that mandate use (that is, referral is automatic for all or a specified set of cases). Judges have authority to order ADR in half the districts that authorize ENE, as well, and in half of those that provide general authorization to use ADR.

* * *

Referral Methods Authorized by the Federal District Court

Most district courts include information about referral to ADR in their ADR rules, orders, or other documents. The methods authorized can generally be grouped into three categories. Some districts authorize mandatory referral of cases to ADR, some permit use of ADR only if all parties consent, and the great majority leave the referral decision to the judge. The referral information in the third group of districts typically authorizes the judge to order referral to ADR at the judge's initiative without party consent or at the request of one party. To cover the cases in which a judge does not order referral to ADR sua sponte or at a party's request, the rules in these districts typically also include authorization for parties to use ADR at their own discretion if all parties consent. Table 3 shows the number of districts authorizing each type of referral by the type of ADR process authorized in the district. * * *

For arbitration, the picture is somewhat different, with more districts authorizing voluntary use, rather than authorizing required use. Voluntary use is in compliance with the 1998 ADR Act. . . . Although the 1998 ADR Act expressly requires consent, a number of other districts authorize their judges to refer cases to arbitration without party consent.

Types of Neutrals Authorized by the Federal District Courts

In their written ADR documents, many district courts provide information that tells litigants about the neutrals authorized by the district. Among the kinds of information commonly provided are the types of persons who serve as neutrals, the requirements for being listed on a district's panel of neutrals, and the fees, if any, that litigants are expected to pay neutrals. Table 4 shows the number of districts that authorize several different types of neutrals for the principle types of ADR authorized in the district courts. The table does not include settlement conferences because district and magistrate judges are always the neutrals.

The principle story in Table 4 is that most districts authorize creation of a panel of neutrals to provide ADR services. Among the sixty-three districts that authorize mediation, for example, forty-two of them, or more than two-thirds, authorize creation of a panel of neutrals who can serve as mediators. The great majority of districts that authorize arbitration and ENE procedures also rely on panels of neutrals. District court ADR documents typically set out the qualifications that must be met by applicants to the panel, such as years of bar membership and hours of mediation training.

A number of districts authorize outside neutrals for their ADR procedures. For mediation, arbitration and ENE, these outside neutrals may be a panel authorized by the state courts or any neutral the parties wish to select. For districts that provide a general authorization to use ADR, the outside neutrals are typically as unspecified as the type of ADR authorized. Although most districts rely primarily on panels of neutrals, a handful authorize judges to serve as ADR neutrals and a similarly small number have staff who can serve as ADR neutrals. Of the eleven districts that have staff neutrals, two authorize the clerk of court to serve as a generalized ADR neutral and nine have professional staff mediators. A small number of districts provide no information at all about the types of persons that are authorized to serve as neutrals in their ADR programs.

Table 4
Number of Districts That Authorize Each Type of ADR Neutral by Type of ADR Procedure Authorized

ADR Procedure (Number of Districts That Authorize)	Number of Districts That Authorize Each Type of Neutral[a]				
	Judges	Court Staff Neutral	Panel of Neutrals	Outside Neutral	No Information
Mediation (63)	4	9	42[b]	12	8
Arbitration (23)	-	-	21	2	1
ENE (23)	4	-	15	2	3
General Authorization (27)	8	2	3[c]	13	7

Types of Fees Authorized by the Federal District Courts

When the district courts first developed ADR procedures, most provided ADR services pro bono. This arrangement worked because ADR was a new and untested procedure, one for which neither courts nor neutrals could claim particular expertise. In the formative years, ADR neutrals were generally satisfied with the honor of being listed on a federal district court panel and the opportunity to gain experience.

The picture is quite different today, as Table 5 shows. Most district courts now authorize payment of ADR neutrals and place responsibility

---

[a] The total number of districts authorizing neutrals may be greater than the number of districts authorizing each type of ADR procedure because some districts authorize more than one type of neutral, depending on the type of ADR procedure authorized (for example, a district may authorize both a staff mediator and a panel of neutrals to provide mediation services.)

[b] Includes eight districts where the panel includes judges (in addition to attorneys and, in some districts, non-attorneys.)

[c] Includes one district where the panel includes judges (in addition to attorneys and, in some instances, non-attorneys.)

for neutral's fees on the parties. Of the sixty-three districts that authorize mediation, for example, only six provide non-court mediators at no cost to the parties. Thirty-nine of these fifty districts require parties to pay the mediator's market rate fee or a fee set by the court. Eleven of these districts have set up a tiered scheme, under which parties receive some pro bono service, typically between four and six hours, after which they must pay the mediator's market rate fee or a fee set by the court.

* * *

Table 5
Number of Districts By Type of Compensation Authorized for ADR Neutrals and Type of ADR Procedure Authorized

ADR Procedure (Number of Districts That Authorize)	Number of Districts that Authorize Each Type of Compensation Arrangement[a]						
	Judges Serve as Neutrals	Court Staff Serve as Neutral	Party Pays the Fee	Non-Court Neutral Serves Pro Bono	Court Pays the Fee	Tiered Scheme[b]	No Information
Mediation (63)	3	9	39c	6	-	11	5
Arbitration[d] (23)	-	-	8	1	12	1	1
ENE (23)	3	-	11d	2	-	3	4
General Authorization (27)	8	2	11	-	-	-	15

A number of district courts recognize that some litigants may not be able to pay the neutrals' fees. These twenty-eight districts provide for reduced fees or waiver of fees for such litigants. Some of these districts state that pro bono service is expected of neutrals in exchange for being listed on the district's panel of neutrals.

* * *

---

a   The total number of districts authorizing a fee arrangement may be greater than the number of districts authorizing each type of ADR procedure because some districts authorize more than one type of fee arrangement, depending on the type of neutral used.

b   In a tiered scheme, the parties receive a small number of hours, typically between four and six, as a pro bono service. After this, the parties may continue the ADR process but must pay a fee to the neutral unless the neutral waives the fee. Some districts permit the neutrals to charge their market rates; others place limits on the fees that may be charged.

c   Includes seven districts that have set an upper limit on mediator fees.

d   Includes one district that has set an upper limit on neutral evaluator fees.

Number of Cases Referred to ADR

The federal courts are not required to report the number of cases referred to ADR or the number disposed of by ADR, and therefore we do not have a full picture of ADR activity in the district courts. The districts are, however, invited each year to submit their number of referred cases to the Administrative Office in application for an ADR staffing supplement. These applications provide a count of referrals for the subset of districts that seek funding.

Table 7
Number of Cases Referred to ADR in Forty–Nine Federal District Courts[a] (Twelve–Month Period Ending June 30, 2011)

ADR Process	No. of Cases
Mediation	17,833
Arbitration	2,799
CA-N multi-option program[b]	4,222
Early neutral evaluation	1,320
Settlement week	522
Summary jury trials	0
Mini-trials	0
Other[c]	1,571
Total	28,267

Table 7 shows the number of ADR referrals for the twelve-month period ending June 30, 2011. * * * We know of at least a few district courts with active ADR programs, however, whose cases are not counted in the table. And, of course, a great deal of settlement activity, which takes place in judicially-hosted settlement conferences, is also not included.

For the forty-nine districts for which we do have information, it is clear that mediation is the most commonly used ADR procedure, with many times more referrals than other forms of ADR. Arbitration also has a noticeable number of referrals, due largely to the three districts that continue to mandate referral for all cases meeting the statutory criteria (cases not alleging violation of a Constitutional or civil right and not

---

[a] Source: Applications to the Administrative Office of the U.S. Courts for supplemental funding for ADR staff.

[b] In the submission from the Northern District of California, the number of referrals is reported as a total for the Multi-Option Program and is not broken down into the several different types of ADR offered under this program.

[c] "Other" includes primarily judicially-hosted settlement conferences.

claiming damages greater than $150,000). Early neutral evaluation has clearly taken root in more districts than the one where it originated.

Over the ten years of the funding program, the total number of cases referred to ADR in the applicant districts has ranged from the mid-to-high 20,000s. Of all civil cases filed in these forty-nine districts in the twelve-month period ending June 30, 2011, the ADR referrals represent fifteen percent of the filed cases. Many civil cases are not, however, either by definition or by early termination, eligible for ADR. Thus, the true rate of referral is higher, by an unknown amount, than the fifteen percent suggested by the referral numbers.

* * *

Following are three observations based on the number of cases referred to the various ADR procedures.

First, among the subset of districts for which we have referral numbers (which may or may not differ systematically from other districts), more forms of ADR are authorized than are used; * * * Second, we can see that neighboring districts may have quite different ADR cultures, at least as shown by the number of cases referred to ADR; * * *. There also appear to be differences by circuit—again, as surmised from the submissions for funding; in the Fifth and Seventh Circuits, for example, few districts requested funding to support ADR whereas in the Third Circuit all did and in the Second Circuit all but one did. With current information about ADR, it is difficult to know just what the state of ADR is in the federal district courts today. We know that three-quarters of the districts have authorized a specific ADR procedure, while the remainder have provided only a general authorization or authorization for settlement conferences only. We know that some ADR programs are actively used and others are not, as reflected in the referral numbers submitted by forty-nine districts. We know that these referrals represent a fairly small, but not insignificant, portion of the civil cases filed in these districts. We do not know, however, whether this referral rate is representative of the district courts generally or might be lower if referrals in the other forty-five districts were counted. Nor do we know the number of cases disposed of by ADR, and therefore we cannot calculate a settlement rate or get a sense of the impact of ADR on court caseloads or judicial workloads. All that said, the referral numbers and the profile of authorized procedures provide a great deal of information in themselves and may help give direction to future questions.

NOTES AND QUESTIONS

1. While there have been studies of court ADR programs in individual states, there are no systematic studies analyzing ADR programs in all state courts. Still, it is widely believed that many if not most state courts have incorporated at least some ADR into their program of court services. Further,

the pattern is generally understood to be similar to what Ms. Stienstra described for the federal courts, with mediation being by far the most common form of ADR used in state court ADR programs.

Court-related ADR programs in both spheres face similar problems in terms of funding, bureaucratic resistance to change, negative perceptions about ADR, and the lack of leadership and political will. Some suggest that these pressures might be more pronounced at the state level. Why might that be the case? For a discussion, see Christine N. Carlson, *ADR in the States: Great Progress Has Been Made, But There is Still Much to Do*, 4 Disp. Resol. Mag. 4, 4–5 (2001).

2. If you read between the lines of the Stienstra excerpt you can see the enormous challenge that researchers face in even being able to describe what is happening in the courts. Each courthouse is its own sovereignty in many respects, and ADR processes came to each of them at different times and in different ways, and with different sets of concerns. As a result, there is no uniformity with respect to programs, processes, or even terminology. As difficult as this is at the federal level, it is worse at the state level.

3. There are many different and sometimes conflicting purposes for supporting court-annexed ADR programs. These include reducing court loads, saving litigants time and money, and providing a dispute resolution process that is more satisfying than litigation and that produces better outcomes for parties. Which of these do you view as more legitimate for a court-annexed program? Less legitimate? How would you prioritize them? What should be the goal of court-related ADR program?

4. While certainly not unanimous, federal and state judges have generally been supportive of ADR. As long ago as 1994, a survey of federal judges by the Federal Judicial Center found that

- 66% of district court judges disagreed with the proposition that courts should resolve litigation through traditional procedures only;

- 86% disagreed with the proposition that ADR should never be used in the federal courts;

- 56% thought that ADR should be used in the courts because it produces fairer outcomes than traditional litigation in some cases; and

- 86% thought that the role of the federal courts should be to assist parties in resolving their dispute through whatever procedure is best suited to the case.

WILLIAM W. SCHWARZER, ADR AND THE FEDERAL COURTS: QUESTIONS AND DECISIONS FOR THE FUTURE, 7 FJC DIRECTIONS 2 (1994).

Why might some judges be resistant to ADR?

5. Former U.S. Magistrate Judge Wayne Brazil has described five different models for the delivery of ADR services by courts: full-time in-house neutrals who are full-time employees of the court, neutrals who work with

non-profit organizations under a contract with the court, private neutrals paid by the court or who perform services for free, as well as private neutrals who charge the parties market rates. Which of these models do you think is most likely to provide the highest quality of neutrals? Which is most likely to inspire confidence and trust in the courts and the rule of law? Which is most likely to be perceived as fair? *See* Wayne D. Brazil, *Comparing Structures for the Delivery of ADR Services by Courts: Critical Values and Concerns,* 14 Ohio St. J. on Disp. Resol. 715 (1999).

6.   Donna Stienstra's research finds that most district courts now use outside lawyers as neutrals for cases they refer to ADR. These lawyers typically apply to be on a court's "roster" of neutrals, and are often required to meet certain conditions for eligibility, including being a member of the Bar, have a certain number of years of litigation or subject matter experience, and completing specific training provided or approved by the court. For attorneys interested in mediation practices, positions on these rosters are coveted sources of cases and prestige. Charles Pou Jr. describes the tension this can create with respect to both quality assurance and ethics:

> Decisions over roster admissions and referrals can occasion strong feelings, given the potential to affect egos and livelihoods. There have even been a few bouts of litigation in the arbitration context, where panel composition can be critical.

> In all settings, there is inherently some tension between providers, users and administrators. Providers may seek workloads, opportunities and rewards comparable to their peers, and are not always objective about their own strengths and weakness. Meanwhile, many users may just want some assurance that they are getting a neutral for their dispute who possesses appropriate ability and style, with minimal transaction and economic costs.

> Roster managers tend to agree with the general consensus that it is difficult to define objectively what constitutes a "qualified" mediator or other neutral. Lacking broadly agreed on standards or certification procedures—and given the controversy that many efforts to address these issues have raised—some entities have "ducked" the issue, and have made no effort to limit or prequalify their rosters. * * *

> Most programs . . . have established some admission standards in an effort to provide some assurance that listed practitioners possess the necessary competence. As one administrator puts it, "I'd rather risk a few disgruntled neutrals than disgruntled agencies."

> Criteria tend to vary depending upon program goals, which in turn affects decisions as to what constitutes "quality practice." Most rosters place relatively low hurdles before neutrals wishing to be listed, except for a few "elite" programs. Roster managers typically focus on standbys like ADR experience, training, mentoring, reputation, recommendations by peers and/or parties, and substantive knowledge in some situations.

* * *

Most roster programs have been considerably less formal, and more subjective, in selection. A few programs have generated comment over "old boy" lists allegedly compiled on a basis of friendship or worse. An extreme case involved a former head of the Wisconsin Employment Relations Commission, who aroused great unhappiness during the 1980s by allegedly exercising his discretion over panel selections so as to eliminate systematically certain experienced arbitrators from all panels. The ensuing scandal, fueled by the agency head's destruction of pertinent public documents, led to a criminal investigation and his resignation.

Charles Pou Jr., 'Wheel of Fortune' or 'Singled Out?': How Rosters 'Matchmake' Mediators, Disp. Resol. Mag, Spring 1997, at 10, 12.

What factors should be considered in establishing a roster and eligibility for inclusion? What controls should be in place to guard against cronyism? How frequently should a roster be updated? How much information should be made available to parties about roster composition?

7.   The rise of court-annexed ADR has meant a shift in the nature of what judges do. The "managerial judge" model assumes that judges are expert dispute resolvers, and, "can analyze each dispute, suggest the appropriate methodology for achieving an efficient and fair resolution, and monitor the progress of conflicts to ensure that additional intervention is not necessary." Francis E. McGovern, *Toward a Functional Approach for Managing Complex Litigation*, 53 U. Chi. L. Rev. 440, 442–43 (1986). Professor Judith Resnik has expressed doubts:

I am deeply skeptical of the capacity of individual judges to craft rules on a case-by-case basis. * * * I do not believe that * * * judges can perform their adjudicatory tasks and still have sufficient time to ascertain which mode of procedure is best suited to each individual case. Moreover, * * * [d]eciding how to mold procedures to a given case may well involve a judge so deeply in managerial and adversarial events that it undermines the ability of the judge to adjudicate—should that become necessary.

Judith Resnik, *Failing Faith: Adjudicatory Procedure in Decline*, 53 U. Chi. L. Rev. 494, 548 (1986). What do you think? Can judges both craft rules and assess cases for the appropriate procedure for dispute resolution? Should they?

8.   Should judges also mediate cases? Many courts have systems in which judges do mediate cases. However, the more critical issue is whether they should mediate cases that may come before them. Most academics conclude they should not because of concerns about judicial coercion in the mediation and the risk of prejudice that could flow from an unsuccessful mediation. *See, e.g.* James Alfini, *Risk of Coercion Too Great: Judges Should Not Mediate Cases Assigned to Them for Trial*, Disp. Resol. Mag., Summer 2004, at 10. To address this problem, many courts have instituted so-called "buddy judge" systems, in which a judge is assigned just to handle the mediation of filed cases. Still, Professor Peter Robinson's survey of California

judges indicates that nearly half of the judges who responded to the survey personally mediate during settlement conferences or formal mediations in cases before them as judges. Peter Robinson, *Adding Judicial Mediation to the Debate About Judges Attempting to Settle Cases Assigned to Them*, 2006 J. Disp. Resol. 335.

9. ADR proponents historically sold ADR on efficiency grounds—i.e., that it is faster and less expensive than traditional litigation—and much of the early empirical research focused on such issues. For a compilation and analysis, see Jennifer Stack, *Mediation Can Bring Gains, But Under What Conditions?*, DISP. RESOL. MAG., Summer 2003 (analyzing the findings of 62 studies of court-related mediation regarding cost, pace of litigation and satisfaction). Many, but not all, of these studies supported efficiency claims. Among the more critical studies are JAMES S. KAKALIK, TERENCE DUNWORTH, LAURAL A. HILL, DANIEL McCAFFREY, MARIAN OSHIRO, NICHOLAS M. PACE & MARY E. VAIANA, AN EVALUATION OF JUDICIAL CASE MANAGEMENT UNDER THE CIVIL JUSTICE REFORM ACT (1996) ("The CJRA pilot program, as the package was implemented, had little effect on time to disposition, litigation costs, and attorneys' satisfaction and views of the fairness of case management"); Lisa Bernstein, *Understanding The Limits of Court–Connected ADR: A Critique of Federal Court–Annexed Arbitration Programs*, 141 U. Pa. L. Rev. 2169, 2176 (1993) (mandatory court-connected arbitration "will tend to systematically disadvantage poorer and more risk-averse litigants"); Kim Dayton, *The Myth of Alternative Dispute Resolution In The Federal Courts*, 76 Iowa L. Rev. 889, 915 (1991) ("[C]laims concerning ADR's potential to reduce costs and delays are exaggerated"); Neil Vidmar & Jeffrey Rice, *Observations About Alternative Dispute Resolution In An Adversary Culture*, 19 Fla. St. U. L. Rev. 89, 97 (1991) (the summary jury trial "largely fails").

10. Professor Deborah Hensler suggests that the reason parties may find greater satisfaction in ADR proceedings has less to do with the efficiency interests that have captivated the courts, and more to do with the process-control issues that have made ADR attractive to businesses and those interested in community justice.

> Interestingly, empirical research on the outcomes of court-annexed ADR procedures suggests a rather different picture of the costs and benefits of these procedures than either ADR proponents or opponents have anticipated. The efficiency gains from court-annexed arbitration and court-mandated family mediation in custody suits appear mixed: The fiscal savings to courts from diverting cases from trial may be outweighed by the costs of running an efficient ADR program, and savings in lawyer time are often modest and not necessarily passed on to litigants through lower legal fees. But the gains in quality of process, at least as assessed by the disputants, appear significant: Because ADR procedures frequently offer litigants with small value cases and modest resources their only practical opportunity for a day in court, parties whose cases are diverted from the traditional negotiation-settlement-trial track to an ADR track are more likely to feel that they have been

treated fairly by the justice system and more likely to be satisfied with the process and outcomes than parties whose cases are negotiated to a conclusion, with or without judicial intervention, in the form of a settlement conference. In sum, while the main impetus for ADR in the court context appears to be a desire for efficiency—that is, reductions in cost and delay—the parties' reactions to ADR speak more to the objectives of gaining control over the litigation process that have been associated with the enthusiasm for ADR expressed by the community justice movement and the corporate community.

Deborah R. Hensler, *A Glass Half Full, A Glass Half Empty: The Use of Alternative Dispute Resolution In Mass Personal Injury Litigation*, 73 Tex. L. Rev. 1587, 1593–94 (1995).

11. Assume that you are a member of the local advisory committee for the state court of the jurisdiction in which you practice and that the judges of the court are considering the adoption of a local court rule providing for some form of court-annexed ADR. The judges have asked the committee for recommendations on whether there should be such a court rule, and if such a rule is adopted, which processes should be included in the court rule, and whether participation should be mandatory or voluntary. What position will you take on each of these issues? For additional discussion of designing dispute systems, see Chapter VII, beginning at page 916.

11. Assume that your client has a dispute with a video production company that he hired to tape his lavish wedding. A technician inadvertently destroyed the master tape and no copies are available. Your client had foregone arranging for photographs because of his confidence in the video production company, which has now offered to refund the $10,000 fee. Your client is despondent and furious at the production company. He tells you he is not very concerned about the money, but is motivated principally by revenge—he wants to drive the production company out of business. After you file suit, the director of the court's ADR program sends you a letter indicating that you are required to participate in one of the following court-annexed dispute resolution programs: non-binding arbitration, early neutral evaluation, or mediation. How would you go about helping your client choose?

2. COURT–ANNEXED MEDIATION

Overwhelmingly, mediation has come to be the most popular form of alternative dispute resolution in the state and federal courts. In this Section, we take a more focused look at how mediation is practiced in civil courts, as well as some unique problems associated with it. In the first section, we take a general look at court-annexed mediation, beginning with a reading by Professors McAdoo, Welsh, and Wissler, which synthesizes the vast accumulation of empirical research that has been conducted in the state and federal courts, and provides practical advice for court program administrators. In the second section, we consider whether courts should require participants to mediate disputes, as well as related problems of how to assure quality participation in court-mandated mediations, and the exceptions to mandatory mediation.

a. An Overview

BOBBI MCADOO, NANCY A. WELSH & ROSELLE L. WISSLER, INSTITUTIONALIZATION: WHAT DO EMPIRICAL STUDIES TELL US ABOUT COURT MEDIATION?
DISP. RESOL. MAG., WINTER 2003, AT 8, 8–9

Most court-connected mediation programs seek successful institutionalization, which we define here as regular and significant use of the mediation process to resolve cases. Voluntary mediation programs rarely meet this goal because they suffer from consistently small caseloads. In contrast, programs that make mediation mandatory (at the request of one party or on a judge's own initiative) have dramatically higher rates of utilization.

Significantly, mandatory referral does not appear to adversely affect either litigants' perceptions of procedural justice or, according to most studies, settlement rates. Further, judicial activism in ordering parties into mediation triggers increased voluntary use of the process, as lawyers begin to request it themselves in anticipation of court referral. An additional benefit of exposing lawyers to mediation is that they are more likely to discuss and recommend the process to their clients.

Another program design option involves requiring lawyers to consider mediation as an integral part of their usual litigation planning. For example, some courts require lawyers to discuss the potential use of mediation or other ADR processes and report the results of that discussion to the court early in the life of a case. Other courts require lawyers to discuss ADR with their clients. These court rules face less lawyer opposition than mandatory case referral and can give lawyers more control over the logistics of mediation (e.g., choice of mediator and timing). Adopting these rules (combined with active judicial support and willingness to order mediation when deemed appropriate) tends to increase requests to use mediation.

The local legal and mediation cultures influence how quickly mediation is integrated into the court system, as well as which program design features are more (or less) acceptable. Knowledgeable leadership from the bar and the judiciary contribute to the growth of mediation programs.

* * *

Which Cases Should Mediate

Many courts have adopted civil mediation programs in order to encourage and obtain the settlement of cases. And, importantly, both lawyers and litigants view mediation more favorably and as more procedurally just when settlement is achieved.

Although it has been suggested that certain general categories of civil cases (e.g., employment, contract) are "best" handled by mediation, there is no empirical support for this notion. Neither settlement rates nor litigants' perceptions of the procedural justice provided by mediation vary with case type. (There is some limited evidence, however, that medical malpractice and product liability cases may be somewhat less likely to settle than other types of tort cases.)

Interestingly, the level of acrimony between the litigants in non-family civil cases does not seem to affect the likelihood of settlement in mediation. Not surprisingly, the cases most likely to settle in mediation are those in which the litigants' positions are closer together, the issues are less complex, or the issue of liability is less strongly contested. Litigants' perceptions of procedural justice do not seem to vary with the tenor of the relationship between the litigants or with these other case characteristics.

Thus, because no case characteristics have been identified for which mediation has detrimental effects, mediation programs do not need to exclude certain types of cases. Some programs may be tempted to exclude the cases that seem likely to reach settlement on their own, without the assistance of a mediator. This choice, however, is likely to limit not only the rate of settlement achieved but also the opportunity to improve litigants' perceptions of the procedural justice of the settlement process and to enhance their views of the courts.

When to Mediate

Without a statute or court rule to the contrary, mediation tends to occur late in the life of a case and often after all discovery is completed. Holding mediation sessions sooner after cases are filed, however, yields several benefits. Cases are more likely to settle, fewer motions are filed and decided, and case disposition time is shorter, even for cases that do not settle in mediation.

Local litigation customs and case management practices affect lawyers' comfort with the early use of mediation, and the chance of settlement is reduced somewhat if lawyers lack critical information about their cases. Discovery does not have to be completed, however, for cases to settle. In addition, the status of dispositive and other motions tends to affect the likelihood of settlement in mediation. If motions are pending, settlement is less likely. Litigants' perceptions of the procedural justice provided by mediation, meanwhile, do not seem to vary with the timing of the session.

Thus, program designers should consider scheduling mediation sessions to be held at some reasonable point before discovery is completed but only after dispositive or other critical motions have been decided.

Who the Mediators Should Be

Mediation is most likely to be successfully institutionalized if the mediators are drawn from the pool that is preferred by lawyers: litigators with knowledge in the substantive areas being mediated. But neither mediators' knowledge of the subject matter of the dispute nor the number of years they have practiced has proved to be related to settlement or to litigants' perceptions of procedural justice.

One characteristic of the mediators, namely having more mediation experience, is related to more settlements. However, several aspects of mediator training, such as the number of hours of training or whether it included role play, tend not to affect settlement. None of these mediator characteristics seem to be related to litigants' perceptions of the procedural justice of mediation.

Thus, program design options that maximize each mediator's level of experience, such as the use of in-house mediators or a limited roster, may enhance the success of the program more than a roster with many mediators who get no or few cases to mediate. Matching mediators to cases based on subject matter expertise makes lawyers more comfortable with the process, but not doing so has not been shown to have detrimental effects on settlement or on litigants' perceptions of justice.

What the mediators should do

The approach that mediators ought to use (facilitative, evaluative, transformative) has been the subject of much debate. Both active facilitation and some types of evaluative interventions tend to produce more settlements as well as heighten perceptions of procedural justice.

For example, when mediators disclose their views about the merits or value of a case, cases are more likely to settle and litigants are more likely to assess the mediation process as fair. By contrast, when mediators keep silent about their views of the case, cases are less likely to settle and litigants' views of procedural justice are not enhanced. But when mediators recommend a particular settlement, litigants' ratings of the procedural fairness of the process suffer, notwithstanding an increased rate of settlement.

When litigants or their lawyers participate more during mediation, cases are more likely to settle than when they participate less. Moreover, the litigants evaluate the mediation process as more fair. In addition, when the lawyers behave more cooperatively during mediation sessions, both the likelihood of settlement and litigant perceptions of procedural fairness increase.

Thus, the training, ethical guidelines and monitoring tools applicable to court-connected mediation programs should encourage mediators to facilitate participation by both litigants and their lawyers and to enhance the amount of cooperation during the session. Programs need not discourage all evaluative interventions, but should restrict those, such as recommending particular settlements, that reduce litigants' perceptions of the fairness of the mediation process.

Roles for lawyers

In civil mediation sessions, lawyers generally speak on their clients' behalf and, consequently, do more of the talking. Neither settlement nor litigants' perceptions of procedural justice tend to be harmed by this allocation of responsibility between the lawyer and client. As noted earlier, greater participation by both lawyers and clients is beneficial. Litigants' presence during the session is important for several reasons, most notably because litigants who are not present view the dispute resolution process as less fair. Lawyers also perceive that their clients' presence changes the lawyers' role in settlement, makes the clients' interests more relevant and influences ultimate outcomes.

Preparation for the mediation session also is important. The more lawyers prepare their clients for mediation, the greater the likelihood of settlement in mediation and the greater the litigants' perception of procedural fairness. As noted earlier, greater cooperation among the lawyers during mediation also has these benefits. Interestingly, both greater client preparation and more cooperation among lawyers lead attorneys as well as their clients to view the mediation process as more fair.

Thus, court-connected mediation programs should encourage litigants to attend and participate in mediation sessions. Attorneys should be expected to prepare their clients for mediation, and mediation programs should provide information to assist their preparation. Lawyers should adopt a cooperative rather than a contentious approach during the session.

Advice for program designers

In this article, we have presented empirical data that address the effects that important program design choices have on institutionalization, settlement and perceptions of justice. We assume that court-connected mediation programs are concerned about all three of these issues, although courts' desire to institutionalize mediation or encourage settlement should never overwhelm their commitment to justice. The research suggests that the following program design options can enhance one or more of these three components without diminishing any of the others:

To maximize the use of court-connected civil mediation programs:

- Enlist the bench and bar in developing a program that fits the local legal culture.

- Obtain on-going judicial support for referring cases to the program.

- Make mediation use compulsory if one side requests it, or require attorneys to consider mediation early in the litigation process.

To increase the likelihood of settlement in mediation:

- Schedule sessions fairly early in the life of a case.

- Require that critical motions be decided before the session.

- Adopt a system that ensures that the mediators get enough cases to keep their mediation skills sharp.

To heighten litigants' perceptions that the program provides procedural justice:

- Require litigants to attend the session and invite them, along with their attorneys, to participate.

- Urge lawyers to adopt a cooperative approach and prepare their clients for mediation.

- Restrict more extreme evaluative interventions such as recommending a specific settlement.

* * *

NOTES AND QUESTIONS

1. During the 1980s and 1990s, mediation began to expand from the trial courts to the courts of appeal. By 2005, all 13 federal courts of appeal had implemented appellate mediation programs or settlement programs, under Federal Rule of Appellate Procedure 33.2. Each of the programs encourages or requires counsel for the parties to discuss settlement, including settlement discussions in the form of mediation. 3 In most cases referred to mediation, the mediator is a non-judicial court employee or other third-party neutral. The courts' mediation program offices usually schedule mediations before the filing of appellate briefs and, in nearly all cases, before oral argument. Most local appellate court rules or procedures on mediation identify the criteria each court's mediation program office uses to determine whether a case is eligible for the program and whether to schedule mediation.

See generally Robert J. Niemic, MEDIATION AND CONFERENCE PROGRAMS IN THE FEDERAL COURTS OF APPEAL: A SOURCEBOOK FOR JUDGES AND LAWYERS 3 (2nd ed. 2005).

2.   Critical race theorists have long raised the concern that minorities may not be able to get a fair shake in an informal mediation process that does not provide the formal procedural safeguards that are found in trial. For a summary and assessment, see Sharon Press, *Court–Connected Mediation and Minorities: A Report Card*, 39 CAPITAL U. L. REV. 819 (2011) (generally describing a significant need for continued improvement).

The Oklahoma Supreme Court crafted Oklahoma's court-connected mediation rules to respond to these concerns through a standardized court mediator training manual emphasizing cultural sensitivity; a court-sponsored process for mediator supervision; continuing mediator education to reinforce program best methods; party feedback on satisfaction with services rendered; and an administrative mechanism offering parties a venue to enforce claims of bias in the mediation process. For a discussion, see Phyllis E. Bernard, *Minorities, Mediation, and Method: A View from One Court–Connected Mediation Program*, 35 Fordham Urb. L. J. 1 (2008).

Similarly, Professor Michael Green argues in favor of greater inclusion of minorities in the design of employment dispute resolution programs. "As part of an overall approach to a healthy conflict resolution system, mediation must include safeguards that support a realistic opportunity for legal representation, a fair selection of mediators from a core and critical mass of qualified people of color and women, and an opportunity for employees to have a role in its design of reasonable and balanced procedures." Michael Z. Green, *Tackling Employment Discrimination with ADR: Does Mediation Offer a Shield for the Haves or Real Opportunity for the Have–Nots?*, 26 Berkeley J. Emp. & Lab. L. 321, 325 (2005). *See also* Julia Ann Gold, *ADR Through a Cultural Lens: How Cultural Values Shape Our Disputing Processes*, 2005 J. Disp. Resol. 289.

3.   Although there haven't been many cases, courts split early in the modern ADR movement on the question of media access to court-related ADR proceedings. In *Cincinnati Gas and Electric Co. v. General Electric Co.*, 854 F.2d 900 (6th Cir. 1988), the Sixth Circuit rejected an argument by the Cincinnati Post that the First Amendment required the court to permit the newspaper to attend a summary jury trial. The court stressed that the summary jury proceeding would not result in a binding determination. The court reaffirmed its holding that a summary jury trial could be closed to the public in *In re Cincinnati Enquirer, a Division of Gannett Satellite Information, Inc.*, 94 F.3d 198 (6th Cir. 1996).

On the other hand, in *Bank of America National Trust & Savings Association v. Hotel Rittenhouse Associates*, 800 F.2d 339 (3d Cir. 1986), the Third Circuit afforded access to a settlement agreement in spite of the fact that the agreement had been filed under seal at the parties' request. The court asserted that "[e]ven if we were to assume that some settlements would not be effectuated if their confidentiality was not assured, the generalized interest in encouraging settlements does not rise to the level of interests that we have recognized may outweigh the public's common law right of access."

Id. at 346. The dissenting judge said the majority had reached "an illogical and impractical result." *Id.* at 352.

What factors should be considered in deciding whether the public's right to know will prevail over the parties' need for privacy? *See* STEPHEN B. GOLDBERG, FRANK E.A. SANDER, NANCY H. ROGERS & SARAH RUDOLPH COLE, DISPUTE RESOLUTION 464–73 (5th ed. 2007); Edward D. Sherman, *Policy Issues for State Court ADR Reform,* Alternatives to the High Cost of Litig., Nov. 1995, at 142, 142–43. The case for courthouse confidentiality under appropriate circumstances is made in Arthur R. Miller, *Private Lives or Public Access?,* A.B.A. J., Aug. 1991, at 65.

b. Mandatory Mediation

As you have seen, parties are often required to mediate cases that have been filed in federal and state courts. The excerpt from Trina Grillo's article, *The Mediation Alternative: Process Dangers for Women,* in Chapter IV beginning at p. 536, introduced some of the challenges associated with mandatory mediation where the power disparities between the parties is great, such as may be the case with women in domestic violence situations.

In this subsection, we begin with an article that provides a helpful summary of the arguments for and against mandatory mediation. We then focus on two issues that arise from the employment of mandatory mediation in court-related programs: the need for exceptions and the problem of good faith participation.

DORCAS QUEK, MANDATORY MEDIATION: AN OXYMORON? EXAMINING THE FEASIBILITY OF IMPLEMENTING A COURT–MANDATED MEDIATION PROGRAM
11 Cardozo J. Conflict Resol. 479, 480–89, 498–500 (2010)

I.   Introduction

* * *

Mandatory or court-mandated mediation has been used in multiple ways in the relevant literature. This is especially true as mediation has become increasingly used as an adjunct to civil proceedings and as many different permutations of mediation programs have emerged in various states. Professor Frank Sander has formulated a useful way of navigating the different usages of the term court-mandated mediation.[7] He distinguishes between categorical and discretionary referral to ADR. The former approach applies when statutes provide that certain classes of disputes must undergo ADR, whereas the latter approach refers to judges

---

[7]   Frank E. A. Sander, H. William Allen & Debra Hensler, Judicial (Mis)use of ADR? A Debate, 27 U. Tol. L. Rev. 885, 886 (1996); Frank E. A. Sander, Another View of Mandatory Mediation, Disp. Resol. Mag., Winter 2007, at 16.

who are given the authority to refer any case they deem appropriate to any of a listed number of ADR options. This paper will examine the utility of court-mandated mediation from both perspectives.

III. The Necessity of Court–Mandated Mediation

. . . [M]andatory mediation appears to be a glaring contradiction. Formality is eschewed within mediation because this mode of dispute resolution emphasizes self-determination, collaboration and creative ways of resolving a dispute as well as addressing each party's underlying concerns. Any attempts to impose a formal and involuntary process on a party may potentially undermine the raison d'être of mediation. In view of this danger, there must be compelling reasons to introduce mandatory mediation.

A.   Empirical Studies on the Benefits of Mediation

The issue of whether to introduce mandatory mediation presupposes that mediation yields benefits that are both verifiable and well-accepted. However, some writers opine that these benefits are over-stated and have not been subject to rigorous empirical scrutiny. Some studies have also revealed that the parties who attempted mediation did not necessarily view the mediation process more favorably than the litigation process. Furthermore, other studies have found that mediated agreements did not increase the level of compliance or reduce subsequent disputing.

Notwithstanding the need for further advanced research to be conducted, recent studies have adequately established the general benefits of mediation. Parties endorse mediation because of the opportunities to participate in the process, to tell their side of the story and to contribute in determining the outcome of the dispute. Attorneys have found that mediation has improved communication between the parties and the attorneys. Furthermore, a majority of the studies show that mediated cases have a higher rate of settlement than cases that did not undergo mediation. A number of studies also show a greater compliance rate for judgments resulting from mediation rather than from judgments arrived through the litigation process. The available research indubitably establishes the utility and benefits of mediation. The residual gaps in empirical studies concern relatively peripheral aspects of mediation, such as whether mediation produces more creative solutions. It is therefore submitted that the general benefits of mediation are not in doubt.

B.   Mandated Mediation: A Temporary Expedient

Despite its documented advantages, mediation may well be under-utilized in certain jurisdictions. Parties and their attorneys are still accustomed to treating litigation as the default mode of dispute resolution; initiating mediation may also be perceived as a sign of weakness. In many jurisdictions, the rates of voluntary usage of mediation have been low. For instance, in England's Central London County Court system in which mediation occurred only with the parties' consent, only 160 mediations took place out of the 4,500 cases in which mediation was offered. In contrast, after England introduced the Civil Procedure Rules, which empowered the courts to encourage the use of ADR (with cost sanctions), the number of commercial disputes referred for mediation increased by 141 percent. Hence, the full benefits of mediation are not reaped when parties are left to participate in it voluntarily.

Where the parties' reticence towards mediation is due to unfamiliarity with or ignorance of the process, court-mandated mediation may be instrumental in helping them overcome their prejudices or lack of understanding. Studies show that parties who have entered mediation reluctantly still benefited from the process even though their participation was not voluntary. It has been observed that parties probably get "swept along by [mediation's] power and forget how they got there initially." The need to increase awareness and the usage of mediation services is probably the most compelling reason for introducing mandatory mediation. It may not be ideal to implement what appears to be an uneasy contradiction in terms. However, as Professor Sander has noted, mandatory mediation is needed as a temporary expedient because individuals do not use mediation voluntarily and therefore should be given the opportunity to experience the benefits of mediation. One critic has opined, in this respect, that mandatory mediation might have been appropriate in the United States as a remedial measure to get the ADR ball rolling in the 1970s and 1980s, and that court compulsion is no longer needed since the ADR movement in the United States is more mature. It is thus submitted that court-mandated mediation should only be a short-term measure utilized in jurisdictions where mediation is relatively less well-developed, and that this expedient should be lifted as soon as the society's awareness of mediation has reached a satisfactory level.

IV. Whether Mandatory Mediation is an Oxymoron

Although mandatory mediation may be beneficial, considerable criticism has been leveled against the movement towards compulsory mediation. The principal objection is that mandatory mediation impinges upon the parties' self-determination and voluntariness, thus undermining the very essence of mediation. Mediation, according to the U.S. Model Standards of Conduct for Mediators, is a process that emphasizes voluntary decision-making and focuses on self-determination as a controlling principle. Coercion into the mediation process therefore seems inconsistent with, and even antithetical to, the fundamental tenets of the consensual mediation process.

A.   Coercion "into" vs. Coercion "within" Mediation

The apparent paradox of mandatory mediation has sparked diverse opinions on whether coercion into mediation may realistically be distinguished from coercion within mediation. Some writers adamantly contend that coercion into the mediation process invariably leads to coercion to settle within the mediation process, which leads to unfair outcomes. In this regard, a mediation study has shown that disputants are most satisfied with the mediation process when it is non-coercive and attentive to parties' interests. Critics of mandatory mediation are of the opinion that there cannot possibly be a neat demarcation or even a semantic difference between coercion into and within mediation. One writer has opined that from a broad perspective, the mediation process cannot exist separate from the preceding sequence of stages leading to the mediation, and that "the expectation of an imposed settlement will inevitably alter the meaning of the [mediation] event for all the actors." * * *

Other observers, including Professor Frank Sander, however, share the opinion that mandatory mediation is not an oxymoron because there can be a clear distinction between coercion within the mediation process and coercion into mediation. An individual may be told to attempt the process of mediation, but that is not tantamount to forcing him to settle in the mediation. As two writers put it, the coercion in mandatory mediation only "relates to requiring that parties try to reach an agreement to resolve their dispute." Furthermore, the individual is not being denied access to court because mandatory mediation is not being ordered in lieu of going to court. Instead, the parties' access to court is only delayed; the parties have the liberty to pursue litigation once again if mediation fails.

The above debate is partially resolved by empirical studies showing no major difference between the rates of settlement in mandatory mediation and voluntary mediations. If the critics' hypothesis were true, mandatory mediation could possibly have yielded higher settlement rates than voluntary mediation as the parties who participate in a mandated mediation process would feel compelled to arrive at a settlement. On the contrary, certain other studies indicate that not only did mandatory mediation fail to increase settlement rates, but resulted in lower rates of settlements than cases in which the parties voluntarily participated in mediation.

Nonetheless, the empirical research may arguably be equivocal and fail to show a clear correlation or nexus between mandatory mediation and the likelihood of coercion within mediation. The lower settlement rates for mandatory mediation in the above studies could well be attributable to other factors and need not necessarily demonstrate that mandatory mediation does not readily lead to coercion to settle. It is equally possible that lower settlement rates are the result of the negative ramifications of mandatory mediation associated with undue pressure. For instance, there could be the lack of frank communication because parties perceive the mediator as having an effect on the adjudicated outcome and consequently act strategically within the mediation.

In one study of New York state mediation centers, mediation program staff revealed that disputants often agreed to participate in mediation because they wished to impress the judge and they thought that their case would not be damaged if they told the judge that they made an effort to mediate; it was found that court referrals to mediation led to a lower likelihood of settlement compared to referrals from other agencies and lower settlement rates for mandatory vis-à-vis voluntary mediation established that the litigants and certain attorneys gave negative ratings regarding their satisfaction with the process in mandatory mediation. Empirical studies may therefore be less than conclusive in this debate. Evidently, settlement rates alone cannot be an indicator of whether coercion exists, and other factors such as the parties' level of satisfaction and response to the entire mandatory mediation process have to be considered to reach an accurate and holistic conclusion. Furthermore, there may be limited utility in comparing settlement rates between mandatory and voluntary mediation, since it is highly plausible that parties who voluntarily enter into mediation are more amenable to reach a settlement to begin with; any comparison with the purpose of finding a correlation between mandatory mediation and the likelihood of settlement may thus be meaningless. In short, more nuanced research is probably required to specifically establish the link between mandatory mediation and coercion (or lack thereof).

In the light of the equivocal and provisional results of empirical studies, it is submitted that the above concerns concerning the level of coercion within the mediation process may not be totally unwarranted. Since mediation is often closely linked to the entire court process, parties could easily associate coercion from the judge with a reduction in the level of autonomy that they may exercise within the mediation process. In short, there could be a very faint distinction between coercion to enter mediation and coercion within mediation.

* * *

B.   The Continuum of Mandatoriness

The resolution of the above issue ultimately hinges on the degree of mandatoriness of any mediation program. A program that has a high degree of compulsion is more likely to blur the distinction between coercion to enter into mediation and coercion within mediation. As pointed out above, mandatory mediation may take the form of either discretionary or categorical referral of cases for mediation. For both categories, there can be differing levels of compulsion being imposed on the parties. This "continuum of mandatoriness" is diagrammatically summarized below. * * *

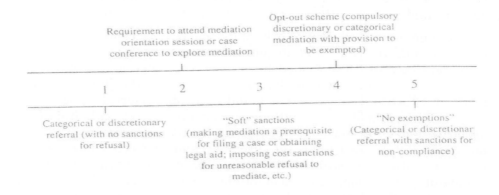

* * *

V.   The "Case Against Mandatory Mediation:" Other Objections

While this paper focuses principally on whether mandatory mediation impinges on the parties' autonomy, there are also the following objections to compulsory mediation, which should be taken into account when designing any mandatory mediation program:

A.   It Hampers the Parties' Access to Justice

Critics have highlighted that parties who are forced to mediate are being deprived of their day in court and made to incur additional litigation costs against their will. Along this line, the U.K. courts have decided that compelling a party to mediate against his will may unduly restrict an individual's right of access to court which is guaranteed under Article 6 of the European Convention of Human Rights. Also, Professor Sander has noted that making the parties pay for court-annexed ADR may run counter to the fundamental idea of creating a justice system that provides litigants with a range of dispute resolution options. He raises the pertinent question of whether it is fair to compel parties to use alternative processes and also to pay for these processes.

It is submitted that mandatory mediation does not deny access to justice, but merely defers it. * * * A more significant issue with regard to this objection is ensuring that such access to justice is not unduly deferred (through, for instance, draconian sanctions), as well as ensuring that the quality of mandatory mediation is monitored closely so as not to unfairly compel parties to incur additional costs for mediation.

B.   It Leads to General Inefficiency

There is also the concern that the mandatory mediation program leads to satellite litigation concerning issues such as whether the parties complied with the obligation to mediate and the appropriate sanctions to be imposed for non-compliance. Such litigation ultimately increases the costs for litigants and results in general inefficiency within the court system. In this regard, it has been noted that court time may be used in deciding on an issue which has been initially designed to save court time. This objection, as in the case of the issue of voluntariness, has implications on how participation standards and sanctions for non-compliance should be designed.

C. There is Unfairness in Administering the Mandatory Mediation Program

This objection relates principally to the difficulty in arriving at fair and clear criterion concerning issues such as when the obligation to mediate has been fulfilled or when one can opt out of mandatory mediation. As stated above, an amorphous standard of good faith or satisfactory participation results in great difficulties in enforcing the parties' obligations. Inconsistent results and a general lack of clarity may ensue as a result.

VII. Conclusion

* * * There may well be an acute danger that mandatory mediation could undermine the essence of mediation when accompanied by excessive coercion by the judge without exercise of his or her discretion, unduly strict sanctions for non-compliance or participation requirements that are amorphous and entail scrutiny of the parties' conduct within mediation.

It must be recognized that mandatory mediation, as a temporary expedient, has to be carefully implemented in any jurisdiction with the penultimate aim of increasing the awareness of mediation in a society. The "mandatory" aspect of this scheme has to be delicately handled so that mediation does not become enmeshed in excessive technicalities or rigid requirements that are in contradistinction with the fluid nature of mediation. As a temporary measure, mandatory mediation ultimately has to be complemented by education and other steps to increase the general awareness of mediation in the society.

NOTE AND QUESTIONS

1. As the earlier Stienstra review of the federal district courts demonstrates, federal court ADR programs typically let individual judges decide which cases to refer to mediation instead of mandating mediation by the nature of the claim. Many state court systems, however, do mandate that some classes of cases be mediated, often as a condition for proceeding to trial. For example, California requires mediation for all civil cases valued at $50,000 or less before they may be heard at law. Cal. Civ. Proc. Code

§ 1141.11(a) (West 2008). Florida and Texas also permit courts to require mediation for all civil cases. *See* Fla. Stat. ch. 44.102 (West 2008); Tex. Civ. Prac. & Rem. Code Ann. §§ 154.022–022 (West 1997).

2.   Professor Richard Reuben offers additional arguments against mandatory mediation, including that it allows for the exploitation of power imbalances, creates collateral problems (such as the need for good faith requirements), shifts mediation practice toward a narrower, more evaluative model; all of which undermine the legitimacy of court-related mediation. Richard C. Reuben, *Tort Reform Renews Debate Over Mandatory Mediation*, Disp. Resol. Mag., Winter 2007, at 13. Which of these sets of reasons seems most persuasive to you? If none, what are your counter-arguments? Professor Frank Sander suggests that parties can be compelled into mediation, but can't be compelled to settle. *See* Frank E.A. Sander, *The Future of ADR*, 2000 J. Disp. Resol. 3, 7–8. Does that resolve the problems Reuben identifies?

3.   Concluding a study of medical malpractice mediations in North Carolina, researchers paint a stark picture of the mediations they observed. As you read their conclusions, consider whether their findings make you more or less favorably disposed toward mandatory mediation.

[Mediation] is one event in a series of events that leads either to trial, abandonment, or settlement of the case. Given the complexity and the high-stakes nature of most medical malpractice cases, a settlement rate much lower than the state-wide average for mediated settlement conferences should not be a surprise. Because the process is dominated by the attorneys for the parties, it is not surprising that the researchers consistently observed typical, distributive bargaining patterns at the conferences. Interests (other than the payment or receipt of money) were simply not discussed.

Cases involving death were more likely to settle, as were cases in which the plaintiff was willing to discount its opening demand substantially. Very little that the mediator said or did, or that counsel said or did, affected case outcome. Reaching settlement took time and effort. The joint session followed a predictable ritual, and it was characterized by its understated quality. The private sessions were less predictable, but also followed a certain order. The mediator usually met with the plaintiff first, and then with the defendant. There were no "magic phrases" that, when spoken, virtually guaranteed settlement or impasse.

The shorter average length of time of the opening session for cases that settled, compared to cases that reached impasse (48 minutes versus 71 minutes) suggests that the attorneys, going in, had a good idea of the likely case outcome. If settlement was a real possibility, there was less reason to waste time on the formalities of the opening statements. Reaching settlement?when settlement was a possibility?took time. How long the conference lasted was a function of the level of interest in reaching a settlement on that particular day.

The findings here suggest a sort of predestination was at work in these sessions. The parties knew, going in, whether a settlement was a distinct possibility. Even if it was, however, settlement required both persistence and hard work.

Ralph Peeples, Catherine Harris & Thomas Metzloff, *Following the Script: An Empirical Analysis of Court–Ordered Mediation of Medical Malpractice Cases*, 2007 J. Disp. Resol. 101, 117–18.

4.   Would you support a mandatory mediation program for your local court? Would you limit it to certain claims? Would you prefer a local rule that would authorize the court's judges to refer a case to mediation?

1.   Exceptions to Mandatory Mediation

Most if not all mandatory mediation programs have at least some exceptions to compelled participation. Trina Grillo's *The Mediation Alternative: Process Dangers for Women* was an early call for an exception for cases involving domestic violence. The following reading discusses how states have responded.

LAUREL WHEELER, COMMENT, MANDATORY FAMILY MEDIATION AND DOMESTIC VIOLENCE
26 S. ILL. U. L.J. 559, 563–70 (2002)

* * *

III. ANALYSIS OF THE PROBLEM

A.   *Domestic Violence Exceptions to Mandatory Mediation*

Most states have developed mandatory family mediation programs, and many of them have addressed the domestic violence problem, although the approaches differ. "Currently, court-connected mediation plans vary widely from state to state, with no consensus among jurisdictions on the role mediation should play when domestic violence somehow taints the process."[30] To deal with cases involving domestic violence, many states force courts to exempt a couple from mediation because of a domestic violence history. The four states that will serve as examples of the various approaches are: Colorado, Ohio, Illinois, and California.

Colorado provides a domestic violence exemption for situations where one party alleges abuse and states that he or she is unwilling to mediate. In *Pearson v. District Court*, one of the few examples of case law on the subject, the Colorado Supreme Court held that a trial court is precluded from ordering a spouse who claims to be victim of domestic violence to participate in mediation with the other spouse, regardless of when the

---

[30] Holly Joyce, Comment, *Mediation and Domestic Violence: Legislative Responses*, 14 J. AM. ACAD. MATRIM. L. 447, 448 (1997).

declaration of abuse was filed. The trial court had ordered Karen Sanders to mediate disputes with her former husband in post-dissolution of marriage proceedings. She immediately appealed this order and alleged that "during the course of the marriage [her former husband] was physically and emotionally abusive, and that she 'suffer[ed] severe anxiety episodes when interacting' with her former husband and 'sh[ook] uncontrollably' when in his presence." The court found that "[t]he plain and obvious statutory language forbids a court from ordering mediation where a party claims physical and psychological abuse."

The Colorado rule removes the discretion of the court in all cases where domestic abuse is alleged. Whether or not those charges are substantiated is irrelevant. This ruling creates a system open for manipulation. Parties wishing to avoid mediation could make false allegations of domestic violence. However, mediation has been widely praised in the area of family law because of the need for a "non-adversarial environment in which to decide family law issues." Therefore, it is unlikely that this exception would harm mandatory family mediation programs as a whole.

Ohio law does not offer as complete an exception to parties claiming domestic abuse. Where there is evidence of domestic violence, "Ohio courts must determine that [mediation] is in the best interest of the parties and make specific written findings of fact to support their determinations." The court is able to order mediation even if one parent has been convicted of domestic violence, as long as mediation is still in the parties' "best interest."

California allows local courts to establish their own rules for family mediation programs. Until recently, San Luis Obispo County required only that cases involving allegations of domestic violence "with current restraining orders ... be screened by a mediator for determining the necessity of the presence of a support person during mediation, separate waiting areas for the parties, and separate mediation to insure safety and facilitate mediation." Therefore, not only were domestic violence situations not exempt from mandatory mediation, but even where there was a current restraining order in place, the mediation continued with only minimal safety precautions.

Illinois does not go to the extreme to which certain counties in California have gone. For example, the Thirteenth Judicial Circuit, which includes Bureau, Grundy, and LaSalle Counties, allows courts to waive mandatory mediation "for good cause." This gives judges very broad discretion. Domestic violence cases would fall under this exception because the rules also state that every case filed will be ordered to mediation where "there is a reasonable likelihood that mediation can aid the parties in resolution of the dispute." If there is unequal bargaining power, and one party is unwilling to participate because of past domestic violence, this would obviously decrease the likelihood that mediation would be successful in moving these parties towards a resolution. * * *

Whether a jurisdiction chooses to completely exempt domestic violence cases from mediation, as in Colorado, leaves the decision to the court, or leaves cases to be screened by the mediator, it is clear that all programs realize that mandatory mediation poses very real threats to the victim where there is a history of domestic abuse. Domestic violence advocates argue that mediation in these cases is never safe, and could never be in the best interest of the abused. When there is unequal bargaining power, it becomes difficult for even the most talented mediator to reduce differences in power, and the ability of the parties' to effectively engage in mediation is reduced. Advocates for mediation believe that where there is truly unequal bargaining power, the courts would recognize the problem and would not send the couple to mediation in the first place. However, those cases that are not excused by the court are left to the mediator to screen for domestic violence issues. States differ on screening requirements and mediator training in the area of domestic violence, as much as they differ on domestic violence exceptions.

B.   *The Impossible Job of Mediators: How do You Train Mediators to be Investigators?*

Unlike attorney regulation, there are no national requirements or professional standards regarding mediator training. In all jurisdictions, the role of the mediator during the mediation is multifaceted. In a normal mediation, mediators are required to manage the mediation, open communication, keep negotiations moving forward, probe for facts, help parties understand ramifications of agreements reached, and remain neutral. Mediators in the family law arena must not only be trained in the profession of mediation, but must also be knowledgeable about other areas, such as legal, sociological, and psychological issues.

"Mediators should receive sufficient training in the preparation process to enable them to encounter these dynamics and seek appropriate information from the parties when considering the family violence quotient." The courts have established mandatory family mediation programs, and many have determined that mediators may still mediate such difficult cases as those involving domestic violence. Being forced to mediate such cases puts a huge burden on mediators, requiring them to act neutral, while simultaneously searching for psychological clues that one party is a victim of violence.

It is crucial that family mediators be trained, especially in jurisdictions where deciding whether mediation is in the best interests of parties is left to the mediator. "[T]he mediator is often untrained to deal with the psychological complexities of a domestic violence relationship."

Training and educational requirements vary from jurisdiction to jurisdiction. [The Model Standards of Practice for Divorce and Family Mediators require] . . . that family mediators be educated so that they would be knowledgeable in family law, and "aware" of the impact family conflict has on "parents, children, and other family members." This would include "education and training in domestic violence and child abuse and neglect."

To provide some guidance as to exactly what level of education and training should be required, the Association of Family and Conciliation Courts adopted the "Model Standards of Practice for Divorce and Family Mediators." The very first standard, which establishes the ultimate goal of mediation, states that "[m]ediation is based on the principle of self-determination by the parties." The mediator's job is to facilitate the parties' assessment of their ability to mediate, their goals, and possible agreements. Self-determination depends on whether the parties have the ability to mediate fairly and on equal footing. In order for both parties to have their needs met, they must have the ability to be advocates for their own needs.

The second standard set out by the Model Standards of Practice is that "[a] family mediator should be qualified by education and training to undertake the mediation." There are no specific training programs outlined, but the Model Standards specify that mediators must be knowledgeable about family law, the psychological impact of family conflict on parents and children, education and training in domestic violence, child abuse and neglect, and special education and training in the process of mediation.

Standard X and XI state that a family mediator "should recognize" family situations which involve child abuse or domestic violence. In the case of child abuse or neglect, Standard X requires the mediator to report abuse to the proper authorities. In cases of domestic violence, however, the mediator is only required to "shape the mediation process accordingly." Neither situation absolutely requires the mediation to end; notwithstanding, some jurisdictions do require the mediation to terminate as soon as this information is learned by the mediator, regardless of whether the parties were willing to mediate. Both Standards X and XI require the mediator to be knowledgeable about the "symptoms and dynamics" of both forms of abuse, and they should not undertake the mediation unless they have "adequate training." The Model Standards are intentionally vague as to what level of training would be considered "adequate" in order to permit individual jurisdictions to draft more specific standards for its mediators. However, this has proven to be a difficult task.

The only time the Model Standards require a mediator to withdraw from mediation is in Standard XII, which states that "[a] family mediator should withdraw from further participation in the mediation process when the mediator reasonably believes that further participation will not further the parties' self-determination." Many argue that if there is a history of violence and abuse between the couple, there are doubts as to the ability of the abused to make decisions free of coercion.

The Model Standards recommended extensive training so that mediators will be able to "recognize a family situation involving child abuse or neglect, report it to the proper authorities, and shape the mediation process accordingly." Critics argue that no amount of training can make a mediator able to discern all signs of domination and abuse in a relationship. More importantly, no person would ever be skilled enough to put a victim on the same power level as her abuser, no matter how "in tune" the mediator is to the dynamics of the relationship. This argument would call for a complete exclusion of all cases where domestic violence has been alleged.

Even if mediators could be trained to put the parties on equal levels and help them reach a voluntary, uncoerced agreement that is in both parties' best interests, the biggest problem is discerning which cases this "screening" is needed. Even experts on domestic violence disagree as to the signs of domestic violence, how the victim will react during a mediation, and even what should be considered "domestic violence." Every victim reacts differently, and every mediator will react differently to those situations.

Until mediators begin to understand, and are properly trained, skilled, and educated to recognize the velocity, force, and coercive power of even a simple involuntary movement (a hand gesture, a blink) and the effect it can have on a victim of intimate violence, they will never understand how the balance of power is inextricably changed with an episode of violence.

It would be next to impossible, no matter how extensively trained the mediator is, to be able to understand that a slight hand movement or word has created a serious level of fear in the victim, and will ultimately impact the outcome of the mediation.

Also, a common tactic used by abusers is reduction of their victim's self-esteem. One of the reasons abused individuals have such a difficult time leaving their abusive spouses is that they have become convinced that they "deserve" the abuse, or that no one will care or help them if they try to leave. Once victims are able to muster the courage to file for divorce, the most dangerous thing for their self-esteem is to carry on a face-to-face conversation with their abuser, especially when the third-party in the room is constrained to complete neutrality. In that situation, abused parties have no advocate, and abusers constantly search for ways to regain control over victims and the outcome of the mediation.

In the worst cases, the batterer also is able to gain control over the mediator. In cases where domestic violence is known by the mediator, the mediator cannot condemn the violent behavior, or the mediator's neutrality will be compromised. Yet, "if the mediator does not condemn the abuse, the batterer's belief that his behavior is acceptable is maintained and the battered woman is disempowered." One mediation participant reported that she "was forced to sit down with the man who for the past twelve years [had] abused me, intimidated me, controlled me by threats and scare tactics, emotionally torn me down and whom I truly fear." She felt the mediator became his advocate because the mediator's reported (sic) to the court that "there had been no physical violence since [he] stopped drinking in 1982, yet hours earlier [her] husband had described in detail to [the mediator] how he had broken into [the] home [about two weeks prior to the mediation session]."

The victim attributed the mediator's lack of neutrality to the fact that her husband had no attorney and was a wonderful "con-artist." These issues arise repeatedly because the abuse almost always stems from a need to control the victim, which leads to a need to control the mediator and the process itself. One way the abuser is able to "con" the mediator is that abusers are usually the best mediation participants. The victim will often be unwilling to talk openly, to share the children, and to make any concessions as to visitations or giving up any information. The abuser on the other hand is willing to share the children and discuss multiple options because this "assures his ongoing access to his partner and allows him to continue to manipulate and intimidate her," while at the same time making "him appear the more attractive candidate for custody" and mediation.

Mediators are human. To expect them to be aware of all the dynamics unfolding before them is simply too great a burden on the system. Family mediation does a great deal of good, but by leaving cases with violent pasts in the framework, the workability of the entire system is jeopardized. Looking at all these human complications, it becomes clear that the Colorado approach might be the safest for all involved.

NOTES AND QUESTIONS

1.   As Wheeler states, exceptions are common for situations involving domestic violence. Taking a contrary view, Professor Andrew Schepard has argued that mediation programs should not have exceptions for domestic violence, but rather should screen cases for domestic violence, and then permit parties to opt out after hearing about the pros and cons of mediation. Schepard's concern is that if mediation isn't mandated, parties won't know they have the opportunity to opt out of the adversarial process of litigation. Moreover, he says, mediation may be more helpful than litigation in actually reaching and addressing the problems that lie beneath the dispute, but that parties will not have that opportunity under a rule of automatic exclusion of

such cases. *See* ANDREW I. SCHEPARD, CHILDREN, COURTS, AND CUSTODY 105 (2004). Is this a better approach?

2.   Because of the prevalence of domestic violence, mediation professional standards generally call for the screening of such cases. As the Wheeler excerpt notes, mediation programs often leave this function to mediators. But is this realistic? Wheeler thinks not, that it is beyond the capacity of mediators to adequately screen for domestic violence, or to manage the problem once it is identified. Do you agree? For more on screening, see Eduardo R.C. Capulong, *Family Mediation After Henderschott: The Case for Uniform Domestic Violence Screening and Opt–In Provision in Montana*, 74 MONT. L. REV. 273 (2013); Nancy Ver Steegh, *Yes, No, and Maybe: Informed Decision Making about Divorce Mediation in the Presence of Domestic Violence*, 9 Wm. & Mary J. Women & L. 145, 151 (2003).

3.   What other types of mandatory mediation exceptions might be appropriate? How liberally should they be construed as a general matter?

4.   In addition to exceptions, some mediation programs permit parties to opt out of a mandatory referral to mediation. However opt-out provisions vary widely in their permissiveness and breadth of coverage. For example, rules for courts in the city of St. Louis permit parties to opt out of mediation simply by advising the court and providing an explanation. In such cases, the rule states "The matter shall not thereafter be referred by the court to alternative dispute resolution absent compelling circumstances, which shall be set out by the court in any order referring the matter to alternative dispute resolution." Mo.22d Cir.R. 38.5(1). Similarly, an Oregon mandatory mediation program permits parties to opt out if they are represented by counsel and counsel recommends against mediation. *See* Multnomah County Local R. 18.035. By contrast, however, the mandatory mediation rule for the U.S. District Court for the Western District of Missouri provides that "Cases will not normally be allowed to opt out of the program. However, there may be cases where good cause can be demonstrated for opting out." *See* W.D. Mo., Early Assessment Program, § II(C).

5.   Even where mediation is mandatory or expected in civil cases, judges sometimes decline to order parties into the process. Some of the reasons that researchers have compiled include the judges' belief that the case would settle without mediation, concerns about significant power imbalances (such as in domestic violence cases), severe enmity between the parties, or the fact that there was only small amount in dispute. If you were a judge, what other reasons might persuade you not to send a case to mediation? *See* Bobbi McAdoo, *All Rise: The Court is in Session: What Judges Say About Court–Connected Mediation*, 22 Ohio St. J. on Disp. Resol. 377 (2007).

2.   *The Problem of Good Faith Participation in Mediation*

One problem that flows from the mandatory mediation of disputes is the assurance that parties in fact will use the mediation process to attempt to resolve their disputes in good faith. Good faith participation can be an issue in voluntary mediation, but the agreement by the parties to use the process helps assuage concerns about potential abuse. When compelled into mediation by court programs, however, it may well be that neither party really wants to be at the mediation, or may want to use the mediation for exploitation rather than settlement.

One way that some states have addressed this problem, either by statute or court rule, is by requiring the parties to mediate in good faith. In an important article, Professor Kimberlee Kovach argued that states should impose good faith requirements, either through statutes or court rules, to preserve the integrity of the mediation process as a vehicle for resolving disputes according to the underlying interests of the parties. *See* Kimberlee K. Kovach, *Good Faith in Mediation—Requested, Recommended, or Required? A New Ethic*, 38 S. Tex. L. Rev. 575, 580–96 (1997).

Kovach contends such a requirement is necessary to promote reciprocal good faith participation, which is especially important since many mediation participants come to the process from an adversarial mindset. She writes: "[I]f during a mediation, one party fails to cooperate, perhaps by withholding information, how can other parties be expected to cooperate? When participants come to mediation from an adversarial context, often tactics which emphasize and continue adversarial behavior are employed; if good faith participation is not required, the entire procedure will be frustrated." *Id.* at 575. She contends the presence of lawyers in the mediation only worsens the problem, as many may be tempted to abuse the mediation process for as a vehicle for discovery or as a forum for intimidation or other dilatory tactics. Says Kovach: "If good faith is not present, all we will be left with is a pro forma mediation, one more procedural task to be checked off of the long list of items to be covered in order to get to the trial." *Id.*

Kovach's proposal drew strong reactions from supporters and critics, but the idea of a good faith requirement has had legislative appeal. More than 20 states have enacted some form of good faith requirement for court-annexed mediations. At least twenty-one federal district courts and seventeen state courts also have local rules requiring good-faith participation. Several federal district courts have relied on Rule 16 of the Federal Rules of Civil Procedure as the basis for a good-faith requirement in mediation.

In the following excerpt, Professor Lande examines some of the problems with such requirements.

JOHN LANDE, USING DISPUTE SYSTEM DESIGN METHODS TO PROMOTE GOOD–FAITH PARTICIPATION IN COURT–CONNECTED MEDIATION PROGRAMS

50 UCLA L. REV. 69, 70, 86–89, 93–95, 98–99, 102–04, 106–08 (2002)

What can be done to prevent people from behaving badly in mediation? One litigator described his approach to mediation this way:

"If . . . I act for the Big Bad Wolf against Little Red Riding Hood and I don't want this dispute resolved, I want to tie it up as long as I possibly can, and mandatory mediation is custom made. I can waste more time, I can string it along, I can make sure this thing never gets resolved because . . . I know the language. I know how to make it look like I'm heading in that direction. I make it look like I can make all the right noises in the world, like this is the most wonderful thing to be involved in when I have no intention of ever resolving this. I have the intention of making this the most expensive, longest process but is it going to feel good. It's going to feel so nice, we're going to be here and we're going to talk the talk but we're not going to walk the walk."[2]

Legislatures and courts have adopted rules requiring good faith in mediation, and courts have sanctioned violators. * * *

* * *

C. Problems with Good–Faith Requirements

1. Problems Defining and Proving Good Faith

The definition of good faith in mediation is one of the most controversial issues about good-faith requirements. Legal authorities establishing good-faith requirements and commentators' proposals do not give clear guidance about what conduct is prohibited. As a result, mediation participants may feel uncertain about what actions mediators and judges would consider bad faith. This uncertainty could result in inappropriate bad-faith charges as well as a chilling of legitimate mediation conduct.

In practice, the courts have limited their interpretation of good faith in mediation to attendance, submission of pre-mediation memoranda, and, in some cases, attendance of organizational representatives with adequate settlement authority. Despite the narrow scope of courts' actual application of good-faith requirements, good-faith language in the legal

---

[2] Julie Macfarlane, Culture Change? Commercial Litigators and the Ontario Mandatory Mediation Program, 2002 J. Disp. Resol 241, 267 (quoting a Toronto litigator) (first alteration in original). * * *

authorities and commentators' proposals go far beyond these specific matters.

Commentators agree that the definition of good faith needs to be clearly and objectively determinable so that everyone can know what conduct is considered bad faith. Commentators disagree, however, about whether the definition of good faith can be clear, objectively determinable, and predictable, and whether good faith is a function of the reasonableness of participants' offers or their state of mind.

[Professor Kimberlee] Kovach argues that "without an explanation or definition of just what is meant by the term good faith, each party may have in mind something different. It is important that the parties are clear about the term." She maintains that "judging a party's state of mind is too complex and subjective" to be appropriate in determining good faith in mediation. She also contends that bad faith does not include failure to make an offer or "come down enough," stating that "the economic aspects of the negotiations—the offers and responses, in and of themselves—may not create a bad faith claim."

Most of the elements of good-faith definitions do not satisfy Kovach's criteria. Virtually all good-faith elements depend on an assessment of a person's state of mind, which is, by definition, subjective. Consider the following definition from *Hunt v. Woods*:

> A party has not "failed to make a good faith effort to settle" under [the statute] if he has (1) fully cooperated in discovery proceedings, (2) rationally evaluated his risks and potential liability, (3) not attempted to unnecessarily delay any of the proceedings, and (4) made a good faith monetary settlement offer or responded in good faith to an offer from the other party. If a party has a good faith, objectively reasonable belief that he has no liability, he need not make a monetary settlement offer.[87]

Good faith under this definition is not objectively determinable, readily predictable, or independent of parties' states of mind or their bargaining positions. To assess their risk evaluations, courts must determine the merits of the case, whether parties' evaluations are objectively reasonable, and whether their negotiation strategies are acceptable by the courts. Courts make these assessments at subsequent hearings in which there is a great temptation to take advantage of hindsight. Obviously parties' understandings of the law and the facts evolve during the course of litigation so that some things do not become clear for a period of time, perhaps not until trial or even later. To make fair

---

[87] Id. at 3 (quoting *Kalain v. Smith*, 495 N.E.2d 572, 574 (Ohio 1986)). Cf. Black's Law Dictionary 701 (7th ed. 1999) (defining good faith as a "state of mind consisting in (1) honesty in belief or purpose, (2) faithfulness to one's duty or obligation, (3) observance of reasonable commercial standards of fair dealing in a given trade or business, or (4) absence of intent to defraud or to seek unconscionable advantage") * * *.

decisions, courts would need to reconstruct the information available to the parties at the time of the mediation. Courts also would need to consider the negotiation history up to the point of the alleged bad faith. Given the norms of negotiation in litigated cases, parties rarely begin negotiations by offering the amount that they believe "the case is worth." The timing and amount of offers often depend on the context of prior offers and the conduct of the litigation more generally. Parties vary in negotiation philosophy; some prefer to negotiate early and make apparently reasonable offers whereas others prefer to engage in hard bargaining, taking extreme positions and deferring concessions as long as possible. Although Kovach argues that hard bargaining should not be considered bad faith, courts applying the *Hunt* definition could easily interpret it as bad faith. In any event, to determine parties' good faith fairly, courts would need to assess and second-guess the parties' offers and their states of mind. * * *

2.   *Overbreadth of Bad–Faith Concept*

Kovach's and [Professor Maureen] Weston's proposed good-faith requirements are so broad that they effectively would prohibit defensible behaviors in mediation. Under Kovach's proposed statute, if one side claims that the other participated in bad faith, the moving party could use the legal process to investigate whether all participants adequately prepared for the mediation, "followed the rules set out by the mediator," engaged in "direct communication" with the other parties, "participated in meaningful discussions with the mediator and all other participants during the mediation," and "remained at the mediation until the mediator determined that the process is at an end or excused the parties." Under Weston's proposed "totality of the circumstances" test, this wide-ranging inquiry would be limited only by the court's discretion.

Both proposals raise many problems. Mediators typically establish "ground rules" at the outset of a mediation, such as a requirement that the participants treat each other with respect and not interrupt each other. Under Kovach's proposed statute, courts could be required to adjudicate whether someone disobeyed the mediator's rules by being disrespectful or interrupting others during the mediation.

Kovach states that "if the parties refuse to share particular knowledge, they should not be compelled to do so. However, it is important that some information be exchanged which would provide an explanation for, or the basis of, the proposed settlement or lack thereof." Under a duty to engage in direct communication and meaningful discussions, parties could be confused about what information they would be compelled to disclose to the mediator and opposing parties. In sensitive mediations, parties often want to withhold information justifying their bargaining strategies. Although exchanging such information in mediation can be helpful and appropriate, court-connected mediation should not be a substitute for formal discovery. Kovach presumably does not intend her proposed statute to be interpreted as such, but that could be the result. * * *

3. *Inclusion of Settlement–Authority Requirement*

Although mediations generally work better when organizational parties send representatives with a reasonable measure of settlement authority, courts have difficulty strictly enforcing such a requirement—and regularly doing so can stimulate counterproductive mediation tactics. Slightly more than half of the courts have found bad faith when entities fail to send representatives with sufficient settlement authority. * * *

When courts focus heavily on settlement authority, participants may be distracted from various ways that mediation can help litigants achieve goals other than reaching final monetary settlements. Settlement-authority requirements typically focus only on monetary resolutions; mediation can be useful to explore nonmonetary aspects of disputes. These requirements also assume that cases should be settled at a single meeting; in some cases it may be appropriate to meet several times, especially when organizational representatives need to consult officials within the organization based on information learned at mediation. Moreover, settlement-authority requirements do not recognize benefits of exchanging information, identifying issues, and making partial or procedural agreements in mediation. * * *

4. *Questionable Deterrent Effect and Potential Abuse of Bad–Faith Sanctions*

Sanctioning bad faith in mediation actually may stimulate adversarial and dishonest conduct, contrary to the intent of proponents of a good-faith requirement. Proponents argue that a good-faith requirement would cause people to negotiate sincerely, would deter bad-faith behavior, and, when people violate the requirement, would provide appropriate remedies.

Although a good-faith requirement presumably would deter and punish some inappropriate conduct, it might also encourage surface bargaining, as well as frivolous claims of bad faith or threats to make such claims. Proponents seem to assume that participants who might act in bad faith but for the requirement would behave properly in fear of legal sanctions. It seems at least as likely that savvy participants who want to take inappropriate advantage of mediation would use surface bargaining techniques so that they can pursue their strategies with little risk of sanction. This would be fairly easy given the vagueness of a good-faith requirement. Participants can readily make "lowball" offers that they know the other side will reject and generally go through the motions of listening to the other side and explaining the rationale for their positions. Although attorneys often are quite sincere, making arguments with feigned sincerity is a skill taught in law school and honed in practice. Because mediators are not supposed to force people to settle, participants who are determined not to settle can wait until the mediator gives up. This scenario illustrates how a good-faith requirement could ironically induce dishonesty, when providing more honest responses might put participants in jeopardy of being sanctioned.

Similarly, tough mediation participants could use good-faith requirements offensively to intimidate opposing parties and interfere with lawyers' abilities to represent their clients' legitimate interests. Given the vagueness and overbreadth of the concept of bad faith, innocent participants may have legitimate fears about risking sanctions when they face an aggressive opponent and do not know what a mediator would say if called to testify. In the typical conventions of positional negotiation in which each side starts by making an extreme offer, each side may accuse the other of bad faith. Without the threat of bad-faith sanctions, these moves are merely part of the kabuki dance of negotiation. With the prospect of such sanctions, bad-faith claims take on legal significance that can spawn not only satellite litigation, but satellite mediation as well. After a volley of bad-faith charges in a mediation, mediators may need to focus on bad faith as a real issue rather than simply a negotiation gambit. Moreover, the mediator could be a potential witness in court about the purity of each side's faith in the mediation, further warping the mediator's role. * * *

5.   *Weakened Confidentiality of Mediation Communications*

Establishing a good-faith requirement undermines the confidentiality of mediation. The mere prospect of adjudicating bad-faith claims by using mediator testimony can distort the mediation process by damaging participants' faith in the confidentiality of mediation communications and the mediators' impartiality.

Proponents of a good-faith requirement cite the need for an exception to rules providing for confidentiality of communications in mediation. Weston contends that a good-faith requirement is "essentially meaningless if confidentiality privileges restrict the ability to report violations." Noting the existence of some exceptions to confidentiality in mediation, she argues that reports of bad faith should be added to the list of exceptions. Weston and Kovach assert that an exception for bad-faith participation can be clearly and narrowly limited, and that the need for an exception outweighs the general need to encourage open discussion in mediation through confidentiality protections.

          * * *

The proponents have identified correctly concerns that a good-faith requirement could undermine participants' trust in the confidentiality of mediation because of uncertainty about what might later be used in court.

An exception for bad faith does not seem as narrow and definite as the proponents suggest, however. The vagueness and overbreadth of the concept contribute to participants' uncertainty about whether their statements in mediation would be used against them.

Proposals for admitting mediators' testimony presume that courts need such testimony to pursue their mission of seeking truth and justice and that mediators' testimony is highly probative and reliable because mediators are the only source of disinterested, neutral evidence about conduct in mediation. Certainly mediators' testimony can be helpful, but one can overstate its value. Much discussion in mediation does not focus on facts strictly relevant to legal issues and often involves feelings, interests, expected consequences of various options, negotiation strategy, and even analysis of hypothetical situations. Moreover, if called to testify at such hearings, mediators may have significant biases even if the mediators have the highest integrity. Mediators would be interested in presenting themselves and their actions in mediation in a favorable light. If a mediator reports that a participant has not participated in good faith, courts should expect that the mediator might emphasize facts consistent with that conclusion and downplay inconsistent facts. Thus, one should not simply assume that mediator testimony is necessarily neutral, probative, and reliable. * * *

6. *Encouragement of Inappropriate Mediator Conduct*

A good-faith requirement gives mediators too much authority over participants to direct the outcome in mediation and creates the risk that some mediators would coerce participants by threatening to report alleged bad-faith conduct. Courts can predict abuse of that authority given the settlement-driven culture in court-connected mediation. The mere potential for courts to require mediators' reports can corrupt the mediation process by instilling fear and doubt in the participants.

    * * *

NOTES AND QUESTIONS

1. Professor Lande notes that only one of the 22 states that have enacted good faith statutory requirements at the time of his writing had included a definition of "good faith." *Id.* at 77. He further points out that, at the time his article was written, there were 27 reported cases dealing with bad faith in mediation, and most of them arose out of court-connected mediation programs. The number of reported cases increased in the 1990s, and it can be speculated that the increase was caused by the expanding use of court-mandated mediation and an accompanying legalization of the process.

The behaviors alleged to constitute bad faith in the 27 cases fell into five categories: (1) failure to attend; (2) failure of an organizational party to send a representative with sufficient settlement authority; (3) inadequate preparation for a mediation—including failure to submit a pre-mediation memorandum or to bring experts to a mediation; (4) insincerity of efforts to resolve the dispute—including claims that a party had not made any offer or any suitable offer, had made inconsistent legal arguments, or had not provided requested documents; and (5) miscellaneous allegations, including failure to sign a mediated agreement and failure to release living expenses pending farmer-lender mediation. *Id.* at 82–83. Professor Lande describes the final outcomes in these cases as follows:

> The final court decisions in these cases generally have been quite consistent in each category. The courts have found bad faith in all the cases in which a party has failed to attend the mediation or has failed to provide a required pre-mediation memorandum. In cases involving allegations that organizational parties have provided representatives without sufficient settlement authority, the courts have split almost evenly. In virtually all of the other cases in which the courts ruled on the merits of the case, they rejected claims of bad faith. In effect, the courts have interpreted good faith narrowly to require compliance with orders to attend mediation, provide pre-mediation memoranda, and, in some cases, produce organizational representatives with sufficient settlement authority. *Id.* at 84.

2.   Professor Kovach suggests the following court rule as an example of what a good faith requirement might look like. Would you support it if it were under consideration by your court?

Rule 1.7 Good Faith in Mediation

> A lawyer representing a client in mediation shall participate in good faith.

>> (a) Prior to the mediation, the lawyer shall prepare by familiarizing herself with the matter, and discussing it with her client.

>> (b) At the mediation, the lawyer shall comply with all rules of court or statutes governing the mediation process, and counsel her client to do likewise.

>> (c) During the mediation, the lawyer shall not convey information that is intentionally misleading or false to the mediator or other participants.

3.   Would you add a requirement that the participants have settlement authority to Kovach's good faith requirement? How much authority would you require the participant to have?

4.   Professor Lande suggests that the concerns raised by Kovach and other supporters of good faith requirements can better be addressed through better design of court-annexed mediation programs. In particular, Lande suggests key stakeholder groups—including litigants, attorneys, courts, and mediators—work together to develop policies that address the problem, including collaborative education about good mediation practice, pre-mediation consultations and submission of documents, a limited and specific

attendance requirement, and protections against misrepresentation. If faithfully implemented, he suggests, these policies will enhance the integrity of mediation programs and satisfy the interests of the stakeholder groups without the problems caused by good-faith requirements. *See* John Lande, *Using Dispute System Design to Promote Good–Faith Participation in Court–Connected Mediation Programs*, 50 UCLA L. REV. 69, 108–39 (2002). What benefits would you see with this approach? What problems would you see?

5. Ulrich Boettger, a German legal scholar, provides a comprehensive critique of good faith requirements in mediation, writing:

> What started out as an idea to combine efficiency and party-empowerment has shown not to work in practice. Although courts use mandatory mediation all the time, the participants often do not comply with the mediators' and judges' ideas of educating the parties. Although no statistical data exists about the number of participants refusing to engage meaningfully in mediation, it seems that the horse, led to water by the courts that mandate mediation, still refuses to drink. Instead of learning and using mandatory mediation to negotiate, many participants treat mandatory mediation like another part of litigation. Parties and lawyers, as ordered by the court, often show up at the mediation table, but do not participate in a meaningful way. In many mediations, groups of participants show the same adversarial behavior as they do in the courtroom. The expectations that, once in mediation, most of the cases will settle, and that working on a solution for the future always trumps sorting out the past, has often not worked out according to plans. Assuming that participant behavior is a problem in mandatory mediation, it seems that many parties have not applied their self-determination to become educated or to participate, even though forced to the mediation table by the court. Although not supported by empirical data, one can assume that the participants behave uncooperatively because they have been forced to mediate. The courts' power to refer cases to mediation does not provide a substitute for participants being convinced that mediation will help settle the dispute.

Ulrich Boettger, *Efficiency Versus Party Empowerment—Against a Good–Faith Requirement in Mandatory Mediation*, 23 REV. LITIG. 1 (2004)

6. In place of a good-faith requirement, Professor Edward Sherman proposes a "minimal meaningful participation" requirement. This requirement would include requiring the parties to provide each other and the third-party neutral with position papers and other relevant information that lays a basis for meaningful consideration of the case without mandating specific forms of presentation or interaction with the other party. For example, Sherman says "a reasonable order would be that the parties provide a position paper in advance of the ADR proceeding which would include a plain and concise statement of: (1) the legal and factual issues in dispute; (2) the party's position on those issues; (3) the relief sought (including a particularized itemization of all elements of damage claimed); and (4) any offers and counter-offers previously made." On the other hand, Sherman

argues program designers should take care not to impose requirements that interfere with trial strategy, such as one that would require the disclosure of privileged attorney work product. *See* Edward F. Sherman, *Court–Mandated Alternative Dispute Resolution: What Form Of Participation Should Be Required?*, 46 SMU L. Rev. 2079, 2101–03 (1993). Does this approach do a better job of getting at the underlying problem? What benefits and problems do you see?

7.   The ABA Section of Dispute Resolution in 2004 adopted a policy on good faith participation that responds to many of the concerns described above. It provides that "sanctions are appropriate for violation of rules specifying objectively-determinable conduct. Such rule-proscribed conduct would include but is not limited to: failure of a party, attorney, or insurance representative to attend a court-mandated mediation for a limited and specified period or to provide written memoranda prior to the mediations. These rules should not be labeled as good faith requirements, however, because of the widespread confusion about the meaning of that term." It also calls for limits on mediator reports to courts about good faith participation, and cites the Uniform Mediation Act with approval. Finally, it calls for greater collaborative planning of court-mandated mediation programs, such as that suggested by Professor Lande. The policy may be found on the ABA Section of Dispute Resolution's web site at http:// www.americanbar.org/con tent/dam/aba/migrated/2011_build/dispute_resolution/draftres2.authcheck dam.pdf (last visited Nov. 3, 2013).

3.   COURT–ANNEXED "MIXED PROCESSES"

As we indicated in Chapter I, "mixed" dispute resolution processes are those that include elements of more than one of the basic processes. This section presents several mixed processes that combine elements of adjudication and negotiation, sometimes in order to foster negotiated settlement.

a.   Court–Annexed Arbitration

Arbitration is relatively rare in the courts. As you may recall, in her 2011 study of the federal district courts, Donna Stienstra found that "no district courts authorize only arbitration." She also found:

. . . twenty-three districts, or nearly a quarter, include it among other forms of authorized ADR. Among these twenty-three districts are seven of the ten that were authorized in 1988 to mandate use of arbitration and seven of the ten that were authorized to offer voluntary use of arbitration; nine additional courts authorize use of this procedure. Today only three of the ten mandatory arbitration districts continue to require use of arbitration for the full portion of their caseload that meets the statutory requirements; four others have made arbitration an ADR option, and three no longer authorize this procedure.

DONNA STIENSTRA, ADR IN THE FEDERAL DISTRICT COURTS: A
SOURCEBOOK FOR JUDGES AND LAWYERS 9 (Federal Judicial Center 2011).

As a historical matter, The Civil Justice Reform Act of 1990 did not
include arbitration among the listed ADR methods recommended for
consideration by district courts. This omission led the General Counsel of
the Administrative Office of the U.S. Courts to conclude that "the CJRA
does not appear to authorize arbitration in other courts." ELIZABETH
PLAPINGER & DONNA STIENSTRA, A.D.R. AND SETTLEMENT IN THE
FEDERAL DISTRICT COURTS: A SOURCEBOOK FOR JUDGES AND LAWYERS 5
n.2 (1996).

Constitutional concerns offer one reason for the reluctance of courts
to impose. In Article III, the U.S. Constitution vests the federal judicial
power in the judiciary. While the Constitution also authorizes Congress to
establish inferior courts and tribunals, neither Congress nor the courts
have pushed the boundaries of this power beyond the specialty courts and
administrative tribunals, which the U.S. Supreme Court has specifically
upheld against a constitutional challenge. *Crowell v. Benson*, 285 U.S. 22
(1932).

Unlike private arbitrations discussed in Chapter V, which sometimes
are unilaterally imposed on parties, court-annexed arbitrations are often
voluntary and almost always non-binding. For these reasons, federal and
state courts have routinely rejected constitutional challenges to court-
annexed ADR programs based on the Seventh Amendment right to a jury
trial in civil cases and on the Fourteenth Amendment Due Process
Clause. *See, e.g., Riggs v. Scrivner, Inc.*, 927 F.2d 1146 (10th Cir. 1991);
Kimbrough v. Holiday Inn, 478 F.Supp. 566 (E.D. Pa. 1979); *Firelock Inc.
v. District Court*, 776 P.2d 1090 (Colo. 1989); *American Universal Ins. Co.
v. DelGreco*, 205 Conn. 178, 530 A.2d 171 (1987). In *New England
Merchants Nat'l Bank v. Hughes*, 556 F.Supp. 712 (E.D. Pa. 1983), the
defendant failed to appear at a mandatory court-annexed arbitration
hearing and offered no explanation. The District Court granted the
plaintiff's request for a summary judgment and held that failure to
comply with the local arbitration rule precluded the defendant from
demanding a trial *de novo*. *Id.* at 716.

In *Making Alternative Dispute Resolution Mandatory: The
Constitutional Issues,* 68 Or. L. Rev. 487 (1989), Professor Dwight Golann
concluded that "[s]ubject to specific comments articulated in this article"
mandatory, non-binding ADR "may be applied to almost any kind of civil
dispute without violating the provisions of the federal constitution or
most of its state counterparts." *Id.* at 568. *See also* Lucy V. Katz,
*Compulsory Alternative Dispute Resolution and Voluntarism: Two–
Headed Monster or Two Sides of the Coin?*, 1993 J. Disp. Resol. 1, 22–31.
For a more recent treatment of the issues, albeit set more broadly in the

context of international arbitration, see Peter B. Rutledge, *Arbitration and Article III*, 61 VAND. L. REV. 1189 (2008).

NOTES

1.   Some states court systems continue to use court-connected arbitrations, especially for smaller cases. In a study of court-connected arbitration in Arizona, researchers found that arbitration actually saved court resources in only 5% of civil cases arbitrated, but resulted in faster dispositions (three to five months faster than non-arbitration cases) and high lawyer satisfaction with the process. Virtually all lawyers (93%) felt they could fully present their case; 82% percent felt the hearing process was fair; 82% said the other side participated in good faith, and 79% felt the arbitrator was completely unbiased. But they also expressed concerns about the adequacy of arbitrators' knowledge of the issues, arbitration procedures, and civil procedure more generally; interestingly, arbitrators themselves also had similar concerns. Accordingly, a majority of lawyers felt that arbitrators should be assigned to cases based on their substantive expertise and should receive arbitration training before serving. *See* Roselle Wissler & Bob Dauber, *Court–Connected Arbitration in the Superior Court of Arizona: A Study of its Performance and Proposed Rule Changes*, 2007 J. Disp. Resol. 65.

2.   Professor Richard Reuben has argued that court-related ADR programs operate under the aegis of state action, and therefore still require programs to provide participants with "minimal but meaningful" due process protections, which vary depending upon the nature of the process. For court-related arbitration, these minimal but meaningful due process standards include the right to a neutral forum, the right to present and confront evidence, and a qualified right to counsel. *See* Richard C. Reuben, *Constitutional Gravity: A Unitary Theory of Alternative Dispute Resolution and Public Civil Justice*, 47 UCLA L. Rev. 949, 952–60 (2000).

b.   Summary Jury Trial

THOMAS LAMBROS, THE SUMMARY JURY TRIAL AND OTHER ALTERNATIVE METHODS OF DISPUTE RESOLUTION[*]
103 F.R.D. 461, 468–69 (1984)

* * *

It is clear that settlement of cases prior to trial provides a cost savings in terms of litigation. One aspect of this savings is the elimination of the need to empanel a jury. Some cases, however, are not amenable to settlement through the usual pretrial methods of dispute resolution, or the alternative methods mentioned above. There may be a variety of reasons for this inability to settle. Litigants may refuse to accept a compromise because emotionally they need a "day in court" to tell their

---

[*]   Reprinted from 103 F.R.D. 461 with permission of West Publishing Company.

story. Absent the opportunity to hear both sides of the case presented to the finders of fact, a lawyer and his client may be unable to objectively recognize the weaknesses in their position. The lawyer and his client may believe they can "pull off" a weak case if only they can get it in front of a jury. These reasons, among others, act as barriers to settlement; barriers which often result in protracted litigation and expense.

The Summary Jury Trial (SJT) provides a means by which to decimate these barriers to settlement. Alternatively, SJT can aid in streamlining jury trials so that the trial process undergoes a more efficient use of time. * * * SJT is the only alternative dispute resolution technique which utilizes the age old jurisprudential concept of trial by jury. It is this concept, the expression of opinion by a jury of peers, which has molded our judicial system and which permits the parties to believe that their story has been told, and a decision reached. No other alternative allows for the use of this basic foundation of our present system.

Initiated in 1980, SJT is counsels' presentation to a jury of their respective views of the case and the jury's advisory decision based on such presentations. It is a flexible pretrial procedure that aids appreciably in the settlement of trial-bound cases.

The SJT can be an effective predictive process for ascertaining probability of results. It is my perception that the sole bar to settlement in many cases is the uncertainty of how a jury might perceive liability and damages. Such uncertainty often arises, for example, in cases involving a "reasonableness" standard of liability, such as in negligence litigation. No amount of jurisprudential refinement of the standard of liability can aid the resolution of such cases. Parties' positions during settlement negotiations in cases of this type are based on an analysis of similar cases within the experience of counsel as to juries' determinations of liability and findings of damages. Such comparison is usually of little value, however, as parties tend to aimlessly grope toward some notion of a likely damages award figure upon which to base their negotiating positions. The parties and the court may become frustrated in cases, especially where neither party wants to fully try the case on the merits and the only roadblock to a meaningful settlement is the uncertainty of how a jury might perceive liability and damages.

The half-day proceeding is designed to provide a "no-risk" method by which the parties may obtain the perception of six jurors on the merits of their case without a large investment of time or money. The proceeding is not binding and in no way affects the parties' rights to a full trial on the merits. SJT is a predictive tool that counsel may use to achieve a just result for their clients at minimum expense.

After preparation and presentation of the case at an SJT, the possibility of a settlement becomes much more real to both sides.

Unreasonable demands and offers are reevaluated, and mutually agreeable compromises are worked out in light of the jury's findings.

NOTES AND QUESTIONS

1.   One advantage to summary jury trials is that lawyers are typically permitted to question or talk with jurors after they issue their verdict. What other advantages do you see to the summary jury trial? What disadvantages do you see? Describe a situation in which you would recommend that a client participate in a non-binding summary jury trial. A binding summary jury trial.

2.   The power of a federal district court to order a party to participate in a summary jury trial at one time was open to question. Prior to the 1993 Amendments to Rule 16 of the Federal Rules of Civil Procedure, the Sixth and Seventh Circuits held that federal courts do not have the power to require participation in a summary jury trial. *In re NLO, Inc.*, 5 F.3d 154 (6th Cir. 1993); *Strandell v. Jackson County*, 838 F.2d 884 (7th Cir. 1987). However, the 1993 Amendment made clear that district courts have the power to require parties and their attorneys to attend pre-trial conferences for purposes of "facilitating the settlement of the case." Fed. R. Civ. Proc. 16(a)(5). Since then, courts have consistently held that courts may order parties to a summary jury trial when there is a court rule authorizing the reference. *Ohio ex rel. Montgomery v. Louis Trauth Dairy, Inc.*, 164 F.R.D. 469, 471 (S.D. Ohio 1996) (ruling that *In re NLO, Inc.*, had been "effectively overruled" by the 1993 amendment). *See generally* Amy M. Pugh & Richard A. Bales, *The Inherent Power of Federal Courts to Compel Participation in Nonbinding Forms of Alternative Dispute Resolution*, 42 Duq. L. Rev. 1 (2003).

3.   Should the jury in a summary jury trial be told that its verdict will be advisory only? If so, should the jurors be told at the outset or after the jury has recorded its verdict? *See* Avern Cohn, *Summary Jury Trial—A Caution*, 1995 J. Disp. Resol. 299, 300.

4.   If you were a U.S. district judge, would you support the adoption of a local court rule giving judges the discretion to "set any appropriate civil case for summary jury trial"? Would you have a different view if you were a lawyer representing clients before the court?

5.   Professor Thomas Metzloff has proposed a stronger version of the summary jury trial, one that is binding. The theory of the binding SJT rejects the common assumption that the process is intended for cases in which conventional negotiations have failed. Instead, it seeks a broader role by providing an ADR option for litigants presently forced to settle, but who would prefer a binding adjudication if the process could be made less expensive and more predictable. The process allows litigants to obtain a binding adjudication of their dispute at a reasonable cost without the risks inherent in the current jury system. Thomas B. Metzloff, *Improving the Summary Jury Trial*, 77 Judicature 9, 11–12 (1993).

6.   The summary jury trial enjoyed some popularity in federal district courts in the years following the publication of Judge Lambros' article. A joint study by the Federal Judicial Center and the CPR International Institute for Conflict Prevention and Resolution found that, "[j]ust over half the [federal district] courts report authorization or use of the summary jury trial. . . . The level of usage reported by most courts is, however, very low—generally around one or two cases a year." DONNA STIENSTRA & ELIZABETH PLAPINGER, ADR AND SETTLEMENT IN THE FEDERAL DISTRICT COURTS: A SOURCEBOOK FOR JUDGES AND LAWYERS 5 (1996).

c.   Early Neutral Evaluation

JOSHUA D. ROSENBERG & H. JAY FOLBERG, ALTERNATIVE DISPUTE RESOLUTION: AN EMPIRICAL ANALYSIS[*]

46 Stan. L. Rev. 1487, 1488, 1489–92, 1493 (1994)

INTRODUCTION

* * *

This article adds to the empirical research by reporting on a quantitative and qualitative study of the ADR program of the United States District Court for the Northern District of California. The Northern District is one of six courts designated as demonstration districts in the Civil Justice Reform Act of 1990 (CJRA). Prior to the enactment of the CJRA, the Northern District had generated significant national interest in its design and use of an ADR procedure known as early neutral evaluation (ENE). Pursuant to the CJRA, the court retained the authors to evaluate its mandatory ENE program and suggest improvements.

Our most important findings include the following: (1) Approximately two-thirds of those who participated in the mandatory ADR program felt satisfied with the process and believed it worthy of the resources devoted to it (dissatisfaction with the program resulted primarily from dissatisfaction with the particular neutral assigned to the case); (2) while the percentage of parties who reported saving money approximately equaled the percentage who reported that the process resulted in a net financial cost, the net savings were, on average, more than ten times larger than the cost of an ENE session; (3) approximately half the participants in the program reported that participation decreased the pendency time of their cases; (4) the majority of parties and attorneys reported learning information in the ENE session that led to a fairer resolution of their case; and (5) the ENE process varied significantly from case to case and from neutral to neutral, and the most important factor in determining the success of the process in any one case was the individual

---

neutral involved. Consequently, we focused many of our suggestions for improvement on ensuring the quality of the neutrals. While these findings and suggestions are based on the Northern District's ENE program, we believe that they are likely to be relevant for other court-based ADR.

* * *

I.   HISTORY AND OPERATION OF EARLY NEUTRAL EVALUATION

A.   *History of the Program*

* * *

The court established a pilot ENE program in 1985. It handled about a dozen cases assigned by Wayne Brazil, the magistrate who administered the program at that time. An early study of the pilot program revealed promising results. In the second phase of the ENE experiment, the court assigned 150 cases in specified subject areas to the program, with sixty-seven actually proceeding through the ENE process. A study of these cases concluded that most ENE participants strongly believed ENE was worthwhile. Based on the apparent success of the experimental program, the court further expanded and refined the ENE program in 1988 and again in 1989.

B.   *Design of the ENE Session*

Absent a waiver granted by the court, every party in a case assigned to ENE must attend the ENE session, together with the attorney who will be lead counsel should the case go to trial. If a party is a corporation, it must be represented at the session by a person (other than outside counsel) who has authority both to enter stipulations and to bind the party to the terms of a settlement. Prior to the ENE session, each side must submit to the neutral a statement identifying session participants, major disputed issues, and any discovery that would be a necessary prelude to meaningful settlement discussions. The session is expected to last approximately two hours, during which the following events are expected to take place:

1.   The evaluator explains the purposes of the program and outlines the procedures.

2.   Each side in turn presents a 15–minute opening statement, either by counsel, client, or both, without interruption from the evaluator or the other party. The statement presents the side's case and legal theories and describes the supporting evidence.

3.   The evaluator may then ask questions of both sides to clarify issues, arguments, and evidence, to fill in evidentiary gaps, and to probe for strengths and weaknesses.

4.   The evaluator identifies the issues on which the parties agree (and encourages them to enter stipulations where appropriate) and also identifies the important issues in dispute.

5.   The evaluator adjourns to another room to prepare a written case evaluation. The evaluation assesses the strengths and weaknesses of each side's case, determines which side is likely to prevail, and establishes the probable range of damages in the event the plaintiff wins.

6.   The evaluator returns to the ENE conference room, announces that she has prepared an informal evaluation of the case, and asks the parties if they would like to explore settlement possibilities before she discloses the evaluation to them. If either party declines the offer to begin settlement discussions, the evaluator promptly discloses her written assessment. If, on the other hand, both sides are interested in working on settlement, the evaluator facilitates these discussions.

7.   If the parties do not hold settlement discussions or if discussions do not produce a settlement, the evaluator helps the parties develop a plan for efficient case management. This aid may include scheduling motions or discovery that would put the case in a position for rapid settlement or disposition.

8.   After the ENE session, the parties may agree to a follow-up session or other activity. With the consent of the court, the parties may engage the evaluator for additional sessions on a compensated basis.

C. *Administration of the Program*

1. *Selection of cases.*

Most ENE cases enter the program pursuant to an automatic assignment system set forth in the court's General Order 26. Subject to certain specific exceptions, the order assigns to the ENE program every even-numbered case in eighteen "nature of suit" categories, as identified by counsel on the cover sheet that must be filed with every complaint. Attorneys whose cases are administratively assigned to ENE may petition the court to have their cases removed from the ENE program. Written petitions are submitted to Magistrate Judge Wayne Brazil, who will grant such petitions upon a showing of good cause. Cases not automatically assigned to ENE may enter the program by stipulation among the parties with approval of a judge, or by referral from the judge assigned to the case, either at a party's request or sua sponte.

In cases automatically assigned to ENE, the plaintiff must serve on all defendants a copy of General Order 26 and other papers describing ENE. Once an evaluator has been appointed, the court notifies the parties of the appointment, and the evaluator then schedules the ENE session and notifies the parties. Absent an order from the ENE magistrate or the judge to whom the case is assigned, General Order 26 mandates that

ENE sessions be held within forty-five days from the notice of the evaluator's appointment and within 150 days from the filing of the complaint.

    2.   *Selection and training of evaluators.*

Judges, magistrates, and members of the ADR task force initially recommended evaluators for the ENE program based on their temperament, judgment, intelligence, and subject matter expertise. Later, the ADR task force selected additional attorneys, many of whom were recommended by judges or by respected peers. Some of these attorneys initially volunteered and were later recommended by judges or attorneys already involved with the program.

Early in the life of the ENE program, the ADR task force required all evaluators to attend a training session lasting approximately two and one-half hours. After the first experimental stage of ENE, program organizers videotaped the training session so that evaluators who were unable to attend could watch the tape. Evaluators also received written materials describing the program generally and suggesting how they could best perform their roles.

II. METHODOLOGY

This study is based on a review of all cases filed from April 1988 through March 1992 that met the subject matter criteria for automatic referral to ENE.

* * *

We received questionnaire responses from 377 (52.4 percent) of the 720 lead attorneys who had attended an ENE session. Of these, 191 had represented plaintiffs and 186 had represented defendants. We received responses from attorneys for all parties in 115 of the 326 cases (35 percent) in which an ENE session was held, and we received responses from a single attorney (either plaintiff's or defendant's) in another 147 cases (45 percent). Overall, we received a reply from at least one side in 262 cases (80 percent).

* * *

NOTES AND QUESTIONS

    1.   Rosenberg and Folberg found significant variation in the conduct of the neutral evaluators. They also concluded that levels of attorney satisfaction with ENE depended substantially on the identity of the evaluator. Why might this be the case? Assume you are an attorney whose case has been assigned to ENE and that a specific attorney has been designated the evaluator. Would you be concerned about what to expect in the hearing and how to prepare for it? How might you determine, or take part in the decision to determine, the kind of process the evaluator would conduct?

Do you suppose it would be appropriate for you to call the evaluator and inquire about her or his approach? Note that it is generally acceptable for parties or lawyers to have private contact with mediators but not arbitrators.

2.   Is it troublesome to you that different neutral evaluators might evaluate the same case differently? Is such a result consistent with our notions of justice? Should ENE program designers try to standardize the approaches of neutral evaluators? Would such an effort produce a kind of rigidity that would be counterproductive to settlement?

Assuming it would be desirable to standardize the approaches of neutral evaluators, how could this be done? Would more extensive training help? Most mediation training programs are longer than the ENE training program described by Rosenberg and Folberg. Would it be possible to identify persons to serve as neutral evaluators who are likely, by virtue of their backgrounds or personalities, to take an evaluative rather than facilitative approach?

3.   Some mediation scholars have argued that "evaluative mediation" is not really mediation but more closely resembles neutral evaluation. Kimberly K. Kovach & Lela P. Love, *Evaluative Mediation is an Oxymoron*, Alternatives to the High Cost of Litig., Mar. 1996, at 30, 30–31. What might Professors Kovach and Love say about "non-evaluative early neutral evaluation"?

4.   Remember the term "evaluation" can cover a range of activities. In a portion of the article not reprinted here, Rosenberg and Folberg indicate that lawyers felt more satisfied with the ENE process when the mediators "[g]ave views on the merits" than when they "[p]redicted a specific dollar amount for a verdict" or "[s]uggested a specific dollar figure for settlement." Joshua D. Rosenberg & H. Jay Folberg, *Alternative Dispute Resolution: An Empirical Analysis*, 46 Stan. L. Rev. 1487, 1529 (1994). What are likely explanations for this finding?

5.   Does anything in the excerpt from Rosenberg and Folberg suggest that evaluators helped the parties broaden the scope of the problem to be addressed in the session? Is this desirable in the ENE process?

6.   ENE has not proven nearly as popular as mediation in court-annexed programs. Why might this be the case? Should ADR program administrators give greater emphasis to ENE?

d.   Innovative Processes for Mass Personal Injury Litigation

Massive tort claims raise special management problems for courts. The following excerpt discusses several different models for handling mass claims. As you read these materials, consider the costs and benefits of the bulk processing of mass claims, and the degree to which the models that have been tried strike the right balance.

George W. Conk, Diving into the Wreck: BP and Kenneth Feinberg's Gulf Coast Gambit

17 Roger Williams L. Rev. 137 (2012)

Since the United States Supreme Court in *Amchem Products v. Windsor* effectively ruled out class actions in mass tort claims, the federal courts have continued to develop systems for management of large-scale claims. * * *

In the aftermath of the Deepwater Horizon catastrophe BP moved dramatically to get control of the process—hoping to use the prestige, creativity, and capability of Kenneth Feinberg and his firm to effectively pre-empt the complex, protracted, and costly litigation process. The purportedly independent method developed by BP and Feinberg could be labeled "the pseudo-fund model" of global settlement.

* * *

We begin with a look at the history of mass torts and some of the reforms that have moved us away from the common law system of trial by judge and jury. The [Gulf Coast Claims Facility] is unlike workers compensation systems, the administrative fund claims for childhood vaccine injuries, the mass tort global settlements of drug product liability cases, and the World Trade Center cleanup workers cases. All of those yield awards that are the product of open and adversarial processes with transparent measures of damages. But the GCCF is entirely private, its liability principles obscure, and its damages measures stated with such generality as to leave the Administrator with wide discretion. Like the September 11 Victims Compensation Fund to which it is otherwise inaptly compared, the GCCF is characterized by the broad, generally undefined discretion exercised by its administrator: Kenneth Feinberg.

* * *

[But] after one year, the GCCF has failed to garner the credibility as a neutral forum that BP sought, federal public regulatory authority has been faint, and state regulation has consisted of Attorneys Generals' laments. By default the [Multi-District Litigation] court has been pressed into service by private litigants. That government which governs least has not governed best.

* * *

The Emergence of Mass Tort Claims: Industrial Illness—A Modern Epidemic

We have been troubled by mass torts for over a hundred years. Tort reform arose in the early twentieth century when the emerging labor movement and social reformers forged a response to the grievous epidemic of industrial accidents. The common law presented formidable obstacles to employer liability for industrial accidents. But, driven by the railway workers unions' political force, Congress in 1908 passed the first Federal Employers Liability Act. * * *

Although FELA was the first modern tort reform measure, it was an anomalous one. The much broader thrust was one that bypassed the jury system: state workers' compensation laws. * * * [W]orkers' compensation largely replaced the jury trial system with a no-fault or strict liability system administered by administrative law judges. It abolished the defenses of negligence of a fellow employee, or that the injured employee assumed the risks inherent in or incidental to or arising out of his employment, or the failure of the employer to provide and maintain safe premises and suitable appliances. It modified the burden of proving proximate cause by use of the phrase "arising out of and in the course of employment" to describe the requisite causal link to the employment.

Unlike the common law tort system with its lump sum awards at the conclusion of the litigation, workers compensation systems assured injured workers of receiving interim wage loss claims during treatment and recovery for work-related injuries. It provided a reasonably efficient system of paying for their medical bills, replacing their wages during the time of their injury, and finally compensating them for permanent loss (partial or total) of working ability. Although the adjudication systems are administrative, not common law, they are generally adversarial systems with both employer and worker represented by counsel.

* * *

In the 1970's, modern mass tort claims arose when a liberal spirit encouraged third party litigation against asbestos product manufacturers. * * *

As the massive epidemic manifested itself, workers compensation and third-party tort causes of action arose against dozens of asbestos-containing product manufacturers and the companies that used their products. They were handled one by one, primarily in state workers compensation and trial courts. Thousands of cases were tried before juries, and thousands were settled. Delays were substantial due to heavy trial calendars, legal obstacles, vigorous defense tactics, and then, the insolvency of many manufacturers, some of which collapsed under the weight of their liability to injured workers. The force of these claims pushed relentlessly toward aggregate settlements, rather than the individual case-by-case resolution, which still characterizes workers' compensation claims, as well as tort claims for medical malpractice, and automobile accident injuries.

Focused Mass Tort Claims

Vioxx: Global Settlement after Case Management and Bellwether Trials

In the past twenty-five years, some of the most difficult mass tort claims have been associated with heedless mass marketing of little-studied drugs like the diet drug fen-phen, Zyprexa, and Vioxx. In those cases, thousands of events were aggregated through litigation, thrusting thousands of litigants into an unexpected and complex group dynamic, which tested the outside limits of the individual claim model of tort litigation. Courts responded with consolidation techniques like the federal MDL panels and state mass tort courts. The result was the now familiar pattern of case management, consolidated discovery, bellwether trials, and settlement grids. Despite the formation of judicially administered ad hoc litigation-management bureaucracies laden with lawyers, through selected bellwether trials juries have continued to provide an important measure of community judgment of the conduct of claimants and defendants in such mass tort pharmaceutical product liability cases.

But the pressures toward aggregation are enormous. Mass marketing done heedlessly yields mass litigation. Thus it was with the anti-inflammatory medicine Vioxx that was approved for marketing by the FDA in April 1999. The mass marketing campaign was very successful (sales reached two billion dollars per year). But anecdotal reports of heart attacks among users turned into a tsunami of epidemiological reports and meta-analyses dissecting the risk factors and results among Merck's millions of arthritic customers. Merck announced a "try every case" strategy. Merck's lawyers focused on the difficulties of proof of causation in each individual case—the drug's users were, after all, an older, arthritic, and therefore sedentary group. Merck's defense otherwise mirrored its aggressive sales strategy: its drug was good, there was some slight risk after eighteen months of use, we studied the drug's uses carefully, and prudentially withdrew it from the market.

But the evidence showed that its marketing-led pharmaceutical division had downplayed dramatic evidence of health risks, concealed data from a medical journal and the FDA, and had tenaciously—and largely successfully—fought every effort by the FDA to warn patients of the growing evidence of elevated risk of heart attacks and strokes. The result was a record at trial of two-thirds won by Merck (twelve out of eighteen). Most defense victories were on individual causation. There were four punitive damages awards and five major awards of compensatory damages, three awards of consumer fraud damages and attorneys' fees. With defense costs approaching $200 million per year and thousands of cases in the hopper—each theoretically entitled to a trial by jury—Merck finally conceded and offered $4.85 billion for a global settlement.

The Vioxx litigation and settlement is an exemplar of successful consolidated case management. After the $4.85 billion settlement was announced in November 2007, as of February 29, 2008, more than 44,000 of 47,000 eligible claimants had enrolled in the program. That constitutes over ninety-three percent of all eligible claimants. In order for Merck's offer to vest, plaintiffs' lawyers had to recommend the settlement to every client and achieve acceptance by eighty-five percent of those who claimed they had suffered a heart attack or stroke over twelve months usage of Vioxx. If a client rejected the recommendation the lawyer was bound to withdraw from further representation. The phrase "offer that cannot be refused" comes to mind. Indeed the Vioxx settlement has been sharply criticized for granting so much leverage to the lawyers who struck the bargain that client consent was improperly compromised.

* * *

The success of the plaintiffs' lawyers in selling the global settlement to their clients has many causes. But high among them is the experience of the bellwether trials. Through that experience, counsel for both plaintiffs and defendants learned something of their strengths and weaknesses. Their clients saw that the cases had been presented and tested vigorously, and that they were met with explainable success and failure. . . . It was, thus, the jury verdicts that were the ultimate guarantor of the legitimacy of the settlement.

9/11 Victims Compensation Fund: Secrets of its Success

The next example of successful global settlement is the September 11, 2001 Victims Compensation Fund, of which Kenneth Feinberg served as Special Master. The success of that project boosted Feinberg to iconic status as a Solomon among lawyers, a compassionate judge, a sort of Walter Cronkite swimming among the sharks. The reputation was well-earned.

Congress responded to the entreaties of the airlines in the days after the catastrophe. The air carriers were insured for negligence verdicts involving passenger deaths, but were utterly unprepared for the deaths of the victims on the ground. That there would be evidence of negligence, of sleeping at the switch, no one doubted. The airline manufacturers and airlines had reflexively resisted regulators who sought to require hardened cockpits for fear an airplane would be hijacked by terrorists. As one historian observed, "[I]n the face of a clear warning, alert measures bowed to routine." Congress responded with the Air Transportation System Stabilization and Safety Act.

The third "S" is a sop. It was system stabilization that drove the Congress to authorize the Attorney General to name one person who would, without budgetary limit, achieve a global settlement, which would save the airlines and our national passenger airplane manufacturer,

Boeing, from insolvency. That person, as we all know, was Kenneth Feinberg. He achieved nearly complete acceptance of his offers of settlement, and he did it without interference from the courts, without trials by jury, in an administrative process that proceeded parallel to the multi-district litigation managed by Judge Alvin Hellerstein (another Solomonic sort) in the federal district court in lower Manhattan. As time went on and Feinberg got signatures on bottom lines, the numbers of plaintiffs on Hellerstein's 9/11 catastrophe docket dwindled.

When making settlement offers, the statute directed the Special Master to consider:

> (i) the extent of the harm to the claimant, including any economic and non-economic losses; and (ii) the amount of compensation to which the claimant is entitled based on the harm to the claimant, the facts of the claim, and the individual circumstances of the claimant.

Feinberg faced formidable obstacles in designing a scheme of compensation for the 9/11 victims. Although the national treasury was his for the purpose, Congress had constrained Feinberg in certain respects: he was required to make individually tailored awards and deduct from each anything received from a collateral source, which Congress defined broadly to include life insurance, pension funds, death benefit programs, and payments by Federal, State, or local governments. Feinberg, as Special Master, was a one-man federal administrative agency. He interpreted the statute very loosely, concluding that "all" life insurance proceeds did not include the cash value that employee contributions represented in the life insurance policy benefits.

* * *

Kenneth Feinberg's ninety-seven percent success rate established him as the master of the global settlement. Working with virtually complete autonomy he had resolved the 9/11 claims through the flexibility shown in his willingness to relax statutory provisions, meet with claimants face-to-face, and set flexible, little-specified norms in order to accomplish both distributional equity and complete closure.

Feinberg's now peerless prestige as healer/lawyer who had served the nation pro bono, brought his next high profile public service appointment—by President Obama as the (nearly powerless) "payroll czar" for companies receiving Troubled Asset Relief Program "bailout" subsidies after the financial crisis of 2008.

The BP Deepwater Horizon Catastrophe:
GCCF—The Pseudo-Fund Model

When on April 20, 2010 the Deepwater Horizon rig burned and the largest oil spill in history began, BP was designated a "responsible party" by the Coast Guard under the OPA. BP's statutory obligations ranged from cleanup to interim and final payments to those who suffered losses due to the spill. The country was transfixed and BP was in its sights. While oil still flowed from the blowout well, BP announced that it would commit twenty billion dollars to meeting its statutory obligations under the OPA. When the spill erupted BP soon saw the value in the brand-name Feinberg had developed. BP decided to hire Kenneth Feinberg to administer its compensation plan. President Obama concurred in BP's decision to hire Feinberg to carry out its duties as a "responsible party" under the OPA. BP's appointment of Feinberg was said by the White House to be a guarantee of independence.

With that decision BP signaled its intention to seek a global solution to claims arising from the still untamed spill. Feinberg would be the independent claims administrator. But unlike special masters appointed by courts or legislators, Feinberg's operation—the Gulf Coast Claims Facility (GCCF)—answers only to BP, which was obligated to answer to the nation under the OPA, which imposed strict liability for the spill's consequences.

Funds have been (or will be at the anticipated rate of five billion dollars per year) transferred to bank accounts owned by BP and announcements made on what has been paid, but there is no "fund" if what one means by a fund is an entity with meaningful juridical independence, such as a trust fund. Here the obligations remain BP's and any funds that remain at the close will revert to BP.

Although the "Gulf Coast Claims Facility" that Kenneth Feinberg operates is commonly referred to as a "fund" there is in fact nothing to make that so. There is no escrow, no supervision, no accounting, no independent review, no regulatory oversight, no regulations with which the GCCF must comply. There is only the commitment to "pay all legitimate claims"—a meaningless statement since the company, designated as a "responsible party" under the OPA, is legally obligated to pay all legitimate claims.

Only if BP defaults on its obligations will the Coast Guard-administered Oil Spill Liability Trust Fund come into play to pay for "uncompensated" damages and clean-up costs. So long as BP is paying claims it operates free of government supervision.

* * *

Feinberg has been exercising this broad settlement authority within the scope of the OPA and general tort law in exchange for an initial $850,000 per month flat fee, now increased to $1,250,000 per month. Feinberg has devoted the efforts of his law firm, his judgment, and deployed his considerable reputation to successful management of the massive undertaking of overseeing BP's claims-processing centers. In March 2011, Feinberg announced that:

"Since the end of the Emergency Payment period on November 23, 2010, the GCCF has received approximately 256,000 individual and business claims seeking Final Payments, Interim Payments or Quick Payments." The GCCF had processed 138,874 (54.2%) of these claims.

* * *

Future Loss Claims

The causal relationship and estimation of future losses is a difficult proposition. Catch landings are reported to have been high for the latter part of 2010, when the fisheries were reopened, according to a report by a Texas A&M scientist. Feinberg has offered final settlements to fishermen of double their demonstrated 2010 loss. The report estimated certain fisheries will recover by 2012.

Feinberg therefore has estimated—with evidence that would ordinarily not be admissible because it is excessively speculative—that the fisheries will be at thirty percent of normal in 2011, at seventy percent of normal in 2012, and 100 percent of normal the year after that. He has therefore offered double the 2010 loss in exchange for a general release in favor of BP.

In comments posted online by the GCCF (with identifiers redacted) BP protested Feinberg's alleged generosity. But its continued retention of Feinberg and his firm indicates a recognition that if defendants want to settle early, they must settle on the high side.

Feinberg and his law firm took over management of a massive effort. As of March 19, 2011, the thirty GCCF offices had received 828,225 claims, the bulk of them for emergency assistance and other interim claims. The services rendered by Feinberg Rozen for BP's "Gulf Coast Claims Facility" have been broad in scope. The firm undertook, pursuant to its contract with BP, claim intake, review, evaluation, settlement, and payment services, and "[c]laim administration services including maintenance of appropriate databases and information technology systems therefor." The GCCF has done that work and has processed a huge number of claims. As of March 11, 2011, total payments were said to be approximately one billion dollars.

* * *

NOTES AND QUESTIONS

1. Do you agree with Mr. Conk's critique of the Gulf Coast Compensation Fund? If so, what advice would you have given Ken Feinberg if you had been given an opportunity to review his plan for the program before he finalized it?

2. What concerns do you have about these programs? Which models seem more troubling to you, and which are less problematic? The September 11th Victim Compensation Fund used a no-fault approach in the sense that claimants were entitled to recovery under the fund once they established their relationship to a 9–11 victim; the only question would be how much they would be entitled to recover. Significantly, Congress did not place any limits on overall disbursements from the fund. Feinberg measured economic losses by determining each victim's lost income from September 11, 2001 (the date of death) through his or her retirement, based on the victim's previous three years' income, with reductions for payments from life insurance, pension funds, death benefits programs and other such collateral sources of compensation. He also fixed noneconomic damages for all victims at $250,000 per victim plus $100,000 for each of the victims' surviving children and spouses.

Neither Feinberg's regulations nor his awards in individual cases were subject to appeal. After a slow start, 97% of the persons eligible for recovery ultimately chose to file claims with the fund rather than pursue remedies in court. The structure of the fund has been widely criticized by families of the victims and observers. *See, e.g.,* Robert M. Ackerman, *The September 11th Victim Compensation Fund: An Administrative Response to a National Tragedy*, 10 Harv. Negot. L. Rev. 135 (2005); Janet Cooper Alexander, *Procedural Design and Terror Victim Compensation*, 53 DePaul L. Rev. 627 (2003); George L. Priest, *The Problematic Structure of the September 11th Victim Compensation Fund*, 53 DePaul L. Rev. 527 (2003). What problems do you see? How would you describe Feinberg's role as a dispute resolution professional? What changes to this structure would you recommend? An empirical study found that claimants were satisfied with the procedural aspects of the fund, but were dissatisfied with the distributive dimensions. Brian H. Bornstein & Susan Poser, *Perceptions of Procedural and Distributive Justice in the September 11th Victim Compensation Fund*, 17 Cornell J.L. & Pub. Pol'y 75 (2007).

3. Science can often play an important role in mass tort, environmental, and other large cases. Indeed, as the Toms River, New Jersey childhood cancer case demonstrates, it can be virtually dispositive. The dispute involved allegations that several corporations had contaminated the drinking water and air in Toms River. While thousands of plaintiffs were involved in class actions, a relatively small band of 69 plaintiffs came together to try to find scientific answers before seeking redress. Working together with the companies and a mediator, the families set up a "scientific dialogue" process to assess the scientific issues that shifted the nature of the Toms River debate over several months. As Professor Eric Green tells the story:

> Somewhat surprisingly, however, settlement of the Toms River childhood cancer cases was reached relatively easily through mediation, with no judicial involvement whatsoever. The reason for the success of the Toms River mediation process was that it was grounded in the

scientific information exchange that preceded actual mediation. When mediation came, the parties' first settlement proposals were based so much on the scientific exchange that they were immediately perceived as reasonable, legitimate, coherent, and even elegant. When it became clear that both sides were operating with reciprocal reasonableness based on the scientific and technical information exchanged by the experts, the remaining differences between the parties were bridgeable through the use of conventional mediatory processes. The only judicial involvement in the Toms River childhood cancer cases was the shadow of law.

In the Toms River childhood cancer cases, the participants overcame the low odds of success because the initial conceptual design of the scientific process was so well conceived and then implemented by the many people who played key roles in the scientific dialogue that it created huge positive momentum and good will, which carried the participants through the transition from dialogue to resolution. Incrementally, the mediator introduced suggestions and steps that might lead to a resolution growing integrally out of the scientific process. When these suggestions were positively received, the foundation was laid for more conventional mediatory procedures that ultimately led to a complete global resolution of all the childhood cancer cases, utilizing a methodology founded on the scientific dialogue in which the participants had so strongly invested. Once the parties entered the conventional mediation phase of the process, resolution was almost inevitable.

Eric D. Green, *Re-examining Mediation and Judicial Roles in Large, Complex Litigation: Lessons from Microsoft and Other Megacases*, 86 B.U. L. Rev. 1171, 1197–98 (2006). For a proposal on how to integrate scientific evidence into mediation more effectively, see Deborah M. Hussey Freeland, *Maieusis Through a Gated Membrane: "Getting the Science Right" in Public Decisionmaking*, 26 Stan. Env. L. J. 373 (2007).

4. ADMINISTRATIVE AGENCIES

ADR has seen explosive growth in administrative agencies. Former U.S. Attorney General Janet Reno was a strong supporter of ADR during her tenure in the Clinton Administration, and ADR has enjoyed bipartisan support since then. One reason might be the extraordinary number and range of disputes with which administrative agencies get involved. One class of disputes includes those that arise during the course of the fulfillment of their statutory regulatory obligations. For example, the Internal Revenue Service administers the federal tax laws, and now uses mediation to help settle disputes with taxpayers. However, agencies are also involved in disputes in their capacity as employers, and most federal agencies now have alternative dispute resolution programs for the handling of such claims. Finally, administrative agencies are involved in disputes in their capacity as consumers of good and services, and have made extensive use of ADR to resolve public contract disputes.

ADR is also used in other types of disputes, from inter-agency disputes to military combat operations, but the materials that follow address the primary governmental contexts. The first reading, a 2007 federal government-wide report on the use of ADR by government agencies—excluding the courts—demonstrates the remarkable breadth and depth of the institutionalization of ADR within the administrative state. The second reading elaborates upon a topic touched on in Chapter IV, beginning at page 371, the use of dispute resolution during the public rulemaking process of administrative agencies, so-called "reg negs." The third reading is an analysis of one of the government's largest, and most ambitious, employment dispute resolution programs, the U.S. Postal Service's REDRESS program.

a. An Overview

REPORT FOR THE PRESIDENT ON THE USE AND RESULTS OF ALTERNATIVE DISPUTE RESOLUTION IN THE EXECUTIVE BRANCH OF THE FEDERAL GOVERNMENT

April 2007

Executive Summary 1–15

* * *

A.   A Brief History of Federal Alternative Dispute Resolution

The first uses of ADR processes began experimentally in the 1970s as a potential remedy for disabling court backlogs, and as resolution techniques for environmental and natural resource disputes. In 1985, the Attorney General issued an order recognizing the need for ADR to reduce the time and expense of civil litigation. A few years later the Department of Justice again recognized the benefits of ADR in the Congressional testimony of its Assistant Attorney General, Office of Legal Counsel, who supported the first ADR legislation enacted by Congress in 1990.

In the 1990s, Congress passed three statutes (the Administrative Dispute Resolution Acts of 1990 and 1996, and the Alternative Dispute Resolution Act of 1998) which, collectively, required each agency to adopt a policy encouraging use of ADR in a broad range of decision making, and required the federal trial courts to make ADR programs available to litigants.

In 1996, the President issued Executive Order 12988 on Civil Justice Reform, directing federal litigation counsel to consult with the referring agency and suggest ADR where benefits might be derived from its use. On May 1, 1998, the President issued a Memorandum directing the Attorney General to lead an Interagency Alternative Dispute Resolution Working Group ("Working Group") to promote and facilitate federal ADR.

* * *

C. Survey of Federal Alternative Dispute Resolution Programs

The Working Group Steering Committee in mid–2005 began surveying every agency in the Executive Branch about their ADR operations. Responsive data was submitted by over 100 agencies and agency components. . . .

II. Alternative Dispute Resolution Programs: Enhancing Agency Missions

The ADR programs and policies of the 15 Cabinet agencies and 31 independent agencies are summarized, and the nexus between programs and the agency missions is shown, in this section of the Report. The Report demonstrates that, increasingly, agencies such as the Federal Energy Regulatory Commission are expanding their ADR options to provide a menu of resolution choices that are better able to enhance the missions of government and agencies, and serve the needs of citizens.

* * *

Here are a few examples of the types of success stories that are seen in Cabinet agencies:

- The Department of Commerce/National Oceanic and Atmospheric Administration used consensus building and public participation throughout the development of the natural resource damage assessment regulations promulgated pursuant to the Oil Pollution Act of 1990.

- The Department of Education/Office of Federal Student Aid Ombudsman works with federal student aid recipient loan holders, guarantee agencies, and schools to prevent loan foreclosures.

- The Department of Health and Human Services/Departmental Appeals Board uses ADR to provide less contentious and quicker resolution of disputes involving Medicare and Medicaid program exclusions, imposition of civil sanctions against health care providers and nursing homes, and disputes with grantees (including States and universities) concerning disallowances of funds.

- The Department of Homeland Security/Federal Emergency Management Agency provided arbitration for more than 130 Los Alamos fire claim victims who wanted an alternative to court proceedings.

- The Department of Justice/Civil Rights Division's Americans With Disabilities Act Mediation Program uses ADR to resolve, quickly and voluntarily, discrimination complaints about architectural, communication, and attitudinal barriers for people with disabilities throughout the country.

- The Department of Transportation/Federal Aviation Administration has integrated a Neutral Evaluation program into the negotiated grievance process for all labor disputes between the Air Traffic Controllers Association and the Federal Aviation Administration. The program promotes collaboration and resolution early in the process by presenting disputes to an independent neutral, with expertise in the particular subject matter at issue, to provide a non-binding advisory decision.

- The Department of the Treasury/Office of the Comptroller of the Currency's Office of the Ombudsman, through the Customer Assistance Group, addresses disputes between consumers and national banks or their subsidiaries, and provides a user-friendly Web site of resources, answers, and formal complaint forms for consumers.

The independent agencies shared a similarly impressive track record of success stories, some of which are these illustrative examples:

- The Consumer Product Safety Commission utilized mediation to resolve a major dispute involving a risk to the public of carbon monoxide poisoning.

- The Environmental Protection Agency/Office of Administrative Law Judges uses a mediation program to facilitate settlement of administrative civil penalty enforcement cases under a set of federal environmental laws. The agency's Office of the Small Business Ombudsman resolves disputes with the small business community in the development and enforcement of environmental regulations.

- The Federal Energy Regulatory Commission provides a menu of ADR options such as facilitation of collaborative pre-license processes, mediation, settlement judges, and the use of early neutral evaluation.

- The Federal Maritime Commission facilitates the flow of U.S. ocean commerce by using ADR to quickly resolve disputes involving ocean shipping transactions, violations of shipping statutes, and freight charges.

- The Nuclear Regulatory Commission employed collaborative, facilitated ADR processes to involve the public in decision making about revision of agency rules and guidance on emergency planning in the wake of 9/11.

* * *

III. Advantages of Alternative Dispute Resolution

ADR has been instrumental in promoting a citizen-centered government, managing the costs of government, and supporting the strategic management of government resources.

A.   Promoting a Citizen–Centered Government

A citizen-centered government is one that is:

- accessible to the citizens it serves;
- responsive to the needs of the citizens it serves; and
- inclusive of the interests impacted by government initiatives.

The inherent design of ADR promotes a citizen-centered government because ADR processes facilitate early and direct communication and interaction among disputants. Federal agencies are capitalizing on technology to enhance the contributions of ADR to citizen-centered government. The National Mediation Board is a forerunner in the use of on-line dispute resolution tools, such as document-sharing software, to bring parties together electronically in their efforts to forge agreement. The Federal Energy Regulatory Commission operates an Enforcement Hotline which gives citizens access to an early neutral evaluation for a range of disputes before complaints are formally filed with the agency. The Department of Justice Civil Rights Division has a comprehensive, interactive, and user-friendly Web site for persons with disabilities and business owners who have questions about their rights and obligations under the Americans with Disabilities Act. The Department of Defense/Department of the Air Force utilizes the Internet as a primary means of dispensing ADR information.

Numerous agencies, such as the United States Agency for International Development, are employing ombuds to provide employees and citizens an opportunity to speak directly with an agency representative about issues of concerns. The ombuds provides timely feedback to the potential disputant and, as importantly, ongoing feedback to the respective agency regarding the impact and effectiveness of its programs.

Countless agencies also are encouraging the use of consensus-building processes to let citizens participate in these agencies' decision making. The Nuclear Regulatory Commission, for example, has convened collaborative processes for developing guidelines regarding the recycling of radioactive materials. The Department of Energy Office of Legacy Management has developed a Public Participation process to target populations—small towns, rural areas, minority and low-income communities—that are limited in their ability to participate in environmental decisions because they lack access to information, technology, expertise, and decision-makers. Such processes serve to identify and dismantle roadblocks to agency initiatives and foster collaborative relationships between agencies and their respective stakeholders, something that can have a long-lasting impact on agency decision making and approval processes.

B.   Managing Costs

ADR contributes to the effective conservation of limited federal resources in several interrelated ways:

- controlling the costs of conflict;
- producing quicker and more durable results; and
- preserving resources for the mission of the agency.

C.   Managing Strategically

ADR contributes to the strategic management of government resources, both monetary and human, by:

- maximizing resources;
- promoting innovation; and
- fostering continuous improvement and expansion.

IV.   Areas of Alternative Dispute Resolution Programs and Use

This section of the Report discusses the specific contributions of ADR to good government, as viewed through the lens of the four major substantive areas of federal ADR applications: civil enforcement and regulatory; claims against the government; contracts and procurement; and workplace.

A.   Civil Enforcement and Regulatory

Promoting a Citizen–Centered Government. In civil enforcement and regulatory disputes, unassisted negotiations and litigation have focused traditionally on which party has the stronger position. Today, many agencies fulfill their statutory mandates with the use of ADR, which is used as a supplemental tool to avoid protracted litigation when unassisted negotiations fail. The public interest is often better served when citizens, nongovernmental organizations, corporations, state and federal agencies, tribal nations, and other entities participate directly in an ADR process that includes them in the development of a result that meets the interests of all concerned. Stakeholders who work toward a shared, positive outcome often achieve better results than they would have received in court and can create long-term productive working relationships. A few examples show how ADR is supportive of citizen-centered government by promoting accessibility, responsiveness, and inclusiveness:

- The Environmental Protection Agency Brownfields Mine–Scarred Lands Initiative is a multi-level effort to engage a broad range of federal partners and local community members in addressing mine-scarred lands across the country.

- The Department of Energy Office of Environmental Management is using ADR to involve stakeholders early and often in decision making regarding the nuclear weapons complex cleanup program.

- The Small Business Administration National Ombudsman acts as a "trouble shooter" between small businesses and federal agencies on problems perceived as unfair and excessive regulatory enforcement.

- The Department of the Interior Office of Environmental Policy and Compliance is advancing greater use of consensus-based decision making in the implementation of the National Environmental Policy Act to engage local communities throughout the analysis process including developing the preferred alternative.

Managing Costs. ADR programs enable better control over resources expended, as well as better outcomes, as these examples reflect:

- The Department of Homeland Security/Federal Emergency Management Agency notes that for every lawsuit avoided, the agency can save thousands of dollars, thus leaving it better able to manage its resources.

- The Federal Energy Regulatory Commission reports faster processing and savings in hydroelectric proceedings where settlement agreements are reached during the pre-filing period.

- The Securities and Exchange Commission, while unable to agree to settlements during the mediation session (because of the need for review and authorization by the Commissioners), emphasizes the benefits that can flow from the process of mediation. For example, the Commission reports that mediation routinely helps to streamline discovery and focus the parties on key issues so that they are able to reach settlement shortly after the mediation concludes.

Managing Strategically. Agencies are building internal capacity to maximize the benefits of ADR, as shown by these practices:

- The Department of the Treasury/Internal Revenue Service Appeals office has an incentive-based training program which enhances the competitiveness of Appeals Officers trained for collateral duty mediation, and 400 of them have been trained as mediators.

- The U.S. Institute for Environmental Conflict Resolution has a national roster of pre-qualified neutrals, searchable on-line, that is used by federal agencies to locate environmental conflict resolution practitioners.

B. Claims Against the Government

Cases involving claims against the government are cases in which the United States is a defendant in a civil action. Since the federal district courts are required to offer some form of ADR, its use is fairly common in many of the cases.

* * *

C. Contracts and Procurement

The application of ADR to contracts and procurement disputes has increased in recent years, as more agencies—and more contracting companies—realize the value of ADR in achieving prompt and fair resolution of contract and procurement-related disputes.

Promoting a Citizen–Centered Government. Agencies across the board are utilizing technology to promote ADR, and as these examples show, that approach is allowing individuals and private sector entities to do business with a government that is accessible, responsive, and inclusive:

- The Department of Defense (the Department of the Air Force, the Department of the Navy, and the Defense Logistics Agency) has developed user-friendly Web sites that provide information on ADR processes, sample forms, and training in how to engage in interest-based collaborative problem solving.

- The Department of Transportation/Federal Aviation Administration has developed a similar citizen-centered Web site.

Managing Costs. The use of ADR in contracts and procurement disputes has resulted in savings of both time and money:

- The Department of Defense/Department of the Air Force reports that its "ADR First" policy in contract disputes has enabled it to avoid an average of $57.6 million in liability in each of the most recent five years (FY 2002 through FY 2006).

- The Department of Transportation/Federal Aviation Administration reports that the use of ADR has resulted in shorter resolution timeframes for the agency: bid protests are resolved through ADR in an average of 24 calendar days, while contract disputes have been resolved by ADR in an average of 67 calendar days.

Perhaps most importantly, agencies report that resolutions reached through ADR are more durable because they reflect the needs and concerns of the parties at the table, including the government. The Department of Veterans Affairs says that as the result of its ADR program, decisions are made with "greater certainty in achieving the Department's mission."

Managing Strategically. Use of ADR is enhancing the effective allocation of resources while promoting innovation in both process and outcome:

- The Department of Defense/National Guard is maximizing its resources by providing contracting officers and other Guard personnel with Claims Avoidance workshops which have contributed to a reduction in problems and disputes arising from the implementation of contracts.

- The Department of Agriculture maximizes resources through ADR process efficiencies such as using internal neutrals, consolidating travel assignments, and using telephonic and video-conferencing in place of travel where possible.

- The Department of Transportation/Federal Aviation Administration provides ADR to parties *before* they file formal bid protests which enables them to resolve concerns before the dispute escalates, and reports that of 79 "pre-dispute" cases where ADR was employed only three proceeded to formal litigation.

D.   Workplace

Across the federal government, agencies have found that the availability of workplace ADR increases the ability of employees and managers to resolve internal disputes quickly and effectively, at the earliest possible time, and at the lowest possible level. This is especially important in the workplace, where festering disputes may distract an employee or manager from fulfilling essential work responsibilities.

ADR Programs Are Successful in Resolving Workplace Disputes. Agencies report ADR settlement rates all above 50% and some reaching 75% and above, with significant cost savings. By comparison, the Equal Employment Opportunity Commission reported the national settlement rate of EEO cases through ADR was 49%.

ADR Programs are Cost–Effective. ADR programs conserve human capital by creating loyalty and longevity in the agency's work environment, and increase productivity.

ADR Saves Agency Funds. Federal agencies report considerable savings of monetary resources through workplace ADR programs:

- The Social Security Administration calculated that the average costs of processing an EEO complaint through a traditional process was approximately $40,000, while the costs of mediating an EEO complaint ran from $50 (if a shared neutral is used) to $1500 (if an outside vendor is used).

- The General Services Administration noted that for every EEO case resolved through mediation, the agency saved $3500—$4500 in investigation fees alone.

- The Department of Justice/Federal Bureau of Investigation calculated that it cost the agency over $2,600 for each EEO investigation and over $250,000 for a Final Agency Decision, but only $1,800 on average for each case resolved through mediation.

ADR Saves Agency Time. Agencies report substantial time savings through the application of ADR to workplace disputes:

- The Department of Defense/Department of the Air Force reports, for example, that workplace disputes resolved through mediation take an average of 27–40 days, as opposed to an average of 390 days for EEO cases which proceed to the administrative phase.

- The Department of Defense/Washington Headquarters Service reported that ADR processes took an average of 39 days, as opposed to EEO formal complaints (federal-wide) which took an average of 469 days in Fiscal Year 2004.

- The Department of Housing and Urban Development reports that processing time is reduced from 802 days in formal EEO cases to 53 days in ADR.

ADR Programs Are Essential to Strategic Management of the Workplace. The availability of ADR options gives both internal and external benefits to the agencies by:

- demonstrating an agency's concrete commitment to fostering a positive long-term working environment for all employees;

- improving relationships between federal managers and employees;

- increasing employee productivity;

- reducing costs with interagency sharing of in-house neutrals; and

- increasing efficiency with interagency sharing of expertise.

Workplace ADR Programs Create Collateral Benefits for the Agency. The benefits to ADR extend beyond the immediate dispute:

- Effective communication, a key ingredient of ADR, enables management to get key input from the employees working with issues that can potentially pose problems for the agency as a whole.

- Addressing causes of employee dissatisfaction can increase productivity.

- ADR processes identify and address recurring issues that lead to systemic problems, making it more likely that similar disputes can be avoided in the future.

* * *

Alternative dispute resolution is a tool for appropriate cases, not a panacea for all cases. The interests of the United States often are unique. Federal officials can resolve cases only in ways that will not undermine important legal issues, jurisdictional defenses, or policy interests. In appropriate cases, ADR has become a common sense option for the federal agencies. It is cost-effective, time-efficient, it gives the parties control over the outcome, and it involves stakeholders in decisions that affect them.

NOTES AND QUESTIONS

1. Are there any agency uses of ADR that you found surprising?

2. As with courts, mediation is overwhelmingly the dispute resolution method of choice among the federal administrative agencies. Indeed, there are significant constraints on the federal government's ability to use arbitration.

Until relatively recently, the federal government was generally prohibited from participating in arbitration because the U.S. Comptroller General took the position that the government had no legal authority to let a private party decide the outcome of a case involving the government. The Administrative Dispute Resolution Act of 1990 explicitly authorized arbitration for federal agencies, but only if it is clearly voluntary. Moreover, agencies cannot require a commitment to arbitration as a condition of entering into a government contract or obtaining a benefit. Finally, unless an agency has explicit statutory authority, it may not use arbitration until it has promulgated official rules prescribing the cases that may be arbitrated and the procedures the agency will follow. *See generally* JEFFREY M. SENGER, FEDERAL DISPUTE RESOLUTION 41–45 (2004). Why might the federal government be stricter about the use of arbitration than mediation?

b. Setting Agency Policy: "Reg Negs"

Administrative agencies sometimes use ADR in the fulfillment of their statutory missions. For example, the Equal Employment Opportunity Commission frequently mediates employee complaints against employers. In such a context, the alternative dispute resolution process is typically substantially the same as is found in other areas, although some context-specific adaptations are sometimes appropriate.

Administrative agencies also use ADR in their policymaking processes, the most significant of which is known as rulemaking. It is through rulemaking that administrative agencies implement the authority that has been vested in the agency by the legislature to carry out a particular policy objective. For example, the Occupational Safety and Health Administration will use a rulemaking process to promulgate workplace safety standards, and the Environmental Protection Agency will use rulemaking to develop air or water pollution standards. The use of ADR principles has helped revolutionize this process.

Traditional agency rulemaking is a three-part process, in which the agency sends out a notice of proposed rulemaking describing the subject matter of the rulemaking and any preliminary proposals it is considering. In the second stage, the agency conducts a hearing process by which affected parties may make comments to the agencies on its proposals. Finally, once the agency decides the rule it wants to promulgate, it sets forth a clear and concise statement of the rule, along with an explanation of the basis upon which the agency made a decision. This process, which can take years and include many different iterations of the first two stages, is often called "notice and comment rulemaking." *See generally* PETER L. STRAUSS, TODD D. RAKOFF & CYNTHIA FARINA, GELLHORN AND BYSE'S ADMINISTRATIVE LAW 483–732 (Rev. 10th ed. 2003).

Regulatory negotiations, or "reg negs," change that process by engrafting a dispute resolution process, such as negotiation or mediation, into the notice and comment rulemaking process. As Professor Harter describes below, rather than simply using the notice and comment process to decide unilaterally what the agency's policy will be, an agency using a reg neg facilitates a policy discussion among interested stakeholders about what the rule should be, and if the group achieves consensus, the agency agrees to use the group's proposal as the basis for its rule.

PHILIP J. HARTER, NEGOTIATING REGULATIONS: A CURE FOR THE MALAISE
71 Geo. L.J. 1, 28–31 (1982)

III. THE ADVANTAGES OF RULEMAKING BY NEGOTIATION

The idea of developing rules through negotiation among interested parties received brief attention when John Dunlop proposed it during his tenure as Secretary of Labor. Interest in the idea largely died before being translated into legal requirements or practice. * * *

Negotiating has many advantages over the adversarial process. The parties participate directly and immediately in the decision. They share in its development and concur with it, rather than "participate" by submitting information that the decision maker considers in reaching the decision. Frequently, those who participate in the negotiation are closer to the ultimate decision makingauthority of the interest they represent than traditional intermediaries that represent the interests in an adversarial proceeding. Thus, participants in negotiations can make substantive decisions, rather than acting as experts in the decision makingprocess. In addition, negotiation can be a less expensive means of decision makingbecause it reduces the need to engage in defensive research in anticipation of arguments made by adversaries.

Undoubtedly the prime benefit of direct negotiations is that it enables the participants to focus squarely on their respective interests. They need not advocate and maintain extreme positions before a decision maker. Therefore, the parties can develop a feel for the true issues that lie within the advocated extremes and attempt to accommodate fully the competing interests. An example of this benefit occurred when a group of environmentalists opposed the construction of a dam because they feared it would lead to the development of a nearby valley. The proponents of the dam were farmers in the valley who were adversely affected by periodic floods. Negotiations between the two groups, which were begun at the behest of the governor, revealed a common interest in preserving the valley. Without the negotiations the environmentalists would have undoubtedly sued to block construction, and necessarily would have employed adversarial tactics. Negotiations, however, demonstrated the true interests of the parties and permitted them to work toward accommodation.

In another example, an environmental group sued a government agency that granted a permit for a uranium mine, alleging that the environmental impact statement (EIS) was defective. The mine, confronted with protracted litigation and the consequent delay, agreed to negotiations. The attorney for the environmental group queried rhetorically what would have happened if the case had been successful? He thought that the mining company would simply beef up the EIS and continue to build the mine. Negotiations enabled the parties to focus on the issues separating them instead of fighting the legal strawman of a defective EIS. A general agreement resulted from the negotiations. More important, both sides were enthusiastic about the process.

Negotiation enables the parties to rank their concerns and to make trades to maximize their respective interests. In a traditional proceeding an agency may be unable to anticipate the intensity with which the respective parties may view the various provisions of a proposed rule. The agency may focus on an aspect of a rule that is critical to one party, but not of particular interest to other parties. An agency simply would have to guess how to reconcile such an issue because it would not know how to rank the parties' concerns. An interested party, however, could easily decide to accommodate another party in return for concession on a critical point. An example of such a trade off process would be when a beneficiary of a proposed regulation argues that the standard should be stringent with early compliance by the regulated company. A company that must comply with the regulation might counter that the standard should be more lenient with a long lead time for compliance. An agency faced with this situation might decide to require a lax standard in response to the company's claims of excessive burdens and require a short deadline in response to the need for immediate protection. Everyone involved, however, may be more content with precisely the opposite result. A rule allowing a longer time to implement a more stringent standard might benefit both parties because the shorter time for implementation might cause disruption that would offset any savings resulting from the reduced level of regulation.

Rulemaking by negotiation can reduce the time and cost of developing regulations by emphasizing practical and empirical concerns rather than theoretical predictions. In developing a regulation under the current system, an agency must prove a factual case, at least preliminarily, and anticipate the factual information that will be submitted in the record. Because the agency lacks direct access to empirical data, the information used is often of a theoretical nature derived from models. In negotiations, the parties in interest decide together what information is necessary to make a reasonably informed decision. Therefore, the data used in negotiations may not have to be as theoretical or as extensive as it is in an adversary process. For example, one agency proposed a regulation based on highly technical, theoretical data. The parties argued that the theoretical data was unnecessary because it simply did not reflect the practical experiences of the parties and of another agency. The agency determined the validity of the assertion and modified its regulation accordingly. The lesson of this example is that the data can emphasize practical and empirical concerns rather than theoretical predictions. In turn, this emphasis on practical experience can reduce the time and cost of developing regulations by reducing the need for developing extensive theoretical data.

Negotiation also can enable the participants to focus on the details of a regulation. In the adversary process, the big points must be hit and hit hard, while the subtleties and details frequently are overlooked. Or, even if the details are not overlooked, the decision maker may not appreciate their consequences. In negotiations, however, interested parties can directly address all aspects of a problem in attempting to formulate workable solutions.

Overarching all the other benefits of negotiations is the added legitimacy a rule would acquire if all parties viewed the rule as reasonable and endorsed it without a fight. Affected parties would participate in the development of a rule by sharing in the decisions, ranking their own concerns and needs, and trading them with other parties. Regardless of whether the horse under design turns out to be a five-legged camel or a Kentucky Derby winner, the resulting rule would have a validity beyond those developed under the current procedures.

Moreover, nothing indicates that the results would be of any lesser quality than those developed currently. Surely the *Code of Federal Regulations* stable has as many camels as derby winners.

Negotiation clearly has distinct advantages. It is therefore easy to fall into a "hot tub" view of negotiation as a method of settling disputes and establishing public policy: if only we strip off the armor of an adversarial hearing, everyone will jump into negotiations with beguiling honesty and openness to reach the optimum solution to the problem at hand. In fact, the process is far more complex than that. Negotiation must be carefully analyzed to determine not only whether it can work at all in the regulatory context, but also to identify those situations in which it is appropriate. Moreover, if a form of negotiation is to be used to develop rules issued by a government agency that determines the rights and obligations of the population at large, the process must be sensitive to methods of conducting negotiations and translating any result into a binding rule. Thus, the complex legal issues of how negotiations would relate to the APA and to the traditional political theories and values underlying rulemaking procedures must be examined. * * *

* * *

NOTES AND QUESTIONS

1.   Getting the right participants to the bargaining table, or convening, is an important part of the reg neg process. Assume the state Department of Natural Resources needs to resolve a longstanding dispute over river flow problems that implicate environmental aesthetics in a state park, certain endangered species, and tourism in a nearby resort area. Why might the agency want to use a reg neg? Who would it want to have at the bargaining table?

2.   How much consensus among stakeholders and interested parties should such a reg neg process require? Absolute? Supermajority? Majority? Should the relative weight of the stakeholders' interests make any difference?

3.   In this excerpt, Professor Harter lists several advantages of the reg neg process. What might be some disadvantages? Under what circumstances would they outweigh the advantages of using the reg neg process for the agency?

4.   Is a reg neg more suitable for some types of issues than others? *See* Gary E. Marchant & Andrew Askland, *GM Foods: Potential Public Consultation and Participation Mechanisms*, 44 Jurimetrics J. 99, 118–19 (2003).

5.   For criticisms of reg negs, see Cary Coglianese, *Assessing Consensus: The Promise and Performance of Negotiated Rulemaking*, 46 Duke L.J. 1255 (1997) (they fail to achieve instrumental goals of saving time and reducing litigation); William Funk, *Bargaining Toward The New Millennium:*

Regulatory Negotiation and the Subversion of the Public Interest, 46 Duke
L.J. 1351 (1997) (they fail to assure adequate role of public interests); Jim
Rossi, *Participation Run Amok: The Costs of Mass Participation for
Deliberative Agency Decisionmaking*, 92 Nw. U. L. Rev. 173, 217–36 (1997)
(they interfere with agency's larger agenda-setting efforts). For responses, see
Jody Freedman & Laura I. Langbein, *Regulatory Negotiations and the
Legitimacy Benefit*, 9 NYU Envtl. L.J. 60 (2000); Philip J. Harter, *Assessing
the Assessors: The Actual Performance of Negotiated Rulemaking*, 9 NYU
Envtl. L.J. 32 (2000). For a repost, see Cary Coglianese, *Assessing the
Advocacy of Negotiated Rulemaking: A Response to Philip Harter*, 9 NYU
Envtl. L.J. 386 (2001).

c.   ADR in the Federal Workplace

As in the private sector, ADR has been particularly popular in the
government workplace. Many federal entities, ranging from the Center
for Disease Control to the U.S. Air Force, have workplace ADR programs,
most of which emphasize mediation. The following reading looks at one
such program, offered by the U.S. Postal Service.

LISA BINGHAM, MEDIATION AT WORK: TRANSFORMING WORKPLACE CONFLICT AT THE UNITED STATES POSTAL SERVICE
IBM Center for the Business of Government
5, 12–23 (2003)

Introduction

Over the past decade, the United States Postal Service (USPS) has
emerged as a national leader in the use of appropriate or alternative
dispute resolution in employment disputes. Employment disputes include
but are not limited to conflict over supervisory decisions (criticism,
demeaning or improper treatment), management policies (for example,
opportunities for detail into supervisory positions or changing crafts),
working conditions, pay and benefits (overtime, leaves of absence, absence
for illness, for example), and discipline. The USPS's innovative program
for employment disputes is named REDRESS (Resolve Employment
Disputes Reach Equitable Solutions Swiftly). * * *

The EEO Complaint Process

The United States Postal Service REDRESS program provides
mediation for equal employment opportunity (EEO) disputes, specifically
those arising out of a claim of discrimination under federal law. Federal
law prohibits discrimination based on race, sex, color, national origin,
religion, age, and disability, and also prohibits sexual or racial
harassment or retaliation for raising a claim of prohibited discrimination
or harassment.

The traditional dispute system design established by the Equal Employment Opportunity Commission for federal discrimination claims is primarily rights-based. An employee may contact an EEO counselor regarding a potential claim. This is called the informal complaint or counseling stage of the process. In USPS and federal agencies, this EEO counselor is a federal employee who will conduct an informal inquiry into the dispute and attempt to resolve it, sometimes in face-to-face meetings between the disputants, but more often through telephone diplomacy. If counseling fails, the employee may file a formal EEO complaint. This triggers a formal investigation into the dispute and may include the taking of sworn statements and depositions. If the complaint is not abandoned or resolved, it may proceed to a formal adjudicatory hearing before an administrative judge. The judge's decision is submitted to the agency for final agency decision. If the employee is dissatisfied with the result, federal court litigation may ensue. This traditional regulatory process is largely rights-based, focusing on legal or contractual rights, obligations, and remedies, although it does provide for conciliation efforts.

This report examines the development and evaluation of REDRESS I, which involves the use of mediation at the informal complaint stage of the EEO process. REDRESS I was designed, pilot-tested, and rolled out nationwide between 1994 and 1999. In November 1999, after the national rollout was complete, the EEOC adopted regulations on standards for federal ADR programs. REDRESS meets, or exceeds, those standards. USPS recently expanded the program to encompass mediation at the formal complaint stage, REDRESS II. * * *

* * *

The Mediation Experiments

* * * The key system design features that continue to be part of the program are that mediation is voluntary for the EEO complainant, but mandatory for the supervisor respondent, who represents USPS as an organizational entity. As required by EEOC regulations, complainants are entitled to bring any representative that they choose to the table. These can include lawyers, union representatives, professional association representatives, family members, co-workers, or friends. USPS, as a party, may also designate a representative. The supervisor respondent must have settlement authority, or be in immediate telephone contact during the process with someone else in the organization authorized to approve the settlement. Mediation occurs during work hours, is private, and generally occurs within two to three weeks of a request.

* * *

The USPS pilot program initially used a facilitative model of practice. After a period of experimentation, USPS chose transformative mediation for the national model. Unlike other models, the USPS model does not permit the mediator to evaluate the case's merits, even if the participants request it. The mediator may not give a personal opinion regarding the merits, any assessment of the likely outcome in court, or specific proposals for settlement. All choices regarding the process, ideas for settlement, and the outcome of mediation are placed in the hands of the parties. This model differs from facilitative mediation in that the parties themselves design the mediation process; the mediator does not structure it for them, but instead asks them a series of questions about how they would like the process to proceed. This model of mediation is essentially participant-designed mediation.

* * *

The National Rollout

* * * The [REDRESS] Task Force created a national roster of experienced mediators. The initial roster of about 3,000 mediators nationwide was the product of a massive outreach effort. USPS REDRESS program staff attended mediator conferences and bar association meetings in an effort to deliver roster application forms (called the ADR Provider Survey) to the most experienced mediators in each geographic area. Minimum qualifications for consideration included at least 24 hours approved mediator training and experience as the lead mediator in at least ten cases. In addition, mediators had to agree to attend at least two additional days (20 hours) of transformative mediation training sponsored by the USPS. Finally, successful applicants had to agree to mediate one case pro bono to afford an opportunity for USPS staff to observe their effectiveness in the transformative framework. Persons who serve as arbitrators for disputes involving USPS or who have brought litigation against USPS within two years prior to application were not eligible for inclusion on the roster. No current or former employees are eligible for inclusion on the roster. This exclusion of current and former employees is intended to maintain the perception of fairness among employees.

In keeping with the transformative model, USPS did not limit the roster to mediators with employment law expertise, because mediators were not expected to evaluate the merits of the cases. Instead, USPS opened the roster to mediators from varied professional backgrounds, including psychology, counseling, and social work. The roster included teachers, academics, human resource professionals, and retirees from these professions. Many of the mediators had extensive experience in family and domestic relations practice. This outreach produced the most diverse roster then available, comprised of 44 percent women and 17 percent minorities.

USPS pays for all program costs, including mediator fees, administration, and training of mediators and participants from the Labor Relations budget at Headquarters. Mediator fees are negotiated locally on an individual basis. The policy is to pay mediators per session—not per case or hour—and also to cover travel expenses. In general, the USPS has recouped its investment in mediator training through the requirement that each mediator do one case *pro bono*.

The USPS took steps to institutionalize quality control. In collaboration with Professors Bush and [Joseph] Folger, it developed specialized advanced 20–hour transformative mediation training for experienced mediators from a variety of different practice models. The USPS identified a cadre of experienced mediation trainers and convened a Train-the-Trainers retreat in March 1998 at which they were taught the REDRESS model. The trainers' job was to fan out across the country to train mediators. * * *

To ensure that mediators did in fact practice the model in which they had been trained, USPS/EEO ADR Specialists observed at least one mediation session for each mediator used from the roster, and often they observed multiple mediation sessions. Surveys of these specialists about what they observed mediators do or say during these sessions indicated both that the specialists understood the model and that they were screening mediators based on implementation of this form of practice. After two years of this screening, the national roster ultimately stabilized at about 1,500 active mediators.

As the trainers fanned out across the country to train mediators, USPS Task Force staff trained key stakeholders and participants. The EEO/ADR coordinators all received 40–hour mediation training and attended the advanced mediator training for potential roster members in their region. Other key stakeholders—including union leadership and shop stewards, plant managers and supervisors, and local postmasters—received four-hour training about mediation and the program. A brochure was mailed to each employee's home. Lastly, supervisors conducted "stand-ups", brief workplace meetings at which they explained the program to craft employees. Information was also provided through the internal USPS video network and through literature in EEO counseling offices.

Institutionalization

A key step in institutionalization was to build an esprit de corps among the EEO/ADR specialists and coordinators, while at the same time fostering cooperation between the REDRESS program staff and EEO Counselors. One source of possible resistance to any new program is a group that feels its job security is threatened by the program. From the outset, the Task Force was identified as a temporary organization and the EEO/ADR positions as temporary assignments. * * *

* * *

A last element of institutionalization was to set an appropriate goal by which to measure the program's success. Typically, programs before REDRESS used *settlement rate*—the percentage of all cases submitted to mediation that resulted in a settlement—as their barometer. However, settlement is explicitly *not* a goal of transformative mediation. Instead, the goal is to provide the participants with opportunities to take control of their own conflict (empowerment) and reach a better understanding of the other participant's perspective (recognition). It is hoped that the process may provide an opportunity for participants to resolve their conflict, but that is not the mediator's objective. Thus, USPS set *participation rate*— the percentage of all employees offered mediation who agreed to participate in the process—as the key indicator of each district's and area's success. The reasoning was that the program could only affect workplace conflict management if people used it: "We knew that to really have an impact, we needed as many people as possible to accept mediation."

In order for people to use it, someone had to have an incentive to encourage them. Participation rate gave everyone associated with the program that incentive. In contrast, had the program used settlement rate as the measure, there would have been a counterincentive; program staff might have counseled what they perceived as hard-to-settle or intractable cases out of the program. With participation rate as the target, it did not matter whether anyone believed mediation had any likelihood of success. The goal was simply to get people to talk to each other in a safe, private environment. If they resolved their conflict, that was a good thing, but if they failed to do so, it did not reflect adversely on the program staff. Initially, USPS set a goal of 70 percent. Subsequently, it raised the bar to 75%. Each time, the program met this national goal. Headquarters staff eventually developed a one-page bar chart showing participation rate graphically for each of the 85 geographic districts, with recognition and awards for those with the highest participation, to create an incentive structure for EEO staff to support the program, market it, and work to maintain its reputation among employees.

The USPS does maintain records on case closure rate, as distinguished from settlement rate. Case closure includes not only cases where the parties reached a resolution in mediation, but also cases where the parties conclude a formal settlement within 30 days thereafter, or where the complaining party drops, withdraws, or fails to pursue the case to the formal EEO complaint stage. The case closure rate varies from 70 percent to 80 percent.

National REDRESS Evaluation Project

* * *

Results after the National Rollout

* * * Overall, formal EEO complaints have declined by over 25 percent since their peak in 1998 at 14,000 formal complaints.

Researchers also examined various aspects of the program design. One study looked at the role that various kinds of representatives play. The program differs from some private sector Dispute System Designs in that it allows employees to bring any representative they choose to the mediation session, including lawyers, union representatives, professional association representatives, and friends or family. Some employees chose not to bring a representative. * * *

Researchers found that representation in some form had a positive impact on settlement. The settlement rate for mediations where neither party was represented was 55 percent, whereas the settlement rate for mediations where both parties were represented was 61 percent, a statistically significant difference of 6 percent. Representation was also associated with longer mediation sessions. The mean duration for mediations where neither party was represented was 152 minutes, but that number rose to 184 minutes for mediations where both parties were represented.

* * *

A second key result from the exit surveys related to participant satisfaction with mediation fairness. Among complainants who were represented by union or professional association representatives, 91 percent reported being very or somewhat satisfied with the fairness of the mediation. Eighty-eight percent of those represented by fellow employees agreed, while only 76 percent of attorneys were satisfied with the fairness of the proceedings. This is not surprising, given that cases with attorney representatives had the lowest rate of partial or complete resolution of the three types of representatives, and resolution correlates with perceptions of fairness. However, complainants with no representation reported a 91 percent rate of satisfaction, with the highest percentage (67 percent) reporting that they were "very satisfied." (Had they been prohibited from bringing a representative, the result would undoubtedly have been different.)

* * *

Before researchers can assess the impact of a program on agency goals, they must verify that the program has in fact been implemented in accord with its design and that it is functioning; this is called a process evaluation. Researchers looked at implementation of the transformative model through a process evaluation using surveys of USPS program. EEO/ADR specialists and coordinators were asked to describe what they had seen or heard mediators do or say that fostered or interfered with party empowerment or recognition between the parties. This provided a rich collection of descriptions and anecdotes about what was happening in mediation, from the perspective of an outside, dispassionate observer. An analysis revealed that the USPS program staff had correctly categorized mediator moves as fostering or hindering empowerment and recognition, in that their descriptions corresponded with the hallmarks of transformative mediation practice described by Folger and Bush (1995).

NOTES AND QUESTIONS

1.   Recall the discussion of the different approaches of mediation in Chapter IV, beginning at page 327. The use of transformative mediation is unusual in federal agencies. Why do you think the REDRESS program designers chose the transformative model? Critics of the transformative model suggest it is not appropriate for many common disputes. Would the results of the REDRESS program give you more confidence in selecting this model for a workplace dispute resolution program?

2.   Professor Bingham stresses the importance of the voluntary character of the REDRESS program for the employees (it was mandatory for the employer). How might the program's implementation and results have been different if the designers had used a mandatory model?

3.   The program's designers also made a deliberate decision to schedule the mediations during the normal workday. What are the arguments for and against taking this approach?

4.   In constructing their rosters, the program's designers elected not to have current or former USPS employees serve as mediators. In other federal agencies, departmental employees are commonly used as mediators. Sometimes these positions are as full-time mediators, but more often mediation is a "collateral duty" appended to other responsibilities. What are the advantages and disadvantages of the REDRESS approach? What are the advantages of the "collateral duty" approach?

5.   The REDRESS program did not require the mediators on its roster to have any special background or expertise, including USPS experience. Yet as noted at the outset of the article, the disputes being mediated often were covered by substantive employment statutes and case law, such as Title VII of the Civil Rights Act of 1964. Do you think the program would be more effective if it required mediators to have more of a substantive background in employment issues, or perhaps even to be lawyers? How might such a design choice have affected the implementation and results of the REDRESS program? What kind of background should the REDRESS program managers have?

6.   Professor Bingham notes that the program designers used participation rates rather than settlement rates as a barometer of success. Do you agree with this choice? What are the advantages and disadvantages of this approach?

7.   Professor Bingham states that "... [S]ettlement is explicitly not a goal of the transformative mediation process. Instead, the goal is to provide participants with opportunities to take control of their own conflict (empowerment) and reach a better understanding of the other participant's perspective (recognition). It is hoped that the process may provide an opportunity for participants to resolve their conflict, but that is not the mediator's objective."

In a recently published second edition of their book, On Transformative Mediation (an excerpt of which appears in Chapter IV beginning at page 344), Bush and Folger provide a reformulation of their view on this issue:

> ... [E]ven though the mediator's job is to support empowerment and recognition shifts, the transformative model does not ignore the significance of resolving specific issues. Rather, it assumes that, if the mediators do the job just described, the parties themselves will very likely make positive changes in their interaction and find acceptable terms of resolution for themselves where such terms genuinely exist.
> * * *

ROBERT A. BARUCH BUSH & JOSEPH FOLGER, THE PROMISE OF MEDIATION: THE TRANSFORMATIVE APPROACH TO CONFLICT (rev. ed. 2005). For additional discussion of evaluating dispute systems, see Chapter VII, beginning at page 942.

8.   The REDRESS model permitted employees to bring in any representative to assist them, if they so chose. Professor Bingham's evaluation found that settlement rates were actually higher in mediations in which both parties were represented than when neither party was represented (61 percent in represented cases versus 55 percent in non-represented cases). Is this result surprising to you? What might explain it?

5.   DISPUTE RESOLUTION AND DEMOCRATIC GOVERNANCE

The foregoing discussion of dispute resolution in the government context has demonstrated the extraordinary breadth and depth that ADR has become institutionalized in the nation's courts and administrative agencies. Does the fact that the government is involved in all of these cases, as opposed to a private party, have any special implications for the process? In the following excerpt, Professor Reuben contends it does. He argues that when dispute resolution is provided by, administered by, or enforced by a democratic government, it should at least have the benefit of furthering rather than undermining democratic governance.

RICHARD C. REUBEN, DEMOCRACY AND DISPUTE RESOLUTION: THE PROBLEM OF ARBITRATION

67 Law & Contemp. Probs., Winter/Spring 2004, at 279, 279–82, 285–95

Scholars have approached arbitration, especially under the Federal Arbitration Act, from a variety of perspectives, including doctrinal, historical, empirical, and practical. One aspect that has not yet been fully considered, however, is the relationship between arbitration and constitutional democracy. Yet, as a dispute-resolution process that is often sanctioned by the government, that sometimes inextricably intertwines governmental and private conduct, and that derives its legitimacy from the government, it is appropriate—indeed, our responsibility—to ask whether arbitration furthers the goals of democratic governance. It is only sensible that state-supported dispute resolution in a democracy should strengthen, rather than diminish, democratic governance and the civil society that supports it.

* * *

[This article] establishes an operative understanding of what democracy is, explores the role of dispute resolution in a democracy, and identifies certain core substantive values of democratic governance that may be used to assess the democratic character of a dispute-resolution method, process, or system, namely: personal autonomy, participation, accountability, transparency, rationality, equality, due process, and the promotion of a strong civil society. [It] suggests that public adjudication represents a high embodiment of these values and that, under U.S. democracy, it constitutes democracy's endowment for dispute resolution.

* * *

II. The Framework for a Democratic Analysis of Arbitration

* * *

B. *Democracy's Substantive Values and the Centrality of Personal Autonomy and Dignity*

Once one acknowledges dispute resolution as a necessary function of democratic governance, the question becomes how to understand, assess, and constructively cultivate the democratic character of a dispute-resolution method, process, or system. The democracy literature is helpful in this regard. While particular formulations and articulations may vary, most scholars who embrace a broader definition of democracy tend to agree upon its core values. Those values are briefly discussed here to provide a common language and context. To move beyond the intellectual seductions of the counter-majoritarian difficulty, it is helpful to cluster them into three categories: political values, legal values, and social capital values. In brief, the political values are participation, accountability and transparency, and rationality. The legal values are due process and equality. And the social capital values are public trust, social connection and cooperation, and reciprocity.

Before describing these values in more detail, two observations are appropriate. First, these values will be treated separately below for purposes of theoretical analysis, but should be understood as much more integrated in practice, often overlapping and mutually reinforcing, and sometimes barely distinguishable. Second, and more substantively, they should be understood as operating to fulfill democracy's ultimate aspiration of enhancing the capacity and competence of personal autonomy and dignity within a system of collective self-government and social responsibility. This is a primary lesson from the birth of modern Western democracy and from the Enlightenment's repudiation of a divinely ordained socio-political hierarchy, its embrace of individual worth and self-actualization, and its deliberate expression in the grand experiment of U.S. democracy.

The Founders viewed their new nation as a laboratory for the potential of human achievement and constructed a government through a written constitution that would limit the worst instincts of man in his state of nature, while at the same time maximizing the potential for personal autonomy and self-actualization. They accomplished this by a structure that promoted individual and collective choice through elected legislative and executive branches, and through the rights to vote, to hold office, and to engage in political expression. They hoped to create a government and, equally important, a society burgeoning with the vibrancy and creativity that ambition and choice could inspire in political, economic, and social structuring. For these reasons, personal autonomy should be seen as a unifying and synthesizing value that can have a dominating or trumping effect when other supporting democratic values are in tension.

1. *Political Values*

The first, and largest, set of core democratic values may be understood as those primarily intended to foster collective self-governance by enhancing the capacity of individuals to participate in that governance effectively. These include participation, accountability, transparency, and rationality.

a. *Participation.* Democracy's essential theory is the consent of the governed, a concept that is implemented through the democratic value of participation. Under this social contract theory, the exercise of coercive government power is seen as legitimate because laws are enacted with the consent of those who will be bound by them. In most democracies, this consent is achieved through representation rather than direct participation.

This individual citizen participation in governance is one of the principle factors distinguishing democratic from authoritarian or totalitarian forms of government, under which the exercise of coercive force is justified through the authority of familial descent, military might, or the raw power of an individual. In the United States, participation in democratic governance is secured through the Constitution's electoral structure for the legislative and executive branches, the decentralization of government through state and local governments, and the rights to vote, to hold office, and to engage in political expression, even if critical of the government or otherwise unpopular.

Majoritarian theorists would generally limit the notion of public participation to the electoral process and the exercise of the franchise. However, a broader understanding of democracy recognizes, fosters, and integrates other aspects of public participation in democratic governance. Jury service is perhaps the most common example of public participation, accepted even by majoritarians, but participation values are also promoted in other areas of the law, such as the notice-and-comment processes in administrative rulemakings.

Deliberative democratists and communitarians would likely go further, considering the public debate on political issues that takes place between and among people, and between and among institutions, as democratic participation.

    b. Accountability and transparency. The accountability of elected officials to the general public interrelates with participation, in that government accountability makes individual and public participation meaningful. In this sense, accountability refers to the degree to which the government can be held responsible to the citizenry for its policies, words, and actions.

In U.S. democracy, accountability is constitutionally assured in part through the vesting of the legislative and executive powers in elective offices, thus conditioning the exercise of these powers on voter approval. Significantly, accountability is also fostered constitutionally through the First Amendment rights of speech, press, and petition, and the availability of legal actions to vindicate these rights in the courts.

Accountability is also furthered by a closely related democratic value: transparency. This generally refers to the openness of government decisionmaking, and in the United States is frequently associated with press freedoms secured by the First Amendment, as well as federal and state open records and open meetings laws. Transparency is closely aligned with accountability as a democratic value because it is transparency that makes accountability possible by permitting witness to government actions.

c.   Rationality. Rationality, in the democratic sense, refers to the consistency of governmental decisions with the law, social norms, or public expectations. It correlates with notions of equal protection and due process, and in the United States is secured by the Bill of Rights and the Fourteenth Amendment, as well as by statutory protections against arbitrary and capricious decisionmaking by government agencies. Rationality also interrelates with transparency and accountability: To the extent that eligible voters view legislative, executive, or judicial decisions as inconsistent with their expectations, values, or other nonbinding social norms, their votes provide a vehicle through which officials may be held accountable.

2.   *Legal Values*

The foregoing political values are complemented by at least two values that pertain to the application of substantive law: equality and due process. Significantly, these legal values also further the central value of personal autonomy by recognizing and protecting the inherent worth and dignity of the individual through fair and equal treatment under the law.

Democracies generally at least aspire to provide equal treatment under the law. This equality, or neutrality, speaks to the notion of the same law being applied in the same manner to all persons, without regard to governmental position, wealth, or social status. Equality in democracy serves to check the influence and power of elites (both governmental and nongovernmental), which in turn helps to assure the stability of the political, social, and economic orders.

In the United States, equality is most prominently enshrined in the Equal Protection Clause of the Fourteenth Amendment. It is also, however, assured through the neutrality and independence of the judiciary, through such means as due process and professional proscriptions against judges receiving compensation from parties. Such protections provide a hedge against factions and capture and rent-seeking in the administration of the rule of law. Due process is closely aligned with equal protection in its operation as a constraint upon arbitrary government action, and is essentially the promise of fair treatment at the hands of the government. While there is considerable debate over the meaning of the term, there seems little question that at least some kind of due process value is embedded deeply in democratic governance.

Due process is enshrined in the Fifth and Fourteenth Amendments to the Constitution. In interpreting those provisions, the Supreme Court has come to distinguish two types of due process: procedural due process (focusing on the procedures required before the government may take one's life, liberty, or property), and the more controversial substantive due process (focusing on the substantive fairness of legislation). Language may vary, but the concepts in these separate strands represent internationally recognized standards.

3. *Social Capital Values*

The final category of core democratic values relates to social capital, in particular the promotion of civil society, a concept that embraces public trust, social connection and cooperation, and reciprocity. While social capital values are familiar to political scientists and organizational behaviorists, their discussion expands democratic theory beyond its traditional governmental moorings in the constitutional law literature.

Civil society is generally recognized as the conceptual space between purely governmental and purely private affairs, where much of our collective societal interaction takes place—"including churches, schools, places of employment, clubs, and other group affiliations." Researchers, led by Harvard political scientist Robert Putnam, have come to recognize that this civil society, spawned by and supporting the structure of democratic governance, is just as important to the consolidation of a healthy democracy as properly functioning political institutions.

In his seminal work, Putnam compared the effectiveness of democracy in the autonomous regions of Italy and found that, measured in terms of institutional efficiency and citizen responsiveness, democracy in some regions was more effective than in others. Putnam found that effective democracies were marked by a civil society that broadly encouraged cooperation, reciprocation, and a sense of common good among citizens at all levels of national life, from social, to political, to economic, and beyond. Such cooperation led to an ever-deepening sense of social trust and order, both horizontally among the citizenry and vertically between the citizenry and its regional and national governmental institutions. In contrast, the less effective democracies were marked by civic traditions of distrust and competition, and a sense of isolation and detachment between and among citizens and their governmental institutions.

The work of Putnam and other social capital theorists strongly suggests that it takes far more than governmental institutions operating according to the substantive political and legal values identified above for a democracy to reach its maximum potential; it also requires the support of a strong civil society, steeped in public trust of governmental institutions, with a sense of social connection and cooperation among citizens and between citizens and their national institutions, as well as a spirit of goodwill, reciprocity, and civic virtue that reinforces this sense of trust and connection. Indeed, it is these seeming intangibles that constitute the foundation upon which a democracy must rest if it is to be sustained, consolidated, and effective.

C. *Democracy's Endowment for Dispute Resolution in the United States*

The core democratic values identified above provide criteria for assessing the democratic character of a method of dispute resolution.

When applied to public adjudication in the United States, one sees a very high capacity for democratic dispute resolution. Indeed, public adjudication can be considered a functional baseline endowment for dispute resolution that shapes obligations and expectations regarding the democratic character of other dispute-resolution technologies, such as arbitration.

Courts promote public participation in the development and administration of the rule of law by allowing parties to bring actions to enforce legal rights, as well as by allowing, or requiring, the citizenry to administer the law through jury service. As noted by Justice Anthony Kennedy, jury service is particularly important because "with the exception of voting, for most citizens the honor and privilege of jury duty is their most significant opportunity to participate in the democratic process." This participation fosters social and political stability by permitting individuals to turn to the law for the resolution of disputes rather than resorting to violence or other such means of destructive self-help, as well as by inspiring trust in the rule of law itself.

Similarly, courts promote equality, due process, and rationality by operating according to specific rules of procedure, evidence, and substantive law that have been enacted pursuant to statutory or administrative prescription, or which have evolved over time at common law. Regardless of whether a trial is held before a judge or jury, public adjudication requires legal standards to be used as the basis and process for decisions, with the principle of stare decisis providing an important constraining mechanism on judicial rulings. In this way, judicial proceedings operate at the highest level of formality, with the greatest level of procedural due process protection available at law. This is particularly significant because empirical research repeatedly confirms that participant perceptions of procedural fairness are crucial to the participant's acceptance of the decisional outcome as substantively fair.

There is also significant accountability and transparency in trial-court decisionmaking. The availability of appellate review helps to assure that legal rules are accurately applied and permits the evolution of legal standards as legal principles are tested in new situations. Similarly, while it is rare, jury decisions that stray too far from legal standards may be set aside by a trial-court judge or reversed on appeal. Both judicial and jury trials are open and accountable to the public (a right often exercised through the proxy of the press), as well as to the other branches of government, most notably the legislature, which has the capacity to reverse most judicial decisions through legislation.

Finally, as instruments of the rule of law, courts help generate a rich reserve of social capital that generally revolves around common compliance with law. Public adjudication constrains the arbitrary exercise of power by elites, the powerful, and other governmental or nongovernmental factions, which in turn promotes a sense of fairness and equality that inspires reciprocal mutual compliance with the law—the belief that we should follow the law because we know that the same rules will apply to all people and because we expect others to follow the law as well. From Nixon to Enron, the court of law is the great equalizer in a democracy. This also promotes both public and private stability—private stability by providing public standards by which citizens can order their private affairs, and public stability by assuring the peaceful use and transition of political power. Finally, courts and the law provide for the legitimacy of the political, economic, and social order by assuring legal constraints, compliance, and stability. This social capital is substantial, but is still capable of diminishment, as we see later in Part IV.

* * *

NOTES AND QUESTIONS

1. Professor Reuben contends that judicial and alternative dispute resolution processes are material factors in democratic governance. For much of the last 50 years, however, legal scholarship has tended toward a narrower view of the role of courts in democratic governance: that of policing access to, and the operation of, the elective branches. The seminal elaboration of this view is JOHN HART ELY, DEMOCRACY AND DISTRUST 87–88, 101–04 (1980) (articulating "representation-reinforcing" theory of American democracy). *See also* JESSE H. CHOPER, JUDICIAL REVIEW AND THE NATIONAL POLITICAL PROCESS: A FUNCTIONAL RECONSIDERATION OF THE ROLE OF THE SUPREME COURT 4–6 (1980) (review appropriate when necessary to vindicate certain individual rights). Which side has the better view?

2. Professor Reuben identifies several criteria for determining the "democratic character" of dispute resolution, grouped into three sets of values. The first set, political values, includes participation, accountability, transparency, and rationality. The second, legal values, includes equality and due process. The third, social capital values, includes trust in government and a strong civil society. Using these criteria, would arbitration have a more democratic or less democratic character than public adjudication? How about mediation? Early neutral evaluation? Other processes? What are the implications for the use of these methods in court-related or administrative programs? For an analysis of the democratic character of arbitration, see Richard C. Reuben, *Democracy and Dispute Resolution: The Problem of Arbitration,* 67 Law & Contemp. Probs., Winter/Spring 2004, at 279, 298–310. For an analysis of the democratic character of mediation, see Richard C. Reuben, *Democracy and Dispute Resolution: Systems Design and the New Workplace,* 10 Harv. Negot. L. Rev. 11 (2005).

3. A key question for the courts concerns the standard for determining whether an arbitration provision constitutes a valid waiver of trial and related rights. Some scholars, such as Professor Jean Sternlight, have argued in favor of a higher constitutional standard, at least when Seventh

Amendment rights to a civil jury trial are at stake. *See* Jean R. Sternlight, *Mandatory Binding Arbitration and the Demise of the Seventh Amendment Right to a Jury Trial*, 16 Ohio St. J. on Disp. Resol. 669 (2001); *see also* Richard C. Reuben, *Constitutional Gravity: A Unitary Theory of Alternative Dispute Resolution and Public Civil Justice*, 47 UCLA L. Rev. 949, 1017–28 (2000). Others, such as Professor Stephen Ware, have argued for a much lower contract standard. *See* Stephen J. Ware, *Arbitration Clauses, Jury–Waiver Clauses, and Other Contractual Waivers of Constitutional Rights*, Law & Contemp. Probs., Winter/Spring 2004, at 167. Does the democratic character of arbitration auger in favor of a higher or lower standard?

4.   Scholars have identified a relationship between trust in the courts and the willingness to comply with law. Several empirical studies by Professor Tom Tyler have consistently found that trust in legal institutions far exceeds other factors—including agreement in the substantive correctness of the law—as the primary determinant of the willingness to comply with legal rules. Tyler's research further suggests that people begin with a trusting posture, or "illusion of benevolence" toward legal institutions, and then test that trust with each interaction with the institution. Tom R. Tyler, *Public Mistrust of the Law: A Political Perspective*, 66 U. Cin. L. Rev. 847, 868 (1998). What might this research suggest for the implications for the design of governmental dispute resolution programs? *See generally* Wayne D. Brazil, *Structures for the Delivery of ADR Services by Courts: Critical Values and Concerns,* 14 Ohio St. J. on Disp. Resol. 715 (1999).

5.   Political scientist Robert Putnam has pioneered so-called "social capital" theory, which generally contends that the relationship between and among the citizenry of a democracy, and between the citizenry and its government institutions is as important to the effectiveness of a democracy as its electoral institutions. *See generally* ROBERT D. PUTNAM, MAKING DEMOCRACY WORK: CIVIC TRADITIONS IN MODERN ITALY (1993). What might be the relationship between Tyler's research on trust and the rule of law, and Putnam's social capital theory? *See* Richard C. Reuben, *Democracy and Dispute Resolution: The Problem of Arbitration*, 67 Law & Contemp. Probs., Winter/Spring 2004, at 279, 309–18.

B. THE PRIVATE SPHERE

As we have seen, the government has provided an important place for expansion and innovation in dispute resolution. The private sector has also seen this growth as well, and in this section, we lay out several of the different ADR techniques that have been used successfully in the private sector.

In Subsection 1, we examine a wide variety of traditional dispute resolution mechanisms that build on the methods discussed in earlier chapters. In this regard, we look first at two different methods of adjudication: the mini-trial (which roughly parallels the summary jury trial) and private judging, which is similar to arbitration except private judges are bound to apply the law, and their decisions are fully appealable as court judgments. We then consider med-arb, a two-step process in which the parties attempt to mediate their dispute, and if they are not successful, move on to arbitration. Finally, Subsection 1 closes with a reading on the ombuds, a unique vehicle for dispute resolution that originated in the public sector but which has seen considerable growth in the private sector in recent years.

In Subsection 2, we look at two more novel forms of dispute resolution processes. The first is collaborative law, a way of altering the structure of negotiation to enhance the possibility of an interest-based outcome. Collaborative lawyering has been popular in recent years in the family law area, and may expand to other areas. But it raises important questions about the roles and obligations of lawyers in the process. We then consider partnering, which is a vehicle for the preventive management of disputes that has been pioneered in the construction industry, but which may have further applications.

Finally, in Subsection 3, we close out this chapter with a look at the application of dispute resolution methods and principles in an entirely different context, online dispute resolution.

1. EARLY PROCESS VARIATIONS

a. The Mini–Trial

ERIC D. GREEN, CORPORATE ALTERNATIVE
DISPUTE RESOLUTION
1 Ohio St. J. on Disp. Resol. 203, 238–42 (1986)

The mini-trial ... essentially structures private negotiation by combining elements of negotiation, mediation, and adjudication in a new way. The mini-trial is used most often in business disputes when the parties are at an impasse because of a good faith disagreement about the likely outcome if the dispute is litigated, the existence of emotional barriers to resolution caused by the parties' (or, sometimes, the lawyers') personal antagonism, or the parties' inability to fashion a settlement that is responsive to all of their needs and rights.

A mini-trial can overcome a negotiation impasse by doing the following:

(a) Focusing the negotiation on the legal merits at the heart of the dispute, thus overcoming the barrier to resolution caused by the parties' differing assessments of the likely outcome of the case in court; and

(b) Reconverting into a business problem what has often been transformed by the litigation process into a technical, lawyers' fight. This reconversion is achieved by bringing in new negotiators—usually high level, non-legal managers who are not emotionally involved in the dispute, but who have authority to settle the case and who can view the dispute in a broader context in which imaginative, integrative solutions are more likely to be found. The presence of these non-legal representatives of the clients also brings together the true parties in interest, who often are better able than the legal representatives to assess the strategic risks and overall importance of the case to the client.

Although the specific procedures of a mini-trial may vary depending on the case and the parties' desires, most mini-trials contain these key elements:

(1) The parties *voluntarily agree* to conduct a mini-trial. There is no statutory, regulatory, or (usually) contractual obligation to participate in a mini-trial. Parties may terminate the mini-trial at any time.

(2) The parties negotiate and sign a "protocol" or *procedural agreement* that spells out the steps and timing of the mini-trial process. This agreement usually specifies the parties' obligations and responsibilities in the mini-trial process, their right to terminate the process, and certain legal matters such as confidentiality of the proceedings and the effect of the process on any pending or future litigation. This agreement may be quite short and simple or it may resemble ad hoc, private rules of civil procedure.

(3) Prior to the mini-trial, the parties *informally exchange key documents,* exhibits, summaries of witnesses' testimony, and short introductory statements in the nature of briefs. If necessary, the parties may engage in shortened, expedited depositions and other discovery without prejudice to their right to take full discovery later if the mini-trial does not settle the case.

(4) The *parties select a mutually acceptable neutral advisor to preside* over the mini-trial. Unlike an arbitrator or judge, the neutral advisor has no authority to make a binding decision, but at the mini-trial, the neutral advisor may ask questions that probe the strengths and weaknesses of each party's case. Also, after the mini-trial the neutral advisor may be asked by the parties' representatives to advise them on what the likely outcome would be if the case went to trial. Selection of a respected neutral advisor with credibility is very important for each side. One of the principal goals of the participants if they cannot obtain a favorable settlement in direct negotiations is to persuade the neutral advisor to advise the opponent that it would be better off settling than taking the case to trial.

In most mini-trials, the parties select a former judge as the neutral advisor because they believe that a person with prior judicial experience is best able to give them sound advice on likely trial outcomes. But parties generally try to select a former judge who recognizes the difference between the adjudicative function and the advisory role the neutral advisor plays at a mini-trial. In some mini-trials, especially those that turn on the resolution of a technical or economic issue, the parties may select a nonjudicial expert in the subject matter as the neutral advisor. In other mini-trials, the parties dispense with the neutral advisor altogether and rely solely on their business representatives to preside over the mini-trial and to conduct the negotiations privately. Another approach used at some mini-trials is to have a less active facilitator set up the mini-trial and chair it, but not advise the parties as to likely trial outcomes. In still other cases, the parties want the neutral advisor to attempt to mediate a resolution of the dispute. The function the neutral advisor is expected to perform will determine the kind of person best suited for the role. As a practical matter, however, it may be difficult to know in advance what will be required of the neutral advisor. Thus, the most successful neutral advisors have been those who are capable of playing the roles of advisor, mediator, and facilitator as the situation dictates and the parties ultimately determine.

(5) At the mini-trial itself, the parties' *lawyers make concise, summary presentations of their best case.* Mini-trials may last from half a day to three or four days (two days is average). Thus, presentations are usually limited to from one to six hours for each side, depending on the complexity of the issues. Generally, each party retains complete discretion over how it will use its allotted time. In some cases, the entire presentation is made by the lawyers, similar to an appellate or closing argument. In others, the lawyers call key witnesses to explain parts of the case. Often, key documents are used to explain the case. Quite often, the parties' experts testify on technical issues. At other mini-trials, parties have used movies, views of the scene, and other imaginative devices to communicate the essence of a case in the short time allotted.

At the mini-trial, rules of evidence do not apply. Thus, if there is testimony by witnesses, it tends to be in a narrative form under informal questioning by counsel rather than in the precise question and answer form of trial examination. In most mini-trials, time is set aside for rebuttal. This may include an opportunity for questions to opposing counsel, witnesses, and experts, again in an informal, modified cross-examination format. It may also include an open question and answer session in which expert may question expert, lawyer may question lawyer, and client may question client, or any variation of these combinations.

Although mini-trial formats may vary considerably, the common goal is to employ a procedure that effectively draws out the strengths and weaknesses of each side, including the persuasiveness of counsel and witnesses, in a short time.

(6) Mini-trial *presentations are made to high-level representatives of the parties* who have clear settlement authority. In most cases, the representatives are nonlawyers who have not been involved in creating or trying to resolve the underlying dispute, but who have authority or at least persuasive power over the decision of whether to settle. In cases involving businesses, the party representatives are generally at least one level higher in the corporate hierarchy than the business people who have been involved in the case prior to the mini-trial.

At the mini-trial, the nonlegal party representatives listen, observe, and ask questions to clarify points, much like a judge or arbitrator would, but they do not sit with or assist the advocates. Immediately after the parties' adversarial presentations on the merits of the case, the nonlegal representatives meet privately and attempt to negotiate a resolution. The theory behind the mini-trial is that the party representatives, armed with a crash course on the merits of the dispute (but without any emotional or face-saving motivations) and aware of the larger interests of their side, will be better able than the advocates or lower-level party representatives to appraise their positions and negotiate a mutually beneficial settlement.

(7) If the nonlegal representatives are unable to negotiate a settlement immediately after the mini-trial, they may schedule further talks or presentations. They may also call in the neutral advisor and ask for the advisor's views on likely trial outcomes. In the negotiation terminology of Fisher and Ury, the neutral advisor's opinion gives both sides an expert's view of its BATNA—"best alternative to a negotiated agreement." Armed with this data, the nonlegal representatives may negotiate further. If a settlement is reached, the dispute is over, as with any negotiated settlement, and any pending litigation is dismissed. If the case is not settled, the parties are free to resume any other dispute resolution process including adjudication. Most mini-trial agreements specify, however, that the entire process, including the opinion of the neutral advisor and any statements made in the course of the mini-trial, is confidential and inadmissible in any subsequent proceeding. The parties also agree that the neutral advisor may not testify or consult with any party in that case.

The hybrid nature of the mini-trial should be apparent from this description. For example, the mini-trial provides the parties the opportunity to present proofs and arguments on the merits of the case— Fuller's classic definition of adjudication—but in a process that has greater capacity to arrive at "win/win" results (negotiation) because the business representatives can work out their own integrative solution. The parties set their own rules of procedure and select a third party to help them resolve the dispute by considering the proper outcome (arbitration). But the third party has no binding decision-making capacity (mediation). The procedure is private (arbitration, mediation, negotiation), but is usually carried on within the structure of an on-going adjudication, and the goal is agreement rather than consistency with substantive law (negotiation and mediation).

The first mini-trial was held in 1977 to resolve a legally and technically complex patent infringement case. Since then it has been used to settle product liability, commercial, contract, distributor termination, insurance, construction, employee grievance, toxic tort, anti-trust, and trade secret cases. Most of the mini-trials have involved multi-party disputes and some have involved cases between individual plaintiffs and businesses. Others have involved governmental entities. While most mini-trials have been conducted under custom-structured ad hoc procedures, there is a growing tendency to attempt to codify the mini-trial. * * *

NOTES AND QUESTIONS

1. What kinds of disputes are most appropriate for mini-trials? Professor Green suggests that the best results are obtained when complex questions of mixed law and fact exist and when litigation is apt to be long and costly. Examples are patent, products liability, contract, antitrust, and unfair competition cases.

When are other processes preferable to mini-trials? Green suggests that other processes should be considered when a case turns solely on legal issues or factual disputes involving credibility, when litigation is used for tactical reasons, and when delay gives one side a substantial advantage over the other.

2. Consider the advantages and disadvantages of mini-trials, binding arbitration, and litigation in disputes between corporations and former executives who allege they were discharged for an improper reason. If you represented the former executive, would you recommend litigation, arbitration, or a mini-trial? If you represented the corporation, would you recommend litigation, arbitration, or a mini-trial? In each instance, if you believe you would need additional information before deciding what to recommend, what would you need to know, and why?

b. Private Judging

BARLOW F. CHRISTENSEN, PRIVATE JUSTICE: CALIFORNIA'S GENERAL REFERENCE PROCEDURE

1982 Am. B. Found. Res. J. 79, 79–82

* * *

A recent response to the problem of court delay has generated some interest and discussion. This innovation is the trial of cases by retired judges under the California general reference statute, a practice which has come to be called "rent-a-judge" by the popular press. The procedure appears to be a useful device, but it raises some questions that perhaps deserve discussion. * * *

II.   THE ELEMENTS OF THE PROCEDURE

The general reference procedure, as it is presently being used in California, includes a number of elements, not all of which derive directly from the statute. One element that does flow from the statute is the need for the consent of the parties. It appears that an entire case can be sent to a referee for trial only when both parties to the case agree to the reference. While the statute empowers the court to select a referee if the parties do not agree, in practice the parties themselves usually choose the referee.

* * *

Trials by referees are conducted as proper judicial trials, following the traditional rules of procedure and evidence. Transcripts are made of the proceedings, and the judgment of the referee becomes the judgment of the court. It is thus enforceable and appealable, as any other judgment would be. One lawyer who uses the reference procedure suggests that parties might agree to submit disputes to retired judges for decision independently, without any court order, but that they use the statutory procedure to preserve their rights of enforcement and appeal. Unlike trials in courts, however, trials by referees are conducted privately, without the presence of either the public or the press. Again, there appears to be no statutory requirement that this be so.

In theory, almost any kind of case might be referred to a referee for trial. The consensual portion of the statute imposes no restrictions. In practice, however, the procedure has been used primarily in technical and complex business litigation involving substantial amounts of money. The case in which the procedure was first used, for instance, was a complicated dispute between a medical billing company and two attorneys who had acquired interests in the company. Other examples have been a suit by major oil companies against a California governmental agency over air pollution control standards, a contract dispute between a nationally known television entertainer and his broadcasting company employer, and an action between a giant motor vehicle manufacturer and one of its suppliers over the quality of parts supplied.

* * *

NOTES AND QUESTIONS

1.   Stargazers may recall that Brad Pitt and Jennifer Anniston used a private judge when they divorced in 2005. *See Brad Pitt and Jennifer Anniston "Hire Private Divorce Judge,"* Hollywood, Aug. 17, 2005, http://www. hollywood.com/news/brief/2444017/brad-pitt-and-jennifer-aniston-hire-

private-divorce-judge? page=all (last visited Dec. 5, 2013). Why would they have done that rather than going through the traditional court system? What does this say about the advantages of this process for the parties and their lawyers? For the courts? For society at large?

2. Recall the critique of settlement by Owen Fiss in Chapter I, beginning at page 15. Do any of the concerns he raised about settlement apply to this essentially adjudicatory process?

3. California's chief justice appointed an advisory committee to study policy issues raised by private judging. The 1990 report of the advisory committee concluded that private judging benefits those who use the procedure and that the various concerns expressed did not warrant its elimination. JUDICIAL COUNCIL OF CAL., THE REPORT AND RECOMMENDATIONS OF THE JUDICIAL COUNCIL ADVISORY COMMITTEE ON PRIVATE JUDGES (1990). The report states:

> [o]n the present state of the evidence, we cannot conclude that the fears about private judging creating a two-tier system of justice, "one for the wealthy and one for the poor," are warranted. Even if they were, the committee is dubious about whether that would justify elimination of the private judging alternative. We believe that private judging is attractive in large measure because the public system is not able to resolve all civil disputes in a timely fashion. Improving the public system, not eliminating the private alternative, is the appropriate response.

Id. at 22–23.

4. If you were a member of the California legislature, would you support legislation prohibiting the referral of cases to private judges? Would you support an amendment requiring trials under the reference procedure to be open to the public? For an analysis of the arguments for and against private judging, see David J. Shapiro, *Private Judging in the State of New York: A Critical Introduction*, 23 Colum. J.L. & Soc. Probs. 275, 310–14 (1990). For a helpful study of the major private ADR firms in Los Angeles, see ELIZABETH RALPH, ERIK MOLLER & LAURA PETERSEN, ESCAPING THE COURTHOUSE: PRIVATE DISPUTE RESOLUTION IN LOS ANGELES (1994).

5. If you were an attorney advising a client on whether to use a private judge pursuant to the California reference procedure, what factors would you consider? *See* Winslow Christian, *Private Judging* §§ 40.4, 40.5, in THE ALTERNATIVE DISPUTE RESOLUTION PRACTICE GUIDE (Bette J. Roth, Randall W. Wulff & Charles A. Cooper eds. 1993).

c. Med–Arb

STEPHEN GOLDBERG, THE MEDIATION OF GRIEVANCES UNDER A COLLECTIVE BARGAINING CONTRACT: AN ALTERNATIVE TO ARBITRATION
77 Nw. U. L. Rev. 270, 281–84 (1982)

MEDIATION AS AN ALTERNATIVE TO ARBITRATION

The Mediation Process

In order to enable employers and unions to accomplish more satisfactorily the goal of resolving disputes in a speedy, inexpensive, and informal fashion which also holds promise of improving those unsatisfactory relationships that contribute to frequent resort to arbitration, I propose that the resolution of grievances through arbitration be substantially replaced by the resolution of grievances through a particular type of mediation.

The Proposal. Under the method here proposed, the parties would have the option of resorting to mediation rather than going directly to arbitration after the final step of the internal grievance procedure. The mediation procedure would be entirely informal in nature. The relevant facts would be elicited in a narrative fashion to the extent possible, rather than through examination and cross-examination of witnesses. The rules of evidence would not apply, and no record of the proceedings would be made. All persons involved in the events giving rise to the grievance would be encouraged to participate fully in the proceedings, both by stating their views and by asking questions of the other participants in the hearing.

The primary effort of the mediator would be to assist the parties in settling the grievance in a mutually satisfactory fashion. In attempting to achieve a settlement, the mediator would be free to use all the techniques customarily associated with mediation, including private conferences with only one party. If settlement is not possible, the mediator would provide the parties with an immediate opinion, based on their collective bargaining agreement, as to how the grievance would be decided if it went to arbitration. That opinion would not be final and binding but would be advisory. It would be delivered orally and would be accompanied by a statement of the reasons for the mediator's opinion. The advisory opinion could be used as the basis for further settlement discussions or for withdrawal or granting of the grievance. If the grievance is not settled, granted, or withdrawn, the parties would be free to arbitrate. If they do, the mediator could not serve as arbitrator, and nothing said or done by the parties or the mediator during mediation could be used against a party during arbitration.

The Proposal's Advantages. If grievances can be resolved through mediation, the advantages to the parties would be significant. First, mediation would be substantially quicker and less expensive than arbitration because the mediator would settle or give an advisory decision on the same day that the grievance is considered. This would eliminate the cost and delay associated with obtaining a transcript, filing briefs, and writing a decision. Furthermore, since the proceedings would be informal, the parties may choose to proceed without attorneys, resulting in still further savings of time and money.

Those parties with a substantial number of grievances could obtain still further savings in time and money by arranging for the mediator to consider more than one grievance per day. In addition, the parties could schedule mediation on a regular basis, with a mediator selected in advance. This would eliminate the wait for a free day in a busy mediator's schedule, and could result in the final resolution of grievances in 15–30 days from the completion of the internal steps of the grievance procedure.

Employees would benefit not only from the promptness with which their grievances would be resolved, they would also benefit from the process itself. Free of the constraints imposed by the quasi-judicial procedure of eliciting facts by direct and cross-examination, employees would have the opportunity to tell their stories as they wished. Furthermore, everyone at the mediation conference, including management personnel, would have the opportunity to talk to each other, not just to an examiner, cross-examiner, or arbitrator. Under this procedure, all the participants should feel that they have been heard fully and dealt with fairly, regardless of the outcome. Mediation thus may achieve more satisfactorily than does arbitration the catharsis and employee acceptability sought by arbitration.

The mediation process also offers hope of alleviating some of the situational characteristics which contribute to a large volume of arbitration. Frequently, such a volume of arbitration results from a combative relationship in which the parties approach grievances in a highly adversarial fashion. The arbitration process is unlikely to alter this attitude because of its adjudicative mode. The mediation process, however, compels a different approach. It eliminates the concept of "winning" a grievance, substituting the concept of negotiations leading to a mutually satisfactory resolution. To the extent that the parties focus on seeking a mutually satisfactory outcome through negotiations, they should develop a mutual understanding of each other's concerns. This mutual understanding, in turn, should lead not only to the resolution of more grievances without resort to mediation or arbitration, but also to the improvement of their entire relationship.

* * *

In addition to potentially improving the relationship of the parties, mediation also offers the prospect of a more satisfactory substantive resolution of contractual disputes than does arbitration. It is a truism of industrial relations that the negotiators of a collective bargaining contract can never anticipate and deal with all the issues which are likely to arise during its term. Hence, some issues inevitably arise which the contract does not clearly address. An arbitrator called upon to determine the "correct" interpretation of the contract in a grievance presenting such an issue will examine the language of the contract, its bargaining history, prior practice, and various canons of construction, and conclude that, if the negotiators had foreseen the particular problem and been able to resolve it, it is more likely that they would have resolved it in one way rather than another.

A resolution of the disputed issue through negotiation at the time the dispute arises is more likely to satisfy the parties, in light of their current interests and concerns, however, than is an arbitrator's probabilistic estimate as to how they would have resolved the dispute had they been able to do so at the time of the contract negotiations. While mediation does not guarantee that the parties will achieve a current solution to a current problem, the likelihood of attaining such a result is one of the strengths of the mediatory approach to dispute resolution.

Finally, the mediation process described here, in which the mediation step is entirely separate from the final and binding arbitration step, offers substantial advantages over the impartial chairman approach, in which the roles of mediator and adjudicator are combined. The fact that the "pure" mediator has no power to issue a binding award means that the parties need not fear that their contractual rights will be overridden to serve the mediator's interest in obtaining a settlement or in furthering their relationship. The separation of the mediatory function from the power to issue a final and binding decision also means that the parties need not fear that facts disclosed to the mediator in an effort to obtain a settlement will be used against them in the event no settlement is reached. This should increase their willingness to be candid with the mediator and so increase the prospects for settlement.

* * *

NOTES AND QUESTIONS

1.   Professor Goldberg's proposal, which was implemented in 1980 in the bituminous coal industry, includes the issuance of a non-binding opinion indicating how the mediator believes the grievance would be decided if it went to arbitration. As an alternative, the mediator could serve as an arbitrator if the mediation fails, with power to issue a binding decision. The position of the mediator-arbitrator in such a process would resemble that of a judge who works to bring about settlement and then presides over the trial.

The parties may take the mediator's recommendations more seriously because they know he will have the power of decision if negotiations fail. Moreover, it may save hearing time because the arbitrator becomes familiar with the case while serving as mediator.

2.   Professor Lon Fuller has articulated several reasons why the same person should not serve as both mediator and arbitrator. He asserted that the essence of an adjudicative process such as arbitration is a guarantee of opportunity to present proofs and argument. He also maintained that private conferences with parties are incompatible with such a guarantee because the party who did not participate in the private conference cannot know toward what she should direct her presentation. In mediation, on the other hand, Fuller thought private conferences usually are essential to success. He also argued that the types of facts that are relevant differ in arbitration and mediation. The differences arise, he thought, because the objective of mediation is a settlement most nearly meeting the interests of both parties while the objective of arbitration is a decision based on the contract. To Fuller, such different objectives call for different facts. Further, Fuller noted that a mediator learns things that should have no bearing on his decision as an arbitrator. For a further discussion, see LON FULLER, COLLECTIVE BARGAINING AND THE ARBITRATOR, PROCEEDINGS, FIFTEENTH ANNUAL MEETING, NATIONAL ACADEMY OF ARBITRATORS 8, 8–9, 24–25, 29–33 (1962).

In *Township of Aberdeen v. Patrolmen's Benevolent Ass'n, Local 163*, 286 N.J.Super. 372, 669 A.2d 291 (App. Div. 1996), the same person served first as mediator and then as arbitrator in a dispute between a local government and a union representing police officers over the terms of a collective bargaining agreement. The trial and appellate courts held that information learned during the mediation process could not be considered during the arbitration process.

If you were representing a client in a mediation, and the mediator offered to change the process to arbitration, would you advise your client to accept the offer?

3.   Professor Goldberg believes that med-arb usually will be faster and cheaper than arbitration. If these goals are important to the parties, can they be achieved just as well by modifying the arbitration process? For example, some contracts provide for expedited arbitration in which the arbitrator issues an oral decision at the conclusion of the parties' presentations and some contracts prohibit the use of lawyers in arbitration hearings.

4.   For a case study of a med-arb with an analysis that responds to critiques of the process, see Stephen B. Goldberg, *The Case of the Squabbling Authors: A "Med–Arb" Response*, 6 Negotiation J. 391 (1990).

5.   "Arb-med" is similar to med-arb, except that it begins as an arbitration, but converts to a mediation after the presentation of evidence to the arbitrator. The arbitrator makes and records a decision, which is withheld from the parties while they attempt to mediate the dispute. If the parties settle, that ends the matter and the arbitrator's decision is never

disclosed to the parties. If the parties do not settle, then the arbitrator's award is disclosed to the parties and is binding upon them. Writing in the context of airline industry strikes, arbitrator Arnold Zack describes the benefits of arb-med:

> [An] advantage of arb-med is that it will encourage greater openness. Because the arbitrator's decision may ultimately decide the merits of the dispute, the parties will have good reason to disclose all pertinent information to the arbitrator. That is not the case under the present system. At this time there is no incentive for the parties to reveal to the mediator potentially damaging information that would encourage settlement. * * * Thus, mediation under the present system places a premium on evasiveness. * * *

> [Moreover, the] arbitration format . . . forces the disclosure that having the mediation first tends to discourage. * * *

> I espouse arb-med for the airline industry because it provides finality while offering the parties the greatest number of options to reach their own agreement. They can . . . reach agreement in direct negotiations to avoid entering the spillway to arbitration. They can agree to settle during arbitration, as they perceive the evidence from the other side winning over the arbitrator. They can also settle during the mediation phase, as they weigh the likelihood of their having done better or worse than the outcome inscribed in that secured envelope. Even if they do not settle during the mediation, they can use the arbitrator's announced award to work out an agreement that better satisfies them both. The parties can even ask the arbitrator to recast the decision to reflect that final agreement. The goal of the arb-med process is settlement, which can be better achieved by the availability of conducting the arbitration hearing first.

Arnold Zack, The *Quest for Finality in Airline Disputes: A Case for Arb–Med,* Disp. Resol. J., Jan. 2004, at 34, 36–38.

Would you consider using arb-med? In what kinds of cases? What kinds of cases might be inappropriate for arb-med?

d. Ombuds

PHILIP J. HARTER, OMBUDS—A VOICE FOR THE PEOPLE
Disp. Resol. Mag., Winter 2005, at 5, 5–6

While the process of oversight and accountability can be traced to antiquity, the modern version of ombuds starts two hundred years ago in Sweden when the Parliament appointed an overseer—the "Justitieombudsman"—to ensure that the royal officers obeyed the law; interestingly, that action followed by a century the King himself appointing someone for the same purpose.

The proliferation of ombuds

Since then, ombuds have sprouted in all sorts of institutions, and they are now a varied lot. A number of them, especially in emerging democracies, are designed to protect civil rights and human dignity.

The Comptroller General of the United States—a de facto ombuds if not one in name—investigates on behalf of Congress to ensure the executive branch performs adequately. Government agencies themselves have established similar offices to investigate allegations of wrong doing or to receive and process complaints over maladministration.

Companies likewise have created ombuds to field complaints, to work out difficult issues in the workplace, and in this era of corporate scandals, to provide a means by which insiders can call potentially difficult issues to the attention of senior management. Newspapers have them to serve as a "watchdog" on behalf of the public. Others investigate complaints filed on behalf of vulnerable people and, if the facts merit, they become advocates for redressing wrongs and securing change.

* * *

Essential characteristics and functions

Given the extraordinary variety of issues ombuds address, the logical question arises as to just what do these people called ombuds have in common and how do they function.

At bottom, an ombuds is authorized to receive complaints and questions from a defined constituency about issues within the ombuds' jurisdiction.

To a very real extent, the foundation of the process is the ombuds' charter that defines the nature of the duties and to whom the office responds. For example, the traditional ombuds that is created by a legislature hears complaints from the citizens about the activities of the executive, whereas in a company it may be that an ombuds would hear only complaints from employees about designated issues or from customers. It is necessary to define this jurisdiction—who complains and what is complained about—in advance and in a publicly available document.

Importantly, the charter should specify whether an ombuds who helps resolve workplace issues can—or cannot—get involved in potentially explosive issues like sexual harassment or racial discrimination. Unlike a court, the ombuds customarily has discretion as to whether or not to accept the complaint and may also act on its own initiative.

The ombuds then develops sufficient information and takes appropriate action, such as issuing a report (which may or may not be public depending on the circumstances) with recommendations; raising the issue to an appropriate level within the organization; working out an agreement addressing the issue; or providing information so that the complainant can take individual action. An ombuds is not limited to addressing just individual complaints, however, but also is in a position to see trends or patterns so the ombuds frequently will point out systemic or general problems or issues. Importantly, an ombuds does not have authority to compel action of any sort.

An ombuds office must possess three essential characteristics to function effectively and with integrity: (1) It must be independent from control of anyone who may be the subject of a complaint or inquiry; were it otherwise, the ombuds is not likely to take strong, appropriate action. (2) The ombuds must conduct investigations or inquiries in an impartial manner, without bias or preconceived orientations; once the facts are determined, however, the ombuds may become an advocate for securing appropriate change. (3) The ombuds must not voluntarily disclose matters provided in confidence, and the establishing institution needs to assure the ombuds and those using the office that it will not seek anything provided confidentially; were it otherwise, those who come to the office could be badly hurt. These are characteristics that all ombuds should share, regardless of where they are located, how they function, or subjects addressed.

Four types of ombuds

In addition, it is helpful to differentiate among several types of ombuds, since as a practical matter how they operate differs slightly by category and to a certain degree they are conceptually distinct. The four types are:

- **Legislative**. A legislative ombuds is created by and is regarded as part of the legislature and the office is designed to hold the executive accountable; it reports to the legislature.

- **Executive**. An executive ombuds may be located in either public or private sector and receives complaints concerning the actions and failures to act of an agency, company, division, or some specified group, including its personnel and contractors. It may work to hold the agency, company, or NGO accountable, or the executive ombuds may work with officials to improve performance.

- **Organizational**. An organizational ombuds works to facilitate the fair and equitable resolution of issues that arise in the workplace. Thus, an organizational ombuds receives complaints and concerns from employees of the institution that employs the ombuds.

- **Advocate**. An advocate ombuds serves as an advocate on behalf of a group that is designated in the charter, usually for a specified vulnerable population. What differentiates an advocate ombuds from simply an advocate on behalf of that population is that an advocate ombuds, unlike a traditional advocate, conducts the investigation into a complaint in an objective, impartial manner and only becomes an advocate for the complainant if the facts support the claim.

An ombuds obviously has a complex relationship with the institution in which it works. Often it is an in-house goad whose job is to make sure those in authority abide by the rules. In the words of one charter, the ombuds is to investigate "abuse or unjustifiable exercise of power or unfair, capricious, discourteous or other improper conduct or undue delay" and "to rectify any act or omission by . . . any . . . means that may be expedient in the circumstances."

In other instances the ombuds serves as a mediator who attempts to work out agreements that would rectify the situation. But for this to work, the ombuds must be seen as impartial and effective. That in turn means that the ombuds must be fairly autonomous within the institution and able to function independently and without interference. In many ways, the same notion applies to an ombuds as underlies the separation of functions that protects the integrity of administrative law judges in government hearings.

* * *

NOTES AND QUESTIONS

1.   Ombuds have been around for generations. But a relatively new, and vibrant, area of growth has been in the organizational context. As Mary Rowe explains:

Corporate ombudsmen handle a wide variety of problems:

Many ombuds offices now keep careful statistics. Pilot surveys indicate that once an office is up and running, it appears to get calls from two to eight percent of the constituent community each year. Practitioners commonly report a considerable fraction of very brief contacts to the office (which may or may not be serious problems).

One practitioner estimates about one-tenth of the contacts to the office concern rather serious problems in terms of (potential) disruption to the individual and/or the company. Another practitioner estimates that, at any given time, the "open" office case load runs at about 12–15 percent of the yearly caseload, indicating that many problems can be resolved rather promptly.

Common topics include salary and benefits; promotion and demotion; performance appraisals; job security and retirement issues; company policies; discipline/termination; discrimination and harassment; safety, ethics and whistle-blowing; transfers; personality conflicts/meanness; information/referral; suggestions; working conditions; personal health, mentoring, and counseling issues; management practices; bizarre behavior and problems. Established offices that are reasonably well-known in a sizable company will see all these kinds of contacts each year. The profile of concerns, however, varies somewhat, company to company.

A majority of ombuds practitioners in companies where at least some employees are unionized, do see bargaining unit employees. Union employees are, however, appropriately referred elsewhere if they bring up concerns that are covered by the union contract. Ombuds offices are typically very respectful of their local unions and practitioners commonly report good relations with bargaining unit officers. In fact many an ombudsman has had union officers as clients in the office.

Mary B. Rowe, *The Corporate Ombudsman: An Overview and Analysis*, 3 Negotiation. J. 127, Apr. 1987, at 135.

For more on the role of ombuds, *see Howard Gadlin & Ellen J. Waxman, An Ombudsman Serves as a Buffer Between and Among Individuals and Large Institutions,* Disp. Resol. Mag., Summer 1998, at 21; Mary B. Rowe, *Options, Functions, and Skills: What an Organizational Ombudsman Might Want to Know,* 11 Negotiation. J. 103 (1995); Merle Waxman, *A Nonlitigational Approach to Conflict Resolution: The Medical Center as a Model,* Arb. J., Mar. 1987, at 25 (describing use of ombuds in a large medical center).

2.   Should communications to an ombuds be confidential? For most ombuds, confidentiality is an article of faith, enshrined in their most significant profession standards. *See* A.B.A. STANDARDS FOR THE ESTABLISHMENT AND OPERATION OF OMBUDS OFFICES (2001). However, the courts have been less sympathetic. In the most significant opinion to date, *Carman v. McDonnell Douglas Corp.*, 114 F.3d 790 (8th Cir. 1997), the Eighth Circuit ruled that communications to an ombuds are not privileged from discovery. The court said:

> We are especially unconvinced that "no present or future [McDonnell Douglas] employee could feel comfortable airing his or her disputes with the Ombudsman because of the specter of discovery." See Appellee's Br. 45. An employee either will or will not have a meritorious complaint. If he does not and is aware that he does not, he is no more likely to share the frivolousness of his complaint with a company ombudsman than he is with a court. If he has a meritorious complaint that he would prefer not to litigate, then he will generally feel that he has nothing to hide and will be undeterred by the prospect of civil discovery from sharing the nature of his complaint with the ombudsman. The dim prospect that the employee's complaint might someday surface in an unrelated case strikes us as an unlikely deterrent. Again, it is the perception that the ombudsman is the company's investigator, a fear that does not depend upon the prospect of civil discovery, that is most likely to keep such an employee from speaking openly.

McDonnell Douglas also argues that failure to recognize an ombudsman privilege will disrupt the relationship between management and the ombudsman's office. In cases where management has nothing to hide, this is unlikely. It is probably true that management will be less likely to share damaging information with an ombudsman if there is no privilege. Nonetheless, McDonnell Douglas has provided no reason to believe that management is especially eager to confess wrongdoing to ombudsmen when a privilege exists, or that ombudsmen are helpful at resolving disputes that involve violations of the law by management or supervisors. If the chilling of management-ombudsman communications occurs only in cases that would not have been resolved at the ombudsman stage anyway, then there is no reason to recognize an ombudsman privilege.

Id. at 794.

Do you agree with the Eighth Circuit? Recall from Chapter IV that the Uniform Mediation Act, echoing the laws of most states, provides a privilege for mediation communications. How are ombuds different than mediators in this regard? Why should the law treat them differently?

3.   The problem of when a communication to an ombuds may constitute notice to the entity for purposes of triggering federal anti-discrimination laws was a difficult issue for the drafters of the ABA Ombuds Standards, promulgated in 2001 and amended in 2004. On one hand, confidentiality is an important part of the ombuds process, which led many professional ombuds to assume that communications to an ombuds could never be notice to the company. On the other hand, attorneys concerned with the rights of workers believed that any communication to the ombuds should constitute notice to the entity because the ombuds works for the entity. How would you resolve this tension? To see how the drafters addressed it, see A.B.A. STANDARDS FOR THE ESTABLISHMENT AND OPERATIONS OF OMBUDS OFFICES § F (2001).

4.   If you were a union secretary, electrician, or lab assistant employed by a company with an ombuds office, would you prefer to go to the ombuds or the union for help with your dispute? Would your answer depend on the nature of your complaint? The nature of your job? Your relationship with your supervisors? Political considerations?

5.   Some ombuds have suggested that the most important personal characteristic of a mediator or neutral, is an interest in fostering the growth of others. Where does this approach to mediation fit on the grid described in Leonard Riskin, *Mediation Orientation, Strategies, and Techniques: A Grid for the Perplexed*, 1 Harv. Negot. L. Rev. 7 (1996) (excerpted in Chapter IV, beginning at page 304). Does this approach seem similar to the "transformative" orientation to mediation described by Robert A. Baruch Bush and Joseph Folger, *The Promise of Mediation: Responding to Conflict Through Empowerment and Recognition* (1994) (an excerpt from which appears in Chapter IV, beginning at page 344)?

2.   RECENT INNOVATIONS AND ADAPTATIONS

Different contexts bring different challenges to dispute resolution, and help spur the innovative path of the ADR movement. In this section, we take a brief look at three permutations on the cutting edge. The first explores collaborative lawyering, a way of changing the structure of legal negotiations to maximize the potential for interest-based solutions. The second looks at partnering, a way of restructuring business relationships with respect to disputes on large projects that involve many different parties, such as in the construction industry. The third section provides an overview of the new field of online dispute resolution, in which the traditional methods are applied to a very different context.

a.   Collaborative Lawyering

JOHN LANDE, POSSIBILITIES FOR COLLABORATIVE LAW: ETHICS AND PRACTICE OF LAWYER DISQUALIFICATION AND PROCESS CONTROL IN A NEW MODEL OF LAWYERING
64 Ohio St. L.J. 1315, 1315–30 (2003)

Is collaborative law (CL) a revolutionary idea whose time has come? CL proponents say that it constitutes a "paradigm shift" in dealing with legal cases and that it is the "next generation" of family dispute resolution. CL practitioners seek to provide a more civilized process than in traditional litigation, produce outcomes meeting the needs of both parties, minimize costs, and increase clients' control, privacy and compliance with agreements. CL encourages spouses to honor the positive connections between them so that they can divorce respectfully and maintain good relationships with children and other relatives.

In CL, the lawyers and clients agree to negotiate from the outset of the case using a problem-solving approach in negotiation. Despite widespread interest in problem-solving by academics and professional leaders and rhetorical support by practitioners, in practice, much legal negotiation and mediation apparently relies on traditional positional negotiation processes.

CL lawyers and parties negotiate primarily in "four-way" meetings in which all are expected to participate actively. Lawyers are committed to "keep the process honest, respectful, and productive on both sides." The parties are expected to be respectful, provide full disclosure of all relevant information, and address each other's legitimate needs. Under CL theory, parties have "shadow" feelings (such as anger, fear, and grief), which are "expected and accepted, but not permitted to direct the dispute-resolution process." CL theory provides that each lawyer is responsible for moving parties away from artificial bargaining positions to focus on their real needs and interests to seek "win-win" solutions. Some theorists suggest that the CL agreement effectively "amounts to a 'durable power of attorney,' directing the lawyers to take instructions from the client's higher-functioning self, and to politely disregard the instructions that may emerge from time to time during the divorce process when a less high-functioning self takes charge of the client." If a lawyer determines that his or her client is participating in bad faith, the lawyer must withdraw. As a result, the lawyer's continued participation effectively vouches for the client's good faith.

Under CL theory, CL creates a metaphorical "container" around the lawyers and clients to help focus on negotiation. CL creates this container through a mutual withdrawal agreement that disqualifies both lawyers from continuing to represent their clients if either party chooses to discontinue with CL and proceed in litigation. This agreement is intended to align parties' and lawyers' incentives to promote settlement. Virtually all CL practitioners believe that this agreement is the "irreducible minimum condition" for calling a practice collaborative law.

CL proponents contend that CL can avoid structural flaws in mediation. Mediation is often inadequate, they argue, due to mediators' difficulties in managing power imbalances and emotional dynamics of the parties. Parties presumably receive limited legal input from the mediators, who are supposed to be neutral and are not supposed to provide legal advice. Some parties in mediation do not have consulting lawyers. Even when parties do have such lawyers, the lawyers often do not participate, are limited to advising "from the sidelines," and may undo mediated agreements. As a result, Pauline Tesler argues that mediation is appropriate only for a relatively small group of "high-functioning, low-conflict" spouses whereas CL is appropriate for the vast majority of divorcing couples, excluding only a relatively small proportion of couples who are so low-functioning or have so much conflict that they require traditional adversarial lawyers to litigate and judges to make decisions.

The CL movement has grown rapidly and legal authorities have embraced it with remarkable speed. Professional leaders recognize CL as a major innovation in dispute resolution practice barely a decade after it was first developed in 1990. In the 1990s, CL practitioners developed practice groups in many localities to train and socialize CL practitioners, publicly identify CL lawyers, develop local CL practice protocols, build demand for CL, and form referral networks for CL cases. During this period, CL proponents wrote articles in professional journals to describe CL and advocate its use. In 1999, the American Institute of Collaborative Professionals began publishing a journal, The Collaborative Quarterly. In 2000, Harvard Law Professor Robert H. Mnookin and his co-authors recommended that lawyers use CL to create incentives for problem-solving. In 2000, a California court established a "Collaborative Law Department." In 2001, the American Bar Association Section of Family Law published a CL manual with practice forms. In 2001, Texas enacted the first statute authorizing CL. In 2002, the American Bar Association Section of Dispute Resolution bestowed its first "Lawyer as Problem Solver" Award, to honor two CL founders-Stuart Webb, a Minneapolis family lawyer, and Pauline Tesler, a Northern California family lawyer and the author of the ABA CL manual. In 2003, several law schools started offering courses on CL including Hamline University, Santa Clara University, and the University of British Columbia. Major dispute resolution organizations have featured sessions about CL at their annual conferences.

Much CL theory and practice clearly is valuable. CL leaders and practitioners deserve great credit for promoting protocols of early commitment to negotiation, interest-based joint problem-solving, collaboration with professionals in other disciplines, and intentional development of a new legal culture through activities of local practice groups. If CL practice becomes firmly institutionalized, it could influence traditional legal practice, which might be its most significant impact.

Although CL promises to provide significant benefits, some aspects of CL theory and practice may be quite problematic. This Article focuses particularly on the disqualification agreement, which CL practitioners argue is essential to create a positive negotiation environment and encourage parties to settle. Though this encouragement is undoubtedly helpful in many cases, it also can invite abuse. This agreement creates incentives for lawyers to pressure their clients to settle inappropriately and leave clients without an effective advocate to promote their interests and protect them from settlement pressure. Indeed, the disqualification agreement may violate ethical rules designed to protect clients from being pressured by their lawyers. Thus this Article identifies a major paradox of CL: the feature that CL practitioners believe to be indispensable may actually conflict with ethical norms and harm some clients. In particular, this Article analyzes how the disqualification agreement may effectively increase lawyers' control of negotiation and decrease clients' control. Even if courts and ethics committees do not determine that the disqualification agreement violates ethical rules, its operation raises serious concerns about the nature and effects of CL practice. Moreover, although CL practitioners would dearly love to extend CL practice to general civil and business disputes, the disqualification agreement is a major barrier to acceptance by major businesses and law firms.

This Article offers only conditional conclusions about the merits of the disqualification agreement and CL practice generally because most courts and bar association ethics committees have not yet grappled with difficult cases involving CL and there is virtually no empirical research analyzing how people have used it and what the results have been. [T]raditional rules of legal ethics do not clearly answer questions about the propriety of disqualification agreements and thus recommends that courts and ethics committees should approve them if they find that these agreements do not produce a significant risk of serious harm to clients. This Article urges CL groups to experiment by offering clients similar processes with and without disqualification agreements to provide clients greater choice and to test the effects of the disqualification agreements.

QUESTIONS

1.   Stuart Webb, a founder of the collaborative law movement, notes that collaborative law participation agreements typically include other commitments besides the disqualification provision:

> "Attorneys do not deceive or intentionally mislead. Welfare of children is paramount. Attorneys explore reconciliation. Attorneys do not to threaten to withdraw from the collaborative process for tactical reasons. Attorneys do not impair the neutrality of experts. Attorneys respect other dispute resolution approaches."

Stu Webb, *Collaborative Law: A Practitioner's Perspective on Its History and Current Practice*, 21 J. Am. Acad. Matrim. Law. 155, 162 (2008).

Other common features of participation agreements include terms committing parties to negotiate in good faith, act respectfully toward each other, disclose all relevant information, use jointly retained experts, protect confidentiality of communications, and refrain from formal discovery and contested litigation during negotiation

2.   Would you feel your obligation to represent your clients zealously would be compromised, or enhanced, by a collaborative law agreement?

3.   Recall the different models for the attorney-client relationship discussed in Chapter II (traditional, client-centered, and collaborative). Which of the three might lend itself to collaborative lawyering? How would a collaborative law arrangement affect negotiations between the attorney and the client? Would the lawyer have more or less control?

4.   Would you advise your client to be forthright with respect to sensitive information during a collaborative law negotiation?

5.   Collaborative lawyering was largely pioneered in the family law area. What other types of disputes might lend themselves to a collaborative law arrangement? What types would not? *See, e.g.,* Kathleen Clark, *The Use of Collaborative Law in Medical Error Situations,* Health Lawyer, June 2007, at 19.

6.   What barriers might there be to establishing a collaborative law group in your community? For an empirical study of collaborative law in Canada, see Julie Macfarlane, *Experiences of Collaborative Law: Preliminary Results of the Collaborative Lawyering Research Project*, 2004 J. Disp. Resol. 179.

7.   The American Bar Association has weighed in on the disqualification provision, holding in 2007 that a disqualification provision in

a collaborative law participation agreement does not violate ethics rules under the Model Rules of Professional Conduct, which have been adopted in a majority of states:

> Before representing a client in a collaborative law process, a lawyer must advise the client of the benefits and risks of participation in the process. If the client has given his or her informed consent, the lawyer may represent the client in the collaborative law process. A lawyer who engages in collaborative resolution processes still is bound by the rules of professional conduct, including the duties of competence and diligence.

American Bar Association Standing Committee on Ethics and Professional Responsibility, Formal Opinion 07–447, Ethical Considerations in Collaborative Law Practice (2007).

For critiques of the ABA ethics opinion, see Scott R. Peppet, *The Ethics of Collaborative Law*, 2008 J. Disp. Resol 131 (2008); John Lande & Forrest S. Mosten, *Collaborative Lawyers' Duties to Screen the Appropriateness of Collaborative Law and Obtain Clients' Informed Consent to Use Collaborative Law* (forthcoming).

The Ethics Committee of the Colorado State Bar has taken the opposite view, finding that the disqualification provision violates standards of client loyalty required by the state's rules of professional conduct. Ethics Committee of the Colorado Bar Association, Formal Ethics Opinion 115, Ethical Considerations in the Collaborative and Cooperative Law Context (2007). For a critique, see Scott R. Peppet, *Colorado Ethics Opinion 115: Next Steps for Colorado's Collaborative Lawyers*, Colo. L., Sept. 2007, at 37.

8.   The National Conference of Commissioners on Uniform State Laws moved quickly to embrace collaborative law, and adopted the Uniform Collaborative Law Act in 2009, and amended it in 2010. The act's critical features include a privilege for collaborative law communications, a section specifying what must be in a participation agreement in order to qualify as a collaborative law agreement, and a definitions section that provides a common understanding of the basic terms of the process. As of this writing, the act had been adopted by Alabama, Utah, Nevada, Texas, Hawaii, Ohio, the District of Columbia, and Washington State. For the latest developments, see the Uniform Law Commission web site at http://www.uniformlaws.org/ Act.aspx?title=Collaborative%20LawÄct.

Unlike most other uniform laws, however, the American Bar Association House of Delegates refused to endorse the act for submission. Why not, do you suppose? On the other hand, a relatively new movement in dispute resolution, it already has spawned another dispute resolution process: cooperative law. Cooperative law is similar to collaborative law in that it is a process whereby the parties agree to negotiate cooperatively, but the process is less structured and does not include a disqualification provision in their participation agreements. *See generally* John Lande, *Practical Insights From an Empirical Study of Cooperative Lawyers in Wisconsin*, 2008 J. Disp. Resol.

203. Would you feel more comfortable as a cooperative lawyer than as a collaborative lawyer?

b. Partnering

JOHN G. BICKERMAN, PARTNERING IN THE CONSTRUCTION INDUSTRY: TEAMING UP TO PREVENT DISPUTES
Prob. & Prop. Mar./Apr. 1995, at 61, 61, 61–63, 64

Construction projects involve a complex web of relationships among owners, developers, general and subcontractors, architects, suppliers and future users such as tenants or purchasers. Success of a project often requires close teamwork, cooperation and flexibility to adapt to constantly changing circumstances. Not long ago, projects involved local participants who knew each other and had long-term relationships. They shared a certain level of trust and interdependence. The economic well-being of one depended on the profitability and success of its contracting partners.

Today, relationships among construction parties have broken down. Technological improvements make building projects more complicated and mandate greater sophistication and expertise. Because projects are less likely to be local or even regional, parties frequently do not know each other and are unlikely to maintain continuing working relationships.

* * *

Partnering can realign relationships in a cooperative and economically beneficial manner. Lawyers also can thrive by advising clients on maximizing the benefits of these new relationships instead of protecting clients against all real or imagined risks.

Preventing Disputes Through Partnering

The success of ADR techniques depends on identifying the needs and interests of parties and maximizing solutions that recognize those needs and interests—in other words, finding "win-win" outcomes. Partnering applies the "win-win" philosophy to construction projects by reforming the working relationships of the complex network of project participants. Rather than promoting competition for the moment, value is placed on long-term relationships that extend beyond a single project. Long-term profitability is prized above the profit of a single job. Instead of responding to the four corners of the specifications in a bid proposal, parties learn the needs and advance the objectives of one another. Innovation and deviation from specifications are encouraged. Thus, the concept of partnering can be summarized in three dimensions: trust, shared vision and longterm commitment. All parties hold stakes in the successful outcome of the project and share risks and rewards.

Reversing 100 Years of Learned Behavior

Partnering is not pie in the sky. Fortune 500 companies—including Bechtel, Shell Oil, Union Carbide, DuPont, Procter & Gamble and IBM—have been entering into partnering relationships for the last decade. The United States Army Corps of Engineers uses partnering frequently and credits partnering with the success of such large projects as the $70 million Tombigbee Waterway, the multimillion dollar Bonneville Navigation Lock renovation and the construction of the Cape Canaveral Test Operation Control Center project. The Corps has used partnering at least 18 other times. The United States Air Force salvaged a multimillion dollar construction project at Patrick Air Force Base through partnering.

The mechanics of partnering are surprisingly simple. First and most critically, the parties must agree to adopt the process. Senior management must understand the concept and commit the company. Managers must comprehend the implications of the partnering arrangement positively, judge partnering's value to the organization and make an endorsement to proceed.

Second, the intent to use partnering must be communicated to prospective bidders as early as possible—ideally, in the request for proposals or the bid invitation. As finalists are identified through the bidding process, the partnering arrangement must be explained to senior management of potential contractors. Final awards should be based, in part, on the commitment of bidders to embrace a partnering arrangement.

Third, senior management of all organizations that have agreed to partnering must communicate their commitment to staff who will be responsible for performing the design and construction tasks. Partnering starts at the top and must emanate through the organization to reach the multitude of significant individuals who, because of their constant interaction, make or break the partnering arrangement.

Fourth, the parties should select a neutral facilitator to assist the partnering process. Partnering depends on trust and open communication. Particularly at the outset, when participants' needs and objectives must be articulated clearly to other organizations, a neutral's participation could be essential to the success of the partnering arrangement.

Fifth, shortly after contract award and before start-up, all parties should meet to develop a charter. The charter is a non-contractual statement embodying the objectives and expectations of the parties and setting forth principles by which all signatories agree to conduct themselves. The process of creating a partnering charter is intended to fuse members of different organizations into a cohesive unit that shares common goals.

Partnering Differences

The partnering charter that expresses the parties' joint expectations and shared vision can change the behavior and accepted practices of the parties. For example, partnering can alter the way participants allocate risk, share rewards and resolve disputes.

Over time, risk allocation has shifted steadily downstream to smaller and smaller parties that frequently are least able to absorb the risk and most often have inferior bargaining power to negotiate otherwise. Owners, particularly public owners, have become more averse to risk in recent years. Owners have sought to "fix" the costs of a project at the outset and thus have shifted the risk of surprises to other parties.

Typically, owners can shift risk in three ways. First, they may use contractual provisions that deny contractors damages for delay. Under normal conditions, contractors base their bids on being able to perform according to a pre-ordained work schedule. Although some contingencies may be built into the bids, if an owner substantially interferes with a contractor's start-up or access, the unintended delays increase the contractor's cost. Contractors who are unable to recoup increased expenses due to delay through no fault of their own may be resentful and seek other ways to recover lost profit.

Second, owners may seek to avoid responsibility for differing conditions. If actual conditions are different from those a contractor in good faith expected (and based its bid on), then a contractor may reasonably expect additional compensation for additional work. A provision that requires a contractor to assume the risk of differing conditions asks that contractor to pay for circumstances over which it has no control.

Third, owners desire global indemnification against all potential claims. Owner indemnification clauses are primarily intended to protect owners against claims from workplace injuries by the contractor's employees. Other claims appear to be relatively insignificant. Although owners may reasonably require contractors to indemnify them against claims for job site injuries to third parties, many clauses now require complete owner indemnification, even for claims caused by owner negligence over which the contractor has no control.

A more sensible allocation of risks achieved through partnering might lessen conflict among construction participants during a project. Satisfied participants are those that can earn a reasonable profit for work performed. The seeds of discord are sown when a participant does not realize a profit because it shouldered an unreasonable share of the risks. A partnering arrangement that acknowledges the rights of all parties to earn a reasonable profit for work performed is more likely to result in a sensible and manageable allocation of risks that, in turn, avoids disputes.

Thus, the product of a partnering agreement might be allocation of the risk of unknown events to all parties. Similarly, a partnering arrangement could include a compensation mechanism for delay that increases contractor expenses.

A partnering arrangement might lead to an agreement by the contractors to carry insurance for owner liability for workplace injuries. This coverage is relatively affordable and would limit the scope of indemnification clauses to the most likely risks. Contractors also could insure architects and other design professionals, thereby effectively indemnifying these parties against claims for workplace injuries. Owners, in turn, might agree to limit the liability of contractors and design professionals and carry insurance for excess risks. The potential solutions to the problems of risk are limited only by the ingenuity of the partnering participants.

Just as risks can be shared in a partnering arrangement, so too can the parties share rewards when goals are met. A partnering arrangement can set out positive incentives that reinforce cooperative relationships. All parties may realize benefits if the project is a success.

For example, increases in revenues or cost savings from early completion or efficient construction could be shared according to a pre-negotiated formula for the parties. Alternatively, an owner could regularly evaluate performance. The contractor's performance could be graded based on objective, predetermined criteria that extend beyond timeliness of completion and include quality criteria. Based on the grades received, the contractor would be entitled to additional payments.

Under a third scheme, in lieu of rewarding individual contractors, incentives could be tied to the work of several different participants. Parties whose joint gain depends on collectively reaching certain goals may work together more cooperatively and effectively.

Finally, rewards can be extended to individual employees. Rewarding key personnel with performance bonuses may encourage success. A partnering arrangement recognizes the desire of all individuals and parties to share in the rewards of a job well done. An incentive scheme is a likely manifestation of a partnering arrangement.

Resolving Disputes as They Occur

By opening communication lines, partnering should reduce conflict, but disagreements during construction are inevitable. No matter how well one plans, disputes occur. Resolving disputes when they arise in the course of construction is cost-effective and, more important, instrumental in maintaining positive working relationships among construction parties. If disputes fester and await resolution until project completion, positions harden. Less expensive solutions that could have been implemented during the course of construction are lost. Informal dispute resolution techniques yield to more expensive formalized procedures such as arbitration or litigation.

Although partnering may not eliminate all arguments, the arrangement provides the foundation for prompt dispute resolutions. For example, "step negotiations" provide for the measured escalation of a dispute to ascending orders of management. If a dispute cannot be resolved by the line staff, the immediate supervisors (who may not be as intimately invested in the decision) are asked to confer and seek a solution. Junior management has a powerful incentive to demonstrate to their superiors their problem-solving abilities and to keep messy problems from moving up the hierarchy. If the immediate supervisors fail, their superiors step in. In that way, more senior management is "on call" to resolve problems before they get out of hand. Under a partnering arrangement, step negotiations are more likely to succeed because senior management has committed itself to cooperate and make conflict settlement a priority.

* * *

The Lawyer's Role

Under the adversarial model of construction contracting, lawyers draft and implement contractual provisions that protect their clients from such uncertainties as the untoward behavior of other parties and shift the consequences of the unknown to others. The goal, of course, is to maximize the client's profit on each project. When contract language is not followed, lawyers attempt to vindicate their client's rights through lawsuits, arbitration or ADR.

The same skills that make lawyers so good in the adversarial model have application to the cooperative model associated with partnering. Lawyers are trained to identify client needs and interests. They can be skilled communicators through the written and spoken word. Lawyers may also be able to lend a more objective eye to critical issues than a client blinded by its partisan perspective. In a partnering arrangement, lawyers can be valuable resources to clients, using these skills to develop the partnering charter. When disputes arise, lawyers may be more likely to understand the needs of other parties and craft solutions that address those needs while meeting the client's interests as well. In addition, experienced lawyers could make excellent facilitators or job site neutrals.

c. Online Dispute Resolution

LOUIS DEL DUCA, COLIN RULE AND ZBYNEK LOEBL, FACILITATING EXPANSION OF CROSS–BORDER E–COMMERCE—DEVELOPING A GLOBAL ONLINE DISPUTE RESOLUTION SYSTEM

1 Penn. St. J. L. & Int'l Aff. 59, 59–74 (2012)

I. THE GROWING NEED FOR ONLINE DISPUTE RESOLUTION (ODR)

A. *Birth of the Internet—Origin and Evolution of ODR Systems*

The advent of the Internet and subsequent development of the World Wide Web (or "the Web") ushered in a new era of understanding about the world in which we live and forever changed peoples' conceptions of human interaction. Today, individuals can communicate their ideas across continents, retrieve their news from multiple sources simultaneously, and conduct their business in a global marketplace. However, just as disputes can arise in the context of real-world interactions, so too can they arise in the context of online-world interactions.

* * *

B. *Developments in e-Commerce and ODR*

The real driver for the expansion of ODR was and is commerce. Business-to-business (B2B) and business-to-consumer (B2C) e-commerce has grown exponentially in the past decade, due in large part to the rising number of individuals connected to the Internet. In the late 1990s roughly between 2% and 5% of the world's population used the Internet. By 2010, however, that percentage had increased to nearly 30%, with users dispersed over every geographic region around the globe. The acceptance of the Internet as a commercial trading platform also increased and continues to increase as the number of commercial transactions that consumers complete online continues its meteoric rise, so too does the amount these consumers are spending.

From 1999 to 2009, for example, the value of e-commerce in the United States alone expanded nearly 400% from $33 billion in 1999, at best, to $182 billion in 2009. At the same time, internet usage in the United States expanded from 36.6% of the population to an enormous 78.1%. For the period 2009–2015, as indicated in the graph which follows, e-commerce sales in the United States are projected to rise 10% a year to a total of $279 billion by 2015.

For the period of 2010–2015 worldwide, e-commerce sales are projected to rise at the rate of 19% per year from a total $572.5 billion to $1.4 trillion in 2015, as indicated in the graph, which follows.

This significant growth of e-commerce in the last decade and the projected continuing growth has spurred the development of various public and private initiatives aimed at providing redress to both businesses and consumers involved in domestic disputes arising out of online transactions.

Disputes arising in the online context can vary considerably and are often extremely difficult for courts to handle for a number of reasons, including: the high volume of claims, the contrast between the low value of the transaction and the high cost of litigation, the question of applicable law (in both e-commerce and consumer protection contexts), and the difficulty of enforcement of foreign judgments. For years, courts all over the world have been promoting the use of Alternative Dispute Resolution (ADR) as an effective, and even preferred, substitute for litigation. ADR has been praised for its speed, flexibility, informality, and its solution-oriented (as opposed to blame-oriented) approach to conflict resolution. However, traditional ADR methods, such as arbitration, have proven to be less than helpful tools for addressing the complications inherent in judicial resolution of web-based transactional disputes.

Unlike other dispute resolution processes, ODR is a fast, efficient, flexible, and inexpensive mechanism for handling e-commerce disputes, both at the domestic level and across borders. ODR processes provide businesses and consumers with a simple and reliable process through which to resolve conflicts arising out of their online interactions. ODR works the way the internet works, with resolutions built directly into websites and transaction flows, as opposed to being imposed by a central judicial authority that is completely separate from the online environment where the issue arose. ODR is also cross-jurisdictional and independent of any single set of laws or regulations, which is a better fit with the global nature of the internet. ODR offers clear benefits to both buyers and sellers: consumers appreciate the ability to get their issues resolved quickly and painlessly, and merchants like how consumers are more willing to make purchases (and pay higher prices) when they know a fair and painless resolution process is available to them. ODR also unlocks new demand from cross-border buyers who might have been averse to making purchases outside of their home geography without a clear resolution process. In essence, ODR is the best approach to providing redress and justice on the internet.

II.   EXISTING AND PROPOSED ODR SYSTEMS— SUBSTANTIVE PRINCIPLES FOR LOW–VALUE/HIGH– VOLUME FAST TRACK CLAIMS

A.   *eBay*

eBay, an American Internet company launched in 1995 with experience in B2B, B2C, and consumer-to-consumer transactions, has made numerous acquisitions over the years, including the PayPal payment service in 2002. In 2009, eBay added to the dispute resolution services available through PayPal and initiated an on-eBay ODR platform for resolving "item not received" and "item not as described" claims. Today, the eBay platform handles over 60 million e-commerce disputes annually. These disputes have an average value of $70–100 and each are processed through a Resolution Center that enables parties to resolve their problems amicably through direct communication. The number of disputes being resolved through eBay's online platform is expanding steadily as the transaction volume on the site increases at about 13% per year. More than $45 billion in merchandise is sold on eBay each year and eBay has more than 90 million active buyers and sellers, in 16 languages and 36 countries around the globe as well as Hong Kong.

eBay also provides information to facilitate identification of reliable sellers. eBay makes extensive use of a Feedback system, which keeps market participants honest and avoids possible disputes. Currently, eBay houses more than four billion feedback ratings left by transaction participants for each other. The system allows participants to make informed choices about whom they will trade with based on reports of positive or negative experience. eBay assigns parties a "star" based on how many positive reviews they have received. For example, if the seller has 10 to 49 positive ratings, they get a yellow star and if the seller has 50 to 99 positive ratings they get a blue star. A seller with a million or more positive ratings is entitled to a "shooting silver star." This system allows buyers to see at a glance, how trusted the seller is by other market participants. Merchants have a strong incentive to take good care of their buyers so as to avoid receiving negative feedback, which can harm their future commercial prospects.

In the feedback system, like the dispute resolution system, buyers and sellers are treated differently. Buyers can leave positive, neutral, or negative ratings while sellers can only leave short comments and positive ratings. Although this is a system, which exacts honesty from sellers by the threat of a negative rating, eBay is very clear, that feedback extortion and manipulation is not allowed. For example, buyers cannot use threats of poor feedback to demand a refund or some additional good or service, which was not included in the purchase price. Similarly, sellers are not allowed to demand positive Feedback from buyers in return for expedited shipping or other services. While eBay does not issue trustmarks to vendors, prospective buyers nevertheless are able to identify reliable vendors in any one of the thirty-six countries plus Hong Kong in which eBay operates based on the billions of feedback ratings left by previous transaction participants. This achieves two of the main goals of any trustmark system: 1) empowering buyers with information; and 2) facilitating compliance of vendors with awards, so that they will receive positive ratings in the feedback system.

Under the eBay Buyer Protection Policy, buyers can file a report when they have not received an item they purchased or if the item was received but did not match the seller's description. Only consumers who buy items from the U.S. eBay site and use an eligible payment method may file a claim and that claim must be based on a "good faith dispute" between the buyer and seller of "goods." Sellers can also file through eBay when they have not received a payment or when they need to cancel a transaction. The types of claims for buyers offered for resolution under the policy include:

1.   The buyer did not receive the items within the estimated delivery date; or

2.   The item received was wrong, damaged, or different from the seller's description. For example:

    i.   Buyer received a completely different item;

    ii.   The condition of the item is not as described;

    iii.   The item is missing parts or components;

    iv.   The item is defective during the first use;

    v.   The item is a different version or edition from the one displayed in the listing;

    vi.   The item was described as authentic but is not;

    vii. The item is missing major parts or features, and this was not described in the listing;

    viii. The item was damaged during shipment; or

    ix.   The buyer received the incorrect amount of items.

The eBay Buyer Protection Policy is not a product warranty of any kind and applies only to the transaction. The policy covers only the original purchase price and the shipping cost; it does not cover "damages." The buyer therefore retains rights to bring suit in an appropriate forum to recover "damages." eBay also has a more limited dispute resolution system for sellers, which permits them to file claims against buyers, but only for nonpayment of an item.

       * * *

C.   *Internet Corporation for Assigned Names and Numbers (ICANN)*

Since 2000, the Internet Corporation for Assigned Names and Numbers (ICANN) has been operating an online arbitration system to resolve domain name disputes across borders. Instead of forcing a party engaged in trademark infringement to file suit in court, a party can simply submit a complaint to an ICANN-approved dispute resolution provider and resolve the entire matter online. ICANN's domain name dispute resolution system has been highly successful and it resolves thousands of disputes across borders annually.

ICANN lists the types of claims offered for resolution through its online dispute resolution as follows:

1. A Domain Name Transfer;

2. An Unsolicited Renewal or Transfer Solicitation;

3. Accreditation;

4. An Unauthorized Transfer of Your Domain Name;

5. A Trademark Infringement;

6. A Uniform Domain Name Dispute Resolution (UDRP) Decision;

7. A Registrar Service;

8. Inaccurate Who is Data;

9. Spam or Viruses; and

10. Content on a Website.

Although ICANN offers an array of online dispute proceedings, the remedies are very limited. The remedies are primarily limited to the cancellation or change of a registered name. ICANN has an approval process for selecting providers and requires that a provider have a track record, list of potential panelists, and requested limitation on the number of proceedings.

To initiate a dispute, the Complainant must give the Respondent actual notice about the complaint. Once the Respondent has received actual notice, he has twenty days to respond. The Complainant is responsible for all fees. The selected panel will initiate and conduct the proceedings. Panelists are required to be impartial and independent. The panel can determine which remedies to grant. All decisions by the panel are published over the internet. The panel must forward its decision to the provider within fourteen days and the provider must relay the decision to the opposing parties within three days.

D. Better Business Bureau (BBB)

"The Council of Better Business Bureaus (CBBB) is a not-for-profit organization representing its 122 member Better Business Bureaus throughout the United States and Canada." A local Better Business Bureau (BBB) office is a nonprofit organization supported by local businesses. BBBs assist in the resolution of disputes between a business and its customers. When a marketplace dispute arises, BBBs work with the business and the customer to reach a resolution using various dispute resolution processes. Each process provides an alternative to going to court. Through the use of an online complaint system, BBBs help to resolve thousands of complaints each year.

Most BBBs offer several dispute resolution methods to help resolve disputes, such as conciliation, mediation, informal dispute resolution, conditionally binding arbitration, and binding arbitration. The BBB Online Complaint System handles disagreements between businesses and their customers; it will not resolve workplace disputes, discrimination claims, matters that are or have been litigated, or claims about the quality of health or legal services.

A customer's submitted claim is forwarded to the business within two business days. The business is then asked to respond within fourteen days. If a response is not received, a second request is made. The customer is notified of the business's response once the BBB receives it, or is notified that no response was sent. Complaints are usually closed within thirty business days.

The BBB also uses a trustmark system to help consumers in identifying reliable vendors. The BBB allows vendors who meet the BBB's standards to be "accredited." These standards include being "trustful," "honest in advertising," and "transparent." Additionally, vendors agree to "fulfill contracts signed and agreements reached as well as honor representations by correcting mistakes as quickly as possible." Accredited businesses are allowed to display BBB Accredited Business marks (*i.e.* trustmarks in their stores, online, or in other advertising). This trustmark signals to the consumer that the business meets BBB standards and that BBB dispute resolution will be available to him if he transacts with that business.

* * *

F. *Chargeback Procedures*

Chargebacks are ODR procedures which can be used by buyers if a credit card is used for payment of any type of purchase whether in a store or online. Chargebacks can also be used for purchases made in the service industry, such as at a hotel or restaurant. While each credit card company uses a slightly different process, the general process used by all companies is very similar. Consumers initiate a chargeback after an issue arises following a purchase. Examples of transaction issues that might lead to chargebacks are non-delivery of goods or delivery of substantially different goods. After the consumer contacts their credit card issuer and files a chargeback, the funds are immediately reversed from the seller's merchant account back to the buyer. The merchant has the ability to "re-present" the charge, disputing the buyer's assertions, which results in another immediate reversal of the funds back to the seller. The process can continue in this manner for several iterations with fees charged for each additional reversal. Cases that continue back and forth may eventually be arbitrated by the card network (e.g. Visa or MasterCard), but that arbitration can be quite expensive, so there is a strong incentive to either resolve or give up the case prior to reaching that point.

In the United States, federal law requires credit card companies to allow chargebacks. To take advantage of this system, a buyer must notify the credit card company of the disputed charge within sixty days of receiving notice of the charge from the credit card company. If the buyer alleges that the charge is incorrect because the goods were not delivered "in accordance with the agreement made at the time of the transaction," the credit card company must undertake an investigation to determine whether or not that is true. Under these regulations chargebacks extend only to consumer and not to business transactions. In Europe, credit card companies are not required to provide chargeback services. Although chargebacks are not as prevalent in Europe as in the United States, they are still used fairly frequently. The availability of chargebacks in countries where such a mechanism is not mandated indicates their popularity and usefulness to both credit card issuers and credit card users.

Each credit card company currently has a slightly different chargeback system. For example, the types of claims that the companies process vary. Visa, MasterCard, and Discover for example, have claims for "Illegible transaction receipt," while American Express does not. However, generally the companies have claims for the same types of transactions. Examples of these universal transactions include fraudulent and counterfeit transactions, declined authorizations and failure to receive merchandise.

While many of the reasons for a chargeback do not include any buyer-seller interaction, there are a number of situations in which the buyer-seller interaction may lead to a chargeback. The four most common reasons for a chargeback are a) non-delivery, b) delivery of non-conforming goods or services, c) charges after cancellation of a recurring transaction, and d) duplicate processing of a single transaction.

Consumers cannot receive damages in a chargeback process. They will either be re-billed, with the new bill showing an absence of the disputed charge, or their account will be credited with the disputed amount.

Quite often a payment facilitator is also involved in the chargeback process. For example, PayPal, a company which helps consumers pay electronically online, does not begin or administer chargebacks, but does facilitate the process from the seller's side. After a buyer has independently initiated a chargeback with their credit card issuer, the card network contacts PayPal and PayPal places a hold on the seller's PayPal funds related to the chargeback. PayPal then requests information from the seller that could help to determine whether the charge should be "re-presented" to the buyer, effectively disputing the buyer's account of the issue. PayPal uses the chargeback system as a separate process, distinct from another dispute resolution process handled entirely by PayPal. Buyers must choose which system to use, the PayPal claims process or the credit card chargeback process. The buyers may not pursue claims using both systems, so if the buyer initiates a PayPal claim process and subsequently files a chargeback through their card issuer, the PayPal claim is immediately shut down and the chargeback process takes precedent. In dealing with Chargebacks, PayPal works only with the seller, because the buyer is working through their card issuer. PayPal specialists help sellers by disputing the chargebacks on their behalf, because PayPal is actually the merchant of record in the transaction. Some credit card companies also have detailed instructions on their websites dedicated to helping sellers avoid and dispute chargebacks.

NOTES AND QUESTIONS

1.   The internationalization of commerce begs for a unitary means of resolving conflict that arise from online transactions involving parties from different nations. The United Nations Commission on International Trade Law (UNCITRAL) Working Group III has been negotiating international ODR procedures since 2010. As of this writing, its proposed rules establish a two-tiered binding dispute resolution process—one for consumer disputes and the other for business-to-business—that exists apart the transaction channel (i.e., not with the payment intermediary or another online intermediary). They rules would require disputants to use an automated negotiation process first, and if no resolution is reached, proceed to binding online arbitration. The arbitrator would have the authority under the rules to broker a settlement before issuing a final, binding award. Do you see any problems with this structure? For a critique, see Vikki Rogers, *Managing Disputes in the Online Global Marketplace: Reviewing the Progress of UNCITRAL's Working Group III on ODR*, 19 DISP. RESOL. MAG 20 (Spring 2013). For the latest, see http://www.uncitral.org/uncitral/commission/working_groups/3On line_Dispute_Resolution.html (last checked Aug. 24, 2013).

2.   Confidentiality is a concern with online dispute resolution. There are at least four sources of confidentiality in online dispute resolution: encryption, which prevents the interception of data or renders intercepted data meaningless; laws that preclude the interception of electronic communications; private confidentiality agreements, which bar the disclosure of dispute resolution communications; and professional industry standards. For a general discussion, see Llewellyn Joseph Gibbons, *Private Law, Public "Justice": Another Look At Privacy, Arbitration, and Global E–Commerce*, 15 Ohio St. J. on Disp. Resol. 769, 773–78 (2000).

3.   Many mediators believe that there is an intangible quality or dynamic that arises "in the room" of a traditional "face-to-face" mediation session, where the parties (and the mediator), are able to evaluate the credibility of statements and to assess options that emerge during the meeting. Under this view, non-verbal communication can often be as important as verbal communication. *See generally* BARBARA MADONIK, I HEAR

WHAT YOU SAY, BUT WHAT ARE YOU TELLING ME? THE STRATEGIC USE OF NONVERBAL COMMUNICATION IN MEDIATION (2001). Online mediation is only textual, however, meaning that parties do not have the opportunity to assess, for example, tone of voice, or body language, or reactions to statements. How would the absence of this information affect a mediation? Would your answer depend upon the subject matter of the mediation?

4.   As the authors describe, ODR has been effective in handling disputes involving online providers like EBay. Are there other types of disputes that ODR might be less suited for? Would it be helpful to integrate online technology into a broader dispute resolution effort? For example, in a public policy mediation, might it be helpful to use web-based preference polling to assess the relative strengths and weaknesses of specific proposals? How about using email to facilitate a dispute between business partners?

5.   What are the implications of online mediation for mediator style? Would an online format necessarily lend itself to a more elicitive or directive style? SquareTrade mediators may not evaluate, for example. Is there something about the online environment that might have led the program designers to include this prohibition?

6.   Time and geography appear to be two dimensions in which online dispute resolution adds potential value. There is no need for simultaneous convening of the parties, since the parties can respond to mediation communications from their homes, offices, even internet cafes. That means ODR can be used by people in different parts of the country, and indeed the world. Similarly, parties might have greater choice with respect to mediators because the mediators need not come from the same community (assuming the ODR provider permits consumers to know the identity of the neutral). Moreover, the fact that the online mediation may not be conducted in "real" time might give parties more time to reflect on statements made during the mediation. What disadvantages might this flexibility create? For a nice summary of the pros and cons of using online dispute resolution, see Orna Rabinovich, *Going Public: Diminishing Privacy in Dispute Resolution in the Internet Age,* 7 Va. J.L. & Tech. 4, 89–109 (2002).

7.   How might online mediation affect power disparities between the parties? *See* Robert C. Bordone, Note, *Electronic Online Dispute Resolution: A Systems Approach—Potential, Problems, and a Proposal,* 3 Harv. Negot. L. Rev. 175, 185–93 (1998).

8.   Would you expect online mediation to improve or exacerbate cultural barriers to dispute resolution? *See* Orna Rabinovich, *Going Public: Diminishing Privacy in Dispute Resolution in the Internet Age,* 7 Va. J.L. & Tech. 4, 107 (2002).

9.   As we saw in Chapter III, the establishment of rapport between negotiators can be helpful in overcoming interpersonal friction and finding cooperative agreements. Social scientists have found that rapport-building also facilitates negotiations conducted by email. *See* Michael Morris, Janice Nadler, Terri Kurtzberg & Leigh Thompson, *Schmooze or Lose: Social*

Friction and Lubrication in E–Mail Negotiations, 6 Group Dynamics 89 (2002). However, empirical research has also demonstrated that email negotiators also suffer from various psychological biases, including the "burned bridge" bias (tendency to engage in some riskier interpersonal behaviors they would when negotiating face to face), the "squeaky wheel" bias (tendency to adopt more aversive emotional style when negotiating by email than might be used during face-to-face negotiations), and the "sinister attribution" bias (tendency to attribute diabolical motivations to the other persons behavior). *See* Leigh Thompson & Janice Nadler, *Negotiating Via Information Technology,* 58 J. Soc. Issues 109 (2002).

CHAPTER VII

DESIGNING AND SELECTING DISPUTE RESOLUTION PROCESSES

■ ■ ■

Lawyers design and select dispute resolution processes at multiple levels. At the most general level, lawyers are involved in developing broad systems for resolving a range of disputes. For example, lawyers may participate in the creation or reform of the processes by which disputes are resolved through a court system. Lawyers also help individual clients to devise broad systems for resolving the types of disputes in which they are involved. For instance, a corporate client may need assistance developing a structure within which the client can resolve broad classes of consumer complaints, employee conflicts, and disputes with suppliers. In addition, lawyers are involved in helping individual clients select mechanisms for resolving individual disputes either before—e.g., helping a client draft a dispute resolution clause in a contractual agreement—or after the dispute arises—e.g., advising a client about the mechanisms available to help resolve a divorce. As we have seen in previous chapters, the selection of a dispute resolution process and decisions about how that process is to be organized and conducted are inextricably connected. Decisions about how the process is to be carried out may take place before the process begins, as the process unfolds, or both.

The interests and values one wishes to foster have a substantial influence on how one constructs or selects a dispute resolution process. These interests and values are likely to vary with one's circumstances and role. Thus, a proposal to establish a mandatory court-annexed mediation program might be seen quite differently by the Governor, by judges at various levels, by court staff, by lawyers concerned about their profession, by lawyers representing particular clients or classes of clients, by the litigants themselves, and so on. And, of course, perspectives will differ among individuals in each of these categories. If a system or process for resolving disputes is to function appropriately, it is important to consider each of these sets of interests. As you work through this chapter, keep in mind the perspectives of these important constituents.

The considerations involved in building and choosing dispute resolution processes have been implicit issues in each of the preceding chapters. Chapter I introduced the issues in broad terms. Chapter II considered the interviewing and counseling processes that an attorney can use to assist a client in selecting a method for resolving a particular dispute. In Chapters III through VI, we persistently inquired into the circumstances under which a particular dispute resolution method—or one of its many possible variants—was preferable to other methods. This chapter draws on these previous discussions, concentrating both on how to create a system for resolving disputes generally and on how to choose a dispute resolution mechanism for an individual dispute. Examining these topics builds on the reader's accumulated knowledge of particular processes and the comparative strengths and weaknesses of these processes.

In Section A, we reflect on several overarching considerations that come into play when designing and selecting dispute resolution processes. In Section B, we explore the processes by which systems for resolving disputes are designed and evaluated. In Section C, we examine the issues surrounding how to advise individual clients about dispute resolution processes. Finally, in Section D, the chapter ends with an exercise that requires the student to advise a client about dispute resolution options.

A. OVERARCHING CONSIDERATIONS

1. IN GENERAL

Whether one is thinking about designing a system for resolving many disputes over time or attempting to select a dispute resolution process to resolve a particular dispute, many common issues arise. First, the building blocks of a dispute resolution system and the options available to select from are the mechanisms that you have learned about in the previous chapters of this book. Whether designing a comprehensive system to resolve disputes or selecting a mechanism to resolve a particular dispute, the relative advantages and disadvantages of the various mechanisms are important factors to consider. System designers or attorneys advising clients about dispute resolution processes must also consider the appropriateness of a particular dispute resolution process given the circumstances of the system or case. The first excerpt in this section, the Report of the Ad Hoc Panel on Dispute Resolution and Public Policy that was convened in 1983 by the National Institute for Dispute Resolution, provides a comparative analysis of various dispute resolution processes.

Second, when designing a system or selecting a process, attention must be paid to how the process will be perceived by the participants. Research on how disputants assess the procedural fairness of a dispute resolution process demonstrates that judgments of procedural justice have a strong influence on disputants' willingness to use the process, their satisfaction with the process, and their willingness to comply with the outcome of the process. In the second excerpt in this section, Professor

Nancy Welsh summarizes the findings of research on procedural justice and points to its importance for dispute resolution.

Third, important issues of public policy arise when designing dispute resolution systems or selecting dispute resolution processes for particular disputes. In thinking about appropriate mechanisms for resolving particular kinds of disputes, attention should be paid to concerns that have been raised about, for example, the need for precedent, the need to protect the rights of those who are disadvantaged, or the need to protect the public interest. The final two excerpts in this section, one by Judge Harry Edwards and one by Professors Frank Sander and Stephen Goldberg, address these public policy questions.

As you read these excerpts consider the following questions: What are the advantages and disadvantages of different dispute resolution mechanisms? Under what circumstances is one or another dispute resolution process more or less appropriate? How should choices among alternatives be made? What problems might be solved or created by increased resort to the different dispute resolution processes? Consider these questions, but do not expect clear or final answers to all of them.

NAT'L INST. FOR DISPUTE RESOLUTION, PATHS TO JUSTICE: MAJOR PUBLIC POLICY ISSUES OF DISPUTE RESOLUTION
3–4, 8–18, 30, 34–35 (1983)

CHOOSING AMONG DISPUTE RESOLUTION OPTIONS

No one approach is best for resolving all disputes. The nature of the dispute and the disputants will, in large measure, determine which dispute resolution method is most appropriate. Among the characteristics that might suggest one approach over another are whether the relationship among disputants is of a continuing nature, the disputants' financial circumstances, their desire for privacy and control of the dispute resolution process, and the urgency of resolving the dispute.

One must be wary of ascribing particular attributes to one or another method of dispute resolution, however. Litigation is not always final, although that is a commonly perceived benefit; mediation may not enable parties to work together in the future, as is often suggested; arbitration may not always be less expensive than pursuing a case in court. And all dispute resolution methods may have unanticipated consequences that make them more or less desirable in particular instances.

With that caveat, the Panel reviewed the advantages and disadvantages of three major kinds of dispute resolution methods: litigation, arbitration, and mediation.

ADVANTAGES AND DISADVANTAGES OF THE COURTS

The concern expressed repeatedly by the Panel is that courts are simply too expensive and too time consuming. Although the government subsidizes a great deal of the cost of running the courts, their full use requires expensive lawyers and the time of the disputants. These costs mean that courts are generally inaccessible to all but the most wealthy parties. Hence, the courts tend to be the province of large organizations and concomitantly the ten-year anti-trust case consumes a disproportionate share of judicial resources. Thus, although courts are vitally important for protecting private rights and concerns, the delay and costs may render them ineffective in discharging this critical duty.

— Because of the relatively structured approach courts use, the range of remedies available to the court may be quite limited. Indeed, lawyers may have to reframe the issues separating the parties to fit a particular legal doctrine and, thus, may change the nature of the dispute. As a result, the court is often not able to address the real issues and tailor an appropriate remedy.

— Courts largely rely on a formal adversarial process that may further antagonize the disputing parties. Thus, a judicial approach may not be the preferred forum for settling disputes in which the parties will continue to have a close working or living relationship. Further, because the process is also somewhat mystifying to many laymen, they may become estranged from the court.

— Some disputes require a technical expertise for their resolution and, since judges are necessarily generalists, courts may be inappropriate for some controversies. In others, even though courts could be educated sufficiently to make the decision that may not be an efficient use of resources. Moreover, the existing expertise of the parties is generally not tapped in shaping a resolution because of the way roles are defined. . . .

These concerns notwithstanding, courts continue to provide indispensable services to society. They are the appropriate forum when the purpose is to establish a societal norm or legal precedent. Thus, for example, if the underlying cause of a dispute is not a disagreement over how to apply an accepted norm but rather a need to create such a principle, then courts—or the legislature—are the appropriate forum. Groups and individuals who lack economic power or social status are likely to need the courts to protect their rights and preserve their leverage in dealing with others.

Courts are also the preferred method of establishing a record of something that happened in the past. If the resolution of a dispute turns on reconstructing the facts—or at least on developing an authoritative version of the facts—then courts best serve that function. They also provide the official recognition and basis for enforcement which society demands in the resolution of some disputes, such as divorce and bankruptcy, for example.

Some cases get to court not because they have these characteristics that commend them for judicial resolution, but because of the exigencies of the situation. Some issues are sufficiently controversial that at least one of the disputants does not want to take the responsibility for voluntarily participating in its resolution. Instead, the dispute will be submitted to adjudication to deflect responsibility for the eventual, possibly unpopular, decision. School desegregation and other sensitive cases involving elected officials often fall into this category. Another example is the corporate dispute where the stakes are too high for a middle level officer to take responsibility for losing and, hence, the matter is submitted to a court to neutralize responsibility. Courts are also used sometimes when one party wants to delay a decision for as long as possible.

Most cases that are filed do not go all the way to judicial resolution. Nevertheless, filing a lawsuit may serve important functions and be a necessary prelude to using other methods for resolving disputes. It crystallizes the issues and provides the disputants with ways of compelling participation, procedures for sharing information, motivation for taking action, and deadlines for doing so. Thus, many cases are resolved through "bargaining in the shadow of the law."

* * *

ADVANTAGES AND DISADVANTAGES OF OTHER FORMS OF DISPUTE RESOLUTION

Arbitration and mediation are the two most widely known nonlitigative methods of dispute resolution. Arbitration, widely accepted and used in labor and management grievances and in some commercial settings, has special advantages over the courts, among them:

— It can be initiated without long delays; the procedure is relatively short; and a decision can be reached promptly.

— Relaxed rules of evidence enhance flexibility and the process is more streamlined than a judicial proceeding.

— The parties may select the applicable norms—that is, they can specify a particular body of law as a basis for a decision that might not be relevant in a court setting.

— The parties are able to choose the arbitrator.

— The arbitrator can be required to have expertise in the subject matter of the dispute.

— The resolution can be tailored to the circumstances.

— The dispute can be kept private since the decision is not necessarily a public document, as it would be in a court proceeding.

— Arbitration may be less expensive than going to trial.

— An arbitrator's decision is final and may be binding on the parties.

— The award in binding arbitration usually is enforceable by a court with little or no review.

In sum, with arbitration, decisions can be reached with relative speed and finality. Arbitration has proved especially valuable to parties that have a large number of disputes which must be resolved during the course of a contractual relationship. Labor-management and contractor-subcontractor relationships are examples.

But the efficiency of arbitration sometimes may be achieved at the expense of the "quality of justice" in an individual decision. In commercial and labor cases, where there is a high volume of cases with fairly low stakes, trade-offs between an expeditious, inexpensive arbitration process and the assurance of a more studied decision in each case may be acceptable. In other types of disputes, parties may not agree to arbitration because they want the protection offered by the courts, or they want to maintain control over a settlement through a process of negotiation. Thus, for example, a party may be more willing to use arbitration to determine the amount in controversy than initially to establish liability.

Further, arbitration has become so formalized in labor relations that it has developed some of the problems of procedure and delay present in judicial process. It should be noted, too, that an arbitration hearing may be more expensive and time consuming than the negotiated settlement which might otherwise have occurred.

Mediation is a valuable approach to the many disputes that are better settled through negotiation than adjudication. Among the benefits of mediation:

— It may provide an opportunity to deal with underlying issues in a dispute.

— It may build among disputants a sense of accepting and owning their eventual settlement.

— It has a tendency to mitigate tensions and build understanding and trust among disputants, thereby avoiding the bitterness which may follow adjudication.

— It may provide a basis by which parties negotiate their own dispute settlements in the future.

— It is usually less expensive than other processes.

But mediation, too, has potential shortcomings. It can be time consuming, lack an enforcement mechanism when done outside the courts (although agreements may be enforceable as contracts), and depends on the voluntary participation of all parties to a dispute and their willingness to negotiate in good faith. It does not always result in an agreement and, therefore, the resolution of a dispute.

It also raises a series of considerations related to the role of the mediator. In general, mediation works best when the parties have a rough parity of power, resources, and information. But, what is the responsibility of the mediator if there is a significant power imbalance among parties or if one party is uninformed or misinformed about the law or facts needed to make a sound decision? Should the mediator, or anyone else, have the responsibility to make certain an agreement has a principled basis and is not reached out of ignorance or fear? Should a mediator refuse to take part in resolving a dispute if one or another party may be hurt in the process or have their confidences disclosed? What are the consequences if the mediator becomes interventionist and is not perceived as impartial? In sum, assuming they can be defined, how are the ethics of the mediator assured? And, what is the appropriate role for the lawyer when a client is attempting to reach a mediated settlement?

Beyond the specifics of arbitration and mediation, there are general concerns about nonjudicial methods of dispute resolution. These methods, which might reach settlements without the use of lawyers or counselors, may lead disputants to make choices they would avoid if they were better informed. . . . Further, nonlitigative methods may merely give the appearance of resolving some disputes while avoiding a finding of more extensive liability or leaving fundamental issues unsettled (e.g., an individual settlement in a products liability case while the company keeps manufacturing the defective part or an individual settlement of a discrimination complaint while the organization continues the prohibited practice).

* * *

It should also be noted that efforts to settle disputes may not be productive if the parties have not sufficiently narrowed the issues, developed the facts, and concluded that compromise is in their best interests. Disputes somehow must be ripe for resolution before they can be settled satisfactorily. . . .

DISPUTE RESOLUTION PRINCIPLES

Comparison of various methods of dispute resolution raises complex issues. More empirical information is needed before any definite statements can be made about the appropriateness of one method over another in a particular kind of dispute. The Panel was able to conclude, however, that there are a number of major criteria by which a dispute resolution mechanism can be judged:

1.   It must be accessible to disputants. This means that the forum for resolution should be affordable to disputants as well as accessible in terms of physical location and hours of operation. Parties should be comfortable in the forum and feel that it is responsive to their interests.

2.   It must protect the rights of disputants. In cases where there is a parity of resources, influence, and knowledge, this may not be a concern. But where one party is at a disadvantage, his or her rights may be jeopardized by choice of the forum. For instance, the poorer litigant may not be able to afford full discovery, expert witnesses, etc. Similarly, a party may unnecessarily forfeit rights in mediation if without counsel.

3.   It should be efficient in terms of cost and time and, so, may have to be tailored to the nature of the dispute. Time is very important in many instances, and the forum for settlement should respond to this imperative. For example, it is obviously vital to the elderly that their disputes be settled quickly. Some disputes, especially those involving highly charged emotional issues, may take some time to settle; factual disputes may be more amenable to expeditious handling.

4.   It must be fair and just to the parties to the dispute, to the nature of the dispute, and when measured against society's expectations of justice.

5.   It should assure finality and enforceability of decision. Although the mechanism itself can discourage appeals, it may be that disputants' belief that the process was fair that will be the principal component of finality. In coercive situations, due process concerns will require that there are proceedings for review of decisions.

6.   It must be credible. The parties, their lawyers, and other representatives must recognize the forum as part of a legitimate system of justice. People who practice the alternatives, especially as judicial adjuncts, must be competent, well-trained, and responsible. Society, too, must have faith in the alternative and recognize its legitimacy.

7.   It should give expression to the community's sense of justice through the creation and dissemination of norms and guidelines so that other disputes are prevented, violators deterred, and disputants encouraged to reach resolution on their own.

The Panel recognized that it is unlikely that any dispute resolution mechanism will be equally strong in all of the seven criteria. Rather, choices will have to be made concerning which qualities are the most essential with respect to particular kinds of disputes. It is through this process of decision making and monitoring outcomes that some assessment can be made of the real implications of various forms of dispute resolution.

* * *

APPENDICES

APPENDIX 1: TABLES

General Observations on the Comparison and Evaluation of the Various Dispute Resolution Mechanisms

• Dispute mechanisms do not exist in isolation, but in close proximity to one another. They interact with and influence one another. Thus, for example, many mechanisms that work by agreement depend on the threat of resort to institutions with coercive powers. And much of what coercive institutions do, in fact, is to induce and ratify agreements between disputants.

• We usefully distinguish pure types like adjudication and mediation, but institutions usually do not operate in accordance with a single prototype. In practice, these types are combined, and much dispute processing deviates from the avowed prototype. This is particularly true of courts, where what starts as adjudication may end up as a form of mediation. And, generally, the mechanisms employing third parties with the power to make binding decisions often create a setting for negotiations between the disputants.

• Each of the types listed on the tables that follow is a composite, spanning a wide range of actual instances. For example, arbitration includes court-annexed arbitration, arbitration by standing bodies of experts within trade associations, commercial arbitration by ad hoc arbitrators supplied by the American Arbitration Association, etc. Hence the list of qualities associated with a particular mechanism can only be general and suggested and must be reassessed in relation to any specific stance of the type.

• In accounting features as strengths (advantages) or weaknesses (disadvantages), we should recall that this depends on what we want to achieve. For example, absence of a constraint to decide according to pre-existing rules may be accounted an advantage if we seek primarily resolution of the dispute at hand but may be a disadvantage if we seek to set a precedent for resolution of large numbers of claims or to forward public policy embodied in a rule.

• We must examine the advantages and disadvantages of the alternative mechanisms in both the public and private sectors. In seeking such comparisons, we must avoid false comparison between the ideal functioning of one institution and the actual functioning of another.

* * *

Table 4: Advantages/Disadvantages Associated With Dispute Resolution Mechanisms Court Adjudication

Table 4: Advantages/Disadvantages Associated With Dispute Resolution Mechanisms

1. Court Adjudication	2. Arbitration	3. Mediation/Negotiation	4. Administrative Decision-Making	5. Ombudsman	6. Internal Tribunal
– announces and applies public norms	– privacy	– privacy	– defines problem systematically	– not disruptive to ongoing relations	– privacy
– precedent	– parties control forum	– parties control process	– devises aggregate solution	– flexible	– responsive to concerns of disputants
– deterrence	– enforceability	– reflects concerns and priorities of disputants	– flexibility in obtaining relevant information	– self-starting	– enforceability
– uniformity	– expeditious	– flexible	– can accommodate multiple criteria	– easy access	
– independence	– expertise	– finds integrative solutions			
– binding/closure	– tailors remedy to solution	– addresses underlying problem			
– enforceability	– choice of applicable norms	– process educates disputants			
– already institutionalized		– high rate of compliance			
– publicly funded					
– expensive	– no public norms	– lacks ability to compel participation	– no control by parties	– not enforceable	– not independent
– requires lawyers and relinquishes control to them	– no precedent	– not binding	– not independent	– no control by parties	– no due process safeguards
– mystifying	– no uniformity	– weak closure	– not individualized		– not based on public norms
– lack of special substantive experience	– lack of quality	– no power to induce settlements			– may reflect imbalance within organization
– delay	– becoming encumbered by increasing "legalization"	– no due process safeguards			
– time-consuming		– reflects imbalance in skills (negotiation)			
– issues redefined or narrowed		– lacks enforceability			
– limited range of remedies		– outcome need not be principled			
– no compromise		– no application/development of public standards			
– polarizes, disruptive					

Table 5: Partial Listing of Characteristics That May Argue for One or Another Type of Mechanism as Appropriate

	Adjudication	Arbitration	Mediation/Negotiation
ARGUES FOR	- need to create a public norm	- high volume	- desire to preserve continuing relations
	- need to offset power imbalance	- premium on speed, privacy, closure	- emphasis on future dealings
	- need for decision on past events		- need to avoid win-lose decision
	- need to compel participation		- premium on control by disputants
			- multiple parties and issues
			- absence of clear legal entitlement
ARGUES AGAINST	- high volume, low stakes	- need for precedent	- need to compel participation
	- continuing relations		- need to enforce agreements
	- need for speedy resolution		- need to create a public norm

NOTES AND QUESTIONS

1. What factors characterize disputes that are best suited for mediation? For arbitration? For litigation? Despite the apparent simplicity of Table 5 in the preceding reading, such questions are difficult to answer in the abstract. As we have seen in previous chapters, goals, styles, and practices will vary among creators of and participants in dispute resolution processes. In addition, within each broad category of dispute resolution method, we find many quite different processes. For example, we have seen that in some negotiations and mediations, parties have no opportunity to participate directly and no one makes an effort to address underlying interests. In some courts—such as small claims courts—it is common for lawyers not to appear. Mediation can be voluntary or mandated by a court, mediation may come at different stages of the process, mediators may be selected and paid differently, and mediators and other participants may exercise differing degrees of influence. Arbitration can involve one or three arbitrators, pre- or

post-hearing briefs or no briefs. Ask yourself how these differences in form might influence the dispute resolution process and decisions about what dispute resolution processes to offer or select.

2.   In an excerpt in Chapter I, beginning at page 4, Bernard Mayer, a well-known mediator, suggests that it is valuable to consider conflict along three dimensions—cognitive, emotional, and behavioral—and that true resolution occurs only if there is resolution in all three dimensions. To what extent do the various dispute resolution processes have the potential to address each dimension? For a given case or category of cases, who should decide which dimensions should be addressed or how they might be prioritized? Should such decisions be made by program designers or by participants in the processes?

3.   Note that the processes described here are not mutually exclusive. A system for resolving disputes may incorporate several of these processes under the appropriate circumstances. *See infra* at pages 982–984. Similarly, the parties to an individual dispute may utilize several different processes before the dispute is ultimately resolved. As Professor Jean Sternlight notes:

> I see that an intertwining between litigation and other forms of dispute resolution is inevitable. Some disputants will always choose to settle their disputes, and there seems to be no way that a society could force them to resolve the dispute through litigation rather than through settlement. Just as settlements occur in the "shadow of the law," that is, that the possibility of a litigated solution is often what drives disputants to resolve the dispute through mediation or negotiation, so too does litigation take place in the shadow of settlement. As lawyers and disputants litigate cases they do, or at least should, always keep in mind the possibility of negotiation or mediation. Thus, it is generally a mistake to consider that one form of dispute resolution is entirely a substitute for others.

Jean R. Sternlight, *ADR is Here: Preliminary Reflections on Where it Fits in a System of Justice*, 3 Nev. L.J. 289, 295–96 (2002/2003).

4.   Professor Nancy Welsh calls attention to the need to understand both the available options and their variations, but also the "need to be aware that the use of *any* dispute resolution procedure or set of procedures may predictably involve particular legal problems." She points out that in order to design and choose creative and workable alternative processes, attorneys need to understand the substantive law at issue and how the alternatives considered fit (or do not fit) with existing processes. Nancy Welsh, *Integrating "Alternative" Dispute Resolution into Bankruptcy: As Simple (and Pure) as Motherhood and Apple Pie?*, 11 Nev. L.J. 397 (2011).

2.   PROCEDURAL JUSTICE

Several of the criteria the Panel gives for judging a dispute resolution mechanism relate to the fairness, justice, and legitimacy of the process. To be viewed as legitimate, a process for resolving disputes must not only result in just substantive outcomes (i.e., distributive justice), but must also consist of procedures that are perceived to be fair (i.e., procedural justice). In designing and choosing processes for resolving disputes, it is important to consider the experiences and reactions of the individuals who participate in the procedure. Below, Professor Nancy Welsh discusses the role of procedural justice in dispute resolution.

NANCY A. WELSH, MAKING DEALS IN COURT–CONNECTED MEDIATION: WHAT'S JUSTICE GOT TO DO WITH IT?
79 Wash. U. L.Q. 787, 817–26 (2001)

II. UNDERSTANDING PROCEDURAL JUSTICE

What does "justice" mean? What types of justice must or should the courts provide? This Article focuses primarily upon one type of justice— procedural justice. Procedural justice is concerned with the fairness of the procedures or processes that are used to arrive at outcomes. Distributive justice, in contrast, focuses on perceptions of and criteria to determine the substantive fairness of the outcomes themselves.

* * *

A. The Effects of Procedural Justice

Although issues of procedural justice often do not attract as much public attention as concerns about distributive justice, research has shown that when people experience dispute resolution and decision-making procedures, they "pay a great deal of attention to the way things are done [i.e., how decisions are made] and the nuances of their treatment by others." As a result, perceptions of procedural justice profoundly affect people's perceptions of distributive justice, their compliance with the outcomes of decision-making procedures and processes, and their perceptions of the legitimacy of the authorities that determine such outcomes. Perhaps surprisingly, perceptions of distributive justice generally have a much more modest impact than perceptions of procedural justice.

Research has repeatedly confirmed that people's perceptions of procedural justice mediate or influence their perceptions of distributive justice. Disputants who believe that they have been treated in a procedurally fair manner are more likely to conclude that the resulting outcome is substantively fair. In effect, a disputant's perception of procedural justice anchors general fairness impressions or serves as a fairness heuristic. Further, research has indicated that disputants who have participated in a procedure that they evaluated as fair do not change their evaluation even if the procedure produces a poor or unfair outcome.

The perception of procedural justice also serves as a shortcut means of determining whether to accept or reject a legal decision or procedure.

Disputants who believe that they were treated fairly in a dispute resolution procedure are more likely to comply with the outcome of that procedure. This effect will occur even if outcomes do not favor the disputants or they are actually unhappy with the outcomes.

Disputants' perceptions of the procedural justice provided by a decision-making authority also affect the respect and loyalty accorded to the authority. This effect is particularly strong for the courts. Thus, litigants' reactions to the institution of the judiciary and their compliance with decisions arising out of court-mandated procedures do not depend simply (or even primarily) upon whether they feel that they won or lost their cases. Rather, litigants' reactions depend largely upon their "experience of legal procedures."

B.   Process Characteristics That Enhance Perceptions of Procedural Justice

Several rather specific process characteristics enhance perceptions of procedural justice. First, perceptions of procedural justice are enhanced to the extent that disputants perceive that they had the opportunity to present their views, concerns, and evidence to a third party and had control over this presentation ("opportunity for voice"). Second, disputants are more likely to perceive procedural justice if they perceive that the third party considered their views, concerns, and evidence. Third, disputants' judgments about procedural justice are affected by the perception that the third party treated them in a dignified, respectful manner and that the procedure itself was dignified. Although it seems that a disputants' perceptions regarding a fourth factor—the impartiality of the third party decision maker—also ought to affect procedural justice judgments, it appears that disputants are influenced more strongly by their observations regarding the third party's even-handedness and attempts at fairness.

Through a long series of experiments involving many different settings and situations, disputants' opportunity for voice has been found to "reliably affect" perceptions of procedural justice. "[W]hen disputants [feel] that they [have] been allowed a full opportunity to voice their views, concerns, and evidence, the disputing process [is] seen as fairer and the outcome [is] more likely to be accepted." Concerns regarding the opportunity for voice apply in a variety of settings, including the courtroom, arbitration proceedings, contacts with the police, political decision making, and decision making in work organizations. Even in countries where the judicial systems typically use nonadversarial procedures, citizens often prefer procedures that allow a full opportunity for voice. Perhaps most surprisingly, both field and laboratory studies have demonstrated that the opportunity for voice heightens disputants' judgments of procedural justice even when they know that their voice will not and cannot influence the final outcome.

These research results are helpful as we consider the application of procedural justice to court-connected mediation, but they raise several important questions: What counts as a full opportunity for voice? How much freedom and time must disputants be given? What represents sufficient control by disputants over the presentation of their views, concerns, and evidence? Can an agent's presentation fulfill the disputants' opportunity for voice? Many of the procedural justice studies deal with these questions, directly or indirectly. * * *

The other three process characteristics that influence procedural justice judgments center upon the behavior of the third party. In particular, disputants assess the extent to which the third party hears and considers their presentations, treats them with dignity and respect, and tries to be fair and even-handed. Disputants seek assurance that the decision maker has given adequate consideration to their presentations. Apparently, while disputants care very much about having the opportunity for voice, they also wish to know that they have been heard. In one study examining citizens' interactions with police and judges, researchers found that the effect of providing an opportunity for voice was significantly enhanced if citizens also believed that the police and judges considered their views before they made decisions. Indeed, a third party's behavior, including the third party's consideration of the disputants' views, independently affects perceptions of procedural justice and "acts as a filter for . . . and an amplifier of" the disputants' subjective assessments of their control over both the outcome and the process within a particular procedure.

Disputants' perceptions of procedural justice also are influenced by how the third party interacts with them on an interpersonal level. In particular, disputants assess the degree to which the third party treats them in a polite and dignified fashion and tries to be fair and even-handed. Research has shown that disputants' procedural justice judgments are strongly influenced by the dignity or lack of dignity in decision-making proceedings. For example, in one study comparing litigants' reactions to the third-party processes of trial, arbitration, and judicial settlement conferences, the litigants gave much higher procedural justice rankings to trial and arbitration, even though these proceedings required the litigants to surrender decision-making control. Most litigants perceived trial and arbitration as dignified and careful. In contrast, settlement conferences were more likely to strike litigants as undignified and contrary to the litigants' sense of procedural fairness. Dignified and respectful treatment demonstrates to citizens that authorities recognize their own role as that of "public servants and [recognize] . . . the role of citizens as clients who have a legitimate right to certain services." Interestingly, while authorities' politeness and respect for citizens' rights have been found to influence all citizens' perceptions of procedural justice, some research suggests that minority group members particularly value the existence of these qualities in their interactions with authorities.

Significantly, several studies have shown that disputants value these process characteristics as much as, or even more than, control over the final decision (also termed "decision control"). Disputants particularly have identified the opportunity for voice as just as valuable as decision control. Other studies have demonstrated that disputants actually prefer processes in which they surrender decision control (e.g., trial and arbitration) if they perceive that these processes provide more opportunity for voice and more dignified treatment than the available consensual processes. This finding is consistent with other studies that have found that disputants' procedural justice judgments are affected much more strongly by variations in process control than by variations in decision control.

NOTES AND QUESTIONS

1.   "The procedural justice hypothesis goes against the strong intuition of many people that they and others are motivated by [monetary] self-interest. Lawyers in particular are often found to hold this view of human motivation quite vigorously." Tom R. Tyler, *Procedural Justice, in* JURY PSYCHOLOGY: SOCIAL ASPECTS OF TRIAL PROCESSES 25, 29 (Joel D. Lieberman & Daniel A. Krauss eds., 2009). But procedural justice research such as that described by Professor Welsh has demonstrated that perceptions of procedural justice play a significant role in disputants' willingness to use dispute resolution processes, their satisfaction with such processes, and their willingness to comply with the outcomes of such processes. For example, in a study of 411 felony defendants, Professor Tom Tyler and his colleagues found that defendants' assessments of the procedural fairness of their experience more strongly influenced their views of legal authorities than did the length of their sentences. Tom R. Tyler, Jonathan D. Casper, & Bonnie Fisher, *Maintaining Allegiance Toward Political Authorities: The Role of Prior Attitudes and the Use of Fair Procedures*, 33 Am. J. Pol. Sci. 629 (1989). In another study, Professor E. Allan Lind and his colleagues studied individual and corporate civil disputants who were required to participate in court-annexed nonbinding arbitration programs. Disputants could either accept the arbitration award or could reject it and proceed to a trial. The researchers found that the disputants' decisions were more strongly influenced by their perceptions of the procedural justice of the arbitration proceeding, than by the size of the arbitration award. E. Allan Lind, Tom R. Tyler, Carol T. Kulik, Maureen Ambrose, & Maria V. de Vera Park, *Individual and Corporate Dispute Resolution: Using Procedural Fairness as a Decision Heuristic*, 38 Admin. Sci. Q. 224 (1993). This is not to say that people are happy to lose: "On the contrary, no one likes to lose. However, people recognize that they cannot always win when they have conflicts with others. They accept 'losing' more willingly if the . . . procedures used to handle their case are fair." Tom R. Tyler, *Procedural Justice and the Courts*, 44 COURT REV. 26 (2007–2008).

For further reading on procedural justice, see Rebecca Hollander–Blumoff & Tom R. Tyler, *Procedural Justice and the Rule of Law: Fostering Legitimacy in Alternative Dispute Resolution*, 2011 J. Disp. Resol. 1; E. ALLAN LIND & TOM R. TYLER, THE SOCIAL PSYCHOLOGY OF PROCEDURAL JUSTICE (1988); Robert J. MacCoun *Voice, Control and Belonging: The Double–Edged Sword of Procedural Fairness*, 1 Ann. Rev. L. & Soc. Sci. 171 (2005); Tom R. Tyler & E. Allan Lind, *Procedural Justice*, in HANDBOOK OF JUSTICE RESEARCH IN LAW 65 (Joseph Sanders & V. Lee Hamilton eds., 2001).

2. The factors identified by research on the determinants of procedural justice can be used to design and select systems for resolving disputes that maximize or enhance participants' views of procedural justice. How would you assess each of the dispute resolution processes you have studied for their potential effects on perceptions of procedural justice? Within each broad category of dispute resolution process, how might these effects change with variations in procedures?

3. Psychological research indicates that the effects of procedural justice occur in two different ways. As Professor Welsh explains:

> Two theories—the "social exchange" theory and the "group value" theory—together explain the importance of procedural justice. According to the social exchange theory, disputants value the opportunity for voice because this provides them with the opportunity to influence the decision maker and indirectly influence the final outcome. Disputants "evaluate procedures in terms of the immediate financial and social benefits they receive from the procedure." Thus, procedure is important because it serves the disputants' goals of achieving favorable outcomes. As previously noted, however, research has shown that disputants value voice even when they know they cannot influence outcomes. This suggests that voice has a significance that is independent of its effect upon the outcome.

> A second theory, the "group value" theory, supplements the social exchange theory and helps to explain the inherent value of voice. The group value theory views procedures as something more than a means to achieve outcomes. The theory "emphasize[s] the symbolic and psychological implications of procedures for feelings of inclusion in society and for the belief that the institution using the procedure holds the person in high regard." By focusing on the symbolism and psychological implications of procedures, the group value theory explains the overwhelming importance of voice in affecting perceptions of procedural justice, even when such voice will not affect the outcome of a decision-making forum. The theory also provides a means for understanding the importance of dignified treatment and consideration of the views expressed by the disputants. All of these cues send powerful messages to disputants regarding their status in society, which then "validates their self-identity, self-esteem, and self-respect."

Nancy A. Welsh, *Making Deals in Court–Connected Mediation: What's Justice Got to Do With It?* 79 Wash.U.L.Q. 787, 826–27 (2001).

4.   In a RAND Corporation study of tort litigants' views of traditional trials, court-annexed arbitration, and judicial settlement conferences, the researchers concluded that litigants viewed trials and court-annexed arbitration as more fair and dignified than bilateral settlement negotiations. Judicial settlement conferences, in contrast, were viewed with more discomfort than the process of bilateral settlement negotiation, possibly because the litigants were often excluded from the conferences. E. Allen Lind, Robert MacCoun, Patricia Ebener, William L.F. Felstiner, Deborah R. Hensler, Judith Resnik & Tom R. Tyler, *In the Eye of the Beholder: Tort Litigants' Evaluations of their Experiences in the Civil Justice System*, 24 Law & Soc'y Rev. 953 (1990). Recent work by Professors Donna Shestowsky and Jeanne Brett has examined disputants' preferences and satisfaction over the course of a dispute. They find that disputants' ultimate satisfaction with adjudicative versus non-adjudicative processes varies in relation to the disputants' initial preferences for how control over the process should be allocated (i.e., controlled by the disputants or by a third-party). *See* Donna Shestowsky & Jeanne M. Brett, *Disputants' Perceptions of Dispute Resolution Procedures: A Longitudinal Empirical Study*, 41 Conn. L. Rev. 63 (2008).

5.   Consider the desires of disputants as articulated by Professor Jean Sternlight:

> Unfortunately, some people who opine on dispute resolution issues have a tendency to say that they or we know what disputants really want, when in fact the evidence is quite sparse. Thus, some mediation advocates overstate their case, suggesting that most everyone would prefer a conciliated, non-legal solution to a trial. Along somewhat the same lines, an increasing number of judges and lawyers tend to say that trials are terrible, and too much of an uncontrollable gamble for disputants, although it is not clear disputants actually share this view. Some lawyers feel it is their responsibility to educate disputants as to the failings of our litigation system. At the same time, some trial advocates also overstate their case, suggesting that most, or all, litigants would prefer to resolve their disputes in the public and adversarial courtroom.

* * *

> I believe [research] will ultimately show that disputants are generally looking for three benefits from a dispute resolution system: (1) a system that provides them with a substantively fair/just result; (2) a system that meets the procedural justice criteria of voice, participation, and dignity as set out above; and (3) a system that helps them to achieve other personal and emotional goals, such as reconciliation, or that at least does not leave them feeling worse, emotionally and psychologically. The first two points seem fairly obvious. It is hard to imagine that any system can be tolerated as fair and just in the long term if it in fact

consistently yields unfair results. In addition, although the social science literature on procedural justice needs to be developed further, and while its applicability to other kinds of societies needs to be verified, as a preliminary matter, it seems clear that the perception of justice is quite important to disputants.

The third goal is the least obvious, at least to those of us who are used to Western conceptions of justice. We recognize that disputants have emotional needs and desires. They may seek revenge, forgiveness, or reconciliation, among other things. However, we in the West have been trained to think that these emotional needs should not necessarily be served by a system of justice, or at least by a system of law. Instead, since the Enlightenment, we have become accustomed to thinking of a justice system in an almost mechanical fashion, as an institution designed to resolve disputes fairly, effectively, and according to neutral legal principles. Yet, not all societies share this limited vision as to the goals of a system of justice. Instead, many see the purposes of justice more broadly, as bringing the members of society back into balance or harmony. I believe there is no reason why we should not continue to have our system of justice serve these emotional needs, as well as the other goals set out above. Why should we not take into account psychological and emotional factors, as well as other social policies, when we set up our legal system? Surely these factors can be considered in drafting our legal procedures, just as they are considered when we adopt substantive laws. Indeed, given the inevitability that the manner in which we structure a system of procedure will impact disputants, psychologically and emotionally, do we not have an obligation to try to make this impact positive rather than negative?

Jean R. Sternlight, *ADR is Here: Preliminary Reflections on Where it Fits in a System of Justice*, 3 Nev. L.J. 289, 297–300 (2002/2003).

6. Consider the September 11th Victim Compensation Fund of 2001, Pub. L. No. 107–42, § 401 (codified at 28 C.F.R. § 104 (2003)), as a process for resolving disputes in an alternative forum. The Fund was created in the aftermath of the September 11, 2001 terrorist attacks on the World Trade Center and the Pentagon to provide compensation to injured victims and the families of deceased victims. In exchange for waiving their right to sue for damages, eligible persons were entitled to compensation for economic and non-economic losses as determined by a schedule, based on factors such as age, income, and number of dependents and reduced by collateral sources of funds such as life insurance. Tom Tyler and Hulda Thorisdottir argue that both the process of designing the Fund and the dispute resolution mechanisms initially employed by the Fund were inconsistent with principles of procedural justice:

The Fund lacks many of the procedural features that have been shown to facilitate the willingness to accept decisions made by third-party authorities:

(1) The manner in which the Fund was initially created lacked these features, because there were no hearings or other forums in which people could articulate their views about what type and level of compensation was appropriate. People did not have the opportunity to have input into creating the Fund and establishing its operating principles. Instead, Congress established the Fund in a short period of time without public hearings, and the initial design of the plan did not call for hearings involving the families of victims to discuss how compensation should be determined.

(2) The manner in which the Fund was to be implemented also lacked features such as participation, transparency, and accountability, that are typically viewed as part of fair procedures. Victims' families were not entitled to hearings, nor were the rules of allocation clearly stated. Further, there were no appeal mechanisms. Placing most of the authority for implementation in the judgments of one person, no matter how competent or well motivated, does not reflect procedural justice.

Tom R. Tyler & Hulda Thorisdottir, *A Psychological Perspective on Compensation for Harm: Examining the September 11th Victim Compensation Fund*, 53 DePaul L. Rev. 355, 375–76 (2003).

For more on the design of the Victim Compensation Fund, see Janet Cooper Alexander, *Procedural Design and Terror Victim Compensation*, 53 DePaul L. Rev. 627 (2003); Stephan Landsman, *A Chance to be Heard: Thoughts About Schedules, Caps, and Collateral Source Deductions in the September 11th Victim Compensation Fund*, 53 DePaul L. Rev. 393 (2003). Distribution of payments from the Fund was completed in June 2004 with approximately $7 billion having been paid to more than 5000 families. David W. Chen, *After Weighing Value of Lives, 9/11 Fund Completes Its Task*, N.Y. Times, June 16, 2004, at A1. How might the Fund have been designed differently to take into account the findings of procedural justice research and principles of dispute systems design?

7.   Compare the 9–11 Fund to the Gulf Coast Claims Facility created in the wake of the 2010 British Petroleum oil spill.

The GCCF established a process where claimants could file petitions for compensation from the $20 billion trust fund in exchange for waiving the right to sue the company. The volume of claims to the fund was large, and included fisherman, seafood companies, those associated with the tourism industry-like hotels, stores, and restaurants-oil workers, and state governments, which incurred cleanup costs and lost tourism revenues. Litigation also proceeded against the company in a consolidated class action including private and governmental plaintiffs. The private plaintiffs in the case reached a settlement with BP in March 2012, for $7.8 billion. The agreement replaces the GCCF fund with a new fund to be administered by the court. By this time, the company had paid out more than $8 billion to claimants and spent over $14 billion responding to the spill.

Tracy A. Thomas, *Introduction, Symposium, Remedies for Big Disasters: The BP Gulf Oil Spill and the Quest for Complete Justice*, 45 Akron L. Rev. 567, 568–69 (2012). Do the circumstances of the respective disasters affect your assessment of the procedures?

For more on the design of the Gulf Coast Claims Facility, see Symposium, *Remedies for Big Disasters: The BP Gulf Oil Spill and the Quest for Complete Justice*, 45 Akron L. Rev. 567 (2012); Linda Mullenix, *Prometheus Unbound: The Gulf Coast Claims Facility as a Means for Resolving Mass Tort Claims—A Fund Too Far*, 71 La. L. Rev. 819 (2011).

8.   Procedural justice researchers have also studied the effects of assessments of procedural justice on compliance with the law. Interestingly, these studies have consistently shown that trust in legal institutions far exceeds other factors—including agreement in the substantive correctness of the law—as the primary determinant of compliance with law. Tom R. Tyler, *Public Mistrust of the Law: A Political Perspective*, 66 U. Cin. L. Rev. 847, 856–58 (1998). More specifically, the research suggests that people are most willing to comply with the law when it is perceived to be legitimate and that the primary determinants of this entitlement or legitimacy are perceived procedural fairness and trust in the motives of legal authorities. *Id.* at 859–66. *See also* Irina Elliott, Stuart D. Thomas, & James R.P. Ogloff, *Procedural Justice in Contacts with the Police: Testing a Relational Model of Authority in a Mixed–Methods Study,* 17 Psychol., Pub. Pol'y, & L. 592 (2011). Is this consistent with your experience? Why might the core values of procedural justice resonate so deeply? Professor Reuben suggests one reason might be the consistency of these values with fundamental democratic values, including personal autonomy, participation, transparency, equality, and due process. Richard C. Reuben, *Democracy and Dispute Resolution: The Problem with Arbitration,* 67 Law & Contemp. Probs., Winter/Spring 2004, at 79.

9.   The influence of procedural justice on disputant decision making also raises the possibility that disputants will be manipulated or misled by procedures with which they are satisfied, but that lead to arguably unjust or objectively disadvantageous results—sometimes referred to as "false consciousness." What ethical issues might be raised about the use of procedural justice as a technique for social influence? *See* Tom R. Tyler, *Procedural Strategies for Gaining Deference: Increasing Social Harmony or Creating False Consciousness?* in SOCIAL INFLUENCES ON ETHICAL BEHAVIOR IN ORGANIZATIONS (John M. Darley, David M. Messick, & Tom R. Tyler eds., 2001).

3.   PUBLIC POLICY IMPLICATIONS

In addition to the procedural justice implications of a method of dispute resolution, it is also important to consider public policy implications of using alternative dispute resolution mechanisms. The final two excerpts in this section address important public policy issues that are raised by the use of alternatives to traditional litigation. First, U.S. Court of Appeals Judge Harry T. Edwards, a prominent labor arbitrator and law professor before his appointment to the bench, asserts that society's approach to ADR should vary depending on whether ADR is being proposed as an adjunct to or separate from the courts, and whether the disputes submitted to an ADR system involve significant public rights and duties. He is least concerned when private disputes are resolved in ADR systems annexed to courts and most concerned when public law issues are resolved in ADR systems that are independent of the courts. Second, Professors Frank Sander and Stephen Goldberg discuss considerations that are relevant when process selection is viewed from a public perspective.

HARRY EDWARDS, ALTERNATIVE DISPUTE RESOLUTION: PANACEA OR ANATHEMA?

99 Harv. L. Rev. 668, 671–72, 675–82 (1986)

Given the inadequacy of traditional responses to the manifold problems with our court systems, it is not surprising that many commentators believe that we must develop new approaches for dispute resolution in lieu of litigation. Generally, I concur, but I think that there are two critical threshold inquiries that we must make before we leap to embrace any system of ADR. First, we should consider whether an ADR mechanism is being proposed to facilitate existing court procedures, or as an alternative wholly separate from the established system. Second, we must consider whether the disputes that will be resolved pursuant to an ADR system will involve significant public rights and duties. In other words, we must determine whether ADR will result in an abandonment of our constitutional system in which the "rule of law" is created and principally enforced by legitimate branches of government and whether rights and duties will be delimited by those the law seeks to regulate. Perhaps the best way to conceptualize these critical issues is by reference to a simple matrix:

	Private Disputes	Private Disputes
ADR in Court	Private Disputes Resolved by Adjuncts to Courts	Public Law Issues Resolved by Adjuncts to Courts
ADR Outside Court	Private Disputes Resolved by Independent Mechanisms	Public Law Issues Resolved by Independent Mechanisms

Obviously, many disputes cannot be easily classified as solely *private* disputes that implicate no constitutional or public law. Many commentators have tried to distinguish "public" and "private" disputes; but, in my view, no one has been fully successful in this effort. The problem is that hidden in many seemingly private disputes are often difficult issues of public law. In this Commentary, I offer no easy solution to the definitional problem of public/private disputes. I do suggest, however, that there are a number of public law cases that are easily identifiable as such. These include constitutional issues, issues surrounding existing government regulation, and issues of great public concern. The latter category might include, for example, the development of a legal standard of strict liability in products liability cases. Although less easily identifiable than constitutional and regulatory issues, such issues of great public concern can be accommodated so long as ADR mechanisms are created as adjuncts to existing judicial or regulatory systems, or if these issues can be relitigated in court after initial resolution pursuant to ADR.

My purpose in creating a public/private law matrix is not to give court administrators a fool-proof method of assigning cases to appropriate dispute resolution systems. Instead, the matrix helps to illuminate those aspects of ADR that should give rise to the greatest concern. In particular, we must focus on the quadrant of the matrix that would allow for the resolution of public law disputes in ADR systems that are totally divorced from courts. ADR mechanisms falling within this quadrant, I believe, are wholly inappropriate.

* * *

If we can assume that it is possible to finance and administer truly efficient *systems* of dispute resolution, then there would appear to be no significant objections to the use of even wholly independent ADR mechanisms to resolve private disputes that do not implicate important public values. For instance, settling minor grievances between neighbors according to local mores or resolving simple contract disputes by commercial norms may lead to the disposition of more disputes and the greater satisfaction of the participants. In strictly private disputes, ADR mechanisms such as arbitration often are superior to adjudication. Disputes can be resolved by neutrals with substantive expertise, preferably chosen by the parties, and the substance of disputes can be examined without issue-obscuring procedural rules. Tens of thousands of cases are resolved this way each year by labor and commercial arbitration, and even more private disputes undoubtedly could be better resolved through ADR than by adjudication.

However, if ADR is extended to resolve difficult issues of constitutional or public law—making use of nonlegal values to resolve important social issues or allowing those the law seeks to regulate to delimit public rights and duties—there is real reason for concern. An oft-forgotten virtue of adjudication is that it ensures the proper resolution and application of public values. In our rush to embrace alternatives to litigation, we must be careful not to endanger what law has accomplished or to destroy this important function of formal adjudication. As Professor Fiss notes:

> Adjudication uses public resources, and employs not strangers chosen by the parties but public officials chosen by a process in which the public participates. These officials, like members of the legislative and executive branches, possess a power that has been defined and conferred by public law, not by private agreement. Their job is not to maximize the ends of private parties, not simply to secure the peace, but to explicate and give force to the values embodied in authoritative texts such as the Constitution and statutes: to interpret those values and to bring reality in accord with them.

The concern here is that ADR will replace the rule of law with nonlegal values. J. Anthony Lucas' masterful study of Boston during the busing crisis highlights the critical point that often our nation's most basic values—such as equal justice under the law—conflict with local nonlegal mores. This was true in Boston during the school desegregation battle, and it was true in the South during the civil rights battles of the sixties. This conflict, however, between national public values reflected in rules of law and nonlegal values that might be embraced in alternative dispute resolution, exists in even more mundane public issues.

For example, many environmental disputes are now settled by negotiation and mediation instead of adjudication. Indeed, as my colleague Judge Wald recently observed, there is little hope that Superfund legislation can solve our nation's toxic waste problem unless the vast bulk of toxic waste disputes are resolved through negotiation, rather than litigation. Yet, as necessary as environmental negotiation may be, it is still troubling. When Congress or a government agency has enacted strict environmental protection standards, negotiations that compromise these strict standards with weaker standards result in the application of values that are simply inconsistent with the rule of law. Furthermore, environmental mediation and negotiation present the danger that environmental standards will be set by private groups without the democratic checks of governmental institutions. Professor Schoenbrod recently has written of an impressive environmental mediation involving the settlement of disputes concerning the Hudson River. According to Schoenbrod, in that case private parties bypassed federal and state agencies, reached an accommodation on environmental issues, and then presented the settlement to government regulators. The alternative to approval of the settlement was continued litigation, which was already in its seventeenth year, with no end in sight.

The resulting agreement may have been laudable in bringing an end to protracted litigation. But surely the mere resolution of a dispute is not proof that the public interest has been served. This is not to say that private settlements can never produce results that are consistent with the public interest; rather, it is to say that private settlements are troubling when we have no assurance that the legislative- or agency-mandated standards have been followed, and when we have no satisfactory explanation as to why there may have been a variance from the rule of law.

In the Hudson River example, we should be concerned if private negotiators settled the environmental dispute without any meaningful input or participation from government regulators, or if the private parties negotiated a settlement at variance with the environmental standard that had been established by government agencies. If, however, government agencies promulgated the governing environmental standards pursuant to legislatively established rulemaking procedures (which, of course, involve public participation), and if the private parties negotiated a settlement in accordance with these agency standards and subject to agency approval, then the ADR process may be seen to have worked well in conjunction with the rule of law. Indeed, the environmental negotiators may have facilitated the implementation of the rule of law by doing what agency regulators had been unable to achieve for seventeen years.

A subtle variation on this problem of private application of public standards is the acceptance by many ADR advocates of the "broken-telephone" theory of dispute resolution that suggests that disputes are simply "failures to communicate" and will therefore yield to "repair service by the expert 'facilitator.'" This broken-telephone theory was implicitly illustrated in a speech by Rosalynn Carter describing the admittedly important work of the Carter Center at Emory University in Atlanta. The Carter Center recently conducted a seminar that brought together people on both sides of the tobacco controversy. According to Rosalynn Carter, "when those people got together, I won't say they hated each other, but they were enemies. But in the end, they were bringing up ideas about how they could work together."

This result is praiseworthy—mutual understanding and good feeling among disputants obviously facilitates intelligent dispute resolution—but there are some disputes that cannot be resolved simply by mutual agreement and good faith. It is a fact of political life that many disputes reflect sharply contrasting views about fundamental public values that can never be eliminated by techniques that encourage disputants to "understand" each other. Indeed, many disputants understand their opponents all too well. Those who view tobacco as an unacceptable health risk, for example, can never fully reconcile their differences with the tobacco industry, and we should not assume otherwise. One essential function of law is to reflect the public resolution of such irreconcilable differences; lawmakers are forced to choose among these differing visions of the public good. A potential danger of ADR is that disputants who seek only understanding and reconciliation may treat as irrelevant the choices made by our lawmakers and may, as a result, ignore public values reflected in rules of law.

We must also be concerned lest ADR becomes a tool for diminishing the judicial development of legal rights for the disadvantaged. Professor Tony Amsterdam has aptly observed that ADR may result in the reduction of possibilities for legal redress of wrongs suffered by the poor and underprivileged, "in the name of increased access to justice and judicial efficiency." Inexpensive, expeditious, and informal adjudication is not always synonymous with *fair* and *just* adjudication. The decisionmakers may not understand the values at stake and parties to disputes do not always possess equal power and resources. Sometimes because of this inequality and sometimes because of deficiencies in informal processes lacking procedural protections, the use of alternative mechanisms will produce nothing more than inexpensive and ill-informed decisions. And these decisions may merely legitimate decisions made by the existing power structure within society. Additionally, by diverting particular types of cases away from adjudication, we may stifle the development of law in certain disfavored areas of law. Imagine, for example, the impoverished nature of civil rights law that would have resulted had all race discrimination cases in the sixties and seventies been mediated rather than adjudicated. The wholesale diversion of cases involving the legal rights of the poor may result in the definition of these rights by the powerful in our society rather than by the application of fundamental societal values reflected in the rule of law.

Family law offers one example of this concern that ADR will lead to "second-class justice." In the last ten years, women have belatedly gained many new rights, including new laws to protect battered women and new mechanisms to ensure the enforcement of child-support awards. There is a real danger, however, that these new rights will become simply a mirage if all "family law" disputes are blindly pushed into mediation. The issues presented extend beyond questions of unequal bargaining power. For example, battered women often need the batterer ordered out of the home or arrested—goals fundamentally inconsistent with mediation.

Some forms of mediation, however, would protect the public values at stake. Professors Mnookin and Kornhauser suggest, for example, that divorce settlements can be mediated successfully despite disparities in bargaining power by requiring court review of settlements that deviate from a predefined norm. Additionally, some disputes that are not otherwise subject to court review also might be well suited for mediation. Many cases, however, may require nothing less than judicial resolution. At the very least we must carefully evaluate the appropriateness of ADR in the resolution of particular disputes.

Even with these concerns, however, there are a number of promising areas in which we might employ ADR in lieu of traditional litigation. Once a body of law is well developed, arbitration and other ADR mechanisms can be structured in such a way that public rights and duties would not be defined and delimited by private groups. The recent experience of labor arbitrators in the federal sector, who are required to police compliance with laws, rules, and regulations, suggests that the interpretation and application of law may not lie outside the competence of arbitrators. So long as we restrict arbitrators to the application of clearly defined rules of law, and strictly confine the articulation of public law to our courts, ADR can be an effective means of reducing mushrooming caseloads. Employment discrimination cases offer a promising example. Many employment discrimination cases are highly fact-bound and can be resolved by applying established principles of law. Others, however, present novel questions that should be resolved by a court. If the more routine cases could be certified to an effective alternative dispute resolution system that would have the authority to make some final determinations, the courts could devote greater attention to novel legal questions, and the overall efficiency of an anti-discrimination law might be enhanced.

* * *

Finally, there are some disputes in which community values—coupled with the rule of law—may be a rich source of justice. Mediation of disputes between parents and schools about special education programs for handicapped children has been very successful. A majority of disputes have been settled by mediation, and parents are generally positive about both the outcome and the process. At issue in these mediations is the appropriate education for a child, a matter best resolved by parents and educators—not courts. Similarly, many landlord-tenant disputes can ultimately be resolved only by negotiation. Most tenant "rights" are merely procedural rather than substantive. Yet tenants desire *substantive* improvement in housing conditions or assurances that they will not be evicted. Mediation of landlord-tenant disputes, therefore, can be very successful—often more successful than adjudication—because both parties have much to gain by agreement.

In both of these examples, however, the option of *ultimate* resort to adjudication is essential. It is only because handicapped children have a statutory right to education that parent-school mediation is successful. It is only because tenants have procedural rights that landlords will bargain at all.

ADR can thus play a vital role in constructing a judicial system that is both more manageable and more responsive to the needs of our citizens. It is essential—as the foregoing examples illustrate—that this role of ADR be strictly limited to prevent the resolution of important constitutional and public law issues by ADR mechanisms that are independent of our courts. Fortunately, few ADR programs have attempted to remove public law issues from the courts. Although this may merely reflect the relative youth of the ADR movement, it may also manifest an awareness of the danger of public law resolution in nonjudicial fora.

FRANK E.A. SANDER & STEPHEN B. GOLDBERG, FITTING THE FORUM TO THE FUSS: A USER–FRIENDLY GUIDE TO SELECTING AN ADR PROCEDURE
10 Negot. J. 49, 60–61 (1994)

When a process selection is made from a public perspective, the public interest must also be considered. If the dispute is one in which a trial is likely to be lengthy, and so consume precious court time, there may be a public interest in referring the dispute to *some* form of ADR. Beyond that, one must ask if there is a public interest in having the dispute resolved pursuant to a *particular* procedure. For example, the referral of child custody disputes to mediation is required by law in several jurisdictions. The disputing parents may believe that they have no interest in a better relationship, but only in vindication, and hence prefer court to mediation. However, many states believe that a better relationship between the parents serves the public interest by improving the life of the child, and so mandate that child custody disputes go first to mediation.

The final question that must be asked in the public context is whether the public interest will be better served by a court decision than by a private settlement. If, for example, the dispute raises a significant question of statutory or constitutional interpretation, a court resolution might be preferable to a private settlement. While a court normally has no power to prevent parties from settling their own dispute, it does not follow that the court, as a public agency, should encourage or assist settlement in such a case.

Litigation may also serve the public interest better than mediation in cases of consumer fraud, which are often handled by the consumer protection division of an attorney general's office. Here not only the issue of *precedent,* but also the related issue of *recurring violations,* is key. The establishment of a general principle or a class remedy, by means of a class action, is clearly preferable to a series of repetitive and inconsistent mediations.

Another situation in which public adjudication is called for is when there is a *need for sanctioning.* If the defendant's conduct constitutes a public danger (assault with a deadly weapon, say, or maintaining a building in a grossly unsafe condition), ADR is inappropriate.

Finally, two more situations may militate against any use of ADR. First, *one or more of the parties may be incapable of negotiating effectively.* An unsophisticated pro se litigant, for example, may be vulnerable to exploitation in an ADR process. (On the other hand, such an individual, if not represented by a lawyer, may not fare better in court.) Second, court process may be required for some other reason: for example, *when serious issues of compliance or discovery are anticipated.*

* * *

NOTES AND QUESTIONS

1. From a public policy perspective, how would you react to proposals for mandatory mediation of all civil actions or all personal injury claims? What would be the costs and benefits? Would your answers be affected by what you assume about the approaches to mediation that would be employed or available?

2. Judge Edwards' principal concern about the use of ADR is that public disputes will be resolved through private means. He cites the controversy over the regulation of tobacco as an example of the kind of disagreement that "cannot be resolved simply by mutual agreement and good faith." Consider the similar controversy over the regulation of firearms. Assume that Congress authorized the Bureau of Alcohol, Tobacco, Firearms, and Explosives (ATF) to set up a negotiated rulemaking process (discussed in Chapter VI, beginning at page 827) to develop rules for the regulation of firearms. The agency will hire an outside mediator to conduct the proceedings and to determine that all appropriate interests are represented. The ATF, which will be represented in the proceedings, will agree to base its regulations on the proposal produced by this process. As a citizen, how would you react to such an announcement? What concerns might you have? As a citizen, again, how would you react if the terms of settlement of a products liability case against a gun manufacturer were filed under seal at the parties' request?

3. Professor Richard Delgado and his co-authors argue that informal processes may foster racial and ethnic prejudice, since studies show that people are more apt to act on prejudicial attitudes in informal than in formal settings. They believe that ADR should be reserved for disputes between parties with comparable status and power and that steps should be taken to reduce bias when the issue to be adjudicated touches a sensitive or intimate area of life. Richard Delgado, Chris Dunn, Pamela Brown, Helena Lee, & David Hubbert, *Fairness and Informality: Minimizing the Risk of Prejudice in Alternative Dispute Resolution*, 1985 Wis. L. Rev. 1359, 1402–1403. Recall also the findings of the Metrocourt study excerpted in Chapter IV, at page 523.

4. The Administrative Dispute Resolution Act of 1990 included a provision stating that "An agency shall consider not using a dispute resolution proceeding if—

(1) a definitive or authoritative resolution of the matter is required for precedential value, and such a proceeding is not likely to be accepted generally as an authoritative precedent;

(2) the matter involves or may bear upon significant questions of Government policy that require additional procedures before a final resolution may be made, and such a proceeding would not likely serve to develop a recommended policy for the agency;

(3) maintaining established policies is of special importance, so that variations among individual decisions are not increased and such a proceeding would not likely reach consistent results among individual decisions;

(4) the matter significantly affects persons or organizations who are not parties to the proceeding;

(5) a full public record of the proceeding is important, and a dispute resolution proceeding cannot provide such a record; and

(6) the agency must maintain continuing jurisdiction over the matter with authority to alter the disposition of the matter in the light of changed circumstances, and a dispute resolution proceeding would interfere with the agency's fulfilling that requirement."

5 U.S.C. § 582(b) (1994) (*repealed by* Administrative Dispute Resolution Act of 1996, Pub. L. No. 104–320, § 4). Although § 582 was repealed, the Act added 5 U.S.C. § 572(b) (2000), which contains the same language.

What do these recommendations for situations in which it may be best not to use ADR suggest about the relationship between alternative dispute resolution and the law? Under what circumstances are rule of law values more desirable than dispute settlement values?

5. The articles by Judge Edwards and by Professors Goldberg and Sander raise the notion that litigation consumes public resources (e.g., courts, judicial resources) and produces public benefits (e.g., precedent, application of public values). Making a comparison to public roads and the phenomenon of "induced traffic," Professors Tracey George and Chris Guthrie argue that courts are impure public goods and that the availability of additional court resources might serve to induce more litigation:

Courts and roadways might appear to be pure public goods because each has an aspect (or output) that is enjoyed by the whole community equally. The highway system appears to be a pure public good in that the availability of roadways allows for the economic growth and development of a city, state, and nation. Likewise, the justice system appears to be a pure public good because the courts resolve disputes peacefully and articulate legal rules that enable people to order their lives. Those benefits (or outputs) are nonexcludable and nonrival.

Both courts and roadways, however, have aspects (or outputs) that are not purely public. The individualized use of either good (i.e., the resolution of one person's complaint or one commuter's use of the road) is inherently divisible and rival, as one person's presence precludes others from using the same part of the good during that period. The larger the number of person using courts or roads, the greater the effect on the use by others due to congestion and crowding. Thus, the judicial and highway systems are more appropriately categorized as impure public goods, comprised of both pure and impure aspects.

* * *

Because roadways are generally available free of charge, drivers do not pay an explicit price to use them. When they think of price in this way, policymakers ignore what we might call the implicit price of driving; yet, it is also relevant. Drivers pay an implicit price in the form of opportunity costs. Driving, in short, takes time, and the implicit price of driving is higher when the roads are congested than when they are not. Because drivers are likely to respond not only to changes in explicit prices, but also to changes in implicit prices, changes in roadway supply are likely to influence driver demand. When the state adds a lane to a congested roadway, for example, the implicit price of driving on that roadway drops. This drop in implicit price then leads more drivers to travel on the roadway, causing the implicit price of driving to rise again as travel times return to, and often surpass, pre-expansion levels. This phenomenon—induced traffic—"is one of the most troubling [issues] facing transportation planning today."

* * *

Congestion is a problem not only on the nation's roadways, but also in the nation's courts. Court reformers, like transportation planners, often contend the perfect decongestant is an increase in supply. By increasing the number of courts and judges, the court reformers argue that the judicial system will be able to accommodate existing demand without stimulating new demand. In fact, however, the addition of judicial resources may induce new demand.

* * *

Court reformers may face an unwelcome surprise if they allocate additional resources to courts. Rather than facilitating the efficient resolution of existing cases, they might actually induce litigation. More courthouses, more courtrooms, and more judges may simply mean that more litigants bring their disputes to court.

* * *

Thus, we believe that society should think about courts not in isolation but rather as one of many dispute resolution processes that claimants can use to seek redress for harms allegedly suffered. We support, in other words, the erection of literal or figurative "multi-door courthouses" containing "a flexible and diverse panoply of dispute resolution processes (or combination of processes)" for disputants.

Tracey E. George & Chris Guthrie, *Induced Litigation*, 98 Nw. U. L. Rev. 545, 555–56 (2004).

6. Consider several other important public policy issues: How should we fund the study and implementation of alternatives to traditional litigation? What incentives do you imagine could be provided to encourage the use of alternative dispute resolution processes?

B. DESIGNING AND EVALUATING CONFLICT MANAGEMENT SYSTEMS

In this section we move from the general considerations important to both designing and selecting dispute resolution processes to explicit consideration of the techniques used in designing and evaluating dispute management and resolution systems.

1. SYSTEMS DESIGN

The field of dizspute systems design (or conflict management systems design) explores how processes or programs for managing and resolving conflict are created and developed. This section will explore how many different types of dispute resolution systems may be designed for a variety of settings—e.g., systems for resolving disputes under the auspices of a court, systems within organizations for resolving internal disputes, systems created by an organization for dealing with disputes with outside parties such as customers or suppliers, systems created to deal with disputes that arise during the operation of a contract, or systems to address conflict in international settings. Dispute systems designers consider questions such as: What types of disputes occur in the organization or community? How does the organization or community currently handle conflict? How can the system be designed to prevent the unnecessary escalation of conflict? What dispute resolution processes should be used and how will these processes interrelate? How will the system be structured? How will the system be funded? Under what conditions will people access and use the system? How will the system be evaluated?

a. Basic Concepts

The first two excerpts in this subsection offer two approaches to dispute systems design.

In the first excerpt, the pioneers of the field, Professors Jeanne Brett, Stephen Goldberg, and William Ury describe their principles for designing systems to resolve disputes. In the second, Cathy Costantino advocates what she and a co-author, Christina Sickles Merchant, call "interest-based conflict management systems design," which emphasizes involving stakeholders (end-users, customers, labor unions, and others) in the creation of conflict management systems.

JEANNE M. BRETT, STEPHEN B. GOLDBERG & WILLIAM L. URY, DESIGNING SYSTEMS FOR RESOLVING DISPUTES IN ORGANIZATIONS

45 Am. Psychologist 162, 162–63, 165–69 (1990)

Two oil companies, about to engage in a joint venture, agree in advance to try to resolve all disputes in a partnership committee. If direct negotiations fail, senior executives from each company who are otherwise uninvolved in the joint venture will try to resolve the dispute by using a mix of mediation and negotiation procedures. If they cannot, the dispute will be sent to arbitration.

At the Catholic Archdiocese of Chicago, school administrators, looking for a better way to resolve disputes about teacher dismissals and student suspensions, designed a multistep dispute resolution system that requires negotiation between disputing parties, provides advice from a school conflict-management board, and offers the services of a trained mediator.

IBM and Fujitsu, after disputing for years over hundreds of charges that Fujitsu had wrongfully used IBM software, negotiated a system that allowed Fujitsu to examine and use IBM software in exchange for adequate compensation. Future disputes about use will be resolved by a neutral technical expert; future disputes about compensation will be resolved by arbitration.

In these situations managers and the consultants who worked with them designed multiprocedure systems for resolving disputes without resort to litigation. Their dispute systems designs were intuitive, based on their recognition that an ongoing series of disputes was inevitable and that currently available procedures were costly.

In 1980 we found ourselves in a similar situation. We had been asked to consult at Caney Creek (a pseudonym), a coal mine in eastern Kentucky, where conflict had reached monumental proportions. In the prior two years there had been 27 wildcat strikes, management had regularly taken the union to court for breach of the no-strike clause in the contract, and 115 miners had been jailed overnight. There had been bomb threats, sabotage, and theft. Productivity was so low that management was considering closing the mine.

The Union contract provided for a four-step procedure for the resolution of grievances: (a) negotiation between miner and supervisor; (b) negotiation between local mine management and a committee that represented the miners; (c) negotiation between a representative of the company and a district-level representative of the union; and (d) binding arbitration. At Caney Creek, as at other high strike mines, little serious negotiation occurred at the local level, and miners had little confidence that arbitration would resolve disputes satisfactorily. Working with union and management officials, we designed a program of changes intended to encourage miners and managers to resolve their disputes by negotiating the interests underlying their positions rather than focusing on intractable positional differences and then helped them put the program into practice. Afterward, bomb threats ceased, sabotage and theft decreased, and productivity improved. There were no wildcat strikes until the national contract expired, nearly a year later.

At the same time we were working at Caney Creek, we began an experiment in mediating grievances in the coal industry. On the basis of our prior research and Stephen B. Goldberg's own experience as an arbitrator in the industry, Goldberg thought that mediation inserted between the negotiation (third) and arbitration (fourth) steps of the coal industry grievance procedure would be able to uncover and resolve the problems underlying a grievance, problems that seldom surfaced at arbitration where grievances were typically dealt with exclusively on contractual terms. One of Goldberg's arbitration cases illustrates this point. A miner filed a series of grievances claiming that his foreman was doing work that should have been done by union members. Goldberg denied the miner's grievances and only learned later that the miner believed that his frequent assignments to shovel muck from the mine's sump hole were unfair, but because he had no grounds to file a grievance on the job assignment, he sought other contractual grounds on which to file a grievance against his foreman. Arbitration neither resolved the real problem, the miner's job assignments, nor did anything to improve the relationship between the miner and his foreman.

The mediation of grievances experiment, too, was successful and led us to reflect on just what it was from the perspective of the theory of dispute resolution that we and others were trying to do. We were not mediators—that is, we were not helping to settle specific disputes. Rather we were dispute systems designers—helping disputants change the way they handled disputes. Our interventions were not limited to suggesting new procedures, but extended to organizing procedures into a sequence and working with the parties to help them acquire the motivation, negotiation skills, and resources to use their new system successfully.

* * *

Cutting the Costs and Reaping the Benefits of Conflict: Principles of Dispute Systems Design

* * *

Our six principles of dispute system design are guidelines for cutting the costs of conflict and realizing the benefits and are applicable to disputes within and between organizations.

Principle 1: Consultation Before Disputing, Feedback After

Our assumptions that conflict is inevitable in organizations and is often an early warning of need for change imply that organizations should make a significant effort to discuss issues that may cause disputes and to learn from those disputes that do occur. Consultation before disputes erupt can minimize the occurrence of unnecessary disputes. Feedback after a dispute has occurred helps managers take action to prevent reoccurrence. Two examples illustrate these points.

Consultation. When Pacific Bell went through the transition of deregulation, the company and the union formed Common Interest Forums to discuss ways to work together and prevent unnecessary disputes. These forums provided opportunities for management to consult with the union before initiating action. Management was not committed to negotiate over such intended actions but could do so if the union raised unexpected oppositions.

Feedback. Managers and lawyers at some consumer-product companies regularly analyze consumer complaints to determine what changes in product design might reduce the likelihood of similar disputes in the future. In some states consumer mediation agencies keep records of complaints against each merchant. The agency alerts the proper state authorities when repeated complaints are lodged against the same merchant. In this way state action to prevent the merchant from continued unlawful practices can be instituted.

Principle 2: Put the Focus on Interests

Negotiation is almost always available to disputants. The challenge lies in using negotiation to reconcile interests. Framing negotiations as a cooperative rather than competitive exercise facilitates interests-based resolutions, as does an exchange of information about interests, either directly by sharing information or indirectly through the exchange of proposals. Providing negotiation skills training that focuses on techniques for reconciling interests may not only increase skills but may also establish norms about how disputes are to be handled within an organization. Additionally, successful resolution of disputes in simulated negotiations training may generate expectations that interests-based negotiations can be successful and may thus motivate disputants to use interest-based procedures.

* * *

Principle 3: Build in "Loop–Backs" to Negotiations

Sometimes negotiations fail because the parties' perceptions of who is right or who is more powerful are so different that they cannot establish a range in which to negotiate. Information about how rights standards have been applied in other disputes can serve to narrow the gap between the parties' expectations of the outcome of a rights contest and thus make agreement possible.

For interorganizational disputes advisory arbitration (in which a third party provides a nonbinding decision concerning how a case would be resolved in court) may be the simplest procedures for acquiring rights information. Disputants within organizations may use information about corporate norms to help them establish a bargaining range. An example illustrates this point.

Two strategic business units of an organization were negotiating over what one would pay the other in return for the transfer of some magnet technology. When negotiations broke down, the directors of the two units could have turned the dispute over to the corporation's president, but this was risky in absence of information about what the president might do. Instead, they went to the director of another unit, whom they asked about previous transfers of technology between units, in particular, how profits had been shared. Precedent provided a norm to help them define the bargaining range and negotiate a resolution.

There are also loop-back procedures that help avoid power contests. Rarely does a negotiated agreement look so attractive as when the parties are on the verge of a costly power contest. For this reason a cooling-off period, a specified time during which the disputants refrain from a power contest, can be effective. Such periods are mandated by the Taft–Hartley Act and the Railway Labor Act before strikes that threaten to cause a national emergency, but they are just as applicable to small-scale conflict. For example, "sleeping on" a decision or talking it over with an uninvolved third party before taking action are practical rules of thumb that let emotions cool and rationality reassert itself.

* * *

Principle 4: Provide Low–Cost Rights and Power Procedures

In some disputes interests are so opposed that agreement is not possible. Thus, effective dispute resolution systems have low-cost procedures for providing final resolution of disputes on the basis of rights or power. Joint-venture agreements ... often provide for arbitration. Management hierarchy provides the same mechanism for final resolution of disputes within organizations. Voting resolves proxy battles like the one between Texaco and Carl Icahn, the corporate raider.

Principle 5: Arrange Procedures in a Low-to-High Cost Sequence

Our designing principles—consultation before disputing, feedback after—put the focus on interests, provide procedures that loop back to negotiations, and provide low cost rights and power procedures; the principles suggest creating dispute resolution systems in which procedures are arranged in a low-to-high cost sequence. These principles are the building blocks of a dispute resolution system. Table 1 shows a menu of procedures to draw on in designing such a sequence.

Table 1. Menu of Procedures Least Costly to Most Costly

Procedure	Example
Prevention procedures	Consultation
	Feedback
Interest-based procedures	Negotiation
	Mediation
"Loop-back" procedures	Rights
	Information procedures
	Advisory arbitration
	Power
	Cooling-off periods
	Third-party intervention
Low-cost rights and power	Rights—arbitration
Procedures	Power—voting

Depending on the characteristics of the organization or interorganizational relationship in which the new dispute resolution system is to be embedded, the designer may wish to select more than one procedure from a category. For example, in our grievance-mediation experiment in the coal industry, we added interests-based mediation to a system that already provided for negotiation. Our decision about where to place the mediation in the coal industry's sequence of procedures for resolving grievances was based both on considerations of costs and the effect of the new procedure on the old ones. Mediation at the mine site would not only be prohibitively expensive but also would likely encourage disputants to treat negotiation as pro forma and become dependent on the mediator instead of themselves for resolving disputes. Thus, a sequence of procedures, each only slightly more costly than the previous one, may have the paradoxical effect of encouraging use of higher procedures. The best means to guard against this is to space procedures sufficiently far apart that increased transaction costs are noticeable.

Principle 6: Provide Disputants with the Necessary Negotiation Skills, Resources, and Motivation

Designing procedures according to these principles is not sufficient to reduce the costs of dispute resolution and to realize its benefits. Disputants must have the negotiation skills, the resources, and the motivation to use the system.

Issues in training negotiation skills. A dispute resolution system that meets our costs criteria is one in which a relatively high proportion of disputes are resolved through interest-based procedures. The Achilles heel of our system may be negotiation skills. Negotiators seem to be better at maximizing their own gains (distributive bargaining) than they are at maximizing joint gains (integrative bargaining). It is intuitive to many that when negotiating over a single issue, say the purchase price of a company, the buyer makes a low initial offer, the seller makes high initial demand, and the two make concessions in a reciprocal fashion until they reach agreement or impasse. Negotiators also seem to know intuitively how to compromise by splitting the difference between their positions. What they do not do very well is to find agreements that integrate interests, agreements by which they receive more than they would have had they simply compromised on each issue.

* * *

Overcoming cognitive biases that limit effectiveness of interests-based negotiations may take rather sophisticated negotiation training. Does this mean that dispute systems design is limited to situations in which such training is possible or to people whose attitudes or abilities indicate that they would benefit from training? We do not think so. In many seriously distressed dispute resolution situations, like Caney Creek mine, schools, or even penitentiaries, disputes are normally resolved by power contests, such as strikes or fights. Dispute systems design coupled with training that does little more than expose disputants to interest-based negotiations has been successful in getting disputants to talk their disputes through to resolution instead of fighting them out. Although these resolutions may show signs of cognitive biases, transaction and other costs of disputing have been reduced.

* * *

Motivating disputants to use new low-cost procedures. One of the most difficult issues in dispute system design is motivating the parties to use interests-based procedures, procedures that loop back to negotiations, and low-cost rights or power procedures. Parties often engage in procedures that generate high costs and fail to use procedures that would seem to be less costly and potentially more beneficial. Why? Sometimes interests-based procedures are not available, parties lack negotiation skills to use them successfully, or they do not have the necessary resources. Often, however, the problem is one of motivation.

At Caney Creek mine we were faced with frequent wildcat strikes despite the availability of a contractual grievance procedure that provided for three stages of negotiation and binding arbitration. We found some miners were reluctant to raise grievances with their foreman because of fear of retaliation. Others felt that the grievance procedure deprived them of a voice. Union and company representatives would argue about contractual technicalities far removed from the actual problem as the miner perceived it. Miners were passive observers at arbitration and often would have to wait months for the arbitrator's decision. Any miner, in contrast, could instigate a wildcat strike and receive immediate attention. Even if the strike failed to get the miners what they wanted, their voice would be heard, and they would receive the emotional satisfaction of revenge. In many instances the motivation to strike outweighed the motivation to use the contractual grievance procedures.

We are doubtful that a Caney Creek miner with a grievance weighed the pros and cons of alternative courses of action before striking. However, for a dispute systems designer who is trying to understand why parties are using what seems to be high cost procedures, it is useful to analyze the incentives associated with the use of alternative procedures. Some incentives have to do with expected outcomes, others with characteristics of the procedures themselves.

Incentives associated with outcomes. Disputants prefer procedures that generate outcomes that meet their interests and avoid those in which they believe outcomes are risky. As a result, powerful parties who believe they have been winning with old procedures may be extremely reluctant to cooperate with dispute systems design. It may be that the weaker party will have to champion the dispute system design and the focus on interests. In the long run, however, the stronger party should also prefer a system that preserves its strength but reduces transaction costs and increases satisfaction with outcomes. The costs of imposing one's will can be high. Threats must be backed up by actions from time to time. The weaker party may fail to comply fully with the settlement imposed by power and thereby force the more powerful party to engage in expensive policing. Thus, even for a party who has been winning, a focus on interests, within the bounds set by power, may be more desirable than would appear at first glance.

Incentives associated with process. Empirical research has identified several procedural characteristics that affect parties' procedural preferences. Two of these are outcome control and voice. Evidence from a wide variety of contexts indicates that disputants prefer procedures in which they retain outcome control or final authority over the resolution of the dispute. Furthermore, despite laboratory evidence to the contrary, mediation, an interest-based procedure in which disputants retain outcome control, appears to be quite effective in resolving disputes when parties have an ongoing relationship and even when they do not. Other research suggests that procedures in which disputants simply have a veto, for example, advisory arbitration in which the third party makes recommendation after hearing evidence presented in an adjudicative format, are not particularly successful in resolving disputes, possibly because the parties do not participate in formulating the resolution and, therefore, feel little ownership of it.

Parties also prefer procedures that give them voice, the opportunity to present their side of the dispute or to frame the dispute from their own perspective. However, it is not entirely clear whether it is voice qua voice that is important or whether having voice results in perceptions of greater influence over ultimate decision.

Another aspect of voice that has not received empirical attention is the opportunity to express emotions. It may be that in emotionally charged disputes parties prefer procedures that provide for the controlled expression of emotion and the acknowledgment by the blamed party of the validity of such emotions. An apology, for instance, can often defuse emotion and make problem solving negotiation possible.

* * *

NOTES AND QUESTIONS

1. In their book, GETTING DISPUTES RESOLVED: DESIGNING SYSTEMS TO CUT THE COSTS OF CONFLICT (1988), Professors Ury, Brett, and Goldberg shifted the focus from the resolution of individual disputes to resolving streams of disputes that arise over time. *See also* ASS'N FOR CONFLICT RESOLUTION, DESIGNING INTEGRATED CONFLICT MANAGEMENT SYSTEMS; CATHERINE CRONIN–HARRIS, BUILDING ADR INTO THE CORPORATE LAW DEPARTMENT: ADR SYSTEMS DESIGN (1997); DAVID B. LIPSKY, RONALD L. SEEBER & RICHARD D. FINCHER, EMERGING SYSTEMS FOR MANAGING WORKPLACE CONFLICT (2003); NANCY H. ROGERS, ROBERT C. BORDONE, FRANK E.A. SANDER, & CRAIG A. MCEWEN, DESIGNING SYSTEMS AND PROCESSES FOR MANAGING DISPUTES (2013); KARL A SLAIKEU & RALPH H. HASSON, CONTROLLING THE COSTS OF CONFLICT: HOW TO DESIGN A SYSTEM FOR YOUR ORGANIZATION (1998).

2. Many court-annexed dispute resolution programs effectively have "loop-backs" to negotiation. Moreover, it is common in litigated cases to "loop-back" to negotiation between (and especially right before) formal legal proceedings. *See* Thomas B. Metzloff, *Resolving Malpractice Disputes: Imaging the Jury's Shadow*, Law & Contemp. Probs., Winter/Spring 1991, at 43, 59 n.54 (finding that many cases settle right before trial).

3. Cathy A. Costantino and Christina Sickles Merchant advanced the growing field of dispute systems design in their book, DESIGNING CONFLICT MANAGEMENT SYSTEMS (1996). They suggest that an emphasis on the expertise of the outside dispute system designer can result in a failure of the organization itself to study what is wrong with the existing way of processing disputes. *Id.* at 47. They advocate what they call "interest-based conflict management systems design," which emphasizes involving stakeholders (end-users, customers, labor unions, and others) in the creation of conflict

management systems. *Id.* at 48, 78. Consider the following description of their comprehensive approach to dispute systems design.

CATHY COSTANTINO, USING INTEREST–BASED TECHNIQUES TO DESIGN CONFLICT MANAGEMENT SYSTEMS

12 Negotiation J. 207, 207–14 (1996)

As practitioners and dispute systems designers, how often have we used our expertise to create a dispute resolution program that we think is effective, accessible, even elegant—only to discover that no one uses it? Our wonderful design for resolving disputes quicker, cheaper, and more amicably may look great on paper, in a sheaf of corporate policies and procedures or in a box on some organizational chart; but unfortunately, it never sees the light of day. It is a field of dreams that becomes a field of despair.

In working with organizations and doing large-scale dispute systems design projects, many of us have discovered that one of the keys to creating "successful" conflict management systems (not merely dispute resolution programs) that are actually *used* by disputants (and that continue to be used) is to involve *all* the stakeholders in the design process. That is, the designer works with both organizational and individual stakeholders to gather information, identify interests, develop options, and build together to create a design that satisfies everyone's needs for fairness, participation, and resolution.

In effect, a conflict management systems designer is really the mediator of a system: facilitating the creation of a conflict management system *with* the stakeholders, not *for* them, and ensuring that the necessary parties are at the design table. By doing so, the designer not only assures that alternative dispute resolution (ADR) methods are made available to disputants, but also that the design process itself is interest-based.

In our recent book (Costantino and Merchant 1996), we argue that if there is an incongruity or dissonance between the dispute resolution method and the design method (that is, when an interest-based method such as mediation is imposed on disputants through a rights-based design such as mandatory mediation), there is greater likelihood that the disputants will resist using the system or may even sabotage it. Based on our works over the years with large-scale organizational designs in both the public and private sector, we have come to the conclusion that integrated, interest-based conflict management systems created through participative, interest-based design processes hold the greatest potential for durable, usable, and effective methods to resolve disputes on a systematic, rather than a case-by-case basis.

This interest-based design model uses principles from organization development, dispute systems design, and ADR, and builds on the work of Ury, Brett, and Goldberg (1988) and their paradigm of interests, rights, and power as methods to resolve disputes. Our "next generation" model of "interest-based conflict management systems design" urges maximum participation by stakeholders in the design process.

But how does a practitioner actually "do" an interest-based design? How does one translate these lofty principles into practice? Unlike the slogan used by Nike in its ubiquitous advertising campaign, we cannot urge practitioners to "just do it." There's far more to it than that.

At least six tasks (not necessarily linear) are necessary to facilitate an effective, interest-based conflict management system: entry and contracting, organizational assessment, design architecture, training and education, implementation and evaluation.

Entry and Contracting

How one enters the system—whether as an internal design specialist or an external consultant—affects the system. Even if the organization chooses not to change its conflict management system as a result of the designer's intervention, the designer's entry into the system has an impact.

For the system to choose to initiate change, there must be both a presenting problem and a perceived opportunity. The presenting problem might include a backlog of cases, negative publicity, or the increased cost of disputes. Perceived opportunities might include reduction of financial exposure, improving public perceptions of the organization, or improving relations with customers, employees or the community.

Once the designer enters the system, the contracting process begins among the designer, leadership, and key stakeholders. Among the questions to be considered are: Which key stakeholders need to be involved in the design process (end-users, customers, unions)? Is there a commitment that leadership will allow these stakeholders to participate in the process? Do the stakeholders understand the basic change principles, including the possibility that there may be no need for change? Will the parties accept evaluation and feedback throughout the design process? Are they willing to serve as partners with one another in collaborative problem identification and resolution? Is there agreement as to who (leadership, committee, collective consensus) will make the final decision about revising the conflict management system?

During the entry/contracting process, the designer serves several roles: *catalyst* for triggering change within the system without becoming part of the reaction; *educator* to teach the organization and its stakeholders about conflict and change; *facilitator* in assisting the system to work together to identify interests and create options; *translator* to interpret various interests and options to other parts of the system; and *agent of reality*, to identify those areas where change may be difficult, where resistance can be expected, or where there may be constraints which inhibit change.

At this stage of the process, several traps and pitfalls may ensnare the designer. These dangers include: *enabling*, which involves the organization and its stakeholders becoming dependent upon the designer for approval, feedback and options rather than relying on themselves; *being the bad guy*, or management using the designer as the messenger to deliver "bad news" and-or to tell the other stakeholders what is not possible and what is not negotiable; *playing the savior*, a situation where the designer believes he or she is indispensable and can control the ultimate success or failure of the design; and *letting it fail*, where the designer resists the temptation to "fix" the system or to force it to change.

Organizational Assessment

This stage is often skipped over by designers who imprudently want to jump right into the "fun" part of the process—inventing options and solutions. However, organizational assessment, similar to gathering information in a mediation, is critical not only because it helps determine what is necessary for the intervention, but also because it establishes the goals of any new or revised system so they can be evaluated.

The designer needs to assess the *organization* (its culture, customers and attitude towards conflict); the *disputes* (types, numbers, nature and cost); the *resolution methods* (prevention, use of formal or informal techniques, and who decides which method to use); and the *results* (cost, durability, satisfaction and effect on the organization and its stakeholders). A solid organizational assessment is accomplished through the use of such techniques as surveys, interviews and focus groups (the designer must be able to guarantee a safe environment for stakeholders to disclose information, without fear of reprisal). The information gathered from the assessment is then collated and presented to the responsible decision maker(s), who can either choose to revise the system or maintain the status quo.

Design Architecture

Once a decision has been made to revise the conflict management system, design architecture looks at the *whether*, *when* and *how* of the new system. Whereas entry and contracting and organizational assessment involve the big picture, or "macro" aspects of the design, design architecture focuses on the disputes themselves and methods of resolution—the "micro" aspects of managing conflict. In general, system designers should follow six principles of design architecture:

Whether to Use ADR:

- Principle 1: *Develop guidelines for whether ADR is appropriate.* Although ADR is an acronym for alternative dispute resolution, we prefer to think of it as "appropriate dispute resolution." Is ADR appropriate for this type of conflict, and if so, what type of ADR? The method must be congruent with the culture of the organization, further the organizational goals and mission, and have some benefit for the disputants.

- Principle 2: *Tailor the ADR process to the particular problem.* Aside from the organizational fit, there must also be a process fit: The ADR method should meet the interests of the particular dispute and the particular disputants. For example, choosing mediation when, in fact, the nuances of the particular case and the interests of the disputants indicate that neutral fact-finding would be more appropriate can lead to a conclusion that ADR is not effective when the mediation is not effective. In actuality, it may be that ADR was appropriate, but mediation was not. The appropriate process will depends on a variety of factors, including the goals of the disputants, their tolerance for risk and the relationship of the parties.

When to Use ADR:

- Principle 3: *Build in preventative methods of ADR.* As practitioners, we often forget that preventive ADR methods such as partnering, joint problem solving, and negotiated rulemaking can be effective. It may be useful for the designer to think of developing a range of preventative methods in a variety of contexts, such as the individual, the group, the organization, and the community, and within the global environment. As organizations continue to adopt "best practices" in their day-to-day operations and relationships—to compete, to control costs and to maximize resources—dispute prevention becomes increasingly important.

- Principle 4: *Make sure that disputants have the necessary knowledge and skills to choose and use ADR.* For example, labor and management need to know how to engage in interest-identification processes, brainstorming and consensus decision making in order to use interest-based negotiation. A dissatisfied customer needs to know what mediation is (and what it is not) before deciding to choose it. Disputants need to know not only what the process is, but also how to participate in it effectively. Much of this can be taught and modeled in appropriate training and educational sessions.

How to Use ADR:

- Principle 5: Create ADR systems that are simple to use and easy to access, and that resolve disputes early, at the lowest organizational level, with the least bureaucracy. For disputants to choose ADR, it must be easier to use, faster, and more effective than the current dispute resolution method. As practitioners know, the introduction of new processes in organizations tends to generate an almost irresistible tendency to over-control. To make ADR difficult to use and impossible to access, a design architect should follow this recipe: Require multiple levels of approval, increase the bureaucratic paperwork requirements as the process proceeds, make it difficult to get approval to use ADR by having only one or two people who can make the decision, do not give line or staff personnel the authority to commit to use ADR or to a settlement, send messages that the organization does not support ADR, that it is "risky" behavior. Voila—you have created a system that is ready to boil over!

- Principle 6: Allow disputants to retain maximum control over choice of ADR method and selection of neutral whenever possible. Not surprisingly, practitioners have found that disputants are likely to be more resistant to an ADR process if they are not involved in selecting it, and even more resistant if they have little or no voice in determining who the neutral will be. When an organization imposes a certain resolution method on disputants, practitioners have discovered that disputants are somewhat less resistant as long as they retain a degree of control over the selection of the neutral. * * *

Training and Education

Although the terms are used interchangeably, training and education are not the same. ADR education is a dynamic, ongoing process of increasing awareness about conflict, responses to it, and choices about conflict management. ADR training is more skills-based and competency-based. Several myths about ADR training and education are rife in organizations today, including the following.

All stakeholders need identical ADR training and education. There is a misrepresentation that all stakeholders (including senior and midlevel management) need to be skills-trained as mediators or neutrals of some type. The result is that organizations are often spending exorbitant amounts of money training personnel as mediators, when these people will be overseeing ADR programs, selecting cases for ADR or sitting at the table during ADR proceedings as a user/consumer. Our experience has shown that, if people are trained in skills that they have little chance to use, they become frustrated and reluctant to use the system at all.

ADR training and education is best conducted by outside ADR experts and consultants. Not only is this myth expensive, it can also be a form of rights-based design. That is, the outside vendors decide what kind of training and education is best for the organization, and decide what types of "problems" or "role plays" will be used. As a result, the training strategy is often inappropriate or irrelevant for the particular organization. This is particularly true where vendors are using "off-the-shelf" training modules. We have found it helpful to use team teaching and partnering arrangements that pair an outside consultant with a stakeholder or organizational representative, not just to design the training, but to actually teach it. The consultant provides the architectural and technical part of the training (subject matter and technique) and the stakeholder adds the organizational and cultural components (process and context). It is also useful to design organization-specific training problems similar to the types that participants will actually face.

Only organizational stakeholders should be trained and educated. Those who are designing ADR training and education often forget that organizational stakeholders are only half the equation: To engage in ADR approaches, one needs *all* the disputants engaged, educated and in some cases trained. Many will raise their eyebrows at this suggestion: Why train and educate one's "opponents"? The answer is simple: Without bilateral (and ideally joint) training and education, the program's projected timed efficiencies, cost savings, enhancement of satisfaction levels, and durability of results are unlikely to become reality.

Once they are trained and educated, stakeholders will use ADR. Just because they have the skill and knowledge to use the system does not mean that stakeholders will do so. If you build it, it is not necessarily true that they will come; they must have a reason to come. We are constantly amazed at the number of organizations that assume that once they provide ADR training and education, people will somehow magically begin to use ADR. In addition, disputants must be able to figure out that use of the system offers rewards and incentives to them—they must know the answers to the "What's–In–It–For–Me?" questions.

Once these myths are dispelled, designers can recommend one or more of five types of ADR training and education:

Marketing Efforts. The purpose here is to get "buy-in" for ADR from stakeholders and managers. Typically, this education is limited to one or two hours, and includes examples and "success" stories.

Awareness education. Here, the purpose is to educate stakeholders about what ADR is, how it is used in the particular organizational setting, and guidelines for using ADR. We have found that half-day sessions with an interactive component work well.

Conflict management and communication training. This type of training is generic and not geared towards a particular form of ADR. The purpose is to introduce skills that can be used in day-to-day life, or serve as the foundation for additional ADR training. We believe such training is most effective if it is no more than one day in length and interactive.

Consumer/User training. Aimed at the stakeholders who will actually be using ADR procedures, this training targets those who will be sitting at the table negotiating or participating in an ADR proceeding. It offers practical guidance on such areas as: how to select a neutral, how to identify interests, and how to develop strategies and options. We believe that it is critical for students to participate in a mock ADR proceeding; such training typically involves a full day, and no more than two.

Training of third-party neutrals. This intensive skills training is targeted only for those who will actually serve as neutrals: mediators, arbitrator, evaluators. It is usually of longer duration (no less than three days), more intensive and more interactive, and limited in size (ideally no more than 12 students per instructor).

Implementation

Starting small and thinking big can be useful at this stage of the design process. Starting with a small, time-limited, clearly defined pilot project helps to determine the willingness of stakeholders to change, makes it safer for individuals in the old system to experiment with new behaviors and rewards, and tests the suitability of the design to see whether it fits the organization. In addition, a pilot effort can uncover unknown costs, expectations, and attitudes that may impede adoption of the new system. In setting up this kind of small-scale experiment, it is useful to:

- select individuals to be responsible for the administration of the pilot;
- look to other sources for experience, expertise, and success stories;
- identify stakeholders who will be affected by the pilot;
- choose a pilot linked to organizational goals; and
- select the site of the pilot project with success in mind.

Once the experimental effort has been completed and evaluated, we recommend the "4–T Approach" to expand the pilot to the full organization: Tout the Pilot (promote publicity and results); Test the Pilot (do not assume that because it worked in one part of the organization it will necessarily work in another setting); Tailor the Pilot (reassess and make sure that the disputes in the expanded arena are appropriate for ADR, and that the appropriate method of ADR is chosen); and Team the Effort (use an ADR team, task force, or steering committee).

Evaluation

A common belief these days is that ADR is "better." The obvious questions are: Better at what, and if it is better how do you know? There are several components to evaluating a conflict management system, a task that should take place throughout the life of the design process, rather than being just tacked on at the end. These include: clarify goals, determine evaluation baseline data, chart progress towards goals, modify the system in response to feedback, measure the results, reclarify the goals, and start the evaluation cycle again. Two distinct measurements can be the focus of ADR evaluation:

ADR's effectiveness and impact. In this case, the evaluation deals with the success or failure of the ADR process: its efficiency (change in costs and time); effectiveness (nature of outcomes, durability of resolutions; effect on organizational environment); and satisfaction levels of the system's users (with process, relationships and outcomes).

ADR program administration and operation. This kind of evaluation gauges the merits of the particular ADR programs: its administration/operation (structures and procedures, guidelines and standards, lines of responsibility, sufficiency of resources and coordination of relationships); service delivery (access to system, procedures in use, and selection of cases); and program quality (training and education, selection of neutrals, and competence of neutrals).

In Conclusion

When these six tasks are combined with an interest-based design process that actively involves stakeholders through openness, participation and feedback, the likelihood of a durable, effective conflict management system increases.

Perhaps as designers we *can* plant a field of dreams and not a field of despair in our work and in the processes we help to create, if we apply the very interest-based principles that we have been espousing for so long. Perhaps it is time that as designers we become personally congruent and "walk-the-walk" of interest-based processes in our design work.

NOTES AND QUESTIONS

1.   Importantly, the sequence that Costantino describes includes more than just the "off-the shelf" design of a dispute resolution system that is provided by a consultant. Instead, she describes a process that is attuned to the differences among organizations, that involves the participants in creating the new system, that recognizes and addresses barriers to the adoption of a new system, and that highlights the need for on-going assessment and evaluation.

2.   In practice, the design processes that Costantino describes—entry and contracting, organizational assessment, design architecture, training and

education, implementation, and evaluation—may unfold in a non-linear or recursive fashion. For example, participants may need to be informed about the design method early in the process, may need to be educated about conflict and dispute resolution on an on-going basis, and may need to be trained to use the system once it is developed. Similarly, consideration of how the new system will be evaluated should start at the beginning of the process as the old system is assessed, processes for data collection are incorporated in the design of the system, and baseline data is collected.

3. How do the principles of design architecture described by Costantino compare to the principles of dispute systems design articulated in the excerpt by Brett, Goldberg, and Ury? How might the differences in their approaches to dispute systems design influence their views of the role of the dispute systems designer? Which approach would you be more likely to use?

4. When designing a system for resolving disputes, the designer and the stakeholders should consider all aspects of the system including:

- type(s) of dispute resolution processes that are appropriate for the organization or community

- the progression of dispute resolution processes that will be employed

- the types of cases that will be eligible and how they will be selected

- how the neutrals will be selected, trained, and paid

- what parties will have a role and what those roles will be

- what resources are available

- how participants will be informed about and trained to use the system

- whether the program will be voluntary or mandatory

- how the system will be evaluated.

These factors can be used both for assessing the current system for resolving disputes and for designing and evaluating any new system that is implemented. In considering these design elements, the designers and stakeholders ought to consider how the system is likely to affect the cognitive, emotional, and behavioral aspects of conflict and its resolution as described in Chapter I, beginning at page 4.

5. Management guru Peter F. Drucker and others have argued that the fundamental nature of the American workplace has changed in the last quarter of a century, and in a way that has important implications for dispute resolution systems within these organizations. *See* Peter Drucker, *The New Society of Organizations*, Harv. Bus. Rev., Sept./Oct. 1992, at 95, 100; Katherine Van Wezel Stone, *Dispute Resolution in the Boundaryless*

Workplace, 16 Ohio St. J. on Disp. Resol. 467, 471–79 (2001). In this view, the "old" workplace could be characterized by fixed, clearly defined jobs and career paths, job security in exchange for corporate loyalty, and hierarchical command. Katherine Van Wezel Stone, *The New Psychological Contract: Implications for the Changing Workplace for Labor and Employment Law*, 48 UCLA L. Rev. 519, 534 (2001). The "new" workplace, however, is more of a partnership, with employers and employees seen as stakeholders sharing opportunities for the satisfaction of mutual interests, employees enjoying much greater mobility outside of the firm, and no expectation of long-term employment by either labor or management. *Id.* at 568–72. Professor Reuben argues that the values that support the new workplace are consistent with many deeply rooted democratic values, including self-determination, participation in governance, and equality and due process in treatment. Richard C. Reuben, *Democracy and Dispute Resolution: Systems Design and the New Workplace*, 10 Harv. Negot. L. Rev. 11 (Spring 2005). Reuben contends that mediation, nonbinding arbitration, and other ADR methods further these principles by expanding the range of options available for dispute resolution, by allowing for integrative results, and by contributing to the creation of more productive, more effective, and more stable workplace environments. *Id.* at 39–66. Do you agree? Think of your own work history.

6.   Both the excerpt by Brett, Goldberg, and Ury and the excerpt by Costantino note the importance of providing incentives to encourage people to use the system. Social psychologist Kurt Lewin has described individuals as existing within a force field, subject to a variety of pressures on their behavior. He argues that behavioral change should be considered in this context. As Costantino and Merchant explain:

> As most practitioners have frequently witnessed, the status quo of any system is the result of forces driving change in opposition to forces restraining change. This balanced driving/restraining equation describes a system in its steady state at any point in time. Lewin suggested that the system's status quo can be changed by one of three methods: (1) increasing the forces driving change, (2) reducing the forces restraining change, or (3) converting restraining forces into driving forces. Common use of force field analysis in [organizational development] change efforts has revealed that focusing on the second method—reducing the forces that restrain change—often yields faster and more effective results than any other. Force field analysis is particularly useful in designing conflict management systems because it is often a series of specific restraints that operate to prevent or inhibit those with a dispute from using dispute resolution procedures. For example, in an organization where the chief dispute resolution mechanism is litigation, a manager's decision to pursue something other than litigation, perhaps some form of alternative dispute resolution (ADR), may be most strongly influenced by the number of additional "permission memos" that have to be written to justify ADR use (a restraining force). This restraining force may have a greater impact on an employee deciding whether to recommend ADR

than possible recognition in the company newsletter for saving litigation costs (a driving force).

CATHY A. CONSTANTINO & CHRISTINA SICKLES MERCHANT, DESIGNING CONFLICT MANAGEMENT SYSTEMS 28–29 (1996). *See also* KURT LEWIN, FIELD THEORY IN SOCIAL SCIENCE (1951).

7.   Shauhin Talesh examines (in the context of consumer lemon laws) how the design of dispute resolution processes has implications for what values are transmitted to neutrals, how the meaning of the law is constructed, and how the processes operate in practice—for example, what fact-finding is done, what voice is allowed, and what experts are consulted. Shauhin A. Talesh, *How Dispute Resolution System Design Matters: An Organizationl Analysis of Dispute Resolution Structures and Consumer Lemon Laws*, 46 Law & Soc'y Rev. 463 (2012).

8.   For discussion of the design of several other programs, see *Dispute Systems Design: A Special Section*, 5 Negotiation J. 355 (Stephen B. Goldberg, Jeanne M. Brett & William L. Ury eds., 1989); KENNETH FEINBERG, WHAT IS LIFE WORTH? THE UNPRECEDENTED EFFORT TO COMPENSATE THE VICTIMS OF 9/11 (2006); John Lande, *Using Dispute Systems Design Methods to Promote Good–Faith Participation in Court–Connected Mediation Programs*, 50 UCLA L. Rev. 69 (2002); David O'Connor, *The Design of Self–Supporting Dispute Resolution Programs*, 8 Negotiation J. 85 (1992); Andrea Kupfer Schneider & Natalie C. Fleury, *There's No Place Like Home: Applying Dispute Systems Design Theory to Create a Foreclosure Mediation System*, 11 Nev, L.J. 368 (2011).

9.   Commentators have begun to consider a range of ethical issues associated with conflict management systems design. Important questions focus on identifying the parties or entities to whom the designer owes a professional duty (i.e., who is the client?), specifying the purpose of the design process (recognizing the potential for divergence among the stated, perceived, and actual purposes), considering the role of the systems designer, clarifying the responsibility of the designer for what happens after the system is designed (e.g., implementation, evaluation, or enforcement), and identifying the potential for problems related to confidentiality or privilege, immunity, and conflicts of interest. *See* Cathy A. Costantino, *Second Generation Organizational Conflict Management Systems Design: A Practitioner's Perspective on Emerging Issues*, 14 Harv. Negot. L. Rev. 81 (2009); Carrie Menkel–Meadow, *Are There Systemic Ethics Issues in Dispute System Design? And What We Should [Not] Do About It: Lessons from International and Domestic Fronts*, 14 Harv. Negot. L. Rev. 195 (2009). Cathy Costantino raises a range of sticky design scenarios:

A few examples of actual problems faced by practitioners may be instructive here. What does a designer do if she learns that an organization is using the ADR process to keep evidence of systemic discrimination confidential? What if the designer becomes aware that one of the stakeholders (perhaps one without rank, power, and privilege) has been subjected to reprisal as a result of participating in the design process? What if the designer discovers that she is the second (or third, or fourth, or fifth) designer to be brought into the organization because the organization does not like what it is being told? And what if she suspects that those in power are "consultant shopping" for a particular result or recommendation? Does it matter whether the organization is consultant shopping with regard to the organizational assessment or with regard to the suggested design product or recommendation? What if the designer uncovers evidence of criminal wrongdoing or fraud during her organizational assessment? What does the designer do if he is later asked to testify about information he learned doing the design intervention (and does it matter whether his testimony is sought in the criminal or civil context)? On what basis and under what circumstances can the designer promise confidentiality to stakeholders since there is no designer privilege? What if an entity other than the organization itself (for example, a regulatory body or government agency) initiates the design process—should the designer provide the regulator or agency with information learned during the design process? In the corporate context, what is the interplay between the design process and fiduciary obligations to shareholders or corporate governance bodies? As the [conflict management systems design] literature develops and as our profession matures, there is striking need for practitioners to begin to discuss these and other ethical dilemmas.

Cathy A. Costantino, *Second Generation Organizational Conflict Management Systems Design: A Practitioner's Perspective on Emerging Issues*, 14 Harv. Negot. L. Rev. 81, 98 (2009).

Carrie Menkel–Meadow proposes the following 10 ethical "commandments" of dispute systems design:

1. Do no harm—do not make the parties worse off than they were before you were hired. Don't make waste (Cost and expenses without benefits).

2. Do not become a "tool" of a client or organization or government that wants to use process design to achieve inappropriate or illegitimate ends (deterring rightful complaints, manipulating workers or customers, "cooling" out or ignoring claims).

3. Be sure that the end users of any dispute system have had input into the design. (This suggests full participation and bottom-up sensitivity, rather than control by "top-down" officials of organizations, institutions and governments).

4. Attempt to ensure that any process you design can actually accomplish what it was designed to do. Take some responsibility for implementation and evaluation.

5. Know what participants' legal rights are (and what they might be giving up or waiving to participate in a particular system).

6. Be sure, as much as you can, that a system of dispute resolution does not systematically discriminate against or harm particular individuals.

7. Be prepared and be competent. Learn about particular organizations, cultures, groups, and histories before embarking on a design project.

8. Consider whether processes should include multiple choices, menus, gateways or tiers. One size does not fit all, even within the same organization, nation-state, and culture. Individuals will have different preferences even within affinity or other groups.

9. Ensure that any process designed can be adequately explained to and understood by its users.

10. Suggest that any system designed should be evaluated and revised as conditions change.

Carrie Menkel–Meadow, *Are There Systemic Ethics Issues in Dispute System Design? And What We Should [Not] Do About It: Lessons from International and Domestic Fronts*, 14 Harv. Negot. L. Rev. 195, 229–230 (2009). How would you evaluate these principles? Are they implementable? Are there other principles that you would include? Any that you would exclude? *See also* Lisa Blomgren Bingham, *Designing Justice: Legal Institutions and Other Systems for Managing Conflict,* 24 Ohio St. J. on Disp. Resol. 1 (2008) (discussing the importance of being "designers of justice").

b. Self–Determination in Systems Design

Central to Costantino and Merchant's approach to dispute systems design is the notion of disputant self-determination. Chapter IV described the importance of disputant self-determination in mediation. Self-determination at the level of designing the system for resolving disputes is similar but distinct, as Professor Lisa Bingham explains below.

LISA B. BINGHAM, SELF–DETERMINATION IN DISPUTE SYSTEM DESIGN AND EMPLOYMENT ARBITRATION
56 U. Miami L. Rev. 873, 879–80, 881–86 (2002)

There is an issue underlying these efforts, a current of tension in the discussions, that concerns one of the core values underlying ADR: disputant self-determination. Proponents of alternative or appropriate dispute resolution often argue its chief value is disputant control over the process. This notion of disputant control or self-determination is distinct from legal consent. It is not the same concept as voluntary consent for purposes of imputing agreement to an adhesive arbitration clause.

Instead, self-determination includes procedural justice notions of a disputant's perceptions of control and fairness. I argue here that dispute systems vary across two separate dimensions of disputant self-determination. Those dimensions are disputant self-determination in the design of the system as a whole, and disputant self-determination within a given case using a specific dispute resolution process provided by the overall system design. Self-determination in dispute system design includes making choices regarding what cases are subject to the process, which process or processes in sequence are available (mediation, early neutral evaluation, and binding arbitration, for example), what due process rules apply, and other structural choices for setting up a private justice system. Self-determination at the case level includes whether the process results in a voluntary, negotiated settlement agreement or an imposed binding third party decision. It includes self-determination as to process and outcome within a given dispute involving a single set of parties. Most discussions of self-determination in dispute resolution tend to ignore the system design level, or assume that self-determination is present, or conflate the two levels.

* * *

I.   SELF–DETERMINATION WITHIN A SINGLE CASE CONTRASTED
     WITH SELF–DETERMINATION IN DISPUTE SYSTEM DESIGN

The Model Standards of Conduct for Mediators provide in several sections for party "self-determination." They suggest that mediation is based on the principle of self-determination, that mediators must have qualifications necessary to satisfy the reasonable expectations of the parties, that mediators must conduct the process in a manner consistent with party self-determination, and that they have a duty to improve the practice of mediation. These standards do not define self-determination, nor do they distinguish between self-determination at the case level and self-determination in system design. I use self-determination at the case level to refer to a single set of disputing parties in conflict within a given dispute resolution process, for example, a single mediation case or a single arbitration case. Self-determination at this level refers to the parties' experience of control over both process and outcome in a single dispute.

Self-determination in dispute system design refers to control over the structure of a process or set of processes to handle a series of disputes. There is an established and growing body of literature on dispute system design that focuses primarily on a dispute resolution program within an organization, not the courts. Most of these discussions assume that the sponsoring company, organization, or agency will make the ultimate choices about the final dispute system design. Since the leading professional organizations approved Model Ethical Standards at a time when courts had already implemented mandatory mediation programs, it is reasonable to conclude that its drafters contemplated self-determination as to outcome at the individual case level. In mandatory court-annexed programs, legislatures and courts effectively make dispute system design choices for the parties before the parties use mediation for a given case. The legislatures authorized courts to mandate mediation and the courts are exercising that power.

* * *

Relatively little commentary discusses self-determination in the area of dispute system design. Increasingly, commentators advocate requiring that counsel inform clients of alternative or appropriate dispute resolution generally, and the different kinds of processes in particular. This provides an opportunity for party self-determination in dispute system design, if only the design of a process for a single case. Scholars advocate fully informed consent by clients; this requires that lawyers and their clients understand the difference between mediation and arbitration, and the differences among various models of mediation. However, there is often an unstated assumption that the client is represented by counsel and has a choice in how to design an ADR process for the case. Many disputants act pro se. The most controversial new systems give employee or consumer disputants no choices in ADR system design and may even prohibit representation by counsel.

* * *

In parallel to this commentary is the increasingly heated discussion among arbitration scholars regarding the legitimacy of adhesive arbitration clauses, or "mandatory arbitration." The current state of the law is that the stronger contracting party may require the weaker contracting party to participate in arbitration of any disputes arising out of the contract through an adhesive clause, provided that clause meets the standards for enforcing a contract in that jurisdiction. These standards include defenses such as duress, unconscionability, fraud, and, to a limited extent, public policy. In this context, if the weaker party proceeds with the economic relationship (employment, health care treatment, purchase of consumer goods and services), the weaker party is deemed to have consented to the clause. The entire economic relationship is presented as a take it or leave it offer; dispute system design is part of this larger whole. This is consent as a legal concept. A variety of disgruntled would-be litigants would assert forcefully that it is not voluntary consent or self-determination as a subjective, psychological concept. In this context, it is clear that the weaker party and its counsel have no control over dispute system design—at least that is the case after the parties have entered into the economic relationship. The economically more powerful party has already made all the design choices in adopting the arbitration plan. Some scholars argue that arbitration in these contexts should not be called appropriate or alternative dispute resolution at all. Professor Fiss's argument against settlement is most forceful here because the disputants who might be motivated to make new law or set precedent are contractually disabled from doing so.

This debate illustrates the tension between self-determination as an underlying core value of ADR and the notion of legal consent as a historical reality. Distinguishing between self-determination at the case level and self-determination in system design can foster a more productive discussion of this tension. Table 1 is an effort to illustrate the different dimensions of self-determination in ADR.

Table 1. Self–Determination at the Case Level and in Dispute System Design

Self–Determination in System Design	Self–Determination in Individual Case	
	Parties Control Outcome	Third Party Controls Outcome
Both/All Parties	A. Ad hoc mediation Ad hoc non-binding evaluative processes	D. Ad hoc arbitration Labor arbitration Negotiated binding processes
One Party	B. Mandatory or voluntary Mediation Mandatory or voluntary non-binding processes	E. Adhesive binding arbitration
Third Party	C. Court-annexed mediation or non-binding processes (mandatory or voluntary) Public sector labor mediation	F. Court or administrative adjudication Legislated binding arbitration

* * *

NOTES AND QUESTIONS

1.   Professor Bingham distinguishes between self-determination at the system design level and at the case level. At the case level, she combines self-determination as to process and outcome. In an article excerpted in Chapter

IV at page 317, Professor Leonard Riskin proposed grids to address three categories of decision making in mediation: substantive, procedural, and meta-procedural. Leonard L. Riskin, *Decisionmaking in Mediation: The New Old Grid and the New New Grid System*, 79 Notre Dame L. Rev. 1 (2003). His "new new grid system" emphasizes that a mediation participant can exercise quite different degrees of influence in each category of decision making. That system also makes it clear that many procedural decisions—which could be called dispute resolution design decisions—can be made moment to moment during a mediation.

2. In a recent article, Adam Kinon argues that developing an understanding of the underlying power dynamics (formal and perceived) in an organization and how to address them is essential to a designer's ability to implement an interest-based design process. Adam B. Kinon, *Power Before Interests in Dispute Systems Design*, 17 Harv. Negot. L. Rev. 273 (2012).

3. Professor Donna Shestowsky argues that courts ought to work to learn more about disputants' preferences with regard to dispute resolution procedures—individually and in the aggregate—and should take these preferences into account when determining the range and type of dispute resolution processes to offer:

> Insofar as lawyers strongly influence client decisionmaking with respect to ADR, it becomes important that legislatures and courts protect party autonomy at the front-end by mandating or suggesting procedures that align with aggregate disputant preferences. They should then build flexibility into the governing rules so that the parties can exercise some design preferences on a case-by-case basis.

Professor Shestowsky also reviews the empirical research exploring disputant preferences for different dispute resolution processes and offers suggestions for more nuanced ways to study such preferences. Donna Shestowsky, *Disputants' Preferences for Court–Connected Dispute Resolution Procedures: Why We Should Care and Why We Know So Little*, 23 Ohio St. J. Disp. Resol. 549, 572–73 (2008).

4. Dispute systems can be designed for individual organizations, courts, agencies, or even countries. Consider the following: "Imagine a society emerging from some sort of armed conflict. Though a peace agreement has been negotiated to halt the violence, the more significant challenge is to design a set of institutions that will allow this society to manage peacefully the ongoing conflicts about the shape of political, economic, and social life into the future. The commission charged with designing this set of political institutions quickly realizes that although these institutions must achieve several goals, their principal purpose is to create a permanent institutional capacity for collective problem solving. They turn to the dispute resolution literature to seek advice on the details of institutional design: how should the institutions be structured, who should the members be, what processes should be centralized, how should decisions be made, how should issue areas be disaggregated and assigned? Can they use the fruits of dispute resolution

literature to 'hardwire' the institution in ways that will maximize its chances for peacefully resolving disputes?" Khalil Z. Shariff, *Designing Institutions to Manage Conflict: Principles for the Problem Solving Organization*, 8 Harv. Negot. L. Rev. 133 (2003).

2. EVALUATING DISPUTE RESOLUTION SYSTEMS

Essential to any evolving system is a process of evaluation to determine how the system is functioning. Questions that might be addressed by evaluation include:

- How is the system functioning?
- What needs is it meeting?
- What needs is it failing to meet?
- Has the program been implemented as intended?
- How is the program operating?
- What effects is the program having?
- Under what circumstances and for which types of cases, does the program have these effects?
- What unintended effects are occurring?
- How satisfied are participants?
- Is the program operating efficiently?

Deborah Hensler has noted: "As legislatures and courts continue to expand mandates for ADR in federal and state courts, the need to know what in fact the ADR revolution has wrought for good or ill becomes more pressing. The urge to protect the infant innovation from too careful scrutiny needs to give way to hard assessment of potential gains and losses from the new vision of legal dispute resolution." Deborah Hensler, *A Research Agenda: What We Need to Know about Court–Connected ADR*, Disp. Resol. Mag., Fall 1999, at 15.

a. The Process of Evaluation

In the following excerpt, Donna Stienstra, a senior analyst for the Federal Judicial Center, the research arm of the federal judiciary, describes the process of evaluation. The following notes and questions explore the importance of the evaluation function.

DONNA STIENSTRA, EVALUATING AND MONITORING ADR PROCEDURES

FJC Directions, Dec. 1994, at 24, 24–25

Courts considering for the first time whether to adopt an alternative dispute resolution procedure are often frustrated by a lack of good information about whether ADR "works." Courts that already have ADR programs in place often face a different frustration—lack of information about whether their particular ADR procedure is working. In addition, policy makers who wish to consider broad policy questions related to ADR often lack adequate empirical information to assist their deliberations. In response to these problems, individual courts and others have begun to consider how to collect more and better information about how ADR works and what its effects are.

Recognizing the need for good information is, of course, far easier than collecting it. To carry out a sound and reliable data-collection project requires careful planning at the outset and close attention throughout. This may seem a daunting task to courts whose resources are already taxed. Yet the reward for carefully planned evaluations can be a wealth of information useful not only to the individual court undertaking the evaluation but also to others who need to know more about the effects of ADR.

How, then, can a court collect useful information about its ADR procedures? It may be helpful to think about this process as having three principal tasks: identifying the appropriate data, preparing the data collection methods, such as questionnaires, and establishing the evaluation design, or the road map for collecting the data.

Identifying the appropriate data

While it is tempting, when conducting an evaluation, to ask for information on many aspects of the litigation process, an evaluation can quickly go off track if a court does not have a good idea of what it needs to know. To narrow the possible choices—and to make certain that all necessary information is obtained—a court should look to the nature and purpose of its ADR program. What is it supposed to accomplish for the court? What is it supposed to do for the litigants? For example, if the purpose of a court's mediation program is to save litigant costs, time to disposition—though interesting—is the wrong information to use when assessing the program's impact. The more explicit a court has been at the outset in defining the purpose of its ADR program, the more guidance it will provide to those who have to determine whether the program is working.

Equally important, a court should consider very carefully the different dimensions of the effects it wants to measure. Litigant costs, for instance, may be thought of solely as the number of dollars spent on fees and other legal expenses, but this narrow focus excludes other costs, such as absence from work or emotional toll of the litigation process, that may [be] of equal significance to litigants. Similarly, in programs that seek to reduce litigation delay, a court must determine whether it needs to measure the actual number of hours spent (by judges, attorneys, or whomever) or the time that elapses between stages of a case (e.g., from filing to disposition).

Preparing the data collection methods

Once a court has determined what to measure, it may find that several different types of data collection methods are needed. Some ADR effects, such as time to disposition, can be evaluated though routinely collected caseload statistics, but others may best be evaluated by questionnaires or interviews that ask those involved in the ADR procedure how they think it's working. Still other effects, such as delay, may best be measured through both methods. Some concepts—quality of justice, for instance—simply may not be measurable at all, at least not by standard data collection methods.

Designing the data collection instruments themselves is another important aspect of an evaluation. Questionnaires are one of the most frequently used methods because they are inexpensive relative to the amount of information obtained, but they present many pitfalls and should be used carefully. They are generally used when one wants to generalize about a population—for example, attorneys who litigate in the district—and such generalization is risky if response rates are low or questions are imprecise. (To feel more confident of questionnaire results, courts should consider working with someone trained in designing questionnaires who can help craft questions.)

Courts should not overlook the usefulness of other methods, such as focus groups, which are helpful when generalization is not needed, or collecting information from dockets. Finally, it is very important to decide on data collection methods early, even as the ADR procedure is designed, so that important information is not lost. Some evaluations may require information that is not routinely collected, such as the identity of the mediator or arbitrator or the names and addresses of litigants with cases in mediation, and new docketing procedures may have to be developed to record such data.

Establishing the evaluation design

Although data collection tools are important, they are more useful if guided by an overall evaluation design that tells court personnel when and how to use them. Evaluations of new programs are generally of two types: evaluation of program *implementation* and evaluation of program *effects*. To evaluate implementation, a court would look at how its program is used. Do judges and parties submit cases to the procedure, or is it ignored? If other litigation activities are to be tolled, does this in fact happen? For this type of evaluation, the court might examine the dockets in a sample of cases to identify just what happens in these cases.

If a court can assume that successful implementation—that is, faithful use—necessarily leads to the desired effects, evaluation of program implementation may be sufficient. But if this assumption cannot be made, or if the court wants to understand whether the program has other unanticipated effects, it will need to conduct an evaluation of effects as well. Ascertaining what effects were caused by the program or procedure necessarily requires a basis for comparison. For instance, data showing that cases in the program take an average of nine months from filing to disposition do not reveal whether the program has increased or decreased the disposition time—or had an effect on it at all. What is needed is some idea of what these cases' average time to disposition would have been absent the program.

The best design for making such a determination is to compare a group of cases not subject to the program, a "comparison" or "control" group, with a group of cases subject to the program, an "experimental" group. In this design, every case eligible for the ADR program is randomly assigned to one or the other of these two groups. This means all cases are exposed to the same conditions *except for* the ADR program, which is applied only to the experimental cases. If after following this procedure the court finds a difference between the two groups on some measure—average disposition time, for example—it can infer the program had an effect. (For guidance on the ethical considerations of using experimental designs in court settings, *see Experimentation in the Law: Report of the Federal Judicial Center Advisory Committee on Experimentation in the Law* (1981), available on WESTLAW as well as from the Center.)

A number of courts have used random assignment to determine the effectiveness of their ADR procedures, and any court planning an evaluation should at least consider using this design. An assessment that relies on some other kind of comparison group—say, a comparison of cases terminated before the programs began with cases terminated after going through the program—may reflect influences other than those of the program. For instance, there might be a change over time in the type of case filed or a difference in the economic conditions in which they were litigated. Random assignment accounts for those influences and therefore permits more powerful conclusions about the causal effect of an ADR program.

While comparisons are critical for making causal inferences, they are reliable only if apples are compared with apples. A common error is to compare cases selected for a program to cases not selected, where the selection relied on judicial or staff discretion rather than random assignment. For example, when judges are called on to select suitable cases for an arbitration program, they will chose cases they believe are amenable to arbitration and leave cases they consider less suitable to be resolved by other means. Comparing these two groups of cases, which are clearly different, will not give reliable conclusions about the effect of arbitration.

One final point: Decisions about overall evaluation design and data collection methods are linked, and neither should be made without considering the other. For example, asking attorneys for their subjective assessments of cost savings is an unreliable measure of impact of an ADR program on litigation costs. The quality of these subjective evaluations can be enhanced, however, by combining random assignments of cases with an objective question to all attorneys about litigation costs: "What were the fees and costs for this case?" By comparing the answers of attorneys whose cases were and were not subject to the ADR program, the court would obtain a far better measure of the program's impact on costs than by addressing subjective questions only to the attorneys subject to the program.

In undertaking evaluations of their ADR programs, courts should keep in mind that just as these programs have their own unique context and purposes, so may their evaluation approaches differ from others. Further, courts may find it helpful to use experts from sources like the [Federal Judicial] Center's Research Division or local colleges and universities. Whatever the approach used, ensuring quality dispute resolution services requires that those adopting ADR understand the effects of their programs. This information, when shared with others, will also help build a body of knowledge that will enable us all to assess the costs and benefits of ADR for the courts and litigants.

NOTES AND QUESTIONS

1.   Evaluative research is useful in order to find out what is actually going on in a program, how the parties understand and experience the processes, what the effects of a process are, which processes participants prefer, and so on. *See* EMIL J. POSAVAC & RAYMOND G. CAREY, PROGRAM EVALUATION: METHODS AND CASE STUDIES (7th ed. 2006).

2.   Systematic evaluation is particularly important given the limits of our casual observation of the world. Much of human intuition and perception is unconscious, unsystematic, and limited by our capacities to perceive, pay attention to, and remember what happened. This can, on occasion, lead us to reach incorrect conclusions. Thus, if we think that a dispute resolution process is effective, it is likely that our casual observation of the process will confirm our belief. Systematic evaluation allows us to attempt to more objectively explore those beliefs. *See generally* THOMAS GILOVICH, HOW WE KNOW WHAT ISN'T SO (1991); HEURISTICS AND BIASES: THE PSYCHOLOGY OF INTUITIVE JUDGMENT (Thomas Gilovich, Dale Griffin & Daniel Kahneman eds., 2002).

3.   Importantly, psychological research suggests that we are prone to perceiving relationships where none exist, a phenomenon referred to as illusory correlation:

Imagine yourself participating in a pioneering study of how people associate events. Psychologists William Ward and Herbert Jenkins show you the results of a hypothetical fifty-day cloud seeding experiment. They tell you for each day whether clouds were seeded and whether it rained. The information is a random mix: sometimes it rained after seeding, sometimes not. If you *believe* that cloud seeding works, might you be more likely to notice and recall days with both seeding and rain? In Ward and Jenkins' experiment, and in many others since, people have become convinced that they really see precisely what they expected. An overstated Chinese proverb has the idea: "Two-thirds of what we see is behind our eyes."

"Illusory correlations"—perceiving relationships where none exist— help explain many a superstition, such as the presumption that more babies are born when the moon is full or that infertile couples who adopt are more likely to conceive. Salient coincidences, such as those who conceive after adopting, capture our attention. We focus on them and are less likely to notice what's equally relevant to assessing correlations— those who adopt and never conceive, those who conceive without adopting, and those who neither adopt nor conceive. Only when given all this information can we discern whether parents who adopt have elevated conception rates.

Such illusory intuitions help explain why for so many years people believed (as many still do) that sugar made children hyperactive, that cell phones caused brain cancer, that getting cold and wet caused colds and that weather changes trigger arthritis pain. Physician Donald Redelmeier, working with Amos Tversky, followed eighteen arthritis patients for fifteen months. The research recorded their subjects' pain reports, as well as each day's temperature, humidity, and barometric pressure. Despite the patients' beliefs, the weather was uncorrelated with their discomfort, either on the same day or up to two days earlier or later. Shown columns of random numbers labeled "arthritis pain" and "barometric pressure," even college students saw an illusory correlation. We are, it seems, eager to detect patterns, even when they're not there.

* * *

Shortly after I wrote this, a journalist called, seeking help with a story on why so many famous people (Bill Clinton, Hillary Clinton, Jimmy Carter) have embarrassing brothers. Do they? I responded. Or is it our attention is just drawn to salient conjunctions of famous people and boorish brothers? Is boorishness less frequent among men with unfamous siblings, or just less memorable? If we easily deceive ourselves by intuitively seeing what is not there, the remedy is simple: Show me the evidence. Gather and present the comparison data.

DAVID G. MEYERS, INTUITION: ITS POWERS AND PERILS 113–14 (2002). How might "illusory correlation" interfere with an intuitive assessment of the effectiveness of a dispute resolution process or system?

4. In addition, psychological research suggests that we intuitively tend to seek out information that confirms our theories, rather than systematically attempting to gather accurate information:

We also actively seek information that confirms our ideas, a phenomenon known as "confirmation bias." Peter Wason demonstrated our preference for confirmation bias in a famous experiment with British university students. He gave students the three-number sequence 2–4–6 and asked them to guess the rule he used to devise the series. First, however, he invited them to test their hunches by generating their own three-number sequences. Each time Wason told them whether their sets conformed to his rule. (Stop: If Wason walked in on you right now, what three numbers might you try out on him? If he answered "yes," what additional three numbers might you put to him?) Once they had tested enough to feel certain they understood the rule, they were to announce it.

The result? Often wrong but seldom in doubt. Only one in five of these confident people correctly discerned the rule, which was simply any three ascending numbers. Typically, Wason's students formed a wrong idea ("counting by two's?") and then searched only for confirming evidence, for example by testing 6–8–10, 31–33–35, and so forth. (Perhaps you, too, would have tested your hunch by seeking to confirm rather than disconfirm it?) Experiments on our preferences for belief-confirming evidence would not have surprised Francis Bacon, whose 1620 *Novum Organum* anticipated our modern understanding of the limits of intuition: "The human understanding, when a proposition has been once laid down . . . forces everything else to add fresh support and confirmation."

Try another of Wason's classical little problems, one that has been the subject of much research and debate: Which cards must you turn over to determine whether this rule is true or false: "If there is a vowel on one side, then there is an even number on the other side."

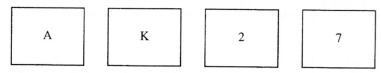

Like everyone else responding to this problem, you probably first wanted to turn over the A. So far, so good. Some stop there, but we need to turn over one more card. Most folks, seeking to confirm the rule, want to turn over the 2. But if there's a consonant on the other side, this card would be irrelevant to the rule ("If there is a *vowel* on the other side . . ."). Only 4 percent of people correctly turned over the 7. (If there's a vowel on the other side, the rule is false; if not, it's irrelevant.) Our confirmation bias on these tasks suggests that natural human reasoning is flawed, or at least better suited to assessing probabilities than executing logic.

DAVID G. MEYERS, INTUITION: ITS POWERS AND PERILS 116–17 (2002). How might you explain how "confirmation bias" compounds the need for systematic research into the effects of dispute resolution procedures?

5.   When conducting evaluation research it is important to consider data obtained from a variety of sources using a variety of methods:

> Each technique for gathering information has its shortcomings. Experimentation is limited by artificiality, observation by unreliability, interviews by interviewer bias, and so on. There is no ideal research technique in the behavioral sciences. The advantages may lie along one dimension, such as economy; the disadvantages along another, such as objectivity. The goal of the researcher is not to find the single best method.
>
> For most problems, several procedures will be better than one. Even though each has its limitations, these tend not to be the same limitations. The artificiality of the laboratory can be supplemented by observation, which is high on naturalness but low on reliability; the questionnaire, which can be given to many people quickly, can be supplemented by detailed interviews with a few people to probe more deeply into significant issues. This has been described as the methods of converging operations. A number of different research techniques are applied, each with somewhat different limitations and yielding somewhat different data.

ROBERT SOMMER & BARBARA SOMMER, A PRACTICAL GUIDE OF BEHAVIORAL RESEARCH: TOOLS AND TECHNIQUES 6–7 (5th ed. 2002).

6.   What variables might it be useful to measure in evaluating an ADR program? What are the strengths and weaknesses of each variable? How would you measure each variable and where would you obtain the data? Be specific. Consider the utility and difficulty of measuring the following:

- time savings
- cost savings
- parties' satisfaction (with the process? with the outcome? with the mediator?)
- attorneys' satisfaction (with the process? with the outcome? with the mediator?)
- settlement rates
- parties' compliance with the settlements reached
- perceived fairness (according to whom? parties? outside expert?) (of process? of outcome?)
- effects on relationships
- changes in social values about disputing
- changes in the role or behavior of lawyers.

The American Bar Association Section of Dispute Resolution's Research and Statistics Task Force identified the "Top Ten Pieces of Information Courts Should Collect on ADR":

1. Was ADR used for this case (yes/no)?

2. What ADR process was used in this case? (mediation, early neutral assessment, nonbinding arbitration, fact-finding, mini-trial, summary jury trial, other)

3. Timing information (the date the claim was docketed; date of referral to ADR; date of first ADR session; date of close of ADR referral period; at what point in the docket duration did ADR occur (before suit, after filing suit, before discovery, just before trial); the final disposition date of the case; the date of post-trial motions)

4. Whether the case settled because of ADR. If settled, wether the case settled in full or settled in part.

5. What precipitated the use of ADR (court order sua sponte, party consent to the process, party motion with one or more parties opposed and a court order for ADR following, automatic referral per court rule due to kind of case)?

6. Was there a settlement without ADR (yes/no)? If so, how was the case terminated—e.g., dispositive motion, settlement in ADR, settlement by some other process, during or after trial, removal to another court etc.

7. Case type (general civil, criminal, domestic, housing, traffic, small claims).

8. The cost of the ADR process to the participants (cost of neutral, filing fees, attorneys' fees of disputants, time spent by disputants in ADR, costs of experts, etc.).

9. Did the disputants use more than one form of ADR? If so, which?

10. Satisfaction data: How satisfied are the participants with the process, the outcome, and the neutral?

American Bar Association Section of Dispute Resolution Task Force on Research and Statistics, Memorandum, Top Ten Pieces of Information Courts Should Collect on ADR (2006), available at http://www.americanbar.org/con tent/dam/aba/events/dispute_resolution/cle_and_mtg_planning_board/telecon ferences/2012–2013/May_2013/topten.authcheckdam.pdf.

What do you think of these measures? Are there others you would include? How might you design a mechanism for collecting such data? What constraints might you face?

7. For discussion of criteria to use for evaluating procedures for public participation in regulatory processes—acceptability, robustness, consensus, procedurality, and nonfairness related issues, how various processes stack up against these criteria, and the implications of empirical research for the design of procedures, see Tom Tyler & David Markell, *The Public Regulation of Land Use Decisions: Criteria for Evaluating Alternative Procedures*, 7 J. Empirical Legal Stud. 538 (2010); David L. Markell & Tom R. Tyler, *Using Empirical Research to Design Government Citizen Participation Processes: A*

Case Study of Citizens' Roles in Environmental Compliance and Enforcement, 57 U. Kan. L. Rev. 1 (2008).

8. Tom Stipanowich proposed an "Arbitration Fairness Index" aimed at facilitating comparison among consumer or employment arbitration programs. He posits the following criteria (each to be assessed on a 5–point scale from "terrible" to "very good"):

Meaningful Consent, Clarity, and Transparency

>   Meaningful consent to arbitrate

>   Adequate notice and disclosure

>   Clear guidance of program users ("roadmap") and access to helpline

>   Ease of court oversight

>   Published program statistics

Independent and Balanced Administration

>   Independent and impartial administration

>   Balanced input in rules and policies

Quality and Suitability of Arbitrators

>   Balanced input in roster of arbitrators

>   Diversity

>   Experience and training

>   Disclosure and challenge mechanism

>   Ethics standards and complaint mechanism

Fair Hearing

>   Reasonable costs and fees

>   Legal Counsel

>   Reasonable hearing location

>   Access to information and discovery

>   Limitations period

>   Expeditious process

>   Fair hearing

>   Availability of class action

Fair Outcomes (Awards and Remedies)

>   Access to remedies available in court

>   Publication of reasoned awards

>   Outcomes

Thomas J. Stipanowich, *The Arbitration Fairness Index: Using a Public Rating System to Skirt the Legal Logjam and Promote Fairer and more Effective Arbitration of Employment and Consumer Disputes*, 60 U. Kan. L. Rev. 985, 1031 (2012). What benefits and challenges might such a ratings system entail? What do you think of the items included?

9.   Ideally, researchers would conduct field experiments in which cases are randomly assigned to either the dispute resolution program or a control group of cases that do not participate in the program. Such field experiments are infrequent. One notable exception is the Early Assessment Program in the U.S. District Court for the Western District of Missouri, a demonstration program that was established under the Civil Justice Reform Act. The court permitted cases to be randomly assigned to three different groups: 1. cases that were required to use the Early Assessment Program; 2. cases in which the parties were allowed to voluntarily choose whether to use the Early Assessment Program; and 3. cases that were not allowed to use the program. *See* DONNA STIENSTRA, MOLLY JOHNSON & PATRICIA LOMBARD, A STUDY OF THE FIVE DEMONSTRATION PROGRAMS ESTABLISHED UNDER THE CIVIL JUSTICE REFORM ACT OF 1990, FEDERAL JUDICIAL CENTER 215–53 (1997). As Stienstra notes, using this type of experimental design allows the researcher to attribute different outcomes among the groups to the operation of the program.

10.   Professor Deborah Hensler draws an analogy between the type of empirical research that is needed in the field of ADR and the research that has become commonplace in the field of medicine:

> As I consider the state of ADR research today, I often think of the evolution of modern medicine. Over the last century, much has been learned about the nature of disease and antidotes for illness. This progress was a result of applying rigorous and objective investigative techniques (in particular, randomized clinical trials), reporting research results accurately and completely, and engaging in freewheeling debate about the meaning of the findings. Of course, not all health care providers nor all manufacturers of drugs and devices have applauded these investigations or their results; some of modern medicine's failures are traceable to inadequate research, flawed reporting, or unwillingness to heed research results. But over time, the patent medicines and folk therapies of yesterday have been replaced by products and therapies whose claimed benefits and side-effects have an evidentiary basis. Some of these products and therapies will be set aside, as new empirical research reveals their shortcomings, or produces better alternatives. As a result, some practitioners and manufacturers will suffer a temporary loss of revenue, while they adjust their practices to newly available evidence. Some of them may wish that the research had turned out differently. Others may long for the days when a single bottle held the promise of curing-all. But most of us would agree that we are better served by knowing more about the complexities of disease and health, and about the benefits and limitations of alternative health care

regimes. I think it would be good for all of us if we could adopt this model of knowledge-building for the ADR field as well.

Deborah R. Hensler, *ADR Research at the Crossroads*, 2000 J. Disp. Resol. 71, 77–78 (2000). Consider our experience with this model in medicine—what do you see as the advantages and disadvantages of this approach? What are the implications for designing systems for dispute resolution?

b. The Value of Evaluation Research

As you can see, the process of evaluating dispute resolution systems can be demanding. In the following excerpt, Professor Robert MacCoun and his colleagues demonstrate why such work is worth the effort—that is, the value of evaluation research.

ROBERT J. MACCOUN, E. ALLAN LIND, DEBORAH R. HENSLER, DAVID L. BRYANT & PATRICIA A. EBENER, ALTERNATIVE ADJUDICATION: AN EVALUATION OF THE NEW JERSEY AUTOMOBILE ARBITRATION PROGRAM
v–xi (1988)

Executive Summary

BACKGROUND

In recent years, legislators and court officials have become increasingly interested in the use of alternative dispute resolution (ADR) procedures to dispose of civil lawsuits. ADR programs divert certain cases from the regular trial court calendar to some form of arbitration or mediation process. The goals of these procedures are to reduce congestion on trial calendars, to diminish court costs, to speed case disposition, and to reduce costs and time for litigants.

In court-based ADR programs, the courts retain administrative control of the cases. One court-based ADR procedure that has been particularly popular with legislators and court officials is *court-annexed arbitration*. These programs divert certain classes of cases to a relatively informal hearing before one or more experienced attorneys, who provide a decision on liability and damages. Typically, the parties to the case may then either accept the award or reject it and demand trial *de novo*. If they choose the latter, the case returns to the court's calendar and moves along to trial.

In 1983, New Jersey introduced mandatory arbitration of automobile injury lawsuits in Burlington and Union counties as an experimental procedure. The Institute for Civil Justice was asked to help design the experiment and evaluated the pilot program in 1984. The program was adopted statewide in 1985. The New Jersey Administrative Office of the

Courts asked ICJ to evaluate the program's effectiveness, and evaluation began in 1986.

RESEARCH APPROACH

The ICJ's evaluation posed five basic questions:

- How was the program working?
- Did it change disposition patterns?
- Did it speed disposition?
- Did it reduce litigant's costs?
- Do participants like it?

To address these questions, we needed to:

1. Examine lawsuits representing the entire range of auto negligence cases filed in New Jersey;

2. Include cases from multiple courts, reflecting the diversity of caseload composition, resource constraints, local legal culture, and arbitration program implementation statewide;

3. Compare auto cases filed before the program was implemented with those filed after its implementation to ascertain whether the total system of auto negligence litigation had changed during that period;

4. Investigate differences in the postarbitration period between cases assigned to arbitration and those unassigned (presumably because of ineligibility); and

5. Collect data from multiple sources to measure the key program outcome variables.

To implement this evaluation scheme, we randomly sampled more than 1,000 auto negligence cases filed in eight New Jersey courts in the second half of 1983 (before the program's inception) and the second half of 1985. The latter included cases assigned to arbitration as well as cases that were not. We sampled cases by the date at which they were filed (rather than the date at which they were arbitrated or terminated) because this strategy allowed us to examine whether a change in the litigation environment provided by the courts—the arbitration program—influenced the manner in which cases were litigated from the day they were filed. For each case sampled, we collected two kinds of data: (1) we abstracted data from court records, and (2) we surveyed attorneys to obtain data from their records.

To obtain data about how participants evaluated the arbitration program in which they were involved, we conducted a survey of approximately 300 litigants and 400 attorneys immediately after their arbitration hearings. The sample for this survey was drawn from all eight courts.

CONCLUSIONS

Effects on Program Functioning

* * * The following conclusions can be drawn from these data:

The program captures a significant fraction of auto negligence cases, but relatively few are disposed of by an arbitration judgment. In our sample, about 68 percent of the cases were assigned to the program, but many of them settled before they reached an arbitration hearing. Just over half of the assigned cases (about 55 percent) were actually arbitrated, and about 40 percent of those were terminated by the arbitration judgment.

More than half of the arbitrated cases are appealed, but trials de novo *are rare.* Only 10 percent of the arbitrated cases actually went to a trial *de novo*; this is only 3 percent of all the cases that were assigned to the program, or 2 percent of all the auto negligence filings. Disputants may file an appeal primarily as a bargaining tactic; we found that over 80 percent of appealed cases settled before a trial took place.

Effects on Litigation and Disposition Patterns

We were unable to detect a significant effect of the program on the trial rate. However, trial rates were initially quite low (less than 5 percent), making it difficult to measure any further reduction. We estimate that our sample size was large enough to allow us to detect a fairly modest effect on the trial rate, but we would have needed a considerably larger sample to detect a reduction of 1 or 2 percent. It should be noted that a small reduction in the trial rate might be sufficient to bring about meaningful reduction in judicial workload.

Cases that are assigned to the program are more likely to be adjudicated. Before the program was introduced, most answered cases settled or were dismissed without an adjudicatory hearing—that is, without a trial. The arbitration program has provided disputants with an alternative adjudicatory option: an arbitration hearing.

Assigned cases terminate at a slower rate; the delay appears to be linked to the scheduling of arbitration hearings. Cases assigned to the arbitration program in 1985 terminated at a significantly slower rate than either the unassigned cases or the cases filed in 1983. This effect was especially pronounced in the first 12 months after filing. However, the assigned cases began terminating more rapidly after this point, and the assigned cases had almost closed the gap 18 months after filing. We believe that this later acceleration may have occurred because many disputants postponed settlement negotiations while waiting for an arbitration hearing.

Effects on Case Activity and Private Costs

The program appears to have slightly increased case activity by attorneys and court staff. We believe that this increase reflects a new set of litigation activities brought about by the introduction of the arbitration program: scheduling, preparing for, and participating in an arbitration hearing.

The program has not had a measurable effect on attorney hours and fees.

Litigant and Attorney Evaluations

Disputants were generally quite favorable in their evaluation of arbitration. Both litigants and attorneys viewed arbitration hearings as fair procedures and felt that their cases had received high-quality treatment by the arbitrators. Disputants rarely reported that the arbitrators had been unprepared, had shown favoritism, or had simply "split the difference" instead of reaching a principled judgment on the merits of the case. Moreover, the majority of litigants and attorneys rated arbitration as a more efficient procedure than either trial by jury or trial by judge.

On average, plaintiffs and their attorneys were more favorable in their evaluation of arbitration than defendants and defense attorneys; this discrepancy appeared to reflect the fact that the arbitrators usually awarded at least some money to the plaintiffs. Also, attorneys were more favorable than litigants in their evaluation of arbitration. Nevertheless, although most attorneys viewed arbitration as a fair procedure, about half of them felt that a jury trial was even fairer.

IMPLICATIONS FOR COURT POLICY

Efficiency and Expediency Claims Reconsidered

Our findings illustrate the importance of systematic empirical evaluation of ADR programs. The claim that arbitration is a mechanism for expediting tort litigation is intuitively plausible and is often viewed as self-evident; however, our data suggest a more complicated story. While we found no evidence to dispute the claim that arbitration is a more efficient form of adjudication than trial, this ignores the fact that *very few cases ever go to trial.* If an ADR program diverts a significant number of cases from trial, then it is likely to reduce public and private litigation costs as well as court congestion and delay. However, if the perception that trial is prohibitively time-consuming and expensive is motivating litigants to settle cases privately, then a program that offers an informal alternative might induce many of them to change their minds and wait for a hearing. As a result, the program will divert cases from private settlement. Since more cases were settled privately than were tried, the net result may be an increase in the proportion of cases that are disposed of through court involvement. We suspect that this scenario characterizes the introduction of court-annexed arbitration in New Jersey.

Lessons for Implementation

Without a controlled experiment, we cannot be certain about our suggestions for improving implementation; however, the following conclusions appear plausible:

Prescreening appears to reduce trial de novo *requests.* Administrators in courts that are not currently prescreening cases might consider whether the potential decrease in trial *de novo* requests justifies the additional effort.

Early hearings can expedite the termination of cases. We found a significant relationship between the time a case took to reach an arbitration hearing and the amount of time a case took to terminate. We believe that assigned cases might terminate more quickly if the litigants, attorneys, and court personnel cooperate to bring about earlier hearings.

The size of the arbitration panel and the method of rescheduling cases for trial had minimal effects. We found little evidence to justify strong policy recommendations regarding either the size of the arbitration panel or the manner in which arbitrated cases are scheduled for trial.

Arbitration Meets a Demand for Informal Adjudication

It appears that the New Jersey arbitration program is providing a service to disputants involved in auto negligence suits, albeit a service somewhat different from what the designers might have envisioned. The program appears to be meeting a demand for informal adjudication. Disputants want a hearing—an opportunity to present their case before an impartial third party and to receive a judgment based on the merits of the case. Moreover, they want a hearing to be dignified, respectful, and impartial, and they feel that arbitration hearings in New Jersey meet these criteria. Attorneys do not appear to mind the fact that arbitration hearings are informal, and litigants actually see this informality as a plus. In fact, it appears that disputants who might otherwise settle privately are willing to wait a year or more to take their case to arbitration. Thus, the arbitration program is providing an opportunity for more cases to be adjudicated, and it appears to be doing so without adding to private litigation costs.

NOTES AND QUESTIONS

1. How would you interpret the findings of the New Jersey arbitration study? Was the program "successful"? Note that how you answer this question may depend on what you see as the goals of the program—for example, was the program intended to save time and money, to provide "access to justice," or to satisfy some other interest?

2.   The importance of a study such as the New Jersey arbitration evaluation is not to answer a simple question about whether or not court-annexed arbitration "works." Instead, the significance of evaluation studies such as the one described here is to help illuminate the circumstances under which a process has particular effects. Accordingly, the study sheds lights on design issues such as the role of pre-screening and early hearings. In 1996, the RAND Corporation released the results of an evaluation of ADR in six federal courts under the Civil Justice Reform Act. The study concluded that there was "no strong statistical evidence that the mediation or neutral evaluation programs, as implemented in the six districts studied, significantly affected time to disposition, litigation costs, or attorney views of fairness or satisfaction with case management." JAMES S. KAKALIK, TERENCE DUNWORTH, LAURAL A. HILL, DANIEL MCCAFFREY, MARIAN OSHIRO, NICHOLAS M. PACE & MARY E. VAIANA, AN EVALUATION OF MEDIATION AND EARLY NEUTRAL EVALUATION UNDER THE CIVIL JUSTICE REFORM ACT, xxxiv (1996). Professor Craig McEwen proposes reframing these findings as follows: "Lawyers and parties in federal courts fail to make effective use of mediation and early neutral evaluation to speed resolution and reduce costs." Craig McEwen, *Managing Corporate Disputing: Overcoming Barriers to the Effective Use of Mediation for Reducing the Cost and Time of Litigation*, 14 Ohio St. J. on Disp. Resol. 1, 3 (1998). How might this reframing change the nature of the response to the report's findings? Compare these findings to those from the study of the Early Assessment Program in the U.S. District Court for the Western District of Missouri. DONNA STIENSTRA, MOLLY JOHNSON & PATRICIA LOMBARD, A STUDY OF THE FIVE DEMONSTRATION PROGRAMS ESTABLISHED UNDER THE CIVIL JUSTICE REFORM ACT OF 1990, FEDERAL JUDICIAL CENTER 215–53 (1997) (finding savings in time and money).

3.   The results of the MacCoun et al. research in New Jersey highlight the importance of defining a comparison group with which to compare cases resolved through a dispute resolution process. Professor Chris Guthrie notes: "In a system where a tiny fraction of cases is actually tried, what matters most is not how litigants rate mediation relative to *trial* but how they rate mediation relative to the *litigation processes that are actually likely to lead to the resolution of the dispute*. Data from federal and state courts show that litigants are likely to resolve their disputes not through trials on the merits but rather through pre-trial motions or settlement. In 2011, the federal district courts "terminated" 302,922 civil cases. Only 1.1% of these cases (3,194) went to trial. Rather, 18% (54,440) were terminated without any court action, the majority (72%; 218,131) were terminated pre-trial, and 9% (27,157) were terminated during or after the pre-trial period without reaching trial. Federal Judicial Caseload Statistics, Table C–4A, http://www. uscourts.gov/uscourts/Statistics/JudicialBusiness/2011/US_District_Courts— Civil_all.pdf. *See also* Chris Guthrie, *Procedural Justice Research and the Paucity of Trials*, 2002 J. Disp. Resol. 127, 128–29 (2002).

4.   For other research evaluating dispute resolution processes, see, for example, E. Allen Lind, Robert MacCoun, Patricia Ebener, William L.F.

Felstiner, Deborah R. Hensler, Judith Resnik & Tom R. Tyler, *In the Eye of the Beholder: Tort Litigants' Evaluations of Their Experiences in the Civil Justice System*, 24 Law & Soc'y Rev. 953 (1990); Bobbi McAdoo, *A Report to the Minnesota Supreme Court: The Impact of Rule 114 on Civil Litigation Practice in Minnesota*, 25 Hamline L. Rev. 401 (2002); Joshua D. Rosenberg & H. Jay Folberg, *Alternative Dispute Resolution: An Empirical Analysis*, 46 Stan. L. Rev. 1487 (1994) (excerpted in Chapter VI, beginning at page 804); Roselle Wissler, *The Effects of Mandatory Mediation: Empirical Research on the Experience of Small Claims and Common Pleas Courts*, 33 Willamette L. Rev. 565 (1997). For a review of empirical research assessing mediation and neutral evaluation, see Roselle L. Wissler, *The Effectiveness of Court Connected Dispute Resolution in Civil Cases*, 22 Conflict Resol. Q. 55 (2004).

5.   For additional information about how to do evaluation research, see for example, DAVID L. FAIGMAN, DAVID H. KAYE, MICHAEL J. SAKS, & JOSEPH SANDERS, SCIENCE IN THE LAW: STANDARDS, STATISTICS, AND RESEARCH ISSUES (2002); JEFFREY KATZER, KENNETH H. COOK, & WAYNE W. CROUCH, EVALUATING INFORMATION: A GUIDE FOR USERS OF SOCIAL SCIENCE RESEARCH (4th ed. 1998); ROBERT M. LAWLESS, JENNIFER K. ROBBENNOLT, & THOMAS S. ULEN, EMPIRICAL METHODS IN LAW (2009); MELINDA OSTERMEYER & SUSAN L. KEILITZ, MONITORING AND EVALUATING COURT–BASED DISPUTE RESOLUTION PROGRAMS: A GUIDE FOR JUDGES AND COURT MANAGERS (1997); ELIZABETH ROLPH & ERIK MOLLER, EVALUATING AGENCY ALTERNATIVE DISPUTE RESOLUTION PROGRAMS: A USER'S GUIDE TO DATA COLLECTION AND USE (1995); BARBARA SOMMER & ROBERT SOMMER, A PRACTICAL GUIDE TO BEHAVIORAL RESEARCH: TOOLS AND TECHNIQUES (5th ed. 1997); ADR Program Evaluation Recommendations, 65 Fed. Reg. 59,200 (Oct. 4, 2000), *available at* http://www. epa.gov/adr/evalu.pdf (last visited Nov. 18, 2013).

C. ADVISING CLIENTS IN SELECTING A DISPUTE RESOLUTION PROCESS

Next we turn to the process of advising an individual client about the available dispute resolution processes. Specifically, we examine how a lawyer can gain a deeper understanding of the client's situation and needs in order to advise the client about what would likely happen in court and about the potential advantages and disadvantages of various methods of dispute resolution. In a world of "process pluralism," both the attorney and the client must have an expanded understanding of the interests involved and the likely outcomes in order for the client to effectively reach a decision about which course to pursue.

In the first excerpt, Professor Roselle Wissler describes some potential barriers to attorneys' discussion of ADR with clients, and presents empirical research describing the role of these barriers in practice. In the second excerpt, we examine the nature of the discussion of dispute resolution processes with clients. The factors identified by Professors Frank Sander and Lukasz Rozdeiczer can be used in assisting such clients in choosing an appropriate process for resolving a particular dispute. The final excerpt discusses the use of dispute resolution clauses in business agreements.

1. BARRIERS TO DISCUSSION AND USE OF ADR

ROSELLE L. WISSLER, BARRIERS TO ATTORNEYS' DISCUSSION AND USE OF ADR

19 Ohio St. J. on Disp. Resol. 459, 462–68, 470–72, 493–97, 500 (2004)

Various methods to increase voluntary ADR use have been proposed and adopted, including providing ADR information or education to attorneys, encouraging or requiring attorneys to discuss ADR options with clients, and requiring attorneys to discuss possible ADR use with opposing counsel. Underlying these approaches is the assumption that certain factors operate as barriers that constrain attorneys from regularly considering and using ADR processes. Commonly cited impediments include attorneys' lack of knowledge about ADR processes, attorneys' unfavorable views of ADR, attorneys' concerns that proposing ADR will be seen as a "sign of weakness," the routines and economics of law practice, and the lack of judicial involvement.

* * *

II. A REVIEW OF POTENTIAL BARRIERS TO ATTORNEYS' DISCUSSION AND USE OF ADR

A. Attorneys' Knowledge of ADR Processes

Commentators maintain that attorneys should be informed about ADR in order to be able to counsel clients about litigation and ADR options and to participate effectively in a range of dispute resolution processes. Attorneys who do not feel sufficiently familiar with ADR processes to discuss them with clients and opposing counsel and to participate in them might be reluctant to discuss or use ADR.

* * *

B. Attorneys' Views of ADR

Attorneys' views of ADR, negotiation, and litigation are thought to play a role in their willingness to discuss and use ADR. Attorneys who view ADR as offering few advantages, while creating disadvantages relative to negotiation and trial, might be hesitant to consider ADR.

Attorneys' concerns about ADR could reflect misperceptions as a result of unfamiliarity with ADR. In addition, attorneys might not see the appropriateness or value of ADR because their training, "philosophical map," and practice emphasize an adversarial rather than a problem-solving perspective. And for some attorneys, negative perceptions of ADR could be the direct result of experience with a poor quality ADR session.

Several cognitive barriers that hinder negotiation and settlement also might affect attorneys' views and impede their use of ADR. For instance, if "optimistic overconfidence" leads to overestimates of the likelihood of favorable case outcomes, attorneys will be less likely to see a need to use ADR to facilitate settlement. If their consideration of ADR is "framed" in terms of what will be lost relative to litigation rather than what will be gained, attorneys will be less likely to use ADR. And if their opponent proposes ADR, "reactive devaluation" will lead attorneys to suspect that using ADR will be to their disadvantage and to view it less positively.

In addition, attorneys' economic interests could color their views of the relative benefits of ADR and litigation. Attorneys who are paid on a contingent-fee basis might give insufficient weight to the importance of their client's non-monetary goals and, thus, attach less importance to ADR's potential for addressing those interests. And because contingent-fee lawyers have an interest in resolving modest cases quickly, they might view ADR as producing a more expensive and slower resolution than a negotiated settlement. By contrast, attorneys paid on an hourly fee basis might attach extra weight to full, formal discovery and to the benefits their clients can derive by delaying settlement or threatening to go to trial. And attorneys' estimates of whether their long-term compensation, advancement, and prestige would benefit more from clients' increased use of ADR or of litigation also could affect their views of these options.

The structural and strategic aspects of litigation that are thought to impede early settlement are also likely to affect attorneys' views of when or whether to discuss ADR. The demands of numerous other active cases and the lack of early court deadlines contribute to not assessing cases early for their ADR or settlement potential. The virtually automatic progression of litigation and the inertia of following the usual process, combined with the escalation of commitment and strategic moves in negotiation, make it difficult to stop the process and propose ADR.

One specific view of ADR that is frequently mentioned as a barrier is the concern that proposing ADR is viewed as a sign of weakness. Attorneys might be reluctant to discuss ADR if they think it will be interpreted by clients as a lack of commitment to their case or by opposing counsel as a lack of confidence or resolve. In addition to strategic considerations in the instant case, some attorneys might have a more general interest in establishing a reputation for being a fierce litigator and, thus, might not propose ADR if they think doing so will make them look weak.

* * *

C. *Judicial Involvement*

Given the many impediments to ADR use discussed above, judicial involvement in the consideration of ADR processes might be needed to overcome them. Judges' support for the use of ADR can enhance attorneys' views of the value and appropriateness of ADR. Of course, some of the same factors that are thought to keep attorneys from discussing ADR might also act as barriers to greater judicial encouragement of ADR. For instance, judges might be reluctant to suggest ADR if they themselves are not knowledgeable about or supportive of ADR. In addition, judges are likely to be hesitant to discuss ADR with litigants due to concerns about interfering with the attorney-client relationship. And unless the discussion of ADR options is integrated into an existing case management system, caseload and scheduling pressures are likely to prevent judicial involvement.

* * *

III. THE PRESENT STUDY: SURVEY PROCEDURE AND RESPONDENT CHARACTERISTICS

Questionnaires were mailed to all members of the Trial Practice Section of the State Bar of Arizona in June 2001. At that time, Arizona attorneys had no explicit obligation to consider ADR. The questionnaire asked the attorneys about their discussions and use of ADR in the context of their Arizona state court civil practice during the preceding two years. The attorneys also were asked about their knowledge of different ADR processes, potential benefits of and barriers to using ADR, and the nature of their law practice.

Four hundred forty-six completed questionnaires were received, for a response rate of 45%. * * * Because we assumed that attorneys whose practice involved a greater proportion of civil litigation would provide more informed judgments, we limited the analyses reported in this Article to those attorneys who devoted half or more of their practice to civil litigation. This excluded 17 (4%) of the respondents. Thus, the findings reported in this article are based on the 426 Trial Practice Section members who devoted at least half of their practice to civil litigation. On average, these attorneys devoted 94% of their practice to civil litigation.

* * *

VI. SUMMARY AND IMPLICATIONS OF THE RESEARCH FINDINGS FOR ADR POLICY

A. *Summary*

Discussing ADR processes has become a common practice for Arizona civil litigation attorneys, although not in all of their cases. Three-fourths of attorneys discussed ADR with their clients in three-fourths or more of their cases. Attorneys discussed ADR with opposing counsel less frequently, with nearly half of the attorneys doing so in three-fourths or more of their cases. These ADR discussions generally did not take place early in the life of a case. Nor did ADR discussions automatically translate into ADR use: one-fifth of attorneys used voluntary ADR processes in three-fourths or more of their cases. Although attorneys who more frequently discussed ADR with clients and opposing counsel used voluntary ADR processes more often, those who tended to discuss ADR early were not more likely to use ADR.

The findings are consistent with assumptions that certain ADR-specific factors constrain attorneys' voluntary discussion and use of ADR. Attorneys who reported less judicial encouragement of ADR, a lower rate of settlement in ADR cases, less familiarity with ADR, less favorable views of ADR, and less support for mandatory ADR policies tended to discuss and use ADR in a smaller proportion of their cases. Taken together, these factors were strongly related to how often attorneys voluntarily discussed and used ADR. Attorneys' views regarding whether ADR provided free discovery or whether the supply of qualified neutrals was sufficient were not related to how often they discussed or used ADR.

Only a subset of these factors—attorneys' views regarding ADR's benefits, their familiarity with the processes, and the degree of judicial encouragement of ADR use—were related to how often attorneys first discussed ADR early in a case, and their combined impact was small. These ADR-specific factors apparently play less of a role in the timing of ADR discussions than do other factors, such as those that affect the timing of the negotiation process more generally.

Despite the strong relationship between these factors and attorneys' discussion and use of ADR, most of the barriers were not widespread. That is, fewer than one-fifth of the attorneys were unfamiliar with the various ADR processes, thought others viewed proposing ADR as a sign of weakness, reported that fewer than half of their ADR cases had settled, or thought ADR did not offer substantial benefits, greater client satisfaction, and earlier settlements. A larger proportion of attorneys, however, reported a low rate of judicial encouragement of ADR and were opposed to mandates requiring the discussion and use of ADR.

B.   Implications for Policies to Increase Voluntary ADR Use

In this section, we discuss what the findings of the present study and other empirical studies suggest about the potential effectiveness of two approaches for increasing voluntary ADR use, namely expanded ADR education and mandated ADR consideration. First, however, we must note a caution in extrapolating from the findings of the present study, based on data regarding voluntary discussions, to situations that involve mandatory consideration of ADR. Once the voluntary aspect of ADR discussions is removed, the comparative and the combined impacts of the various factors on ADR use could be dramatically different.

1. *Expanding ADR Education and Information*

One set of proposals to increase voluntary ADR use focuses on increasing attorneys' familiarity with ADR, either through the expansion of law school or continuing education course offerings or through ADR information provided by the court at the time of filing. The present study found that attorneys who were less familiar with ADR were less likely to discuss and use ADR. In addition, attorneys who were less knowledgeable about ADR were less likely to think ADR offered benefits and were more likely to think proposing ADR signaled weakness, and attorneys who held these views discussed and used ADR less often.

Thus, these findings suggest that efforts to increase attorneys' familiarity with ADR processes might increase how often they discuss and use ADR. And, presumably, educational efforts also would enhance the effective use of ADR by giving attorneys a better understanding of which processes address which sources of impasse or client goals and how the different processes could be structured or combined to address case-specific needs. The findings of other studies, however, suggest that the impact of increased ADR education on ADR use might be small, and smaller than if the increased familiarity had been acquired instead through direct experience with ADR processes.

The impact of ADR information, education, and training might be enhanced if it is targeted not only at attorneys but also at judges and regular users of legal services. In the present study, judicial encouragement of ADR use was the factor that had the strongest impact on the frequency of attorneys' discussion and use of ADR. Judges' greater familiarity with the various ADR processes might enhance their ability to discuss ADR with attorneys and their willingness to suggest the use of ADR. Efforts to inform "repeat player" litigants about ADR processes might lead them to be more receptive to their attorneys' presentation of those options, although direct experience with ADR is likely to have an even greater effect. Educational efforts alone, however, are likely to have a limited impact on ADR use because they address only a subset of the barriers to considering ADR.

2. *Mandating ADR Discussions with Clients or Opposing Counsel*

Other proposed approaches to increase voluntary ADR use are to encourage or require attorneys to discuss the possible use of ADR with their clients, with opposing counsel, or with both. These duties have been incorporated in aspirational creeds, professional responsibility or ethics codes, and statutes or court rules. The nature of the obligation to consult with clients about ADR ranges from simply advising clients of the availability of ADR processes or giving them the court's ADR brochure, to providing an assessment of the advantages and disadvantages of available ADR options and assistance in selecting the most appropriate process.

Will these suggestions or requirements increase the frequency of attorneys' ADR discussions and, if so, will that result in increased voluntary ADR use?

* * *

Overall, the findings [of existing research] seem to suggest that the components of a mandatory discussion rule that would enhance its effectiveness include: a requirement that attorneys provide their clients ADR information and discuss ADR with opposing counsel; a deadline by which the discussions must take place, a reporting requirement, and enforcement; a court conference to assist attorneys in choosing an ADR process; and active judicial involvement. The findings of the present study shed further light on why these components seem likely to enhance the effectiveness of mandatory ADR discussion requirements in increasing voluntary ADR use, and on what other components might be helpful.

NOTES AND QUESTIONS

1.   What other barriers to discussing ADR with clients or using ADR can you think of? Make a list of these barriers. Think about how each barrier might be addressed in the design of a dispute resolution system. Do the barriers vary when considered at the client, firm, and professional levels?

2.   A study of the use of ADR in Missouri explored the reasons that some attorneys had not used ADR. The most common reasons cited were that their cases were "not appropriate" for ADR, that the court did not actively encourage or order ADR, that they preferred trial, that they settle cases as well or better without ADR, and that ADR would impose an unnecessary expense. Bobbi McAdoo & Art Hinshaw, *The Challenge of Institutionalizing Alternative Dispute Resolution: Attorney Perspectives on the Effect of Rule 17 on Civil Litigation in Missouri*, 67 Mo. L. Rev. 473, 489 (2002).

3.   Many commentators have argued that attorneys should have the ethical responsibility to discuss with clients the differing methods by which they can resolve their disputes. *See e.g.*, Carrie Menkel–Meadow, *Ethics in ADR: The Many "Cs" of Professional Responsibility and Dispute Resolution*, 28 Fordham Urb. L.J. 979, 981 (2001) (arguing for "an ethical obligation to counsel clients about the multiple ways to resolving problems and planning transactions"). The Model Rules of Professional Conduct provide:

Rule 1.2 Scope of Representation and Allocation of Authority Between Client and Lawyer

(a) . . . a lawyer shall abide by a client's decisions concerning the objectives of representation and, as required by Rule 1.4, shall consult with the client as to the means by which they are to be pursued . . .

Rule 1.4 Communication

(a) A lawyer shall . . . reasonably consult with the client about the means by which the client's objectives are to be accomplished . . .

Rule 2.1 Advisor

Comment

(5) . . . Similarly, when a matter is likely to involve litigation, it may be necessary under Rule 1.4 to inform the client of forms of dispute resolution that might constitute reasonable alternatives to litigation . . .

Some jurisdictions *encourage* lawyers to counsel their clients about alternative methods of dispute resolution. *See, e.g.,* Ark. Code Ann. § 16–7–204 ("An attorney . . . is encouraged to advise his or her client about the dispute resolution options available to him or her and to assist him or her in the selection of the technique or procedure, including litigation, deemed appropriate for dealing with the client's dispute, case, or controversy."). Many jurisdictions *require* lawyers to counsel their clients about the availability and appropriateness of alternative methods of resolving disputes. *See, e.g.,* Minn. Gen. Prac. Rule 114.03(b) (2004) (requiring attorneys to "provide clients with . . . ADR information"); N.D. Rules of Court 8.8(b) (2011) (requiring the filing of a statement certifying "that the parties have discussed ADR participation with each other and that the parties' lawyers have discussed ADR with their clients"). *See* Marshall J. Breger, *Should an Attorney Be Required to Advise a Client of ADR Options?*, 13 Geo. J. Legal Ethics 427 (2000); Kristin L. Fortin, *Reviving the Lawyer's Role as Servant Leader: The Professional Paradigm and a Lawyer's Ethical Obligation to Inform Clients About Alternative Dispute Resolution*, 22 Geo. J. Legal Ethics 589 (2009). Professor Robert Cochran has argued for "the extension of malpractice liability to attorneys who fail to allow clients the choice of whether to pursue mediation or arbitration." Robert F. Cochran, Jr., *Legal Representation and the Next Steps Toward Client Control: Attorney Malpractice for the Failure to Allow the Client to Control Negotiation and Pursue Alternatives to Litigation*, 47 Wash. & Lee. L. Rev. 819, 869 (1990).

4.   Some law firms have not only overcome the barriers described above, but have specifically decided to provide ADR services. *See* CATHERINE CRONIN–HARRIS, BUILDING ADR INTO THE LAW FIRM: ADR SYSTEMS DESIGN (1997); Kevin R. Casey, Law Firm ADR Departments Can Respond to Market Challenges, 25 Alternatives to High Cost Litig. 1 (2007); Kevin R. Casey, Getting Past Setup Obstacles, and Moving to Implementation, For Law Firm ADR Groups, 25 Alternatives to High Cost Litig. 17 (2007). In addition, it is the practice of some law firms to appoint "settlement counsel" for a particular case. This involves appointing an attorney, separate from the trial counsel, whose role is to focus on the settlement discussions. William F. Coyne, *The Case for Settlement Counsel*, 14 Ohio St. J. on Disp. Resol. 367 (1999); James

E. McGuire, *Why Litigators Should Use Settlement Counsel*, 18 Alternatives 107 (2000). As we saw in Chapter VI, some attorneys now practice "collaborative law" in which the attorneys for both sides agree to work with the parties to resolve the dispute. The attorneys agree, however, that they will not represent the clients in court and will withdraw if the case is litigated. Pauline H. Tesler, *Collaborative Law Neutrals Produce Better Resolutions*, 21 Alternatives 1 (2003). *See also* John Lande, *Possibilities for Collaborative Law: Ethics and Practice of Lawyer Disqualification and Process Control in a New Model of Lawyering*, 64 Ohio St. L.J. 1315 (2003) (raising ethical and other questions about collaborative lawyering) an excerpt of which appears in Chapter VI at page 865.

5. If you were a member of the management committee of a large law firm, would you support any or all of the following steps:

- establishing an ADR practice group to act as advocates for clients in ADR proceedings and assist clients in building and choosing dispute resolution processes;

- establishing an ADR practice group that would provide neutrals for mediation, arbitration, and various mixed processes;

- hiring an ADR specialist to advise and assist the lawyers in the firm?

Might some law firms shun ADR procedures because they produce fewer billable hours than litigation? Eric Green, who was a mediator in the antitrust case brought by the U.S. Justice Department against Microsoft Corp., has a response to such concerns: " 'Don, baby, if you don't do it, Jack will do it, and your client will end up going to him.' You have to get across that the long-term interests of all lawyers are to serve the needs of their clients." David Berreby, *Thoughts on ADR: An Interview with a Veteran Neutral*, Alternatives to High Cost Litig., May 1986, at 3, 14.

2. SELECTING A PROCESS

The next excerpt offers an approach for selecting among the most common procedures for resolving disputes.

FRANK E.A. SANDER & LUKASZ ROZDEICZER, MATCHING CASES AND DISPUTE RESOLUTION PROCEDURES: DETAILED ANALYSIS LEADING TO A MEDIATION– CENTERED APPROACH
11 Harv. Negot. L. Rev. 1, 10–29 (2006)

[W]e believe three lenses are key to focusing the analysis: goals, facilitating features, and impediments.

Goals. The first question regarding the choice of the most appropriate process relates to the kind of objectives the party would like to achieve during, or at the end of, this process. In other words, this future-oriented approach asks what should happen as a result of the choice of the particular dispute resolution process. As a party will usually have more than one objective, she should also prioritize her various goals.

Facilitating Features. When the party determines the desired (future) outcome, she should reflect on her present resources, i.e., the attributes of the case that make it particularly suitable or unsuitable to solving the case. We therefore propose that the party should focus next on the attributes of the process, the case, and the parties that are likely to facilitate reaching effective resolution. For example, if the dispute involves lower-level representatives of the parties, but requires a broader view of the problem from the perspective of the whole company, this might suggest the use of a minitrial, which involves high-level officials.

Impediments. In the third step of the analysis, we suggest that one should focus on the ability of various procedures to overcome impediments to effective resolution. This is a focus on the forum.

* * *

B.   The Goals of the Parties

One of the most basic aspects of finding the appropriate dispute resolution procedure is to look to the goals of the parties and how they can be satisfied by various processes. As the example below makes clear, the determination of the goals leads to the particular process or processes that will achieve those goals.

1.   Assessing Goals

One of the most essential tasks of a party and her counsel is assessing appropriate goals. We illustrate that by the example that follows.

Anna is going through a divorce with John. She brings her problem to you—an attorney—and asks for your advice on how to proceed. Her choice of procedure will partly depend on the goals that she wants to achieve. Does she want to preserve a good relationship with John? Does she want John to participate in raising their children, or on the contrary, does she want to prevent him from seeing them? How important is it for her to maximize her monetary income from the divorce? How important is her financial concern when balanced against the relationship with John and other concerns? Does she want to keep divorce matters private? Does she have a desire for public vindication?

Before knowing what Anna really wants, it is impossible to make an informed decision about the preferable process. The table below shows some of the possible goals that Anna or other parties may want to achieve, and the degree to which various processes satisfy them. See Table 2.

Anna's analysis. In the divorce case described above, probably the first question Anna has to answer is what kind of a relationship she wants to have with John after the divorce. If they have children, she should also consider what parental relationship would be best for the children. As indicated in Table 2 (Goals), mediation gives the highest chance of preserving and even improving the relationship. On the other end of this spectrum, litigation often threatens to destroy the relationship. According to research, thirty percent of couples that mediated their divorces felt that mediation actually improved their relationship. By contrast, only fifteen percent felt that litigation improved their relationship and fifty percent believed that it worsened it. The benefits of mediation are also salient in the context of commercial contracts—fifty-nine percent of attorneys in the Cornell Survey stated that an important reason for choosing mediation over adjudication was "preserving good relationship."

However, a future relationship with John may not be what Anna desires. To the contrary, she may prefer her children to have as little exposure as possible to John. In such a case, she should probably go to court and request that the court grant very limited visitation rights to John or even issue a restraining order against him if the situation warrants one.

If Anna decides that her most important goal is to maximize her monetary income from the divorce, the suggested forum to best realize such a goal would probably be court. However, the question of the highest payoff is a complicated one. At first sight, winning a case in litigation might secure the highest possible payoff. There are, however, three caveats. First, losing the case may result in the highest loss rather than the highest gain, and, therefore, considering the risk of loss, this procedure may turn out to be not so beneficial after all. Additionally, a monetary outcome of litigation will probably be offset by higher transactional costs compared to other procedures. Thus, due to a risk of high loss and to high transactional costs, the expected value of litigation may be lower relative to its alternatives. Second, the outcome of a court case likely will assume a constant pie and disregard the possibility of increasing the payoffs. Thus, parties often could get higher payoffs through a pie-enlarging settlement (via mediation) than in court. This would be the case where, in exchange for higher alimony, child support, or a lump sum, Anna offers John something he could not get through the court. For example, Anna could agree not to reveal some of John's business or private secrets or she could agree to more convenient visitation times than would otherwise be set by the court. Hence, through problem-solving and value-creating opportunities, one or both parties could achieve an outcome more favorable than the court alternative. Third, winning in litigation may win the battle but lose the war if Anna is unable to collect on the judgment against John.

Table 2. Goals

0 = unlikely to satisfy goal   2 = satisfies goal substantially
1 = satisfies goal somewhat   3 = satisfies goal very substantially

	Process Goal	Mediation	Mini-Trial	Summary Jury Trial	Early Neutral Evaluation	Arbitration/ Private	Adjudication
1	Speed	3	2	2	3	0 – 2	0
2	Privacy	3	3	1	2	1	0
3	Public Vindication	0	1	1	1	2	3
4	Neutral Evaluation	1	1	2	2	3	3
5	Minimize Costs	3	2	2	3	0 – 2	0
6	Maintain/ Improve Relationship	3	2	2	1	1	0
7	Precedent	0 – 1	0 – 1	0 – 1	0 – 1	2	3
8	Max/Min Recovery	0 (3)	1	1	1	2	3
9	Create New Solutions	3	3	1	2	1	0
10	Party Control of Process	3	2	1	1	1 – 2	0
11	Party Control of Outcome	3	3	1	2	1	0
12	Shift Responsibility for Decision to a Third-Party	0 – 1	1	2	2	3	3
13	Court Supervision or Compulsion	0 – 2	0	1	1	2	3
14	Transformation of the Parties	3	1	0	0	0	0
15	Provide Satisfying Process	3	3	2	2	2	0
16	Improve Understanding of the Dispute	3	3	1	2	2	1
	OTHER						

Another important question that Anna needs to ask herself is whether she wants the case to become publicly known or whether she would prefer to keep it confidential. If John's behavior would be dangerous to their children, or if Anna wanted to publicly shame John, she might want to make the case public. The court would be the best place to do so. If, however, her intention is to keep the case private and confidential, non-court mediation or another private, non-court process like case evaluation would be more suitable.

One of the key issues that Anna needs to contemplate is whether the mediation agreement should be enforceable as a private contract or as a court judgment. If the parties want to use a more facilitative process and still benefit from the enforcement of the court, they can settle through a facilitative court-annexed process such as mediation. Then the settlement, after being confirmed by the court, can be embodied in a court decree.

On the other hand, research shows a higher compliance rate with consensual agreements than with decrees that are forced upon the parties. Therefore, particularly when the parties desire continued cooperation in the future, they may prefer voluntary agreements to court decisions.

It should be noted that court enforcement should be balanced against the party's goal to keep the dispute and its result confidential, and, thus, parties must decide which objective is paramount.

2. Other Possible Goals

A particular challenge arises when the dispute is one of a group of disputes or centers on one event in a series. Not only does the party have to consider the future relationship with the other side, but the party must also determine how this case relates to other cases, which may completely change the goals of the party. For example, a party may care less about the outcome of a particular case than about such factors as precedent, future claims, economies of scale, chronology of the cases, or relationships with other parties (repeat players). Thus, when the perspective of the party widens from one specific case to a few linked cases, her goals, and hence the analysis of the most appropriate procedure, will shift as well.

It is very important that parties treat the goals given in Table 2 (Goals) just as examples among many possible objectives. The list of goals is far from exhaustive, and, in each dispute, the parties should ask themselves which particular goals are salient under the circumstances. For example, in this case Anna may not want her children to testify in court, and she may therefore strongly prefer mediation or other processes that are private and confidential. In commercial and other cases, a party may prefer to collect a lower amount sooner rather than a higher amount later. This situation may arise where a company has liquidity problems or where an accident victim needs money now for medical treatment.

Fairness is another goal that may occasionally be salient. For example, Anna, for reputational reasons, may say that her primary goal is to reach a fair settlement with John. Fairness, however, is an elusive concept that different individuals value differently. Fairness of process and fairness of outcome are also traditionally distinct. In light of these ambiguities, it will be difficult to pinpoint the process implications for Anna in such a case. Given the prevailing evidence of high satisfaction with mediation, as well as its flexibility, that process would generally be a good starting choice. More generally, consensual processes (i.e., mediation, minitrial, summary jury trial, and ENE) would seem to provide the best opportunity of achieving what disputants define as fairness. However, some parties may view inclusion of a third-party decision-maker as essential to fairness, which would point towards arbitration or court adjudication.

The reader will note that some of these goals pertain to a process outcome (e.g., to control process, to maintain privacy, etc.), and others are related to a substantive outcome (e.g., to create new solutions, to minimize or maximize recovery). Some goals include objectives that have both a substantive and a procedural impact (e.g., to minimize costs). These categories may serve as a helpful guide when looking for additional goals not listed in Table 2.

3.   Prioritizing and Weighting the Goals

After deciding which goals the party wants to achieve, one might add together the values in Table 2 (Goals) and "determine" which process best satisfies her goals. Such an approach, however, assumes that all of these concerns are of equal value to the party, which may not be true. A better approach would consist of both ranking and weighting the goals. Therefore, a party could assign a weight, in points, to each of her concerns, and then multiply them by the measure by which such procedure satisfies these goals, as indicated in Table 2 (Goals). For example, Anna might decide that since it would be best for the children that she and John maintain a good relationship, this should be her highest priority. She would therefore assign a weight of 3 to this goal.

It may also be very important to Anna that the procedure be kept private. Although everybody thinks of her only as a victim now, she is convinced that if outsiders knew all the facts about the breakdown of their marriage, she would have to bear part of the blame for it. Since it is less important than maintaining the relationship, she could assign a weight of 2 to the goal of privacy.

On the other hand, she is not quite sure whether she will manage to be tough enough in settlement negotiation with John; moreover, according to her lawyer, the law is on her side. For these reasons, she has a slight preference for shifting the responsibility for making the decision to a third party. Her last concern is to resolve this matter at a minimal cost. Since shifting responsibility for a decision to a third party and minimizing costs are less important to her than the first two goals, which she weighed at 3 and 2, she should assign a weight of 1 to each of the latter ones.

Assigning weights to these different goals should then be followed by multiplying the assigned weight by the effectiveness of each procedure in satisfying this goal. For example, weight 3 for "Maintaining/Improving Relationship" (from Table 2, Goals) would translate to the weighted "power/strength" of: 9 (3x3) for mediation; 6 (3x2) for minitrial; 6 (3x2) for summary jury trial; 3 (3x1) for early neutral evaluation; 3 (3x1) for arbitration; and 0 (3x0) for adjudication. After multiplying weights assigned to the selected goals, a party would then add up the numbers representing the strength of the weighted goals for each of the available procedures. For example, after adding weighted power/strength of goals selected by Anna: (Maintain/Improve Relationship x 3) + (Privacy x 2) + (Minimize costs x 1) + (Shift Responsibility for Decision to a Third Party x 1) the appropriate power/strengths of the processes are as follows: mediation (18–19), minitrial (15), summary jury trial, (12), early neutral evaluation (12), arbitration (8–10), and litigation (3). Therefore, Anna could conclude that mediation would probably best realize her objectives and that the worst choice in this case would be adjudication.

Although this example and proposed method involves a lot of counting and weighing, we still think that this method is more art than science. It is very important to remember that the outcomes of these calculations should not be taken literally, but rather that they only provide guidance for evaluating the parties' goals. Sometimes the primary benefit will be the exercise of going through this process rather than the numerical result reached.

4. The Goals of the Other Party?

Parties who have consistent goals probably can be convinced easily to use one process. However, what if the goals of the other party are inconsistent and would suggest another process? One option might be that they would agree to start from mediation, which seems to be a "safe" procedure (no commitment) for both parties, unless the case is one when even mediation is not appropriate. Another approach is suggested by the New Hampshire court rules. When the parties' ADR preferences are incompatible, the court will utilize the least binding process (e.g., mediation over arbitration).

C. Features of the Process, the Case, and the Parties that Facilitate Effective Resolution

Certain features of the case and the parties can facilitate reaching effective resolution. However, only with an appropriate dispute resolution procedure will they be triggered. For example, a good relationship and trust between the parties' attorneys can facilitate communication and lead to a better settlement. These facilitating features would not be maximally utilized if the parties selected litigation. Moreover, litigation could quickly destroy both a good pre-existing relationship and trust, creating an impediment to settlement later. Therefore, it is crucial for the parties to recognize the attributes of the case that may facilitate effective resolution, and to match these attributes with the process (e.g., mediation) that may trigger them.

Generally speaking, every procedure is capable of activating some of the facilitating features of the case or the parties. For example, mediation and minitrial can facilitate communication and maximize the parties' chances for a value-creating resolution. Summary jury trial and early neutral evaluation may provide an opportunity to make an early assessment of the strengths and weaknesses of the case, allowing the parties to make a more informed decision about a possible settlement. Adjudication (and binding arbitration) provides certain procedural tools that can serve parties' needs, including court enforcement during the dispute resolution process and at the decision-implementation stage.

In our mixed approach of fitting the forum to the fuss and the fuss to the forum, we think it is crucial not only to analyze the features of the case and the parties, but also to recognize the individual features of each procedure that can benefit the party. For example, if discovering assets of the defendant is important, or if a third party needs to appear at the proceedings, a party may prefer litigation, which offers ways of achieving these objectives, such as through discovery or impleader. In cases where the specific expertise of a neutral is needed, litigation may not be the best option. Other procedures like mediation, minitrial, or case evaluation, where parties can choose an expert-neutral, will be more advantageous. Each procedure may have many strengths. In Table 3 we present just a few of them, but in each case, parties should carefully consider the existence of other beneficial characteristics of the procedures.

1.   John's Business Dispute

One of the things that has been distracting John from his home and that has indirectly caused many quarrels with his wife, Anna, is his ongoing involvement in a messy business dispute.

Six years ago, John started a small commercial printing company, which has been operating with modest success. Last year, Jim, a college friend and computer whiz, approached John about providing sophisticated computer services for John's printing company, which he assured John would significantly enhance productivity. John was intrigued, and following extensive discussions, a contract was drawn up by their respective lawyers. Before it was formally executed, John, preoccupied by his divorce, got cold feet and called the whole deal off. Considering the long-standing relationship between the two of them, John was immensely surprised and hurt when he was served with a writ for a breach of contract suit filed by Jim. To make matters worse, in this document Jim accused John of getting a divorce for the sole purpose of immunizing some of his assets against possible claims by Jim. He demanded that the court freeze John and Anna's shared bank account and some other assets. Jim also accused John of dealing behind his back with someone else and asserted that John refused to talk to him and did not reply to his phone calls or any other messages.

Table 3. Facilitating Features

Process Feature	Problem–Solving	Reality–Checking			Adjudicating	
	Mediation	Mini Trial	SJT	ENE	Arbitration/Private Judging	Adjudication
1 Good Relationship Between the Attorneys	3	2	1	1	0	0
2 Good Relationship Between the Parties	3	2	1	1	0	0
3 Case/Parties Seem Apt for Problem–Solving	3	2	1	1	0	0
4 One or Both Parties are Willing to Apologize	3	3	1	1	0	0
5 Eager to Settle (or Engage in ADR)	3	2	2	2	0	0
6 High–Rank Agents Involved	2	3	2	2	1	1
7 Many Issues in Case	3	3	1	1	1	0
8 Party Would Benefit from Procedural Features of Litigation	0–2	1	2	1	2	3
9 Specific Expertise of a Neutral Required	3	3	1	3	3	1

OTHER

In the following paragraphs, we analyze some of the most important facilitating features of a procedure (litigation or arbitration), a case (suitability for problem solving), and the parties (relationship between the parties and their counsel).

2.   Features of the Procedure

Procedural features of litigation or arbitration. Before deciding which process might be most useful in promoting a party's interests, a party (or more often her counsel) should reflect on the procedural advantages and disadvantages of various procedures. Since among contemplated processes only litigation and arbitration have formalized procedures, those procedures will be our main focus here. As civil procedure is a large, complex subject, we will limit our remarks to only a few selected issues: discovery, formal hearing, and third-party involvement.

Discovery can either help or hinder a party's position. Unlike private dispute resolution forums, courts, through judicial orders, can compel a disclosure or protect against it. If Anna suspects her husband of concealing assets, a court process may be appropriate. However, a party must also account for the possibility of discovery abuse; as noted by Dauer, "discovery abuses are among the most frequently cited causes of excess cost and dissatisfaction with the formal judicial system." Even if there are no abuses in the discovery process, its costs can escalate and its results are sometimes unpredictable.

An alternative to formal discovery can be a private process of neutral (expert) fact-finding where the parties conduct their discovery according to their own rules. Parties in mediation or any other private procedure could, for example, limit their discovery to certain agreed-upon key issues and choose not to formally decide the remaining ones. In mediation and other facilitative processes, the parties could go so far as to avoid the entire discovery process, and choose instead to focus on their future relationship.

Another feature of litigation that may provide strategic advantage (or disadvantage) is a formal hearing. Because this involves the adversarial process, it can lead to discovery of the truth about particular issues in the case, or it could lead to a deterioration of the parties' relationship. Court hearings can also lead to witness examination, which can be very stressful for individuals (e.g., Anna's children in a divorce case) and harmful to parties. Litigation can be very advantageous in a case where joining a third party would be necessary. This can be compelled only in court or in court-annexed programs like mediation or arbitration.

3.   Features of the Case

Suitability for problem-solving. A problem-solving approach to dispute resolution suggests that the parties "focus on their actual objectives and creatively attempt to satisfy the needs of both parties, rather than [ ] focusing exclusively on the assumed objectives of maximizing individual gain." A problem-solving solution is a result the parties have not contemplated previously which is better than otherwise achievable results. These solutions are only possible where parties can create and freely choose from new potential outcomes. Sometimes suggestions by mediators may aid this process, but decisions imposed by neutrals are not likely to be based on attempts to enlarge the pie. As reaching a creative solution is one of the greatest advantages of processes where parties control the outcome (e.g. mediation or minitrial), it is crucial to recognize which cases might have the greatest potential for problem-solving.

Although it is not easy to predict which cases can be "problem-solved," certain features of the case and the parties can indicate a higher or lower probability of such a resolution. A reliable indicator of a high chance for a problem-solving resolution is a cooperative approach of the parties and their counsel and the trust that the parties and counsel have towards each other. In order to come up with new, creative options and to solve problems, parties usually have to share information, which can either create more value or cause harm to the disclosing party. Thus, trust and a cooperative relationship are needed.

On the other hand, certain features of the case or the parties may make it more difficult to arrive at a problem-solving resolution. Frequently such difficulties exist

(1) when the parties:

(a) Are certain they will prevail in court (or arbitration);

(b) Have sensitive information, which could harm the disclosing party when shared;

(c) Want to secure public vindication;

(d) (Or leaders on each side) Are unreceptive to the general idea of problem-solving; or

(2) when the case:

(a) Turns on the existence of a fundamental principle; or

(b) Involves a single issue.

4.   Features of the Parties

The relationship between the parties and between their counsel. As noted by Edward Dauer, "[t]he relationship between the parties is at once a resource, an objective, a constraint, and a source of a future contention." Maintaining or improving a good relationship between the parties often can be one of their goals following the dispute. It is also an important factor in choosing the dispute resolution procedure that would provide the best substantive results (not only in terms of the relationship). As previously mentioned, a good relationship between the parties, including trust and a cooperative approach, is a positive indication of effective communication and problem-solving. There is data showing that low to moderate levels of conflict, distrust, and tension between the parties produce the best outcomes. On the other hand, a number of impediments described later in this article, such as poor communication, excessive emotionality, or fear of disclosing true interests, are the result of a poor relationship. A good relationship is important between the parties; research shows, however, that attitudes of counsel may be even more important for effective resolution. Many commentators and practitioners agree that in all of these circumstances, processes in which the parties control the outcome are recommended.

Another issue that can determine the relationship between the parties and the choice of procedure is the dispute resolution styles of the parties and particularly their counsel. According to empirical research, much evidence shows that different results follow from the choice of a cooperative or a competitive style. Consequently, a competitive style of the other party and particularly her counsel is an argument against choosing a negotiation-based procedure (like mediation or minitrial). On the other hand, a cooperative style of the other party will suggest a higher probability of a problem-solving solution. The problem-solving solution depends not only on the negotiating styles of the parties, but also on their eagerness to get involved in ADR and their negotiating skills. Parties who feel that they have strong negotiation skills should be more eager to engage in mediation; conversely, inability to negotiate is a counter-indication for mediation.

When analyzing personal features and opportunities of the dispute, one should also consider the positions of the engaged individuals in their respective organizations. When an opponent on the other side of the table is relatively low in the hierarchy of the organization that she represents, her power may be narrowly defined and she may not be able or willing to agree to a solution that was not pre-approved. The higher the position of the official, the broader picture of the dispute she may have and the more flexible and creative she may be with respect to the resolution of the dispute.

A bad relationship between the parties will not only decrease the chance of effective resolution, but it can also be the reason for a legal dispute in the first place. If this is the case, facilitative processes like mediation are better suited for improving the relationship and getting to the root of the problem. This may be particularly true where the legal dispute is only a symptom of a deeper conflict or when parties could benefit from the improved relationship in the future.

D. Capacity of a Procedure to Overcome Impediments to Effective Resolution

The vast majority of cases ultimately settle. At least, most parties try to settle, for they often perceive settlement as more beneficial than the binding decision of a third party. Therefore, in considering impediments to resolution, parties and their counsel should mainly focus on impediments to settlement and particularly on the capacity of different procedures to overcome such impediments.

Table 4. Capacity of a Process to Overcome Impediments to Effective Resolution

0 = unlikely to satisfy goal	2 = satisfies goal substantially
1 = satisfies goal somewhat	3 = satisfies goal very substantially

	Process Impediment	Mediation	Mini–Trial	SJT	ENE	Arbitration	Adjudication
1	Poor Communication	3	2	1	1	1	0
2	Need to Express Emotions	3	1	1	1	1	0
3	Different View of Facts	2	2	3	3	2	2
4	Different View of Law	1	2	3	3	2	2
5	Important Principle Constituent	1	0	0	0	0	3
6	Pressure	3	2	2	2	0	0
7	Linkage to Other Disputes	2	1	1	1	1	0
8	Multiple Parties Different	2	1	1	1	1	1
9	Lawyer–Client Interests	2	1	1	1	1	1
10	Jackpot Syndrome	0	1	1	1	3	3
11	Fear of Disclosing True Interests, Negotiator's Dilemma	3	2	1	1	0	0
12	Psychological Barriers	2	2	1	1	0	0
13	Inability to Negotiate Effectively	2	2	1	1	2	2
14	Unrealistic Expectations	2	2	3	3	0	0
16	Power Imbalance	1	1	3	3	2	2
17	Other						

There are cases in which impediments can be better overcome by some adjudicative procedure (e.g., important principle, "jackpot" syndrome, or different view of facts). For that reason, and in order to give the parties the full spectrum of procedures from which to choose, adjudicative procedures are added to the table below. There are other instances where settlement is not an appropriate resolution of a case. This problem is described in Part III.B of this Article dealing with cases where mediation is not appropriate because of private or public perspectives.

This list of impediments is not exhaustive. Parties should be encouraged to look for other impediments in their particular case.

NOTES AND QUESTIONS

1.   What problems might arise as you try to use the Sander–Rozdeiczer model? When using the system that Professors Sander and Rozdeiczer recommend, remember that variations in procedures within the broad categories of dispute resolution can influence the utility of this methodology and the ratings assigned in each category. Keep in mind also that more than one process may be used at different stages of a dispute. Indeed, Sanders and Rozdeiczer note the importance of flexibility and taking the opportunity to revisit choices that have been made:

> Probably the most important process choice takes place when the parties first choose their dispute resolution process. That original choice, however, may not continue to be optimal. Due to possible changes of conditions throughout the dispute and gains in understanding of the dispute pending its resolution, the parties could profit from changing their dispute resolution procedure during the processing of the dispute. Thus, they should continually question their choice of procedure throughout the process and keep a flexible mind attuned to possibly changing or modifying the selected procedure.

Frank E.A. Sander & Lukasz Rozdeiczer, *Matching Cases and Dispute Resolution Procedures: Detailed Analysis Leading to a Mediation–Centered Approach*, 11 Harv. Negot. L. Rev. 1, 4 (2006).

2.   Another option might be to structure the screening analysis in the form of a questionnaire that explores the client's situation and goals. *See* CPR INST. FOR DISPUTE RESOLUTION, ADR SUITABILITY GUIDE (2001), available at http://www.cpradr.org/Portals/0/Resources/ADR%20Tools/Tools/cpr%20suita bility%20guide.pdf. *See also* Wayne D. Brazil, *Early Neutral Evaluation or Mediation? When Might ENE Deliver More Value?*, Disp. Resol. Mag., Fall 2007, at 10 (detailing factors to consider in choosing between mediation and ENE).

3.   Consider whether, and how, as part of the screening process you might discuss with clients the cognitive, emotional, and behavioral dimensions of their conflict and its resolution as described in Chapter I, beginning at page 4. What kind of discussion might you have with a client to explore these three dimensions? How might you discuss the ways in which a

particular conflict is discernible in each of these dimensions and how the conflict might be resolved along each dimension? What implications might that discussion have for the selection of a dispute resolution process or for decisions about how the process is to be carried out?

4.   It is not always easy to select a dispute resolution procedure through asking the kinds of questions suggested by Sander and Rozdeiczer or those in the CPR Screen. One goal may be so important that it virtually dictates which process is most desirable. In addition, the clients or lawyers may not know, before a dispute resolution process begins, exactly what their goals are, what sorts of processes (problem-solving as opposed to adversarial) are possible or desirable, or what obstacles are likely to impede a consensual resolution. Do these factors raise any doubts in your mind about the value of the process proposed by Sander and Rozdeiczer? Do they—combined with the "participatory" model of professional-client relations advocated in Chapter II—suggest that a dialogue between lawyer and client would lead to the best decision by the client? Consider how you might apply the client counseling and interviewing techniques that you learned about in Chapter II to help you gather the information and to counsel your client about the appropriate dispute resolution options.

5.   If, in a given case, parties and lawyers are having difficulty knowing the parties' precise goals and obstacles, how should they proceed? Will they be best off beginning with a mediation—because it offers more potential for fulfilling goals and overcoming obstacles than do the other processes? If so, who should influence procedural decisions, such as whether the mediator should evaluate, and who should influence substantive decisions, such as the definition of the problem? *See* Leonard L. Riskin, *Decisionmaking in Mediation: The New Old Grid and the New New Grid System*, 79 Notre Dame L. Rev. 1 (2003), excerpted in Chapter IV, beginning at page 317.

6.   Just as with the evaluation of ADR programs, see *supra*, beginning on page 942, when choosing among processes it is important to define the appropriate comparison:

> Because civil case mediation occurs in the midst of a "litigotiation" process that seldom ends in trial, its most likely role is to facilitate settlements that would otherwise have occurred rather than to substitute for trial. Therefore, we should be skeptical of focusing our comparisons of "what parties want" on their choice or assessments of mediation and trial. In this context, the significant research and policy questions turn on comparisons between lawyer-assisted mediation and lawyer-driven negotiation.

Craig A. McEwen & Roselle L. Wissler, *Finding Out If it is True: Comparing Mediation and Negotiation through Research*, 2002 J. Disp. Resol. 131, 133–34 (2002).

7.   Client counseling about alternative methods of resolving disputes may also take place prior to the time at which a specific dispute arises. Transactional attorneys in particular are often involved in helping clients to

plan ahead in selecting mechanisms by which to resolve their disputes. Consider the following excerpt:

KATHLEEN M. SCANLON & HARPREET K. MANN, A GUIDE TO MULTI–STEP DISPUTE RESOLUTION CLAUSES

ADR Counsel In–Box, No. 8, 20 Alternatives (centerfold pullout September 2002)

Dispute resolution planning is becoming a critical function of corporate law departments, law firms, and public sector legal departments. Powerful economic incentives, increased emphasis on risk management, and the growing complexity of dispute resolution options are among the reasons that compel private and public sector lawyers to engage in dispute resolution planning.

Predispute resolution clauses are an important component in dispute resolution planning for business-to-business transactions. Agreeing upon a process to manage disputes before they arise yields multiple benefits, including efficiency, predictability, and controlled risks. . . .

OVERVIEW

For many decades, simple, stand-alone, standardized arbitration clauses had been the extent of ADR clause drafting in many business-to-business agreements. If litigation, rather than arbitration, was contemplated to resolve future disputes, provisions relating to forum selection, choice-of-law, and a few other select items may have been addressed in the contract. Presently, much more sophisticated drafting techniques exist. Most notable is the use of the multi-step, or multi-tiered, dispute resolution clause.

A multi-step clause provides for sequential stages of dispute resolution. Negotiation and mediation are commonly used prior to the parties resorting to arbitration or litigation. The rationale underlying this sequential use of negotiation and/or mediation in the first instance is that it provides the parties with an opportunity to develop creative, business-oriented solutions before investing time and money in an adversarial process, such as arbitration or litigation. The use of multi-step clauses to manage disputes effectively and efficiently reflects sound legal and business judgment in many circumstances. Companies across a cross-section of industries are using some form of multi-step dispute resolution clause in their agreements when appropriate.

CPR MODEL MULTI–STEP CLAUSE

(Negotiation–Mediation–Arbitration)

(A) The parties shall attempt in good faith to resolve any dispute arising out of or relating to this [Agreement] [Contract] promptly by negotiation between executives who have authority to settle the controversy and who are at a higher level of management than the persons with direct

responsibility for administration of this contract. Any person may give the other party written notice of any dispute not resolved in the normal course of business. Within [15] days after delivery of the notice, the receiving party shall submit to the other a written response. The notice and response shall include (a) a statement of that party's position and a summary of arguments supporting that position, and (b) the name and title of the executive who will represent that party and of any other person who will accompany the executive. Within [30] days after delivery of the initial notice, the executives of both parties shall meet at a mutually acceptable time and place, and thereafter as often as they reasonably deem necessary, to attempt to resolve the dispute. All reasonable requests for information made by one party to the other will be honored.

All negotiations pursuant to this clause are confidential and shall be treated as compromise and settlement negotiations for purposes of applicable rules of evidence.

(B) If the dispute has not been resolved by negotiation as provided herein within [45] days after delivery of the initial notice of negotiation, [or if the parties failed to meet within [20] days,] the parties shall endeavor to settle the dispute by mediation under the CPR Mediation Procedure [then currently in effect OR in effect on the date of this Agreement], [provided, however, that if one party fails to participate in the negotiation as provided herein, the other party can initiate mediation prior to the expiration of the [45] days]. Unless otherwise agreed, the parties will select a mediator from the CPR Panels of Distinguished Neutrals.

(C) Any dispute arising out of or relating to this [Agreement] [Contract], including the breach, termination or validity thereof, which has not been resolved by mediation as provided herein [within [45] days after initiation of the mediation procedure] [within [30] days after the appointment of a mediator], shall be finally resolved by arbitration in accordance with the CPR Rules for Non–Administered Arbitration [then currently in effect OR in effect on the date of this Agreement], by [a sole arbitrator] [three independent and impartial arbitrators, of whom each party shall designate one] [three arbitrators of whom each party shall appoint one in accordance with the "screened" appointment procedure provided in Rule 5.4] [three independent and impartial arbitrators, none of whom shall be appointed by either party]; [provided, however, that if one party fails to participate in either the negotiation or mediation as agreed herein, the other party can commence arbitration prior to the expiration of the time periods set forth above.]

The arbitration shall be governed by the Federal Arbitration Act, 9 U.S.C. §§ 1–16, and judgment upon the award rendered by the arbitrator(s) may be entered by any court having jurisdiction thereof. The place of arbitration shall be (city, state).

For additional model CPR multistep clauses and corporate examples, see CPR Drafter's Deskbook (CPR, 2002) (Appendix A & Section 3).

WHEN TO CONSIDER USING MULTI–STEP CLAUSES

When to consider using a multistep clause requires an assessment of the potential benefits and concerns: * * *

AT A GLANCE

Advantages . . .

Providing for a negotiation or mediation period is highly desirable because there is a process in place to keep everyone talking early in a dispute.

Although the people involved in a deal today may have an excellent relationship, they may not be at the company in the future when a dispute arises.

Offering any of the new people a means to resolve a dispute other than litigation may enable them to constructively resolve a dispute which otherwise could deteriorate into adversarial litigation. Avoids the situation of "What do we do now?" when a dispute arises.

Multi-step approach gives the parties a concrete reason to fully explore whether a consensual, potentially more satisfactory resolution is possible before investing the significant resources typically required by arbitration or litigation.

Concerns . . .

Prevents a case-by-case determination of an appropriate ADR process and conceivably a dispute that may not be amenable to negotiation or mediation, for example, may end up in such a process. Such an outcome could result in delay and needless costs. But the parties can always jointly agree to forgo or limit participation under such circumstances.

Can raise the possibility of strategic participation (e.g., only to obtain free discovery) and tangential enforcement litigation. Parameters of good-faith participation are evolving. Moreover, examples exist of parties seeking to stay arbitration or litigation until negotiation or mediation is held pursuant to a multi-step clause. While the case law is not extensive, there is authority that agreements to engage in consensual processes can be enforceable. Also can raise the possibility of precluding enforcement of an arbitration clause when both parties fail to request mediation.

NOTES AND QUESTIONS

1. Additional issues that might be addressed in the contract include procedures for the selection of a neutral, confidentiality, discovery, statutes of limitation, which disputes are subject to the clause, and other variations in

the procedures desired. For sample dispute resolution provisions, drafting checklists, and discussion of the various alternatives, see CORINNE COOPER & BRUCE E. MEYERSON, A DRAFTER'S GUIDE TO ALTERNATIVE DISPUTE RESOLUTION (1991); KATHLEEN M. SCANLON, DRAFTER'S DESKBOOK FOR DISPUTE RESOLUTION CLAUSES (2002). *See also* JAY E. GRENIG, ALTERNATIVE DISPUTE RESOLUTION WITH FORMS (2d ed. 1997). You should note that to the extent parties to a contract craft a set of procedures for resolving disputes under the contract, they have engaged in a form of dispute systems design. How might you apply the dispute systems design principles detailed in the previous section in this context?

2.   It is becoming increasingly necessary for transactional lawyers and litigators to work together to provide appropriate dispute resolution to clients. Consider the following:

> [T]ransaction lawyers and trial lawyers can provide the best client service to business entities by working together, from the drafting state through to advising the client how to conduct the mediation.

> The transaction lawyer needs to know much more today then years ago to draft an ADR clause that will satisfy client goals, needs and interests. Consultation with ADR-knowledgeable trial counsel at the drafting stage is essential on matters such as the parameters for enforceable confidentiality and many outcome-influencing clause provisions. Such consultation at the mediation stage also is important to the client and trial counsel because the transaction lawyer knows the deal, the client and probably the other parties. It makes sense.

Donald Lee Rome, *Business Mediation's Orientation Focuses Detail on Printed Words*, 21 Alternatives 21, 21 (2003).

3.   Professor Amy Schmitz explores the tension between statutory and common law approaches to the enforcement of ADR clauses. She argues that ADR clauses providing for nonbinding processes ought to be clearly distinguished from clauses providing for binding arbitration (the enforcement of which is governed by the Federal Arbitration Act and the Uniform Arbitration Act) and makes the case that "[c]ontract and remedy law provide courts with the tools to develop a coherent and refreshed approach for determining proper enforcement of these [nonbinding] ADR agreements." Amy J. Schmitz, *Refreshing Contractual Analysis of ADR Agreements by Curing Bipolar Avoidance of Modern Common Law*, 9 Harv. Negot. L. Rev. 1, 74 (2004).

4.   Recall the discussion in Chapter V over the use of mandatory and binding arbitration provisions, beginning at page 620. Would you include a mandatory arbitration provision as part of a multi-step dispute resolution provision? Why? Why not?

5.   How should attorneys approach the task of drafting ADR clauses? What ethical obligations should they have with regard to drafting and enforcing such clauses? *See* Amy J. Schmitz, *Ethical Considerations in*

Drafting and Enforcing Consumer Arbitration Clauses, 49 S. Tex. L. Rev. 841 (2008).

6. You have been asked to draft a proposed dispute resolution clause for the three clients of your law firm described below. Summarize the principal features of the clauses you will recommend for each.

a. A client has been selected as the general contractor for a multi-million dollar office building that will serve as the home-office for an insurance company. The client is likely to do other construction work for this company in the future. The construction contract will contain a provision for dealing with disputes that arise.

b. Susan, your client, and John, her husband of five years, are divorcing. They have agreed that the two children will remain with Susan during the school year but will spend their Christmas and summer vacations with John.

Susan is concerned about the environment in which her children will live while with John, especially if he remarries, and where John will take them on trips. Living with John has convinced her that he may take the children to places where they might not be safe. John has agreed to "consult" with Susan on proposed trips with the children, to have the children call Susan at least once a week while they are with him, and to allow Susan to visit his home once each summer vacation and make "suggestions" regarding the children's safety and needs. Susan is concerned that disputes will arise in the implementation of these arrangements. John has agreed to consider including in the separation agreement a dispute resolution clause covering such disputes.

c. An insurance company client is reviewing the language of its policies covering products liability of large manufacturers. It is considering adding a dispute resolution clause to deal with disagreements involving issues such as coverage and duty to defend.

D. CHOOSING AND BUILDING DISPUTE RESOLUTION PROCESSES

The Daily Bugle*

GENERAL INFORMATION FOR BOTH PARTICIPANTS

Two weeks ago, the *Daily Bugle,* its editor, and one of its reporters, Terry Ives, were sued for defamation by John Roark, M.D. The article that was the basis of the suit described the latest in a series of fires in

---

* The role-play instructions were prepared by Professor Nancy Rogers, based upon *Tape IV: The Roark v. Daily Bugle Libel Claim,* Dispute Resolution and Lawyers Video Tape Series (Distributed by West Publishing Co. (1991)), which was based upon Nanette Laughrey and Sandra Davidson Scott, "The Doctor and the Daily Bugle: A Process Selection Exercise," in the Instructor's Manual for Tape IV. Confidential Instructions for both participants appear in the Instructor's Manual for Tape IV, and on the casebook's TWEN web site at www.lawschool.westlaw.com.

slum housing, pointing out that the building in which the fire took place was so poorly managed that some tenants lacked heat. It contained the following language, which includes statements that Roark alleges to be false and defamatory:

> The destroyed building is owned by slum landlord Dr. John Roark, county property records reveal. Dr. Roark is a prominent orthopedic surgeon. . . . A source in the Fire Marshall's office indicated that the office is not ruling out the possibility of arson because it is not uncommon for owners of tenements to intentionally burn them to collect insurance.

Roark alleges that the reporter was negligent—property records show that he was only a limited partner in the group owning the property—and that the reporter acted with malice. He states that the newspaper refused his request for a retraction. He seeks $250,000 in actual damages for harm to his reputation, lost income in his medical practice, aggravation of a serious health problem, and mental anguish. He also seeks $1 million in punitive damages.

Defamation is a communication of an untruth to a third person that harms a person's reputation or causes harm in that person's business. Truth is a defense. Public figures must show that the defendant acted with actual malice in order to recover. In this jurisdiction, private individuals need only show negligence in order to recover actual damages. Actual malice must be shown in order to recover punitive damages.

In this jurisdiction, the reporter has a privilege to refuse disclosure of a source who has been promised confidentiality. However, under the privilege statute, the judge decides in each instance whether the need for disclosure outweighs the harm caused by disclosure, specifically the harm to the public interest in promoting dissemination of news by assuring the anonymity of sources.

Exercise 1: Counsel for Dr. Roark is to meet with Dr. Roark, explain the options for resolving the dispute, and help the client decide which option(s) the lawyer should promote in a forthcoming meeting with counsel for the *Daily Bugle*.

Exercise 2: Like any newspaper, the *Daily Bugle* must deal with defamation claims as an on-going part of its business. Work in teams to design a system that the *Daily Bugle* can use to address these conflicts in the future.

CHAPTER VIII

LOOKING AHEAD

▪ ▪ ▪

In the preceding chapters, we have covered a lot of ground about the nature of the various methods of dispute resolution, their potential advantages and disadvantages, and the challenges of integrating them into our roles as lawyers. But as we have seen, the field of dispute resolution is dynamic, not static, and is constantly evolving with new applications, insights, and skills. We covered some of this innovation in Chapter VI, in our discussion of such recent adaptations as collaborative lawyering, partnering, and online dispute resolution.

In this short, concluding chapter, we continue taking a brief look at the road ahead. We first will look at new connections for the field, in particular exploring how the modern ADR movement fits within other movements in the law to humanize the process of conflict resolution. We then turn to new skills that ADR professionals are coming to use to improve their practices and quality of life, focusing on the use of mindfulness mediation as a vehicle for expanding self-awareness and fostering other virtues of so-called emotional intelligence. Finally we explore how interested students may get started in the field, beginning with a general discussion of the professional organizations that can provide for initial entrée, and then providing several personal stories of current practitioners.

A. NEW CONNECTIONS

As we saw in Chapter I, the modern ADR movement was born of many forces, including the recognition by leaders and pioneers within the legal profession that traditional litigation may not be the best vehicle for the resolution of some problems. This casebook has focused primarily on the resolution of formal legal disputes, and the degree to which the methods we have discussed are capable of resolving the behavioral, cognitive, and emotional dimensions of conflict. Yet, the development of the dispute resolution field is only part of a larger tapestry of efforts to make conflict resolution more responsive to human needs. In the following excerpt, Professor Susan Daicoff provides a sense of this terrain, discussing several "vectors" of what she calls "the comprehensive law movement."

SUSAN DAICOFF, THE COMPREHENSIVE LAW PRACTICE: OVERVIEW OF THE MOVEMENT, THE VECTORS, AND THEIR COMMON GROUND
49–61 (2011)

Vector Definitions

* * *

Therapeutic jurisprudence is one of the most well-known vectors, with the broadest applications. Since around 1990, it has focused on the therapeutic or countertherapeutic consequences of the law and legal procedures on the individuals involved, including the clients, their families, friends, lawyers, judges, and community. It attempts to reform law and legal processes in order to promote the psychological well-being of the people they affect. Its website explains that TJ "concentrates on the law's impact on emotional life and psychological well-being. It is a perspective that regards the law (rules of law, legal procedures, and roles of legal actors) itself as a social force that often produces therapeutic or anti-therapeutic consequences. It does not suggest that therapeutic concerns are more important than other consequences or factors, but it does suggest that the law's role as a potential therapeutic agent should be recognized. . . ." TJ has been applied to almost every area of law, including mental health law, family law, employment law, health law, elder law, appellate practice, criminal law, criminal sentencing, litigation, and estate planning. It has been applied to police work and become very popular with judges. Its founders are David B. Wexler, Professor of Law at University of Arizona and University of Puerto Rico and the late Bruce Winick, Professor of Law at University of Miami. * * *

Preventive law has been around for many years. Like preventive medicine, it explicitly seeks to intervene in legal matters before disputes arise and advocates proactive intervention to head off litigation and other conflicts. It emphasizes the lawyer-client relationship, relationships in general, and planning. In recent years, its lawyering techniques were integrated with TJ concepts in order to describe "how to" practice TJ-oriented law, thus resulting in therapeutically-oriented preventive law. Its founder was the late Louis Brown and it is associated with Professor and Dean Emeritus Edward Dauer at the University of Denver College of Law. California Western School of Law houses the National Center for Preventive Law and it has its own textbook, reporter. * * *

Procedural justice refers to Tom Tyler's research finding that, in judicial processes, litigants' satisfaction depends more on (1) being treated with respect and dignity, (2) being heard and having an opportunity to speak and participate, and (3) how trustworthy the authorities appear and behave, than it does on the actual outcome (e.g, winning vs. losing) of the legal matter. It is being used to re-engineer dispute resolution processes (litigative and nonlitigative) to incorporate these three important features. * * *

Creative problem solving is a broad approach to lawyering that is explicitly humanistic, interdisciplinary, creative, and preventive. Its website explains that "clients and society are increasingly asking lawyers to approach problems [not always as fighters, but] more creatively." CPS seeks to prevent legal problems if possible and creatively solve those that exist. It "focuses both on using the traditional analytical process more creatively and on using nontraditional problem solving processes, drawn from business, psychology, economics, neuroscience, and sociology." CPS is associated with the McGill Center for Creative Problem Solving at California Western School of Law, which sponsors a number of law school courses on CPS, national and international projects, and periodic conferences. The merging of the vectors is clear in CPS's use of preventive law and transformative mediation.

Holistic justice is a grass-roots movement among practicing lawyers which "acknowledge[s] the need for a humane legal process with the highest level of satisfaction for all participants; honor[s] and respect[s] the dignity and integrity of each individual; promote[s] peaceful advocacy and holistic legal principles; value[s] responsibility, connection and inclusion; encourage[s] compassion, reconciliation, forgiveness and healing; practice[s] deep listening, understand[s] and recognize[s] the importance of voice; contributes[s] to peace building at all levels of society; recognize[s] the opportunity in conflict; draw[s] upon ancient intuitive wisdom of diverse cultures and traditions; and [encourages the lawyer to] enjoy the practice of law." It is explicitly interdisciplinary, allows the lawyer to incorporate his or her own morals and values into client representation, and seeks to "do the right thing" for the lawyer, clients, and others involved. Like holistic medicine, it takes a broader view of legal problems and possible solutions. It is associated with the International Alliance of Holistic Lawyers, whose founder is practicing lawyer William Van Zyverden in Vermont. **Collaborative law** is a nonlitigative, collaborative process employed mainly in divorce and family law, where the spouses and their respective attorneys and neutral experts resolve the issues outside of court in a four (or more) party process. No litigation is usually instituted until settlement is reached. The attorneys are contractually forbidden from representing their clients in court should the agreement process break down. Basically, it puts the divorcing spouses with their respective attorneys into a collaborative, series of discussions designed to resolve the issues without litigation. Because the attorneys must withdraw if the process breaks down, the attorneys' financial interests are the same as the clients'—to reach settlement. This contrasts with the usual process, where the lawyers "win" whether the clients settle or not, since they simply litigate if negotiations break down. There is a strong psychological component to the lawyer-client relationship in that emotions, needs, transference, etc. are openly acknowledged and dealt with in order to maximize results of the 4-way conferences. Interdisciplinary models use a "team" of mental health, financial, and other professional as well. Collaborative law can be appropriate for other areas, such as employment. Leading trainers include practicing attorneys Pauline Tesler (Bay Area, California) and Stuart G. Webb (Minnesota) * * *

Transformative mediation is a form of alternative dispute resolution set forth in Bush and Folger's 1994 book, *The Promise of Mediation*. TM views conflict as a destabilizing "crisis in human interaction" rather than a violation of rights or conflict of individual interests. Its three-person mediations seek to restore balance between self and other, transform conflict into a positive, constructive process, and encourage parties to do two things: (1) regain their sense of strength and self-confidence (the "empowerment" shift) and (2) expand their responsiveness to each other (the "recognition" shift, much like empathy, or the ability to stand in the other's shoes). By focusing on these goals, the parties are moved towards increased personal development and enhanced personal and interpersonal skills. Baruch Bush is a law professor at Hofstra University School of Law and Joseph Folger is a communications professor at Temple University. * * *

Restorative justice refers to a movement employed most often with juvenile offenders in the U.S., although it is more widely used in Australia, Canada, and the United Kingdom, in which criminal justice and criminal sentencing are done by the community, victim, and offender in a collaborative process. It may be as simple as post-sentencing victim-offender mediation or as complicated as sentencing that is done in a community conference with all parties present. It emphasizes relationships between the offender, victim, and community instead of a top-down, hierarchical system of imposing punishment. The website for The Center for Restorative Justice & Peacemaking at the University of Minnesota School of Social Work explains that "[t]hrough restorative justice, victims, communities, and offenders are placed in active roles to work together to. Empower victims in their search for closure; Impress upon offenders the real human impact of their behavior; Promote restitution to victims and communities. Dialogue and negotiation are central to restorative justice, and problem solving for the future is seen as more important than simply establishing blame for past behavior. Balance is sought between the legitimate needs of the victim, the community, and the offender that enhances community protection, competency development in the offender, and direct accountability of the offender to the victim and victimized community." One of its leaders is Mark Umbreit, who is a social work professor at the University of Minnesota. * * *

The **problem solving court movement** resulted from judges' enthusiastic application of TJ to the adjudication process. Frustrated with recidivism and repeat performances, judges developed specialized, multidisciplinary "problem solving" courts focused on resolving the interpersonal issues underlying the legal problems instead of punishing defendants or assigning fault. They take a long-term, relational, interdisciplinary, healing approach to judging. In the criminal setting, judges create collaborative and ongoing relationships with offenders and helping professionals and supervise the offenders' rehabilitation efforts. Examples are drug treatment courts, mental health courts, domestic violence courts, and unified family courts. Drug treatment courts are reporting impressive drops in recidivism as a result of their changed focus and approach. The nonadversarial nature of these courts is consistent with the approach to civil matters taken by vectors like collaborative law and transformative mediation.

* * *

Common Ground

While intuitively the vectors of the comprehensive law movement may appear similar, it is important to examine the precise ways in which they resemble each other, as well as the ways in which they differ. Professor Bruce Winick, one of the two founders of therapeutic jurisprudence, described the vectors beautifully when he said they are like members of an extended family. He explained that some have red hair, some have brown hair and brown eyes, some have blue eyes, but when you put them all together for a group photo, a striking family resemblance is evident in each member. Yet, each member has his or her own distinctive features that are peculiar to that member only. The beauty of the movement is evident not only in the features that unify the vectors, but also in their distinct and individual differences; they remain separate and vibrant movements of their own, while sharing common ground.

Law schools traditionally teach students to sift through facts and issues to eliminate "irrelevant" concerns and focus only on what is "relevant" to the rule of law. The emotional and interpersonal dynamics of a matter are deemed irrelevant to the pure legal analysis learned in the first year of law school. Sometime during the third year of law school or first few years of practice, lawyers are left to their own to rediscover their ability to evaluate these dynamics and somehow incorporate that assessment into their work as lawyers, but this process (if it occurs) happens haphazardly and without direction. It may not happen at all. * * *

Certainly, in law school, emotional and interpersonal concerns are strongly de-emphasized, if not blatantly ignored. Empirical research indicates that law school actually fosters two shifts in values that echo this de-emphasis. First, during law school, law students tend to either intensify their rights orientations or move from a care ethic to a rights orientation.

The second shift that occurs during law school is away from an emphasis on "growth/self-acceptance, intimacy/emotional connection, and community/societal contribution," which have been called "'intrinsic' values," and towards an emphasis on "appearance/attractiveness," "money/luxuries, popularity/fame, and beauty/attractiveness," which have been called "'extrinsic' value[s]."

Both shifts appear among law students as early as the first year of law school. In both shifts, a movement away from valuing interpersonal harmony, connectedness, and emotional wellbeing is evident. The comprehensive law movement values these concerns, in contrast. It asks lawyers to focus on these concerns and issues that are traditionally ignored, if not actively silenced, in law school and law practice. In this way, it differs from traditional approaches to law and lawyering. While "good," traditional lawyers may implicitly or unconsciously take these concerns into account in their representation of clients, the comprehensive law movement differs from traditional lawyering in that it *explicitly* values interpersonal, emotional, psychological, and relational concerns. It elevates the importance of these concerns in the law and seeks to consciously train lawyers to effectively deal with these concerns. The revolutionary nature of the movement is thus evident. * * *

Optimizing Human Wellbeing

First, the vectors of the comprehensive law movement seek legal solutions that make things better, or at least not worse, for the people involved in the legal matter. They explicitly or implicitly attempt to optimize the psychological and emotional wellbeing of the individuals involved. All of the vectors seek to resolve the legal dispute or matter in a way that prevents harm to, preserves, or enhances individuals' interpersonal relationships, psychological wellbeing, opportunities for personal growth, mental health, or satisfaction with the process and outcome of the matter.

While the vectors may initially focus on the wellbeing of the individual client at hand, they often seek to preserve or enhance the wellbeing of all of the individuals involved in the matter. They intuitively understand the well-known social science finding that positive relationships and good connections with one's family, friends, colleagues, peers, and community lead to enhanced psychological wellbeing and functioning and, as a result, they often work to preserve, maintain, restore, or create good interpersonal relationships.

Because of the emotional devastation that can result from traditional adversarial litigation, many of the vectors explicitly seek nonlitigious solutions to legal problems. Some vectors are explicitly therapeutic to the individuals involved and some are indirectly therapeutic. Many utilize collaborative methods in solving legal problems; however, some explicitly acknowledge that litigation, uncompromising positions, and legal force can themselves be healing and they use these methods in achieving their goals.

Social scientists might call this feature "optimizing human functioning." They might define the vectors' goal as "satisfaction with the legal process" or "good mental health." Jurisprudents might call the goal therapeutic or curative. Others might describe the goal as a search for healing or restoration. Native American tradition might call the goal "harmony" and then define harmony as three-part wholeness, meaning harmony within oneself (intrapersonal harmony), harmony between self and a Supreme Being, if one so believes (vertical harmony), and harmony between self and others (horizontal or interpersonal harmony). Whatever moniker is used, the concept is focused first on people and second on leaving people in the best possible internal, psychological, emotional, moral, relational, and spiritual state at the conclusion of their legal matter.

"Rights Plus:" Considering Extra-Legal Factors

The second unifying feature is that all of the vectors take into consideration, when assessing or resolving a legal problem, more than just the strict legal rights, liabilities, obligations, duties, and entitlements presented. While law school teaches us to focus only on the law and what facts are relevant to the legal tests used in courts, the comprehensive law approaches explicitly go above and beyond the law to incorporate a consideration of one or more extra-legal factors. The factors considered include: the social, psychological, and emotional consequences of various courses of action, the communities in which the individuals involved exist, and the parties' emotions, feelings, needs, resources, goals, psychological health, relationships, values, morals, and financial concerns. Pauline Tesler, one of the founders of the collaborative law movement, calls this feature "rights plus."

Every traditional lawyer probably takes his or her client's financial concerns into account, so that at least one extra-legal factor is usually considered beyond the client's legal rights or duties. In fact, focusing on the economic bottom line is rather characteristic of attorneys, as compared to non-attorneys. Unlike a more traditional approach, however, the comprehensive law approaches also consider the psychological, social, emotional, and relational consequences of various legal courses of action.

These two main areas of common ground appear to be the unifying characteristics of the otherwise somewhat diverse main vectors of the movement. Other features are shared by some but not all of the vectors, such as: nonlitigative or collaborative approaches to dispute resolution, a focus on spirituality and faith, explicitly therapeutic goals, interdisciplinary approaches, shared equal power instead of a hierarchical top-down power structure, a focus on interpersonal relationships, and a focus on process rather than outcome.

Organizational Chart of the Movement

* * *

Until now, the legal system offered only one "lens," the traditional approach to lawyering. This lens typically focuses on legal rights, duties, and responsibilities and on resolution of legal matters and disputes. The comprehensive law movement adds at least five more "lenses." Each of these new lenses focuses on concerns, beyond legal rights, through which to view legal matters.

Lenses		
Traditional (Win/Lose-Binary)	Therapeutic Jurisprudence	Procedural Justice
	Creative Problem-Solving	Holistic Justice
		Religious/Spiritual
Processes		
Problem Solving Courts	Negotiation/Settlement	Collaborative Law
	Evaluative Mediation	Restorative Justice
Arbitration	Facilitative Mediation	TJ/PL
Litigation and Other Judicial Processes	Transformative Mediation	Preventive Law

Despite perhaps being limited to one "lens," the existing legal system offers a number of "processes" which can be used to carry out the goals identified by the traditional "lens." The existing processes include: litigation, mediation (facilitative and evaluative forms thereof), arbitration, private adjudications, private trials, and old-fashioned negotiation and settlement. The comprehensive law movement adds at least five more "processes" to the lawyers' toolkit, each of which is consistent with a different paradigm for resolution of legal matters. * * *

Parallel Developments

While many of the vectors of the comprehensive law movement have been developed by practicing lawyers and judges, some parallel developments have emerged in legal education, primarily through the work of various like-minded law professors. These academic developments are related to the comprehensive law movement because of their emphasis on humanism, values, and enhanced interpersonal and intrapersonal sensitivity. They also assist law students to develop or preserve core skills and attributes necessary to effectively practice law comprehensively.

The Humanizing Movement

Energized by the leadership and enthusiasm of law professor Lawrence Krieger, a group of law professors have banded together to make law school and legal education a more humane environment. Aware of common complaints about the competitive and intimidating nature of the law school environment and painfully aware of the empirical data demonstrating that law students are "normal" before they enter law school but rapidly develop depression and other psychiatric distress thereafter, which does not abate after graduation, these professors began sharing information, teaching techniques, and research on how to humanize legal education. While the thrust of this movement has focused on humanizing the experience of law school for law students, its values are consistent with comprehensive law's intention of humanizing legal process for participants. The humanizing movement also encourages law students to identify, evaluate, and maintain their own personal morals, values, beliefs, and standards during law school. This exploration of values may prepare or propel some students to practice law comprehensively rather than traditionally.

Mindfulness Meditation

Law professor Leonard Riskin, author and legal commentator Steven Keeva, and others have written about the importance of the lawyer's mental state to the efficacy of his or her work. One strategy that many attorneys and law students are experimenting with, to improve their professional efficacy, is "mindfulness meditation." Some have incorporated the principles and insights of mindfulness meditation into their preparation for professional practice. These concepts have been introduced to law students through such avenues as the Yale Law School project for Meditation and the Law and programs sponsored by the Fetzer Institute. Being more aware of and able to manage and monitor one's mental state, emotions, and reactions can assist lawyers in their daily work, particularly if they are practicing comprehensive law, due to its emphasis on the ability to identify and cope with the emotions and mental states of others.

Law and Spirituality

Law and religion is a familiar topic, but some recent commentary has focused on the concept that one's spiritual beliefs, values, and practices are relevant to law, legal education, and law practice. Specifically, they are important for preparing one's mental state or legal work, maintaining one's mental health, the professional choices one makes as a lawyer, and the way in which one interacts with clients. Lawyers who have personal spiritual practices or who are explicitly faith-based themselves may be drawn to comprehensive law practice, due to the easy interface of the goals of comprehensive law with their personal values.

NOTES AND QUESTIONS

1.   The aim of the comprehensive law movement is to "optimize human well-being and focus on extra-legal concerns, including the emotions of those involved and relationships." *See* Carolyn Copps Hartley & Carrie J. Petrucci, *Justice, Ethics, and Interdisciplinary Teaching and Practice: Practicing Culturally Competent Therapeutic Jurisprudence: A Collaboration between Social Work and Law*, 14 Wash. U. J.L. & Pol'y 133, 171–73 (2004).

2.   As you recall from Chapter I, Professor Frank E.A. Sander is widely credited with heralding the dawn of the modern ADR movement with his speech calling for what has been come to be known as the "multi-door courthouse." Is the comprehensive law movement an extension of that concept?

3.   Which, if any, of the vectors are likely to become part of the mainstream of American law? What barriers do you see to this progression?

4.   Restorative justice has been a particularly active vector within the comprehensive law movement. For other applications, *See, e.g.*, Ann Skelton, *Restorative Justice as a Framework for Juvenile Justice*, 42 Brit. J. Criminology 496 (2002); Carrie J. Niebur Eisnaugle, *International Truth Commission: Utilizing Restorative Justice as an Alternative to Retribution*, 36 Vand. J. Transnat'l L. 209 (2003); Kristen F. Grunewald & Priya Nath, *Defense–Based Victim Outreach: Restorative Justice in Capital Cases*, 15 Cap. Def. J. 315 (2003). For a thorough treatment, see Symposium, *The Restorative Justice Conference*, 2003 Utah L. Rev. 1.

5. The restorative justice concept has also been adapted to the administrative context. For example, some agencies have experimented with a New Zealand innovation called the Family Group Conference, in which a social worker for an agency investigating juvenile delinquency or child abuse, for example, convenes a meeting of all immediate family members and relevant professionals to address the presenting problem. For a discussion, see Susan M. Chandler & Marilou Giovannucci, *Family Group Conferences: Transforming Traditional Child Welfare Policy and Practice*, 42 Fam. Ct. Rev. 216 (2004); Allison Morris, *Youth Justice in New Zealand*, 31 Crime & Just. 243 (2004).

6. There has been considerable experimentation with specialized courts to deal with drug offenses. For a discussion of so-called "drug courts," see John S. Goldkamp, *The Drug Court Response: Issues and Implications for Justice Change*, 63 Alb. L. Rev. 923 (2000); JAMES L. NOLAN JR., REINVENTING JUSTICE: THE AMERICAN DRUG COURT MOVEMENT (2001). For a critique, see Martin B. Hoffman, *The Drug Court Scandal*, 78 N.C. L. Rev. 1437 (2000).

B. NEW SKILLS

Much of our aim in this book has been to raise your awareness of the various issues that need to be taken into account when considering a dispute resolution option, such as the different approaches to negotiation and mediation and their implications, doctrinal issues in arbitration, and empirical questions in evaluation. Such awareness elevates our capacity to use the dispute resolution methods appropriately, effectively and wisely, whether we are negotiating a matter on behalf of a client, representing a client in a mediation, serving as an arbitrator, designing a dispute resolution program for a court, or engaging in another form of dispute resolution or conflict management.

We have also sought to provide the skills with which to practice dispute resolution, skills such as listening, inquiry, analysis of interests and other issues, and the management of power imbalances. These are foundational skills that in some respects are easily taught, but take a lifetime to master.

As the excerpt on the mediator's "presence" by David Hoffman and Daniel Bowling in Chapter IV indicates, beginning at page 456, dispute resolution professionals are joining business, education, and other professionals in recognizing the importance of self-awareness, and other aspects of "emotional intelligence."

A concept pioneered by Yale psychologist Peter Salovey and popularized by pscychologt and journalist Daniel Goleman, emotional intelligence may be understood as the set of competencies that arise from our understanding of our emotions, our physiological systems, and the interactions we have with other people, situations, events, etc. *See* DANIEL GOLEMAN, EMOTIONAL INTELLIGENCE: WHY IT CAN MATTER MORE THAN I.Q. (1995); Peter Salovey & John D. Mayer, *Emotional Intelligence*, 9 Imagination, Cognition & Personality 185–211 (1989). These competencies lie in essentially two domains. The first is our personal competencies, which include not only self-awareness, but also self-management—how we conduct ourselves in light of the qualities and characteristics about ourselves about which we have become self-aware. The second set of competencies deal with how we manage our interactions with others, including our basic awareness of social relationships and our capacity to manage those relationships. Applied to conflict and dispute resolution, emotional intelligence means that the better we understand ourselves, our emotions, our relationships with others, etc., the better we will be able to handle ourselves when we are involved in conflict or engaged in a process of dispute resolution.

There are a variety of skills based on emotional intelligence, such as empathy, communication, and leadership, many of which can be cultivated with practice and training. Self-awareness is a foundational part of this skill set, and in the following excerpt, Professor Riskin discusses the use of mindfulness meditation as a technique for fostering such awareness, as well as empathy, presence of mind, and the capacity for connecting with others effectively as lawyers, dispute resolution professionals, and people.

LEONARD L. RISKIN, MINDFULNESS: FOUNDATIONAL TRAINING FOR DISPUTE RESOLUTION
54 J. Leg. Educ. 79 (2004)

I want to begin with a profound problem that afflicts all of us as teachers, students, and practitioners of dispute resolution. It was brought home to me about two weeks after the attacks of September 11, 2001, in an e-mail message I received from a friend who lives in Washington, D.C., not far from the Pentagon. My friend told me that he had been abroad on September 11, and on his return he found an e-mail message that included the following reading:

If you can start the day without caffeine or pep pills,

If you can be cheerful, ignoring aches and pains,

If you can resist complaining and boring people with your troubles,

If you can eat the same food every day and be grateful for it,

If you can understand when loved ones are too busy to give you time,

If you can overlook when people take things out on you when, through no fault of yours, something goes wrong,

If you can take criticism and blame without resentment,

If you can face the world without lies and deceit,

If you can conquer tension without medical help,

If you can relax without liquor,

If you can sleep without the aid of drugs,

Then you are probably a dog.

[Robert D. Hutchison, Untitled]

A Problem: Mindlessness in Counseling, Negotiating, and Mediating

It is a fact of the human condition that we are suffused with fears, insecurities, passions, impulses, judgments, rationalizations, assumptions, biases, and the mental shortcuts that some academics call "heuristics." These can be more or less available to our conscious awareness, and we can be more or less able to resist them.

Such mental and emotional influences, of course, help guide us through life and through professional activities, including teaching, resolving disputes, and lawyering. The problem is that they also can interfere with our ability to do these activities well. They can, for instance, draw our attention away from where we want it to be. When we want to listen to a client or read a document, we may be distracted by worries about whether the client likes us, or by thoughts (or chains of thoughts) about almost anything: the laundry, whether we made the right career choice, or why we didn't schedule that trip to Hawaii. The less conscious awareness we have of these impulses, fears, passions, thoughts, and habitual assumptions and behaviors, the more likely we are to succumb to them.

The mind tends to wander, and very often we do not realize where it has gone. Usually it is dwelling in the past or future, keeping us from paying attention to the present moment. Understood in this way, intermittent mindlessness can affect and afflict just about everyone in conducting virtually any activity.

Mindlessness impairs our work as practitioners of dispute resolution in several ways. For example, it could mean that a mediator or negotiator is not very "present" with the other participants or with himself, i.e., not fully aware of what is going on. This diminishes the professional's ability to gather information and to listen to, and understand, others and himself, and even to achieve satisfaction from his work. The second problem is that, in the grip of mindlessness, we sometimes rely on old habits and assumptions, rather than deciding what behavior is most suitable in the precise circumstances we are encountering. To Harvard psychology professor Ellen Langer, mindlessness means "the light's on but nobody's at home." Manifestations include being "trapped by categories," "automatic behavior," and "acting from a single perspective." As mediators, for instance, we might routinely impose the same rules of procedure (e.g., that we caucus immediately after the first joint session, or that we never caucus), case after case, irrespective of the differences in issues and parties.

* * *

A Potential Solution: Mindfulness in Practice and Mindfulness Meditation

Mindfulness, as I use the term, means being aware, moment to moment, without judgment, of one's bodily sensations, thoughts, emotions, and consciousness. It is a systematic strategy for paying attention and for investigating one's own mind that one cultivates through meditation and then deploys in daily life. The meditation practice begins with developing concentration, usually by focusing on the breath. Next the meditator directs his attention to bodily sensations, emotions, and thoughts, then works toward "bare attention," a nonjudgmental moment-to-moment awareness of bodily sensations, sounds, thoughts, and emotions as they arise and fall out of consciousness. Mindfulness meditation (also known as insight meditation and vipassana meditation) both requires and produces a measure of equanimity, which reinforces the ability to fix attention where we want it to be.

The practice has a number of other potential benefits that motivate people to participate. It commonly helps people deal better with stress, improve concentration, develop self-understanding (which helps them clarify their own goals and motivations) and understanding of others, and feel compassion and empathy. Recently scientists have documented that mindfulness meditation also improves the functioning of the meditator's immune system and even produces "happiness," as measured by brainwave activity, actually shifting a person's disposition, not just her mood. In Buddhist philosophy, meditation is an important part of the quest for freedom from the suffering caused by craving and aversion.

It also seems likely to improve performance in virtually any kind of activity. The kinds of outcomes it fosters correlate with success in a variety of fields. Daniel Goleman—a psychologist, journalist, and authority on meditation—has articulated the concept of emotional intelligence, which he distinguishes from academic intelligence, the basis for the IQ and most other intelligence tests. This idea of emotional intelligence entails five "basic emotional and social competencies": self-awareness, self-regulation, motivation, empathy, and social skills. Goleman argues, marshaling a great deal of empirical evidence, that emotional intelligence is much more important than academic intelligence in predicting success at virtually any occupation or profession—assuming, of course, an adequate level of academic intelligence.

As I have shown above, mindfulness meditation can help develop the first four of these emotional intelligence competencies: self-awareness, self-regulation, motivation, and empathy. These, in turn, are likely to help produce the fifth emotional intelligence competency: social skills.

Although mindfulness meditation derives from ancient practices taught by the Buddha, in recent years it has found employment in a variety of secular settings. In the U.S., for instance, specialized programs have appeared for medical patients in chronic pain; professional basketball players; journalists; undergraduate, nursing, and medical students; corporate and foundation executives; and Green Berets. Most important for our purposes, extensive meditation instruction has been offered to lawyers in at least three large law firms (the Boston offices of Hale and Dorr and Nutter, McClennan & Fish and the Minneapolis office of Leonard, Street & Deinard) and to persons who work in the criminal justice system. A variety of programs, ranging widely in length, intensity, and scope, have been offered to law students at Cardozo, Columbia, Denver, Hamline, Harvard, Hastings, Miami, Missouri–Columbia, North Carolina, Stanford, Suffolk, and Yale. Mindfulness meditation also has been a central focus of many programs for lawyers across the U.S., ranging from five-day retreats to brief introductory sessions, some of which have carried CLE credit. Some of the law school and post-law school efforts have had a range of focuses, including managing stress, developing spiritually, clarifying motivations, or enhancing skills in law school, law practice, or law teaching.

In recent years mindfulness meditation has appeared in a variety of programs in connection with teaching negotiation or mediation. Mindfulness can help negotiators and mediators in several ways. It provides methods for calming the mind, concentrating, experiencing compassion and empathy, and achieving an awareness of, and "distance" from, thoughts, emotions, and habitual impulses that can interfere with making good judgments and with building rapport and motivating others. Thus, it can help us make appropriate strategic decisions, moment to moment. In a negotiation, for instance, when our counterpart issues a threat and we feel an impulse to retaliate, mindfulness helps us to "insert a wedge of awareness" and to examine that impulse and decide whether retaliation is more appropriate than another move that would more likely foster value creating, understanding, or healing. In addition, there is evidence that a positive mood enhances performance in problem-solving negotiation. And it seems reasonable to suspect that mindfulness could help negotiators be more aware of certain deep assumptions, including those based on ethnicity or culture, and of psychological processes that can interfere with wise decision making, such as reactive devaluation, optimistic overconfidence, risk aversion, and anchoring.

Mindfulness allows mediators to make better judgments about how the mediation process should work because it enables them to keep a focus on goals and to maintain a moment-to-moment awareness (to be "present" with themselves and others). In addition, a mediator's presence, especially her degree of calm, can dramatically affect the participants' moods and conduct.

* * *

The education and training programs that deal with mindfulness and negotiation or mediation include mindfulness meditation instruction and practice as well as exercises and discussions on how to bring mindful awareness into professional practice and other aspects of daily life. They generally begin with the basics: meditating on the breath (in part to enhance the ability to concentrate) and on sound, bodily sensations, emotions, and thoughts. All of this helps prepare the student for what is called "bare attention," an awareness of whatever passes through one's consciousness. Most of these programs present a very brief introduction to a small range of meditative practices, sometimes including yoga. Although students typically learn some techniques they can employ immediately, the leaders of such programs also hope the students will be inspired to develop their mindfulness through continued meditation and study, alone and with groups.

Exercises on listening (active or not) often form important parts of such programs. Students, already in a reasonably mindful state, are asked to engage in activities in which their ability to listen is challenged by emotional or other distractions, and they are asked to be aware of these distractions. The programs also include exercises on negotiation that encourage the students to notice and examine the assumptions about negotiation that they hold and implement. Similarly, in mediation training, exercises are intended to examine assumptions, strategies, and techniques, at many levels of the decision-making process. In addition, students notice the related bodily sensations and emotions.

* * *

In this brief essay I meant to demonstrate the potential value of mindfulness meditation and to suggest questions to address as we move forward. The future of this work is not clear to me. It seems counter to many established practices and perspectives in our field. But there is reason for optimism. The use of mindfulness and other contemplative practices is growing rapidly in society and in the legal profession. Numerous organizations have supported programs in mindfulness for lawyers or mediators. These include established entities, such as the AALS Section on Dispute Resolution, the ABA Section of Dispute Resolution, the CPR Institute for Dispute Resolution, the Association for Conflict Resolution, and prominent law firms and law schools. In addition, many established meditation organizations and teachers are available to provide training and practice opportunities. Some of these—such as the Center for Mindfulness in Medicine, Health Care and Society; the Center for Contemplative Mind in Society; and the Spirit Rock Meditation Center—already provide meditation instruction to lawyers. And two newly created programs—the Harvard Negotiation Insight Initiative and the Initiative on Mindfulness in Law and Dispute

Resolution at the University of Missouri–Columbia School of Law—will bring additional energy and people into this work.

In order to plan and implement programs in mindfulness and dispute resolution—or to decide not to do so—we must be clear about our intentions. Mindfulness meditation can serve a range of goals, from lightening up, to improving our professional practices and our lives, to a kind of spiritual freedom. And, of course, nothing is more helpful in understanding our goals and the mental and emotional obstacles to achieving them than the nonjudgmental awareness that is the essence of mindfulness.

NOTES AND QUESTIONS

1.   Can you remember a time when you read a few pages of a book—perhaps even this book—and then realized that you had no idea was those pages said? Your eyes covered the words, but where was your mind? This is the experience of what Professor Riskin refers to as mindlessness.

To get a sense of mindfulness, try this exercise: Close your eyes and focus on the sensation of the breath as it enters and leaves the nostrils. To help you stay focused, count each exhalation up to ten. When you reach ten, or when you realize you have lost track, begin again at one. All the while, notice, as best you can—without judging—whatever pulls your attention away from the breath, including thoughts, sounds, smells, emotions, and sensations in the body. This kind of non-judgmental awareness is the essence at mindfulness, and as Professor Riskin's article suggests, may be cultivated through a meditation practice. It's very simple, but not easy.

2.   Mindfulness and other forms of meditation are the subject of active study by psychologists, neurologists, and other scientists. In just the past decade, researchers have found that mindfulness meditation has had positive effects on cancer patients and their partners, healthcare providers, working adults, primary school teachers, breast cancer survivors, aging adults, parents of children with chronic conditions, sufferers of generalized anxiety disorder, and even child abuse survivors. *See generally*, DANIEL J. SIEGEL, THE MINDFUL BRAIN: REFLECTION AND ATTUNEMENT IN THE CULTIVATION OF WELL–BEING 3–28 (2007) (summarizing the literature and citing studies).

While there are no published studies on lawyers or law students, some studies have shown that mindfulness training can help medical students, who like law students also evidence mental health declines during the first year. *See, e.g.,* C. Hassed, S. de Lisle, G. Sullivan, & C. Pier., *Enhancing the health of medical students: outcomes of an integrated mindfulness and lifestyle program.* 14 Advances in Health Sci. Educ. Theory & Prac. 387–398 (2008). Research has also shown that even a relatively small amount of mindfulness training and practice over a two-week period improved the Graduate Record Examination (GRE) verbal scores of participants by an average of 60 points. Michael D. Mrazek, Michael S. Franklin, Dawa Tarchin Phillips, Benjamin Baird & Jonathan W. Schooler, *Mindfulness Training*

Improves Working Memory Capacity and GRE Performance While Reducing Mind Wandering, 24 Psych. Sci. 776–81 (2013).

3.   University of Wisconsin neuroscientist Richard Davidson has spent years studying the neurology of constructive and destructive emotions. This research has narrowed in on the prefrontal cortex as the region of the brain in which emotions are processed. More specifically, his research has found that when people have high levels of brain activity in the left prefrontal cortex, they simultaneously report positive feelings such as happiness, enthusiasm, joy, high energy, and alertness. By contrast, people with a higher level of activity in the right prefrontal cortex tend to report more distressing emotions, such as sadness, anxiety, and worry. Through such experiments, Davidson concludes that each of us has an emotional set-point that is based on the ratio between left and right prefrontal cortex activity, and that this set point provides something of a barometer of the daily moods we are likely to experience.

Davidson also conducted a now-famous series of functional MRI (fMRI) tests on a Tibetan monk, Lama Öser, to determine the degree to which Öser's meditation affected the activity of his left and right prefrontal cortex. Öser used six different forms of meditation, including clear mind meditation, visualizations, and lovingkindness meditation, in which the meditator seeks to generate compassionate or well-wishing thoughts toward himself or herself, or toward others. The fMRI data clearly indicated that large networks in Öser's brain changed with each mental state he generated. Such shifts in brain activity between mind states are unusual, except for significant shifts in consciousness, such as between sleeping and wakefulness. Davidson takes this evidence to support his thesis that with significant practice, meditation techniques can allow people to push their emotional set-points in more constructive directions. *Id.* at 11–13. From a dispute resolution perspective, such an effort would contribute to personal conflict management, as well as the capacity of a dispute resolution professional to work effectively with disputing parties.

4.   Davidson and his colleagues also did research on high tech executives in Madison, Wisconsin, who meditated a fraction as much as the Tibetan Lama. They found that during the course of their eight-meditation practice, these executives increased they level of brainwave activity in the left prefrontal cortex—and also improved their immune functions. Richard J. Davidson, et al., *Alterations in Brain and Immune Function Produced by Mindfulness Meditation*, 65 Psychosomatic Med. 564 (2003).

5.   Mindfulness can help students transfer skills from the classroom simulations into actual practice.

> Students learn from each of these [classroom] activities, of course. They do so partly in the same way that football players learn from practice drills in blocking and tackling, followed by critiques of their performance. But football players cannot execute blocks and tackles well unless . . . they have a certain minimal amount of strength. For that

reason, football training routinely includes weightlifting and other methods of building muscles.

Similarly, for a person to appropriately implement the strategies associated with the new approaches to mediation and negotiation and lawyering, she must have a set of foundational capacities, including awareness, emotional sophistication, and understanding. * * *

Leonard L. Riskin, *Mindfulness: Foundational Training for Dispute Resolution,* 54 J. Leg. Educ. 79 (2004).

6.   In recent years, mindfulness has made inroads into the legal community. It was introduced to law schools in the 1980s and 1990s through retreats for Yale Law School students, and picked up steam after a 2002 symposium edition of the Harvard Negotiation Law Review on the topic. *Symposium, Mindfulness in Law and ADR*, 7 Harv. Negot. L. Rev. 1 (2002), Several law review articles and books followed. *See, e.g.,* Rhonda V. Magee, *Educating lawyers to meditate?*, 79 UMKC L. Rev. 3 (2011) and SCOTT ROGERS, MINDFULNESS FOR LAW STUDENTS: USING THE POWER OF MINDFULNESS TO ACHIEVE BALANCE AND SUCCESS IN LAW (2010). In 2012, the *Journal of Legal Education* published a symposium on mindfulness in legal education. *Symposium, The Mindful Lawyer*, 61 J. Legal. Educ. 634 (2012). and a year later, a Mindfulness Affinity Group for legal educators formed in the Association of American Law Schools Section on Balance in Legal Education.Several law schools have launched mindfulness initiatives for students as well, including the law schools at Berkeley, Miami, San Francisco, Missouri, CUNY, Hastings, Florida, Georgetown, George Washington, Northwestern, Roger Williams, and Vanderbilt. Researchers at Missouri began the first empirical study of mindfulness and law students at the Missouri School of Law in 2013.

C. NEW OPPORTUNITIES

For many students, the study of ADR presents an unfamiliar picture of what life as a lawyer might be like. A common question is what ADR practice is like in "the real world," and how can I get started? In this section, we try to answer those questions by referring readers to the experiences of others who have asked those same questions. We begin with brief overview of the professional organizations that support dispute resolution practitioners, attorneys, and others interested in the field. We then conclude this chapter, and the book, with excerpts from a collection of personal stories telling how some dispute resolution professionals came to work in the field, with several writers addressing particular aspects of the question.

1. ENTERING THE STREAM: PROFESSIONAL ORGANIZATIONS

Like many other endeavors, a dispute resolution practice can be difficult when going alone. Many dispute resolution practitioners connect with the field through state and national dispute resolution professional organizations.

Through these organizations many working in dispute resolution share their professional experiences, learn new skills, and develop professional networks for support and advancement that may assist in a wide variety of ways. These organizations also often help define professional standards on pressing issues by studying and/or drafting professional guidance standards themselves, or by participating in the research and drafting of such standards by others.

As of this writing, there are two major national organizations—the American Bar Association Section of Dispute Resolution and the Association for Conflict Resolution (ACR)—which seek to serve a broad array of areas within the profession. There are several other smaller but important organizations that are more focused on a particular area or type of practice, such as the National Association of Family and Community Mediators and the Victim Offender Mediation Association.

Both the ABA SDR and ACR have student divisions, and encourage the creation and growth of chapters at individual law schools. The ABA Section of Dispute Resolution is the larger of the two, with approximately 17,000 members as compared to about 3,500 members of ACR. Both organizations welcome lawyers and non-lawyers, but, not surprisingly, the ABA tends to attract those with law backgrounds while ACR tends to attract those with non-law backgrounds.

Despite these differences, many ADR professionals belong to both organizations, so each includes members from across the field, including: full and part-time practitioners and trainers, educators, judges, and public and private program managers, among others. Both have large and informative annual meetings, with the ABA's typically in the Spring and ACR's in the Fall. Both the ABA SDR and ACR have multiple standing committees (such as committees on mediation, arbitration, and legislation) as well as special committees and task forces to focus on particular problems (such as professional training and certification), and sometimes participate jointly on policy-setting committees for the field, such as with the drafting of the Model Standards of Conduct for Mediators. ACR has regional organizations and chapters in many states chapters, including: Arizona, California, Florida, Georgia, Delaware, Georgia, Hawaii, Illinois, Maryland, Michigan, Minnesota, New England, New Jersey, New York, North Carolina, Pennsylvania, Texas, Virginia, and Washington, D.C. More about these two organizations can be found on their web sites. The ABA's web address is www.abanet.org/dispute. ACR's web address is www.acrnet.org. State and local bar associations also tend to have committees or sections on dispute resolution, which work with courts and present programs on ADR topics.

Other professional organizations of note include:

• **National Association for Community Mediation.** NAFCM supports the maintenance and growth of community-based mediation programs and processes, participates in policy making, and encourages the development and sharing of resources for these efforts.

• **Victim Offender Mediation Association.** VOMA is an international membership association that supports and assists people and communities working at restorative models of justice. VOMA provides resources, training, and technical assistance in victim-offender mediation, conferencing, circles, and related restorative justice practices.

• **Academy of Family Mediators.** AFM members provide mediation services to families facing decisions involving separation, divorce, child custody, parenting, visitation, property division, wills and estates, elder care, spouse support or alimony, child support, family business, pre-nuptial agreements, and many other disputes, conflicts, or issues involving the family.

• **Association of Family and Conciliation Courts.** AFCC is an association of family, court, and community professionals.

• **Chartered Institute of Arbitrators.** The Institute is an international organization dedicated to the advancement of international commercial arbitration.

2.   PERSONAL STORIES

The following excerpts, drawn from *ADR Personalities and Practice Tips*, by James Alfini and Eric Galton, give a sense of how others have traveled the path into dispute resolution, and include many practical suggestions for getting started.

JAMES J. ALFINI & ERIC GALTON, ADR PERSONALITIES AND PRACTICE TIPS
6–8, 13–14, 50–53, 104–07, 136–39 (1998)

Dana L. Curtis

Ms. Curtis tells the story of how interest in dispute resolution sparked during law school turned into a career, thanks to some mentoring by an accomplished practitioner.

I knew I wanted to be a mediator when I was introduced to mediation in a second-year law school course. My other courses, though interesting intellectually, minimized the role of the human being behind the legal claims. Mediation focused on the individuals involved and on the meaning they attached to the dispute. The parties' priorities could be the most important reference point for resolution. In addition to, or instead of, the rule of law, their concerns, needs, fears, hopes and desires all mattered. As well as seeing how mediation could better meet the needs of the parties than a litigated resolution, I realized that mediation better utilized my strengths. As a mediator, I could use relationship and communication skills I had developed in my first career as a teacher.

Full of enthusiasm for mediation, I asked my professor where to learn about mediating as a career. He referred me to Gary Friedman, a pioneer lawyer mediator and Director of the Center for Mediation in Law in Mill Valley, California. I sought Gary's advice about mediating employment and other commercial disputes. He encouraged me, but warned that such a career would be difficult to forge, as the application of mediation in civil disputes was uncommon at that time. He also noted that I seemed to have what it would take—the commitment to mediation and an entrepreneurial spirit, evidenced by the fact that I had entered law school as a single mother after moving to California from Idaho with my three children.

Gary advised me to remain committed, to be patient and to get litigation experience to enhance my credibility with lawyers and my understanding of the legal process. Following his advice, after law school I clerked for a California Supreme Court associate justice and thereafter joined a large San Francisco law firm, practicing commercial and employment litigation in San Jose and San Francisco. I began as an enthusiastic associate and during much of my first year of practice seriously considered a long-term litigation career. Before long, my enthusiasm abated. The enormity of financial and human resources spent on litigation astounded me. The inefficiency of the discovery process (where the object, it seemed to me, was to provide the other side with as little information as possible), the lack of predictability and fairness of jury trials, and the failure of litigation to address the clients' true needs all left me disaffected.

In addition, the demands of big firm practice, the often sixty and sometimes eighty hour work weeks, and the isolation I experienced among 200 other big firm lawyers convinced me that I was not willing to sacrifice more years of "being" for "becoming." The idea of partnership became unthinkable. As one of my law school friends put it, partnership is like a pie eating contest where the prize is more pie.

I dreamed of mediating. Although I had trained as a mediator and had been teaching mediation for several years, I was unable to see a way to make the transition. During this time of profound dissatisfaction with my career, I spent an evening with four dear women friends, as I had been doing on a bimonthly basis for several years. That night I spoke of my life consumed with work, of the months without a day off, of the weeks in a hotel room, of the frustrations of a difficult trial and of the day-to-day failure of my career to provide deep, personal meaning for me. What followed caused me finally to initiate change in my life. One of my friends looked me in the eye and said, "Dana, you will die if you don't leave your job." I knew she was right. If not physically, I was dying spiritually. The next day, without knowing what else I would do, I gave notice that I would be leaving the firm.

A few days later, I ran into Gary Friedman on the street in San Francisco. When he discovered I was leaving my law practice, he invited me to meet with him. Over a series of meetings, I learned that he was becoming increasingly interested in mediation of civil disputes and would like to work closely with lawyers who were pursuing commercial mediation. Within a few months, I hung out my mediation shingle (literally!) at Gary's office in Mill Valley. There, I practiced mediation for two years with Laura Farrow, another lawyer who left the firm at the same time I did. It was an exciting time—the invigoration of moving from a high-rise Financial District office to a renovated house with rose bushes, even an apple tree, in the yard, where at last my whole heart was in my work, as well as the uncertainty of whether a mediation practice could actually support my family.

The years I spent at Mediation Law Offices enabled me to develop a successful practice and to build a foundation that has been important in my practice and in my teaching. By working closely with Gary, I became more effective and more reflective. Following most mediations, I would write a critique of the process and meet with Gary to reflect on the dynamic between the parties and within myself. I was also able to consult with Gary on the spot. At the outset of one early divorce mediation, for example, a couple told me they had come to ask me to write up an agreement they had already reached. Essentially, the agreement provided the husband would have custody of the children and all but $10,000 of their community property assets, which totaled about $300,000. I had been ready to launch into the first phase of mediation, discussing the process and helping the parties to decide if they wanted to go forward, but I was thrown by this request. Excusing myself to get some papers, I ducked into Gary's office and in three minutes worked out an approach that engaged the parties in discussion about the efficacy of their agreement without compromising my neutrality.

After two years at Mediation Law Offices, I had the opportunity to become a Circuit Court Mediator for the U. S. Court of Appeals for the Ninth Circuit in San Francisco. I was persuaded to leave private practice by the promise of an endless array of Federal cases to mediate and steady paycheck. In the Ninth Circuit Mediation Program, I worked with five other full-time mediators to resolve cases on appeal. It was a mediator's dream come true. We selected our caseload from hundreds of diverse civil appeals. On any day, we might conduct a telephone mediation in a securities case, an employment discrimination dispute, a products liability matter, an IRS appeal, a bankruptcy case or an insurance coverage dispute. Several times a month, I would mediate in person, often in complex multi-party disputes. It was a time of applying my experience and knowledge of a face-to-face mediation model, where the parties could reach understanding in order to craft a resolution that addressed their priorities, not just their assessment of their legal positions. I sought to provide more than a settlement conference. In fact, when I began to speak of legal argument in mediation as an *option*, not a *given*, I was surprised by how frequently the parties, and even their lawyers, agreed that discussing the law would not be productive. The first time I suggested that we may not want to discuss the law, the plaintiff (in an employment discrimination case) said, "Thank God! If I had to listen for five more minutes to the company's lawyer telling me what a rotten case I have, I'd leave!"

During the three years I worked at the Ninth Circuit, I mediated hundreds of appeals. I learned that it is never too late for mediation. It was not unusual for a case to have been in litigation for ten years or more—and still settle! I also learned the approach required of an appellate mediator: how to unravel a long history of misunderstanding; how to address the harm the parties inflict upon one another in litigation, which often eclipses the original grievance; how to use the parties' experience with numerous failed negotiations, settlement conferences and mediations to structure a mediation process that avoids repeating their failures. On a more practical note, I learned how to discuss the law, and especially legal issues unique to appeals, without crowding out other reference points for decision; I learned about effective facilitation of both distributional and interest-based negotiations; and I learned how to turn mandatory mediation into a voluntary process—and to believe in it!

Eric R. Galton

It is common for dispute resolution professionals to begin by "hanging out a shingle." Mr. Galton provides some suggestions for getting started.

Mediation Markets

Basically, you will enter one of three distinct ADR markets: first, a "no market situation" in which no one makes a living "doing ADR"; second, a developing ADR market; or, third, an oversaturated ADR market (yes, they really do exist). The realities of developing an ADR practice depend upon which sort of market you are entering.

On the other hand, regardless of which market you are confronting, you should not make an ADR practice commitment until you first do the following things:

- Visit with at least three neutrals who are in fact engaged in a full time ADR practice. . . .
- Take the required mediation training.
- Observe three live mediations conducted by experienced neutrals.
- Conduct five pro bono mediations.

While these steps will not guarantee whether you will make it or succeed as a neutral, you will undoubtedly develop a strong feeling whether this kind of work is or is not for you. If you remain convinced this work is something you wish to do, your practice development steps will vary depending upon the type of market.

Oversaturated Market.

An oversaturated market is one in which several generations of mediators have entrenched themselves. This market has already ferreted out mediators who are deemed "unsuccessful." The remaining mediators have identifiable sectors of loyal clients. This market may have even, perhaps not expressly, identified mediators by style and the grade of complexity of a case (routine, complex, impossible). Mediators may be perceived as interchangeable within these subgroups or stratas. I am also assuming that in such a market and in court annexed cases the *lawyers* select the mediator (in some venues, this is not the case).

In such markets, I see two wildly different approaches. They are as follows:

Develop a Niche. Certain types of disputes require a neutral with specific skills or expertise; i.e. family law, intellectual property, tax etc. Or, certain services, even in an oversaturated market, may not be available.

Permit me to provide an illustration of the latter. Jane Meddler, a budding and hopeful neutral, determines she has three hundred competitors with established practices. Jane also notices that these mediators offer full-day or half-day rates. Jane further realizes that certain cases do not require that time commitment, need a lower rate, and also need a more evaluative approach. Jane offers two hours [of] assisted settlement conferences, charging $400.00 per party. She provides a case evaluation, and a service at a cost which is substantially less than a full day rate with an experienced mediator.

Patience: Cream Rises to the Top. Alternatively, you do not want to be identified in a niche and you believe that you can compete heads up with the local talent. I would suggest the following plan:

- Be patient. Do not quit your day job.

- Contact lawyers you really know well, advise them of your training and commitment, and ask for a tryout. Inevitably, their preferred neutrals will have scheduling conflicts.

- When you finally get the call, excel and resolve the dispute. As a general rule, each successful mediation creates four new ones. I know. . . success, from the mediation perspective, does not always mean or require the matter to settle. Success in the marketplace is defined as the consistent ability to resolve disputes. More blatantly stated, if you obtain and resolve four cases in your first month, you should be seeing eight to nine referrals per month by your twelfth month.

Developing Market

In a developing market, others have gone before you, created the potential for the market, and have developed something of a following.

Assuming you have received your training and made an informed decision that mediation is for you, I would suggest the following approach:

- Keep your day job. You do not know how the market will respond to your efforts nor do you know whether you will succeed as a mediator or enjoy the practice.

- Do a direct mail piece to those colleagues you really know. Outline your training, your commitment, and specify your fee structure.

- Follow-up the direct mail with telephone calls and office visits. Letters may be easily dismissed or forgotten.

- Contact practicing mediators you know and make them aware that you are prepared to accept their conflicts or cases they do not have the time to handle. Most mediators enter into informal cross-referral pacts, usually without a referral fee being paid.

- Should the courts in your jurisdiction maintain a list of qualified mediators, do what is necessary to get on such a list.

- Consider developing an identity as a "specialist" in a particular area.

No Market

If you think about it, the maximum opportunity and greatest difficulty in creating a mediation practice exists in a venue in which no one has established a viable mediation practice.

In these venues, most people will advise you that you cannot succeed. Depending upon your personality, such naysaying may be music to your ears. But, you need to exercise your communication skills and find out why people believe you will not succeed.

Again, my frame of reference is court-annexed mediation, so the questions I would ask are in that context and are as follows:

- Are the local judges opposed to mediation and why? If judges, are opposed, you need to educate the judges about the value of the mediation process.

- Are local lawyers opposed to mediation and why? Most lawyers oppose what they do not understand. Again, your mission is to educate lawyers and explain that mediation is good for both their clients and them.

- Have others before you attempted to develop a mediation practice and failed? If so, why?

Your primary job will be to educate those who are in a position to refer cases. Anticipate skepticism, distrust, and ignorance. But, as a bright beacon in the fog, keep this one unmistakable truth in mind—most of the greatest skeptics and naysayers about the process become the most outspoken proponents of the process after a successful mediation. These people will tell countless friends, "I did not believe in mediation, I never thought this case would settle, and it did." The only thing you need are a few opportunities to prove the process works to these skeptics. If you are able to be given a few chances, your work will market itself.

Public Service and Professional Development Considerations

Regardless of which of the three markets you enter, you will underscore your commitment to the practice by devoting some time to public service ADR projects and professional development matters. Such activities will enrich your new life as a mediator and allow you to give something back to the community. You might consider any of the following:

- Make a point of handling at least four cases per year on a pro bono basis. Many cases are appropriate candidates for mediation, but the parties may not be able to afford the services of a mediator.

- Volunteer to create a peer mediation program in a local elementary, junior high, or high school. If such programs already exist, adopt a school and train a class of students.

- Certain community, public policy matters may need the volunteer services of a qualified mediator.

- If your local courts have a Settlement Week program or are initiating one, volunteer.

- Join any local ADR groups or sections. Cross-talk with your colleagues is both necessary and helpful.

- Join national ADR groups or associations (e.g., the ABA Section of Dispute Resolution or Society of Professionals in Dispute

Resolution [SPIDR]). In addition to providing necessary collegiality and insight into the experiences of other neutrals from a nationwide perspective, these groups, among others, are leaders in the development of ADR!

• Make a commitment, whether required or not, to at least twenty hours per year of continuing education in mediation. One never stops learning and it is beneficial to learn the perspectives and techniques of others.

Kathy Fragnoli

Ms. Fragnoli provides more tips for getting started in mediation and arbitration, including the incorporation of training into one's dispute resolution practice.

Mediation

Volunteer until you are really good. In my opinion, it usually takes about 30 mediations to even approach a point where you are ready to charge for your services. When you are there, you will know it. Only then should you start introducing yourself as a mediator for hire. Attorneys who use you in a volunteer setting will recommend you to others. Most attorney mediators charge $1,500 per day in Texas. As with any business, word of mouth takes time. Plan to eat macaroni and cheese for two years. If you do not use professional mediation rooms, nice stationery and a good voice mail system, plan to eat macaroni and cheese for six years.

For local court ordered disputes, I have become associated with a local mediation firm called Burdin Mediations. Burdin markets six mediators and is a full service mediation company with two locations, very upscale space and three full time administrators. They schedule my local mediation cases (around my obligations to other clients), and handle all billing. In exchange, I pay them a portion of my fee from each case.

It is difficult to become associated with most services like Burdin unless you already have a following or a niche market. New mediators may want to join together to share space and administrative help if they are unable to become a member of an established mediation firm.

Another option for mediators is to look for opportunities with state and federal agencies who contract for mediation services. Ask your local Small Business Administration Office to help you search for such opportunities.

Arbitration

Without substantive experience in a particular field, it is difficult to get started as an arbitrator. However, many labor arbitrators are willing to let those who are interested in entering the field serve as interns and observe hearings. After interning, the American Arbitration Association in New York will list you as a labor arbitrator if you provide letters of recommendation from four different management representatives and four unions. Labor arbitrators typically bill about $1,600 per case which includes travel, hearing and writing time.

The National Association of Securities Dealers will list you as an arbitrator even if you have very limited experience. They pay only $200 per day, but you sit on a panel with two other arbitrators and do not have to write a lengthy decision—only a few sentence award. Serving on one of these panels is a good way to see if you enjoy the process. Without a listing on panels such as the one AAA maintains, it is nearly impossible to serve as a private arbitrator.

ADR Training

Training is, by far, the most rewarding segment of my practice. Besides being financially profitable, it is extremely satisfying to "create" new mediators or to teach organizations conflict resolution skills. In addition to mediator training, I provide seminars on interest based negotiation skills designed especially for women in law or business.

ADR practitioners who think they would enjoy the platform should start developing their public speaking skills by volunteering at a local dispute resolution center. Another way to get started is to call local business clubs about volunteering to give an after dinner speech on ADR. Soon you may find, as I did, that businesses will be interested in paying you to teach a full day (or week long!) seminar.

Jeffrey G. Kichaven

Mr. Kichaven describes the transition to commercial mediation from a traditional business litigation practice.

An ADR practice—as a professional mediator—is not for the faint of heart. Too often, when I ask aspiring mediators what attracts them to the field, they tell me that they are, in some way or to some degree, averse to the "conflict" inherent in litigation and other aspects of law practice, and want to get away from that. These people are not likely to make it as mediators.

First, there is no career, as a mediator or anything else, that will provide satisfaction if it is an "escape" from something else rather than something to which you are drawn in its own right. Relationships "on the rebound," whether in romance or career, rarely succeed over the long haul. If one seeks a career as mediator just to escape from the conflict inherent in litigation, without a passion for what mediation has to offer, the likelihood of enhanced career satisfaction, to me, is small.

Second, though, and perhaps more importantly, mediation is not an alternative to "conflict" at all. It is the essence of conflict. In mediation, the parties can bare their souls; there are no rules of evidence or civil procedure, no concept of courtroom decorum, no transcription of the record, to keep the discussion tightly and unemotionally focused on the legal claims and defenses set forth in the pleadings. The parties can plumb the depths of their business and personal relationships. And, if the mediator is any good, that discussion is not only tolerated, it is encouraged. The deeper the parties' relationship is explored, the more likely the parties will achieve a high degree of clarity, and a durable, comprehensive, mutually-satisfying resolution. The road to this kind of resolution is generally not easy to tread. The effective mediator must model, among other things, the courage to look the conflict square in the eye, and say the things which have for too long gone unsaid. A mediator whose goal is to "smooth over" the conflict, and require "nice-nice" behavior all around, is unlikely to give the parties or the process what they all deserve.

When I graduated from Harvard Law School in 1980, I joined a rough, tough, take-no-prisoners business litigation firm in my home city, Los Angeles. I was one of the youngest members of my graduating class; I received my J.D. about two weeks before my 24th birthday.

In my mid–20s, the scorched-earth style of litigation was great fun. I fashioned myself as a kind of "Errol Flynn of litigation," swashbuckling my way through conflicts, heroically swinging in on the chandelier, sword drawn, thrusting it through the chest of the "bad guy" as I pounced. This almost always provoked retaliation from the other side, and hence became very expensive for the clients; it was also consuming of my time and psyche. In the highly adversarial mode, nobody cuts anybody else any slack. This razor's edge between "perfection" and "disaster" produced a high degree of anxiety.

In addition, I found it hard to "turn it on" at the office and "turn it off" at home. In part, that is because there was relatively little time at home. Before I was married, and then before we had children, it was no big deal to work around the clock as needed, which seemed to be almost all the time.

As I got older (and, if I dare say so, more mature), my thoughts changed. Time with my family became a higher priority as my family expanded (we have 3 kids) and grew. But at least as important was the perspective I began to develop on the litigation process itself. Yes, there ARE some cases in which the take-no-prisoners approach is required. And, if you are involved in one of those cases, you must fight fire with fire. But not every case calls for that approach. Indeed, the number of such cases on any given lawyer's desk is likely smaller than that lawyer might at first perceive. When you are in the middle of the war, however, it is difficult to see that there might be another way, which might serve the client's interests even better.

Many times, I would question my partners as to whether there was another way. "This litigation is awfully expensive and time consuming for the client," I often thought, "and the parties to this lawsuit, who once had a solid business relationship, will probably never do business with each other again once we are done with the hostility this litigation is engendering." It just seemed to me that there must be a better way to serve the client's interests; the client, after all, was not in the business of prosecuting or defending lawsuits; the client was in one type or another of widget business, and we rarely looked at how the litigation would affect the client's long- and short-term interests in the overall health and prosperity of its business.

These questions did not particularly endear me to my partners, some of whom perceived mediation as little more than a foolish means of resolving cases less remuneratively. The rainmakers stopped asking for me to work on their cases, since I persisted in asking whether "another way" might better serve the client's interest, and, incidentally, reduce the amount of rainfall per cloud. Eventually, my partners and I came to realize that the situation, which had worked so well for all of us in previous years, was no longer working, and so, amicably, I left to make my way in the world.

I joined three friends, also big-firm veterans, in a small-firm practice. At first, I tried to pursue big-ticket business litigation cases, but with an ADR-oriented twist—in essence, taking my old practice as a base, and "fixing" what I didn't like about it. At the same time, I started to take on cases as a mediator, through court panels on which I had volunteered. It soon became apparent to me—and even more apparent to my wife—which type of work I preferred. My wife commented that, when I came home at night, she could tell which days I had been mediating and which days I had been litigating. When I had been mediating, I was happier and more relaxed. In one stretch, in the spring of 1996, she said to me that it had become obvious which type of work I preferred; that, for months, I had been "flirting" with the idea of becoming a full-time neutral; and that I should stop trying to "fix" my old practice, and have the courage to create something totally new, a mediation practice. With her encouragement, I took that plunge in mid–1996, and have not looked back.

There are plenty of pressures on a mediator, just as there are plenty of pressures on a litigator. But they are different pressures, and I greatly prefer the one over the other.

As a litigator, I always found it difficult to leave my work at the office, to put it down and relax, when it was time to spend time with my family or pursue other activities. When cases take years to resolve, they consume a prominent part of the litigator's (or at least THIS litigator's) mind-space. I was always concerned that some tyro on the umpteenth floor of some big office building was staying up late working on ways to outsmart me. Many times, I was right! So I felt I had to spend my time fighting back—generally, ALL of my time! I felt that I was always "on."

As a mediator, that pressure is gone. My involvement with most cases is relatively brief—a few days, a week at most. When one case is done (whether settled or brought to impasse), I am done, too, until the next case starts. This makes for infinitely better evenings, weekends and vacations.

The other pressure, though, also arises from the fact that my involvement with cases is relatively brief. That is the pressure to keep new cases coming in all the time. As in the semiconductor industry, my "book to bill" ratio is critical. New cases must be brought in as rapidly as current cases are handled, if the business is to prosper. So, I spend a huge amount of time marketing. Fortunately, most of the marketing activities are things I enjoy—meeting people and talking to them about how ADR can help them, whether as transactional lawyer, litigator or client; writing and speaking; and bar activities. As my "computer guy," Dan Turner, said when we were discussing our respective passions, for computer technology and dispute resolution, "find something you love to do, and never work another day in your life!"

Ironically, I think that my 15 years in rough-and-ready business litigation uniquely prepared me for service as a mediator, and is my biggest marketing plus. The reason is that ADR professionals are changing their perception about their "clients." We now understand that, in a very significant sense, *other lawyers ARE our clients*, no less than the underlying business clients who are parties to the dispute.

In my experience (and I think this fairly mirrors the experiences of others), it is other lawyers who make our phones ring with new business. The underlying business clients may have an inchoate sense that the processes of traditional litigation are not getting them where they want to be going with their dispute (or at least not getting them there as quickly, affordably or smoothly as they want), but likely do not have the knowledge that mediation may be the way out of their box. It is other lawyers—in-house counsel as well as law firm partners—who are aware of the specific alternatives, and who know that we mediators are the people to call.

But other lawyers will not call us if they perceive that we do not appreciate them, their situations, and their problems. And to be sure, lawyers often have just as many "problems" as the underlying business clients. The client-with-unrealistic-expectations and the hard-to-collect-receivable are just two on a much longer list. So, from a business sense and a professional sense as well, we must acknowledge that the lawyers are stake-holders in the dispute, too, and we have to deal with them and their interests straight-up.

In marketing my mediation practice, I have found that my past experience gives other lawyers confidence that I will do the job for them as well as for their clients; that I can and will understand and deal with their concerns, interests and problems. Other lawyers know that I have walked miles in their shoes. They are comfortable that I am "like them" in material ways.

QUESTIONS

If you hope to incorporate work as an ADR neutral into your professional practice, which of these stories seems most helpful to you? What else would you like to know about developing a neutral practice? For more, see FORREST S. MOSTEN, MEDIATION CAREER GUIDE: A STRATEGIC APPROACH FOR BUILDING A SUCCESSFUL PRACTICE (2001).

APPENDIX A

FEDERAL RULES OF CIVIL PROCEDURE RULE 16

■ ■ ■

Rule 16. Pretrial Conferences; Scheduling; Management

(a) Pretrial Conferences; Objectives. In any action, the court may in its discretion direct the attorneys for the parties and any unrepresented parties to appear before it for a conference or conferences before trial for such purposes as

(1) expediting the disposition of the action;

(2) establishing early and continuing control so that the case will not be protracted because of lack of management;

(3) discouraging wasteful pretrial activities;

(4) improving the quality of the trial through more thorough preparation; and

(5) facilitating the settlement of the case.

(b) Scheduling and Planning. Except in categories of actions exempted by district court rule as inappropriate, the district judge, or a magistrate judge when authorized by district court rule, shall, after receiving the report from the parties under Rule 26(f) or after consulting with the attorneys for the parties and any unrepresented parties by a scheduling conference, telephone, mail, or other suitable means, enter a scheduling order that limits the time

(1) to join other parties and to amend the pleadings;

(2) to file motions; and

(3) to complete discovery.

The scheduling order may also include

(4) modifications of the times for disclosures under Rules 26(a) and 26(e)(1) and of the extent of discovery to be permitted;

(5) the date or dates for conferences before trial, a final pretrial conference, and trial; and

(6) any other matters appropriate in the circumstances of the case.

The order shall issue as soon as practicable but in any event within 90 days after the appearance of a defendant and within 120 days after the complaint has been served on a defendant. A schedule shall not be modified except upon a showing of good cause and by leave of the district judge or, when authorized by local rule, by a magistrate judge.

(c) Subjects for Consideration at Pretrial Conferences. At any conference under this rule consideration may be given, and the court may take appropriate action, with respect to

   (1) the formulation and simplification of the issues, including the limitation of frivolous claims or defenses;

   (2) the necessity or desirability of amendments to the pleadings;

   (3) the possibility of obtaining admissions of fact and of documents which will avoid unnecessary proof, stipulations regarding the authenticity of documents, and advance rulings from the court on the admissibility of evidence;

   (4) the avoidance of unnecessary proof and of cumulative evidence, and limitations or restrictions on the use of testimony under Rule 702 of the Federal Rules of Evidence;

   (5) the appropriateness and timing of summary adjudication under Rule 56;

   (6) the control and scheduling of discovery, including orders affecting disclosures and discovery pursuant to Rule 26 and Rules 29 through 37;

   (7) the identification of witnesses and documents, the need and schedule for filing and exchanging pretrial briefs, and the date or dates for further conferences and for trial;

   (8) the advisability of referring matters to a magistrate judge or master;

   (9) settlement and the use of special procedures to assist in resolving the dispute when authorized by statute or local rule;

   (10) the form and substance of the pretrial order;

   (11) the disposition of pending motions;

   (12) the need for adopting special procedures for managing potentially difficult or protracted actions that may involve complex issues, multiple parties, difficult legal questions, or unusual proof problems;

   (13) an order for a separate trial pursuant to Rule 42(b) with respect to a claim, counterclaim, cross-claim, or third-party claim, or with respect to any particular issue in the case;

(14) an order directing a party or parties to present evidence early in the trial with respect to a manageable issue that could, on the evidence, be the basis for a judgment as a matter of law under Rule 50(a) or a judgment on partial findings under Rule 52(c);

(15) an order establishing a reasonable limit on the time allowed for presenting evidence; and

(16) such other matters as may facilitate the just, speedy, and inexpensive disposition of the action.

At least one of the attorneys for each party participating in any conference before trial shall have authority to enter into stipulations and to make admissions regarding all matters that the participants may reasonably anticipate may be discussed. If appropriate, the court may require that a party or its representative be present or reasonably available by telephone in order to consider possible settlement of the dispute.

(d) Final Pretrial Conference. Any final pretrial conference shall be held as close to the time of trial as reasonable under the circumstances. The participants at any such conference shall formulate a plan for trial, including a program for facilitating the admission of evidence. The conference shall be attended by at least one of the attorneys who will conduct the trial for each of the parties and by any unrepresented parties.

(e) Pretrial Orders. After any conference held pursuant to this rule, an order shall be entered reciting the action taken. This order shall control the subsequent course of the action unless modified by a subsequent order. The order following a final pretrial conference shall be modified only to prevent manifest injustice.

(f) Sanctions. If a party or party's attorney fails to obey a scheduling or pretrial order, or if no appearance is made on behalf of a party at a scheduling or pretrial conference, or if a party or party's attorney is substantially unprepared to participate in the conference, or if a party or party's attorney fails to participate in good faith, the judge, upon motion or the judge's own initiative, may make such orders with regard thereto as are just, and among others any of the orders provided in Rule 37(b)(2)(B), (C), (D). In lieu of or in addition to any other sanction, the judge shall require the party or the attorney representing the party or both to pay the reasonable expenses incurred because of any noncompliance with this rule, including attorney's fees, unless the judge finds that the noncompliance was substantially justified or that other circumstances make an award of expenses unjust.

(As amended Apr. 28, 1983, eff. Aug. 1, 1983; Mar. 2, 1987, eff. Aug. 1, 1987; Apr. 22, 1993, eff. Dec. 1, 1993.)

APPENDIX B

SELECTED PROVISIONS OF THE MODEL RULES OF PROFESSIONAL CONDUCT (2002)

■ ■ ■

PREAMBLE: A Lawyer's Responsibilities

[1] A lawyer, as a member of the legal profession, is a representative of clients, an officer of the legal system and a public citizen having special re-sponsibility for the quality of justice.

[2] As a representative of clients, a lawyer performs various functions. As advisor, a lawyer provides a client with an informed understanding of the client's legal rights and obligations and explains their practical implications. As advocate, a lawyer zealously asserts the client's position under the rules of the adversary system. As negotiator, a lawyer seeks a result advantageous to the client but consistent with requirements of honest dealings with others. As an evaluator, a lawyer acts by examining a client's legal affairs and reporting about them to the client or to others.

* * *

Client-Lawyer Relationship

Rule 1.1 Competence

A lawyer shall provide competent representation to a client. Competent representation requires the legal knowledge, skill, thoroughness and preparation reasonably necessary for the representation.

Rule 1.2 Scope of Representation and Allocation of Authority Between Client and Lawyer

(a) Subject to paragraphs (c) and (d), a lawyer shall abide by a client's decisions concerning the objectives of representation and, as required by Rule 1.4, shall consult with the client as to the means by which they are to be pursued. A lawyer may take such action on behalf of the client as is impliedly authorized to carry out the representation. A lawyer shall abide by a client's decision whether to settle a matter. In a criminal case, the lawyer shall abide by the client's decision, after consultation with the lawyer, as to a plea to be entered, whether to waive jury trial and whether the client will testify.

(b) A lawyer's representation of a client, including representation by appointment, does not constitute an endorsement of the client's political, economic, social or moral views or activities.

(c) A lawyer may limit the scope of the representation if the limitation is reasonable under the circumstances and the client gives informed consent.

(d) A lawyer shall not counsel a client to engage, or assist a client, in conduct that the lawyer knows is criminal or fraudulent, but a lawyer may discuss the legal consequences of any proposed course of conduct with a client and may counsel or assist a client to make a good faith effort to determine the validity, scope, meaning or application of the law.

Rule 1.4 Communication

(a) A lawyer shall:

(1) promptly inform the client of any decision or circumstance with respect to which the client's informed consent, as defined in Rule 1.0(e), is required by these Rules;

(2) reasonably consult with the client about the means by which the client's objectives are to be accomplished;

(3) keep the client reasonably informed about the status of the matter;

(4) promptly comply with reasonable requests for information; and

(5) consult with the client about any relevant limitation on the lawyer's conduct when the lawyer knows that the client expects assistance not permitted by the Rules of Professional Conduct or other law.

(b) A lawyer shall explain a matter to the extent reasonably necessary to permit the client to make informed decisions regarding the representation.

Rule 1.6 Confidentiality of Information

(a) A lawyer shall not reveal information relating to the representation of a client unless the client gives informed consent, the disclosure is impliedly authorized in order to carry out the representation or the disclosure is permitted by paragraph (b).

(b) A lawyer may reveal informa tion relating to the representation of a client to the extent the lawyer reasonably believes necessary:

(1) to prevent reasonably certain death or substantial bodily harm;

(2) to prevent the client from committing a crime or fraud that is reasonably certain to result in substantial injury to the financial interests

or property of another and in furtherance of which the client has used or is using the lawyer's services;

(3) to prevent, mitigate or rectify substantial injury to the financial interests or property of another that is reasonably certain to result or has resulted from the client's commission of a crime or fraud in furtherance of which the client has used the lawyer's services;

(4) to secure legal advice about the lawyer's compliance with these Rules;

(5) to establish a claim or defense on behalf of the lawyer in a controversy between the lawyer and the client, to establish a defense to a criminal charge or civil claim against the lawyer based upon conduct in which the client was involved, or to respond to allegations in any proceeding concerning the lawyer's representation of the client;

(6) to comply with other law or a court order; or

(7) to detect and resolve conflicts of interest arising from the lawyer's change of employment or from changes in the composition or ownership of a firm, but only if the revealed information would not compromise the attorney-client privilege or otherwise prejudice the client.

(c) A lawyer shall make reasonable efforts to prevent the inadvertent or unauthorized disclosure of, or unauthorized access to, information relating to the representation of a client.

Rule 1.7 Conflict of Interest: Current Clients

(a) Except as provided in paragraph (b), a lawyer shall not represent a client if the representation involves a concurrent conflict of interest. A concurrent conflict of interest exists if:

(1) the representation of one client will be directly adverse to another client; or

(2) there is a significant risk that the representation of one or more clients will be materially limited by the lawyer's responsibilities to another client, a former client or a third person or by a personal interest of the lawyer.

(b) Notwithstanding the existence of a concurrent conflict of interest under paragraph (a), a lawyer may represent a client if:

(1) the lawyer reasonably believes that the lawyer will be able to provide competent and diligent representation to each affected client;

(2) the representation is not prohibited by law;

(3) the representation does not involve the assertion of a claim by one client against another client represented by the lawyer in the same litigation or other proceeding before a tribunal; and

(4) each affected client gives informed consent, confirmed in writing.

Rule 1.9 Duties to Former Clients

(a) A lawyer who has formerly represented a client in a matter shall not thereafter represent another person in the same or a substantially related matter in which that person's interests are materially adverse to the interests of the former client unless the former client gives informed consent, confirmed in writing.

(b) A lawyer shall not knowingly represent a person in the same or a substantially related matter in which a firm with which the lawyer formerly was associated had previously represented a client

(1) whose interests are materially adverse to that person; and

(2) about whom the lawyer had acquired information protected by Rules 1.6 and 1.9(c) that is material to the matter;

unless the former client gives informed consent, confirmed in writing.

(c) A lawyer who has formerly represented a client in a matter or whose present or former firm has formerly represented a client in a matter shall not thereafter:

(1) use information relating to the representation to the disadvantage of the former client except as these Rules would permit or require with respect to a client, or when the information has become generally known; or

(2) reveal information relating to the representation except as these Rules would permit or require with respect to a client.

Rule 1.12 Former Judge, Arbitrator, Mediator or Other Third–Party Neutral

(a) Except as stated in paragraph (d), a lawyer shall not represent anyone in connection with a matter in which the lawyer participated personally and substantially as a judge or other adjudicative officer or law clerk to such a person or as an arbitrator, mediator or other third-party neutral, unless all parties to the proceeding give informed consent, confirmed in writing.

(b) A lawyer shall not negotiate for employment with any person who is involved as a party or as lawyer for a party in a matter in which the lawyer is participating personally and substantially as a judge or other adjudicative officer or as an arbitrator, mediator or other third-party neutral. A lawyer serving as a law clerk to a judge or other adjudicative officer may negotiate for employment with a party or lawyer involved in a matter in which the clerk is participating personally and substantially, but only after the lawyer has notified the judge or other adjudicative officer.

(c) If a lawyer is disqualified by paragraph (a), no lawyer in a firm with which that lawyer is associated may knowingly undertake or continue representation in the matter unless:

(1) The disqualified lawyer is timely screened from any participation in the matter and is apportioned no part of the fee therefrom; and

(2) Written notice is promptly given to the parties and any appropriate tribunal to enable them to ascertain compliance with the provisions of this rule.

(d) An arbitrator selected as a partisan of a party in a multimember arbitration panel is not prohibited from subsequently representing that party.

Counselor

Rule 2.1 Advisor

In representing a client, a lawyer shall exercise independent professional judgment and render candid advice. In rendering advice, a lawyer may refer not only to law but to other considerations such as moral, economic, social and political factors, that may be relevant to the client's situation.

Comment: Offering Advice

[5] In general, a lawyer is not expected to give advice until asked by the client. However, when a lawyer knows that a client proposes a course of action that is likely to result in substantial adverse legal consequences to the client, the lawyer's duty to the client under Rule 1.4 may require that the lawyer offer advice if the client's course of action is related to the representation. Similarly, when a matter is likely to involve litigation, it may be necessary under Rule 1.4 to inform the client of forms of dispute resolution that might constitute reasonable alternatives to litigation. A lawyer ordinarily has no duty to initiate investigation of a client's affairs or to give advice that the client has indicated is unwanted, but a lawyer may initiate advice to a client when doing so appears to be in the client's interest.

Rule 2.4 Lawyer Serving as Third-Party Neutral

(a) A lawyer serves as a third-party neutral when the lawyer assists two or more persons who are not clients of the lawyer to reach a resolution of a dispute or other matter that has arisen between them. Service as a third-party neutral may include service as an arbitrator, a mediator or in such other capacity as will enable the lawyer to assist the parties to resolve the matter.

(b) A lawyer serving as a third-party neutral shall inform unrepresented parties that the lawyer is not representing them. When the lawyer knows or reasonably should know that a party does not understand the lawyer's role in the matter, the lawyer shall explain the difference between the lawyer's role as a third-party neutral and a lawyer's role as one who represents a client.

Rule 3.3 Candor Toward the Tribunal

(a) A lawyer shall not knowingly:

(1) make a false statement of fact or law to a tribunal or fail to correct a false statement of material fact or law previously made to the tribunal by the lawyer;

(2) fail to disclose to the tribunal legal authority in the controlling jurisdiction known to the lawyer to be directly adverse to the position of the client and not disclosed by opposing counsel; or

(3) offer evidence that the lawyer knows to be false. If a lawyer, the lawyer's client, or a witness called by the lawyer, has offered material evidence and the lawyer comes to know of its falsity, the lawyer shall take reasonable remedial measures, including, if necessary, disclosure to the tribunal. A lawyer may refuse to offer evidence, other than the testimony of a defendant in a criminal matter, that the lawyer reasonably believes is false.

(b) A lawyer who represents a client in an adjudicative proceeding and who knows that a person intends to engage, is engaging or has engaged in criminal or fraudulent conduct related to the proceeding shall take reasonable remedial measures, including, if necessary, disclosure to the tribunal.

(c) The duties stated in paragraphs (a) and (b) continue to the conclusion of the proceeding, and apply even if compliance requires disclosure of information otherwise protected by Rule 1.6.

(d) In an ex parte proceeding, a lawyer shall inform the tribunal of all material facts known to the lawyer that will enable the tribunal to make an informed decision, whether or not the facts are adverse.

Rule 3.4 Fairness to Opposing Party and Counsel

A lawyer shall not:

(a) unlawfully obstruct another party's access to evidence or unlawfully alter, destroy or conceal a document or other material having potential evidentiary value. A lawyer shall not counsel or assist another person to do any such act;

(b) falsify evidence, counsel or assist a witness to testify falsely, or offer an inducement to a witness that is prohibited by law;

(c) knowingly disobey an obligation under the rules of a tribunal except for an open refusal based on an assertion that no valid obligation exists;

(d) in pretrial procedure, make a frivolous discovery request or fail to make reasonably diligent effort to comply with a legally proper discovery request by an opposing party;

(e) in trial, allude to any matter that the lawyer does not reasonably believe is relevant or that will not be supported by admissible evidence, assert personal knowledge of facts in issue except when testifying as a witness, or state a personal opinion as to the justness of a cause, the credibility of a witness, the culpability of a civil litigant or the guilt or innocence of an accused; or

(f) request a person other than a client to refrain from voluntarily giving relevant information to another party unless:

(1) the person is a relative or an employee or other agent of a client; and

(2) the lawyer reasonably believes that the person's interests will not be adversely affected by refraining from giving such information.

Rule 3.9 Advocate in Nonadjudicative Proceedings

A lawyer representing a client before a legislative body or administrative agency in a nonadjudicative proceeding shall disclose that the appearance is in a representative capacity and shall conform to the provisions of Rules 3.3(a) through (c), 3.4(a) through (c), and 3.5.

Transactions With Persons Other Than Clients

Rule 4.1 Truthfulness in Statements to Others

In the course of representing a client a lawyer shall not knowingly:

(a) make a false statement of material fact or law to a third person; or

(b) fail to disclose a material fact to a third person when disclosure is necessary to avoid assisting a criminal or fraudulent act by a client, unless disclosure is prohibited by Rule 1.6.

Comments to Rule 4.1

Misrepresentation

[1] A lawyer is required to be truthful when dealing with others on a client's behalf, but generally has no affirmative duty to inform an opposing party of relevant facts. A misrepresentation can occur if the lawyer incorporates or affirms a statement of another person that the lawyer knows is false. Misrepresentations can also occur by partially true but misleading statements or omissions that are the equivalent of affirmative false statements. For dishonest conduct that does not amount to a false statement or for misrepresentations by a lawyer other than in the course of representing a client, see Rule 8.4.

Statements of Fact

[2] This Rule refers to statements of fact. Whether a particular statement should be regarded as one of fact can depend on the circumstances. Under generally accepted conventions in negotiation, certain types of statements ordinarily are not taken as statements of material fact. Estimates of price or value placed on the subject of a transaction and a party's intentions as to an acceptable settlement of a claim are ordinarily in this category, and so is the existence of an undisclosed principal except where nondisclosure of the principal would constitute fraud. Lawyers should be mindful of their obligations under applicable law to avoid criminal and tortious misrepresentation.

Crime or Fraud by Client

[3] Under Rule 1.2(d), a lawyer is prohibited from counseling or assisting a client in conduct that the lawyer knows is criminal or fraudulent. Paragraph (b) states a specific application of the principle set forth in Rule 1.2(d) and addresses the situation where a client's crime or fraud takes the form of a lie or misrepresentation. Ordinarily, a lawyer can avoid assisting a client's crime or fraud by withdrawing from the representation. Sometimes it may be necessary for the lawyer to give notice of the fact of withdrawal and to disaffirm an opinion, document, affirmation or the like. In extreme cases, substantive law may require a lawyer to disclose information relating to the representation to avoid being deemed to have assisted the client's crime or fraud. If the lawyer can avoid assisting a client's crime or fraud only by disclosing this information, then under paragraph (b) the lawyer is required to do so, unless the disclosure is prohibited by Rule 1.6.

Maintaining the Integrity of the Profession

Rule 8.3 Reporting Professional Misconduct

(a) A lawyer who knows that another lawyer has committed a violation of the Rules of Professional Conduct that raises a substantial question as to that lawyer's honesty, trustworthiness or fitness as a lawyer in other respects, shall inform the appropriate professional authority.

(b) A lawyer who knows that a judge has committed a violation of applicable rules of judicial conduct that raises a substantial question as to the judge's fitness for office shall inform the appropriate authority.

(c) This Rule does not require disclosure of information otherwise protected by Rule 1.6 or information gained by a lawyer or judge while participating in an approved lawyers assistance program.

Rule 8.4 Misconduct

It is professional misconduct for a lawyer to:

(a) violate or attempt to violate the Rules of Professional Conduct, knowingly assist or induce another to do so, or do so through the acts of another;

(b) commit a criminal act that reflects adversely on the lawyer's honesty, trustworthiness or fitness as a lawyer in other respects;

(c) engage in conduct involving dishonesty, fraud, deceit or misrepresentation;

(d) engage in conduct that is prejudicial to the administration of justice;

(e) state or imply an ability to influence improperly a government agency or official or to achieve results by means that violate the Rules of Professional Conduct or other law; or

(f) knowingly assist a judge or judicial officer in conduct that is a violation of applicable rules of judicial conduct or other law.

APPENDIX C

UNIFORM MEDIATION ACT (2003)

■ ■ ■

SECTION 1. TITLE. This [Act] may be cited as the Uniform Mediation Act.

SECTION 2. DEFINITIONS. In this [Act]:

(1) "Mediation" means a process in which a mediator facilitates communication and negotiation between parties to assist them in reaching a voluntary agreement regarding their dispute.

(2) "Mediation communication" means a statement, whether oral or in a record or verbal or nonverbal, that occurs during a mediation or is made for purposes of considering, conducting, participating in, initiating, continuing, or reconvening a mediation or retaining a mediator.

(3) "Mediator" means an individual who conducts a mediation.

(4) "Nonparty participant" means a person, other than a party or mediator, that participates in a mediation.

(5) "Mediation party" means a person that participates in a mediation and whose agreement is necessary to resolve the dispute.

(6) "Person" means an individual, corporation, business trust, estate, trust, partnership, limited liability company, association, joint venture, government; governmental subdivision, agency, or instrumentality; public corporation, or any other legal or commercial entity.

(7) "Proceeding" means:

    (A) a judicial, administrative, arbitral, or other adjudicative process, including related pre-hearing and post-hearing motions, conferences, and discovery; or

    (B) a legislative hearing or similar process.

(8) "Record" means information that is inscribed on a tangible medium or that is stored in an electronic or other medium and is retrievable in perceivable for

(9) "Sign" means:

(A) to execute or adopt a tangible symbol with the present intent to authenticate a record; or

(B) to attach or logically associate an electronic symbol, sound, or process to or with a record with the present intent to authenticate a record.

SECTION 3. SCOPE.

(a) Except as otherwise provided in subsection (b) or (c), this [Act] applies to a mediation in which:

(1) the mediation parties are required to mediate by statute or court or administrative agency rule or referred to mediation by a court, administrative agency, or arbitrator;

(2) the mediation parties and the mediator agree to mediate in a record that demonstrates an expectation that mediation communications will be privileged against disclosure; or

(3) the mediation parties use as a mediator an individual who holds himself or herself out as a mediator or the mediation is provided by a person that holds itself out as providing mediation.

(b) The [Act] does not apply to a mediation:

(1) relating to the establishment, negotiation, administration, or termination of a collective bargaining relationship;

(2) relating to a dispute that is pending under or is part of the processes established by a collective bargaining agreement, except that the [Act] applies to a mediation arising out of a dispute that has been filed with an administrative agency or court;

(3) conducted by a judge who might make a ruling on the case; or

(4) conducted under the auspices of:

(A) a primary or secondary school if all the parties are students or

(B) a correctional institution for youths if all the parties are residents of that institution.

(c) If the parties agree in advance in a signed record, or a record of proceeding reflects agreement by the parties, that all or part of a mediation is not privileged, the privileges under Sections 4 through 6 do not apply to the mediation or part agreed upon. However, Sections 4 through 6 apply to a mediation communication made by a person that has not received actual notice of the agreement before the communication is made.

Legislative Note: To the extent that the Act applies to mediations conducted under the authority of a State's courts, State judiciaries should consider enacting conforming court rules.

SECTION 4. PRIVILEGE AGAINST DISCLOSURE; ADMISSIBILITY; DISCOVERY.

(a) Except as otherwise provided in Section 6, a mediation communication is privileged as provided in subsection (b) and is not subject to discovery or admissible in evidence in a proceeding unless waived or precluded as provided by Section 5.

(b) In a proceeding, the following privileges apply:

(1) A mediation party may refuse to disclose, and may prevent any other person from disclosing, a mediation communication.

(2) A mediator may refuse to disclose a mediation communication, and may prevent any other person from disclosing a mediation communication of the mediator.

(3) A nonparty participant may refuse to disclose, and may prevent any other person from disclosing, a mediation communication of the nonparty participant.

(c) Evidence or information that is otherwise admissible or subject to discovery does not become inadmissible or protected from discovery solely by reason of its disclosure or use in a mediation.

Legislative Note: The Act does not supersede existing state statutes that make mediators incompetent to testify, or that provide for costs and attorney fees to mediators who are wrongfully subpoenaed. See, e.g., Cal. Evid. Code Section 703.5 (West 1994).

SECTION 5. WAIVER AND PRECLUSION OF PRIVILEGE.

(a) A privilege under Section 4 may be waived in a record or orally during a proceeding if it is expressly waived by all parties to the mediation and:

(1) in the case of the privilege of a mediator, it is expressly waived by the mediator; and

(2) in the case of the privilege of a nonparty participant, it is expressly waived by the nonparty participant.

(b) A person that discloses or makes a representation about a mediation communication which prejudices another person in a proceeding is precluded from asserting a privilege under Section 4, but only to the extent necessary for the person prejudiced to respond to the representation or disclosure.

(c) A person that intentionally uses a mediation to plan, attempt to commit or commit a crime, or to conceal an ongoing crime or ongoing criminal activity is precluded from asserting a privilege under Section 4.

SECTION 6. EXCEPTIONS TO PRIVILEGE.

(a) There is no privilege under Section 4 for a mediation communication that is:

(1) in an agreement evidenced by a record signed by all parties to the agreement;

(2) available to the public under [insert statutory reference to open records act] or made during a session of a mediation which is open, or is required by law to be open, to the public;

(3) a threat or statement of a plan to inflict bodily injury or commit a crime of violence;

(4) intentionally used to plan a crime, attempt to commit or commit a crime, or to conceal an ongoing crime or ongoing criminal activity;

(5) sought or offered to prove or disprove a claim or complaint of professional misconduct or malpractice filed against a mediator;

(6) except as otherwise provided in subsection (c), sought or offered to prove or disprove a claim or complaint of professional misconduct or malpractice filed against a mediation party, nonparty participant, or representative of a party based on conduct occurring during a mediation; or

(7) sought or offered to prove or disprove abuse, neglect, abandonment, or exploitation in a proceeding in which a child or adult protective services agency is a party, unless the

[Alternative A: [State to insert, for example, child or adult protection] case is referred by a court to mediation and a public agency participates.]

[Alternative B: public agency participates in the [State to insert, for example, child or adult protection] mediation].

(b) There is no privilege under Section 4 if a court, administrative agency, or arbitrator finds, after a hearing in camera, that the party seeking discovery or the proponent of the evidence has shown that the evidence is not otherwise available, that there is a need for the evidence that substantially outweighs the interest in protecting confidentiality, and that the mediation communication is sought or offered in:

(1) a court proceeding involving a felony [or misdemeanor]; or

(2) except as otherwise provided in subsection (c), a proceeding to prove a claim to rescind or reform or a defense to avoid liability on a contract arising out of the mediation.

(c) A mediator may not be compelled to provide evidence of a mediation communication referred to in subsection (a)(6) or (b)(2).

(d) If a mediation communication is not privileged under subsection (a) or (b), only the portion of the communication necessary for the application of the exception from nondisclosure may be admitted. Admission of evidence under subsection (a) or (b) does not render the evidence, or any other mediation communication, discoverable or admissible for any other purpose.

Legislative Note: If the enacting state does not have an open records act, the following language in paragraph (2) of subsection (a) needs to be deleted: "available to the public under [insert statutory reference to open records act] or".

SECTION 7. PROHIBITED MEDIATOR REPORTS.

(a) Except as required in subsection (b), a mediator may not make a report, assessment, evaluation, recommendation, finding, or other communication regarding a mediation to a court, administrative agency, or other authority that may make a ruling on the dispute that is the subject of the mediation.

(b) A mediator may disclose:

(1) whether the mediation occurred or has terminated, whether a settlement was reached, and attendance;

(2) a mediation communication as permitted under Section 6; or

(3) a mediation communication evidencing abuse, neglect, abandonment, or exploitation of an individual to a public agency responsible for protecting individuals against such mistreatment.

(c) A communication made in violation of subsection (a) may not be considered by a court, administrative agency, or arbitrator.

SECTION 8. CONFIDENTIALITY

Unless subject to the [insert statutory references to open meetings act and open records act], mediation communications are confidential to the extent agreed by the parties or provided by other law or rule of this State.

SECTION 9. MEDIATOR'S DISCLOSURE OF CONFLICTS OF INTEREST; BACKGROUND.

(a) Before accepting a mediation, an individual who is requested to serve as a mediator shall:

(1) make an inquiry that is reasonable under the circumstances to determine whether there are any known facts that a reasonable individual would consider likely to affect the impartiality of the mediator, including a financial or personal interest in the outcome of the mediation and an existing or past relationship with a mediation party or foreseeable participant in the mediation; and

(2) disclose any such known fact to the mediation parties as soon as is practical before accepting a mediation.

(b) If a mediator learns any fact described in subsection (a)(1) after accepting a mediation, the mediator shall disclose it as soon as is practicable.

(c) At the request of a mediation party, an individual who is requested to serve as a mediator shall disclose the mediator's qualifications to mediate a dispute.

(d) A person that violates subsection [(a) or (b)] [(a), (b), or (g)] is precluded by the violation from asserting a privilege under Section 4.

(e) Subsections (a), (b), [and] (c), [and] [(g)] do not apply to an individual acting as a judge.

(f) This [Act] does not require that a mediator have a special qualification by background or profession.

[(g) A mediator must be impartial, unless after disclosure of the facts required in subsections (a) and (b) to be disclosed, the parties agree otherwise.]

SECTION 10. PARTICIPATION IN MEDIATION

An attorney or other individual designated by a party may accompany the party to and participate in a mediation. A waiver of participation given before the mediation may be rescinded.

SECTION 11. INTERNATIONAL COMMERCIAL MEDIATION

(a) In this section, "Model Law" means the Model Law on International Commercial Conciliation adopted by the United Nations Commission on International Trade Law on 28 June 2002 and recommended by the United Nations General Assembly in a resolution (A/RES/57/18) dated 19 November 2002, and "international commercial mediation" means an international commercial conciliation as defined in Article 1 of the Model Law.

(b) Except as otherwise provided in subsections (c) and (d), if a mediation is an international commercial mediation, the mediation is governed by the Model Law.

(c) Unless the parties agree in accordance with Section 3(c) of this [Act] that all or part of an international commercial mediation is not privileged, Sections 4, 5, and 6 and any applicable definitions in Section 2 of this [Act] also apply to the mediation and nothing in Article 10 of the Model Law derogates from Sections 4, 5, and 6.

(d) If the parties to an international commercial mediation agree under Article 1, subsection (7), of the Model Law that the Model Law does not apply, this [Act] applies.

Legislative Note. The UNCITRAL Model Law on International Commercial Conciliation may be found at www.uncitral.org/en-index. htm. Important comments on interpretation are included in the Draft Guide to Enactment and Use of UNCITRAL Model Law on International Commercial Conciliation. The States should note the Draft Guide in a Legislative Note to the Act. This is especially important with respect to interpretation of Article 9 of the Model Law.

SECTION 12. RELATION TO ELECTRONIC SIGNATURES IN GLOBAL AND NATIONAL COMMERCE ACT

This [Act] modifies, limits, or supersedes the federal Electronic Signatures in Global and National Commerce Act, 15 U.S.C. Section 7001 et seq., but this [Act] does not modify, limit, or supersede Section 101(c) of that Act or authorize electronic delivery of any of the notices described in Section 103(b) of that Act.

SECTION 13. UNIFORMITY OF APPLICATION AND CONSTRUCTION

In applying and construing this [Act], consideration should be given to the need to promote uniformity of the law with respect to its subject matter among States that enact it.

SECTION 14. SEVERABILITY CLAUSE

If any provision of this [Act] or its application to any person or circumstance is held invalid, the invalidity does not affect other provisions or applications of this [Act] which can be given effect without the invalid provision or application, and to this end the provisions of this [Act] are severable.

SECTION 15. EFFECTIVE DATE

This [Act] takes effect . . . .

SECTION 16. REPEALS

The following acts and parts of acts are hereby repealed:

(1)

(2)

(3)

SECTION 17. APPLICATION TO EXISTING AGREEMENTS OR REFERRALS.

(a) This [Act] governs a mediation pursuant to a referral or an agreement to mediate made on or after [the effective date of this [Act]].

(b) On or after [a delayed date], this [Act] governs an agreement to mediate whenever made.

APPENDIX D

MODEL STANDARDS OF CONDUCT FOR MEDIATORS (2005)

■ ■ ■

AMERICAN ARBITRATION ASSOCIATION

(ADOPTED SEPTEMBER 8, 2005)

AMERICAN BAR ASSOCIATION

(APPROVED BY THE ABA HOUSE OF DELEGATES
AUGUST 9, 2005)

ASSOCIATION FOR CONFLICT RESOLUTION

(ADOPTED AUGUST 22, 2005)

SEPTEMBER 2005

The Model Standards of Conduct for Mediators was prepared in 1994 by the American Arbitration Association, the American Bar Association's Section of Dispute Resolution, and the Association for Conflict Resolution.[1] A joint committee consisting of representatives from the same successor organizations revised the Model Standards in 2005.[2] Both the original 1994 version and the 2005 revision have been approved by each participating organization.[3]

Preamble

Mediation is used to resolve a broad range of conflicts within a variety of settings. These Standards are designed to serve as fundamental ethical guidelines for persons mediating in all practice contexts. They serve three primary goals: to guide the conduct of mediators; to inform

---

[1] The Association for Conflict Resolution is a merged organization of the Academy of Family Mediators, the Conflict Resolution Education Network and the Society of Professionals in Dispute Resolution (SPIDR). SPIDR was the third participating organization in the development of the 1994 Standards.

[2] Reporter's Notes, which are not part of these Standards and therefore have not been specifically approved by any of the organizations, provide commentary regarding these revisions.

[3] The 2005 version to the Model Standards were approved by the American Bar Association's House of Delegates on August 9, 2005, the Board of the Association of Conflict Resolution on August 22, 2005 and the Executive Committee of the American Arbitration Association on September 8, 2005.

the mediating parties; and to promote public confidence in mediation as a process for resolving disputes.

Mediation is a process in which an impartial third party facilitates communication and negotiation and promotes voluntary decision making by the parties to the dispute.

Mediation serves various purposes, including providing the opportunity for parties to define and clarify issues, understand different perspectives, identify interests, explore and assess possible solutions, and reach mutually satisfactory agreements, when desired.

Note on Construction

These Standards are to be read and construed in their entirety. There is no priority significance attached to the sequence in which the Standards appear.

The use of the term "shall" in a Standard indicates that the mediator must follow the practice described. The use of the term "should" indicates that the practice described in the standard is highly desirable, but not required, and is to be departed from only for very strong reasons and requires careful use of judgment and discretion.

The use of the term "mediator" is understood to be inclusive so that it applies to co-mediator models.

These Standards do not include specific temporal parameters when referencing a mediation, and therefore, do not define the exact beginning or ending of a mediation.

Various aspects of a mediation, including some matters covered by these Standards, may also be affected by applicable law, court rules, regulations, other applicable professional rules, mediation rules to which the parties have agreed and other agreements of the parties. These sources may create conflicts with, and may take precedence over, these Standards. However, a mediator should make every effort to comply with the spirit and intent of these Standards in resolving such conflicts. This effort should include honoring all remaining Standards not in conflict with these other sources.

These Standards, unless and until adopted by a court or other regulatory authority do not have the force of law. Nonetheless, the fact that these Standards have been adopted by the respective sponsoring entities, should alert mediators to the fact that the Standards might be viewed as establishing a standard of care for mediators.

STANDARD I.   SELF–DETERMINATION

A.   A mediator shall conduct a mediation based on the principle of party self-determination. Self-determination is the act of coming to a voluntary, uncoerced decision in which each party makes free and informed choices as to process and outcome. Parties may exercise self-determination at any stage of a mediation, including mediator selection, process design, participation in or withdrawal from the process, and outcomes.

    1.   Although party self-determination for process design is a fundamental principle of mediation practice, a mediator may need to balance such party self-determination with a mediator's duty to conduct a quality process in accordance with these Standards.

    2.   A mediator cannot personally ensure that each party has made free and informed choices to reach particular decisions, but, where appropriate, a mediator should make the parties aware of the importance of consulting other professionals to help them make informed choices.

B.   A mediator shall not undermine party self-determination by any party for reasons such as higher settlement rates, egos, increased fees, or outside pressures from court personnel, program administrators, provider organizations, the media or others.

STANDARD II. IMPARTIALITY

A.   A mediator shall decline a mediation if the mediator cannot conduct it in an impartial manner. Impartiality means freedom from favoritism, bias or prejudice.

B.   A mediator shall conduct a mediation in an impartial manner and avoid conduct that gives the appearance of partiality.

    1.   A mediator should not act with partiality or prejudice based on any participant's personal characteristics, background, values and beliefs, or performance at a mediation, or any other reason.

    2.   A mediator should neither give nor accept a gift, favor, loan or other item of value that raises a question as to the mediator's actual or perceived impartiality.

    3.   A mediator may accept or give de minimis gifts or incidental items or services that are provided to facilitate a mediation or respect cultural norms so long as such practices do not raise questions as to a mediator's actual or perceived impartiality.

C.   If at any time a mediator is unable to conduct a mediation in an impartial manner, the mediator shall withdraw.

STANDARD III. CONFLICTS OF INTEREST

A.   A mediator shall avoid a conflict of interest or the appearance of a conflict of interest during and after a mediation. A conflict of interest can arise from involvement by a mediator with the subject matter of the dispute or from any relationship between a mediator and any mediation participant, whether past or present, personal or professional, that reasonably raises a question of a mediator's impartiality.

B.   A mediator shall make a reasonable inquiry to determine whether there are any facts that a reasonable individual would consider likely to create a potential or actual conflict of interest for a mediator. A mediator's actions necessary to accomplish a reasonable inquiry into potential conflicts of interest may vary based on practice context.

C.   A mediator shall disclose, as soon as practicable, all actual and potential conflicts of interest that are reasonably known to the mediator and could reasonably be seen as raising a question about the mediator's impartiality. After disclosure, if all parties agree, the mediator may proceed with the mediation.

D.   If a mediator learns any fact after accepting a mediation that raises a question with respect to that mediator's service creating a potential or actual conflict of interest, the mediator shall disclose it as quickly as practicable. After disclosure, if all parties agree, the mediator may proceed with the mediation.

E.   If a mediator's conflict of interest might reasonably be viewed as undermining the integrity of the mediation, a mediator shall withdraw from or decline to proceed with the mediation regardless of the expressed desire or agreement of the parties to the contrary.

F.   Subsequent to a mediation, a mediator shall not establish another relationship with any of the participants in any matter that would raise questions about the integrity of the mediation. When a mediator develops personal or professional relationships with parties, other individuals or organizations following a mediation in which they were involved, the mediator should consider factors such as time elapsed following the mediation, the nature of the relationships established, and services offered when determining whether the relationships might create a perceived or actual conflict of interest.

STANDARD IV. COMPETENCE

A.   A mediator shall mediate only when the mediator has the necessary competence to satisfy the reasonable expectations of the parties.

    1.   Any person may be selected as a mediator, provided that the parties are satisfied with the mediator's competence and qualifications. Training, experience in mediation, skills, cultural understandings and other qualities are often necessary for mediator competence. A person who offers to serve as a mediator creates the expectation that the person is competent to mediate effectively.

2. A mediator should attend educational programs and related activities to maintain and enhance the mediator's knowledge and skills related to mediation.

3. A mediator should have available for the parties' information relevant to the mediator's training, education, experience and approach to conducting a mediation.

B. If a mediator, during the course of a mediation determines that the mediator cannot conduct the mediation competently, the mediator shall discuss that determination with the parties as soon as is practicable and take appropriate steps to address the situation, including, but not limited to, withdrawing or requesting appropriate assistance.

C. If a mediator's ability to conduct a mediation is impaired by drugs, alcohol, medication or otherwise, the mediator shall not conduct the mediation.

STANDARD V. CONFIDENTIALITY

A. A mediator shall maintain the confidentiality of all information obtained by the mediator in mediation, unless otherwise agreed to by the parties or required by applicable law.

1. If the parties to a mediation agree that the mediator may disclose information obtained during the mediation, the mediator may do so.

2. A mediator should not communicate to any non-participant information about how the parties acted in the mediation. A mediator may report, if required, whether parties appeared at a scheduled mediation and whether or not the parties reached a resolution.

3. If a mediator participates in teaching, research or evaluation of mediation, the mediator should protect the anonymity of the parties and abide by their reasonable expectations regarding confidentiality.

B. A mediator who meets with any persons in private session during a mediation shall not convey directly or indirectly to any other person, any information that was obtained during that private session without the consent of the disclosing person.

C. A mediator shall promote understanding among the parties of the extent to which the parties will maintain confidentiality of information they obtain in a mediation.

D. Depending on the circumstance of a mediation, the parties may have varying expectations regarding confidentiality that a mediator should address. The parties may make their own rules with respect to confidentiality, or the accepted practice of an individual mediator or institution may dictate a particular set of expectations.

STANDARD VI. QUALITY OF THE PROCESS

A.   A mediator shall conduct a mediation in accordance with these Standards and in a manner that promotes diligence, timeliness, safety, presence of the appropriate participants, party participation, procedural fairness, party competency and mutual respect among all participants.

1.   A mediator should agree to mediate only when the mediator is prepared to commit the attention essential to an effective mediation.

2.   A mediator should only accept cases when the mediator can satisfy the reasonable expectation of the parties concerning the timing of a mediation.

3.   The presence or absence of persons at a mediation depends on the agreement of the parties and the mediator. The parties and mediator may agree that others may be excluded from particular sessions or from all sessions.

4.   A mediator should promote honesty and candor between and among all participants, and a mediator shall not knowingly misrepresent any material fact or circumstance in the course of a mediation.

5.   The role of a mediator differs substantially from other professional roles. Mixing the role of a mediator and the role of another profession is problematic and thus, a mediator should distinguish between the roles. A mediator may provide information that the mediator is qualified by training or experience to provide, only if the mediator can do so consistent with these Standards.

6.   A mediator shall not conduct a dispute resolution procedure other than mediation but label it mediation in an effort to gain the protection of rules, statutes, or other governing authorities pertaining to mediation.

7.   A mediator may recommend, when appropriate, that parties consider resolving their dispute through arbitration, counseling, neutral evaluation or other processes.

8.   A mediator shall not undertake an additional dispute resolution role in the same matter without the consent of the parties. Before providing such service, a mediator shall inform the parties of the implications of the change in process and obtain their consent to the change. A mediator who undertakes such role assumes different duties and responsibilities that may be governed by other standards.

9.   If a mediation is being used to further criminal conduct, a mediator should take appropriate steps including, if necessary, postponing, withdrawing from or terminating the mediation.

10. If a party appears to have difficulty comprehending the process, issues, or settlement options, or difficulty participating in a mediation, the mediator should explore the circumstances and potential accommodations, modifications or adjustments that would make possible the party's capacity to comprehend, participate and exercise self-determination.

B. If a mediator is made aware of domestic abuse or violence among the parties, the mediator shall take appropriate steps including, if necessary, postponing, withdrawing from or terminating the mediation.

C. If a mediator believes that participant conduct, including that of the mediator, jeopardizes conducting a mediation consistent with these Standards, a mediator shall take appropriate steps including, if necessary, postponing, withdrawing from or terminating the mediation.

STANDARD VII. ADVERTISING AND SOLICITATION

A. A mediator shall be truthful and not misleading when advertising, soliciting or otherwise communicating the mediator's qualifications, experience, services and fees.

1. A mediator should not include any promises as to outcome in communications, including business cards, stationery, or computer-based communications.

2. A mediator should only claim to meet the mediator qualifications of a governmental entity or private organization if that entity or organization has a recognized procedure for qualifying mediators and it grants such status to the mediator.

B. A mediator shall not solicit in a manner that gives an appearance of partiality for or against a party or otherwise undermines the integrity of the process.

C. A mediator shall not communicate to others, in promotional materials or through other forms of communication, the names of persons served without their permission.

STANDARD VIII. FEES AND OTHER CHARGES

A. A mediator shall provide each party or each party's representative true and complete information about mediation fees, expenses and any other actual or potential charges that may be incurred in connection with a mediation.

1. If a mediator charges fees, the mediator should develop them in light of all relevant factors, including the type and complexity of the matter, the qualifications of the mediator, the time required and the rates customary for such mediation services.

2.   A mediator's fee arrangement should be in writing unless the parties request otherwise.

B.   A mediator shall not charge fees in a manner that impairs a mediator's impartiality.

1.   A mediator should not enter into a fee agreement which is contingent upon the result of the mediation or amount of the settlement.

2.   While a mediator may accept unequal fee payments from the parties, a mediator should not allow such a fee arrangement to adversely impact the mediator's ability to conduct a mediation in an impartial manner.

STANDARD IX. ADVANCEMENT OF MEDIATION PRACTICE

A.   A mediator should act in a manner that advances the practice of mediation. A mediator promotes this Standard by engaging in some or all of the following:

1.   Fostering diversity within the field of mediation.

2.   Striving to make mediation accessible to those who elect to use it, including providing services at a reduced rate or on a pro bono basis as appropriate.

3.   Participating in research when given the opportunity, including obtaining participant feedback when appropriate.

4.   Participating in outreach and education efforts to assist the public in developing an improved understanding of, and appreciation for, mediation.

5.   Assisting newer mediators through training, mentoring and networking.

B.   A mediator should demonstrate respect for differing points of view within the field, seek to learn from other mediators and work together with other mediators to improve the profession and better serve people in conflict.

APPENDIX E

FEDERAL ARBITRATION ACT (1925)

■ ■ ■

9 U.S.C. § 1 et seq. (1994).

CHAPTER 1—GENERAL PROVISIONS

§ 1. "Maritime Transactions" and "Commerce" Defined; Exceptions to Operation of Title

"Maritime transactions", as herein defined, means charter parties, bills of lading of water carriers, agreements relating to wharfage, supplies furnished vessels or repairs to vessels, collisions, or any other matters in foreign commerce which, if the subject of controversy, would be embraced within admiralty jurisdiction; "commerce", as herein defined, means commerce among the several States or with foreign nations, or in any Territory of the United States or in the District of Columbia, or between any such Territory and another, or between any such Territory and any State or foreign nation, or between the District of Columbia and any State or Territory or foreign nation, but nothing herein contained shall apply to contracts of employment of seamen, railroad employees, or any other class of workers engaged in foreign or interstate commerce.

§ 2. Validity, Irrevocability and Enforcement of Agreements to Arbitrate

A written provision in any maritime transaction or a contract evidencing a transaction involving commerce to settle by arbitration a controversy thereafter arising out of such contract or transaction, or the refusal to perform the whole or any part thereof, or an agreement in writing to submit to arbitration an existing controversy arising out of such a contract, transaction, or refusal, shall be valid, irrevocable, and enforceable, save upon such grounds as exist at law or in equity for the revocation of any contract.

§ 3. Stay of Proceedings Where Issue Therein Referable to Arbitration

If any suit or proceeding be brought in any of the courts of the United States upon any issue referable to arbitration under an agreement in writing for such arbitration, the court in which such suit is pending, upon being satisfied that the issue involved in such suit or proceeding is referable to arbitration under such an agreement, shall on application of one of the parties stay the trial of the action until such arbitration has been had in accordance with the terms of the agreement, providing the applicant for the stay is not in default in proceeding with such arbitration.

§ 4. Failure to Arbitrate Under Agreement; Petition to United States Court Having Jurisdiction for Order to Compel Arbitration; Notice and Service Thereof; Hearing and Determination

A party aggrieved by the alleged failure, neglect, or refusal of another to arbitrate under a written agreement for arbitration may petition any United States district court which, save for such agreement, would have jurisdiction under Title 28, in a civil action or in admiralty of the subject matter of a suit arising out of the controversy between the parties, for an order directing that such arbitration proceed in the manner provided for in such agreement. Five days' notice in writing of such application shall be served upon the party in default. Service thereof shall be made in the manner provided by the Federal Rules of Civil Procedure. The court shall hear the parties, and upon being satisfied that the making of the agreement for arbitration or the failure to comply therewith is not in issue, the court shall make an order directing the parties to proceed to arbitration in accordance with the terms of the agreement. The hearing and proceedings, under such agreement, shall be within the district in which the petition for an order directing such arbitration is filed. If the making of the arbitration agreement or the failure, neglect, or refusal to perform the same be in issue, the court shall proceed summarily to the trial thereof. If no jury trial be demanded by the party alleged to be in default, or if the matter in dispute is within admiralty jurisdiction, the court shall hear and determine such issue. Where such an issue is raised, the party alleged to be in default may, except in cases of admiralty, on or before the return day of the notice of application, demand a jury trial of such issue, and upon such demand the court shall make an order referring the issue or issues to a jury in the manner provided by the Federal Rules of Civil Procedure, or may specially call a jury for that purpose. If the jury find that no agreement in writing for arbitration was made or that there is no default in proceeding thereunder, the proceeding shall be dismissed. If the jury find that an agreement for arbitration was made in writing and that there is a default in proceeding thereunder, the court shall make an order summarily directing the parties to proceed with the arbitration in accordance with the terms thereof.

§ 5. Appointment of Arbitrators or Umpire

If in the agreement provision be made for a method of naming or appointing an arbitrator or arbitrators or an umpire, such method shall be followed; but if no method be provided therein, or if a method be provided and any party thereto shall fail to avail himself of such method, or if for any other reason there shall be a lapse in the naming of an arbitrator or arbitrators or umpire, or in filling a vacancy, then upon the application of either party to the controversy the court shall designate and appoint an arbitrator or arbitrators or umpire, as the case may require, who shall act under the said agreement with the same force and effect as if he or they had been specifically named therein; and unless otherwise provided in the agreement the arbitration shall be by a single arbitrator.

§ 6. Application Heard as Motion

Any application to the court hereunder shall be made and heard in the manner provided by law for the making and hearing of motions, except as otherwise herein expressly provided.

§ 7. Witnesses Before Arbitrators; Fees; Compelling Attendance

The arbitrators selected either as prescribed in this title or otherwise, or a majority of them, may summon in writing any person to attend before them or any of them as a witness and in a proper case to bring with him or them any book, record, document, or paper which may be deemed material as evidence in the case. The fees for such attendance shall be the same as the fees of witnesses before masters of the United States courts. Said summons shall issue in the name of the arbitrator or arbitrators, or a majority of them, and shall be signed by the arbitrators, or a majority of them, and shall be directed to the said person and shall be served in the same manner as subpoenas to appear and testify before the court; if any person or persons so summoned to testify shall refuse or neglect to obey said summons, upon petition the United States district court for the district in which such arbitrators, or a majority of them, are sitting may compel the attendance of such person or persons before said arbitrator or arbitrators, or punish said person or persons for contempt in the same manner provided by law for securing the attendance of witnesses or their punishment for neglect or refusal to attend in the courts of the United States.

§ 8. Proceedings Begun by Libel in Admiralty and Seizure of Vessel or Property

If the basis of jurisdiction be a cause of action otherwise justiciable in admiralty, then, notwithstanding anything herein to the contrary, the party claiming to be aggrieved may begin his proceeding hereunder by libel and seizure of the vessel or other property of the other party according to the usual course of admiralty proceedings, and the court shall then have jurisdiction to direct the parties to proceed with the arbitration and shall retain jurisdiction to enter its decree upon the award.

§ 9. Award of Arbitrators; Confirmation; Jurisdiction; Procedure

If the parties in their agreement have agreed that a judgment of the court shall be entered upon the award made pursuant to the arbitration, and shall specify the court, then at any time within one year after the award is made any party to the arbitration may apply to the court so specified for an order confirming the award, and thereupon the court must grant such an order unless the award is vacated, modified, or corrected as prescribed in sections 10 and 11 of this title. If no court is specified in the agreement of the parties, then such application may be made to the United States court in and for the district within which such award was made. Notice of the application shall be served upon the adverse party, and thereupon the court shall have jurisdiction of such party as though he had appeared generally in the proceeding. If the adverse party is a resident of the district within which the award was made, such service shall be made upon the adverse party or his attorney as prescribed by law for service of notice of motion in an action in the same court. If the adverse party shall be a nonresident, then the notice of the application shall be served by the marshal of any district within which the adverse party may be found in like manner as other process of the court.

§ 10. Same; Vacation; Grounds; Rehearing

(a) In any of the following cases the United States court in and for the district wherein the award was made may make an order vacating the award upon the application of any party to the arbitration—

(1) Where the award was procured by corruption, fraud, or undue means.

(2) Where there was evident partiality or corruption in the arbitrators, or either of them.

(3) Where the arbitrators were guilty of misconduct in refusing to postpone the hearing, upon sufficient cause shown, or in refusing to hear evidence pertinent and material to the controversy; or of any other misbehavior by which the rights of any party have been prejudiced.

(4) Where the arbitrators exceeded their powers, or so imperfectly executed them that a mutual, final, and definite award upon the subject matter submitted was not made.

(5) Where an award is vacated and the time within which the agreement required the award to be made has not expired the court may, in its discretion, direct a rehearing by the arbitrators.

(b) The United States district court for the district wherein an award was made that was issued pursuant to section 580 of title 5 may make an order vacating the award upon the application of a person, other than a party to the arbitration, who is adversely affected or aggrieved by the award, if the use of arbitration or the award is clearly inconsistent with the factors set forth in section 572 of title 5.

§ 11. Same; Modification or Correction; Grounds; Order

In either of the following cases the United States court in and for the district wherein the award was made may make an order modifying or correcting the award upon the application of any party to the arbitration—

(a) Where there was an evident material miscalculation of figures or an evident material mistake in the description of any person, thing, or property referred to in the award.

(b) Where the arbitrators have awarded upon a matter not submitted to them, unless it is a matter not affecting the merits of the decision upon the matter submitted.

(c) Where the award is imperfect in matter of form not affecting the merits of the controversy.

The order may modify and correct the award, so as to effect the intent thereof and promote justice between the parties.

§ 12. Notice of Motions to Vacate or Modify; Service; Stay of Proceedings

Notice of a motion to vacate, modify, or correct an award must be served upon the adverse party or his attorney within three months after the award is filed or delivered. If the adverse party is a resident of the district within which the award was made, such service shall be made upon the adverse party or his attorney as prescribed by law for service of notice of motion in an action in the same court. If the adverse party shall be a nonresident then the notice of the application shall be served by the marshal of any district within which the adverse party may be found in like manner as other process of the court. For the purposes of the motion any judge who might make an order to stay the proceedings in an action brought in the same court may make an order, to be served with the notice of motion, staying the proceedings of the adverse party to enforce the award.

§ 13. Papers Filed With Order on Motions; Judgment; Docketing; Force and Effect; Enforcement

The party moving for an order confirming, modifying, or correcting an award shall, at the time such order is filed with the clerk for the entry of judgment thereon, also file the following papers with the clerk:

(a) The agreement; the selection or appointment, if any, of an additional arbitrator or umpire; and each written extension of the time, if any, within which to make the award.

(b) The award.

(c) Each notice, affidavit, or other paper used upon an application to confirm, modify, or correct the award, and a copy of each order of the court upon such an application.

The judgment shall be docketed as if it was rendered in an action.

The judgment so entered shall have the same force and effect, in all respects, as, and be subject to all the provisions of law relating to, a judgment in an action; and it may be enforced as if it had been rendered in an action in the court in which it is entered.

§ 14. Contracts Not Affected

This title shall not apply to contracts made prior to January 1, 1926.

§ 15. Inapplicability of the Act of State Doctrine

Enforcement of arbitral agreements, confirmation of arbitral awards, and execution upon judgments based on orders confirming such awards shall not be refused on the basis of the Act of State doctrine.

§ 16. Appeals

(a) An appeal may be taken from—

(1) an order—

(A) refusing a stay of any action under section 3 of this title,

(B) denying a petition under section 4 of this title to order arbitration to proceed,

(C) denying an application under section 206 of this title to compel arbitration,

(D) confirming or denying confirmation of an award or partial award, or

(E) modifying, correcting, or vacating an award;

(2) an interlocutory order granting, continuing, or modifying an injunction against an arbitration that is subject to this title; or

(3) a final decision with respect to an arbitration that is subject to this title.

(b) Except as otherwise provided in section 1292(b) of title 28, an appeal may not be taken from an interlocutory order—

(1) granting a stay of any action under section 3 of this title;

(2) directing arbitration to proceed under section 4 of this title;

(3) compelling arbitration under section 206 of this title; or

(4) refusing to enjoin an arbitration that is subject to this title.

CHAPTER 2—CONVENTION ON THE RECOGNITION AND ENFORCEMENT OF FOREIGN ARBITRAL AWARDS [omitted]

CHAPTER 3—INTER–AMERICAN CONVENTION ON INTERNATIONAL COMMERCIAL ARBITRATION [omitted]

APPENDIX F

UNIFORM ARBITRATION ACT (1956)

■ ■ ■

7 U.L.A. 1 (1997).

§ 1. Validity of Arbitration Agreement.

A written agreement to submit any existing controversy to arbitration or a provision in a written contract to submit to arbitration any controversy thereafter arising between the parties is valid, enforceable and irrevocable, save upon such grounds as exist at law or in equity for the revocation of any contract. This act also applies to arbitration agreements between employers and employees or between their respective representatives [unless otherwise provided in the agreement].

§ 2. Proceedings to Compel or Stay Arbitration.

(a) On application of a party showing an agreement described in Section 1, and the opposing party's refusal to arbitrate, the Court shall order the parties to proceed with arbitration, but if the opposing party denies the existence of the agreement to arbitrate, the Court shall proceed summarily to the determination of the issue so raised and shall order arbitration if found for the moving party, otherwise, the application shall be denied.

(b) On application, the court may stay an arbitration proceeding commenced or threatened on a showing that there is no agreement to arbitrate. Such an issue, when in substantial and bona fide dispute, shall be forthwith and summarily tried and the stay ordered if found for the moving party. If found for the opposing party, the court shall order the parties to proceed to arbitration.

(c) If an issue referable to arbitration under the alleged agreement is involved in an action or proceeding pending in a court having jurisdiction to hear applications under subdivision (a) of this Section, the application shall be made therein. Otherwise and subject to Section 18, the application may be made in any court of competent jurisdiction.

(d) Any action or proceeding involving an issue subject to arbitration shall be stayed if an order for arbitration or an application therefor has been made under this section or, if the issue is severable, the stay may be with respect thereto only. When the application is made in such action or proceeding, the order for arbitration shall include such stay.

(e) An order for arbitration shall not be refused on the ground that the claim in issue lacks merit or bona fides or because any fault or grounds for the claim sought to be arbitrated have not been shown. Unif.Arbitration Act § 2

§ 3. Appointment of Arbitrators by Court.

If the arbitration agreement provides a method of appointment of arbitrators, this method shall be followed. In the absence thereof, or if the agreed method fails or for any reason cannot be followed, or when an arbitrator appointed fails or is unable to act and his successor has not been duly appointed, the court on application of a party shall appoint one or more arbitrators. An arbitrator so appointed has all the powers of one specifically named in the agreement.

§ 4. Majority Action by Arbitrators.

The powers of the arbitrators may be exercised by a majority unless otherwise provided by the agreement or by this act.

§ 5. Hearing.

Unless otherwise provided by the agreement:

(a) The arbitrators shall appoint a time and place for the hearing and cause notification to the parties to be served personally or by registered mail not less than five days before the hearing. Appearance at the hearing waives such notice. The arbitrators may adjourn the hearing from time to time as necessary and, on request of a party and for good cause, or upon their own motion may postpone the hearing to a time not later than the date fixed by the agreement for making the award unless the parties consent to a later date. The arbitrators may hear and determine the controversy upon the evidence produced notwithstanding the failure of a party duly notified to appear. The court on application may direct the arbitrators to proceed promptly with the hearing and determination of the controversy.

(b) The parties are entitled to be heard, to present evidence material to the controversy and to cross-examine witnesses appearing at the hearing.

(c) The hearing shall be conducted by all the arbitrators but a majority may determine any question and render a final award. If, during the course of the hearing, an arbitrator for any reason ceases to act, the remaining arbitrator or arbitrators appointed to act as neutrals may continue with the hearing and determination of the controversy.

§ 6. Representation by Attorney.

A party has the right to be represented by an attorney at any proceeding or hearing under this act. A waiver thereof prior to the proceeding or hearing is ineffective.

§ 7. Witnesses, Subpoenas, Depositions.

(a) The arbitrators may issue (cause to be issued) subpoenas for the attendance of witnesses and for the production of books, records, documents and other evidence, and shall have the power to administer oaths. Subpoenas so issued shall be served, and upon application to the Court by a party or the arbitrators, enforced, in the manner provided by law for the service and enforcement of subpoenas in a civil action.

(b) On application of a party and for use as evidence, the arbitrators may permit a deposition to be taken, in the manner and upon the terms designated by the arbitrators, of a witness who cannot be subpoenaed or is unable to attend the hearing.

(c) All provisions of law compelling a person under subpoena to testify are applicable.

(d) Fees for attendance as a witness shall be the same as for a witness in the . . . Court.

§ 8. Award.

(a) The award shall be in writing and signed by the arbitrators joining in the award. The arbitrators shall deliver a copy to each party personally or by registered mail, or as provided in the agreement.

(b) An award shall be made within the time fixed therefor by the agreement or, if not so fixed, within such time as the court orders on application of a party. The parties may extend the time in writing either before or after the expiration thereof. A party waives the objection that an award was not made within the time required unless he notifies the arbitrators of his objection prior to the delivery of the award to him.

§ 9. Change of Award by Arbitrators.

On application of a party or, if an application to the court is pending under Sections 11, 12 or 13, on submission to the arbitrators by the court under such conditions as the court may order, the arbitrators may modify or correct the award upon the grounds stated in paragraphs (1) and (3) of subdivision (a) of Section 13, or for the purpose of clarifying the award. The application shall be made within twenty days after delivery of the award to the applicant. Written notice thereof shall be made within twenty days after delivery of the award to the appellant. Written notice thereof shall be given forthwith to the opposing party, stating he must serve his objections thereto, if any, within ten days from the notice. The award so modified or corrected is subject to the provisions of Sections 11, 12 and 13.

§ 10. Fees and Expenses of Arbitration.

Unless otherwise provided in the agreement to arbitrate, the arbitrators' expenses and fees, together with other expenses, not including counsel fees, incurred in the conduct of the arbitration, shall be paid as provided in the award.

§ 11. Confirmation of an Award.

Upon application of a party, the Court shall confirm an award, unless within the time limits hereinafter imposed grounds are urged for vacating or modifying or correcting the award, in which case the court shall proceed as provided in Sections 12 and 13.

§ 12. Vacating an Award.

(a) Upon application of a party, the court shall vacate an award where:

(1) The award was procured by corruption, fraud or other undue means;

(2) There was evident partiality by an arbitrator appointed as a neutral or corruption in any of the arbitrators or misconduct prejudicing the rights of any party;

(3) The arbitrators exceeded their powers;

(4) The arbitrators refused to postpone the hearing upon sufficient cause being shown therefor or refused to hear evidence material to the controversy or otherwise so conducted the hearing, contrary to the provisions of Section 5, as to prejudice substantially the rights of a party; or

(5) There was no arbitration agreement and the issue was not adversely determined in proceedings under Section 2 and the party did not participate in the arbitration hearing without raising the objection; but the fact that the relief was such that it could not or would not be granted by a court of law or equity is not ground for vacating or refusing to confirm the award.

(b) An application under this Section shall be made within ninety days after delivery of a copy of the award to the applicant, except that, if predicated upon corruption, fraud or other undue means, it shall be made within ninety days after such grounds are known or should have been known.

(c) In vacating the award on grounds other than stated in clause (5) of Subsection (a) the court may order a rehearing before new arbitrators chosen as provided in the agreement, or in the absence thereof, by the court in accordance with Section 3, or if the award is vacated on grounds set forth in clauses (3) and (4) of Subsection (a) the court may order a rehearing before the arbitrators who made the award or their successors appointed in accordance with Section 3. The time within which the agreement requires the award to be made is applicable to the rehearing and commences from the date of the order.

(d) If the application to vacate is denied and no motion to modify or correct the award is pending, the court shall confirm the award. As amended Aug. 1956.

§ 13. Modification or Correction of Award.

(a) Upon application made within ninety days after delivery of a copy of the award to the applicant, the court shall modify or correct the award where:

(1) There was an evident miscalculation of figures or an evident mistake in the description of any person, thing or property referred to in the award;

(2) The arbitrators have awarded upon a matter not submitted to them and the award may be corrected without affecting the merits of the decision upon the issues submitted; or

(3) The award is imperfect in a matter of form, not affecting the merits of the controversy.

(b) If the application is granted, the court shall modify and correct the award so as to effect its intent and shall confirm the award as so modified and corrected. Otherwise, the court shall confirm the award as made.

(c) An application to modify or correct an award may be joined in the alternative with an application to vacate the award.

§ 14. Judgment or Decree on Award.

Upon the granting of an order confirming, modifying or correcting an award, judgment or decree shall be entered in conformity therewith and be enforced as any other judgment or decree. Costs of the application and of the proceedings subsequent thereto, and disbursements may be awarded by the court.

§ 15. Judgment Roll, Docketing.

(a) On entry of judgment or decree, the clerk shall prepare the judgment roll consisting, to the extent filed, of the following:

(1) The agreement and each written extension of the time within which to make the award;

(2) The award;

(3) A copy of the order confirming, modifying or correcting the award; and

(4) A copy of the judgment or decree.

(b) The judgment or decree may be docketed as if rendered in an action.

§ 16. Applications to Court.

Except as otherwise provided, an application to the court under this act shall be by motion and shall be heard in the manner and upon the notice provided by law or rule of court for the making and hearing of motions. Unless the parties have agreed otherwise, notice of an initial application for an order shall be served in the manner provided by law for the service of a summons in an action.

§ 17. Court, Jurisdiction.

The term "court" means any court of competent jurisdiction of this State. The making of an agreement described in Section 1 providing for arbitration in this State confers jurisdiction on the court to enforce the agreement under this Act and to enter judgment on an award thereunder.

§ 18. Venue.

An initial application shall be made to the court of the [county] in which the agreement provides the arbitration hearing shall be held or, if the hearing has been held, in the county in which it was held. Otherwise the application shall be made in the [county] where the adverse party resides or has a place of business or, if he has no residence or place of business in this State, to the court of any [county]. All subsequent applications shall be made to the court hearing the initial application unless the court otherwise directs.

§ 19. Appeals.

(a) An appeal may be taken from:

(1) An order denying an application to compel arbitration made under Section 2;

(2) An order granting an application to stay arbitration made under Section 2(b);

(3) An order confirming or denying confirmation of an award;

(4) An order modifying or correcting an award;

(5) An order vacating an award without directing a rehearing; or

(6) A judgment or decree entered pursuant to the provisions of this act.

(b) The appeal shall be taken in the manner and to the same extent as from orders or judgments in a civil action.

§ 20. Act Not Retroactive.

This act applies only to agreements made subsequent to the taking effect of this act.

§ 21. Uniformity of Interpretation.

This act shall be so construed as to effectuate its general purpose to make uniform the law of those states which enact it.

§ 22. Constitutionality.

If any provision of this act or the application thereof to any person or circumstance is held invalid, the invalidity shall not affect other provisions or applications of the act which can be given effect without the invalid provision or application, and to this end the provisions of this act are severable.

§ 23. Short Title.

This act may be cited as the Uniform Arbitration Act.

§ 24. Repeal.

All acts or parts of acts which are inconsistent with the provisions of this act are hereby repealed.

§ 25. Time of Taking Effect.

This act shall take effect. . . .

APPENDIX G

AMERICAN ARBITRATION ASSOCIATION COMMERCIAL ARBITRATION RULES AND MEDIATION PROCEDURES (INCLUDING PROCEDURES FOR LARGE, COMPLEX COMMERCIAL DISPUTES) (2013)

■ ■ ■
* * *

Standard Arbitration Clause

The parties can provide for arbitration of future disputes by inserting the following clause into their contracts:

> *Any controversy or claim arising out of or relating to this contract, or the breach thereof, shall be settled by arbitration administered by the American Arbitration Association under its Commercial Arbitration Rules, and judgment on the award rendered by the arbitrator(s) may be entered in any court having jurisdiction thereof.*

Arbitration of existing disputes may be accomplished by use of the following:

> *We, the undersigned parties, hereby agree to submit to arbitration administered by the American Arbitration Association under its Commercial Arbitration Rules the following Controversy: (describe briefly). We further agree that the above controversy be submitted to (one) (three) arbitrator(s). We further agree that we will faithfully observe this agreement and the rules, that we will abide by and perform any award rendered by the arbitrator(s), and that a judgment of any court having jurisdiction may be entered on the award.*

The services of the AAA are generally concluded with the transmittal of the award. Although there is voluntary compliance with the majority of awards, judgment on the award can be entered in a court having appropriate jurisdiction if necessary.

Administrative Fees

The AAA charges a filing fee based on the amount of the claim or counterclaim. This fee information, which is included with these rules, allows the parties to exercise control over their administrative fees.

The fees cover AAA administrative services; they do not cover arbitrator compensation or expenses, if any, reporting services, or any post-award charges incurred by the parties in enforcing the award.

* * *

COMMERCIAL ARBITRATION RULES

R–1. Agreement of Parties*+

(a) The parties shall be deemed to have made these rules a part of their arbitration agreement whenever they have provided for arbitration by the American Arbitration Association (hereinafter AAA) under its Commercial Arbitration Rules or for arbitration by the AAA of a domestic commercial dispute without specifying particular rules. These rules and any amendment of them shall apply in the form in effect at the time the administrative requirements are met for a Demand for Arbitration or Submission Agreement received by the AAA. The parties, by written agreement, may vary the procedures set forth in these rules. After appointment of the arbitrator, such modifications may be made only with the consent of the arbitrator.

(b) Unless the parties or the AAA determines otherwise, the Expedited Procedures shall apply in any case in which no disclosed claim or counterclaim exceeds $75,000, exclusive of interest, atorneys' fees, and arbitration fees and costs.

Parties may also agree to use these procedures in larger cases. Unless the parties agree otherwise, these procedures will not apply in cases involving more than two parties. The Expedited Procedures shall be applied as described in Sections E–1 through E–10 of these rules, in addition to any other portion of these rules that is not in conflict with the Expedited Procedures.

(c) Unless the parties agree otherwise, the Procedures for Large, Complex Commercial Disputes shall apply to all cases in which the disclosed claim or counterclaim of any party is at least $500,000, or more, exclusive of claimed interest, attorney's fees, arbitration fees and costs. Parties may

---

    * *The AAA applies the Supplementary Procedures for Consumer-Related Disputes to arbitration clauses in agreements between individual consumers and businesses where the business has a standardized, systematic application of arbitration clauses with customers and where the terms and conditions of the purchase of standardized, consumable goods or services are non-negotiable or primarily non-negotiable in most or all of its terms, conditions, features, or choices. The product or service must be for personal or household use. The AAA will have the discretion to apply or not to apply the supplementary procedures and the parties will be able to bring any disputes concerning the application or non-application to the attention of the arbitrator. Consumers are not prohibited from seeking relief in a small claims court for disputes or claims within the scope of its jurisdiction, even in consumer arbitration cases filed by the business.*

    + *A dispute arising out of an employer promulgated plan will be administered under the AAA's Employment Arbitration Rules and Mediation Procedures.*

also agree to use the procedures in cases involving claims or counterclaims under $500,000, or in nonmonetary cases. The Procedures for Large, Complex Commercial Disputes shall be applied as described in Sections L–1 through L–3 of these rules, in addition to any other portion of these rules that is not in conflict with the Procedures for Large, Complex Commercial Disputes.

(d) Parties may, by agreement, apply the Expedited Procedures, the Pocedures for Large, Complex Commercial Disputes, or the Procedures for the Resolution of Disputes through Document Submission (Rule E–6) to any dispute.

(e) All other cases shall be administered in accordance with Sections R–1 through R–54 of these rules.

R–2. AAA and Delegation of Duties

When parties agree to arbitrate under these rules, or when they provide for arbitration by the AAA and an arbitration is initiated under these rules, they thereby authorize the AAA to administer the arbitration. The authority and duties of the AAA are prescribed in the agreement of the parties and in these rules, and may be carried out through such of the AAA's representatives as it may direct. The AAA may, in its discretion, assign the administration of an arbitration to any of its offices. Arbitrations administered under these rules shall only be administered by the AAA or by an individual or organization authorized by the AAA to do so.

R–3. National Roster of Arbitrators

The AAA shall establish and maintain a National Roster of Arbitrators ("National Roster") and shall appoint arbitrators as provided in these rules. The term "arbitrator" in these rules refers to the arbitration panel, constituted for a particular case, whether composed of one or more arbitrators, or to an individual arbitrator, as the context requires.

R–4. Filing Requirements

(a) Arbitration under an arbitration provision in a contract shall be initiated the initiating party (the "claimant") filing with the AAA a Demand for Arbitration, the administrative filing fee, and a copy of the applicable arbitration agreement from the parties' contract which provides for arbitration.

(b) Arbitration pursuant to a court order shall be initiated by the initiating party filig with the AAA a Demand for Arbitration, the administrative filing fee, and a copy of any applicable agreement from the parties' contract which provides for arbitration.

(i) The filing party shall include a copy of the court order

(ii) The filing fee must be paid before a matter is considered properly filed. If the court order directs that a specific party is responsible for the filing fee, it is the responsibility of the filing party to either make such payment to the AAA and seek reimbursement as directed in the court order or to make other such arrangements so that the filing fee is submitted to the AAA with the Demand.

iii. The party filing the Demand with the AAA is the claimant and the opposing party is the respondent regardless of which party initiated the court action. Parties may request that the arbitrator alter the order of proceedings if necessary pursuant to R–32.

(c) It is the responsibility of the filing party to ensure that any conditions precedent to the filing of a case are met prior to filing for an arbitration, as well as any time requirements associated with the filing. Any dispute regarding whether a condition precedent has been met may be raised to the arbitrator for determination.

(d) Parties to any existing dispute who have not previously agreed to use these rules may commence an arbitration under these rules by filing a written submission agreement and the administrative filing fee. To the extent that the parties' submission agreement contains any variances from these rules, such variances should be clearly stated in the Submission Agreement.

(e) Information to be included with any arbitration filing includes:

i. the name of each party;

ii. the address for each party, including telephone and fax numbers and e-mail addresses;

iii. if applicable, the names, addresses, telephone and fax numbers, and e-mail addresses of any known representative for each party;

iv. a statement setting forth the nature of the claim including the relief sought and the amount involved; and

v. the locale requested if the arbitration agreement does not specify one.

(f) The initiating party may file or submit a dispute to the AAA in the following manner:

i. through AAA WebFile, located at www.adr.org; or

ii. by filing the complete Demand or Submission with any AAA office, regardless of the intended locale of hearing.

(g) The filing party shall simultaneously provide a copy of the Demand and any supporting documents to the opposing party.

(h) The AAA shall provide notice to the parties (or their representatives if so named) of the receipt of a Demand or Submission when the administrative filing requirements have been satisfied. The date on which the filing requirements are satisfied shall establish the date of filing the dispute for administration. However, all disputes in connection with the AAA's determination of the date of filing may be decided by the arbitrator.

(i) If the filing does not satisfy the filing requirements set forth above, the AAA shall acknowledge to all named parties receipt of the incomplete filing and inform the parties of the filing deficiencies. If the deficiencies are not cured by the date specified by the AAA, the filing may be returned to the initiating party.

R–5. Answers and Counterclaims

(a) A respondent may file an answering statement with the AAA within 14 calendar days after notice of the filing of the Demand is sent by the AAA. The respondent shall, at the time of any such filing, send a copy of any answering statement to the claimant and to all other parties to the arbitration. If no answering statement is filed within the stated time, the respondent will be deemed to deny the claim. Failure to file an answering statement shall not operate to delay the arbitration.

(b) A respondent may file a counterclaim at any time after notice of the filing of the Demand is sent by the AAA, subject to the limitations set forth in Rule R–6. The respondent shall send a copy of the counterclaim to the claimant and all other parties to the arbitration. If a counterclaim is asserted, it shall include a statement setting forth the nature of the counterclaim including the relief sought and the amount involved. The filing fee as specified in the applicable AAA Fee Schedule must be paid at the time of the filing of any counterclaim.

(c) If the respondent alleges that a different arbitration provision is controlling, the matter will be administered in accordance with the arbitration provision submitted by the initiating party subject to a final determination by the arbitrator.

(d) If the counterclaim does not meet the requirements for filing a claim and the deficiency is not cured by the date specified by the AAA, it may be returned to the filing party.

R–6. Changes of Claim

(a) A party may at any time prior to the close of the hearing or by the date established by the arbitrator increase or decrease the amount of its claim or counterclaim. Written notice of the change of claim amount must be provided to the AAA and all parties. If the change of claim amount results in an increase in administrative fee, the balance of the fee is due before the change of claim amount may be accepted by the arbitrator.

(b) Any new or different claim or counterclaim, as opposed to an increase or decrease in the amount of a pending claim or counterclaim, shall be made in writing and filed with the AAA, and a copy shall be provided to the other party, who shall have a period of 14 calendar days from the date of such transmittal within which to file an answer to the proposed change of claim or counterclaim with the AAA. After the arbitrator is appointed, however, no new or different claim may be submitted except with the arbitrator's consent.

R–7. Jurisdiction

The arbitrator shall have the power to rule on his or her own jurisdiction, including any objections with respect to the existence, scope, or validity of the arbitration agreement or to the arbitrability of any claim or counterclaim.

The arbitrator shall have the power to determine the existence or validity of a contract of which an arbitration clause forms a part. Such an arbitration clause shall be treated as an agreement independent of the other terms of the contract. A decision by the arbitrator that the contract is null and void shall not for that reason alone render invalid the arbitration clause.

A party must object to the jurisdiction of the arbitrator or to the arbitrability of a claim or counterclaim no later than the filing of the answering statement to the claim or counterclaim that gives rise to the objection. The arbitrator may rule on such objections as a preliminary matter or as part of the final award.

R–8. Interpretation and Application of Rules

The arbitrator shall interpret and apply these rules insofar as they relate to the arbitrator's powers and duties. When there is more than one arbitrator and a difference arises among them concerning the meaning or application of these rules, it shall be decided by a majority vote. If that is not possible, either an arbitrator or a party may refer the question to the AAA for final decision. All other rules shall be interpreted and applied by the AAA.

R–9. Mediation

In all cases where a claim or counterclaim exceeds $75,000, upon the AAA's administration of the arbitration or at any time while the arbitration is pending, the parties shall mediate their dispute pursuant to the applicable provisions of the AAA's Commercial Mediation Procedures, or as otherwise agreed by the parties. Absent an agreement of the parties to the contrary, the mediation shall take place concurrently with the arbitration and shall not serve to delay the arbitration proceedings. However, any party to an arbitration may unilaterally opt out of this rule upon notification to the AAA and the other parties to the arbitration. The parties shall confirm the completion of any mediation or any decision to opt out of this rule to the AAA. Unless agreed to by all parties and the mediator, the mediator shall not be appointed as an arbitrator to the case.

R–10. Administrative Conference

At the request of any party or upon the AAA's own initiative, the AAA may conduct an administrative conference, in person or by telephone, with the parties and/or their representatives. The conference may address such issues as arbitrator selection, mediation of the dispute, potential exchange of information, a timetable for hearings, and any other administrative matters.

R–11. Fixing of Locale

The parties may mutually agree on the locale where the arbitration is to be held. Any disputes regarding the locale that are to be decided by the AAA must be submitted to the AAA and all other parties within 14 calendar days from the date of the AAA's initiation of the case or the date established by the AAA. Disputes regarding locale shall be determined in the following manner:

(a) When the parties' arbitration agreement is silent with respect to locale, and if the parties disagree as to the locale, the AAA may initially determine the place of arbitration, subject to the power of the arbitrator after appointment, to make a final determination on the locale.

(b) When the parties' arbitration agreement requires a specific locale, absent the parties' agreement to change it, or a determination by the arbitrator upon appointment that applicable law requires a different locale, the locale shall be that specified in the arbitration agreement.

(c) If the reference to a locale in the arbitration agreement is ambiguous, and the parties are unable to agree to a specific locale, the AAA shall determine the locale, subject to the power of the arbitrator to finally determine the locale.

The arbitrator, at the arbitrator's sole discretion, shall have the authority to conduct special hearings for document production purposes or otherwise at other locations if reasonably necessary and beneficial to the process.

R–12. Appointment from National Roster

If the parties have not appointed an arbitrator and have not provided any other method of appointment, the arbitrator shall be appointed in the following manner:

(a) The AAA shall send simultaneously to each party to the dispute an identical list of 10 (unless the AAA decides that a different number is appropriate) names of persons chosen from the National Roster. The parties are encouraged to agree to an arbitrator from the submitted list and to advise the AAA of their agreement.

(b) If the parties are unable to agree upon an arbitrator, each party to the dispute shall have 14 calendar days from the transmittal date in which to strike names objected to, number the remaining names in order of preference, and return the list to the AAA. The parties are not required to exchange selection lists. If a party does not return the list within the time specified, all persons named therein shall be deemed acceptable to that party. From among the persons who have been approved on both lists, and in accordance with the designated order of mutual preference, the AAA shall invite the acceptance of an arbitrator to serve. If the parties fail to agree on any of the persons named, or if acceptable arbitrators are unable to act, or if for any other reason the appointment cannot be made from the submitted lists, the AAA shall have the power to make the appointment from among other members of the National Roster without the submission of additional lists.

 (c) Unless the parties agree otherwise when there are two or more claimants or two or more respondents, the AAA may appoint all the arbitrators.

R–13.   Direct Appointment by a Party

(a) If the agreement of the parties names an arbitrator or specifies a method of appointing an arbitrator, that designation or method shall be followed. The notice of appointment, with the name and address of the arbitrator, shall be filed with the AAA by the appointing party. Upon the request of any appointing party, the AAA shall submit a list of members of the National Roster from which the party may, if it so desires, make the appointment.

(b) Where the parties have agreed that each party is to name one arbitrator, the arbitrators so named must meet the standards of Section R–18 with respect to impartiality and independence unless the parties have specifically agreed pursuant to Section R–18(b) that the party-appointed arbitrators are to be non-neutral and need not meet those standards.

(c) If the agreement specifies a period of time within which an arbitrator shall be appointed and any party fails to make the appointment within that period, the AAA shall make the appointment.

(d) If no period of time is specified in the agreement, the AAA shall notify the party to make the appointment. If within 14 calendar days after such notice has been sent, an arbitrator has not been appointed by a party, the AAA shall make the appointment.

R–14. Appointment of Chairperson by Party–Appointed Arbitrators or Parties

(a) If, pursuant to Section R–13, either the parties have directly appointed arbitrators, or the arbitrators have been appointed by the AAA, and the parties have authorized them to appoint a chairperson within a specified time and no appointment is made within that time or any agreed extension, the AAA may appoint the chairperson.

(b) If no period of time is specified for appointment of the chairperson and the party-appointed arbitrators or the parties do not make the appointment within 14 calendar days from the date of the appointment of the last party-appointed arbitrator, the AAA may appoint the chairperson.

(c) If the parties have agreed that their party-appointed arbitrators shall appoint the chairperson from the National Roster, the AAA shall furnish to the party-appointed arbitrators, in the manner provided in Section R–12, a list selected from the National Roster, and the appointment of the chairperson shall be made as provided in that Section.

R–15. Nationality of Arbitrator

Where the parties are nationals of different countries, the AAA, at the request of any party or on its own initiative, may appoint as arbitrator a national of a country other than that of any of the parties. The request must be made before the time set for the appointment of the arbitrator as agreed by the parties or set by these rules.

R–16. Number of Arbitrators

(a) If the arbitration agreement does not specify the number of arbitrators, the dispute shall be heard and determined by one arbitrator, unless the AAA, in its discretion, directs that three arbitrators be appointed. A party may request three arbitrators in the Demand or Answer, which request the AAA will consider in exercising its discretion regarding the number of arbitrators appointed to the dispute.

(b) Any request for a change in the number of arbitrators as a result of an increase or decrease in the amount of a claim or a new or different claim must be made to the AAA and other parties to the arbitration no later than seven calendar days after receipt of the R–6 required notice of change of claim amount. If the parties are unable to agree with respect to the request for a change in the number of arbitrators, the AAA shall make that determination.

R–17. Disclosure

(a) Any person appointed or to be appointed as an arbitrator, as well as the parties and their representatives, shall disclose to the AAA any circumstance likely to give rise to justifiable doubt as to the arbitrator's impartiality or independence, including any bias or any financial or personal interest in the result of the arbitration or any past or present relationship with the parties or their representatives. Such obligation shall remain in effect throughout the arbitration. Failure on the part or a representative to comply with the requirements of this rule may result in the waiver of the right to object to an arbitrator in accordance with Rule R–41.

(b) Upon receipt of such information from the arbitrator or another source, the AAA shall communicate the information to the parties and, if it deems it appropriate to do so, to the arbitrator and others.

(c) In order to encourage disclosure by arbitrators, disclosure of information pursuant to this Section R–16 is not to be construed as an indication that the arbitrator considers that the disclosed circumstance is likely to affect impartiality or independence.

R–18. Disqualification of Arbitrator

(a) Any arbitrator shall be impartial and independent and shall perform his or her duties with diligence and in good faith, and shall be subject to disqualification for:

> (i) partiality or lack of independence,

> (ii) inability or refusal to perform his or her duties with diligence and in good faith, and

> (iii) any grounds for disqualification provided by applicable law.

(b) The parties may agree in writing, however, that arbitrators directly appointed by a party pursuant to Section R–13 shall be nonneutral, in which case such arbitrators need not be impartial or independent and shall not be subject to disqualification for partiality or lack of independence.

(c) Upon objection of a party to the continued service of an arbitrator, or on its own initiative, the AAA shall determine whether the arbitrator should be disqualified under the grounds set out above, and shall inform the parties of its decision, which decision shall be conclusive.

R–19.   Communication with Arbitrator

(a) No party and no one acting on behalf of any party shall communicate ex parte with an arbitrator or a candidate for arbitrator concerning the arbitration, except that a party, or someone acting on behalf of a party, may communicate ex parte with a candidate for direct appointment pursuant to Section R–13 in order to advise the candidate of the general nature of the controversy and of the anticipated proceedings and to discuss the candidate's qualifications, availability, or independence in relation to the parties or to discuss the suitability of candidates for selection as a third arbitrator where the parties or party-designated arbitrators are to participate in that selection.

(b) Section R–19(a) does not apply to arbitrators directly appointed by the parties who, pursuant to Section R–18(b), the parties have agreed in writing are non-neutral. Where the parties have so agreed under Section R–18(b), the AAA shall as an administrative practice suggest to the parties that they agree further that Section R–19(a) should nonetheless apply prospectively.

(c) In the course of administering an arbitration, the AAA may initiate communications with each party or anyone acting on behalf of the parties either jointly or individually.

(d) As set forth in R–43, unless otherwise instructed by the AAA or by the arbitrator, any documents submitted by any party or to the arbitrator shall simultaneously be provided to the other party or parties to the arbitration.

R–20. Vacancies

(a) If for any reason an arbitrator is unable or unwilling to perform the duties of the office, the AAA may, on proof satisfactory to it, declare the office vacant. Vacancies shall be filled in accordance with the applicable provisions of these rules.

(b) In the event of a vacancy in a panel of neutral arbitrators after the hearings have commenced, the remaining arbitrator or arbitrators may continue with the hearing and determination of the controversy, unless the parties agree otherwise.

(c) In the event of the appointment of a substitute arbitrator, the panel of arbitrators shall determine in its sole discretion whether it is necessary to repeat all or part of any prior hearings.

R–21. Preliminary Hearing

(a) At the discretion of the arbitrator, and depending on the size and complexity of the arbitration, a preliminary hearing should be scheduled as soon as practicable after the arbitrator has been appointed. The parties should be invited to attend the preliminary hearing along with their representatives. The preliminary hearing may be conducted in person or by telephone.

(b) At the preliminary hearing, the parties and the arbitrator should be prepared to discuss and establish a procedure for the conduct of the arbitration that is appropriate to achieve a fair, efficient, and economical resolution of the dispute. Sections P–1 and P–2 of these rules address the issues to be considered at the preliminary hearing.

R–22.   Pre-Hearing Exchange and Production of Information

(a) Authority of arbitrator. The arbitrator shall manage any necessary exchange of information among the parties with a view to achieving an efficient and economical resolution of the dispute, while at the same time promoting equality of treatment and safeguarding each party's opportunity to fairly present its claims and defenses.

(b) Documents. The arbitrator may, on application of a party or on the arbitrator's own initiative:

> i. require the parties to exchange documents in their possession or custody on which they intend to rely;

> ii. require the parties to update their exchanges of the documents on which they intend to rely as such documents become known to them;

> iii. require the parties, in response to reasonable document requests, to make available to the other party documents, in the responding party's possession or custody, not otherwise readily available to the party seeking the documents, reasonably believed by the party seeking the documents to exist and to be relevant and material to the outcome of disputed issues; and

> iv. require the parties, when documents to be exchanged or produced are maintained in electronic form, to make such documents available in the form most convenient and economical for the party in possession of such documents, unless the arbitrator determines that there is good cause for requiring the documents to be produced in a different form. The parties should attempt to agree in advance upon, and the arbitrator may determine, reasonable search parameters to balance the need for production of electronically stored documents relevant and material to the outcome of disputed issues against the cost of locating and producing them.

R–23. Enforcement Powers of the Arbitrator

The arbitrator shall have the authority to issue any orders necessary to enforce the provisions of rules R–21 and R–22 and to otherwise achieve a fair, efficient and economical resolution of the case, including, without limitation:

(a) conditioning any exchange or production of confidential documents and information, and the admission of confidential evidence at the hearing, on appropriate orders to preserve such confidentiality;

(b) imposing reasonable search parameters for electronic and other documents if the parties are unable to agree;

(c) allocating costs of producing documentation, including electronically stored documentation;

(d) in the case of willful non-compliance with any order issued by the arbitrator, drawing adverse inferences, excluding evidence and other submissions, and/or making special allocations of costs or an interim award of costs arising from such non-compliance; and

(e) issuing any other enforcement orders which the arbitrator is empowered to issue under applicable law.

R–24. Date, Time, and Place of Hearing

The arbitrator shall set the date, time, and place for each hearing. The parties shall respond to requests for hearing dates in a timely manner, be cooperative in scheduling the earliest practicable date, and adhere to the established hearing schedule. The AAA shall send a notice of hearing to the parties at least 10 calendar days in advance of the hearing date, unless otherwise agreed by the parties.

R–25. Attendance at Hearings

The arbitrator and the AAA shall maintain the privacy of the hearings unless the law provides to the contrary. Any person having a direct interest in the arbitration is entitled to attend hearings. The arbitrator shall otherwise have the power to require the exclusion of any witness, other than a party or other essential person, during the testimony of any other witness. It shall be discretionary with the arbitrator to determine the propriety of the attendance of any other person.

R–26. Representation

Any party may participate without representation (*pro* se), or by counsel or any other representative of the party's choosing, unless such choice is prohibited by applicable law. A party intending to be so represented shall notify the other party and the AAA of the name, telephone number and address, and email address if available, of the representative at least seven calendar days prior to the date set for the hearing at which that person is first to appear. When such a representative initiates an arbitration or responds for a party, notice is deemed to have been given.

R–27. Oaths

Before proceeding with the first hearing, each arbitrator may take an oath of office and, if required by law, shall do so. The arbitrator may require witnesses to testify under oath administered by any duly qualified person and, if it is required by law or requested by any party, shall do so.

R–28. Stenographic Record

(a) Any party desiring a stenographic record shall make arrangements directly with a stenographer and shall notify the other parties of these arrangements at least three calendar days in advance of the hearing. The requesting party or parties shall pay the cost of the record.

(b) No other means of recording the proceedings will be permitted absent the agreement of the parties or per the direction of the arbitrator.

(c) If the transcript or any other recording is agreed by the parties, or determined by the arbitrator to be the official record of the proceeding, it must be provided to the arbitrator and made available to the other parties for inspection, at a date, time, and place determined by the arbitrator.

R–29. Interpreters

Any party wishing an interpreter shall make all arrangements directly with the interpreter and shall assume the costs of the service.

R–30. Postponements

The arbitrator may postpone any hearing upon agreement of the parties, upon request of a party for good cause shown, or upon the arbitrator's own initiative.

R–31. Arbitration in the Absence of a Party or Representative

Unless the law provides to the contrary, the arbitration may proceed in the absence of any party or representative who, after due notice, fails to be present or fails to obtain a postponement. An award shall not be made solely on the default of a party. The arbitrator shall require the party who is present to submit such evidence as the arbitrator may require for the making of an award.

R–32. Conduct of Proceedings

(a) The claimant shall present evidence to support its claim. The respondent shall then present evidence to support its defense. Witnesses for each party shall also submit to questions from the arbitrator and the adverse party. The arbitrator has the discretion to vary this procedure, provided that the parties are treated with equality and that each party has the right to be heard and is given a fair opportunity to present its case.

(b) The arbitrator, exercising his or her discretion, shall conduct the proceedings with a view to expediting the resolution of the dispute and may direct the order of proof, bifurcate proceedings and direct the parties to focus their presentations on issues the decision of which could dispose of all or part of the case.

(c) When deemed appropriate, the arbitrator may also allow for the presentation of evidence by alternative means including video conferencing, internet communication, telephonic conferences and means other than an in-person presentation. Such alternative means must afford a full opportunity for all parties to present any evidence that the arbitrator deems material and relevant to the resolution of the dispute and, when involving witnesses, provide an opportunity for cross-examination.

(d) The parties may agree to waive oral hearings in any case and may also agree to utilize the Procedures for Resolution of Disputes Through Document Submission, found in Rule E–6.

R–33. Dispositive Motions

The arbitrator may allow the filing of and make rulings upon a dispositive motion only if the arbitrator determines that the moving party has shown that the motion is likely to succeed and dispose of or narrow the issues in the case.

R–34. Evidence

(a) The parties may offer such evidence as is relevant and material to the dispute and shall produce such evidence as the arbitrator may deem necessary to an understanding and determination of the dispute. Conformity to legal rules of evidence shall not be necessary. All evidence shall be taken in the presence of all of the arbitrators and all of the parties, except where any of the parties is absent, in default, or has waived the right to be present.

(b) The arbitrator shall determine the admissibility, relevance, and materiality of the evidence offered and may exclude evidence deemed by the arbitrator to be cumulative or irrelevant.

(c) The arbitrator shall take into account applicable principles of legal privilege, such as those involving the confidentiality of communications between a lawyer and client.

(d) An arbitrator or other person authorized by law to subpoena witnesses or documents may do so upon the request of any party or independently.

R–35. Evidence by Written Statements and Post-hearing Filing of Documents or Other Evidence

(a) At a date agreed upon by the parties or ordered by the arbitrator, the parties shall give written notice for any witness or expert witness who has provided a written witness statement to appear in person at the arbitration hearing for examination. If such notice is given, and the witness fails to appear, the arbitrator may disregard the written witness statement and/or expert report of the witness or make such other order as the arbitrator may consider to be just and reasonable.

(b) If a witness whose testimony is represented by a party to be essential is unable or unwilling to testify at the hearing, either in person or through electronic or other means, either party may request that the arbitrator order the witness to appear in person for examination before the arbitrator at a time and location where the witness is willing and able to appear voluntarily or can legally be compelled to do so. Any such order may be conditioned upon payment by the requesting party of all reasonable costs associated with such examination.

(c) If the parties agree or the arbitrator directs that documents or other evidence be submitted to the arbitrator after the hearing, the documents or other evidence shall be filed with the AAA for transmission to the arbitrator. All parties shall be afforded an opportunity to examine and respond to such documents or other evidence.

R–36. Inspection or Investigation

An arbitrator finding it necessary to make an inspection or investigation in connection with the arbitration shall direct the AAA to so advise the parties. The arbitrator shall set the date and time and the AAA shall notify the parties. Any party who so desires may be present at such an inspection or investigation. In the event that one or all parties are not present at the inspection or investigation, the arbitrator shall make an oral or written report to the parties and afford them an opportunity to comment.

R–37. Interim Measures**

(a) The arbitrator may take whatever interim measures he or she deems necessary, including injunctive relief and measures for the protection or conservation of property and disposition of perishable goods.

(b) Such interim measures may take the form of an interim award, and the arbitrator may require security for the costs of such measures.

(c) A request for interim measures addressed by a party to a judicial authority shall not be deemed incompatible with the agreement to arbitrate or a waiver of the right to arbitrate.

R–38. Emergency Measures of Protection

(a) Unless the parties agree otherwise, the provisions of this rule shall apply to arbitrations conducted under arbitration clauses or agreements entered on or after October 1, 2013.

(b) A party in need of emergency relief prior to the constitution of the panel shall notify the AAA and all other parties in writing of the nature of the relief sought and the reasons why such relief is required on an emergency basis. The application shall also set forth the reasons why the party is entitled to such relief. Such notice may be given by facsimile or e-mail or other reliable means, but must include a statement certifying that all other parties have been notified or an explanation of the steps taken in good faith to notify other parties.

(c) Within one business day of receipt of notice as provided in section (b), the AAA shall appoint a single emergency arbitrator designated to rule on emergency applications. The emergency arbitrator shall immediately disclose any circumstance likely, on the basis of the facts disclosed on the

---

** The Optional Rules may be found below.

application, to affect such arbitrator's impartiality or independence. Any challenge to the appointment of the emergency arbitrator must be made within one business day of the communication by the AAA to the parties of the appointment of the emergency arbitrator and the circumstances disclosed.

(d) The emergency arbitrator shall as soon as possible, but in any event within two business days of appointment, establish a schedule for consideration of the application for emergency relief. Such a schedule shall provide a reasonable opportunity to all parties to be heard, but may provide for proceeding by telephone or video conference or on written submissions as alternatives to a formal hearing. The emergency arbitrator shall have the authority vested in the tribunal under Rule 7, including the authority to rule on her/his own jurisdiction, and shall resolve any disputes over the applicability of this Rule 38.

(e) If after consideration the emergency arbitrator is satisfied that the party seeking the emergency relief has shown that immediate and irreparable loss or damage shall result in the absence of emergency relief, and that such party is entitled to such relief, the emergency arbitrator may enter an interim order or award granting the relief and stating the reason therefore.

(f) Any application to modify an interim award of emergency relief must be based on changed circumstances and may be made to the emergency arbitrator until the panel is constituted; thereafter such a request shall be addressed to the panel. The emergency arbitrator shall have no further power to act after the panel is constituted unless the parties agree that the emergency arbitrator is named as a member of the panel.

(g) Any interim award of emergency relief may be conditioned on provision by the party seeking such relief for appropriate security.

(h) A request for interim measures addressed by a party to a judicial authority shall not be deemed incompatible with this rule, the agreement to arbitrate or a waiver of the right to arbitrate. If the AAA is directed by a judicial authority to nominate a special master to consider and report on an application for emergency relief, the AAA shall proceed as provided in this rule and the references to the emergency arbitrator shall be read to mean the special master, except that the special master shall issue a report rather than an interim award.

(i) The costs associated with applications for emergency relief shall initially be apportioned by the emergency arbitrator or special master, subject to the power of the tribunal to determine finally the apportionment of such costs.

R–39. Closing of Hearing

(a) The arbitrator shall specifically inquire of all parties whether they have any further proofs to offer or witnesses to be heard. Upon receiving negative replies or if satisfied that the record is complete, the arbitrator shall declare the hearing closed.

(b) If documents or responses are to be filed as provided in Rule R–35, or if briefs are to be filed, the hearing shall be declared closed as of the final date set by the arbitrator for the receipt of briefs. If no documents, responses, or briefs are to be filed, the arbitrator shall declare the hearings closed as of the date of the last hearing (including telephonic hearings). If the case was heard without any oral hearings, the arbitrator shall close the hearings upon the due date established for receipt of the final submission.

(c) The time limit within which the arbitrator is required to make the award shall commence, in the absence of other agreements by the parties, upon the closing of the hearing. The AAA may extend the time limit for rendering of the award only in unusual and extreme circumstances.

R–40. Reopening of Hearing

The hearing may be reopened on the arbitrator's initiative, or by the direction of the arbitrator upon application of a party, at any time before the award is made. If reopening the hearing would prevent the making of the award within the specific time agreed to by the parties in the arbitration agreement, the matter may not be reopened unless the parties agree to an extension of time. When no specific date is fixed by agreement of the parties, the arbitrator shall have 30 calendar days from the closing of the reopened hearing within which to make an award (14 calendar days if the case is governed by the Expedited Procedures).

R–41. Waiver of Rules

Any party who proceeds with the arbitration after knowledge that any provision or requirement of these rules has not been complied with and who fails to state an objection in writing shall be deemed to have waived the right to object.

R–42. Extensions of Time

The parties may modify any period of time by mutual agreement. The AAA or the arbitrator may for good cause extend any period of time established by these rules, except the time for making the award. The AAA shall notify the parties of any extension.

R–43. Serving of Notice and Communicatons

(a) Any papers, notices, or process necessary or proper for the initiation or continuation of an arbitration under these rules, for any court action in connection therewith, or for the entry of judgment on any award made under these rules may be served on a party by mail addressed to the party or its representative at the last known address or by personal service, in or outside the state where the arbitration is to be held, provided that reasonable opportunity to be heard with regard to the dispute is or has been granted to the party.

(b) The AAA, the arbitrator and the parties may also use overnight delivery or electronic facsimile transmission (fax), or electronic (e-mail) to give the notices required by these rules. Where all parties and the arbitrator agree, notices may be transmitted by e-mail or other methods of communication.

(c) Unless otherwise instructed by the AAA or by the arbitrator, any documents submitted by any party to the AAA or to the arbitrator shall simultaneously be provided to the other party or parties to the arbitration.

(d) Unless otherwise instructed by the AAA or by the arbitrator, all written communications made by any party to the AAA or to the arbitrator shall simultaneously be provided to the other party or parties to the arbitration.

(e) Failure to provide the other party with copies of communications made to the AAA or to the arbitrator may prevent the AAA or the arbitrator from acting on any requests or objections contained therein.

(f) The AAA may direct that any oral or written communications that are sent by a party or their representative shall be sent in a particular manner. The failure of a party or their representative to do so may result in the AAA's refusal to consider the issue raised in the communication.

R–44. Majority Decision

(a) When the panel consists of more than one arbitrator, unless required by law or by the arbitration agreement, or section (b) of this rule, a majority of the arbitrators must make all decisions.

(b) Where there is a panel of three arbitrators, absent an objection of a party or another member of the panel, the chairperson of the panel is authorized to resolve any disputes related to the exchange of information or procedural matters without the need to consult the full panel.

R–45. Time of Award

The award shall be made promptly by the arbitrator and, unless otherwise agreed by the parties or specified by law, no later than 30 calendar days from the date of closing the hearing, or, if oral hearings have been waived, from the due date set for receipt of the parties' final statements and proofs.

R–46. Form of Award

(a) Any award shall be in writing and signed by a majority of the arbitrators. It shall be executed in the form and manner required by law.

(b) The arbitrator need not render a reasoned award unless the parties request such an award in writing prior to appointment of the arbitrator or unless the arbitrator determines that a reasoned award is appropriate.

R–47. Scope of Award

(a) The arbitrator may grant any remedy or relief that the arbitrator deems just and equitable and within the scope of the agreement of the parties, including, but not limited to, specific performance of a contract.

(b) In addition to a final award, the arbitrator may make other decisions, including interim, interlocutory, or partial rulings, orders, and awards. In any interim, interlocutory, or partial award, the arbitrator may assess and apportion the fees, expenses, and compensation related to such award as the arbitrator determines is appropriate.

(c) In the final award, the arbitrator shall assess the fees, expenses, and compensation provided in Sections R–53, R–54, and R–55. The arbitrator may apportion such fees, expenses, and compensation among the parties in such amounts as the arbitrator determines is appropriate.

(d) The award of the arbitrator(s) may include:

> (i) interest at such rate and from such date as the arbitrator(s) may deem appropriate; and

> (ii) an award of attorneys' fees if all parties have requested such an award or it is authorized by law or their arbitration agreement.

R–48. Award upon Settlement—Consent Award

(a) If the parties settle their dispute during the course of the arbitration and if the parties so request, the arbitrator may set forth the terms of the settlement in a "consent award." A consent award must include an allocation of arbitration costs, including administrative fees and expenses as well as arbitrator fees and expenses.

(b) The consent award shall not be released to the parties until all administrative fees and all arbitrator compensation have been paid in full.

R–49. Delivery of Award to Parties

Parties shall accept as notice and delivery of the award the placing of the award or a true copy thereof in the mail addressed to the parties or their representatives at the last known addresses, personal or electronic service of the award, or the filing of the award in any other manner that is permitted by law.

R–50. Modification of Award

Within 20 days after the transmittal of an award, any party, upon notice to the other parties, may request the arbitrator, through the AAA, to correct any clerical, typographical, or computational errors in the award. The arbitrator is not empowered to redetermine the merits of any claim already decided. The other parties shall be given 10 calendar days to respond to the request. The arbitrator shall dispose of the request within 20 calendar days after transmittal by the AAA to the arbitrator of the request and any response thereto.

R–51. Release of Documents for Judicial Proceedings

The AAA shall, upon the written request of a party to the arbitration, furnish to the party, at its expense, copies or certified copies of any papers in the AAA's possession that are not determined by the AAA to be privileged or confidential.

R–52. Applications to Court and Exclusion of Liability

(a) No judicial proceeding by a party relating to the subject matter of the arbitration shall be deemed a waiver of the party's right to arbitrate.

(b) Neither the AAA nor any arbitrator in a proceeding under these rules is a necessary or proper party in judicial proceedings relating to the arbitration.

(c) Parties to an arbitration under these rules shall be deemed to have consented that judgment upon the arbitration award may be entered in any federal or state court having jurisdiction thereof.

(d) Parties to an arbitration under these rules shall be deemed to have consented that neither the AAA nor any arbitrator shall be liable to any party in any action for damages or injunctive relief for any act or omission in connection with any arbitration under these rules.

(e) Parties to an arbitration under these rules may not call the arbitrator, the AAA, or AAA employees as a witness in litigation or any other proceeding relating to the arbitration. The arbitrator, the AAA and AAA employees are not competent to testify as witnesses in any such proceeding.

R–53. Administrative Fees

As a not-for-profit organization, the AAA shall prescribe administrative fees to compensate it for the cost of providing administrative services. The fees in effect when the fee or charge is incurred shall be applicable. The filing fee shall be advanced by the party or parties making a claim or counterclaim, subject to final apportionment by the arbitrator in the award. The AAA may, in the event of extreme hardship on the part of any party, defer or reduce the administrative fees.

R–54. Expenses

The expenses of witnesses for either side shall be paid by the party producing such witnesses. All other expenses of the arbitration, including required travel and other expenses of the arbitrator, AAA representatives, and any witness and the cost of any proof produced at the direct request of the arbitrator, shall be borne equally by the parties, unless they agree otherwise or unless the arbitrator in the award assesses such expenses or any part thereof against any specified party or parties.

R–55. Neutral Arbitrator's Compensation

(a) Arbitrators shall be compensated at a rate consistent with the arbitrator's stated rate of compensation.

(b) If there is disagreement concerning the terms of compensation, an appropriate rate shall be established with the arbitrator by the AAA and confirmed to the parties.

(c) Any arrangement for the compensation of a neutral arbitrator shall be made through the AAA and not directly between the parties and the arbitrator.

R–56. Deposits

(a) The AAA may require the parties to deposit in advance of any hearings such sums of money as it deems necessary to cover the expense of the arbitration, including the arbitrator's fee, if any, and shall render an accounting to the parties and return any unexpended balance at the conclusion of the case.

(b) Other than in cases where the arbitrator serves for a flat fee, deposit amounts requested will be based on estimates provided by the arbitrator. The arbitrator will determine the estimated amount of deposits using the information provided by the parties with respect to the complexity of each case.

(c) Upon the request of any party, the AAA shall request from the arbitrator an itemization or explanation for the arbitrator's request for deposits.

R–57. Remedies for Nonpayment

If arbitrator compensation or administrative charges have not been paid in full, the AAA may so inform the parties in order that one of them may advance the required payment.

(a) Upon receipt of information from the AAA that payment for administrative charges or deposits for arbitrator compensation have not been paid in full, to the extent the law allows, a party may request that the arbitrator take specific measures relating to a party's non-payment.

(b) Such measures may include, but are not limited to, limiting a party's ability to assert or pursue their claim. In no event, however, shall a party be precluded from defending a claim or counterclaim.

(c) The arbitrator must provide the party opposing a request for such measures with the opportunity to respond prior to making any ruling regarding the same.

(d) In the event that the arbitrator grants any request for relief which limits any party's participation in the arbitration, the arbitrator shall require the party who is making a claim and who has made appropriate payments to submit such evidence as the arbitrator may require for the making of an award.

(e) Upon receipt of information from the AAA that full payments have not been received, the arbitrator, on the arbitrator's own initiative or at the request of the AAA or a party, may order the suspension of the arbitration. If no arbitrator has yet been appointed, the AAA may suspend the proceedings.

(f) If the arbitration has been suspended by either the AAA or the arbitrator and the parties have failed to make the full deposits requested within the time provided after the suspension, the arbitrator, or the AAA if an arbitrator has not been appointed, may terminate the proceedings.

R–58. Sanctions

(a) The arbitrator may, upon a party's request, order appropriate sanctions where a party fails to comply with its obligations under these rules or with an order of the arbitrator. In the event that the arbitrator enters a sanction that limits any party's participation in the arbitration or results in an adverse determination of an issue or issues, the arbitrator shall explain that order in writing and shall require the submission of evidence and legal argument prior to making of an award. The arbitrator may not enter a default award as a sanction.

(b) The arbitrator must provide a party that is subject to a sanction request with the opportunity to respond prior to making any determination regarding the sanctions application.

EXPEDITED PROCEDURES

E–1. Limitation on Extensions

Except in extraordinary circumstances, the AAA or the arbitrator may grant a party no more than one seven-day extension of time to respond to the demand for arbitration or counterclaim as provided in Section R–5.

E–2. Changes of Claim or Counterclaim

A claim or counterclaim may be increased in amount, or a new or different claim or counterclaim added, upon the agreement of the other party, or the consent of the arbitrator. After the arbitrator is appointed, however, no new or different claim or counterclaim may be submitted except with the arbitrator's consent. If an increased claim or counterclaim exceeds $75,000, the case will be administered under the regular procedures unless all parties and the arbitrator agree that the case may continue to be processed under the Expedited Procedures.

E–3. Serving of Notices

In addition to notice provided by Section R–43, the parties shall also accept notice by telephone. Telephonic notices by the AAA shall subsequently be confirmed in writing to the parties. Should there be a failure to confirm in writing any such oral notice, the proceeding shall nevertheless be valid if notice has, in fact, been given by telephone.

E–4. Appointment and Qualifications of Arbitrator

(a) The AAA shall simultaneously submit to each party an identical list of five proposed arbitrators drawn from its National Roster from which one arbitrator shall be appointed.

(b) The parties are encouraged to agree to an arbitrator from this list and to advise the AAA of their agreement. If the parties are unable to agree upon an arbitrator, each party may strike two names from the list and return it to the AAA within seven days from the date of the AAA's mailing to the parties. If for any reason the appointment of an arbitrator cannot be made from the list, the AAA may make the appointment from other members of the panel without the submission of additional lists.

(c) The parties will be given notice by the AAA of the appointment of the arbitrator, who shall be subject to disqualification for the reasons specified in Section R–18. The parties shall notify the AAA within seven days of any objection to the arbitrator appointed. Any such objection shall be for cause and shall be confirmed in writing to the AAA with a copy to the other party or parties.

E–5. Exchange of Exhibits

At least two business days prior to the hearing, the parties shall exchange copies of all exhibits they intend to submit at the hearing. The arbitrator shall resolve disputes concerning the exchange of exhibits.

E–6. Proceedings on Documents and Procedures for the Resolution of Disputes Through Document Submission

Where no party's claim exceeds $25,000, exclusive of interest, attorneys' fees and arbitration costs, and other cases in which the parties agree, the dispute shall be resolved by submission of documents, unless any party requests an oral hearing, or the arbitrator determines that an oral hearing is necessary. Where cases are resolved by submission of documents, the following procedures may be utilized at the agreement of the parties or the discretion of the arbitrator:

(a) Within 14 calendar days of confirmation of the arbitrator's appointment, the arbitrator may convene a preliminary management hearing, via conference call, video conference, or internet, to establish a fair and equitable procedure for the submission of documents, and, if the arbitrator deems appropriate, a schedule for one or more telephonic or electronic conferences.

(b) The arbitrator has the discretion to remove the case from the documents-only process if the arbitrator determines that an in-person hearing is necessary.

(c) If the parties agree to in-person hearings after a previous agreement to proceed under this rule, the arbitrator shall conduct such hearings. If a party seeks to have in-person hearings after agreeing to this rule, but there is not agreement among the parties to proceed with in-person hearings, the arbitrator shall resolve the issue after the parties have been given the opportunity to provide their respective positions on the issue.

(d) The arbitrator shall establish the date for either written submissions or a final telephonic or electronic conference. Such date shall operate to close the hearing and the time for the rendering of the award shall commence.

(e) Unless the parties have agreed to a form of award other than that set forth in rule R–45, when the parties have agreed to resolve their dispute by this rule, the arbitrator shall render the award within 14 calendar days from the date the hearing is closed.

(f) If the parties agree to a form of award other than that described in rule R–45, the arbitrator shall have 30 calendar days from the date the hearing is declared closed in which to render the award.

(g) The award is subject to all other provisions of the Regular Track of these rules which pertain to awards.

E–7. Date, Time, and Place of Hearing

In cases in which a hearing is to be held, the arbitrator shall set the date, time, and place of the hearing, to be scheduled to take place within 30 calendar days of confirmation of the arbitrator's appointment. The AAA will notify the parties in advance of the hearing date.

E–8. The Hearing

(a) Generally, the hearing shall not exceed one day. Each party shall have equal opportunity to submit its proofs and complete its case. The arbitrator shall determine the order of the hearing, and may require further submission of documents within two days after the hearing. For good cause shown, the arbitrator may schedule additional hearings within seven business days after the initial day of hearings.

(b) Generally, there will be no stenographic record. Any party desiring a stenographic record may arrange for one pursuant to the provisions of Section R–28.

E–9. Time of Award

Unless otherwise agreed by the parties, the award shall be rendered not later than 14 calendar days from the date of the closing of the hearing or, if oral hearings have been waived, from the due date established for the receipt of the parties' final statements and proofs.

E–10. Arbitrator's Compensation

Arbitrators will receive compensation at a rate to be suggested by the AAA regional office.

PROCEDURES FOR LARGE, COMPLEX COMMERCIAL DISPUTES

L–1. Administrative Conference

Prior to the dissemination of a list of potential arbitrators, the AAA shall, unless the parties agree otherwise, conduct an administrative conference with the parties and/or their attorneys or other representatives by conference call. The conference will take place within 14 days after the commencement of the arbitration. In the event the parties are unable to agree on a mutually acceptable time for the conference, the AAA may contact the parties individually to discuss the issues contemplated herein. Such administrative conference shall be conducted for the following purposes and for such additional purposes as the parties or the AAA may deem appropriate:

(a) to obtain additional information about the nature and magnitude of the dispute and the anticipated length of hearing and scheduling;

(b) to discuss the views of the parties about the technical and other qualifications of the arbitrators;

(c) to obtain conflicts statements from the parties; and

(d) to consider, with the parties, whether mediation or other non-adjudicative methods of dispute resolution might be appropriate.

L–2. Arbitrators

(a) Large, Complex Commercial Cases shall be heard and determined by either one or three arbitrators, as may be agreed upon by the parties. If the parties are unable to agree upon the number of arbitrators and a claim or counterclaim involves at least $1,000,000, then three arbitrator(s) shall hear and determine the case. If the parties are unable to agree on the number of arbitrators and each claim and counterclaim is less than $1,000,000, then one arbitrator shall hear and determine the case.

(b) The AAA shall appoint arbitrator(s) as agreed by the parties. If they are unable to agree on a method of appointment, the AAA shall appoint arbitrators from the Large, Complex Commercial Case Panel, in the manner provided in the Regular Commercial Arbitration Rules. Absent agreement of the parties, the arbitrator(s) shall not have served as the mediator in the mediation phase of the instant proceeding.

L–3. Management of Proceedings

(a) The arbitrator shall take such steps as deemed necessary or desirable to avoid delay and to achieve a fair, speedy and cost-effective resolution of a Large, Complex Commercial Dispute.

(b) As promptly as practicable after the selection of the arbitrator(s), a preliminary hearing shall be scheduled in accordance with sections P–1 and P–2 of these rules.

(c) The parties shall exchange copies of all exhibits they intend to submit at the hearing at least 10 calendar days prior to the hearing unless the arbitrator(s) determines otherwise.

(d) The parties and the arbitrator(s) shall address issues pertaining to the pre-hearing exchange and production of information in accordance with rule R–22 of the AAA Commercial Rules, and the arbitrator's determinations on such issues shall be included within the Scheduling and Procedure Order.

(e) The arbitrator, or any single member of the arbitration tribunal, shall be authorized to resolve any disputes concerning the pre-hearing exchange and production of documents and information by any reasonable means within his discretion, including, without limitation, the issuance of orders set forth in rules R–22 and R–23 of the AAA Commercial Rules.

(f) In exceptional cases, at the discretion of the arbitrator, upon good cause shown and consistent with the expedited nature of arbitration, the arbitrator may order depositions to obtain the testimony of a person who may possess information determined by the arbitrator to be relevant and material to the outcome of the case. The arbitrator may allocate the cost of taking such a deposition.

(g) Generally, hearings will be scheduled on consecutive days or in blocks of consecutive days in order to maximize efficiency and minimize costs.

OPTIONAL RULES FOR EMERGENCY MEASURES OF PROTECTION

O–1. Applicability

Where parties by special agreement or in their arbitration clause have adopted these rules for emergency measures of protection, a party in need of emergency relief prior to the constitution of the panel shall notify the AAA and all other parties in writing of the nature of the relief sought and the reasons why such relief is required on an emergency basis. The application shall also set forth the reasons why the party is entitled to such relief. Such notice may be given by facsimile transmission, or other reliable means, but must include a statement certifying that all other parties have been notified or an explanation of the steps taken in good faith to notify other parties.

O–2. Appointment of Emergency Arbitrator

Within one business day of receipt of notice as provided in Section O–1, the AAA shall appoint a single emergency arbitrator from a special AAA panel of emergency arbitrators designated to rule on emergency applications. The emergency arbitrator shall immediately disclose any circumstance likely, on the basis of the facts disclosed in the application, to affect such arbitrator's impartiality or independence. Any challenge to the appointment of the emergency arbitrator must be made within one business day of the communication by the AAA to the parties of the appointment of the emergency arbitrator and the circumstances disclosed.

O–3. Schedule

The emergency arbitrator shall as soon as possible, but in any event within two business days of appointment, establish a schedule for consideration of the application for emergency relief. Such schedule shall provide a reasonable opportunity to all parties to be heard, but may provide for proceeding by telephone conference or on written submissions as alternatives to a formal hearing.

O–4. Interim Award

If after consideration the emergency arbitrator is satisfied that the party seeking the emergency relief has shown that immediate and irreparable loss or damage will result in the absence of emergency relief, and that such party is entitled to such relief, the emergency arbitrator may enter an interim award granting the relief and stating the reasons therefore.

O–5. Constitution of the Panel

Any application to modify an interim award of emergency relief must be based on changed circumstances and may be made to the emergency arbitrator until the panel is constituted; thereafter such a request shall be addressed to the panel. The emergency arbitrator shall have no further power to act after the panel is constituted unless the parties agree that the emergency arbitrator is named as a member of the panel.

O–6. Security

Any interim award of emergency relief may be conditioned on provision by the party seeking such relief of appropriate security.

O–7. Special Master

A request for interim measures addressed by a party to a judicial authority shall not be deemed incompatible with the agreement to arbitrate or a waiver of the right to arbitrate. If the AAA is directed by a judicial authority to nominate a special master to consider and report on an application for emergency relief, the AAA shall proceed as provided in Section O–1 of this article and the references to the emergency arbitrator shall be read to mean the special master, except that the special master shall issue a report rather than an interim award.

O–8. Costs

The costs associated with applications for emergency relief shall initially be apportioned by the emergency arbitrator or special master, subject to the power of the panel to determine finally the apportionment of such costs.

ADMINISTRATIVE FEES

The administrative fees of the AAA are based on the amount of the claim or counterclaim. Arbitrator compensation is not included in this schedule. Unless the parties agree otherwise, arbitrator compensation and administrative fees are subject to allocation by the arbitrator in the award.

In an effort to make arbitration costs reasonable for consumers, the AAA has a separate fee schedule for consumer-related disputes. Please refer to Section C–8 of the *Supplementary Procedures for Consumer–Related Disputes* when filing a consumer-related claim.

The AAA applies the *Supplementary Procedures for Consumer–Related Disputes* to arbitration clauses in agreements between individual consumers and businesses where the business has a standardized, systematic application of arbitration clauses with customers and where the terms and conditions of the purchase of standardized, consumable goods or services are non-negotiable or primarily non-negotiable in most or all of its terms, conditions, features, or choices. The product or service must be for personal or household use. The AAA will have the discretion to apply or not to apply the Supplementary Procedures and the parties will be able to bring any disputes concerning the application or non-application to the attention of the arbitrator. Consumers are not prohibited from seeking relief in a small claims court for disputes or claims within the scope of its jurisdiction, even in consumer arbitration cases filed by the business.

Standard Fee Schedule

These fees will be billed in accordance with the following schedule:

Amount of Claim	Initial Filing Fee	Case Service Fee
Above $0 to $10,000	$775	$200
Above $10,000 to $75,000	$975	$300
Above $75,000 to $150,000	$1,850	$750
Above $150,000 to $300,000	$2,800	$1,250
Above $300,000 to $500,000	$4,350	$1,750
Above $500,000 to $1,000,000	$6,200	$2,500
Above $1,000,000 to $5,000,000	$82000	$3,250
Above $5,000,000 to $10,000,000	$10,200	$4,000
Above $10,000,000	*	*
Nonmonetary Claims**	$3,350	$1,250
Deficient Claim Filing Fee	$350	

Fee Schedule for Claims in Excess of $10 Million

The following is the fee schedule for use in disputes involving claims in excess of $10 million. If you have any questions, please consult your local AAA office or case management center.

Claim Size	Fee	Case Service Fee
$10 million and above	Base fee of $12,800 plus .01% of the amount of claim above $10 million. Filing fees capped at $65,000	$6,000

** This fee is applicable when a claim or counterclaim is not for a monetary amount. Where a monetary claim amount is not known, parties will be required to state a range of claims or be subject to a filing fee of $10,200.

Fees are subject to increase if the amount of a claim or counterclaim is modified after the initial filing date. Fees are subject to decrease if the amount of a claim or counterclaim is modified before the first hearing.

The minimum fees for any case having three or more arbitrators are $2,800 for the Initial Filing Fee, plus a $1,250 Final Fee. Expedited Procedures are applied in any case where no disclosed claim or counterclaim exceeds $75,000, exclusive of interest and arbitration costs.

Parties on cases filed under either the Flexible Fee Schedule or the Standard Fee Schedule that are held in abeyance for one year will be assessed an annual abeyance fee of $300. If a party refuses to pay the assessed fee, the other party or parties may pay the entire fee on behalf of all parties, otherwise the matter will be administratively closed.

Refund Schedule

The AAA offers a refund schedule on filing fees connected with the Standard Fee Schedule. For cases with claims up to $75,000, a minimum filing fee of $350 will not be refunded. For all other cases, a minimum fee of $600 will not be refunded. Subject to the minimum fee requirements, refunds will be calculated as follows:

- 100% of the filing fee, above the minimum fee, will be refunded if the case is settled or withdrawn within five calendar days of filing.

- 50% of the filing fee will be refunded if the case is settled or withdrawn between six and 30 calendar days of filing.

- 25% of the filing fee will be refunded if the case is settled or withdrawn between 31 and 60 calendar days of filing.

No refund will be made once an arbitrator has been appointed (this includes one arbitrator on a three-arbitrator panel). No refunds will be granted on awarded cases.

Note: The date of receipt of the demand for arbitration with the AAA will be used to calculate refunds of filing fees for both claims and counterclaims.

Hearing Room Rental

The fees described above do not cover the rental of hearing rooms, which are available on a rental basis. Check with the AAA for availability and rates.

INDEX

References are to Pages